Feb 1972

RANDALL
DAVIDSON

RANDALL DAVIDSON AGE 68

RANDALL DAVIDSON

ARCHBISHOP OF CANTERBURY

By G. K. A. BELL

BISHOP OF CHICHESTER

THIRD EDITION

GEOFFREY CUMBERLEGE
OXFORD UNIVERSITY PRESS
LONDON NEW YORK TORONTO
1952

Oxford University Press, Amen House, London E.C. 4
GLASGOW NEW YORK TORONTO MELBOURNE WELLINGTON
BOMBAY CALCUTTA MADRAS CAPE TOWN
Geoffrey Cumberlege, Publisher to the University

FIRST PUBLISHED 1935
SECOND EDITION 1938
THIRD EDITION 1952

REPRINTED LITHOGRAPHICALLY IN GREAT BRITAIN

PREFACE TO THIRD EDITION

Since this book was first published Randall Davidson's two immediate successors in the See of Canterbury have died, and have been the subjects of admirable Lives: *Cosmo Gordon Lang* by J. G. Lockhart, and *William Temple* by F. A. Iremonger. The wide welcome which each received testified not only to the understanding and ability of the biographer, but also to the great interest which his theme aroused.

In issuing a third edition of the present biography, I propose, with due regard to those works, to offer a few general reflections on the development of the office of Archbishop of Canterbury during three primacies from 1903 to 1944. And I shall take an occasional glance farther back by way of illustration.

Randall Davidson was enthroned two years after Queen Victoria's death. The end of her reign meant the end of an epoch. The whole character of British life had been transformed between 1837 and 1901. The first Reform Bill of 1832 had already been enacted before she came to the throne. The railway age, the age of coal and iron, had begun. By the middle of the century the industrial and commercial revolution was gathering its full strength. Science was advancing all along the line. Great strides were made in social legislation and in the Trade Union movement. In 1870 a national system of universal primary education was instituted. The Universities were reformed and extended. Before the end of the century the new journalism had arrived. By 1901 the population of England and Wales had risen to over 32 million, as compared with just under 14 million seventy years before. And a fresh epoch began in the range and diversity of the Empire. Added to this there were great changes in the framework of the Church, through the various measures of Church reform. Convocation resumed its Sessions in 1852, after being suppressed for a hundred and thirty five years. The Evangelical party had considerable influence, especially in the early years of the century. There were the Tractarian, the Broad Church, the Christian Social movements. And by the passing of the Matrimonial Causes Act in 1857 the Church of England lost her jurisdiction over marriages, and the re-marriage of divorced persons was made legal.

The Archbishop of Canterbury holds a spiritual office. To this the style of official documents bears witness: 'We [*Randall Thomas*] by Divine Providence Archbishop of Canterbury, Primate of all England and Metropolitan.' His office also gives him a position of immense responsibility and many functions in Church and State. Much has always depended on the personal qualities and attainments of the individual Primate. But the course of these last fifty years, more I think than that of the fifty years preceding, shows that while the prestige of the institution may have waned, the character and gifts of the person count for more and more.

Archbishop Howley died in 1848, the year when Randall Davidson was born, 'in a week of Continental hurly-burly and of disorder at home'. He was the last Prince Archbishop of Canterbury. When he dined out, no one left the room till he rose to go. At the public banquets at Lambeth, 'the domestics of the Prelacy stood, with swords and bag-wigs, round pig, and turkey, and venison'. He drove abroad in a coach and four, and when he crossed the courtyard of Lambeth Palace from the chapel to 'Mrs. Howley's Lodgings', he was preceded by men bearing flambeaux.[1] How different from the picture of William Temple touring the parishes of Croydon on a summer evening with Mrs. Temple, in his chaplain's little car, as the bombs exploded, or sleeping on a sofa in a ground-floor passage at Lambeth during the air-raids of 1944![2]

The contrast between Archbishop Howley and his successors of this century in relation to political and social questions may be judged from this episode. In 1832 popular feeling in Canterbury was very strong against those who had in any way opposed the passing of the Reform Bill, and the Archbishop had been active in opposition. That year, as he arrived in Canterbury for an official visit, he was greeted by a mass demonstration of people congregated in the immediate vicinity of the Guildhall. As soon as his carriage drew up in front of the Guildhall, 'he was greeted by a torrent of hissing and howling and groans, and

[1] 'William Howley', in *Dictionary of English Church History*, G. W. E. R., p. 289.

[2] F. A. Iremonger, *William Temple*, p. 618.

these were followed by mud, rotten eggs, and stones, which fell around the carriage as thick as blackberries'.[1] And he only just managed to escape the anger of the mob and drive to the Deanery in safety. How different from Archbishop Davidson's Appeal from the Churches in 1926, with proposals for the ending of the General Strike; and how strange William Temple would have seemed, as 'the People's Archbishop', to William Howley!

The contrast between the last Prince Archbishop and his modern successors may also be seen by a comparison of their correspondence; though something must be allowed for the personal characteristics of an archbishop, as well as for the introduction of the typewriter. 'In Archbishop Howley's days', (writes Mr. George Lipscoomb, a porter at Lambeth for forty-two years), 'the General Postman, dressed in bright scarlet, brought the country letters every morning, and came round again at five o'clock in the evening to collect the letters. He went to the front door, ringing in his hands a heavy bell to give notice of his coming. He had a guinea a quarter from the Palace. The general-post letters in the morning for the Archbishop and Mrs. Howley were put into a china bowl in the hall. They were scarcely enough to cover the bottom of it. When the Archbishop was at Addington, and I had to forward the letters there, I could put, as a rule, all the letters of the day, servants' included, in a medium-sized envelope.'[2] In 1912, excluding the immense number of official and legal letters, that part of Archbishop Davidson's personal correspondence which was carefully filed at the close of each year (perhaps about one-third of the letters actually received and sent) consisted usually of about 650 or 700 sets of subjects, any one of which might comprise perhaps ten or twenty or even fifty letters.[3] And by 1928 anything from 70 to 100 letters were posted from Lambeth each day, in addition to the private correspondence.

It is time, however, to turn to the development in the position and influence of the Archbishop of Canterbury during the three primacies under review.

The first half of the twentieth century is likely to be regarded

[1] *Chronological History of Canterbury Cathedral*, pp. 345–6.
[2] R. T. Davidson, *Archibald Campbell Tait*, vol. ii, pp. 556–7.
[3] Idem, *The Character and Call of the Church of England*, p. 7.

by historians as even more significant for the people of Britain than the Victorian age; and the social changes which have marked it as not less momentous. During the years covered by the three Primates, Democracy arrived. Already implicit in British self-government, it was accelerated by far-reaching measures passed when Mr. Asquith was Prime Minister. The First World War made it a fact. By the Representation of the People Act, 1918, women were given the vote for the first time, and the electorate was trebled. The Education Act of 1918 introduced ambitious measures designed to equip future citizens for the task of government. The condition of the working classes was much improved, and State control greatly increased. The Labour Party, which held office for the first time in 1924, became more and more powerful; and in the General Election of 1945 returned 396 Members to the House of Commons, as against 11 in 1900. At the same time, the years between the two World Wars were marked by nation-wide labour disputes between 1919 and 1926, and by large-scale unemployment. The number of unemployed in Great Britain from 1924 to 1939 was never less than a million, and averaged 1,744,000. Among other factors influencing the pattern of the common life were the motor-car, the cinema, the wireless, cheap literature, and the pictorial press. A new Matrimonial Causes Act, known as the Herbert Act, greatly extending the grounds for divorce, was passed in 1938. Both at home and abroad the total results of the two World Wars have still to be measured.

Each of the three Archbishops in these forty-one years was a great churchman; but each was also concerned with secular affairs. It may be of service to consider the development of the secular side of the Primate's contact with the life of the nation, before dealing more particularly with ecclesiastical affairs. Therefore, as the Archbishop of Canterbury is the first subject of the Crown, I turn first to his relations with his Sovereign.

Queen Victoria died before Randall Davidson became Primate of all England. But it is safe to say that no modern Bishop was ever so deeply trusted by his Sovereign as Randall Davidson was trusted by her, from the day when he visited Windsor, after Archbishop Tait's death, to the end of the Queen's life. His intimacy with King Edward VII and King George V was different in character. He was always a trusted friend of members of the Royal Family. But so far as King Edward was concerned, Archbishop Davidson was received rather as his Royal Mother's counsellor, to whom great deference was due, than as the chosen confidant of the King. He was greatly respected, but he was not on the same intimate terms—though twice his wisdom was invoked in a political crisis. There was one occasion, the proposed marriage of Princess Eugenie Victoria to the King of Spain in 1906, on which he felt bound to adopt a role which was highly unwelcome to King Edward. Although courteous as ever, and refraining from public intervention, he was both courageous and persistent in his private appeals and protests.[1] Archbishop Davidson was on more intimate terms with King George V. He saw him often, and had a unique personal access through his long-standing friendship with Lord Stamfordham; and in the early days of the reign there were important comings and goings about the Parliament Act. Archbishop Lang knew King George V still more intimately; and there was a real affection between them. Every year he visited the King and Queen at Balmoral. He was with the King frequently at Craigweil House, Bognor Regis (where he was convalescing), and was able to give him spiritual ministrations, rather (he says) 'as a personal friend than officially as the Archbishop'.[2] And he was with him at the end. But with the accession of King Edward VIII, to quote the Archbishop's words, there was 'not only a new reign, but a new régime'.[3] And the fact that conversations had been held with the Prince's father on his own private matters, and were known by the Prince to have been held, was bound to embarrass the relations of King and Archbishop.[4] His attitude to the abdication is well known, though his actual part in the conclusion of the crisis was small. The old close relationship was resumed with King George VI, and gained an added depth through the King's overwhelming sense of religious reality at the solemn service of the Coronation. In the short Primacy of Archbishop Temple there is no specially close link to record, but King,

[1] *Infra*, p. 506.
[2] J. G. Lockhart, *Cosmo Gordon Lang*, p. 320.
[3] Ibid., p. 395.
[4] Ibid., p. 396.

Queen, and Archbishop were naturally brought into contact from time to time through the experiences of the war.

The Archbishop of Canterbury is the chief Spiritual Peer in Parliament. So I turn next to the House of Lords. Randall Davidson, writes Dr. Lang, 'loved the House of Lords and was never more, so to say, at home than when he was there. He liked to be in his place whatever the business in hand might be. He became an institution there, a "House of Lords man".'[1] He was never a party man, though at times, as with the Education Bills brought in by the Liberal Government, and the Bill for the Disestablishment of the Church in Wales, he was engaged in a sharp political conflict, and was on the same side as the Conservative Party. During his Primacy the power of the House of Lords was greatly reduced by the passing of the Parliament Act in 1911. Incidentally it may be noted that his speech at a critical moment during the Third Reading debate was acknowledged by Viscount Morley to have been of crucial importance in determining a majority for the Government.[2] But the second Chamber, though unreformed, continued to exercise great influence both in legislation and through its debates, where the level of speaking was high. The Chamber itself in some ways became more and more a Council of State, in which the wisest and most experienced men spoke as the need required on contemporary affairs. When it was fitting, the Archbishop took an active part in debates on contemporary issues such as the Irish question, Conscription, and Divorce; and on great occasions, or on subjects of special importance, he would always make his contribution. He would himself initiate debates on social and international questions, where matters of moral principle were concerned. To him the House of Lords seemed a very proper place in which the Primate of all England should appeal to the national conscience, or give public support to lay Peers denouncing grave wrongs.

Archbishop Lang, though not quite so frequent in his attendance, took a similar view of the part played by the House of Lords in the nation's life, and of the opportunities afforded to a Primate willing to take them. He had also a quite astonishing

[1] J. G. Lockhart, *Cosmo Gordon Lang*, p. 232.
[2] *infra*, p. 631.

gift of oratory. Lord Quickswood describes him as one of the two or three best speakers he had ever heard; 'whether it was exposition or narrative, exhortation or argument, anecdote or humour, he was pre-eminent in all these arts'.[1] He exercised considerable influence among the Peers, though he was never to quite the same degree as Randall Davidson a 'House of Lords man'. The value attached to his contributions is shown by the fact that he also was created a temporal Peer to enable him to sit after he had resigned.

Archbishop Temple, though his occasional contributions were of high value, and his share in the passing of the Education Act in 1944 was of special significance, came much less often to the House. He took the view that its influence on the life of the nation had declined in recent years. He tended therefore to regard its sessions as of secondary importance in his programme of engagements. Speaking generally, he did not feel greatly at home in the House, and preferred to make the platform, the press, or the B.B.C. the vehicle of his views on secular affairs.

There is a further difference in the approach of Archbishop Davidson and Archbishop Lang from that of Archbishop Temple. Both the former, and Randall Davidson especially, valued the House of Lords for the opportunities it gave for making personal contacts. The fact that the Archbishop was always in his place enabled him to be in constant touch with those in high office, or holding important positions in the nation's life. Dr. Temple had an immense range of contacts, very different in character from those of his two predecessors. And he did not set store by the House of Lords for this purpose. He made the contacts he desired not only in different ways but in different fields; for example in the Universities, the Workers' Educational Association, meetings with Trade Unionists, as well as at groups of economists and representatives of various interests invited as his guests to the Old Palace or elsewhere.

Another test of the Archbishop's connexion with the leading authorities in the State is the closeness of his relations with the Prime Minister of the day. The Archbishop and the Prime Minister are bound to meet in a formal way at national services in Westminster Abbey and St. Paul's Cathedral, at Guildhall dinners and Royal Academy banquets, and on other similar

[1] J. G. Lockhart, *Cosmo Gordon Lang*, pp. 231–2.

public occasions. But this is very different from being on friendly terms, and having easy access. Archbishop Davidson set a remarkable precedent here. He knew all the seven Prime Ministers during his tenure of the See personally, and four of them intimately—Balfour, Campbell-Bannerman, Asquith, and Baldwin. This kind of intimacy had certainly not been equalled for 100 years. In Mr. Lloyd George, however, a new kind of Prime Minister emerged, with different ways and habits of mind from his predecessors, and—this is the important point—much less accessible to Archbishops of Canterbury. With Mr. Baldwin the former intimacy was restored; and it was maintained by Archbishop Lang. Up to and including the premierships of Mr. Baldwin (1924–9 and 1935–7), the personal contacts of Archbishops Davidson and Lang were concerned in various degrees with social and national and even international affairs, and not only with ecclesiastical matters such as appointments to Bishoprics. The same was true when Mr. Ramsay Macdonald became Prime Minister. When Mr. Neville Chamberlain succeeded Mr. Baldwin the links tended to be weaker. And during the Second World War Mr. Churchill saw little of either Archbishop Lang or Archbishop Temple. But the pace of public life has quickened, and the pressure of affairs has greatly increased. Although there is no reason why future Prime Ministers and Primates should not be on terms of intimate friendship, able to discuss affairs of common concern, and the business of the Church, with an interest equal to that shown by Mr. Balfour, Mr. Asquith, and Mr. Baldwin, the signs of the times do not point that way. Indeed, the pressure is now of such a character that, in the business of the Church requiring his attention, the modern Prime Minister is inclined to trust more and more to the skilled help and judgement of those whose duty it is to let their chief have the fullest information in their power. This is a service often admirably performed, but it is not the same thing as the former personal relationship between Primate and Premier.

I have said nothing of relationships with foreign countries or their rulers and statesmen. But one of the most striking features in these 41 years is the growing significance of the Archbishop of Canterbury in the international field. All three

Archbishops counted increasingly here, not only at home but abroad. Archbishop Davidson took an active part in the international developments which followed the First World War. Archbishop Lang was sharply attacked in Germany and Japan for his public pronouncements between the wars. President Roosevelt testified to King George VI of Archbishop Temple that 'as an ardent advocate of international co-operation based on Christian principles he exercised profound influence throughout the world'.[1]

There are many other ways in which the Archbishop of Canterbury exercises influence in relation to the State, or to international affairs. Speeches in Convocation and in the Church Assembly, addresses at public meetings, sermons in Westminster Abbey or St. Paul's Cathedral, broadcasts, communications to the press, and books, especially such books as Temple's Penguin volume, *Christianity and Social Order*, are natural illustrations. But I have chosen the particular points of contact which I have sought to explain because they come to the Archbishop by virtue of his office. And I think there will be little doubt about the inference to be drawn. The new developments in the State and the progress of democracy may diminish the political power of the Archbishop of Canterbury as a national institution. There are also quite new ways (as Archbishop Temple had begun to show) by which the Archbishop can influence the nation. But every Archbishop derives a great potential moral authority from his office, and in the exercise of that moral authority his personal qualities count for more and more.

It is, however, in relation to the Church that the development of the influence of the Archbishop of Canterbury possesses a special interest for the historian. In Dr. Davidson's time the Primate became known as a person, far outside the borders of his diocese or of London. This was due partly no doubt to the increasing circulation of the daily press. But it was also due in no small measure to the creation of the Church Assembly in 1920. The Church Assembly has not fulfilled all the hopes entertained by its most ardent original promoters. It has been criticized for over-complicated or unnecessary legislation, and for the impetus it has given to central administration. It has failed to solve the problems of Prayer Book Revision, or to deal

[1] F. A. Iremonger, *William Temple*, p. 627.

with reforms affecting the Ecclesiastical Courts and certain other important issues in the relationship between Church and State. But it has been the means of giving the laity a far larger share in Church legislation. It has accomplished many valuable practical reforms. And through its sessions in London three times a year, not only has it enabled representatives of the clergy and laity from all over England to meet and work together in a new way, but its chairman has become familiar to the people of the Church of England in a way impossible before.

Again, the moral authority of the Archbishop over the bench of Bishops has greatly increased. In law every Bishop is the ruler in his own diocese, and even when the Archbishop is present in state in a church of another diocese, it is the Bishop who has the right to pronounce the benediction; although few would exercise it, as a Bishop of Chichester once did in Brighton Parish Church, somewhat to the dismay of Archbishop Davidson, who had come for a great festal occasion. In law the Archbishop has no authority to order special prayers in another diocese, or to prescribe forms of public intercession. He may recommend, but it is the Bishop who sanctions. In fact, however, the weight of the Archbishop's recommendation has so increased during the forty-one years that whatever he asks in his province is almost certainly done. More important, the word of the Archbishop of Canterbury goes in Convocation, and at the private meetings of Bishops, in a way and to a degree, which is a little disturbing at times to Bishops (like Dr. Gore and Dr. Henson) who value their independence as diocesans. Meetings of Bishops of the two Provinces seem to have started just before Archbishop Tait became Archbishop of Canterbury, as conversations at the office of Queen Anne's Bounty in Westminster, after a dinner privately arranged. It was Archbishop Benson who in May 1883 arranged that they should be held at Lambeth Palace, and minutes kept. Bishops were more interesting in Archbishop Tait's time, says Archbishop Davidson, and there were sometimes great clashes in the Bishops' Meetings.[1] It is worth noting that the increase in archiepiscopal influence has coincided with the increase in the number of Bishops. In 1903 there were 35 Diocesan Bishops. By 1944 12 new English dioceses had been formed, and the number of Bishops

[1] *Infra*, p. 1155.

fact, if not in form, and one much wider in range and abler in personnel than any ever suggested by 'reformers', whose fertility of suggestion was greater than their acquaintance with the facts. Anyhow, I seemed to get on well without the apparatus of any of those fancy schemes.'[1]

It is beyond dispute that there are countless tasks which only the Archbishop can discharge. No doubt in a sense Archbishop Lang's words in 1935 are only too true. 'The job is really impossible for one man, yet only one man can do it.'[2] The real issue is that of strategy, and on the grievous lack of provision here Dr. Lang's notebooks (so often quoted in the *Life*) speak for themselves: 'his own notebooks, penned almost entirely in his fastness at Ballure, abound in laments at the absence of any breathing-space when he could, as it were, sit down and think out some of the major problems of the Church.'[3]

The plan of a G.H.Q. in relation to the Archbishop has to be considered from two points of view. There is the need of relief in the sheer bulk of administrative work which falls to the Primate's lot. This is of great importance in itself, in relation to the Primate's time and strength. But the need of more adequate provision for planning and strategy is even greater. What Archbishop Benson chiefly desired was help in thought on 'the really grave great questions'. Indeed, when one considers the increasing pace of modern life, the constant exposure to the public gaze, the decline in resources for private hospitality, with opportunity for leisured counsel, and the unceasing pressure for ever greater mobility brought about by modern transport, including the aeroplane, the difficulties in the way of finding space for quiet and unhurried deliberation are almost overwhelming. The whole issue is one which requires the urgent attention of the Church. But in view of the different attitudes adopted by different Primates as to the desirability of any such plan, this also must be remembered. No plan is likely to succeed which is not initiated, or at least heartily welcomed, by the Archbishop of Canterbury of the day.

G. K. A. B.

Christmas 1951

[1] J. G. Lockhart, *Cosmo Gordon Lang*, p. 330.
[2] Ibid., p. 372. [3] Ibid., p. 373.

qualified to attend Bishops' Meetings was 49, including 6 (instead of 4) Welsh Bishops. Even with 35 Bishops, meeting for a day and a half with a full agenda, effective counsel presents its problems. It is much more difficult when there are 49.

In the Anglican Communion at large the Archbishop of Canterbury may be in theory one Metropolitan among many, although admittedly the chief. But the tact and wisdom which Archbishops Davidson and Lang displayed while on the throne of St. Augustine, especially at successive Lambeth Conferences and in various ways, in which Archbishop Temple played his part, have materially increased the influence and prestige of the Archbishopric of Canterbury with the whole Anglican episcopate.

The three Archbishops of Canterbury have rendered outstanding service to their Church in the realm of Christian unity. Relations between the leaders of the Church of England and the leaders of the Free Churches in England were transformed in this period, most of all as a result of the Appeal to all Christian people issued by the Lambeth Conference of 1920. All three Archbishops were active in this work, although less has actually followed from the prolonged conferences on Church relations than many hoped. Archbishop Temple did a notable service in connexion with the inauguration of the British Council of Churches in 1942. Again, many new contacts have been made with foreign Churches. Never before had there been a *rapprochement* on so wide a scale with the Eastern Orthodox Churches, and, in a lesser degree, with other Eastern Churches. New relationships began with the Scandinavian Churches. Personal links were established with individual Lutheran and Reformed Church leaders. The Old Catholics entered into an agreement with the Anglican Church on intercommunion. There was a striking departure from precedent in the conversations which took place between representatives of the Archbishop of Canterbury on the one hand, and Cardinal Mercier and other Roman Catholic divines with the approval of the Holy See, on the other hand, at Malines. And a new step of some importance was taken, under the auspices of Archbishop Lang, by the formation of the Church of England Council on Foreign Relations in 1933.

Last of all comes the Ecumenical Movement. It is 'the great new fact of our time'. Men of many Churches in East and West have played their part in its evolution over many years. Archbishops Davidson and Lang were amongst them. Archbishop Davidson showed his friendship for it at the first World Missionary Conference in Edinburgh in 1910, at which William Temple (then twenty-nine years old) was an usher. Archbishop Lang gave it steady support, and was one of the Presidents of the Oxford Conference on Church, Community, and State in 1937. Archbishop Temple gave his main service before he came to Lambeth. It was as Archbishop of York that he presided over the Edinburgh Conference on Faith and Order in 1937, was appointed Chairman of the Provisional Committee of the World Council of Churches (in process of formation), and helped to frame its constitution as a 'fellowship of Churches which accept our Lord Jesus Christ as God and Saviour'. But he kept in as close touch as possible with foreign col eagues, when at Canterbury, and it was to his guiding hand, up to the time of his death, more than to that of any other Christian man, that the World Council of Churches owed its inauguration at Amsterdam.

It is a far cry back from 1944 to 1848, the year in which Archbishop Howley died and Archbishop Davidson was born. There is no comparison between the burden of the Primacy now and the burden then. It is not surprising, therefore, that the question of providing the Church with its 'G.H.Q., the department devoted to planning and strategy', should have again been raised by Dean Iremonger[1] and others, following the calamity of William Temple's death. The first Archbishop in recent times to have brought it forward was Archbishop Benson. He left a note of a conversation with Bishop Lightfoot and Dr. Westcott in 1887. 'We discussed the unfortunate result in one most important matter of the happy change in Episcopal activity. The diocesan energies now interfere with every Bishops' meeting, or meeting of Convocation, and leave the Church almost destitute of the opportunity of counsel. . . We came to the conclusion that a "Cardinalate" in some form was becoming absolutely necessary. What we thought might be done was the appointment of four or five Bishops, to give at least an annual fortnight of conference, with nothing else to do, on matters proposed by the Archbishop—or otherwise found

[1] F. A. Iremonger, *William Temple*, pp. xi, xii.

necessary. These to be named by the Archbishop.'[1] By 1894 the 'Cardinalate' seems to have developed into something more definite and continuous. His biographer, after quoting a typical day's work in 1894, writes as follows: 'It was such pressure of important business as that of which this day gives an example which used to make my father frequently say that what the Archbishop of Canterbury needed more than anything else was a small strong Council of wise and statesmanlike ecclesiastics to whom he could refer important matters, and who would be at hand and free to deliberate carefully and thoroughly about any matter on which the Archbishop needed advice, besides originating proposals affecting Church matters. He used to speak laughingly of a College of Cardinals.'[2]

Archbishop Benson was not blind to the difficulties which stood in the way of achieving such an inner council. Archbishop Davidson in his turn opposed the plan, as a new departure of a grievous kind. He preferred to rely on personal contacts, and the help of proved counsellors, as occasion required. But the plan which he condemned was described by him as one for 'a group of officially appointed men, call it by what name you will—Council, Curia, Cabinet, Board, Committee—who might jointly bear the burden, and, speaking with collective voice, increase immensely the weight of what is said.'[3] This plan 'for dealing with these larger matters' is rather different in its character from that which some at least of the present advocates of a G.H.Q. at Lambeth have in mind. Archbishop Lang was even more critical of 'a proposal which has taken many shapes'. 'There has been the grandiose conception of a sort of "Abbey of Cardinals"—a precedent which I don't think would commend itself to Anglican churchmen; or it has been advocated that there should be experts in various branches of the work of the Church at home and abroad to assist the Archbishop with their knowledge and counsel.'[4] He describes his own habit of recourse to particular experts or officials or chairmen or secretaries of councils or societies; and he dismisses the matter with these words: 'Thus there was always a Headquarters Staff in

[1] A. C. Benson, *Life of Edward White Benson*, vol. ii, p. 131.
[2] Ibid., p. 357.
[3] *Infra*, p. 711.
[4] J. G. Lockhart, *Cosmo Gordon Lang*, p. 329.

PREFACE TO SECOND EDITION

THE present edition includes an entirely new chapter on The Coronation of King George V (printed as Appendix IV). It is based on material contained in three box files which, in spite of search, could not be discovered when this book was being written. The author desires to express his gratitude to H.M. the King for leave to quote certain documents; and to the Archbishop of Canterbury. Lady Davidson died on June 26, 1936. In *Edith Davidson of Lambeth* by M. C. S. M. (1938) a fitting memorial to her life and character will be found. A Note on relations with the Church of Sweden (page 1015), and a List of Portraits (Appendix III), have also been added; and a number of minor corrections have been made.

August, 1938. G. K. A. B.

PREFACE TO FIRST EDITION

THE author of this work has been greatly assisted in the fulfilment of his task by the ample records and admirably arranged correspondence which Archbishop Davidson left behind him. Indeed, the Archbishop had hoped that after his resignation he might perhaps be able to prepare his own reminiscences. Though this did not prove possible, the preliminary notes which he put together, especially in connexion with the history of his early life, have been of much service to the biographer. Dr. Davidson never kept a diary for any length of time, but five small quarto leather-bound MS. books survive, containing accurate accounts written in from time to time of conversations or incidents which had specially aroused his interest when he was Dean of Windsor, and also when he was Bishop of Rochester. They extend chronologically from January 1888 to September 1895; and though there are considerable periods during which no entry is made, they afford a running commentary on a number of important episodes in which Dr. Davidson was concerned, together with his impressions of many important people whom he met. The first of these MS. books refers to the failure of a series of January attempts to keep a diary in anything like orthodox diary form, and records his decision 'to try something more irregular, with no vacant pages, dated and blank'; and the writer adds 'I know that things *do* happen to me and around me which I ought to be recording and *don't*.' Their contents may be dated thus: (1) January 1888–April 1889: about 100 autograph pages; (2) May 1889–November 1890: about 90 autograph pages; (3) January 1891–February 1892: about 90 autograph pages; (4) April 1892–August 1893: about 90 autograph pages; (5) March 1894–September 1895: about 32 autograph pages (together with half a page for April 1897, a beginning for Winchester, not continued). After he had become Archbishop, during a summer holiday abroad in 1906, Dr. Davidson dictated his recollections of Windsor days and also of his work in the two dioceses of Rochester and Winchester, ending with his appointment to the Primacy; and though he felt afterwards that the recollections were somewhat hurried and unfinished in form, they have proved of considerable value, especially for the light they throw on his relations with Queen Victoria. On this MS. book of 1906, and the smaller leather-bound volumes, the biographer has drawn a great deal.

For the Primacy itself there is a whole series of memoranda of a private character, mostly typed and arranged in large envelopes, dealing as a rule with particular years. They commenced in 1909 and went down to 1930. These were all dictated, often at the time, or occasionally after an interval, when the Archbishop, surveying a period of a few months, picked out certain leading incidents or delivered himself of general reflections. At first they dealt specially with constitutional questions such as The Budget of 1909, and the Parliament Act; but later they covered general church questions as well as matters of general public interest. They also, like the earlier MS. books, form a running commentary on contemporary events and the characters with whom the Archbishop was brought into official relations. There are in addition many separate memoranda of interviews etc. filed with the correspondence on the particular subject. All these documents, whether written or dictated before or during the Primacy, may be described generally as 'the Davidson papers', and the biographer has quoted them constantly in the different parts of this Life. Indeed, it may be assumed that passages commencing 'The Archbishop notes', or having some other similar introduction (not being clearly indicated as letters) are taken from the Davidson papers. They are naturally of great value; since from them it is possible to learn the Archbishop's reactions towards and verdict upon the scenes in which he was a principal actor. The copious extracts from them given in this biography indicate sufficiently their nature and importance. But though quoted considerably, much remains which can hardly be published at present (to quote one of the greatest of all biographers) 'without trespassing against the feelings of distinguished individuals still alive',[1] or causing difficulties of other kinds.

The correspondence of Archbishop Davidson was of a most extensive character, and has been extensively preserved, both as regards letters written to and by him. Year by year it was arranged and filed in excellent order, both in respect of subject and date. It may therefore be supposed that the material con-

[1] Lockhart, *Life of Scott*, Chapter 19.

fronting the biographer is vast and that the difficulty of selecting what is characteristic and outstandingly important has been unusually great.

The author owes a special personal debt to Lady Davidson, not only for kindness and friendship during the ten years when he served as Archbishop's Chaplain at Lambeth, and since, but also for her own vivid recollections, and her generosity and consideration during all the stages of the preparation of this book.

Most grateful acknowledgement is due to H.M. the King for the permission which he has given for the publication of various letters and extracts, not least those belonging to the lifetime of Queen Victoria. One point should be made plain at the very outset with regard to the correspondence and the various other communications which took place between Randall Davidson and Queen Victoria. It is necessary to emphasize it, in order to avoid any possible misunderstanding. The circumstances in which Randall Davidson was introduced to Her Majesty were altogether unusual, following upon the death of his father-in-law, Archbishop Tait. They led, as the biography shows, to an extraordinary trust in Dr. Davidson and to an unusual reliance on his judgement in Church matters. But the consultations which resulted may be justly described as so purely personal in character, and so almost fortuitous in their origin, that they could not rightly be regarded as precedents even within the limited department concerned. In any event the whole situation changed on the Queen's death. And with regard to Dr. Davidson himself, readers of this work will see that the relations between him and King Edward and King George, though never wanting in friendly feeling, were of a quite different kind. The personal factor was completely altered.

The biographer wishes also to express his thanks to the Archbishop of Canterbury, who has been most generous in reading special chapters, in helping with advice, and in contributing a description of the relations between himself, as Archbishop of York, and Dr. Davidson, when Archbishop of Canterbury, besides giving him facilities of every kind at Lambeth Palace.

It would be impossible to thank publicly every one of the many friends and helpers who have assisted in the preparation of this book; sometimes by reminiscences, sometimes by revising passages or chapters in which they were themselves concerned, sometimes by permitting the publication of letters. But a special tribute of gratitude must be paid to some who have given exceptional help. First, the author has to thank Mr. Arthur Sheppard, the Archbishop's Private Secretary for many years, who undertook the task of going through the files of the Davidson correspondence covering nearly 40 years, deposited at Lambeth, with a view to facilitating the work of selection; and has in addition compiled the index. Next, he thanks Miss Mary Mills, without whose help in going through the personal papers, in compiling memoranda and giving aid of all kinds in conjunction with Lady Davidson, this book would have been immeasurably poorer; and Mr. Charles Williams for reading the Life in MS. as well as in proof, and for the most valuable and skilled advice which he has given him as a result—a service which is deeply appreciated. Particular thanks are due to the Rev. Lancelot Mason, the biographer's Chaplain, for help in various ways; and both to him and to the Rev. Norman Sykes, for most useful assistance in reading the proofs, in making many important suggestions, and in the arduous but indispensable work of verification. Last but not least, the biographer desires to express his gratitude to Mr. Humphrey Milford, most patient and considerate of publishers, for his unfailing help and personal interest from the very outset of the task; as well as his appreciation of the attention and scholarship of the printers and readers of the Oxford University Press.

THE PALACE, CHICHESTER. G. K. A. B.
July, 1935.

TABLE OF CONTENTS

VOLUME I

VOLUME II

LIST OF ILLUSTRATIONS

VOLUME I

VOLUME II

VOLUME I

CHAPTER I

EDINBURGH, HARROW, OXFORD

Mrs. Scott . . . liked Dr. Erskine's sermons; but was not fond of the Principal's, however rational, eloquent and well-composed, and would, if other things had answered, have gone, when he preached, to have heard Dr. Davidson. LOCKHART'S *Life of Scott*, ch. iv.

The family of Swinton is very ancient and was once very powerful. Ibid., ch. lv.

RANDALL THOMAS DAVIDSON was born on April 7, 1848, at No. 15 Inverleith Place, Edinburgh. He was the eldest of the four children of Henry and Henrietta Davidson. On May 18, 1848, he was baptized in the same house, according to the Presbyterian form, by Dr. Muir, Minister of St. Stephen's Church. He was of pure Scottish blood on both his father's and his mother's side; and his Scottish character as well as his love for Scotland were conspicuous throughout the eighty-two years of his life. Like many of his fellow countrymen, he attached not a little importance to his family history. His papers indicate both his own feeling for his ancestors and his accuracy as a chronicler. And so a brief chapter from that history may be given at once in his own words.

I

'Go back in thought two centuries and a little more. Queen Anne is on the throne. An eager controversy is in the air. Ought, or ought not, her two kingdoms, England and Scotland, to be united into one? The storm centre lies in Edinburgh, where the strife of tongues in the Parliament House and in the General Assembly finds ready echo on the open pavements of the High Street and the Canongate. The Act of Union struggled painfully into life, but even after it had, in March 1707, received the Royal Assent, the discussions, as Sir Walter Scott has taught us, were carried on with scarcely diminished force and pungency.

'The clergy of the City, intensely concerned for the security of the Presbyterian system, but doubtful whether the Union would strengthen or impair it, were eloquent on either side. Prominent among them was the Rev. Thomas Davidson, lecturer in the Tron Church of Edinburgh, and two years after the Union a Chaplain to Queen Anne. A devoted pastor, as well as a keen controversialist, he was promoted successively to the parishes of Whitekirk, of Stirling, and of the Cross Church, Dundee, where he became a recognised champion of the Church's rights and liberties. Like many Scotsmen of the day, he had close relations with Holland, where older members of the family had for many years held positions of high public trust. (Among these was Sir William Davidson, who had acted as political friend and adviser to William of Orange before he came to England.) During Thomas Davidson's ministry in Dundee his daughter Mary, already a widow, became the wife of the Rev. Thomas Randall, minister of Inchture in the Carse of Gowrie. The son of this marriage, born in 1747, inherited his father's name, Thomas Randall. He was grandfather to the subject of this memoir.

'Besides this daughter, Thomas Davidson had two sons. In view of subsequent history, it is not uninteresting to note that the younger of these, named Hugh, was ordained in the Church of England and became Rector of Kirby [Misperton] in Yorkshire. In the upbringing of the elder son, William, advantage was taken of the ancestral connexion with Holland, and the lad was sent to The Hague to complete his education. Settling in Holland, he became, we are told, "one of the most considerable and opulent general merchants at Rotterdam". He left Holland about 1750, and for the rest of his life resided in London and in Edinburgh. He is described as being "ostentatious and with numerous servants dressed in unsilvered white liveries".

'When in London he seems to have been regarded as a leader in financial circles. His portrait, by Sir Joshua Reynolds, shows a man of striking and dignified appearance. Of equal interest is the portrait of his only child, Susannah, whom Sir Joshua painted with a large lamb upon her lap. At the age of twenty, she died unmarried, and was, for some unexplained reason, buried in Westminster Abbey, where her monument in the North Transept bears a long and laudatory inscription. Her father, though he survived her for nearly thirty years, is said never to have recovered his spirits. Dying in 1794, he left his estates of Muirhouse and Hatton, near Edinburgh, together with a considerable fortune, to the Rev. Thomas Randall, son of his sister Mary, "on the express stipulation that the name of Randall should be for ever abolished, and that of Davidson substituted".

The motive actuating William Davidson in making this bequest seems to have been his desire to found a family of Scottish landed gentry, rather than affection for the nephew whom he thus enriched, or appreciation of his ministerial calling. Indeed the two Thomas Randalls, father and son, had little in common with the opulent merchant, except that they also were connected with Holland. It is necessary to go back a little way.

'In the year 1728, David Randall, who is described by the historian Wodrow as a man of capacity and public spirit,[1] had emigrated to Holland. His son, Thomas, after graduating in the University of Edinburgh, spent some time with his father in the flourishing Scottish settlement in Rotterdam. He then returned to Scotland and was ordained in 1739 as minister of Inchture. His marriage, while there, to Mary Davidson, daughter of the well-known minister of Dundee, has been mentioned above. Mary Davidson, already a widow, seems to have been in every way suited to be the wife of a man of Randall's character and powers. He rapidly became a leader among the clergy of the Church of Scotland. While minister of Inchture he was consulted by those who were promoting the Evangelical revival in England, and he is said to have been visited by John Wesley when he rode through the Carse of Gowrie in 1768.[2] At the same time he was prominent in his advocacy among Presbyterians of the more frequent Celebration of the Lord's Supper. His pamphlet on that subject became famous, and [Sir Henry Moncreiff, afterwards] Sir Henry Moncreiff Wellwood describes Dr. Randall as "a man whose learning, ingenuity and eminence as a Christian pastor entitled him to the first distinctions in the Church to which he belonged".[3] He was the author of the Forty-ninth "Paraphrase",[4] one of the best known of the collection which has for more than a century and a half been the Hymn Book of the Church of Scotland. In 1770, in which year he left Inchture and became minister of Stirling, he issued a Series of Tracts upon the constitution of the Church of Scotland, which is still regarded as a work of standard authority.

[1] See *The Ancestry of Randall Thomas Davidson, D.D.*, by Adam Philip (Elliot Stock, 1903), p. 1. [2] Ibid., p. 14.

[3] See *Life and Writings of J. Erskine, D.D.*, by Sir Henry Moncreiff Wellwood, 1818.

[4] Though perfect eloquence adorned
My sweet persuasive tongue;

This paraphrase was sung when R. T. D. visited the General Assembly in 1919.

'His ministry at Stirling, where again he was in a storm-centre of controversy, lasted for ten years. Dr. Burns, pastor of Kilsyth, speaks of "his more than magisterial command over the populace of the ancient burgh of Stirling and of the awe and dread which surrounded him on Sabbath and week-days".[1]

'At Inchture, in July 1747, was born the son of Thomas and Mary Randall. He, too, was christened Thomas. His early years were spent in his father's manse at Inchture, and, after a College course at Glasgow, he was sent to Holland, where he studied both at Utrecht and at Leyden, devoting himself particularly to the subject of Biblical criticism. He was licensed to preach at Rotterdam in 1769, and in the following year, on the removal of his father to Stirling, he was appointed his successor at Inchture. This was in persistent disregard of the wishes of his rich uncle, William Davidson, who desired that the young man should join the mercantile house over which he ruled. Thomas Randall, however, adhered to his purpose, and in a ministry of fifty-seven years exercised a constantly increasing influence throughout the Church of Scotland. Every writer (and they are many) who sets himself to depict the social and literary life of Edinburgh in the last quarter of the eighteenth century gives a prominent place to the gentle, devout, and charitable minister of the Tolbooth Church. Sir Walter Scott[2] records, in testimony to his mother's piety of conviction, her love of attending his ministrations. His portrait by Raeburn is well known, and has often been reproduced. In 1794, on the death of his uncle, William Davidson, he succeeded, as above mentioned, to the estates of Muirhouse and Hatton, and to a considerable fortune, and was required in consequence to change his name to Davidson.

'By his wife, Elisabeth Cockburn,[3] sister of the well-known Lord Cockburn, one of the leaders of Scotch Liberalism, and a joint founder of the *Edinburgh Review*, he had three sons, the youngest of whom was Henry, born in 1810, who became the father of Randall Thomas Davidson, the subject of this memoir. In his boyhood Henry was designated for the Scottish Bar. Educated in the High School of Edinburgh, and then in the famous

[1] For all this see Philip, *Ancestry*, &c., pp. 13–20.

[2] Lockhart's *Life of Scott*, ch. iii.

[3] He had been previously married to Elisabeth Rutherford, whose son inherited and spent his fortune.

Edinburgh Academy, (the foundation of which, under the auspices of Sir Walter Scott, Lord Cockburn and Francis Jeffrey,[1] has been often recorded,) and subsequently in the University of Edinburgh, where he earned distinction in English literature (under the tutelage of Professor Pillans and others), he decided, when his university days were over, to adopt a commercial rather than a legal career, and became almost immediately a prominent figure in the extensive shipping business of the Port of Leith. His musical powers and social gifts made him a favourite with the literary coterie depicted with graphic detail in Henry Cockburn's *Memorials of his Time*; while his activity as a horseman gave him access to a rather exclusive group among the hunting men of the Lothians.

'In 1845, Henry Davidson married Henrietta, daughter of John Swinton of Kimmerghame, a prominent member of the Berwickshire family of Swinton of Swinton, whose persistent place in Border annals for more than seven centuries is a topic which Sir Walter Scott, who had himself by his grandfather's marriage become one of the family, was fond of recounting both in prose and verse. When Henrietta Swinton was about twelve years old, Sir Walter Scott, in right (he said) of his "cousinship", enlisted the little girl as critic of the *Tales of a Grandfather*, then passing through the press, and she used to recount fifty years later how, to her legitimate pride, he re-wrote the chapter on "The Feudal System" because she found it difficult to understand it fully when he read it to her in its original form.

'Henry Davidson and his wife settled in a house, No. 15 Inverleith Place, Edinburgh, next door to the house, No. 16, occupied by the bride's father, Mr. Swinton, the two houses standing at the west end of Inverleith Place. There, in my parents' house, No. 15 Inverleith Place, I was born on April 7th, 1848, and there I was baptized, as my baptismal certificate shows, on May 18th, 1848, by Dr. Muir, minister of St. Stephen's Church. I read in my Mother's diary:

> *Thursday May 18th.* Fine. Randall was christened by Dr. Muir. My Aunts . . . and Archie, Mrs. J. Cockburn and Mary, Christian Davidson and M. D. being present. The two latter stayed to dinner.'

[1] See, e.g., account given in the *Life of Archbishop Tait*, vol. i, p. 21.

II

The influence of both parents on Randall was marked from the very start. Henry Davidson was a wood merchant in Leith. 'He was a very small man,' says Lord Dunedin, a neighbour and schoolfellow of Randall, 'blind of one eye but very lively, with a most engaging manner, and he was a great favourite.' With his children he shared fun and sport alike in full measure. Indeed, it may well be that from this keen sportsmanship of his father Randall got his own love for sport and for adventures in the open air. Thus he writes in his recollections:

> I was in closest personal friendship with my father from the earliest years. I used to stalk rabbits and magpies as soon as I was able to hold a gun, always under his eager personal tuition. He had been, and in some ways still was, a keen sportsman. He had once been an admirable rider, but he had given it up. He shot very well, and had in schooldays a reputation as a runner.

Both parents were deeply religious, and the simplicity and strength of his father's religion, especially at certain critical moments in the boy's life, made a great impression on Randall. But it was to his mother's teaching that Randall owed most. She, though less eager than her husband, had a resourcefulness and buoyancy of her own, coupled with a poetic gift which added considerable vividness to her lessons. To quote her son's recollections again:

> I do not find it easy to explain the remarkable influence which my mother was able to exercise over and among us all in religious matters and in Bible teaching. I think partly her poetic temperament—she was keenly poetic, and used to read and even write a good deal of poetry—gave her a power of putting things in the sort of way that made them interesting at the moment and rememberable afterwards, and of course her real absorption in the religious side of life, and the dominance which religion exercised upon all her thoughts and plans, domestic and personal, made it a natural thing that she should reveal incidentally to others, and especially to us, her children, what was so essentially the pivot of her own life.

But in addition to these more serious qualities, Randall continues:

> she had the gift of identifying herself with our interests, and even our amusements, which is certainly not very usual among people of her make. For example, the Christmas holidays were always

times when we had every sort of amusement in the way of specially arranged games, and acting and competitions, and in all these things she was indisputably the central moving force.

The immediate family circle to whom father and mother thus gave so much consisted of Randall, his sister Mary (born 1849), his brothers Henry (born 1851) and Ernest (born 1856). All grew up together, and though they followed different paths in later life, all acknowledged to the end the debt they owed to the vitality and religious sincerity of their parents.

The scene of many of the games which children and parents played together was the old home at Kimmerghame where Henrietta had been born. In Randall's boyhood his uncle, Archibald Swinton, the owner of Kimmerghame, made it the festive centre of all sorts of amusements and entertainments, and even the slightest sketch of these years would be at fault without some tribute not only to Kimmerghame but to the part Archibald Swinton played:

> We were often, perhaps generally, at Kimmerghame in the Christmas holidays. I have not recorded what we owe to my uncle, Archibald Swinton, for his unfailing and unending kindness to us all. He was a man who might, if Fortune had favoured him, have been a conspicuous figure in public life, not in Scotland only, but in Parliament or elsewhere. For many years Professor of Law in Edinburgh University, a post which to the best of my recollection he only resigned when his Berwickshire duties made continuous Edinburgh life impossible, he had a wide knowledge of public affairs, and he certainly had a remarkable gift of public speaking. In the General Assembly he was, for many years, one of the foremost, if not the foremost, lay figure; and in county affairs and many other fields of service he was conspicuous. In his earlier Edinburgh days, when a widower, he had made his home for long periods under my Father's roof, my parents being devoted to him and he to them. At Kimmerghame his hospitality was unbounded, and we were always among his spoilt and favoured guests. I and my brother Harry shot there whenever there was any shooting going, and during the winter weeks we had the run of everything in that way.

Randall also, as he grew older, derived

> endless gain from intercourse with him on all kinds of literary, historic, and legal matters in which his stores of cheery information were always forthcoming in the readiest way.

It is said by those who knew both that in his looks Randall resembled the Swintons rather than the Davidsons. Archibald Swinton had one child by his first marriage (for he married again in 1856) whose name was Kate, and of her Randall says:

> Kate and I were in our early years simply like brother and sister—a relationship which in one sense never waned in its character though our lives necessarily lay widely apart.

Miss Swinton, as an old lady in 1917, told the writer a prophetic story of how the English Prayer Book troubled Randall as a child. Once, when he was about seven, he said to her in great anger, 'What do you think those English have done?' She replied that she could believe anything of them. Randall said, 'They've altered the Bible!' He had just seen for the first time the Prayer Book version of the Psalter—the Scotch using the Old Testament version. Randall and Kate both vowed they'd never use the Prayer Book version after that!

Reference has already been made to the general religious teaching which Randall received from his parents and especially from his mother. To make the picture complete it will be well to add his recollections of their relation to the Church:

> As regards Churchmanship, our upbringing was very undenominational, to use a word which had not then been coined. My parents had both been brought up as devout Presbyterians, and in my early childhood they attended St. Stephen's Church, under the ministry of Dr. Muir, a famous old divine. It was he who baptized me in Inverleith Place, on 18 May, 1848, and I know that he tried to get my Father to become one of his Elders. Why my Father declined at that time I do not know, but I know that a little later on when similar requests came he always said he was more of an Episcopalian than a Presbyterian, and declined. When we were in Atholl Crescent (i.e. from 1854 onwards), my parents began to attend St. Thomas's Episcopal Church, the minister being the Rev. D. T. K. Drummond. Drummond had separated himself from the Scotch Episcopal Church, and had joined the little body of English Episcopalians. . . . When at Muirhouse we used to drive to Edinburgh on most Sundays to attend St. Thomas'; but pretty often we walked to Cramond Parish Church near Muirhouse, which my Father had loved from his boyhood, and which was then served by an odd, rather remarkable man, Dr. Colvin. . . . I have no recollection of receiving any

teaching upon Churchmanship, either Episcopal or Presbyterian, the religion taught us being wholly of the personal sort, but beautiful in its simplicity and reality. My Father absolutely declined to limit himself to one denomination. I remember the eagerness with which he answered someone who had made the remark that a man must be, surely, either a Presbyterian or an Episcopalian by saying emphatically, 'I am both: and if I were one or other only I should be false to my deepest beliefs.'

All through his life Randall Davidson was the possessor of a remarkable memory. He has left not a few reminiscences of his early days as a child in Edinburgh. The first thing he remembered was the return home of his father and mother after the Duke of Wellington's funeral, when he was four years old; and the picture of the hearse and great black plumes from an illustrated paper of the day. Another recollection was connected with the death of his great-uncle, Lord Cockburn:

> He and my father were devoted to one another (he was my father's uncle, brother of my grandmother) and I distinctly recall the sorrow of our house when he died (April 26, 1854). I was just six years old. I was perplexed as to how to reconcile this sorrow with the religious teaching my mother sedulously gave me, and I asked her bluntly why she was sad if he, Lord Cockburn, had gone to Heaven. She didn't answer and I persevered. 'Was he a good man? Is he in heaven?' Her honesty made her, I suppose, hesitate to reply very certainly about one who could hardly, for all his charm, be described as pious, and she left on my mind, without at all knowing it, the impression that he had been a bad man. I remember always connecting him (why I don't know) with 'Jeroboam, who made Israel to sin'—a most unfair parallel!

III

In May 1854, the family moved from Inverleith Place to 6 Atholl Crescent, a larger house nearer the centre of Edinburgh, from which Randall somewhat irregularly attended Mr. Oliphant's School for Boys and Girls in Charlotte Square ('I remember always thinking that the girls did much better than the boys'). But in May 1857 they left Edinburgh for Muirhouse, on the shore of the Firth of Forth, about four miles from Edinburgh and three miles from Dalmeny, Lord Rosebery's place. The house stood in an estate of some 240 acres, in the parish of Cramond about a mile from the village of Davidson's Mains. It was a substantial modern mansion built in the Gothic style by William Davidson, Henry's eldest brother, in 1830, on the site of the old seventeenth-century mansion, of which only two round towers survived. There were beautiful views and just the kind of garden and park to appeal to boys.

> From the first [writes Randall Davidson] we boys were indoctrinated in all sorts of country things. I have never known other children who kept such quantities of rabbits for whose tending they are personally responsible. We had about fifty, and used to drive them into the field on the west side of the approach, to eat in the early morning. We also became, for little boys, really knowing about birds and marine beasts, though never in the scientific way children would be taught to understand things now.

And there was always a pony.

The lessons which had begun in a mild form under Mr. Oliphant in Edinburgh were continued by governesses at Muirhouse, with the help of divinity students from the University, who acted as tutors before more serious schooling commenced.

In 1860, at the age of twelve, Randall was sent to a private school at Worksop, kept by the Rev. William Bury. He was there for two years, which were not very profitable. The motto of the school was curious—'Faint but pursuing'. Mr. Bury was a kind elderly man of strong Evangelical opinions, possessed of a large family, to which he added some twenty or twenty-five pupils with a view to increasing his income. The boys differed greatly in age and knowledge, and, as there was only one assistant, not much real education could be expected. A correspondence was maintained between Mr. Bury and Mr. Henry Davidson, from which it appears that Randall was like most boys, high-spirited, and even possessed (a terminal report runs) of 'an undue volatility at improper times'. On the other hand, Randall occasionally criticized his headmaster. Thus he said once, writing home:

> Mr. Bury is getting more addicted to caning now instead of giving tasks.

Looking back in later years, he wrote:

> I do not remember learning anything very thoroughly at Worksop, and yet I see by a letter which my Father preserved that Mr. Bury regarded me as, in some respects, his best pupil.
>
> I have all my life suffered from not having been thoroughly well grounded in Latin and Greek grammar in the way boys are

grounded now in good preparatory schools; also the school was too small for producing good results at games, and the successive ushers during my two years were anything but capable men or competent teachers.

The Scripture teaching was wearisome in the extreme after the stimulating lessons he had received at home. One taste he seems, however, to have been able to gratify, his delight in country sports, and the following experience, narrated in his own words, made a lasting impression:

Mr. Bury was a naturalist, and we learnt a great deal about butterflies and birds' eggs, and we used to take long walks through the neighbouring Dukeries, Mr. Bury having been a friend of the Duke of Newcastle, and I think of the Duke of Portland. He was also Chaplain to Mr. Foljambe at Osberton, a place about three miles from Worksop. We used to walk there on Sundays and by surreptitious arrangements did some birdnesting on the way. I remember my perplexity on being forced to kneel upright during the Litany in church with my trouser pockets full of water-hens' eggs from Osberton Lake.

A number of letters of this period have been preserved, and the ties which bound father and mother and their eldest son together were clearly of the strongest sort. Both parents wrote in an intimate and affectionate strain. Both entered to the full into his boyhood's tastes and difficulties. With his father, Randall had

an almost brotherly friendship through school and college days. Keenly athletic and intensely amusing, he had withal a deep personal religion which was impressed upon us in the frankest manner every day.

In more than one letter his father urged him to stand on his own ground. Thus he wrote:

HENRY DAVIDSON, ESQ., *to* RANDALL

14 March 1862.

I would strongly urge on you my dear Randall, always to stand *on your own ground.* You know right and wrong—better I am sure than many boys do, at any school you may go to—for few Mothers have taken the pains and loving labour yours has done with you—don't you be moved—*shoved—pushed—driven—laughed* off your own ground by any boy, or any number of boys. There is plenty of *fun*, without evil—and very soon one finds there is no *fun* in evil!

but it may be found too late. I believe NOTHING creates such respect, as for either boy or man *to stand on his own ground, and keep it*—and show you are keeping it too. And when you feel it difficult, just like Nehemiah before the King, silently ask God's help, and I cannot believe you won't get it—only of course, you must bear a bit of the burden yourself—it won't be made *so easy*, that you will have no farther trouble—but above all things be consistent.

Randall himself always wrote in a good straightforward way. Here is a regular schoolboy letter, picked out of many.

RANDALL DAVIDSON *to his* FATHER

Worksop. Wednesday.

My dear Papa

Thanks to Mary and Harry for their letters of yesterday.

Do you really intend to buy us a pony?

When do you expect Miss Turner home again?

I hope dear Mama is quite well again now.

I think my lessons are getting on very well. My favourite lesson is Latin verses, which we do from ¼ past 9 till 10.

Vickers is my greatest friend now that Houldsworth has left. I do not like sleeping with Dalton at all, but today Vickers has asked Mrs. Bury if he may change rooms with Dalton and as yet she has given no certain answer. There are many boys who appear very kind and friendly one day, and then again you find them speaking ill of you and teasing you as if you were their enemy: they make me think of the hymn

'Earthly friends may pain and grieve thee
One day kind the next day leave thee'

I have no more time today so good bye. Give my love to all at home. I am ever your very affectionate son

RANDALL.

P.S. I am very anxious to hear about the Pony.

At the end of the summer of 1862, it was decided that Randall should go to Harrow. But the very week before term began came the first of the many almost fatal accidents or illnesses which marked the whole of his career. The accident is thus described by Randall's father in a letter to his daughter Mary. Willy is a cousin and Master Ice the pony.

HENRY DAVIDSON, ESQ., *to* MARY

Do you know we nearly lost Randall on Saturday—he might now no more have been in the land of the living. All the party and Willy had taken the pony cart to the shore with cut branches

—and after tumbling them out, they *all* got into the cart and thought they would wash Ice's legs in the sea. Master Ice however wished a better bathe than this—he took the bit in his teeth and went straight out to sea. The cart floated up off its wheels and sank of course with so many in it. Randall jumped out in order to save Ernest by getting him out, and found the water up and over his chin. Willy put Ernest out to him. Poor fellow he tried to *carry* him, instead of dragging him in the water, but could not—stumbled and fell—the tide, which was ebbing, took him further out and he could do no more for Ernest but told him to lie still on his back with his arms out—which the brave little man did and floated perfectly. Randall called to Willy who was then out of the cart too to save Ernest—which he did. Harry stuck by the cart as he had the reins, and when Ice was fairly swimming he turned him to the shore, and then jumped out to get Ernest from Willy, that Willy might try and save Randall—he got off his coat, and little able to swim at all he went out to him—he had then sunk. Willy was afraid he might seize him so went near carefully, got hold of the hair of his head, but by this time Randall was insensible, so he was dragged to shore, and laid down on the wet sand, face down and Willy beat his back, and Harry rushed up to the house for help—met your Mamma at the door and told her in great agitation that *Randall was drowned.* But as we know Harry's little keen statements she asked him if he was out of the water and learned he was lying on the beach. I suppose the distance from the house to the gate was never travelled faster than by your Mother and Charlton. When the former got down Randall began to recover consciousness and spoke. Charlton came and *blew* into his mouth, which Randall declared afterwards was vastly abominable—and worked at him to make him breathe. Ice meantime with the wheelless cart stood as pacific as usual. Charlton walked in, to complete the matter, to save *the wheels* which were also recovered!—and so what might have been a very sad and tragical affair mercifully ended well—and more than that—for *all* even to Ernest, seem to have acted so well and so plucky, as to have really gained great praise. Randall and your Mother were both '*queer*' yesterday, but nothing worse. Now this is a very long story—but it has been a very narrow escape, and but for Willy being there both Randall and Ernest would apparently have been lost. Not a creature was on the shore to help.

Randall got sea water into his lungs, and this did him harm for long afterwards. Otherwise there were no ill effects. But it was his first narrow escape from death.

IV

In September 1862, he entered Harrow. Of the choice of his school he writes as follows:

> What led my Father to choose Harrow I forget, if I ever knew. He knew nothing about English Public Schools, and if he had had wise advice he would not, I think, have sent me, as he did, to a small House.
>
> It had, however, the advantage of beginning my life-long friendship with Arthur Watson, who then had a small House (Byron House) occupied in after years by Matthew Arnold. I happily retained the friendship of Arthur Watson for many years, and his kindness to me was unvarying during nearly half a century. He was a Rugbeian under Tait, was then at Balliol, and was afterwards a Fellow of All Souls. He at once opened for me new channels of thought; he was a cultivated Radical, and I had not been much in touch with Radicals.
>
> I remember to this day the impression made on me by his talk at meals on political subjects, and my inward revolt against the silly scorn with which my companions, and I with them, thought it our duty to regard Liberal opinions. He set me thinking upon many subjects in a way which has borne fruit ever since.

Arthur (known as Vanity) Watson, though a layman, also prepared Randall for confirmation. Scarlet fever prevented his being confirmed with the rest of the boys at Harrow; and he was in fact confirmed by Bishop Tait (his future father-in-law) in St. George's, Hanover Square, on June 16, 1865. He was seventeen at the time; but he says, 'It was by my own wish that I was delayed rather beyond the usual age.' He liked relating afterwards how a kinsman found him in the church, the solitary occupant of a large pew—the said kinsman going up and down the church, looking into the pews and saying repeatedly in a loud voice, with strong Scotch accent, 'Is Randall Davidson here? Is Randall Davidson here?' Afterwards he was taken off to a high-class restaurant for lunch, and given cutlets done in champagne, a dish he never tasted again!

Byron House consisted of only six or seven boys, and the loss in games and companionship was so great that Davidson persuaded his father to move him for his last year to Westcott's, where he had many friends. To change from one house to another required a little care on the part of those concerned; for no housemaster likes to lose a promising pupil, and the very suggestion was a difficult one for the pupil to make. The negotiations were, however, so capably handled by Davidson that he got his way and yet retained his friendship with Watson. The following letter, while revealing the schoolboy, is most characteristic of that ability to get his own way without hurting other people's feelings which was to be so remarkable a quality of his later life:

RANDALL DAVIDSON *to his* FATHER

Byron House. Saturday, May 26[, 1866.]

. . . I have been feeling lately, more than I ever did before, a craving for the society and companionship of other fellows well up in the school, and desire for *intellectual* friends *in the house*. Poor old Mahon though an excellent fellow has about as much *thought* in him, on any subject, as this quill pen. All the VIth Form fellows in Westcott's house keep begging me to come into their house, and I really feel that I would give anything to do so. Then comes the question. Could Westcott receive me, either in September or January? *This* I should like to ascertain, before saying anything to Watson on the subject, and if he could *not* receive me, I would let the subject drop and never tell him (Watson) that I had thought of leaving him. But I am sure that Westcott would make an effort to do so, and if he could I should be *so* thankful. I know you will think me awfully *turncocky*, but I know my mind now, and my motive for the wish. The more I see of Westcott and of the fellows in the house, the more I feel what a *superior lot* they are and the more I long to be one of them. As to Watson's feelings on the subject, I feel sure that were I to explain to him my motives he would sympathize fully with me—and would not be offended. If *you* approve, don't you think the best way would be for *you* to send a line to Westcott asking him to *speak to me* on the subject, as I think that would have more weight with him than if I were to go and ask him myself? At the same time you begging him not to mention it to Watson, if he could *not* receive me at all.

Sunday Night, May 27.

I have been walking today with Tupper, who thinks it very probable that Westcott will manage somehow to receive me, at Christmas if not next term. If you write, perhaps it would be better to send the letter *through me*. In that case I should give it him at some time when he could not possibly see Watson before he saw me again. I know he would say nothing till he had thought over it.

But you manage that as you think best. If you don't approve of the change, then never mind, as I have no doubt I shall get on all right where I am—and can console myself by thinking that 'Distance lends enchantment to the view'.

The petition was successful, and the last year of his Harrow life was spent in Westcott's House, where he shared a room with Graham Murray (later Lord Dunedin), whose parents were intimate friends of Randall's parents at Edinburgh. Lord Dunedin described him later as 'not having any special position in the school, but very easy to live with, as he was good natured and not quarrelsome or even argumentative'.

The two greatest influences on Davidson at Harrow were the headmaster, Dr. H. M. Butler, and his new housemaster, B. F. Westcott. He was under Butler in the Upper Sixth from September 1864 to July 1867, and found his teaching 'a constant source of interest and gain'. Butler's sermons also impressed him quite remarkably, and there is many a letter written on the Sunday or Monday giving a full account of Butler's Sunday sermon and showing how much it meant to the boy—though there were occasional exceptions. The friendship which began at Harrow grew in after days and lasted nearly sixty years.

A deeper impression still was made by Westcott, 'for whom I entertained from the first a kind of reverence which never left me till he died'. He writes:

> Westcott was to us VIth Form boys very much what he has always remained to me—the Prophet to whom we looked for intellectual guidance on every subject, human and divine. I would give a great deal now to have over again the kind of talks he used to give to us advanced boys on subjects lying quite outside the then School Curriculum, e.g. the leading Features of the Middle Ages, the Growth and Character of Christian Architecture, the Influence of Great Men upon their Times, and so on. He was often quite over our heads, at least over mine, but that was all the better. I think he did really give us a spur which was bound to be lifelong towards the better understanding of things outside the run of schoolboy literature. He was the first to make any of us think about Browning, and, indeed, I know of no one else at Harrow who ever mentioned Browning. And he utterly bewildered us by his plunges into Kant and Comte and hagiology.

Westcott was not, however, by any means always at his best

similar books on the Old Testament, and my interest in the Old Testament became very keen.

In the summer holidays, August 1866, just before Randall's last year at Harrow, came the accident which influenced the whole of his life. It is so important, that the Archbishop's own description must be given in full:

I had been shooting rabbits with my brother and another friend at Muirhouse, and on our return into the house my friend, by some accident, let off his gun into my back. He said he was taking out the cartridges, but what exactly happened we never knew. He was only a few feet from me. We knew that the whole charge had gone in in a lump, making a hole big enough, as my Father always put it, to hold an average orange. In the confusion of treatment pending the arrival of a doctor, they threw everything away, and were unable to say afterwards how many shot had been taken out of the wound in the rush of blood, etc. The wound was so fearful that when the surgeon, Spence, who had been summoned from Edinburgh, arrived an hour later, he thought my life hopeless, and consequently, as I have always understood, abstained from doing what he would otherwise have tried to do, taking my right leg off or 'out' by the socket—a fearful operation.

(Strange to say, the facts came to light nearly fifty years later. When I was ill in 1913, there was some desire to investigate internal conditions, and the Röntgen rays were applied. This revealed a condition of things which the surgeons found to be of supreme interest. The surgeons were excited about it, and sent for me to see the skiagraph of my inside, pointing out that we could clearly count 164 shot, and that there were black patches which might contain more. That these should have been carried unconsciously by me for half a century, and not one of them should have interfered with ducts or other little organs, was surely an amazing thing! They were widely scattered through the whole of the lower trunk.)

The treatment was extraordinarily unlike what would have been given me in the way of nursing, etc., a generation later. Except my Mother, the only nurse was a Mrs. Barr, a monthly nurse, who had never had anything to do with surgery of the wound type and was simply a worthy old lady, who took all pains possible but knew nothing. My Mother was devoted to the last degree, but the absence of antiseptic treatment—universal, I suppose, since these years, but then comparatively unknown—contrasts strangely with what one has been accustomed to in surgical patients for the last

HENRY DAVIDSON
Father of R. T. D.
(*After* 1878)

HENRIETTA DAVIDSON (*née* SWINTON)
Mother of R. T. D.
(*About* 1878)

in preaching to boys, and the following letter gives an amusing as well as a shrewd account of the favourite master's defects.

RANDALL DAVIDSON *to his* FATHER

Rev. B. F. Westcott's. Feb. 17th, 1867.

. . . We had a very learned sermon from Westcott this morning, which might possibly have been intelligible had one been thoroughly well up in the Ecclesiastical histories of Rome, Greece, and Syria for the first 5 centuries A.D. As it was I don't suppose 10 fellows in the school could follow it. Not above 100 could hear it! His voice is feebler than ever. He is certainly a nice little fellow to talk to, and does one no end of good. He lets the most extraordinary, not to say ludicrous, remarks fall from him in a sort of soliloquy. The other day I was speaking to him of Trevelyan's Book on the Indian Mutiny (Cawnpore) and he said, 'Yes . . . yes . . . yes . . . that was the book—yes. . . . I could not shake off the idea that it was the prophet Ezekiel done into bad English,' and all this said not to me but to himself. He cries out lustily against my ale and hot meat—of course to no avail. He says 'look at me! I *lived* on cold meat when I was at Cambridge almost entirely'. I think to *look at him!* is quite enough!

Davidson's careful attention to sermons has already been noticed, and among the masters whose preaching impressed him we should not forget the Rev. John Smith, whose religious influence was of an unusual kind. In one of his letters to his father he said, 'We have had a most beautiful sermon this morning from Mr. Smith', and he gave an account of a sermon on two standards of religion. His father wrote to him with regard to the same preacher: 'I have been delighted with two accounts you have sent your Mother of sermons from Mr. Smith and Mr. Butler. Cultivate the acquaintance and society of the former as much as possible.'

The Archbishop summed up his own impressions in la[illegible] years, as follows:

People complained then, as they do now, of the lack of [illegible] religious life in the Public Schools. I can only say that my [illegible] tion of Harrow is a recollection of continuous and helpf[illegible] influence. Watson, though a layman, prepared his b[illegible] for Confirmation; he was a follower of Jowett in T[illegible] keen student of the Bible, and especially interes[illegible] of thought as are followed in Stanley's *Jewish*

quarter of a century. But it was strongly in my favour that my physical health was so good: I was in the best possible training, was absolutely temperate and healthy, and the vitality of that age of life is, I suppose, difficult to estimate. I can, however, remember details which would seem almost incredible now, and I marvel a good deal that the high medical and surgical authorities who looked after me were satisfied even in those days with the manner of things. Strange to say, I fancy that those were the very years in which Lister was inaugurating his antiseptic treatment in Edinburgh itself.

However, by degrees I recovered, although I was laid up for many months, the latter part of the time being spent in the back drawing-room at Muirhouse, which was transformed into a bed-room for me. I got about at first on crutches, which I had to use for a long time, and it was supposed that my leg would always be more or less helpless; but by degrees this went away, and I got back full power, save for a permanently weak ankle, which seems a strange effect to follow from a wound in the hip. There were also other troubles inaugurated, which have never passed away, though I have been able to ignore them more or less. Had anyone prophesied in those autumn months that I should a couple of years later be winning a cup at racquets at Oxford, it would have been ludicrous.

Randall returned to Harrow, entering Westcott's House, in January 1867, more or less a cripple. Just after seeing him off, his father wrote him a letter:

HENRY DAVIDSON, ESQ., *to* RANDALL

Muirhouse, Davidson's Mains, Edinburgh — Friday night, 25 Jany. [1867]

. . . I went to your room last night—deserted, black and cold. I always think of these rooms on the nights you leave, as if they were the former abodes of those now gone from earth. It is somehow so like this. On this occasion I sat down and thought of the memories of which that room was *full*—the suffering, the anxieties, the little bed and Barr—the softly-shutting door—the way in which we used to steal in to look at you—the cradled bed—the cradle still hanging, a memento—it was all like a dream—as life will soon be—life itself with *all* its memories—and there were the crutches hanging, belonging to a later scene of the story—and you are gone, and able to go—without a wrecked body, or injured health, but with a life marvellously preserved. May it be preserved for real good and usefulness—to be the means of preserving others from worse than your sufferings and trial. I thank God for it all. I am sure it has only the more endeared you to us all—how different might it not have been this night. I was calling at Granton to-day, and, speaking of you, Sir John said you within an ace escaped the femoral artery being struck; had it been, death would have ensued within 15 minutes! These are all things to think of. We could then see how near you were to loss of life and limb—but how often must we in our lives be near the same, and all unknown to us.

He had a hole in his thigh, Lord Dunedin bears witness, having seen it himself at the time in the room they shared, that 'a small child could have put his fist in'. Other games were denied him, but he managed to keep up squash racquets with some success. As to prizes, Davidson writes:

My accident came at the very moment when I was most keen about some of the great School Prizes, and of course put me out of the running. I obtained the Prize for English Verse, a Poem on Sir Walter Scott, and was near the top in several other competitions. In competing for the Beaumont Prize for Scripture, I had been the Prize Winner in the Vth Form, and Second in the Senior. I had hoped without fail to obtain the First in the Autumn of 1866,[1] but the accident intervened.

V

His accident also spoilt his chance of a scholarship at Oxford:

I had hoped for a scholarship at Oxford, and probably, but for my accident, I might have counted upon one. I entered for a Corpus scholarship, which was won by Abbot. Failing a scholarship it had been intended that I should go to Balliol, but owing to some mistake or change about dates, particulars of which I

[1] There is a photograph in *The Harrow Life of Dr. Butler* (p. 150) giving the members of the Harrow School Debating Society 1866. The twenty-one portraits show an exceptionally distinguished set of senior boys, amongst whom were A. G. Murray, Solicitor-General, Lord Justice-General of Scotland, afterwards Viscount Dunedin, G.C.V.O.; T. H. Ponsonby, Manager of St. James's Street Branch of Lloyds Bank, afterwards Ponsonby-Fane; H. H. Montgomery, Bishop of Tasmania, Secretary to S.P.G., Prelate of the Order of SS. Michael and George; C. B. Heberden, Fellow and Principal of Brasenose College, Oxford; R. T. Davidson, Archbishop of Canterbury; C. L. Tupper, Member of the Legislative and Executive Councils of the Punjab; B. Bosanquet, Professor of Moral Philosophy at St. Andrews; R. G. Tatton, Fellow of Balliol, Member of Council of Toynbee Hall; H. N. Abbot, Head of the School 1866–7, C.C.C. Oxford, 1st Mods. and Finals, Solicitor, a leading citizen of Bristol.

forget, no room could be found there for me as a Commoner, and I accordingly went to Trinity. (Why Trinity was selected I do not remember.) To Trinity I went for matriculation in October 1867. My exact contemporary—I walked side by side with him to the Vice-Chancellor for matriculation—was Edgar Gibson, afterwards Bishop of Gloucester. He had come up from Charterhouse, and he, too, was, I think, disappointed at being a Commoner when he might have been expected to be sure of a scholarship.

Davidson always looked back upon his Oxford career as a time of disappointment, and the disappointment began in his very first term:

My health was at that time in a very odd state. Many of the things that I, with other boys, had done I had to give up, both as regards games and books; learning repetition became curiously difficult, and my memory failed in the oddest way for days altogether. There was an idea that I should vegetate abroad for a year before going to Oxford, but I strongly deprecated this as severing me from all my friends who were going straight from school to Oxford.

However, after one term I was, without being actually laid up, so unwell—headaches, loss of memory, etc., that I was peremptorily ordered to go abroad. After discussion in the Christmas holidays of 1867, my parents arranged that we should all go together. Accordingly they, and my sister and I, and a young widow, Mrs. Lockhart, whom my father wanted to befriend, went off together.

It is true that he travelled, and travelled delightfully, but:

Everybody who knows University life [he said later] will realise the almost unmendable mischief which arises from an undergraduate being absent from Oxford during his second and third terms; he gets out of touch with College and University life at the very time when it matters most he should become a part of it.

The President of Trinity in 1867 was Mr. Samuel Wayte, for whom Davidson had not much respect. He describes him as very small, fat, sulky, ugly, and a stammerer. He adds: 'Without exception he is the most silent man I know... he walks sideways.' The Dean was the Rev. A. Plummer, 'a pleasant, jovial, round-faced, dark individual with bushy whiskers and considerable ideas of his own dignity. I do not think much of his Bible lectures.' The youngest Don, and the man Davidson liked best, was

R. W. Raper, 'very handsome and quite an undergraduate in spirit still'.

The Trinity set to which he belonged was not composed mainly of very thoughtful men, nor were his contemporaries on the whole men who distinguished themselves in after life, though there were two future bishops amongst them, Edgar Gibson, Bishop of Gloucester, and W. W. Perrin, Bishop first of Columbia and then of Willesden.

His letters show him to have taken a good deal of interest in political issues. He spoke sometimes at the Union, and was a keen supporter and member of the Canning Club. He played racquets and fives, but rowing and violent exercise were forbidden on grounds of health. He kept in close touch with his old school, and on one occasion in his first term had 'a very jolly day' with a somewhat perilous conclusion when he rode in a four-in-hand with post-boys to Harrow.

RANDALL DAVIDSON *to his* FATHER

Sunday, Novr. 17th, 1867.

I spent a very jolly day yesterday *at Harrow*—I was asked on Friday night to fill a vacant place in a drag which was to take a football eleven from Paddington down to Harrow. We did the thing in style with 4 spanking greys and post boys. The latter got rather the worse for liquor towards night, and, having forgotten to bring lamps, considerably perilled our limbs in taking us up to Paddington (in 55 minutes) at 8 o'clock p.m. We ran into one cart and one *bus*, but no damage done. The horses too had a propensity to get the traces between their legs. This occurred no less than 3 times on our return. Everyone at Harrow seems to be flourishing.

His wish 'to be ultimately ordained' went back as far as he could 'remember anything' in his life. He looked forward to ordination all the time he was at Oxford. But the great Church questions which interested men who were contemporary at Oxford and afterwards became close friends, like Edward Talbot and Henry Scott Holland, troubled him not at all:

It now seems to me quite odd how entirely outside the thoughts of myself and my friends at Oxford were the big ecclesiastical questions which were agitating great sections of Oxford men—reverberating memories of Newmanism; controversies about Jowett and his beliefs; Liddon's clericalism; Edward King's influence, which everybody now speaks about—as belonging to those very years, were wholly ignored by our Trinity folk. I can scarcely remember anyone there who cared about these questions. My home upbringing had been quite off what are ordinarily called *ecclesiastical* lines, though religion was its very backbone.

Sermons such as those of Wilberforce, Dean Burgon, Liddon, and Pusey he attended with profit, and he found special stimulus in Liddon's series of lectures on the Epistle to the Hebrews in the Hall of Queen's College. 'They touched the religious note, which was after all the deepest in my life.'

Indeed, Scot that he was, he liked sermons and constantly wrote home his criticisms of the preacher as he had done at Harrow. Thus, in 1869, he referred to Archbishop Tait, whose appointment as Archbishop, he said in an earlier letter, 'is very popular among those who have *broad* Church tendencies (a considerable and increasing majority), also among Evangelicals. But *Highs* (or Popes as they are called here) cannot abide it'.

RANDALL DAVIDSON *to his* MOTHER

The Archbishop preached here this morning [May 16, 1869] a long, very careful, slightly pedantic, rather dry and strikingly unattractive discourse. Such at least was *my* opinion. This afternoon we had a contrast in Goulburn, whose eloquence, fervour and practicability were all remarkable. He was very bold in his remarks on the English Church generally and used strong language with regard to Disestablishment.

On one occasion at least, on the eve of the Vatican Council, October 1869, he went to the Roman Catholic Church.

RANDALL DAVIDSON *to his* MOTHER

Oct. 16, 1869.

I went the other night to hear the great Monsignor Capel preach on the coming Council. His subject then was 'infallibility', a very interesting topic on which to have heard him—and if what he said is all that can be said for it, it is a very weak point. However it is scarcely fair to judge him by a sermon addressed in Church to a congregation supposed to consist only of R. Catholics. He referred to Cumming, fully allowing the crimes of the various Popes, but accurately distinguishing between infallibility and impeccability. I should like to have been able to get up and ask him some questions.

The sermons in the College chapel were disappointingly few. In his first letter home as a freshman, October 14, 1867, he wrote: 'I am much disappointed with the *Chapel* here. There are only *two* sermons in the term! and *no organ*!!!'

Outside his work for the Schools, he did a good deal of desultory reading, and there are some interesting letters to his cousin Kate Swinton on Tennyson's *Idylls of the King*. His main study, however, was History:

> After returning from abroad in 1868, I decided to read for Honours in History and did read pretty widely, though never, I think, under very close direction. We had no history tutor or lecturer in Trinity, and my instructors were Lang of Corpus, Newman of Balliol, George of New College, and Creighton of Merton. I remember no other lecturers than these, and no one of the four took any particular interest in my studies.
>
> In my last year I attended lectures from Bryce on Roman law, and incidentally got a great deal of historical information and guidance from him as he became a very real personal friend. I had some private coaching from Jayne of Jesus, and from Knox of Merton, but, looking back now upon the whole training, I seem to realise how different it might have been if I had had some friend or tutor who had taken me more thoroughly in hand and advised me more in detail what to read, and how. The fault may have been my own, for I was probably desultory and was certainly, owing to ill health, irregular, but there was a total lack of system in the course I followed.

His health was very poor throughout his time at Oxford. He was very near a break-down, and was nervous and unhappy. At one time he had hoped for a First, but as the Schools drew near he was again really unwell, and on the second day of the examination in May 1871 he collapsed. He had, however, done so well in the little that he had been able to attempt, that the examiners gave him a Third. What even this must have meant to a boy as able and as anxious to succeed as Randall, may be judged from the letter written a year before to his cousin Kate Swinton.

RANDALL DAVIDSON *to* KATE SWINTON

Feb. 20, 1870.

Pray don't be unhappy about my reading—I shall not yet give up *thoughts* of honours though I may draw back when the time

> comes. If I had due humility and contentment I should prefer a '*third* CLASS' to a mere 'pass', but as I haven't I prefer the '*pass*'! Perhaps I may get meeker as the time goes on.

On the final result he says:

> I have had a great many disappointing periods and incidents in my life, but none were equal to the disappointment of those days, when I contrasted them with the hopes and resolves and expectations which had been mine both at Harrow and in the early Oxford days.[1]

[1] Even as late as 1920 the sense of disappointment remained. Thus, writing to his old friend Bishop Edward Talbot (of Winchester) on the occasion of the latter's golden wedding, he said (June 27, 1920): 'Fifty years is a long long time. Fifty years ago I was a poor, rather feckless, but aspirant invalid undergraduate. Another year had to pass before I could present myself to the examiners, and in 1870 I was still hopeful, and didn't foresee the collapse which was to make the "Schools" a humiliation! Already you were a potentate and you were off with your Lady to the German Army!' Davidson was, however, made an Honorary Fellow of Trinity on June 8, 1903; and Dr. H. E. D. Blakiston (President of Trinity) has informed the biographer that he was the *first commoner* to receive that distinction, which began with Cardinal Newman, ex-President Wayte, Lord Lingen, and others who had been either Scholars or Fellows, such as A. V. Dicey (Fellow) and James Bryce (Scholar).

CHAPTER II

THE TEMPLE. DARTFORD TO LAMBETH

Every Scotchman, with very few exceptions, holds country exercises of all kinds to be part of his nature. LOCKHART's *Life of Scott*, ch. lii.

He would not allow Scotland to derive any credit from Lord Mansfield; for he was educated in England. 'Much (said he) may be made of a Scotchman, if he be *caught* young.' BOSWELL's *Life of Dr. Johnson* (1772).

RANDALL DAVIDSON was already twenty-three years old when he left Oxford. But three more years were to pass before he entered the ministry. He was a delicate man, and certainly he had not yet sufficient strength to start on his life's work. It was therefore of great importance that he should now devote himself to the task of regaining his health. And the prescription for his recovery involved both plenty of fresh air and a change of scene.

I

For the first few months after taking his degree, he spent a very happy outdoor life on Tweedside, where his father was the tenant of Yair. There was plenty of sport, and he thoroughly enjoyed fishing for salmon, and shooting grouse; with his brother Harry as his constant companion, he was out all day from morning till night. The months in the open air in the same place were followed by more months of foreign travel. Early in 1872, Randall and his father and mother made a tour of Italy. There was plenty of sightseeing—in the Italian Lakes, Florence, Naples, and Pompeii. But the chief portion of the holiday was spent at Rome. And it is remarkable that, though often visiting other parts of Italy in later life, and though fascinated by the history and the architecture of Rome, yet his visit of this year was the first and last he ever paid to the city. He loved the buildings, and the pictures, and took much trouble in learning the language. He was taught by a famous Italian professor who, at his first application, refused, as his whole time was occupied, but had then sent for him and offered to give him lessons at the hotel at which Lord Randolph Churchill was staying. The professor said that Lord Randolph had engaged him at 9 a.m. on alternate mornings, but he was never up when he came; and so he offered to take Davidson at the same hour, if he cared to take his chance! Davidson took his chance, received his lessons at the hotel for many weeks, and never once did Lord Randolph appear! He could give a very good account of his experiences, storing them in his wonderful memory, so as to be able to check by what he had seen the stories others told him in later years. He kept a careful diary throughout the tour. One entry records his visit to the Vatican to see Pope Pius IX:

> *Friday, March 1*. . . . We spent the morning in being presented to the Holy Father. Mr. Maynard, Duff and I, together with Miss Edwards. . . . After miles of ascending stairs we were ushered by scarlet chamberlains into a mighty and gaunt waiting-room, with hard-backed wooden chairs. After half an hour of this we were removed to one of the 'Loggie', which was full of chairs on either side, and here we awaited his Holiness a full hour. At length he appeared with his Cardinals and marched down one side and up the other looking as jolly and comfortable as possible and addressing a few words in French to most of the foreigners present. But I was disappointed with the ceremony and had looked for something more imposing in the way of a Court. It is a dreary thing to spend a morning in dress clothes.

Six weeks later, at the end of the Italian tour, Davidson paid his first visit to Canterbury. He crossed from Calais to Dover, and on the early morning of April 15, breaking his journey to London, started with a single companion for the cathedral of the successor of St. Augustine, the Apostle of the English. He noted in his diary that he spent four most profitable hours in the city, and fresh from all his Italian travels he added:

> I don't think any foreign Cathedral I have seen surpasses this in beauty.

The very next day he started on his regular training for Holy Orders at the Temple under Dr. Vaughan.

The plan of reading, as one of Vaughan's 'Doves', in the purlieus of the Temple, had been suggested to Davidson by his old Harrow teachers, Dr. Butler and Dr. Westcott. It was to be a trial trip—if his health stood the tax of six months' consecutive study in London, the way might then be considered open for ordination.

Dr. Charles Vaughan had begun training young men for the ministry when Vicar of Doncaster, and he continued the work as Master of the Temple. He was an excellent scholar, a good parish priest, and above all a most remarkable expositor and preacher, whose sermons were not only brilliant in phrasing and delivery, but also charged with a strong moral appeal. He was a Broad Churchman, whose contact with the Benchers at the Temple gave him a special opportunity for appreciating the lay attitude to religion. And he was a master of the treasures of the Bible. His method of training his young men (from whom he took no fees) was to give them rooms in and about the Temple—assign them districts, in which the parochial clergy superintended their work, secure that they had some training in Sunday schools, and then himself give them lectures, see them personally, make them write sermons for him and criticize them freely. Davidson himself had lodgings first in 16 Devereux Court, and later in Thanet Place. He writes:

All this life was wholly unlike the routine of an ordinary theological college. Indeed Vaughan spoke with scant respect—though with marked reserve—about theological colleges, of which practically, as one must be honest, he knew very little. The teaching he gave us was personal, not according to any examination system. . . . He gave us very little history, either primitive or later; scarcely anything philosophical; but he had an extraordinary power of bringing out from the text of scripture things new and old; thoughts basic after all in the best theologies, and practical in their ceaseless referring of us back to the teachings of the Bible itself. . . .

We wrote sermons for him every week, and he used to read out to the assembly one or more of these after he had carefully examined and annotated them all. I was not infrequently subjected to the rather trying ordeal of having one of my crude productions thus set forth in all the smoothness of Vaughan's manner of speech. But sometimes we were allowed to send, not an actual sermon, but just our carefully arranged notes for it, and he would then give us his own notes on the same subject. Besides all this he used to set us the task of writing on subjects like the Atonement, Forgiveness, or the like, and in these we could speak freely about our thoughts and beliefs without fear of jarring upon him. Nor would he at all object, unless it were with placid humour and wit, to our putting forth opinions of an ecclesiastical sort with which

Feb 1972

RANDALL DAVIDSON

RANDALL DAVIDSON AGE 68

RANDALL DAVIDSON

ARCHBISHOP OF CANTERBURY

By G. K. A. BELL

BISHOP OF CHICHESTER

THIRD EDITION

GEOFFREY CUMBERLEGE
OXFORD UNIVERSITY PRESS
LONDON NEW YORK TORONTO
1952

Oxford University Press, Amen House, London E.C. 4
GLASGOW NEW YORK TORONTO MELBOURNE WELLINGTON
BOMBAY CALCUTTA MADRAS CAPE TOWN
Geoffrey Cumberlege, Publisher to the University

FIRST PUBLISHED 1935
SECOND EDITION 1938
THIRD EDITION 1952

REPRINTED LITHOGRAPHICALLY IN GREAT BRITAIN

PREFACE TO THIRD EDITION

SINCE this book was first published Randall Davidson's two immediate successors in the See of Canterbury have died, and have been the subjects of admirable Lives: *Cosmo Gordon Lang* by J. G. Lockhart, and *William Temple* by F. A. Iremonger. The wide welcome which each received testified not only to the understanding and ability of the biographer, but also to the great interest which his theme aroused.

In issuing a third edition of the present biography, I propose, with due regard to those works, to offer a few general reflections on the development of the office of Archbishop of Canterbury during three primacies from 1903 to 1944. And I shall take an occasional glance farther back by way of illustration.

Randall Davidson was enthroned two years after Queen Victoria's death. The end of her reign meant the end of an epoch. The whole character of British life had been transformed between 1837 and 1901. The first Reform Bill of 1832 had already been enacted before she came to the throne. The railway age, the age of coal and iron, had begun. By the middle of the century the industrial and commercial revolution was gathering its full strength. Science was advancing all along the line. Great strides were made in social legislation and in the Trade Union movement. In 1870 a national system of universal primary education was instituted. The Universities were reformed and extended. Before the end of the century the new journalism had arrived. By 1901 the population of England and Wales had risen to over 32 million, as compared with just under 14 million seventy years before. And a fresh epoch began in the range and diversity of the Empire. Added to this there were great changes in the framework of the Church, through the various measures of Church reform. Convocation resumed its Sessions in 1852, after being suppressed for a hundred and thirty five years. The Evangelical party had considerable influence, especially in the early years of the century. There were the Tractarian, the Broad Church, the Christian Social movements. And by the passing of the Matrimonial Causes Act in 1857 the Church of England lost her jurisdiction over marriages, and the re-marriage of divorced persons was made legal.

The Archbishop of Canterbury holds a spiritual office. To this the style of official documents bears witness: 'We [*Randall Thomas*] by Divine Providence Archbishop of Canterbury, Primate of all England and Metropolitan.' His office also gives him a position of immense responsibility and many functions in Church and State. Much has always depended on the personal qualities and attainments of the individual Primate. But the course of these last fifty years, more I think than that of the fifty years preceding, shows that while the prestige of the institution may have waned, the character and gifts of the person count for more and more.

Archbishop Howley died in 1848, the year when Randall Davidson was born, 'in a week of Continental hurly-burly and of disorder at home'. He was the last Prince Archbishop of Canterbury. When he dined out, no one left the room till he rose to go. At the public banquets at Lambeth, 'the domestics of the Prelacy stood, with swords and bag-wigs, round pig, and turkey, and venison'. He drove abroad in a coach and four, and when he crossed the courtyard of Lambeth Palace from the chapel to 'Mrs. Howley's Lodgings', he was preceded by men bearing flambeaux.[1] How different from the picture of William Temple touring the parishes of Croydon on a summer evening with Mrs. Temple, in his chaplain's little car, as the bombs exploded, or sleeping on a sofa in a ground-floor passage at Lambeth during the air-raids of 1944![2]

The contrast between Archbishop Howley and his successors of this century in relation to political and social questions may be judged from this episode. In 1832 popular feeling in Canterbury was very strong against those who had in any way opposed the passing of the Reform Bill, and the Archbishop had been active in opposition. That year, as he arrived in Canterbury for an official visit, he was greeted by a mass demonstration of people congregated in the immediate vicinity of the Guildhall. As soon as his carriage drew up in front of the Guildhall, 'he was greeted by a torrent of hissing and howling and groans, and

[1] 'William Howley', in *Dictionary of English Church History*, G. W. E. R., p. 289.

[2] F. A. Iremonger, *William Temple*, p. 618.

these were followed by mud, rotten eggs, and stones, which fell around the carriage as thick as blackberries'.[1] And he only just managed to escape the anger of the mob and drive to the Deanery in safety. How different from Archbishop Davidson's Appeal from the Churches in 1926, with proposals for the ending of the General Strike; and how strange William Temple would have seemed, as 'the People's Archbishop', to William Howley!

The contrast between the last Prince Archbishop and his modern successors may also be seen by a comparison of their correspondence; though something must be allowed for the personal characteristics of an archbishop, as well as for the introduction of the typewriter. 'In Archbishop Howley's days', (writes Mr. George Lipscoomb, a porter at Lambeth for forty-two years), 'the General Postman, dressed in bright scarlet, brought the country letters every morning, and came round again at five o'clock in the evening to collect the letters. He went to the front door, ringing in his hands a heavy bell to give notice of his coming. He had a guinea a quarter from the Palace. The general-post letters in the morning for the Archbishop and Mrs. Howley were put into a china bowl in the hall. They were scarcely enough to cover the bottom of it. When the Archbishop was at Addington, and I had to forward the letters there, I could put, as a rule, all the letters of the day, servants' included, in a medium-sized envelope.'[2] In 1912, excluding the immense number of official and legal letters, that part of Archbishop Davidson's personal correspondence which was carefully filed at the close of each year (perhaps about one-third of the letters actually received and sent) consisted usually of about 650 or 700 sets of subjects, any one of which might comprise perhaps ten or twenty or even fifty letters.[3] And by 1928 anything from 70 to 100 letters were posted from Lambeth each day, in addition to the private correspondence.

It is time, however, to turn to the development in the position and influence of the Archbishop of Canterbury during the three primacies under review.

The first half of the twentieth century is likely to be regarded

[1] *Chronological History of Canterbury Cathedral*, pp. 345–6.
[2] R. T. Davidson, *Archibald Campbell Tait*, vol. ii, pp. 556–7.
[3] Idem, *The Character and Call of the Church of England*, p. 7.

by historians as even more significant for the people of Britain than the Victorian age; and the social changes which have marked it as not less momentous. During the years covered by the three Primates, Democracy arrived. Already implicit in British self-government, it was accelerated by far-reaching measures passed when Mr. Asquith was Prime Minister. The First World War made it a fact. By the Representation of the People Act, 1918, women were given the vote for the first time, and the electorate was trebled. The Education Act of 1918 introduced ambitious measures designed to equip future citizens for the task of government. The condition of the working classes was much improved, and State control greatly increased. The Labour Party, which held office for the first time in 1924, became more and more powerful; and in the General Election of 1945 returned 396 Members to the House of Commons, as against 11 in 1900. At the same time, the years between the two World Wars were marked by nation-wide labour disputes between 1919 and 1926, and by large-scale unemployment. The number of unemployed in Great Britain from 1924 to 1939 was never less than a million, and averaged 1,744,000. Among other factors influencing the pattern of the common life were the motor-car, the cinema, the wireless, cheap literature, and the pictorial press. A new Matrimonial Causes Act, known as the Herbert Act, greatly extending the grounds for divorce, was passed in 1938. Both at home and abroad the total results of the two World Wars have still to be measured.

Each of the three Archbishops in these forty-one years was a great churchman; but each was also concerned with secular affairs. It may be of service to consider the development of the secular side of the Primate's contact with the life of the nation, before dealing more particularly with ecclesiastical affairs. Therefore, as the Archbishop of Canterbury is the first subject of the Crown, I turn first to his relations with his Sovereign.

Queen Victoria died before Randall Davidson became Primate of all England. But it is safe to say that no modern Bishop was ever so deeply trusted by his Sovereign as Randall Davidson was trusted by her, from the day when he visited Windsor, after Archbishop Tait's death, to the end of the Queen's life. His intimacy with King Edward VII and King George V was different in character. He was always a trusted friend of members of the Royal Family. But so far as King Edward was concerned, Archbishop Davidson was received rather as his Royal Mother's counsellor, to whom great deference was due, than as the chosen confidant of the King. He was greatly respected, but he was not on the same intimate terms—though twice his wisdom was invoked in a political crisis. There was one occasion, the proposed marriage of Princess Eugenie Victoria to the King of Spain in 1906, on which he felt bound to adopt a role which was highly unwelcome to King Edward. Although courteous as ever, and refraining from public intervention, he was both courageous and persistent in his private appeals and protests.[1] Archbishop Davidson was on more intimate terms with King George V. He saw him often, and had a unique personal access through his long-standing friendship with Lord Stamfordham; and in the early days of the reign there were important comings and goings about the Parliament Act. Archbishop Lang knew King George V still more intimately; and there was a real affection between them. Every year he visited the King and Queen at Balmoral. He was with the King frequently at Craigweil House, Bognor Regis (where he was convalescing), and was able to give him spiritual ministrations, rather (he says) 'as a personal friend than officially as the Archbishop'.[2] And he was with him at the end. But with the accession of King Edward VIII, to quote the Archbishop's words, there was 'not only a new reign, but a new régime'.[3] And the fact that conversations had been held with the Prince's father on his own private matters, and were known by the Prince to have been held, was bound to embarrass the relations of King and Archbishop.[4] His attitude to the abdication is well known, though his actual part in the conclusion of the crisis was small. The old close relationship was resumed with King George VI, and gained an added depth through the King's overwhelming sense of religious reality at the solemn service of the Coronation. In the short Primacy of Archbishop Temple there is no specially close link to record, but King,

[1] *Infra*, p. 506.
[2] J. G. Lockhart, *Cosmo Gordon Lang*, p. 320.
[3] Ibid., p. 395.
[4] Ibid., p. 396.

Queen, and Archbishop were naturally brought into contact from time to time through the experiences of the war.

The Archbishop of Canterbury is the chief Spiritual Peer in Parliament. So I turn next to the House of Lords. Randall Davidson, writes Dr. Lang, 'loved the House of Lords and was never more, so to say, at home than when he was there. He liked to be in his place whatever the business in hand might be. He became an institution there, a "House of Lords man".'[1] He was never a party man, though at times, as with the Education Bills brought in by the Liberal Government, and the Bill for the Disestablishment of the Church in Wales, he was engaged in a sharp political conflict, and was on the same side as the Conservative Party. During his Primacy the power of the House of Lords was greatly reduced by the passing of the Parliament Act in 1911. Incidentally it may be noted that his speech at a critical moment during the Third Reading debate was acknowledged by Viscount Morley to have been of crucial importance in determining a majority for the Government.[2] But the second Chamber, though unreformed, continued to exercise great influence both in legislation and through its debates, where the level of speaking was high. The Chamber itself in some ways became more and more a Council of State, in which the wisest and most experienced men spoke as the need required on contemporary affairs. When it was fitting, the Archbishop took an active part in debates on contemporary issues such as the Irish question, Conscription, and Divorce; and on great occasions, or on subjects of special importance, he would always make his contribution. He would himself initiate debates on social and international questions, where matters of moral principle were concerned. To him the House of Lords seemed a very proper place in which the Primate of all England should appeal to the national conscience, or give public support to lay Peers denouncing grave wrongs.

Archbishop Lang, though not quite so frequent in his attendance, took a similar view of the part played by the House of Lords in the nation's life, and of the opportunities afforded to a Primate willing to take them. He had also a quite astonishing

[1] J. G. Lockhart, *Cosmo Gôrdon Lang*, p. 232.
[2] *infra*, p. 631.

gift of oratory. Lord Quickswood describes him as one of the two or three best speakers he had ever heard; 'whether it was exposition or narrative, exhortation or argument, anecdote or humour, he was pre-eminent in all these arts'.[1] He exercised considerable influence among the Peers, though he was never to quite the same degree as Randall Davidson a 'House of Lords man'. The value attached to his contributions is shown by the fact that he also was created a temporal Peer to enable him to sit after he had resigned.

Archbishop Temple, though his occasional contributions were of high value, and his share in the passing of the Education Act in 1944 was of special significance, came much less often to the House. He took the view that its influence on the life of the nation had declined in recent years. He tended therefore to regard its sessions as of secondary importance in his programme of engagements. Speaking generally, he did not feel greatly at home in the House, and preferred to make the platform, the press, or the B.B.C. the vehicle of his views on secular affairs.

There is a further difference in the approach of Archbishop Davidson and Archbishop Lang from that of Archbishop Temple. Both the former, and Randall Davidson especially, valued the House of Lords for the opportunities it gave for making personal contacts. The fact that the Archbishop was always in his place enabled him to be in constant touch with those in high office, or holding important positions in the nation's life. Dr. Temple had an immense range of contacts, very different in character from those of his two predecessors. And he did not set store by the House of Lords for this purpose. He made the contacts he desired not only in different ways but in different fields; for example in the Universities, the Workers' Educational Association, meetings with Trade Unionists, as well as at groups of economists and representatives of various interests invited as his guests to the Old Palace or elsewhere.

Another test of the Archbishop's connexion with the leading authorities in the State is the closeness of his relations with the Prime Minister of the day. The Archbishop and the Prime Minister are bound to meet in a formal way at national services in Westminster Abbey and St. Paul's Cathedral, at Guildhall dinners and Royal Academy banquets, and on other similar

[1] J. G. Lockhart, *Cosmo Gordon Lang*, pp. 231–2.

public occasions. But this is very different from being on friendly terms, and having easy access. Archbishop Davidson set a remarkable precedent here. He knew all the seven Prime Ministers during his tenure of the See personally, and four of them intimately—Balfour, Campbell-Bannerman, Asquith, and Baldwin. This kind of intimacy had certainly not been equalled for 100 years. In Mr. Lloyd George, however, a new kind of Prime Minister emerged, with different ways and habits of mind from his predecessors, and—this is the important point—much less accessible to Archbishops of Canterbury. With Mr. Baldwin the former intimacy was restored; and it was maintained by Archbishop Lang. Up to and including the premierships of Mr. Baldwin (1924–9 and 1935–7), the personal contacts of Archbishops Davidson and Lang were concerned in various degrees with social and national and even international affairs, and not only with ecclesiastical matters such as appointments to Bishoprics. The same was true when Mr. Ramsay Macdonald became Prime Minister. When Mr. Neville Chamberlain succeeded Mr. Baldwin the links tended to be weaker. And during the Second World War Mr. Churchill saw little of either Archbishop Lang or Archbishop Temple. But the pace of public life has quickened, and the pressure of affairs has greatly increased. Although there is no reason why future Prime Ministers and Primates should not be on terms of intimate friendship, able to discuss affairs of common concern, and the business of the Church, with an interest equal to that shown by Mr. Balfour, Mr. Asquith, and Mr. Baldwin, the signs of the times do not point that way. Indeed, the pressure is now of such a character that, in the business of the Church requiring his attention, the modern Prime Minister is inclined to trust more and more to the skilled help and judgement of those whose duty it is to let their chief have the fullest information in their power. This is a service often admirably performed, but it is not the same thing as the former personal relationship between Primate and Premier.

I have said nothing of relationships with foreign countries or their rulers and statesmen. But one of the most striking features in these 41 years is the growing significance of the Archbishop of Canterbury in the international field. All three

Archbishops counted increasingly here, not only at home but abroad. Archbishop Davidson took an active part in the international developments which followed the First World War. Archbishop Lang was sharply attacked in Germany and Japan for his public pronouncements between the wars. President Roosevelt testified to King George VI of Archbishop Temple that 'as an ardent advocate of international co-operation based on Christian principles he exercised profound influence throughout the world'.[1]

There are many other ways in which the Archbishop of Canterbury exercises influence in relation to the State, or to international affairs. Speeches in Convocation and in the Church Assembly, addresses at public meetings, sermons in Westminster Abbey or St. Paul's Cathedral, broadcasts, communications to the press, and books, especially such books as Temple's Penguin volume, *Christianity and Social Order*, are natural illustrations. But I have chosen the particular points of contact which I have sought to explain because they come to the Archbishop by virtue of his office. And I think there will be little doubt about the inference to be drawn. The new developments in the State and the progress of democracy may diminish the political power of the Archbishop of Canterbury as a national institution. There are also quite new ways (as Archbishop Temple had begun to show) by which the Archbishop can influence the nation. But every Archbishop derives a great potential moral authority from his office, and in the exercise of that moral authority his personal qualities count for more and more.

It is, however, in relation to the Church that the development of the influence of the Archbishop of Canterbury possesses a special interest for the historian. In Dr. Davidson's time the Primate became known as a person, far outside the borders of his diocese or of London. This was due partly no doubt to the increasing circulation of the daily press. But it was also due in no small measure to the creation of the Church Assembly in 1920. The Church Assembly has not fulfilled all the hopes entertained by its most ardent original promoters. It has been criticized for over-complicated or unnecessary legislation, and for the impetus it has given to central administration. It has failed to solve the problems of Prayer Book Revision, or to deal

[1] F. A. Iremonger, *William Temple*, p. 627.

with reforms affecting the Ecclesiastical Courts and certain other important issues in the relationship between Church and State. But it has been the means of giving the laity a far larger share in Church legislation. It has accomplished many valuable practical reforms. And through its sessions in London three times a year, not only has it enabled representatives of the clergy and laity from all over England to meet and work together in a new way, but its chairman has become familiar to the people of the Church of England in a way impossible before.

Again, the moral authority of the Archbishop over the bench of Bishops has greatly increased. In law every Bishop is the ruler in his own diocese, and even when the Archbishop is present in state in a church of another diocese, it is the Bishop who has the right to pronounce the benediction; although few would exercise it, as a Bishop of Chichester once did in Brighton Parish Church, somewhat to the dismay of Archbishop Davidson, who had come for a great festal occasion. In law the Archbishop has no authority to order special prayers in another diocese, or to prescribe forms of public intercession. He may recommend, but it is the Bishop who sanctions. In fact, however, the weight of the Archbishop's recommendation has so increased during the forty-one years that whatever he asks in his province is almost certainly done. More important, the word of the Archbishop of Canterbury goes in Convocation, and at the private meetings of Bishops, in a way and to a degree, which is a little disturbing at times to Bishops (like Dr. Gore and Dr. Henson) who value their independence as diocesans. Meetings of Bishops of the two Provinces seem to have started just before Archbishop Tait became Archbishop of Canterbury, as conversations at the office of Queen Anne's Bounty in Westminster, after a dinner privately arranged. It was Archbishop Benson who in May 1883 arranged that they should be held at Lambeth Palace, and minutes kept. Bishops were more interesting in Archbishop Tait's time, says Archbishop Davidson, and there were sometimes great clashes in the Bishops' Meetings.[1] It is worth noting that the increase in archiepiscopal influence has coincided with the increase in the number of Bishops. In 1903 there were 35 Diocesan Bishops. By 1944 12 new English dioceses had been formed, and the number of Bishops

[1] *Infra*, p. 1155.

qualified to attend Bishops' Meetings was 49, including 6 (instead of 4) Welsh Bishops. Even with 35 Bishops, meeting for a day and a half with a full agenda, effective counsel presents its problems. It is much more difficult when there are 49.

In the Anglican Communion at large the Archbishop of Canterbury may be in theory one Metropolitan among many, although admittedly the chief. But the tact and wisdom which Archbishops Davidson and Lang displayed while on the throne of St. Augustine, especially at successive Lambeth Conferences and in various ways, in which Archbishop Temple played his part, have materially increased the influence and prestige of the Archbishopric of Canterbury with the whole Anglican episcopate.

The three Archbishops of Canterbury have rendered outstanding service to their Church in the realm of Christian unity. Relations between the leaders of the Church of England and the leaders of the Free Churches in England were transformed in this period, most of all as a result of the Appeal to all Christian people issued by the Lambeth Conference of 1920. All three Archbishops were active in this work, although less has actually followed from the prolonged conferences on Church relations than many hoped. Archbishop Temple did a notable service in connexion with the inauguration of the British Council of Churches in 1942. Again, many new contacts have been made with foreign Churches. Never before had there been a *rapprochement* on so wide a scale with the Eastern Orthodox Churches, and, in a lesser degree, with other Eastern Churches. New relationships began with the Scandinavian Churches. Personal links were established with individual Lutheran and Reformed Church leaders. The Old Catholics entered into an agreement with the Anglican Church on intercommunion. There was a striking departure from precedent in the conversations which took place between representatives of the Archbishop of Canterbury on the one hand, and Cardinal Mercier and other Roman Catholic divines with the approval of the Holy See, on the other hand, at Malines. And a new step of some importance was taken, under the auspices of Archbishop Lang, by the formation of the Church of England Council on Foreign Relations in 1933.

Last of all comes the Ecumenical Movement. It is 'the great new fact of our time'. Men of many Churches in East and West have played their part in its evolution over many years. Archbishops Davidson and Lang were amongst them. Archbishop Davidson showed his friendship for it at the first World Missionary Conference in Edinburgh in 1910, at which William Temple (then twenty-nine years old) was an usher. Archbishop Lang gave it steady support, and was one of the Presidents of the Oxford Conference on Church, Community, and State in 1937. Archbishop Temple gave his main service before he came to Lambeth. It was as Archbishop of York that he presided over the Edinburgh Conference on Faith and Order in 1937, was appointed Chairman of the Provisional Committee of the World Council of Churches (in process of formation), and helped to frame its constitution as a 'fellowship of Churches which accept our Lord Jesus Christ as God and Saviour'. But he kept in as close touch as possible with foreign col eagues, when at Canterbury, and it was to his guiding hand, up to the time of his death, more than to that of any other Christian man, that the World Council of Churches owed its inauguration at Amsterdam.

It is a far cry back from 1944 to 1848, the year in which Archbishop Howley died and Archbishop Davidson was born. There is no comparison between the burden of the Primacy now and the burden then. It is not surprising, therefore, that the question of providing the Church with its 'G.H.Q.,'the department devoted to planning and strategy', should have again been raised by Dean Iremonger[1] and others, following the calamity of William Temple's death. The first Archbishop in recent times to have brought it forward was Archbishop Benson. He left a note of a conversation with Bishop Lightfoot and Dr. Westcott in 1887. 'We discussed the unfortunate result in one most important matter of the happy change in Episcopal activity. The diocesan energies now interfere with every Bishops' meeting, or meeting of Convocation, and leave the Church almost destitute of the opportunity of counsel. . . We came to the conclusion that a "Cardinalate" in some form was becoming absolutely necessary. What we thought might be done was the appointment of four or five Bishops, to give at least an annual fortnight of conference, with nothing else to do, on matters proposed by the Archbishop—or otherwise found

[1] F. A. Iremonger, *William Temple*, pp. xi, xii.

PREFACE TO SECOND EDITION

THE present edition includes an entirely new chapter on The Coronation of King George V (printed as Appendix IV). It is based on material contained in three box files which, in spite of search, could not be discovered when this book was being written. The author desires to express his gratitude to H.M. the King for leave to quote certain documents; and to the Archbishop of Canterbury. Lady Davidson died on June 26, 1936. In *Edith Davidson of Lambeth* by M. C. S. M. (1938) a fitting memorial to her life and character will be found. A Note on relations with the Church of Sweden (page 1015), and a List of Portraits (Appendix III), have also been added; and a number of minor corrections have been made.

August, 1938. G. K. A. B.

PREFACE TO FIRST EDITION

THE author of this work has been greatly assisted in the fulfilment of his task by the ample records and admirably arranged correspondence which Archbishop Davidson left behind him. Indeed, the Archbishop had hoped that after his resignation he might perhaps be able to prepare his own reminiscences. Though this did not prove possible, the preliminary notes which he put together, especially in connexion with the history of his early life, have been of much service to the biographer. Dr. Davidson never kept a diary for any length of time, but five small quarto leather-bound MS. books survive, containing accurate accounts written in from time to time of conversations or incidents which had specially aroused his interest when he was Dean of Windsor, and also when he was Bishop of Rochester. They extend chronologically from January 1888 to September 1895; and though there are considerable periods during which no entry is made, they afford a running commentary on a number of important episodes in which Dr. Davidson was concerned, together with his impressions of many important people whom he met. The first of these MS. books refers to the failure of a series of January attempts to keep a diary in anything like orthodox diary form, and records his decision 'to try something more irregular, with no vacant pages, dated and blank'; and the writer adds 'I know that things *do* happen to me and around me which I ought to be recording and *don't*.' Their contents may be dated thus: (1) January 1888–April 1889: about 100 autograph pages; (2) May 1889–November 1890: about 90 autograph pages; (3) January 1891–February 1892: about 90 autograph pages; (4) April 1892–August 1893: about 90 autograph pages; (5) March 1894–September 1895: about 32 autograph pages (together with half a page for April 1897, a beginning for Winchester, not continued). After he had become Archbishop, during a summer holiday abroad in 1906, Dr. Davidson dictated his recollections of Windsor days and also of his work in the two dioceses of Rochester and Winchester, ending with his appointment to the Primacy; and though he felt afterwards that the recollections were somewhat hurried and unfinished in form, they have proved of considerable value, especially for the light they throw on his relations with Queen Victoria. On this MS. book of 1906, and the smaller leather-bound volumes, the biographer has drawn a great deal.

For the Primacy itself there is a whole series of memoranda of a private character, mostly typed and arranged in large envelopes, dealing as a rule with particular years. They commenced in 1909 and went down to 1930. These were all dictated, often at the time, or occasionally after an interval, when the Archbishop, surveying a period of a few months, picked out certain leading incidents or delivered himself of general reflections. At first they dealt specially with constitutional questions such as The Budget of 1909, and the Parliament Act; but later they covered general church questions as well as matters of general public interest. They also, like the earlier MS. books, form a running commentary on contemporary events and the characters with whom the Archbishop was brought into official relations. There are in addition many separate memoranda of interviews etc. filed with the correspondence on the particular subject. All these documents, whether written or dictated before or during the Primacy, may be described generally as 'the Davidson papers', and the biographer has quoted them constantly in the different parts of this Life. Indeed, it may be assumed that passages commencing 'The Archbishop notes', or having some other similar introduction (not being clearly indicated as letters) are taken from the Davidson papers. They are naturally of great value; since from them it is possible to learn the Archbishop's reactions towards and verdict upon the scenes in which he was a principal actor. The copious extracts from them given in this biography indicate sufficiently their nature and importance. But though quoted considerably, much remains which can hardly be published at present (to quote one of the greatest of all biographers) 'without trespassing against the feelings of distinguished individuals still alive',[1] or causing difficulties of other kinds.

The correspondence of Archbishop Davidson was of a most extensive character, and has been extensively preserved, both as regards letters written to and by him. Year by year it was arranged and filed in excellent order, both in respect of subject and date. It may therefore be supposed that the material con-

[1] Lockhart, *Life of Scott*, Chapter 19.

fronting the biographer is vast and that the difficulty of selecting what is characteristic and outstandingly important has been unusually great.

The author owes a special personal debt to Lady Davidson, not only for kindness and friendship during the ten years when he served as Archbishop's Chaplain at Lambeth, and since, but also for her own vivid recollections, and her generosity and consideration during all the stages of the preparation of this book.

Most grateful acknowledgement is due to H.M. the King for the permission which he has given for the publication of various letters and extracts, not least those belonging to the lifetime of Queen Victoria. One point should be made plain at the very outset with regard to the correspondence and the various other communications which took place between Randall Davidson and Queen Victoria. It is necessary to emphasize it, in order to avoid any possible misunderstanding. The circumstances in which Randall Davidson was introduced to Her Majesty were altogether unusual, following upon the death of his father-in-law, Archbishop Tait. They led, as the biography shows, to an extraordinary trust in Dr. Davidson and to an unusual reliance on his judgement in Church matters. But the consultations which resulted may be justly described as so purely personal in character, and so almost fortuitous in their origin, that they could not rightly be regarded as precedents even within the limited department concerned. In any event the whole situation changed on the Queen's death. And with regard to Dr. Davidson himself, readers of this work will see that the relations between him and King Edward and King George, though never wanting in friendly feeling, were of a quite different kind. The personal factor was completely altered.

The biographer wishes also to express his thanks to the Archbishop of Canterbury, who has been most generous in reading special chapters, in helping with advice, and in contributing a description of the relations between himself, as Archbishop of York, and Dr. Davidson, when Archbishop of Canterbury, besides giving him facilities of every kind at Lambeth Palace.

It would be impossible to thank publicly every one of the many friends and helpers who have assisted in the preparation of this book; sometimes by reminiscences, sometimes by revising passages or chapters in which they were themselves concerned, sometimes by permitting the publication of letters. But a special tribute of gratitude must be paid to some who have given exceptional help. First, the author has to thank Mr. Arthur Sheppard, the Archbishop's Private Secretary for many years, who undertook the task of going through the files of the Davidson correspondence covering nearly 40 years, deposited at Lambeth, with a view to facilitating the work of selection; and has in addition compiled the index. Next, he thanks Miss Mary Mills, without whose help in going through the personal papers, in compiling memoranda and giving aid of all kinds in conjunction with Lady Davidson, this book would have been immeasurably poorer; and Mr. Charles Williams for reading the Life in MS. as well as in proof, and for the most valuable and skilled advice which he has given him as a result—a service which is deeply appreciated. Particular thanks are due to the Rev. Lancelot Mason, the biographer's Chaplain, for help in various ways; and both to him and to the Rev. Norman Sykes, for most useful assistance in reading the proofs, in making many important suggestions, and in the arduous but indispensable work of verification. Last but not least, the biographer desires to express his gratitude to Mr. Humphrey Milford, most patient and considerate of publishers, for his unfailing help and personal interest from the very outset of the task; as well as his appreciation of the attention and scholarship of the printers and readers of the Oxford University Press.

THE PALACE, CHICHESTER. G. K. A. B.

July, 1935.

TABLE OF CONTENTS

VOLUME I

TABLE OF CONTENTS

VOLUME II

LIST OF ILLUSTRATIONS

VOLUME I

VOLUME II

VOLUME I

CHAPTER I

EDINBURGH, HARROW, OXFORD

Mrs. Scott . . . liked Dr. Erskine's sermons; but was not fond of the Principal's, however rational, eloquent and well-composed, and would, if other things had answered, have gone, when he preached, to have heard Dr. Davidson. LOCKHART'S *Life of Scott*, ch. iv.

The family of Swinton is very ancient and was once very powerful. Ibid., ch. lv.

RANDALL THOMAS DAVIDSON was born on April 7, 1848, at No. 15 Inverleith Place, Edinburgh. He was the eldest of the four children of Henry and Henrietta Davidson. On May 18, 1848, he was baptized in the same house, according to the Presbyterian form, by Dr. Muir, Minister of St. Stephen's Church. He was of pure Scottish blood on both his father's and his mother's side; and his Scottish character as well as his love for Scotland were conspicuous throughout the eighty-two years of his life. Like many of his fellow countrymen, he attached not a little importance to his family history. His papers indicate both his own feeling for his ancestors and his accuracy as a chronicler. And so a brief chapter from that history may be given at once in his own words.

I

'Go back in thought two centuries and a little more. Queen Anne is on the throne. An eager controversy is in the air. Ought, or ought not, her two kingdoms, England and Scotland, to be united into one? The storm centre lies in Edinburgh, where the strife of tongues in the Parliament House and in the General Assembly finds ready echo on the open pavements of the High Street and the Canongate. The Act of Union struggled painfully into life, but even after it had, in March 1707, received the Royal Assent, the discussions, as Sir Walter Scott has taught us, were carried on with scarcely diminished force and pungency.

'The clergy of the City, intensely concerned for the security of the Presbyterian system, but doubtful whether the Union would strengthen or impair it, were eloquent on either side. Prominent among them was the Rev. Thomas Davidson, lecturer in the Tron Church of Edinburgh, and two years after the Union a Chaplain to Queen Anne. A devoted pastor, as well as a keen controversialist, he was promoted successively to the parishes of Whitekirk, of Stirling, and of the Cross Church, Dundee, where he became a recognised champion of the Church's rights and liberties. Like many Scotsmen of the day, he had close relations with Holland, where older members of the family had for many years held positions of high public trust. (Among these was Sir William Davidson, who had acted as political friend and adviser to William of Orange before he came to England.) During Thomas Davidson's ministry in Dundee his daughter Mary, already a widow, became the wife of the Rev. Thomas Randall, minister of Inchture in the Carse of Gowrie. The son of this marriage, born in 1747, inherited his father's name, Thomas Randall. He was grandfather to the subject of this memoir.

'Besides this daughter, Thomas Davidson had two sons. In view of subsequent history, it is not uninteresting to note that the younger of these, named Hugh, was ordained in the Church of England and became Rector of Kirby [Misperton] in Yorkshire. In the upbringing of the elder son, William, advantage was taken of the ancestral connexion with Holland, and the lad was sent to The Hague to complete his education. Settling in Holland, he became, we are told, "one of the most considerable and opulent general merchants at Rotterdam". He left Holland about 1750, and for the rest of his life resided in London and in Edinburgh. He is described as being "ostentatious and with numerous servants dressed in unsilvered white liveries".

'When in London he seems to have been regarded as a leader in financial circles. His portrait, by Sir Joshua Reynolds, shows a man of striking and dignified appearance. Of equal interest is the portrait of his only child, Susannah, whom Sir Joshua painted with a large lamb upon her lap. At the age of twenty, she died unmarried, and was, for some unexplained reason, buried in Westminster Abbey, where her monument in the North Transept bears a long and laudatory inscription. Her father, though he survived her for nearly thirty years, is said never to have recovered his spirits. Dying in 1794, he left his estates of Muirhouse and Hatton, near Edinburgh, together with a considerable fortune, to the Rev. Thomas Randall, son of his sister Mary, "on the express stipulation that the name of Randall should be for ever abolished, and that of Davidson substituted".

The motive actuating William Davidson in making this bequest seems to have been his desire to found a family of Scottish landed gentry, rather than affection for the nephew whom he thus enriched, or appreciation of his ministerial calling. Indeed the two Thomas Randalls, father and son, had little in common with the opulent merchant, except that they also were connected with Holland. It is necessary to go back a little way.

'In the year 1728, David Randall, who is described by the historian Wodrow as a man of capacity and public spirit,[1] had emigrated to Holland. His son, Thomas, after graduating in the University of Edinburgh, spent some time with his father in the flourishing Scottish settlement in Rotterdam. He then returned to Scotland and was ordained in 1739 as minister of Inchture. His marriage, while there, to Mary Davidson, daughter of the well-known minister of Dundee, has been mentioned above. Mary Davidson, already a widow, seems to have been in every way suited to be the wife of a man of Randall's character and powers. He rapidly became a leader among the clergy of the Church of Scotland. While minister of Inchture he was consulted by those who were promoting the Evangelical revival in England, and he is said to have been visited by John Wesley when he rode through the Carse of Gowrie in 1768.[2] At the same time he was prominent in his advocacy among Presbyterians of the more frequent Celebration of the Lord's Supper. His pamphlet on that subject became famous, and [Sir Henry Moncreiff, afterwards] Sir Henry Moncreiff Wellwood describes Dr. Randall as "a man whose learning, ingenuity and eminence as a Christian pastor entitled him to the first distinctions in the Church to which he belonged".[3] He was the author of the Forty-ninth "Paraphrase",[4] one of the best known of the collection which has for more than a century and a half been the Hymn Book of the Church of Scotland. In 1770, in which year he left Inchture and became minister of Stirling, he issued a Series of Tracts upon the constitution of the Church of Scotland, which is still regarded as a work of standard authority.

[1] See *The Ancestry of Randall Thomas Davidson, D.D.*, by Adam Philip (Elliot Stock, 1903), p. 1.

[2] Ibid., p. 14.

[3] See *Life and Writings of J. Erskine, D.D.*, by Sir Henry Moncreiff Wellwood, 1818.

[4] Though perfect eloquence adorned
My sweet persuasive tongue;

This paraphrase was sung when R. T. D. visited the General Assembly in 1919.

'His ministry at Stirling, where again he was in a storm-centre of controversy, lasted for ten years. Dr. Burns, pastor of Kilsyth, speaks of "his more than magisterial command over the populace of the ancient burgh of Stirling and of the awe and dread which surrounded him on Sabbath and week-days".[1]

'At Inchture, in July 1747, was born the son of Thomas and Mary Randall. He, too, was christened Thomas. His early years were spent in his father's manse at Inchture, and, after a College course at Glasgow, he was sent to Holland, where he studied both at Utrecht and at Leyden, devoting himself particularly to the subject of Biblical criticism. He was licensed to preach at Rotterdam in 1769, and in the following year, on the removal of his father to Stirling, he was appointed his successor at Inchture. This was in persistent disregard of the wishes of his rich uncle, William Davidson, who desired that the young man should join the mercantile house over which he ruled. Thomas Randall, however, adhered to his purpose, and in a ministry of fifty-seven years exercised a constantly increasing influence throughout the Church of Scotland. Every writer (and they are many) who sets himself to depict the social and literary life of Edinburgh in the last quarter of the eighteenth century gives a prominent place to the gentle, devout, and charitable minister of the Tolbooth Church. Sir Walter Scott[2] records, in testimony to his mother's piety of conviction, her love of attending his ministrations. His portrait by Raeburn is well known, and has often been reproduced. In 1794, on the death of his uncle, William Davidson, he succeeded, as above mentioned, to the estates of Muirhouse and Hatton, and to a considerable fortune, and was required in consequence to change his name to Davidson.

'By his wife, Elisabeth Cockburn,[3] sister of the well-known Lord Cockburn, one of the leaders of Scotch Liberalism, and a joint founder of the *Edinburgh Review*, he had three sons, the youngest of whom was Henry, born in 1810, who became the father of Randall Thomas Davidson, the subject of this memoir. In his boyhood Henry was designated for the Scottish Bar. Educated in the High School of Edinburgh, and then in the famous

[1] For all this see Philip, *Ancestry*, &c., pp. 13–20.

[2] Lockhart's *Life of Scott*, ch. iii.

[3] He had been previously married to Elisabeth Rutherford, whose son inherited and spent his fortune.

Edinburgh Academy, (the foundation of which, under the auspices of Sir Walter Scott, Lord Cockburn and Francis Jeffrey,[1] has been often recorded,) and subsequently in the University of Edinburgh, where he earned distinction in English literature (under the tutelage of Professor Pillans and others), he decided, when his university days were over, to adopt a commercial rather than a legal career, and became almost immediately a prominent figure in the extensive shipping business of the Port of Leith. His musical powers and social gifts made him a favourite with the literary coterie depicted with graphic detail in Henry Cockburn's *Memorials of his Time*; while his activity as a horseman gave him access to a rather exclusive group among the hunting men of the Lothians.

'In 1845, Henry Davidson married Henrietta, daughter of John Swinton of Kimmerghame, a prominent member of the Berwickshire family of Swinton of Swinton, whose persistent place in Border annals for more than seven centuries is a topic which Sir Walter Scott, who had himself by his grandfather's marriage become one of the family, was fond of recounting both in prose and verse. When Henrietta Swinton was about twelve years old, Sir Walter Scott, in right (he said) of his "cousinship", enlisted the little girl as critic of the *Tales of a Grandfather*, then passing through the press, and she used to recount fifty years later how, to her legitimate pride, he re-wrote the chapter on "The Feudal System" because she found it difficult to understand it fully when he read it to her in its original form.

'Henry Davidson and his wife settled in a house, No. 15 Inverleith Place, Edinburgh, next door to the house, No. 16, occupied by the bride's father, Mr. Swinton, the two houses standing at the west end of Inverleith Place. There, in my parents' house, No. 15 Inverleith Place, I was born on April 7th, 1848, and there I was baptized, as my baptismal certificate shows, on May 18th, 1848, by Dr. Muir, minister of St. Stephen's Church. I read in my Mother's diary:

> *Thursday May 18th.* Fine. Randall was christened by Dr. Muir. My Aunts . . . and Archie, Mrs. J. Cockburn and Mary, Christian Davidson and M. D. being present. The two latter stayed to dinner.'

[1] See, e.g., account given in the *Life of Archbishop Tait*, vol. i, p. 21.

II

The influence of both parents on Randall was marked from the very start. Henry Davidson was a wood merchant in Leith. 'He was a very small man,' says Lord Dunedin, a neighbour and schoolfellow of Randall, 'blind of one eye but very lively, with a most engaging manner, and he was a great favourite.' With his children he shared fun and sport alike in full measure. Indeed, it may well be that from this keen sportsmanship of his father Randall got his own love for sport and for adventures in the open air. Thus he writes in his recollections:

> I was in closest personal friendship with my father from the earliest years. I used to stalk rabbits and magpies as soon as I was able to hold a gun, always under his eager personal tuition. He had been, and in some ways still was, a keen sportsman. He had once been an admirable rider, but he had given it up. He shot very well, and had in schooldays a reputation as a runner.

Both parents were deeply religious, and the simplicity and strength of his father's religion, especially at certain critical moments in the boy's life, made a great impression on Randall. But it was to his mother's teaching that Randall owed most. She, though less eager than her husband, had a resourcefulness and buoyancy of her own, coupled with a poetic gift which added considerable vividness to her lessons. To quote her son's recollections again:

> I do not find it easy to explain the remarkable influence which my mother was able to exercise over and among us all in religious matters and in Bible teaching. I think partly her poetic temperament—she was keenly poetic, and used to read and even write a good deal of poetry—gave her a power of putting things in the sort of way that made them interesting at the moment and rememberable afterwards, and of course her real absorption in the religious side of life, and the dominance which religion exercised upon all her thoughts and plans, domestic and personal, made it a natural thing that she should reveal incidentally to others, and especially to us, her children, what was so essentially the pivot of her own life.

But in addition to these more serious qualities, Randall continues:

> she had the gift of identifying herself with our interests, and even our amusements, which is certainly not very usual among people of her make. For example, the Christmas holidays were always

times when we had every sort of amusement in the way of specially arranged games, and acting and competitions, and in all these things she was indisputably the central moving force.

The immediate family circle to whom father and mother thus gave so much consisted of Randall, his sister Mary (born 1849), his brothers Henry (born 1851) and Ernest (born 1856). All grew up together, and though they followed different paths in later life, all acknowledged to the end the debt they owed to the vitality and religious sincerity of their parents.

The scene of many of the games which children and parents played together was the old home at Kimmerghame where Henrietta had been born. In Randall's boyhood his uncle, Archibald Swinton, the owner of Kimmerghame, made it the festive centre of all sorts of amusements and entertainments, and even the slightest sketch of these years would be at fault without some tribute not only to Kimmerghame but to the part Archibald Swinton played:

> We were often, perhaps generally, at Kimmerghame in the Christmas holidays. I have not recorded what we owe to my uncle, Archibald Swinton, for his unfailing and unending kindness to us all. He was a man who might, if Fortune had favoured him, have been a conspicuous figure in public life, not in Scotland only, but in Parliament or elsewhere. For many years Professor of Law in Edinburgh University, a post which to the best of my recollection he only resigned when his Berwickshire duties made continuous Edinburgh life impossible, he had a wide knowledge of public affairs, and he certainly had a remarkable gift of public speaking. In the General Assembly he was, for many years, one of the foremost, if not the foremost, lay figure; and in county affairs and many other fields of service he was conspicuous. In his earlier Edinburgh days, when a widower, he had made his home for long periods under my Father's roof, my parents being devoted to him and he to them. At Kimmerghame his hospitality was unbounded, and we were always among his spoilt and favoured guests. I and my brother Harry shot there whenever there was any shooting going, and during the winter weeks we had the run of everything in that way.

Randall also, as he grew older, derived

> endless gain from intercourse with him on all kinds of literary, historic, and legal matters in which his stores of cheery information were always forthcoming in the readiest way.

It is said by those who knew both that in his looks Randall resembled the Swintons rather than the Davidsons. Archibald Swinton had one child by his first marriage (for he married again in 1856) whose name was Kate, and of her Randall says:

> Kate and I were in our early years simply like brother and sister—a relationship which in one sense never waned in its character though our lives necessarily lay widely apart.

Miss Swinton, as an old lady in 1917, told the writer a prophetic story of how the English Prayer Book troubled Randall as a child. Once, when he was about seven, he said to her in great anger, 'What do you think those English have done?' She replied that she could believe anything of them. Randall said, 'They've altered the Bible!' He had just seen for the first time the Prayer Book version of the Psalter—the Scotch using the Old Testament version. Randall and Kate both vowed they'd never use the Prayer Book version after that!

Reference has already been made to the general religious teaching which Randall received from his parents and especially from his mother. To make the picture complete it will be well to add his recollections of their relation to the Church:

> As regards Churchmanship, our upbringing was very undenominational, to use a word which had not then been coined. My parents had both been brought up as devout Presbyterians, and in my early childhood they attended St. Stephen's Church, under the ministry of Dr. Muir, a famous old divine. It was he who baptized me in Inverleith Place, on 18 May, 1848, and I know that he tried to get my Father to become one of his Elders. Why my Father declined at that time I do not know, but I know that a little later on when similar requests came he always said he was more of an Episcopalian than a Presbyterian, and declined. When we were in Atholl Crescent (i.e. from 1854 onwards), my parents began to attend St. Thomas's Episcopal Church, the minister being the Rev. D. T. K. Drummond. Drummond had separated himself from the Scotch Episcopal Church, and had joined the little body of English Episcopalians. . . . When at Muirhouse we used to drive to Edinburgh on most Sundays to attend St. Thomas'; but pretty often we walked to Cramond Parish Church near Muirhouse, which my Father had loved from his boyhood, and which was then served by an odd, rather remarkable man, Dr. Colvin. . . . I have no recollection of receiving any

teaching upon Churchmanship, either Episcopal or Presbyterian, the religion taught us being wholly of the personal sort, but beautiful in its simplicity and reality. My Father absolutely declined to limit himself to one denomination. I remember the eagerness with which he answered someone who had made the remark that a man must be, surely, either a Presbyterian or an Episcopalian by saying emphatically, 'I am both: and if I were one or other only I should be false to my deepest beliefs.'

All through his life Randall Davidson was the possessor of a remarkable memory. He has left not a few reminiscences of his early days as a child in Edinburgh. The first thing he remembered was the return home of his father and mother after the Duke of Wellington's funeral, when he was four years old; and the picture of the hearse and great black plumes from an illustrated paper of the day. Another recollection was connected with the death of his great-uncle, Lord Cockburn:

> He and my father were devoted to one another (he was my father's uncle, brother of my grandmother) and I distinctly recall the sorrow of our house when he died (April 26, 1854). I was just six years old. I was perplexed as to how to reconcile this sorrow with the religious teaching my mother sedulously gave me, and I asked her bluntly why she was sad if he, Lord Cockburn, had gone to Heaven. She didn't answer and I persevered. 'Was he a good man? Is he in heaven?' Her honesty made her, I suppose, hesitate to reply very certainly about one who could hardly, for all his charm, be described as pious, and she left on my mind, without at all knowing it, the impression that he had been a bad man. I remember always connecting him (why I don't know) with 'Jeroboam, who made Israel to sin'—a most unfair parallel!

III

In May 1854, the family moved from Inverleith Place to 6 Atholl Crescent, a larger house nearer the centre of Edinburgh, from which Randall somewhat irregularly attended Mr. Oliphant's School for Boys and Girls in Charlotte Square ('I remember always thinking that the girls did much better than the boys'). But in May 1857 they left Edinburgh for Muirhouse, on the shore of the Firth of Forth, about four miles from Edinburgh and three miles from Dalmeny, Lord Rosebery's place. The house stood in an estate of some 240 acres, in the parish of Cramond about a mile from the village of Davidson's Mains. It was a substantial modern mansion built in the Gothic style by William Davidson, Henry's eldest brother, in 1830, on the site of the old seventeenth-century mansion, of which only two round towers survived. There were beautiful views and just the kind of garden and park to appeal to boys.

> From the first [writes Randall Davidson] we boys were indoctrinated in all sorts of country things. I have never known other children who kept such quantities of rabbits for whose tending they are personally responsible. We had about fifty, and used to drive them into the field on the west side of the approach, to eat in the early morning. We also became, for little boys, really knowing about birds and marine beasts, though never in the scientific way children would be taught to understand things now.

And there was always a pony.

The lessons which had begun in a mild form under Mr. Oliphant in Edinburgh were continued by governesses at Muirhouse, with the help of divinity students from the University, who acted as tutors before more serious schooling commenced.

In 1860, at the age of twelve, Randall was sent to a private school at Worksop, kept by the Rev. William Bury. He was there for two years, which were not very profitable. The motto of the school was curious—'Faint but pursuing'. Mr. Bury was a kind elderly man of strong Evangelical opinions, possessed of a large family, to which he added some twenty or twenty-five pupils with a view to increasing his income. The boys differed greatly in age and knowledge, and, as there was only one assistant, not much real education could be expected. A correspondence was maintained between Mr. Bury and Mr. Henry Davidson, from which it appears that Randall was like most boys, high-spirited, and even possessed (a terminal report runs) of 'an undue volatility at improper times'. On the other hand, Randall occasionally criticized his headmaster. Thus he said once, writing home:

> Mr. Bury is getting more addicted to caning now instead of giving tasks.

Looking back in later years, he wrote:

> I do not remember learning anything very thoroughly at Worksop, and yet I see by a letter which my Father preserved that Mr. Bury regarded me as, in some respects, his best pupil.
>
> I have all my life suffered from not having been thoroughly well grounded in Latin and Greek grammar in the way boys are

grounded now in good preparatory schools; also the school was too small for producing good results at games, and the successive ushers during my two years were anything but capable men or competent teachers.

The Scripture teaching was wearisome in the extreme after the stimulating lessons he had received at home. One taste he seems, however, to have been able to gratify, his delight in country sports, and the following experience, narrated in his own words, made a lasting impression:

Mr. Bury was a naturalist, and we learnt a great deal about butterflies and birds' eggs, and we used to take long walks through the neighbouring Dukeries, Mr. Bury having been a friend of the Duke of Newcastle, and I think of the Duke of Portland. He was also Chaplain to Mr. Foljambe at Osberton, a place about three miles from Worksop. We used to walk there on Sundays and by surreptitious arrangements did some birdnesting on the way. I remember my perplexity on being forced to kneel upright during the Litany in church with my trouser pockets full of water-hens' eggs from Osberton Lake.

A number of letters of this period have been preserved, and the ties which bound father and mother and their eldest son together were clearly of the strongest sort. Both parents wrote in an intimate and affectionate strain. Both entered to the full into his boyhood's tastes and difficulties. With his father, Randall had

an almost brotherly friendship through school and college days. Keenly athletic and intensely amusing, he had withal a deep personal religion which was impressed upon us in the frankest manner every day.

In more than one letter his father urged him to stand on his own ground. Thus he wrote:

HENRY DAVIDSON, ESQ., *to* RANDALL

14 March 1862.

I would strongly urge on you my dear Randall, always to stand *on your own ground.* You know right and wrong—better I am sure than many boys do, at any school you may go to—for few Mothers have taken the pains and loving labour yours has done with you—don't you be moved—*shoved—pushed—driven—laughed* off your own ground by any boy, or any number of boys. There is plenty of *fun*, without evil—and very soon one finds there is no *fun* in evil!

but it may be found too late. I believe NOTHING creates such respect, as for either boy or man *to stand on his own ground, and keep it*—and show you are keeping it too. And when you feel it difficult, just like Nehemiah before the King, silently ask God's help, and I cannot believe you won't get it—only of course, you must bear a bit of the burden yourself—it won't be made *so easy*, that you will have no farther trouble—but above all things be consistent.

Randall himself always wrote in a good straightforward way. Here is a regular schoolboy letter, picked out of many.

RANDALL DAVIDSON *to his* FATHER

Worksop. Wednesday.

My dear Papa

Thanks to Mary and Harry for their letters of yesterday.

Do you really intend to buy us a pony?

When do you expect Miss Turner home again?

I hope dear Mama is quite well again now.

I think my lessons are getting on very well. My favourite lesson is Latin verses, which we do from ¼ past 9 till 10.

Vickers is my greatest friend now that Houldsworth has left. I do not like sleeping with Dalton at all, but today Vickers has asked Mrs. Bury if he may change rooms with Dalton and as yet she has given no certain answer. There are many boys who appear very kind and friendly one day, and then again you find them speaking ill of you and teasing you as if you were their enemy: they make me think of the hymn

'Earthly friends may pain and grieve thee
One day kind the next day leave thee'

I have no more time today so good bye. Give my love to all at home. I am ever your very affectionate son

RANDALL.

P.S. I am very anxious to hear about the Pony.

At the end of the summer of 1862, it was decided that Randall should go to Harrow. But the very week before term began came the first of the many almost fatal accidents or illnesses which marked the whole of his career. The accident is thus described by Randall's father in a letter to his daughter Mary. Willy is a cousin and Master Ice the pony.

HENRY DAVIDSON, ESQ., *to* MARY

Do you know we nearly lost Randall on Saturday—he might now no more have been in the land of the living. All the party and Willy had taken the pony cart to the shore with cut branches

—and after tumbling them out, they *all* got into the cart and thought they would wash Ice's legs in the sea. Master Ice however wished a better bathe than this—he took the bit in his teeth and went straight out to sea. The cart floated up off its wheels and sank of course with so many in it. Randall jumped out in order to save Ernest by getting him out, and found the water up and over his chin. Willy put Ernest out to him. Poor fellow he tried to *carry* him, instead of dragging him in the water, but could not—stumbled and fell—the tide, which was ebbing, took him further out and he could do no more for Ernest but told him to lie still on his back with his arms out—which the brave little man did and floated perfectly. Randall called to Willy who was then out of the cart too to save Ernest—which he did. Harry stuck by the cart as he had the reins, and when Ice was fairly swimming he turned him to the shore, and then jumped out to get Ernest from Willy, that Willy might try and save Randall—he got off his coat, and little able to swim at all he went out to him—he had then sunk. Willy was afraid he might seize him so went near carefully, got hold of the hair of his head, but by this time Randall was insensible, so he was dragged to shore, and laid down on the wet sand, face down and Willy beat his back, and Harry rushed up to the house for help—met your Mamma at the door and told her in great agitation that *Randall was drowned.* But as we know Harry's little keen statements she asked him if he was out of the water and learned he was lying on the beach. I suppose the distance from the house to the gate was never travelled faster than by your Mother and Charlton. When the former got down Randall began to recover consciousness and spoke. Charlton came and *blew* into his mouth, which Randall declared afterwards was vastly abominable—and worked at him to make him breathe. Ice meantime with the wheelless cart stood as pacific as usual. Charlton walked in, to complete the matter, to save *the wheels* which were also recovered!—and so what might have been a very sad and tragical affair mercifully ended well—and more than that—for *all* even to Ernest, seem to have acted so well and so plucky, as to have really gained great praise. Randall and your Mother were both '*queer*' yesterday, but nothing worse. Now this is a very long story—but it has been a very narrow escape, and but for Willy being there both Randall and Ernest would apparently have been lost. Not a creature was on the shore to help.

Randall got sea water into his lungs, and this did him harm for long afterwards. Otherwise there were no ill effects. But it was his first narrow escape from death.

IV

In September 1862, he entered Harrow. Of the choice of his school he writes as follows:

> What led my Father to choose Harrow I forget, if I ever knew. He knew nothing about English Public Schools, and if he had had wise advice he would not, I think, have sent me, as he did, to a small House.
>
> It had, however, the advantage of beginning my life-long friendship with Arthur Watson, who then had a small House (Byron House) occupied in after years by Matthew Arnold. I happily retained the friendship of Arthur Watson for many years, and his kindness to me was unvarying during nearly half a century. He was a Rugbeian under Tait, was then at Balliol, and was afterwards a Fellow of All Souls. He at once opened for me new channels of thought; he was a cultivated Radical, and I had not been much in touch with Radicals.
>
> I remember to this day the impression made on me by his talk at meals on political subjects, and my inward revolt against the silly scorn with which my companions, and I with them, thought it our duty to regard Liberal opinions. He set me thinking upon many subjects in a way which has borne fruit ever since.

Arthur (known as Vanity) Watson, though a layman, also prepared Randall for confirmation. Scarlet fever prevented his being confirmed with the rest of the boys at Harrow; and he was in fact confirmed by Bishop Tait (his future father-in-law) in St. George's, Hanover Square, on June 16, 1865. He was seventeen at the time; but he says, 'It was by my own wish that I was delayed rather beyond the usual age.' He liked relating afterwards how a kinsman found him in the church, the solitary occupant of a large pew—the said kinsman going up and down the church, looking into the pews and saying repeatedly in a loud voice, with strong Scotch accent, 'Is Randall Davidson here? Is Randall Davidson here?' Afterwards he was taken off to a high-class restaurant for lunch, and given cutlets done in champagne, a dish he never tasted again!

Byron House consisted of only six or seven boys, and the loss in games and companionship was so great that Davidson persuaded his father to move him for his last year to Westcott's, where he had many friends. To change from one house to another required a little care on the part of those concerned; for no housemaster likes to lose a promising pupil, and the very suggestion was a difficult one for the pupil to make. The negotiations were, however, so capably handled by Davidson that he got his way and yet retained his friendship with Watson. The following letter, while revealing the schoolboy, is most characteristic of that ability to get his own way without hurting other people's feelings which was to be so remarkable a quality of his later life:

RANDALL DAVIDSON *to his* FATHER

Byron House. Saturday, May 26[, 1866.]

. . . I have been feeling lately, more than I ever did before, a craving for the society and companionship of other fellows well up in the school, and desire for *intellectual* friends *in the house.* Poor old Mahon though an excellent fellow has about as much *thought* in him, on any subject, as this quill pen. All the VIth Form fellows in Westcott's house keep begging me to come into their house, and I really feel that I would give anything to do so. Then comes the question. Could Westcott receive me, either in September or January? *This* I should like to ascertain, before saying anything to Watson on the subject, and if he could *not* receive me, I would let the subject drop and never tell him (Watson) that I had thought of leaving him. But I am sure that Westcott would make an effort to do so, and if he could I should be *so* thankful. I know you will think me awfully *turncocky*, but I know my mind now, and my motive for the wish. The more I see of Westcott and of the fellows in the house, the more I feel what a *superior lot* they are and the more I long to be one of them. As to Watson's feelings on the subject, I feel sure that were I to explain to him my motives he would sympathize fully with me—and would not be offended. If *you* approve, don't you think the best way would be for *you* to send a line to Westcott asking him to *speak to me* on the subject, as I think that would have more weight with him than if I were to go and ask him myself? At the same time you begging him not to mention it to Watson, if he could *not* receive me at all.

Sunday Night, May 27.

I have been walking today with Tupper, who thinks it very probable that Westcott will manage somehow to receive me, at Christmas if not next term. If you write, perhaps it would be better to send the letter *through me.* In that case I should give it him at some time when he could not possibly see Watson before he saw me again. I know he would say nothing till he had thought over it.

But you manage that as you think best. If you don't approve of the change, then never mind, as I have no doubt I shall get on all right where I am—and can console myself by thinking that 'Distance lends enchantment to the view'.

The petition was successful, and the last year of his Harrow life was spent in Westcott's House, where he shared a room with Graham Murray (later Lord Dunedin), whose parents were intimate friends of Randall's parents at Edinburgh. Lord Dunedin described him later as 'not having any special position in the school, but very easy to live with, as he was good natured and not quarrelsome or even argumentative'.

The two greatest influences on Davidson at Harrow were the headmaster, Dr. H. M. Butler, and his new housemaster, B. F. Westcott. He was under Butler in the Upper Sixth from September 1864 to July 1867, and found his teaching 'a constant source of interest and gain'. Butler's sermons also impressed him quite remarkably, and there is many a letter written on the Sunday or Monday giving a full account of Butler's Sunday sermon and showing how much it meant to the boy—though there were occasional exceptions. The friendship which began at Harrow grew in after days and lasted nearly sixty years.

A deeper impression still was made by Westcott, 'for whom I entertained from the first a kind of reverence which never left me till he died'. He writes:

> Westcott was to us VIth Form boys very much what he has always remained to me—the Prophet to whom we looked for intellectual guidance on every subject, human and divine. I would give a great deal now to have over again the kind of talks he used to give to us advanced boys on subjects lying quite outside the then School Curriculum, e.g. the leading Features of the Middle Ages, the Growth and Character of Christian Architecture, the Influence of Great Men upon their Times, and so on. He was often quite over our heads, at least over mine, but that was all the better. I think he did really give us a spur which was bound to be lifelong towards the better understanding of things outside the run of schoolboy literature. He was the first to make any of us think about Browning, and, indeed, I know of no one else at Harrow who ever mentioned Browning. And he utterly bewildered us by his plunges into Kant and Comte and hagiology.

Westcott was not, however, by any means always at his best

HENRY DAVIDSON
Father of R. T. D.
(*After* 1878)

HENRIETTA DAVIDSON (*née* SWINTON)
Mother of R. T. D.
(*About* 1878)

in preaching to boys, and the following letter gives an amusing as well as a shrewd account of the favourite master's defects.

RANDALL DAVIDSON *to his* FATHER

Rev. B. F. Westcott's. Feb. 17th, 1867.

. . . We had a very learned sermon from Westcott this morning, which might possibly have been intelligible had one been thoroughly well up in the Ecclesiastical histories of Rome, Greece, and Syria for the first 5 centuries A.D. As it was I don't suppose 10 fellows in the school could follow it. Not above 100 could hear it! His voice is feebler than ever. He is certainly a nice little fellow to talk to, and does one no end of good. He lets the most extraordinary, not to say ludicrous, remarks fall from him in a sort of soliloquy. The other day I was speaking to him of Trevelyan's Book on the Indian Mutiny (Cawnpore) and he said, 'Yes . . . yes . . . yes . . . that was the book—yes. . . . I could not shake off the idea that it was the prophet Ezekiel done into bad English,' and all this said not to me but to himself. He cries out lustily against my ale and hot meat—of course to no avail. He says 'look at me! I *lived* on cold meat when I was at Cambridge almost entirely'. I think to *look at him!* is quite enough!

Davidson's careful attention to sermons has already been noticed, and among the masters whose preaching impressed him we should not forget the Rev. John Smith, whose religious influence was of an unusual kind. In one of his letters to his father he said, 'We have had a most beautiful sermon this morning from Mr. Smith', and he gave an account of a sermon on two standards of religion. His father wrote to him with regard to the same preacher: 'I have been delighted with two accounts you have sent your Mother of sermons from Mr. Smith and Mr. Butler. Cultivate the acquaintance and society of the former as much as possible.'

The Archbishop summed up his own impressions in later years, as follows:

People complained then, as they do now, of the lack of definite religious life in the Public Schools. I can only say that my recollection of Harrow is a recollection of continuous and helpful religious influence. Watson, though a layman, prepared his boys carefully for Confirmation; he was a follower of Jowett in Theology, but a keen student of the Bible, and especially interested in such lines of thought as are followed in Stanley's *Jewish Church* and other similar books on the Old Testament, and my interest in the Old Testament became very keen.

In the summer holidays, August 1866, just before Randall's last year at Harrow, came the accident which influenced the whole of his life. It is so important, that the Archbishop's own description must be given in full:

I had been shooting rabbits with my brother and another friend at Muirhouse, and on our return into the house my friend, by some accident, let off his gun into my back. He said he was taking out the cartridges, but what exactly happened we never knew. He was only a few feet from me. We knew that the whole charge had gone in in a lump, making a hole big enough, as my Father always put it, to hold an average orange. In the confusion of treatment pending the arrival of a doctor, they threw everything away, and were unable to say afterwards how many shot had been taken out of the wound in the rush of blood, etc. The wound was so fearful that when the surgeon, Spence, who had been summoned from Edinburgh, arrived an hour later, he thought my life hopeless, and consequently, as I have always understood, abstained from doing what he would otherwise have tried to do, taking my right leg off or 'out' by the socket—a fearful operation.

(Strange to say, the facts came to light nearly fifty years later. When I was ill in 1913, there was some desire to investigate internal conditions, and the Röntgen rays were applied. This revealed a condition of things which the surgeons found to be of supreme interest. The surgeons were excited about it, and sent for me to see the skiagraph of my inside, pointing out that we could clearly count 164 shot, and that there were black patches which might contain more. That these should have been carried unconsciously by me for half a century, and not one of them should have interfered with ducts or other little organs, was surely an amazing thing! They were widely scattered through the whole of the lower trunk.)

The treatment was extraordinarily unlike what would have been given me in the way of nursing, etc., a generation later. Except my Mother, the only nurse was a Mrs. Barr, a monthly nurse, who had never had anything to do with surgery of the wound type and was simply a worthy old lady, who took all pains possible but knew nothing. My Mother was devoted to the last degree, but the absence of antiseptic treatment—universal, I suppose, since these years, but then comparatively unknown—contrasts strangely with what one has been accustomed to in surgical patients for the last

he had little or no sympathy. Of course, it was an extraordinary example of a man making his personality felt in his pupils.

Looking back at it now, I honestly think that it would have been difficult to find any other plan of preparation for Orders which would have suited me so well as Vaughan's arrangements did. I did not take kindly to the notion of a Theological College, and I cannot honestly say that this was in my judgement due to any fault on my part. The three years which passed between my graduating and my Ordination were in a very real sense a time of development and thought; I had begun to feel a keen interest in things ecclesiastical, as well as maintaining my old interest in things religious, and the friends with whom I was in closest touch —Craufurd Tait and others—had awakened a care about Church questions as such.

The district assigned to him was Denzil Street, Clare Market, a poor and squalid neighbourhood, north of the Strand, under the charge of the Rev. Brook Deedes, then Curate of St. Mary, Golden Lane, himself an old 'Dove' and afterwards Archdeacon of Hampstead. Davidson found real difficulty in the visiting of the district, owing partly to shyness, which hampered him again, he used to say, in his curacy days, and partly to the difficulty, which most young laymen would have found, in explaining his identity and mission to a suspicious occupant of a slum dwelling. His studies included Hebrew, but the Rabbi who taught him was only able to congratulate him at the end of his course upon his application, for (said he) 'ability you have none'. He worked hard and read hard—though from time to time he drove about with Craufurd Tait in his wagonette, and had lunch with the Archbishop, noting in his diary that the Taits were 'very hospitable—pressing me to come again'. He also paid visits to St. George's Hospital 'to see operations performed as a bit of training for my nerves'!

But unhappily Davidson's health was still far from robust; and hardly three of the proposed six trial months had passed when he again began to suffer from headaches and exhaustion after much reading. Once more he was ordered to rest; and the former prescription of open-air life and foreign travel was repeated—the travel to take the form of a long tour in the East with Craufurd Tait (the Archbishop's son and his close friend at Oxford and the Temple), George Courthope, Claude Hankey, and George

Horner. The close friendship which had already been formed in these few weeks between Davidson and Vaughan is indicated in the following letter written only a week after Davidson's departure from the Temple.

The REV. C. J. VAUGHAN *to* RANDALL DAVIDSON

The Temple, E.C. 23 July 1872.

You would think me very weak if you knew how much my thoughts have been fixed upon a letter from you, ever since that dear parting in my Study, which I shall never forget. It is come now, and Oh I trust you will not let it be the only one to fill up what seems to be such a long long interval till June 1873. It looks *worse*, I think, as you write it thus in *years* 'A.D.', than if you had described it by its real duration.

I shall be used to it in time. And of course you know how many things and persons I have to occupy me—so that I ought not to make you think that I care too much about it. Only I had got to think of you as one who could feel as I felt and who *anticipated* half of my thoughts ere they were uttered.

May God ever help you. If I *never* had you here again, still I should always think of you as my friend. . . .

Once more the autumn was spent in the open air on Tweedside, this time at Drygrange, a few miles lower down the Tweed between Melrose and Dryburgh, a place renowned for salmon and trout fishing and with good shooting as well.

It was then [writes Davidson] that the spell of the Border country set its firmest grip upon me. I like to dwell a little upon the Berwickshire life there in the irresistible charm and a kind of glamour attaching to the Border Country which Sir Walter Scott has made so familiar. It is not easy to describe, but I never re-visit Tweedside, or Kimmerghame, or the Cheviot country, without feeling a sort of patriotic enthusiasm for it, and indeed our Berwickshire days were to me one of the happiest periods of my life. . . . I cannot now open *The Monastery* or *The Lay of the Last Minstrel*, or other bits of Walter Scott, without feeling the air and freshness and the very smells of that Borderland. The fact that we had a great deal of partridge-shooting, and that I became a first-rate shot and was consequently invited to all kinds of rather select shooting-parties, uplifted me at the time, and dented my memory with thoughts which live and breathe for me still.

The start for the East was made in November, and on the 28th of that month the party landed at Alexandria.

Davidson kept a full diary of these months of travel, and further detailed accounts of his adventures are recorded in an interesting series of letters to his people at home. All show the extraordinary thoroughness with which he mastered the history and the geography of the places visited. In later life Davidson wrote of these travels:

> We were all keen about the things we were to do and see, and were well armed with books and money, and intent on doing the thing thoroughly. We went up the Nile in a Dahabiah—there were in those days no steamers either public or private except one belonging to the Khedive. The Dahabiah gave us ample opportunities for reading and we used it. . . . We really worked hard at the temples and history, and also gained a smattering of colloquial Arabic. . . . We had a great deal of shooting, especially pigeons, but also water-fowl of different kinds, including geese—now I believe quite unapproachable. We were on the Nile from December 9th until February 3.

The distinguishing feature of the tour no doubt was the journey through the Desert and through the Petra country. He explored the heights of Sinai and saw the sun rise from the top of the Mount (Jebel Katerina). In both letters and journals he gives vivid pictures showing how deep an impression his experiences were making on his mind. Recalling these days as Archbishop he wrote:

> The Sinai Peninsula was . . . brimful of interest every day, but we were resolved to go farther East, and succeeded at Akabah in making a bargain with the wilder Alawin Tribe to escort us through the Petra Country. Strangely enough I found in 1906 in the House of Lords that I was apparently the only man there who had been at Akabah, at that moment the centre of diplomatic strife and discussion. Our journey through the Petra region was not without adventure, but we had no real perils of a grave sort.

The exploration of the Petra country was an unusual feat, and, as a long and interesting letter to his father shows, the journey, if not accompanied by actually serious danger, was risky and hazardous:

RANDALL *to* HENRY DAVIDSON, ESQ.

Akabah. 15 March, 1873.

The list of travellers who have been turned back by force from Petra is nearly as long as the list of those who have been robbed when there. . . . There is no other town in the world the least like it, and above all it contains almost the only very interesting site of ancient Bible history about which there is and can be no dispute. I mean Mount Hor and the actual grave of Aaron. . . .

Since I wrote the last portion of this we have passed along the old Roman route from Akabah. This route is one which has never yet been described properly, as it has only been open for the last 3 or 4 years, even theoretically; and practically the Bedoueen feuds have closed it for the last two. . . . We have had some extraordinary scenes with quarrelling Sheikhs and their wild Bedoueen retainers. . . . We know that we are liable to be robbed at any time, and yet I suppose our *persons* are as safe as they would be at home. . . . But they are not reassuring individuals to look upon. Wild, unkempt savages, lithe and bony and semi-naked, and each one armed with an ancient and very huge matchlock and a yet more ancient sword.

And here he recounts the marvels of the rose-red city of Petra:

On glancing over what I have said about Petra I don't seem to have made enough of what is I suppose the most wonderful among its many wonders, the *colours*. Remember then that all the precipices and *all* the columns, and all the caves, in short everything except the actual soil is of a deep thorough red, not always bright, but always red—and that everywhere it is crumbling and cracking and wearing, and every inch of worn or crumbled surface is streaked with purple and blue and yellow unlike any rocks anywhere else in the world. Among these colours we wandered all day—never getting into a more sombre atmosphere till Petra was far behind. Imagine also what these be-carved rocks must have looked like when fitfully lighted up by the flickering of the huge bonfires lighted by the many Arabs who spent their night in squabbling and singing round our tents. Sometimes it was all aglow from top to bottom. . . .

The tour ended in Palestine, which the party reached on March 30, when Davidson paid his first visit to Jerusalem. But he was again unwell, and was unable to spend the time he had planned in the Holy Land. He returned to England, and arrived home in June. After a few months in Scotland, he went back to the Temple. And here he continued his training without further disturbance, from October 1873 until his ordination the following March. In later years, looking back at the years 1871–4 and their varied experiences, he used to maintain that all had played their part in equipping him for the ministry—the months spent in Scotland, and the visits to Italy and the East, no less significant in their way than the actual course of theological training under the Master of the Temple. And he thought that just because the training was less professional it fitted him more than that given to most young students of theology for understanding the layman's point of view. Had he received the more normal training, or gone into retirement with his books like Edward Talbot or Edgar Gibson, he would probably have been (he said) better as a preacher and as a teacher of young men —but not necessarily better equipped for the work of life:

> I have persistently through life found the gain of my thought about religious and literary matters having reached their undergraduate maturity in surroundings which taught me instinctively to grasp the lay view, and sometimes the sporting view, on all sorts of questions on which people have got to think and act with such capacities as they possess. So I should by no means be prepared to put down as a blank space in life's preparation days the many months which I spent of those years on the hills of Dunira or the Spey or the Tweed at Yair and at Drygrange. And still less could I regard as blank spaces the months at Rome or in Northern Italy. . . .

II

It was arranged, chiefly through his friendship with Craufurd Tait, that Davidson should be ordained for work in the diocese of Canterbury, and that he should serve as curate at Dartford in Kent. He notes the Ordination (on March 1, 1874) and its circumstances thus:

> I had had opportunity of getting to know Dr. Lightfoot, who was examining Chaplain to Archbishop Tait, and after my many disappointments in competitive fields it was a satisfaction to me when he told me that I had done best in the Ordination Examination and was to read the Gospel, my papers on Butler's Analogy and the Epistle to the Hebrews having especially pleased him.
>
> I have a vivid recollection of Lightfoot speaking to three or four of us about the papers in the Archbishop's study (to be for more than a quarter of a century my own) and of the way in which he

told me, with his hand on my shoulder, that he had no hesitation in wishing that I should read the Gospel. I can remember the very spot in the room where this occurred.

Craufurd Tait had been preparing for Ordination at the same time, and we were both to be ordained with some fifteen other men, by the Archbishop either at Addington or Lambeth. Unfortunately the Archbishop was taken ill shortly before the Ordination day and was obliged to depute the task to Edward Parry, Bishop of Dover. The Ordination accordingly took place, not at Addington or Lambeth, but in St. Mark's Church, Kennington, Edmund Fisher, Vicar of St. Mark's, being one of the Archbishop's Chaplains. There I was ordained on the second Sunday in Lent, 1874, little thinking that seventeen years later I should be living as Bishop of Rochester near that Church. For the sake of the associations of the place I arranged in 1891 to hold there my first Confirmation as Bishop, two or three days after my Consecration.

Dartford, where he went to work, is in the north of Kent, fifteen miles from London and about seven miles from Gravesend. It was a town of some size, and its importance consisted in its industrial life with its paper and powder mills and ironworks. He had two vicars during his two and a half years. For the first six months his vicar was Canon Bowlby, 'a capital Vicar under whom to start'. Bowlby was 'methodical and somewhat rigid in his Church manner and usages, keen about efficient pastoral work', 'an old fashioned and staunch High Churchman of the moderate sort'. For the rest of his time Davidson served under the Rev. F. S. Dale, 'a Birmingham vicar of marked evangelical opinions'. From each he learned a great deal, both in pastoral work and in piety. He was ordained priest by Archbishop Tait on February 21, 1875, in Croydon Parish Church, and celebrated the Holy Communion for the first time on Sunday, March 7, at Dartford.

Long after, Davidson wrote thus of his happiness at Dartford—and note should be taken of his nursing of the smallpox patients:

I do not think any years in my life have been happier, and none, I think, have been more useful than those which I spent at Dartford. I enjoyed all departments of the work, except for the shyness which has always hampered my house-to-house visitations. In my second year at Dartford the work was immensely helped by the fact that a serious outbreak of smallpox of a particularly virulent type raged in the town. There was a good deal of foolish panic about it among the people, and undoubtedly we obtained access, both to houses and to hearts, which would in ordinary years have been very unwelcoming. There were a great many deaths, and I became familiar for the first time with case after case of confluent or 'Black smallpox', the most horrid I suppose of all human ills.

Nowadays when the science and system of nursing have been developed, one looks back with amazement to those days when we had in all this epidemic no nurses, and it is literally true that we curates frequently had to help in tending the sick and dying (and even the dead!) for lack of other people—the friends being often panic-stricken.

He also took an active part in the life of the neighbouring Home of St. Mary's, Stone, for preventive and rescue work, and came to the fore in Rural Deanery organizations.

Thirty years later Miss Armes, the headmistress of the National School, wrote some interesting reminiscences of Davidson at Dartford, showing amongst other things his interest in schools:

Once, when I was ill, he kept School for me (Oct. 30th, 1874). He had no difficulty about order, as the Verger at his Church testified—'I should think he can keep the Boys quiet; but then, he 's got such a eye, and he does leer at 'em'. . . . He was one of the Managers of the National Schools, and took a load off the Vicar's shoulders by acting as Correspondent, Secretary, and Treasurer at various times. He was instrumental in getting the School premises in better order, and having them better furnished, for they were not elegantly equipped; and I remember his saying 'We've got you a new ceiling, a new floor, new desks, and a harmonium—what more can we do for you?'

He was so good in visiting the sick, even the worst cases—we had several during his stay here. On one occasion a child was suffering from fever, and it was a severe case. Mr. Davidson ascertained from the Doctor when the crisis would be; and on that night about 11 o'clock, he went to the house to enquire how Florrie was. After looking at the child a little while, he prevailed on the Mother to take a rest, and he would watch instead. He did so, and when at last the child sank into a quiet sleep, he knew the fever had turned, and there was hope. Afterward, he told the Mother he did not like to think of her sitting there alone, to see the little one die; and a very true thanksgiving was offered up for the child's recovery. . . . It was a very big cloud that came over Dartford when Mr. Davidson told us he was going to leave us, and, for a while, everybody was lamenting.

He was serious, known among his fellow curates as 'the Dean', and Miss Armes records that 'generally he seemed to take the serious side of life and be so much in earnest that he did not descend to frivolity and fun'. But he had his relaxations and of these he writes:

> I was fortunate in having been able to take over from Fisher [George Carnac Fisher, his predecessor] not his work only, but his house and his housekeeper, Mrs. Richards. It was a villa in Miskin Road with a largish garden behind it. This Fisher had stocked with roses, being himself an expert. I felt this to be part of my heritage, and acquired in the early mornings the art of budding roses, and was so successful that I obtained a 1st Prize in the West Kent County Show held near Dartford. Nowadays I could no more bud a rose than I could shoe a horse!

In the middle of his Dartford life came a second visit to Palestine. He writes:

> In 1876, my fellow-curate, Arkwright, who was rich, proposed that he and I should go together to Palestine at his expense. We did so, and I had all the satisfaction which so peculiarly belongs to one's second visit to a region of absorbing interest. We left England on March 6th, but we had not been more than, I think, a week in Palestine, having visited the Jordan Valley and the Dead Sea, when he was taken ill. I did not realise at first how serious it was, and we struggled back to Jerusalem, where we were encamped outside the Damascus Gate, when, in the middle of the night, I found him raving in delirium. A thunderstorm came on at the time, and I had literally to struggle with him in the tent while I called in vain for help. Next day we got a doctor, who thought him most gravely ill; none of the then inns, such as they were in Jerusalem, would receive him, and finally we got a stone room over a Greek drinking shop. There he was laid up for weeks with most serious typhoid fever. I shared the room with him all the time, and was his only nurse, except for such aid as the Dragoman occasionally gave.
>
> The English doctor, Dr. Chaplin, was most kind, and told me afterwards that he daily expected to find me down with the fever myself. I kept myself well by taking long hard rides in the early morning and at sundown, so that I came to know the country for six or seven miles round Jerusalem better almost than any part of England or Scotland. No nurse was obtainable; the German deaconesses offered to take him into their Hospital, but none of them could speak anything but German or Arabic; he knew no word of

either, and as they refused to let me go there, he would not hear of going alone. We declined the offer.

I had not at all realised till afterwards how terribly serious his illness had been. Ultimately, as the heat became unbearable and Dr. Chaplin had to leave for England, we decided to run the risk of moving him, ill as he was. There was no road from Jerusalem to Jaffa, but we got a sort of litter, slung between two mules, one in front of it and the other behind, and carried him down through a hot night to Jaffa, although he had not previously left his bed. The litter got into difficulties and tilted him during the night. The Dragomen were lingering somewhere behind. When I dismounted to help to pick him up, my horse ran away in the darkness, and I felt that I could have sat down and cried, so hopeless did the whole matter seem. We got him, however, on board ship more dead than alive, and next day at Alexandria his brother, M.P. for Derbyshire, met him and released me. He soon got well.

This time it was his fellow traveller who was ill, and, as the account just quoted shows, very seriously ill, depending for his life during part of the time on Davidson's unremitting and devoted attention as 'his only nurse'. But it will also be noted that Davidson during these weeks acquired a most unusually perfect knowledge of Jerusalem and its surroundings, by means of 'long hard rides in the early morning and at sundown'. And fifty years later he was able to discuss the exact geography of this part of Palestine, with soldiers and administrators who were stationed there in and after the Great War, with a knowledge the freshness and accuracy of which amazed them: though he never visited the Holy Land again.

The day came, however, when Davidson had to leave Dartford. He had been a curate for three years when the move was made which was to determine the whole course of his life. It is true that one or two proposals had already been received, including the offer from the Archbishop of the living of St. Andrew and St. Mary Breadman, Canterbury, which he had declined, feeling his unsuitability for the post. The change he was destined to make was not to another parish.

One Sunday, late in 1876, Craufurd Tait came down to Dartford. He was then acting as his father's Resident Chaplain; but he was hoping to be married and would shortly leave Lambeth. A successor would be needed, and Craufurd was commissioned to inquire of Randall whether he would be ready to take his place. Randall was willing, and after some period of uncertainty the Archbishop made the offer, and it was at once accepted. By Whitsuntide 1877, Randall Davidson had taken up his abode as Resident Chaplain to the Archbishop of Canterbury at Lambeth Palace.

III

We may pause a moment to consider what manner of man it was who thus began an association with the central life of the Church of England which lasted more than fifty years.

In personal appearance Davidson was slight, though broad-shouldered. He had worn a heavy moustache before ordination, but the Archbishop had then asked him to remove it. He was now clean shaven, except for the side-whiskers customary at the time. His hair was thick and of a dark reddish-brown. But his eyes were his most conspicuous feature—clear deep-set eyes, overshadowed by great eyebrows which as time went on became more and more predominant. He had even a hungry look about him; for, while his face was not specially gaunt, his eyes seemed to pierce what was before them. And though the hungry look did not last, the deep piercing gaze remained throughout his life, looking steadily forth from under the shaggy eyebrows.

In manner he was active and energetic. He loved sport, whether fishing or shooting, and, as we have seen, he was devoted to Scotland. He had a real grace of his own, and was both kind and sociable. He had a passion for information, and a remarkable memory. He was not philosophic or poetic, but a sturdy lover of facts; and he was not at all averse from catching people out who talked in a large and rhetorical way, or had failed to verify their statements. And certainly he was prepared to make the most of any opportunities which Providence gave him. Above all, he was deeply interested in human beings, and in the work he had to do for its own sake.

To go to Lambeth as Archbishop's Chaplain is to open a door into a large new world; and while Randall no doubt missed the personal work in the parish and its schools, he quickly found all sorts of fresh, far wider, interests awaiting him in the daily programme. It was not only the diocese, nor even the Province, that demanded attention, but the whole Church overseas with all sorts of missionary problems; the relations of the Church of England with other Christian communions; critical issues in the life of the Church at home, and great national questions. He soon discovered a natural taste for affairs—and negotiations both by letter and interview—and he soon came to see at close quarters the men whose names he had known as prominent in the life of the Church and the Nation. His letters home show how quickly he took hold of his new duties, which, as Craufurd Tait had gone on a visit to the United States, covered the whole of the secretarial work. He wrote thus to his father, July 22, 1877:

The Rev. R. T. Davidson *to* Henry Davidson, Esq.

I am now bound to see and do everything. . . . I am certainly enjoying my life here hugely and making many friends. I had two nights ago an interesting little dinner at Dean Stanley's. He very kindly asked *me*, without the Archbishop, to meet a few delightful people, and a more enjoyable evening I never spent. I think Stanley himself about the most brilliant man I have ever met, much more sparkling than I had imagined. . . .

Two postscripts were added to this letter, both showing the pleasure and pardonable pride which the young man was taking in his sudden change of outlook and new touch with public matters:

Did you read the —— Correspondence? The letters were mainly my handywork.

and:

. . . I am off to coach Lord Beaconsfield's secretary upon the working of the Public Worship Regulation Act.

His very handwriting changed, and gradually acquired the beauty of form which it retained almost to the end of his life. And his manner of expressing himself on paper also matured and assumed a new sense of responsibility. And as to his health, looking back in later years he was able to say:

Notwithstanding all the hard work, that was, I think, the time of my own life at which I was stronger and healthier than at any other. My days were very busy and my nights very short, but I do not remember being laid up at all. Gradually I was getting the Chaplaincy work better and better in hand. . . .

His first big task was the Church Congress which met at Croydon in October 1877—only a few months after his arrival. The main arrangements were left in the young chaplain's hands, and at the close of the Congress Week he wrote to his father:

The Rev. R. T. Davidson *to* Henry Davidson, Esq.

Sunday night. Oct. 14, 77.

A few lines before I go to bed. This has been a quiet day after a week of ceaseless turmoil and excitement.

The Congress has more than answered the highest hopes formed for it. In answer, I am very sure, to faithful prayers. . . . We have had a most interesting week in this *house*. Most of the notorieties have been here more or less. Several are here still. We have a curious bevy of great preachers now in the house. The two great Irish orators, the Bishop of Derry and Archdeacon Reichel. Then Dean Stanley, Dean Howson of Chester, Dean Lake of Durham. Imagine my having to hold forth—extempore—in Addington Church this evening—in presence of Archbishop, Bishops and Deans, not to speak of other big people. Lord Hatherley strikes me as one of the finest specimens of a Christian man of genius I have ever seen. . . . But the hand to hand encounters of argument between the Dean of Durham (Lake)—a vigorous logical fiery sensible high-Churchman (Gladstone's friend) and Dean Stanley have been our most remarkable episodes in the household. . . .

Some notes of conversation during that Congress include the following:

Dean Stanley wholly disapproves of Church Congresses. He says he would not ever have thought of consenting to be present save for a personal desire to support the Archbishop. He could not go thither after praying 'Lead us not into temptation'. . . . Beresford Hope recounted a conversation in which Gladstone deliberately selected the four greatest men, in his opinion, in mediaeval history. They were Dante—Aquinas—Charlemagne—Innocent III. . . . Nobody agreed with G.!!

Side by side with the official work was the home life—and the Archbishop and Mrs. Tait were able to blend the two in a remarkable way. The year was divided between the two Archiepiscopal residences at Lambeth and Addington, and Stonehouse, a private house which Archbishop Tait had bought on the North Foreland. The Taits were a wonderfully united family: and the tragic loss of five little daughters in a single month twenty-one years before (March–April 1856), through scarlet fever, at the Deanery of Carlisle, had bound them all even closer to each other.

There were three daughters, all young, Lucy (21), Edith (18), and Agnes (17), and one son Craufurd (27), and they all made Randall Davidson (29) a very welcome member of the circle. In the autumn months of the first year, a new light began to dawn in the young chaplain's life, and love sprang up between him and the second of the Archbishop's daughters. She was very young, just turned nineteen—ten years younger than Davidson; but for four years she had known him as Craufurd's friend. Davidson spent Christmas 1877 in Scotland with his parents; and told his father what he was daring to hope might come to pass. A few days after returning to Addington he asked Edith Tait to be his wife. On the late afternoon of January 10, 1878, they became engaged, the Archbishop and Mrs. Tait gave their blessing; and Randall wrote joyfully home to his father:

The REV. R. T. DAVIDSON *to* HENRY DAVIDSON, ESQ.

10 Jan., 1878.

I do feel that the words 'thank God' are no empty form with me to-day—and I feel well assured that when you know something of her whom I may now call *mine*, you will join with me with all your heart.

Nothing on earth could have been kinder in the whole matter than the conduct both of His Grace and of Mrs. Tait. They utterly surprised me by their quiet readiness to accept me as a son. I shall ever feel grateful to them both for their calm wise words before I saw Edith this evening.

And now all is smooth, and *utterly* happy—and my great wish is for you to learn, by experience of *her*, how happy I am. . . .

The Archbishop also wrote—and reminded Henry Davidson of the days when they were schoolboys together at Edinburgh Academy:

ARCHBISHOP TAIT *to* HENRY DAVIDSON, ESQ.

Addington Park, Croydon.
Jan. 14, 1878.

Your kind letter arrived to-day. Randall has those sterling qualities which make me glad to have him as a son-in-law, and seems to promise every prospect of happiness to my daughter. I think both of them much to be congratulated.

He has been a great help to me and I rejoice to have him in a nearer relation.

As to material resources your letter is quite satisfactory, and

Randall, if his health is prolonged, has before him every prospect of great usefulness and eminence in the high profession to the work of which he gives himself with so much zeal and wisdom.

I trust we shall see you and Mrs. Davidson here very soon.

Edie is only 19—so they must wait till she is 20.

Your letter reminds me how long a time has passed since we were at the Academy, and it is satisfactory to both of us that our children should be settling in life before the close comes upon us.

It was arranged that the marriage should take place at the end of the year, after Edith Tait's twentieth birthday; and there was talk of where the young couple should settle after marriage. But long before the wedding-day came, a new sorrow came to the Taits. Craufurd Tait died at Stonehouse on May 29, 1878—a blow from which Mrs. Tait never recovered.

In July of that year the Lambeth Conference met, and Davidson acted throughout as a sort of additional secretary under the orders of the Bishops of Gloucester and Edinburgh, and Chancellor Brunel, who were the officials of the Conference. It was the second Lambeth Conference so far held; and Davidson was himself destined to be present at four more in four successive decades.

At the close of the summer of 1878, the living of Maidstone fell vacant, and Tait offered it to his future son-in-law. In making the offer the Archbishop was thinking, no doubt, of the new start which Davidson and his own daughter might make together in a home of their own when they were married. And Davidson's own journal shows how attractive such a prospect was to them both. Indeed he was greatly perplexed, as he wrote in his journal in the first days of August.

I don't think I have ever felt more perplexed as to what is right than I do this evening.... Ought I to accept it or not? May God guide me to a right answer. There is so very much to be said on both sides that I am utterly at a loss. On the one hand—an important parish—a grand Church—lots of work—and a delightful curate who would, I think, remain with me (Howson)—such an opportunity for doing God's work may not be again within my reach.

On the other hand to leave His Grace at present seems impossible—and I shrink from it more than I can express. He has no one else ready to come as Chaplain, and at the moment of all others in his life he is least fit to be left in the hands of someone who does not know his ways—and whom he would have to teach. If it were possible and desirable for Max Spooner to come to him again it might answer. But I do not see how it is possible. In his unselfishness he may very likely press me to go to Maidstone, and if he does so with authority I shall have no choice but to obey. But I trust he won't do so. The sum of my inclinations to-night leads me to the conclusion that it would be far better that I should stay here and help His Grace to the best of my ability.

O God direct and guide me what I ought to do! I love the Archbishop more dearly every day, and at the moment with the halo of a sacred sorrow about him he is more lovable than ever. . . .

It was Craufurd's death that made the difference, in his own judgement, as in that of those whom he consulted. He took counsel of Dr. Vaughan and Dean Stanley; and his father came specially from Scotland to advise. Henry Davidson also interviewed Dean Stanley (who had already expressed the same view to Randall)—and he said plainly, so Henry Davidson told his wife in a letter of August 7, 1878:

I would really look on your son's leaving the Archbishop at this time, heavily burdened by a great sorrow, and shaken in system, as nothing short of a National Evil!! For the sake of the Church, and the valuable life *for it* of His Grace, I would quite deplore such a thing at this time. . . . I cannot contemplate too gravely, the gravity of the loss at this moment.

Randall's decision was made—to decline Maidstone and stay at Lambeth. There was indeed another side:

There must certainly be a disagreeable side to living on in a house after marrying a daughter thereof, and if Craufurd had lived I think I should have been very unwilling to consent to stay here.

Nevertheless his judgement was clear:

God has ordered it otherwise—and as Craufurd is not visibly with us I think it my clear duty to do everything in my power to help His Grace, and to enable him more easily to carry on his work.

And there is this far-seeing note about his future wife:

My mind is now at rest, as I am sure we have come to the right decision. As for Edith she is now as always so absolutely ready to do what is shown to be *right* that self never seems to come into the case at all. I positively *dread* her unselfishness after our marriage.

One will need to be very watchful to prevent her from giving way over-much. I do thank God for her love! and all my countless other mercies.

During the next four years further offers came at intervals from the Archbishop or others—including the vicarage of Croydon and a residentiary canonry at Canterbury. But Davidson used to say in later years that, except for the offer of Maidstone in 1878, when he was really perplexed, he never had any real doubt that, so long as Tait lived, his place was by his side.

His marriage with Edith Tait took place in Lambeth Palace Chapel on November 12, 1878, and the bridegroom and his bride started off for their honeymoon to Florence. But within three weeks of the wedding-day they were called home. Mrs. Tait was suddenly taken ill on November 29. She died, fifty-nine years old, on Advent Sunday, December 1, and was laid to rest in Addington Churchyard on December 7, the twentieth birthday of her married daughter. So, doubly bereaved in a single year, the old Archbishop came to turn more than ever before to his chaplain and 'true son' for a help which never failed.

IV

The story of his chaplaincy has been told by Davidson himself in the penultimate chapter of his *Life of Archbishop Tait.* He speaks there of the affection which he felt for his chief, an affection that increased in a measure he had not expected with every month of his remaining years. And he describes how the 'sacred principle of delegation', as Tait called it, became with him a fine art, and how he applied it with a success to which Davidson knew no parallel; rarely writing a letter himself, and yet retaining even in small matters a control and recollection which frequently surprised them all. But there were many letters both written and signed by Davidson, notably the correspondence with the Rev. S. F. Green, imprisoned for contempt of court in a ritualist controversy, March 1881, which admirably illustrate Davidson's characteristic power of sticking to the point and pressing a correspondent. The following letter is a good example, and at the same time prophetic of the issues which it was to be Davidson's task to try to get the Church to face for many years to come:

The Rev. R. T. Davidson *to the* Rev. S. F. Green[1]

Addington Park. Croydon
20th Jan. 1882.

My dear Sir,

Your letter, just received, makes it clear, if I understand you rightly, that no authority, ecclesiastical or civil, exists to which you would feel yourself at liberty to defer with respect to the practical action which you found upon your own interpretation of the Ornaments Rubric. If I am mistaken in this, please set me right, in order that the Archbishop may clearly understand your position. His Grace now directs me to ask you further: Does any authority exist, ecclesiastical or civil, at the command of which you would be willing, under protest if necessary, to abstain for a time from officiating in the church of Miles Platting, if you were now at liberty?

You will, I am sure, excuse the formulating of the question in this abrupt form, with a view to a clear understanding of the facts of your position.

Believe me to remain, yours very sincerely,

Randall T. Davidson
Chaplain.

Readers of the *Life of Tait* will also remember Davidson's share in the correspondence between Tait and the Rev. A. H. Mackonochie in the last weeks of the Archbishop's life, when the chaplain helped to pave the way for Mr. Mackonochie's resignation of St. Alban's, Holborn, and the termination by this means of the proceedings against him in a court the jurisdiction of which he had so long refused to recognize.[2] It is perhaps worth noting, even thus early in the present work, a comment by Davidson in his *Life* of his father-in-law which throws a good deal of light on his own attitude to ritual disputes:

It is necessary to remember that the space occupied by the narrative [of the Ritual controversy] is out of all proportion to the Archbishop's estimate of its direct importance. His speeches and letters must have made it clear how anxious he always was to relegate the subject of ritual details to the comparatively insignificant place which he thought to belong to it, in face of the great problems of faith and morals which were claiming the attention of the Christian Church. The question was forced into prominence by the far larger subject which had become connected with it—

[1] See *Life of Archbishop Tait*, vol. ii, p. 460.
[2] Ib., vol. ii, pp. 474–80.

nothing less than the whole question of authority and discipline within the Church.[1]

There are references in his papers to the missionary side of the work at Lambeth, and to his relationship to Church Societies:

I have already in Archbishop Tait's *Life* said a good deal about my Chaplaincy years, though of course the things which happened had to do with him rather than with me. . . . I was from the first led to concern myself actively with the work of different Church Societies in London. . . . [Archbishop Tait] had never taken an active part, for example, in S.P.G. work or, indeed, in missionary administration. There had been great episodes like Copleston's troubles in Ceylon, or the Madagascar rivalries of French and English, in which he had been forced to act, and had acted with supreme wisdom, but, speaking generally, I was the first at Lambeth to become active in the daily administration of missionary questions. I was on committees and sub-committees of S.P.G., and a few extracts from my rough journal will show how ceaselessly I was in Delahay Street.

Again, the Junior Clergy Society, which was then rather an important body of the more active of the young clerics in London, made considerable trespass on my time and thoughts. The active men in the thick of it with me were J. W. Horsley, Stewart Headlam, and Dawes—afterwards Bishop of Rockhampton. I was elected to be chairman and attended without fail. I soon came to see the gain for the Archbishop's chaplain being thus in touch with what these young men were doing and saying, and I have since tried, when myself Archbishop, to encourage my chaplains to a like course, and certainly Macmillan, Bell, and Haigh, and to some extent others also, have carried on the tradition. . . .

It was, it may be added, through his membership of the Junior Clergy Society that Davidson first came into contact with the Trade Union Movement. Stewart Headlam, the well-known reformer and educationalist (whose fag Craufurd Tait had been at Eton), was on the extreme Left of this Society, and the founder in 1877 of the Guild of St. Matthew with its strong Christian Socialist programme. It was Headlam and a few like-minded members who arranged meetings between the Clergy and the Trade Union leaders, in which Davidson also took part. In those days such an ardent championship of Labour as Headlam's was very unpopular with Churchmen; and Davidson's sympathy at

[1] *Life of Archbishop Tait*, vol. ii, p. 473.

such a time must not be forgotten, nor the fact that he intervened on Headlam's behalf in his struggles with the Bishop of London (Dr. Jackson) over a telegram which Headlam had sent to Charles Bradlaugh, the radical free thinker, in prison. In the *Life of Stewart Headlam* it is noted a few years later, after Davidson had ceased to be Chaplain at Lambeth, that Headlam, an enthusiastic disciple of the works of Henry George, in a letter to a friend, one of his left-wing colleagues in the Junior Clergy Society, states:

> Davidson told me that he had got the Queen to read *Progress and Poverty* which she found difficult.[1]

Davidson also took a special interest in the Salvation Army, and acted as Archbishop Tait's intermediary. Thus he attended all sorts of meetings in connexion with the Army, and obtained information of every kind, officially and otherwise, about its agencies and modes of work. It was he who supplied Tait with the material for his speeches in Convocation and in the House of Lords, and it was he too who sent the contribution of £5 on the Archbishop's behalf to General Booth 'for the purpose of acquiring a site, at present occupied by a theatre, tavern and dancing gardens', for the religious work of the Salvation Army, especially on its rescue side. And there is an even more interesting point. Randall Davidson, while full of appreciation of 'the straightforward ability and earnest zeal of the leaders of the Army', fastened at this early date on what was to prove the principal cause of difficulty for the Army in the future. In an article on the Salvation Army, in *The Contemporary Review* for August 1882, he wrote as follows:

> I pass on now to notice some of the characteristics of the work, which, if uncorrected, must tend, as it seems to me, to impair its usefulness as a permanent agency for God's glory and man's good. Some of them may at present be mere symptoms of possible danger ahead. If so, the more reason they should now be considered and examined, both by the 'Army' and by those who wish it well.

[1] *Stewart Headlam. A Biography*, by F. G. Bettany, 1926, pp. 38, 40, 84. To Headlam, in his last illness on October 22, 1924, Randall Davidson wrote a warm letter in which were these words: ' "What a many" years you and I look back across to our London experiences. I vividly recall the old Junior Clergy days in St. Martin's vestry, with Horsley and Dawes and Thomas and Hancock and Hill, and a great many more' (ib., p. 239). The links between Headlam and Davidson were thus maintained to the end.

> The point which naturally suggests itself first, though I do not think it is the most important, is the *Autocracy of the General in Command.* Few outsiders, probably, are aware how absolute is his rule. He is the sole trustee for all the buildings and property of the Army; he is empowered to nominate his successor in the trust; and he can by his mere fiat dismiss any officer in the service, or transplant him to another station or to new work. . . . Now this may work very well so long as Mr. Booth is alive and able for all his duties, but the experience of history does not lead us to anticipate that it will of necessity work equally well when he is gone. . . . It is understood, if not yet definitely enacted, that 'General' Booth is to be succeeded by his eldest son, already a prominent officer upon his father's staff. If the system of arbitrary generalship is—judging by the experience of history—a dangerous one for the common good, the danger in the case of a religious organisation is certainly not diminished by introducing the notion of hereditary rule. Unless it be in some of the smaller and more benighted Eastern Churches, where the Patriarch is necessarily succeeded by his nephew, I doubt whether an analogous system can be found in any religious community in the world. It may possibly be said that the results should be left to God, who will guide and protect His own. But a like plea might of course be put forward for any honest system which could be devised, and the problem is not by any means thus easily disposed of.

The latest biographer of General Booth, though critical of Davidson's efforts in other ways with regard to the Army, has called attention to the remarkable accuracy of this prophecy. He says:

> [Dr. Davidson] criticized the Army's government and, with singular penetration and prescience, foretold the impasse to which that government brought Bramwell Booth and the Army in 1929. This is one of the few prophetic articles which can bear republication without fear, since its forecastings have not been refuted.[1]

During these years Davidson also gained a remarkable position among the Bishops, and much of their business was done through him instead of direct with the Archbishop. With Bishop Lightfoot of Durham he had a special link from his ordination, and he took it as a very particular honour that this great scholar invited him to become one of his Examining Chaplains; and, still feeling the disappointment of his third class at Oxford, it

[1] See *God's Soldier*, by St. John Ervine, vol. ii, p. 838 (1934).

ARCHBISHOP TAIT, EDITH DAVIDSON,
RANDALL DAVIDSON
(*About* 1879)

was with the utmost diffidence that he accepted. Another Bishop for whom he conceived a growing admiration was Bishop Benson. He and Mrs. Davidson stayed with the Bensons at Truro in 1881—and Davidson noted in his journal that he 'is a grand man, whom I would give much to see Bishop of London some day . . . full of fresh sympathy with all forms of Church life from Ritualism to Methodism'. In days when Church meetings were far less frequent than they are now, a convenient place of meeting was the House of Lords, where the senior Bishops have a special Bench which was more constantly filled then than it is to-day. Tait made much use of the Archbishops' room at the House, and Davidson acquired for himself the right, as Chaplain, to stand with the private secretaries of Cabinet ministers and other official assistants, just by the steps of the Throne, beside the Bishops' Bench, a right which has been accorded to the Chaplains of the Archbishop of Canterbury ever since.

As domestic chaplain in the strict sense of the word, Davidson carried out his duties with quietness and efficiency. He held a Bible class for the members of the household; and he prepared them for Confirmation. He effected reforms in the Embertide arrangements preceding the Ordination Sundays. By his suggestion the examination of the candidates was held some time before the Ember Days, instead of during those days, as was then the common custom: thus allowing a time of peace and devotion under the Archbishop's roof immediately before the men were ordained, unharassed by the writing of their papers or anxiety as to the result. The help and sympathy he gave those who came for Ordination was very marked, and by some long remembered.[1]

His personal relations with the Archbishop were, as we have already suggested, as those of a son to his father. Occasionally Tait's calmness and dislike of anything approaching 'hustle' would make his zealous and eager chaplain anxious, but on such occasions Tait would merely remark 'It is only Dibson in a fuss'. And his grave references to his young son-in-law as 'that eminent

[1] When R. T. D. first went to Lambeth as chaplain the result of the Ordination examination was announced on the Saturday, on the very eve of ordination. He changed this—and developed the personal relations between the candidates and the Archbishop. In the Diocese of Ely R. T. D. related, in connexion with a Canterbury Embertide of 1920, how Bishop Turton's (Bishop 1845–64) one personal touch with his candidates was at dinner after the Ordination, when he would call out, e.g. to the gospeller, 'Mr. Smith, a glass of wine with you!'

divine' show that the leaven of humour was not lacking in their relationship. But it must be confessed that the pressure was considerable, and work always came first—as was somewhat ruefully recognized by Edith Tait even before their marriage. So at least the following note suggests:

EDITH TAIT *to* RANDALL DAVIDSON

26 June, 1878

Then I shan't see you till Saturday! I can't help a little wishing in the bottom of what I am pleased to call my heart that you and Father weren't quite so 'devoted and excellent'. But of course you will say that this is very wicked and it is all for the good of the Church and I don't know what. Well then I submit, as there's nothing else to do.

And after their marriage the Rector of Lambeth used to shake his head and say, 'She wants more cherishing. Davidson is too austere—too much wrapped up in affairs.'

As a recognition in the diocese of his service to the Church, the Archbishop appointed Davidson one of the Six Preachers of Canterbury Cathedral. He was invited to do a good deal of preaching away from Lambeth, and spoke at more than one Church Congress. He was sufficiently well known outside to make it natural for the Dean of Windsor (Wellesley) to nominate him as sub-almoner to the Queen in 1882, and for the Lord Chamberlain (Lord Sydney) to recommend him for a chaplaincy to Her Majesty.

Randall's mother died in 1881, after a long illness. Though they were devoted to one another, Davidson had never felt that his mother cared for or understood his chaplaincy work. She feared indeed that the secretarial and administrative duties might outweigh the pastoral life—the winning of souls—to which she had dedicated him in her heart. But it is significant of the close spiritual tie which bound them that often he wrote and asked for his mother's prayers for some important meeting or conference. On one such occasion he wrote '... *Don't* neglect to pray for us definitely on *Friday* soon after you get this. We meet at 11.30.' And as he prayed beside her as she lay dying, the words that came to her lips again and again were 'Randall, Randall'.

A year later it became clear that Archbishop Tait's life could not be prolonged, and in the autumn of 1882 the long weeks of gradually lessening strength began. On December 1, Davidson wrote to his father, 'The doctor thinks it must come *to-night*. He is quite calm and like himself . . . God is strengthening him and all about him, and when the change comes it will find him "prepared" if ever man was. . . .'

The 'change' came on the morning of Advent Sunday, December 3,[1] three weeks before his seventy-first birthday. His son-in-law ministered to him to the end, and received both blessing and charge from the dying Archbishop in the parting words, 'My dear Randall. Dear dear boy. You have been a true son to me ever since Craufurd died. Take care of them all.'

[1] Archibald Campbell Tait, born at Harviestoun, Dec. 21, 1811; died at Addington, Dec. 3, 1882.

CHAPTER III

FROM LAMBETH TO WINDSOR

I write again praying you that ye will be at the court as shortly after Easter as ye can, for the Queen will see you; and for as much as Mr. Betts is departed, I think her mind is to have you to her chaplain. I pray you resist not your calling. 23rd March, 1534–5. JOHN SKYPP, *the Queen's Almoner, to the* REV. MATTHEW PARKER (*Correspondence of Archbishop Parker*).

It is after all most difficult to judge when the Queen likes a person or what sort of person she will like. DEAN WELLESLEY *to* LADY DERBY, *September* 1874.

FOR some months before the Archbishop's death, many of the foremost leaders in Church and State had been considering the question of his successor. The names most prominent in such private discussions were those of the Bishop of Winchester (Harold Browne, aged seventy-two), the Bishop of Durham (J. B. Lightfoot, aged fifty-four), the Dean of St. Paul's (R. W. Church, aged sixty-seven), and the Bishop of Truro (E. W. Benson, aged fifty-three). Mr. Gladstone was Prime Minister, and it was known that he would act with a high sense of responsibility, whatever the recommendation he thought right to make to the Queen. It was also natural that the dying Archbishop himself should consider the question. But the Archbishop, though having views of his own, was most anxious not to express them in any way which would have even the appearance of a desire to influence the Prime Minister in his decision; indeed, he quite definitely said, some two months before his death, in answer to his chaplain's specific inquiry as to whether he desired him to make a statement to the authorities about his own view:

> No; not, at all events, as a message from me. God has not laid on me that responsibility. It is in other hands, and I have no wish to assume it.[1]

It is clear, however, that Tait's own judgement led to a choice between the Bishop of Winchester and the Bishop of Truro. The Bishop of Truro stayed at Addington in September, and the Archbishop told him then that he hoped he would succeed him. But he was unwilling to make a specific recommendation. And, perhaps with some consideration of the Bishop of Truro's

[1] *Life of Archbishop Tait*, vol. ii, p. 592.

comparative youth, he said, only a few days before his death, November 23:

> I should be truly thankful to think it certain that the Bishop of Winchester would succeed me at Lambeth. He could do more than any other man to preserve the Church in peace for its real work against sin. I pray God he may be appointed and may accept the call.

Indeed, Tait went so far as to request his chaplain to write to the Bishop of Winchester about the wisdom of his continuing Bishop Parry as Bishop-Suffragan of Dover. Davidson felt that such a statement was too grave for him to keep locked up in his own breast. He accordingly informed Dean Bradley of Westminster, with whom, as well as with the Deans of Durham (Lake) and St. Paul's, Mr. Gladstone was likely to be in touch. He also informed the Queen through Lady Ely; and thus began that long and remarkable association with Her Majesty which was to mean so much for his whole life. The following are the first letters which passed between the Queen and the Chaplain:

The Rev. R. T. Davidson *to the* Queen

3 Decr. 1882
Madam, Addington Park, Croydon.

In accordance with Your Majesty's gracious wish, expressed through Lady Ely, on Friday last, I beg leave dutifully to lay before Your Majesty some of the details as to the last days of the Archbishop's life.

Last Thursday evening he told us repeatedly that he felt sure it was to be his last night on earth, and longed it might be so.

I took down a few words of the prayer which he, as usual, offered with us, before going to sleep.

'Father into Thy hands I commend My spirit: Myself, with all my sins, forgiven for Jesus' sake,—All my dear ones—All whom I love here—The Church with all its difficulties—The Queen in Her Person, Her Family, Her Office,—Our orphan Home,—Keep them all under the shadow of Thy wings for Jesus Christ's sake—Amen.'

At three o'clock on Friday morning, we were called to his bedside. He had had a slight convulsive fit, but had not lost consciousness, and was then quite himself.

He thought, as we did, that he was just dying. I reminded him that it was the anniversary of Mrs. Tait's death, and he called out 'O *is it*? What a blessed thing!' He said a few farewell words to each of his Daughters, and to me, and then asked for the Commendatory prayer from the 'Visitation service'.

When I had read it he gave the benediction, and then added quite in his usual manner, 'And now that is all. It isn't so dreadful after all. My beloved children—God keep you—and my friends—and my servants—and all whom I love. How many there are that I love, and don't forget!'

Afterwards he rallied somewhat, and had some broken sleep for several hours. At ten o'clock on Friday morning he asked to receive the Holy Communion. He followed the service throughout, and—speaking with some difficulty—gave the benediction at the close.

We did not expect him to live through the day, but he lay in a drowsy state, not suffering much, and quite conscious when roused.

Lady Ely's visit with Your Majesty's kind message touched him very deeply.

Of that Your Majesty has already received an account.

He did not speak much more during the afternoon or evening, but referred twice to Your Majesty's gracious message.

We were again summoned about three o'clock yesterday morning as he seemed to be dying. But he once more rallied and then for twenty-four hours he lay still—breathing very heavily but seldom sleeping and apparently conscious of all that went on. He was able to answer if we spoke to him, but it seemed rather to disturb him. We read short passages of Scripture and said hymns and prayers at intervals, and he was always aware of it, and it seemed to soothe him.

Early this morning a change came over his face, and his breathing became much quieter—until at last, at a quarter past seven, it simply ceased, without any struggle or pain whatever.

Your Majesty was good enough to ask that I should state how the Archbishop's daughters were—when the Archbishop had gone.

They are all perfectly well and cheerful—thanking God for this quiet end to an illness which seemed as though it might close with violent pain.

We all attended Church this morning and remained for Holy Communion.

I need not say how great a help has been afforded by Your Majesty's gracious and touching kindness.

I have the honour to remain, Madam,

Your Majesty's Most obedient humble Servant,

RANDALL T. DAVIDSON.

The QUEEN *to the* REV. R. T. DAVIDSON[1]

Windsor Castle. Dec. 5, 1882

I have been deeply touched by your beautiful account of the last days and hours of the beloved Archbishop, who had ever been so kind to me and mine and for whom I had the greatest respect, esteem, and sincerest affection! That he should have thought and spoken of me, so near the end of his exemplary, useful, and valuable life, is most gratifying to me and will help to reconcile me to the great disappointment of being unable to go and see him. Nothing but the distance from Addington and the overwhelming number of public duties could prevent me from doing so. It was also most painful to me to be unable to put off yesterday's Ceremony. [This refers to the opening of the new Law Courts.]

Lady Ely has forwarded to me your letter and I am most grateful to you for what you tell me as to the dear Archbishop's views, respecting his successor, painful as it is to think of such a thing. I may however say that I had heard just the same from Mr. Gladstone, who had heard it from the Dean of Durham, *not* as a message, but from what he (Mr. G.) had *gathered* from the Dean. These views, I may in confidence state, will be followed, the Bishop of Winchester's age being perhaps the only difficulty. It is a great comfort to know the dear Archbishop's opinion on such a momentous question.

I shall be most grateful for the engraving you mention and have a request to make, which is whether I might have a little of his hair?

Would it suit you to come and see me on Saturday, either at ¼ to 3 or ½ past 5? I am most anxious to make your acquaintance having heard so much of you.

Pray say everything most kind from me to dear Miss Tait and her sisters. You have been so devoted to him that the thought of this and his present happiness must be a comfort in the midst of the great sorrow for the loss of such a Father!

The interview took place on December 9. The impression made by Davidson was immediate, as the extract from the Queen's Journal for that day clearly reveals.[2]

December 9, 1882.

A fine morning, without much frost.—After luncheon, Leopold and Helen left.—Saw Mr. Davidson, the Arch Bishop's son-in-law, and was seldom more struck than I have been by his personality. He had written me a most striking account of the Arch Bishop's death,

[1] *Letters of Queen Victoria*, 2nd Series, vol. iii, p. 367. [2] Ibid., p. 368.

and said he believed there had been but little suffering. They had been 3 times called up, when it was thought he was dying, but he had rallied again. The Arch Bishop, Mr. Davidson said, had been much attached to me, and always used to pray specially for me every night. Mr. Davidson alluded to the letter the Arch Bishop had written me, and to the strong hope he had expressed (though he would not leave it exactly as a message) that the Bishop of Winchester, or Bishop of Truro, might succeed him. The former was rather old, but would command the respect and acquiescence of all the Bishops. The Arch Bishop had seen him several times during his illness, also the Bishop of Truro, and had had a great deal of conversation with him and entered most fully into his views and plans. The Bishop of Truro, Mr. Davidson said, was a man of singular power, firmness, and at the same time, gentleness. He, Mr. Davidson, had been during 6 years, Chaplain to the Arch Bishop, and for 4 years, his son-in-law. For the last 2, he had written everything for the Arch Bishop from dictation, and latterly he had only got directions as to what he was to say. The 3 months illness had been much blessed to them, for they had been able to talk over and discuss everything, nothing being omitted. A cast, after death, had been taken, and they hoped to get a statue made, either for Canterbury or Westminster. No Arch Bishop, since Cardinal Pole, had been buried at Canterbury, hence the idea of his being laid at Westminster Abbey, but they greatly preferred Addington. We went over various topics, and I feel that Mr. Davidson is a man who may be of great use to me, for which I am truly thankful.—Lenchen and Christian, Lord and Lady De Vesci, (both handsome) Mr. Boyd Carpenter, a very nice clever little man, Sir J. McNeill, Lady Abercromby and Lord Dalhousie, dined.

Sir Henry Ponsonby's comment, when Davidson returned to his room at the end of an hour's talk (in which, says Davidson, 'she certainly startled me by the openness of her confidence, and by her genuine anxiety to hear all that I had to say'), was 'What on earth has been happening? I don't know when the Queen has had such a long interview with anybody.'

The next step concerned Mr. Gladstone, who had very soon made up his mind that the Bishop of Winchester was too old, and, in Dean Lake's words, 'on the whole decidedly inclined to Truro'. Dean Lake, who reported this to Davidson, after a long bedside talk with Mr. Gladstone, went on to make the following suggestion in a letter of December 4:

The Dean of Durham *to the* Rev. R. T. Davidson

Athenaeum. Dec. 4

Most private

This being the case, I feel sure you will allow me to suggest, that if you say anything of the Archbishop's views as to his successor to the Queen, it might be right in itself and might diminish the possibility of difficulties, if the Archbishop's decided preference for Truro *next to Winchester* were mentioned. You mentioned to me the Archbishop's unwillingness to interfere with Gladstone's responsibility,—and yet there might be danger of his doing so, if the Queen, in her present keen feeling of affection for him, imagined that his wishes were entirely set upon Winchester.

It must also be remembered with regard to Truro's difficulties with Bishops, that a very few years may probably see an important accession of younger Bishops to the Bench.

The Queen, as Dean Lake had prophesied, desired the appointment of the Bishop of Winchester. Mr. Gladstone in a long memorandum stated his conviction that the Bishop of Winchester was 'no longer equal to such duties as the Primacy would entail' and recommended the Bishop of Truro. The Queen persisted in pressing the Bishop of Winchester, and objected to the Bishop of Truro's youth. The following letter was written to Mr. Gladstone:

The Queen *to the* Rt. Hon. W. E. Gladstone

Windsor Castle. Dec. 10, 1882.

Though the Queen will see Mr Gl. tomorrow she thinks it may facilitate a decision which will have to be come to now—as to who is to succeed the beloved and excellent Archbishop of Canterbury—if she writes these few lines.

She has thought a great deal about it and feels convinced that to place a man of only 53, excellent as he is, above all the other Bishops would create a very bad and angry feeling in the Church and that the Bishop of Winchester is far the fittest to be appointed now.

He could resign in two years if he were unable to go on—but for that time he surely could undertake it—and should be pressed to do so. In the last letter the dear Dean W. ever wrote to the Queen he spoke of this as the best arrangement and said he thought Mr. G. likewise thought so.

The dear Archbishop by what Mr. Davidson wrote and told the Queen certainly hoped this.

The Bishop of Truro should go to Winchester which is far harder work than the Archiepiscopal see.

The Queen was very much struck with Mr. D. with whom she had a long interview yesterday. He is singularly pleasing both in appearance and manner, very sympathetic and evidently very intelligent—wise and able.

At the same time the Queen instructed Davidson to obtain the most accurate information possible respecting the health and physical strength of the Bishop of Winchester; and in response to his suggestion entrusted Davidson with the very delicate mission of going to Farnham with a view to a confidential talk with Mrs. Harold Browne about her husband's health. The result of his difficult embassy is recorded in the following letter:[1]

The REV. R. T. DAVIDSON *to the* QUEEN

Addington Park, Croydon.
Dec. 13, 1882

I have the honour to report, in accordance with Your Majesty's direction, the result of my confidential interview this afternoon with Mrs. Harold Browne. I merely told Mrs. Browne that your Majesty having certain names under consideration, had directed me to find out as accurately as possible what is the present condition of the Bishop of Winchester's health and physical vigour. I feel quite sure that Mrs. Browne will respect absolutely the confidential character of the communication.—I learn from her that the Bishop of Winchester is really stronger at this moment than he has been for some time past, and that he finds himself quite competent for the discharge of any reasonable amount of work *upon his present lines.* He suffers from no actual complaint of any sort, except that he is subject from time to time to really severe colds which lay him temporarily aside—At the same time Mrs. Browne shrinks from the responsibility of saying decidedly that the Bishop, who will be 72 next March, would be physically strong enough to enter upon all the somewhat unknown duties of the Primacy—should the post be offered to him. She naturally sees that his strength and vigour are likely to grow yearly less; and she tells me that she and the Bishop would alike recoil from the idea of his entering upon such vast and new responsibility unless with a reasonable prospect of his being able to discharge its duties for some years at least. On this point, were the Primacy to be offered to him, the Bishop would—Mrs. Browne thinks—take a competent

[1] *Letters of Queen Victoria*, 2nd Series, vol. iii, p. 375.

medical opinion before accepting or declining. I tried to explain to Mrs. Browne as fully as I could the actual character of the work done during the course of the year by the late Archbishop; and while she thinks the Bishop's strength would be husbanded by his having as Primate so much less travelling than the Diocese of Winchester demands, she evidently has some fear as to his very nervous temperament being proof against the exceptional anxieties which must press upon the Archbishop of Canterbury. In short, Madam, Mrs. Browne is unable to form a clear opinion of the Bishop's physical capabilities for the post, although on the whole she would look hopefully to his being able for it.—Your Majesty will perhaps allow me to say that my protracted conversation with Mrs. Browne led me to attach somewhat more weight than I had previously given to what I have certainly heard in more than one quarter as to the Bishop's decreasing vigour. Nor would it be right for me to lead Your Majesty to suppose that the late Archbishop before expressing the private opinion which has been communicated to Your Majesty and to Mr. Gladstone, had given special and minute consideration to the *physical* qualifications or disqualifications of the Bishop of Winchester for the work of the Primacy—I have now, I think, had the honour of laying before Your Majesty with my humble duty all the information within my reach as to the health of the Bishop of Winchester—Your Majesty has been pleased to direct me also to answer another question to the best of my humble ability—viz 'What would the feeling of the Bishops be, looking to the *possibility* of the Bishop of Truro being chosen?'

The knowledge I have gained from the private correspondence and the episcopal and other meetings of the last five years at Lambeth enables me, I think, to answer Your Majesty's question with tolerable certainty. The Bishop of Winchester is probably the only Bishop whose Presidency, were his health known to be equal to it, would fall in with the general wish of the entire Episcopate. His gentle wisdom and unobtrusive learning have long commended him in a marked degree to all the Bishops, even to those who would naturally be most afraid of his supposed High Church views. I have again and again had opportunity of observing the respect with which his views have been received on subjects where the difference of opinion had been marked.—Next to him, IN THE VIEW OF THE EPISCOPATE, would undoubtedly stand the Bishop of Durham. His position is so unique a one, and his reputation in certain fields so unrivalled, that with two dissentients only among the Bishops I believe he would be received with emphatic favour as their chief.

The Bishop of Truro would, as I believe, stand next in Episcopal favour. He is only a few years younger than the late Archbishop was on his appointment to the Primacy, and I cannot recall a single instance, either at a Lambeth Meeting or in Convocation, in which he has met with anything but cordiality and admiration among the assembled Bishops. The Archbishop often spoke to me of his remarkably sudden access to Episcopal favour and reputation—But undoubtedly there are three (or probably four) Bishops who would feel hurt and angry at his appointment to the Primacy and this it would tax all his remarkable geniality and grace and goodness to overcome.

I have felt it my duty, Madam, to endeavour, to the best of my ability, to answer frankly the important question Your Majesty did me the honour of putting to me. I cannot find words to express the natural diffidence I feel, on being thus called upon to give, however humbly, an opinion on matters involving such momentous issues. Your Majesty's most gracious letter left me, however, no alternative, and I have tried, in humble reliance on the guidance of Almighty God, to answer your Majesty's questions by as plain and simple a statement as possible of what I believe to be the truth.

Almost simultaneously came a note from Mr. Gladstone:

The RT. HON. W. E. GLADSTONE *to the* QUEEN

10 Downing Street. Dec. 14, 1882

Mr. Gladstone with his humble duty submits to Your Majesty a list of the ages of the Archbishops of Canterbury at the time of appointments, complete for 220 years, with the insignificant exception of Archbishop Hutton's Archiepiscopate. Your Majesty will not fail to observe 1. That no Archbishop has ever been appointed at or over the age of 70. 2. That seven Archbishops have been appointed under 60, and two of them in the reign of George the Third were appointed at 50.

Mr. Gladstone believes that if earlier records were examined, either before or after the Reformation, they would exhibit a range of younger appointments.

By December 16, the appointment was settled.

The QUEEN *to the* REV. R. T. DAVIDSON

Windsor Castle. Dec. 16, 1882.

I hasten to say that it is definitively settled to be the Bishop of Truro. I suppose there is no doubt of his acceptance? At the same time I find that Mr. Gladstone himself wished as I had suggested to write himself to the Bishop of Winchester to mention that but for his age and not very vigorous health or something to that effect, the offer of this very high and important office would have been made to him.

I hope and think our dear Archbishop would have approved.

I have heard the Bishop of Winchester's sons very well spoken of. Are they promising?

The Queen never withdrew the trust she thus placed in Randall Davidson in so conspicuous a manner. He was practically at once installed in the post of Dean Wellesley's successor as adviser on ecclesiastical appointments, and the extent of Her Majesty's confidence is shown in the following letter:[1]

The QUEEN *to the* REV. R. T. DAVIDSON

Osborne. Dec. 20, 1882.

I am very grateful for your kind letter. As there will be two vacancies on the Episcopal Bench and a Deanery (if not two!) I should be *most thankful* if you could *help* me with names. I need not say that *your* name will *never be mentioned*, but losing, as I have done, the two dear Deans, Stanley and Wellesley, I am left without any one to turn to for advice and help—when sometimes names are submitted which I often feel would *not* be suitable. And I feel you have had such immense opportunities of knowing *all* the Clergy that I could *not* look to *any* one *more likely* to help me than yourself.

Both extremes of High and Low Church are to be avoided.

To this letter Davidson wrote a long and exhaustive reply in which he not only suggested clergy who might be appointed to the three vacant posts but gave a list of ten others worthy of consideration when important vacancies occurred. At the same time the Queen's Private Secretary, Sir Henry Ponsonby, was permitted to establish a short cipher code with him for use in case of necessity.

II

There was, however, Davidson's own future to consider. The Bishop of Truro, immediately on receiving Mr. Gladstone's letter, had telegraphed to Davidson and begged him to continue for a while as chaplain at Lambeth. This arrangement,

[1] *Letters of Queen Victoria*, 2nd Series, vol. iii, p. 380.

which was very desirable on all counts, had the Queen's warm approval. But Davidson had served Archbishop Tait with remarkable ability for six years; and he was married. Clearly it was desirable that he should soon be placed in a post of independent responsibility.

The new Archbishop came to Lambeth in February 1883. Davidson had naturally a great deal to do in helping him to undertake the very varied work of the Archbishopric for the first few months. In the later spring, the question of the future became practicable. On the very day of Archbishop Tait's funeral, he had been offered by Bishop Lightfoot the canonry at Durham filled afterwards by the appointment of the Rev. George Body, but he had declined this, feeling that his real work and interests belonged to the South. He had also declined an offer of the vicarage of Maidstone, made during the vacancy of the Archiepiscopal See. The appointment of the Rev. G. H. Wilkinson as Bishop of Truro left the important parish of St. Peter's, Eaton Square, vacant, and there was a good deal of discussion as to the possibility of his serving there. Wilkinson showed him the parish books, discussed the services, and, in all sorts of ways, without definitely saying so, led him to think he wished Davidson to succeed him. Davidson, writing in 1906, said, 'Why he changed his mind I do not know, but I think it was the result of a conversation with Mary Gladstone (or Drew, I forget if she was yet married) who took a keen, not to say, a dominant interest in such matters.'

On February 23, 1883, Wilkinson wrote a letter to Davidson which shows that a doubt of his suitability as a churchman had reached his ears.

The REV. G. H. WILKINSON *to the* REV. R. T. DAVIDSON

Someone who ought to know better has, I am told, been saying that you could not carry on the work here in the spirit in which it has been begun because you are so 'Broad Church'. On the strength of our talk in the Park, I shall contradict this unless I hear from you to the contrary.

On March 6, 1883, Wilkinson wrote again:

The *impression* which I gathered yesterday is that, *after a while*, a parish will be offered to you, but not St. Peter's.

Sir Henry Ponsonby wrote to Davidson (April 7, 1883):

> I believe . . . that Mr. Gladstone objects on the ground that you have never had charge of a parish. . . .

Thus though there were many comings and goings the offer never came. Instead Mr. Gladstone, on April 27, wrote and invited Davidson to become Vicar of St. Mary's, Bryanston Square, in succession to the Hon. and Rev. W. H. Fremantle. At the same time news came that Dean Connor, who had only been Dean of Windsor for six months, was dying. Davidson had already been warned 'by a well-informed friend' to wait before taking any decisive step. Let him tell the story himself.

> Just then I heard that Dean Connor was dying. I was in some perplexity and returned Mr. Gladstone a dilatory answer; after a week he wrote once again for a definite 'yes' or 'no'. By that time Dean Connor had died. On Sunday, May 6, I was staying at Lord Stanhope's, at Chevening, with Archbishop Benson, who was confirming in the neighbourhood. On the Sunday morning the Archbishop's bundle of letters was brought to me in bed. There was one from the Queen, which I sent to his room unopened. At breakfast he said nothing to me about what it contained, but before starting for the Confirmation he wrote a long reply, which he left with Mrs. Benson to copy.

The letters follow:

The QUEEN *to the* ARCHBISHOP OF CANTERBURY

Very Confidential. Osborne. May 4th, 1883.

I write in the first person, as I can better express myself and wish to consult you on a subject, *of very great importance* to myself. It is about the successor to good kind Dean Connor, whose loss is in many ways a great one. I appointed him to the Deanery, as I had a high opinion of his upright, kind and sympathetic nature, and because I had known him long and felt he was no stranger. Alas! I have now lost almost all of those who were associated in any way with my altered and saddened life since Decr. 61. and I must look around for other helps. It is however therefore *most* important, nay *imperative* that I should *find someone* who possess's a kindly sympathetic nature—who could be a comfort to me, now that I get older, and have been sorely stricken as Mr. Davidson can tell you!

I may mention *that I know of only two* people who personally would at all possess these qualities, combined with just intellectual ones as well.—these are Mr. Davidson himself—and Mr. Boyd Carpenter! And I would ask you to answer me *openly* which of these two, *you* would think the best choice? I myself, can think of no one more fitted than Mr. Davidson (if you could give him up!) from his great knowledge of *society* and of the Clergy generally, and his great charm of manner. The only thing that might be said against his appointment is his youth. But surely that is a fault which recedes quickly, and he has had so much experience, and is so much liked—that I should think this would be no insurmountable obstacle.

Pray answer me openly and think of my sadly lonely position and of the great need I have of loving and sympathetic help and of some one to lean on. May I ask you to consider this as most *strictly confidential*?

The appointment of Dean of Windsor would go through The Prime Minister, but it is *understood* that I should select him. The position at Court is one requiring tact—and it is not desirable that the Domestic Chaplain should interfere with the Servants (who are of a superior class)—unless they seek his advice and assistance.

You should answer me in the first person also.—I would have preferred waiting till after the last sad Duties of to-morrow, but there seems so much speculation as to the Choice that I feel it necessary not to delay longer in writing to you.

I omitted to mention that I think Mrs. Davidson would be of great use at Windsor, which is a place of rather a gossiping nature, requiring tact and Judgment.

The ARCHBISHOP OF CANTERBURY *to the* QUEEN

On Monday and after, Lambeth.
Chevening, Sevenoaks.
May 6. 1883. Sunday Morning.

I am much grieved that Your Majesty's most important letter has only this moment reached me.

I will indeed write with perfect openness. I know and feel that the appointment to the Deanery of Windsor is of utmost moment to Your Majesty's Service and Happiness. And upon the point of whether I could give up Mr. Davidson, I will only say that nothing which concerns me should ever for a moment be kept back or withheld from its proper devotion to Your Majesty.

I have grieved most deeply to see friend after friend removed by the Hand of God in His wisdom from that service, and have prayed that He would raise up others to fill their places—especially if it were possible those three whom I have so long loved and mourned—and again of these especially the place of Dean Wellesley. One could not but trust that the kind goodness of Dean Connor might be such a help. But God has again seen otherwise.

And now of the two whom Your Majesty names, I will, as I am desired, speak quite freely.

I do not know Mr. Boyd Carpenter. But I think this is owing to a point which is important in the consideration. I believe that his acquaintance with men, even clergymen, is rather limited. I know very few who do know him personally. He is on few or no Committees of a general kind. I have heard of odd little misjudgments of his about people arising from want of knowledge of them. In all other respects I should think him delightful. *But* is not this of *very great* importance? I should have thought the Dean of Windsor ought to know everyone, so to speak. But if Your Majesty thinks my own want of knowledge of Mr. Boyd Carpenter is a hindrance in the way of my own judgment, I will at once contrive through friends to see him and have one or two conversations about affairs which would help my judgment. Only I am sure of what I *have* said so far.

With regard to Mr. Davidson,—he has a most wide and a very thorough knowledge of the clergy and others; he has a remarkably good, sober and at the same time a kindly judgment; his advice, as well as his power of executing business, is always not only carefully weighed but is prompt; and then he is of a deeply sympathetic and loyal nature. His affectionateness makes him *wholly* at service, whatever he has to do. It is done with the heart as well as with the head. And a sounder head and warmer heart I do not know.

With regard to his youth—I think Your Majesty can wholly set aside whatever might be said about that. *His* youth has all the advantage of spring and freshness, while it does not carry him away into any intemperate expression even, at any time—much less into any rashness. Besides it is a shortcoming of which he is daily being cured as Your Majesty says, and it will be cured all too soon. With his particular carefulness of judgment I think it an advantage.

I am writing this from my daily experience and sense of his value. I should, knowing it well, give him up at once to what is so far more precious to us all, and all that I feel I should lose in him makes me only more honestly glad of Your Majesty's gain.

What may I do more? I will see Mr. Boyd Carpenter before firstly giving an opinion, if it is wished. But so far as I have written, it is from knowledge and I trust it may be of use. I am sorry that my letter is so long, owing to the shortness of time in which I write—And I earnestly hope that I have not written too freely.

On May 7 (to quote Davidson's dairy):

the Archbishop received a telegram from the Queen asking him to find out whether I would accept the Deanery of Windsor!! . . . He then dissuaded me from answering Gladstone definitely about St. Mary's, Bryanston Square.

O God give me grace for this great responsibility. Thou knowest how it is needed! And yet the call comes so unexpectedly—so solemnly—that there is no alternative left as to acceptance.

Two days later came the Prime Minister's offer.

The RT. HON. W. E. GLADSTONE *to the* REV. R. T. DAVIDSON

10 Downing Street, Whitehall.
May 9, 1883.

Dear Mr. Davidson

I have received the permission of Her Majesty to propose to you that you should now fill the vacancy so sadly created by the death of Mr. Connor, in the Deanery of Windsor, and I am sure that, if you accept the office, you will preside in a Chapter, over most of whose members you have so much the advantage in point of age, with a courtesy and consideration which will show the circle of your gifts is complete.

Believe me
with all good wishes
Very faithfully yours
W. E. GLADSTONE.

The REV. R. T. DAVIDSON *to the* RT. HON. W. E. GLADSTONE

Lambeth Palace, S.E. 10 May 1883

I have the honour to acknowledge, with respectful thanks, the receipt of your kind letter proposing, with the sanction of Her Majesty, that I should succeed to the post vacated by the sad death of Dean Connor.

It is an offer to which, under all the circumstances, only one reply seems possible. With fear and trembling, under a deep sense of the responsibility of the position, I accept the call, and I venture to ask at once, not, I am sure, in vain, for your prayers, that I may be enabled by God's Grace to discharge aright the great duties of the office.

The fact of my inferiority in age and experience to those with whom I am called to work, and the deep sense of my many deficiencies for a position of such a kind will lead me, I humbly trust, to a more absolute reliance upon the strength which comes from above. I need hardly assure you that it will be my earnest endeavour to listen and to learn rather than, at first, to lead.

For your own kind words I thank you from a full heart and once more I ask your prayers.

The appointment gave rise to a good deal of talk in ecclesiastical circles, the new dignitary's youth (according to the *Manchester Guardian*) being the chief ground of complaint among those who objected to his nomination. Scott Holland, a contemporary (who was later to join Liddon at St. Paul's), writing in his free way to Mrs. Drew, the Prime Minister's daughter, expressed himself thus:

The REV. H. S. HOLLAND *to* MRS. DREW

I have been immensely amused at the Dean of Windsor. It set me staring and amazed, more than anything else that has lately happened; but I expect it may do wonderfully. Only it is indeed bold.[1]

Truth was also somewhat caustic. A week before the announcement it had commented on the attractions of the 'most desirable piece of preferment' which Dean Connor's death had vacated; and, after dealing with the somewhat large salary and the number of canons and minor canons who would assist in the duty, described the whole office as 'perhaps the closest approximation to doing nothing obtainable in these days'. In the next issue it expressed its chagrin at Mr. Davidson's appointment. 'He would have done very well for St. Peter's, Eaton Square, where there would have been a fine scope for his very considerable administrative talents, but it is not right that at thirty-five he should be promoted to the luxurious indulgence of Windsor.' On the other hand, by most of those who knew Randall Davidson's abilities and personal qualities, as well as the special opportunities of the post, the appointment was very cordially approved. 'Dear Davidson, conscience of the Empire', one epistle (from R. W. Raper) began. Many were the episcopal congratulations, but here it will be of greater interest to print two letters from a different point of view.

[1] *A Forty Years' Friendship: Letters from H. S. H. to Mrs. Drew*, ed. Ollard (1919), pp. 32-3.

The REV. BENJAMIN JOWETT *to the* REV. R. T. DAVIDSON

Oxford. May 11, 1883.

I congratulate you heartily on your new preferment. The Deanery of Windsor is one of the most considerable positions in the Church of England, though a peculiar one. I used to think that my dear friend Hugh Pearson would have held it: may I venture to think that it is still held by a friend?

PROFESSOR B. F. WESTCOTT *to the* REV. R. T. DAVIDSON

6 Scrope Terrace, Cambridge.
May 11th, 1883.

My dear Davidson,

May I once again use the old address? In spite of the Archbishop's loss, which must be most serious, I rejoice more than I can say in the appointment which I have just seen. We had perhaps rather confidently anticipated it, but royal appointments are uncertain. There is no place, I think, in which you could have had a nobler opportunity of doing good service. The few conversations which I had with Dean Wellesley enabled me to feel what a power for good there is in an office where Christ's minister can speak with simple and direct counsel to those who have the heavy burden of sovereignty.

May God guide you in the work which has to be done in a critical time. But all times are critical, and they are in His hand.

ἔστω μεθ' ὑμῶν πάσας τὰς ἡμέρας.

Even more practically useful, as well as personally gratifying, were the kindly and generous greetings of the canons at Windsor and the Queen's personal staff. To the former Her Majesty had taken pains to cause special letters to be sent, preparing them for the news and expressing the hope that the new Dean would be welcome.

III

Randall Davidson was installed as Dean of the Free Chapel of St. George's, Windsor, on June 25, 1883. There was 'much trouble beforehand as to the possibility of having any special service of any sort', Lord Wriothesley Russell objecting on the grounds that it would be a 'reflection' upon previous installations. However, 'after much discussion in private' it was resolved that there should be a special service for the new Dean. He was the fifty-fourth holder of an office which had been occupied by not a few distinguished men, amongst whom might be counted many bishops; one Archbishop of Canterbury, Manners Sutton, who owed his Primacy to the favour of George III; and one Archbishop of Spalato, Marcus Antonius De Dominis, 1618–22, who, in an unusually romantic career, forsook the Church of Rome, held the Deanery for four years, and then returned to Rome, where the Pope refused the promised pardon.

The Chapter was composed almost entirely of old men. Of the four canons, Lord Wriothesley Russell had been appointed in 1840, the Rev. Frederick Anson in 1845 (both before their new Dean was born), the Hon. C. L. Courtenay in 1859, a cousin of Lord Halifax and an ardent High Churchman (who had withstood Temple's appointment to Exeter, in 1869) but most ready to take his share with the Evangelical Lord W. Russell in preparing the choristers for confirmation. The Rev. W. Boyd Carpenter, appointed in 1882, was alone near the new Dean's age. Even the minor canons were not young. When Dean Davidson came to Windsor (said a minor canon of the day) 'he was, I believe, the youngest on the staff of clergy'.

It is difficult to realize the difference which such an arrival meant to the intimate life of the Cloister and the Castle, a difference increased by the youth and charm of the wife he brought with him, only twenty-four years old, ten years younger than himself.

Sir Walford Davies, a later organist of St. George's, writing of the three deans he knew as a chorister, says:

> I came to Windsor in January 1882, and have a vivid recollection of three successive Deans. Dean Wellesley had a deep, rolling, resonant way of reading the Communion Service. He always stood at the North End of the Communion Table, where we could (as Decani choristers) clearly see his stern, rugged face, and feel something like awe at the sight. He recited the service on or near a low A flat or G ()
>
> Then came Dean Connor, with a very gentle face and manner. He seemed always to wear his Garter blue ribbon (which Dean Wellesley did only on Sundays); so his face and the bright ribbon are quite inseparable in my memory. Then in 1883, after what seemed a very little while, he died; and there came a young Dean, —so young that I remember a minor canon expatiating vigorously in the Vestry (as we waited to go in to service) as to the appointment

> of a 'Boy-Dean'. But though Dean Davidson (as he then was) brought youth and freshness with him, he never seemed young to us as choristers. He had the dignity and authority of Dean Wellesley himself; but he had a grace and quiet friendliness as well, which gave us great confidence. The Deanery became a new place to us as boys; for Mrs. Davidson and Miss Agnes Tait (afterwards Mrs. Ellison) read to us, played games with us, and gave us homely Sunday lessons; and the long room in the Deanery became something of a choristers' paradise.

But if the choristers were conquered, the members of the Chapter and the community at large equally fell victims to the spell of the Dean and his wife. Where an old man in failing health, with a team of old men, has ruled for long, especially in a cathedral or collegiate church, affairs tend to become slack. It required, therefore, knowledge and courage to handle the situation in the way required, but the new Dean was very wise and very considerate in presiding over the Chapter in its little room above the cloister.

'In manner', said Canon Dalton[1] (appointed in 1885) to the writer, 'he was quiet and cheerful, very self-restrained, but so natural, a charming Chairman'; and again, 'He did everything so thoroughly. There was no pretence about him, yet he could be firm when the need arose, and when he said a thing had to be done it was done.'

Those who have not been members of a Chapter would be surprised at the amount and variety of actual business which such a body has to get through. A very serious responsibility falls upon the Dean, and it may test the skill and patience of a new Dean sometimes to persuade a Chapter composed of his elders that certain business is very urgent. One of the first things to which the Dean had to attend was the repair of the roof of St. George's, and later it turned out that very considerable repairs were required for the vaulting of the nave, and for the mullions of the windows in the clerestory of the nave. Again, it was found that the Chapel and the collegiate buildings were gravely under-insured against fire and that the apparatus for dealing with fire was sadly out of date; that the Chapel was inadequately warmed; that the respective shares of the Office of Works, which was responsible for the out-

[1] Canon Dalton (d. 1932) gave the writer great help in a long conversation at Windsor in January 1931.

side of the fabric, and the Chapter, which was responsible for the inside, in protecting the Chapel, required very careful investigation. All these things and many others the Dean took quietly in hand; amongst them the conditions under which the minor canons and the lay clerks served. Sometimes, of course, a canon thought the Dean went too far, but the Dean always won. Once the very Evangelical canon, Lord W. Russell, expressed his fury because *Hymns Ancient and Modern* had been introduced into the Chapel. He stormed: 'I shall burn every book in the Chapel. There was no Chapter order.' But he stormed in vain.

The Dean was indeed an irresistible Dean; not because he fought (he never fought), still less because there was anything dramatic about him (he was never dramatic), but because he was so cool and Scotch and right and always to the point. It hardly requires to be said that the charm of his wife made him doubly irresistible, and that their combined thoughtfulness, friendliness, and hospitality in the Deanery and outside it, their kindness, their natural spontaneous interest in the lay clerks, the minor canons, and everything that went on, won all hearts.

A study of the diaries intermittently kept during the first five years at Windsor reveals a life quite extraordinarily full. But the activities were by no means confined to Windsor—as we shall see in the chapters which follow. Nevertheless, in and near Windsor he did a great deal. There is constant evidence throughout the Dean's diary and his papers of the pains he took in preaching wherever he was asked to preach. He preached university sermons of a practical character; he preached on occasions outside Windsor, and in the Chapel itself he took particular pains, remembering the variety of his congregation, and feeling, as one who remembers his sermons at the time realized, a particular responsibility in view of the masters and their wives and others who often came up from Eton.

It was, however, to the Ladies' Bible Class that his own and Mrs. Davidson's thoughts used to go back. 'The at that time comparatively modern way of studying the Bible' (said a lady mentioned in the Archbishop's note below) 'opened one's eyes and seemed to give the key to so much that happens in the world of today.' This was what the young members of the class felt, though some of the older ones, and there were several quite elderly, did not always quite approve:

> One of the interesting points about that Bible Class [said the same member] was the unconscious self-revelation of the lecturer. His faith, sympathy, insight, wide views (and humour) made one realise what manner of man was giving of his best to us and influencing many lives.

The Dean's own memorandum is as follows:

> One more important matter belonging to the Windsor time I ought to allude to. From an early period of my tenure of the Deanery up to the time I finally left it, I conducted a Ladies' Bible Class which was to me a matter of constant interest and about which I took a great deal of trouble week by week. Reference to the current diaries of that period will show the amount of time I was giving to the preparation of these lectures. Among those who came to them (and there were many, at one time I think more than a hundred) were a good many really intelligent and cultivated ladies, wives of Eton masters and others of that type. There were also some devout and oldfashioned ladies of worth and piety, and these last I was constantly told that I should inevitably frighten away by dealing as I did with questions of Higher Criticism, but to the best of my belief no single member of the Class ever left on that account, though some of them doubtless shook their heads over my opinions. The lectures were on the general structure and growth of the Bible. Miss Ella Ellison, afterwards Mrs. Bliss, a most capable woman, took very full notes and of these I was ultimately allowed to have a transcript made so that the lectures remain in a rough form on record.
>
> Biblical criticism has moved rapidly during the last few years, and some of the things which I then said I should express differently now; but I am quite sure of the real gain which ensued from these lectures, both to myself and to the ladies who attended them. They gave me a constant subject of study, and awakened and maintained in the minds of many of the ladies a vivid interest in the Bible the fruits of which have frequently come under my notice since.
>
> The authorities of the Oxford Diocesan Higher Religious Education Society begged me to adopt their syllabus and lecture on the subjects therein prescribed, and they would also have liked me to throw the lectures open to men as well as women, but I did not think either course was desirable. The lectures began by being held in the Deanery, but when the large dining-room there became

too small we migrated to the Chapter Library where the lectures were continued during my subsequent years.

I also undertook a class for the lay clerks, or singing men, which I held in the Deanery, and which, though at its start it laboured heavily and the men did not much care to come, grew in interest, and I think we had a really keen Bible Class, fruitful I believe of actual good, and certainly interesting to myself.

CHAPTER IV

THE QUEEN AND HER CHAPLAIN

I do think that ye have received or this a letter from Mr. Secretary, willing you to come up immediately, if your health will suffer, for certain weighty matters touching the Queen's service. 4th January 1558–9. SIR NICHOLAS BACON *to* DR. MATTHEW PARKER (*Correspondence of Archbishop Parker*).

THE Queen first spoke to Randall Davidson on December 9, 1882. In January, 1883, he was sent for to Osborne, and he has described in his diary how within an hour of his arrival on January 20 he received a message from the Queen, followed very soon by a summons to the Presence.

At 6. o'clock had a kind visit from Lady Ely who came from the Queen to ask whether I had any objection to dining with her own circle—being in such mourning. I reassured her.

At 7.45 I was sent for to see the Queen. She received me in a dressing room. Washingstand, towels, hot water in a kettle—looking glass, brushes etc. and a set of nice pictures—miniatures etc. about the room. She stood all the time (about 20 minutes) I was with her. She asked about Edith and the girls, and then passed on to wider topics—the new Archbishop—his earnestness and vigour—the *memorial*, that *dreadful* scheme—the new Bishops—Wilkinson suited for Truro—'I never myself liked him much—but perhaps I dont do him quite justice. It is commonly supposed I dislike him because he preached at Windsor against painting and false hair and so forth. Not at all!—I respect him for his courage in saying it, though it was singularly out of place *there*! But I dont like some of his teaching—inclined to the confessional etc. But he will suit Truro very well. But he is too *sacerdotal* for me! As to the Welsh see, I have had such a "*to do*". All the *ladies* have been writing to me, and saying there was nobody suitable except their pet man. Lady Llanover—Lady Londonderry etc. Gladstone took great pains about it all—and quite tried to get the best men—apart from his personal church sympathies. I think he (Gladstone) is *very* unwell'—etc. Then other subjects. 'Do you know who is to succeed Mr. Wilkinson?' Full enquiry as to the parish &c. She had evidently not had the matter before her, and didn't at all refer to me for that or any other post. Then she discussed Farrar his feeling of being 'wronged' etc. Then Henry Villiers, whom she happened to have seen. 'Can you imagine a young lady wanting to marry that man? He may be *good*, but his personal appearance is terribly against him.' Then *Wilberforce's Life* with which she is very angry indeed. 'Perfectly disgraceful.' 'But then Mr. Wilberforce is an unsatisfactory man . . . was a great trial to his father' etc. I told her some of the things in the book (she had not read it) which would be likely to make mischief. She was much amused about Denison and the Archbishop of York. But then Bishop Wilberforce *hated him*. He wanted to be Archbishop of York himself.

Next day he preached to the Queen on 'The Faithful Creator', after being 'initiated by Sir John Cowell in the mysteries of the strange service'—in the drawing-room. That night there was another long interview with the Queen in the same room as before, though 'for the first time she sat down', and the diary narrates 'she told me she was *specially* pleased and interested in my sermon, which had "suggested many quite new thoughts to her"'. Thus the trust which the Queen instinctively reposed at first sight in the late Archbishop's chaplain was deepened, and it is safe to say that for the rest of the Queen's life her belief in Randall Davidson as a man, her dependence on his counsel in the affairs of the Church, and her confidence in his general ministry and judgement were unwavering.

I

The office of Dean of Windsor in Queen Victoria's reign was possessed of a character and possibilities altogether its own. The Queen divided her time more or less equally between Windsor, Osborne, and Balmoral. But Windsor possessed a special importance ever since the Prince Consort's death on December 14, 1861. She was at Windsor every year for a couple of months from the middle of February; then again after Easter (spent at Osborne) for two or three weeks; then another three weeks or a month in those June and July days when the business of the session was wont to prove critical; and finally, after a few weeks at Osborne and a long spell at Balmoral, back for the autumn Cabinets in November until after the anniversary of the Prince Consort's death on December 14.[1] Osborne and Balmoral were for the less busy times—and provided opportunities of withdrawal. Thus Windsor Castle (hallowed also for Her

[1] *Letters of Queen Victoria*, 2nd Series, vol. i, Preface, pp. xi, xii.

Majesty by her husband's tomb) had become in a special way the centre of the royal authority. The appointment, therefore, of a Dean of Windsor, who was an independent person touching the life of the world outside on the one hand and touching the life of the household so closely on the other hand, might mean much to the happiness of the Sovereign. It might mean much if the holder of the office were a man possessed of the right gifts. But it might mean nothing, for the office was an office with opportunities rather than rights.

Dean Davidson's immediate predecessor was Dean Connor, who only held the post for some seven months. He was a worthy and devoted parish priest, but he was not suitable for the quite peculiar position at Windsor. He had lived quietly as vicar of Newport, in the Isle of Wight, and was quite outside the circle of such knowledge as the Queen had a right to expect in her confidential adviser.[1]

It was Dean Wellesley who had really created the position. He was nephew of the great Duke of Wellington and a personal friend of Mr. Gladstone. In twenty-eight years he had acquired such an influence with the Queen as to give him an almost commanding authority in all Church affairs in which the Crown was involved.[2] Indeed, Mr. Gladstone once suggested that he should be offered the Primacy,[3] and it is to this approach that Mr. Gladstone referred in the epitaph which he composed for the monument to Wellesley in St. George's Chapel—an epitaph which was founded upon an English epitaph by Dean Vaughan:

Episcopatus etiam summi gradum
Pro sua modestia
Strenue detrectavit.

Dean Davidson writes of Dean Wellesley:

> If the holder of the office so desired he need have practically no active duties at all. On the other hand opportunities of usefulness abound in all directions and in the Queen's time the personal relations between herself and the Dean had for many years been

[1] The offer of the Deanery was actually made to Dean Connor not by Mr. Gladstone but in the Queen's name by Prince Leopold on October 3, 1882.

[2] Extract from the Queen's Journal: Balmoral, September 18th, 1882 (on the news of Dean Wellesley's death): 'By degrees and imperceptibly he had grown to be our best friend' (*Letters of Queen Victoria*, 2nd Series, vol. iii, p. 335).

[3] Morley, *Life of Gladstone*, vol. iii, p. 93.

the closest possible. Dean Wellesley had been among the most trusted of her friends.

It was Dean Wellesley who, as adviser to the Queen, secured the appointment of Tait as Archbishop of Canterbury in succession to Longley, notwithstanding Lord Beaconsfield's strong and persistent pressure for Bishop Ellicott. It was Dean Wellesley on whom in all ecclesiastical affairs the Queen leaned. And though the difference was great between Wellesley's seventy-three years and Davidson's thirty-five, it was to Wellesley's relation to the Queen that Davidson succeeded. It is therefore of no little interest to know that only three weeks before his own death Wellesley, reporting to the Queen how he paid his last visit to the dying Tait on September 1, added these words:

DEAN WELLESLEY *to the* QUEEN

Just at the time when he was taken ill, the Dean offered the place of Sub-Almoner to his [the Archbishop's] son-in-law, Mr. Davidson, both as a mark of respect to the Archbishop and because the young man himself is most highly esteemed. The delight this gave to the Archbishop threw a gleam of sunshine over his sick-bed. Now as to the successor . . . .[1]

When Dean Davidson began his residence at Windsor in June 1883, the Queen was sixty-four years old. She was 'very little in stature' but had an extraordinary dignity, and also irresistible charm.

I have always regarded her as embodying to a degree I have never known in other people a combination of the best sort of common sense, persistent industry, genuine and whole-hearted devotion to duty, and affectionate sympathy with people who were in trouble. It was her common sense which welded together the other attributes and enabled her (though not in the ordinary sense of the words a really clever woman) to do far more than most clever women could have accomplished.

What exactly it was which constituted the irresistible charm attaching to her I have never been able quite clearly to define to myself, but I think it was the combination of absolute truthfulness and simplicity with what had become an instinctive realisation of her position and what belonged to it. I have known many prominent people, but I have never known one of them with whom it was so easy and so natural to speak freely and frankly after even

[1] *Letters of Queen Victoria*, 2nd Series, vol. iii, p. 330.

a very short acquaintance. I imagine it would be difficult to name any attribute more valuable to a sovereign than the possession of this particular power. This must perhaps be qualified in one respect. She hated conversational controversies about matters wherein she differed acutely from the person to whom she was speaking. It was not exactly resentment against contradiction; she disliked contradicting as much as being contradicted, and if the subject was really an unpleasant one, on which one was bound to point out that she was mistaken or wrong (and I had several such marked occasions), she obviously disliked it very much, and would be apt to end the conversation and then write a note about it. Similarly, she would not find fault with people directly, but made somebody else do it for her. This came out oddly when she wished severely to criticize things done by e.g. one of her sons or daughters, and she would make me, for my sins, go to them with peremptory statements of her emphatic objection to something they had done or said. I could give examples of this—some of them funny—some of them almost tragic.

One wonders a little whether the same combinations and qualities would have been possible in a person of stately or splendid appearance, or whether the lack of those physical qualifications, combined with the reality of her dignity in word and movement, did not itself constitute a sort of charm because of the very way in which it took people by surprise.

In the early eighties, the Queen was a very solitary woman. Her mother, the Duchess of Kent, had died in March 1861, and the Prince Consort the following December. Of the Royal Family there was no one member, when Davidson went to Windsor, who was continually with the Queen: though Princess Beatrice was her mother's most constant companion to the end of her life, and it was to Princess Beatrice that it fell, as her mother grew older, to read her the confidential communications from ministers and other people every day, and to do much of her writing. The Dean also saw a great deal of Princess Christian and her daughter, and the Duchess of Albany, and others very close to the Queen. It is very interesting to read his account of the Prince of Wales:

So far as my own experience goes, the member of the family who showed the most unswerving loyalty to the Queen was the Prince of Wales. Difficult as his position was, and real as were sometimes the grounds of complaint as to the position either allowed or not allowed to him in discussions and decisions, I have

> personally never heard him say anything but what was absolutely respectful and loyal about the Queen. . . . The position of a man, who, when sixty years of age, is still only Prince of Wales, presents difficulties of a very grave sort. The Queen personally had fears, about which she has more than once spoken to me, about the mistake which is committed when the heir-apparent is given responsibilities respecting political or public matters. What she used to say is, I think, true; but she certainly in my judgment overdid it, and when she was known to be consulting a younger member of the family about public matters on which she did not invite the counsel of the Prince of Wales, it was very easy for jealousy and misunderstandings to arise in more than one quarter.

The Master of the Household was Sir John Cowell, 'a man of deep religious earnestness', a friend of General Gordon, and a capable soldier of the scientific sort. He was (wrote the Dean) 'essentially something of a martinet, and strangely lacked adaptability or ingenuity in effecting his excellent purposes for and in the Royal Household. His splendidly high tone and serious views of life were appreciated by the Queen although, I think, she came personally to be tired of him and certainly did not follow his advice.'

The two ladies most closely attached to the Queen were Lady Ely and Miss Stopford, who shared the secretarial labours between them—the latter a very religious woman with strong High Church sympathies but over-nervous. There were many more—among them the Duchess of Atholl, full of vigorous common sense and with plenty of courage, Lady Waterpark, Lady Churchill, and Lady Errol, 'keen and eager, a hot Evangelical, a supporter of all kinds of odd philanthropic causes'.

Without a doubt the foremost member of the staff was Sir Henry Ponsonby, Private Secretary to the Queen and Keeper of the Privy Purse. He had the help of an extraordinarily clever wife. 'I imagine,' wrote Davidson, 'although I do not know this, that he told her everything and consulted her about everything. She had had many years' experience of Court surroundings, and her natural gifts were of a high order.' Ponsonby was about sixty when Davidson became Dean, and throughout his tenure of the Deanery they were on terms of the closest friendship. Every day when the Court was at Windsor, after the service in the private chapel at 9 a.m., Davidson and Ponsonby used to pace up and down the Castle walks, discussing most things in the Castle and out of it. Nor is there any doubt that while the Dean learnt much from his intercourse with Sir Henry, the latter came to rely more and more on the younger man's shrewd judgement for help in all manner of political and general problems. Ponsonby was a man of great charm, a letter-writer of remarkable wit and skill and considerable insight. To quote Davidson's words: 'Ponsonby showed, I think, great capacity in all political matters, advising the Queen admirably, and communicating with her Ministers in exactly the right sort of way....' Both Lord Salisbury and Mr. Gladstone 'entertained for him a high respect and regard'. But there was one quality missing:

> He distinctly lacked courage, and seldom, if ever, stood up bravely to oppose the Queen in things in which he thought she was wrong. He would cleverly try to get her out of doing wrong things, but I think he might have done far more sometimes by a direct appeal, as she had, rightly, full confidence in his judgment. I do not remember his ever doing so, although many a time he would discuss with me how best to prevent this or that plan of hers being effected.

Ponsonby had as assistants, though he used them but little,

> two men whom it is impossible to over-praise, Sir Fleetwood Edwards and Sir Arthur Bigge. In selecting these two, the Queen had shown her extraordinarily acute perception, for each of the men had been more or less accidentally brought to her notice. I think I am right in saying that Edwards had been selected as an equerry to the Duke of Albany, and on his coming to Windsor to be approved by the Queen . . . the Queen had on the same evening told the Duke that she did not intend him to have Captain Edwards as she meant to retain him herself. Sir Arthur Bigge, a keen artillery officer, had been in South Africa in the Zulu war, and was, I think, deputed to take out the Empress Eugénie to see her son's grave. The Queen in a similar way spotted him when appointed to that service and herself retained him. Edwards and Bigge became two of my closest friends

It was during the rides with Captain Bigge, in Windsor Park particularly, that the seeds were sown of that intimate friendship between the future Archbishop of Canterbury and the future Lord Stamfordham, which lasted for nearly fifty years.

Such was the family into whose circle the new Dean came, winning their friendship and confidence with remarkable speed.

Very soon he was the recipient of all sorts of confidences. As one of the ladies of the Court once wrote to him:

> If I thought that you felt an 'outsider' to anything of ours, I tell you it would make me very unhappy, as I could never come again with utter confidence, as I do, and tell you anything, from the shape of the kitchen-maids' new caps to some of the deepest padlocks of my soul!

It so happened that two great sorrows which the Queen suffered drew Her Majesty and the Dean together at once in a very unusual way.

> I never at any later period had more intimate private talk with her than I had in my first year at Windsor. She from the very first opened out to me upon big subjects, religious and secular. This was in part due to the fact that during that year she was twice in deep distress, once at my very outset, and again in the following Spring, in consequence of the death of the Duke of Albany. She felt that sorrow very acutely and it gave new opportunities of really confidential talk and even ministry. I think I got at that time to understand thoroughly her rather unusual religious position and holding.

One of the earliest entries in his diary describes his first experience of St. George's Chapel, on May 20, 1883, and shows how the Queen turned to him only two months after the death of her faithful servant, John Brown:

> *May 20.* 7.15-8.15. Interview with the Queen. Most touching, solemn and interesting, but terribly difficult. Oh God give me guidance and grace if I am to be called on thus to counsel and strengthen in spiritual things.
>
> Dined with household. A most important talk with Miss Stopford, which filled me with deep thankfulness and anxious fear.

When Prince Leopold, Duke of Albany, died in March 1884, Randall Davidson felt keenly for the unhappy Queen and did everything in his power by word and deed to help her bear her grief. After the funeral the Queen wrote to him as follows:

The QUEEN *to the* DEAN OF WINDSOR

April 9, 1884.

> . . . Let me however express to you *now* from the *bottom of my* poor bleeding heart, which has been so cruelly torn of late—for all your great and tender kindness and thought on this most

solemn and overwhelming occasion! You have been such a help to us, and we feel it the more as you had not the long acquaintance with us and experience of our dear old friend Dean Wellesley! The Services were most touchingly beautiful and the spirit in the memorial chapel partook more of Heaven than Earth. . . .

Realizing Her Majesty's need of and demand for sympathy, Davidson never let an anniversary of a great grief in the Queen's life pass by without a letter of sincere and tender feeling. Thus the assurance of this sympathy led the Queen to talk to Davidson freely about spiritual things in a way which those who knew her best had never witnessed before. 'Until you both came to Windsor,' wrote Miss Stopford in 1884 of the new Dean and the new Canon, Boyd Carpenter, soon to be Bishop of Ripon, 'the Queen had literally no one whom she ever spoke of these matters to.'

The circumstances of her life after 1861 [the Dean's memorandum continues] threw her religious thoughts to the life beyond the grave. Upon this she was constantly dwelling; she liked allusions to it in sermons, and constantly brought it up in conversation.

There is an instance of her interest in the future life recorded in the Dean's diary at the time, just after the sudden death of Agnes Ellison, Mrs. Davidson's newly married, younger sister, and with reference also to the death in the same year of the Emperor Frederick:

January 20, 1889, Osborne. I have had a pleasant visit here and a great deal of talk this evening with the Queen, both before and after dinner. She was most kind about Agnes and we talked long over the general questions of this life and the next. She asked me if there ever came over me (as over her) waves or *flashes* of doubtfulness whether, after all, it might be all untrue. 'And yet', she added, 'these feelings never last, for it is simply *impossible* to believe that lives we have seen cut short in the full swing of activity (e.g. Prince Consort, Emperor Frederick, and others she had named) can really have come then to an utter end, or that we shall not see and know them hereafter. The Empress', the Queen said, '*never* feels these sudden qualms, and I am so thankful it is so.'

To continue the memorandum:

With her the thoughts about it were very real and were not, I think, mawkish. Indeed, she used to be specially indignant with the mawkishness of a good many of what she called 'consolatory letters'. She used to quote to me some of those she had received when the Prince Consort died as examples. . . . I remember one special letter to which she more than once alluded. I do not know who was the writer, but from the terms she used about him he must have been a person of some importance religiously. He had used what seems to me an atrociously wrong expression: 'Henceforth you must remember that Christ Himself will be your husband.' This she used to repeat to me with indignation, and say 'That is what I call twaddle. The man must have known, or ought to have known that he was talking nonsense. How can people like that comfort others or teach anybody?'

I was often surprised by the definiteness with which she held her beliefs about the intercourse in the other world of those who have been friends here. It did not correspond with the sort of common sense test which she liked to apply to theological teachings even about matters upon which we have ampler biblical authority than we have about this. She used to denounce as amazing any disbelief or hesitation about the assurance we ought to have of such maintenance beyond the grave of the relations we have held to one another upon earth.

Upon many other subjects she used to say, 'I suppose the orthodox belief is so and so; do you think we have really ground for holding it firmly? Do you really and truly believe it yourself or is it only a pious opinion?' But about this particular branch of ordinary Christian opinion or belief she never seemed to have any hesitation or questioning.

People entitled to put the question have sometimes asked me 'Do you think that the Queen, besides being a good woman, was a really religious one?' and I have never had any hesitation in answering 'Yes'. The talks I have had with her were much too genuine, too unconventional, too simple in diction, too untheological, I might almost say too matter-of-fact, to justify one in doubting that the religious impulse in her life was definite as well as deep. She had not I think been very wisely taught as a child in these matters. I do not suppose that her mother had much religion in her character, though perhaps I have no right to say so, and from the account she has given me of her other instructors, male and female, I should not expect to learn that any of them really helped her in religious matters. Bishop Davys, of Peterborough, who taught her many things, she evidently never liked. She used to say he had two or three daughters on whom he practised the lessons he was going to give her, and that they were so stupid that he was in a bad temper by the time her lesson began. How far this corresponds with fact I have no means of knowing.

The Prince Consort brought into her life a large religious element, but I should think it was, in his case, of a very nebulous sort so far as Christian dogma goes. His intellectual powers were, of course, far greater than hers, and she would not, I think, have attempted to follow him in metaphysical speculations on credal subjects. . . .

I should certainly say that her life was fashioned and carried on upon a religious basis, and that her shrewdness and common sense combined with her genuine and prayerful anxiety to do right at every juncture, made religion a more potent force in her conduct, both public and private, than either she herself or some of her family and friends probably realised.

There is one little point to which I ought to allude.

People were constantly puzzled or irritated by the Queen's rather morbid dwelling upon the details of the past, and especially upon the actual physical surroundings of those who were gone. About this I would say, first, that the facts were even more odd than most people had any idea of, secondly that the explanation is more reasonable and less morbid than is ordinarily realised. As to the facts—nothing that the Prince Consort had had or used in daily life was allowed to be set aside, and his room at Windsor remained as he had left it, with his old-fashioned white hats and gloves and canes lying about. Odder still at Osborne—I do not know whether it was so at Windsor—hot water was actually brought to his dressing-room at dressing-time forty years after his death, and this room she used as a sitting-room or interview-room for intimate people as it was conveniently situated next to her own set of rooms, and I have again and again had talks to her there before dinner with the hot water actually steaming.

The Queen acted in a similar way with regard to the sitting-room of the Duchess of Kent, her mother, at Frogmore. The practice was indeed odd, but

the explanation is not any fantastic or morbid idea about retaining memorials of the dead, still less, as was sometimes suggested, a sort of spiritualistic notion of their still haunting the rooms. It was simply this. She had at the time of these successive deaths given orders that nothing was to be moved or touched until she gave orders to that effect. Then these orders were not given. There was nothing to bring pressure to bear upon her, nothing to force her, so to speak, to make a decision, yes or no, by one particular day.—The rooms were not wanted for any other purpose, and it rested therefore with her to take the initiative in directing any change to be made. I remember two of the old pages, Searle and another, speaking to me about it in the nicest way. 'Such a pity Her Majesty does not give us orders to stop this; it makes people mock, and yet nobody likes to say anything to her about it.'

Such is, I am convinced, the simple explanation of what was sometimes ignorantly exaggerated by those who described it as a morbid craze. It is exactly one of the cases I have before referred to in which a sovereign suffers from having nobody on the appropriate terms with her for friendly remonstrance or even raillery of a kindly sort.

The services in the private chapel were, of course, the Dean's special and regular care. Every morning there were prayers at 9 a.m. for the household. On Sundays there was a service, with a sermon, at 10.30.

When I began at Windsor, the Queen used to give me minute instructions as to what ought and ought not to be done with respect to the services in her Private Chapel, the relation of the Domestic Chaplain to the servants, both indoor and outdoor, and the management of occasional functions, such as a baptism or a marriage. The curious aloofness of her life from the ordinary current of English ways showed itself in her wishes and arrangements about Divine Service. When she came to the Throne, English Ritual, in the large sense of the word, was at its lowest ebb and ordinary Church services were dreary in the extreme. The Prince Consort brought with him the traditions of Lutheran services, which he liked, and what was called the Ritual Revival, then in its mildest forms, surplices, chanted psalms, eastward position, turning eastward at the creed, found no recognition or even toleration in the Royal chapel.

Forty years later, when I began my Windsor life, these things had become usual elsewhere, but the Queen never saw them, and I remember her incredulous surprise one day when I was discussing these matters with her and contrasted the usages of the Private Chapel at Windsor with common usages elsewhere. Even the very Protestant ritual of Whippingham Parish Church was thought by herself to be rather advanced because the clergy preached in a surplice. The black gown never departed from the Private Chapel at Windsor, though bishops of course preached in their episcopal dress. In the Private Chapel we used Mercer's hymn-book, a most dreary compilation. Fortunately she took a fancy to some special hymn *tunes* in *Hymns Ancient and Modern*, and I suggested incidentally one day that we might have both hymn-books in the Chapel. She agreed, the new hymn-books came and Mercer was never used again. She was however very particular about the hymns and would deprecate or forbid any that she disliked. It was the custom, still maintained I believe by King Edward, that the preacher should write out his text and that it should be placed in her seat, together with a paper showing the hymns to be sung.

With regard to sermons, and her likes and dislikes thereon, a great deal of nonsense has been talked by people who knew little about it. She was in my opinion a very reasonable and sensible judge of sermons. She actively disliked to have in the Private Chapel sermons of an ambitious public character, dealing largely with great affairs. On the other hand she always wished that some allusion should be made to personal incidents, specially those connected with the Royal household, and it was her constant use to send to the preacher an intimation, perhaps ten minutes before service, that she wished an allusion made to the death of so-and-so, or the illness of somebody else.[1] This was very disquieting to many men. What I used to urge upon preachers who asked my advice was that they should preach as they would to the household, simple sermons with something to attract attention or awaken interest. It was her very common habit to ask to have in writing a copy of a sermon which had interested her.

Most of the preaching was done by the Dean himself, by the Queen's special command. On certain anniversaries, notably December 14, the anniversary of the Prince Consort's death, there were memorial services in the Mausoleum at Windsor, and on those occasions the Queen always desired some special reference to be made to recent happenings and recent sorrows. The first time that Davidson had to conduct that service, he says:

> I was directed to prepare prayer for the special Mausoleum service and to introduce reference to the Duke of Connaught in India, successive deaths of Wellesley and Connor, and above all J.B., a very difficult task. But it must be done.

According to the entry in the Dean's diary for the day the 'Queen afterwards expressed herself, through Miss Stopford, completely satisfied'.

[1] 'February 19, 1886. Though very possibly the Dean may have thought of it himself, the Queen wishes to say she hopes he will make an allusion tomorrow to the death of dear Principal Tulloch, one of our most distinguished men, noble, brave, most intelligent, large-hearted and liberal-minded, and a great personal friend of the Queen, who is deeply grieved at his loss, which is irreparable for our beloved Scotland and her Church. He was one of the Queen's Chaplains and Dean of the Order of the Thistle.'

The Dean was sometimes rather embarrassed by the Queen's requests that he would print his sermons:

The QUEEN *to the* DEAN OF WINDSOR

Windsor Castle. May 10, 1885.

The Queen *must* ask the Dean of Windsor to let his admirable sermon of to-day *be printed.* It was so true and would be *so* useful. Indeed there is none of his which she would not like to see printed for the benefit of *high and low.* Why not have several printed in a small volume for the benefit of some charity? . . .

The DEAN OF WINDSOR *to the* QUEEN

May 11, 1885.

I had the honour to receive yesterday Your Majesty's most gracious and encouraging letter with reference to the sermon I preached in the Private Chapel yesterday morning—and with allusion to other sermons also.

With my humble duty I venture most respectfully to thank Your Majesty for the kindly words of approval with which Your Majesty has honoured me.

It is a high privilege to be allowed from time to time to preach before Your Majesty, and any wish Your Majesty may express respecting any sermon of mine ought, of course, to be regarded as a command which, as in duty bound, I will gladly obey.

And yet after waiting for 24 hours so as to think it all over, I ask Your Majesty to pardon me if I venture to give expression to the exceeding difficulty I find in bringing myself to believe that it would be a gain that such sermons of mine should be reproduced in a permanent shape.

I write with all submission, but it does appear to me that so many indifferent sermons are constantly published, that I shrink immensely from what (notwithstanding Your Majesty's most gracious words) I cannot but feel would be adding to the number!

I hope I am not too bold in saying that I would very greatly prefer not publishing—or even privately printing—any such volume at present, unless it be Your Majesty's special wish that I should do so.

It is not so much the difficulty of recalling such sermons (though they have never been written) that daunts me. *That* I would gladly undertake at Your Majesty's desire. But I honestly cannot help thinking that Your Majesty's kindness overrates the merit of the sermons, and as I have unhappily a great lack of facility in reproducing in writing words which I have spoken, I fear that even such merit as any of them possess would disappear in print.

I must ask pardon for my presumption in thus questioning, however humbly, Your Majesty's gracious suggestion, and, of course, should Your Majesty, after what I have said, still desire me to print a little volume, I will do my best to give effect to Your Majesty's kind wish. But perhaps Your Majesty will at least permit me to delay the matter for awhile, and to see, by degrees, what may be practicable.

Once more I must, with my humble duty, thank Your Majesty for words of encouragement and kindly approbation which are an incentive of no ordinary kind.

I return herewith, with my dutiful thanks, the very interesting letter from the Archbishop of Chambéry which Your Majesty has allowed me to read.

I hope it will become known in Ireland as well as in England how strong a protest the respect shown to Your Majesty by the French clergy has practically raised against the bad conduct and disloyalty of the Roman Catholic clergy in Ireland. It must have been a source of satisfaction to Your Majesty to find how warmly the consideration shown to Roman Catholics in England has been appreciated in France. Certainly the cordial respect shown by the monks is eloquent in no ordinary degree.

I thank Your Majesty much for telling me of these very interesting and important facts, and I have the honour . . . .

The Queen disliked new faces, and, on the rare occasions on which strange preachers were in fact invited, Bishop Magee, Dean Vaughan, and Bishop Boyd Carpenter were the favourites. Norman McLeod, Principal Tulloch, and Matheson, the blind Presbyterian minister (in Scotland), Dean Stanley and Dean Vaughan were all of them men whose opinions she was fond of quoting on religious topics, though (Davidson writes) 'in talking of Dean Stanley, she always distinguished between his delightfully liberal sympathies and his theological holdings, with which she repeatedly told me that she had no sympathy'.

The Queen's views on other preachers, when they came, were usually at least decisive.

Sir Henry Ponsonby *to the* Dean of Windsor

Osborne. August 3, 1886.

The Queen tells me to let you know she was well pleased with the sermon preached by the poor but prolific ——.

I am to add that on the previous Sunday R. preached a long and most tedious rambling discourse. He lost his place, repeated himself, and Her Majesty thought it would never end. She cannot let him preach again, though if you consider it necessary he may read the service here.

The Dean's help was sought by various members of the Royal Family in religious questions. Thus on Christmas Day 1885 he wrote to Mrs. Davidson from Osborne:

The DEAN OF WINDSOR *to his* WIFE

The Duchess of Albany was most refreshing and *un*royal. She wants me to go to her for an hour tomorrow to solve sundry vexatious problems which are vexing her in religious matters: 'If I am to bring up my children to understand these things surely I must first learn them better myself.'

He also had the special task of preparing the younger members of the Royal Family for Confirmation. On one occasion a difficulty had arisen about the suitability of the particular clergyman chosen by the Prince and Princess of Wales for the preparation of their daughter, Princess Louise. On the Dean's telling the Queen that he had undertaken the duty, she wrote:

The QUEEN *to the* DEAN OF WINDSOR

Windsor Castle. June 28, 1884.

The Queen has to thank the Dean for his letter received yesterday morning and cannot sufficiently express her great satisfaction at its contents. Her son and daughter had not mentioned the subject to the Queen but she knew that in talking to the Princess of Wales about it, she felt anxious on the subject, not liking that Mr. T. should continue to teach the Princess (in which she entirely agreed) and yet feeling a delicacy and difficulty about it.

The Queen is therefore greatly rejoiced that one so kind, so intelligent and enlightened as the Dean of Windsor should be entrusted with this charge. And from being the Queen's domestic Chaplain as well as Dean of Windsor nothing could be better, and the Queen thinks that this must have softened the fact of the *cessation* of Mr. T.'s duties to him. . . .

With respect to the household (in Davidson's words):

The Queen's views were of a similarly old-fashioned and restrictive kind. She had a quite extraordinary fear of clericalism in any form and above all of such confidences as might lead, as she used to say, 'to the very border of Confession', and it was with her discouragement rather than approval that any really pastoral relationships either in health or sickness could be maintained. What exactly she was afraid of I never could tell, but I had some odd counsels from her about the danger of my visiting too much, even her old coachman, who specially liked me to come when he was ill.

There were many other matters on which the Queen spoke or wrote to the Dean, for he was constantly at her service, whether at Windsor or Osborne or Balmoral or on occasional expeditions to Italy. There are a great number of letters in the Queen's handwriting, and her directions or questions to him were various and frequent. Now the subject was the birth of a great-granddaughter:

The QUEEN *to the* DEAN OF WINDSOR

Windsor Castle. February 27, 1885.

The Queen thanks the Dean of Windsor very much for his extremely kind letter received yesterday. The birth of this dear little *great*-granddaughter is a source of gratitude, and recalls many a day and hour in her past life, especially the birth of dear Victoria herself—in this very place. The Queen is not feeling very strong yet and her anxiety about the War and her brave Troops prevents her being as well as otherwise she might, added to the sad and harassing recollections of this season. The Queen asks the Dean to have collect-prayer on Sunday to thank for dear Princess Louis of Battenberg's safety and the birth of the Queen's great-granddaughter. Unlike many people, the Queen does *not* rejoice greatly at these constant additions to her family. . . .

Now, again, she would discuss a character in a novel:

The QUEEN *to the* DEAN OF WINDSOR

May 18, 1887.

We have been (or indeed are *still*) reading that really beautiful book *We Two* (we read *Donovan* last year)[1] and the Queen wishes to know if the character and life of Raeburn are not taken from some real atheist Orator and leader. The Queen thought the Dean might know.

The DEAN OF WINDSOR *to the* QUEEN

Deanery. Windsor Castle.

I am extremely interested in the fact that Your Majesty should have enjoyed that most remarkable book *We Two*. Considering how young the authoress is, she seems to me to have promise of

[1] By Edna Lyall.

the very highest order, and her books are already in immense circulation. I think the character of Luke Raeburn is an entirely idealised one, although no doubt different men—whose teaching professed to be anti-Christian but was really more Christian than they knew—may have suggested many of the episodes. I will however find out incidentally, as I can easily do, whether any one life formed the basis of her picture. She has, as I think you will feel, done good service in calling attention to the fact that real Christianity is utterly *misunderstood* by so many who oppose it, and that if we can get a wider and more wholesome and rational Christianity to take the place of the narrow and rather sour creed which turns so many minds against it, very much of the present opposition will disappear.

On another occasion she put straight a curious story of her accession, in which it was stated that Lord Melbourne, on coming to announce William IV's death to the young Princess, opened a Bible and read to her 1 Kings iii. 5–14:

The QUEEN *to the* DEAN OF WINDSOR

November 11, 1886.

The Queen hastens to answer the Dean's letter, and Dr. Plumptre's story. From beginning to end it is a *complete invention*, and the Queen *never heard* of it even, during these nearly 50 years of her reign. It was always stated (which was the *fact*) that the Archbishop of Canterbury (Howley) and the Marquis of Conyngham (Lord Chamberlain) came to announce to the *Princess* Victoria her Uncle, the King's death, for which we had been prepared for some days.—The Queen was asleep, as it was quite early in the morning—in the Duchess of Kent's Bedroom (where she always slept) and was woke by her Mother. She got up *at* once and hastily put on a Dressing-gown and went into her (the then Princess') Sitting-room, where she found the 2 above-named gentlemen. The Lord Chamberlain knelt down and handed to Princess Victoria the paper on which was written the fact of the King's death, signed by the Physicians. The Archbishop then gave the Princess some details of her poor Uncle's last hours. Both knelt down and kissed the young *Queen*'s hand, and left.

The Queen has *since writing this* referred to her Journal written at the time, which she has had copied out, and sends to the Dean. He may copy it or get it copied, and send the copy to Dr. Plumptre *to read.* It is exactly as she wrote the account today. It shows the value of keeping a Journal, laborious and often overwhelming as she frequently finds it.

It contradicts the *whole story* from *beginning* to *end.* She was NOT nervous. Perhaps some of the details in the extract need not be copied and the Queen has put a pencil mark where it might stop.

On reflection the Queen has *not* marked anything—as it is as well to have the whole account of that *memorable day.*

II

The Dean's confidential relations with the Queen, to use his own words, 'brought me sometimes into rather sharp conflict with her, when I wanted to press some point of which she disapproved, or still more to object to something which she wished'. The most notable instance occurred very early in the Dean's time at Windsor. It concerned a proposal on which the Queen's mind was set for a further volume of *Leaves from the Journal of a Life in the Highlands.* This addition to what had already appeared caused no small anxiety amongst those nearest Her Majesty. The Queen had just published *More Leaves from the Journal of a Life in the Highlands* early in 1884. She gave the Dean a copy of the book and told him of her further intention. He had already heard of the plan from Dr. Cameron Lees of St. Giles', Edinburgh, who was at that time much in her confidence in Scotland, and had been entrusted with the editing of the memoranda concerned. The Dean read the volume and the memoranda, and at once felt that publication, or even the printing of anything of the sort suggested, would be injudicious. Indeed, he had told Dr. Lees that in his judgement such a course would be most undesirable, and had urged him, in vain, to communicate with the Queen himself. It was, however, obvious that Dr. Lees was afraid to express his real opinion about it to Her Majesty, though as a matter of fact he shared the Dean's view. Accordingly the Dean wrote the following letter to the Queen:

The DEAN OF WINDSOR *to the* QUEEN

The Deanery, Windsor.
6 March, 1884.

I have delayed, perhaps unduly, in writing, according to Your Majesty's kind permission, to thank Your Majesty again for the copy of the recent Volume of *Leaves,* which arrived while I was absent from Windsor. The reason of my delay was that I have been anxious to re-read the whole with all the care which is its due.

I have done so, with an ever-deepening interest, and Your Majesty will permit me to say once more how much there is in these 'leaves' which must, as I think, do real and permanent good. To feel sympathy with human sorrow is good for all people. To be the means of evoking such sympathy is a privilege which for more than 20 years has been Your Majesty's in no common measure, and the privilege, however sad a one, is a sacred power for good. The people of England would have lost much had the books been withheld from them whereby Your Majesty has admitted them to a closer share in the lifelong sorrow which clouded both the Nation and the Royal Home more than 20 years ago.

And the little volume which has now been given to your Majesty's loyal subjects contains in a simple form much that is calculated to keep alive that wholesome flame, as well as to strengthen other sorrowing hearts, in the darker hours of life, whether of bereavement or of anxiety.

If I may venture to particularize I would refer specially to the good which must accrue to many from the records Your Majesty has allowed to become public with regard to the tragic death of the Prince Imperial, to the drowning of the little boy in the spate at Balmoral, and to the details of the day on which Your Majesty received intelligence of the battle of Tel el Kebir. The constant and appreciative tribute, spoken and unspoken, which Your Majesty has borne to the faithfulness and loyal affection of those with whom Your Majesty has been surrounded, ought to have a powerful effect for good in more than one class of Society.

May I be pardoned by Your Majesty if I take courage to add, in this connection, something more. I have taken great pains during the last few weeks to ascertain by all such means as are available without direct enquiry what is the actual reception with which the volume has met among the thousands who are reading it. The ordinary upper class newspapers of course convey some picture of this public opinion, but, as Your Majesty is aware, it is usually possible to know pretty accurately beforehand what such newspapers will say, and they write under a conventional restraint which diminishes to some extent the value of their testimony.

I have tried to gather, in addition to such testimony, some view of the reception the volume is meeting with among other classes of Society.

I am pleased, but not surprised, to be able to tell Your Majesty that beyond all question these *Leaves* have in the main been received and read, among the humbler classes of Your Majesty's subjects in the very spirit in which Your Majesty has given them to the world—a spirit on the readers' part of that loyal and dutiful sympathy which it has been so long Your Majesty's privilege to evoke.

At the same time Your Majesty will readily understand that such a spirit of ready response to the gracious confidences so frankly given, is not always to be found, and I should be deceiving Your Majesty were I not to admit that there are, especially among the humbler classes, some, (perhaps it would be true to say *many*) who do not shew themselves worthy of these confidences, and whose spirit, judging by their published periodicals, is one of such unappreciative criticism as I should not desire Your Majesty to see. —These facts, which are, I fear, beyond dispute, do not in any way detract from the respectful sympathy with which all the better natures among Your Majesty's subjects accept this volume from Your Majesty's hands—but the facts remain and give a special point to words which I venture to quote from the letter Your Majesty was good enough to write to me a few weeks ago:

> 'the sacredness of deep grief may be desecrated by unholy hands, and when it is for the loss of a friend that is far more the case as it is much more one's own alone'.

I feel I should be wanting in my honest duty to Your Majesty who has honoured me with some measure of confidence were I not to refer to this, for Your Majesty's consideration, in connection with what Your Majesty in the same letter was good enough to tell me as to some further publication which Your Majesty has in contemplation.

I humbly trust Your Majesty will not deem me presumptuous in saying this much—and will indeed believe in the earnest gratitude and loyalty which alone prompts me to be so bold. I feel well assured that in this as in other things the prayers of a devoted people will be answered as heretofore by the gift from God to Your Majesty of a right judgement in all things, and that He will bless and prosper Your Majesty in every way.

Once more I would express to Your Majesty my very earnest thanks for the gift of a volume calculated in so many ways to promote the Christian simplicity of English and Scottish homes and to awaken afresh among the truer hearted of Your Majesty's subjects the loyal devotion to Your Majesty's person which finds daily expression throughout the land.

The letter was, to use the Dean's own epithet, 'a careful letter', but it was also very brave. The effect on the Queen was immediate. Her Majesty expressed her surprise that the Dean should hold such a view, and let those about her know that, notwithstanding what he had said, the book should go forward.

The Dean then sent a further letter, in which he declared that he felt so strongly about the inappropriateness of any such publication that he would feel bound to take every means of persuading her if possible to desist. The Queen replied, through a third person, asking Davidson to withdraw what he had said, or at least apologize for the pain he had given. The Dean answered that, while he was quite willing to write a letter expressing his distress at causing the Queen pain, he would be bound at the same time to reiterate his view as to what was right, and having said this he wrote the letter and offered his resignation.

> I wrote the letter, adding an assurance that, if I was unduly or unfairly taking advantage of my privileged position as her confidential Chaplain and counsellor, I would without a moment's demur resign the position so that she might get someone else whose presence would not recall to her mind this unfortunate incident. I promised to do this without giving anyone a word of explanation, and I thought it could be quite easily arranged—but as to the suggested book, I repeated that I must adhere to everything that I had said.

The letter was met by complete silence. The Dean did not see the Queen for a fortnight, and by his own suggestion another preacher took his place on the next Sunday. But at last the strain was over.

> A few days afterwards she sent for me on some matter of a totally different nature, and was more friendly than ever, and we have never heard another word about the proposed book. To the best of my recollection Dr. Cameron Lees heard next Spring that the matter was postponed for the present.

The following comment is added in Davidson's memorandum dealing with the whole incident. It shows the significance of the episode in the relations between the Queen and her Chaplain, and not least the sound common-sense judgement of the Queen.

> This was only one, though the most serious, of several occasions of difference or remonstrance on my part towards her. In the long run her sound common sense judgement always prevailed, and she was much too good *au fond* to let things continue to rankle harmfully. My belief is that she liked and trusted best those who occasionally incurred her wrath provided that she had reason to think their motives good.

III

There were, of course, many other problems which came to the Dean, of varying degrees of gravity. Often they were put in a somewhat pungent way by Sir Henry Ponsonby, with regard not only to ecclesiastical appointments, of which we shall speak later, but to problems of charitable relief and points of ritual and doctrine, e.g. about turning to the east for the creed, or the state of the departed.

SIR HENRY PONSONBY *to the* DEAN OF WINDSOR

Windsor Castle. December 6 1884.

Do we officially believe in Purgatory?

Canon Luckock of Ely wrote a book about the future state. He apparently knows all about it.

He states that the Queen has expressed herself warmly in favour of his book (??).

And so wants to send another—

An appeal once reached him from the Public Schools, a little staggered at the unexpected largesse of a week's holiday on the occasion of the Jubilee, asking the Dean to act as intermediary to protect them against future bounty of the same kind!

On not a few occasions he had to act as ambassador between the Sovereign and the Archbishop of Canterbury. Thus he was asked to let Archbishop Benson know the Queen's wishes with regard to the Deceased Wife's Sister Bill[1] in 1883, of which she was a strong supporter in opposition to the Archbishop. This led to the Dean's suggesting a letter from the Archbishop to Her Majesty, justifying his position. Sir Henry Ponsonby's comment was: 'Your reply about the message to the Archbishop did very well, though the Queen "deplores his views" and hopes to beat him on Monday next.'

Once he had to explain the proposals for services at the Abbey and St. Paul's in memory of General Gordon, and show that they had no political character.

On another occasion the Queen was anxious about a Bible class of Society ladies, which the Archbishop had started at Lambeth Palace, intended, the Queen believed, to reform 'Society'. The Dean, after consultation, wrote to Sir Henry

[1] *Letters of Queen Victoria*, 2nd Series, vol. iii, pp. 422–7, 429.

Ponsonby. He said (March 6, 1885) that he was quite sure that some mistaken report of what had taken place must have reached Her Majesty. He repeated twice in the letter that there was no sort of idea of any general scheme for the improvement of Society or anything of the kind. All that had happened was this:

The DEAN OF WINDSOR *to* SIR HENRY PONSONBY

Windsor Castle. March 6, 1885.

A few ladies came to the Archbishop some months ago and told him they thought they and some of their friends would find it helpful if he could give them an opportunity this Spring of something a little systematic in the way of religious *teaching*, or addresses, adapted specially for educated people. He agreed to do so, in the quietest way possible. The notion was *theirs*, not his. They said they would find out which of their friends would like to come, and it ended, as I understand, in some invitation cards being printed, showing the hour at which he would hold such a service weekly in Lambeth Chapel. These invitations were given in a quiet way through the ladies themselves to those of their friends who would, they thought, care for it—and the result has been that for the last few weeks these ladies have met on Friday afternoons in Lambeth Chapel, had a little service, prayers, hymn, address—and gone away again. That is all.

The Dean offered to see the Queen, and give her any further explanation as to who attended, and anything else 'including what had happened about the Princesses'—through whom, or an invitation to whom, the news had apparently reached Her Majesty.

The Deanery, with Mrs. Davidson as hostess, was, it need hardly be said, a considerable addition to the charm and effectiveness of the Dean's influence in the Castle. It was not only visited by the Royal family (on one celebrated occasion, at the time of the Jubilee, 1887, five present or future Sovereigns took tea with the Davidsons), but it was the means of bringing other people, among them American bishops, into direct or indirect touch with the Queen of England. And there was a very general impression abroad, most helpful for all, that the Deanery was a centre of friendship, and a home where everybody could meet.

IV

St. George's Chapel contains the tombs of kings, and there was one remarkable event, recorded at the time by Dean Davidson, in which one famous king of England of the past and the future King Edward VII were brought into a close association.

In the centre of the Chapel, midway between the Sovereign's stall and the high altar, lies a vault under a pavement made of squares of black and white marble. Within the vault are four royal coffins. The large leaden coffin of Henry VIII lies in the centre. On its south side, with a space of about three inches between their shoulders, lies the coffin of Charles I, covered still with a black velvet pall, which seems to be in good preservation. Upon the coffin of King Charles, near the foot, lies a little coffin covered with black cloth, containing the remains of an infant child of Queen Anne. At the north side of Henry VIII lies the small leaden coffin of Queen Jane Seymour.

In 1813, in the reign of King George III, the coffin of Charles I had, apparently with the connivance of the Dean of the day (Legge), been opened for inspection by the Prince Regent, Sir Henry Halford,[1] his physician, and others. It would seem that certain articles were removed at the time, namely (1) a portion of the cervical vertebra cut transversely with some sharp instrument, (2) a portion of the beard of the King of auburn colour, with a bit of linen cerecloth attaching to it, (3) a tooth. In 1888, these relics were in the possession of Sir Henry Halford's grandson, Sir Henry St. John Halford. He desired to restore them, and presented them in a small ebony box to the Prince of Wales. The box contained the following inscription, engraved on a plate inside the lid:

En
Caroli I^{mi} Regis
Ipsissimum os cervicis
Ferro eheu! intercisum
1648
Et regiam insuper barbam

[1] Cp. Lockhart's *Life of Scott*, ch. xxvi, where it is stated that at Dr. Baillie's request Sir Henry Halford transmitted to Scott a lock of the hair of Charles I, taken 'when the royal martyr's remains were discovered at Windsor in April 1813'. Scott wore a ring containing the lock for some years (vol. iv, p. 141).

Dean Davidson, with a view to their safety in the future, suggested to the Prince of Wales that he might think it right to replace these relics in the vault or grave from which they had been abstracted. The Prince of Wales agreed. The Queen was consulted and her consent obtained, on condition that no one entered the vault or disturbed the coffin. The Prince handed the ebony box to the Dean on Tuesday, December 11; and the Dean had a leaden casket prepared, which was enclosed in a stout oaken case, fitting closely, and all firmly closed with screws, with the following inscription on the lid of the leaden casket:

> The relics enclosed in this case were taken from the coffin of King Charles I on April 1, 1813, by Sir Henry Halford, Physician to King George III. They were by his grandson Sir Henry St. John Halford given to H.R.H. Albert Edward Prince of Wales.
>
> On December 13th, 1888, they were replaced by H.R.H. in this vault, their original resting-place.

The day appointed for the restoration was Thursday, December 13. After the service of Evensong, the Dean, with Canon Eliot, as Canon in Residence, and Canon Dalton, superintended the removal of the pavement stones above the vault. This was done with the utmost care and reverence by Mr. A. Y. Nutt, Surveyor to the Dean and Canons, and three workmen, and occupied a very short time. Six of the small squares of black and white marble were raised, with the mortar that lay between them, and the brick arch of the vault was removed. From this about twenty bricks were taken out with the greatest care so that no débris should fall on the coffin beneath. By this means an aperture of about eighteen inches square was made immediately over the centre of King Charles's coffin. The workmen retired from the Chapel as soon as the aperture had been made.

The Prince of Wales then came to the Chapel. It was just past seven o'clock and the choir was wrapped in darkness on the winter evening. Only a long coil of magnesium wire served to light the narrow chamber, in which the Martyr King and his royal companions lay. All was silent as the little company of watchers gazed within; but no foot was allowed to enter. The Prince of Wales stooped down and lowered the ebony casket in its oaken case, with the relics, and placed it near the centre of King Charles's coffin. The Prince then withdrew. The workmen re-entered the Chapel, and the aperture into the vault was closed. The opening in the brick arch was rebuilt from above, each brick being held in place by hand till the mortar had set. The marble pavement was relaid, and by half-past nine that night all had departed from the Chapel.

CHAPTER V
THE DEAN AS CHURCHMAN

Is it not whimsical that the Dean has never once written to me? And I find the Archbishop very silent to that letter I sent him with an account that the business was done. I believe he knows not what to write or say; and I have since written twice to him, both times with a vengeance. DEAN SWIFT, *Journal to Stella* (Nov. 25, 1710).

WHEN Edward White Benson became Archbishop of Canterbury he expressed a particular wish that Randall Davidson should remain at Lambeth to help him. And though Davidson's actual service as chaplain lasted for only a few months, he was as much behind the scenes during the whole of Benson's primacy as he had been in the later years of Tait. The contrast between Tait and Benson was great indeed. Like Tait, Benson had been headmaster of a public school and member of a cathedral chapter, but he had none of Tait's ways or his manner of looking at the world. He was a churchman and a poet—in one; a lover of pageantry; a master of curious language, delighting in beauty, revelling in old chronicles, fascinated by the constitution, ritual, and archaeology of the Church; with a very high sense of the dignity and prestige of the see of St. Augustine (*Papa alterius orbis*). His interests lay not so much in the defence of orthodoxy as such, or in keeping the stream of the Church's teaching fresh with the currents of new thought, as in the setting forth of the Church's law, establishing historic precedents, declaring the Church's system, and making the Church tell as a spiritual society—as the Catholic Church of England in the midst of the modern world. He was not at home in Parliamentary proceedings, and always felt himself a stranger in the House of Lords. On the other hand, when vexed with ritual troubles he met these troubles by the unexpectedly bold and successful vindication of the ancient Court of the Archbishop of Canterbury as an independent spiritual tribunal with an authority and jurisdiction of its own.

I

To an Archbishop of this quality the aid of a man with Davidson's training was of unusual value. But from the very circumstances of his previous service Davidson also gained from Benson an experience and outlook which were likely to count for a good deal when the time came for him in his turn to take his place upon St. Augustine's marble throne. The relationship between the two men was very different from that between Davidson and Tait. To Davidson, Tait had been a father who had given and taught him almost all that he had. But Davidson was rather the counsellor of Benson, his partner and intimate friend. Davidson always looked at Benson as Archbishop and Master—and loved him as his 'dearest Lord'; and he knew that Benson was rich in gifts and qualities different from his own. But he did not in any sense become his spiritual heir, as he was certainly Tait's. He received much and he learned much; as a junior partner learns from the head of the firm. But he brought his own resources also to the common stock. He gave unreservedly all the knowledge he possessed; and the large correspondence between them, which still survives, reveals the magnitude of his contribution to Benson's work, not only his stored knowledge of the past but his extraordinary skill. Indeed, Davidson got the nickname of *Sapum* from the Benson family because he was 'more subtle than all the beasts of the field'! There is a story told of Canon Carter of Clewer which illustrates this. He had got into some kind of trouble over his teaching about the Eucharist. Davidson went to see him and said, 'Don't you mean so and so?' using an entirely different phraseology from that in dispute, which conveyed what Carter wanted and yet could not be fairly rejected by others. Carter said, 'I suppose it is what I mean', and after a little reflection agreed. 'May I tell the Archbishop so?' asked the Dean. Carter again agreed. Davidson went to Benson and told him what had happened. Benson looked at Davidson and said 'The old serpent!' and everything was settled happily.

Davidson himself writes thus about the correspondence, much of it preserved amongst his own papers, and more still at Trinity College, Cambridge:

> Practically every day there arrived a packet from him containing the most important items of his correspondence with brief annotations or queries, and I returned the documents with further comments, suggestions, etc. Forcible as he was in correspondence, and weighty as his opinions were upon all ecclesiastical matters,

R. T. D. and HARRY DAVIDSON
(*About* 1862)

AT HARROW, 1867
R. T. D., A. G. MURRAY (afterwards VISCOUNT DUNEDIN), H. N. ABBOT

R. T. D. CHAPLAIN AT LAMBETH
(*About* 1878)

R. T. D. as DEAN OF WINDSOR
(*About* 1885)

he was not a quick worker, and he was a man who specially sought counsel and help from somebody else before finally dealing with big questions. Bishop Lightfoot during his life, and Dr. Westcott both then and afterwards, Canon Mason in Benson's earlier years of episcopal duty, and, in some branches, Lord Selborne and Sir Richard Webster, were his constant counsellors. Sir Lewis Dibdin also helped him greatly on certain matters of Church patronage and the like, but there is I think no doubt that it was to me that he chiefly looked for daily aid, and it was I think a happy thing that my Windsor duties were of a kind which left me full opportunity for giving him such help.

Of course the mass of these annotations are either not preserved at all or are buried in the official correspondence bundles, but besides this I have a very large number of letters from him, all of which were placed at Arthur Benson's disposal for the purpose of the biography. The confidence with which he honoured me, and the opportunity he gave me for keeping in touch with the matters which had afforded me my main work in the Chaplaincy years, have been among the happiest episodes of my life.

There were continuous conversations, as well as the unbroken stream of correspondence, and all manner of topics public and personal tumble in and out of the letters. Drafts of Benson's Charges and of his Diocesan Letters used to come to Windsor, and Davidson made detailed comments upon them, and suggestions, even to the very syllables.[1] And there is a letter of April 12, 1887, about a clergyman ('Whatever you do with B. dont try to appeal to his commonsense') which Benson annotated in the top left-hand corner, 'The Dean really gets too cautious'. One or two specimens may be given by way of illustrating the importance and variety of the problems on which counsel was sought. His methods in advising the Archbishop were the very same that he used with the Queen.

In view of a Radical Disestablishment Campaign during the General Election of 1885, which in fact flared out, the Dean had suggested a manifesto in the name of the united Episcopate. The Dean's letter comments on a form of this manifesto which the Archbishop sent for his criticism. Eventually a Statement signed by the two Archbishops appeared in the press November 2, 1885:

[1] *Life of Archbishop Benson*, ii, p. 383.

The DEAN OF WINDSOR *to the* ARCHBISHOP OF CANTERBURY

17 October 1885.

I have, in the midst of a whirl of other important things, been giving all available thought to the Yorkist packet herewith returned.

The suggested manifesto is *not* what I had myself anticipated or desired. There is too little about the general duty of electors—too little of the serious WEIGHT which such an utterance emanating from two Archbishops ought to carry—and, in my opinion, too much about disestablishment. It is undoubtedly ably written and effective in its way, and as an address from a Bishop or Archbishop to his Diocese I should have no special fault to find. But what is wanted in this case is, to my mind, something different. An appeal from the Archbishop*s* as representing the accredited teachers of Christianity in the nation—calling on the citizens at large to realize their responsibilities towards God and man. But it is obviously easier to criticise than to manufacture such an address!

I confess I think the Bishop of Peterborough's[1] marvellously telling pronunciamento has a good deal changed the case. IT is now (necessarily and rightly) regarded as the foremost existing exposition of the Church's case against disendowment in 1885–90!! and if, as I suppose, the Church Defence Institution is reprinting it as a pamphlet to go forth by thousands, a fresh address by the Archbishops, of a necessarily much milder and less partisan sort, will surely be apt to fall flat. I should have thought it might have been said, (in your joint appeal to the electorate) that you abstained from going *here* into the question of disestablishment (earnestly as you deprecated so terrible a national calamity) because you did not want your solemn counsel to have even the appearance, far less the reality, of political or ecclesiastical partisanship. You could thus, as it appears to me, throw much more weight into the few plain and straightforward paragraphs, which should simply urge on the voter—in the very simplest available Saxon—the duty of thoughtfulness, earnestness, and caution; the danger of giving rash promises of support, or of crediting rash promises of special legislation, and should at the same time press on the employer the wrong he would do by trying to coerce voters. I think the opening and closing passages of W. Ebor's[2] draft are capable of being worked well into such a document.

I honestly confess that I think more of such a manifesto for the

[1] William Connor Magee, Bishop of Peterborough, 1868–90.

[2] William Thomson, Archbishop of York, 1862–90.

recognition it claims for the Voice of the National Church at a National crisis, than for the actual difference it is likely to make in the votes given!

Bosworth Smith's most admirable letter in last Thursday's *Times* is of real importance. He tells me he is getting the thanks of Liberals by every post. He is, of course, not a 'Churchman' in any technical sense, and some would call him rather a lax 'Christian'. All the more are his words weighty. If you have not written anything to W. Ebor before we meet on Tuesday, I should greatly like to talk the manifesto over with you further—and express my growing conviction of what is wanted.

I will try to put on paper before Tuesday what I mean.

The following letter deals with the Trial of Bishop King and other matters, annotated in Benson's hand 'Assessors—Southwell —Booth':

The DEAN OF WINDSOR *to the* ARCHBISHOP OF CANTERBURY

9 Jan. 1889.

I return herewith the *very* important and interesting packet you have sent me. I need not say how intensely I feel for you the burden and difficulty of the position in which at this moment you are placed. But I do most honestly believe that in such a matter as this we have no shoulders in the Church which could have carried so well as you can this particular load. You seem to me to have *throughout* acted in a way which is less susceptible of unfavourable criticism from fairminded men than anyone prior to experience would have deemed possible. (What a clumsy sentence!) May God continue to you the grace for a right judgement in the face of what is no ordinary mountain of difficulty and anxiety.

As regards the particular letters you sent me, may I say a word on each.

1. *Winton*[1] is what you would have expected. He is a 'grand old man' although he cant be of any great use to you if real *complications* should arise. His name is a tower of strength (among the clergy). . . .

4. As to *Southwell*,[2] I think he wants his ears boxed. The notion of writing in that fashion and then going off up the Nile is monstrous. If he had been in England, I think there is enough in some

[1] Edward Harold Browne, Bishop of Winchester, 1873-90.

[2] George Ridding, Bishop of Southwell, 1884-1904.

of the points he raises to have made it worth your while to have seen him—and shown him the facts and heard his criticisms thereon.

I should suggest for your consideration whether you should not now write to him in something of this vein:

> The points you raise are interesting and important. If I could now see you I think I could show you that you have misapprehended the case—which you admit not to have studied at all. But you wont expect me to enter into a discussion by letter which may be months before it reaches you—I wish you had been able to tell me your views by word of mouth, that I might have seen whether your objections have any residuum after I have explained the facts to you. As it is I haven't a notion what you expect me to do—I have taken the best advice in England and have weighed the matter with the whole facts before me. Have you the effrontery to suggest that I should throw all this advice overboard and start upon a new tack altogether because of the criticisms of *one* of my brethren which he fulminates at my head and then goes off for an African holiday!

That, put into civil language, is the sort of answer he should get, I think. I should certainly not try, if I were you, to argue or explain the details to him further on paper, and I should make the fact of his being on the Nile a sufficient reason.

You might add that the fact of floating on the Nile in an ark does not of necessity make him a Divine Lawgiver.

I thank you for your prompt and kind regard to my note about Birkbeck. It is of course possible that your original letter to the Kieff folk may provoke criticism—but it is better perhaps to be criticised for what you really said than for some imaginary version of it made public because people cant get the original.

Have you seen *Booth*'s statement in today's *Times* as to your supposed 'visit' to him?? You will see it is even referred to in the Leader. What can he mean? Does he refer to the day you went with me to Clapton in 1881? If much notice should be taken of the statement Booth has made, it might *possibly* be well for you to send to 'a correspondent' in answer to an enquiry, a few lines to say that you have no notion what Booth can mean. But I should not think you ought to send a contradiction direct to the papers. Possibly you have had some later communications with Booth whereof I know nothing.

I also return herewith the Natal letter you sent me, and (in a separate packet) the Australian Paper about Bp. Barry's 'return'.

Neither seem to call for much remark. The Natal letter you will, I imagine, merely acknowledge with thanks.

What a specimen of the variety and bigness of the Archbishop's work this letter gives:

Salvation Army
Bp. Lincoln Trial
Russo-Greek Synod at Kieff
South African troubles
Australian Primacy

II

But, busy as Davidson was in helping the Archbishop in all manner of problems, he was making his own independent and individual contribution to the work of the Church in addition. The representative assemblies of the Church were the Convocations, with their two Houses of Bishops and Clergy. After a disuse of 138 years (since 1717) Canterbury Convocation had been revived, notwithstanding opposition, in 1855. Dean Wellesley, however,

> had shared the old-fashioned dislike of Convocation as a new-fangled thing . . . and a curious correspondence exists at Windsor in which the Dean and Canons indignantly declined to receive from the Bishop of Oxford, or indeed from anybody, a summons to attend Convocation. Times had changed however, and I was naturally anxious to take my part in Convocation work, and, on consulting the old precedents, I found that there was no doubt at all that the Deans of Windsor had sat—as such—both before and after the Reformation. . . . Archbishop Benson duly summoned a Dean and a Canon in the first year of my tenure, and they have sat ever since.[1]

The Dean's first appearance was in February 1884. At that time the Lower House met in Westminster School Hall, and the Dean of Windsor sat at the end of the Prolocutor's table looking (says a Proctor of those years) 'so wise, so quiet'. The main debate of that session was concerned with the composition of the Final Court of Appeal in ecclesiastical suits, a subject to which Davidson was to devote much attention for the whole of his life. The Report of the Royal Commission on Ecclesiastical Courts, in the

[1] Till 1921, when a new canon was passed limiting the representation of Cathedral and Collegiate Chapters to the Dean or in his absence a Canon.

chairmanship of which Benson succeeded Tait, had just been issued. Davidson spoke, upholding the right of the lay judge to deal with ecclesiastical matters, as well as the cleric, in opposition to the followers of the fiery Archdeacon of Taunton (Denison), who maintained in the following May that 'it was not the layman's province to be trained in theology', and 'that Our Lord gave jurisdiction not to laymen but to the Apostles'. Of the Dean's speech on this occasion the *Church Times*, not usually his supporter,[1] wrote:

> The most noticeable incident of the week was the début of the Dean of Windsor, who at once took a high place amongst the debaters of the Lower House. Mr. Davidson is an excellent and judicious speaker, and is likely to form a great acquisition.

A glance through the *Chronicle of Convocation* (1884–91) shows that Davidson was always 'in' things at Convocation, and an active debater. Though of course not yet in a position to lead, or openly determine Church policy, he made contributions of no small value from the point of view of shrewd common sense, not unmingled with a liking for catching people out on the questions of the day, anticipating on certain points the line he pursued as Archbishop. Thus, in speaking of Church Councils (1886), Davidson was not afraid to reprove even so learned a speaker as Dr. William Bright for some words he had used a little carelessly, and observed:

> There was a way of speaking of the relation of Parliament to Church questions as though Parliament was a body altogether common and unclean. . . . An immense deal of harm was being done to the Church because Churchmen declined to expect that any good thing could come out of Parliament.

To some again who urged a multiplication of Diocesan Bishops (1888) he opposed the counsel *Audi alteram partem*; and suggested to those who wished to get rid of the old Bishops' Palaces that:

> Those who sit here a generation hence would look back with very mixed feelings upon our work when they saw Fulham Palace perhaps become a candle factory and Farnham Castle a Jesuit seminary.

It is also significant for the future that Davidson's last speech as

[1] After his speech at the Church Congress in 1882, against the falsehood of extremes, the *Church Times* had remarked on his 'sneering, especially ungraceful in a young man'.

Dean of Windsor in the Lower House was made in February 1891, when he persuaded the House to negative outright the motion of Archdeacon Denison, asking for a committee to examine the volume of essays *Lux Mundi*, of which the editor was Charles Gore, dealing (it was thought dangerously) with the doctrine of the Incarnation. The Archdeacon was then 86, and the Dean 43. Thirty years before, to the month, he reminded the House, the same fiery Archdeacon had persuaded the Lower House to appoint a committee to examine an earlier collection, *Essays and Reviews*, which he had described then as containing 'all the poison which is to be found in Tom Paine's *Age of Reason*, while it has the additional disadvantage of having been written by clergymen'. Indeed Davidson, in the course of his speech, through a suggestion that no member of the present Convocation, save the Archdeacon, would now be likely to sign the Report which the Committee on *Essays and Reviews* had produced, drew a remark from the Archdeacon which, with the Dean's conclusion, is worthy of reproduction:

> *Archdeacon Denison*: I wish to say that I should not myself be willing now to append my signature to it.
> *The Dean of Windsor*: Could there be a stronger support for my argument than that observation of the Archdeacon's? The report then drawn up was of such a character that even its author would now disown it. Now, is that the sort of process which if this Committee be granted, the Archdeacon wishes to see repeated now?

In 1884 the Queen appointed Davidson a Trustee of the British Museum,[1] in succession to Prince Leopold. One of the earliest questions with which he had to deal in this capacity was that of the Sunday opening of museums. The objection to the opening was partly on the score of Sunday labour for the museum staff, but it was also based on the view that, apart from the question of attendance at public worship, it was wrong 'to provide for our people on that day amusements or occupations which are not religious and spiritual'. Such was the objection of the Lord's Day Observance Society, as expressed in a letter from its Secretary to the Dean. And here again we find him handling a matter much more controversial than it afterwards became in very much the same way as he was often to handle it in later

[1] In 1884-1903 he served as the Crown's nominee; 1903-28 as Principal Trustee; 1928-30 as Permanent Trustee. See *infra*, p. 1195.

days; and (what is of equal interest) taking a line of his own in opposition to Archbishop Benson and (it was supposed) to Archbishop Tait.

He wrote thus to his father:

The DEAN OF WINDSOR *to* HENRY DAVIDSON, ESQ.

19 Jan. 1885.

On Saturday we had our British Museum debate on the Sunday Question. I did not have to initiate the matter, as it came up in the form of a report by the Secretary.

But I did finally move the resolution whereon we voted.

I moved that a letter be written to the Treasury to say that in the opinion of the Trustees it is desirable that, as an experiment, the Natural History Museum at Kensington should be opened on Sunday afternoons from 2–6 o'clock and that the Treasury be asked for a sum not exceeding £500 to meet the expense.

I made a full speech which was very well received. Sir F. Leighton seconded me. I was supported by Lord Rosebery—Sir John Lubbock—and the Prince of Wales (who was in the Chair and said only a few words) and we carried the motion, though the Archbishop (not very vehemently) and Beresford Hope were potent opponents.

Some of those who voted with me did so because they thought it certain that the Treasury won't vote the money unless Parliament reverses its previous decisions, and they wished to press the question on Parliament by means of *our* decision.

What will come of it, it is hard to say. The more I look into it the more do I feel sure we are doing right—and that Our Lord Himself would have been—under modern circumstances—on that side.

I have not another moment—Please let me hear soon how you are going on.

When his aid to resist the decision of the Trustees in favour of an experimental opening of the Natural History Museum on Sundays was invoked by the Lord's Day Observance Society, the Dean replied as follows:

The DEAN OF WINDSOR *to the* SECRETARY OF THE LORD'S DAY OBSERVANCE SOCIETY

Jan. 28, 1885.

I am in receipt of your letter about the British Museum and the possibility of its being opened to the public on Sunday afternoons. I am afraid our views on that subject would not be altogether in agreement, as I am one of those who believe that it is a mistake, both on religious and other grounds, to keep the doors of the Museum closed when so many other doors, leading to evil and not to good, stand open. I am well aware of the difficulty of the problem, and of the wide issues it raises, and I know how much is to be said from your point of view. It is, it seems to me, a case wherein no absolute law of right and wrong can be laid down with certainty, and we must therefore act, by the help of God, in such way as we believe to be most in accordance with His will, and most after the example of our Blessed Lord. I have, as a trustee of the British Museum, taken part in the movement for making an experiment in the direction of Sunday opening, for the benefit of those now debarred from such opportunities, and driven, by force of circumstances, into an evil mode of spending Sunday.

I do not refer so much to what are popularly called the 'working classes' as to the classes a little above them, many of whom feel, to my knowledge, the help towards good which would thus be given them. I fear I dare not expect that you will agree with me in this view, but it is not lightly or thoughtlessly that I have arrived at it. I am, however, most anxious that nothing should be done in the direction I desire without the fullest and fairest consideration of all that is so truly said by you and others upon the opposite side, and I hope you will use every effort to ensure the due discussion of the question by those in authority before any final step is taken. I entirely approve myself of your proposal to memorialize the First Lord of the Treasury on the subject, and also to bring about a discussion in Parliament. I imagine that you are sure, under present circumstances, of the efficient aid of Mr. Broadhurst and others to secure a majority in the House of Commons, and that, no doubt, will effectually prevent, for a time, the fulfilment of the wish I and others have at heart. I cannot complain of this though I personally regret it. But I have felt it impossible as a Trustee of the British Museum to face the terrible responsibility of aiding in keeping the Museum doors locked, in the face of the evils which I believe their opening will tend to counteract. If, in the course of the controversy which is now likely to be raised on this most difficult subject, you perceive any risk that your side of the question is not being fully presented or patiently heard, I shall be glad if you will let me know, and I can promise you that I will do all that I reasonably can to secure the fullest consideration of anything you bring forward.

May God give to us in these matters the 'right judgement' so hard for us to attain to. The 'Sunday Question' was certainly a burning one during our Master's earthly life, and the religious

> authorities of His day believed the action He took to be dangerous and wrong. One can but ask Him to be with us still, and to guide our authorities towards such a decision, on whichever side it be, as may most conduce to the advancement of His Kingdom.

The Dean's attitude, as thus explained, was a great disappointment to the Lord's Day Observance Society. Its Secretary demurred to the suggestion that their

> Sabbatic opposition to the free handling of the Lord's Day by the Sunday Society and those who are doing the work of that Society is to be compared with the opposition shown to our gracious Lord by the pharisaic Sabbatarians of the gospel period.

He also added:

> The Committee are very sad that they should find on the side of a movement such as led to our correspondence one by whose hand they had not unfrequently received communications on the question from the late revered Archbishop Tait and one to whom they had looked as likely to use any position he might hold in the Church of God on the same side as that on which the Archbishop ranged himself.

The Dean sent a civil reply. He could hardly refute the charge that he was not on the same side as 'the late revered Archbishop Tait'; and contented himself with the following comment:

> Your reference to Archbishop Tait was, I am ready to believe, kindly meant. I think however I may claim to have known pretty thoroughly his views on all such matters. Perhaps you have not noticed how marked a line he drew between a Parliamentary vote and the decision of the Museum Trustees.

III

The year 1885 was a very heavy year. It was the year of the General Election, the Disestablishment Campaign, the *Pall Mall Gazette* revelations and the passing of the Criminal Law Amendment Act, the Dynamite Outrages, the death of General Gordon, the marriage of Princess Beatrice, the completion of the Revised Version, the appointments of Bishop Temple to London and Bishop Moorhouse to Manchester—to name only some of the important events with which Davidson was definitely associated in one way or another. For some months of it Mrs. Davidson was away, and we get some interesting sidelights on the heavy demands made upon the Dean in letters written to her during her absence abroad:

The DEAN OF WINDSOR *to his* WIFE

June 18, 1885.

All Windsor is upside down. It is on the one hand ASCOT *Cup Day* and on the other hand Ministers are coming and going. Yesterday I went in to see Ponsonby and rushed in upon Lord Salisbury who was shut up in Ponsonby's room composing his cabinet. . . . One cannot help wondering whether Lord S. has some deep plan for making the Tories *popular* before the General Election comes.

The DEAN OF WINDSOR *to his* WIFE

44 Grosvenor Road
12 July, 1885.

I have treated you very badly in the matter of letters for the last few days, but it really has not been wholly my fault. I got last night your letter of Friday. Of course I shall not get one tonight.

Yesterday I greatly enjoyed the Harrow and Eton match which had the most exciting finish that has been seen in such a match for years, and which kept the whole thousands in a state of enthusiasm on one side or the other for at least an hour. The match had in any case to stop precisely at seven o'clock in accordance with rules—and Harrow, which was winning, had to try whether it was possible to make the necessary runs (93) in an hour and three quarters. During the first hour they only made about 20 and then it became a race against time. Finally Harrow won by getting the 93rd run at ONE *minute to seven o'clock.* Had they been two minutes slower in getting their runs the match would have been drawn. The boy who most distinguished himself was Arthur Watson (Vanity's son), and Teddy Butler, as Harrow Captain, was the hero of the second innings and finally won the match. Both these *fathers* will be in a state of supreme content. I enjoyed it all extremely.

This morning I went with Lucy to early service in Lambeth Chapel and officiated with the Archbishop, Monty being absent. We breakfasted there and then I went on alone to *Spurgeon*'s. Lucy was to have gone with me—but at the last we decided she should not go—thinking that Spurgeon would be sure, after all the horrors which have been revealed this week—to preach a coarse and trying sermon. The Archbishop quite approved of *my* going, in order to see what line Spurgeon was taking on this horrible but, at present, all absorbing topic. As it turned out he never directly alluded to it at all—but preached a most powerful sermon on final judgement—with a running reference throughout to all that has been published—but did not say one word which was indiscreet or coarse or harmful. I disagreed with nearly all he said about the Day of Judgement—but I could find no cause for censure with respect to his taste in the matter of these awful revelations or statements.

In case you don't know what all this is about, I will tell you briefly. Last Saturday week the *Pall Mall warned* its readers that it proposed to begin on Monday a series of revelations of the wickedness now going on with respect to very young girls, as the result of an enquiry they had themselves (the Staff of the paper) set on foot, to show the necessity of passing the Act for which we have all been petitioning and which seemed in danger of being again allowed to collapse in the House of Commons. It therefore bid them beware of its own pages for a few days. On Monday the first chapter of these Revelations was published and was so sickening and horrible in its ghastly revelations that an hour after its publication all the bookstalls were forbidden by W. H. Smith to sell it. This created huge excitement and troops of men and boys were selling it in the streets and the price went up to 6d. or 1/- per copy in some streets.

On Tuesday the excitement was still greater and the paper was selling in hundreds of thousands as fast as it could be printed. It was less revolting than Monday's, but was still most terrible. It was attempted to prosecute the sellers in some of the streets, but that failed, as the Lord Mayor said it was not *their* fault. Questions were asked in the House of Commons and still the sale went on The other newspapers who noticed it at all abused the Editor and declared the whole thing to be abominably false, but that won't do. From the first the Editor has said he will submit all his facts *with the names* to any three of the following—The Archbishop of Canterbury—Lord Shaftesbury—The Bishop of London—Samuel Morley—Lord Dalhousie (as in charge of the Bill)—the Lord Mayor—Cardinal Manning—Mr. Howard Vincent—in order that they may testify whether he is a liar. At present no names are published—but Mr. Stead declares that if he is prosecuted (as is threatened) he will rejoice—inasmuch as he will then, in self-defence, summon into the witness box in open court all the people of whose awful wickedness he now possesses proof, and will confront them '*princes, peers, and M.P.s*' with the victims of their sin. After this, probably he won't be prosecuted! He professes to long for prosecution.

The last chapter appeared on Friday—and yesterday had only comments on the whole—and statements as to the means used for discovering the evils and a repeated request for investigation into the truth or falsehood of the charges made.

I can't, of course, go into the particulars, but the general gist and outcome of the whole charge is this—That a deliberate trade is going on for the inveigling and capture and horrible treatment of young girls who are quite innocent and know nothing of what is going to be done with them—and who are bought and sold like slaves at so much a head. Such is his charge, and he professes to know names, places, etc. etc. and to be prepared to reveal them if he is prosecuted—or to tell them privately to any three of those whom he has selected as leading men, on the understanding that the three judges are only to testify to whether the charges are lies or not, and are to promise not to prosecute or expose the guilty men. You can well believe what a difference of opinion there must be as to whether the publication of such things is right or not. He has certainly gone fearfully far in the way of plain speaking and hideous details, and certainly the paper must have done harm to many who were pure and innocent. But I cannot myself doubt that, on the whole, the good outweighs the evil, and that the wave of moral wrath and indignation which has been evoked will sweep things before it, and will go far to prevent such hideous things going on unchecked. For example, the Criminal Law Amendment Bill, which was supposed to be hopelessly doomed in the House of Commons was carried on Thursday night *without a division* though it is to be again very carefully considered and discussed in Committee next Tuesday. His *immediate* purpose therefore already bids fair to be accomplished. Pray God it may all turn out well—and that He may bring good out of the evil.

Enough (perhaps too much!) of such a subject.

It was perhaps after the receipt of this letter that Mrs. Davidson put in the plea for more quiet, to which the following letter refers:

The DEAN OF WINDSOR *to his* WIFE

17 July 1885.

As the days lessen in number which separate us from one another I keep thinking about you more and more. May God bless and keep you in body and soul. You will come back refreshed in all senses, to give some of your refreshment to your rather be-jaded husband who wants above all things to get into his life some of that peacefulness which you have been writing about and which is the sure producer, I suppose, of better strength. I don't want to be overrestless and overbusy—indeed I don't—but I seem to have somehow so many more sides open to such attack than most people have, and I don't think it is quite my fault that *I*, or rather *we*, have so little time of quiet refreshment. But I will try, please God, to make these things more manageable. The real difficulty lies in the fourfold character of my present duties, no one of which, I suppose, can possibly be really shoved aside—except for a time:

Duty as Queen's Chaplain and Adviser.

Duty to *Windsor*, as Dean, Head of Chapter, and Lecturer to class etc. etc.

Duty to public matters in the Church wherein I have had so unusual an apprenticeship and about which your father felt so strongly.

Duty with my *pen*—especially at present in the matter of the *Life*! This last is growing upon me with a kind of night-mare bigness—and if I only could see a fair Genie rise out of the earth and undertake the work for me I should feel as if a veritable burden were lifted off my shoulders.

Nobody else, so far as I see, has so many quite different duties of the very first importance pressing on him—and as I am not clever enough to discharge them with the ease and rapidity which some men would exhibit, the burden squeezes me down and prevents me (and you too) from having the time for the refreshing and beautiful side of life which you so rightly feel the lack of for us both. Ask God to guide us rightly that we may see how to rearrange the days and hours in some wiser mould.

In 1886 and 1887, there was a considerable agitation in Church circles about the Anglican Bishopric in Jerusalem. In its original form it was jointly financed, and the Bishop was alternately nominated, by England and Prussia. From the start it had been bitterly opposed by most of the leaders of the Oxford Movement. Bishop Barclay, the third Bishop, died in 1881. The Prussian Government then withdrew from its share in the arrangement; and a very strong body of High Churchmen, headed by Dean Church and Canon Liddon, set their faces against any revival. Liddon went out to Jerusalem and wrote to tell the Archbishop that the Orthodox Patriarch was very strong against a Jerusalem Bishopric of the Anglican Church. Davidson had been himself in touch with the Bishop of Gibraltar, who was of an entirely different opinion about the views of the Patriarch. 'He thinks' (Davidson wrote, November 7, 1886) that 'Liddon, of whose views he was quite cognisant, tried when at Jerusalem to force an unfavourable opinion, first into, and then out of, the Greek Patriarch.'

On March 2, 1887, the appointment of Archdeacon Popham Blyth as Bishop in Jerusalem was announced. On the same day, Davidson wrote to the Archbishop, who had heard of a threatened memorial against the appointment of what Mr. Athelstan Riley described as 'the episcopal resident in Jerusalem —this seems to be the title which gives least offence':

The DEAN OF WINDSOR *to the* ARCHBISHOP OF CANTERBURY

March 2, 1887.

I return herewith Riley's letter and his three enclosures.

I greatly hope they won't get up such a Memorial to you as Liddon foreshadows, as it is by no means to be desired that you should now have to prophecy in detail all that is or is not to be done hereafter by a man who won't, after all, be under your direct command though you have the main voice in his appointment. You have two colleagues who are not apt to be ignored and one of them would very likely take the opportunity of answering in a very different spirit from that which the Memorialists profess to find in *you*. Liddon would like nothing better than to evoke from Bishopthorpe[1] something which he would parade as justifying all his violent language.

As far as I understand him, he wants to denounce Blyth simply because he (Blyth) won't use his own bad language about C.M.S.

It may be difficult for you, without doing harm, to choke off such a memorial as is suggested. But, if it comes, I hope it will receive the briefest and most dignified of replies.

It is intolerable that you should be pecked at by outsiders till they force you into some declaration upon a matter in which they are in no way concerned, and for which nobody asks them to be responsible. I wish somebody would ask Liddon to give the dates and circumstances of the personal visits of inspection at Jerusalem on which he bids Riley rely!

The memorial was, however, presented with a formidable list of signatures and was duly acknowledged.

The DEAN OF WINDSOR *to the* ARCHBISHOP OF CANTERBURY

Deanery, Windsor Castle
22 March, 1887.

I thank you much for sending me your strong, dignified, and as it seems to me most satisfactory letter. It is *very much* superior—

[1] Bishopthorpe, York—the residence of the Archbishop of York (Thomson).

as is meet—to the rough draft I ventured to send as an element for consideration. . . . As to Talbot's private reply, herewith returned, I think its frankness does him credit. He is evidently writing with utmost honesty and I think you will probably have sent him a line of genuine thanks without much difficulty. But its very honesty betrays a sad lack of grip of the real facts! . . .

Bishop Blyth was consecrated and received a very cordial welcome from the Orthodox authorities, to whom he was officially commended by the Archbishop of Canterbury. He ruled long (1886–1914) and wisely.

The Jubilee year, 1887, made many demands on the Dean of Windsor, as was to be expected; and he took a full part in the various celebrations—at the Abbey, at Buckingham Palace, and at Windsor itself. The following is the entry in his Diary for June 21, the Jubilee day:

At 7.30 a.m. Alice[1] arrived, from G.N. Hotel.

She was to go with me to the Abbey in lieu of Edith, as E. had received a second ticket admitting her to the Queen's Gallery, a special place on S. of Sacrarium. Lucy and Agnes had places on N. side of Sacrarium. We all went to Abbey together about 8.30 and got easily to our several places. The best by far was where Alice and I were, as we looked straight westward from above the Altar. The whole service and scene impressed me far more than I had at all anticipated, and I was also most agreeably surprised to see how comparatively little the beauty of the Abbey was marred by all the erections once they were filled with people.

The Archbishop read most clearly and well, and the Dean was also, I suppose, fairly audible. So soon as the Queen left, people began to move, and Alice and I soon went out and walked by the back streets to Buckingham Palace, missing Edith at the door where we had hoped to find her. We overtook Courtenay by the way and took him with us. We were nearly alone in the great forecourt of Buckingham Palace and could see the whole procession most admirably, after waiting rather a long time for it while we could trace its position by the cheering. By 3, we got back to Grosvenor Road, baked and hungry. Alice and Edith soon afterwards went off to Windsor. I dined again at Buckingham Palace where all was on a bigger and grander scale than last night and there was in the evening a very brilliant small reception by the Queen in the Ball room. The foreign Ambassadors and the Papal Nuncio!! and the Indians and the Queen of Hawaii were in an

[1] His sister-in-law, wife of Henry Davidson.

ascending scale the things most admired! Few others save the Household were present. The Queen was most gracious. I got away at 11.30 and walked and 'trammed' home.

The year 1888 opened at Sandringham. It was the Dean's third visit, but the first with Mrs. Davidson. He preached at Sandringham Church on the Sunday morning (Jan. 1), and at dinner that night sat next the Princess of Wales:

Had much very interesting talk to her. She described her first coming to England 25 years ago and the (most reasonably) alarming character of her visit to Osborne 'to be inspected' a few months before the marriage, when the Queen was in deepest mourning and the poor girl had to visit her for several days without anybody to break the gloom. She had not even a lady in waiting, and was terribly frightened at the whole process. Then the great triumphal entry into London came a few months afterwards. She had not been in London before, having gone straight to Osborne to see the Queen, and being bidden to avoid London. Then she described to me with the utmost enthusiasm her brother's going to the throne of Greece.[1] Her account of it was that Lord Palmerston and Lord Russell, one night at Marlborough House soon after her marriage, asked him half-jokingly whether he would like to go to Greece as King, and he, being then in the Navy 'and not good at his examinations' answered at once that he would like it immensely. Thereupon (so says the Princess) the then King of Denmark was privately consulted by the English Foreign Office, and, before either the boy's father or mother had heard a word about it, he was officially nominated as King and his consent made known in Europe. Then, she says, he had four years of tremendous hard work in the midst of cliques and abuses of all sorts, which he, as a lad, was powerless to stop, and he worked like a horse at learning his duties, but hated the dreariness of it all, till he married in 1867 'and lived happily ever after'. Nothing could be nicer than her sisterly enthusiasm about her brother's work.

On January 12, Mrs. Davidson's sister Agnes was married in Lambeth Palace Chapel to the Rev. J. H. J. Ellison, who had been Assistant Chaplain to Archbishop Tait from 1881 to 1882, and was then vicar of St. Gabriel's, Pimlico. On January 14, the Dean went to Osborne to see the Queen:

On Saturday, 14th, I went to Osborne. The fog had been terrific for days, but had happily lifted, and the boats were again crossing.

[1] King George of Greece, who at the age of eighteen succeeded King Otto, who had been deposed.

I had a pleasant 36 or 40 hours there—the Queen in good spirits. I dined with her both nights and had much talk at and after dinner. (Music by Alec Yorke and Miss Cochrane.) The Queen discussed the Lambeth Conference, and I explained why I had undertaken to serve. Also she spoke much of the schemes for more Bishoprics. I urged the encouragement of *suffragans* rather than the multiplication of sees. I don't think she much likes *either* plan—but she is dead against the multiplication of sees.

The spring found the Dean, Mrs. Davidson, and Miss Tait at Florence for a quiet holiday, he reading a good deal, including *Ecce Homo* and Addington Symonds on the Renaissance. Then came the chief event of the year—the Lambeth Conference, to which Davidson acted as Assistant Secretary to the Episcopal Secretary, Bishop Ellicott of Gloucester. A history of the Lambeth Conferences of 1867 and 1878 had been prepared and published by him beforehand. From his knowledge of the past he had of necessity a 'very large say in arranging what the subjects should be, as also in fixing . . . who should be the speakers invited to open each subject'.

The Archbishop steered wisely and cleverly through some of the initial difficulties—such as an endeavour by some extreme Bishops to get it privately arranged that they should appear in copes and mitres for the processions at Canterbury and Westminster. To stop this, a circular was issued saying that a question had arisen (as it had) whether the red or black chimere should be worn, and that the Archbishop recommended black chimere, lawn sleeves, and red hood for all the Bishops, to secure uniformity. I don't think anybody outside ourselves knew what had been planned and how it had been stopped.

The opening service was at Canterbury, and the Dean notes the contrast in manner between his former chief and Benson:

The Archbishop's address from St. Augustine's Chair was wise and generous if somewhat obscure. Seldom to my mind has the contrast been more remarkable than between the big simplicity of the words *spoken* from the Chair in 1878 and the somewhat eager, apologetic and involved utterance *read* from the same chair in 1888. But it was thoroughly *good* all the same—and no-one is more effective *looking* in a function of this sort, or more genial and kindly as the centre of such a gathering.

The Conference contained two crises. One related to the

recognition of Presbyterian Orders; and the other concerned the definite teaching of the Faith, the report, drafted by the Bishop of London (Temple), being rejected 'after a stormy and most unfortunate debate'. The Encyclical Letter, drafted in July by Archbishop Benson for the approval of the Conference, was, as regards its actual wording, the handiwork of Bishop Lightfoot of Durham and Bishop Stubbs of Oxford.

> I well remember sitting up with them almost the whole night, certainly until after daylight, while the actual wording and even transcription of the document went on.

The Report of the Conference was published in record time, and the Dean received the following appreciation of his work from old Bishop Ellicott of Gloucester and Bristol:

The Bishop of Gloucester and Bristol *to the* Dean of Windsor

August 3, 1888.

> We all owe you a very deep debt of gratitude, and I say this most deliberately, that the great success of the Conference is to a very large degree due to your unflagging energy and rapidity of successful labour.

In the middle of the Conference Davidson was 'distraught... by a very private but important communication asking me whether in the event of Barry resigning [the Archbishopric of] Sydney I would allow my own name to be ... put before the Committee of Synod'. But with the full approval of the Archbishop he declined.

When the Conference was over, the Dean noted in his journal 'an absurd and really disgraceful letter from the Bishop of Liverpool' in *The Times* about the Lambeth Encyclical; and added, 'the Archbishop had a reply in the next day's *Times* (*cujus pars magna fui*), as I went over to Addington with the letter already drafted and he accepted and inserted it'.

Immediately after this entry, the Journal gives a long and careful account of two conversations between Davidson and two American Bishops, in succession, on the Race question. The account is significant as showing the Dean's interest in this problem even in these early days. He describes the views of Bishop Thompson of Mississippi, who dined at the Deanery on two nights running and 'talked magnificently'. His view was that the negroes had not got it in them to be the dominant race whatever their *numerical* superiority. Bishop Whipple of Minnesota, whom Davidson saw in between the two nights on which Bishop Thompson came to dinner and 'pumped . . . on the same question', held the opposite opinion: 'He is of course the champion of the inferior races and he rose at once to the occasion and proclaimed to us his real belief in the possibility, aye the certainty, that the negro has all the latent capacity, if only you will give him time and opportunity.' Davidson's comment at the end of these talks is as follows:

> It is to be noted that there are very few negroes in Minnesota, and that this question in no way presses there: while in Mississippi it is vital.

For the rest of the year he was kept busy with the *Life of Archbishop Tait*, and with the preparation for the Lincoln case, which was soon to be almost overwhelming in its demands; and in addition to this and his regular duties he found time to write an article for the *Contemporary Review* on Religious Novels, with special reference to Mrs. Humphry Ward's *Robert Elsmere*.

The year ended in tragedy for the Dean and Mrs. Davidson. The young bride of the previous January, Agnes Ellison, had died quite suddenly on December 19, two months after the birth of her child. She was only twenty-eight, the life and soul of Lambeth in old days, and on her mother's death she had been everything to Archbishop Tait: vivacious, brilliant, beautiful, sparkling, in quite indescribable ways.

> No sorrow in my life has been to compare with the death of dear Agnes last month. The death of my Mother, and of the Archbishop were so different in kind from this that I can't compare them: and of course in each case they had, so to speak, finished their course. Craufurd was very dear to me: but not to compare in any way whatever with the intense love I had for this dearest of sisters.

Then follows in Davidson's journal a long and interesting study of Agnes Ellison's character and development. She was the youngest, but in some ways the most remarkable, of the three surviving sisters—Lucy, Edith, and Agnes—and Randall was almost as often with Lucy and Agnes at Grosvenor Road as they were with him and his wife at the Deanery. The note in the journal continues:

> No one could know of the work she had done among the Lambeth girls—or, still more, the work she had *planned* for St. Gabriel's folk, both rich and poor, without feeling that she might hereafter, with a combination of her father's Christian common sense, her mother's warmth of sympathy, and [her aunt] Lady Wake's vivacity and attractiveness and originality, have become a real power for good, of the best and freshest sort. Truly 'in a short time she fulfilled a long time': compressing into the last few years of her life what for most people would be spread out by degrees over a much bigger space. A life like hers affords, as it seems to me, the very best conceivable evidence of a continuance of Life, and Work, and energy, beyond the river. It is simply impossible to me to conceive the position of the man who would say that her personality came quite to an end a fortnight ago and ceased to be. I can only believe—and I do believe—that if such a man had known Agnes as we knew her he would perforce have reconsidered his creed.

CHAPTER VI

THE ARCHBISHOP'S COURT AND THE LINCOLN JUDGEMENT

He that cares not though the material church fall, I am afraid is falling from the spiritual. . . . He that undervalues outward things in the service of God, though he begin at ceremonial and ritual things, will come quickly to call Sacraments but outward things, and Sermons and Public Prayers but outward things in contempt. Beloved, outward things apparel God, and since God was content to take a body, let us not leave Him naked and ragged. JOHN DONNE.

ONE of the great problems with which the Church of England was confronted during the primacies of Archbishops Tait and Benson was the problem of authority. This especially affected ecclesiastical discipline in ritual questions. Several causes combined to produce the situation. Partly, as Davidson used often to maintain, under the influence of Walter Scott, 'with no necessary doctrinal purpose', church-people were coming to have a new respect for order, for history, for venerable buildings, and to rebel against slovenliness in public worship. Partly as a result of the Oxford Movement, a new sense of the continuity of the Church of England was created, with a resulting emphasis upon the doctrine of Apostolic succession. This led to a new interest in the Sacraments, together with a desire to make the Eucharist the clear centre of the Church's worship, and to restore (as it was claimed) the ancient vestments of the minister and ornaments of the sanctuary.

It was inevitable that what some proclaimed as an Anglican Revival should be denounced by others as a betrayal of the very principles of the Reformation. The outward matters at issue, though taken by themselves they might seem small, were in reality far from small, for a whole philosophy of the Christian life was ultimately involved. It was therefore natural that, as strong sides were taken by clergy and laity alike, certain of the points in dispute should be challenged in the only forum where a decision could be reached—the ecclesiastical courts. The difficulty, however, lay in the Final Court of Appeal. Prior to 1832 this had been the Court of Delegates. An Act of 1832 abolished the Court of Delegates and substituted for it the Privy Council itself. An act of 1833 transferred appeals from the Privy Council to the Judicial Committee of the Privy Council. To High Churchmen, whatever might be their views of the lower courts, this was a most unsatisfactory body. It was composed of lay judges who neither occupied such an official position in the Church of Christ as would give spiritual authority to their decisions, nor possessed any special training in religious learning as a necessary qualification of office. Since 1833, it had heard many important appeals involving questions of doctrine and ritual. In deciding those cases it had acted on its own view of doctrine and ritual, as stated in the formularies of the Church of England, without seeking to obtain the opinion of the Bishops as a body. The objection to the Judicial Committee as the Final Court of Appeal in doctrine was stated at the time of the Gorham litigation (1850)[1] by Bishop Blomfield (of London) as follows:[2]

> In all matters requiring judicial acuteness and calmness, impartiality and firmness, for the discovery of the truth of facts, and for the explanation and application of the law, nothing more is to be desired. It is only when questions of doctrine arise, and points of faith are to be determined, that I object to that tribunal as incompetent; it is competent to decide all questions of ecclesiastical law, but not matters purely spiritual, involving questions of divine truth; for this office it is not properly qualified, with reference either to the Church's original constitution, or to the personal qualifications of the judges. . . . But, my Lords, I would not be understood to rest my case entirely upon the probabilities of superior fitness in point of theological learning. I rest it also, and in the first place, on the inherent and indefeasible right of the Church to teach and maintain the truth by means of her spiritual pastors and rulers; a right inherent in her original constitution, and expressly granted to her by her Divine Head, on the terms of the Apostolical Commission. . . . I cannot conclude without protesting against an inference . . . that I think lightly of what is in truth the fundamental and vital principle involved in this subject, namely, the inherent and inalienable right of the Bishops of the Church of England to be the judges of questions of its doctrine duly submitted to them. (House of Lords, June 3, 1850.)

[1] The Judicial Committee held that the Rev. C. T. Gorham's teaching with regard to Baptism, that the grace given depended (in part at least) on worthy reception, was not contrary or repugnant to the declared doctrine of the Church of England.

[2] See *Report of the Royal Commission on Ecclesiastical Discipline*, 1906, pp. 66–7.

The objection to the Judicial Committee as the Final Court of Appeal in questions of ritual and ceremonial also grew steadily—notably from the time of the Purchas Judgement of 1871.[1] Hostility to its proceedings had also been increased by the series of imprisonments which followed the passing of the Public Worship Regulation Act (1874), when four High Church clergymen successively were sent to jail for refusing to obey the order of the court.

I

It was in the year 1888, while the imprisonment of yet a fifth clerk in Holy Orders (the Rev. J. Bell Cox)[2] was still fresh in people's minds, that the Church Association decided to appeal to a new and indisputably spiritual court, and to make, not an ordinary incumbent, but a Diocesan Bishop, the object of a prosecution. If it be granted (and it is of course a large concession) that litigation was for any reason desirable, there is much to admire in the courage of the Church Association in going to the Archbishop's Court, and in attacking a Bishop who was one of the most devoted and beloved of the Bishops on the Bench.

In 1888, Edward King, Bishop of Lincoln, was fifty-eight years old. For ten years he had been Principal of Cuddesdon College, where he had done a wonderful work in training young men for ordination. For another twelve years he had exercised an even wider influence among undergraduates of many kinds as Professor of Pastoral Theology and Canon of Christ Church, Oxford. In 1885 he succeeded Bishop Wordsworth at Lincoln, chosen for this see as a foremost leader of the High Church school. In his first three years as Bishop he had obtained a great hold alike on the clergy and the laity, and was as popular with the villager as with the

[1] The Judicial Committee in the case of the Rev. John Purchas held that Vestments were illegal and the Eastward Position illegal, and forbade the use of the Mixed Chalice and of wafer bread.

[2] The Rev. J. Bell Cox of St. Margaret's, Liverpool, was prosecuted for ritual offences in 1887. Dean Church, writing to Archbishop Benson (26 May 1887), spoke thus of this prosecution and consequent imprisonment: 'This Bell Cox case has come home to my sense of justice far more strongly than any of the previous imprisonments. They were in the thick of battle, and of hot blood. This comes after all has cooled down. . . . And what all see is, that while Mr. Bell Cox goes to prison for having lighted candles, and mixed water with the wine, and refusing to give up such things, dignified clergy of the Church can make open questions of the personality of God, and the fact of the Resurrection, and the promise of immortality.' *Dean Church's Life and Letters*, pp. 323–4.

working man of the town. In 1887 his action in taking on the duties of prison chaplain in order to minister to a young Grimsby fisherman, condemned to death for the murder of his sweetheart, touched the imagination of England and served to show the public that a new type of spiritual ministry had arisen in the Church.

Such was the Bishop against whom the Church Association presented a petition to the Archbishop of Canterbury in June 1888, on the ground that he had been guilty of certain ritual acts and practices which had been declared illegal. And the court to which the petitioners appealed was that of the Archbishop of Canterbury himself, as having jurisdiction over his suffragans.

The full story of the trial of Bishop King belongs to the *Life of Archbishop Benson*. But (as is constantly stated in that *Life*) the Dean of Windsor was throughout an adviser on whom the Archbishop specially relied. Moreover, since the ultimate questions behind the trial have their own connexion with latter developments in which Randall Davidson was destined to play a very large part, we may properly describe certain events with which he was practically connected in the two years during which the trial proceeded.

The first is the conspicuous interest taken by the Dean at this juncture in the nature of the Final Court.

The full bearing of the case was only recognized by degrees, and the friends of Bishop King could hardly believe that the Archbishop would give it serious treatment. The Archbishop was indeed implored to refuse to hear it. There is thus a letter from the Rev. E. S. Talbot, Warden of Keble, to the Dean, who is clearly recognized to be very close to the Archbishop from the start; and the Dean's reply is full of interest.

The Rev. E. S. Talbot *to the* Dean of Windsor

June 21, 1888.

Isn't this little cloud which has risen out of the sea *re* Bishop of Lincoln threatening to become a big storm? I confess to feeling most seriously alarmed. We have all come, have we not? for some time past to the feeling that the *status quo* must in some shape be maintained as the condition of peace, and of life. When you spoke to me in 1885 you entirely recognized this, and urged the withdrawal of Bell Cox on the ground that a strange conjuncture, unlikely to recur, threatened to break up the *status quo*.

The present matter gives a rude shock to all such ideas.

All the points of moderate ritual, from the Eastward Position onwards, are directly challenged, and if the case is allowed to proceed, and the decision is unfavourable, there must be (the Church Association will take care that there is) war along the whole line.

I hear that the Archbishop has urged the Bishop of Lincoln to concede three of the main points. But I shall not believe till I know it that you, my dear Davidson, can think that he *could* do this. Just think of his relations to people all up and down the country. Could anything be more cowardly or more mean than for him to yield points which with his full knowledge and support they have adopted? It would be an incredible course.

But—if he did it—what could conceivably follow? Can any one really think that you can unravel history to that extent, that we can go back now without catastrophe to Bishop Blomfield's Ritual? enforced all round, or at least on High Churchmen?

Yet if the Archbishop allows the case to proceed, how can he, upon your principles, decide the points otherwise than as the Privy Council has decided them, because it has so decided them?

Conceive what this means, the strife, the trouble, the strain to consciences.

Surely the only course is for the Archbishop to decline to take up the case. I know that it may involve risks first of attack by way of application for mandamus, then through Parliament.

But even if these are possible (and the latter is most doubtful) surely the risks are well worth running. He would be fighting for what on every ground of policy and principle we should desire—the right of the Church's chief Officer to independence and discretion in the exercise of his functions (a right which in his place every Bishop has even by the P.W.R.A.).

And he would be standing out clearly and boldly for the only one policy which for the sake of fairness and religion is really to be accepted—the policy I mean of insisting that the two great parties should live side by side without mutual molestation.

I do not see how any other policy can possibly save the Establishment.

Surely we may think that Archbishop Tait would have seen this: it is his last policy.

Unless it is *certain* that the Archbishop has no discretion (and surely that cannot be) we should be infinitely better off if he claimed it. If he were driven in the last resort by mandamus to act, this would not necessarily be nearly so disastrous: and he would have a great force of sympathy and support on which to rely.

I do trust that I shall find that you see the force of this which must be all clearly present to your mind. I do not *think* that I exaggerate the least.

The DEAN OF WINDSOR *to the* REV. E. S. TALBOT

June 22, 1888.

I need not tell you that I have read your letter with the greatest care, and have pondered over what you say. Not that pondering does much good in this case, for, as far as I can see, there is practically nothing to be done by us, and I should shrink extremely from pressing the Archbishop upon a subject of such a character—and especially upon what may have passed between himself and the Bishop of Lincoln in an interview of such an absolutely confidential, and even solemn character. The Archbishop has, I am certain, reported to no one his conversation with the Bishop. I suppose, from what you say, that the Bishop of Lincoln has been less reticent, though I cannot suppose he has told many people, and I most earnestly trust he will not. It surprises me to learn from you that the Archbishop has definitely asked the Bishop to give up certain points of ritual. I should have thought any such request most unlikely, at all events at this stage. But of course I cannot tell, and no doubt you have authority for what you say. The whole subject is evidently one at this moment of intensest difficulty and complexity and obscurity, and a rash or irregular step on the Archbishop's part may plunge the Church into trouble for many a day. I do not believe he will be either rash or irregular, for though I know no more than other people know and read for themselves about it, I can see what infinite and earnest pains the Archbishop is taking to act with caution and 'in order'. I am not sure from your letter whether you recognize what seems to me to be almost the most important point of all in the matter. Perhaps you do, and deem it of less importance than it seems to me to have, or you may see and know some answer to it which I do not. It is this: The Archbishop, if the accounts which are made public in conversation and otherwise be true, is found to possess a jurisdiction to try certain cases of ritual HIMSELF—a strictly spiritual court if ever there was one. The movers in this matter have, according to common report, satisfied themselves that such is the case—that it is a power inherent in his office. But it is not certain by any means, I should imagine, that the Queen's Bench, if the question were argued before them, would agree that he has such a jurisdiction. It is said to be the immemorial practice of the Queen's Bench to minimise or deny all jurisdiction (outside their own) which is questioned. Now suppose the Archbishop to be formally asked to hear this ritual case in this 'spiritual' court of his, and suppose him to reply that he declines to let the case be so tried, and declines on the ground (not that he has no jurisdiction, but) that it is inexpedient to have such a trial.

Then suppose the promoters to go, as they would, to the Queen's Bench to ask for a *Mandamus*, what do you think would be the result? There are various possibilities, of course, but to me it seems likely that they would say:

'This imaginary "spiritual court" which has been so rarely called into exercise is a very dubious and unsatisfactory sort of thing. We don't believe in its existence. We won't grant a Mandamus because we deny the existence or jurisdiction of any such Court.'

Now is that what we should desire? I suppose this court (which if it exists at all, may surely be independent of the Privy Council, which is part of an organised Act of Parliament system) to justify its existence and its power of action. May we not have gained, by a side wind, but very really, some restitution of a spiritual authority, the area of which might perhaps be hereafter extended.

Nobody that I have heard speak on the subject (except a silly and ill-informed writer in the *Guardian*) supposes that it is Lord Penzance before whom the Bishop of Lincoln is to be brought. Are the High Churchmen wise if they object to the Archbishop's exercise of this (so suddenly exhumed but perhaps quite regular) distinctly spiritual jurisdiction?

That is the point which seems to me to be almost more important than any other at this moment. It may be that my facts are wrong —nobody seems to understand them—or that I have misunderstood the process whereby the thing would work. But surely we had better be cautious how we 'madly cast away' the power of exercising a distinctly spiritual jurisdiction, if such there be.

As I have told you—I have not sought, and will not seek, to extract from the Archbishop on such a subject one word more than he chooses to tell any of us, whose counsel he might desire. He is placed, in such a matter, in one of the most difficult positions in which a man can stand, and the difficulty he must always have in talking over such a thing with anyone consists largely in the danger that he as judge prejudges the case he has to try by expressing an opinion upon the merits of the case. But nobody can doubt that he is the very last man in England who would wish to narrow, by any act of his, the fair and legitimate liberty of Bishops or clergy in any direction consistent with our formularies, and we have a right surely to expect that he will have wisdom from above for the exercise of functions so serious in a matter of this kind.

I don't quite follow your allusion to what I tried to urge on you and others in connection with the Bell Cox case. My view was that (1) *That* could not be regarded as a typical case, likely to recur all over England; (2) An exhibition, on Bell Cox's part, of the spirit of obedience, and loyalty to his Bishops *as such*, even at some sacrifice of what he cared for, would have an immense effect, in the public mind, in favour of the school he represents. How does this apply now? You say 'A rude shock is now given to any such ideas'—I don't see it a bit. For surely (1) No two cases could be less alike in their inception, character, and probable issue, than that of Mr. Bell Cox and that of Bishop King; and (2) Bell Cox *didn't* do what I and so many others tried to urge. Canon Carter —as you know—tried hard to get a few leading men of like views to join him in urging such a course on Bell Cox. But, as he told me, with the utmost sorrow, the fiery party prevailed, and Bell Cox would not budge an inch. Surely then you cannot urge now that the idea (of which Mr. Carter in precept and in action has been so warm an exponent) 'has received a rude shock'. It has not been tried. Would to God that it had. However, that is quite beside the mark. I don't want to go off into the past.

I don't think I need to tell you how intensely and whole-heartedly I am myself in favour of the *toleration* line, and how I should use every possible opportunity in favour of it. But a case of this sort—the relation between the Archbishop and one of his best-loved suffragans, is holy ground indeed, upon which I, for one, could not try to 'rush in'. The Archbishop has of course spoken about it. But in the most guarded way (especially as to any communications between Bishop King and himself). I can scarcely doubt, he would be helped by anything the Dean of St. Paul's could say to him. But I can imagine (though I don't at all know) the difficulty—which as a potential judge—he must feel in talking about it to even his closest friends—who might afterwards be called as witnesses to what he had said.

I am going to Lambeth tomorrow for some *Lambeth Conference* work with the Archbishop, and it is quite possible (I don't at all know, but it is *possible*), that he will speak to me about this most serious matter in its details. *If so, should you object to my showing him your letter to me?* It puts one side of the case most forcibly, and though of course he would see it was to *me*, and not to him you were writing—he might be glad to have read it. But this is *as you like*. Will you send me a note to LAMBETH PALACE upon that point and any others.

One principal point to be settled was the authority and even the existence of the Court before which the prosecution was made. It appeared that only one precedent was forthcoming for the exercise of the Archbishop's jurisdiction over his suffragans —the case of *Lucey* v. *Bishop Watson* (of St. David's), 1699, in which the Archbishop of Canterbury (Tenison), attended by six episcopal assessors, tried the Bishop, who was a man of scandalous conduct in various ways, for simony, and passed sentence of deprivation upon him. As such a precedent seemed hardly sufficient by itself to dispose of all objections, Archbishop Benson decided after much consultation 'especially with the Dean of Windsor' that before exercising jurisdiction he would wish for some instruction from a competent Court that the jurisdiction referred to in the *Lucey* v. *Watson* case was applicable.

The Judicial Committee of the Privy Council[1] were accordingly approached by the prosecutors, and on August 3 gave their opinion 'that the Archbishop had jurisdiction in the case'. They were also of opinion that the abstaining by the Archbishop from entertaining the suit was a matter of appeal to Her Majesty. 'They desired to express no opinion whatever whether the Archbishop had or had not a discretion as to whether he would issue the citation.' They humbly advised Her Majesty 'to remit the case to the Archbishop to be dealt with according to law'.

The Lord Chancellor (Halsbury) told the Archbishop, just after the judgement, that amongst the points agreed by the five judges and their assessors was this:

> That the Archbishop had jurisdiction over his Suffragan Bishops; that he ought to exercise it in person. It is not proper that he should merely remit it to his judge, the Vicar General, *propter dignitatem* of the Bishops.[2]

The Archbishop decided that he would exercise his jurisdiction and hold the trial, though 'Davidson gathers that the whole party are ominously banded to frustrate it'.

The Dean had a good deal of discussion with various members of the High Church party; and he caused some irritation, at times, by his persistence—as once when he came to Dean Church on a mission from Archbishop Benson. 'Master Davidson',

[1] The Judicial Committee on this occasion consisted of five judges with five episcopal assessors.

[2] *Life of Archbishop Benson*, ii. 329.

Church exclaimed, 'mustn't fancy he can always get his own way!' He was also much concerned to secure that Bishop King and his friends should not rely on what Benson called 'the confessed loveliness of the Bishop', but get the best legal help they could obtain.

The citation was issued by the Archbishop on January 4, 1889, and the trial was opened on February 12 of that year. Five Bishops were chosen as assessors, after a good deal of difficulty.[1] The charges against the Bishop were seven, as follows:

1. Mixing water with the sacramental wine during the service and subsequently consecrating the Mixed Cup.
2. Standing in the 'Eastward Position' during the first part of the Communion service.
3. Standing during the prayer of Consecration on the West side of the table, in such manner that the congregation could not see the manual acts performed.
4. Causing the hymn *Agnus Dei* to be sung after the Consecration prayer.
5. Pouring water and wine into the paten and chalice after the service and afterwards drinking such water and wine before the congregation.
6. The use of lighted candles on the Communion table or on the retable behind, during the Communion service, when not needed for the purpose of giving light.
7. During the Absolution and Benediction making the sign of the Cross with upraised hand facing the congregation.[2]

There had been some doubt as to whether the Vicar-General, Sir James Parker Deane, should sit by himself or whether the Archbishop should sit with the Vicar-General beside him.

Davidson writes (Friday, Feb. 8, 1889, 4 Warwick Square):

This morning I was summoned to Lambeth by telegram to meet the Archbishop, the Bishop of London, the Vicar General and Hassard,[3] to discuss the Lincoln case arrangements. The Archbishop, the Bishop of London, and I had half an hour's talk first, and decided that the Archbishop should not yield to Dr. Deane's wish to sit *alone* (as Vicar General) when the Court opens next Tuesday. The Archbishop felt that in the present excitement amongst the clergy, and especially after Lord Halifax's violent

[1] The Bishops of London (Temple), Rochester (Thorold), Oxford (Stubbs), Salisbury (Wordsworth), Hereford (Atlay).

[2] *Life of Archbishop Benson*, vol. ii, p. 354.

[3] Sir John Hassard, K.C.B., Registrar of the Province of Canterbury.

Clifton speech, it would never do to let it be said that the Bishop of Lincoln was simply brought before Dr. Deane. But we knew the Vicar General would not like it, for he had set his heart on sitting alone in the purely formal business which must precede the hearing of the case on its merits. Nor *did* he like it! When he and Hassard came in (Baynes being also there as Chaplain) the Archbishop and the Bishop of London both told him their view very strongly. He gave way at once, like a gentleman—(as he always is) and if he was not *convinced* he at least yielded with a good grace—though it was clear that he was disappointed. The Bishop of Lincoln's solicitors have written some very slippery and dodgy sort of letters and evidently mean to give all the trouble they can. It is a very black look-out, however one regards it. Dr. Deane said to me privately, in the most emphatic manner, 'I do not believe, after this prosecution, that the Church of England will last for five years'. We settled the details as to dress (Convocation Robes), place for *public* in the Court, and a few more particulars, and I arranged to meet Hassard at Lambeth next Monday morning to help him to get these all put straight.

At the opening of the trial Bishop King made a formal protest against the jurisdiction of the Court, and demanded that if tried at all he should be tried by the Archbishop sitting with the Bishops of the Province. Davidson's diary gives the following account (Tuesday evening, Feb. 12, 4 Warwick Square):

This morning I idiotically fell while dressing (missing a 'supposed' chair!) and hurt my back which made me less fit for work. But I have had a busy day nevertheless. At 10, Edith and Lucy and Beatrice Ellison were taken by me to Lambeth, that they might see something of the Trial. I had a good deal of private talk with the Archbishop in his dressing room and with the Vicar General also. Everybody was pleased by the long memorandum in big type which had appeared in the *Times* (nobody knows whence!).[1] It formed the basis of a leading article also, and I think it will do good. The 'trial' opened successfully. I met the Bishop of Lincoln on the stairs, on his way into the Court with Halifax, Randolph, Clements, and other friends. I ventured to ask him if he was going to speak, and he said *yes*, he would make a statement, and would then leave all to his Counsel. He also said 'I suppose I am right not to be in robes? Who wears robes?' I answered 'Only the Judges I believe. I think you are right as you are.' I told the Archbishop and Vicar General of the Bishop's intention to make

[1] The memorandum was written by R. T. D.

a protest himself, and the Archbishop and Deane thereupon asked the Bishop to come out and speak to them. He asked if he might bring Phillimore—and he did—and the four had a confab. in the guard room simply as to the order of proceedings—whether the Bishop should say his say *before* or *after* the Court was formally 'opened'. It was agreed it should be *before* and they retired. The Archbishop then told his assessors and the Vicar General that he intended to open with prayer. (He wisely asked no advice from the lawyers as to *this* 'formality'.) On the Bishops and Deane taking their places on the Dais—the same which was used for the Metropolitans at the Lambeth Conference—the Archbishop *standing* used three collects and the Lord's Prayer. Then the Bishop of Lincoln read his protest, and the rest went on, precisely as is reported in to-day's *Times*. On the whole I think things were smooth and satisfactory. The trouble will (I anticipate) be with the *assessors* who seem all to have fads of their own as to what ought to be done. Rochester (being on the high seas) was the only absentee. The Bishop of London was admirable—strong and clear and helpful; but, in the conversations both before and after the case, Stubbs[1] (as usual) was quietly sneering and carping at the whole thing from the strength of his very conscious omniscience. Wordsworth was quietly critical and implied that he could easily settle such things himself. Dear old Winton had started a hare of his own—some rather obscure argument as to the non-liability of Bishops to obey rubrics at all, as they had, of old, a dispensing power. We shall probably hear more of this a month hence.

The Archbishop did his part well, I thought, and *looked* so well! He has been much cheered since he had (yesterday) a long talk with the Attorney General (Webster) who has encouraged him in every way to go on and who is very hopeful as to the good which will come out of the suit, and the opportunity given for a wise and clear and strong judgement going more to the root of matters than the Privy Council has ever done. This took place, by arrangement, at the Athenaeum yesterday and I met the Archbishop there afterwards to hear the result.

The protest of the Bishop of Lincoln mentioned above, against trial by the Archbishop of Canterbury as such instead of before all the Bishops of the Province, was duly argued in March. Then the Archbishop took time to give his judgement. In the interval Dean Davidson saw Bishop King and others, including Lord Halifax, and pointed out the mischief 'the Bishop of Lincoln or

[1] He is said to have continually muttered: 'It is not a court. It is an Archbishop sitting in his Library.'

his lawyer may do if they allow the case on some technicality of jurisdiction to get out of the hands of the Archbishop and into the Queen's Bench or elsewhere'. In the end he succeeded. The Bishop of Lincoln made up his mind to accept the Archbishop's decision and to free himself from the lawyers.

II

But the most conspicuous action taken by the Dean was through a letter to *The Times*, as a sort of challenge to make the High Church party face realities and state what kind of Court they would accept if the Archbishop's Court, so obviously spiritual, was unacceptable. He privately consulted the Archbishop, who wrote the following note:

The ARCHBISHOP OF CANTERBURY *to the* DEAN OF WINDSOR

23 March 1889.

As regards this Trial—undoubtedly the Laity (those who are not merely disposed to banter about it) do take the view you mentioned. They divide the Clergy into Romanizers and Puritans and are angry with both. A letter such as you well planned would do good in two ways. It would open the eyes of the laity as to the existence of the broad plateau of central sensible clergy—and it would encourage many clergy to stick to that centre instead of joining either Romanizers or Puritans which the attitude of the laity and others tends to make them do. They are very likely to become what they are told they are.

On April 2 (six days after the conclusion of the argument about jurisdiction before the Archbishop) a letter appeared over the Dean's name in large type in *The Times*, under the title 'Ritualists and the Law'. It was of considerable length. It urged that the real question at issue was that of authority. The Dean declared:

The DEAN OF WINDSOR *to the* EDITOR *of 'The Times'*

Rightly or wrongly, they [i.e. the 'Ritualists'] are persuaded that every decision of an ecclesiastical Court is at present invalidated, to say the least, by the fact that the existing Court of final appeal, the Judicial Committee of the Privy Council, sitting with episcopal assessors, is not properly qualified to decide cases in which a question of ritual or doctrine may be involved.

He gave a full résumé of the proposals which had been made for reform, particularly through the Royal Commission of 1883. He showed how all these proposals had been rejected by High Churchmen, and challenged the rejecting party to produce a scheme which was a practical substitute—i.e. a substitute compatible with the Establishment and therefore one that might be proposed in Parliament with some chance of success. The letter ended:

> If the Ritualist leaders have indeed arrived at a solemn conviction that they cannot, without disloyalty to Christ, obey, even for a time, either the Court which has existed since 1833 or any final Court now obtainable, and that they prefer disestablishment, then the Church and nation have a right to be told of their resolve, and their followers above all should understand clearly and without delay what is the path upon which they are being led. If no such resolve has been arrived at, we have an equal right to know in plain, unmistakable terms what is the plan proposed. The moment for considering it is opportune, and it will receive in every sense a favourable hearing. The great central body of the Church, both clergy and laity, is weary of these strifes. Its members, I believe, care comparatively little for any of the points directly raised, and are anxious to have their minds set free for their larger work—the promotion of the social, moral and religious progress of the people of England. And the strife, such as it is, turns less, after all, upon ritual than upon authority. Once let us secure somewhere an unchallenged jurisdiction, and the ritual problems will be quickly and quietly solved.

The publication of this letter caused a sensation, not least because the Dean was known to be in the inner counsels of the Archbishop. In addition to scores of private communications, a long correspondence followed in the Press. The *Rock* spoke of the Dean's pluck; the *Church Times* attacked what it described as the Dean's 'Eristikon'; the *Guardian* and the High Church papers generally disliked it.

Lord Halifax expressed the views of the High Churchmen on the crucial point thus in a letter to *The Times* of April 8:

VISCOUNT HALIFAX *to the* EDITOR *of 'The Times'*

> There was [when the Royal Commission reported in 1883], so far as 'the disaffected section of High Churchmen' are concerned, a very general acceptance of the recommendations of the Commission with respect to all the Episcopal and Provincial Courts. The difficulty arose as to the nature of the appeal contemplated

> from the Provincial Courts of Canterbury and York to the Crown. Upon this point there was an ambiguity in the recommendations of the Commission.
>
> Was the appeal from the Archbishop's Court to the Crown of the nature of an *appel comme d'abus* and affecting only temporal consequences, leaving the Archbishop free, when the case was remitted to him, to reassert, if he saw no reason to modify it, his original judgment; or was he bound to amend his decision, even in the most spiritual matters, in accordance with the finding of the civil tribunal?
>
> If the latter, it was obvious that the recommendations of the Commission left matters exactly where they were, and had done nothing to meet the difficulties entertained by such men as Mr. Keble. If the former, there could be no question of opposition on the part of those whom the Dean mentions, since not only in public but in private Lord Addington, myself, and others repeatedly said that the recommendations of the Commission afforded the basis for a settlement which we could thankfully accept.

The crux was, as the Dean pointed out in a further letter (April 9), to preserve both the principles of the Church and the principles of the Establishment. ('Lord Halifax desires to preserve both. So do I.') The correspondence ended on April 20, when the Dean made a general reply. Many champions on both sides had taken part in the controversy, and he claimed that a considerable amount of agreement had been reached. In this he was perhaps too sanguine. So a leading article in *The Times* surmised. For the real question, it pointed out, was whether the decisions of the Final Court proposed by the Royal Commission were to be really final. The Royal Commission had proposed a Court of Appeal which should consist of not less than five lay judges, members native of the Church of England, who should be empowered, and in some cases bound, to consult the Bishops of the Province before giving a decision. It further provided that 'when on appeal to the Crown the judgment of the Church Court is to be varied, the case shall be remitted to the Court the judgment of which is appealed against, in order that justice may be done therein according to the order of the Crown'. Then came the question—when the Final Court disagreed with the Church Courts was the Archbishop to be free to adhere to his former judgement, or must he alter it? If the former, the Final Court was a superfluity. If the latter, the Civil Court ruled the

Spiritual Court and all the objections of the Ritualists remained unabated.

> Of course [*The Times* concluded] if the Dean of Windsor is content to reduce the functions of the Final Court to the cognizance of an *appel comme d'abus*, or of an appeal in plea of excess of jurisdiction, and to surrender its authority altogether in matters of faith he may find it easy to come to an understanding with the Ritualists. But it has never been difficult to come to an understanding with them on those terms. The difficulty has always been, and still is, to reconcile their claim to spiritual independence with an Establishment over which the authority of the Crown is, in the last resort, supreme.

From the point of view of argument towards agreement, therefore, *The Times* would say no progress had been made. But it is very clear that, from the point of view of opening the eyes of the laity, and forcing the friends of Bishop King to show where they stood, and the difficulties of agreement on their side, there had been great gain.

The Dean's own comments at the time, and seventeen years later (when himself Archbishop) are as follows:

Note by DEAN DAVIDSON, *April 15, 1889*

I am the recipient of a great deal of abuse from some people and a good deal of praise from others. I do not think either is very much deserved. . . . On the whole I incline to think the correspondence has done good, though I am not sure I should have plunged into it had I foreseen the amount of work and worry it would involve.

Note by ARCHBISHOP DAVIDSON, *1906*

Looking back upon it all now I am not quite clear that I acted rightly or justifiably in thus plunging into controversy while occupying the known position I did (*a*) as the Queen's confidential adviser and (*b*) as the constant correspondent and friend of Archbishop Benson, who was at that time engaged in the Lincoln case about which I had myself as was well known to many people given him important advice. But I had consulted him on the point and he entirely approved of what I was doing, though of course holding himself quite aloof from the controversy, nor do I think that what I said was in itself other than right.

III

On May 11, Archbishop Benson delivered his judgement, which concluded as follows:

> The Court finds that from the most ancient times of the Church the Archiepiscopal jurisdiction in the case of Suffragans has existed; that in the Church of England it has been from time to time continuously exercised in various forms; that nothing has occurred in the Church to modify that jurisdiction; and that even if such jurisdiction could be used in Convocation for the trial of a Bishop, consistently with the ancient principle that in a synod bishops could hear such a cause, it nevertheless remains clear that the Metropolitan has regularly exercised that jurisdiction both alone and with Assessors. . . . There is no form of the exercise of the jurisdiction in this country which has been more examined into and is better attested and confirmed. . . .
>
> This Court decides that it has jurisdiction in the Case and therefore overrules the protest. (*Life of Archbishop Benson*, ii. 347.)

A good deal of correspondence followed with Lord Halifax, in which the Dean urged the importance of arguing the whole case on behalf of the Bishop of Lincoln with the greatest thoroughness, and rather vigorously objected to a warning given by Lord Halifax in the course of a letter:

VISCOUNT HALIFAX *to the* DEAN OF WINDSOR

June 11, 1889.

> Depend upon it, the Oxford Movement was God's message to the Church of England—and the decision which the Archbishop has to make is whether so far as in him lies—he will ponder it or reject it.

The Dean replied:

The DEAN OF WINDSOR *to* VISCOUNT HALIFAX

17 June 1889.

> I do not think however that he [the Archbishop] is likely, in the actual trial of the cause, to look intentionally beyond the historical and other facts which can be adduced as argument on either side. The business surely is to decide fairly upon the facts and not to consider what is 'wanted' or whether 'it will hinder or assist the Oxford movement' or be 'a safe position to take up'. As a man, and as a Churchman, he may be feeling the pressure of all or any of these points and have a very clear notion of what would be 'politic' and helpful. As a Judge however he has surely a solemn obligation to avoid consideration of *policy* altogether.

> I gather from your letter that you would not quite agree in this, and I own some of your words surprise me. Nor have I any sort of right or means of conjecturing what line the Archbishop is likely to take. I only know that he is certain to do his duty as a Judge with the most absolute and straightforward impartiality, and with a knowledge of the subject perhaps unrivalled among English Churchmen.

Lord Halifax in his answer said that he had not meant quite what Davidson supposed—only that in his view a certain line of action 'would be contrary to the mind of the Church of England'!

On the resumption of the trial on July 23, Bishop King's Counsel objected that the word 'Minister' in the Rubrics to the Communion Service did not include a Bishop, and therefore that the Bishop was not bound by them. The Archbishop dismissed this plea. All the preliminary obstacles were now removed, and the course was clear for the trial in the following spring.

For the remainder of the trial, though the Dean was without doubt in close touch with the Archbishop, it would not appear from the correspondence that he played as active a part in immediate connexion with the proceedings as he had clearly played in the preliminary, vitally important stages. But outside the precincts of the Court he found himself engaged in defending the Archbishop against continuous criticism both of himself and of his Court from various points of view.

From the Diocese of Ely there had already come an 'address of sympathy' to the Bishop of Lincoln from Ely Theological College in which past and *present* students—Davidson underlines 'present' with a blue pencil in his copy—expressed their 'profound regret' that the Primate had allowed the case to proceed and their 'most earnest gratitude' to Bishop King for his 'unflinching attitude against the medieval and monarchical mode of exercising the metropolitan jurisdiction of the see of Canterbury'—(this also is strongly marked with Davidson's blue pencil). Another document came from the same diocese in the autumn of 1889, signed by doctors of divinity and others in Cambridge, in which Bishop Gray's dealings with Bishop Colenso,[1] who was deposed by him as Metropolitan from the

[1] The Rt. Rev. J. W. Colenso, Bishop of Natal, deposed by the Bishop of Capetown (the Rt. Rev. Robert Gray) as Metropolitan, sitting with two assessors, for heresy. See *Life of Archbishop Tait*, i. 326–64.

Bishopric of Natal in 1863, were favourably compared with Archbishop Benson's methods with Bishop King. Other protests were threatened from clergy in other dioceses. There was much correspondence in the *Guardian* to which Davidson himself contributed, and there were various exchanges with Dr. William Bright, Regius Professor of Ecclesiastical History at Oxford, who took a leading part in a protest in the Diocese of Oxford.

The following letter from Canon T. T. Carter, the eminent Warden of the Clewer Sisterhood, gave Davidson particular pleasure:

CANON T. T. CARTER *to the* DEAN OF WINDSOR

Clewer. Sunday, Nov. 17, 1889.

. . . I cannot see how the Archbishop could have done otherwise than he has done unless he could have vetoed the attack at the beginning. But I have supposed that if he had attempted it his hand would have been forced which would have been worse. I think he could not but have claimed jurisdiction though it might not be the only method. Certainly precedents seemed in favour of such increase of archiepiscopal powers. I hardly see how as a practical way of dealing as the Church spreads it could be otherwise. The difficulty as to synods thus acting I believe would be that the synodical principle is against delegation. Proxies are possible but proxies cannot vote and as you say to expect the 25 Bishops to sit week after week is ridiculous. I am unable to go along with these protests. The one now being circulated in our Diocese seems the best and most respectful and I see Bright takes a lead in it, but I cannot sign it. I am afraid there is a tendency to 'bespatter' any court that could now be formed. I am afraid I cannot hope to live to see what will escape.

The DEAN OF WINDSOR *to the* ARCHBISHOP OF CANTERBURY'S CHAPLAIN

20th November, 1889.

. . . I think he [the Archbishop] will like to see the enclosed from old Canon Carter. I wish the old boy would say publicly what he says privately. But he won't.

The Dean was certainly very pertinacious, and his interrogations were not always appreciated, as when Dr. A. J. Mason, Archbishop Benson's close personal friend, turned on him once, when they were both at Bishop Lightfoot's funeral in December 1889, with the strong protest: 'What business have you to catechize me?'

IV

Shortly after this, Davidson made it his business to deal with a strong agitation from various Protestant associations, directed partly against the Ritualists and partly against the policy of the Bishops. He thus found himself, as he was often to find himself through his long life, answering extremes on either side and explaining formally and courteously what he felt to be the real facts of the situation.

On February 13, 1890, the Rev. T. Davis, Vicar of St. John's, Harborne, sent Davidson a leaflet about the Church Association, containing the following statement:

> About thirty years ago, what is now known as Ritualism had begun to manifest itself in the diocese of Norwich, and some clergy began to introduce unlawful practices in Divine Services, all in imitation of the services of the apostate Church of Rome. An appeal to the Bishop was made to put these practices down, and he resorted to the Ecclesiastical Courts. To defend in these courts the breakers of the law, the English Church Union was formed in 1859.... The law-breaking clergy, now called the Ritualists, stated through their own organs that if the matter were decided in a court of law, they would willingly obey. The Bishops said that if the law were only clearly defined, they would gladly enforce the law. *Some of them, alas! were insincere in this statement.* At this point the Protestant laity of England, guided by godly clergy, came forward and, at a COST OF MORE THAN FIFTY THOUSAND POUNDS, undertook to have the points in dispute legally tested; and so in the year 1865, six years after the formation of the English Church Union, the Church Association was founded.... Case after case was tried in the very highest courts of the realm, and the law upon fifty-nine points fully declared. Every hindrance was thrown in the way by the law-breakers which could possibly be devised, some utterly disgraceful to them as men, to say nothing as clergymen, but they were beaten all along the line. *And now comes the melancholy issue.* The Bishops almost entirely sided with the criminal clergy, refusing to enforce the law, and in some cases, notably the Bishop of Lincoln, have joined the ranks of the law-breakers themselves;... Of the Church Association let me say at once, it is neither a prosecuting society, nor is it a persecuting society.

The DEAN OF WINDSOR *to the* REV. THOMAS DAVIS

18th February, 1890.

It has fallen to me as the Biographer of Archbishop Tait to examine with a good deal of care the historical facts of the last quarter of a century, and I cannot honestly say that I am led with you to the conclusion that the Church Association is adhering in its present course of action to the lines on which it was originally founded. . . . Perhaps you are hardly aware how frequently it was stated by those who were concerned in the earlier work of the Association that its business was to ascertain the law, and when this was done it would be for the officers of the Church, Episcopal and other, to administer according to their due responsibilities the law which had been ascertained. It was and is of course open to those who had at first been engaged ascertaining the law to criticise afterwards the over vehemence or over laxity of its administrators. Nor can it be called necessarily wrong that a man who has the legal right to prosecute some clergyman for ritual irregularity, should exercise that right even in the most ruthless and wholesale manner. But such a course of action is a totally new departure and does not correspond with the aims and objects set forward in public and in private by those who founded the Church Association or who supported it in its earlier days. To say, as your paper says, that the Association in its present attitude 'is not a prosecuting Society' is certainly a little startling. If it is not the prosecutor in all or nearly all recent suits, it has certainly been wickedly misrepresented. If it is the prosecutor in these suits, how can it be said that it is not a prosecuting society? That it was not founded upon such lines or with such views I am well aware, and it is precisely because of its having departed from the lines of its earlier days that it has forfeited the support of so many who were in full agreement with its early desire that the law should be authoritatively ascertained. I gather from your sending me the paper that you desired to invite such criticism as I have ventured to trouble you with. You will see that I have carefully abstained from any expression of opinion as to how far it is the duty of the authorities in the Church, Episcopal or other, to enforce *vi et armis* the rigid letter of every law. Some people think such is their duty, others do not; but to most of us it certainly seems obvious that the responsibility for administering ascertained law rests with the authorities to whom God has committed the care and governance of the Church, and not with any independent Society or Association.

Mr. Davis, while thanking the Dean for his 'kind and courteous reply', qualified the statement to which exception had been taken, saying that the Church Association 'does not exist for mere prosecution'. But when Davidson referred him to the evidence given by the Church Association before the recent Royal Commission on Ecclesiastical Courts, he was reduced to the remark:

The REV. T. DAVIS *to the* DEAN OF WINDSOR

March 1, 1890.

It has never prosecuted except for the purpose of testing some point, or to see if the law would not be enforced.

If the Bishops only had fulfilled their promise, or the law-breaking clergy theirs, all would have been well. But it was the Bishops who took a new departure, and instead of enforcing the law as they ought, some of them have joined the law-breakers. These are facts that cannot be denied.

The Dean replied:

The DEAN OF WINDSOR *to the* REV. T. DAVIS

March 3, 1890.

I thank you for your letter of the 1st inst. I gather from it that you have found on inquiry that you were mistaken when you said in your letter of February 20 that the Association 'has never prosecuted a second clergyman for the breakage of the law on any point which had previously been tried'. You now tell me that the object of the Society is either to test some point of law 'or to see if the law would not be enforced'. This was precisely what I criticised before, and I still venture to think that the Society departs altogether from the original intention of its promoters when it seeks to take out of the hands of the constituted authorities the duty of enforcing law which has already been declared. I have myself no doubt whatever that a very large part of the extreme Ritualism now in use has been distinctly fostered by the irritation not unnaturally felt by earnest men against the particular modes adopted by the Church Association. . . . I ought to add that in my opinion the further result has followed that Bishops have found themselves hampered and thwarted in the exercise of their legitimate authority by the action which the Society has taken professedly for their help.

In the summer of the same year another memorial was circulated, this time requesting the Archbishop of York (Thomson) to introduce into Parliament a Bill substituting deprivation for imprisonment in cases of clerical contumacy. The covering letter was signed by five lay peers including Lord Grimthorpe, and three Deans, including the Dean of Canterbury (Dr. Payne-Smith). The movement was not one with which the Bishops generally sympathized; but the Archbishop of York, popular in many ways though he was, did not altogether agree with the others on the matter, nor with his brother Primate, who had referred to him in a letter to Davidson a little before this date as 'William the Hinderer':

The DEAN OF WINDSOR *to the* DEAN OF CANTERBURY

Amsterdam. June 7, 1890.

Private.

Will you pardon me for writing to you upon a matter which has surprised and perplexed me more than I can say.

Among the letters which have just reached me forwarded from Windsor, whither I hope to return on Tuesday, is a printed one from yourself and one or two others, asking me to append my name to a memorial to the Archbishop of YORK, requesting *him* to introduce a Bill to substitute Deprivation for Imprisonment. I imagined it had come to be a matter of general agreement that Archbishop Tait was right in his oft repeated opinion that a Bill *to that sole effect* would defeat its own object, and that the provision would only form part of far wider and larger measures to meet present needs. Of course I know that a mere partisan cry of the Grimthorpe order is easily raised to proclaim that such a Bill is both workable and desirable—but I thought calmer folk had come to see the fallacy of this. This however is not what I meant to write about—Why do *you* ask us to address the Archbishop of YORK?

I know why Lord Grimthorpe does. He has stated in private that he will do all he can to hamper and hinder Archbishop Benson, whom for some reason he dislikes—and he wants to make him seem to the public an Anti-Protestant. Now, you and I know that Archbishop Benson has done and is doing more perhaps than any man living to restrain and regulate High Church excesses and follies. Could his difficulties of a personal sort be made public, he would win deserved applause at the expense of others whom he is too chivalrous to throw over and expose, badly as they have treated him. But for the Dean of his own Cathedral (pray pardon my presumption) to say to the world—'We can't trust Archbishop Benson so we ignore him altogether, and turn to the Archbishop of the other Province for help'—will surely bewilder the faithful beyond all measure, not to mention the pain and distress it must of necessity cause to the Archbishop of Canterbury himself. I am glad to see that most of the signatures printed on the paper which accompanies your letter are those of clergy of the Northern Province who are, of course, perfectly in their rights in asking their own Archbishop for such legislative aid as they desire. It is *your* name which is to me the puzzle and distress (knowing the pain it must cause at Lambeth), and at the imminent risk of seeming impertinent and presumptuous I do venture to appeal to you to consider the effect it will produce, as coming from one occupying both personally and officially such a position as yours.

I do not of course know yet—having been abroad—whether the Archbishop has seen your printed letter—but I suppose it will soon reach him if it has not already done so. Why could not the petitioners be invited to address the TWO Archbishops? Lord G. would of course not approve because he means this to be a weapon for damaging Archbishop Benson in the eyes of Protestants—though he knows perfectly well how grossly unfair such a representation of him is. But must others therefore follow the same envenomed course?

I feel you may be reasonably angry with me for writing thus freely—especially as I am away from friends and may be ignorant of something that has passed, but I have felt bound with all most true and genuine respect *liberare animam* and I half think you will pardon me.

The DEAN OF CANTERBURY *to the* DEAN OF WINDSOR

June 13, 1890.

Nothing could be further from my wishes than to show any disrespect to the Archbishop of Canterbury for whom I have not respect only but a strong personal attachment. But as regards imprisonment of clergymen for theological views I have the strongest possible objection to it. It is a remnant of a barbarous age of jurisprudence and is silly as well as useless. If a man is so disobedient as to refuse to obey the constituted courts and authorities, let him finally after every method of patience is exhausted, be treated as a solicitor would be, and struck off the rolls. As for anything stopping ritualism, I for one believe in no public remedies. Probably there will come a turn in public opinion in due time, and I think that reasonable men now are in a large majority. As for this blot of imprisonment, I would rather see someone else bring in a bill to remove it, when the matter would be fully discussed, and the air cleared; but any such bill would be roughly dealt with probably in the Commons' House, and our Archbishop should hold the place of umpire rather than combatant. A bill brought in by the two Archbishops would be too serious a matter, and would be right only on some point which commanded general assent, and besides our Archbishop's judgment in the Bishop of Lincoln's case, however fair and wise, is sure to lead to troubles, and I would not put any fresh load upon him. He is doing much by quiet influence and guidance, and that, I believe, to be his wisest course.

During the busy months which followed the close of the proceedings Archbishop Benson was occupied with the preparation of his judgement—a task at which Davidson would often find him in 'his dressing-room at Lambeth . . . surrounded with stacks of books, deep in liturgiology as if he had nothing else to do'.[1] He completed the Judgement in Switzerland in August and September. On November 21, the Judgement was delivered—a judgement in which all the Assessors concurred save on one point in which there was one dissentient. The Judgement was very fully argued—learned and independent, showing a careful consideration for recent decisions of the Privy Council, but taking a different line on some of the points at issue.

The Court decided:

(1) that the ceremonial mixing of water with the sacramental wine, in and as part of the Service, is against the law of the Church, but finds no ground for pronouncing the use of a cup mixed beforehand to be an ecclesiastical offence.

(2) that pouring wine and water into the paten and chalice after the Service and afterwards drinking it before the Congregation is lawful.

(3) that it is lawful to stand in the 'Eastward position' during the first part of the Communion Service.

(4) that the manual acts during the Prayer of Consecration must be visible to the communicants properly placed.

(5) that singing of the hymn *Agnus Dei* after the consecration prayer is lawful.

(6) that the use of two lighted candles, when not wanted for the purpose of giving light, standing on the Holy Table continuously through the Service, is lawful.

(7) that the making of the sign of the cross in giving the Absolution, and in giving the final Benediction, is unlawful.

[1] *Life of Archbishop Benson*, ii. 355.

The Judgement was received with gratitude and admiration, as a work of rare excellence and wisdom.

Dean Church voiced the thanks of the High Churchmen when he said, 'It is the most courageous thing that has come from Lambeth for the last 200 years.' The Church Association appealed, but the Judicial Committee of the Privy Council dismissed the Appeal in August 1892. The Archbishop's Court had thus been declared able to exercise its ancient authority to the general satisfaction. On two points in particular Benson set an especial value. The first was that history had been proved admissible in the interpretation of the substance of rubrics. The second was that the judgement of the Privy Council could be reversed.

CHAPTER VII

PAGES FROM A JOURNAL; THE LIFE OF ARCHBISHOP TAIT

We talked of biography.—*Johnson*. It is rarely well executed. They only who live with a man can write his life with any genuine exactness and discrimination; and few people who have lived with a man know what to remark about him. The chaplain of a late Bishop, whom I was to assist in writing some memoirs of his Lordship, could tell me scarcely anything. BOSWELL'S *Life of Dr. Johnson*, 1776.

IT has been necessary for the sake of clearness to tell the story of the Lincoln trial without any break. But it will not be supposed that the Dean had nothing else to do but watch the various proceedings within the Court, and champion the Archbishop without. We have already given instances of other occupations, and we shall see very soon that during many months of these years the whole question of his future was agitating not only his own mind but that of the Queen.

I

An intermittent Journal was kept in 1889, and we can gather from it some illustrations of the Dean's various interests and duties during the spring and summer of 1889.

The Dean attends a dinner at Nobody's Club:

Wednesday, Feb. 13. Dined this evening at 'Nobody's Club' where we had a big muster to greet *Liddon*, who made his début, along with Wace and Bernard. Liddon's speech was disappointing.

He has a long talk with the Empress Frederick, full of sorrow at the thought of returning to Germany:

Sunday night, Feb. 17. This morning I preached in the Private Chapel on Genesis i. 1. and this evening I dined with the Queen—sitting between the Empress and Princess Beatrice.

At dinner the Empress was full of interesting talk—tackling me about my sermon this morning wherein I had said that before the time of the Exodus there was no real history in the true sense of progress. She thought both Nineveh and Babylon were evidence to the contrary, and she poured forth much—in a somewhat crude shape—about ancient Egypt as the source of Mosaic Law. Some of her statements would have astonished *Ebers* on whom they were fathered by her—e.g. she said that Ebers had himself found a mummy—of a period long anterior to Moses—on whose swathing clothes were written *exactly* 'the ten commandments', word for word as we have them in Exodus!

We had also much talk at dinner about the Lincoln prosecution —the Queen showing much interest in the subject, and objecting equally to the Bishop's doings and the prosecutors! After dinner I had much further talk both to the Empress and the Queen. The Empress spoke very freely about the trial of returning to Germany and of leaving England where her visit had done her so much good. She said it was hard to know what in her case *forgiveness* ought to mean. 'She would not pretend to say she was not full of anger and "unforgivingness" towards the traducers of her husband. Ought she to regard such feelings as *wrong*? etc. etc.' She said it was not so much Bismarck himself against whom she felt anger, as he was only carrying out the unscrupulous policy which he had pursued so long. 'It is a quarrel of thirty years' standing.' The people against whom her real indignation was most keen were the much smaller folk who had for years received favours at her husband's hands and who now traduced him 'in this cowardly way, because they know I am helpless and can't answer them'. She said emphatically that her anger and 'unforgivingness' did not mean that she bore them illwill or would not be glad to meet them half way if they would make some approach or amends. Altogether there was much that was both interesting and touching in what she said.

The question of his own future is raised in a talk with the Bishop of Ripon (Boyd Carpenter).

Friday, March 8. 89. Yesterday and the day before I had two very important talks with the Bishop of Ripon who came here each day to see me. He is very unhappy at the silence of all moderate men in the present difficulties and wishes I think for some protest or declaration. In this I don't agree with him. I have been in correspondence on the subject with Dean Vaughan, Sir Walter Farquahar, Kitto of St. Martin's, and others, and all, as it seems to me, tends to shew that it would be impossible to draw up such a declaration in any form that would be effective. E. G. H. McNeile of Manchester wanted Vaughan to head a Memorial to the effect that those who sign it pledge themselves to abide by the Archbishop's decision whatever it may be. I don't see how we could—with the possibility of an *appeal* lying ahead—agree to such a declaration without making the mischief worse than now. I now hear that Kitto is going to get up a meeting of some sort to assert the loyalty of moderate folk. I can't say I feel very hopeful of its effecting much.

But what the Bishop of Ripon is far more keen and unhappy about is the general drift in the direction of moving heaven and earth to include Ritualists, and yet taking no step to include Broad Churchmen or Nonconformists, but the reverse. He feels the responsibility of having got into Parliament and yet having no scope for *moving* in that wider direction. He says he is always in a minority of one at Bishops' meetings and clerical gatherings and so forth, because everybody is organisation-mad and is working upon a different line altogether to what seems to him (Ripon) to be most essential. Huxley is hammering at the gate with the cry of No God—and we are worrying about ritual details of the smallest sort. Can he, ought he to, DO anything? That is his view. 'Surely', he says, 'somebody in authority ought publicly to declare that we are not *all* concentrating our thoughts on these trivialities.' I discussed it all with him very fully but I can't, for my life, see how at this moment any definite *public action* can be usefully taken. I think he and all who agree with him should keep on saying it, but that is all I can regard as possible. That was the point of our first day's talk (on Wednesday). Yesterday his line was a more personal one. What can be done to get upon the Bench of Bishops some men of wider sympathies and different views? Men like Wilson, and Farrar, and so forth? And then a very strong pressure (which he said was his real point in wanting to see me) as to the need of making *me* a Bishop, so as to bring the views of Archbishop Tait forward, and have them pressed on the Church with the force which comes from my knowledge of the Church History of our time. I honestly think he quite overrates and exaggerates the power I should have of doing this. I don't think he has had means of judging of the feebleness which would in many ways mark any public utterances of mine. But it would be affectation to deny that I do want often to be unmuzzled by some more independent position where one could speak out freely what one felt instead of being, as now, trammelled by the responsibility of not bringing 'the Queen' into party politics. But anyhow, as we agreed, there is nothing that can be practically done, and one must work on *behind the scenes*, so far as it may be, and do one's best for the cause of freedom and wider sympathies. If I know myself, I think I can say quite honestly that I have no personal ambition for great office, and that I am well content to do what is set before me from day to day, my *only* discomfort and dissatisfaction being that I am *muzzled* at the very time when the numbers in favour of outspoken freedom of sympathy are so few, and when every voice, however weak, might help.

The contrast between Huxley's vigorous campaign against Christian dogma and the Church's absorption in ritualist controversy was much in Davidson's mind at this time:

March 10. Read in the train Wace's article on Agnosticism in this month's *XIXth Century* in answer to Huxley's attack on him in last month's. Wace is very strong in such argument, but spoils it by a sort of bad-temper which underlies it all.

A note of a visit to the House of Commons, and speeches by Mr. Herbert Asquith and the Hon. George Curzon:

March 29. 10 p.m. I had a very interesting four hours in House of Commons from 3–7, and heard the interesting *Bright*[1] discussion well (W. H. Smith, Gladstone, Hartington, Justin McCarthy, Chamberlain). Gladstone and Justin McCarthy were both admirable, and the flexibility and ease of the former is a standing marvel. Also an interesting discussion on the payment of members—A capital, rattling speech from Asquith, whom I had never heard before, seconding Fenwick's proposal. He was opposed in a similar (but far less thoughtful) speech by George Curzon, who is a slashing young debater but with overmuch self-assumption for my taste.

'A strange sort of life!'

April 7. 11. [Private Chapel] when I preached on Luke xix. 10, with allusion to the old Duchess of Cambridge who died yesterday. Then much reading and writing till 5 o'clock Chapel. Then more ditto, and talks with Ethel Smyth and Etta McArthur. Then I dined in the Castle very quietly—sitting next the Duchess of Albany at dinner and having a great deal of talk with her both then and afterwards. Also with the Queen, who is very full of her visits to the Bernardine Convent and Reformatory at Biarritz and who has today written me a long letter on the subject. The Queen very well and lively.

My birthday today—no less than 41! More than half—probably two-thirds—of life already gone—and very little done. Mine is a strange sort of life, with very much that is unlike other people's.

A conversation on Religion and Science:

May 18. Professor Flower, of the British Museum, has been staying here for the last two days and I have had a great deal of talk with

[1] After John Bright's death, March 27, 1889.

him on many subjects, and specially on the question of the present relation of scientific opinion towards religious thought. He is very warm upon the subject, and seemed indignant at the popular notion that there is some antipathy on the part of scientific men generally towards any definite statement of the Christian faith. He says it is very hard and very unfair that, because Huxley and Tyndall happen to be scientific men of the first order, and happen also to be opposed in some sense to the truths of religion, that scientific men generally should be ticketed as though they belonged to the same school of thought. He says that both Huxley and Tyndall were anti-religious in a dogmatic sense long before they had made any mark in science, and that their views on these subjects cannot therefore be regarded as the legitimate outcome of scientific thought and scientific knowledge. In evidence of this he refers to a little autobiography of Huxley just published, of which he promises to send me a copy. Even with respect to Huxley himself, he maintains that there has been more religious belief than Huxley is perhaps himself aware of. He tells me that on one occasion when he (Flower) was President of the Biological Section of the British Association at Dublin, and concluded his address by quoting the words 'Lord, how manifold are Thy works: in wisdom hast Thou made them all,' he afterwards remarked to Huxley: 'I said that, not in order to please or displease anybody, as some suppose, but simply because it is what I firmly believe.' And Huxley replied 'Well, I am not sure that I do not believe it myself' —or words to that effect. In Flower's opinion Huxley's present rather solitary life, with friends only of his own way of thinking, tends to make him go further in the wrong direction than he would naturally be inclined to go, and Mrs. Huxley encourages him in doing so. The bitterness of his recent articles, in answer to Wace, have been a distress, Flower says, to very many of Huxley's best friends. . . . His own acquaintance with scientific men is of course immense, and he says emphatically that he knows not the slightest reason for thinking that unbelief is more rife among them than it is in other professions—*e.g.* barristers. Among the younger men, for example, in the British Museum, he says, there is abundance of belief, and that anything like aggressive unbelief is at a discount. And he believes the same to be true of scientific men generally.

In the summer of 1889, Davidson got right away from England and all the problems of the Lincoln trial. With Mrs. Davidson, Lucy Tait, and John Ellison he visited Denmark and Sweden via Belgium. Wherever he travelled, Davidson always found the people, the country, and their institutions of absorbing interest. As a memorial of this tour two small notebooks remain filled with graphic accounts of things seen and persons met.

The most interesting part of the holiday was spent in Sweden from the middle of August. At Lund he acquired a great deal of knowledge about the University. The Cathedral 'is ten times finer than any of the guide-books say'. The place generally 'is very like one of the Scottish Universities and must be doing a great deal for the life of Sweden generally'. From Lund the Davidsons passed to Jönkoping, where Ernest Davidson joined them; thence to Motala, Linkoping, and Stockholm. Here he pursued his explorations, and on Sunday after Church took the opportunity of seeing how the Sunday opening of museums worked in Sweden.

> We went to the National Museum, which is full of interest. It is open 1.–3. on Sundays (i.e. *not* in Church hours) and I wanted to see how the Sunday opening answers here. Certainly the right sort of people, working men and women of all sorts, were thronging it. I never saw a museum being better patronised.

There is further a long and interesting account of the conditions and constitution of the Swedish Church, the number and the payment of the clergy, etc., the method of appointing bishops, patronage, ritual, etc. Another place the Dean visited was Upsala, a university town and the seat of the Primate of Sweden, whom he was anxious to see. It was a real regret to him that the Primate did not find it possible to arrange for an interview. The following letters passed between them—of no little interest when we remember the close friendship which came to exist between the Dean, as Archbishop of Canterbury, and a later Archbishop of Upsala, Dr. Nathan Söderblom:

The ARCHBISHOP OF UPSALA *to the* DEAN OF WINDSOR

Upsala, 3 Sept. 1889.

Very Reverend Sir!

At this time of the year I am much occupied, and it is often very difficult to say what day I certainly can be ready to receive visitants. When I sended my last letter to you, reverend Sir, I believed that I would be at home 10th September, but the circumstances are altered, and I fear now that I probably will become an unsteady traveller during the whole month. Best therefore to leave all hope of our meeting. I deplore that my answer on your honored letter of Aug. 28 not is more satisfying for us both; but can not help it. May God bless yourself and your Church!

With greatest esteem your thankful and dutiful servant

A. A. SUNDBERG
Archbishop of Upsala.

The DEAN OF WINDSOR *to the* ARCHBISHOP OF UPSALA

At Leksand. 7 Sept. 89.

My Lord Archbishop,

I am greatly obliged to Your Grace for the kind letter I have here received. I confess it is a disappointment to me that Your Grace has not been able to arrange for my having the privilege of an interview with you, and the Archbishop of Canterbury, who is very keenly interested in the Swedish Church, will also, I know, be disappointed that I have not been able to communicate more directly with Your Grace as to the important matters which were treated of in the recent Conference of Anglican Bishops. But I shall be able to explain to him that Your Grace's numerous and pressing avocations rendered such an interview impossible for you, and I will take care to convey to him your expressions of esteem and good will.

I have the honour to be etc.
Your obedient and dutiful servant
R. T. DAVIDSON.

On his journey home, Davidson returned through Copenhagen and lunched with Bishop Fog, the Bishop of Seeland, the foremost ecclesiastic of the Danish Church, 'a really good old man of deep and earnest personal piety, many of his expressions and lines of talk being like Archbishop Tait's'. It was another opportunity for acquiring information and was fully used. The Bishop's description of an ordination made a profound impression on Davidson.

The Bishop described with emotion the impressiveness and beauty of an ordination—dwelling specially on the custom of hand-giving by the ordinands. They are asked as they kneel at the altar rail, whether they will promise to observe all that belongs to their office (in words not unlike those of our ordinal). They answer 'Yes'. 'Then', says the Bishop 'give me your hand upon it.' And each of them solemnly takes the Bishop's hand in turn—and then turning to the great row of clergy of the Diocese who are sitting round the choir behind, the candidate takes the hand of each

> Priest in turn. It is not till after this that the 'laying on of hands' takes place—the priests present assisting, as with us, in thus ordaining the new Priest.

Bishop Fog also told him 'of a quasi High Church movement inaugurated in the present century by a priest named Grundtvig who seems to have been a man of the utmost pugnacity, earnestness, and force (a sort of Archdeacon Denison)—who lived in a fray from first to last'!

The party reached Hamburg on September 17. But their holiday was brought to an abrupt end by a telegram announcing 'the sudden death to-day of our dear Father—a strangely solemn and, for us, sad ending of our tour'. All returned home at once, and the two brothers, Randall and Ernest, with Ernest's wife went straight to Edinburgh from London. The Dean's journal continues:

> How different from the happy arrivals here of so many former years. What scores of times I have driven to the door, and seen *him* looking out for me—from Worksop—Harrow—Oxford—travels—Dartford—Lambeth—Windsor: and now, one could only go up again to his little room—where he lay, looking so peaceful and like himself that one could hardly believe it possible he was dead. I never saw so little change in the face of one whose spirit had fled.

It was the break-up of the old home, and the entry in the little Journal ends with a note of pathos:

> We were all together for this *final* Muirhouse week.

The DEAN OF WINDSOR *to the* ARCHBISHOP OF CANTERBURY

Muirhouse,
Davidson's Mains, Midlothian.
27 Sept. 1889.

I thank you with all my heart for your kind and affectionate words. We are indeed passing just now through rather 'deep waters'. One grows angry with oneself for not being able to let the sunshine conquer the mist, but the sense of what we have lost in him comes surging across one again and again, and the melancholiness of breaking-up an old home with all its manifold associations does not make it easier to look upon it as one tries to do. To sorrow for *him* is impossible. He was I think the most simply 'pure in heart' of any man I ever knew, and he has stepped in a moment —as he always said he would wish to do—into the fuller sunshine beyond, without pain of parting, probably without even the consciousness of death.

I can recall no period in my life, from little-childhood till now, in which he has not been my most intimate and trusted confidential counsellor and friend, and the *blank* is now proportionately great.

We are here for another week (during which however I have to go to Banffshire to marry our friend Helen Gordon Duff) and hope to be at Windsor about the 7th or 8th of October.

I feel somehow as if I had been cut off from you for a long time, and there are hundreds of things I long to know and to ask you about—besides all I would fain tell you about the Swedish Church and its apparent possibilities (which seem to me much less than I had expected to find them). I wonder what is happening about your *Charge*—I have kept on wondering how you are going either to say or to leave unsaid the things which must be trembling on your lips as to our present troubles. I wonder when I shall see you. Might we go for a night to Addington when you get back from the Congress? Is the Charge to be in type before it is spoken? But if I began to ask questions I should have a wearisome list to inflict upon you—Lincoln, Australia, Tithes, Perowne, Liverpool, Manning *versus* F. Londin., and scores of other matters. So I forbear.

After his father's death, Randall Davidson, as the eldest of the family, had much to do, and there are a few notes in his journal of the plans he had to make 'for the not very easy-looking future'. But he paid a visit to his old uncle, Archibald Swinton, with his wife.

On October 5th Edith and I went to Kimmerghame for a few days. I thought Uncle A. a good deal weaker than last year. I preached in Dunse on October 6th and shot some partridges on the 7th.

And he noted particularly, with regard to the weeks which followed after the return to Windsor:

Edith was all through these weeks busy with the foundation of an Association for the care of friendless girls and the rescue of those who need *that* form of help. She seems to me to have managed splendidly and to have steered with all her tact and graceful skill through a shoal of petty difficulties and materials for possible strifes. I do think there is no other woman quite like her.

II

The following year (1890) was much taken up with the last stages of the writing of the *Life of Archbishop Tait*. Indeed a great part of the Dean's time at Windsor was spent on that task. It was not entirely his own handiwork, for a second name appears on the title-page, that of Canon William Benham. But though Benham worked hard and was most amenable in letting Davidson use the facts and quotations he had collected, the amount of his actual composition which survived in the published volumes is very small. Davidson's own notes, as he looked back from a distance when himself Archbishop, are as follows:

> Few people, I think, realise how much labour the writing of that book involved. It is a comparatively simple thing to edit the letters and record the facts about an individual who has left large material behind him, and it is often easy to fit into such biography an account of the surroundings and the life, or, as is commonly said, to tell of a man's 'times' as well as his personal life, but usually this is easy because the facts relative to those times are already accessible in a published form, political or ecclesiastical History or the like.
>
> As regards Archbishop Tait, this was for the most part not so; of course the ordinary sources of information, e.g. files of the newspapers etc., were available for a great many leading facts, for the verification of dates etc., but I aimed at telling the story of each controversy, in which he bore a part, in such manner as to give the record a permanent interest as a book of reference. For this purpose I had to make out afresh the full story of such things as the controversy about *Essays and Reviews*, the earlier Ritual Disputations, the Colenso question, the Athanasian Creed Controversy, Burial Bill, and a good many more such things, and no existing book except Archbishop Tait's *Life* contains any considerable or consecutive story of these incidents.
>
> It was for example of great interest and satisfaction to me to find in the discussions of the Royal Commission on Ecclesiastical Discipline which issued its Report some years ago that the standard Book of Reference for the Church History from, say, 1860–1880 was Archbishop Tait's *Life*, and the care which I took in furnishing references and authorities and in verifying them, is I think amply justified. But the labour was immense.

A few extracts from the journal of 1890 may be given.

> *April 13, 1890.* I find a great gain from having been elected (*tandem*, for my name was put down in 1875) into the Athenaeum—so that I can see friends, Episcopal and other, more easily.
>
> *Sunday, May 4, 1890.* On Saturday I had a busy day. First, the

funeral of Miss Gale who died last Tuesday—a touching ceremony, as the little girl Maud was led to the grave by her big brother etc. Then a luncheon in the Castle and the Baptism of the Duke of Portland's infant daughter (Victoria Alexandrina Violet), the Queen standing sponsor. There was some mistake between Her Majesty and me about the Pronouncement of the babe's names by the Royal Godmother—and she was vexed about it and somewhat angry; and said I had quite misunderstood her Pronouncement. [I thought she said to me on giving me the babe 'Have you got the name?' meaning that *she* hadn't—whereas it seems she had really said 'Have you got the baby safe?'!!]

Then I went to town for the Royal Academy dinner—the first time I had attended that function—Lord Salisbury's speech seemed to me one of the cleverest things I ever heard, and contrasted markedly with most of the others which I thought poor—barring always Sir F. Leighton whose elaborated periods are, to my mind, somewhat *too* finished and polished up. The gathering as a whole supremely interesting. I sat 'twixt Sir Dighton Probyn and Mr. Tate, the . . . rather interesting rich benefactor of South London. But opposite were other folk of higher order. Sir E. Bradford just back from showing Prince Albert Victor over India—and Ouless, the portrait painter—and (very interesting man) Calderon, the R.A., with whom I had very much talk on Sunday Opening, and other kindred questions.

Caught the 11.30 train, and worked hard at preparation of sermon for today. Preached this morning (May 4), in private Chapel unwritten—(not unsatisfactorily I think) on 'Manifestation of Spirit given to *every* man to profit withal'.

This evening Edith, Etta, and I have been reading carefully the first part of *A Death in the Desert.*

Tuesday, May 6th. This morning to Convocation, where we had a dull day with little matter for important discussion, and I hurried back to Windsor in afternoon so as to be in time for the reception of Stanley,[1] who was to arrive at 7 o'clock on a visit to the Queen. But he had anticipated matters, and arrived earlier, before he was expected.

Finding he was going to give a sort of lecture at night, I went into the Castle for dinner with household, and then we had an hour's discourse from him in the white drawing room. He was on the whole very interesting. Lord Salisbury and Lord Knutsford were also there—and it was intensely amusing to me to see the former's obvious dislike at being thus brought to Windsor to swell

[1] Sir H. M. Stanley, the explorer.

Stanley's triumph. He sat gloomy and *uneasy*, but listening most attentively. All the Royal party possible were present—and some 20 of household. Nobody else. Then when the Queen had retired about 11.15 we adjourned to the smoking room, and Stanley held forth, in the midst of an admiring circle, for nearly two hours more, answering all our questions and discussing the position, especially about Emin,[1] most fully and freely.

Saturday, 21st June. Mr. Bentley the publisher came, by appointment, to luncheon, and formally invited me to undertake the continuation of Hook's *Lives of the Archbishops*—He pressed it very strongly—and would not take a final refusal, leaving it open for me to write to him after 'further consideration'. [The Dean was unable to undertake the task.]

Tuesday, 22nd July. Spent the morning with Mr. Gladstone, going over portions of the Archbishop's *Life* in proof, in order to get his sanction to the publication of certain letters of former years. A very curious interview full of interest. He was anxious to hold forth upon the questions raised in each of the letters—and then upon the 'Gospel of Wealth' as enunciated by Mr. Carnegie. A most extraordinary and pointless outburst against Lord Selborne for permitting the publication of a certain letter. I offered *not* to publish. But Mr. Gladstone said that if Lord Selborne consented, HE most readily did, as it could only damage Lord Selborne himself and nobody else. A curious scene altogether.

[1] Emin Pasha, German naturalist and one-time governor of a province in Equatorial Africa, who had been abandoned in command of the Egyptian army, when the Mahdi overran the Sudan. Stanley had been sent to rescue him 1887–9.

CHAPTER VIII

THE PATRONAGE OF THE CROWN

The Duke of Ormond has told the Queen he is satisfied that Sterne should be Bishop, and she consents I shall be Dean; and I suppose the warrants will be drawn in a day or two. DEAN SWIFT, *Journal to Stella* (April 7, 1713).

THERE are few things more important in the general life of the Church of England than the securing of the right men to be Diocesan Bishops. From very early days the Sovereign has claimed a considerable say in their appointment. Indeed, it has been said on high authority that while in most countries the questions between the Pope and the Sovereign were ultimately settled by the system of concordats, in England from very early days appointments to bishoprics were practically at the disposition of the Crown.[1] In theory the Chapter elected and the Pope confirmed or even provided—but in each case the person chosen was the person nominated by the King. Indeed, so great was the power of the King in such matters that Pope Clement VI actually exclaimed, 'If the King of England were to petition for an ass to be made Bishop we must not say him nay.'[2]

After the breach with Rome, the King was left in sole possession. The actual procedure was laid down by statute in 1534 (25 Henry VIII, c. 20), the Crown being empowered on a vacancy of a bishopric to send the Chapter a *licence to elect* with a *letter missive*, containing the name of the person whom they shall elect. If the Chapter fail to elect within twelve days, the Crown shall appoint by *Letters patent*, and the Chapter failing to elect, or the Archbishop failing to consecrate, are subject to the penalties of *Praemunire* (16 Richard II, c. 5—1393) including the loss of civil rights, forfeiture of lands, goods, and chattels, and imprisonment during the King's pleasure. Thus refusal to elect and refusal to consecrate were both recognized as possible, though on pain of dire penalties. The King at first had the power of choosing the

[1] Stubbs, *Constitutional History*, iii, ch. xix. See also *Les Élections épiscopales dans l'Église de France du* IXe *au* XIIe *siècle*, par Imbart de la Tour, ch. v; Jervis, *History of the Gallican Church*, i. 165 f.; *Catholic Encyclopaedia*, Article: Concordat, pp. 196 seq.

[2] Stubbs, op cit., iii. 324.

person to be elected. But later he came to be advised in his personal choice, and as a rule by the Secretary of State. Thus Cecil undoubtedly advised Queen Elizabeth, as is clearly shown by Parker's correspondence. During the later seventeenth and eighteenth centuries, more especially after the growth of the organized parties of Whig and Tory, the sovereigns tended necessarily to pay more regard to the advice of their chief ministers; but there is indeed plenty of evidence in Hanoverian times of a successful claim on the part of the King to make his own nominations. The most famous case is the appointment of Manners Sutton to be Archbishop of Canterbury in 1805. Pitt had recommended the Bishop of Lincoln (Pretyman) to succeed Moore; but the King, George III, on receipt of the letter, rode over to Windsor where Manners Sutton was, and offered him the archbishopric on the spot, telling Pitt the next day what he had done. Pitt 'was exceedingly angry at having been over-reached by the King'. Lord Sidmouth told Dean Milman that he believed such strong language had rarely if ever passed between a Sovereign and his minister.[1] It was not until 1821, in the reign of George IV, that the Prime Minister of the day (Lord Liverpool) succeeded, under threat of resignation, in enforcing his will, the post at issue being a Windsor canonry, for which the King's nominee was the Rev. C. R. Sumner,[2] subsequently Bishop of Winchester.

I

Queen Victoria, throughout her long reign, took a deep interest in all matters of Church patronage. For nearly thirty years (1854–82) Dean Wellesley was her trusted adviser, and with his help the Queen exercised a great influence in most of the important ecclesiastical appointments. It was on Dean Wellesley's advice, and against the wishes of Mr. Disraeli, that Tait was appointed Archbishop of Canterbury in preference to Bishop Ellicott.[3] When Dean Wellesley died Randall Davidson succeeded to the role of the Queen's confidential counsellor; and for the eighteen years from the date of his appointment to the

[1] Jervis, *Memoirs of George III*, iii. 414; Convocation of Canterbury, *Report of Joint Committee on Crown Nominations to Ecclesiastical Offices*, 1920, Appendix II.

[2] See *Life of Bishop Sumner*, p. 61 f.; Lord Liverpool's *Life*, iii. 150.

[3] See *Life of Bishop Wilberforce*, iii. 269.

Deanery of Windsor until the Queen's death in 1901 the Queen was constantly asking his counsel.

In the memorandum which he drew up in 1906—five years after the death of Queen Victoria—and revised in later years, Randall Davidson described the practice of the Queen as follows:

> The Queen's usage was this; when an ecclesiastical post of any importance—a Bishopric, a Deanery, sometimes even a Canonry—was vacant, the Queen would ask me to advise her as to the sort of man who ought to hold such and such a position. About this she took a really continuous interest and did not like to wait until a recommendation should arrive from the Prime Minister before forming opinions of her own about the vacant position and the sort of man who was to fill it. I say the sort of man, for I always deprecated any endeavour upon the Queen's part to shift to her own shoulders the responsibility belonging to the Prime Minister, as representative of the English people, of nominating the particular man who should fill the vacant office. I was always impressed by her ready appreciation of the quite different men who were wanted for the different positions, apparently, though not really, identical in their requirements. I remember being struck by hearing her blurt out with reference to an appointment at Manchester: 'The man seems to think he is making an appointment to Wells or Ely and not to a great industrial capital.' I always tried to impress upon her that the Prime Minister of his day holds office because he is the man the English people want to have in that position, and therefore we are bound to regard his judgement as expressing the contemporary judgement of the nation as a whole. This, though she admitted its truth, she used to regard as a rather troublesome dogma of mine. 'Lord Palmerston with Shaftesbury at his elbow, was a very different adviser', she used to say, 'than Lord Salisbury or Mr. Gladstone.' But she agreed that, for the time being, the Prime Minister's opinion, if persisted in, must be taken as the *Vox Populi*, so far as we could get at it. I remember this coming up markedly when Lord Salisbury[1] made a concurrent nomination of Edward King to the See of Lincoln and Edward Bickersteth to the See of Exeter.
>
> The usage was this. As soon as the Prime Minister's recommendation reached her she used to send it to me, or if I were at a distance it was telegraphed to me. . . . Sometimes the . . . telegrams were long and elaborate. This depended greatly upon who was doing her Secretarial work. Ponsonby and Bigge wrote more fully than Edwards. I then gave her in writing a full memo-

[1] It was really Mr. Gladstone. See pp. 172 ff.

randum about the recommendation which had been made, unless indeed, as often happened, I was able simply to say that I thought it the best possible.

A kind of conventional reticence was observed between herself and the Prime Minister about these communications with me, which were not supposed to exist although Lord Rosebery, I remember, when Prime Minister, made no bones about it. . . .

Sometimes I advised her to accept nominations which did not seem to me very good ones, but I never scrupled to advise her to veto nominations if they were really unsuitable or bad, and during my years of advising her the veto was exercised a great many times.

My view always was that she might exercise the veto as often as she liked with regard to the Prime Minister's suggestions for filling a vacancy, but that it was not desirable that she should initiate recommendations for a particular place. I always thought it suitable that she should occasionally put before the Prime Minister names of men who ought to be considered when opportunities should arise, but I thought she was placed in a false position if she initiated suggestions as to specific appointments which the Prime Minister did not like and which he declined to be responsible for.

The MS. calendar of Church of England papers in the Royal Archives at Windsor gives abundant evidence of the consultations thus described between the Queen and Randall Davidson, and also of the unfailing reliance which she placed on Davidson's judgement.

For the two years following Davidson's appointment as Dean, Mr. Gladstone was Prime Minister.[1] Davidson describes him as, of the four Prime Ministers who held office during his years of advisership to the Queen (Gladstone, Salisbury,[2] Rosebery,[3] and Balfour[4]), 'the most painstaking in regard to appointments'. But he adds: 'He was also the most determined to adhere, if possible, to his own opinion.'

The Queen's insistence on her right to consultation, even before formal submission, is illustrated in the following correspondence between Mr. Gladstone's private secretary and Sir Henry Ponsonby, about the appointment of the Rev. W. Boyd

[1] Mr. Gladstone was Prime Minister for the second time 1880–5; again (on Lord Salisbury's failure to secure a majority in the House of Commons at the beginning of 1886) for five months in 1886; and for a fourth time 1892–4.

[2] Lord Salisbury, Prime Minister 1885–6; 1886–92; 1895–1902.

[3] Lord Rosebery, Prime Minister 1894–5.

[4] Rt. Hon. A. J. Balfour, Prime Minister 1902–5.

Carpenter, Canon of Windsor, a close friend of Her Majesty, to the Bishopric of Ripon:

E. W. HAMILTON, ESQ., *to* SIR H. PONSONBY

10, Downing St., Whitehall.
May 10, 1884.

I don't think Mr. Gladstone quite clearly understood the objection which Her Majesty had taken to the submission of Canon Carpenter—whether it was because he had not communicated with Her first before making a submission, or because he had not accompanied the submission with an explanation.

He does not remember to have suggested a name for a See, previously to and independently of a formal submission. But he is of course most ready to furnish Her Majesty with a statement of reasons why he thinks Canon Carpenter suited for a Bishopric and for this particular Bishopric. He only abstained from doing this, thinking that, as Her Majesty was so well acquainted with Canon Carpenter, he would be troubling Her unnecessarily.

There is one letter which bears the mark of a dispute about the merits of a particular clergyman whom Mr. Gladstone, not for the first time, was pressing for a canonry. The memorandum submitting this particular name is annotated by Her Majesty in her own hand, in blue pencil, 'Consult the Dean. If it is granted it should be with the understanding that it is final.'

II

At the beginning of 1885, a series of episcopal appointments had to be made which were, for various reasons, of more than ordinary interest. They reveal the Queen's own powers of intervention. They also throw a very clear light on the manner in which the Dean was consulted. Two sees had to be filled—London and Lincoln—and if London were filled by translation there would be three. The Bishop of London (Jackson) died suddenly on January 6, 1885. The story begins with the following letter from Sir Henry Ponsonby to the Dean:

SIR HENRY PONSONBY *to the* DEAN OF WINDSOR

Osborne. 7th January, 1885.

Henry.
So then our good ~~Arch~~bishop Theobald
Lies dying.

Becket.

I am grieved to know as much.

Henry.

But we must have a mightier man than he
For his successor.

Becket.

Have you thought of one?

Would you answer the above question?

Her Majesty wants to learn your thoughts. I told her I thought the Bishop of Bedford??[1] I must show your letter in reply to the Queen—so if you quote Tennyson, as I have done, it must go before the Royal eye.

Bigge told me that retired Bishops weren't called Bishops. I said Hurrah—then A. can be Chaplain General—But you have upset his wild theories. All the same the Clergy list doesn't call them Bishops.

Telegram from Sir Henry Ponsonby *to the* Dean of Windsor

8th January, 1885.

With reference to the work mentioned in first part of my letter I find a wish here that your late carpenter[2] should be employed.

The Dean of Windsor *to* Sir Henry Ponsonby

8th January, 1885.
The Deanery, Windsor.

Confidential.

On returning here this evening after spending 48 hours in Scotland with my Father, who is ill, I found your letter and telegram on the subject of the vacant Bishopric of London.

The vacancy now created is more difficult, I consider, to fill properly, than any other (except the Archbishopric itself) which could have occurred.

I do not think that any man among the present bishops stands out as *markedly* suited above all others for the position. What is wanted is not merely a man of great power, and ability, and liberality of view on Church questions, but a man who adds to these qualities the *weight*, and recognized position among English clergy which will enable him to hold his own and to make way. He must also have marked *business* powers, for the Bishop of

[1] Rt. Rev. Walsham How.

[2] The Rt. Rev. W. Boyd Carpenter, Bishop of Ripon; formerly Canon of Windsor.

London is the principal Manager of the enormous business of the Ecclesiastical Commission, in addition to all his other duties.

For many reasons one would have desired to see there Dr. Boyd Carpenter of Ripon, our late Canon here. But, immensely as I like and honour him, I cannot think this particular post is one which is at present suited to his peculiar gifts. He is *par excellence* a *preacher*, and it is not the preaching power of the Bishop of London which is most important. Archbishop Tait was a very bad preacher; but he was an admirable Bishop of London. . . .

It is much less easy, however, to say who ought to go to London, and, to tell the truth, I shrink greatly from giving, at present, without further thought, a decided and definite opinion. If I were obliged to give some positive opinion I should say that three possible men suggest themselves:

1. The Bishop of Durham (Lightfoot)
2. The Bishop of Exeter (Temple)
3. The Bishop of Carlisle (Goodwin).

No one of the three is one's *ideal* for the post, but all the three possess *many* of the necessary qualifications.

The Bishop of Durham stands indisputably first among the theologians and scholars of England, and he combines with his scholarship and culture, a wide liberality of thought and action in religious matters, of which I am quite sure the Queen must approve. As a Bishop he is every day gaining in popularity and influence in his Diocese as he gains in experience of Episcopal work. He would be quite invaluable as an adviser and helper to the Archbishop, and his speeches in the House of Lords and elsewhere would be of immense weight and would all be on the side of a wholesome and liberal theology like that of Archbishop Tait. The great *dis*advantage under which he labours, for the Diocese of London, is that he is unmarried, but I doubt whether this ought to outweigh the other considerations. His appointment would be universally welcomed.

2. Bishop Temple of Exeter has entirely lived down the foolish cry once raised against his theological opinions, which have turned out quite 'safe' after all, as Archbishop Tait and Dean Stanley always said they would. . . .

3. Bishop Harvey Goodwin of Carlisle is one of the most popular speakers and preachers in England, and is withal a great (Mathematical and Scientific) scholar—and possessed of a huge fund of experience on all Church questions. He would I think be less good for the post than either of the others I have named, but he would in many respects be an admirable Bishop of London. . . .

Please understand that all these views are somewhat crude. I give you them for what they are worth, as I understand from you that Her Majesty was good enough to ask you what I thought. . . .

It is impossible to exaggerate the importance of the occasion.

Communications then passed between Dean Davidson and the Archbishop of Canterbury, who had heard from Mr. Gladstone, and had informed him already that he would welcome the appointment of the Bishop of Exeter to London—and found no disposition on the Prime Minister's part to substitute the Bishop of Durham or any one else for Temple. He commented thus on the Bishop of Durham:

The ARCHBISHOP OF CANTERBURY *to the* DEAN OF WINDSOR

Addington Park, Croydon. 15 January, 1885.

Private.

. . . I should be well content with either. I do not wonder that you think J. B. D.[1] would be the best counsellor for me. So he would, if he would counsel. But of late years his caution has grown upon him so exceedingly that I can get nothing out of him. 'I can't advise' has become a fixed phrase with him. The oldness of our friendship has made this rather a trial to me, and lately when he has been at Lambeth it has been almost impossible to get him across the threshold from Lollards Tower. He was always doing some bit of work which would not allow him to breakfast at 8.30 instead of 8 or to dine. Consequently all the opportunities for talk which are so essential were lost—and I got next to none. One wants to learn his view of things in casual ways, and not by direct interrogation always—for the latter fails, while it's of no use looking for the former. He is what you might call terrifically selfish in pursuit of utterly unselfish ends. Also it is said that he is guided himself by younger people almost entirely: that they have an unfailing influence over him, and that the real Bishop of Durham just now is named Watkins.

Hence I don't feel so sure that his sagacious perceptions, thorough consideration, and sound conclusions would have a fair chance of helping the archbishopric work and counsel. Also if he applied himself to London in the spirit in which he applies himself to Durham, it would of course cut off a good many of my pressures, but it wouldn't help those that were left me. I think there would be a very clean cut.

Temple would often wound and bruise one without knowing it

[1] J. B. Lightfoot (Bishop of Durham). He was at King Edward's School, Birmingham, with Archbishop Benson.

—and think if he knew you were hurt that it was your own fault—more brusque than people would like, or I should find pleasant. But one could always depend on having hearty sympathy, outspoken counsel, and any amount of time and trouble.

It is a very nice balance. It seems a *little* in favour of Temple to me—a very little. And a little would turn it. It was a great pity that the question came to me in so narrow a form, and with such injunctions to secrecy. The secrecy only lasted over the time when it would do harm.

On receipt of this, the Dean wrote as follows to Sir Henry Ponsonby:

The DEAN OF WINDSOR *to* SIR HENRY PONSONBY

The Deanery, Windsor. 17 January, 1885.

With respect to the Bishopric of London, the more I think of it the more doubtful do I feel whether, after all, Bishop Temple of Exeter might not be quite as good a man for the post as Bishop Lightfoot of Durham. The bachelorhood of the Bishop of Durham is now certain to be permanent, and would be a very serious drawback to a man who has already a shrinking from Society.

Bishop Temple is certainly not so great a man as Bishop Lightfoot—but he is a first rate administrator and a born leader.

Either of the two would be an admirable Bishop of London, and if I were suddenly called upon to make responsible choice between them I should feel myself in a very serious difficulty.

P.S. I hear some papers speak of Edghill (Chaplain General) as being an advanced High Churchman! I believe him to be one of the most moderate of men.

Important, however, as the see of London was, the Prime Minister could not disregard the other see or sees which would also require to be filled. There was a considerable discussion about Canon Liddon, the great preacher of St. Paul's Cathedral, and pronounced by Lord Acton to be 'the greatest power in the conflict with sin and in turning the souls of men to God that the nation now possesses'.

Although, when sounded, in the end Liddon begged not to be nominated,[1] there is a letter from Davidson about his relations with Tait, which is too interesting to be omitted. On January 9, Mr. Gladstone wrote to the Archbishop of Canterbury describing

[1] See *Life of H. P. Liddon*, p. 314.

Liddon as 'The first champion of belief', and asking whether he would welcome him as a bishop: but at the same time referring to the perplexity which he felt about a statement of which he had just heard that Dr. Liddon had declined to work with the late Archbishop,[1] and asking for enlightenment. The Archbishop accordingly wrote to the Dean, who replied as follows:

The DEAN *to the* ARCHBISHOP OF CANTERBURY

The Deanery, Windsor. 12 January, 1885.

Private.

You ask me to tell you definitely, to the best of my belief what were the relations of Canon Liddon towards Archbishop Tait.

I should greatly have preferred to say nothing on the subject. When it has come up, as frequently happens, in conversation I have always endeavoured to avoid it, but since *you* ask me it is my duty to tell you exactly what I know or believe—*valeat quantum.*

I remember, just after I became Archbishop Tait's Chaplain in Spring of 1877, being sent by him to see Mr. Bullock, the then Secretary of S.P.G., on some matter connected with the S.P.G. controversies then going on, about which a somewhat stormy meeting was anticipated. Bullock, who was the gentlest of men, was speaking of those likely to be present at the meeting, and I asked if there was any chance of Canon Liddon being there. He answered, No, I wish he would come—but *it would be of no use to ask him, as the Archbishop is to be in the Chair.* I looked enquiringly, and he simply replied, 'The relations there are quite impracticable.' I remember the words because they surprised me so much that on returning to Lambeth I asked Craufurd Tait what Bullock could have meant, and he answered that Liddon, to the best of his belief, would attend no meeting, if he could help it, where Archbishop Tait was to preside.

Twice that same year (in August and December) the Archbishop invited the leading men of all parties to come to Lambeth for a quiet devotional meeting. The invitation was accepted by Canon Carter, Montagu Villiers, Murray of Chislehurst, Herbert Bristow, and many other extreme High Churchmen. *Many* also wrote expressing their great regret at being unavoidably kept

[1] In 1871 Liddon informed Tait, who desired the disuse of the Athanasian Creed in the public service of the Church, that 'if this most precious Creed is either mutilated by the excision of the so-termed damnatory clauses, or degraded by an alteration of the rubric which precedes it from its present position in the Book of Common Prayer, I shall feel bound in conscience to resign my preferment and to retire from the ministry of the Church of England', *Life of Tait*, ii. 137.

away by engagements. I think about 150 invitations were issued. The one only man who *declined to attend* was Canon Liddon. Of this I speak from personal knowledge, and I know how keenly his refusal to be present was felt by the Archbishop, who was striving by these meetings to draw men together.

During the six years that I was Chaplain, Canon Liddon never, as a matter of fact, attended any meeting, public or private, at which the Archbishop presided. Nor, I think, was he ever present in St. Paul's at any of the many Episcopal Consecrations held there by Archbishop Tait. On this last point I cannot speak with absolute certainty, but I knew Archbishop Tait to have believed, and to have sorrowed over this belief, that Canon Liddon did not wish to be present when he (the Archbishop) celebrated the Holy Communion.

When Archbishop Tait, shortly before his death, dictated from his bed an article upon his Oxford reminiscences, he spoke, in the first draft of his article, with some severity of a recent sermon preached by Canon Liddon before the University. When I read over the article to him in proof, he stopped me at the passage and said, as nearly as I can remember, 'Stop. I must alter that. It is not kind. He has striven against my efforts after unity, but all the more I must beware of speaking unkindly of him.' And the words were softened down.

I write these reminiscences, trivial as they appear, as the best means of answering your question. I have purposely not dwelt upon the, I suppose unquestionable, fact that people generally *believed* Canon Liddon to have practically declined of late years to meet the Archbishop on any official occasion. The belief may be an erroneous one and I wish the question had not been asked of me, because I fear lest, even unconsciously, I should be doing some wrong to so great and good a man as Canon Liddon. Please set your own value upon what I have said. Whatever be your Grace's object in asking the question, the less weight you give to my words the more thankful shall I be.

Mr. Gladstone made his formal submission to the Queen for the three sees of London, Lincoln, and Exeter, as follows:

The RT. HON. W. E. GLADSTONE *to the* QUEEN

January 23, 1885.

The Bishop of Exeter (whom failing, the Bishop of Durham) is humbly recommended to Your Majesty to succeed Bishop Jackson in the See of London.

Mr. Bickersteth, recently approved by Your Majesty for the Deanery of Gloucester, is in like manner humbly recommended to be named for the See of Exeter, in the event of its becoming vacant.

And the Rev. Dr. King, Professor of Pastoral Theology (Regius) in Oxford, for the See of Lincoln.

The Rt. Hon. W. E. Gladstone *to the* Queen

Memorandum to accompany the present Episcopal Submissions

1. *See of London.* Inasmuch as the names of the Bishops of Durham and Exeter were those which had already suggested themselves to Your Majesty, Mr. Gladstone will only trouble Your Majesty by stating that he has been prompted to submit first the name of Bishop Temple:

a. by the great eminence of the See which Bishop Lightfoot already holds, and by the desire to avoid a double translation;

b. by the likelihood that the offer, if made, might be declined;

c. by a sense of the value of Bishop Lightfoot's studies to the Church, and by the high probability that acceptance of the See of London would put an end to them.

2. *See of Exeter.* Should Your Majesty accede to the recommendation just given, the great appointment will, with the two last Episcopal nominations, have been given in one and the same line. For Your Majesty was undoubtedly most accurate in the appreciation of Bishop Boyd Carpenter, as more nearly related to what is termed the Broad School than to that called Evangelical. (Bishop Ridding was of the same colour.)

Searching among the clergy who bear the last named designation, Mr. Gladstone, after taking pains to inform himself, believes that the claim of Mr. Bickersteth, who has recently received a conspicuous mark of Your Majesty's favour, is upon the whole the best.

3. *See of Lincoln.* It has been since the death of Bishop Jackson that this See has been placed at Your Majesty's disposal. Bishop Wordsworth had a short time ago announced his intention to resign not later than Lady Day: but he has taken the present opportunity to anticipate the resignation, and a Deed has been prepared accordingly, which will have been executed before this Memorandum has reached Your Majesty's hands. The Bishop desired Mr. Gladstone to convey to Your Majesty his humble gratitude for Your Majesty's goodness, especially in allowing him,

many years ago, to be relieved of a portion of his labours through the appointment of a Suffragan. It was this announcement, which widened the field of operation, and somewhat retarded these submissions to Your Majesty.

Dr. King as to opinion would be reputed a Divine of the High Church. At the time when he received his important Professorship from Your Majesty, he had by a wise and loving spirit attracted confidence and attachment from many, Bishops and others, within a wider circle than that of any special party. No occupant of a Theological Chair in Oxford has, as Mr. Gladstone believes, ever done more than Dr. King for the maintenance of practical and earnest religion among the younger members of the University, and few indeed have done so much. Dr. King is also an accomplished modern scholar, with a noteworthy gift of languages; and a person who would in all respects do honour to the Bench, and be a worthy successor to Dr. Wordsworth, who has undoubtedly attracted as a Diocesan Bishop much veneration and affection.

Mr. Gladstone refrains from troubling Your Majesty, unless so commanded, with further particulars.

The Dean was asked to report on these names, and wrote as follows:

The DEAN OF WINDSOR *to* SIR HENRY PONSONBY

The Deanery, Windsor. 25 January, 1885.

You bid me report upon the three recommendations which have been made for Bishoprics. I will do so, in order:

1. Bishop *Temple* for London. I have already, as you will recollect, written about him. I believe him to be (with the single exception of the present Bishop of Durham, if he *is* an exception) the fittest man in England to become Bishop of London.

Notwithstanding his rough exterior and harsh voice he has proved himself to be eminently qualified to lead and influence men. He has gained the confidence of all those whose confidence is best worth having to whatever party they belong. Possibly the extreme Evangelicals don't like him much, but that is all. He is distinctly a broad Churchman in theology—but the outcry which formerly arose about his connexion with *Essays and Reviews* has entirely died away. His personal friendship (from early days onwards) with Archbishop Benson will tend, if Her Majesty appoints him, to make everything work with utmost smoothness —and Mrs. Temple's links with so many men prominent in the political world will be a clear advantage socially. He is a man remarkable for earnestness of purpose and terse vigour of expression, and though now 63 years old is physically very strong and active, a most necessary qualification for London.

2. The Rev. E. H. Bickersteth, who had just been nominated to the Deanery of Gloucester, is a most *liberal-minded* Evangelical, of no party bias whatever, a man acceptable to all who know him as a refined Christian gentleman. He is *58* years old. His University career was a distinguished one—and he has since been widely known as the author of much religious and other poetry of a high order—and as a vigorous and earnest parish clergyman. The narrow partisan Evangelicals regard him as too lax and wide in his sympathies to please them—and for that very reason he is the better suited—as I believe Her Majesty will think—to be placed in a position of authority and influence.

I have every reason to think he will make, if appointed, a good and wise Bishop, and his nomination would certainly be acceptable to a large and important section of English Churchmen. Indeed if a man of his school of thought has now to be selected for a Bishopric I do not know what other name would be so suitable as his.

3. Canon King—now professor of Pastoral Theology at Oxford—is a remarkable man in every way. He has a strangely winning power, and has at Oxford succeeded beyond any other theological teacher in gaining the confidence of young men of all sorts of opinions. His own views are very decidedly High Church, but he has never thrown himself actively into the *public* controversies on these subjects, and he is so bright and cheery that he has done much to counteract the rather severe and gloomy views both about present and future, which have characterized some of the other teachers who share his Church opinions. Next to Canon Liddon he probably stands foremost among the representative and popular High Churchmen—but he has a much greater power than Canon Liddon has of getting on with all sorts and conditions of men. He is extremely popular, and as a Bishop his winning manners, and his power of ready sympathy would be valuable.

He openly and emphatically avows decided High Church opinions, and must be distinctly classed as belonging to that school. But I imagine that Her Majesty will feel it to be necessary or desirable that there should be among the Bishops some representative of a body so largely represented among the parochial clergy, and supposing Her Majesty to approve of the two other recommendations which have now been made the High Church party would only have had *one* representative among the *five* Bishops last appointed.

Bishops *Carpenter*, *Ridding*, and *Temple* are all Broad Churchmen and Mr. *Bickersteth* is a liberal *Low* Churchman. Canon King would thus be the only High Churchman among them.

Her Majesty will judge best how far it would be desirable to exclude this modicum of representation. I confess to being myself a little surprised that Mr. Gladstone in recommending a High Churchman, did not submit the name of Canon Liddon with whom he is on such terms of friendship.

Canon King, however, would, I think, be very decidedly a better *bishop* than Canon Liddon—and perhaps Mr. Gladstone also thinks so, and does not mind the outcry which some High Churchmen may possibly make at Canon Liddon being apparently passed over in favour of a lesser man. An excluded leader is sometimes a source of danger and difficulty, but all this Her Majesty will judge of far better than I can.

What I have endeavoured to do is simply to state the *facts* about the various men named, leaving the issue to Her Majesty's judgement.

I rather wonder that Mr. Gladstone should have wished to send Mr. Bickersteth to *Exeter* and Canon King to *Lincoln*. The former is much more of a High Church *Diocese* than the latter—notwithstanding the characteristics of their present Bishops. But this has doubtless been weighed.

I am afraid my letter has run to an inordinate length.

SIR HENRY PONSONBY *to the* DEAN OF WINDSOR

Osborne. 27 January, 1885.

The Queen has approved the Episcopal nominations and was very much pleased by your excellent letter upon them. . . .

III

In June 1885, a new Prime Minister, Lord Salisbury, was in office, and the following month, at Osborne, Davidson 'got a very interesting talk with Lord Salisbury, who was very ready to discuss some of his Church Patronage problems and talked about them as if he was certain to be Prime Minister for at least a generation or two'. To the Queen, Lord Salisbury did not seem to be very judicious or well informed.

> Lord Salisbury on many occasions [writes Davidson] consented without a murmur to the Queen's veto to some suggestion which he made.

His first experience was discouraging. He had obtained the

Queen's leave to offer the Bishopric of Salisbury to Dr. Inge, Provost of Worcester College.[1] The Provost declined, Lord Salisbury reported to the Queen, 'most resolutely—in terms which would be unnecessarily strong if he had been asked to go to Sierra Leone'. The name of Dr. B. was then submitted and referred to the Dean of Windsor, who wrote:

The DEAN OF WINDSOR *to* SIR HENRY PONSONBY

Most Confidential. Deanery, Windsor Castle.
5 August, 1885.

. . . I am very sorry Dr. Inge has declined. His appointment would have been good in all ways. He is a scholar, and a man of real intellectual power as well as a good and vigorous man, who would in every way have done credit to Lord Salisbury's very wise selection.

Of Dr. B. it is, I fear, impossible to say the same, however much one may desire to do so.

Personally, I like him. I have always found him a kindly, amiable gentleman. But that is all! What qualifications he has for a Bishopric it is really very hard to see, and we do, at this moment, so sadly lack men of real intellectual power and scholarship on the Bench that every one had hoped the Salisbury vacancy would be used to give an accession of new *intellectual* power to the Bench of Bishops. . . . It was stated in the newspapers that he was likely, as Lord Salisbury's old colleague and friend, to be nominated, and instantly I received letters from men, high and low, saying, 'Can this be true?'

One most competent judge, who might have been expected to think the nomination a desirable one, writes to me, 'Such an appointment would be a disaster: he has no claim: he preaches feebly, speaks in wearisome fashion, he has written nothing, done nothing, organised nothing.'

I should not myself have spoken quite so strongly but the words are substantially true. . . .

It costs me something to say this about a clergyman whom personally I esteem highly.

I wonder what his episcopal qualifications are *supposed* to be?

The name was withdrawn, and Bishop John Wordsworth, one of the first scholars of the day, was appointed.

The Queen had a strong wish, emphasized by the controversies on ritualism, that Bishops should be nominated who were not only

[1] His son, W. R. Inge, in later years became Dean of St. Paul's.

ecclesiastics but also statesmen. The Dean made the following entry in his journal for November 21, 1889—in the very midst of the trial of the Bishop of Lincoln:

November 21st. Got back to Windsor on same day as the Queen and in the following three weeks saw rather more of Her Majesty than has of late been usual. She was very much exercised about the ritual and other difficulties and most eager about the appointment of some new and stronger sort of Bishops who should be statesmen as well as ecclesiastics. . . . My business is to try to put the *good* side of High Churchmanship before her. She hears and thinks plenty on the other side without my help!

In the course of his association with ecclesiastical appointments as adviser to the Queen, Davidson became the recipient of a great many letters from other people who wished their views taken into account. Sometimes the letters were critical of the trend of recent appointments. There were not a few correspondents who expressed their profound disappointment, for example, with Lord Salisbury in his supposed neglect of Evangelical clergy.

To one of these who had written about 'the rising discontent with the ecclesiastical patronage of the Government', Davidson replied as follows:

The DEAN OF WINDSOR *to the* REV. F. GELL

The Deanery, Windsor Castle. 11 Mar. 1890.

Private.

I thank you for your letter. I am well aware of the existence of such a feeling as you describe on the part of some Evangelical clergy. But I thought it had been confined to the less thoughtful and the less well-informed. It is a simple delusion to suppose that there is any disinclination on the part of the authorities to give due prominence, in Church appointments, to men who belong to the Evangelical School. The difficulty is to find the right men, and they must be men not only of piety, learning, and power, but of physical strength sufficient for the daily increasing burdens of Episcopal work. Some of the best men are growing old. The younger generation is not overstocked with clergymen possessing all these qualifications.

I do not gather that you had yourself given credence to so utterly absurd a rumour as that the great Diocese of Bangor would be used as a place of exile wherein to confine a man 'who is too strong to be kept in England'. You quote it, I imagine, as showing the length to which some men will go in such arguments.

I speak that which I know when I say that the notion that there is a determination not to promote Evangelicals is the merest delusion.

There was much correspondence about Welsh bishoprics. The appointment to Bangor (just mentioned) had very special difficulties of which Davidson heard full details from all sides. There were letters also about the appointment of a successor to Bishop Walsham How[1] as Suffragan Bishop in the Diocese of London, when, owing to special circumstances, the Queen, on Lord Salisbury's advice, made a departure from the usual custom by selecting the second name of the two proposed. There were also a few, but very few, letters from clergy who felt that their own claims had been disregarded. There was, for example, a long letter from the well-known preacher Canon *** enclosing a news-cutting giving an unfounded report that he had been chosen for the Deanery of Manchester. The letter was long and full of feeling. It was docketed by Davidson, on the back of the envelope containing it, '***, Canon (his woes!)'. A short extract may be given:

I do not think that I have been idle, or unfaithful or unsuccessful. Is it right that appointments should be mainly influenced by the wives, daughters, and sisters-in-law of Premiers? It is, of course, useless to hope that Lord Salisbury who, I am told, has been so often urged to promote me, that my very name makes him *angry*, will ever notice me. (*17 June 1890.*)

Davidson's reply was kind and disarming. His attitude may be summed up in the following sentence:

My own position in the matter is one of the utmost delicacy and I have practically no *initiative* voice whatever. If I had you need not doubt how it would be used. (*21 June 1890.*)

The last appointment to which we need refer is the bishopric of Durham, vacated by the death on December 21, 1889, of Bishop Lightfoot—a great scholar and a bishop for whom Davidson always entertained a special honour and affection. The Archbishop of Canterbury and Dean Davidson were, from the beginning, most anxious to secure the appointment of Dr. Westcott as his successor. Davidson was summoned to Osborne on December 28 and dined with the Queen:

She talked long and earnestly . . . telling me of her real wish to have *wise* Bishops appointed, and recounting with a good deal of

[1] Appointed first Bishop of Wakefield, 1888.

satisfaction how entirely it was she herself who had got Archbishop Tait appointed to the Primacy, how earnestly Dizzy had pressed Ellicott, and how Dizzy had often thanked her in later years for having taken the line she did! She thinks Lord Salisbury not very wise in his nominations and means 'decidedly to take the matter largely into her own hands, while leaving the initiative *always* with him'. Lord Salisbury, she said, 'is so sensible and liberal-minded in political matters, and so ready to give up the foolish points of old-fashioned Conservatism, that it is a great pity he should so lack liberality in his view of Church appointments'. She told me of her recent correspondences and conversations with him about several people (in which she seems to me to have shown great wisdom) and quite approves of my wish that Westcott should go to Durham.

Sir Henry Ponsonby was instructed to write to Lord Salisbury. Lord Salisbury, however, was not very well, and on January 10, 1890, Lady Salisbury wrote to Sir Henry Ponsonby promising to give him some notes about Episcopal appointments after his fortnight's rest, adding:

LADY SALISBURY *to* SIR HENRY PONSONBY

10 January, 1890.

I always find that anything to do with the appointment of Bishops has a special power of worrying and tiring him.

At the end of the month, Lord Salisbury wrote a long letter objecting to Dr. Westcott as 'too learned for Durham'. A considerable correspondence took place between Sir Henry Ponsonby on behalf of the Queen, and Lord Salisbury; Dean Davidson being consulted throughout, and maintaining throughout the great superiority of Westcott. Dr. Walsham How (Wakefield) and Dr. Jayne (Chester) both declined. When Dr. Ridding's (Southwell) name was proposed, Davidson suggested a letter from Her Majesty 'to the effect that, although the Bishop of Southwell is not a High Churchman, his action at Clumber, and still more the letters which he had written in answer to remonstrants, had so irritated the Evangelicals that he is now regarded as a foremost offender and protests have been everywhere got up. Is it a wise moment for sending him to Durham? Also the Queen feared his health was bad. But if Lord Salisbury, knowing this, persists, the Queen will not refuse him.'[1]

[1] See also *Letters of Queen Victoria*, 3rd series, vol. i, pp. 553–63, 575, 577.

The final result appears in the following memorandum by Davidson, showing the persistence of the Queen, which culminated in her sending for Lord Salisbury to Buckingham Palace:

> The ultimate facts were these. The Bishopric having been refused by the Bishops of Wakefield and Chester to whom it was quite formally offered, much correspondence took place. I have preserved the letters which explain themselves. The only point of importance which they don't, I think, say, is that Lord Salisbury was told by the Queen that he might certainly nominate Maclagan of Lichfield as he would do well. He replied that he had already sounded him (doubtless through Lord Barrington, his own private secretary and Mrs. Maclagan's brother) and found that he would not accept. He kept on suggesting Bishop Boyd Carpenter again and again, and the Queen said she didn't think him suitable. At last they had an interview and long conversation at Buckingham Palace on Tuesday, March 4th, and at this interview the Queen again said to Lord Salisbury that she was surprised he didn't accept the notion of Dr. Westcott for Durham which she had throughout desired—*whereupon he consented.* Had he refused, the Queen would have pressed, or even insisted, on his appointing *me*—as she said she was determined there should be no more refusals.

On March 16 the Dean dined at Windsor Castle with the Queen, and noted in his journal as follows:

> Much talk with the Queen about the Bishoprics etc. She is greatly amused by Lord Salisbury's jubilation with which Westcott's appointment is received. 'He talks as if he had done it, instead of having opposed it with all his might for weeks!'[1]

[1] In his papers (1906) Davidson also noted: 'A year or two later the Queen sent me in great triumph a letter from Lord Salisbury to herself in which, after Bishop Westcott's intervention in the Coal Strike (1892), Lord Salisbury took special credit to himself for the acumen he had shown in selecting Westcott for that office.'

CHAPTER IX

FAREWELL TO WINDSOR

I hope you occupy yourself with the several great questions which agitate parties. I think a good mode will be to talk concerning them sometimes with the Dean. He is a good moderate man, and still well able to give you sufficient information. KING LEOPOLD *to* PRINCESS VICTORIA, April 1837.

IT has been convenient in the survey of the different departments of the work done by Dean Randall Davidson to give a separate treatment to each. But it would be a complete missing of the character of his seven years at Windsor to forget, even for a moment, that all these different activities were in fact going on together. He was Dean, and therefore had the necessary duties which the office involved in the care of the services of St. George's Chapel, the preaching, the music, in the pastoral charge of the members of the society which sang or ministered within its walls, in the leadership of the Chapter and the administration of the Chapter business. He was Chaplain to the Queen—her religious counsellor and, in an uncommon degree, her spiritual pastor and teacher: and also her invariable and deeply trusted adviser in the exercise of the patronage of the Crown and in all manner of questions which might come up concerning the Church. He was besides, outside Windsor, an active member of Convocation and deeply involved in the central affairs and policies of the Church of England. Again, he was in practically daily communication with the Archbishop of Canterbury, and the counsellor on whose experience and judgement His Grace instinctively relied with regard to the main Church questions which poured into Lambeth Palace. He was therefore Dean, Chaplain to the Queen, and Archbishop of Canterbury's trusted lieutenant, all at once: and though a particular claim might be uppermost at a particular time, he could not, and he would not, forget the others.

One of the things which made it possible for him to do so much, and to do it so well, was his vivid interest in everything that was going on. He was extraordinarily alive. He never, as we should say, missed anything. He extracted all that he could out of the particular matter before him, and he was ready to give his whole mind to it at the moment when it claimed his attention. Thus he possessed a remarkable faculty of concentration. He was absorbed in the problem for the time, and, when the problem was finished, he passed with equal interest and equal zest to the next, treating it in the same way. Moreover, he never forgot, but stored up events, precedents, and facts of all sorts and kinds, in a wonderful memory, ready to bring them out whenever the need came. Above all he was deeply interested in people—individual human beings, just as human beings. The Queen commented on his warm, affectionate, sympathetic nature, the Archbishop of Canterbury on his charm, and the two were thinking of the same thing. Certainly he had a great gift, which was to remain with him throughout his life, of drawing people to him, winning their confidence, and communicating to them a conviction of his sincere desire to be of use.

I

But time slipped by, and in 1889 Randall Davidson had been Dean of Windsor for six years. The days were critical for the Church. The trial of Bishop King was still proceeding, a trial in the course of which the whole question of Authority in the Church was raised—a question, as we have seen, of the deepest moment to Davidson. Again, the end of 1889 saw the publication of *Lux Mundi, a Series of Studies in the Religion of the Incarnation*, edited by Charles Gore; and 'great stir' was caused by the liberal views on Inspiration which the Editor expounded. And though not specially attracted by the Catholic tradition which bound the authors together, Davidson would certainly respond to the claim made in the Preface that 'theology must take a new development', together with the statement that the 'true development of Christian doctrine' does not mean 'a narrowing and hardening of theology by simply giving it greater definiteness or multiplying its dogmas. The real development of theology is rather the process in which the Church, standing firm in her old truths, enters into the apprehension of the new social and intellectual movements of each age: and because "the truth makes her free" is able to assimilate all new material, to welcome and give its place to all new knowledge, to throw herself into the sanctification of each new social order'.[1]

On another side there was 'Huxley . . . hammering at the gate with the cry of No God—and we are worrying about ritual details of the smallest sort'.[2] It was not unnatural that Davidson, with his strong sense of the multitude of problems facing the Church, should sometimes wonder whether those were right who, like Bishop Boyd Carpenter, urged the need of making him a Bishop 'so as to bring the views of Archbishop Tait forward and have them pressed on the Church with the force which comes from my knowledge of the Church history of our time'.

To quote his own words (1906):

> The question of my own acceptance of a Bishopric was a difficult one, and I had a great deal of hesitation about what was right. In early years at Windsor it would obviously have been inappropriate either to leave the Deanery or to rule a Diocese, but as the years went on the Queen frequently said to Sir H. Ponsonby and others that she did not wish to stand in the way of what was right.

There was a genuine clash of duties in his mind. He owed much to the Queen, who in various ways relied greatly upon him. He did not want to fail her; and he knew too that through his relations with her he could do considerable service to the Church. At the same time there were those who believed that he could make a special contribution as a Bishop at a moment 'when every voice, however weak, might help'.

The question had been first tentatively raised in December 1889—actually in connexion with the see of Durham, for which Lord Salisbury mentioned him to the Queen. The Queen rejected the idea (though ready to adopt it, as we have seen, had Dr. Westcott's name been refused). She told Davidson that she had rejected it and 'that both the Bishop of Ripon and Lord Salisbury without knowing what the other's opinion was, told the Queen how very fit the Dean himself was for a Bishopric. But she hopes the Dean will not think she acted selfishly or against the Dean's interests, when the Queen said she *could not spare him*—at any rate for some time to come—and she trusts that he will feel that she is right and that he should not forsake his post?' (22 Dec. 1889).

[1] Preface to first edition of *Lux Mundi*. Signed C. G. (Charles Gore), Pusey House, Michaelmas, 1889.

[2] See *supra*, ch. vii, p. 152.

The Dean's reply was not quite what the Queen expected. It ran as follows:

The DEAN OF WINDSOR *to the* QUEEN

Windsor. 23 December 1889.

. . . As regards myself, it is not necessary that I should assure your Majesty how deeply I feel the kindness of your Majesty's words, or that I should repeat that it is my one desire to do just that which may be given me to do, for the glory of God, for your Majesty's service, and for the promotion, in whatever way I can, of the good of the Church and Realm.

The present position is a critical and complex one, in which I shall be intensely grateful for such direction as your Majesty may be pleased to give me. Most assuredly your Majesty may rely on my anxiety simply to serve your Majesty in whatever way God may enable me, and the generous and kindly words your Majesty has now used must be to me a strength and stimulus whatever I should be called upon to do here or elsewhere.

The Queen was somewhat disturbed by the Dean's words. She explained to Sir Henry Ponsonby what had happened and added:

The QUEEN *to* SIR HENRY PONSONBY

Osborne. 24 December 1889.

The Queen . . . is sure Sir Henry will agree that, after only six years, he ought *not* to be taken away so soon. In short the Deans never were moved. But she *owns* that the Dean's answer is not *quite what* she expected. She knows of no one whatever who could at all take his place. . . .

The Queen wonders if the Dean is at all an ambitious man. She wishes she had said nothing to him about this idea of Lord S's, but she did it from a (perhaps mistaken) sense of straightforwardness. Silence is however generally the best. 'Least said soonest mended.'

Sir Henry Ponsonby[1] acted as intermediary, and very sympathetically explained the Dean's position to the Queen, the desire of the Archbishops and others who 'remonstrated with him for remaining in this quiet and comfortable place when others were doing their utmost for the Church and devoting themselves to work', and his own wish to be of use to the Church as a Bishop 'not in ecclesiastical matters so much as in social and national

[1] *Letters of Queen Victoria*, 3rd series, vol. i, pp. 544–5.

points of view'—coupled with his conviction that he could still be of equal use to the Queen as adviser.

The Queen reflected much; saw the force of what was urged; and wrote thus to the Archbishop of Canterbury:

The QUEEN *to the* ARCHBISHOP OF CANTERBURY

Osborne. 3 January 1890.

. . . I have been told by various people that the Dean of Windsor would be admirably suited to be made a Bishop. You will easily understand that I do not wish to lose him, as besides his merits as a preacher, and his great suitableness for the position, which as the Queen's Chaplain and Dean of Windsor is one of great importance, he is socially most agreeable, which is also of importance. My first impulse was to say that I *could not* give him up, but when it was represented to me by people of influence and experience how much good he could and would do, I felt I could not, from selfish motives—though I *do* think *all underrate* the *importance* of his present position, even for the good of the Church—refuse to allow his name to be submitted to me when the time comes for new Bishops.[1]

There were many discussions and much searching of heart. The Dean was greatly perplexed—and full of anxiety as to the path of duty. There were soundings about St. Albans, a see which was in fact offered to and declined by Dr. Talbot. But this was not to be, and Davidson wrote to Captain Bigge:

The DEAN OF WINDSOR *to* CAPTAIN BIGGE

January 11, 1890.

It is an unaffected satisfaction to me to feel that my leaving Windsor is not—at the very worst—an immediate thing, and perhaps it may never come about at all. If not I am thoroughly well satisfied to stay where I am. I must own the wrench of leaving Windsor would have been to me very severe, and this is greatly due to the strong links of affection and regard I have been allowed to feel binding me to so many friends in the Household. I can say without a spark of humbug that your own kindness to me in this matter—and what you said as to the possible usefulness, in the present, of our Windsor life, gave me a new notion of it in more ways than one.

Lord Salisbury's comments on the Dean's powers, and also on the character of his future influence, are full of interest:

[1] *Letters of Queen Victoria*, 3rd series, vol. i, p. 554.

The Marquess of Salisbury *to* Sir Henry Ponsonby

January 26, 1890.

If a third Diocese fell vacant, I should recommend the Dean of Windsor. He has not the influence over High Churchmen which Talbot would have. On the other hand his power of dealing with men is very great indeed. He ought to have a southern Diocese as he would be constantly wanted in London. I have no doubt that in time he would establish new influence over the Church, not unlike that which Bishop Wilberforce possessed towards the close of his life.

A little later Sir Henry Ponsonby told the Queen that the Archbishop and Dean Vaughan wanted the Dean of Windsor to go to Durham, 'or at any rate that he should soon come into the House of Lords, where his presence is so much required' (February 22, 1890).

In his journal for April 13, 1890, Davidson wrote:

I was for a time greatly worried and 'difficulted' by the announcement in the papers that *I* was appointed to Durham.

On May 1, he was present at the consecration of Dr. Westcott as Bishop of Durham in Westminster Abbey:[1]

I attended the Archbishop of York (the consecrating Primate) as an extra chaplain in order to be close to the ceremony. . . . The day altogether—and especially the whole consecration service suggested to me very many thoughts in connection with all the discussions and searchings of heart that I went through a few months ago. It seemed to me nearly impossible, and altogether unsuitable, to picture myself in the position occupied that morning by B.F.W. Full of thankfulness, we may well be, that such a man goes to such a post, and that others do not!

II

In August it was known that two sees were about to be vacant—Winchester and Worcester. Lord Salisbury recommended the Bishop of Rochester for the former, with a view to offering Rochester to the Dean. The Queen wrote to Lord Salisbury on August 20, to press the Dean of Windsor for Winchester, on the ground that this see had special associations with the Sovereign

[1] Archbishop Benson was present in a stall. The consecration was held in the Abbey, as Westcott had been a Canon of Westminster.

and that, as Bishop of Winchester, Davidson would at once take his seat in the House of Lords:

The QUEEN *to the* MARQUESS OF SALISBURY[1]

August 20, 1890.

Everyone in the Church, High and Low, has confidence in Dean Davidson's great intelligence, knowledge, and straightforwardness, and *all* desire his promotion. Of course he will be a serious loss to the Queen in many ways; but she would feel consoled if he were placed in a *post* of real usefulness, which in a small Bishopric like Rochester he would not be.

The Dean was at Osborne August 17–18, two days before the Queen sent this letter. On Sunday he preached on Cardinal Newman, and then went for a walk with Captain Bigge. On Monday (he writes in his journal):

In the forenoon at Osborne I had a very long talk with the Queen, who sent for me to her tent in the shrubbery for the purpose. She discussed Newman, Pusey, the Archbishop's Biography, and a great many other subjects, including the relative powers and characters of many Ecclesiastics—Farrar—Barry—Spence—Liddon etc. etc. For a long time she made no reference whatever to the impending Episcopal vacancies. Then she said—'The Bishop of Winchester is, I suppose, going to resign immediately? Lord Salisbury thinks Bishop Thorold of Rochester should succeed him. What do you think?' I answered that I had the greatest respect and esteem for Bishop Thorold, but that his health was so bad that I could hardly think him equal to so big a task—the Diocese of Winchester having been long in the hands of an old man, not up to much work, and needing a vigorous stirring up. She was interested, and we discussed it for some time. Then she said 'Failing him, what do you think of the Bishop of Ripon for it?' I answered that she knew my admiration and love for the Bishop, but that I feared the appointment would not be a very popular one, at all events with the clergy.

Further conversation followed about the suitability of other names for Winchester, also for Worcester, and the Dean continues:

All this conversation puzzled me a good deal, for I knew from Sir H. Ponsonby that the Queen had been discussing the question of *my* leaving Windsor and going to some Bishopric, and Sir Henry thought her wish was that I should go to Winchester straight. This

[1] *Letters of Queen Victoria*, 3rd series, vol. i, p. 632.

had been the outcome, as he believed, of what had occurred in the spring about Durham etc. and of her correspondence at that time with Vaughan and with the Archbishop. The perfect absence therefore of any sort of constraint or reserve in her talk about these Bishoprics (for she had spoken also of the Worcester vacancy) surprised me a little. I was not at all surprised at her being perhaps unwilling that I should go straight to Winchester, on her *personal* nomination, knowing that she isn't fond of these *personal* responsibilities for particular appointments. What did surprise me was her apparent unreserve in speaking about the different vacancies, as though my name had never been under discussion at all, whereas I knew this was not so.

The perplexity remained until the end of September, when Sir Henry Ponsonby came to Windsor for his holiday:

On Thursday evening, Sept. 25th, Edith and I dined quietly with the Ponsonbys—no other man being there. After dinner I had a very long and important talk with Sir Henry. He told me that he had that morning had a telegram from the Queen from Balmoral, bidding him narrate to me all that had passed and take my advice as to what She ought to do. The story he then told me was this. The Queen had from the first wished that I should go straight to Winchester and had been pressing this repeatedly upon Lord Salisbury. When she saw me at Osborne on Aug. 18th she was already taking this line, but, as she told Sir Henry, she 'felt it was better not to talk to the Dean about himself, and so she conversed about other names instead'. In short she *acted*—and acted so well that she quite took me in. It was touching to hear of this really considerate thoughtfulness which was quite of a piece with all that followed.

After seeing me at Osborne she wrote again to Lord Salisbury, and finding that he raised objections on account of my youth and inexperience and of the offence which would be given to the older Bishops she wrote to the Archbishop of Canterbury who was then in Switzerland, and to Vaughan of Llandaff.

The QUEEN *to the* ARCHBISHOP OF CANTERBURY[1]

Balmoral Castle. September 1, 1890.

I have another object in writing to you to-day and that is with respect to Dean Davidson. You, and I believe many others in the Church, are very desirous that he should be promoted to the Episcopate. Of course he will be a very serious loss to me at

[1] Ibid., p. 634.

Windsor; at the same time I quite feel the great necessity of having able, young, good, courageous and large-minded men on the Episcopal bench. Now two vacancies are likely to occur soon by the resignations of the Bishops of Winchester and Worcester. Lord Salisbury I know wishes to place the Bishop of Rochester at Winchester and the Dean of Windsor to go to Rochester or Worcester. I had however thought (of course *without any* consultation with the Dean *himself*) that it would have been such a good thing to promote him at once to the See of Winchester, as Windsor[1] and Osborne are in the diocese, the Bishop of Winchester is Prelate of the Order of the Garter, and the connection with the Royal Household would thus be maintained, besides the great advantage of his entering at once into the House of Lords. I have pointed this out in 2 strong letters to Lord Salisbury but he won't agree; and says if the 2 great Bishoprics were given to Broad Churchmen it would be thought by the 2 parties of the Clergy, High and Low Church, that we were rationalizing the Church. A very extraordinary idea I must say. I am not aware what your feelings on this subject are, but should YOU agree with me about Winchester, I think a letter from you, as from *yourself* and *without mentioning* me, to Lord Salisbury recommending this, would have much weight; and perhaps others, Dr. Vaughan for instance and any one else of weight, writing in the same way to Lord Salisbury, might remove the prejudice in his mind. He seems to undervalue the talents and power of Dean Davidson and thinks he is unknown.

The Archbishop strongly supported the Queen's view:

The ARCHBISHOP OF CANTERBURY *to the* QUEEN[2]

8 September, 1890.

The Dean is now *very well known*, and the appointment would be well received. His practical good-sense, unsparingness of self, and earnest purpose are appreciated by the Clergy of both sections, and he is just the person whom the laity will like. He makes himself felt when he speaks. Indeed we must have in the House of Lords men who see, and will care to use, its great opportunities, and have the power to do so. We must have in London men who will enter into the great social questions which are stirring, with sympathy and yet with a good sense which will not be run away with by mere cries of uninformed sympathy. All this requires judgment, intelligence, vigour and, I should say, youth. I know *no-one* so well adapted as the Dean for these works. . . . When I say '*we*

[1] Windsor is in fact in the Diocese of Oxford.

[2] *Letters*, 3rd series, vol. i, p. 635.

must' have such men, I mean that if we do *not*,—if we are to have tired, gentle, good men, uninterested in social questions, the Church *cannot* do her duty, or fill her position as a national Church.

Lord Salisbury, however, persisted in his refusal to nominate the Dean to Winchester; and the Queen, though writing him a very frank letter in reply, acquiesced, and agreed that Davidson should have the offer of Rochester or Worcester.

The QUEEN *to the* MARQUESS OF SALISBURY[1]

27 September, 1890.

The Queen was much surprised to receive from Lord Salisbury yesterday the accompanying submission. . . . She fears that Lord Salisbury has been much misinformed on the subject; for the Dean is certainly particularly well-known. . . . As however, unfortunately as the Queen must think, Lord Salisbury persists in taking a contrary view, she will no longer withhold her consent to the appointment of the Bishop of Rochester to the See of Winchester, and the choice of Rochester and Worcester being offered to the Dean, who will be a very serious loss to the Queen at Windsor. She cannot help reminding Lord Salisbury that when the question of naming a Bishop for the Diocese in which Hatfield is situated arose, the Queen, out of consideration to Lord Salisbury and to what might be agreeable to him, made no objection to what was proposed whatever, though Canon Liddon was one mentioned. But in this case of Winchester, which borders on Windsor and includes Osborne, the Queen's personal wishes and convenience are overlooked. It is painful to the Queen to say all this; but Lord Salisbury knows that she is always frank in all her dealings with him.

Private Memorandum by the DEAN OF WINDSOR

Sir Henry Ponsonby sent me (I received it on Oct. 9) a long letter from Lord Salisbury to the Queen dated Oct. 3 which seems to shew that she had, before receiving back the draft which I saw at Hull and which I returned to Edwards in my letter of Oct. 1, written—in similar terms—to Lord Salisbury. He says in this letter to the Queen that he is sorry to differ from her or to seem to put her to inconvenience, but that (1) Rochester is as near Windsor as Farnham is and therefore the Queen can see me as well from Rochester as from Winchester. (2) That Thorold's

[1] Ibid., p. 639.

nomination is a public move, to please the Evangelicals, and that Thorold is an admirable and moderate implement for that purpose, an 'unexceptionable candidate' he calls him.

He goes on:

'The fact that Dean Davidson's high qualifications are not known much, outside his own acquaintance, and that he has no celebrity as a preacher, an author, or a parish priest and is still young, would tend to aggravate the disappointment as his promotion would seem forced and unnatural.

His moral strength in the Church would not be increased by an unexplained rapidity of promotion. If he distinguishes himself, as he probably will, in one of the ordinary sees he will have a claim to promotion to the highest offices, which any minister will be glad to press upon Your Majesty.'

After reading this, I replied to Sir Henry Ponsonby (in a form which he could show.)

Oct. 9. 90.

Many thanks for sending the letter which I return herewith. I am bound in fairness to say that in Lord Salisbury's personal remarks about myself, from first to last, I entirely concur, and think he has stated the facts very correctly. The Queen's constant personal kindness to me has, I think, led Her Majesty to take an over-favourable view of anything I may have been able to say or do.

I also quite see Lord Salisbury's point about the need of appointing some Evangelical etc. . . .

I suppose from Lord Salisbury's letter that I am now to regard it as certain that Rochester will be offered to me.

R. T. D.

The Dean had in the meantime been sounded as to whether he would accept Worcester or Rochester if they were offered to him. He consulted the Archbishop, but both he and the Archbishop agreed that he would be wrong to refuse Rochester. He wrote as follows in his Journal, while staying at Muirhouse after the Church Congress in Hull.

October 5, 1890.

So now it seems as though I am almost certain to be offered the charge of what is I suppose the second largest Diocese in the world—with all the biggest problems of social life and difficulty, stirring and seething there almost more than anywhere else. It is an overwhelming prospect—and one can but cast oneself in utter feckless helplessness upon the LORD who knows all—and resolve, in humble reliance on Him, that we two will together face what He sends us, and strive to do His will in such way as He may show it to us.

It has been a big burden of thought and anxiety to carry through these Congress days—as one sat quietly listening to the casual allusions of one speaker after another to South London, as THE problem of our time, THE place where 'Christianity is not in possession'—where needs are greatest and agencies weakest, etc. etc. I don't know that it was unhelpful—and GOD seemed to give me thoughts (at times) of hopefulness and energy and courage to try (with Edith alongside) to see what we can by His grace do, however feebly. I had a ten minutes talk with the Bishop of Durham in a Congress interval, and he was as clear as every other counsellor has been that the call was one to which no other response was possible than an answering submission thereto. May the LORD give us grace and guidance, if indeed it so comes about—I cannot doubt that our own dear Archbishop would have said 'Go, in the strength of the Lord!'

After the Church Congress at Hull the Davidsons went to Scotland, first to Muirhouse, then to Kimmerghame, the home of the Swintons, where Davidson had spent so many holidays as a boy. On Monday, October 13, just as Davidson and his cousins were about to start out partridge-shooting, came the letter from Lord Salisbury.

On Monday we shot partridges (George and Alan and I) for a very short day. But before starting, came the momentous letter which we had been expecting, Lord Salisbury, in kind terms, offering me the choice between Worcester and Rochester. I merely acknowledged it, and said I would write fully next day, though of course, after all that had passed before, there was no real doubt in our minds as to what the decision ought to be. On Tuesday, before going out shooting, I wrote fully to Lord Salisbury accepting Rochester (copy preserved) and told him also that I would next day write to some of my friends. After a few hours shooting we went off in the afternoon to the Pitmans at Gala House.

The MARQUESS OF SALISBURY *to the* DEAN OF WINDSOR

Foreign Office.
Oct. 10, 1890.

Private.

My dear Dean,

I have the Queen's permission to inform you that she desires that you should take your place on the Episcopal Bench, and to ask you whether you would accept either of the Sees of Rochester or Worcester which are now vacant. I should think Worcester perhaps would suit you best as being connected with a more stirring and influential population. But that is entirely a matter for your own judgment.

Perhaps you would kindly keep this matter to yourself for the moment.

Believe me,
Yours very truly,
SALISBURY.

The DEAN OF WINDSOR *to the* MARQUESS OF SALISBURY

(written at Kimmerghame)
Address Deanery, Windsor Castle.

Gala House,
Galashiels, N.B.
14 Oct. 1890.

My dear Lord,

I have given the fullest consideration to the subject of your Lordship's very important and kind communication yesterday received. I have come to the conclusion that as the Queen graciously consents to my leaving Windsor and entering upon the higher work of the Episcopal Office, it is my duty, in reliance upon the help of Almighty God, to accept the position thus offered me, and to set myself, with whatever powers I possess, to endeavour to discharge its responsibilities. I have to thank your Lordship much for the kind terms of your letter, and for giving me the privilege of choosing in which of the two vacant sees my work shall lie. I appreciate to the full what your Lordship has said with reference to the vast importance of the Diocese of Worcester, but I feel quite sure that, upon the whole, I should be less able to do good service there than in the Diocese of Rochester. Rochester, containing, as it does, all South London, has an even larger population than Worcester, and so much of my work, during my years of residence at Lambeth, lay in that Diocese, and I have so large a knowledge of its clergy, that I feel no hesitation in believing that such powers as I possess would be more appropriately exercised there than in the, to me, almost unknown regions of Worcestershire and Warwickshire. I venture therefore, though with fear and trembling, and in reliance upon a strength which is not my own, to accept the Diocese of *Rochester*; and I have once more to express my sense of the kindness and confidence shewn to me by your Lordship in offering to nominate me to a position of such importance.

I remain, my Lord, with much respect, very truly and dutifully yours,

RANDALL T. DAVIDSON.

Your Lordship will not, I hope, consider that I am forgetful of the request you made that the offer should, for the moment, be regarded as confidential, if I communicate the fact in strictest confidence tomorrow to a *very few* of my most intimate friends and relations in order that they may not hear of it first through the public press. I can guarantee that the few individuals to whom I write thus privately will not allow the matter to become prematurely public.

Extract from Journal, Oct. 19, 1890

I have not found that these days of open air walking (without conversation, for the most part) were at all adverse to a quiet thoughtfulness about these great new responsibilities and all that they imply. I think I was able—though perhaps it seems strange to say so—to make them really days of prayer. We got to Gala on Tuesday Evening and I told Ernest and Mary and Mr. and Mrs. Pitman—not the others—what had happened. Wednesday was a day of showers and the River was too big for fishing, so I stayed at home all day and wrote some 40 letters to friends in anticipation of the announcement which I knew would appear on the following day. On Thursday morning I had telegrams (as requested) from J. Ellison and other friends in London to say that the appointment was officially announced in *The Times*. None the less I spent the day fishing (vainly) for salmon, with plenty of time for quiet thought and devotion.

The DEAN OF WINDSOR *to the* QUEEN[1]

Deanery,
Windsor Castle.

Gala House,
Galashiels, N.B.
14 Oct. 1890.

Madam,

Now that I have received Lord Salisbury's formal letter offering me, in Your Majesty's name, the choice of the See either of Worcester or Rochester, and have replied to him accepting the See of Rochester, I am not I hope and believe, acting wrongly in

[1] *Letters of Queen Victoria*, 3rd series, vol. i, p. 647.

writing, with my humble duty, direct to Your Majesty, to express, with my whole heart, the grateful sense I entertain of the immense kindness and consideration which has, from first to last, been shown to me by Your Majesty in this matter, to me so momentous as to be almost overwhelming.

Your Majesty will, I hope, believe me when I say that nothing in my life has ever affected me more deeply than this characteristic evidence of the gracious readiness of Your Majesty to consider the interests of others whether public or private, rather than Your Majesty's own personal convenience and comfort.

It is thus that Your Majesty has for fifty years, whether in joy or sorrow, won the *hearts* of those whose privilege it has been to be among Your Majesty's more immediate servants.

For myself, I can say in all sincerity that my desire to serve Your Majesty with loyal honesty and devotion has gone on, steadily increasing, during each year of my Windsor life, and I do most earnestly trust that our removal to London—where my home as Bishop of Rochester will probably lie—will not prevent Your Majesty from exercising to the fullest extent whatever claim upon my personal services may be to Your Majesty's convenience in any way whatever.[1] No claims of other duties, to whomsoever due, can ever in my mind compete with the privilege of Your Majesty's personal service, and I shall be more than ready at any moment to render by word or deed all and every service which may conduce to Your Majesty's convenience.

The kindness which Your Majesty has shown, in an unbroken course, both to Mrs. Davidson and to me, ever since the day when Your Majesty sent for me at Christmas *1882* upon the death of Archbishop Tait, has made an ineffaceable mark upon our hearts, and each sorrow which in these eight years has fallen upon Your Majesty in the loss of those whose affection and loyal service had been a source of strength and comfort in former years, has, if possible, strengthened the sense of loyal personal devotion to Your Majesty which will endure with us while life shall last.

I trust Your Majesty will pardon the freedom of this letter, which comes from a full heart, and will believe that I am at all times . . .

I have to thank Your Majesty most cordially and with my very humble duty, for a most kind letter received from Your Majesty yesterday at Kimmerghame.

[1] The passage 'No claims . . . shall last' is not printed in *Letters of Queen Victoria, loc. cit.*, but appears in MS.

The Queen *to the* Dean of Windsor[1]

Balmoral Castle. Oct. 17, 1890.

The Queen has been much touched by the kindness of the Dean of Windsor's letter. She is naturally much grieved that he should leave Windsor where She hoped he would and could have remained and been of such use to herself and others.

But when She saw and heard how useful he would be to the Church in another position, She felt She had no right to be selfish; and therefore gave her consent to a Bishopric being offered him. The Queen must honestly confess that She has (excepting in one case, the Bishop of Ripon) never found people promoted to the Episcopate remain what they were before. She hopes and thinks this will not be the case with the Dean. Many who preached so well before, did no longer as Bishops—excepting the Bishop of Ripon. The whole atmosphere of a Cathedral and its surroundings—the very dignity itself which accompanies a Bishopric—seems to hamper their freedom of speech. The Dean must not [be] discouraged or hurt by what She says here, but She cannot help just mentioning this, as it strikes her from experience. She feels sure that the Dean will not let himself be hampered by his future position, and most truly and sincerely does the Queen wish him all possible success and happiness in his new elevation. The Queen's only fear is that the work may be too much for his health, and She trusts he will ask for assistance if that should be the case. He must take exercise and try and get out of London as much and as often as he can.

The choice of a successor will be a serious difficulty.

She fears the persons mentioned will hardly do.

The Dean of Windsor *to the* Queen

Muirhouse, Davidson's Mains,
Midlothian.
20 Oct. 1890.

I have the honour to thank Your Majesty, with my humble duty, for the very kind and gracious letter which I have to-day had the honour of receiving from Your Majesty, and I can assure Your Majesty of my anxiety that in no way whatever shall the fact of my having become a Bishop, interfere with my free exercise of whatever powers God may have given me for serving

[1] *Letters of Queen Victoria*, 3rd series, vol. i, p. 648. (The last two lines are omitted by the Editor.)

Your Majesty, whether as a preacher in the Royal Chapels or otherwise.

I can promise to be on my guard against any such danger as Your Majesty's experience suggests, and I am most grateful to Your Majesty for writing to me so kindly and fully on the subject.

With respect to what Your Majesty has said about suitable names to be thought of for succeeding to the Deanery of Windsor, it is a very great distress and anxiety to me to learn that Your Majesty does not feel that any of those whose names have been suggested would fill that office properly. I could easily bring forward other names for Your Majesty's consideration if desired, but I shrink from suggesting strangers, as I did not understand that Your Majesty wished me to do so. I hope Your Majesty will pardon me for saying that I am perfectly ready, even now, to withdraw from the proposed arrangement for my going to Rochester, and to place my services again unreservedly at Your Majesty's disposal as Dean of Windsor and Chaplain, rather than that Your Majesty should suffer any inconvenience.

I simply could not bear to feel that I was, by any action of mine, leaving Your Majesty's service inadequately or unsuitably provided for. . . .

The Queen's public spirit and genuine unselfishness throughout had been very striking. She had a real and deep affection for the Dean, on whom she had learnt to rely so much. And now she became full of concern lest the Dean's health might prove insufficient for the great strain of the work in South London. 'Her motherly heart', said the Dean, 'is all taken up about her fears that the strain of the work will be too much for my physical strength.' And there was the further problem of the Dean's successor at Windsor:

CAPTAIN FLEETWOOD EDWARDS *to the* DEAN OF WINDSOR

Balmoral Castle.
4 Oct. 1890.

Private.

Since writing to you this morning[1] the Queen has been discussing the matter of your departure from Windsor which, as I am sure you know, She deeply regrets. Her Majesty desired me to write to you again on the subject of your successor. . . . You know however the sort of man that is required: not only a good preacher,

[1] This refers to a letter of the same date from Captain Fleetwood Edwards, in the course of correspondence on the question whether R.T.D. should go to Worcester or Rochester—prior to Lord Salisbury's formal offer.

but a man of various qualities, clerical, individual and social. Will you consider and report. She also don't want too young and rising a man appointed who would soon be taken away for a bishopric! . . .

Shortly after this the Dean was at Balmoral and had a long talk with the Queen. He noted (October 25, 1890):

I dined with the Queen, and after dinner had a very long talk to her on the whole subject. Her anxious motherliness on the subject of my health was again very striking! She thought that on *that* ground it was doubtful whether I ought to accept—but that on all other grounds it was now clearly right that I should go forward as she had quite made up her mind to it. I told her that I was quite strong and able for work and could not possibly refuse on any such ground, but that if she were to be placed in a real difficulty by my departure nothing should induce me to go away. Then we discussed the various people possible. She was afraid A. was a 'very narrow low Churchman'—as to which I was able to set her mind at rest. She was afraid he was 'a terribly dull preacher' and I pointed out to her that it really didn't matter much, as he needn't preach a bit more than she liked, and I promised to come and preach as often as ever she summoned me, and to tell the Diocese that I must regard her commands as paramount.[1] She agreed that B. would not be a suitable man for Windsor, even as a Canon, and that the same applied to C. I pointed out that there can be no need of settling at present who should succeed to Eliot's vacated canonry.[2] Nothing could be kinder or more affectionate and even *motherly* than she was about it all. I was immensely touched and impressed and felt the same enthusiasm for the dear old lady which I have many times felt before on occasions of some earnest conversation of this sort.

At night I had a long and interesting talk about it all with Bigge, and today I have again gone into the whole matter both with him and with Sir Henry. We all feel the strong advantage of having a man as Dean who is already (through his wife) more or less behind the scenes as to Castle difficulties and complications rather than an 'outsider' who would have everything to learn. It is very clear that, whoever is appointed, she will expect me to go on

[1] 'She discussed the possible advantage of separating the Deanery from the Chaplaincy, a course which seems to me to have really nothing to recommend it—and which had, I think, only occurred to her secretary. She was in a fuss about the whole matter.' [R.T.D.]

[2] The Rev. P. S. Eliot was appointed Dean of Windsor in succession to Dean Davidson.

'taking the lift' of things, in the way of advice—and this, God helping me, I must try to do. It is a very solemn thing to feel that she is thus dependent on my counsel even after I have gone, and surely the load of responsibilities gathers into bigger volume every day. May God give me grace and guidance.

The decision was taken. But the wrench in leaving Windsor was very great, and there was much lamentation. Congratulations from those outside the Windsor circle came, and came in abundance. But in Windsor itself, whether in the Castle or the College, in the inner circle of friends and neighbours or among the Eton masters, and in the Royal Holloway College at Englefield Green which he had done so much to help as one of the original Governors, regret was very deep.

III

There are many references in the letters to the Deanery itself, to Mrs. Davidson, and to the welcome which she and the Dean always so readily gave to everybody: making a real fellowship within the Castle walls, and a hospitable harbour for friends and strangers from outside. If we were to express the general affection and trust and loss in a single message it should be through this poem of their gifted neighbour, Mrs. Oliphant:

Valedictory Address to the Very Rev. The Dean of Windsor

Mr. Dean, oh Mr. Dean
How can you have the heart
To leave—I do not say the Queen
For 'tis that Lady's part
To summon by command
Any bishop in the land
To come and dine and sleep
And discourse on questions deep.
But us: who never may
To his Grace of Roffen say
Oh Bishop, come and dine!
Come and preach, oh sound divine!
Come and pleasant lore impart?
Mr. Dean, oh Mr. Dean
To leave us can you really mean?
How could you have the heart?

To leave us in the lurch
When we all know that the Church
Is by times a little slow
And old and lothe to go
With the movement life demands;
And the world is rather weary
And the royal borough dreary
And there's nobody that understands!

. . . .

Yet Goodbye we'll say and mean
Mr. Dean!
Fare you well, with wishes true
And a gracious bishop be:
But if as well as we loved you
You had loved us, sure are we
That no knife that e'er was made, no Prime Minister so free
Could e'er have cut those loves in two!

It was always those who came into personal touch with Randall Davidson who valued him most. He was little known to the general public. No wonder, therefore, that some newspapers at least should accompany their announcement of his appointment to Rochester with a somewhat frank criticism. 'No man in the Church', says the *World*, 'has had a record which justified his rapid promotion less than the new Bishop of Rochester. His qualifications may be roughly summed up in the words that he is "le mari de sa femme". Had he not married Archbishop Tait's daughter, he would have been content with a fat country Living, and thought himself well off.' The *Pall Mall Gazette* devoted a leading article to what it described as 'A Royal Job', which led up to a vigorous correspondence in which Lord Halifax intervened on Davidson's side:

VISCOUNT HALIFAX *to the* EDITOR *of the* '*Pall Mall Gazette*'

Hickleton, Doncaster. October 17, 1890.

The *Pall Mall* ought not to be ungenerous, and your article upon the Dean of Windsor's nomination to the see of Rochester is ungenerous. The Dean is giving up a position which has everything to recommend it—opportunities of influence, historical association, means of usefulness greater, as some might think, than those enjoyed by almost any other clergyman in England, together with everything that makes life agreeable and interesting, for an overburdened diocese, and for hard work among the masses of South and East London. Surely the editor of the *Pall Mall*, who appreciates so often and so well the higher side of things, might see something better in such a nomination than a 'Royal Job'.

There were, however, other papers, like the *Daily Graphic*, which took a different point of view. One thing at least Randall Davidson made clear from the start. It was no post of ease to which he was going. Not without reason might Bishop Ridding (of Southwell) write, in his caustic vein, to the Dean, 'Leaving your fatness, your sweetness, your good fruit and wine, to be promoted over such a forest—what a plunge from the comfortable to the un!' Not without reason might Bishop Thorold, his immediate predecessor, declare, 'South London needs a Titan.'

IV

The consecration of the new Bishop was fixed for April 25, 1891. During the intervening months, apart from the pangs of good-bye, there was much work to be done, and through these weeks Davidson, as ever, was in constant consultation on Church affairs with the Archbishop of Canterbury. The Archbishop of York (Thomson) died, and a successor must be appointed. There was discussion, often protracted, on the schemes of General Booth and others for relief work amongst the London poor in a time of great distress.

On Septuagesima Sunday, January 25, Davidson preached at Osborne for the last time as Dean of Windsor:

> It was on Septuagesima Sunday 1883 that I *first* preached at Osborne (or anywhere) to the Queen. In the intervening years I have preached to her more often by far than any other clergyman ever did in her life. She says that Dean Stanley would come next in frequency. Dean Wellesley, of course, hardly ever preached.

From the end of February till the beginning of March was a time of farewell. The Queen showed constant kindness of every sort:

> On February 17 the Canons, Minor Canons, Lay Clerks etc. of St. George's presented me with the beautiful ring which had cost them so much pains (and so much money!) . . . On Sunday, March 1, we had the Empress Frederick, the Prince of Wales

etc. to tea after Chapel. We dined with the Queen and had much talk about our departure, etc.

... On Wednesday, March 11, the Queen came to tea to bid us a formal farewell. She was full of kindness.

On Friday, March 13th, I had my final Ladies' Bible Class, but did not wish them any very formal farewell. I felt the close of this endeavour very keenly. Nothing that I have ever in my life tried to do has met with a warmer welcome than this Bible Class, and its numbers have never fallen off during all these years ...

On Sunday, March 15th, I preached my last sermon to the Queen as Dean of Windsor, but did not make of it a formal farewell. I preached on 'The letter killeth, the spirit giveth life'. ... We dined in the Castle and the Queen was most kind in her farewells. She gave Edith a brooch and wrote to me afterwards to say that she had not felt equal to bidding me a regular 'goodbye'.

The DEAN OF WINDSOR *to the* QUEEN

Athenaeum Club, 18 March, 1891.
Pall Mall.

I hope Your Majesty will not think I am taking an undue liberty if I ask leave to send to Your Majesty, with my humble duty, a single line of most dutiful and loyal and heartfelt gratitude at this eventful moment in my life. The resignation of the Deanery of Windsor involved in my acceptance of the See of Rochester, is to me a *wrench* of no ordinary kind, and it is not until the time of leaving that I have fully realised all the painfulness of our departure from what has been to us so happy, as well as so interesting a home. But most of all do I feel at this moment the strain and trial of giving up that more immediate service of Your Majesty which has been, during these eight years, not less of a pleasure than a high privilege and honour.

I cannot attempt to put into words my sense of Your Majesty's unvarying kindness towards me, and of the confidence Your Majesty has been pleased to shew me. I feel it from the very bottom of my heart; I can only ask GOD to enable me, in the years to come, to use to the utmost any such opportunities as may occasionally arise for serving Your Majesty, or those dear to you, in any way direct or indirect in which I can be of the smallest use.

It is not a light thing for any man to lay down a responsible office which he has held for eight years, but the gravity and even *solemnity* of such a change is increased a hundredfold in my case by the vivid remembrance of all Your Majesty's goodness to me, time after time, and of the unmeasured consideration and favour which in these last few weeks Your Majesty has shown me, in connection with my change of work and scene. Nothing would have induced me to consent to such a change, but that I knew Your Majesty was of opinion that, under all the circumstances, it was right that I should go.

I need not, I am sure, add how entirely my wife shares with me these feelings of reverent and affectionate gratitude, which Your Majesty's kindness has inspired. It is our earnest desire and hope that no inconvenience or discomfort of any sort or kind may be caused to Your Majesty by this change in the Office of Dean of Windsor, and I pray with all my heart that Almighty GOD may be pleased to bless and keep Your Majesty day by day for many years to come.

We hope to start tomorrow for Italy, and I have tonight the honour of dining with the Prince of Wales.

The QUEEN *to the* DEAN OF WINDSOR

Windsor Castle.
March 20, 1891.

The Queen was intending to write to the Dean when she received his very kind and touching letter, for which she wishes to thank him very much. She could not take leave on Sunday evening. It would have been too painful. She now repents having ever listened to the proposals of raising him to the Bench—for really for his sake as well as for hers she cannot think it is a good thing. But we know not yet what the advantages may be, what Dean Davidson's power to do good may be—which naturally would somewhat reconcile her to his departure. . . . She would now wish to mention what she hopes he would be able to do, viz. —always to preach in the Mausoleum once in the summer (this year perhaps the 1st Sunday)—that he would perform the services on the 14th Dec.—and that he would preach once at least in the winter and once in the summer at Osborne.—She hopes he and Mrs. Davidson will stay here for 2 nights at the time he does homage. What has he arranged with Canon Eliot as to Preachers in May?

The Queen trusts the Dean will enjoy his time at Perugia.

On March 19, after two most trying days ('The farewells at every turn upset us both'), the Dean and Mrs. Davidson left for Italy. They visited Florence (where Davidson was extremely unwell, though the doctor did not understand his symptoms), Siena, Perugia, Pisa, and were greatly refreshed:

On the whole nothing could have been better than these weeks abroad. They gave us both just what we wanted in quiet and thinking time and reading and preparation for all that was to follow. How little we knew what the next few months were to be! But all our lives we shall thank God for those special weeks in Italy at such a turning-point.

The consecration took place in Westminster Abbey on St. Mark's Day, April 25. Dr. Mandell Creighton was consecrated Bishop of Peterborough at the same time. Dr. Butler, Master of Trinity, his old Headmaster, preached the sermon with a sensitive word or two about the old Archbishop (Tait) and his relation to his former chaplain and son. 'The voice of the dead is a living voice to-day.' Many bishops were present, including the Bishop of Minnesota, who had travelled specially from Cairo. Davidson wrote, looking back a few weeks later:

> No two hours in all my life—not my Ordination as Deacon, not my Marriage, not my Mother's death, or my Father's, or the news of my appointment to Windsor, or the news of my nomination to Rochester,—ever conquered or took possession of me so completely as those hours in the Abbey.

Such was the beginning of Randall Davidson's episcopate.

Eleven days later, May 6, he was taken gravely ill. Dr. Barlow, whose advice they sought, found that he had a very serious ulcer in the stomach, and decided that he must at once go to bed and remain a complete invalid for at least three months to come. The seeds of the illness had been sown long before. They were present during the last months at Windsor, and had been still more evident on the Italian tour. It was a wonder that, in the last few days, just before breaking down, when he had gone for a ride in Windsor Park with Dr. Warre, 'thinking it would perhaps do me good', the adventure had not proved fatal.

The blow was terrible. The new Bishop at once thought of resignation, but the Archbishop, the doctor, and certain clergy whom he consulted in the Diocese, persuaded him to put the idea on one side. Yet the illness was so severe that he used to say in later years that had the collapse come ten days before the consecration instead of ten days after, not only would the consecration never have taken place but he himself would never have been a Diocesan Bishop, as it would always have been said that his health was too poor to stand such a strain.

Nevertheless, with his extraordinary capacity for getting things done, Davidson managed to see the chief diocesan officials in his bedroom, and to transact all the business of the diocese from a bed covered with letters. The work did not stop, and what was more significant, there can be no doubt that the severity and length of the illness had its own silent effects on the character of the man. The Bishop got through a good deal of reading, he and Mrs. Davidson then, as their habit was through life, reading many books aloud to one another. He tried thus to fill up many blank spaces in his knowledge of facts, of men and of nations; and he made a special study of the Bible. He had then, in his own words, 'more opportunity for quiet thought and quiet prayer and quiet reading, such as it is, than I have had for many years or perhaps ever, and more than I ever expected to have again'. After the first few days at Lambeth Palace, where he had been staying, he was moved to the new home—two rather dingy-looking houses knocked into one in the Kennington Park Road—and there remained till the middle of July.

During this time, the long-expected *Life of Archbishop Tait* was published. It was in two volumes. It had occupied the best part of nine years and had cost Davidson much toil, research, and thought, the work having had to be done at intervals and with many interruptions, yet governed all through by the author's passion for accuracy and thoroughness. It was an immediate success. The reviews were full of admiration, and the book was proved at once to be, not only a mine of information accessible nowhere else, but a fine study of Tait's development and character which secured for Tait himself a new place in the thoughts of many, and thoroughly established his position as one of the greatest Archbishops of Canterbury—if not the greatest—since Archbishop Laud.[1]

So the convalescence progressed—first at Windsor, then at Osborne Cottage, finally in Scotland. And all through he kept in close touch with the Archbishop, who still sent him a succession of queries and drafts for his criticism. Here is an interesting note from Benson at Pontresina, thanking him for replies and introducing a later Primate:

[1] Benson wrote to the author, June 12, 1891: 'Your happier work—the Life—is simply done *ad unguem*. I cannot conceive how you bring such a thread out of such a τολύπη. . . . And then you keep out of sight in the most interesting way' (*Life of Archbishop Benson*, ii. 401).

The ARCHBISHOP OF CANTERBURY *to the* BISHOP OF ROCHESTER.

26 August 1891.

Thank you for your information about the Colombo papers and your excellent impartial advice about Jerusalem. *Lang*[1] is here. What a fine fellow he is!

At the end of September, he and Mrs. Davidson returned home to Kennington, and on Michaelmas Day he took his part in the Consecration of Bishops at St. Paul's Cathedral, one of the Bishops being a new Suffragan to help his own labours—Huyshe Yeatman, Bishop of Southwark.

[1] The Rev. Cosmo Gordon Lang, Fellow of All Souls College, Oxford, and Curate of Leeds; afterwards Archbishop of Canterbury.

CHAPTER X

THE BISHOP OF ROCHESTER

I verily believe your lordship and I are both of the same religion, if we were thoroughly understood by one another; and that all honest and reasonable Christians would be so, if they did but talk enough together every day, and had nothing to do together, but to serve God, and live in peace with their neighbour. ALEXANDER POPE *to the* BISHOP OF ROCHESTER, 1717.

WHEN Lord Salisbury offered Randall Davidson, at the age of forty-two, his choice between the two dioceses of Worcester and Rochester, he expressed the view that the Dean would probably choose the former as connected with a more stirring population. It is true that in 1890 Worcester contained within it the great industrial towns of Birmingham and Coventry. But Rochester was not only more industrial but it also had a much larger population. It included all London south of the Thames from Woolwich to Kingston, 'a region which has very little of the wealth of London', and growing steadily poorer every day. It was also a very difficult diocese in which to lead the work of the Church; and a recent inquiry, which had aroused great public interest, had started the cry that in South London Christianity was not in possession.

The new Bishop had been ill for six months, when he first met the clergy and laity in the Diocesan Conference at the end of October 1891. He at once showed that he meant to enter on the field with spirit and courage. He had taken great care beforehand to study the local social conditions, in such books as the newly-published *Life and Labour in London* volumes by Charles Booth. He was probably over-sanguine, as some of his critics said, when he declared that at present he saw no sort of ground, or even of excuse, for the cry which has just been quoted. But his speech revealed the kind of temper in which he wished to tackle his task; and some elderly clergy, not given to enthusiasm, remarked that they had heard nothing which inspired them so much since they had been ordained. He had of course an immense amount to do in the way of meetings, sermons, committees, and correspondence; and, as he knew full well, the evening work for a London Bishop was bound to be very exacting. But 'the presence of the Bishop', he used sometimes to reply to the remonstrances of his doctor, 'at meetings where funds had to be raised, might make the difference of a £10 note, which a poor diocese could not afford to disregard'. There were countless interviews with clergy and laity, and a considerable number of young men came his way as candidates for Holy Orders. Indeed he took a particular care with his ordination candidates, and one of the pieces of work on which he looked back with some satisfaction was the trouble taken to make Embertide a really devotional experience. In view of later events, it is not a little interesting to note that one of the younger clergy, who came to see him about work in South London, was the Rev. C. G. Lang, whom the Bishop invited to be Wilberforce Missioner. Fresh from the slums of Leeds, where he was curate for three years (1890–3), the future Archbishop of Canterbury, as he has told the writer, was much struck by this first interview with Dr. Davidson, whom he saw on his sick-bed, and by the conviction he received that here in the Diocese of Rochester, with South London, was the real thing! Nor has he ever forgotten how deeply the Bishop's understanding of pastoral training and the needs of ordination candidates impressed him. A particular quality which the clergy at once noticed about Bishop Davidson was that personal interest in the individual on which we have already remarked; and, as an old clergyman said in a time of illness, men were 'greatly encouraged by their letters being answered as you answer letters, and by their mole-hills of trouble being looked into by their Diocesan taking the trouble to go into them'. The laity noticed it as well, and one rather well-known but by no means ecclesiastical layman, when thanking him for his humanity, wrote: 'One touch of nature in a Bishop does more to make his clergy kin to him than any amount of official repellence.'

I

To write a complete record of his diocesan work is not possible, and indeed there is a very great deal in which his activities were exactly the same as those which fall to the share of most bishops. But certain things stand out in the brief four and a half years of his Rochester episcopate.

First, the Bishop's House. He considered well 'the weighty and tempting arguments' (as he called them in his *Charge*, p. 3) in favour of a country home—a Bromley, a Danbury, a Selsdon—to which those who were jaded with the noise of 'dusty lane and wrangling mart' might be invited, from time to time, for rest, for fresh air, or for quiet conference *sub tegmine cedri*. But he firmly decided that for the Bishop of South London the proper place to live was in the very heart of South London itself. The following is his account of the steps taken:

> It may be well to explain what the position was as regards a See House. The Act of Parliament which had re-arranged the See of Rochester made no immediate provision for a house for the Bishop. Bishop Claughton, ex-Bishop of St. Albans, was retaining Danbury during his life. At his death it was to be sold, and the proceeds were to go to provide a house for the See of Rochester. I therefore had been called upon to choose a temporary place of residence, and I had no hesitation in deciding that the centre of South London was the proper place for the Bishop of Rochester to live in.
>
> I therefore decided to go there at once and to leave the question of a permanent residence to be settled when the money should be forthcoming and it should be necessary to make a decision. The two end houses of Kennington Park Road—173 and 175—were therefore taken by me and doors knocked through so as to make one house. It was quite comfortable but singularly inconvenient for the public side of a Bishop's work. There however we lived until I was translated to Winchester, but before that time came Danbury was sold, and with the proceeds a site was bought within fifty yards of the house we had thus occupied, and under our directions a new house was built by Norman Shaw, who fell in with every suggestion of ours, and produced an Episcopal House which is, I think, of its sort, the best in England, combining possibilities of economy with possibilities of hospitality, and with Chapel and Examination Room etc. complete.
>
> The money available was not sufficient to build the house and provide what I thought an adequate garden, available for us on occasions of gatherings etc., and I accordingly contributed £800 to make possible the purchase of an adequate site.

Bishop Davidson was not able, however, to do very much with regard to St. Saviour's, Southwark:

> Bishop Thorold, with characteristic energy, enthusiasm and hopefulness, had taken in hand the great work of restoring that Church as a future Cathedral for South London. I succeeded to the work

and carried it forward exactly upon his lines, but I am afraid without his power of obtaining big financial aid. We had big gatherings and functions at successive stages as the work went forward, but it has been left for my successor to inaugurate there a true Cathedral life, and he is doing this with greater effectiveness, I think, than I should ever have been capable of, but the whole story is so well known that I need not dwell upon it here.

Next, we may put two special pieces of work (besides the Embertide occasions already mentioned) on which he laid stress as he looked back in later years—the work for the revival of Deaconesses, and the visitation of individual parishes. We have his own recollections of each:

I found the Deaconess work in full swing. Bishop Thorold, whose heart was in the cause, had been especially fortunate in securing as Head Deaconess Mrs. Gilmore, a widow sister of William Morris, the Socialist Poet, a woman of remarkable capacity, enthusiasm and perseverance. The whole subject was new to me, but as soon as I looked into it I felt persuaded that if the Deaconess order could be wholesomely and vigorously revived it would mean more than almost anything else could mean for the practical efficiency of the ministry in poor parishes. I think I grappled with the subject on more definite Church lines than had previously been thought possible or desirable. I worked at the early History of Deaconess life as well as at the Story of its modern Restoration, and I believe that those who were most keen about the matter in Rochester Diocese, where Deaconess work, as such, was certainly at its best, would say that its strongest impulse forward had come during the years of my Episcopate.

The Deaconesses were in a little house in Clapham and during my time they removed to far larger and better premises on the other side of the Common and acquired the freehold of them. Head Deaconess Gilmore and I worked together in completest harmony, my only difficulty being that Bishop Yeatman was not wholly, if at all, in sympathy with our endeavour, and certainly did not work to promote it. He started instead his admirable system of Grey Ladies, though that idea was really borrowed from what had been done in St. Paul's, Walworth, under C. H. Simpkinson who had there a small body of 'Brown Ladies'.

He describes how he ordained Cecilia Robinson (sister of Dr. Armitage Robinson) and a great many more, and adds:

Thanks to the active co-operation of an eager and capable set of men and women, I left the Rochester Deaconesses well established on true historical lines, with a clear distinction between their position as Deaconesses and the position of those who, as Members of a Sisterhood, owe their first allegiance to the Community and are only indirectly connected with the Bishop of the Diocese.

The visitation of individual parishes was a practice to which he attached considerable importance. His custom was, sometimes from Kennington, sometimes from the country, sometimes from a vicarage in Rochester, to spend whole days in seeing parishes, probably in a group, and in the evenings to dictate to his secretary the facts and impressions which he had gleaned. Before he left Rochester he had visited the majority of the parishes both in London and Kent.

> I managed this in what is, I believe, an unusual, certainly an unconventional way. I had always wished to take it in hand but it did not become possible until I was well advanced in my Rochester Episcopate. During that period I visited the larger number of the London Parishes in the Diocese, taking two or sometimes three in a day, visiting the schools, talking individually to the schoolmasters and mistresses and Heads of Sunday schools and other work, and giving a short address to Church workers gathered in Church to meet me. I saw the Churchwardens separately from the Vicar, and in all ways tried to get a fresh and natural knowledge of what was happening in the particular parish. These visitations were only a part of my systematic endeavour to understand and, if possible, relieve the extreme difficulty of the work in a great poor town area like South London. Life in those parishes, and the almost insuperable obstacles to making it religiously bright and buoyant, weighed upon my thoughts by day and night.

There was one special piece of work to which Davidson gave much more of a Diocesan character than had hitherto belonged to it in his or most Dioceses—Rescue and Preventive work among women and girls. He formed a Diocesan Association with a woman of experience to guide it. Both the Bishop and Mrs. Davidson gave it their active support from the start.

It is also, perhaps, not unimportant (though Davidson does not make a special point of this himself) that, at the very beginning of his episcopate, there were letters from prominent Free Church leaders, such as the Rev. J. Scott Lidgett, who had just started the

Bermondsey Settlement, and the Rev. J. Guinness Rogers; and replies from the Bishop, which show a readiness for co-operation in Christian work which was to become much more widely developed in later years. The following letter is typical:

The BISHOP OF ROCHESTER *to the* REV. J. GUINNESS ROGERS

Private. Kennington, 9 July, 1891.

Will you kindly pardon the delay which has occurred in my replying to your letter received some days ago. I am mainly confined to bed (save for a short time each day in the open air) and writing is extremely difficult. Most cordially do I appreciate the kindness of your letter and the sympathy you have been good enough to express with me in my enforced postponement of all active work. It is a strange and unlooked for beginning, but it is rich in disciplinary lessons, and my task just now is to learn to interpret these aright. You are certainly not wrong in believing that it is my earnest wish to co-operate in all possible ways with fellow-workers outside the Communion of the Church of England. No man, as it seems to me, can rightly study either the English history of the last two centuries, or the 'signs of the times' in our own day, without recognising the duty and the privilege of such brotherliness and fellow-feeling as shall unite for efforts in the cause of godliness and truth all those who love the Lord Jesus Christ in sincerity; and it will be my earnest endeavour, if God shall grant me opportunity, to promote such unity of aim, and such mutual respect and charity, as may soften, instead of embittering and emphasising, the lines of demarcation which keep Christian men apart. Again asking you to pardon a rough and 'bed-written' note.

Two other general statements from the Davidson papers may also be quoted here, by way of illustrating the claims upon the new Bishop outside the Diocese.

The Archbishop was continuous in his demands for counsel:

During the whole Rochester time I had, besides my own Diocesan work, been in daily touch with Archbishop Benson and his central responsibilities. He consulted me constantly about it all, indeed there were times when I did almost as much work for him week by week at Kennington as I had done in the previous years at Windsor. This meant a very heavy addition to labour, but it of course kept one in touch with the larger affairs of the Church and with its labourers both clerical and lay.

The Queen again, who had made him Clerk of the Closet,[1] April 27, 1891, two days after his consecration, was constantly requiring his services:

> Besides these duties and controversies I was in my Rochester days in very close touch with the Queen. She showed me continuous kindness and confidence. After my first great illness in 1891, she lent us Osborne Cottage, now Princess Beatrice's home, for a part of my convalescent time, and I went very frequently both to Windsor and Osborne to preach, nor were any ecclesiastical appointments made without my being consulted in the way I have described in the Windsor period.

II

Dr. Davidson had three serious illnesses as Bishop of Rochester: the first in May 1891, the second in March 1894, and the third in February 1895, each of the last two coming at the conclusion of a winter's labours. The period of good health, therefore, in which his active work could be done was only too short. We may select a few incidents and occasions which have a special interest.

It was the Bishop's fate in after years to meet various challenges in the field of Biblical criticism. The following exchange between himself and Dr. Cheyne, the eminent Hebrew scholar and a Canon of Rochester, has a quality of its own. It arose out of a complaint made by Dr. Hole, Dean of Rochester. A report of the Canon's most recent sermon had been placarded in the local newspapers as 'Sermon on the life of David . . . combat with Goliath a myth'; and the Dean wrote in his letter to the Bishop: 'We hear that the reports in the placards and newspapers remark that they cannot see why, if some parts of the Bible are untrue, they should believe anything.' Dean Hole was a famous rose-grower, and his books upon roses were delightful and widely read, but he had not kept abreast of the latest Biblical scholarship. Canon Cheyne was one of the most distinguished Biblical scholars of his day, and had an eager desire to communicate the fruits of his research to the ordinary educated public; but he certainly had eccentricities, which became much more marked in his later life. On learning of the Dean's complaint, and receiving a letter of inquiry from the Bishop, he wrote thus:

[1] As Clerk of the Closet the Bishop was entitled to the Entrée—'the only reward for the arduous duty of that office' (S. Ponsonby Fane, April 21, 1891).

CANON T. K. CHEYNE *to the* BISHOP OF ROCHESTER

Rochester. August 27, 1891.

Upon reflexion, I think my right course is to throw myself on your Lordship's protection. At Oxford there is no one but Mr. Ffoulkes to do these things; but when I come to Rochester it is not right that I should be exposed to these attacks, even if made in private. Our Dean is an old man, frank, impulsive, and injudicious (as is well-known to the Canons). I therefore ask no apology from him; but I nevertheless must bring before your Lordship the circumstance that he sent in hot haste to two influential persons (yourself and the Archbishop) copies of an injurious placard, without inquiring whether the words on the paper were justified by facts, and aware that his imperfect hearing made it impossible for him to judge fairly of any sermon in our Cathedral. I venture to describe this act as unbecoming in the head of a Society. But the Dean is an old man, and brought up from a country rectory, where he never absorbed any new facts or ideas in theology. It is otherwise with another person,—with whom I am on friendly terms and towards whom, knowing his infirmity, I have always shown deference,—Canon Jelf. I suspect him of having stirred the Dean up to take action; some one, I know from what the Dean said, fomented his excitement, if he did not rather cause it. It was Canon Jelf who did the mischief before, and led the Dean on to take unjustifiable steps, which I must now, once for all, explain to your Lordship in anticipation of any further attacks.

I am not really angry with Mr. Jelf; we all have our weaknesses, which have to be guarded against. Mr. Jelf's special weakness is the desire to make every one do as he conscientiously thinks every one ought to do. From the Minor Canons downwards this is pretty well known in the Cathedral. He has also tried the plan on with me, writing letters about sermons which he has failed to agree with. I have perhaps been too kind, always hoping to overcome his prejudices by gentle argument. Of course, this delusion is at an end now.

It was Canon Jelf who, as soon as he had resigned St. Mary's, Chatham, undertook the functions of fault-finder in relation to the Oriel Professor-Canon. The very Sunday (or else the next after it) on which for the first time he appeared in the Cathedral, he took offence at a Sermon on Psalm xvi, in which the Davidic theory was not indeed attacked but quietly put aside, the psalm being regarded as a late Church-psalm, a vastly more edifying theory! He then proceeded (as the Dean frankly admitted) to stir the Dean up: No, he first of all sat down in the Chapter House with a great Bible, as I was unrobing after Evensong, and proceeded to catechize me. That having no result, he stirred up the Dean. A day or two afterwards came a singular short letter from Dr. Hole,

> 'Dear Canon Cheyne, Will you tell me how you reconcile your sermon with St. Peter's speech?
>
> Yours very truly, S. R. Hole, *Dean.*'

I, believing in people (as is my wont), thought even this old man, so good, so devoted, but so prejudiced, would give way to such evident grounds as I could offer. But no. And now comes his second error:—his first being that of picking holes in a sermon of a Canon, and so sowing strife, where he ought to promote peace and love. He violated the laws of courtesy which prevail among gentlemen, and sent my letter off to the Bishop. The issue you know; the Bishop was not quite so ignorant as the Dean and the Canon, though for form's sake he asked me to consider whether I could not confine myself to simple evangelical truth. I then wrote to the Dean, proposing to bury the past in oblivion. The Dean (who is not quick of comprehension) did not see that this was meant as an act of forgiveness on my part; however, he agreed that we should start fresh on both sides.

Of course, I expected the Dean to keep the peace henceforth. This expectation has not been realized. But knowing what I do of Canon Jelf, I think it highly probable that he is partly responsible for this attack.

With regard to the choice of David,—your Lordship will I think see at once that if people are to learn to read the O.T. narratives in a more historical manner, public teachers must go gently to work and not begin with Genesis. Besides I could not say farewell to the Psalter without David. The Dean of course is utterly incompetent to consider these things; he ought to have thanked me for my gentle dealing. There is on all hands a cry for help on the *narratives*. I feel that I have not been too bold, but in the past not bold enough. All that your Lordship says, I heartily accept; I have said it myself long ago. I ought not to give way to the Dean, who in fact owes me, as does Canon Jelf, an apology for repeated ill-treatment. Of their many excellent qualities, and services to the Church, I am well aware, and I will willingly forget and forgive the past. Also I will willingly take all due care to avoid hurting any one unnecessarily:—*I ought not however to have to say this.*

PS. This letter is not meant as private. I leave its contents in your Lordship's hands.

The following was the Bishop's reply:

The BISHOP OF ROCHESTER *to* CANON T. K. CHEYNE

Kennington Aug. 29. 91.

I have received your two letters of Aug. 27th. The subject as a whole—nothing less than the best mode of presenting to a generation brought up under a different type of teaching the results of the newer O.T. criticism—is so vast and momentous that one shrinks from dealing with it in letters of this sort. It is perhaps in some ways *the* most important Church problem of our time. Speaking generally—without touching on the criticism itself—I imagine that my standpoint as regards the duty of outspokenness in our teaching is not widely different from your own. But everything of course depends upon the degree of wisdom—reverence—tact—considerateness—with which the duty is performed; and it is upon these points that I look forward to the advantage of having a full talk with you before very long. You have now considerable experience in the matter and I am most anxious to hear from you, in such detail as is possible in a conversation; what your experience has been both with University congregations and with mixed congregations elsewhere. You have done me the real favour of writing very frankly about the particular difficulties which have met you at Rochester—and I hope you will not be hurt if I venture, with similar candour, to say that your letters leave in my mind a certain doubt whether you fully appreciate the attitude of those to whom —as for example to Canon Liddon or Bishop Wordsworth—such a treatment of O.T. subjects as you feel to be necessary and right gives pain and distress of the acutest sort. I cannot personally share their feeling, but there is surely no doubt of its existence in many of the religious teachers to whom we owe the highest respect, and for whose feelings—or prejudices if you will—we are bound to show a tender consideration.

The existence of this difficulty does not of course relieve those of us whose studies or sympathies have led us to a different view of the history of O.T. Revelation, from the duty of being honest and outspoken in teaching what we believe to be true. But it ought surely, to lead us to treat with something more than patience—rather with tender respect—the comments which the modern criticism of the O.T. evokes from such men as those to whom I have referred. May it not be that your experience of a University congregation has led you possibly to expect too ready a tolerance from those whose life and work for Christ and His Church has tended to stereotype their views upon other lines?

Like other teachers of truths which are new, the modern students of the O.T. may be called upon to 'endure hardness' for the sake of what they believe to be true, and I venture to think they ought not to be either surprised or angered thereat. I feel sure you will pardon my saying this with a candour reciprocal to your own.

After thinking it well over, I cannot feel that any good purpose would be served by my writing further to the Dean upon the subject at present. Perhaps our conversation to which I am looking forward may throw some new light upon the position, and I do not fail to ask that The Lord of all truth may guide you alike in your teaching and in your relation to your colleagues in these solemn and difficult matters.

P.S. You will understand that I am not expressing any individual opinion—indeed it would be presumptuous for me to do so—upon the critical problems raised in your sermons.

As there are no further letters upon this subject from Dean or Canon, we must suppose that the matter was allowed to rest; and certainly the last letter from Canon Cheyne in the Rochester period recalls a grateful appreciation of the Bishop's support. 'One Canon', he says, 'who does not find himself on a bed of roses, has to thank you for much kindness.'

Bishop Davidson was also able to give practical illustration of his friendly attitude to Nonconformists very early in his episcopate. In February 1892, the famous Baptist preacher, the Rev. C. H. Spurgeon, who had died abroad after a long illness, was buried in Norwood cemetery. The Tabernacle at Newington was only a short distance from the Bishop's house at Kennington, and the Bishop wrote at once to Spurgeon's brother:

The BISHOP OF ROCHESTER *to the* REV. JAMES SPURGEON

February 18, 1892

It is not I hope necessary that I should assure you how deeply I share the feeling which at present animates our whole community in South London and elsewhere as to the loss we have sustained in the death of so stalwart a champion of Christianity, so great a preacher, and so good a man, as he was who has just been called to his rest and his reward. I should have felt it deeply at any time, but in the position of responsibility which I have been called to hold in South London his death has to me an increased and solemn significance. I am anxious to have some opportunity, if it may be, of sharing in the general expression of respect and regard for the memory of one who has worked so long and so manfully in his Master's cause, and of thus bearing witness to the substantial unity in Christ which underlies our differences. Although it would not, I fear, be possible for me, holding the position I do, to take part in the public memorial services which I understand are to be held in the Metropolitan Tabernacle on Wednesday next, I should deem it a high privilege if you would allow me to be present at Norwood and to take a place among the friends who stand beside his grave. May I ask you kindly to let me know whether this would be in accordance with your wishes, and, if so, to give me any necessary directions as to the hour?

The Bishop's offer was accepted. He joined the procession at the cemetery gates, and pronounced the benediction as described in the following extract from his Journal; and he was entirely unperturbed by the charge that thus he had been guilty of 'an indirect approval of the sin of schism'.

On February 11th I attended Mr. Spurgeon's funeral—a deed which has ever since given opportunity to *Guardian* letter-writers and others. I suppose the main *gravamen* was my pronouncing the benediction by the grave. As a matter of fact this had not been pre-arranged in any way—but, as we approached the grave and saw the crowds gathered there, Mr. James Spurgeon said to me 'Will you pronounce the blessing? There is a huge multitude of people and you are Bishop of the Diocese', and I accordingly did so—not in robes—and not by any means with the view of formally 'taking part in the Service' as it is recounted!

Of problems connected with worship and ritual, the Bishop seems to have had comparatively few. But as an example of his method, on a small scale, the case of an attack on a clergyman in Hatcham may be quoted. The clergyman having been charged with introducing *Hymns Ancient and Modern*, and also with refusing to have Evening Communion, the parish committee of the mother church protested against the innovation in a temporary church in that very populous district.

The Bishop took endless trouble to discover the actual grievances, interviewed the committee and the clergyman, and in the end pointed out, most politely, how very slight were the real grounds for any complaint. The letter was accepted as final by the parish committee, though the committee deplored that 'his Lordship has missed a very valuable opportunity of restoring peace'. The Bishop's letter acknowledged the right of the parishioners to request the use of his influence with the vicar, and proceeded as follows:

The Bishop of Rochester *to the* Parish Committee of St. Catherine's, Hatcham

Bishop's House, Kennington Park, S.E. November 10, 1892.

... In such circumstances I am compelled to examine carefully not so much the legal aspect of the question as the amount of actual grievance from which those who have addressed me are personally suffering. In this connection it is not unimportant for me to notice that the first name upon the committee . . . is that of a gentleman who is at present church-warden of another parish and therefore can scarcely claim to be entitled to a voice in such questions as the hours of divine service or the hymn-book in use in St. Catherine's church, which he presumably would not at present in any circumstances attend. I do not wish, however, to make too much of such a point as this . . . but when I look further as to what sort of advice it is wished that I should press upon Mr. Truscott I find that I am asked to bid him discontinue the use of *Hymns Ancient and Modern*, a book which in your opinion 'should not be tolerated'. I am further asked to insist that Mr. Truscott, whatever be his personal opinions upon the subject, should celebrate the Holy Communion in the evening. You explained to me at our recent interview that you have yourself ceased to attend divine service at a neighbouring church, where the services are of a markedly Evangelical character, because of the introduction in that church of an early morning celebration of the Holy Communion . . . in your letter you further specify particular acts on Mr. Truscott's part and you ask me 'to order him immediately to discontinue these acts inasmuch as they have been declared by competent authority to be illegal'. I have looked carefully into these particular items . . . upon some of the points you mention you are, I venture to think, mistaken as to the facts, and upon others as to the law . . . I deplore as deeply as anyone can the self-will and at times the defiance of authority which some few clergymen have exhibited in ritual matters during recent years. You have mistakenly classed Mr. Truscott among those who have so behaved. I believe you to have acted in the matter with perfect good faith and I have the deepest sympathy with all who are endeavouring to maintain the doctrines and discipline of our reformed Church against encroachments either in the direction of superstition or infidelity; did I see any such danger in St. Catherine's parish I should say so and in my conversation with Mr. Truscott I have told him exactly what I think.

Throughout this year, and again in 1893 and 1894, the Bishop continued his advocacy of a more liberal attitude to Sunday observance. In May 1892, he presented a petition to Convocation from the Sunday Society for the Sunday opening of Museums, public libraries, and art galleries. He made a speech, described by the *Guardian* as one of great courage and importance, achieving 'with remarkable success' the very difficult task of putting a subject which had been under debate for years in a totally new light. He dealt successively with the objections that the working classes did not want Sunday openings, that it would mean more Sunday labour, and that this was the thin end of the wedge towards a Continental Sunday. One forcible point concerned the needs of the shop assistants, clerks, and others educationally a grade or so above that of the working classes:

> I remember [he said], having a conversation on the subject several years ago with an intelligent young fellow, who was then a clerk upon a very small salary in a London office. He lived in rather comfortless lodgings with a brother clerk as poor as himself. 'I want to know,' he said, 'how you clergy think that a man like me ought to spend a wet Sunday.'

As a result of the debate which followed, a joint committee of bishops and clergy was appointed to investigate the subject of the petition and to report.

The Report was presented to Convocation in July 1893. The Bishop, as Chairman of the Joint Committee, approached the matter historically, not theoretically, and with characteristic thoroughness set out a complete list of the existing Statutes which bore, in whole or part, upon the subject of Sunday Observance from 1448 to 1887, and also the findings of Parliamentary Select Committees, together with a statement of the facts in the British Colonies, the United States, and the Protestant countries of northern Europe.

The report also showed from the evidence of many English towns that many libraries and institutes were open on Sundays and widely appreciated. Five resolutions were attached to the report, the first two emphasizing the character of Sunday as a day of worship and rest, the last three dealing cautiously with the library problem itself:

> III. That since it is evident that an increasing number of persons, for whom Sunday is the only day of leisure, find the

reasonable use of Libraries, Picture Galleries, and Museums on that day to be wholesome and profitable, it is necessary, in the highest interest both of visitors and attendants, that such Sunday Opening should be carefully guarded against unfairness or misuse.

IV. That in no circumstances ought any Library, Institution, Gallery, or recreative resort to be permitted to be open on Sundays for payment.

V. That, if these conditions be observed, the cause of true religion has, in the opinion of this House, nothing to fear from the reasonable and careful extension of the system of Sunday Opening described in the Report.

The Bishop's speech in commending the Report and Resolutions concluded as follows:

To me the evidence before us shows conclusively that the cause of religion has nothing really to fear from the reasonable and careful extension of the principle to which we have referred. Some of those who read the Report may think that its compilers have suppressed the evidence furnished to them by the Clergy and others opposed to such Sunday opening. On the contrary, we have endeavoured to make the very most of it, and have anxiously wished for more, but we cannot obtain it. . . . I confess to have been greatly surprised by the overwhelming preponderance upon one side of the clerical opinion furnished to us. Scarcely any disapproval is expressed by any one, and this notwithstanding our endeavours to elicit it wherever it exists. We do believe, my lords, that the Church has nothing to fear, or rather that the deposit intrusted to her keeping will be in no way harmed, if more institutions than now should be opened for a time upon Sunday.

The older bishops, however, seemed to be more or less afraid of the subject, and the debate was adjourned for a year. In July 1894, the three main resolutions were rejected. Even the Bishop's caution, as the *Westminster Gazette* pointed out, in slipping in the main point parenthetically, instead of moving a resolution frankly in support of Sunday opening (with safeguards), had failed to persuade his brethren. The Bishop himself notes:

I was disappointed by the line taken by some of the bishops, notably London,[1] Southwell[2] and Peterborough.[3] They all spoke as men belonging to another generation than ours. Of course Exeter,[4] Gloucester[5] and Chichester[6] did so, but this was to be expected. Nobody save Legge of Lichfield voted with me.

[1] Dr. Temple. [2] Dr. Ridding. [3] Dr. Creighton.
[4] Dr. Bickersteth. [5] Dr. Ellicott. [6] Dr. Durnford.

The social conditions under which the people of his diocese lived, formed another matter in which Bishop Davidson took a deep and thoughtful interest. In November 1892 he played an active part in the conference convened by the Archbishop of Canterbury at Lambeth, to consider the duty of the National Church to the aged poor. A Royal Commission at about the same time had been announced to deal with the Poor Laws and especially Old Age Pensions. Amongst those who had spoken at the Lambeth meeting were Lord Halsbury, Lord Coleridge, and Mr. Charles Booth. The last named had expressed his strong sense of the extraordinary amount of knowledge of the needs of the poor possessed by the parochial clergy. The Bishop of Rochester, after the meeting, wrote to his old tutor, Mr. James Bryce, then Chancellor of the Duchy of Lancaster, suggesting that the Royal Commission should include some clergy:

The BISHOP OF ROCHESTER *to the* RT. HON. J. BRYCE, M.P.

Kennington, 11 Dec. 1892.

You will let our long friendship be my excuse for writing you a few lines upon what seems to me a matter of considerable importance, less perhaps in itself than as part of a larger question. I allude to the announcement made and uncontradicted that no clergyman is to be a member of the forthcoming Royal Commission on the Aged Poor.

People are writing to me about it, I suppose because of my known identification, speaking generally, with liberal principles and policy. I can very easily understand that whoever appoints the Commission will greatly *simplify* his task by the omission of all clergy; but I do think he will thereby materially weaken the Commission. What I imagine is wanted, and probably intended, in such a Commission is not the representation of any class interests —or technical knowledge of poor laws—or of minute administrative details—(all these things can be furnished as evidence by witnesses)—but rather the mature general knowledge of the facts of English life, and especially of English life among the poor: their manner of living, in health and sickness, their family claims and responsibilities, etc. etc.

Now it is, I suppose, simply indisputable that there exists no body of educated men whose knowledge on these subjects is to be compared with the knowledge necessarily possessed by the parochial clergy, whose lives have been in no small degree spent in the homes of the poor, and who have therefore an acquaintance with poor men's needs and possibilities which no other class of educated men has had the means of acquiring in the same natural and quite unartificial way.

Is it really the case that sectarian jealousies, or political exigencies, are to be allowed on a question like this to deprive the Commission of that sort of knowledge, except when given in the evidence of witnesses?

You know me too well I think to suppose that I am writing thus from what may be called a mere *denominational* point of view. I should say exactly the same if it were Nonconformist Ministers, instead of National Church Clergy, whose special knowledge seemed to me to be in danger of being wasted. I want to see one or two clergy on such a Commission, not sitting *qua* clergy but *qua* citizens and men of education who have had absolutely unique opportunities of becoming hourly familiar with the matters which such a Commission must consider. It will be for experts to give evidence as witnesses upon the details of poor-law administration etc., but among those who, as Commissioners, weigh that evidence, should surely be one or two men of the class whose knowledge of English poverty is, from the very nature of the case, unique.

So much for the Commission itself. I do not enter on the larger question raised of necessity in the minds of clergy who are also liberals by the adoption of such a policy of exclusion of competent men *because they are clergy* from helping to weigh the evidence given on a topic which is specially forced on their own attention every day of their lives. If we are to regard this as significant of the attitude of the Liberal Government towards the Church upon matters in no way connected with Disestablishment, it certainly gives us food for thought.

It may be you have nothing to do with the matter, but you will at least pardon I think the frank outpourings of an old friend.

Mr. Bryce agreed with the Bishop in principle, and wrote to the President of the Local Government Board, Mr. Henry Fowler, but his representations were unsuccessful.

A public question of a different kind which engaged the Bishop's attention in 1893 was Welsh Disestablishment. A private Conference was summoned at Lambeth on March 4, 1893, to discuss the Welsh Church Suspensory Bill with Lord Salisbury, who emphasized the gravity of the situation. Lord Salisbury begged the Bishops to issue Pastorals, which should be against Disestablishment in general, and not particularly against the Welsh Bill, and argued that it was a time for ecclesiastics rather than politicians to come to the front. There were six bishops in the room besides the Archbishop and Lord Salisbury:

> The Bishop of Chester asked whether we should say 'Rather than let Wales be disestablished we would ourselves in England submit to it also'? Everybody (save the Bishop of St. Asaph who was silent) was against any such line being taken. Lord Salisbury said 'No good in urging a man "If you rob me of my rubies, I will throw my diamonds at your head!"'

The result of the conference was a mass meeting in the Albert Hall on May 16 to protest against Disestablishment. It was an immense demonstration, attended by Bishops, members of the Lower Houses of the Convocations, the Houses of Laymen, and churchwardens from all over England. The meeting was a success, so far as numbers and oratory were concerned, but, considering that the Welsh Bill had made practically no progress owing to the Home Rule agitation, Davidson was doubtful as to its ultimate value. He notes in his journal:

> Suppose there were a real and urgent danger of Disestablishment in England as well as in Wales, what should we now have left us to do? May we not have fired our big guns too soon?

The industrial situation also aroused his keen interest. A great cotton strike, which had begun in November 1892, came to an end the following spring with an agreement as to the means of settling disputes which marked a big step forward. In the late summer of 1893, a disastrous coal strike commenced. The Government, under Lord Rosebery, successfully intervened in November. But, with these various clashes between Capital and Labour, there was a growing feeling that some united action should be taken by the Church. 'Could not something', it was asked, 'be done by the various sections of the Christian Church, with a view to putting an end to, or at least diminishing, the evils of the present system of industrial warfare?' A conference was summoned by the editor of the *Daily Chronicle*, for November 14, in the Jerusalem Chamber. The Bishops of Rochester and Ripon, Cardinal Vaughan, Dr. Marshall Lang, Moderator of the Church of Scotland, Dr. Clifford, Canon Scott Holland, Mr. Charles Gore, and others, were to meet under the chairmanship of Mr. G. W. E. Russell, Under-Secretary of State for India. A series of resolutions had been agreed, dealing especially with the living wage.

But when the day for the meeting came 'for unexplained reasons the Cardinal was absent, the Moderator was absent, and the Dean of Westminster took the chair instead of Mr. Russell, and begged the conference on no account to pass any resolutions'. The Bishop of Rochester took the Cardinal's place in introducing a resolution, which he was not allowed to press, to the effect that in the opinion of this conference the principle of the maintenance of a standard of decent living should be recognized as an essential condition in the settlement of labour disputes. 'He spoke up manfully,' said the *Chronicle* in its extremely candid account of the proceedings, 'while the Bishop of Ripon, with coalfields in his diocese, objected to all resolutions and was most doleful.' The general effect of the meeting showed the extraordinary nervousness of Church opinion at that time. Though the Bishop of Rochester was annoyed at the inclusion of his name without his leave in connexion with a large public meeting a fortnight later, it is an interesting note on the spirit of nervousness of the times, that he was the only Bishop whom Scott Holland, Adderley, and their friends could find to say anything in public, however guarded, about a standard of decent living.

III

In 1894, the Bishop summed up the experience so far gained in his Primary Charge. A few months before its delivery he had been seized by the second grave illness of his Rochester period. Various newspapers discussed the possibility of his resignation. On June 15, he was asked to go and see the Prime Minister, Lord Rosebery, who strongly pressed him to go to Bath and Wells, as a lighter diocese than Rochester, and a 'more sanitary See', in succession to Lord Arthur Hervey. But after reflection and consultation he refused. He gave his Charge in October 1894, and he was able to express some of his views on the principal subjects of the day, notably the conception of a National Church, arising out of the campaign for the Disestablishment of the Church in Wales. He had much to say about the National Church—something also with regard to the Ritual Controversy and Loyalty to the Prayer Book. But there was a special reference to the duty of the clergy with regard to economic questions, in the light of the recent strikes, that showed not only a true disciple of Bishop

Westcott, whom he constantly quoted, but a man looking forward to crises and strikes still to come, and the duty of the Church with regard to them:

> On us then, the clergy of the National Church, it devolves to bring home to the minds of men and women these fundamental principles; to correct or condemn every custom or theory or law which implies that some province of life or conduct lies outside the operations of the law of Christ. So to teach little children that they may grow up to feel and know this as a matter of course. So to influence, bit by bit, the public opinion of average folk that any other principle than this may come to be looked upon as base and wrong. That is our business day by day. 'It is the office of the State to give effect to public opinion, it is the office of the Church to shape it.'[1]
>
> Be this our task, and men by degrees will cease to talk of social questions which affect the homes, and so the characters, of tens of thousands of English men and women and children, as lying outside the province of the clergy. The bishop, priest, or deacon who thinks he can define in any trade, or group of trades, the limits of a 'living wage', and prescribe the mode of its enforcement, must be venturesome indeed; but the Christian man belies his creed, who fails to recognise the law of Christ as laying an absolute obligation upon us all to accept our responsibility for the lives of others, and to see that, if we can help it, no family in Christian England shall live, perforce, in such a home as must degrade and stunt the life.

The Charge also expounded Bishop Davidson's attitude on religious education—a subject with which he had much to do in view of the election to the London School Board in November 1894. He spoke strongly for Church schools, but he also emphasized 'our sense of common responsibility for the teaching our children receive in Board Schools', and he said:

> No effort must be spared to secure, so far as in us lies, that in every Board School such religious education as the law allows shall be honestly and reverently given, and, further, that the teaching shall be Christian in fact as well as in name. In this endeavour, which we must make with all our might, we may surely count upon the support of every thoughtful Christian man. We are happily unfamiliar in Kent and Surrey with the bitter sectarianism which, in the profaned name of religious equality, has

[1] Westcott, *The Incarnation and Common Life*, p. 23.

banished even Bible lessons from nearly a hundred Board Schools in Wales and Northern England. The lamentable controversy in the London School Board has not been as to whether or no religious teaching shall be given; it has turned on the question how best to secure the Christian efficiency of such teaching without hardship to the few individual teachers who find conscientious difficulty in giving it. We have of course no guarantee of its permanence, and therein lies a grave peril; but it is to me almost inconceivable how any Christian man who knows the facts can speak of the religious teaching at present given under the London Board as 'worthless' because it is—to use a sorely battered term—'undenominational'.

At the end of Bishop Davidson's Charge, there was a reference to 'English Orders and Rome'. Cardinal Vaughan had just been proclaiming to the public that Anglican bishops and clergy 'can only be considered as so many laymen'. The Bishop's answer was:

> This is merely to repeat what was said in other words by Cardinal Patrizi on behalf of the Pope nearly thirty years ago, in reply to approaches which had been made to him by Clergy of the Church of England in connection with the Association for the Promotion of the Unity of Christendom.[1]

But while expressing the desirability of the authorities of the Church of Rome being on these, as on other matters, better informed, the Bishop pointed out:

> What separates us from the Church of Rome is another set of considerations altogether than questions about her view of the validity of Anglican Orders; and men are surely forgetting the mighty issues which depend upon those differences, when they talk as though Western Christendom might be again at one if only Rome admitted the truth about our Orders.

A change was necessary in the principles and practice of Rome, before such reconciliation could take place, and he concluded:

> Meantime, alas, the words still remain true which were spoken by Archbishop Laud two centuries and a half ago, when he was approached with proposals of reconciliation and friendship: 'somewhat dwelt within me which would not suffer that, till Rome were other than it is'.[2]

[1] See the full documents in Archbishop Manning's Pastoral Letter, 1866: *The Reunion of Christendom: A Pastoral Letter*. See also *The Life of Cardinal Manning*, by E. S. Purcell, Macmillan, 1896, vol. ii, pp. 276–88.

[2] *Diary*, August 17, 1633.

These words were particularly opportune at a time when a new attempt had just been begun by Lord Halifax and the Abbé Portal for a *rapprochement* between Canterbury and Rome. The story is told in detail in Archbishop Benson's *Life*. But a short account is necessary here, as on certain points Davidson's advice was of the greatest importance.

Portal had published a book *Les Ordinations Anglicanes*, and had been brought by Lord Halifax to see the Archbishop of Canterbury at Addington in the summer of 1894. He then went to Rome, and saw the Pope and Cardinal Rampolla. On his return he paid a further very sudden visit with Lord Halifax, quite unannounced, to the Archbishop at Dulverton. He had hoped to bring a letter from the Pope himself to the Archbishops of Canterbury and York. But the Pope had, on reflection, felt such a step to be incautious, and what Portal actually brought was a letter to himself from Cardinal Rampolla, 'nice,' as Benson said, 'but very general'. The Archbishop did not conceal his annoyance that the interview with an emissary of the Pope should have been forced upon him by Lord Halifax, who had not said a word of Portal's presence when asking the Archbishop to see him. The Archbishop was also aware that, in fact, between Portal's first interview with him in the summer and his later visit at the end of September, the head of the Roman Catholic hierarchy in England, Cardinal Vaughan, had gone out of his way to attack the Church of England, and to declare at Preston that the only conceivable kind of reunion was individual or corporate submission.

The ARCHBISHOP OF CANTERBURY *to the* BISHOP OF ROCHESTER

Private. Baron's Down. 3 October 1894.

I send you some papers which I think will rather astonish you. The history of them is that Halifax wrote to say he had some news which would 'both please and astonish me *very much*' and wanted to come with it to Addington. Being told I was here taking holiday, he telegraphed on Thursday that he would come down next day Friday 28 Sept. He came and brought the Abbé Portal! They travelled two whole nights hither and back from Doncaster. And then took place the interview, of which I send you Mason's notes with my additions in correction. Mason was staying here a few days. I enclose you Cardinal Rampolla's letter (French translation) to Portal—a draft of a letter which a chaplain might write to Halifax

—Mason's improved version of the same. I prefer my own, slightly touched up.

Of course all this must be most private. And I should greatly value your opinion on the whole. I was much taken aback naturally by having the 'emissary' face to face. And we must remember that my letter is quite certain to appear sooner or later. Hence, as well as on its account, the utmost care is needed.

You will conclude, what is the fact, that Halifax has taken the greatest care of M. Portal. He has seen and heard nothing but with H's eyes and voice. Has been to St. Paul's, to the Ritualistic churches, to Cowley, etc. His poor Holiness may well have been surprised.

The Archbishop's original draft for a letter to Halifax which might be communicated to Rampolla was of a very stiff character and intended to be signed by a chaplain. It was also very general. The final letter actually sent, and printed in Benson's *Life*,[1] owed all its main points to Davidson. It took the form of a letter from the Archbishop himself, and, after some general words, pointed out the lack of consideration for the Archbishop's position, in not informing him beforehand either that Portal was to be with Halifax, or of the subject of the interview. It also pointed out that it was a practical impossibility for the Archbishop of Canterbury to enter privately and unofficially into communication on such subjects with the authorities of another branch of the Church Catholic—especially when Cardinal Vaughan was at that very moment publicly declaring the absolute repudiation by the Church of Rome of Anglican Orders.

The disappointment of Lord Halifax was very great. At the same time he kept urging the Archbishop to negotiate directly or indirectly with the Holy See on the matter of a possible conference on the validity of English Orders. Indeed Davidson used to say in later years that the Archbishop was in effect invited to ask the Pope, 'Are Anglican Orders valid?' And this was an impossible question for a self-respecting Archbishop of Canterbury to ask, as the Bishop pointed out vigorously at the time. Lord Halifax did not mend matters by writing a long letter on behalf of the Council of the English Church Union to the Archbishop of Toledo, in which he repudiated the action of the Archbishop of Dublin, who had recently consecrated Señor Cabrera a bishop of

[1] Vol. ii, pp. 604 ff.

the Reformed Church of Spain! The letter only opened the way for a further attack on Anglican Orders by Cardinal Vaughan, on the Church of England generally, and on 'the marvellous communication presented to Your Eminence by Lord Halifax'!

In the following February, a debate took place in Convocation on the Spanish consecration, in the course of which the Bishop of Rochester spoke. He agreed that the circumstances of a comparatively small movement hardly justified the Archbishop of Dublin's action, but maintained that, 'whether we look to the old authorities of the Church of England of the High Church school (Laud, Wake, etc.) or whether we look to the authorities of to-day, corporate or individual (e.g. Christopher Wordsworth and the Old Catholics), we have a practically unanimous witness to the fact that, in case of extreme necessity', such interference as the Archbishop of Dublin's may be justified.

A week later Lord Halifax made a very important speech to a Bristol branch of the English Church Union on 'England and Rome'. He then went to Rome, saw the Pope and Cardinal Rampolla and others, and found that Portal's pamphlet and visit and the articles of the Abbé Duchesne had been a great surprise, and a great source of irritation, to many of the English Roman Catholics. From Rome he wrote to Davidson:

VISCOUNT HALIFAX *to the* BISHOP OF ROCHESTER

April 17, 1895.

I have never thanked you as I ought for your most kind and help-ful letter, or written to tell you what I had been doing here—but the truth is I have not had a moment to myself. Writing Memorandums in French, translating letters, and seeing people all day, leaves little time for anything.

The accompanying papers will, however, I think put you in possession, substantially, of what has occurred and the present position of affairs. I shall be glad if Your Lordship will show them *privately* in any quarter where they are likely to be useful—and let me, at your leisure, have them again to 79 Eaton Square where I hope to be by May 2 or 3?

I translated Your Lordship's letter into French *in extenso* and showed it to the Pope together with some others which I thought likely to be useful. There is no doubt at all that with prudence—some self-restraint and patience, we have *a great opportunity*—not perhaps so much at this exact moment as a little later on—if nothing is done to check what, if all goes well, will develop of itself *here* out of existing circumstances. The misfortune is that our way of looking at things, and doing our business, is so entirely opposed to Italian methods that it will be quite easy to throw away what might, if properly managed, be turned to the greatest advantage of all we have most at heart.

I go to Florence tomorrow to stay with Lady Crawford, so I shall hope to see the Archbishop. If Your Lordship is well enough I would come any day that suited you to expand any information I am in a position to give. The French Ecclesiastics and Baron Von Hugel have been invaluable. The Pope's Mass this morning was most touching.

Davidson at once wrote to the Archbishop, and urged him to write a letter to Halifax saying that he (the Archbishop) utterly repudiated the representation given of his position, that he never invited the interview, that Portal came without warning, and that he (the Archbishop) was by no means of Halifax's opinion as to all the blessings which would ensue from a mere recognition of the validity of Anglican Orders by an unreformed Papal Church. He also wrote himself to Lord Halifax, very thoroughly explaining his own position:

The BISHOP OF ROCHESTER *to* VISCOUNT HALIFAX

Saltwood, Hythe. April 24, 1895.

I am grateful to you for kindly giving me such ample information with regard to your action in the matter of a Roman recognition of Anglican Orders, in connexion with the desires you entertain for a future corporate reunion with the Roman Church. I have read with the closest attention all the memoranda you have sent me, and I will take care that they are duly returned to you as you desire. It is not easy, I think, to exaggerate the possible importance of what you have done, but you will pardon me for saying that I cannot regard that importance exactly as you do yourself. To me it seems that the perils attaching to *this sort* of communication with the Roman authorities are at least as great as is the probability of possible advantage. I know you would wish me to express my views to you explicitly, and that you will not take offence at what I say.

1. I do not think that you yourself realise adequately the strength and depth of the present Protestantism of England. For myself—if the word 'Protestantism' be used in its proper sense—I rejoice that it is both strong and deep. The *principles* which

underlay the Reformation—as contrasted with the mere surface agitations and the mistakes of individual workers—are in my opinion sound and true principles, and I confess I think they need assertion now—in opposition to the principles and policy of Rome—as truly as they did in the sixteenth century. Our wish in the Church of England, as all our best representatives testify, has always been for *daylight*, *fresh air*, outspoken truthfulness and candour—the unswerving assertion of what we believe to be true without concealment or reserve, and, so far as possible, with a frank disregard of the diplomatic expediency and so forth which has taken so large a place in the words and acts of Roman controversialists ever since the middle ages. To adopt your own words in your letter to me, 'Our way of looking at things and of doing our business is so entirely opposed to Italian methods'. I agree with you in that statement, but whereas you speak of it as a 'misfortune', I thank God for it as an evidence of His guidance and blessing upon the Church of England. I believe this principle, this 'way of looking at things and doing our business' to be deeply and I hope ineradicably rooted in us as Englishmen and English Churchmen. It is not the Roman way of 'looking at things and doing business', and the contrast is, to my mind, admirably illustrated by your account of the scheming and counter-scheming and wire-pulling and diplomacy of which you have been witness in these late weeks at Rome, where the thought of the ecclesiastical authorities seems to be so much more 'what will be *effective*?' what will advance the interests of the Church of Rome?' than 'what are the plain facts of history? what is the truth?' *We*, as it seems to me, have nothing to conceal, nothing to 'diplomatise' about. We are ready to publish to the world all the facts in our possession, and we invite and desire the fullest and freest criticism thereupon, and a plain, straightforward judgement by the ordinary use of common-sense and reason, and in answer to the prayers of us all that God will enlighten and guide us.

2. Now such an endeavour as that in which you have been engaged seems to me to have a perilous tendency to force you into modes of action which are *theirs* rather than ours—to make you consider *policy* rather than principle, and give a subordinate place to the consideration of what is straightforwardly and simply *true* either as to the history of the past, the facts of the present, or the doctrines and character of the Church of England. I do not of course mean that you would yourself for one moment compromise or conceal or distort what you believe to be the simple truth—you are as incapable of it as man can be—but, for that very reason, you are attempting to take up an impossible position if, as a loyal

member of the Church of England, you try to negotiate with the Roman Ecclesiastical diplomatists on their own ground. It seems to me that this is already apparent in the impossibility one finds in expressing in plain words any clear and indisputable step which has yet been taken either by the Pope or his official advisers in the direction you desire. He has seen you, heard your statements, received the books and letters you gave him, including a large number, I suppose, of most confidential documents (which his representatives may hereafter use as they will!) and has given you kind words and benedictions. But beyond the very guarded letter written by Cardinal Rampolla to Abbé Portal, they have, as it seems to me, committed themselves to nothing whatever of a definite sort. Your letter to Rampolla made a definite request that he would put certain things in writing. He has not done so. All they have said (*valeat quantum*) might be disavowed tomorrow, and called a mere misunderstanding on your part of kindly expressions which were never intended to have an operative force. It is this sort of diplomatic dealing on matters of sacred doctrine and practice which seems to me so perilous.

3. Then, further, what does it all come to even at the best? You may be right in thinking you have smoothed the way for a declaration on the part of Rome that she recognises the validity, historically, of Anglican Orders. *From the point of view of Rome* I can see the advantages which might accrue to her were she, while retaining all her distinctive doctrines and corruptions, to admit the truth of certain facts of history which indeed can hardly be gainsaid by any fair-minded man. And, as you truly say, this would remove one barrier to the ultimate reunion of Christendom. One barrier, out of so many. So far it would be indisputably to the good, and one can be honestly thankful for any step on the part of Rome which admits daylight into what had been hitherto kept artificially dark. But surely so long as the Roman accretions upon the true, primitive, Scriptural faith of the Church remain, and are asserted as dogmas *de fide*, the mere admission that Archbishop Parker was validly consecrated is an admission of *comparatively* small importance. And have you seen or heard a single thing which would make you believe in any coming disclaimer on the part of Rome of those distinctive and unscriptural doctrines which bulk so large in the Roman system as a whole? If so, there is, I think, no reference to such expectation in the papers you have sent me. Do not suppose I wish to minimise the importance and value of a distinct declaration on the part of Rome that she will henceforth recognise our Orders as fully and frankly as we have always recognised hers. I should welcome it with all my heart as (1) an

enlargement of our common ground of action, (2) an admission of possible, or certain, error on Rome's part in the past, (3) a contribution to the value and strength of historic evidence as such. For all these reasons it would, I think, do real good and remove a *needless* source of irritation. You remember perhaps a sentence in one of Maurice's letters: 'I know the kindling of heart which I feel towards a Dissenting or Romish controversialist who frankly disavows, not to his own class, but to the public and to me, dishonest artifices to which his party and he have resorted. I know what a prepossession he causes me in favour of himself and his cause. I love a man who does this' (*Life*, i. 476). (I don't mean to apply the words 'dishonest artifices' in this case, but the principle of the sentiment is the same.) And yet I should not be honest with you if I did not say that while I should thankfully recognise the gain, so far as it goes, even for us (and should see it very clearly indeed for the Romans), I should at the same time regard such *démarche* (to use your word) as having an element of danger for the Church of England, as leading the unwary and uninformed to make less than they ought of the deep and even fundamental differences which would still remain. This feeling would, I am certain, prevail strongly in England, and I, for one, should share it. However *magna est veritas*; and by all means let us encourage and welcome, whatever be the consequence, any honest attempt to know and proclaim what is historically true.

4. One more point and, to my mind, a most important one. I wonder whether you have fully weighed the possible results *in England* of the documents you have sent me becoming known to even a limited circle. The French memorandum which (so far at least as we in England are concerned) is much the most important, was I presume prepared for the information not of those in England but of the Pope and his friends. Indeed, it bears this impress upon its face, nor does it profess to recount in detail the interviews or communications which may have taken place between M. Portal and yourself on the one hand and English ecclesiastical authorities on the other. It refers, for example, to letters as 'appended' which do not appear in your document as sent to me, and it summarises the general result of these letters in very decided terms (page 8 of your memorandum), while it gives us no means of judging whether we should quite agree in your opinion of what the letters may be regarded as showing. If my own letter to you is among those thus summarised, I should demur to your description of its tenour, and it is *possible* the same may be the case with others of your correspondents. With regard to the letters and opinions of the Archbishops, which you describe of course much

more fully, you have presumably taken steps to secure that the summary is sanctioned as accurate. But do you quite realise how grave is the peril of some wide misunderstanding as to the attitude of e.g. the Archbishops, arising on the part of those who in England read your memorandum? If the kind confidence you have shown in me, in authorising me to show the papers privately 'in any quarter where they are likely to be useful', has been also extended to others, a good many eyes may perhaps ere long have seen the documents; and you know the strange way in which things *do* leak out and get misrepresented, however unintentionally. The consequence of any such misrepresentation might be simply incalculably grave. But all this you must have weighed, and perhaps I am mistaken in supposing that you have sent copies to more than one or two friends. I have myself shown the papers at present to *one* trusted friend only, in whom I have complete confidence. He feels as strongly as I do the risk I refer to. Of course if the actual words of the Archbishops had appeared in the document in their entirety it would be another matter. Whatever they may have said or written was doubtless well weighed. But the responsibility (in a matter at once so grave and so liable to be misconstrued) of circulating, even to a few, an independent summary of their words is one which cannot be overrated, and I confess I feel not a little anxious to know how far the possible risks I refer to are guarded against.

I know you will excuse me for speaking thus plainly. Your confidence invites it. Since I received your letter (on the 22nd) I have thought of little else. I write now, while all is fresh in my mind, but as you do not return till May 2, and I know not where you are, I shall not post this for a few days, and if aught else occurs to me I will add it.

I fear you will think me cold and unsympathetic in the endeavour you are making for Christian reunion. It is not so. No man in England is more keen than I for such reunion as is based upon *truth.* I long for it, and pray for it with all my heart. But I cannot at present share your hopes as to the *way* in which a real reunion of Christendom as a whole—not of the Roman and Anglican Churches only—is to be brought about. I fear on the contrary that anything which seems to advocate a corporate reunion between the Church of England and the unreformed Church of Rome may and will really retard the grander reunion for which we hope and pray. I do not expect you to share this opinion, but I should not deal honestly with you or reciprocate aright your confidence if I did not say what I think. Nor would you desire me to do otherwise. I do dread the Roman *way* of doing things,

> and most earnestly desire that we in England may keep clear of it. I confess I see little, if any, change in this respect since the days when the diplomacy of the Fathers at Constance was opposed to the straightforward open honesty of Huss, or the craft of Cajetan was opposed to the rough, brusque, mistaken (if you will, but) HONEST Luther. These seem to me the same weapons which are being employed to-day, and I cannot bear to think that we should be tempted to try ourselves to employ them. The documents you send me appear, to my judgement, to show the persistence of these characteristics on the part of Roman controversialists. You will not, probably, agree with me, but I have told you frankly what I think and what I dread, and that is what you would have wished me to do.

A conversation of the friendliest kind followed between Davidson and Halifax. The latter was indeed the most grateful and eager of ambassadors. He was also the most transparently innocent. As Cardinal Vaughan wrote to the Archbishop of Toledo, 'I believe his Lordship to be incapable of deceiving anyone'. But his fundamental defect as an ambassador lay in a complete inability to see the real difficulties, as others saw them, or to imagine any other picture of the Church of Rome than the picture which he saw, or any other picture of the Church of England than that on which he desired the Pope to gaze. As Archbishop Benson said, 'Halifax is like a solitary player of chess, and wants to make all the moves on the board himself, on both sides'.[1]

That very same week (April 22) the Pope's encyclical *Ad Anglos* appeared, urging the English nation to come back to the Church, and showing no sign of recognition that there was such a body as the Church of England.

A year later, in September 1896, the Papal Bull *Apostolicae Curae* was published, condemning Anglican Orders. All hopes of any response to the Halifax overtures were destroyed. The wisdom of those who had urged the Archbishop to have nothing whatever to do with an inquiry into Anglican Orders was proved to the hilt. In due course the *Responsio*, a Vindication of Anglican Orders by Archbishops Temple and Maclagan, was given to the world. But the chapter was closed, and the next chapter was not to begin until thirty years later, with the help of the same principal collaborators, under the auspices of Cardinal Mercier at Malines.

[1] *Life*, vol. ii, p. 608.

CHAPTER XI

THE BISHOP AND THE QUEEN. FAREWELL TO ROCHESTER

Lord Treasurer is at Windsor too: they will be going and coming all summer, while the Queen is there and the town is empty. DEAN SWIFT, *Journal to Stella*.

THROUGHOUT his four and a half years at Rochester, as the quotations from his private papers have already made plain, Bishop Davidson was in close and continuous touch with the Queen and the Royal Family.

I

Early in 1892, the Duke of Clarence died, a victim to a terrible epidemic of influenza. As the Archbishop of Canterbury was in Algiers and was told by the Prince of Wales himself on no account to return, the Bishop of Rochester took the funeral. Davidson notes the great dignity of the Prince in his grief.

> The Prince of Wales behaved splendidly. Devout, reverent, grave, and courteous to everyone, though showing all the while how his heart was rent. He said to me with tears in his eyes 'Well, I *am* glad you were able to officiate. It is what we all wished from the first. You are now a friend of so many years.'

He was at Osborne with the Queen in February, and by the Archbishop's wish discussed with Her Majesty the question of a Day of Humiliation or Prayer which had been suggested in connexion with the epidemic. But, he reported to Dr. Benson (February 7, 1892):

> This has not at present become a practical question, and the Queen was very guarded about it. It would be necessary to approach her again about it when the time comes, as I hope it may not come.

In the following summer came the marriage of Prince George (afterwards King George V) to Princess May (afterwards Queen Mary).

On June 10, 1893, the Bishop was at Richmond, and had a good deal of talk with Princess May and her mother, as they sat in the royal box at the horse-show, watching the jumping.

> I confess to feeling very hopeful indeed of her [Princess May] being

a success in her great position. There is a quiet energy and common sense about her which distinguish her. . . . I am glad to have had an opportunity of a good talk of this sort. Prince George too was most agreeable and ready to talk, and full of recollections of some talks he and I had before both at Windsor and at Sandringham, especially about the lives of working men and kindred subjects.

Thursday, July 6 was the day of the Royal Marriage. Sheppard, the subdean, who was in a great fuss about the whole proceedings, insisted on our going to St. James much too early, and we had a terribly long stand in the Chapel—in a position neither very dignified nor very pleasant—crowded beside the Altar. The Bishop of London with Dalton and Hervey on one side; myself with Sheppard and Glyn on the other; and the Archbishop in the middle. *He* had to utilise the occasion for preparing his little address. He had been told the day before by Prince George that there was to be no address. But on the morning of the wedding day the Queen sent *me* an autograph note to bid me be sure that the Archbishop knew all about the Service, and that he was to give an address! I could only send the note on to him by the messenger. He did wondrous well, and the address was perhaps better than it would have been, if the opportunity given had been greater.

At the end of July he went to Osborne.

Saturday, July 29. In the afternoon the Queen sent for me for a talk and I went with her into all sorts of subjects, including Prince George's marriage. . . . She also poured forth upon political subjects, and upon the German Emperor and his doings, and upon her own reminiscences of former years, and upon very private and personal thoughts indeed. I have seldom had a more interesting talk with her and I do feel for her the keenest possible affection and respect and sympathy.

The next entry shows the German Emperor himself in a very interesting light. Dr. Davidson often used to refer to the incident twenty years later, during the European War, pronouncing the words in italics with great gusto.

Sunday, July 30. I went with Bigge and Clarke and Munthe to leave our names on the Emperor's yacht, which was then in Cowes together with the Prince of Wales' and many others. The Emperor was himself on deck, and the Duke of Connaught who was with him saw me and came at once to say the Emperor wished to talk with me. I found him most agreeable and genial—very odd and opinionative, full of himself and his doings, full of the glory of the

German army and navy. He had been preaching that morning on board, he said, but the sermon was *mainly* written by his chaplain-general, only he altered it to suit his congregation of sailors, '*leaving out all dogmatic trash*'. (Those were his words.) He also spoke of the good done by the German army chaplains going *into action* with the troops and 'blessing them before they charge, just as in the Middle Ages'. Also of the friendship subsisting between the Roman Catholic and the Protestant chaplains. 'They do not both of them think the other a damned heathen you know'; and a great deal more to the like effect. I enjoyed my talk with him very much.

On July 7, 1894, the Bishop and Mrs. Davidson went to Windsor, where he preached in the mausoleum and had a long talk with the Queen.

She poured forth upon both public and private matters, making me (as an invalid) *sit* beside her. She spoke of the Cesarewitch and his marriage, and the question of the Greek Church. Also of the whole question of the marriages of Princesses and its difficulty, illustrating her views by all sorts of anecdotes and facts about the marriages and *non-marriages* in her own family and grand-children, too private for recording even here. . . . In the evening after dinner I had a long talk to the Cesarewitch. . . . He gave me the best account I have ever heard of the position and history of the Greek Church in modern times and its relation to the State, and he expressed repeatedly and strongly his own ardent wish for a reunion between the Eastern and Anglican Churches.

Early in 1895 the Bishop was in close consultation with the Queen about changes on the Staff, due to the death of Sir John Cowell (in August 1894) and also the hopeless illness of Sir Henry Ponsonby. But, after being unwell for some time, on February 12, 1895, he was seized with the old symptoms, and a very violent attack of haemorrhage; and he wrote 'I imagine that on February 12 I very nearly died'. He could not therefore go with the Queen to the Riviera and officiate as her Chaplain:

It was a great disappointment not to go to Cimiez. I had been having much confidential work with respect to the Queen's re-arrangement of her staff in consequence of Sir Henry Ponsonby's hopeless illness, which had come suddenly in January. In particular at Osborne January 19–22 I had one very delicate and confidential job assigned me after another. The Queen wrote me afterwards an exceedingly kind and appreciative letter as to the help I had given her and the value to her of my friendship. All this had made me specially eager to be with her on the Riviera when the new arrangements as to Bigge and Edwards were to be tested. But it was not to be. I spent [four] weeks in bed—Edith was, as always, *the* most useful, helpful, and inspiring of wives that any man—sick or whole—could have, and the tax on her was necessarily great.

II

Dr. Davidson's advice was also still continually asked in connexion with ecclesiastical appointments. There was, for example, the case of Dr. Percival and the See of Hereford.[1] The Bishop had his alarming third illness, but his Journal says:

> I had during my illness a grave responsibility with regard to the appointment of Percival to the Bishopric of Hereford.

The Queen was not at all disposed to favour the appointment of a Welsh Church disestablisher to an English see. The Bishop of Rochester, however, urged that while the appointment by the Prime Minister was a grave risk, it was a risk for which the Prime Minister was responsible, and he said, writing to Sir Arthur Bigge:

The BISHOP OF ROCHESTER *to* SIR ARTHUR BIGGE

Kennington. 23 January, 1895.[2]

> Considering the high qualities and merits of Dr. Percival, I certainly see great difficulty in the Queen giving an absolute refusal, on the single ground of his opinions upon one political question of the hour.

He suggested that, instead, the Queen should raise the issue of acceptability:

> What would certainly happen would be that he would be placed in grave difficulties with his own clergy, and this I think the Queen might—as in the draft I have sketched—point out to Lord Rosebery, and ask him for some reassurance—(which he will find it difficult to give in any cogent form).
>
> This course appears to me perfectly fair both to Lord Rosebery and to the Church, and in complete accord with the attitude the Queen has, I think, always taken with respect to ecclesiastical appointments.

Lord Rosebery, in reply to the Queen, who had written on the

[1] 'By the death of Bishop Atlay of Hereford I succeeded to a seat in the House of Lords, and took my seat on the day of the opening of Parliament' (Journal, Jan. 1895).

[2] *Letters of Queen Victoria*, 3rd series, vol. ii, pp. 468–72.

lines suggested by Davidson, did not touch on the objection of acceptability. He simply stated that in Wales, though not in England, the Church of England had lost her authority over the mass of the people and therefore, as the diocese of Hereford contained some thirteen Welsh parishes, it would not be possible for Lord Rosebery, as in the case of Bath, to submit the name of a prelate in favour of the Church Establishment in Wales. On the Bishop of Rochester's advice, the Queen then wrote reiterating the objection as to acceptability, but concluded by telling Lord Rosebery that the responsibility must rest with him.

A few months later there was another battle of letters, on the political character of Lord Rosebery's appointments, arising out of the recent nomination of Dr. Fremantle to the Deanery of Ripon:

The BISHOP OF ROCHESTER *to* SIR ARTHUR BIGGE

Saltwood, Hythe. 8th April 1895.

I am much interested in what you tell me about Ripon Deanery. I know Fremantle intimately. He was once Chaplain to Archbishop Tait. He is a thorough gentleman in all ways, and this commends his Liberal sentiments to many who would not otherwise find them acceptable. He is a strong Liberal, politically, and eke ecclesiastically, and Mrs. Fremantle is the same. . . .

If Rosebery should nominate for the Canterbury Deanery another strong political Liberal, I venture to think the Queen might with great appropriateness point out to him that he has been somewhat markedly political in his nominations. The Bishopric of Hereford, and the Deaneries of Hereford, Durham, Winchester, and Ripon having all been filled by men noted as his political partisans, (though excellent in themselves). So with his Canonries, both at Westminster and Canterbury.

No recent Prime Minister has I think made his political bias quite so prominent in his ecclesiastical nominations.

Sir Arthur Bigge followed the Bishop's suggestion, and Lord Rosebery 'who cannot help being chagrined at the views expressed' in Sir Arthur Bigge's letter, caused a detailed reply to be sent, incidentally remarking (April 16, 1895):

G. H. MURRAY, ESQ., *to* SIR ARTHUR BIGGE

For this question of political church appointments has been unfortunately pressed to the front not by Lord Rosebery, but by the late Conservative Administration. Lord Salisbury practically ostracised Liberal Churchmen, and during the whole of his Administration no one had a chance of preferment who was not a supporter of his Government.

This, I think, would not be denied by Lord Salisbury himself; and yet Lord Rosebery cannot help wondering if any such remonstrance was ever addressed to that Prime Minister on the one-sided character of his Church appointments.

The Bishop of Rochester replied by drawing up a list of Mr. Gladstone's appointments (2 Deans, 1 Canon), followed by Lord Rosebery's appointments (1 Bishop, 4 Deans, 3 Canons), as a consecutive series, all of them belonging to the 'distinctively Liberal' Party;[1] and suggesting that Lord Rosebery's attention be called 'to the danger of prolonging unduly a series of appointments of men who are many of them *marked* as political partisans'. He added (April 23, 1895):

The BISHOP OF ROCHESTER *to* SIR ARTHUR BIGGE

But I do think it will be well Lord Rosebery should be told that he is mistaken in supposing no similar remonstrance or rather *suggestion* was made to Lord Salisbury. I could name off-hand three cases at least in which the Queen definitely *vetoed* nominations of Lord Salisbury's because the men seemed SIMPLY to be political supporters and *all* these were to *Bishoprics*! It would also be most untrue to say that all Lord Salisbury's appointments were political supporters in the true sense. What of Westcott at Durham, or Creighton at Peterborough, or Perowne at Worcester, or even myself?

The suggestion was taken.[2]

In July there are two interesting extracts from the Journal just after the change of Government, when Lord Rosebery had made way for Lord Salisbury, the first describing a dinner with Rosebery, the second a talk with the Queen:

Windsor Castle. Sunday night 7 July 1895.

Since the last entry we have had a stirring week in public affairs. The new Government is formed and I have many friends in high places therein.

On Monday last I dined with Rosebery. The dinner was to have been in Downing Street, but he had left office! and his private

[1] '. . . and Bishop Kennion [Bath and Wells] has certainly in no way marked himself to the contrary, except as to Disestablishment.'

[2] See *Letters of Queen Victoria*, 3rd series, vol. ii, p. 498 (for Lt.-Col. Bigge's letter).

house is under repair. So we dined at the Reform Club, the party being—Rosebery, Lord Acton, Professor Powell (Rosebery's nominee to Oxford History Chair), Farrar, Lecky, Dean Stephens, Henry James (Novelist), Spencer Walpole, Sir J. Lubbock, myself, Traill the journalist, and Sir Alfred Lyall. I sat next Rosebery and had a great deal of talk about Abdul Karim and many other matters. I was amused by a slip of Acton's. Speaking across the table with reference to a discussion on Westminster Abbey and the burial therein of many inferior men, Rosebery commented on the big statues—the large space required and the present fulness—and someone alluded to Dizzy's statue. Acton replied 'Yes—At all events there is no room for *primroses*'. Nobody said aught. . . .

I came here yesterday—Arthur Balfour and Sir M. White Ridley here last night—Much good talking. The Queen not very lively, being sadly upset by the illness (and now the death) of Francis Clark, who has been her 'Highland attendant' for 24 years. . . . I dined both last night and this evening with Her Majesty and had a good bit of talk. She is not specially happy I think at the change of government. In her heart I think she *personally* likes Rosebery, Bannerman, Spencer and Fowler better than their successors. She told me of her talks with Rosebery—and her letters to him and remonstrances against extreme words and deeds. She has persuaded herself that Rosebery told her some time ago not to be alarmed by the attack on House of Lords, as it didn't really mean anything. But I think she must either have exaggerated or misunderstood his words. He could hardly have so committed himself!

On the whole I don't think the Queen looking very well, and her blindness is evidently a sore trial, though she says it is not increasing much if at all.

I had much quiet talk on the personal side of the political changes—but must not put it down.

III

During June 1895, Bishop Davidson was gradually recovering from the last of the three grave illnesses which marked the Rochester episcopate. Among the letters of encouragement, which he received at the time, was a very warm one from his predecessor, Bishop Thorold, welcoming his 'clear, strong and tranquil handwriting', and bidding him take a whole year's rest. 'Your life, my dear Bishop, is in my mind one of the three most important on our Bench.'

On July 28 Bishop Thorold himself died, and Bishop Davidson attended his funeral in Winchester Cathedral. Lord Rosebery had gone out of office at the beginning of the month, and Lord Salisbury was now Prime Minister.

> I knew that it would be the Queen's personal wish that I should succeed him as Bishop of Winchester. I was not so sure that this would be Lord Salisbury's wish and I felt that such an appointment might not be generally acceptable.

The Davidsons went north on July 30. While at Durham he received in cipher the following telegram from Osborne:

Telegram to the BISHOP OF ROCHESTER

What do you think of Talbot for Rochester?

BIGGE.

The telegram puzzled him, and he wired back to that effect. Next morning a telegram came as follows:

Telegram to the BISHOP OF ROCHESTER

Queen wishes me to say you will hear if not done so already offering you Winchester which she hopes you will accept and Talbot to succeed you.

BIGGE.

Bishop Davidson returned immediately to London, and saw Dr. Barlow and the Archbishop of Canterbury. Both were emphatically in favour of acceptance. Dr. Barlow 'was most clear and strong on medical grounds that Farnham and the open air work in the diocese of Winchester would be far less perilous in all ways'.

It appeared that the delay had been due to the fact that 'Lord Salisbury's submission of my name to the Queen had been *crossed* by the Queen's letter to Lord Salisbury asking him to consider my name':

The MARQUESS OF SALISBURY *to the* BISHOP OF ROCHESTER

Hatfield House, Hatfield, Herts.
August 3. 1895.

I am authorised by Her Majesty to propose to you that you should be translated to the See of Winchester in place of the most lamented Bishop Thorold. I have naturally received the expression of many opinions from persons connected with the Diocese; and I believe that your acceptance of the see would be generally welcomed with great satisfaction.

The Bishop accepted the Prime Minister's offer, and in a letter to the three Archdeacons, made public at the time, explained the reasons which had led to his acceptance, as follows:

The BISHOP OF ROCHESTER *to the* ARCHDEACONS OF ROCHESTER, SOUTHWARK, *and* KINGSTON-ON-THAMES

Kennington. 7th August, 1895.

Among the gifts required for the due discharge of our town work is physical strength of a peculiar sort. To name one point only out of several. The demand upon the Bishop for *evening* work in this poorest region of London increases steadily, and, as I think, most rightly. In no other way can our multiplying Confirmations take their proper place in the life of each parish: at no other hours can our gatherings, great and small, of working men and women be appropriately held. But my recent illness has proved that from such evening duty I must, for some time to come, be largely debarred. In other ways too it has become clear to those by whose advice I am necessarily guided that the conditions of Episcopal work in South London, if that work be adequately performed, are such as involve a real risk of a return of the incapacitating illness which has already caused so much inconvenience to the Diocese.

On the other hand, I am led with confidence to believe that in the somewhat different conditions of work which belong to such a Diocese as Winchester I may reasonably hope to be able—so far as physical strength is concerned—to discharge to the full the duties, both Diocesan and general, belonging to the Bishop of that great See. I have the deliberate assurance of my medical adviser, before whom the facts have been carefully laid, that the anxiety with which he would regard my return to full work in the Diocese of Rochester does not apply to the work, equally absorbing and important, but different in character, which is required of a Bishop of Winchester.

In these circumstances my right course has seemed no longer doubtful.

CHAPTER XII

THE BISHOP OF WINCHESTER. A GENERAL CHAPTER

The Bishop is like a man that is surety for his friend; he is bound for many and for great sums. JEREMY TAYLOR. (A Sermon preached at the consecration of Two Archbishops and Ten Bishops, Dublin, 1660.)

FARNHAM CASTLE, to which Randall Davidson now went, is one of the most lovely of all episcopal houses, and, long after they had left, the Davidsons always returned to it with delight. It stood in a great park, at the head of the town, a beautiful building of fair red brick, with a Norman keep, most romantic of castles. All round was beautiful country; and in the park ranged fallow deer, which certainly the new Bishop had no desire to surrender. It was an old and famous castle, and not a little history of a secular kind had been made within its walls. Again, for a thousand years it had been the official residence of the Bishops of Winchester. All these things—history, beauty of architecture, country scenery, country activities, and the deer themselves—were the very things bound to fascinate and impress the spirit of Randall Davidson. And the purpose with which he went to Farnham, so very different a residence from the two houses knocked together in Kennington Park Road, is indicated in the letter which he wrote to his wife from Auckland Castle in September 1895:

The BISHOP OF WINCHESTER *to* MRS. DAVIDSON

29 Sept., 1895.

Certainly a river is worth a great deal in such a park. But I wouldn't exchange Farnham for this house, grand as it is. Farnham is far more interesting and I should say quite as convenient. I long to make Farnham as much of a loved centre for Winchester Diocese as this is for Durham. I don't see why we shouldn't, though of course our distances are greater and we haven't the same sort of stirring *mining* population to deal with. If YOU set your mind to it—and you will—I think it will be done if we live yet a bit.

One thing we may remark at once is the difference which the new home made to Davidson's health. Farnham and the Farnham air and exercise, and the journeying all over the diocese, by carriage, by steamer, and by rail, through Hampshire and West Surrey, across to the Channel Islands and the Isle of Wight, made him a new man. In later years Davidson smilingly declared, remembering the critics' fears, 'Whatever else the Diocese may have suffered from during my episcopate, it did not suffer from an invalid Diocesan.' And there is something further that must be said about the Castle and the Davidsons. Canon T. G. Gardiner, who was Rector of Farnham during most of the Davidsons' reign, writes as follows:

> The hospitality of the Davidsons knew no bounds. Then, as now, Church people were heard to complain that as Bishops were no longer feudal lords they should not reside in Castles or in Palaces! As a matter of fact the Castle, which could accommodate large numbers, was constantly, almost continuously, filled with guests. If Church workers, deaconesses, or rescue workers needed peace and quiet, Farnham Castle became their home for longer or shorter periods. If incumbents' wives were in danger of breaking down owing to the strain of an unpaid curacy and hard work, if problems of their children's education became insistent, if clergymen needed comfort, cheer, guidance or encouragement, they stayed for a week or more, and returned home helped in many ways. If missionaries returning from an extended spell of work overseas were in doubt as to whether they should return or undertake work in England, prolonged interviews 'in the study' coupled with the home life of the Castle helped to make plain the path that should be trod.

The Castle also came to be a centre of friendship for the town as well as for the diocese. Here the people of Farnham found an eager welcome from the Bishop and his lady. And from its walls and walks Mrs. Davidson, practical, strong, full of happiness and charm, used to sally forth to the town to visit and cheer. He was forty-eight and she just ten years younger—and their vitality and buoyancy were all the more positively felt by contrast with the age and failing health of the previous two Bishops of Winchester.

I

Randall Davidson did homage to the Queen at Balmoral on October 2, 1895. He was enthroned in Winchester Cathedral on October 15, as sixty-seventh successor to St. Swithun. In the same afternoon he was received as Visitor of Winchester College

Ad Portas, replying to the Senior Prefect's Latin speech of welcome in a speech of singularly felicitous Latin himself, for which he had secured the aid of the Master of Trinity, Dr. Butler. Two months later he was present at another kind of school function, for he opened two new Board Schools in Farnham and took the opportunity to express his satisfaction at the system of Board Schools and Church Schools working side by side in Farnham 'which is England in miniature'. There was not a little comment in Church quarters on his action at the time.

Looking back in 1906, three years after his Winchester episcopate had closed, the Bishop commented as follows:

> It is not very easy to summarise the work which I attempted or accomplished in my Winchester years 1895–1903. My hands were very full, and I can say without any doubt at all that what I enjoyed most was the purely Diocesan work—Confirmations and such-like duties. . . .

It is therefore to his diocesan work that we first turn.

We have already referred to his travels in the diocese. He was away constantly for a week at a time, as he moved about. He stayed in different houses, sometimes using a house as a centre from which to visit various parishes. And as the method of travel had to be slow—before the time of the motor-car—he used the opportunities of his nights, as well as his days, for getting a close personal knowledge of the clergy and the leading laymen. Many were the long waits in stations, and many the friendships he made with stationmasters on the line, who lent him their offices, where he wrote hundreds of letters. Besides, while he often had to go to Osborne to see the Queen, he was very skilful in fitting in diocesan work with his royal visits.

Here is his own description of the scene of his labours:

> The diocese is, I imagine, one of the most difficult in England to handle satisfactorily, perhaps the most difficult of all, combining as it does an immense area, with singularly awkward means of communication. The Solent is a most troublesome barrier between the Isle of Wight and the rest of the diocese, and the Channel Islands are an accretion of the most inconvenient sort possible, especially to Bishops who are not good sailors. Besides this it has quite other characteristics than those which usually belong to a country diocese. Portsmouth, Southampton, Aldershot, Bournemouth have extreme difficulties of their own, but with the problems

of town life I was better familiar than with the problems of English country life in rural parishes. I think I succeeded fairly well, and I certainly did my best to enter into those country parish difficulties and to advise the clergy how to meet them; but the task of visiting all the country areas proved more than I could overtake during my tenure of the See, and there are many parts of the diocese into the corners of which I never penetrated.

With this picture of the diocese before us, let us follow the method adopted in the case of Rochester and group together in this chapter certain special features of the diocesan work which stand out most clearly.

At Farnham itself, the most conspicuous result of his episcopate was the foundation of the Hostel for the training of young men for ordination. Right preparation for the ministry was one of the things for which the Bishop cared most deeply. He remembered his own training at the Temple, and believed that something rather different from the regular professional course was required for certain types of men:

Ordinations were among the happiest, perhaps quite the happiest of our duties at Farnham. The Castle is splendidly adapted for such gatherings and we were able there to arrange the Ember weeks in a way that had never been possible in Rochester Diocese with the inconveniences I have described. . . . My intercourse with the ordinands impressed upon me the need of more preparation places for the future clergy, many of whom are men who do not fit happily or usefully into the life of an ordinary Theological College.

The sense of such a need led him to give a very warm support to the venture of the new Rector of Farnham, the Rev. T. G. Gardiner, in July 1899, who, with material help from a well-to-do friend, Mr. Bolton, secured an adequate house in West Street, and started the Bishop's Hostel. In some notes on the Hostel written during the last year of his life, Davidson says:

In seeking for a Warden I consulted Westcott, but I forget whether the suggestion of B. K. Cunningham's name came from me or from him. Anyhow he knew Cunningham and wrote me a strong letter, saying that . . . his personality was such that it would be worth anything to secure him, and this decided me in favour of inviting him. He accepted. . . . Of course I could not myself give much time to the Hostel, but I determined that the men should be in close touch with me somehow. Accordingly they came on

Sunday evenings, and at other times too, to the Castle. . . . Cunningham undertook the training of the men, and Gardiner ranged in and out and gave superintendence and inspiration to the whole. We were, I think, very fortunate in the men who came as students, but we owe profound thanks to Cunningham for the teaching he gave. . . . He was absolutely free from any partisan allegiance within the Church and attracted men of widely differing sentiments and attainments. True, he was very deaf, but he possessed the power more than I have known in any other deaf man of overriding it by his beaming power of affection and sympathy. . . . The men did a good deal of theological work for him, and so far as I could judge his teaching was really excellent. During all my later years at Farnham I found one of my chiefest joys in this Farnham Hostel or Brotherhood. It was quite different from any Theological College I have known, and yet it is a little hard to define exactly what made it unlike other Colleges. There was more freedom; there was less ecclesiastical formality, and the numbers were small. With two such guides as Thory Gardiner and B. K. Cunningham, the very notion of formality and conventional regulations were alien to the place. . . . It was more like what I had myself experienced in the Temple under Dr. Vaughan though there were of course marked differences. . . .

. . . I tried never to be out of touch with any part of the life, and our Sunday evenings remain vivid in my memory.

Canon T. G. Gardiner writes:

. . . The entrance to the Hostel was through Farnham Castle, that is to say all applications for admission were considered, approved or rejected, by Dr. Davidson himself. He interviewed all candidates. So far as the time at his disposal allowed he saw much of individuals, and on Sunday evenings all members of the Hostel supped at the Castle. Difficulties and questions which had not been solved satisfactorily in the Common Room at the Hostel were, after notice, brought up for frank and free discussion. With singular patience, with great frankness, he was prepared to give his own views emphasising the Church of England position, the very greatest help to men preparing to make of their lives a great adventure, in which to undertake a measureless responsibility. . . . These Sunday evenings at the Castle stand out in the memory of many men in country parsonages and overseas to-day, who look back with gratitude and affection to their time at the Hostel. . . . Sometimes the Bishop read aloud such books as George Herbert's *Country Parson*, and serious discussion was illuminated by touches of pawky Scotch humour which tended to banish diffidence and self-consciousness, setting everyone at his ease.

Mrs. Davidson shared the Bishop's interest in all that concerned the Hostel; and all those who resided there went out to their work with a clear insight into the foundations of a Christian home of the highest type.

As Bishop of Winchester he again had much to do with the revival of the order of Deaconesses in the Church of England. The Winchester diocese had been concerned in the early stages of that revival, though on somewhat different lines from Bishop Thorold's plans in Rochester:

A little body of Deaconesses had been established at Farnham under Bishop Harold Browne, who took a keen interest in the question of the revival of the Order. But when the deaconesses had become established as a community, the community itself took a somewhat different form and became virtually a Sisterhood, very much as has happened in London diocese, where the Deaconesses are really Sisters first and Deaconesses afterwards.

A beautiful house was ultimately built and equipped in Portsmouth, mainly by the allocation thereto of money placed in the hands of Bishop and Mrs. Harold Browne, and when I came to the diocese the community was flourishing there in its somewhat hybrid character of something between a Sisterhood and a Deaconess Community. At its head was that admirable and capable lady, Emma Day, who, originally Deaconess Emma, had become Sister Emma and ere my time had developed into Mother Emma, with all the insignia appropriate to the Superior of a Sisterhood.

I set myself to make the best of these conditions and struggled long to believe that it was possible to have Deaconesses who were also Sisters and yet to preserve the Deaconess character in its true elements, but my emphasis on the Deaconess side of the question, though it raised the ideal of what a Deaconess should be, and facilitated the examinations as to the study and training acquired by each woman during the probationary period, did not please everybody, and though I personally had retained the friendliest relations with them all, and threw myself earnestly into their interests and their work, it was impossible to prevent elements of friction becoming developed, and since Bishop Ryle succeeded me the Community has been somewhat largely reconstituted upon lines more definitely in accord with the Deaconess idea.

Into the details of this I need not enter, but no record of the work I tried to do in Winchester Diocese would be complete without some such reference as I have given to the question of these ladies and their work which occupied a considerable portion of the time and energies both of myself as Diocesan and of Bishop Lyttelton of Southampton.

It is I think through such experimental endeavours as these that the Church of England will win its way to the right solution of a very difficult problem—what are the true lines upon which Deaconess life can rightly and usefully be revived in England in our own day.

He had a large correspondence with Sister Emma, and the following letter is typical both of his considerateness and of his sense of proportion:

The BISHOP OF WINCHESTER *to* SISTER EMMA

Osborne, 14 Aug. '97.

One point in what you told me yesterday has, as you will know, been giving me some cause for thought, though it is not a great matter.

If I rightly understand, the point is this. You have noticed of late a little departure from the uniformity of usage hitherto followed by all the Sisters in the matter of personal attitude and procedure during the Celebration and administration of Holy Communion.

I gather that the divergence is a purely personal thing in no way affecting, of course, the conduct of Divine Service—mere details as to genuflexion before going forward to receive, and an attitude of unusual prostration at the time of reception, and possibly other similar details. These are trifling matters, the usages being probably almost instinctive on the part of those who adopt them, who are perhaps accustomed so to do in their parish Churches. I should be the last to wish to lay down authoritatively any *rule* as to such details and in an ordinary congregation in a parish Church one would *expect* such small divergences to be common and to attract no attention, so different are the lives, habits, opinions, etc. of different families or individual worshippers many of whom may be strangers belonging to different congregations. But in a Community like ours there is not of course the same variety as in a parish congregation and divergences of usage and manner will obviously be more noticeable if they occur, and may be—nay rather *must* be—distracting to some communicants. I do feel strongly that in such a Community as ours there ought to be as little as possible of such diversity in noteworthy outward things. That there should be some diversity as to the precise personal devotions used, or the small unobtrusive details of personal action, is inevitable—nor is such diversity in *unobservable* trifles to be deprecated. But I think the feeling of those best able to judge will probably be unanimous that it is distracting and may even become slightly mischievous should divergence of usage become common in the more noticeable things.

One knows well that each is simply acting as she feels to be most conducive to her own soul's good and that there is no sort of *intention* to create petty differences. But it is precisely one of those cases in which St. Paul's principles as to *mutual* consideration and *mutual* help in trifles comes to the front—and a Community as I have said differs widely in such respects from an ordinary mixed congregation where uniformity of use would practically be unobtainable.

We adhere to our rule of conforming in our several parishes to the parish usage where such usage can be said to exist. This may involve for some Sisters a slight effort of personal care, or even a slight sacrifice of personal inclination. If so, let us be very sure that 'He who seeth in secret' accepts the devotion as offered to Him whatever its precise outward form.

Apply the same principle to our services and congregational use in our Community chapel. Please let me make it quite clear that I am in no way whatever prescribing in such details the exact 'use' which should be followed. I greatly prefer to leave such small details to the Christian good sense of the Community. All I ask is that, so far as possible, we should follow *one* usage even at the sacrifice—either in one direction or the other—of individual taste and inclination.

In larger matters you will I hope always find me ready to give positive direction and guidance where it is wanted. I regard my association with St. Andrew's as one of the very highest privileges of my office, and I thank God every day for the blessing He is vouchsafing to your manifold works—and pray with a full heart that His Presence may abide among you.

You will use your own discretion as to making any use of this letter.

The Bishop tried to do the main part of the Confirmation work himself—though this did not in fact prove possible. But he delighted in his Confirmations wherever they were held—and there is an interesting note of the parent's gratitude for the Bishop's sympathy, in the following letter written after an Epsom confirmation, by Lord Rosebery:

The Earl of Rosebery *to the* Bishop of Winchester

The Durdans, Epsom.
April 9, 1896.

How can I thank you enough for your kindness to my little girls. I am quite stupefied. To find time to write to either is surprising, but I am dumbfounded by your writing to both, and such beautiful, heartfelt, simple letters.

You have won all hearts here.

Another illustration of the strong personal sympathy both of the Bishop and Mrs. Davidson is found in the special plans for clergy wives:

Among the most delightful and profitable of our endeavours at Farnham I should place what we called 'Clergy Wives Days'. I do not know that in any other Diocese, gatherings had been held by the Bishop corresponding to those which we inaugurated at Farnham. We took a portion of the Diocese and invited the wives of all the Clergy resident therein to visit us at Farnham for a couple of days. They were not what is technically known as 'quiet days'. Those are common enough, but we tried to combine the advantages which a quiet day offers with something rather more stimulating intellectually, and calculated to cheer and brighten up lives which often have rather too many quiet days of a prosaic sort.

The response which this endeavour met with, and the enthusiastic and almost embarrassing warmth of the gratitude evinced by those ladies who had taken advantage of them gave abundant evidence of their genuine usefulness. Here again we were preeminently fortunate in having such a home as Farnham Castle wherein to gather the ladies. The house and its surroundings are ideally well fitted for the purpose.

Bishop Arthur Lyttelton's help, as Suffragan Bishop, has already been mentioned in connexion with Deaconesses. There were at different times four Suffragan Bishops—of whom Bishop Davidson writes thus:

When I came to the Diocese I found Bishop Sumner of Guildford, nominally a Suffragan, but practically doing very little work owing to failing health. He had not, I think, greatly appreciated Bishop Thorold, and he showed a readiness to do more for me than he had done for him. Also there was Bishop Awdry as Bishop of Southampton, but he was appointed to be Bishop in Japan in the following Spring, so I had little advantage from his help. As his successor I nominated my old friend, George Fisher, who had preceded me in my curacy at Dartford, and until his health gave way and his domestic anxieties . . . told upon his nerves, he was both popular and effective. Then I secured as his successor Arthur Lyttelton, who soon became one of my fastest friends, and whose qualifications and merits it is impossible to exaggerate. I believe him to have been a man fit for any position whatever in the Church. His intense goodness, his sound judgement, his wide literary knowledge, and his attractive personality, set him apart from most other men whom I have known. His fatal illness began during my last year at Winchester, and he died just when I was leaving the Diocese. The account of him in the preface to his essays edited by Bishop Talbot is in every way worthy of him.

A single word should also be said about the Bishop's relations with the Cathedral authorities. In 1900, Dr. Davidson conducted a Visitation of Winchester Cathedral, and the letters and records show that at Winchester (just as at Rochester) Bishop and Dean were on the most cordial terms. The following passage in a letter from the Dean,[1] in answer to a kindly act of co-operation on the Bishop's part, shows the confidence and affection existing between them:

The DEAN OF WINCHESTER *to the* BISHOP OF WINCHESTER

October 28, 1900.

In reply to your extremely kind letter received this morning I will only say that I thank you most heartily for it, and assure you that it is one of the greatest comforts of my life in this place to have a Bishop for whom, and with whom I can work with such entire cordiality, and on whom I can rely with such perfect confidence for wise and friendly counsel in all matters of difficulty and doubt.

Bishop Davidson does not say much actually of himself in his reminiscences of the Farnham days. But as we read his reflections on the different aspects of his work, and watch him grappling with some of his problems, we can see a development, and an increasing sureness of his strength. At Windsor he had been alert and eager, and had proved perhaps a little more actively influential behind the scenes than those outside the inner Lambeth circle altogether relished. At Rochester he received a series of shocks, and disappointments, caused by his bouts of grave ill-

[1] Dr. W. R. W. Stephens.

ness—and these had shaken him much. He therefore entered on his labours as Bishop of Winchester with much less sureness, and something more of apprehension, than he would have displayed had he passed immediately from the Deanery of Windsor to Farnham Castle. There was a certain puzzled look at times on his face. It was with him for a while at Lambeth also, though increasingly an inner peace and strength found their outward expression. But the point is worth just this passing note. And it may be best brought out through a sketch drawn by an old friend, Sir Michael Sadler, with the graphic touch at the end. Like other people Sir Michael was struck by Bishop Davidson's eyes—and he writes:

> His eyes, brave and faithful as a dog's, were a little strained by uncertainty and apprehension. To a stranger his expression at times wore the appearance of discomposure and almost of intellectual distress. He saw, no one saw more clearly, the dislocation of things. In the inner chamber of his heart and mind he was at peace. But on the plane of logical definition he (like all of us) was often at a loss how to reconcile beliefs which he knew to be true with facts which cannot be ignored. The strain of this dubiety left its mark on his countenance. I remember once getting into a train which had reached Weybridge from Farnham and Winchester. I found Sir Edward Grey, as he then was, sitting at one window, the future Archbishop at the other. They did not converse. But when Dr. Davidson had got out at Vauxhall, Sir Edward Grey asked me 'Who was that Bishop with such a puzzled face?'

II

Last, we note the Bishop's sense of responsibility with regard to Diocesan Conferences, and his utterances at such times:

> I found it worth while to take great pains with my central utterances in the Diocese. In 1899 I held a visitation and delivered a Charge wherein I tried to deal with thoroughness as well as fairness with two great questions;—Eucharistic worship, and Confession. I spent the summer holiday at Farnham working hard upon this Charge, and as I re-read it now I am inclined to think that it is a really good bit of work and that I ought to republish its permanent and non-local parts as a book. What I had said upon Confession was I believe taken as the textbook in the Conference which took place a few years later at Fulham upon that

subject, and my Catena of quotations and references is, so far as I know, the most complete thing of its kind now published. . . .

I also every year, except the Visitation year (1899), delivered a very carefully prepared Address at the opening of the Diocesan Conference. To these I devoted a good deal of time and I know that some of our wisest men thought it had been worth while. Parts of these also I might I think with advantage republish as a book.

In a note added later Dr. Davidson, then Archbishop of Canterbury, referred as follows to that portion of his Charge of 1899 which dealt with the Holy Communion:

With the other subject, Eucharistic Worship, I also dealt with great care, but as I re-read it in later years I find it very inadequate in its treatment, if treatment it can be called, on the objective side of the Holy Eucharist. It is all about Communion, and I have no wish to alter what I said on that part of the question; but I pass far too lightly over the other ground and deal most insufficiently with the sort of question which has led since then to the movement for Reservation etc.

It is also interesting—and was perhaps disquieting even at the time to Bishop Davidson—to note that Sir William Harcourt, who was then engaged in a long correspondence with the Bishop, wrote a letter on November 4, 1899, thanking him for his Charge and praising it warmly, and adding with regard to Holy Communion:

The Rt. Hon. Sir William Harcourt *to the* Bishop of Winchester

Your chapter on the 'Holy Communion' places that which is the keystone of the whole matter on a firm footing and vindicates the Protestant 'Communion of the faithful' against the Romish doctrines of the 'Priestly Sacrifice' in a manner more satisfactory than I have yet seen it done. It is sound and thorough Anglicanism, worthy of Hooker.

Sixty-seven pages in all, that is over one-third of the whole Charge, were devoted to 'The Holy Communion'. And as the doctrine of the Eucharist was to play so large a part in the whole question of the Prayer Book and its use during the next thirty years, it may be well to give a brief summary of the position which Davidson held in 1899. The treatment is extensive and contains a remarkable series of extracts from leading Anglican Divines from Cranmer to Benson. The Bishop stated the contrast between the unreformed and the reformed Order of Holy Communion as follows:

> What, then, speaking generally and omitting unimportant details, were the principal differences between a Celebration of Holy Communion in the reign of Charles II, and the corresponding Service in the reign of Henry VIII? Or, if you will pardon me for putting it in such a form, what contrasts would have been apparent to Sir Thomas More if he could have returned from the unseen world to be present at a Celebration of Holy Communion, say, by Bishop Morley, in Winchester Cathedral?
>
> Primarily, and most obviously, four: the Service was said in English, not in Latin: it was simplified in many of the accompaniments which strike the eye: it was a general Communion of the people: and lastly, the Office itself was altered and re-arranged.[1]

And he reduced the principles on which the compilers of our Prayer Book acted to three:

> The Reformers set themselves:
>
> I. To restore the original idea of Communion as an essential part of the Sacramental rite.
>
> II. To provide that everything done or said should be visible and easy to be understood by all.
>
> III. To remove sternly whatever had been found by experience to lead to superstition or to a materialistic view of the Sacrament.[2]

First then, he emphasized the great importance of Communion,—and claimed that 'the whole structure of the Service, as it grew into the form with which we are familiar, has evidence stamped upon it that it was meant and fashioned for those who then and there were themselves the Communicants'.[3]

He also maintained that this principle of making the Communion of the people an essential part of the Eucharistic Service 'was deliberately adopted, and continuously supported by High Churchmen no less than by Low Churchmen, as a return to Scriptural and primitive teaching about the Holy Sacrament'.[4] He recalled the almost scornful words of Bishop Andrewes:

> "Partake"—how? By receiving and eating, as the Saviour commanded; for as to "partaking by praying", it is a modern and new-fangled kind of partaking, newer even than your Private Mass.'[5]

[1] *A Charge delivered to the Clergy of the Diocese of Winchester*, 1899, by Randall T. Davidson, Bishop: Macmillan & Co., 1899, p. 54.

[2] Ibid., p. 55. [3] Ibid., p. 68. [4] Ibid., p. 74.

[5] Ibid., p. 71. See *Responsio ad Bellarmine*, p. 250: Anglo-Catholic Library.

Next he laid stress on 'openness' as the tenor of the Book of Common Prayer:

> The Reformers set themselves to clear away, so far as possible, the cloud of mystery in which the Ritual of the Mass had been shrouded from popular understanding.[1]

He quoted Archbishop Benson's striking words in the Lincoln Judgement with whole-hearted approval:

> 'By the use of the mother tongue; by the audibleness of every prayer; by the Priest's prayers being made identical with the prayers of the congregation; by the part of the clerks being taken by the people; by the removal of the invisible and inaudible ceremonial, the English Church, as one of her special works in the history of the Catholic Church, restored the ancient share and right of the people in Divine Service.'[2]

He finally laid great stress on the danger of superstition. He acknowledged his sense of the mysteriousness of the question of 'the manner in which the Lord uses the Consecrated Elements of bread and wine so as to make us verily and indeed partakers of His Body and His Blood'.[3] He expressed his view of the peril and difficulty against which the Reformers worked and guarded thus —and the quotation is crucial for a proper understanding of the later controversies with regard to Reservation:

> The peril or difficulty centred, as was to be expected, in the attitude both of Priest and people towards the Consecrated Elements themselves. It was not for nothing that the sweeping change was made by which all such rubrics as the following were clean removed from the Office of Holy Communion. I quote from the Sarum Missal:
>
> > 'These words [*Hoc est enim Corpus Meum*] ought to be said in one and the same breath without pause. After these words let the Priest incline to the Host, and afterwards elevate It above his forehead, that It may be seen by the people; and reverently replace It before the chalice, making a cross with the same.'[4]

[1] *A Charge delivered to the Clergy of the Diocese of Winchester*, p. 77.

[2] Ibid., p. 77.

[3] Ibid., p. 80.

[4] '*Debent ista verba proferri cum uno spiritu et sub una prolatione, nulla pausatione interposita. Post haec verba inclinet se Sacerdos ad hostiam,* [*et capite inclinato illam adoret*] *et postea elevet eam supra frontem ut possit a populo videri; et reverenter illam reponat ante calicem in modum crucis per eandem factae.*

The clause within brackets was added to the Sarum Missal in 1554, after the reconciliation with Rome.' [Footnote in Charge.]

It would be as easy as it is needless to multiply such quotations.

It is difficult to picture a greater contrast than that which the whole series of these elaborate rubrics presents to the simple directions in our successive Prayer Books. Nor, I am persuaded, can any man who looks calmly into the facts have any doubt that the absence of the old directions from the new Book was an absence due to determined and deliberate rejection. People may approve or disapprove of what Cranmer and his colleagues did, but that their action in this particular respect was intentional and significant is placed beyond question by the existing letters and sermons of the men themselves.* They set themselves, by deliberate changes both in the Rubrics and in the text of the Prayers, to lop off unsparingly what they deemed the 'dangerous deceits' which had grown out of the doctrine of Transubstantiation. We have seen that the new Service was made pre-eminently a Communion, and a Communion in both kinds. We have seen that it was popularised and translated and simplified. But these things might have been effected without any marked change of actual doctrine. Not so the changes of which we are now speaking. They were distinctly intended, and thoughtfully and soberly framed, to render impossible the sort of 'element-worship' (I use the words of Archbishop Benson),† which had in the popular mind replaced the true doctrine of the Holy Sacrament.

This protest against a materialistic doctrine of the Presence of Christ in the Consecrated Elements, and against the adoration superstitiously paid to them in consequence, was reiterated, as we know, by nearly every leading English Reformer throughout the Sixteenth Century.‡[1]

With this principle firmly declared, Davidson gave expression to some strong criticism of certain mischievous manuals in use at the time; and spoke thus of the 'Central Service' of the day:

What we all desire to see is that the Holy Communion may indeed become for all the great Service of the Lord's Day, and that every Christian man, by taking his full part therein, may show the Lord's

* See, e.g., Cranmer, *Answer to the Devon Rebels*, Art. iv; *Works*, Park. Soc. i, p. 173; and *Answer to Gardiner*, iv. 9, Park. Soc., p. 229, &c., &c.

† *The Seven Gifts*, p. 167.

‡ See, e.g. Cranmer, *On the Lord's Supper*, Park. Soc., pp. 228–9, 234–5; Jewel, *Sermon on 1 Cor. xi. 23; Works*, Park. Soc. i. 15, 16; and *Controversy with Harding*, Art. VII, ib., pp. 512–13; Art. VIII, pp. 514–552; and *Sermon on Haggai i. 2*, ib., p. 990; Becon, *Catechism*, Part V, Park. Soc., pp. 251, 265–7, 283, &c. Ridley and Latimer, *Conference*, Park. Soc., pp. 106–7. Examples might easily be multiplied.

[1] *A Charge delivered to the Clergy of the Diocese of Winchester*, pp. 84–6.

death till He come. But we are very far as yet from realising in England that Scriptural and primitive ideal.

As a matter of fact, what has happened in a good many of our town parishes, and in a few country parishes, has unhappily been this. To magnify the honour of the Sacramental Service—to 'place it in its proper central position'—all have been urged to attend it, though the Communicants are few: nay, sometimes actual Communion thereat has been even discouraged. This, surely, however excellent the intention, is a fundamental and grievous error. To teach people better to value and to use the Holy Sacrament, it is being celebrated in a way against which our Church of England has emphatically set its face. The act of the people's Communion, one of the main essentials of the Rite, is slighted, and the seeds of a false doctrine of the Eucharist are week by week sown in the minds of the ignorant and the young.[1]

And he uttered a final warning:

The history of the Church in other lands rings out for us a warning note. The sturdy common-sense of most English Churchmen will, I think, respond to that warning. We have a wholesome dislike of needless obscurity or of a recondite esoteric symbolism in our Eucharistic Rite. Superstition does not fit in well with the national characteristics God has given us. . . . We have inherited in our Liturgy a Service strong in its Scriptural phraseology and tone, strong in its genuine and reverent simplicity, strong in its tacit appeal to the reason and intelligence of the worshipper. Do not, I beseech you, do anything to mar these characteristics. Does any one allege that, by omitting the elaboration of gesture and act prescribed in Rubrics other than our own, we diminish the reverence paid to our Blessed Lord present with us in His Sacrament? Rather we multiply that reverence tenfold, if we are worshipping Him aright. Simplicity can help, not hinder, the deepest possible devotion of body, soul, and spirit. It consists with the most eager care for seemliness and decorum in every particular. Such characteristics are distinctive, in all Christendom, of our English Liturgy. *Spartam nactus es: hanc exorna.*[2]

[1] *A Charge delivered to the Clergy of the Diocese of Winchester*, pp. 105–6.
[2] Ibid., pp. 118–19.

CHAPTER XIII

THE CLASH WITH FATHER DOLLING

The wise minister sees, and is concerned to see further, because government has a further concern: he sees the objects that are distant as well as those that are near, and all their remote relations, and even their indirect tendencies. . . . He considers his administration as a single day in the great year of government; but as a day that is affected by those which went before, and that must affect those which are to follow. BOLINGBROKE, *The Idea of a Patriot King*.

IT was a singular misfortune that Bishop Davidson, at the very outset of his Winchester episcopate, found himself in conflict with one of the most remarkable clergy in the Diocese of Winchester, or in any diocese of that day. Robert Radcliffe Dolling was an Irishman of a most unconventional kind. He went to school, like Davidson, at Harrow. As a young man, in the interval of looking after some difficult property in Ulster, he did slum work in Dublin and slum work in London with a head-quarters of his own in Borough Road, Southwark, where he was known as Brother Bob. At the age of thirty-two, he was ordained and ran a short-lived mission in the East End with what he called 'a sort of Chapel and music-hall combined'. Two years later, he found himself Vicar-designate of St. Agatha's, Landport, and Priest-in-charge of the Winchester College Mission. He has written an account of his life at Landport in *Ten Years in a Portsmouth Slum*. His work was magnificent. The heart of it was the Parsonage, and the Mission Chapel was its soul. The Parsonage had a gymnasium attached with cubicles and hammocks for sailors to sleep in at night. It had also a common table where all sorts and conditions rubbed shoulders with one another—soldiers, sailors, unemployed, Winchester College men, emigrants, down-and-outs. And Father Dolling presided over all, rotund, laughter-loving, affectionate, wearing a cassock and a biretta, with a cigar or clay pipe sticking out of his mouth. At the end of six years, he was able to claim that, besides much else, he had reformed 25 thieves just out of jail, rescued 144 fallen women, started in life 100 young men living in the Parsonage, and closed 50 brothels in the district. No wonder that Mr. John Pares, a well-known layman of the diocese, should write to Bishop Davidson at the end of Father Dolling's time:

I have seen one of the worst 'slums' of Portsmouth completely changed in character, and hundreds of souls brought to Christ by Mr. Dolling's life and devotion.

With the College itself, which supported the Missioner, he was no less successful. As the Headmaster, Dr. Fearon, said: 'His relation to Winchester College was pure, unbroken sunshine.' Wykehamists loved him, and he loved them. He was himself a boy to the end of his life, and he revelled in the fun and the jokes of boys. He touched their hearts. He did not talk much about the Mission, but he got the boys to visit it year after year for week-ends. He was astonishingly good in his talk to the boys in the Big School, in the Chapel and the Chantry, and in their studies. He was a great rollicking, serious, irrepressible Christian gentleman—one of the institutions of Winchester during the ten years he was their missioner.

Such was the man who, on September 28, 1895, only a week after Davidson was confirmed as Bishop of Winchester, wrote to tell him, as he was getting ready to settle in Farnham, that he, Dolling, proposed to take possession of his new church on October 27. Up to that time the soul of the Mission had been a stuffy little brick church, with mission services, extempore prayer, gospel preaching—and incense, acolytes in scarlet cassocks, and the Mass. Very evangelical, very unconventional, and very ritualistic! But now a fine new permanent church, for which Dolling had raised the money, or most of it, was about to be opened. Dolling hoped that the services which had been going on in the little mission church would continue exactly as before, in the new permanent building, without any further question of formal sanction. 'It practically is joined by the vestries to the old church which was licensed for celebrations by Bishop Harold Browne, and so your predecessor did not think that it would require a new licence.'

But, for weal or woe, the coming of the permanent church inevitably altered the situation. Bishop Thorold, who was very fond of Dolling but did not like his ritualistic ways, had feared that a crisis was bound to come whenever the question of a permanent church building arose. It was tragic indeed that Davidson, almost before he had had time to turn round in his house, should be brought straight up against the issue without chance of escape. He promised to consider the question whether a licence was in the circumstances necessary, and in the meantime consulted Canon Jacob, Vicar of Portsea and Rural Dean. Here was another stroke of bad luck, for Canon Jacob and Father Dolling were as poles apart from one another in human sympathy. Canon Jacob sent a memorandum to the Bishop which began in this ominous way:

Mr. Dolling—New Church.

Oct. 12 1895.

IF Bishop Thorold said (did he?) a new licence was not required, I am sure he was mistaken. . . . The licence can't cover 2 churches.

EDGAR JACOB.

The Bishop accordingly wrote to Dolling, and told him that a licence would be necessary, and that therefore, in accordance with custom, he would ask the Rural Dean to visit the church and report that all was in order. When the visit took place a few days later, Father Dolling, with a malicious glee, delighted in pointing out all the most ritualistic points on which the eye could be fastened, in order that nothing whatever might be missed by the inquisitor. The Rural Dean reported to the Bishop that all would be in fit and proper order for the due ministration of the services of the Church of England, save for one feature.

CANON JACOB *to the* BISHOP OF WINCHESTER

Oct. 23 1895.

There is however one feature of the church which I told Mr. Dolling I should have to report to the Bishop, leaving with him all responsibility of decision.

It is proposed to place a third altar in the middle of the S. aisle surmounted by a 'Calvary', i.e. crucifix with the usual figures, taken from the old temporary church. . . . On either side of this altar will be tablets with the names of those belonging to the church who have died 'in religion', arranged according to months, and the altar is avowedly to be used for 'Masses for the Dead'. Mr. Dolling said that Bishop Thorold saw this in the temporary church (there it was simply the second altar, corresponding to that in the E. end of the S. aisle of the new church) and intensely disliked it. Here however it assumes a far greater prominence, for it is not the altar for ordinary daily use—as in the temporary church—but simply to be used for 'Masses for the Dead'. Mr. Dolling laid the greatest stress on this. . . .

The Bishop was compelled to take notice of such a report, and he wrote at once to Father Dolling asking him to come and see him about this particular point. The day on which the letter was received was October 24. The great service for the dedication of the new church was fixed for October 27.

On October 25, Father Dolling came up to Farnham Castle for the interview. It was an extraordinary occasion. Dolling had publicly protested against the appointment of Dr. Davidson to Winchester, both in the *Church Times* and at his own Men's Service in Landport, on the ground that the new Bishop was an invalid and could never get to know the people of Portsmouth, 'understand their ways . . . and lead them into truer understanding of what the Church was'. And now he came to see the Bishop, armed with a sheaf of telegrams to the Headmaster, the Bishop of Southwell (Dr. Ridding, a former Headmaster), and many others, which were to announce that the opening services were all postponed and that the church was to be locked up for the next few months until he himself had given up the mission.

The Bishop, however, disarmed Dolling by his kindness, and the pistol-full of telegrams was not fired. It took two hours to come to a provisional settlement. The crucial feature was the third altar. But Dolling said:

> Canon Jacob had misunderstood him when saying that the third altar was to be simply used for 'Masses for the Dead'. There would probably be twelve celebrations at this altar every week . . . and only one of these would, in ordinary cases, be for the Dead. At the same time he did not wish to disguise the fact that the significance of the altar and of the teaching associated with it would have special relation to the prayers for the Dead.

The Bishop explained his own position as follows:

> I explained to him my position, namely, that he and I were neither of us at liberty to act in matters of this kind upon our mere personal opinions, but were subject to the order and rules of the Church of England as properly and constitutionally interpreted. Our membership in the corporate life of the Church involved this loyalty, and neither sentiment, personal inclination, sympathies, or modes of teaching could be allowed to settle a practical question so definite and important as whether or not, in a great new church, a third altar should be allowed to stand in the position proposed with the special objects he had described. He fully admitted this, and said that his difficulty lay in the fact that no proper decision

could he believed be at present arrived at, as the question of an informal licence could not properly come before the Courts but would be for the Bishop's private discretion. The decision would be mine and mine only, and this seemed to him inadequate. Had it been a question of consecration he would gladly have brought it formally before me for the Court to decide, and he would have been ready to appeal to the Higher Courts (he did not specify this) from the judgement of the Chancellor. On my suggestion that the alternative he preferred seemed to be that he (Mr. Dolling) should decide the question, he said that this had always been the way in which of recent years victories for the cause of Catholic truth had been won in the Church of England.

In the end, after much further discussion, the following memorandum was agreed:

Memorandum read to MR. DOLLING *and assented to by him.*

The alternatives I suggest are as follows:—

1. Open the Church for Divine Service next Sunday as arranged, screening off by some temporary arrangement the site of the proposed third altar. Send me the plans showing what is designed, and I will immediately take such steps as are necessary for approving them or otherwise. Meantime I will informally sanction the use of the Church. Announce to any who are interested in the matter that a question has been raised as to the legality or propriety of what was intended, and that pending the Bishop's decision upon the subject the final arrangements in that part of the aisle are postponed. [I am ready to write you a letter for publication if you desire it, to show that you are acting with perfect propriety and in accordance with due order in thus submitting the question to the Bishop for decision. Such a letter would prevent or answer any possible allegation that the Bishop is disapproving of your action.]

2. Withdraw the proposed third altar and a licence will at once be issued, subject of course to the question of the legality of the arrangements, fittings, or ornaments in the Church being sanctioned by the Diocesan Court before the Church is consecrated.

In the course of the conversation Dolling 'earnestly disclaimed any wish to seem to hold up his resignation as a sort of threat, and he desired to emphasize the fact that in any case he proposes without fail to leave his present position a few months hence—say before Easter—and that therefore if my decision when given should involve his resignation, it would merely mean that it would expedite a little what was already arranged'. Nevertheless Dolling went back to Landport, told everybody that a crisis had arrived, and that if the Bishop was unable, after consideration, to license the third altar (he said this to the congregation in church), 'I am at once to resign so that a successor may be appointed who will remove the altar and the memorial'.

Canon Jacob, as we have seen, was not the most sympathetic Rural Dean for a priest of Dolling's impulsive temperament. He wrote to the Bishop:

CANON JACOB *to the* BISHOP OF WINCHESTER

The Vicarage, Portsea. Oct. 26, 1895.

. . . Dolling has hitherto got his way by threatening resignation. He tried it on with the Bishop of London but did not succeed there and so left London—Bishop Billing told me this. He refused any conditions from Bishop Harold Browne and that dear good Bishop, not liking to offend Fearon, let him go on unlicensed and had nothing more to do with him. He refused to conform to Bishop Thorold and said he was willing to resign. I have told you the line the Bishop took. This seemed to me a curious idea of episcopal responsibility. . . .

The Headmaster also knew that the Rural Dean and the Missioner were hardly a harmonious pair, and that with a Missioner like Dolling the College and everybody connected with it were always living on the edge of a volcano.

The REV. W. A. FEARON *to the* BISHOP OF WINCHESTER

The College, Winchester. Oct. 27, 1895.

I am most grateful to you for your letter—nothing could be possibly kinder or more considerate. I confess that lately I have been dreading some such crisis as seems to be impending in the Mission; and only regret deeply that even indirectly we should be the cause of bringing you anxiety and trouble in such early days of your Episcopate among us. There is one consolation, that we have managed to survive similar crises before: in fact, with all his merits, with Dolling one has to accept perpetually the prospect of a crisis. One can only pray that now the vast good he has done may not be undone by want of self-control in the last act.

As far as any question of fighting Ecclesiastical questions goes, I do not see that Dolling has any legal status to afford a basis for any legal claim of any kind whatsoever. No doubt it is desirable to avoid a 'Paper' war. But if he feels bound to make a fight for his cause, that I take it is the only form it can assume. I would only say 3 things, with all respect.

1. There is an unfortunate personal element in the present controversy; and the more Jacob can be kept out of the matter, the more chance there is of peace. Jacob is like a 'red rag' to Dolling. There have been faults on both sides: but the fact is the 2 men's temperaments are such that they can hardly help being in antagonism: and they certainly have not helped it.

2. On every ground the College Mission field is not the place on which Dolling or anyone ought to raise any anxious questions. This I have said plainly to him; but I cannot hope to influence him.

3. Both by desire, and by policy, we are absolutely loyal to our Bishop. We have of course been obliged to acquiesce in much that we did not like. But you may confidently rely on our sympathy and assistance, as far as they can be given, in any difficulty.

Pardon my writing freely to you in this way—the kindness of your letter challenged it.

The new church was duly opened with great outward jubilation on October 27—though hearts were heavy both at the parsonage and in the castle. After more correspondence, a second interview took place on November 15 between the Bishop and the Missioner at Farnham. The following is the memorandum prepared at the time by the Bishop:

Full conversation about the facts of his services and his views about prayer for the dead etc. . . . The number of his communicants is large. . . . There is never any communicant at the 11 o'clock service. The Celebrant always knows at the time of the offertory whether there will be communicants or not, as communicants are directed to kneel at a special bench. When no one is going to communicate, the Celebrant omits Exhortation, Confession, and Absolution, and goes straight from the Prayer for the Church Militant to Sursum Corda. On Weekdays, unless they are festivals, neither the Creed nor the Gloria is ever said. (He was unable to recollect the reason for this, but said it had long been the use.) With regard to the special identification of the third altar with Masses for the Dead, Mr. Dolling said that if he were starting afresh in another church, he thought he would probably be less anxious to (so to speak) localise the teaching at one particular altar; but in the present case the proposed altar, from the facts of its history and the manner by which it came to be erected, is so connected with this particular teaching that it has come to be locally identified with it in the minds both of clergy and people. With regard to the utility and meaning of what he has described as 'Masses for the Dead' his views may be thus expressed:

> 'At the moment of death some souls go directly into the beatific state, others into a state of "preparation" or purgation. I do not use "purgatory" to my people, because I think they would connect it with notions of physical flames etc., but I do not personally object to it. The Mass for the Dead, as I understand it, is to benefit the souls in that state of "preparation". We benefit them by our Mass because our prayer for them shortens —we know not how—their remaining in the state of "preparation", and hastens their admission to the beatific state.'

The foregoing is taken from a rough note made by me during our interview, and assented to by Mr. Dolling as a correct record of his view.

I pressed him as to what he regarded as the distinction between England and Rome with regard to what the Articles describe as (*a*) the doctrine concerning Purgatory, (*b*) the Sacrifices of Masses. He seemed to mix the two thoughts together and said that in his mind the difference turned almost entirely upon a question as to the manner in which Christ's sacrifice is on the altar offered or repeated—Romans, as he believed, regarding it (at least popularly) as being repeated at each Mass. He did not think there was any marked distinction between his view and that of Rome with regard to the effect of the Mass upon the condition of the departed. He did not consider that the doctrine we repudiate respecting Masses had anything to do with the question of payments for such Masses, although he thought that practice a very terrible one.

It did not seem to me that his views on these doctrinal subjects were at all clear, but the above is what he said.

He promised to send me the books that he uses at his Mass for the Dead, and also at his Vespers of the Blessed Sacrament etc., as well as those used at his Children's Service.

I explained to him the legal position with regard to the question of the Consecration of his Church, namely, that it rests in the Bishop's discretion to give or to withhold Consecration just as to give or to withhold Licence, and that if he desires to appeal from the Bishop to Diocesan or Provincial Courts, or to the Privy Council, with regard to such a question as the third altar, his proper course would be to wait until the Church is consecrated, and then to apply for a Faculty to introduce the structures or ornaments in question. Were this Faculty to be withheld, he would then have full right of appeal. He quite saw and understood the point.

I purposely refrained from asking him whether he still adhered to his intention to resign in the event of my deciding against licensing the Church with the proposed third altar.

We also spoke shortly of his wish to introduce a fourth altar in the Baptistery. This had been suggested to him by a member of his Mothers' Meeting, who had remarked that a certain niche in the Baptistery would be suited for an altar, and that a Celebration might be held there on the day a child was to be baptised, so that its parents might communicate. He was taken with the idea, and would wish, when the time comes, to apply for this also, but he does not press for it at present.

Throughout our interview nothing could be more frank and cordial than his whole manner, and I was impressed by his readiness, or even anxiety, to conceal nothing from me, and to state his full position to the best of his power.

The interview was of the friendliest and kindest description; for when they were together Dolling would get on with the Bishop quite well, though swayed by other influences when he got back to the Mission. But the Bishop, as an officer of the Church, was forced to consider the law of the Church and the teaching and practice of the Book of Common Prayer, not forgetting what had been in fact, as well as what might be, declared by competent ecclesiastical courts. Father Dolling was not a theologian. Moreover, he had never disguised his poor opinion of the Book of Common Prayer, as a handbook for missioners seeking to convert poor ignorant souls in a slum. Besides all this, he was suffering from a bad attack of influenza, though he wrote to the Bishop on the day after the interview that he was none the worse, and also said:

The REV. R. R. DOLLING *to the* BISHOP OF WINCHESTER

16th Nov. 1895.

Our conversation of yesterday was so different from what I have had with Bishops in former days. They seemed to desire to deal with things concerning which complaint had been made to them and so when I had ventured on other details as to the service here they stopped me as though to say, 'That question is not before me; I do not desire to know it.' It seemed to me yesterday that your attitude was the very opposite of this.

He was, however, not at all himself, and, on November 22, wrote to say that he was trying to get well and had gone away for eight days, while waiting full of anxiety for the Bishop's decision. The Bishop was also much harassed—'the whole work of the Diocese to learn, the house to get into, and all manner of people, from Ordination candidates onwards, to see'. The final decision was conveyed to Dolling in the following letter:

The BISHOP OF WINCHESTER *to the* REV. R. R. DOLLING

Farnham Castle. 7 Dec. 1895.

I am now able to write to you definitely upon the question which has arisen with regard to St. Agatha's Church, and as you may probably wish to make my letter public, it will be convenient that I should briefly recall what has taken place.

On October 2nd, a few days after I had become Bishop of Winchester, I heard from you that you had made arrangements to open the new Church for Divine Service on Oct. 27th. With a view therefore to your receiving the necessary licence, I directed Canon Jacob as Rural Dean to pay the customary preliminary visit to the Church and to report to me whether all was in due order. On Oct. 24th I received his report. He told me of the beauty and dignity of the building and its general suitableness for Divine Service in a great Parish. The fittings and ornaments were not yet *in situ*, and he was therefore unable to report upon them in detail. But he directed my attention, as in duty bound, to the structural arrangements for Holy Communion. These, as shown in his report and in your subsequent explanations to me with appended plans, are as follows: One large Holy Table or Altar in the usual position in the centre of the East end of the Church; a second (for less largely attended Services) at the East end of the South Aisle; and a third in the South Aisle, placed against the side wall of the church. It is also your wish to place a fourth in the Baptistery at the West end of the North Aisle, but that question is not at present before us.

When Canon Jacob paid his official visit to the Church, the proposed third Altar had not yet been erected; and, after full correspondence and conversation between yourself and me upon the subject, it was decided that the opening Services should be held in accordance with the arrangements you had already made before I became Bishop, but that the site of the proposed third Altar should be temporarily curtained off, and its erection, at the least, postponed so that I should have time, before issuing formal

Licence for the conduct of Divine Service in the building, to consider the arrangements proposed.

You urged me to give you an answer as speedily as possible, as in the event of my being unable to sanction the proposed arrangements you would feel it necessary to withdraw immediately from St. Agatha's instead of remaining until Easter next, when you proposed in any case to resign.

As it is not proposed that the Church should be consecrated at present, the question raised does not, and indeed cannot, now come formally before the Diocesan Court. Pending consecration, it rests with the Bishop to grant or withhold at his discretion the necessary licence for the conduct of Divine Service in the new building. In order therefore to understand in all its bearings the question to which you attach so much importance, I have, in addition to our correspondence, had two prolonged interviews with you, and I am anxious again to express to you my appreciation of the honest and straightforward readiness you have throughout shown to give me all possible information as to your usages and the opinions on which they are based. In a matter of this kind, where we have but one object—namely, to arrive at a right conclusion in accordance with the doctrines and laws of the Church of England—it is of paramount importance that there should be no concealment or reserve in setting the facts before the Bishop on whom lies the grave responsibility of decision. I am cordially grateful to you therefore for freeing me from any difficulty of that sort.

After deliberately weighing all that you have put before me, I have come to the conclusion that I should act wrongly were I, on my personal authority, now to sanction the erection and use of the proposed third Altar in the situation and for the purposes you have described to me. When the Church is consecrated it would of course be possible for you or your successor to apply to the Diocesan Court for a faculty for the erection of such a third Altar, and, were the faculty refused, you would have the opportunity, which you tell me you desire, of bringing the question before the higher Courts on appeal from the decision of the Chancellor. In the meantime, as I have fully explained to you in conversation, I cannot, in exercising my discretion upon a proposition so unusual, regard the question as merely the technical one,—may there be three Altars or Holy Tables in one Church? It is easy to conceive a Church or Cathedral of such dimensions or construction as to render it desirable to extend yet further the principle upon which a second Altar or Holy Table has been sanctioned in so many of our Churches for more convenient use when the number of communicants is small, and, whatever might be the legal decision on such a point, no question of doctrine or principle need thereby be raised. But such is not the case at St. Agatha's. You do not ask for my sanction of the third Altar on grounds of convenience (in the ordinary sense of the word), and indeed it is obvious that in that respect it would have no advantage over the second or subsidiary Altar, to which I have raised no objection. You have explained to me that your wish for the addition rests in the main on quite different grounds. The Altar in question is intended to have special association with a deceased friend whose memory is rightly cherished in the parish. You desire that it should be surrounded with memorials of the dead, and that its special, though not exclusive, use should be for the celebration of what you describe as 'Mass for the Dead'.

I endeavoured in our recent conversation to ascertain exactly what you mean by this term, and you explained candidly and clearly what it is that you believe and teach. You regard the Celebration of Holy Communion 'for the dead' as having the effect [you add 'we know not how'] of shortening the period during which the souls of the faithful departed are in a state of 'purgation' or 'preparation', and of hastening their admission to the beatific state.

Now I have no wish to dictate to you, or to dogmatise, upon the mysterious and difficult question of what is known as 'prayer for the dead',—a term obviously capable of a great variety of meaning, ranging from the words we use in the Prayer for the Church Militant to doctrines of quite another sort. The whole subject is of great importance and I will gladly discuss it with you hereafter; but, whatever liberty of private opinion and individual devotion may be permissible, I have no hesitation in saying that I should depart both from the spirit and the letter of our Church's formularies were I definitely to sanction the addition of a third Altar to St. Agatha's with the knowledge that one main purpose of its erection is that it should be a centre for services and teaching of the character above described. I myself believe your teaching on this subject to be contrarient to some of the distinctive principles of the Church of England, and I am bound to add further that I am unable to reconcile your usages in celebrating the Holy Communion with the specific directions in the Book of Common Prayer, which both you and I have solemnly pledged ourselves to follow. You tell me, for example, that in St. Agatha's Church, where you have about twenty Celebrations of the Holy Communion every week, more than half the Celebrations on weekdays, 'perhaps eight out of fifteen', are in ordinary circumstances without communicants. You have so arranged that the celebrant shall know beforehand if any desire to communicate, and, if not, the celebrant omits the Exhortation, Confession, and Absolution from the Service. On week-days, unless they are festivals, the Creed and the Gloria in Excelsis are always omitted.

It is impossible for me to disregard these facts in coming to a decision as to what I ought at this juncture to do. You have, as it seems to me, dealt practically at your will with our Church's Rules. I do not for a moment doubt that your motive is a good one. Your Services are those which, in your individual opinion, are best calculated to lead your people into a knowledge of what you believe to be the truth. But the Church of England does not allow us thus to deal at our will with the Book of Common Prayer, and in the event of your deciding to remain at St. Agatha's I must carefully discuss with you what modifications are required in order to bring your Services into harmony with the Prayer Book.

I need not repeat to you what I have so often said as to my sense of the value of your devoted work in the midst of special difficulties. Many of your distinctive Church Services seem to me to have a special value, as bringing home to the minds of unlearned people, by the use of anniversaries and memorials and otherwise, the links which bind us to the world unseen. These are, as I believe, compatible with perfect loyalty to the Book of Common Prayer. I earnestly trust you may not think it necessary to sever yourself at present from a parish in which God has signally blessed your energy, your self-devotion, and your enthusiasm; and you may rely upon my constant endeavour to help and further your work in every legitimate way.

There was no doubt that the Bishop felt keenly the pain of such a decision, and hardly less the pain of the answer which it quickly drew from the Missioner:

The REV. R. R. DOLLING *to the* BISHOP OF WINCHESTER

St. Agatha. Dec. 9, 1895.

I have to-day sent to Dr. Fearon my resignation. I think that your account of our interviews is quite correct, except in one detail. I did not intend to say that I did not know how the Service of the Holy Communion affected the state of the Dead.

There is however one practical question. I must conduct the services as I have for the last 10 years.

Do you wish me and my staff to go away at once, or to wait till Dr. Fearon has appointed my successor? I am ready to follow either course, only, for fear of mistakes arising, I should like to say that as long as I am in charge the Sunday and daily services remain the same.

The shock to Portsmouth—to Winchester—it is hardly too much to say to the Church at large—was instantaneous.

More letters passed—friendly and considerate on both sides—the Bishop more than once pointing out to Dolling, as also to others, that he had no wish that Dolling should resign.

The BISHOP OF WINCHESTER *to the* REV. R. R. DOLLING.

13 Dec., 1895.

A grave question of Church order has come formally before me for decision as Bishop of the Diocese. With anxious care and with an earnest wish to consider your difficulties, I have decided in accordance with what seems to be my duty, and therefore, to my great regret you have resigned at once instead of waiting until the time you had publicly announced. I can scarcely conceive that anyone who studies our ordinal and realises a Bishop's obligations and responsibilities could wish me to have acted otherwise than I have.

I must, in all kindness, remonstrate against your representing your resignation—even at a time of excitement—as though it were my act rather than your own. Few things in my life have caused me more sorrow and anxiety than this.

But Dolling's view was equally clear that he had no other course, and that his resignation was due to the Bishop's act.

Public sympathy was deep and widespread. Dolling was an old favourite, while the Bishop was still new to the county. The Bishop taking, and taking bravely, an unpopular course, because he believed it his duty, felt keenly and deeply for Dolling as well as for the Mission and its friends.

What of the College? The boys were all, or practically all, on Dolling's side; and who would wish it otherwise when the friend of the whole school was in trouble? Never again was the Mission the same after Dolling left it. But the old Warden, who had long been opposed to Dolling, wrote to express his pleasure to the Bishop:

The REV. GODFREY B. LEE *to the* BISHOP OF WINCHESTER

Winchester College. Dec. 13, 1895.

The correspondence which has appeared in the newspapers relative to Mr. Dolling induces me to inform Your Lordship that our Governing Body, i.e. the Warden and Fellows, have nothing whatever to do with the Mission, which would be more appropriately named the Winchester *School* Mission. I withdrew my support from the Mission some years ago owing to Mr. Dolling's papistical doctrines and practices. I had frequent conversations with Bishops Harold Browne and Thorold on the subject, from which I learned that Episcopal advice and remonstrance are thrown away on Mr. Dolling and I should be very glad to hear that he had left Portsea.

The Headmaster, who could look at the matter from the boys' point of view as well, wrote in a different strain, and showed Dolling himself how clearly he appreciated the Bishop's position:

The REV. W. A. FEARON *to the* REV. R. R. DOLLING

The College, Winchester. Dec. 13, 1895.

I don't see how your suggested 'compromise' is any solution of the difficulty, or indeed touches the main question at all,—even supposing we were prepared to make the enormous sacrifice of giving up the new church, on which our money and care has been expended.

But in fact we are absolutely loyal to the Bishop, and should desire to carry out his wishes, which seem to us all to have been very considerately and wisely expressed. Indeed you have always recognised that the School Mission was the last place in the world where it would be fair or right to raise any agitation, or fight any battle. We have submitted to a considerable straining of our position in order to give you large liberty in matters in which we could not go with you. I hoped you would make the return to our affection of being willing to withdraw quietly, and to do your utmost to allay an agitation which is already doing us much harm.

As a matter of fact, I was of course prepared to act; and I have already, with the Bishop's consent, offered the post to another man.

I am sure it is wisest both for you and for us that we should part, bitter as the parting is.

Letters poured in to Farnham. Some of Dolling's friends tried to secure a *modus vivendi*. But no *modus vivendi* could in the circumstances be permanent. It was urged, with Dolling's leave, that the third altar might be removed 'provided the services in the church remained the same as hitherto'. But this, the Bishop pointed out, would only mean that he would 'by the issue of a formal licence give official sanction to the very arrangement for Divine Service, apart from the local question of the third altar, to which I took exception in my published letter to him of 7th December'. The problem could not be solved thus. The resignation took effect. A new Missioner was in due course appointed. Father Dolling retained—the Bishop was eager to make this plain—episcopal permission to minister in the diocese whenever invited by an incumbent, but he left Landport, and the College and the sailors and the soldiers and the slum and the men and women, bad and good, of Portsmouth knew him no more.

Could such a catastrophe have been avoided? Certainly there were very many unhappy circumstances about it. The Bishop, a newcomer; the Rural Dean, a curiously unfortunate person for this particular Missioner at this particular job; Dolling himself in a state of great strain, and in any case—so he told the Bishop—after ten years' work at Portsmouth, about to retire! All these things made for unfavourable conditions. If only there had been a little more time, a little more patience, perhaps another twelve months before the new church had to be opened!

But, after all, decisions have to be taken when the particular case arises. And in this instance let us see why it was that the Bishop felt bound to decide, unpopular as the decision must be, in the way that he did.

The root of the matter lay in the erection of this fine new church, large enough to hold a thousand, in place of the little brick chapel. The services which Dolling held—admittedly outside the Book of Common Prayer—inevitably came up for consideration when the necessary licence for the new church was sought. In the Mission Chapel much might go on of an unusual character, but it was not a permanent place of worship on the way to consecration as a parish church, and Dolling was such a remarkable man that a Bishop would not be too severe. In passing however from the temporary to the permanent, personal questions ceased to have the old meaning, and the Bishop was obliged to consider whether the various types of service, admittedly outside the Prayer Book, were sufficiently near the Prayer Book standard to justify him in giving them, by his licence, the stamp of Episcopal authority. The Bishop came to the conclusion, which certainly at that time it would have been impossible to avoid, that, with the best will in the world, certain things could not be so brought into the comprehensive ambit of Anglican teaching. He did not issue any deliberate judgement of his own that saying Masses for the Dead was unlawful, or that the doctrine of the Eucharistic Sacrifice for the faithful departed must be ruled out of court. He was most careful to say that he deplored an individual Bishop's *ipse dixit*. Thus he wrote to Canon Gore at the time:

The Bishop of Winchester *to* Canon Charles Gore

Dec. 26, 1895.

With regard to the doctrinal question of Prayer for the Departed, or of the relation of such prayer to the Holy Eucharist, I have deliberately refrained from attempting to dogmatise, or indeed to make any statement whatever. My letter to Dolling was as careful in what it left unsaid as in what it said. No-one feels more strongly than I the danger of individual Bishops making such formal declarations—unless with the utmost care and consultation; and I am persuaded of the need of a wide elasticity as to individual opinion and practice. Dolling's case was *sui generis*.

What Bishop Davidson felt bound to do was to restrain Dolling, as he put it to Canon Carter, 'from dealing absolutely at his will with the directions of our Prayer Book'. It was, in the last resort, a question of authority and Church order; and as such it was judged by the most famous missioner of the day, himself a leading High Churchman, Canon Body of Durham.

The Rev. Canon Body *to the* Bishop of Winchester

The College, Durham.
Dec. 14, 1895.

May I write one line of sympathy to you in your troubles with Dolling, and of most sincere gratitude to you for your action in this matter? I believe strongly in your wisdom and am now justified in this belief—conspicuously. I am as glad for what you have not said as for what you have said: for what you have not done as for what you have done. Bishops so often in dealing with High Church extravagances say and do what hits, not self-willed and Romanising men only, but loyal Anglo-Catholics (*e.g.* the Bishop of Exeter's regrettable charge). You give us no pain: you cause us no perplexity. As one whose loyalty to Anglo-Catholicism has been proved and tested, I thank you for your letters and action in this matter.

Of course it is most regrettable for us to jeopardise the services of such a man as Dolling who has found so many dead stones and quickened them into life, and with them built the Temple of the Lord in such a parish as St. Agatha's. Yet for his sake and for that of *the English* Church the reintroduction of the Romish Doctrine of Purgatory and of its system of Masses for the Dead must be resisted. And even more his uncatholic spirit of disobedience must be contended with. To tolerate this *Doctrine*, spirit and system is too great a price to pay even for his strength and zeal. For the sake of Christendom and the Recovery of its Unity the distinctive witness of the English Church to Primitive Doctrine 'Order' and Practice must be preserved at any and every cost.

CHAPTER XIV

A NEW PRIMATE

Honesty. I am, as you see, an old man, and have been a traveller in this road many a day, and I have taken notice of many things. JOHN BUNYAN, *Pilgrim's Progress.*

DURING the first year at Farnham Archbishop Benson was alive, and Bishop Davidson enjoyed the same close touch with Lambeth as before. But a great change was now to take place.

On October 11, 1896, at the age of sixty-seven, the Archbishop of Canterbury died with dramatic suddenness at Morning Prayer in Hawarden Parish Church while visiting Mr. Gladstone. The news was telegraphed to Farnham. To quote Davidson's words:

> Lucy Tait and I started that evening for Hawarden and travelled by the newspaper train leaving London about 3 a.m. We thus reached Hawarden about 10 a.m. She left the next day with Mrs. Benson, and I remained on until the Thursday, when I accompanied the body on its removal to Canterbury, Arthur Benson being my companion throughout. It was a curious experience in more ways than one. The tragic interest and solemnity of the occasion suggested large thoughts, and besides this I had the curious opportunity of three or four days' intercourse with Mr. Gladstone. The other guests had of course left the house and it was a time of leisure for him, and he talked ceaselessly to me for the three days, walking in the park or sitting in his sanctum. The conversation was largely about Manning, whose *Life* by Purcell had just been published and had absorbed Mr. Gladstone's interest.

As we have seen, the relations between Benson and Davidson were close and affectionate. Throughout the whole of Benson's Primacy, Davidson, whether as Chaplain, Dean, or Bishop, was his counsellor in almost everything he did. Scores, if not hundreds, of letters which passed between them survive, and the very difference of their temperament contributed to the health and value of the partnership.

The following letter of deep gratitude was written by Arthur Benson after the funeral:

A. C. BENSON, ESQ., *to the* BISHOP OF WINCHESTER

Addington, Oct. 17th.

It would be too ungrateful of me if I were not to write you a few words—because it is so much easier to write deliberately than to speak—to thank you from my heart for all that you have done for us this last week: your presence and your readiness to advise and be consulted was an inexpressible relief, at a time when as a rule even one's best friends shrink from all the strain that such situations demand. I am never likely to be able to repay you for what you have done and been, but I do want you to know that I have felt an affection and honour for you all this sad week which exceeds all the esteem which I had before—and even that was very great.

I have written a great many letters today, and this letter may seem tainted by formality and the hyperboles of grief, but it is not so at all and I feel very deeply every word I say—and so do all in this household.

The Bishop replied (October 19, 1896), that he could not 'bear to think of the word "gratitude" being used by you or yours as regards any relationship of mine to the sad doings and arrangements of this last week—the most sad to me, I think, of any in my life'.

He spoke of the contrast between the quiet gathering of Archbishop Tait to his rest and reward, when his work was done, and this sudden taking of Edward White Benson at a moment when there was so much more for him, as it seemed, to do. And he added:

The BISHOP OF WINCHESTER *to* A. C. BENSON, ESQ.

What he has been to me as friend and guide and teacher in the deepest things I cannot even try to say. I have had nothing else quite like it in my life, partly I suppose because the lines on which he helped and taught me were so utterly different from my own natural lines.

I

There were many who thought that Randall Davidson himself might succeed to the Primacy; and there is no doubt at all that this was what the Queen desired. Her Majesty, after several telegrams had passed on the news of Benson's death, asked Davidson to give her his views on the succession, as she had already been approached by Lord Salisbury. In a letter of October 18, 1896, he named 'the qualifications desirable at all times and specially needed at this moment':

The Bishop of Winchester *to the* Queen

Farnham Castle. October 18, 1896.

1. A real devotion of the highest sort to the spiritual part of the great Office.

2. Such capacity, and knowledge of the world and of men as will enable him to take his proper place in the public affairs of the Church and Realm.

3. Such learning and reputation as shall ensure real weight for his words apart from the position he holds.

4. A large hearted and liberal sympathy with men of other 'schools of thought' than his own, both inside and outside the Church.

It is further clear that, if it be possible, the new Archbishop should be a man of ripe years, and of the sort of experience to ensure for him the *ready* and not merely the *dutiful* allegiance of those who have long been Bishops.

He named as 'foremost beyond question both in power and in influence' the Bishop of London. 'But he is 75 years old, and his eyesight is failing.' He also mentioned the Archbishop of York (Dr. Maclagan) and the Bishop of Manchester (Dr. Moorhouse), each seventy, and three younger bishops, of whom he put easily first Bishop Talbot. He followed up the letter with a telegram on October 21, pressing Temple as the man who would 'alone command real confidence at this juncture and serve the best interests of Church and nation'.

Lord Salisbury was clear for Temple. Let Davidson describe how he heard the decision:

I returned to Farnham [from Benson's funeral at Canterbury] and was in considerable anxiety as to what might be occurring, having in the last days heard nothing either from the Queen or from Lord Salisbury. We had on one evening in the following week a great meeting in the Hall at Farnham in connection with the Home Reading Union, and somebody was lecturing to a full hall. A telegram was brought to me, it was long [*sic*], and in cipher. I was in the Chair and could not move, so I had to get hold of paper and then and there work out the cipher in use between the Queen and myself. It took a little time, and the newspaper report commented on the careful notes I had taken of the lecture! My wife was sitting in the audience, and the relief which my face showed told her what had happened. It was the Queen's intimation that to her surprise Bishop Temple had accepted the Primacy.

Telegram from the QUEEN *to the* BISHOP OF WINCHESTER

Balmoral. 24 October 1896.

Somewhat to my surprise London has accepted Canterbury.

V. R.I.

It was followed by a letter, October 24, 1896:

The QUEEN *to the* BISHOP OF WINCHESTER

Balmoral Castle.

I have 3 very kind and interesting letters to thank you for.

You will perhaps have guessed what I wished for the Primacy? It was *yourself*, and for the following reasons: 1. my opinion is that you possessed the necessary qualities for that important Post, and above all because your great intimacy with the 2 last great Primates enabled you to know their views and their work. In fact I think *their* mantle has fallen upon you.

Lord Salisbury, though speaking of you in the highest terms, says that you are the youngest of the Bishops and you have had rapid preferment, and thinks it would be an advantage to you if the Bishop of London became Archbishop for a short while, my wishes would then be accomplished. I do not like the choice at all, and think the Bishop of London's presence eminently *unsuited* to the post.

Then comes the choice for the Bishop of London, quite as important a Post! The Archbishop of York and the Prince of Wales were very anxious that the Bishop of Peterborough [Dr. Creighton] should be the Primate. Perhaps that would not have done, though it might for London.

Bishop Davidson telegraphed and wrote words of warm welcome to Temple and received this reply:

The BISHOP OF LONDON *to the* BISHOP OF WINCHESTER

Fulham Palace, S.W. 24 Oct. 1896.

Thank you much for your generous warmhearted Letter. I did not expect to be called to Canterbury, though of course I knew that it was possible. But I thought that a younger man would have been preferred. But I think I can do some service and I will try to do it.

I shall lean much on such help as yours.

May God be with us both.

In the meantime there was the question of the vacancy at London, which Lord Salisbury very much wished Davidson to fill:

The MARQUESS OF SALISBURY *to the* QUEEN

October 26, 1896.

The Bishop of Winchester in most respects is the most deserving of Your Majesty's selection. His knowledge of Church matters, the confidence that was reposed in him by successive Archbishops, his great breadth and liberality of mind which makes him acceptable to all parties in the Church, his high ability, and the general charm of his manner, point him out as specially fitted to fill the vacant see. His rule will be in some respects a contrast to that of the present Bishop. His defects will probably arise from too great gentleness and moderation: while those of Bishop Temple have arisen from too great energy. But the change will not be hurtful.

There are only two serious objections to his appointment. One is the state of his health: for the work of London is much harder than that of Winchester. He is however a very sensible man, as well as a very good man: and he may be trusted not to accept the office if he is physically unequal to its duties. The other objection arises from the relations of the See of Winchester to Your Majesty. He is undoubtedly singularly well fitted to discharge them: and possibly Your Majesty may not wish to part with him. That is a point which Your Majesty alone can decide.

But the Queen rejected the proposal.

Telegram from the QUEEN *to the* BISHOP OF WINCHESTER

Balmoral. October 29, 1896.

Lord Salisbury wished for you to go to London but feared for your health. I said it must not be offered to you as it would be utter ruin to your health, and have appointed Peterborough, the only other proposed. Glyn to be offered Peterborough.

The following letters passed between Lord Salisbury, who knew nothing of this telegram, and the Bishop of Winchester:

The MARQUESS OF SALISBURY *to the* BISHOP OF WINCHESTER

Hatfield House, Hatfield, Herts.

Oct. 31. 96.

The newspapers will have informed you that the Bishop of Peterborough has been nominated to the See of London. I hope you will not think me impertinent if I refer to the grounds which led me in the recommendation I made to the Sovereign to name him rather than yourself. I abstained from the latter course with very great reluctance, and after some hesitation—and only for one reason. Great as are the Bishop of Peterborough's claims in respect of learning, character, and position in the Church, they certainly do not surpass your own. There is alas! one point in which you are inferior—and that is in the kind of physical robustness which enables a man to endure the strain which ministrations in a huge crowded city involve, where much of the work must be done late. This was a consideration which I could not overlook. If I rightly estimated it, the effect of your nomination would have been (supposing you had accepted it)—not that we should have had you as Bishop of London, but that we should have lost you altogether.

The Queen desired me to write to you on this subject: and I may say so much as this, that I should not have written this letter, had I not known that she entirely shares the opinions I have expressed in it.

The BISHOP OF WINCHESTER *to the* MARQUESS OF SALISBURY

The Athenaeum. 3 Nov. '96.

Most cordially do I thank you for the more than kind terms in which you have written. I cannot however receive without a respectful protest what I honestly believe to be quite an over-estimate of any powers or capacity I may myself possess. In no way whatever could I regard myself as qualified for such a position as the see of London, and with regard to the prosaic but very necessary qualification of physical strength, the reasons which led me last year to consent to leave S. London for Farnham, would, even by themselves, disqualify me absolutely for the arduous physical strain which the Diocese of London involves.

None the less do I, with all my heart, thank your Lordship for your exceedingly kind words, while I join in the universal acclaim which welcomes to Fulham the strong man—strong in every sense—whom your Lordship has so wisely recommended to the Queen as Bishop Temple's successor. Shall I be impertinent if I express further, in my own name, and I believe I might add in the name of almost every Bishop on the Bench, our intense gratitude to you for your action in the matter of the Primacy. Age notwithstanding, Bishop Temple is indisputably the strongest man among the English Bishops—the one man whom we can every one of us welcome as our leader at a moment when a strong leader is so pre-eminently necessary. The Lambeth Conference of next year may have far reaching issues, and no hand upon the helm could be comparable to his.

II

At the conclusion of the letter just quoted, the Bishop of Winchester went out of his way to thank Lord Salisbury for the appointment of Dr. Temple to the See of Canterbury. How little can he have expected the change in his own relations with Lambeth which the appointment brought about!

In his recollections of 1906, Dr. Davidson writes:

> He was in many ways one of my heroes, and when Archbishop Benson's unexpected death occurred, I had not a single hour's hesitation as to his being the proper person to succeed to the Primacy. . . .
>
> In many respects he towered above all other members of the then Episcopate, and for him to have served as Bishop under any one of them as Archbishop would have been incongruous in the last degree. To myself he had always been exceedingly kind; for abundant kindness there was under his rugged and at times rude exterior and manner. Archbishop Benson had given us rooms in the Lollards' Tower and these had greatly facilitated my constant intercourse with him. When Archbishop Temple was appointed I offered to give up the rooms, but he genuinely, though brusquely, bade us stay on. . . .
>
> Thereupon my direct association with Lambeth work, as regards its correspondence etc., came absolutely to an end.

Before the end of November (less than six weeks after Benson's death) he wrote thus to the Rev. E. L. Ridge, who, after four years as chaplain to Benson, continued for another four years as chaplain to Temple:

The Bishop of Winchester *to the* Rev. E. L. Ridge

Farnham Castle. November 21, 1896.

Many thanks for your letter. It is a real pleasure to hear from you. Mind you keep me in touch so far as you can with what goes on, for to me it is the strangest of all the changes of my life to find myself out in the cold as regards the central affairs of the Church of England, after nearly 20 years of closest knowledge.

The 'nearly 20 years of closest knowledge' had begun when Davidson went to Lambeth as Tait's chaplain in 1877.

It was indeed the strangest of experiences. But the experience was made even more painful by the remarkable idea firmly planted in the Archbishop's mind that Davidson had himself been hoping for the Primacy, and had been passed over. The facts, however, are clear enough, as the following letters reveal.

A. C. BENSON, ESQ., *to the* BISHOP OF WINCHESTER

January 22, 1897.

I had a long and curious talk with Ridge on Sunday in town. . . . T. himself is in high spirits, and looks upon the change to Canterbury as a headmaster might accept a Deanery. . . . *But*—and this is a very serious matter which I feel bound to tell you—Ridge says that it is obvious that their view of yourself is that you intended to obtain the Primacy, and were passed over, to your own chagrin, for himself, and that you are disappointed and vexed. These are hard and disagreeable statements, but I cannot involve them in any periphrasis, because they seem to me to be dangerous.

Considering that you enacted the part of Warwick, and that T. would not have had a moment's consideration but for yourself, I cannot help feeling that he ought to be disabused of this idea.

I write to you fully and I hope discreetly—at least I trust that I am not only making mischief and causing uncomfortable feelings. Ridge says that it is quite *obvious* that this is his view.

I did not see exactly who else was to tell you this—so, though I don't like handing on such statements—*liberavi animam meam.* You have shown me such confidence, and especially in this particular matter, that I felt bound to repay it. I should like to do anything, if I could. But after weighing the respective merits of silence and speech in the case, I have thought I might do more harm by being silent than by speaking out.

You may scold me if I have done wrong.

The BISHOP OF WINCHESTER *to* A. C. BENSON, ESQ.

Farnham Castle, Surrey.

Private

23 Jan '97.

I thank you cordially for your thoughtful kindness in telling me what I should not have been so likely to learn from others—while I most certainly ought to know it!

Its importance lies in this—that, if the great man really believes what you think he believes, he must be regarding me as the most doubledyed humbug and hypocrite unhanged, as he has received and apparently welcomed from me letters and telegrams and spoken words expressing my belief that none other than he could rightly have taken the position—and has responded thereto in cordial terms. If he really regards me as capable of writing and speaking thus while *thinking* the opposite, his conduct to me is simply inexplicable.

The mystery is so great that I can't help thinking Ridge must be under some total delusion. Mrs. Temple has been, and is, as warm as her husband.

Ridge and I know one another so intimately that I think I must —unless you positively forbid it—have it out with him privately next week, when we shall meet in Convocation.

Many thanks for writing as you did.

The Bishop saw Ridge, and found that there was no delusion; but for the moment it did not seem that anything could be done to disabuse Temple's mind. A year or two later, however, possibly through Mrs. Benson's offices, the Archbishop was disabused and the old kindly relations were resumed. But even then the resumption of friendship did not mean the resumption of the former position of intimate counsellor.

Such were the facts as to the cessation of the intercourse between Lambeth and Farnham, as Bishop Davidson saw them. There were also other reasons why Bishop Davidson no longer found himself a partner in the work at Lambeth. Temple had never got over the shock which he received when Tait, his old tutor at Balliol, lent the weight of his name, as Bishop of London, to the agitation against *Essays and Reviews* in 1861. Temple had written the opening Essay in that volume. He had been deeply wounded by the public censure inflicted upon him and his collaborators by the two Archbishops, by Dr. Tait, and the whole Bench of Bishops, including this declaration, 'We cannot understand how these opinions can be held consistently with an honest subscription to the formularies of our Church.' And what had hurt Temple most was that Tait (who had in former days urged the undertaking of the critical study of the Bible, 'a dangerous study but indispensable'), after speaking kindly to him in private at Fulham about his share in the book, should then, without warning, in deference to a popular clamour, join in an act of unexampled severity.[1] To the end of his days Temple remained critical of

[1] The correspondence is printed in Davidson's *Life of Archbishop Tait*, i. 287–301.

Tait; and perhaps, therefore, was inclined to be less welcoming than he would otherwise have been to Tait's chaplain and son-in-law as a helper in the archiepiscopal labours. And there was a further reason. Readers of the *Memoirs of Archbishop Temple* will remember what is there said about one special tendency which showed itself markedly in Dr. Temple's Primacy, 'the isolation of a powerful mind'. Dr. Benson had been his 'most intimate friend for forty years'; and throughout Dr. Benson's Primacy, the two minds, dissimilar as they were, 'had been in close concert on the large affairs of the Church, and also in comparative isolation from other minds'. And then the writer of the *Memoir*, himself a diocesan Bishop (Dr. Forrest Browne, Bishop of Bristol), continues:

> When Dr. Benson was removed, there was no one left with whom Dr. Temple had been accustomed to take counsel on the greatest questions; and with his long experience, his unrivalled knowledge of the ins and outs of different matters, and his consciousness of adequate powers of mind, the isolation from the rest of the Bishops of the province continued.[1]

It is well, therefore, to remember this general tendency of Archbishop Temple to isolation from all the Bishops, in estimating the special severance of the link with Lambeth from which Bishop Davidson suffered, though Frederick Temple and Randall Davidson were, no doubt, extraordinarily unlike one another in their whole point of view. In the Davidson papers there is the following description of Archbishop Temple's methods:

> Archbishop Temple took a line wholly different from his predecessors. The splendid work which he did for many years as Bishop of Exeter, Bishop of London, and Archbishop, consisted, if I understood it aright, in the vigorous carrying through of various obligatory duties devolving upon the holder of the post which he occupied. For a diocesan Bishop, who means to be diocesan almost exclusively, this gives ample opportunity of strenuous service. The daily round of Confirmations, preachings and other branches of diocesan administration is his, whether he will or not, and the difference between a good diocesan Bishop and a bad one depends upon how far he really rises to the adequate discharge of duties which in some form or other, adequately or inadequately, have got to be discharged.

[1] *Frederick Temple, Archbishop of Canterbury*: Memoirs by Seven Friends, ii. 247–9.

For example, the Confirmation list for the year must be carried through, the men appointed to benefices must be instituted, the letters about parish disputes must be attended to, visitations must be periodically held, and so on. In all such work Frederick Temple excelled. He was strong, thoughtful, self-reliant, forcible in speech and action, a great educationalist, and above all an enthusiastically earnest Christian man. His energy was quite untiring, and in his earlier days no task was beyond his strength. When duties other than diocesan came in natural course to him to be performed he performed them better than anybody else.

The Bishop goes on to give an account of Temple's practice at Lambeth:

The former intercourse about public matters in the way of daily correspondence was ended. Temple neither sought, nor could have used any such help. His habit of doing everything for himself extended from petty trifles, such, I believe, as carefully sorting and tidying his dressing room every morning before he left it, folding, hanging up towels etc., to the biggest things in Church and State. His Chaplains had no knowledge of his correspondence, though a certain number of letters, not many, were given them to write. He told them little or nothing, and they had to pick up facts as best they could. Obviously the kind of help I had given Archbishop Benson would have been not only useless but even offensive to him, and henceforth anything that I was to know about what was happening in the Church's life I had to pick up as best I might. As a matter of fact he practically abandoned, so far as I am able to judge, any real correspondence about overseas affairs. It had for many years been customary that Colonial Bishops and Missionaries should consult the Archbishop upon points of perplexity, and the Archbishop had usually taken counsel with the Church Societies and with individual Bishops—e.g. with Temple himself as Bishop of London, before replying. He brushed aside all that help and answered everything of the sort with his own hand, so far as it was answered at all. I fear that generally in his later years the reply was merely that the matter would receive consideration, and nothing more was heard of it.

My own correspondence files during the years of his Primacy show how constant was the complaint made to myself and others by those who had written to him from across the sea, that they could not get an answer, or an answer of a really helpful kind—still less did he himself initiate enquiries or consultations upon those big matters outside England in the way that had been customary before. His strength, as I have said before, lay in doing thoroughly the thing which was obligatory and could not be put aside.

But then Bishop Davidson shows how something more than this thorough performance of obligatory tasks was required of an Archbishop of Canterbury:

> To a great part of the proper Lambeth work this description does not apply. The Archbishop must of his own accord keep himself abreast of what is happening, must then on his own account take counsel about it and thus fit himself for giving real help to those who ask for it. Whether Temple could have done this or would have consented to do it had he become Primate at an earlier age I cannot tell. Certainly he did not do it coming to the Primacy when he did. His physical power as regards eyesight was already impaired, and was to be increasingly impaired, and his ruthless refusal to let anybody help him rendered it practically impossible that he could master the details required for what ought to have been done. It would be easy to give abundant instances of the mischief which ensued, but it would be invidious and I shall not attempt it. The West Indian Problems present a noteworthy example about which the Archbishop of Jamaica could say much.
>
> His self-reliance sometimes stood him in good stead, and it gave to everyone an impression, a true impression, of his real strength and power, but many a time mischief might have been averted if he had condescended to take counsel with one or two men whom of course he could have chosen according to his own wish.

It would be difficult to bring out the contrast in method between Archbishop Temple and his successor more clearly than it is brought out in these extracts; and certainly the conception of the office of Archbishop of Canterbury which Davidson here expressed was one to which, a few years later, he did abundant justice himself.

III

A curious incident occurred in connexion with the Confirmation of the new Archbishop, in which Bishop Davidson played an important part. He was one of the Commissioners appointed to execute the Royal Commission from the Queen for the confirmation of the Archbishop-elect, at Bow Church, December 22, 1896. In the course of the proceedings a protest was made by the Rev. S. D. Brownjohn, formerly chaplain to the Bishop of Bath and Wells, appearing as 'opposer' to the confirmation, 'on the ground that the said Dr. Frederick Temple is a self-confessed believer in the full doctrine of evolution, and because I believe acceptance of the teaching of evolution concerning the origin of man to be absolutely incompatible with fidelity to the teaching of the Book of Common Prayer and of the Articles of Religion of the Church of England'. The Vicar-General (Sir James Parker Deane) ruled, in pursuance as he stated of a Judgement by the Queen's Bench in the case of Dr. Hampden's confirmation as Bishop of Hereford in 1848, that the Court had no power to hear the objection. The protest had been most quietly, and, by the Archbishop of York as First Commissioner, on the Vicar-General's authority, most courteously disregarded. But the incident raised important questions with regard to the real significance of the whole ceremony. On the following day a letter from Davidson appeared in *The Times*, side by side with the report of the proceedings:

The BISHOP OF WINCHESTER *to the Editor of 'The Times'*

Farnham Castle. 22 Dec. 1896.

I was one of the Commissioners who in Bow Church to-day took part in the 'confirmation' of Archbishop Temple's election. As your report will doubtless tell, a protest against the confirmation was handed in by a clergyman, objecting to what he believes to be the Archbishop's opinion on the subject of evolution.

On the judicial or *quasi*-judicial authority of the Vicar-General the protest was courteously disregarded, its author being informed that he could not then be heard upon the subject. I have no doubt this ruling was legally correct, but the incident, though of the quietest and most unsensational character, serves to emphasize the necessity of the revision of the existing form of 'confirmation'. Its wording, including the 'citation of opposers', is certainly calculated to mislead the uninformed and to create a belief that any and every protest, whatever its character, may legitimately be heard and discussed on such occasions.

I am not so rash as to attempt, without preparation, to describe accurately the historical, canonical, and legal significance of a ceremony about which so much has been written. It is, I suppose, true that its original object was to secure that the person about to be consecrated or admitted to the privileges of his See was the identical person who had been elected by the chapter, and that the election had been in all respects duly and canonically performed. No one will, I believe, contend that it was ever the proper occasion for discussing the opinions of the Bishop-elect or his special fitness for his new office. But the 'form' used is in its wording so misleading that I trust the incident of to-day may enable us to secure by due process its revision and amendment. This I, for one, shall certainly endeavour to promote.

The interest in the protest was not lessened by the fact that Dr. Temple's confirmation as Bishop of Exeter had been similarly opposed. Hardly anybody on this occasion sympathized with the grounds of the objection. It was the manner of ignoring the objection which aroused profound dissatisfaction, freely expressed in the columns of the daily and weekly press. Davidson at once gave notice that he would bring the whole subject of the Confirmation of Bishops' elections before Convocation in January. Meantime, according to his wont, he made exhaustive inquiries into the history and the facts in libraries and elsewhere, with the help of many friends—especially Chancellor Dibdin and Canon Gore. Chancellor Dibdin had written an admirable article in the *Record* pointing out that Confirmation was the regular name for a process in two parts: (1) a preliminary inquiry into the fitness of the person nominated to the vacant See, and (2) the sentence of Confirmation which followed upon it, assuming the inquiry to end satisfactorily. By way of explaining the fitness the article referred to the petition which alleged that the person nominated 'is a prudent and discreet man and eminent for his knowledge of the Holy Scriptures, for his life and morals deservedly commended, of a free condition, born in lawful wedlock, of a lawful age, and an Ordained Priest'. 'The essence of the proceeding is that it is a safeguard.' The Chancellor wrote to the Bishop:

CHANCELLOR DIBDIN *to the* BISHOP OF WINCHESTER

25 December 1896.

I am very sorry for what happened. I do not mean that the Commissioners could do otherwise than follow the octogenarian advice they received, but the advice I greatly deplore . . . I hope you will not abolish confirmation.

The Bishop of Winchester tried to induce the Vicar-General to give notice at the Confirmation of Dr. Creighton as Bishop of London, on January 15, that the form of Confirmation was under consideration—but without success. There was a disgraceful scene arising out of a protest, this time on Ritualist grounds by

Mr. Kensit; and the Vicar-General was physically incapable of dealing with the proceedings so as to maintain decorum.

On January 27, a full debate took place in the Upper House of Canterbury Convocation on the motion of the Bishop of Winchester. His speech was a masterly survey of the situation before and after the Reformation. He pointed out that the question had not really been settled in 1848, as the four judges of the Queen's Bench, to whom application had been made for a *mandamus* to the then Vicar-General, Dr. Burnaby, were equally divided. He also maintained that the decision of Sir Travers Twiss, Vicar-General in 1869, that objections could only relate to defective form in the election or the identity of the person presented, was unsound. And he urged the Archbishop, with whom alone the decision lay, to 'consider afresh whether or not the precise manner in which Confirmation is at this moment carried out conforms exactly to what was originally intended and is intended now by the Sovereign who issues the Order'. The Archbishop, at the unanimous request of the Upper House, promised that he would look into the matter. By the Archbishop's desire, after the debate, Bishop Davidson sent him a memorandum of suggestions:

Suggestions as to the procedure in 'Confirmation'

I. Let the Bishop's formal acceptance of his Election take place either at his own house or elsewhere quite unconnected with the Confirmation ceremony. This was always the custom until quite recently.

II. Let the Confirmation ceremony proceed in the ordinary way, but without the presence of the Bishop-Elect, down to the end of the reading of the second Schedule, including the double citation of opposers and the hearing of them, if any. This will involve a slight modification in the wording relating to the presentation or production of the Bishop-Elect in person, but no other change.

III. Let the Court then adjourn to a subsequent day, on which the Bishop-Elect shall himself be present to take the oath, etc., in exact accordance with the Form as at present observed.

Of course in the event of opposers appearing and offering some material and reasonable objection, the hearing of it might involve more than one day, especially if no notice had been given beforehand and the Vicar-General was unaware of what was coming. But in any case such hearing, whether for one day or more, would be in the absence of the Bishop-Elect. This of itself would diminish the probability of any opposition being made.

In the covering letter, he begged the Archbishop not to avoid the difficulty by making a fundamental change in the form of citation, but to give the proper opportunity for objections inherent in the present proceedings, and so make the Confirmation itself a reality:

The BISHOP OF WINCHESTER *to the* ARCHBISHOP OF CANTERBURY

Farnham Castle. 1 Feb. 1897.

... I imagine that if Your Grace were now to modify the form of citation in the fundamental way which (as you tell me) has now been suggested to you, it would make it impossible ever hereafter to return to what I for one believe to be the true interpretation of the law and to allow opposers to be heard. That such a step would raise a storm, as it certainly would, is comparatively unimportant, if the decision were in itself indisputably right legally, historically, and ecclesiastically. But my own opinion is so convinced that it would be *wrong* in all these respects that I feel bound—as the mover of the resolution we unanimously passed in Convocation—to say so to Your Grace though I repeat what I there said that I regard the question (*quoad* the Confirmation of Bishops as contrasted with Archbishops) to belong to *you* and not to us.

I am sure you would wish me to say out what I feel on a subject to which I have been giving close attention, and however unimportant my own judgement it is no small matter that such men as the Bishop of Oxford, Dibdin, and others of different schools and opinions, who have studied the matter, are in agreement about it.

That there is an element of danger in giving a possibly new opportunity for 'heresy hunting' as Your Grace described it, I do not of course deny. But I believe such danger to be exceedingly small, and anyhow far less serious than a new departure in the direction of formally limiting—in a way that has never been done before in the Church of England—the area within which a protest is allowed to be brought forward. . . .

The correspondence which survives contains no record of any reply from the Archbishop, or evidence as to how or where the matter was concluded, save the copy of a letter to the Archbishop himself from Bishop Stubbs:

The Bishop of Oxford *to the* Archbishop of Canterbury

The Palace, Cuddesdon, Oxford.
Feb. 4, 1897.

I think that it may be said with confidence that there is no case in England, before the Reformation, of any Bishop being refused Confirmation on the ground of heresy. I do not think that, in the case of unconfirmed Elections, matters ever got so far as an attempt at formal Confirmation.

The objection was raised on the Election, and appeal was at once made to the Pope, who decided what was to be done and generally did it himself. There is a case, that of Bishop Stretton of Lichfield, about 1360, whom the Archbishop refused to confirm because he could not read. The King and Pope insisted upon its being done, and the Archbishop had to allow, or commission, two of the Bishops to consecrate, and did not do it himself.

I had to conclude, whilst I was on the Courts Commission, that the Court of Rome did not favour appeals on heresy; and I then hunted up every case of heresy that was to be found in books or registers. None of them touched any Bishop. Indeed Reginald Pecock, under Henry VI, is the only one against whom heterodoxy was ever formally alleged, and his history is the only one that can be really made to throw any side light on the matter. He was not put on trial until he had been a bishop for 13 years: all his adventures are in print.

The appeals on Elections were owing to divided votes, alleged unfitness, illegitimacy, and other non-doctrinal causes.

The next chapter of the story had to wait for the Confirmation of Bishop Gore in 1902.

Two smaller incidents affecting the property of the See of Canterbury may be mentioned here, for, though they were decided a little later, the decisions were the result of deliberation by Archbishop Temple very early in his reign. Archbishop Benson had been devoted to Addington Park—a beautiful estate near Croydon—as the country house of the Archbishops of Canterbury But Temple regarded it as an expensive luxury, and also desired that the Archbishops should have their country residence in Canterbury itself. He therefore sought to sell Addington and rebuild the Old Palace at Canterbury, with the knowledge, of course, that the consent of the Ecclesiastical Commissioners was necessary for the transaction. Addington Park was in fact sold for £70,000 in 1897. There was much opposition in Addington and Croydon, and Bishop Davidson was pressed to intervene, as an Ecclesiastical Commissioner. The Queen also was approached, and telegraphed expressing her hesitation as to the wisdom of the step, on the eve of a meeting of the Privy Council, at which she was to be asked to approve the sale. Davidson, who had throughout refused to take action against the sale, gave his views on the subject in the following telegram in reply:

Telegram from the BISHOP OF WINCHESTER *to* SIR ARTHUR BIGGE

2 Feb. 1898.

The subject has been under consideration for many months but I think present occupant rather hasty in his decision. Ecclesiastical Commissioners have had full discussions. Archbishop Benson was strongly opposed to any sale and wished place retained by future Primates. Archbishop Tait never considered or discussed the question. I cannot personally defend retention of so expensive a place besides Lambeth but I think terms now obtained very unsatisfactory and that delay would have been desirable. Am writing to explain my view.

The order was signed.

The case of Lambeth Field, however, was in Davidson's judgement a different matter. It had been the practice with successive Archbishops to give the use of 10 acres of land adjoining the Palace to the people of the neighbourhood. Some 7,500 tickets had been issued annually, each ticket admitting a whole family, excluding boys over eight years old. The field was used for school-treats, football and cricket clubs, an annual flower-show, a donkey-show, Volunteers' drill, and a variety of other purposes, and the personal relation between the Archbishop and the people of Lambeth secured by this arrangement was, it was claimed, of very real value. But the new Archbishop took the view that it would be far better used as a public open space, and agreed with the London County Council to hand it over to the Council without charge, on condition that it was open free for the use of the public all day, properly laid out and controlled.

Bishop Davidson and a majority of the Commissioners opposed the Archbishop, but their appeals and signed memorials to His

Grace were all in vain. The Archbishop found that the sanction of the Ecclesiastical Commissioners to a lease during the Archbishop's pleasure was not required, and as the Chairman of the L.C.C. (W. H. Dickinson) correctly stated in public on October 9, 1900, though 'for technical reasons the fee simple of the land was not transferred . . . for all practical purposes this valuable space was now secured to the public for ever'.

No friendship, however, was forfeited:

The Archbishop of Canterbury *to the* Bishop of Winchester

October 23, 1900.

It never occurred to me that what you said was either impertinent or in bad taste. I thought your pertinacity unwise. . . .

Do not let us quarrel because we cannot agree on such a matter as this. If you can stop what I propose to do, by all means stop it. I shall be vexed, but I shall not feel any resentment, nor rely less on your friendship.

IV

We have already referred to Archbishop Temple's relations with the overseas work of the Church. It may be well to conclude this chapter with some notes of Bishop Davidson's impressions as Episcopal Secretary of the Lambeth Conference, for they also illustrate his own view of the office of Archbishop of Canterbury.

The Lambeth Conference—a decennial gathering of the Bishops of the Anglican Communion—gives a special opportunity for knitting the various provinces and dioceses of the Anglican Church together in mutual counsel. It was Archbishop Temple's duty to preside over the fourth of these Conferences, while Bishop Davidson acted as its Episcopal Secretary. We propose to give a particular instance of action taken by Bishop Davidson, consulted on a matter of first-rate importance, and then Bishop Davidson's own general impressions of the Conference and the part played by Temple.

We quote first the letters which passed between Bishop W. C. Doane of Albany and Bishop Davidson on the subject of a Central Consultative Body and a Tribunal of Reference for the Anglican Communion. The letters have considerable importance historically in connexion with the development of the Anglican Communion and the attitude of the American Bishops to anything like a Canterbury Patriarchate or a centralization at Lambeth. It is to be noted that the item had been placed on the Agenda of the Conference by Benson, whose method certainly tended to draw all things to Lambeth.

The Bishop of Albany *to the* Bishop of Winchester

Albany, N.Y. Feb. 19, 1897.

I have concluded, after a good deal of thought and anxiety, to write confidentially to you about a matter, which I find is more and more exciting a good deal of interest and anxiety in this country. I mean the subject which is set down among the agenda of the Conference under No. 2 as b and c.[1] Of course it is a very easy matter to discuss and decide any one of the three points a, b, or c, as far as the colonies of the Church of England are concerned, but there is a very decided objection and a very strong opposition to any idea of attempting to establish any authoritative relation to the See of Canterbury in America, and I know there is also in the Church of Scotland. The feeling here is so strong that I know some of our Bishops, who otherwise would have gone, have given up the idea. I have myself the very deepest convictions that in the light of all historical experience, and in the existing conditions of the Church to-day, it is most unwise to attempt and would be absolutely impossible to create anything like a Canterbury Patriarchate, to which National Churches would be willing either to refer, or with which they would be willing to consult, or to which they would be willing to establish any relation. I am sure that we have shown here in America, and I am sure that you know how strongly my own feeling runs in that way, the strongest reverence and regard for the old See and for the Church of England. I am very clear in my own mind that the suggestion of this subject for discussion has been injurious to the best interests of the Conference; that its discussion would be inevitably painful; and that if it could, now that the change has come, (alas, alas,) in the personality of the Archbishopric, be dropped from the list of subjects; or, if that cannot be done, if only the words 'or elsewhere' could be taken out of clause c, I think it would give a very much better impression at the beginning, and secure a very much better feeling throughout the Conference and conduce to far better results in its delibera-

[1] A Committee of the Lambeth Conference, 1897, was appointed to 'consider and report upon the subject of the organisation of the Anglican communion—(*a*) a Central Consultative Body; (*b*) a Tribunal of Reference; (*c*) the Relation of Primates and Metropolitans in the Colonies and elsewhere to the See of Canterbury; (*d*) the Position and Functions of the Lambeth Conferences' (*The First Six Lambeth Conferences*, *1867–1920*, S.P.C.K., p. 212).

tions. I write this in the confidence of very sincere affection, and in the belief that you will recognize and realize at any rate the motive and reason of my writing.

The Bishop of Winchester *to the* Bishop of Albany

Farnham, April 6, 1897.

Private.

You must, I fear, have been wondering what can have happened to bring about my taciturnity! Your very important letter of (I fear) many weeks ago respecting the Lambeth Conference programme has been constantly in my thoughts, and I have often wondered whether I ought to speak to the Archbishop of Canterbury confidentially about it. But on the whole I have considered that I should do more harm than good by so speaking. *Ere your letter reached me* the formal programme of the Conference (including the names of suggested speakers specified *by you* on behalf of the Presiding Bishop) had been posted to every Bishop of our Church entitled to attend, and it was clearly too late to change the programme even if it had been desirable. And, notwithstanding all your weighty and most kindly words, the importance of which I cordially appreciate, I do still doubt whether such a change would be desirable. That anything of the nature of a Canterbury *Patriarchate* will receive the support of the Conference I do not for a moment believe. Some would wish for it, but they will be few. On the other hand the idea of some central tribunal of reference, for disputes on doctrinal or even disciplinary questions, has got a firm hold on the minds of very many, perhaps I ought to say of *most* of the Colonial and Missionary Bishops. I did not realise that it was wholly unpopular even in the United States, though of course it is suggested for the help of our South African, Australian, and Missionary Bishops rather than with any direct thought of *your* branch of our Church, a branch eminently capable of taking care of itself! I believe the S. African and Antipodean Bishops regard the question as quite the most important of any that are to come up for discussion, and, considering the immense weight of authority with which the subject was *suggested*, I don't see how dear Archbishop Benson could do otherwise than place it on our agenda. I suppose it would be perfectly in order for the American Bishops, should they so desire, to say that they preferred to be left out of consideration in that matter and to take no part in forming any such tribunal of reference or consultative body.

I am writing to you in strictest confidence, believing such to be your wish. Do, if you can, let me have a few lines again on the subject. No one can for a moment doubt the generous and brotherly—if I may not say filial—attitude you have always taken towards the Chair of St. Augustine, or suppose you could have any but the highest and most public spirited desire for the good of the *corporate* life of our Anglican Communion as a whole.

You suggest the omission of the words 'or elsewhere'. I don't think the United States were in the mind of those who drafted the heading. The 'elsewhere' includes (1) India, (2) All our Missionary work, (3) All such Dioceses as Gibraltar, Jerusalem, &c. &c.

In the result it was decided by the Conference not to set up any Tribunal of Reference as proposed by the Committee. The Archbishop of Canterbury was, however, 'requested to take such steps as he may think most desirable' for the creation of a consultative body 'to which resort may be had, if desired, by the National Church, Provinces, and extra-Provincial Dioceses of the Anglican Communion either for information or advice'. It was to the Tribunal of Reference that the American Bishops most objected: but they were still somewhat suspicious of the informal Consultative Body. Perhaps we may add another letter from Bishop Doane, written after the Conference was over, which shows Bishop Davidson as a skilful mediator in a more personal matter—the gift from the Bishops to the President. The first proposal appears to have been a mitre, and the reference is to the great reopening ceremony at Glastonbury Abbey during the month of the Conference:

The BISHOP OF ALBANY *to the* BISHOP OF WINCHESTER

Northeast Harbor, Maine,
Aug. 23d, 1897.

I am most grateful to you for your note of the 9th of August. I was quite sure myself that the suggestion about the mitre would not be agreeable to the Archbishop. Indeed, my impression of him, after Glastonbury, is, that he never wants to have anything on his head at all. I beg you will assure him that you have succeeded in stopping my 'kindness', as he calls it, and at the same time, thank him for his kindly way of putting it. It is the greatest pleasure to know of something that he wants, and it will be a still greater pleasure to all of us to see that what he wants is sent to him. I shall take it in hand at once. Why should we not have the brightest and most delightful memory of England, after a month that was crowded so full with every sort of kindness and pleasure and delight, to all of which you contributed so much?

Mrs. Doane joins me in most warm regards to Mrs. Davidson.

Bishop Davidson's general impressions of Archbishop Temple and the Lambeth Conference are as follows:

At its very outset he had to arrange for and preside over the Lambeth Conference of 1897. It had been summoned by his predecessor who had thrown himself with enthusiasm into all its details and identified himself with the things it was going to do. It was his characteristic idea that the Conference should be held not in its natural year 1898 but in 1897 as the thirteen hundredth anniversary of the landing of St. Augustine, a fact to which Temple never alluded in any part of the Conference proceedings.

I had been appointed the Episcopal Secretary and was conversant with everything, yet he hardly consulted me about anything, leaving me a perfectly free hand about things that were in any sense within my province and saying absolutely nothing to me, unless under pressure, about the policy, or the plans, or the order of proceedings, for which he would have to be when the time came technically responsible, but in which I was necessarily closely concerned. The whole thing was done by him like other things in his life, vigorously, brusquely, and effectively but with no attempt to touch any vein of sentiment or to recognise the work of Archbishop Benson in the programme laid down or the matters selected for discussion.

In his opening address at Canterbury everyone had supposed that his main theme would be the absence of the master mind to whom the Conference in its details was due. He made a speech about duty and did not allude in the remotest way to Archbishop Benson's existence. Everyone spoke of this, and I made bold on the morning of the day when the Conference was to meet for discussion to say something as to our hopes that he would allude to Benson in his opening address. I did it gingerly not knowing what answer I might receive. I simply asked him whether it would be his wish that the American Bishops should make such allusion as was appropriate to Archbishop Benson or whether he would do it himself. He replied that he thought nothing of the sort was necessary. I said that I knew some of the Bishops would wish for it and he answered 'Then I will do it' and spoke some admirable and telling sentences.

It would be easy to give scores of other instances as to his curiously direct way of keeping always to the exact point then before him and urging the plain duty of the hour without the

> admission of anything of a sentimental or illustrative sort. Whether that element in life was absolutely trampled under foot or was simply ignored because the thoughts were absent from his mind I do not know. . . .

It cannot be denied that these reflections by Bishop Davidson on his predecessor at Lambeth are critical in character. All the more striking therefore is the tribute with which he concludes:

> It may have been that the hold he obtained upon men, and the glamour he undoubtedly had for the public in the later years of his life, was due to his single-hearted outspoken devotion to the sacred principle of duty, inspired by a quite overmastering sense of the presence and help of God.

CHAPTER XV

THE BISHOP OF WINCHESTER AND THE QUEEN

There is an admirable epistle written by Petrus Blesensis, in the name of the Archbishop of Canterbury, to P. Alexander III, in the defence of the bishops of Ely, Winchester, and Norwich, that attended the court upon service of the king. 'It is no new thing for bishops to be counsellors to princes,' saith he; 'their wisdom and piety, that enables them for a bishopric, proclaims them fit instruments tó promote the public tranquillity of the commonwealth: they know how to comply with oppressed people, to advance designs of peace and public security; it is their office to instruct the king to righteousness, by their sanctity to be a rule to the court, and to diffuse their exemplary piety over the body of the kingdom, to mix influences of religion with designs of state, to make them have as much of the dove as of the serpent.' JEREMY TAYLOR, *Episcopacy Asserted*, Section 49.

THE Queen, when staying in the Isle of Wight, was in the Bishop of Winchester's diocese. We have already seen how he fitted in his own work with his various visits to Osborne. The calls Her Majesty made on his time were still numerous. It was not only that his counsel or comfort were needed in personal sorrow or perplexities—as when he was recalled by telegram from Cannes, in January 1896, on the death of Prince Henry of Battenberg of fever in Sierra Leone. There were public questions as well—though the written recollections are not so full in these days as they were during the life at Windsor or in South London.

In September 1896, the Bishop's influence with the Queen was solicited by Canon Scott Holland and others, for the purpose of gaining her interest with the Tsar on behalf of the suffering Armenian Christians, in view of the approaching visit of the Tsar to Balmoral:

The BISHOP OF WINCHESTER *to* CANON SCOTT HOLLAND

Private and Confidential. [Edinburgh]
19 Sept. 1896.

Farnham Castle,
Surrey.

I received Mr. Hecht's packet last night. I have done, am doing and will continue to do everything I can in the delicate and difficult matter on which you invite my aid. But from the nature of the case it is well to say as little as possible about what I *do* do! and I am writing briefly to Mr. Hecht to that effect.

I am going this afternoon to Dalmeny to spend Sunday under Rosebery's roof with Prince of Wales and Duke of Connaught who are awaiting the Czar's arrival.

The Princes and Rosebery may perhaps be helpful and you may rely on my anxiety to be of any use I possibly can.

We observe the Bishop's immediate action—and the skill with which he uses the link of the Diamond Jubilee, the preparations for which were already beginning.

The Bishop wrote at once to the Queen. He began by offering 'a few lines of dutiful and loyal affection and thankfulness' for the longest and most beneficial reign in English annals. Then he noted 'a rich significance in the fact that at the hour when all previous records of English History are eclipsed by the length of Your Majesty's gracious rule, Your Majesty should also wield a personal and domestic influence over the thrones of Europe absolutely without precedent in the History of Christendom'. The heart of the letter is contained in the following paragraph:

The Bishop of Winchester *to the* Queen

19 September 1896.

It can be no small matter to the world's life that the occupants of the Imperial thrones of Germany and of Russia should at such a juncture bear the relation they do to Your Majesty and, during the present fearful stirring of men's minds in view of Eastern violence and wrong, nothing surely is more touching than the simple belief which those unlearned in political complications hold that somehow or other 'The Queen will set things right when she sees the Czar'.

The letter concludes:

It betokens a genuine and loyal trust born of long experience—and, however mistaken the notion of simple hearts that matters can thus readily be set straight, the fact that people say and think it is in itself a striking evidence of what Your Majesty is to tens of thousands of English men, women, and children who know nothing of public life but know and trust and reverence their Queen and believe in her influence for all that is good.[1]

[1] *Letters of Queen Victoria*, 3rd series, vol. iii, p. 77 (for the full text).

In view of the hope which the Bishop expressed in his letter to Scott Holland that 'Rosebery may perhaps be helpful', it is interesting to note the surprising form which that helper's action took.

In October, a Liberal crisis had been forced by an extraordinary speech made by Lord Rosebery in the very height of a public agitation about the Armenians and Turkey. Here is a note on a talk by Davidson with John Morley at the Athenaeum on October 10, 1896, on its significance.

> This act of Rosebery's has smashed up for a generation to come the organisation known as the Liberal Party. We shall now have one pope at Dalmeny and another at Malwood, each with his followers, and no coherence possible. (I asked 'Which is Rome and which is Avignon?' But he declined to say!) It also gives the *quietus* to all the agitation, for it tells the Turkish and the European Statesmen that all the agitation means nothing—will lead to nothing—and that the Turk may go on as he likes.
>
> (I urged the effect on Foreign peoples.)
>
> I don't believe in the public opinion of Foreign peoples. In Germany it is crushed and kept down by authority. In France nobody really cares about Armenia except the bondholders, who are numberless in France and who don't want Turkey disturbed. I agree in the main with what Rosebery says, but why say it? Why tell them we shan't go to war alone? Why not leave it in the haze in which *Mr. G.* always leaves such things? Lord Salisbury, I believe, encouraged and desired these meetings—but he won't like this action of Rosebery's, which practically tells the Turk that English opinion is divided and that he may discount the meetings and 'feelings' as much as he likes.

With the Diamond Jubilee itself, the Bishop was involved in various ways. There was the school holiday appeal, almost inevitable at such times, which commended itself to the Queen, but not to Archbishop Temple or Bishop Davidson.

The ARCHBISHOP OF CANTERBURY *to the* BISHOP OF WINCHESTER

51 Lennox Gardens, S.W.
5th February 1897.

Advise me how to stop the Queen from giving an extra week holiday to Rugby, Harrow, Winchester etc. this year. The Holidays at the Public Schools have grown very much of late years and are really as long as is wholesome.

Could it not be suggested that a whole holiday on the 22nd June would be the right thing?

Tell me the right course to take.

The Bishop agreed with the Archbishop, though he found some difficulty in persuading the Queen.

The difficulty about the Jubilee Service at St. Paul's was of slightly larger proportions. It included the problem of Sir George Martin's setting for the *Te Deum* at the west door. This involved some delicate negotiations with Sir George Martin and even a visit to Farnham in which the last difficulties were settled. It was not easy altogether, for there were some very important persons who did not want a service at all, but thought that thanksgivings on Sunday June 20th would be sufficient. The character of the service was considerably affected by the fact that the Queen could not get out of her carriage, so that a service, however short, inside St. Paul's was impossible. The following letters tell their own tale:

The BISHOP OF WINCHESTER *to the* DEAN OF ST. PAUL'S[1]

2 March 1897.

The Queen has been talking to me very fully about the plans for the service outside St. Paul's on June 22.

She is evidently nervous about its *length*—and, unless she were satisfied it can be kept *within* the limits of time we spoke of at our recent Committee, she would I think be tempted to give it up.

'About a quarter of an hour—or at all events well under 20 minutes' she repeated several times. She dreads sitting there in her carriage long, with all the Princes on horseback round her.

She quite approves of the sort of service we planned, but she says emphatically

'Tell the Dean to arrange with Dr. Martin that the *Te Deum* is simple with no additions or "flourishes"' (whatever that may mean!).

I promised to communicate all this to you and I reassured her as to the length. She has apparently been counting or measuring how long an average *Te Deum* takes (say in St. George's chapel), and is assured it can be *within* ten minutes—leaving thus a full five or six minutes for the rest of the service.

[1] Robert Gregory, Dean of St. Paul's, 1890–1911.

Will you send me a line to Farnham (which I can show or quote), assuring me that you will see to this? It would be disastrous if the plan for such a service were now to be given up.

The Queen is about to intimate publicly her hope that on Sunday June 20th. there shall be everywhere a religious service of praise and thanksgiving. This is in order to make it clear that *that* is to be regarded as the great National *religious* function throughout the Empire.

On Tuesday the 22nd. the *gist* of the matter, the 'objective', will be the great procession in full pomp through the streets of the capital of the Empire—the religious service at St. Paul's being—so to speak—an *incident* in the day's procession and not its main feature.

She feels that if it were to be said 'The Queen is on that day going *to St. Paul's for a thanksgiving service*' the service ought to be a far grander and longer thing than *this* can possibly be.

So she is anxious to emphasise that *the* religious service of the occasion is on the Sunday, and that the Tuesday Service is merely to make it clear that we recognise in that 'Function of state' the religious element.

I am sure you will understand and appreciate all this, and will explain it to any who are puzzled or vexed (as some are) by what is planned.

I mark this private as it is of course not for publication—but pray show it to anybody you like who is concerned in the matter. I have tried to represent the Queen's views as clearly as I can—and not to import my own sentiments in any way.

The Bishop of Winchester *to the* Dean of St. Paul's

Farnham, 9 March 1897.

I am grateful to you for sending me Dr. Martin's letter. But either I must have written awkwardly in my former letter, or Dr. Martin has misunderstood my words, or both.

Dr. Martin's proposal now is that the *Te Deum* should be simply chanted to an old chant, *without accompaniment*, the choir being merely your own 18 men and 30 boys.

Now, as it seems to me, this would be quite different from what was formally laid before the Queen as the proposal of our Committee, and has been approved by her. It was distinctly proposed that the *Te Deum* should be of a more dignified sort—that there should be a strong force of men's voices, and that two military bands should accompany it. In my view we are not now competent to alter those arrangements unless by the Queen's commands. And surely, apart from our 'competence' to do so, it would be a very great pity? In a crowd so immense on pavement and at windows, and with horses trampling all round in hundreds etc., it will be essential surely to have a huge volume of sound for the *Te Deum* if it is not to be despicable? The Queen spoke especially of the *bands* as a feature in the service.

Again, surely it would cause wide disappointment to everybody (I should *think* to the Queen also, though I have no authority to say so) if we did not have *Dr. Martin*'s special *Te Deum.* We are all looking forward to it. Or, if he prefers that *that* should be inside St. Paul's, and by his own splendid choir alone, he would, better than anybody, choose some other *Te Deum*, be it in form of Chant or of 'Service', which would enlist the powers of band and of *many* voices.

From what he says as to his own *Te Deum* already written taking not more than ten minutes, I should have imagined it was the very thing, and (if I don't misunderstand the Queen's wish) all Her Majesty meant by deprecating 'flourishes' would be long instrumental passages without words.

I can easily ask for further information or commands if necessary, but I have so often had to arrange for services to suit the Queen's wish that I can speak pretty positively; or, if Dr. Martin would be helped by the counsel of a musical expert accustomed to these 'Royal' arrangements (sometimes very trying and inconvenient!) let him consult Sir W. Parratt, whom he knows well, and who could, I am certain, give him any information he desires.

I feel convinced the Queen would be disappointed, if not *pained*, if the Service were reduced to the dimensions Dr. Martin suggests, and I can't believe that in the midst of such a noisy open-air multitude, civil and military, the *Te Deum* could be dignified if chanted as he proposes by your own unaccompanied choir.

I can fully appreciate the difficulties with which Dr. Martin has to contend, and no one is so well able as he to overcome them. If I can in any way be helpful to him, or to you, by again writing to the Queen (who goes abroad to-morrow), or by any other step, you have only to command me. But I think it would be best that we should if possible arrange matters without further appeal to the Queen personally.

There is an excellent photograph of the Queen at the west door of St. Paul's on the great day, and the Bishop of Winchester on the steps in his Garter robes not far away. Davidson used to repeat with some satisfaction at times the Queen's remark at the end of the Jubilee day, that she supposed that the procession through London had been a very fine procession, but that she herself had been in a bad position for seeing it.

Easter 1898 was spent at Cimiez with the Queen:

The BISHOP OF WINCHESTER *to* MRS. DAVIDSON

Cimiez:
1 p.m. Easter Sunday, 1898.

I have your Thursday letter here this morning, sent on from Cannes. I am so distressed to hear that Mike Chapman is not so well, but 'glands' sounds less alarming than the former ails.

I look forward to Friday when I shall I hope find you safe at Rochmount.

Meantime the weather here is heavenly. Sun a little hot, but a delicious air. This Cimiez is an odd place! The biggest Hotel I think, I ever saw. I am housed sumptuously 'au premier' in the public part of it. The Queen's part is one end of the building and one can pass to and fro. There is a really beautiful Chapel, in which there is service for the Hotel when Her Majesty is not here—but when she is here the public have to go to Church in Nice, where—as you know—Erskine Knollys is chaplain. I hope to see him at evening service today. I went to early service this morning in the other Church (*Langford's*) in Nice—with Princess Christian and Princess Beatrice. Since our service (at 11) I have had a walk with Fritz Ponsonby and Reid. The views are splendid. The glare and dust however are considerable. You will be glad to hear I have secured a sleeping berth for Wednesday night, so I hope to get to St. Malo fairly fresh on Thursday night and to sleep there before the Friday crossing.

I am looking forward now to a good many quiet times before I leave the Riviera—as I have done my *work* and have no more responsibilities. This morning in the Chapel, Sir Arthur Sullivan played the Harmonium, and *Signor Tosti* sang the responses—in a loud voice—knowing no English. He is an R.C.

The poor old Queen is terribly worried by domestic and family wrongdoings, and last night Princess Christian sent for me to prepare me for a talk with Her Majesty thereon today.

The Duke of Edinburgh (Coburg) is very ill still—*here* on board ship—but is mending.

Other household worries seem to be rather less than usual! I must try and help if I can.

I think this respite, in midst of hurrying work, has been wholesome all round—I will try to use it to my best profit. I like to have time for weighing matters, and for prayers, and for thoughts of you and all your work for other folk. I think your plan of having that poor Alice Trigg taught by somebody is good. But what a depressing outlook at the best! Truly the world is a very puzzling place!

A note just come in to say the Queen wishes to see me after luncheon.

I am so well and feeling so freshened up already!

In October 1899, the South African War broke out. This made special claims on a Bishop in whose diocese the great military centre of Aldershot lay. In the early months we find him preaching in All Saints' Church to the troops before they set forth for service with the Sixth Division, and his engagement-book shows conferences with the Chaplain-General and many more as to the soldiers' religious needs. He was also later appointed Chairman of the Church Navy and Army Board, which had been formed on the initiative of Convocation, with its agencies in the dioceses, for promoting the moral and religious welfare of sailors and soldiers.

There were two special instances in which the Queen's help was sought by the Archbishop, both applications being referred to Bishop Davidson. The first was the proposal for a special collection in all churches, under the Queen's auspices, for sufferers in the war. To this the Queen agreed, though requiring some reassurance as to the need. A 'Queen's Letter to the Archbishop of Canterbury' for a general collection in the Churches of England and Wales on behalf of sufferers in the War, on January 7, 1900, was officially issued and forwarded to the Archbishop by the Home Secretary—the last instance, we believe, of a Royal Brief.

When, however, a second suggestion was made to the effect that a special day of intercession should be appointed, the Bishop was less successful. The following correspondence passed between Sir Arthur Bigge and the Bishop of Winchester:

SIR ARTHUR BIGGE *to the* BISHOP OF WINCHESTER

Windsor Castle. Decr: 22. 1899.

I have telegraphed to say the Archbishop of Canterbury suggests that a special day for intercession should be appointed.

The Queen is strongly opposed to the idea, and would prefer

that the Archbishops and Bishops should throughout their Dioceses inculcate the necessity for special prayer and praise not *on one day* but throughout these times of national anxiety—but *not* of humiliation.

As the 7th January has been appointed for special collections, the Queen suggests that the intercessory prayers might be then used if the Archbishop is inclined to press for the 'day'.

Please let me know if you can represent to His Grace how disinclined the Queen is to approve of the proposal.

The Queen entirely sympathises with memorial services and prayers on behalf of all who are engaged in or suffering through the War: but Her Majesty objects to the concentration of these into one 'by order' occasion!

The Bishop of Winchester *to* Sir Arthur Bigge

Farnham Castle, Surrey.
23rd Dec. 99.

I have this morning a very important telegram telling me of the Archbishop's request that a day of intercession be appointed in connection with the war. The subject is a most difficult one. On the one hand it seems to me quite vital that nothing should be done which could have the effect at home or abroad of making people think or say that our attitude at this juncture is 'We are losing ground or losing courage and losing men and *therefore* we appeal for Divine aid against our enemies'. The appointment of anything which could be called a 'Day of *Humiliation*' would inevitably so far as I can see have that result and appearance and nothing could be more disastrous. I do not know what are the grounds on which the Archbishop bases his request or who are the representative persons, if any, whom he has consulted. (He has not communicated with me about it. It is his way to do things independently.) I myself receive letters by every post, as, I suppose, do all the Bishops, expressing distress and dismay that no recognition by the *nation as such* of the duty of prayer in connection with our war has been put forth, and a great number of people who would feel as strongly as I do against a 'Day of Humiliation' are yet of opinion that a day of general intercession on the part of the nation and recognition of our duty towards God ought to be appointed. If it be appointed it seems to me quite vital that the directions given on the services authoritatively sanctioned should be so worded as to be equally applicable had our victories been continuous and complete from the first. It ought not I think to be impossible for the Archbishops or other authorities to secure such wording. Tens of thousands of people are in a condition of strain and of anxiety about those they love best. This does not mean that they are losing heart or courage but it makes them want some public national recognition of the Divine Governance of our Nation's Life, and they feel that a day set apart for this purpose would be helpful to everybody. Columns of the *Times* have shewn that this feeling though by no means a unanimous one is strong on the part of many who are certainly neither apt to whine or to cringe and who represent the robust side of English public life. I doubt whether they all see the *difficulties* so strongly as I seem to see them, but I do think a wise course might be steered and these difficulties thus evaded or overcome.

You suggest, as I understand your telegram, that if some appropriate service were drawn up for use on Jan. 7th, when national collections will be made, it would meet the demand. I don't think it would satisfy those who desire a day appointed for prayer. For one thing there are an immense number of churches, perhaps the majority, in which the collections have been already made, and in these cases the 'Queen's letter' directing collections would not apply. If independently of the question of collections the first Sunday of next year were directed to be a day for special prayer *and the lines were laid down in the way I have suggested*, the fact that in a great many churches there would also be collections for the Soldiers' Families etc. would not be an objection, but the prayers ought not in my judgement—if there is to be a National authorization of them—to be a mere appendage to the collections.

I feel terribly unhelpful in giving counsel in this matter, on account of my total lack of knowledge as to the communications on which the Archbishop bases his request, or as to what may have passed between him and responsible statesmen about it. I do not even know in what way he has made his request to the Queen—but I believe the wish for a day (preferably a Sunday so as to avoid making it a holiday) is real and widespread though not unanimous, and I think, with properly safeguarded wording the notion of 'humiliation under defeat' could be eliminated.

In the end the proposal for a Day of Prayer, by appointment of the State, was dropped. The Bishops agreed to advise the use of special prayers in their dioceses on Septuagesima Sunday, February 7, on their own initiative; care having been taken by Davidson, on behalf of the Bishops, to see that no objection was likely to be made to this proposal by the Government or by the Queen.

At the end of January, when Lord Roberts and Lord Kitchener had arrived in Capetown as Commander-in-Chief in South Africa and Chief of the Staff, things having gone ill for the British under the command of Sir Redvers Buller, a delicate personal mission was entrusted to the Bishop by the Queen. A letter came from Osborne to the Bishop, asking him to give a special message of sympathy to Lady Audrey Buller, wife of Sir Redvers, 'as you know her well and often see her'. The Bishop wrote at once and received a most grateful reply.

The Bishop of Winchester *to* Lady Audrey Buller

Farnham Castle, Surrey.
1 Feb 1900.

In a letter I have just received from Osborne the Queen requests me to take an opportunity of saying to you that while she 'cannot well write to you direct' (owing I suppose to official custom in such matters) she is anxious you should know how much she feels for you in all this anxious time, and for all that it must be to you, and that she has all faith in Sir Redvers. As it would be nearly impossible for me in the next few days to arrange to call upon you—so heavy is my work—I write this at once, as I feel sure you would like to know it. I have given you the message exactly as it comes to me.

Need I assure you how entirely what the Queen has said in this private communication gives expression to the feeling which the whole nation is entertaining at this time.

Our thoughts and prayers are constantly with you. God grant we may soon have bright and cheering news.

If you should think well to send me a private note which I could enclose to the Queen I feel sure it would please her.

Lady Audrey Buller *to the* Bishop of Winchester

Government House, Farnborough, Hants.
Feb. 2 1900.

I am indeed grateful and touched beyond words by the Queen's words of true kindness and sympathy, and above all, by her expression of faith in Sir Redvers.

It was so wonderfully good and thoughtful of Her Majesty to send this message and to *think* of me in this time of dreadful and *peculiar* anxiety. I do feel it more than I can say—this great kindness.

I am writing to Sir Redvers by this mail, and I hope I shall not be doing wrong in sending him your letter. I am sure it will do him great good. In all my great anxiety, I *know* that whatever happens, the best that *can* be done will be done by *him*. But certainly there never was a General who had more to struggle against than he has had—all that could possibly happen to frustrate his plans *has* happened not only since his arrival in S. Africa, but *before* he set foot there.

Thank you very, very much for your most kind and helpful words—I know how you and Mrs. Davidson *do* think of me and feel for me, and for *him*. I should like you to read the enclosed, as I have quoted some words of Sir Redvers, which I should like *you* to see. I must thank you so very much for the very fine haunch of venison you have so kindly sent.

Enclosure for the Queen.

From Lady A. Buller to the Queen.

2 Feb. 1900.

I have had a great wish to copy a few words out of one of Sir Redvers's letters (Dec. 18) which I think will interest Your Majesty and I now venture to send them. They were written to explain the reason for going to Natal.

'I regarded the attempt to relieve White as a forlorn hope, and did not want anyone to take the risk of a failure that I ought to be responsible for. So I came, and I can truly say I did what I thought right.'

CHAPTER XVI

THE BISHOP OF WINCHESTER AND THE HOUSE OF LORDS

A desire to serve the Nation in Parliament is an *English* Man's Ambition, always to be Encouraged, and never to be disapproved. THE MARQUESS OF HALIFAX.

The Lower Chamber is a chamber of eager politicians; the Upper (to say the least) of *not* eager ones. WALTER BAGEHOT, *The English Constitution.*

IT was only a week or two before the South African War began that Bishop Davidson gave his Charge to the Clergy of the Diocese (September 28—October 5, 1899). We have already referred, and shall have to refer again, to the main portion of its subject-matter—the doctrinal and ritual difficulties in the Church of England. But he wished to call attention now to his conception of the duties of a Bishop in the 'secular' field—a conception expressed with great emphasis at the very opening of the Charge, before he turned to the ecclesiastical controversy. The Bishop, he said (speaking in the choir of Winchester Cathedral), has his immediate diocesan responsibilities, and must be in touch day by day with the strangely varied needs and interests of each of his parishes ('We have 566 parishes in all'), and find time for looking personally into their circumstances:

> This is all as it should be. It is one main purpose for which a Bishop exists. But he is, besides, and not less rightly, expected to be giving time and thought to a whole multitude of central things in the life of the Nation or the Church, things quite other than Diocesan. Look back into any period you will of English History, and see the part which the Bishops whose tombs surround you in this Choir have always taken, as in duty bound, in such central matters as affected at the time the wellbeing, and especially the moral and religious wellbeing, of the English people. Unless I am strangely mistaken, it is not the wish of contemporary Churchmen, whether lay or clerical, that their Bishops should now for the first time in our history be so exclusively local officers as to have neither time nor opportunity for interests which are larger still.
>
> To evolve a working plan for the combination of these conflicting duties is no doubt a task to baffle any man. As I try to do it month by month I gratefully recognise that it is what you, whose claim upon your Bishop's time and energy stands indisputably

first, desire him to do. He is set in this peculiar office, which has its duly assigned niche in our National history past and present, to be in some sense your representative and mouthpiece for dealing with moral as well as with religious questions in the public life of England.

To give practical examples of what I mean. When questions directly affecting the affairs of the Clergy, or the system of our Church Schools, or the observance of Sunday, and so forth are under discussion, it is expected, as a matter of course, that the Bishops should take an active part. But in my judgment they are not less truly called upon—especially while they have a place in the National Legislature—to accept and use their responsibility in other matters which concern the social and moral health of our citizens and their children, say the protection of infant life from cruelty and wrong—or such amendment of our prison laws as shall make them remedial as well as punitive, or provision for the cases of workmen who are injured in the discharge of duty—or enactments for checking commercial immorality—or arrangements for promoting the health of shop assistants.

Bishops, in short, are entrusted, as I believe, with a place in the Legislature not only for what are technically called Ecclesiastical questions, but for whatever things directly concern the moral life and the social well-being of the English people.

These words express some of the deepest convictions of Randall Davidson regarding the responsibility of his office, which he held from the beginning to the end of his episcopate.

I

We are not surprised, therefore, that Bishop Davidson should take his duties as a member of the House of Lords very seriously. He was a member of the House as Bishop of Rochester for a few months, taking his seat in 1895, only four years after his consecration. But it was as Bishop of Winchester that he first spoke and began to play that active and public part in the debates of Parliament which continued without a break for thirty-five years until his death. He had been brought up to follow the proceedings of the House by Archbishop Tait; and we have already seen how he secured the special post in the corner of the Chamber for the Archbishop's chaplain. He came, therefore, with a far better acquaintance with the atmosphere of the House than is possessed by most bishops, or indeed most peers; and he knew the kind of approach and argument which would weigh with their lordships.

He was also deeply interested in human beings, not only those about whom he had to talk but those whom he met in the House. One of the great pleasures of the House of Lords, he used to say, was the opportunity it gave for friendly intercourse with the responsible leaders in public life. Davidson enjoyed people, and when a man enjoys the company which he finds day by day in the regular course of his work it makes his own part in the work not only more agreeable but also more effective. And there could be no doubt that regular attendance at the House when he became Archbishop enabled him to know things, and to do things, or get them done, through personal contact, which would have been quite impossible without it.

He also took immense pains with everything he did in the House. He knew his subject. He scoured London, and if need be the provinces, and even the Dominions, for help if he wanted to press a particular point home. He missed nothing, and was not only ready, but eager, to see workers, Government officials, representatives of public bodies, or anybody, whether for or against some particular opinion, from whom he could get light on the subject under discussion. He was thorough, and he was absolutely fair.

What was he like as a speaker? He spoke almost invariably from full notes carefully marshalled on long strips of paper, as often as not supplemented by quotations copied out in full from his authorities. Sometimes he would have more than enough material for a speech, and a packet is still preserved which he took to the House of Lords for one of the Temperance debates, unused, labelled '*Bona fide* travellers, surplus evidence'. People sometimes complained that in speaking he was apt to address his remarks much more to the reporters in the gallery than to the lords on the floor of the House. Some of those who heard him in those early days as Bishop of Winchester, describe him as turning his back on his brother bishops and the Lord Chancellor and levelling his voice straight at the reporters' gallery. They also remarked on his vigorous, clear, ringing voice. His previous experience in listening to the debates, as chaplain to Archbishop Tait, stood him in good stead; and he was thus enabled to get accustomed to the atmosphere of the House, and to gain the ear of its members, more quickly than the majority of Bishops.

We have already noted his interest in the Sunday question. A Bill for the legalization of Sunday entertainments was before Parliament. The Bishop had proved himself in favour of opening museums and galleries on Sundays, but he drew the line at the provision of lectures and music in public places for money, though the Bill proposed that the money taken should be for the good of the community and not for the profit of the promoters. In June 1897 he successfully moved the rejection in a striking speech, including a description of a sacred concert in New York, which caused the Lord Chancellor to 'shake and mumble ominously' on the Woolsack.

In July 1898, the Benefices Bill passed into law. It dealt with the transfer of patronage, and matters of clerical discipline. Bishop Davidson paid a tribute in the House of Lords to the indefatigable perseverance of Archbishop Benson as responsible, together with the eloquence of Archbishop Magee, for the placing of the Bill at last on the Statute Book. He also took occasion to condemn the false reports sometimes published as to the morals of the clergy. And as he always enjoyed catching inaccurate or malicious people out, we cannot doubt that it was with a particular relish that he related certain recent experiences of his own. The following account in his speech on July 7, 1898, is an admirable example of his thoroughness in digging things out.

He had noticed (he said), in a newspaper, a letter giving a tabulated statement of cases of wrongdoing among the clergy for twelve months, and according to this there had been 228 gross cases of moral misdemeanour or criminal conduct among the clergy in England. The writer of the letter professed to give his full name and address. The Bishop wrote to him and asked him for fuller information as to the figures upon which the table was based. He received his letter back, after it had wandered through many parts of England, marked to the effect that no such person was known. He then wrote to the editor of the newspaper in which the letter appeared, but owing to a change in the editorship his letter was overlooked; and yet the original letter with its statistics had been copied into many other newspapers! Then, a few months later, he saw a strange statement in the press that, at a gathering for the relief of decayed sandwich-men in the East of London, it was discovered that about one-half of the fourteen or fifteen men present had been in Holy Orders! He wrote to the editor of the newspaper, and, with a candour he hardly expected, the editor favoured him with the grounds upon which the statement had been made. It turned out that a correspondent had listened to some gossip in the smoke-room of his club to the effect that a large number of these people were members of the Church of England! This showed how often it was that scandalous statements concerning the clergy, when inquired into, were found to be absolutely without foundation.

But, as we have already said, Davidson's share in the debates of the House of Lords was by no means confined to ecclesiastical questions. And his action at the time was remarked upon as uncommon.

The earliest instance of his interest in general social welfare is found in his action on behalf of the Seats for Shop Assistants Bill in the summer of 1899. The object of that Bill, which had been brought forward by Sir John Lubbock and other supporters of the Early Closing Association, was to compel the provision of seats in shops or other premises where women assistants were employed. There was no doubt about the suffering endured by women in all too many places of business, where they were compelled by their occupation to stand for too many hours together. At the same time there were not a few excellent employers who disliked the idea of compulsion, and the substitution of legislation for voluntary effort, among those immediately concerned—a point of view sure of a favourable reception in the House of Lords. Bishop Davidson, his sympathies once aroused, tackled the subject with characteristic thoroughness. He interviewed social workers, inspectors, employers, and shop assistants themselves; went into the question of wages as well as leisure and health; and visited shops—some of the larger ones like Gorringe's and Marshall and Snelgrove's as well as the small—nor was he deterred by attacks such as that of Lady Frances Balfour, who poured scorn on this well-meant philanthropy, and described the Bill as the Grandmothers' Armchair Bill!

Accordingly, when it came up before the House of Lords for second reading on July 11, 1899, the Bishop of Winchester spoke with unusual personal authority. He reminded the House of Lord Salisbury's remarks when opposing a former Bill of a similar kind: 'In such matters as sitting down and standing up we trust to human instincts, leaving people to manage it for themselves.' He pointed out that the very object of this Bill was to allow the shop assistants to stand up or sit down as they pleased. We learn also from the report of a watchful observer in the press (*Pall Mall Gazette*, July 12) that the Bishop's narrative of private investigations produced a mild sensation. 'The Bishop', it said, '... but he of Winchester is not altogether as other Bishops are..., during the last fortnight has been on a pilgrimage through certain drapery establishments in London and, to quote his own words which fell with something like a shock upon the nerves of his peers, "I went behind the counter in each shop"!' There were other arguments of a more statistical kind as well, and the Bishop drew a distinction between first-class and second-class shops. In the result, despite a long and emphatic speech from Lord Salisbury against the Bill, the second reading was carried by 73 votes to 28; and on August 9 the Bill received the Royal Assent.[1]

It was perhaps Davidson's notable interest in the fortunes of this Bill which led to correspondence about another measure in which Mr. and Mrs. J. Ramsay MacDonald were interested—a Bill for the better regulation of Home Industries.[2]

Several letters passed on the subject between Mrs. MacDonald and the Bishop in February 1900, but Davidson, though sympathetic, did not see his way to introducing the Bill in the House of Lords.

II

The most important of all Davidson's contributions to social legislation, if we except his work on the Education Bill, 1902, was connected with the reform of the liquor trade.

A Royal Commission of twenty-four persons was appointed by Lord Salisbury in April 1896 under the chairmanship of Lord

[1] Mr. Frank Debenham, of Debenham & Freebody, an opponent of the Bill and himself an admirable employer, wrote after the Debate to the Bishop: 'Whatever our views may be as to remedies, we must all feel deeply grateful for the deep interest yourself and others are taking in these questions. The result of the debate on Tuesday was largely attributable to your own speech, and its influence on public opinion is bound to be great' (14 July).

[2] Lady Laura Ridding was the intermediary between the promoters of the Bill and the Bishop. She wrote to him on February 1, 1900: 'I do thank you most kindly for your thorough plan of going into the Home Work question. If you could see Mr. and Mrs. Macdonald, 3 Lincoln's Inn Fields, W.C., also about it, it would be a very kind and informing step. He has had, I believe, a great deal to do with drafting the Bill.... Mr. Macdonald... is a Labour M.P. candidate for Leicester.'

Peel to investigate this question. It collected an immense amount of evidence and in July 1899 presented its final conclusions in the shape of a majority report and a minority report.

In spite, however, of their apparent independence, out of 99 recommendations 77 were substantially common to the two reports. It was significant of the public disquiet about the general situation that the majority report itself should contain this paragraph:

> It is indisputable that a gigantic evil remains to be remedied and hardly any sacrifice would be too great which would result in a marked diminution of this national degradation.

No sooner were the reports published than a very considerable controversy arose. Lord Salisbury, curiously enough, seemed indifferent whether any action at all were taken on either report. The Temperance party generally ranged itself behind the minority recommendations, which had been signed, amongst others, by the Archbishop of Canterbury. There was, however, real danger that the whole labours of the Royal Commission might be lost. Some who foresaw this, including Davidson, therefore pressed for legislation on that large area where majority and minority were agreed. The matter was debated in the public press, at meetings, sometimes at quarter sessions, and in Convocation.

With a large body of public opinion behind him, Davidson decided to raise the whole question in the House of Lords. He accordingly proposed the following motion on May 8, 1900:

> That it is desirable that legislative effect be given to such of the recommendations contained in the Final Report of the Royal Commission on Liquor Licensing Laws as are common to the 'Majority Report' and the 'Minority Report' of the Commissioners.

It was the first time that the attention of the Lords had been called to the Report, and a large number of peers were present. The Bishop made a most interesting and exhaustive speech. As he pointed out, with some humour:

> One Report is signed by seventeen of the twenty-four members, headed by the vice-chairman of the Commission, that is to say, by the whole of those representing the Trade and by the party who claimed the attribute of approaching the matter with open minds. The second Report was signed by the Chairman of the Commission

and by seven of his colleagues who were ranged upon what is commonly called the 'Temperance' side. One Commissioner of great ability—an Irishman—signed both Reports.[1]

The Bishop laid great weight on the substantial measure of reform on which both Majority and Minority were agreed, and he expressed his regret 'that the matter had not been taken in hand on their own initiative by His Majesty's Government who appointed the Commission . . . and who, it would seem to me, have some measure of responsibility for dealing with the unanimous conclusions to which the Commissioners ultimately came'.

Lord Salisbury, in reply, refused to accept the motion, though inviting the Bishop, if he liked, to produce measures of his own; questioned the meaning and the value of the unanimous recommendations; and spoke somewhat slightingly of the Report of the Commissioners 'who undoubtedly have gone through a labour of extreme severity and have attained results that are perhaps not altogether satisfactory'. The Archbishop of Canterbury not unnaturally asked why, if all the objections urged by Lord Salisbury against any legislation on licensing were well founded, he and his colleagues had appointed the Commission at all. On His Grace's suggestion the Bishop of Winchester's motion was negatived and the following amended motion was put:

> That it is desirable that Her Majesty's Government should at an early date lay before Parliament proposals founded on such of the recommendations contained in the final Report of the Royal Commission with regard to the Liquor Licensing Laws as are common to both the Minority Report and the Majority Report of the Commission.

Lord Salisbury insisted on treating this motion as one of want of confidence, but even so the motion was only lost by a narrow majority (42 to 45).

The Prime Minister's invitation to Davidson to bring in a Bill on his own with the promise of respectful attention did not fall on deaf ears. Lord Rosebery wrote to him, as follows:

The EARL OF ROSEBERY *to the* BISHOP OF WINCHESTER

38, Berkeley Square, W.
June 21, 1900.

I think you are quite right to make even a nibble at legislation. The extent indeed matters little, as nothing will pass.

[1] The chairman was Lord Peel, the vice-chairman Sir Algernon West.

With the help of a Committee of Bishops, he drafted three separate Bills, and in March 1901 introduced them into the House of Lords. By his manner of speech Davidson earned the praise of Lobby Correspondents: 'His Lordship is one of the few prelates who recognize that the art of legislation is learned by steps' (*Nottingham Daily Express*, March 15, 1901). His quietness and pertinacity had their reward. Of the three Bills, one (Intoxicating Liquor Sale to Travellers Bill) was rejected. A second, on Licensing Sessions, was passed by the House of Lords but made no progress with the Commons. The third (Habitual Drunkards Bill) was substantially amended by the Government and passed the Lords, Lord Salisbury in an ironical speech observing: 'I rather wish to push into the foreground the fact that by a strange chance I was able to find myself in agreement with the Right Reverend Prelate. It was rather a satisfaction to know that for once we could pull in the same boat.'[1]

Lord Salisbury had throughout the discussions on Temperance legislation adopted a line which seemed flippant or cynical to his opponents, and he was particularly caustic to the bishops. There is a charming cartoon by F. C. G. in the *Westminster Gazette* (May 16, 1901), called 'The Aged Man', in which Lord Salisbury is sitting on a stile, very sleepy, while the White Knight, in the shape of Lord Rosebery, is trying to pull him about and shake him. The legend below the picture reads thus:

> I shook him well from side to side
>   Until his face was blue.
> 'Come, tell me where's the Bill', I cried,
>   And what you're going to do.'
>
> He said 'I hunt for jibes and pins
>   To prick the bishops' calves,
> And search for Royal Commissions too
>   To use as safety valves.'

The Bills thus introduced by the Bishop of Winchester and amended by the Government for the moment got no farther than the House of Lords. The critics of the Government laughed at the idea of any such legislation going forward. 'In the episcopal bosom', said Lord Rosebery, referring to Davidson, 'a more

[1] Bishop Westcott wrote, March 15, 1901, just before he died: 'To have won praise from Lord Salisbury on questions of Temperance legislation is an unlooked for achievement.'

sanguine spirit may lurk than that which inspires merely secular individuals. He must indeed have it in abundance if he expects any Temperance legislation from this Government.' Randall Davidson was certainly sanguine, but in this case his wild hope of Temperance Reform was rewarded. In the spring of 1902 he had the satisfaction of seeing a full-fledged Licensing Bill introduced into Parliament by the Home Secretary. Indeed it covered a wider field than the Bishop's three Bills, as it also provided, amongst other things, for the registration of clubs. But Davidson's claim when he spoke of the Bill in Convocation on May 2, 1902, was not without its justification.

> The Government has very rightly announced that this Bill is the outcome of prolonged consideration and careful thought on their part in the draft of its various clauses. We are glad to remember, although I do not think that any recognition has been given to the fact, that most of the clauses were, as a matter of fact, drafted in this room and were portions of our Bill which was presented in the House.

The Bishop of Winchester took an active part in the House of Lords debates as the Bill proceeded, and on July 31 it received the Royal Assent.

CHAPTER XVII

THE RITUAL CONTROVERSY AND THE CRISIS IN THE CHURCH

The discourse fell at length upon a point which seldom escapes a knot of true born Englishmen, whether in case of a religious war, the Protestants would not be too strong for the Papists! This we unanimously determined on the Protestant side.
ADDISON, *The Political Upholsterer*.

THE crisis which led to the appointment of the Royal Commission on Ecclesiastical Discipline, and so to the twenty years or more of Prayer Book revision, broke out in 1898. But (apart from its earlier history in the days of Archbishop Tait and Archbishop Benson) we notice an interesting suggestion, in which Bishop Davidson was concerned, for giving legal authority to liturgical revision. It has a special interest as a kind of anticipation of the procedure later adopted under the Enabling Act of 1919.

In February 1896, Davidson brought before the Upper House of Canterbury Convocation a draft Bill to provide facilities for the amendment of the rubrics of the Book of Common Prayer, and for the addition of prayers thereto. The method proposed by the Bill was procedure by scheme through both Houses of Convocation; the scheme to be laid before Her Majesty in Council and to be approved unless either House of Parliament within three months should have presented an address to Her Majesty praying her to withhold her consent. A similar Enabling Bill had been approved by Archbishop Tait and the Upper House in 1879. The present Bill was also approved by the Upper House, and sent down to the Lower House (composed of the inferior clergy), where, however, it met with a sad rebuff. The Lower House in July, on the motion of the Dean of St. Paul's (Dr. Gregory), declared that it was inexpedient to seek for powers to make alterations in the rubrics as proposed by the Bill. The Bishop's disappointment was keen. 'I do not', he said to the Upper House, 'recognize my child on its coming back to me from what I had almost been rude enough to call the gypsy camp.' The Bill was dropped.

In connexion with the Bill, the Bishop had some correspondence with the Rev. T. A. Lacey, a learned clergyman usually associated with the High Church party, who sought his sympathy for a Measure to permit the alternative use of the Prayer Book of 1549 (the First Prayer Book of King Edward VI). The Bishop's objection is significant, for it is very early evidence of his abhorrence of submitting changes in the Church's services to detailed discussion in the House of Commons.

The Bishop of Winchester *to the* Rev. T. A. Lacey

28 March, 1896.

It seems to me that to endeavour at present to obtain such permission as you refer to would (quite apart from any question of its expediency) be putting the cart before the horse. What I am endeavouring to do is to obtain power for the Convocations to suggest changes which should become law without having to be discussed in detail by Parliament. Such a proposal as you make might in due course be made by Convocation if the powers I ask for are granted by law. But if we were now to go to Parliament to ask for a Bill to authorise the use of an alternative Office for the Holy Communion, that Office would require to be itself a schedule to the Act, just as the Prayer Book is a schedule to the Act of Uniformity, and it would thus, *horribile dictu*, have, in its every line, to run the gauntlet of the House of Commons.

I

The crisis, however, so far as the public was concerned, began as we stated, two years later, in May 1898. In that month a petition from Mr. John Kensit was presented by Bishop Creighton to the Upper House of Canterbury Convocation. It was a protest against services in a number of dioceses which, it was alleged, were 'largely those in use in the Church of Rome, and taken from the Roman Missal and other books belonging to that Church'. Mr. Kensit had already made himself notorious by his interruptions of Divine Service, and he gave an undertaking to the Bishop of London that for the next two months he would cease such interruptions and at the same time prepare a memorial setting forth the 'various illegal practices' to which he objected. A debate followed in which the Archbishop and several other Bishops, including Davidson, took part. From that time on the ritual controversy steadily gathered force and held the attention of the public for nearly two years.

The Diocese of Winchester was in no sense the resort of ritualistic clergy, though there were certainly churches in which 'illegal practices' went on. But it was the home of the redoubtable foe of all mutinous priests, Sir William Harcourt, whose seat was at Malwood, near Lyndhurst. He was a stubborn and a strong Churchman, devout in his own way. And he was an Erastian who looked on the Church as a creation of Parliament and the Book of Common Prayer as 'the Schedule of the Statute'. From his pen flew forth prodigious polemics. The pages of *The Times* abound with his letters on 'Lawlessness in the Church', 'The Powers of the Bishops and their Veto', 'The Confessional as it is', 'The Mutiny of the Priests', 'The Laity, their Rights and Powers', and kindred themes.

A voluminous correspondence between Davidson and Harcourt survives among Davidson's papers; and there were encounters also in the Press. One principal feature in the controversy concerned 'special services'. Both Davidson and Harcourt agreed in dismissing Archbishop Temple's interpretation of the words of the Act of Uniformity Amendment Act—allowing special services on special occasions upon the express condition 'so that there be not introduced into such Services anything except hymns or anthems which does not form part of the Holy Scriptures or the Book of Common Prayer'. Dr. Temple claimed that these words meant 'that there must be nothing (in those Services) which contains and nothing which expresses any doctrine which you cannot find the substance of in either the Bible or the Book of Common Prayer'. No other Bishop agreed with the theory of the Archbishop, though they might all appear to act upon it.[1] The point Davidson made, however, was that the Acts of Uniformity only referred to 'open' prayer and to the duly appointed Services of the Church on week-days and

[1] In his evidence before the Royal Commission on Ecclesiastical Discipline in 1905, Davidson referred to Archbishop Temple's interpretation as one held, as far as he knew, by Temple alone. He added (13227): 'If Archbishop Temple's interpretation held good, it would seem that anthems or hymns might be contrary to the teaching contained in the Book of Common Prayer, and that the only things which might not were the prayers. But be that as it may, I am not aware of anyone who defends in theory that interpretation, although in practice I think many of us act almost as though it were the interpretation.'

Sundays alike and did not by any means cover the ground of legitimate worship. In a letter published in *The Times* of August 29, 1898, he wrote:

The Bishop of Winchester *to the Editor of* '*The Times*'

August 26, 1898.

A few generations ago it was usual for Sunday-schools, with the devotions accompanying them, to be held in the parish church, nor was it ever, that I have heard of, suggested that this contravened the Act of Uniformity. Further, what is the authority by which the service for the consecration of the Church is habitually used, in the presence too of the Chancellor, in a form prescribed by each Bishop for his own diocese and modelled usually on the service drawn up by Bishop Andrewes in 1620? When a new incumbent is inducted, by what authority, other than episcopal, is the service used? These, Sir, are not newfangled innovations. They have long prescription in their favour.

I am far from saying that the legal question is a simple one. Still less would I claim for my opinion any other weight than may rightly attach to the opinion of any responsible man who has done his best to consider a difficult question. My position is this. I have to decide, as a diocesan Bishop, whether or not I am under a legal obligation to prohibit such services as I have described. On examining the facts I find that concurrently with the obligatory and continuous use of the services legally and universally prescribed, our parish churches have been utilized for centuries, without suspicion of illegality, for other teaching and devotion appropriate to the needs of the day. In somnolent, dreary Georgian days such use was, no doubt, sparse and broken. But there it was. In face of this fact can it be a Bishop's duty, at a time of welcome activity and life, to put a peremptory stop to the use, for special purposes and at special hours, of wholesome and profitable services submitted in every case for his approval, services based from first to last on Scripture and the Prayer Book, and proved by daily experience to be absolutely required for the modern needs of our people and deeply valued by those who use them? Rather, as it seems to me, ought each diocesan Bishop to redouble his efforts to safeguard the character of every service used, however occasionally, in his diocese. It is, as was pointed out by the Lambeth Conference last year, his bounden duty to take care 'that all such additions or adaptations be in thorough harmony with the spirit and tenor of the whole Book of Common Prayer'. The vagaries of a very few men in a very few dioceses have diverted public attention from the real character of the special services in ordinary use.

Harcourt, writing privately later to Davidson about his remarks on the Reformed Church of England in his Diocesan Conference, with which he agreed, said (Sept. 23, 1898) that whatever might be true of 'special services' in a general way, 'the Ritualists with true Ecclesiastical wile have taken advantage of them as stalking horses to cover their approach to Rome', and added:

SIR WILLIAM HARCOURT *to the* BISHOP OF WINCHESTER

September 23, 1898.

For myself I would willingly trust the present Bishop of Winchester, but I should certainly not have the same confidence in the contiguous Sarum. You would have a special service approved on one side of the road and disapproved on the other side.

The Bishop, in reply, defined his attitude to the special services, and spoke of the general situation thus:

The BISHOP OF WINCHESTER *to* SIR WILLIAM HARCOURT

Baveno, Lago Maggiore.
Sept. 27, 1898.

I am indeed profoundly convinced of our present dangers. Though they are, so far as I can judge, partly the *inevitable* accompaniment of the aesthetic (as contrasted with doctrinal) change which characterises modern modes of worship in all English-speaking Christendom, among Nonconformists as surely as among Churchmen—there is also a weak and sentimental return to emotional rather than intellectual beliefs and forms of devotion. It is I think a mistake to suppose that things can readily be 'set straight' by sheer exercise of authority, either by Bishops or by anybody else. I don't defend the Bishops. I think they have been slack and that too much liberty has been allowed to hard-working and devoted men to do very much as they liked in matters of ritual and even teaching provided only they worked hard. But it has to be remembered that 'sacerdotalism' is not a very *tangible* thing, that some of its worst developments are matters of degree rather than of 'kind'—exaggerations of truth rather than contradictions of it—and that Bishops, like other men, are cautious about issuing ukases which they have no power to enforce.

You speak specially and truly of the dangers arising from Confession. No man, I think, can feel these more strongly than I do. . . . But the wholesale and absolute denunciation of private Confession in any and every form is, so far as I can see, equally incompatible with the Prayer Book words as they stand. . . . I agree with you that the English people is sternly and inflexibly resolved to have no return to the 'System of the Confessional', and in enforcing this resolve they will have nearly all the Bishops enthusiastically on their side. But if we are to carry our best men with us in restraining—sternly if need be—sacerdotal excesses and distortions, we must be on our guard against anything that can be represented as unfair. I believe most of the 'advanced' men (not quite all but most) can be kept loyal or won back to loyalty if we treat them fairly. If we don't, there is no chance at all. The best friend the irreconcileables—the handful of impracticable or disloyal Ritualists—have at this moment is Mr. Kensit.

Meantime the public agitation was increasing, and the Bishops were obliged to deal with the situation by concerted action. Though the Confessional was attacked with some violence from without, the two practices which the Bishops appeared to be resolute in forbidding were the ceremonial use of incense, and—most important of all—Reservation. Davidson was in communication with the Archbishop as to an active policy, particularly with regard to his much cherished plan for reforming Ecclesiastical Courts. The letters show a certain nervousness, as well as persistence, on Davidson's part as to whether Temple was really going not only to take the Courts question out of his hands but, when undertaken, to carry it through. The following letter refers to the proposal adopted at the Bishops' Meeting in January of a twofold policy of reforming the Courts, and making use of the provision at the end of the Preface to the Prayer Book, whereby any Bishop in doubt as to the bearing of the Prayer Book rules on a particular service or ceremony 'may send for the resolution thereof to the Archbishop'.

The BISHOP OF WINCHESTER *to the* ARCHBISHOP OF CANTERBURY

Farnham Castle, Surrey.

Private. Dec. 27, 1898.

I appreciate your kind confidence in the matter of possible 'Court' legislation. . . .

As regards your interesting and I think *new* proposal to make something more formal and more practical of the appeal to the Archbishop provided in the Prayer Book Preface, I think it *admirable*, provided it be not in any way announced as a *substitute* for the legal Courts (reformed or unreformed). If it were proposed and announced as a substitute for these, it would I think play into the hands of the Harcourt party, who already complain that the Bishops keep the matter in their own 'clerical' or 'sacerdotal' hands, and bar out the laymen from any voice.

The Bishops met on January 17, 1899, and duly announced their dual policy in the Press: (1) to submit a Bill for the reform of the Ecclesiastical Courts, drawn on the lines laid down by the Royal Commission of 1883 to the Convocations in February; and (2) to provide for Hearings by the Archbishop of the Province at which those who are concerned in the case may 'argue the matter openly before him, either personally or by counsel', neither Archbishop pronouncing a final decision without first consulting the other Archbishop.

Meantime the controversy raged with increasing fierceness outside the walls of Lambeth. More than ever did ritualism become the absorbing question of the hour. A special attack was levelled on the use by the Bishops of their veto under the Public Worship Regulation Act.[1] It was said that they had used it so deliberately that all prosecutions of disobedient clergy had been stopped and the Courts had been destroyed.

Sir William Harcourt *to the* Bishop of Winchester

Malwood, Lyndhurst.

Private. January 13, 1899.

I have no doubt that you have done and are doing what you can in the way of private communication to restrain unlawful Ritual practices, but unfortunately the results are at present very little apparent to the public eye. . . .

I have recently been in communication with Sir Francis Jeune —the greatest living authority upon this subject—and he writes to me 'the Church Discipline Act was employed in the case of Mackonochie and he was deprived by sentence of the Privy Council in 1883. This action was a complete success and there is every reason to believe that had the Bishops not interfered to close the Law Courts the result must have been that illegal Ritualism

[1] The Public Worship Regulation Act, 1874, gave an express power to a Bishop not to proceed on a representation made to him [against a clergyman] under that Act, subject to the condition that he should consider 'the whole circumstances of the case', and, if he should decide not to proceed, give his reasons in writing (*Report of Royal Commission on Ecclesiastical Discipline, 1906*, p. 69). There were thirty-three cases in which the veto was used between 1874 and 1906.

would have been ended and never would have been revived. It was a great responsibility to take and its assumption could only have been justified by their using some power of their own to better purpose than the ordinary course of Law, but so far from this being the case, they either were never able to stop illegalities or were not able to prevent their coming into existence again. I don't think there could be a doubt that to take away this clearly misused Veto would end illegal Ritualism once for all.' This action of the Bishops by neutralising the law of the Church is the *fons et origo* of the present lawlessness and chaos.

The Bishop of Winchester *to* Sir William Harcourt

Farnham, Jan. 14, 1899.

In your main contention in this controversy, I am, as you well know, in agreement with you. If you will pardon what may seem to you the impertinence of my saying so, I think you underrate the difficulties which beset our *speedy* action, and further that you perhaps do not quite realise the strength of *lay* opinion in support of advanced men. These laymen are, I am thankful to know, a mere insignificant handful among the lay Churchmen of England, but they are good and earnest men who have a right to our consideration, and whom we have no right to 'bully'.

To deal with each such Church and congregation by the process which seems to me the right one—i.e. first privately, by remonstrance, personal influence, and (if need be) formal direction, and then, if these efforts fail, by public 'action', does require time, say a few months, and it is peculiarly difficult at a season of popular excitement on the subject. I am in complete agreement with much of what you say as to the responsibility belonging to those Bishops who have refused to repress excesses on the part of hard-working earnest men. I have urged it repeatedly, and have not I hope myself erred gravely in that direction. But the result of this policy —what has sometimes been called the Gamaliel policy—has been that thousands of laymen have become keenly in favour of usages which public opinion *now* calls on the Bishops to suppress; and I honestly think these men are fairly entitled to sympathy and consideration as to the manner in which they are to be deprived of what they prize. It is to be remembered too that the present hot enthusiasm for repressing vagaries on the part of earnest men has not long been aroused. You may possibly remember that I, on coming into the Diocese, three years ago, was immediately confronted with the case of St. Agatha's, Portsmouth, where Mr. Dolling desired an altar specially for 'masses for the dead'. I absolutely declined to tolerate this, and in the result Mr. Dolling was, as most people put it, 'driven out of Portsmouth by his Bishop'. If you were to consult the Press comments, etc., and still more if you were to see my correspondence files at that time, you would find the outcry which was raised against me 'for letting a hard-working man be harried because of some foolish ritual fads', and so forth.

Harcourt replied in his usual trenchant way:

SIR WILLIAM HARCOURT *to the* BISHOP OF WINCHESTER

Malwood, Lyndhurst.
January 15, 1899.

I confess I am getting rather sick of the 'good and earnest men' who violate the law and break their oaths. It really does not melt my heart, when a man is discovered to be a swindler or a pick-pocket, to be told that he is an admirable family man and goes to church twice on Sunday. . . . I fully recognise the pluck which you showed in the Dolling case, but you stand, like Lot, alone, and without any episcopal family about you. The cause of all mischief is cowardice, and moral cowardice the worst of all. *Misera est servitus*, when the Bench is suffering from this influenza. . . . Half a dozen deprivations of contumacious law breakers will do more good than all the 'talky talky' of well-meaning and weak-acting people and might tranquillize the public mind. If these gentlemen take themselves off to the place where they properly belong so much the better—until these bacilli are got out of the system there will be no health in the Church.

A few days later Davidson was the cause of a considerable amount of speculation in the Press, as he went straight from Osborne to Malwood, whence, the public opined, Harcourt would be given the Queen's own views:

The BISHOP OF WINCHESTER *to the* QUEEN[1]

Lindisfarne, Bournemouth.
25 Jan., 1899.

Your Majesty was good enough to desire me to write about the result of my visit yesterday to Sir William Harcourt.

I had a great deal of conversation with him and while in his general wish to maintain the true Protestant character of the Church of England against foolish innovations, I am in full agreement with him, I yet cannot think his present violent and heated

[1] *Letters of Queen Victoria*, 3rd series, vol. iii, p. 335.

letters are conducive to a wise result. He is stirring up passions which had slumbered, and the result of that will be to make a solution more and more difficult.

I tried to point this out to him but without much effect I fear. I told him, of course, what Your Majesty had said upon the subject.

I am now corresponding with Sir William privately upon some of the points raised in the controversy, and perhaps Your Majesty will graciously afford me some opportunity of reporting further upon the whole subject before very long. The Bishops are placed at present in a most anxious and difficult position, as Your Majesty knows.

The next step in the controversy was taken by the Bishop of Winchester giving notice of a Motion in the House of Lords to call attention 'to statements lately made respecting the actions of the Bishops in dealing with irregularities in public worship'. To some it might be surprising that the Bishops should ask for battle in the House of Lords. But in reality it was a very sound policy, especially when Davidson was able to say at the beginning of his speech that he had challenged Lord Kinnaird to repeat in the House the statement made about the Church and the Bishops in the Albert Hall a week or two before, and that on Lord Kinnaird declining the challenge he had felt it right to come forward himself. The House was crowded. The Bishops were present in force (eighteen out of twenty-four); the galleries full; and among prominent members of the two Front Benches of the House of Commons, on the steps of the throne, were Arthur Balfour and John Morley.

There were many comments on the Bishop's manner in the Press next morning. 'Bishop Davidson knew his House of Lords', 'His Lordship is a cheerful-looking, middle-aged man with very little of the prelate and nothing of the ascetic about him', 'He cooed gently with glib, smooth tongue.' After referring to the attacks in the Albert Hall and the Press, the Bishop dealt with the alleged misuse of the episcopal veto. He stated that, with three trifling but significant exceptions, no living bishop had in any circumstances ever exercised that veto at all. The eloquent indictment had been launched against an imaginary foe. Was this fair in controversy? Was the Bishop not right in taking the first opportunity to call attention to the matter in the House of Lords?

He proceeded to give the facts as to the circumstances in which the veto had been used by Bishops now alive—in 1876, in 1886, and in the case of the St. Paul's Cathedral reredos, more recently. He then said (*The Times*, February 10, 1899):

> It might be asked how it was that there had been no suits for many years past, and that the position of the Dean of Arches had been a sinecure for many years. Simply because the Church of England as a whole—laymen, clergy, and Bishops together—had come to the conclusion that a cessation of these prosecutions was desirable. They found them to be doing incalculable harm. The folly of those who promoted them resulted in the imprisonment of several estimable and worthy men; and if there was one thing which had aroused the feelings of the people against these prosecutions it was these imprisonments. (Hear, hear.) The times had changed since the days of Queen Elizabeth, when it was laid down in the *Reformatio Legum* that a Bishop should have within his jurisdiction 'a prison, or two prisons, or even more' to which to commit offenders. (Laughter.) It was not the Bishops who had stopped prosecutions; prosecutions were not initiated, because the Church at large—Low as well as High—was against them.

After referring to his own action in the case of Father Dolling, and certain particular 'outrageous actions' of individual men to which attention had been called, he went on to say:

> What was the evil that in his opinion was great and growing? It was not the performance of overt acts or outrageous acts. These things were, in his opinion, being speedily suppressed, but the evil, in his opinion, was far more insidious and far more difficult to deal with. It was the exaggeration of a truth rather than the overt act of wrong. It was the growth of mistaken ideas of a materialistic kind with regard to the celebration of the Holy Communion; the perils, which seemed to be very real indeed, with regard to the growth of the practices surrounding confession; the growth of the use of small manuals of devotion and the like, which were circulated by laymen and women quite as much as by clergymen among those who were of tender years. These things, in his opinion, constituted for the Church of England to-day a peril which he did not say was a growing one, but which was at this moment great. They, the Bishops, were entitled to speak on this matter. They desired to support the English laity in dealing with these things quietly, gravely, and steadily, but their power of doing so effectively, of using the powers of guidance and persuasion, which alone could deal with these specific things, which did not come within

the four corners of any Act of Parliament, was directly impaired, just in proportion as he thought those mistaken men were made the objects of violent agitation with scurrilous abuse.

He concluded by emphasizing the comprehensiveness of the Church of England, and said that the meeting at the Albert Hall would have made short work of such men as Andrewes, Wilson, and Keble.

The same day saw a similar debate in the House of Commons; and a month later there was another discussion, mainly on Confessional Boxes, in the House of Lords.

Towards the end of February Davidson issued his own Directions in a letter to each of his 566 incumbents, specifying twelve liturgical points which had given rise to controversy and stating explicitly, 'What is to the best of my judgment the rule of the Church of England':

[*Ritual Irregularity*

The Bishop of Winchester's Directions to Incumbents]

Private. February 22, 1899.

1. No Celebration of Holy Communion ought to take place without, at least, the minimum number of Communicants prescribed in the Book of Common Prayer.

2. No Reservation of the consecrated Elements is permissible.

3. In celebrating the Holy Communion it is not permissible, in ordinary circumstances, to omit the recitation of the Commandments, or to administer the consecrated Elements otherwise than with individual recitation of the full prescribed words. If special arrangements are desired, as for example when, on a great festival, the number of communicants is likely to be very large, my sanction ought to be asked beforehand for what is proposed.

4. In order that there may be no question of using, in the office of Holy Communion, any other form than that prescribed, no books or cards containing other prayers or forms ought to be upon the Holy Table, even if the additional prayers be intended solely for the private devotions of the officiant.

5. If it be desired to use wine mingled with water, the mixing ought to be effected elsewhere than at the Holy Table, and not as a ceremony.

6. The 'Manual Acts' ought not to be intentionally hidden from the view of an ordinary communicant.

7. The habitual attendance of children at Celebrations of the Holy Communion is undesirable. If children are occasionally per-

mitted to be present, with a view to their better understanding of the Service, the Order of Service ought not to be modified in any way, nor ought the children to take any part not ordinarily taken by non-communicants who may be present.

8. The ceremonial use of Incense is not permissible.

9. In any official notice of the Holy Communion no other designation of the Holy Sacrament ought to be used than one of the terms to be found in the Book of Common Prayer.

10. No phrase ought to be used in public notices or Services which carries the idea of prayer or intercession for the departed further than it is carried in the Book of Common Prayer.

11. The Athanasian Creed ought to be said or sung upon the days appointed.

12. The directions of the Book of Common Prayer ought to be followed with regard to the days for which Special Services are appointed.

He asked any who felt a difficulty on any of the twelve points to write to him at once. He received letters from 176 incumbents and wrote a further letter in which he explained that he was not attempting a 'formal and authoritative Direction', but advice. With the letter he sent, as the case required, a memorandum, printed or written. The memorandum (cyclostyled) on Reservation is as follows:

Reservation of the Consecrated Elements

So very few letters have reached me with reference to the above that I print no memorandum.

The subject is an anxious one. The harm that has arisen from abuse of what might in other circumstances have been reasonably sanctioned is real though rare, and adherence to it may occasionally seem hard. After fullest thought and care, I feel bound to say that Reservation, in any true sense of the word, must not take place. Emergencies may arise when a rule ought to give way to a pressing necessity. *Necessitas non habet legem.* In such cases an Incumbent will rightly use his discretion and report to me at once what he has done. I am asked in a very few instances to authorise what cannot be called, in any ordinary sense of the term, Reservation: May the priest carry the consecrated elements straight from Service to a sick bed? I do not wish to prohibit this absolutely in all circumstances. . . .This kind of use of an incumbent's discretion ought to be justified by some exceptional circumstances. It is impossible to prescribe for each detail. I can but rely on wise and loyal adherence to the principles laid down with such emphatic care in the Prayer Book. Among them is the principle that the sick communicant is entitled to the Service specially provided for his use.

Only 15 of the 176 remained unsatisfied with the Bishop's advice on the various points, and with them he dealt personally. He claimed six months later that there were 'only a very few parishes in which ritual matters still remained seriously unsettled'.

II

Meantime the strong feeling evident in the House of Commons crystallized in a debate on a motion by Mr. Gedge on April 11, when the House, by 200 votes to 14, definitely censured the lawlessness of certain members of the Church, and recommended the Crown to refuse preferment to any clergyman who would not obey the Bishops and Prayer Book and the law as declared by the existing Courts.

On May 6, the Archbishops opened their Hearings at Lambeth, on the applications of the Bishops of London and Norwich (in accordance with the provision in the Preface to the Prayer Book for the abolition of doubts), as to the lawfulness of the liturgical use of Incense and of the carrying of lights in procession, and with regard to Reservation.

On May 10, the Church Discipline Bill came up for second reading, and the Government then declared its policy in a motion which was unanimously adopted by the House, to the effect that

> this House, while not prepared to accept a measure which creates new offences and ignores the authority of the Bishops in maintaining the discipline of the Church, is of opinion that, if the efforts now being made by the Archbishops and Bishops to secure the due obedience of the clergy are not speedily effectual, further legislation will be required to maintain the observance of the existing laws of Church and Realm.

In July, the Archbishops gave their decision on Incense and portable lights. It was against both. Unfortunately it was based on a strict interpretation of the Acts of Uniformity, the worst possible grounds for influencing High Churchmen. The following letters passed between the Bishop of Winchester and Sir William Harcourt:

The Bishop of Winchester *to* Sir William Harcourt

Private. 25 Aug., 1899.

I am glad to have the opportunity your letter affords of writing to you on the present position of matters with regard to the recent Lambeth pronouncement. There were I believe 7 churches, and 7 only, in this Diocese in which Incense was used. Since the Lambeth pronouncement I have been in communication with the incumbents of all of these (save one who had already at my direction discontinued the use). The result, roughly, is this. One man says he will obey but resigns. I have accepted the obedience but asked him to reconsider the question of resignation. He has a very small cure in the Channel Islands. Two men (including Tremenheere about whom your correspondent writes) have promised now to discontinue Incense and Lights as directed. One man (absent on his holiday) asks me to wait till his return. Two men are causing me trouble by virtually refusing to obey my direction. But I believe I shall succeed in enforcing obedience on both. . . .

You will not mind my saying that our difficulties in obtaining obedience have been very greatly increased by your own letter to *The Times*. Your attitude is clearly consistent and your words are weighty. But they are so to speak 'rubbing in' upon these men the very thing which makes their obedience most difficult, the notion, namely, that all they have to do is to see what Parliament has said or may say and then to regulate their mode of conducting Divine Service accordingly. I am not now challenging your argument, still less am I saying it is inconsistent with all you have said from 1874 onwards, and no doubt you considered well the *effect* of your letter upon such men before publishing it. All I am saying is that as a matter of fact I honestly believe that if that letter could have been withheld, at a time of extreme difficulty, the number and strength of the recalcitrants would have been diminished, by at least one half. The present number is, I trust, small, and it will be smaller, I believe, a few weeks hence, if we are allowed to use our authority without intervention from outside. But I quite realise that we have no right to ask anybody and least of all *you*, to be guided by our wishes in such a matter.

Sir William Harcourt *to the* Bishop of Winchester

Aug. 27, 1899.

Private.

You do me justice in believing that I did not write my letter to *The Times* without due reflection and with a view to the consequence it might produce.

From the first I have had no object but to bring the Bishops into action to restrain the lawless Priests. As soon as they began to take action I have religiously kept silence awaiting the Resolution of Lambeth. You naturally approach the question in a different point of view from that in which I regard it. You of course look to the effect on the clerical mind, I to that on the opinion of the laity.

The inconclusive shape of the Lambeth procedure, which bound no one, made it necessary to enable the public to understand that it was not really a *brutum fulmen* intended to end in smoke. I therefore thought it right to expound its real inwardness and to demonstrate how it might be made effectual. . . .

Of course we are only yet at the outside fringe of the matter and the really material outrages have still to be dealt with. . . .

I am very glad that the Bishop of London[1] has acted with so much courage and firmness. His position was the most difficult one in which any of the Episcopate found themselves. The condition of the Diocese of London was the result of connivance and *laches* of his predecessor. If Bishop Temple had spoken out 20 years ago, as he has spoken at Lambeth this month, the situation would not be what it is today. He and others have fostered rebellion till it has reached a height from which it will be difficult to displace it. . . .

May I be allowed to say that I consider the future of the Church lies very much in your hands. There is no one who by his youth, experience, character, reputation and judgment can more powerfully affect its fortunes. I look forward to your action and your Charge with great interest and anxiety. This is a critical moment at which the tide may turn either way. . . .

The great battle I suppose will arise upon the condemnation of the Reservation—which is inevitable. I have no doubt many of the Romanisers who give way on Incense will take their stand on that. . . .

The reader will observe Harcourt's hopes of the lead which Bishop Davidson might give in the future. He will also note his prophecy that the great battle was to be fought on the issue of Reservation.

In September of this year, as Harcourt was fulminating in *The Times* against the acts and the braggadocio of Lord Halifax and the English Church Union, correspondence on the crisis passed between the Rev. C. G. Lang, Vicar of Portsea, and the Bishop of

[1] Dr. Mandell Creighton.

Winchester. Unfortunately none of Davidson's letters survive. From Mr. Lang's appeals, however, we can form a shrewd opinion of the somewhat drastic tone which Davidson must have adopted. Mr. Lang put the case for a tolerable use of Incense, a distinction between ceremonies within the limits of the official services of the Church, and ceremonies outside those limits; and took up the cudgels for some of those with whom he was more in sympathy than his Bishop.

REV. C. G. LANG *to the* BISHOP OF WINCHESTER

Largie Castle, Tay in Loan, Argyll, N.B.
Sep. 18, 1899.

Many thanks for so kindly letting me know your thoughts about this Incense complication. . . .

I am not in any way writing a brief for those who wish if possible to retain some use of Incense. I do not say that I agree with all the arguments which they might use. But I would like on behalf of many of my own friends among them—some of whom have been writing to me—to try to put their position in a way which might tend to show that perhaps they do not altogether deserve the very hard words which you deal out to them. I cannot think—knowing some of them as I do—that even the want of a true sense of proportion, which I quite admit the Ritualistic development has often produced, could of itself induce them to urge a mere 'humiliating quibble' or 'shuffling pretence unworthy of a Christian gentleman'. . . . I would not think it worth while to write at such length if I thought that those who are anxious for this modified use of Incense would not be prepared to refer its *manner* of introduction to the sanction of the Bishop: many of them I know would: and would defer at once to his decision. . . . I quite admit that such a way of retaining some devotional use of Incense—or any other ceremony—is most unsatisfactory: but may not the same be said of almost all the arguments in principle by which the rigidity of the Act of Uniformity has been by all Bishops and by all schools of thought mitigated in the interests of the progressive life of the Church? . . .

I easily see the answers which might be made to these considerations. Only I have ventured—and I hope you will forgive my presumption—to lay them before you because the tone of your letter was so very drastic and indignant against a position which it is certain many good men affected will take, and which I think is capable of a kindlier consideration. It would be a great misfortune if by any means the impression got abroad among these men and their people that such a plea would be immediately and almost contemptuously rejected by the Bishops. Such an impression would tend, however wrongly, to make them think that the Bishops were antagonistic to Incense itself, and were paying more heed to the demands of 'Protestants in the street' than to the claims to consideration of those who for so long have been permitted to use an ancient symbol of worship. If on the other hand the plea were considered with some sympathy, even its rejection would be made easier to bear, and so bring less bitterness with it. And, as you so truly say, the *really* important matter in all these difficulties is the firmer and more willing recognition of episcopal authority.

In the autumn the Bishop delivered his Charge, which dealt, as already described, with the main issues at stake in a masterly way. In an important section he urged the reconstruction of the Ecclesiastical Courts:

I have never been one of those who thought that that matter could, with common fairness to lay Churchmen, be allowed to slumber. . . . I have consistently supported the plan which was drafted in the Report signed by a large majority of the Ecclesiastical Courts Commission, and which was, with some modifications, embodied five years later in the Bill prepared by Archbishop Benson, after prolonged discussion with a Committee of leading laymen. It provides, as you will remember, for the strengthening of our Diocesan and Provincial Courts, and for an appeal from the Provincial Court to the Crown, who shall refer the question to a Committee of highly-qualified lay Churchmen, such Committee being bound, before advising the Crown upon the matter, to obtain, upon any particular point of doctrine or Ritual which is in controversy, the opinion of the whole English Episcopate specially summoned for the purpose. . . . A fallacy seems to me to underlie the oft-repeated dictum that spiritual matters must be decided by a spiritual authority. I cordially assent to the proposition if it means that in the last resort a decision affecting Christian Doctrine or the Ritual which expresses Doctrine must, if it is to bind Christian men in *foro conscientiae*, be a decision consistent with the Church's own view of what is true in Doctrine or appropriate in Ritual, and must not be a decision forced upon an unwilling Church by any body or power external to or independent of the Church. But if it means, as it sometimes seems to mean, that the Christian laity, even when acting through duly accredited representatives, have no voice in the decision of such controversies, I believe it to be as false in theory as it would be mischievous in practice. The more determinedly that we force the matter back to 'first principles', the more likely shall we be to arrive at a true, reasonable solution of present problems in the Church of England.[1]

The Charge received a wide and generous welcome from all sorts of people. Sir William Harcourt amongst others approved of its main character most heartily. He took exception, however, to Davidson's views on Ecclesiastical Courts:

SIR WILLIAM HARCOURT *to the* BISHOP OF WINCHESTER

Malwood, Lyndhurst.
Nov. 4, 1899.

... There is one other point to which I must demur, viz. to your views on *Ecclesiastical Courts*. In the first place as an old Parliamentarian I must express my absolute conviction that the House of Commons will not entertain this, or any other large measure of Church Reform, except in the shape of Disestablishment, which is a thing you know I do not desire. I know stress is laid on some expressions of Mr. Balfour, but in this he utters no opinion but his own. His views on Church matters have no echo even on his own side. The present system of the Courts is not in my opinion likely to be improved.

The ecclesiastics have no right to complain. They have (1) the Bishop's Court in which he can pronounce his own judgments either personally or by his Assessor; (2) they have the Court of the Archbishop who can do the same; (3) the final appeal is to the Crown as representing the laity, and even the Royal Commission have admitted that this is to be of exclusively lay composition. From this principle you may be well assured that neither Parliament nor the Protestant laity will allow any departure. It is of the very essence of the Royal Supremacy, which is the corner stone of the Reformation. The idea that this Royal Court is to share its exclusive authority with the 'whole English Episcopate specially summoned for the purpose' does not appear to me to be within the range of practical politics.

(1) It would make all proceedings impossible. The cost, the time and trouble of an appeal where the 'whole English Episcopate' was to be summoned, would exceed even the cumbrousness of the old appeals to Rome.

(2) It is not the least likely that the 'whole English Episcopate' would agree among themselves or with the lay tribunal.

Archbishop Benson's Bill will never reach the House of Com-

[1] A Charge delivered to the Clergy of the Diocese of Winchester, 1899, p. 136 f.

mons (*a*) because the ecclesiastics reject it as giving too much authority to the laity and (*b*) the laity repudiate it as giving too much authority to the ecclesiastics. But if it ever got there I think I could pledge my Parliamentary experience that it would not survive a night's Debate.

He chaffed the Bishop a little on his 'great confidence' in the *mollia tempora fandi*, and still pressed the weapon of prosecution.

In the following May (1900) the Archbishop of Canterbury's decision on Reservation was given:

Archbishop Temple *on* Reservation

. . . In conclusion, after weighing carefully all that has been put before us, I am obliged to decide that the Church of England does not at present allow Reservation in any form, and that those who think it ought to be allowed, though perfectly justified in endeavouring to get the proper authorities to alter the law, are not justified in practising Reservation until the law has been altered.

In the full text of this decision, it is interesting to note (after the outcry against the first hearing), there is no reference to any Act of Parliament.

In July a debate took place in the House of Lords, on Lord Portsmouth's motion, to call attention to the continued lawlessness in the Church and to ask for legislation to make the Clergy obey the law. The request was not granted. Lord Portsmouth was also a layman in the Winchester Diocese, and in August headed a movement which, under the title 'Protestantism before Politics', aimed at returning to Parliament members who were pledged to the maintenance of the Protestant Constitution and amongst other things to abolish the episcopal veto. Some letters of a lengthy character passed between the Bishop and the noble Earl, and though the Bishop succeeded in taking off a little of the edge of Lord Portsmouth's attacks, so far as his own diocese was concerned, he did not satisfy his correspondent that the Bishops as a body might be trusted to maintain the Protestant faith, or even persuade him that there was not a single incumbent in the Diocese of Winchester who was deliberately disobedient.

It was very soon after this that Davidson's intimate acquaintance with Mr. Balfour began. All through the crisis Mr. Balfour had been leader of the House of Commons. He had defended the Bishops and refused to give way to the pressure brought upon him from many sides. But, so far as counsel and sympathy from the leaders of the Church had gone, he had been unsupported. A moment came in December, following upon the use of the veto by Bishop Creighton[1] to stop proceedings against two of his clergy for the use of Incense and Reservation, when even Mr. Balfour's patience was sorely tried. One of Mr. Balfour's private secretaries was Sydney Parry of the Treasury, whose father had been Bishop Suffragan of Dover under Archbishops Tait and Benson, and who had known Davidson ever since he could recollect. Realizing that his chief's repeated appeals to Archbishop Temple for counsel and co-operation had been altogether ineffective, and that Mr. Balfour's long patience had at last reached breaking-point, Parry wrote a strictly confidential and personal letter to his old friend, in which, after rehearsing the House of Commons history of the crisis, he went on to say:

F. S. PARRY, ESQ., *to the* BISHOP OF WINCHESTER

15 December, 1900.

. . . I would now beg you to turn off for a moment and consider what has been, all along, the attitude of Mr. Balfour as Leader of the House. I can assure you that it is not too much to say that, but for his restraining power over both sides of the House, and but for that unique magnetism and attractiveness which he exercises over everyone with whom he comes in contact, the Bishops' sympathisers in the Commons would have been in a pronounced minority. Few people seem to realize the immense weight which any appeal to the 'Law and Order' argument carries with it in the Lower House, and even those who do must often have been astonished at the unanimous condemnation passed by Members not only on the 'lawless' clergy themselves, but also on the authorities who are accused of winking at their lawlessness. They can imagine pretty well what would have happened if the Leader of the House had been a *roi fainéant* like ——, or a bully like ——, or a time-server like ——; but they do not give Mr. Balfour a tithe of the credit he deserves for his steady and successful efforts to induce the great 'Law and Order' party in the House, against its own convictions, to trust the Bishops and give them time. A glance at his speeches on each of the occasions I have men-

[1] See *Life and Letters of Mandell Creighton*, ii. 452.

tioned, will, I think, fully bear out what I say. He has said the same, in the teeth of similar opposition, to the country in general —vide, for instance, his speeches at Bristol (*The Times*, 30 Nov. 1898) and at Manchester (*The Times*, 1 Feb. 1899 and 1 Oct. 1900); and he has avowedly put his principles into force by exacting from every Crown incumbent, before appointment, a pledge of obedience in matters of discipline and ceremonial, not to the Law, as the House of Commons Resolution of 11 April 1899 recommended, but simply to the Bishop.

Meanwhile, what advice or encouragement or even acknowledgment has he received from the Primate or the Bishops generally? . . . We recently learnt, not from the powers spiritual but from common rumours in the press, that proceedings were on foot against 5 London clergymen for breaking the ecclesiastical laws as regards not only non-communicating celebrations, but also two of the practices specifically condemned by the Archbishops' decision—reservation and the ceremonial use of incense. The published accounts now show that the Bishop of London promised at first to proceed in two of the cases; but after receiving a protest from his Archdeacons, he changed his mind and vetoed the actions, not because there was any doubt as to the existence of the practices complained of, but simply because (as he must have known all along) the complainant was not a parishioner. I know, of course, that the Bishop was ill at the time; but surely, after we have been repeatedly told that the Bishops are working together in such matters, his action was not taken without the knowledge and approval of the Primate—or, indeed, of the whole Episcopal Bench! . . .

I believe Mr. Balfour intends to tell the Primate that His Grace really must provide him with *some* 'brief' in the matter; but what I want *you* to understand is that the Archbishop's policy of ignoring both the strained attitude of the great 'Law and Order' party whether inside or outside the House, and also the strenuous and self-denying efforts of the most loyal champion the Established Church possesses, is disheartening and dangerous to the highest degree. No excuse for the Bishop of London's volte-face has been produced that will hold water for a moment; and if it is construed into something like a challenge to the House of Commons to take its own course, and a hint, or more than a hint, to Mr. Balfour that his line of defence was absurd from the first, I fear that no one will be surprised and most men will be delighted.

The Bishop acknowledged the letter, and suggested a confidential talk, which took place a few days later at Canterbury. He added:

The BISHOP OF WINCHESTER *to* F. S. PARRY, ESQ.

December 19, 1900.

So far as the Archbishop is concerned I can never be responsible for anything he does or leaves undone. He is inscrutable—and perhaps most inscrutable of all to *us* who are supposed to have most to do with him. He cannot be regarded as like other men! grand as he is.

At the same time Bishop Davidson defended Archbishop Temple from the charge of ignoring Balfour; and said that it had never been the practice for the Archbishop to volunteer advice to a Minister before being asked. He also justified the Bishop of London's veto in the case of Colonel Porcelli (the complainant in question), since he was not a parishioner, but he added that he could not, and would not, veto such a prosecution if a parishioner demanded it.

More important, however, than this conversation was the fact that it led directly to a visit from Randall Davidson to Balfour at Whittinghame on January 4, 1901. It was the first time the two men had effectively met, though they had been in the same company together before, and it was the beginning of a close friendship which lasted nearly thirty years. The following note of Mr. Balfour's own impression of the interview is full of interest as showing once again Dr. Davidson's extraordinary gift of common sense and understanding. It is also very interesting to observe Mr. Balfour's own view at this early date, that the only fit solution for the present perplexities was some form of ecclesiastical autonomy:

The RT. HON. A. J. BALFOUR *to* F. S. PARRY, ESQ.

January 7, 1901.

I was lucky enough to catch the Bishop for a night and half a day, and had a great deal of talk with him. I rather startled him, I think, by telling him what is certainly the fact, that in all probability the 2nd reading of the new Liverpool Bill will very likely be carried in the House of Commons, which I should regard as a serious misfortune, even though the Bill itself should go no further. I need not trouble you with a report of all the talk we had on matters theological. I found it personally of great profit,—for the Bishop has the art of stating with great clearness and sympathy the gist of opinions from which he differs: so that I really understand more of Halifax's position now than I think I did before.

I am more than ever convinced that the only true solution of our present perplexities lies in the direction of ecclesiastical autonomy, subject of course to Parliament, and I am seriously reflecting whether I cannot induce my colleagues to allow me to prepare the way for legislative action next year.—In the meanwhile I suggested to the Bishop, as a palliative for immediate use, the appointment of, say, a joint Committee of the two Houses, to enquire into the exercise by the Bishops of their veto. He seemed to think the Bench would have no objection to this, but would rather welcome it. I think it might prove of great value.

The Bishop reported the interview to the Archbishop of Canterbury, and was most careful to keep his Grace in touch with everything he did, telling Parry indeed that he would not, and could not, do anything behind Temple's back. The Bishops met as a body a few days later and issued a manifesto, signed by all the Bishops except the Bishops of London and Sodor and Man,[1] addressed to the whole clergy, appealing for obedience to the decisions of the Archbishops 'lately given on questions referred to them in accordance with the direction in the Book of Common Prayer'.

But the letter had hardly been issued before graver causes intervened. The Bishop of London died on January 14; and eight days later, January 22, 1901, a whole epoch came to an end with the death of the Queen.

NOTE

In 1901 only one question on ritual matters seems to have been asked in Parliament—but a good many more in 1902. In the light of later events it is particularly interesting to note a phrase in Mr. Balfour's answer to a question pressing for legislation 'in view of the continuance among a section of the clergy of certain practices and doctrines' (17 February 1902). He said:

> 'As far as I know this House has never dealt with the question of doctrine. It has always concerned itself with the practice of the clergy and not with the doctrine.'

[1] Dr. Straton.

CHAPTER XVIII

THE PASSING OF THE QUEEN

In the death of that Queen, unmatchable, inimitable in her sex; that Queen, worthy, I will not say of *Nestors* years, I will not say of *Methusalems*, but worthy of *Adams* years, if *Adam* had never faln; in her death we were all under one common flood, and depth of tears. JOHN DONNE. *A Sermon Preached at Pauls Cross to the Lords of the Council, and other Honorable Persons*, 24 March, 1616.

IN the last months of 1900, the Queen's health was visibly failing. Personal sorrows and public anxieties had weighed heavy upon her. The New Year came, and one of the last efforts the Queen made was an hour's talk with Lord Roberts (on the progress of the war) on January 14. On the same day the Bishop of London (Creighton) died at Fulham, and Davidson's last letter to the Queen is a description of the impressive funeral service at St. Paul's at which he was present as her representative.[1]

On the Saturday after the funeral Davidson went to see Mrs. Creighton, and at this point we have Davidson's words to describe in graphic manner the course of events.[2]

> On Saturday, January 19th, 1901, I was sitting with Mrs. Creighton at Fulham when a . . . telegram, which had followed me from Farnham, reached me. It was from Sir Arthur Bigge, stating that the Queen's condition had become most serious and that the family had been summoned. . . . I was engaged to preach next day at Holloway College, and was going thither from Fulham, but I decided to go at once to Osborne, though Bigge had not exactly summoned me to do so. I got back to Waterloo and telegraphed to Holloway College, stating that I could not come; to the Dean of Windsor, asking him to provide for my place there; to Sir Arthur Bigge, stating that I would come to Cowes that night and sleep there unless he summoned me to his house at Osborne. Fortunately on Saturday night there is a late boat from Southampton to Cowes. The journey was most unpleasant, as it was a stormy night with some rain, and the train does not on those occasions run from the Dock Station to the Pier. We were packed into some cabs provided by the Railway Company. My companions

[1] The letter, sent to Osborne, was never read by the Queen.

[2] From a long memorandum written immediately after the series of events which it narrates.

were Press men and telegraph clerks, and on the boat we found a great company of footballers, rather boisterous. Altogether it was a strange companionship in an hour of such anxiety.

On reaching Cowes about 11 p.m. I found a letter from Bigge stating that every room in the Osborne houses was full and that the immediate anxiety was relieved. Launcelot Smith met me and I went to his Vicarage. Next morning we heard that no worse reports had been issued. I attended the early Celebration in St. Mary's Church, and then walked to Osborne. It was the day for the commemoration of Prince Henry's death in Whippingham Church, and Parratt had come from Windsor for the occasion. The commemorative service was to take place at 12. I sent a letter from Bigge's house to Princess Beatrice, stating that I should be in Whippingham Church and take part in the Service, and was ready to be of any further use if desired. A message came back begging me to go to Osborne House immediately after the Service. I did so, and had much talk with different members of the Family. The Doctors thought the Queen was rather better and wished to keep her perfectly quiet: even her daughters were not seeing her. I accordingly arranged to sleep at Whippingham Rectory. I attended Whippingham Church at 6 o'clock and preached. There was a good congregation, evidently in anxious strain. We added some special prayers to the Service, and I tried to say something helpful. After I had gone to bed a carriage arrived about midnight bidding me come at once to Osborne and remain there, as the Queen was again worse. I found, however, on arrival at the house, that there had been a further rally, and they again wished her to be kept quiet. In my room I wrote a long letter to E.M.D. and then went to bed for a few hours.

On Monday, Jan. 21st, between 7 and 8 a.m., I went down and found the house quiet and the report unofficially current that the Queen had decidedly rallied. . . . During the morning she brightened up and said to Sir James Reid 'Am I better at all?' He said 'Yes', and then she eagerly answered 'Then may I have Turi?' (her little Pomeranian dog). Turi was sent for, and she eagerly held him on the bed for about an hour. (Turi now belongs to the Duchess of Albany.) Throughout the day I did not go to the Queen's Room at all. I saw most of the members of the Family, either together or separately, and they all talked quietly over the position of matters. It was arranged that I should stay at Kent House (just outside the Queen's Lodge), lent at present to Sir Fleetwood and Lady Edwardes. Princess Victoria of Schleswig-Holstein was there also. She and I had a great deal of conversation in the afternoon. She had just returned to Osborne after a few days' absence, except for which she had been with the Queen for many weeks. . . . The Queen had talked to Princess Tora[1] pretty often lately about illness and even death, which was not according to her wont. . . .

Just after dinner at Osborne I went to the three Doctors (Reid, Powell, and Barlow), who were sitting together in the Stockmar Room I had so often occupied. . . .

After seeing them I had a long talk with the German Emperor and the Duke of Connaught together. They were both keen to know what judgment we all formed about the probabilities! I pointed out that our judgment was surely of no consequence, but I told them with reserve what the Doctors had said. . . .

The Duke of Connaught spoke warmly of the good of my being here with them all, and tried, not very successfully, to describe to the Emperor the accumulated offices I hold as Bishop and otherwise. I returned late to Kent House to sleep, and wrote another long letter home.

On Tuesday, the 22nd, soon after 8 a.m., I was summoned from Kent House, a carriage being sent to bring me as quickly as possible to Osborne. I went straight to the Queen's room. The Family were assembled. . . .

I paid one other visit to the room during the morning, but for some hours Clement Smith and I waited in the Drawing Room downstairs while the Queen slept. . . . She lay very quietly looking white and thin.

While we were at luncheon about 2.15 I was summoned to go at once, and Clement Smith came also. We found her much weaker and the Family again assembled. . . . We remained in the room a long time, Clement Smith and I saying prayers and hymns at intervals. She was not obviously responsive to the words said, but certain things, and specially the last verse of 'Lead, Kindly Light' seemed at once to catch her attention, and she showed that she followed it. About 3 o'clock the room was again cleared, and from 3 to 5 there were intervals of quiet. . . . Twice I was asked to come in for a few minutes. I remained in the Dressing Room and in the adjoining Drawing Room. There I had a good deal of talk with the Emperor, who was full of touching loyalty to 'Grandmamma' as he always described her. 'She has been a very great woman. Just think of it: she remembers George III, and now we are in the Twentieth Century. And all that time what a life she has led. I have never been with her without feeling that she was in every sense my Grandmamma and made me love her as such. And yet the minute we began to talk about political things she

[1] i.e. Princess Victoria of Schleswig-Holstein.

made me feel we were equals and could speak as Sovereigns. Nobody had such power as she.' I spoke of the good his coming to England would do. He said repeatedly, 'My proper place now is here; I could not be away.'

At 6 o'clock we were told that the end was certainly approaching.... The Family wished to see her alone one by one.... Then came a great change of look and complete calmness. I had been mainly in the Dressing Room. At 6.25 Powell summoned me to come in. I said the Commendatory Prayer and one or two texts and ended with the Aaronic blessing at the very moment that she quietly drew her last breath, the whole Family being present in the room. This was just after 6.30....

We left the Family alone for a few minutes. Then the King came out alone. I was in the passage and was the first to greet him as Sovereign. I then went to the Equerries' Room, where Clarendon (Lord Chamberlain), Arthur Balfour, Sir Arthur Bigge, and (I think) Edwards, were present, and told them that the end had come.

In accordance with arrangements already made, the house was at once surrounded by police at intervals to prevent any servant or messenger from taking the tidings outside until telegrams had been despatched to the Prime Minister, the Lord Mayor, and several other potentates. Then, after ten minutes or so, Inspector Fraser took a message to the gate, where a crowd was waiting.

I then walked to Kent House and returned a little later, when I was sent for by the Prince and Princess of Wales (as they still wished to be called till the next day). They expressed a wish that we should have a little Service in the room beside the Queen's bed at 10 o'clock that night. I had a long talk with both.

... At 10.15 we all gathered in the Queen's Room and had a calm and bright little Service. She was lying in the bed where she had died, all being beautifully arranged, with quantities of white lace and a few simple flowers; the little crucifix which had always hung over her head within the bed being in her hand.... They all, I think, liked our little Service....

On Wednesday, the 23rd, I was at Osborne House early, in time to see Arthur Balfour and others before they started with the Prince of Wales for London. The Prince left us directions to arrange the Dining Room as a sort of Mortuary Chapel in which the coffin might be placed next day. I set to work on these arrangements with the Princesses....

To return to the morning: I had a long walk with Dr. Barlow and much interesting talk. Then a series of interviews with most of the Princesses and with the Queen, and then a long one with the Emperor. I paid a visit about 1.30 to the Queen's room. . . . Nothing could be better than the simple arrangements in her room. During the afternoon the servants and tenants were allowed to pass through the room and to see her as she lay.

At 6 o'clock we again had a Service in the room, at which most of the Family were present. It was, at their request, somewhat fuller than the Service of the previous evening. I was greatly struck by the Emperor's demeanour throughout, and again had talk with him afterwards. . . .

On Thursday, the 24th, I was early at Osborne, seeing to what had been done during the night in fitting up the Chapel. . . .

A message came from the King in London saying that he wished to have a Celebration of Holy Communion in the Queen's Room as soon as he arrived from London that afternoon. . . . The King arrived at 2.30, and at a little before 4 p.m. we had the Service he desired. We had not felt it to be right to move the furniture much in the Queen's Room, and as the room was not large and the furniture was plentiful we had some difficulty in arranging for the large number of Royalties who stated that they desired to take part in the Communion Service. But all was ultimately managed. It was altogether a historic scene.

The Bishop then describes the scene, in the centre of which 'lay the little Queen, with fresh flowers arranged on the bed, the small Imperial Crown lying by the side, her face . . . most calm and peaceful'. And he reflects, as the King of England and the German Emperor each received the Sacrament in turn, 'what the memories of that hour might mean for them and for the world'. He notes of the rest of the service, the whole record of which, with its setting, is too intimate for reproduction here:

I shortened the Service, using special Collect, Epistle, and Gospel, and deliberately did not read the Prayer for the King until after the Gloria and just before the Blessing. This gave, I think, and was felt to give, a significance to the whole. . . .

The Bishop left Osborne for a little while in order to take part in the consecration of Herbert Ryle as Bishop of Exeter (January 25) in Westminster Abbey, and to make arrangements with the Duke of Norfolk for the funeral at Windsor. During most of this time he was in close touch with the King, and had constant talks with various members of the Royal Family. The Memorandum proceeds:

Wednesday, the 30th, was a quieter day, as most of the arrangements had now been made. E.M.D. and I had a long walk by the sea in Osborne grounds. At 6 p.m. Parratt, who had arrived from Windsor with some men and boys from St. George's Choir, helped us with a Service in the little Chapel. The choir sang Anthems and Hymns most beautifully. The whole Royal Family were present and appreciated it greatly. . . .

On Thursday, the 31st, we had another fairly quiet day, but a great many detailed arrangements had to be made about the Windsor proceedings. At 6.15 we again had a musical Service in the little Chapel. The Choir did even better than before, and everyone was moved. The Household were invited to be present and were in the Drawing Room adjoining with the doors open. . . .

On Friday, Feb. 1st, I was early at Osborne, after seeing E.M.D. off from Kent House for Windsor, with Parratt and the boys and Lady Edwards. After breakfast I had a long walk with the Bishop of Ripon and much talk. He then left. Then a further interview with the King about matters on which he wished details to be arranged. The Funeral Procession was to start at 1.30. Soon after 12.30 Clement Smith and I went to the Chapel and superintended the final arrangements as to the cushions, etc. for the coffin, bearing the crown, sceptre, and orbs. Then we were left alone in the Chapel for half an hour before the men came to remove the coffin. I felt this to be as solemn a time as any we had had.

At 1.30 the coffin was removed into the Hall at the foot of the Queen's Staircase opposite the large entrance. After a time the Royal Family all gathered there, and we had again a short Service—'Nunc Dimittis', 'Prevent us', a Lesson from St. John, and a few special Prayers. Then the body was carried out, and the rest of the arrangements were public to all and are recorded fully in print. Clement Smith and I (not in robes, but with ribbons, medals, etc.) walked with the late Queen's Household, immediately behind the ladies, to Trinity Pier. Then he returned home, wishing to conduct the Saturday Service in his own Church, and I embarked with the Household on the 'Victoria and Albert'.

The scene crossing the Solent was beyond question the most solemn and moving of which I have ever had experience. Everything combined to make it as perfect as possible. A quite calm sea, the very slow motion of the vessels, which made them seem to glide without visible propelling power, the little 'Alberta' going first (with the coffin on the deck) through the broad avenue of towering battle-ships booming out their salutes on either side, the enormous mass of perfectly silent black-clothed crowds covering Southsea Common and the beach; and then the 'Alberta' gliding silently out of sight into Clarence Yard just as the sun set and the gloom of evening fell. I do not envy the man who could pass through such a scene dry-eyed. . . .

Sunday, Feb. 3rd. . . . At 11 we had full Morning Prayer in St. George's, with Sermon by the Bishop of Oxford. He and I, in ordinary episcopal robes, sat in the Sanctuary, the Dean and Canons in their usual stalls. He was not very audible, being really unwell. All the Royal Family were present, some in the Choir and some in the Royal Pew aloft. In the afternoon, at 3 p.m., I had to go with the King, Lord Esher, Lord Pembroke, and Fritz Ponsonby to the Mausoleum to arrange the details about Monday. . . .

At 6 p.m. we had a Service in the Memorial Chapel, the Dean and I taking Prayers and Lesson, all of a special kind, and Madame Albani singing two solo Anthems. Her voice was too strong for the place, but the general effect of the Service in the darkness was very striking. . . .

Monday, Feb. 4th. In the morning I had to arrange a good many small details with the Dean and with Dalton. . . . The weather was fine until we had left the Mausoleum. The arrangements were admirable, and the Service itself was touching beyond words. The music was beautifully sung, and, for the rest, we simply followed the Prayer Book Service, with the addition of a Prayer of thanksgiving for the Queen's life which I inserted before the Blessing. After the Blessing it had been arranged that the Royal Family should all pass in single file across the platform looking upon the grave in which the two coffins then lay side by side. The King came first alone, but, instead of simply walking by, he knelt down by the grave. Then the Queen followed, leading the little Prince Edward[1] by the hand. She knelt down, but the little boy was frightened, and the King took him gently and made him kneel beside him, and the three, in perfect silence, were there together—a sight not soon to be forgotten. Then they passed on, and the Emperor came and knelt likewise, and so in turn all the rest of the Royal Family in a continuous string. Then the Household or at least the few who had been invited to be present. As we left the building the rain or sleet began to fall. An hour later we drove to Bagshot to catch a train to Farnham, but before we reached Bagshot the snow was lying thickly on the ground, and everyone was commenting on the significant change of weather at the moment when it had ceased to matter.

So ended a fortnight as memorable certainly to me as any I am likely to see this side the grave.

[1] Afterwards King Edward VIII.

CHAPTER XIX

ARCHBISHOP TEMPLE'S LAST YEARS

'Full of years and full of cares, of neither weary, but full of hope and of heaven.'
JOHN HENRY SHORTHOUSE, *John Inglesant.*

THE death of Mandell Creighton, a week before the Queen, was a real calamity to the Church. He was only fifty-seven. He was one of the three younger Bishops whom Davidson had suggested to the Queen as a possible successor of Benson for the Archbishopric; and in the minds of many he was marked for the future Primate. He and Randall Davidson had been consecrated together in Westminster Abbey, less than ten years before. They were men utterly unlike—and, though they had known one another ever since Davidson, as an undergraduate, had attended Creighton's lectures, Creighton's brilliant versatility and slightly caustic, if not cynical, wit were a barrier to anything like real affection between them; while Creighton disliked what he regarded as too great a desire on Davidson's part for his share of public attention. Speaking of their relations generally, Davidson says:

> I never failed to learn much from my intercourse with him, but I was not one of those who had really discovered or appreciated what I now know from his *Life* to have been the deepest and best of his qualities. At the same time I found in his latter days when I knew him best, a frequent touch of something appealing to the deeper spiritual side of things, and it always seemed to me that he had a sound appreciation of the true proportion of great things to small in the Ritual Controversy.

Referring to Creighton's work as Bishop of London Davidson observes:

> In the duties of that Bishopric his versatility had full play; his extraordinary readiness, and thoughtful understanding, and suggestive speech, enabled him to go from place to place on the same day and say something at each which was worth hearing; and few gifts other than the purely spiritual ones would be so valuable as these to a Bishop of London.
>
> He managed his correspondence in a curiously rapid and even airy way, and seemed to keep himself abreast of everything. He

was certainly strangely unlike what any other Bishop of London had been, or is ever likely to be. A great many people who knew him well found it difficult not to believe him to be a cynic, and there were those who doubted his real hold upon the dogmatic side of Christianity. This last was probably due to his endeavour, mistaken and unsuccessful as I personally think it was, to appear as a finished man of the world with social experience and social gifts, who could meet other men of the world on equal terms. My personal belief is that he damaged rather than aided his real influence by this attitude, and it certainly laid him open to the misinterpretations which were widespread.

But he adds, in admiration of Mrs. Creighton's fine *Life* of her husband:

Since those days his *Life* has been published, and I know of no instance in which the publication of a public man's biography has so greatly raised him in the estimation of good and thoughtful people.

I

Who should be the new Bishop of London? The question was all important, for as Tait once said, 'London is the key of the Church'. 'The difficulty of Creighton's position in regard to ritual disputes', says Davidson, 'has been set forth in accurate terms in the Report of the Royal Commission on Ecclesiastical Discipline, and it might have been expressed much more stringently.'

There was a very strong wish in influential quarters that Davidson himself should be appointed. The King at Osborne told him that Lord Salisbury was quite clear in desiring that he should go to London. Davidson says:

I told him that this seemed to be impossible, that all the objections to evening work which had proved fatal to my remaining in South London as Bishop of Rochester were equally strong with regard to the See of London, but I undertook to consult Sir Thomas Barlow, who was then in the house. I had long talks with him about it and he was peremptory in saying that I ought not to go. I then received a direct letter from Lord Salisbury.

The Marquess of Salisbury *to the* Bishop of Winchester

Private. Feb. 2, 1901. Downing St., S.W.

By the strongly worded counsel of the Archbishop of Canterbury —and with the approval of His Majesty—I write to ask you whether you will not accept the vacant See of London. I am aware that you have expressed a reluctance to move from your present diocese—both on grounds of health and on other grounds. But the period is critical—the moral authority of a powerful Bishop is grievously needed by the Church—and there is no Bishop on the Bench that can speak with the authority which you possess.

I venture to break the seal of 'private and confidential' and to submit to you the letter in which the Archbishop disposes of the objections which you might feel bound to make. I am sure the time is *very* critical: and if you feel forced to decline I fear the Church may have much to suffer.

The Bishop writes:

I replied that, after such a letter, conveying as it again did the wish of the King as well as of himself, I was ready to reconsider the position. I consulted Barlow again, and meantime heard from Archbishop Temple who urged me not to decline.

There was not one letter only, but a fusillade of short, sharp commands from Archbishop Temple. Davidson saw the Archbishop and wrote to him as to the unshaken verdict of his doctor. It made no difference to the Archbishop's view:

The ARCHBISHOP OF CANTERBURY *to the* BISHOP OF WINCHESTER

Lambeth Palace, S.E.
Feb. 8, 1901.

I have read your letter and thought about it.

And I am still of opinion that it would be better for the Church at this moment that you should be in London doing nothing more than decide such questions as have to be episcopally decided than that another man should be there doing full work.

But indeed the medical verdict was decisive:

SIR THOMAS BARLOW *to the* BISHOP OF WINCHESTER

February 11, 1901.

The Archbishop of Canterbury thinks you could largely eliminate the night work.

With the greatest deference to his knowledge and judgment I do not believe that your personal equation would permit you to throw all the evening Confirmations on to your suffragans, nor do I believe that you could effectively administer the diocese unless you were able to work along your own lines, which would involve a great deal of personal participation in evening meetings.

I hate overstatement and I don't pretend to prophesy—but I believe, if you go to Fulham, you run the risk of being incapacitated within a couple of years and thereby at the best being obliged to take a long rest. This would be attended with grave inconvenience.

If you keep a certain margin such as you can get at Farnham you can do your work effectively, but without the margin, I doubt if you can.

The Bishop did not lightly decline. The King and Lord Salisbury, both of whom he saw, approved the decision. As Lord Salisbury himself put it at the close of the correspondence:

The MARQUESS OF SALISBURY *to the* BISHOP OF WINCHESTER

Downing Street, S.W.
February 11, 1901.

. . . If Sir T. Barlow distinctly says no, I should not wish, even if I could flatter myself I had the power, to persuade you to say 'Yes': for the Church would lose your present services without gaining anything in exchange.

The see was then offered to and accepted by the Bishop of Stepney, Dr. A. F. Winnington Ingram.

It is interesting to observe that in the very early days of his tenure of the See the new Bishop of London got into close touch with Davidson over the troubles of the Diocese. Davidson told him of the qualms with which he viewed his new and independent plan for the regulation, instead of the prohibition, of Incense:

The BISHOP OF WINCHESTER *to the* BISHOP OF LONDON

27 June 1901.

Considering that the Bishops have resolved not to veto any prosecution, without first communicating with the Archbishop, so that he may invite the counsel and comments of other Bishops, I can't help wishing it had been possible for the Bishops generally to know beforehand that this new departure was imminent or inevitable. . . . I gather that when your action is challenged the defence might be 'It was a choice between giving way (under the euphemism of "regulating"), and open war, and it was wise to choose the first'. I shall be quite ready to say 'The Bishop of London knows the details of each case and I don't, I have complete confidence in him: he sees that by this means and not otherwise he can govern his diocese; our business is to trust him: he no doubt felt it wiser not to tell us beforehand, and depend upon it he knows what he is doing.' That other Dioceses far beyond the London area will have new difficulties in consequence of this new departure goes without saying. But we must bear our burthens; and the mess Benjamin has *inherited*, not *caused*, is ten times greater than the mess of any of his brethren.

The Bishop of London, however, addressing Davidson as 'Dear Elder Brother' and signing himself 'Benjamin', thought that he was too pessimistic and that all would be well. He had, as he said in another letter later in the year, to do his best to deal with 'the twenty churches' and 'Tracy[1] (the leader of the twenty)'.

II

There were other changes this year on the Bench of Bishops, and it is of interest to note that the King, who renewed Davidson's appointment as Clerk of the Closet, pointedly expressed his wish to get just the same counsel from Bishop Davidson on all new Church nominations as he had given to the Queen.

The most striking appointment was that of Canon Charles Gore to the Bishopric of Worcester. The nomination of one who was the founder of a Religious Community[2] known as the Mirfield Monks, and yet had caused so much grief to Dr. Liddon by the liberalism of his views on inspiration, had caused something of a sensation in the Church. He was a close friend of Davidson's, and there are certain letters from Gore himself, giving his point of view of his own difficulties about becoming a Bishop during a crisis in the Church, when he did not at all agree with the regular archiepiscopal leadership.

Here is a letter written after a meeting of the Bishops, which the Bishop-designate had been allowed to attend:

The REV. CANON GORE *to the* BISHOP OF WINCHESTER

4 Little Cloisters, Westminster.

Confidential. Nov. 13.

I find the Consecration cannot be till Jan. 25.

During the meeting yesterday I felt several things. 1. A great desire to stand up and say 'My lords, I have been among ritualists

[1] The Rev. the Hon. A. F. A. Hanbury-Tracy, Vicar of St. Barnabas', Pimlico.
[2] The Community of the Resurrection, at Mirfield, Yorkshire.

and used to their services since 1868. I can tell you, for I know, that to talk of suppressing incense or reservation is to talk about what is impossible. You might have regulated it, you may perhaps still do so:—but suppress it, no'.

But 2. I felt that I must have some *éclaircissement*. I must feel clear what the oath of obedience to the Archbishop means, which the bishop takes. I suppose its interpretation is traditional and historical. Can you direct me to any standard interpretation of it as touches England since the Reformation?

I must in any case let the Archbishop understand that I am prepared to *regulate* incense and reservation, but not prepared to *suppress* it:—that is to say that I am not prepared to regard his Ruling as it stands as 'the Law' or to enforce it.

I am thankful for time to think over these things.

I suppose this attitude, as far as I am concerned, would be anticipated. Still I think I must make my position clear to the Archbishop.

The Bishop of Winchester *to the* Rev. Canon Gore

Farnham. Nov. 16, 1901.

Since your letter of Nov. 13 I have not had one moment for replying. I have noted Jan. 25 as your Consecration Day and you may be sure of my remembering you daily in my prayers from now till then—nor must that day be a terminus.

As to what you say about the Oath of Obedience to the Archbishop, its exact meaning in practical application is not very easy I suppose to define; but most assuredly no Diocesan Bishop, so far as I know, has ever interpreted it as meaning that the Archbishop's Suffragans are bound to follow his lead or command in such details of Diocesan Management as those which formed the subject of our discussion on Tuesday. Indeed the Archbishop has himself made it plain, often and often, that he does not so regard his office, and, so far as the recent Lambeth Opinion goes, he expressly stated publicly that he did not for a moment claim for it a binding force upon any Bishop at all. He had been invited, according to the Prayer Book, to help to resolve a matter 'diversely taken'; he had done his best to resolve it, and the action to follow must depend upon individual Bishops. I don't suppose any Bishop would definitely declare himself against what the Archbishop believes (and publicly says he believes) to be the law, unless he, the Bishop, has, on independent lines, satisfied himself that the Archbishop is mistaken and that those who had declined to obey Bishop Creighton did, in the recent arguments at Lambeth make good their case. So far as I know, no English Bishop does think this, though several may wish the law were other than it is, and presumably we are bound, in controversial matters, to follow, speaking generally, what we believe to be our Church's existing law, even if we dislike it, and would like to see it changed. But this cannot, in the present circumstances, be fairly carried so far as to forbid us to make exceptional arrangements for exceptional cases of difficulty at an exceptional period.

That is how the matter presents itself to me. I entered on the Lambeth Hearing[1] with a mind really open to anything which I might hear, and in good hopes of hearing a better case made out for Incense and for Reservation than I had up to that time been able to find. Instead of that I found every argument against these things being now legal, strengthened, and nothing of any real weight urged on the other side.

I attended the whole Hearing and took careful notes and consulted all the Books. In the end I came without possibility of hesitation to the view that our Church does not at present sanction their usages.

I should not think of resting my conclusions on the arguments or premises used by the Archbishops, but *my conclusion* is identical with theirs. I should *therefore feel* bound by my Consecration and Ordination promises to conform—and generally speaking to promote conformity—to what I conscientiously believe to be the law of the Church and Realm, at the moment. But, if I had come to the opposite conclusion, I certainly should not have felt myself precluded from acting in accordance with that conclusion by the fact of my having promised 'due obedience' to the Archbishop. All this seems so elementary that I shrink from writing it to you—who are far more of a pundit in these things than I am. But you seem to ask me to say how the matter presents itself to me. I suppose in our action as Bishops in these matters we are bound to act in accordance with law—existing law as interpreted by the best authorities available—and not by our view of what ought to be permissible as a matter of expediency in deference to the usages of particular men. The utmost that we can do, consistently with Ordination and Consecration promises, is to make special arrangements for special cases, always supposing we believe the law to be what every single 'Court' or 'Authority' has declared it to be. Of course if we are convinced that they are all mistaken and that the law is other than as hitherto declared, and that this would be proved if it was again tested in Court, we should I suppose be not

[1] For the Lambeth Hearings on Incense and Reservation see pp. 340, 346.

only justified but perhaps bound to act accordingly in administering our Diocese.

I write curtly and perhaps confusedly—under great pressure—but the point is a very important one. Perhaps I have misunderstood you.

Gore's reply to the Bishop brimmed over with gratitude, but he added, about his interview with Temple (November 28): 'I had out my views to the Archbishop at Canterbury yesterday, and I thought he rather slew me than answered me.'

A further difficulty arose with regard to the Confirmation of the Bishop-elect. Sir J. Parker Deane died in January 1902, at the age of eighty-nine, after holding his office of Vicar-General for thirty years. Archbishop Temple appointed Mr. C. A. Cripps, K.C., as his successor, and the whole question, which had been raised five years before but had been left undecided, was raised again in an acute form. A new procedure was adopted by which the citation required opposers to deliver their objections in writing before a date named, and stated that no objector who did not appear in Chambers and establish his right to appear and be heard could appear or be heard during the business of Confirmation. The Vicar-General accordingly sat in Chambers at the Church House, Westminster, at 10 a.m. on January 22, 1902. Certain objectors appeared, all of whom raised questions of doctrine. The Vicar-General informed the objectors that questions of doctrine could 'under no circumstances be entertained at the business of a Confirmation'. At 11 o'clock the public sitting was held in the Lower Convocation hall. Mr. Dibdin, who appeared for the Bishop-elect, stated that he was instructed to say that the Bishop-elect was quite willing to answer any legitimately made and relevant charges. The Vicar-General, however, repeated in public the ruling he had already given in Chambers and, in spite of indignant protests from many objectors present, proceeded with the Confirmation in the usual form.

Two of the objectors then applied for a Mandamus to the Court of King's Bench to compel the Vicar-General to hear the objections, and arguments were heard on February 3, 4, and 5. This involved the postponement of the Consecration—a course insisted upon by Canon Gore, though the Archbishop wished to go forward. The Bishop of Winchester saw a great deal of the

Bishop-elect at this time, and gave him invaluable support when he was suffering from strain and over-excitement ('I am afraid I was over-excited when last I saw you. But my temperature has become normal again'):

The REV. CANON GORE *to the* BISHOP OF WINCHESTER

Westminster. Jan. 25 '02.

You are a great deal too kind to me. You do not know how glad I should be to repay you some of it.

I feel very much confirmed in the sense of having done right. And the Bishop of Coventry,[1] I find to my satisfaction, is thoroughly glad. One thing that presents itself to me more clearly is that, as far as possible legal consequences go, no taking of the responsibility by the Archbishop could have had any effect on my position. The legal difficulties would have remained mine or the diocese's.

Will you tell me whether I may assume that I am *not* to go to Windsor on Tuesday? *I will assume it unless I hear to the contrary.*

I should be very glad if somehow my side of the question could be presented to the King. The statement in this morning's *Standard*, which I am told came from Conybeare[2], is (not *quite* accurate—for I am sure the Court for Confirmation can't try an open question of heresy) tolerable.

Judgement was delivered by the Lord Chief Justice[3] sitting with Mr. Justice Ridley and Mr. Justice Wright on February 10. It was unanimous, each judge reading a separate written judgement dismissing the application. The Court decided that the Vicar-General ought not to entertain, still less adjudicate upon, charges of a doctrinal character in connexion with the Confirmation of a Bishop's election. With regard to other possible objections, the Lord Chief Justice added:

> It is not in my opinion necessary to decide that in no case can any objection be raised at the stage of Confirmation which might have to be investigated by the Vicar-General or the Archbishop, as e.g. an objection to the validity of the election or the genuineness of the documents produced, the identity of the person elected with the person named in the Letters Missive, or possibly some action or conduct of the Bishop-elect since the time of his election.

Canon Gore expressed the view, as the person immediately

[1] The Rt. Rev. E. A. Knox (afterwards Bishop of Manchester).

[2] The Rev. W. J. Conybeare, Resident Chaplain to the Archbishop of Canterbury.

[3] Lord Chief Justice Alverstone.

concerned by the Judgement, that it allowed Confirmation to have a real significance.

The Rev. Canon Gore *to the* Bishop of Winchester

February 10, 1902.

> The judgments give us all we could expect or hope. They are unanimous in refusing the rule. But they leave a real meaning or function to the Archbishop's Confirmation. He can hear objections, as he pleases; and, if he thinks fit, delay consecration and report to the King. So I gather. . . .

But it must be confessed that, though the meaning and function are real, they are confined within a very narrow area indeed.

In the following August the coronation of King Edward VII took place. The date originally fixed was June 26, 1902. But the King was seized with a grave illness a few days before, at Aldershot. Its serious character was not, however, at once detected by the doctors in attendance from June 14. He left for Windsor on June 16, giving up his proposed visit to Ascot. On June 21, all seemed of good augury for the Coronation. On June 23, he travelled to London. A denial of sensational rumours was published by Sir Francis Knollys on the same day. On June 24, however, alarming symptoms appeared. An operation was performed at once and the Coronation was suddenly and dramatically postponed.

This brief record has been given in order to emphasize one aspect of Davidson's own character which must not be forgotten. He was a very just man. He was also a very loyal subject; and he was a patient with good reason to be grateful to the medical profession. The new Bishop of Worcester,[1] preaching in Birmingham on Wednesday, June 25, expressed astonishment in emphatic terms that the public had not been forewarned about what they might expect for weeks past, and added that 'it was not good for them to have to feel that the rumours of the Clubs and the streets were right and the official declarations were wrong'. Sir Thomas Barlow's quick eye saw the reference and wrote to Davidson (in the course of one of his daily letters as to the King's progress):

[1] Dr. Charles Gore, consecrated February 23, 1902.

SIR THOMAS BARLOW *to the* BISHOP OF WINCHESTER

June 26, 1902.

. . . I wonder if you have seen the report in *The Times* of to-day (—under the paragraph head of Birmingham) of the address of the Bishop of Worcester. I should like you to read it if you have not done so.

The Bishop of Winchester wrote off straight to Dr. Gore:

The BISHOP OF WINCHESTER *to the* BISHOP OF WORCESTER

Lollards Tower, Lambeth, S.E.

June 27, 1902.

I have been at Buckingham Palace this morning as usual, and I find rather 'a state of mind' prevailing with regard to the report in yesterday's *Times* of what you said at Birmingham on the previous day. I am not quite sure whether the matter has yet come personally to the King's knowledge, but it certainly would distress him if it did. I have tried to point out that perhaps you have been unfairly or distortedly reported (it is our common lot!) but even when every such discount is allowed, the residuum is important. If there is one thing about which the medical men have been keen from the first beginning of the illness—it has been that they should, when bulletins have to be published, speak the truth simply and straightforwardly and deceive nobody. One of them (Barlow) is my intimate personal friend—one of the straightest and finest fellows I know anywhere—and all of them are men of such character and reputation as to feel intensely the sort of accusation which your words carry. Of course they are accustomed, like the rest of us, to misrepresentation and misunderstanding, or even abuse from the anonymous outside critic in the press; but, as it was put to me this morning 'it is another matter altogether when a man like the Bishop of Worcester takes that line and does it publicly'. You are reported as practically saying that the Doctors had known for weeks past about the King's illness and that they deliberately concealed it, or, as you are made to say, 'that the language of authority had no relation to facts'. This has (surely not unnaturally) caused deep pain and strong indignation in the Doctors, who are doing their level best—as the heads of their profession in England, to give an example of plain straightforward bulletins. They are of course prepared to stand by every word they have said, as written to the best of their knowledge and ability at the time. The full record of the illness given in yesterday's

Times in the ordinary way, as a medical communiqué, states the exact facts. Of course you had not seen it when you spoke as you did, or you would never have launched this charge against them with the great weight of your name. But their contention is that the statement was made by you without knowledge, while they are obviously, so to speak, at your mercy. It is at their request, and at that of Knollys who is familiar in such matters with the opinion of the King and Queen, that *I* write to you, as I pointed out that this would be far better than an *official* letter to you. I feel sure that you will be able to send me some reply which I can shew, to the effect that you did not mean to use words so calculated to give unfair pain. As the account will have shewn you, there was no trace whatever of the approach of the illness until the day when the King went to Aldershot—so any 'ominous rumours of the Clubs' must have been without real foundation, whatever they were. For the first days there seemed no need for any bulletins—so none were published. The doctors kept absolute silence by the express wish of the King, so as to avoid raising disquietude which might, and they fully hoped would, prove to have no *raison d'être*. As soon as it was clear that they must not hope for the disappearance *naturally* of the evil, they published a full and accurate bulletin, and they have done so ever since.

A more personal letter accompanied this reproach:

The Bishop of Winchester *to the* Bishop of Worcester

Private. 27 June 1902.

The enclosed which seems *fiery* is less fiery than that which would have gone, had I not undertaken to write it! I found them on the verge of sending you an official document or formal letter which would have done infinite mischief. Do send me a letter which I can show. It is really hard lines on these good fellows to find themselves charged right and left with lying when they are as keen as you or I could be to be straight and true. Poor Knollys suffers in like manner, e.g. a newspaper agency telegraphs to him 'It is said King has had a paralytic seizure and is lying helpless' or words to that effect. Knollys replies that it is without foundation and instantly a statement is published that Knollys has been asked if *the King was ill* and has said there was no foundation for the rumour!

The Bishop replied, sticking to his guns with regard to the official denial in the Press of June 23, but energetically repudiating the suggestion that his words reflected on the doctors. His final answer was as follows:

The BISHOP OF WORCESTER *to the* BISHOP OF WINCHESTER

St. Martin's Rectory, Worcester.
July 3, '02.

I am exceedingly sorry to have caused you so much trouble. I am at least as sorry to have caused distress to distinguished physicians and surgeons, for certainly there is no class of men in the country whom I honour more profoundly.

I think it is most likely that my words were not well chosen. Possibly, if I go back on the incident a year hence, I shall feel that it was not my business to speak at all. At present I can only feel bothered when I try to reconsider the matter. My motive was simply to try to maintain the honour of the Crown against idle or malignant gossip. Some good I believe I did. Probably if I had been wiser, I could have done the good without accompanying harm. Certainly I never intended to make any accusation against the medical profession. And, of course, I can very well understand how differently matters look from within—from without. I hope I need not say any more. Probably it will be felt by those who strongly condemn what I said that I was not malevolent.

The letters were sent to Sir Thomas Barlow who replied:

[Undated.]

I return Bishop of Worcester's letter. The doctors have no resentment.

It is kind of you to have taken so much pains.

The King recovered. The Coronation took place on August 9. Dr. Davidson acted throughout as intermediary between the Archbishop and the King. With Canon Armitage Robinson (in the Dean's illness) he undertook the re-editing of the Order of Coronation, and in all sorts of ways helped not only the Archbishop, but the Earl Marshal, the Duke of Norfolk, and everybody connected with the ceremony. The following letters tell their own tale:

LORD KNOLLYS *to the* BISHOP OF WINCHESTER

Buckingham Palace. August, 1902.

I am desired by the King to thank you very warmly for all that you have done in connection with the Coronation. The unceasing trouble which you took in regard to the ceremony, with the attention which you paid to every detail, and the personal assistance which you gave him in everything that concerned the part which he had to take in the service, was of the greatest use to him, and he has very highly appreciated it.

As a special mark of the King's satisfaction, the Bishop was awarded the rank of K.C.V.O.

The Archbishop of Canterbury *to the* Bishop of Winchester

Old Palace, Canterbury. 12 August, 1902.

The Coronation is over and there are very few things that have now to be settled. But about these things I should like to say a word or two. What is to be done with the Bible? If the King claims it, of course he must have it, but I do hope he will not give it away to somebody who will deal with it as the Bibles of past Coronations have been dealt with. It is not right to let it go, as it were by haphazard, to wander over the world. I should prefer that it should be held in trust by some permanent Body (say the Chapter of the Abbey) for use at future Coronations. Or it might be deposited in Windsor[1] Palace Library. But to secure this there ought to be an inscription in it very speedily.

Secondly what is to be done with those most useful Scrolls? These ought to be treated in the same way. But here there is another question to be asked. Who paid for them? They were got for me because of my very weak sight, and if they are not paid for out of the general expenses I ought to be allowed to pay for them myself. I have spent very little on the ceremony. The Cope was not my own but lent me by another Bishop. I shall be much obliged if you will tell me how the matter stands. But there must be some letter entrusting them to someone; and I ought to write it.

The success of the Ceremony as a National Ceremony is more largely due to you than to anyone else. But I am conscious that the debt of gratitude for all your labour is due to you from me more than from any other person. I cannot easily express how much I feel that I owe to you. You have been indefatigable in your endeavour to save me from overwork. To the end of my life I shall be sensible of your unselfish kindness.

You will like to know that the King sent for me yesterday and gave me the Collar of the Order of Victoria.

[1] A mistake for Lambeth Palace Library, where it now is.

This letter was much treasured by Bishop Davidson who kept it amongst his papers marked with two crosses 'Very important'. He sent the following letter in reply:

The BISHOP OF WINCHESTER *to the* ARCHBISHOP OF CANTERBURY

Private. Farnham Castle, Surrey. 13 August 1902.

I cannot tell you how deeply I have been moved by the kindness of your letter, just received.

Many a time during the last few months I have wondered whether I was not worrying you unduly and perhaps 'taking too much upon me' about details, and it is an immense relief and happiness to me to have such words from you as you have now written. Many many thanks. We are all so proud of you, and of the way you did it from first to last. I know (and no doubt he himself told you so) how much the King felt it.

During the King's illness and the days before and after the Coronation, the Bishop of Winchester won His Majesty's personal gratitude for the way in which he spoke of the lessons which such an illness at such a time might teach.

III

The latter half of 1902 was also much occupied with work on the new and very important Education Act of that year.

The educational problem in various phases was constantly coming up throughout Davidson's life and a brief word of introduction, therefore, may not be out of place at this point. Ever since the Act of 1870 made elementary education compulsory for all children, the real issue has been the relation of the State schools, at first called Board schools,[1] to Church schools and other schools set up by the Voluntary Bodies. The Board schools were entirely paid for by the State, while the Voluntary schools were simply aided, and, notably, not only appointed but paid their own teachers. Not unnaturally, as the Board schools developed and the standard of education rose, the Voluntary schools found it more and more difficult to compete and to make ends meet. In both Board schools (gener-

[1] School Boards were set up by the Education Act, 1870, with rating powers to establish and maintain public elementary schools, called as a consequence Board schools to distinguish them from Voluntary schools.

ally) and Church schools (always) religious instruction was given: though in Board schools it was given not by legal requirement, could be prohibited, and was of a general and undenominational character,[1] while in Church schools it was guaranteed by Trust Deed and consisted of definite Church teaching. The Voluntary schools and the Voluntary system had an immense advantage in country districts, where for various reasons School Boards were in a difficult position. The question which agitated the public mind was this—should the Voluntary schools be not only aided but practically financed throughout? And, if so, should they be nationally controlled in exactly the same way as the Board schools were controlled, or should they be allowed to retain their denominational character, and, as part and parcel of that, the control of the appointment of their teachers?

Between 1890 and 1902, many conferences were held and many Bills were drafted. The Liberal party steadily supported State control, and the Conservatives were in favour of financing the Voluntary schools and yet allowing them to retain their independence. In 1897, a partial Measure was passed by which the aid given by the State to Voluntary schools was distinctly improved. But the great issue was finally joined in 1902. The Conservative party, under Mr. Balfour, in addition to endeavouring to co-ordinate all forms of education under a single authority, decided to bring the Voluntary schools completely into the national system, so far as maintenance and the payment of teachers were concerned, yet retaining the schools definitely as Church or denominational schools with their full Church or denominational character.

It was a Measure of vast importance and inevitable perplexity. The hero of the Act, without a doubt, was the Permanent Secretary of the Board of Education, Mr. Robert Morant. It was he who, behind the scenes, bore the brunt of the attack and helped his chief to expound, to conciliate, and, where need was, to defeat. But a guide was wanted on the Church side, who could interpret the Church's view to the Government and *vice versa*; no easy task the latter, as the history of the past sixty years makes only too

[1] Under the Act of 1870, where religious instruction is given, what is known as the Cowper-Temple clause provides that 'no religious catechism or religious formulary distinctive of any particular denomination shall be taught in schools which receive rate aid'.

plain. No one could do this better than Davidson, who now, through his dealing with Mr. Balfour on the Church crisis, had completely won his confidence as a man of judgement and a statesman. His help was utilized to the full. At the end of 1901, when the exact nature of the expected Bill was yet uncertain, he wrote thus to Mr. Balfour:

The BISHOP OF WINCHESTER *to the* RT. HON. A. J. BALFOUR

8 Dec. 1901.

I hope I am not doing wrong in troubling you at this juncture with a letter on the position of the Education question. My excuse must be the fact that wherever I go, in this part of England with which I have to do, I find people's minds to be disquieted by a current rumour that in the forthcoming Education Bill the urgent problem of *Primary* Education may, after all, not be seriously grappled with, and that the Bill may be confined wholly or mainly to Secondary Education. Whenever I have heard this said, I have ventured to try to reassure the disgusted folk by the expression of my own firm belief that such a rumour cannot possibly be true, and that the Government is incapable of dealing in such a manner with the mass of its supporters, who have so bravely struggled on for the last few years in the face of ceaseless difficulty—many of them making greater financial sacrifices than anybody will ever know in order, as they believed, to render impregnable the continuance, in Elementary Schools, of Religious Education really worthy of the name. . . .

I do not like to contemplate what I should now have to say to those men were we to learn that all this had been a misapprehension: that no relief was to be given: and that our Voluntary Schools, after all the money we have spent on them—many of the clergy literally denying themselves everything for the sake of the Schools—were to be allowed simply to be closed or handed over to School Boards under the existing regulations. For it is absolutely certain that such would be the result (not of course everywhere but over large areas). We can no longer appeal for Voluntary Subscriptions on the existing scale with any prospect of success. . . .

When one turns from the general principle, that some such relief must be given—to the details or manner of the relief or readjustment, I do not claim that we stand upon such firm ground. The Government has never, so far as I know, made any promise or even held out any definite expectation as to the *mode* in which what we want is to be given. Speaking for myself I have consistently urged that it is our duty, as well as our wisdom, to leave the Government a free hand. We have formulated detailed proposals, but (so far as I and many others are concerned) this has been in order to show that we had our own ideas as to workable schemes and possibilities and were ready to suggest them, and not that we thought our suggestions the only possible ones. You might fairly have said to us 'You assert principles, but you avoid working them out'. We therefore send in a detailed plan which to us seems a reasonable one—leaving the Government to suggest, if it prefers to do so, its own plan instead, and expressing (most of us) our perfect readiness to give a welcome to *any* plan, which gives effect to the *principles* which we advocate.

I may perhaps say that nothing has to me personally been more irritating than to hear and read the sort of language in which some of our Ecclesiastical friends have expressed their 'demands'. They have failed to recognise adequately the extraordinary difficulty of the problem, the opposition which has to be encountered, and the variety of possible ways in which effect might be given to sound principles. But you will know how to discount all this. The mistake would be to suppose that because some of the Resolutions and letters etc. are foolish or intemperate or ask for utter impossibilities, therefore the general demand for readjustment of the existing system can be disregarded.

Such disregard would to many of us seem a withdrawal of virtual pledges given,—pledges on the strength of which we have ourselves spoken and acted and persuaded others to speak and act for years.

Most fully do I see the magnitude and perplexity of the problem and the certainty of opposition, whatever be done. But I believe myself to be right in saying that in the event of the Government making *any* serious and reasonable endeavour to deal with the situation in a manner fair to Voluntary Schools and their friends, they would find an overwhelming majority of Churchmen, lay and clerical, prepared to meet them half way, and to accept loyally the proposals made as a basis for detailed discussion.

We believe ourselves to have established an indisputable claim to relief. We have long understood that that claim, in a large and general way, was admitted by the present Government, and we are counting upon this coming Session for securing to us something at least of what we have been waiting for. . . .

Pardon me again for troubling you with all this. I hope it may be quite unnecessary.

In March 1902 the Bill was read for the first time in the House of Commons, and it showed beyond doubt the Government's desire to tackle both the primary and the secondary school problems. It was welcomed at once by those who spoke for the Church as providing on the whole an equitable settlement of the education question. But it was violently attacked by Nonconformists. In relation both to the Church and to Nonconformists, Mr. Balfour obtained much useful advice from the Bishop of Winchester. They were in constant consultation, and Dr. Davidson was a frequent visitor to Downing Street, and occasionally at Mr. Balfour's home at Whittingehame. He was in close touch, independently, with Lord Rosebery about the violent onslaught of Dr. Clifford upon the Bill.

The BISHOP OF WINCHESTER *to the* RT. HON. A. J. BALFOUR

Davidson's Mains, Midlothian.
17 Sept. 1902.

I am inclined to doubt whether anything substantial would be gained by the publication NOW of your clever and unanswerable reply to the Nonconformist Deputation. So far as it goes it is complete. But they have run off now into so many new paths of objection and criticism that your answer does not cover the ground taken up by your opponents.

The arguments or allegations which you are answering don't of course appear in the pamphlet—and it may therefore be represented (unfairly) as an endeavour to meet all that is said against the Bill. Probably it fairly *did* so at the time, and what you then said remains unshaken and *wants repeating again and again.* But there is now so much more to be said for the meeting of present objections, that I don't think the publication of the speech would be very opportune. It would doubtless do some good, but it would be plausibly attacked, and misrepresented as being your whole case.

I have arranged to see the Archbishop of Canterbury this day week and I am trying to arrest Roffen's[1] departure for Holland until I have seen him (on Monday or Tuesday)

I have written to Dr. Paton in the fashion which you suggested.

I find Rosebery obviously somewhat disquieted by the extravagancies of Dr. Clifford's appeal to the Nonconformist public. He thinks Clifford's absolute misstatements ought to be corrected, lest

[1] Dr. Talbot, Bishop of Rochester.

the lie gets too good a start! My own feeling is that it would be well to let Clifford publish his letters as a pamphlet and thus commit himself more deliberately to them before any attempt is made to show their falsity.

Rosebery is clearly in a position of great difficulty on the question—from his own belief in Municipal bodies and the maintenance or increase of their responsibilities. But I have naturally not felt at liberty to talk the matter over very frankly with him though I have listened to all he had to say, and he has no notion (so far as I can see) of the present complications and of course he is quite unaware of my having had any confidential talk with you about it.

I am most grateful to you for all your kind confidence—and I hope some means may be found for my doing some good among our friends. But it is very difficult to see one's way clearly.

I found Arthur Lyttelton after a full talk rather in favour of B.1 as against B.3. But he had not had time to weigh the position properly before we parted. If left to himself he would I think fully share *our* liking for A.1 as the reasonable and right solution. But he believes the *Church* feeling in favour of restricting the control of the Religious Education to the Clergy—(at all events where the trust so prescribes)—to be very strong.

I won't trouble you with more now—but I will keep you informed of anything that seems important when I have seen or heard from Cantuar or Roffen. I need hardly add that I will take every care to keep the whole thing quite confidential.

Our visit to Whittingehame was full of profit as well as pleasure.

Nine days later the Bishop wrote to thank Mr. Balfour for several letters and memoranda on the Bill, and spoke this time of the difficulties of Churchmen:

The Bishop of Winchester *to the* Rt. Hon. A. J. Balfour

Old Palace, Canterbury.
26 Sept. 1902.

. . . The position, so far as we Churchmen are concerned, has become most perplexing, but speaking for myself and a good many others I may say that we shall of course stand by what you have secured in the House of Commons if you find that, on the whole, it is best to attempt no modification.

At the same time I ought to say that I, for one, am impressed by what in the last few days has been urged upon me by leading

Nonconformists, as to the wish of a large number of the more moderate men to come to some *reasonable* arrangement with us if it can be devised. They are I think irritated by Clifford's violence, and ashamed of his merely pugilistic attitude—and, if this be so, we, who necessarily look at the question from a religious rather than a merely political standpoint, should be thankful to find it possible to meet such men half-way. I am in no way empowered to speak for others, but this is my own view.

I have seen Dr. Paton of Nottingham and have heard from Guinness Rogers—both of whom take this conciliatory attitude—and Paton keeps reiterating that there are thousands of Nonconformists who do the same. He is assured by Hugh Price Hughes that neither he nor the Methodists generally have in any way committed themselves to Clifford's position. Of course there are many Bishops and Clergy and certainly (as you know well) there are many politicians, whose feeling would be strongly against any concession or compromise. I speak merely for myself, but I am very sure that more are with us than is supposed, provided always that the *principle* of maintaining the Denominational system be genuinely (and not merely nominally) maintained.

I had a long talk to Roffen on Tuesday—and then to Gibson[1] of Leeds. I am now with the Archbishop, and on the way here I saw Paton as I have said.

What I have now done is to ask a few very leading men to meet me quite privately and unofficially on Tuesday next to talk over the situation. I shall be guarded in what I say as to what you have told me—but I shall ascertain what is the direction in which concession, if it has to be made, would be least intolerable.

How would it be for me then to run up to Scotland again and report to you what is the outcome? I would do so with pleasure if you wish it—and the matter is so complex that writing about it is not easy. But this is just as you like. Will you let me know what you would desire? I am here till Monday morning and then Farnham Castle, Surrey.

I enclose a Memorandum which tries to boil down some of the confusing matter.

If you were able (or Morant were able) to send me some guiding information as to the *political* 'values' of these concessions, relatively to one another, it would be a very great help to us if we are considering them.

As to a Conference, the Archbishop of Canterbury is *inclined* to

[1] Rev. E. C. S. Gibson, vicar of Leeds (afterwards Bishop of Gloucester).

favour the idea, provided you could preside over it—but he feels that you alone can judge as to its perils or possible gains in a Parliamentary sense.

It is strange how difficult everybody seems to find it to be, to say how far Clifford's diatribes have really affected the minds of the people at large.

I don't trouble you at present with Memoranda upon your Memoranda but I will do so on Monday or Tuesday.

One grave difficulty on the Church side concerned what was known as the Kenyon-Slaney clause, which gave the Managers (two-thirds Churchmen and one-third appointed by the L.E.A.) the control of the religious teaching in the schools. Observe the skill with which the Bishop sets out the clerical case to the lay reader:

The BISHOP OF WINCHESTER *to* J. S. SANDARS, ESQ.

Farnham Castle, Surrey.
October 29 1902.

I am receiving today a great many letters from men entitled to be listened to, as to the panic which may easily 'set in' among the less thoughtful clergy and their friends if it goes out (in the sort of way that a speech from Hugh Cecil will set it out) that the clergy can at any minute and *without appeal* be ousted from the Schools in which they have perhaps taught for years by a vote of a body of Managers whereof two may be hostile Nonconformists and one or two very lukewarm Churchmen. If it is further enacted that these men, again *without appeal*, may decide what is or is not the doctrine of the Church of England the position is not an easy one to defend.

I have always advocated, and do strongly advocate what we knew in our discussions as '*A. 1*'. When we have got our Denominational Majority secured, I should trust them with the full responsibility. For this I am prepared to argue to any extent. But I have always supposed—and indeed said—that there would have to be some arrangement for appeal in extreme cases against what might be a veritable wrong. Surely it can be strongly urged that the granting of such appeal is really a safeguard for the elected *minority*. If the parson were able to get his own three nominees upon a Board of Management to sit and vote with himself, the two men from outside would have little power to prevent extreme teaching should such be the parson's wish. But grant these men an appeal to the

Bishop and they would have an immense access of weight. All this is obvious—pardon my saying it.

It is needless to give further extracts from the correspondence which follows. There was much; and there were many long interviews which showed the constant and most fruitful contact between Bishop Davidson and Mr. Balfour. Indeed Sir Sydney Parry, Mr. Balfour's private secretary during this time, has told the writer that, with the marked exception of the unique help given by Mr. Robert Morant, there was nobody on whom Mr. Balfour leaned more, for his general conduct of the Bill in both Houses and in the country, than Randall Davidson.

When the Bill finally came to the Lords on December 4, the Duke of Devonshire, who introduced it, said that it had occupied more time in Committee than any Measure ever submitted to Parliament up to that date. In the course of the debate, the Archbishop of Canterbury made the last speech of his life, and to the consternation of the House, fell back exhausted on his seat with his closing words. He was helped out of the Chamber and never appeared in public again. On December 5, Davidson made the main speech from the Bench of Bishops. He replied to the spokesman of the Nonconformist opposition outside Parliament, Dr. Clifford, who had used language to the effect that the Board schools were practically to be swept away. The Bishop of Winchester remarked 'that put in that form the words are the wildest distortion of the provisions of the Bill'. After carefully dealing with the main objections to the Bill, that it (1) retained denominational tests, (2) gave control without adequate popular representation, (3) used rates to pay for denominational teaching, he ended his speech, by delivering a sick-bed appeal from the Archbishop to Churchmen to work the Bill in such a way that no hardship should be inflicted on Nonconformists. He opposed the inclusion of the Kenyon-Slaney clause, which gave the control of the religious teaching to the whole body of Managers. He moved an important amendment himself; and, by way of emphasizing his strong central moderating position, it should be sufficient to say that he drew the fire of Dr. Percival, the Liberal Bishop of Hereford, on the one hand, and on the other that of the extreme Tory High Churchman, Lord Halifax, who denounced what he was pleased to describe as the extreme imprudence of the Bishops. In the end the Bill received the

Royal Assent on December 18. It was the last piece of legislative work with which Dr. Davidson was concerned as Bishop of Winchester.

Five days later, December 23, Archbishop Temple passed away at the age of eighty-one, and the Bishop's next appearance in the House was to be as Primate of All England.

CHAPTER XX

THE PRIMACY

. . . Because the fashion of the world changes we think that Heaven is farther off now than in the childhood of the Church. Let our Fathers in God make it clear that every righteous activity is a Divine service, that every aspiration after truth is, consciously or unconsciously, a looking to Christ, that every Article of the Creed is a motive and a help to holiness; . . . let them offer as the scene of human labour a world not left fatherless, echoing with spiritual voices, and bound together through all its parts with underlying harmonies of love; let them keep steadily before the eyes of men the weightier matters of the law, judgment, mercy, and faith, which brings into their true place deep and doubtful questionings, framed of necessity in imperfect language; . . . let them hold forth in all its splendour to eager souls the ideal of that Kingdom in which each earthly achievement finds its consummation and each earthly effort its hallowing. . . .

As the vision rises before us, as we feel that it answers to the inherent power of our Faith, as we confess that it lingers afar off, dim and fleeting, through our great fault, we cry again, bowed down by past failures, disheartened by our present divisions, paralysed by the measures of our hopes, *Who is sufficient for these things?*

There can be but one answer—he who wholly forgets himself in God Who called him; he who lays down at the footstool of God his successes and his failures, his hopes and his fears, his knowledge and his ignorance, his weakness and his strength, his misgivings and his confidences—all that he is and all that he might be—content to take up thence just that which God shall give him.

B. F. WESTCOTT *at Bishop Lightfoot's Consecration*, 1877.[1]

THE close of 1902 was full of sorrow at Winchester. The Bishop's intimate friend and Suffragan, Arthur Lyttelton, lay dying at Petersfield, and the Dean (Dr. Stephens) was near his end under the shadow of Winchester Cathedral. The Bishop's own personal feelings reveal themselves in the following letter:

The BISHOP OF WINCHESTER *to the* BISHOP OF ROCHESTER

Farnham Castle, Surrey
December 20, 1902.

Your tidings are indeed grievous. I have also a note from Barlow which does not, I fear, put matters in a brighter light—(so far as WE count brightness). It is to all of us a sorrow quite beyond words—or it *will* be, when others know. I have not heard from him or from Mrs. L. so I don't write to them. I sent a letter

[1] This extract from the sermon of his old schoolmaster, Bishop Westcott, was printed as the main portion of the Note sent by Davidson to those who wrote him letters of goodwill on his nomination to the Primacy.

to greet him on his arrival, little dreaming of this. He has been, and is, to me a brother in the truest and robustest sense. Seldom have I found anybody on whom to lean so *surely*. God be with them, and with us all. It seems as though all the foundations of the earth were out of course—with that sickbed at Lambeth—and the other in the Deanery at Winchester (also a *very* dear friend)—and now this crushing blow. We have worked so thoroughly happily together. But one dares not grieve over much. The Lord reigneth, and it is one's faithlessness which pulls one's heart down. I am glad rather than sorry that it comes in Ember Week, for one's thoughts are, or ought to be, attuned to a bigger strain than any that can be marred by the changes and chances of this mortal life.

But it is humiliatingly difficult to be preparing aright—at such a moment—the words wanted for our ordinands tonight. We have a noble set of fellows—some of them really big as well as good. Unhappily we have influenza in the Hostel, and three ordinands are 'down'.

God bless you, my brother. You are one of those who seem to be made as a centre and pivot for our Church's life—a support and stay and guide for all of us, especially in deep waters like these.

Four days later he had a letter from the Bishop of London:

So the old Warrior did not last till Christmas. . . . I feel for you, dear Brother, so much at this time, with your Dean dead and dear Southampton going, and you yourself doubtless marked out for the great call, which means so much responsibility.

It was indeed true that Dr. Davidson, in the thoughts of most of those who knew the needs of the Church, was the almost certain successor of Archbishop Temple, as he himself could hardly fail to realize. This is not to say that he was unaware of his own infirmities and limitations. But he could not help perceiving that he knew the work of the Archbishopric of Canterbury better than anybody else. As he put it to a close friend, staying at Farnham during those eventful days, 'I know I am not good enough, but I do know the ropes better than others.' Yet, he said, when the decision was made, writing again to the Bishop of Rochester (January 8, 1903):

It all looms very big and bewildering and I have a good deal of the 'Faint Heart' sense to-day. Yet this is perhaps partly physical, for I am still in bed.

Anyhow you will do what one does *most* want—pray—ora pro nobis—ora ne quid detrimenti capiat Ecclesia Dei. My faintheartedness would be doubled but for the knowledge of friendship and support like yours. On that, more than on any earthly stay, I can, I know, rely.

The Bishop thus describes the actual coming of the offer:

Balfour's idiosyncrasies in the way of not writing letters came out in a peculiar way. He told me, in a letter with reference to the series of appointments which would become inevitable, that it was his intention and wish to nominate me to the King for the Primacy; but he sent no further letter on the subject, and although I had a long interview with Sandars in my bedroom at Farnham, while I was laid up with influenza, I had literally no letter which conveyed to me any definite proposal in the matter, until I had actually to ask for such and then it came readily enough.

The first letters are as follows:

The RT. HON. A. J. BALFOUR *to the* BISHOP OF WINCHESTER

Whittingehame, Prestonkirk, N.B.
December 31, 1902.

Death has been making sad havoc in the Church, and the consequent changes throw a heavy burden of responsibility upon the unfortunate Prime Minister. I mean to propose your name to H.M. for Canterbury. From conversations I have had with him, I have no doubt that he will agree. But, what next?

The BISHOP OF WINCHESTER *to the* RT. HON. A. J. BALFOUR

Farnham Castle, Surrey.
3 Jan. 1903.

Your letter of Dec. 31 with its momentous and to me most solemn intimation, has this morning reached me. You do not need that I should tell you what I feel about the great post now vacant. To dwell however upon one's own quite obvious inadequacies is sometimes paralysing rather than stimulating.

I perfectly realise that you are only *forewarning* me—and that my name has not yet been submitted to the King.

You will I am sure give me notice of the King's decision and allow me at the least 24 hours for final reply on a matter so grave before you allow it to become public. One or two of the foremost Bishops ought to hear about it quite confidentially from myself before (or at least at the same time as) it appears in the papers.

Then came the interview with Mr. Sandars, the Prime Minister's Private Secretary, in the bedroom at Farnham Castle, and the formal offer:

The RT. HON. A. J. BALFOUR *to the* BISHOP OF WINCHESTER

10 Downing Street, Whitehall, S.W.
8th Jan. 1903.

The approval given by the King to the submission of your name for the Archbishopric of Canterbury will I am certain be in consonance with public sentiment. It is also, I feel well assured, in the best interests of the Church. At no period, and under no circumstances can the duties of Archbishop of Canterbury be other than of the utmost importance and difficulty. But, unless I greatly mistake the signs of the times, the occupant of that great post will have a task before him as critical as has fallen to the lot of any of the long line of his predecessors. It will be a fortunate event both for Church and State, should you consent to undertake responsibilities which none can, better than yourself, be qualified to fulfil.

Earnestly hoping that you will not dissent from this view.

The following letters also passed between the Bishop and King Edward:

The BISHOP OF WINCHESTER *to the* KING

Farnham Castle, Surrey.
9th Jan. 1903.

I hope I am not doing wrong in to-day writing direct to your Majesty with reference to the new and high responsibilities which your Majesty has graciously desired, or consented, to entrust me with. I have not until to-day been in a position to write to your Majesty upon this great matter, as I understand that your Majesty's decision was only yesterday finally made, nor have I even now received any such *formal* communication from the Prime Minister to that effect as is now doubtless on its way.

But I feel that to wait longer before writing to your Majesty would be improper now that the formal announcement has been made public.

Your Majesty will, I am sure, understand with what mixed feelings it is that I have expressed my readiness, on your Majesty's call, to take up the work of the great men who have in recent years presided, at Lambeth, over the deliberations and activities of the Clergy and laity of the National Church. My own inadequacies, as compared with any of the three Primates under whom it has been my privilege to serve, are obvious to all men, and to none more obvious than to your Majesty.

But no man, as it seems to me, has a right to refuse to respond to such a summons as has now been conveyed to me from those with whom rests the deep responsibility of decision, and it is in humble reliance upon a strength which comes from no human source that I place myself, in accordance with your Majesty's wish, at the disposal of the Church and people of England for such devoted service as my limited powers are able, while life lasts, to render.

Your Majesty's personal kindness to me has been shown in a hundred ways and on innumerable occasions during the twenty years which have passed since I was called to the Deanery of Windsor, and it is not the least among the privileges which lighten the burden of the Primacy that its holder has ordinarily had some share in those public occasions of a sacred character on which the Sovereign and the Royal Family desire his services.

I hope I may still look forward to being allowed the privilege which your Majesty has so long accorded me, of approaching your Majesty directly upon any matter of public or national importance affecting the life and work of the Church of England, or the religious and moral well-being of the country, and I desire with the most genuine earnestness to express my sense of your Majesty's constant goodness to me, and my desire to be helpful in every possible way as God shall enable me and as occasion shall allow.

Will your Majesty pardon the roughness of this letter, written under some difficulty, as I am only sitting up for the first time to-day after an attack of influenza, now happily over.

With my very earnest prayers for a blessing on your Majesty's person and home, and on the reign which has in this last year been inaugurated with so much that is sacred and significant.

The KING *to the* BISHOP OF WINCHESTER

Sandringham, Norfolk.
January 11, 1903.

Many thanks for your letter of 9th inst:

I am indeed glad to hear that you have accepted the high post of Primate which the Prime Minister has offered you in my name. When he and I discussed the question as to who was to succeed Archbishop Temple, the Prime Minister and I without hesitation came to the conclusion that no one could fill that exalted position more adequately than yourself—and that the whole Church would welcome it!

Your duties will doubtless be most arduous ones and I hope you will have the requisite health and strength for them. You must also nurse yourself—and not let yourself be worked too hard. Most sincerely do I hope that the friendly intercourse which has existed between us for so long will always continue, and I shall always be only too happy to discuss your desires regarding the Church as heretofore.

I regret to hear that you have been suffering from Influenza, which seems very prevalent again, but trust that you will soon quite recover from it, and hope to see you at Windsor on 21st. The musical part of the Service on 22nd has been settled with Sir W. Parratt.

The first of many telegrams of congratulation came, curiously enough, from New York, sent by the Bishop of Albany (Dr. Doane). It arrived 'in the morning before the post came in, and the explanation was that the intimation had been sent to the newspapers late the previous evening, had been then telegraphed to New York where it was still afternoon, and the bishops there had read it and joined in a telegram to me which was the first to reach my hands'.

The telegram ran thus:

Salve dignissime grato animo.

His reply was characteristic of the spirit in which he entered upon his task.

Fratres orate precor frater indignissimus.

More than fifty other telegrams followed. The Bishop received the first batch in his bedroom, for he was still suffering from influenza; and he then gave orders that he should be left in private for the morning. He spent some time with Mrs. Davidson, reading Mozley's sermon on *The Reversal of Human Judgement.* And though his mind was on the Divine judgement to come, it is difficult not to reflect briefly on the curious reversal of human expectations which placed one, who as a boy had been shot within an inch of his life, who was an invalid at Oxford, and had been three times dangerously ill as Bishop of Rochester, on the throne of St. Augustine. Later he came downstairs to lunch, for the first time since his illness. That evening and on the following days the letters poured in. They were from all manner of people and places and from Churchmen of all schools. It is only possible to quote a few. The first shall be from Princess Beatrice, the daughter of Queen Victoria:

(Jan. 9, 1903).

How my dear mother always wished for it and how she would have rejoiced over this appointment!

Mrs. Benson spoke for herself and his old master Archbishop Benson:

(Jan. 9, 1903).

You will let me say 'God bless you' from my uttermost heart I know—for I do not speak for myself alone but also for the one whose blessing at this moment would be singularly dear to you and whose blessing to the fullest I know you have. He always foresaw this and he rejoices.

Archdeacon Sandford wrote in deep appreciation of Davidson's considerateness of Benson's successor Temple:

(Jan. 9, 1903).

As one of the late Archbishop's oldest friends may I thank you for all that you did to lighten and share the burden of these last years. It would be presumptuous in me to say anything about the tact, delicacy and kindness; but I knew the man in his first vigour and strength and I noticed with gratitude the sort of help which you gave.

Here is the judgement of Lord Halifax:

(Jan. 20, 1903).

Except the Pope himself I suppose there is no man in the whole world who will have greater opportunities for influencing the future of the whole Church of Christ than those which will now be yours. It is a terrible responsibility. . . . I do not think that the ideals of St. Anselm or St. Thomas of Canterbury, of Stephen Langton or of Archbishop Laud are likely to be yours. I wish it were otherwise, but I can say with absolute truth that in view of our present circumstances if it had depended on my voice you would be where you now are.

Dr. Guinness Rogers represented the Free Churchmen:

(Jan. 10, 1903).

Possibly it may seem strange that a Dissenting Minister should express such feelings, especially at the present moment. But ours is a conflict of ideas not of persons. To me it is sufficiently painful that we seem to find so much difficulty in understanding each other's ideals and principles. It is well surely to remember that as Christians we have a wide area of common heritage. Once let us see that, and we can at all events learn to respect each other personally. . . . I vividly remember my day at the Castle and the kindly welcome I received from Mrs. Davidson and yourself.

And there is this final note from the Duke of Argyll:

I have always said you are one of the very few preachers who prevent me from falling asleep.

The public on the whole gave the new Primate a very friendly welcome. 'The choice', said the *Guardian*, 'was generally anticipated and has been received if not with enthusiasm at least with wide-spread satisfaction.' There were of course some who complained of an alleged lack of intellectual distinction, others who said that the Bishop's promotion was due to his qualities as a courtier, though both of these charges were demonstrably untrue. *The Times* expressed the considered opinion of thoughtful men when it declared: 'The country may be satisfied that in the prelate who now passes to Lambeth Palace it will have to deal with a shrewd and capable statesman who knows more of the inner history of the close of the Victorian era than many a Cabinet Minister, but who has never lost his spiritual balance in those "slippery" places where much of his life has been passed.'

The Bishop was comparatively young—only fifty-four years old—and the future was to show what manner of Archbishop he should prove. At least, as a friend (Bishop John Wordsworth, of Salisbury) wrote on February 16: 'If God gives you an ordinary lease of life, you may have twenty-five years of archiepiscopal duty before you and you may do many things which others have put off for lack of time.' But at the moment it was his business to get rid of his attack of influenza. So, under doctor's orders, the Bishop and Mrs. Davidson went for a fortnight to Biarritz; leaving the staff behind to prepare for the move from Farnham.

Let us use the pause which Dr. Davidson needs to get well, in order to consider some of the tasks which will await him at Lambeth.

No Archbishop of Canterbury, least of all one who had been brought up in the school of Tait, could fail to be alive to the new era which began with the coming of the twentieth century. Queen Victoria had died in its very first months, and at her passing a whole world seemed to have departed. The South African War had just ceased in 1902. China and the Far East were uneasy, and there were signs of trouble in which Russia was to play its part. At home, the Conservative party had come into power in great force after the Khaki Election, but was already weakened by disputes over tariff reform. The opening years of the new century were therefore disturbed with anxieties on many sides.

The Church of England had its own share of trials. Indeed,

it seemed face to face with a most serious domestic situation. Mr. Balfour, writing to the Bishop of Rochester, spoke with the gloomiest apprehensions as to the future of the Church of England. If he wrote thus as an observer, what would those say who were leaders in the fray? Lord Halifax, the President of the English Church Union, and an old friend, addressed a portentous letter of seventy-six octavo pages to the archbishop-designate, for his quiet meditation at Biarritz. One passage has already been quoted. A few further extracts will show his view of the situation:

'I doubt [he said] if any Archbishop of Canterbury has ever had greater difficulties to contend with than those which are likely to confront you.' The difficulties incidental 'to the whole present position of the Church of England' were, in his judgement, 'well-nigh insuperable'; and he proceeded to arraign most professing Churchmen and practically the whole episcopate, besides giving his estimate of each of the three last Archbishops of Canterbury, praising Benson for 'putting the Protestant party for once more or less in their place', and condemning Tait and Temple for their completely inadequate view of the Catholic Church and therefore of the position and duties of the Church of England. As to the future and the new archbishop, his advice was this:

VISCOUNT HALIFAX *to the* ARCHBISHOP-DESIGNATE OF CANTERBURY

January 20, 1903.

May I add something as to the future? Whatever other people may like to say and think, the Acts of Uniformity are dead. The Church as things are cannot be held by the legal interpretation it pleases the lawyers to put upon those Acts. The State has entirely disregarded one part of them. The Church must disregard the other. Whatever difficulties stand in the way will be best met by ignoring them. The Church has nothing to expect or wish for from Parliament except to be let alone. I do entreat you, and nobody in this world is better qualified than you are, to do what has to be done warily, wisely and successfully in this direction, to take that bull by the horns . . . do everything that is needed for the good of the Church on your own inherent authority and that of the bishops.

Lord Halifax was thinking of the ritualist controversy, and its connexion with the Prayer Book, as annexed to various Acts for the uniformity of common prayer, and administration of the sacraments. But there was also the problem of the interpretation of orthodoxy in his day. These were more fundamental problems, and, it may be added, more congenial to the temperament of Randall Davidson, and therefore, without doubt, more successfully handled on the various occasions when they claimed his attention during the next twenty-five years.

There were other tasks looming ahead—especially that of giving the laity of the Church a greater share in Church government, and the Church itself a greater unity, and larger powers of legislation. There was the little cloud of the disestablishment of the Welsh Church, far off on the horizon. There was the unceasing question of religious education, it being certain that any new Liberal Government would do its best to reverse some of the fundamental provisions of the Education Act of 1902.

In addition to these, and certainly adding greatly to the labours always inevitable to an Archbishop of Canterbury, there was the undoubted fact that in his later years Archbishop Temple had, through age and infirmity, failed to keep pace with the pressure of affairs, and the whole business of the primacy had diminished. Who could wonder, when it is remembered that Temple became Archbishop at the age of seventy-five? Added to this, he had never found it easy to delegate work (as we have already seen), and the amount of correspondence which he had done with his own hand was prodigious. Home affairs, temperance, and the immediate duties of the diocese occupied him day by day. It had not been his custom to take much share in ordinary 'secular' affairs, so that there had been a great lapse in that side of an archbishop's duties, as Tait and Benson had conceived them. The chief failure, however, concerned the various branches of the Anglican Communion, which the two former archbishops had gradually linked up in a particularly close correspondence and friendship with Lambeth. And there were large arrears. The new archbishop had not only to revive the relations between Lambeth and Sydney and Capetown and Ottawa and Calcutta and Zanzibar and the rest, but to cope with the considerable legacy of complicated Church problems in the Colonies (left, by a strange Nemesis, heaped together in a large set of pigeon-holes, called in Tait's days, after the name of the designer, 'Davidson's Folly'), which had, alas, received no attention whatever.

Such were some of the principal tasks with which Randall

Davidson was faced, when he came to the see of Canterbury. It was fortunate that he had the experience and special education which fitted him in a pre-eminent degree to discharge them. He had, indeed, as one of those who knew him best said, been trained by a quite unique life for the Primacy, and had been almost a partner in it.

But there were also other tasks, as yet unnoticed, which an Archbishop of Canterbury has, as it were, to take in his stride. No man has such varied responsibilities as his, or covers so many of the offices of what in parliamentary life would be given to different ministers of state. In regard to the Bench of Bishops, he is in the position of Prime Minister. As President of the Southern Convocation, he occupies a place analogous to that of the Lord Chancellor in the House of Lords. In his dealing with the various provinces of the Anglican Communion, his labours may be compared to those of the Secretary of State for the Dominions. He discharges many of the functions of the Minister of Education. Occasionally he is called upon to act as Judge. He is also a Diocesan Bishop, with all the duties which necessarily fall to the work of governing a diocese, though aided in a special way by the suffragan bishop or bishops. He is a member of the House of Lords, and expected to be the spokesman of the Church in Parliament on national and ecclesiastical questions. He is President of the Ecclesiastical Commission, and takes the chair at the regular monthly meetings of the Board. He is a Principal Trustee of the British Museum, presiding every other Saturday morning at the meetings of the Trustees in Bloomsbury or South Kensington. He is a Governor of at least two Public Schools, a Visitor of two other Public Schools, of three Oxford Colleges as well as of King's College, London, and of St. Augustine's, Canterbury, and he is President of most of the chief Church Societies. In addition to all these, the Archbishop, by virtue of his office, is expected to be the religious spokesman of the country, the man to whom all others, of whatever denomination, naturally look to take the lead on great moral and social issues; and he is also the representative of the Christian religion in Great Britain to all foreign Churches and nations. Such is the daily labour, such the daily responsibility, of the Archbishop of Canterbury!

CHAPTER XXI

THE BEGINNING OF THE PRIMACY

To such men he seemed *commonplace*—not so to the most dexterous masters in what was to some of them almost a science; not so to Rose, Hallam, Moore or Rogers, to Ellis, Mackintosh, Croker or Canning. LOCKHART, *Life of Scott*, ch. xli.

THE new Archbishop arrived in Canterbury in fine spring-like weather on February 11, 1903, and received a most cordial official welcome from the Mayor and Corporation. All but one of the various stages of entering upon the see were completed: election by the Dean and Chapter on January 27; Confirmation in the Church House, Westminster, on February 6; paying of homage to the King at Windsor on February 7. It only remained for him to be enthroned in the Cathedral Church, so familiar to Randall Davidson since his early days as Chaplain to Tait. An immense congregation, including seventeen bishops, a large body of clergy, and representatives of the State, the city, and the nation at large, assisted at the familiar ceremonies on February 12. His old Harrow master, Dr. Farrar, was Dean, but too stricken to take an active part in the service. And another friend of long standing, who had made a point of being present was Lord Rosebery. The enthronement was followed by a luncheon in the library. In the speech responding to the toast of his health, Davidson's thoughts went back to his old chief. 'It so happens', he said, 'that it was in this very room that I performed my first act as Chaplain to Archbishop Tait.' He dwelt on the extraordinary growth of interest in Church affairs and the increasing range of the Archbishop's influence overseas during the past fifty years, paying a happy tribute to the three Primates before him. He said it would be his desire to steer a course between those who looked back to the sixteenth century as though everything in the Church of England depended on that, and 'those on the other side who with equal deficiency of historical knowledge try to make out that what happened in the sixteenth century was a lamentable blunder in Church life'. He said that the difficulties with which the Church was faced had been faced before, and he raised a peal of laughter by quoting the words used by

Archbishop Peckham, at a time of despondency, six hundred and more years before, when he spoke of 'the horrible frauds of Archdeacons, the plague and presumption of Apparitors, and the diabolical craft of Rural Deans'; and he ended on a note of solemn appeal for his friends' prayer and support, 'so that when I am laid "on" sleep, the words may be said that "He at least tried to serve his generation according to the will of God" '.

The day following his enthronement, the Archbishop and Mrs. Davidson returned to Farnham to say farewell to the parish and the Castle in which they had spent seven and a half happy years. It was not easy. Farnham had been the home and the source of inspiration for the diocese. The clergy of the diocese, in saying good-bye three weeks later at Winchester, showed their deep affection for a Father in God whose hold upon them had grown deeper and stronger as year followed year. As the Bishop of Guildford said in the name of them all: 'Never has any one of the Clergy of this Diocese—let alone whether he was a member of the Greater Chapter or not—gone to your Grace for advice, but he has returned happier for his visit to Farnham.' And the relation of the Castle to the town was made specially strong through the personal interest, sympathy, and neighbourliness of Mrs. Davidson. Kind words were spoken at the farewell meeting, when the Archbishop opened the new Council Offices. And the friends and neighbours joined in making Mrs. Davidson and the Bishop a gift which followed a little later in the shape of two cobs—a tribute to the exercise both had enjoyed when riding in the park, and a token that they would continue to enjoy a similar exercise at Lambeth. The gift came from all sorts and conditions of people at Farnham, including the Nonconformist ministers, and the Roman Catholic priest, and some of those who lived in the work-houses and infirmary.

The ARCHBISHOP OF CANTERBURY *to* W. T. COLEMAN, ESQ.

Lambeth Palace, S.E.
9th May, 1903.

Now that Farnham's beautiful gift to me stands actually in our stable as our own, I must write you a few lines to say how intensely we appreciate this further token of a kindness and a brotherliness which have meant so much to us day by day for eight eventful years. We have been profoundly touched, as you know, by the unbroken outflow of the helpful thoughts and words and acts which have given expression to Farnham's goodwill ever since the day when the call came to us to leave the Castle which we have loved and the friends who have surrounded it with the truest kind of friendship.

Day by day, as I rejoice in the strong limbs and the fine paces of the 'high horse' on which you have mounted me, shall I again recall the goodness of our dear friends in the old town, and pray that every highest blessing and happiness may be theirs.

There was of course much left for the Archbishop to do in the way of settling in. Nor are most people aware of the expensiveness of the process, very crippling to a man of slender or even moderate resources. Writing to a friend who most generously helped him with an immediate advance of a large sum, he said:

We shall have to pay just £7000 to Mrs. Temple for furniture and plenishing at Lambeth and Canterbury. I shall have to pay nearly £1000 in fees, and about £700 to Q.A.B. for poor benefices, and perhaps £400 or £500 for Farnham Park dilapidations.

Besides, there were the fees which he was required to pay to civil or government authorities, including a due of £62 to the Home Office, £67 to the Crown Office, £31 to the Board of Green Cloth, and £27 on introduction to the House of Lords—amounting to £398 8*s*. 4*d*. altogether. Well might he say at the end of a letter pointing out these facts to Lord Knollys, the King's Private Secretary:

The ARCHBISHOP OF CANTERBURY *to the* VISCOUNT KNOLLYS

March 2, 1903.

Please understand that I have no sort of wish to be 'stingy' in the matter, or to grudge any legitimate or fair payments. But it is a very grave thing for a man who is not rich to succeed to this sort of office.

I

It was not long before the Archbishop found himself plunged into the very thick of the fray. Certainly his first year was heavy with difficulties enough to tax all his strength and resourcefulness of character, besides giving a very fair picture of the variety and scope of the duties with which an Archbishop has to contend.

The first test was concerned with the Creeds. In the previous December, a Conference of Clergy, under the chairmanship of Dean Wace had passed two Resolutions asking the Bishops for a declaration to reassure the Church, in view of recent statements by Broad Churchmen—Dr. Rashdall, Dean Fremantle, Dr. Cheyne, and others—'as to the Virgin Birth and the Resurrection of Our Lord'. On February 13, the very day after the enthronement, Bishop Gore sent him what was to prove the first of many letters from his pen on similar subjects:

The BISHOP OF WORCESTER *to the* ARCHBISHOP OF CANTERBURY

February 13th, 1903.

. . . Can we not in this Convocation do something to reassure a great number of people that the Bishops would not connive at men being Ordained who do not believe in the Articles of the Creed; particularly the Virgin Birth? I think some such declaration as I enclose would do no harm and much good. Among other things it would make the ritual problem and the *Quicunque Vult much* easier to deal with.

Observe the caution of the Archbishop's reply:

The ARCHBISHOP OF CANTERBURY *to the* BISHOP OF WORCESTER

14th February, 1903.

. . . With respect to the very important question of a Declaration on the Bishops' part about the doctrine of the Incarnation, I am certain that we must proceed with great caution. The history of 1861 (*Essays and Reviews*), and again of 1863–8 (Colenso), furnishes a significant object-lesson as to the perils which surround these Declarations. Look, for example, at the doings in Convocation in Feb. 1863. I am far from saying that we should certainly be wrong in putting out such a Declaration as you suggest, but I am quite clear that we must not do so without adequate notice to every Bishop and time given to him for weighing the whole subject. To raise it next week in Convocation, with a view to action *then*, would be in my judgment most unfair. Our senior Bishop (Gloucester)[1] writes that he is unable to be present, and he certainly would not desire to stand outside such a discussion as must take place.

What I think might be done is this: You might raise the question privately (I mean in the absence of reporters) next week, and furnish us with facts and references (this last is most important) to the books impugned—you mention Cheyne and Rashdall. The

[1] Dr. Ellicott.

> Bishops could then consider the subject before our next group of Sessions, and make up their minds whether or not such a Declaration ought to be put forth. To put it forth is a very grave step: it means virtually an addition to our formularies. Pray prepare your material so that we may have your help and information next week.

The subject was privately raised in the Upper House, and adjourned to a meeting of Bishops. In the long correspondence which followed, the Archbishop made clear his opinion that such a Declaration would be fraught with immense peril. He added, aptly enough:

The ARCHBISHOP OF CANTERBURY *to the* REV. S. BICKERSTETH

30th April, 1903.

> . . . If we merely say that we hold the Creed and wish others to hold it, we surely do what is worse than useless. If, on the other hand, we attempt to define its terms in a particular way, the Church at large may well ask (1) by what right we do so, and (2) what claim our definition has upon the faith of Churchmen.

In May, the Lower House of Convocation, sitting behind closed doors, framed a Resolution praying the Upper House that, 'in order to allay considerable distress and perplexity felt by many at the present time', they would 'consider what measures may seem best to reassure all men that the Church of England holds the Virgin Birth of Our Lord and his Resurrection from the Dead as cardinal doctrines of the Catholic Faith'.

The Bishops' Meeting followed at the end of the month, when it was voted by a majority that the two Archbishops should write a joint letter. Various difficulties, however, arose in carrying out the decision, and the matter was allowed to drop for a while. Certainly one very potent argument against the issue of any declaration was a statement published at the Archbishop's suggestion by the Dean of Westminster with three lectures entitled *Some Thoughts on the Incarnation*[1] in the form of a 'Prefatory

[1] *Some Thoughts on the Incarnation*, J. Armitage Robinson (Longmans), pp. v–xvi. 'If the Bishops were asked to declare that the Incarnation is a cardinal doctrine of the faith, such a statement would be superfluous indeed, but it would be true. But to say that the historical fact of the Virgin-birth is a cardinal doctrine of the faith is to use language which no Synod of Bishops, so far as I am aware, has ever ventured to use. It is to confuse the Incarnation with the special mode of the

Letter to the Archbishop of Canterbury', in which he urged that it was utterly alien to the whole spirit of the English Church to close the doors of inquiry by the hand of authority, and how disastrous would be its results.

II

It was, however, the breaking out afresh of the Ritual controversy, the so-called 'Crisis in the Church', which aroused the greatest public attention, and made the largest demands upon the Archbishop in this first year of office. There had been a pause, due in part to the South African War. But early in 1903, a new movement began in the House of Commons for the 'further legislation' which, in its Resolution of May 10, 1899, the House had said would be required 'if the efforts of the Archbishops and Bishops to secure the obedience of the Clergy are not speedily effectual'. The debates on the Education Bill in the previous year had revealed a considerable distrust of the Clergy, especially in several rural districts, and over a hundred Unionist M.P.s, who were loyal supporters of the Church, asked the two Archbishops to receive them at Lambeth. The Archbishops agreed. Two rival Bills were at the time before the House of Commons. One was the Liverpool Bill, promoted by the Protestant Party, which aimed at taking things out of the Bishops' hands by the abolition of the Bishop's Veto on ecclesiastical prosecutions. The other was fathered by Mr. C. A. Cripps[1] and was designed to strengthen the Bishops by giving them real power in dealing with disobedient clergy by means of a Bishop's monition with legal force, leading in certain circumstances to the voidance of the benefice in case of flagrant disobedience.

The deputation, over a hundred strong, led by Sir John Dorington, waited on the two Archbishops on March 11. It was the Primate's first public function as occupant of Lambeth

Incarnation in a way for which Christian theology offers no precedent. But I let the point of phraseology pass: for it is the act of reassertion by authority of that which is questioned by criticism which I deprecate.... It is quite another thing that some of the theologians amongst [the Bishops] should take natural opportunities of presenting the argument in a way that may reach doubtful minds. Some of them have done so already. But can any one believe that, to offer a single example, the signature of the Bishop of Worcester to a joint episcopal declaration on this matter could effect anything at all for perplexed enquirers in comparison with the writings of Charles Gore?'

[1] Subsequently Lord Parmoor.

Palace. After the introductory speeches, the Archbishop of Canterbury made what was generally regarded as a significant pronouncement. He received the complaints and the appeal with marked courtesy, though not without a word to show that the laity sometimes increased the clergy's difficulties, and he spoke very sympathetically of those country parishes where the wishes of the congregation and parishioners were entirely disregarded by a new incumbent. He pointed out that he had hardly been Archbishop a month, and therefore must not be expected to frame a policy at once. He had (he said) neither seen nor heard from all the Bishops on the subject; and he gave it as his view 'that the cases of flagrant and defiant illegality and disobedience' were very few, and confined almost wholly to the dioceses of London, Chichester, and Exeter. There were, he agreed, in some churches usages of an extreme kind which had prevailed for many years: and though they could not always be stopped on the sudden, arrangements for dealing with them in some way, and restraining them, could be made, and had been made, by the Bishops concerned. 'But', he said, and this was the heart of the pronouncement:

> But, Gentlemen, there is another class. There are a few men defiant of episcopal authority and really reckless of the true Church of England's spirit. You have seen or heard or read about the case of St. Michael's, Shoreditch. You have heard about the Churches at Plymouth and Devonport where things are going on of a like kind. I say to you deliberately to-day that in my view of such cases, tolerance has reached, and even passed its limits. The sands have run out. Stern and drastic action is in my judgement quite essential. . . . It may have been right to give time, after our endeavours began, a few years ago, for further consideration and further appeals to those men, and to make further endeavours by quiet means to bring about the result; but that time is amply past. The initial response must of course in any such case rest with the several diocesan Bishops; but, speaking for myself, so far as in me lies, I assure you, using my words with a full sense of responsibility, I desire and intend that we should now act, and act sternly.

It was a strong statement, and it was made, as *The Times* said next morning, by one 'who knows quite well that history will deal with his tenure of the Primacy in the light of what he said yesterday and of what he may do in fulfilment of what he said'. It was also well received, and though it was expected that the High Church Party would have a great deal to say in reply, in fact it said very little. On the following day the House of Commons listened to a fiery speech from Sir William Harcourt and, in spite of Mr. Balfour's conciliatory appeal, gave a second reading to the Liverpool Bill. There was much correspondence in the Press; many letters passed to and from the Archbishop at Lambeth. At one moment Mr. Balfour was himself contemplating a letter for publication on the Crisis which was submitted in draft to the Archbishop, who made a few pencilled annotations of no great moment, but added:

The ARCHBISHOP OF CANTERBURY *to* J. S. SANDARS, ESQ.

10th April, 1903.

. . . What occurs to me is the question whether the *argument* of the letter is important enough to justify the publication of it as the Prime Minister's view of the situation. It is of course conclusive so far as it goes, and the exposure of the absurdity of the contention put forward by Austin Taylor and Co. is complete and is expressed with characteristic clearness.

But I a little crave for something more of a constructive sort.

The draft got no further. Legislation continued to be talked about both in the House of Commons—where Mr. Cripps's Bill also got a second reading and then died—and in Convocation and the House of Laymen. Indeed there were rumours that the Archbishop himself intended to introduce a Bill in the House of Lords:

SIR JOHN DORINGTON *to the* ARCHBISHOP OF CANTERBURY

30 Queen Anne's Gate,
St. James's Park, S.W.
8th June, 1903.

I congratulate you on having secured the assent of Convocation to the principles of Mr. Cripps' Bill, and so far you are now on sound ground.

May I express a hope that you will find it possible before the close of the Parliamentary Session to bring forward and lay before the public, by the introduction of a Bill in the House of Lords, the measures which you would desire to see pass. In view of the activity of the so-called Liverpool party, and of the uneasiness which prevails generally, it is I think most important that we should have direct and positive guidance from the Heads of the Church as to the disciplinary measures which they would approve of. For want of this guidance so very many are driven to accept the objectionable methods of Church Discipline Bill No. 1, and to vote for it in Parliament, and another six months of inaction will certainly increase the difficulty. It also must I think be recognised that it is only the Government who can pass such a measure, and that it would be a great assistance to them if the approved measure had been before the country in an authoritative manner for some time previously.

The Archbishop of Canterbury *to* Sir John Dorington

9th June, 1903.

Many thanks for your important letter. I think I quite appreciate the view you take, and on the whole I am in agreement with what I understand to be your contention. But I own that I foresee great difficulty with regard to the putting forth by the Episcopate of Mr. Cripps' Bill in anything like its present form. My own main difficulty is not a dislike to the Bill itself, but a feeling that we should certainly be misapprehended if we put out that Bill with the apparent expectation that if enacted it would enable us to get rid forthwith of our existing difficulties. Of course I know that the promoters of the Bill would not make so foolish a claim with reference to it, but outside people would certainly think such to be our anticipation. I tried to make this plain in a speech in Convocation reported in the *Guardian* of May 20th, page 730, and I would ask you kindly to refer to that debate. It begins on page 727 of the *Guardian* and is resumed on page 729. What we did in Convocation was to appoint a Committee to consider the whole subject and to report forthwith. That Committee—a very weighty one—has held at least two meetings and is drafting a report upon the subject. If this report when it appears seems to show us how we could wisely legislate on the lines of Mr. Cripps' Bill, I shall be quite ready to take the necessary steps, if I have the concurrence of the leading men among my Episcopal colleagues. But until that Committee has reported I am not in a position to say anything more than that we are most anxiously considering the whole questions involved. This is no mere form of words; it is the plain truth.

The matter was indeed in the Archbishop's view a much more complicated affair than appeared on the surface, and the debates in Convocation, to which he referred his correspondent, made it clear that not only was a reform of Church Courts required, and a strengthening of the authority of the Bishops, but also a more effective system of self-government in which the laity of the Church should take their part with the Bishops and the clergy.

Discussion continued for a while during the summer. A deputation of High Churchmen of the Moderate school, headed by Mr. H. Russell Wakefield, presented a Declaration of Loyalty, signed by four thousand clergy, to the Archbishop in Lambeth Library in July. Then the fever abated for a time, and the next move was made in the following year by the Crown. But, as the Archbishop had hinted, there was another aspect of the whole question to be considered, the responsibility of the laity in the government of the Church. The same summer saw an important stage in the process of setting up a National Church Council for the Church of England. The proposal had been under discussion intermittently for some years. One part of the proposal consisted of obtaining powers for the reform of Convocation. But the principal purpose was to secure a representative council consisting of bishops, clergy and laity, of the two provinces. The proposal had been discussed in the Northern and Southern Convocations separately, and in the two Houses of Laymen. It had been decided to hold a joint meeting of the members of the Convocations sitting in Committee, and of the Houses of Laymen, in July 1903, to take a definite decision. A good deal of spade work had to be done, and the Bishop of Salisbury[1] was to the fore in the plans that had to be made. The meeting was duly held; the business was complicated; and there was a large body of people not accustomed to meeting together for the Chairman to handle. There were sharp differences of opinion, e.g. as to whether the basis of the lay franchise should be Holy Communion, Confirmation, or Baptism; and whether women should be admitted. And there was a mass of amendments. Patience and leadership were both required in the Chair, if good feeling was to be preserved and clear resolutions adopted.

The joint meeting resolved:

(1) That it is desirable to make provision for the calling together of a representative Council consisting of clergy and laity of the Provinces of Canterbury and York.

(2) That the question of obtaining legal constitution and authority

[1] Dr. John Wordsworth.

for such a Council be reserved for consideration until after the Council has, upon a voluntary basis, come into working order.

(3) That such steps shall be taken as may prove to be necessary for the reform of the two Convocations, and for their sitting together, from time to time, as one body.

It also resolved that the Council should consist of three Houses—Bishops, Clergy, and Laity: the existing Houses of Laymen forming the Lay House for the present; and, as to the franchise:

(6) That the initial franchise of lay electors shall be exercised in each ecclesiastical parish or district by those persons of the male sex (possessing such householding or other vestry qualification in the parish or district as may be defined by the committee to be hereafter appointed) who declare themselves in writing, at the time of voting, to be lay members of the Church of England, and of no other religious communion, and are not legally and actually excluded from Communion, and by such other persons residing in the parish or district as are lay communicants of the Church of England, of the male sex, and of full age.

Thus decisions were taken and agreement was reached. The position and prestige of the new Primate were confirmed. And at the end of the sitting all present rose to their feet and loudly cheered the man who, said *The Times*,[1] 'with much judgment had removed obstacles out of the way of definite resolution, and even in the intervals between the debates, was still guiding events and reconciling antipathies.' It is interesting to read the following letter rejoicing in a decision different from that which led to a very sorrowful letter from the same Dr. Gore[2] fifteen or sixteen years later:

The Bishop of Worcester *to the* Archbishop of Canterbury

July 11, 1903.

Confidential.

May I, with the impression fresh upon me, express my very profound gratitude and admiration for all you have done for me and for the Church in a very few short months and more particularly this week? I only venture to do this, because I fear I am of the nature of a σκόλοψ τῇ σαρκί only too often to you. And I can't promise to amend. This is not to be answered. But I thought you would let me say that if I distress you, it is a great distress to me.

[1] *The Times*, July 13, 1903. [2] See p. 970.

III

Ecclesiastical questions of another kind were coming up in England in connexion with a possible revolt from Rome of a number of laity and clergy, at a time when there was a considerable ferment among Roman Catholics, not only in this country. It seemed natural that such a body of discontented Romans should apply to the Old Catholics in Switzerland or Holland, who had broken away from Rome on the issue of Papal Infallibility in 1870. The organization, headed by a Father O'Halloran, was said to number 150 Roman Catholic priests who were revolting against Cardinal Vaughan.

The BISHOP OF SALISBURY *to the* ARCHBISHOP OF CANTERBURY

Salisbury. 19th March, 1903.

The following is a translation of part of a letter I have just received from the Old Catholic Bishop at Berne, my friend Bishop Herzog. What answer shall I give him?

'The priest Richard O'Halloran, at St. Joseph's and St. Peter's, Mattock Lane, Ealing, desires that an Old Catholic Bishop should come to England in order to confirm about 50 candidates according to the Roman Catholic rite.

'I should be inclined to recommend to my fellow-Bishops to assent to this request. Of course I should not conceive of the act as a practical denial of the legitimacy of the Church of England and her organs, but to place it on the same level as the episcopal actions performed by Bishop Wilkinson on the continent, and that sometimes in congregations, which, as in Holland, no longer understand English. If the assistance asked is not given, O'Halloran and his congregation will shortly have to submit to Cardinal Vaughan; if given it may *perhaps* strengthen the so-called "Revolt from Rome" movement.'

He then goes on to mention the blame he had to bear for consecrating Bishop Koslowski in U.S.A. and does not wish to incur it again. He wishes to know whether I have strong feeling on the matter. If so, he implies, he will go no further.

You probably know much more than I do of O'Halloran. Herzog would be the best man for such an act if you desired anyone to perform it, as he is a true friend.

I hope to see you in the House of Lords.

The ARCHBISHOP OF CANTERBURY *to the* BISHOP OF SALISBURY

Lambeth Palace, S.E.
30th March, 1903.

I have been considering carefully the very important question Bishop Herzog has raised about his possibly coming to England to confirm in the congregations or congregation of recalcitrant Romans. Obviously the utmost caution is necessary before we commit ourselves to sanctioning anything of the kind. Personally I should not regard it as an intrusion on the part of an Old Catholic Bishop were he to come to England and there confirm *in my diocese* Roman Catholics who were genuinely and intelligently desirous of his ministrations and who wished for the Roman rite. But probably other Bishops would take a different view, and would say that any Englishman who, ceasing to be under Cardinal Vaughan, desires still to be a member of the Church Catholic, must become a member of the Church of England and be confirmed according to our rite. In any case I think Bishop Herzog should tell us more fully what is his own view. He must not leave us to decide the matter for him; nor, I imagine, does he wish us to do so. I was quite unaware that Bishop Wilkinson confirmed Dutchmen in Holland, and I find that the Bishop of London was equally unaware of it. I have spoken to both the Bishop of London and the Bishop of Rochester on the matter. Neither of them has any very clear advice to give.

After hearing from you I looked up and read the articles in the *Fortnightly Review* and *Contemporary*, and I also wrote to Arthur Galton, from whom I have an interesting reply. In the first of his articles (*Fortnightly* for 1902, p. 426, etc.) he describes the attitude of the recalcitrants towards the Church of England, and it all seems to leave the matter in a very complicated and hazy condition. I am sure that great caution is necessary. I want to be convinced that Father O'Halloran is not simply a wild Irishman who has evoked personal enthusiasm from his congregation and friends who are prepared to follow him anywhither. I do not at all say that such is the fact, but I want to be convinced of the contrary. I have asked Galton to come and see me about it when he is in London. Big issues may turn on what we do, and big principles are at stake, so I am sure that we ought to be cautious. Any further information that you can send me will be very acceptable.

The Archbishop made a few further inquiries, the result of which fully justified his cautious reply: and further proof of the need of caution will be found a few years later in the curious sequel in which Father O'Halloran was concerned with a certain Bishop Mathew.[1]

IV

In the throng of business of all kinds pressing upon the Archbishop, a pleasant interlude is found in the dinner given him by a number of his friends on April 24, 1903, at the Athenaeum Club. Canon Scott Holland, writing in the *Commonwealth* when Bishop Davidson's appointment to Canterbury was announced, said:

> Bishop Davidson's point of danger is not the Court. He has survived its perils with a singular simplicity. Rather it is to be sought at the Athenaeum. There dwell the sirens who are apt to beguile and bewitch him. They have ceased to be mermaids with harps and have adopted the disguise of elderly and excellent gentlemen of reputation, who lead you aside into corners and, in impressive whispers, inform you what will not do and what the intelligent British public will not stand. The Bishop has a deep veneration for the judgement and the wisdom of important laity of this type.. Yet the Athenaeum is not the shrine of infallibility. Its elderly common sense has no prophetic *afflatus*.

The Club, it was quite true, was one of Davidson's favourite haunts. He was elected in 1890 and remained a member till his death. He made constant use of it, not merely for its library or for business purposes. As a fellow member during many years says:

> Intercourse with his fellow men, especially with those who were themselves leaders in Church and State, in literature, science and art, was eagerly sought by him both as a source of strength and knowledge and as an opportunity of influence; and such intercourse he found in ample measure at the Athenaeum. He soon became, and remained throughout, one of the best known and most esteemed members of the Club. He identified himself with its interests, served when elected on the Committee of Management, and from 1914 till his death was one of its three Trustees. As Trustee he became *ex-officio* member of the Committee, and, in spite of his innumerable engagements, often attended its meetings, particularly on days when there were to be elections under Rule II 'of persons of distinguished eminence in science, literature, or the arts, or for public services'.

[1] See *infra*, p. 1018.

When Canon Scott Holland's criticism was published—to continue the story:

> Some of the Archbishop-designate's lay friends in the Club took it as a challenge; and determined to show by entertaining him at dinner how highly they appreciated his frequent presence among them. As the available room in the Athenaeum could only seat about a couple of dozen, there was a difficulty in selecting the hosts from among so many who would wish to do him honour. The guest, on being sounded, would not go further than to hint that perhaps, on such an occasion, his 'brethren' would hardly be in place. Accordingly there were no bishops present at the dinner on 24th April 1903; and the only two hosts in Holy Orders were men who held positions necessarily in close touch with lay opinion, the Dean of Westminster, Dr. Armitage Robinson, and the Master of the Temple, Canon Ainger.
>
> The then Prime Minister, Mr. Balfour, was in the Chair, with the guest of the evening on his right. The American Ambassador, Mr. Choate, was there among the hosts; so were Lord Roberts, then Commander-in-Chief; the Speaker of the House of Commons, Mr. Gully; and the President of the Royal Academy, Sir Edward Poynter. Four statesmen, two Liberal, two Conservative, attended —Mr. Asquith, Lord Goschen, Lord Knutsford (Sir Henry Holland), and Mr. John Morley, the latter, with Mr. Birrell, representing literature as well. For the law came the Lord Chief Justice (Lord Alverstone), the Master of the Rolls (Sir Richard Henn Collins), and Lord Robertson (Lord of Appeal). Oxford and Cambridge were well represented by Sir William Anson and Sir Richard Jebb. Science had an exponent in Lord Avebury, the principal Trustee of the Club; and the party was completed by Lord Balfour of Burleigh, Sir Henry Craik, Sir Charles Dalrymple, and the then Editor of *The Times*, Mr. G. E. Buckle. One of the hosts, a man of caustic wit, after looking round the big circular dinner-table, said to his neighbour, 'I suppose we here are the kind of folk whom the historian of the future will describe as *alors célèbres*'. At least they were a brilliant representation of the Club at the time; and the Archbishop, in replying to the toast of his health proposed by Mr. Balfour, showed how deeply he felt the compliment, and how highly he valued his intimate association with the Athenaeum.

A month later we see both the pressure on his time, and his attitude to friends of another kind, from a different angle. At the end of May he received a letter from a revered Nonconformist,

Dr. R. F. Horton. He, referring to Davidson's well-known sympathy for those outside the Church of England, sent him an address just given by himself as Chairman of the Congregational Union of England and Wales in the City Temple, and containing incidentally criticisms of 'the appalling mockery of the *congé d'élire*', speaking of the Church of England as 'a branch of the Civil Service', and of the mechanical transmission of ministerial powers:

The ARCHBISHOP OF CANTERBURY *to the* REV. R. F. HORTON, D.D.

Lambeth Palace, S.E., 9 June '03.

I owe you many apologies for my delay in thanking you for an exceedingly kind letter, received I fear more than a fortnight ago, and for sending me a copy of your stirring and helpful address on 'Congregationalism and the Catholic Church'. My excuse—the old one—must be simply the overwhelming pressure of daily work. I have been a busy man all my life, but I have never known such terrible pressure as now. Work as one will, the arrears accumulate, and the very letters one would most desire to write remain unwritten.

You certainly do me no injustice in believing it to be my very earnest desire, GOD helping me, to do something to heal our sore divisions—and it would indeed be to me a source of thankfulness to look forward to additional opportunities, were you ready to afford them, of working side by side with those who like yourself, while not belonging to our Communion, have at heart the simple desire to forward in Christ's Name and by the Holy Spirit's help, the bettering of the world and the advance, here in England, of the Living Kingdom of Our Lord.

With very much that you say in your address I am—perhaps I need scarcely say so—in fullest agreement. I find myself wondering, as I read, what it is that you suppose men like myself to hold when you refer to us as you do. But I may somehow be misunderstanding your meaning and intent, and I at least can rejoice wholeheartedly—nor do I ever lose a suitable opportunity of saying so—in the fact of greater unities, which weld us together at the core whatever the surface 'differentia' on one side or the other.

You will not expect that it should be otherwise than painful to me to find that a brother minister of Christ whom I so sincerely respect, and from whose words I have many a time learned so much, should use respecting the Church of England some of the expressions you do, expressions which I would rather cut my right hand off than use of Congregationalism. But one learns as life goes on, and one's working years draw perhaps near to their close, not to take offence at even the hardest words of a fellow soldier of Christ when he is saying out what he feels to be true and to need saying.

As examples of what I mean, I wonder what prayers you are alluding to in the last line of p. 14, or what you exactly mean by 'mechanically' on page 9 line 19, which would not be applicable to e.g. Acts 8/17 or 2 Tim. 1/6.

I did not however intend when I began this letter to *criticise* your Address but to thank you for it, and to ask you for the help of your prayers in face of the big responsibilities laid upon me—to which you refer so kindly in your letter.

The REV. R. F. HORTON, D.D., *to the* ARCHBISHOP OF CANTERBURY

June 10, 1903.

Your noble and gracious letter touches me to the quick. Believe me, I would not have sent the Address if I had realised that it contained anything which could pain you, or that it was to add a feather weight to your overwhelming burdens. And yet I am glad it went, for it has elicited a letter which comes as a beautiful revelation of Christian character and spirit, and will make me love one whom before I honoured.

And it seems to me that you have forgiven the unintentional wound I inflicted. Perhaps even you are glad to know, however painful it may be, exactly how things strike Nonconformists. I was not expressing an opinion peculiar to myself. These thousands of Nonconformists in the country have suffered, and still suffer, the drawbacks of separation from the Church, simply because they think Christ's Church too Divine an institution to be subjected to a Parliament, or to a Premier, who may not be Christian at all. Certainly we do not feel any animosity to Churchmen or to the Church when we protest against this, which seems to us a degradation of the great ideal.

And with regard to the laying on of hands, we both believe in it and practise it; but we dread the imputation of spiritual powers, which may not be there, simply to the performance of an external act; and we believe that the fearful corruption of Eastern Orthodoxy and of Western Catholicism was due to that very error, which finds its first expression in the idea of such a transmission of orders. —But, O my Lord Archbishop, how I groan under the alienation and separation which lead us to misunderstand and to wound one another—when we are called by His name. Would that I could through your Grace say to the whole Church of England how innocent I was of the intention to grieve.—And may I, not only have the joy of praying for you, but ask very humbly for an occasional remembrance in your prayers?

With respectful and affectionate gratitude for your letter.

This was the time, too, when there was a strong wave of feeling in Nonconformist circles against what was considered to be the unfair placing of Church Schools 'on the rates' by the Education Act of the previous year. And the agitation and the passive resistance were such as to cause great anxiety in various ways: but, though conferences were suggested, and ideas ventilated, it was by no means easy to see how the situation could be relieved. The following letter to the Bishop of Southwark (Dr. Yeatman Biggs) gives a hint of the difficulties. It was written after a talk with Dr. R. F. Horton:

The ARCHBISHOP OF CANTERBURY *to the* BISHOP OF SOUTHWARK

Old Palace, Canterbury,
20 August 1903.

Horton's visit comes to little except perhaps a certain unlikelihood of his being so violent against us as some of his friends are. We had abundant talk. He is against the Passive Resisters but says nobody among Nonconformist Ministers agrees with him therein! It came out again and again in our talk how grossly ignorant these Nonconformists are of the real work of Elementary schools.

He is a fearsome Anti-Roman—and alleges that the fears of our passive resisters are mainly based on the expectation (which he shares) that Rome is going to nobble the Education of the Young in England! I was not so greatly impressed by his 'evidences' of this as he expected. On the whole I trust our talk may have done some good. But he had really no very workable proposals to make.

The Archbishop was also consulted about the proposed *Life* of Queen Victoria, and it is interesting to recall in such a connexion the old association of Dr. Davidson's former service of his Sovereign and his old chief, Archbishop Benson. A certain historian was very eager to write it, but it was Arthur Benson who, to his own great surprise, was actually invited to undertake the task. The Archbishop appears as intermediary both to inform the rejected candidate, and to encourage the other on whom the choice had fallen. In the correspondence of the former with the Archbishop there is an interesting précis of a conversation between him (Mr. D.) and the King which shows one side of the question:

'*Précis of Conversation* with the King on the subject of Queen Victoria's *Life* at Buckingham Palace, July 10, 1903.

After the King's permission had been asked to refer to the subject of Queen Victoria's *Life*, the conversation proceeded.

Mr. D. I have had the advantage of speaking on the subject with a very trusted counsellor of Your Majesty, who also had the entire confidence of the late Queen—the Archbishop of Canterbury.

King. There is no one of whose judgment I have a higher opinion. What did the Archbishop say?

Mr. D. The Archbishop spoke with great reserve. He was reluctant to express an opinion on a matter which, he said, might be deemed not to belong to his province.

King. I know very well that the Archbishop never likes to interfere, but whatever he says has great weight with me and I should like to hear it.

Mr. D. The Primate merely said that it seemed that the time had arrived when it was feasible and even expedient (I do not attempt to quote His Grace's words) to write the *Life* of Queen Victoria down to the death of the Prince Consort. Every one who till then had taken part in public affairs having disappeared no susceptibilities could be hurt etc. etc.

As to the Archbishop's opinion of my capability of writing the *Life* I have no right to say anything.

The King seemed to attach the highest value to the Archbishop's words.

I further said to the King that (1) I was prepared to give up practically my whole life to the task: (2) that, possessed of ample means, I could afford to work slowly and thoroughly: (3) that it would be of great advantage that the work should be begun under the King's personal supervision: and (4) that the *Life* down to 1861 would occupy all my life, so there would be no need to trouble about recent years.

The King ended this part of the conversation by saying "Your proposal is of the greatest interest and is one which I will most carefully consider".'

The following letter from Arthur Benson is an indication of the other side:

A. C. Benson, Esq., *to the* Archbishop of Canterbury

Private. Godolphin House, Eton College, Windsor.
July 6, 1903.

I went over and saw Esher yesterday, and he made me the offer of which you know; and today I have accepted it and have definitely resigned my mastership at Christmas. I have no real hesitation about it, because I have a very deepseated belief in the guidance of Providence. The offer is wholly unexpected, it comes exactly at the moment when I wanted it, and it is exactly the kind of work I desire. At the same time I quite understand the responsibility and difficulty of it; and I can only do my best.

Another point about it is that it is sufficiently important to justify my taking the step of leaving my work here, the giving up of which might have seemed to those who don't know the conditions a piece of whimsical indolence.

I have again, as I have often had cause to do before, to express my gratitude to you for all your *endless* kindness—because I recognise your hand in this—it only adds one more kindness to the debt of gratitude I and mine owe you, which can never be repaid, but is not therefore unmarked or unappreciated.

Will you let the matter remain confidential for a few days? I don't want it to be known here just in this busy time. And please do not answer this.

There was another connexion with the Benson family of a different kind. Archbishop Benson's youngest son, Robert Hugh Benson, after much deliberation, was on the verge of joining the Church of Rome. The Archbishop saw him at Horsted Keynes, his mother's house:

Mrs. Benson *to the* Archbishop of Canterbury

July 29th, 1903.

It is impossible for me (to) thank you as I feel for this last outcome of your love and kindness—and you see I know what it is to ask an Archbishop to give time and thought to one's own special heart's problem—and you have added to it this letter telling me of all—and I *know* under what stress and strain all this has been so lovingly given. Your letter has been everything to me. Hugh has told me his side—it is all one—and he is as grateful to you as I am. I scarcely hope the end can be averted—but I see you have made him *think*, and troubled the waters of his mind.

Hugh was received on September 10. 'He will *not* be re-baptized,' wrote his mother, 'conditionally or unconditionally. They accept my statement as to his complete baptism.'

This is the Archbishop's letter to Hugh on receiving the news from him:

The ARCHBISHOP OF CANTERBURY *to the* REV. R. H. BENSON

Tomatin, Invernesshire. 16 Sep: 1903.

I thank you for writing to me, and it is a genuine satisfaction to me to feel that you have no sense of having been unfairly or unsympathetically treated by those of us to whom you have opened your heart during these momentous (and, to us, inexpressibly sad and anxious) weeks. When I was last at Tremans I purposely refrained from initiating any talk upon the subject, feeling sure, after all our previous conversations, that you would yourself return to the matter if you had felt that there was anything still lacking as to elucidation of possible misunderstandings.

Be very sure that I shall not cease to remember you constantly in my prayers, as you ask me so to do. It would be affectation on my part to pretend that the step you have taken is not a sorrow to us all, and a special grief to those who owe so much as I and many others do to your dear Father.

I retain however the opinion I expressed to you, that it would have been wrong on your part to have allowed reverence for his memory to force you into what would have been a dishonest act or series of acts on your part, your convictions being what they now are. I am quite sure that when the choice lies between a non-natural use of words upon which so much depends and a change of faith—it is an honest man's duty to make the change rather than practise what to me at least seems to be a course of deliberate evasion or deceit.

I should have felt just the same had the alternative before you been the avowal of deliberate disbelief in the doctrines and formularies of the Christian Faith.

Terribly, perilously, false as the doctrines you have embraced seem to me to be, I greatly prefer avowal to concealment on the part of the Anglican Priest who has come to believe them to be true. It is of course possible, though I can hardly expect you to think so at present, that you may come hereafter, as others in like case have, to regard your present step as having been altogether a mistaken one. But, whether or no that should ever come about, you may be certain that I, for one, shall not fail to pray for you, and to welcome every such friendly relation towards us as you are allowed to retain.

You speak most truly of the wonderful power of sympathy and confidence which your Mother has shown in these trying weeks—or months—or even years. It is not the only gift in which she is almost unique. I fear that in some respects it makes the *pain* to her even greater. But upon that I need not dwell, for you know all that I would say.

I rejoice to hear that you have at least been spared what I am bound in honesty to call, when it is practised, the profanity of re-baptism. I have however some cases of it which I can hardly characterise in tolerable words.

For the rest, come what may, your place in our hearts is and will be a warm one—and if ever, in the changes and chances of life with its unexpected developments and disillusionments, the day should come when you feel that counsel or help or guidance from me could be of use to you, you know that to serve your father's son, nay to serve *you* whom I love so well, would be the keenest and most valued privilege and satisfaction.

The Rev. R. H. Benson *to the* Archbishop of Canterbury

Talacre, Prestatyn R.S.O., Flintshire.
Sept. 20, 1903.

I must send a line to thank you most sincerely for your kind letter.

More and more it seems to me, as you say in your letter, that the final convictions I had come to made it impossible to remain where I was. Of course I hope and believe most fervently that I shall always retain them. But if ever I am in trouble, I shall most certainly avail myself of your help and counsel. No one could have been kinder or more sympathetic than you have been to me in every way: and I am most deeply grateful to you for that; and again too for the assurance of your prayers.

As the last letters show, the Archbishop and Mrs. Davidson spent the first of many holidays from Lambeth in Scotland. They took a manse at Tomatin, the Archbishop arriving on September 1, having stayed in town to take Lord Salisbury's funeral at Hatfield. At Tomatin and elsewhere he had opportunities, which he loved, for keeping in close touch with the political crisis—learning, for example, through Lord Balfour of Burleigh of the inner history of the Cabinet difficulties over tariff reform, including Chamberlain's resignation.

Much of the autumn was spent in Kent, with the Old Palace, Canterbury, as head-quarters. And here the question of further help in the diocese came up. Bishop Walsh, who had been appointed Bishop of Dover by Archbishop Temple, continued to act as Bishop Suffragan to the new Archbishop. It had, however, very soon become plain that if both the diocesan and the general work of the Church were to be adequately done, a second Suffragan must be appointed. The main difficulty was finance. The Bishop of Dover received £600 a year from the Archbishop's private purse in addition to the income of his Canonry, and the private purse had to supply the whole cost of the regular staff of Chaplains and Secretaries as well as pay for all correspondence, travelling, hospitality, repairs, maintenance, at Lambeth and Canterbury. In the end, however, the Dean and Chapter of Canterbury agreed to place the city living of All Hallows', Lombard Street, at the Archbishop's disposal, and the Archbishop nominated Canon Pereira for the living, and secured the approval of the Crown for his appointment as first Bishop of Croydon.[1]

This autumn also saw the silver wedding of Randall Davidson and Edith Tait. By a remarkable coincidence, the silver weddings of the Archbishops of Canterbury and York both took place on the same day, November 12, 1903; though Archbishop Maclagan's wife was his second wife and he himself had been born in 1826 and so was twenty-two years older than his brother Primate. At Lambeth the celebrations took place in the very chapel where Randall Davidson and Edith Tait had been married by Archbishop Tait, with a whole host of friends of old days about them. Not the least welcome members of the family gathering were the orphan girls from the Tait Home at Broadstairs, founded by Mrs. Davidson's mother in memory of her own five young children who were so suddenly taken by scarlet fever in the Deanery of Carlisle in 1856. Many friends subscribed to a magnificent silver wedding present, which took the form of three beautiful marble steps[2] of white (for sincerity), black (for contrition), and porphyry (for love), leading to the Altar before which the wedding had been performed.

[1] Consecrated January 25, 1904.

[2] The steps to Purgatory in Dante. These were dedicated on March 22, 1905.

CHAPTER XXII

THE NEAR EAST

I had come, as it were, to the end of this wheel-going Europe, and now my eyes would see the splendour and havoc of the East. A. W. KINGLAKE, *Eothen*, ch. i.

I

IN this chapter will be found the first of the many occasions during the next twenty-five years in which the Archbishop came into contact with the Near East. Among the early correspondence from abroad with which he had to deal were letters from the Eastern Churches with which he was destined to have so much to do throughout his rule. A telegram was received in London, January 19, 1903, from the Patriarch of Constantinople:

The PATRIARCH OF CONSTANTINOPLE *to the* ARCHBISHOP OF CANTERBURY

Inasmuch as the good pleasure of All Holy God has elevated your wise Right Reverence to the great dignity of the Archbishopric of Canterbury, we gladly address to your Lordship brotherly congratulations. May the Lord give your Lordship grace and strengthening for the good of the English Church and people.

The Patriarch JOACHIM.

The telegram was acknowledged, and the following letter, drafted by the Bishop of Salisbury,[1] who was the Archbishop's constant adviser in all dealings with Eastern and foreign Churches, was sent in reply by the Archbishop on the day of his enthronement.

The ARCHBISHOP OF CANTERBURY *to the* PATRIARCH OF CONSTANTINOPLE

12th Feb. 1903.

To His Holiness Joachim III, Archbishop of Constantinople, new Rome, and Oecumenical Patriarch, Randall Thomas by divine Providence Archbishop of Canterbury Primate of all England and Metropolitan, grace and peace be multiplied from God our Father and our Lord Jesus Christ in the power of the Holy Spirit.

[1] Dr. John Wordsworth.

Most reverend Patriarch and beloved Brother in Christ, you have heard that God has been pleased to take away from our head our beloved brother and Primate, Frederick Temple, and you have already expressed your sympathy for us in this bereavement, for which we most heartily thank you, as he was not only a friend to all of us, but a noble example in life and character. You have also been good enough to send to ourselves personally by telegram your brotherly greetings on the occasion of our nomination to the See of Canterbury, to which we have most cordially replied in the same manner. We have now the honour to give official information to yourself and the members of your Synod, that our elevation to this high office, of which we feel ourselves most unworthy, is complete. The election on the part of the Dean and Chapter of the Cathedral Church of Canterbury, to whom this right of old time belongs, took place on Tuesday the 27th day of January. This election was solemnly confirmed by the Archbishop of York and by seven Bishops of our own Province of Canterbury on Friday the 6th day of February. Our enthronement as Archbishop has taken place this very day on which we write, in the Metropolitical Church of Christ in Canterbury, this Thursday the 12th day of February, A.D. 1903.

We are deeply conscious of the difficulties and dangers which attend the office and charge to which the Providence of God has called us, and we humbly and heartily desire the prayers of your Holiness and those of your fellow-bishops as well as those of the whole flock of Christ throughout the important provinces committed to your care, that we may be supported and enlightened by the Divine Grace in this weighty office and charge.

It will be our constant care, beloved brother in Christ, to maintain and promote those friendly relations between the Church of England and the Orthodox Eastern Church, which have long existed, and which were especially dear to our predecessors. We shall endeavour to act in the spirit of the Lambeth Conference of 1897, the resolutions of which on this subject (which we append to this letter) are probably well-known already to your Holiness. They were the foundation of a very friendly correspondence between our late Archbishop and your predecessor, which our Archbishop would gladly have continued if he had not been overwhelmed with work at home too great for his strength.

It was our duty on three occasions (1878, 1888 and 1897) to act as one of the secretaries of the Lambeth Conferences, and we can therefore speak from long experience of the entire goodwill of our brethren in all quarters of the globe to the Orthodox Eastern Church in all its branches.

We have often heard with pleasure from our brethren the Bishop of Gibraltar and the Bishop in Jerusalem of the cordial welcome everywhere given to them by prelates of your Holiness' communion, and of the details of intercourse with them and other members of your body which have been, we believe, from time to time beneficial to both parties.

We earnestly trust that this intercourse may be extended, and we shall be happy to consider any proposals which your Holiness may at any time think fit to make on the subject.

We commit this letter to our trusty and well-beloved Chaplain the Venerable Mark Swabey, who will deliver it to your Holiness with our profound respect.

Given at the Old Palace in Canterbury this 12th day of February in the year of Our Lord 1903.

Your Holiness' affectionate Brother in Christ.

RANDALL (Seal) CANTUAR:

The letter was transmitted to the Patriarch through the Rev. Mark Swabey, Chaplain to the Crimean Memorial Church, who reported the great satisfaction with which it had been received, and also the annoyance of the Russians at the exchange of courtesies, who thought, without the remotest justification, 'that politics must be behind any religious movement'.

The following reply was sent by the Patriarch and read in Canterbury Convocation in May:

The PATRIARCH OF CONSTANTINOPLE *to the* ARCHBISHOP OF CANTERBURY

Most reverend Randall Thomas, Lord Archbishop of Canterbury and Primate of All England, most dearly beloved by us in Christ our God, grace be to you and peace from God our Father and the Lord Jesus Christ. It gave us heartfelt joy to receive from the hands of the reverend priest Mark Swabey the highly esteemed letter which contained the happy news of your Grace's election to the most eminent hierarchical dignity of Archbishop of Canterbury, Primate of All England and Metropolitan, and of your confirmation and enthronement, by the Providence of God and in accordance with ancient practice; and likewise the holy Synod of the most reverend Metropolitans which was about us was delighted with the official reading of your letters, which took place during their session, and with the enrolment of them in our Acts. It afforded us great satisfaction not only to observe the delicate kindness with which you issued your letter, describing these auspicious events, on the very day of your enthronement, but also the revelation of your Christian heart full of evangelical love and of desire for the advancement of the friendly relations already happily existing between our Churches, and for action in reference to the promotion of a more general programme, in consonance with the resolutions of a conference of Bishops, of which you were pleased to subjoin a copy written in Greek. It, therefore, makes us happy to reply that we rejoice with you from the centre of our soul, and pray God, from the bottom of our heart, that He may strengthen and confirm you by His all-invigorating help in the holy, exalted, and anxious office to which He has called you, as your qualifications and your previous distinguished services deserve: and next, we give you due thanks for the expression of your good will towards the Great Church of Christ which is with us here in Constantinople, and towards all the other sister autocephalous Orthodox holy Churches of God, and for your admirable desire for friendly intercommunion (ἐπικοινωνία) with them. We assure your Grace that these kind and benevolent expressions find a deep and hearty echo on our part, inasmuch as they agree both with the spirit of our own Orthodox Church, and with our own private inmost desire to co-operate as far as we can with the Divinely given command. For from the earliest times our Church prays and supplicates in every one of its solemn services for the union of all the Churches: wherefore we saw with pleasure that this prayer, so pleasing to God, was described in the resolutions of the Lambeth Conference as the duty of every Christian of the Anglican Church. This holy purpose formed a favourite subject of our own meditation during the first period of our patriarchate twenty-three years ago, and now, when, having been called to this office a second time, we have given our assiduous attention to the subject, we have invited the brotherly judgement of all the Orthodox Churches, as on other ecclesiastical questions so particularly on this—namely, whether they think it opportune to consider how we may prepare a platform for mutual friendly approach on the part of the different Christian Churches (πεδίον ὁμαλὸν φιλικῆς ἀμοιβαίας προσπελάσεως τῶν διαφόρων χριστιανικῶν Ἐκκλησιῶν). For this cause, since we concur in the same holy Evangelical desire, we readily welcome and highly value the continuance and further development of the friendly relation and intercommunion (ἐπικοινωνία) between the hierarchy of the two Churches, from which we may truly expect mutual advantage, and we shall ever show ourselves zealous in this work. For 'Love is the fulfilling of the law', as the heaven-mounting Paul says, and 'Love edifieth'. In conclusion, praying that your Grace may enjoy unbroken health for a long period of years for the fulfilment of the high ministry committed to you we again salute your Grace with love unfeigned in Christ Jesus our Lord.

In the year 1903, March 11th.

With all respect and affection to your Grace,

Most sincerely yours in Christ Jesus,

✠ JOACHIM of Constantinople.

Messages of congratulation also came from the Churches in Syria, but indirectly; the Greek Orthodox Bishop of Beirut informing the Ven. H. C. Frere, Archdeacon in Syria, that he wished to telegraph his congratulations, but feared that if he did so a notice of the telegram might appear in the newspapers, as telegrams passed through the Turkish officials, which was dangerous.

The Archdeacon, in transmitting the message, also referred to the 'jealousy of the Russian political agents' and their efforts to destroy the national character of this branch of the Orthodox Church. The Archbishop in expressing his thanks thought it therefore well to add:

The ARCHBISHOP OF CANTERBURY *to* ARCHDEACON FRERE

21 February 1903.

It is I hope abundantly clear that our object in thus acting is wholly religious and in no sense whatever political. I have no other aim than the promotion of mutual goodwill among members of the Church of Christ.

It was, the Archbishop always found, extraordinarily difficult to make the Eastern Churches understand that the Archbishop of Canterbury was not a great potentate in the political world, with all sorts of political and even military sanctions behind him. And time after time he had to repeat that the sole object of any dealings he had with the officers of the Orthodox Communions and their followers was purely religious. Throughout his life he was scrupulously careful to avoid any appearance of political action of any kind. When he responded to appeals for help or the exercise of his influence, it was a response to cries for succour from a threatened or distressed people, and for sympathy and comfort in time of danger and tribulation. And the first of many such appeals was addressed to him in his first year of office.

II

In the summer of 1903 an urgent appeal was made to the Archbishop on behalf of the Christians who were enduring terrible suffering and massacre at the hands of the Turkish army in Macedonia. He received letters from the chaplains at Smyrna, from London editors, from leaders of the Christian Social Union, and others, full of entreaty or reproach, begging him to 'rouse the conscience of England to our responsibilities in the Near East'. The Archbishop replied guardedly, disclaiming an intimate knowledge of the intricate and perplexing question, though anxious at the same time to avoid any charge of lack of sympathy. It was, he perceived, clearly a matter on which fuller information as to all the circumstances involved was desirable. He naturally therefore wrote to the Prime Minister, from his holiday rest in a Scottish manse:

The ARCHBISHOP OF CANTERBURY *to the* RT. HON. A. J. BALFOUR

(for a week)—Tomatin, Invernesshire.
17 Sept. 1903.

Private.

I am, as you can well understand, bombarded at present by letters, and appeals of all sorts urging me to come forward and take a lead, on behalf of the Church of England, in some action, or protest, or memorial (their name is legion) on behalf of the Macedonian Christians.

In such emergencies as the present I always shrink from taking such a line as may be likely to hamper the Executive Government upon whom the responsibility rests, and who are, I am persuaded, quite as likely at this moment as any of us clergy can be to be alive to the *horribleness* of what is going on—while their knowledge of details and of possibilities is of course incomparably greater. On the other hand I can't help recalling an occasion, several years ago, when Lord Salisbury expressed to Archbishop Benson a wish that he (as Archbishop) had taken part in a particular meeting or memorial (I THINK it was on behalf of the Armenians), from which the Archbishop had merely abstained because he thought it might hamper rather than help the Government.

With this recollection in mind I cannot help sending you this note, just to say how intensely I share the consternation with which every reasonable man must regard the condition of matters in Macedonia, and to assure you that if you would regard it as any way *helpful* that I should come forward by letter or speech to give expression to such sentiments I am more than ready to do so.

For example, if some great public Meeting were to be held (and I gather that there will be such) would it, or would it not, be a good thing that I should attend it and speak? Or is there any other way in which I could—in the name of our Church—do aught to strengthen your hands in dealing with the awful problems of these unhappy regions?

Mr. Balfour telegraphed in reply, from Balmoral, Sept. 21, 1903:

Am thinking of writing elaborate letter for publication. Would you like it to be addressed to yourself? I'm so pressed with other matters that I fear it may be a day or two before I send it off but will try and despatch it by post.

The Archbishop telegraphed his approval, and followed it up by a letter in which he said:

The ARCHBISHOP OF CANTERBURY *to the* RT. HON. A. J. BALFOUR

21st September, 1903.

Whatever it says, the fact of its being addressed to me will show that it is recognised that the Church of England as such has a sort of 'status' in the matter and responsibility, though an undefined one, as the *religious* mouthpiece of England, when any utterance is desirable.

Mr. Balfour's letter dealt at length with the difficulties of the situation, both external and internal, as well as expressing sympathy with 'the feelings of horror and of indignation which the present position of affairs in South Eastern Europe must excite in the heart of every humane man'. It then proceeded:

The RT. HON. A. J. BALFOUR *to the* ARCHBISHOP OF CANTERBURY

Balmoral, September 24th, 1903.

It is with a problem thus unique in its character and difficulty that Europe has to deal. I cannot think that any man of sober judgement can doubt that the best hope of dealing with it lies in the continued co-operation of Austria and Russia, strengthened by the support and aided by the advice of the other signatories to the Treaty of Berlin.

They possess, if only in virtue of their geographical position, an incomparable influence over the antagonistic forces by which the Balkan Peninsula is rent. No other nation, or group of nations, can do the work as well. No other nation, or group of nations, could do it at all, if Austria and Russia were suspicious or hostile. From this it follows that our best hope at present of ameliorating the condition of Macedonia, as well as of avoiding any international complications, is to support the two Powers. We are obviously not precluded by this support from offering suggestions. We have offered them, and shall continue to offer them, when fitting opportunity presents itself. But it would be folly to forget that there are occasions, and this is one of them, when two Powers are stronger for executive purposes than three, when, indeed, every addition to numbers carries with it a corresponding diminution of efficiency.

These then are the principles by which the Government is directing its policy in the Near East. I do not doubt that they are in accordance with the interests of this country: but they obtain an even higher sanction from the fact that in obedience to them is at present to be found the best hope of improving the condition of Macedonia and the surest security for European peace.

The Archbishop sent a message to a public meeting held the following day, gave his support to the Macedonian Relief Fund, and took other opportunities of expressing his sympathy with the sufferers. But his sense of the dangers of any rash step recoiling on the sufferers themselves prevented him from taking any further marked public action and, as the following letter to the Bishop of Stepney (Dr. Lang) shows, he was unwilling to agree to any central service in St. Paul's Cathedral for the focusing of Christian sympathy and prayer:

The ARCHBISHOP OF CANTERBURY *to the* BISHOP OF STEPNEY

6th October, 1903.

The question of a Special Intercessory Service at St. Paul's about Macedonia is not an easy one. You will have noticed to-day that in some respects the position is technically improved, and that the peril now seems to lie rather in the probability of war than in the continuance of massacres and outrages. But this may be only on paper. I am myself convinced that Balfour is as keen about the matter as we are, and I do not think it would be fair to him were we to seem to say that we are caring and he is callous. The request made to a congregation to pray is a very different thing from a special service in St. Paul's with an address every word of which would be criticised, and rightly criticised, by those who know the details in a way I certainly do not. . . . Personally I am not inclined to believe that a great service at St. Paul's could be appropriately held just now, but I am quite willing to be converted to another view, and I am ready, if you like, to ask the Government what they think. . . .

CHAPTER XXIII

CIVIL AND ECCLESIASTICAL BUSINESS

Went through Lambeth Palace. . . . The palace is noble and has rooms both for civil and ecclesiastical business. *Diary of Frans Burman* (1702).

I

As far back as 1883 Archbishop Benson had written in his diary, after the second reading of the Bill for legalizing marriage with the Deceased Wife's Sister, in the House of Lords, 'This is the first real dissilience of the Law of England and the Law of the Church.'[1] The marriage laws had not in fact been altered, either in that or in any similar direction, for the past twenty years, but efforts were continually being made and Dr. Davidson foresaw that change sooner or later was inevitable, and wished to be prepared. Accordingly, in November 1903, we find him, after consultation with the Archbishop of York, Sir Lewis Dibdin, and others, writing thus to the Prime Minister:

The ARCHBISHOP OF CANTERBURY *to the* RT. HON. A. J. BALFOUR

4th November, 1903.

More than once in recent years a suggestion has been mooted in general terms to the effect that it might be well if a Royal Commission were appointed to consider some of our Marriage Law problems, especially in those directions in which there is opposition, or apparent opposition, between the law of the State and the rules or customs which a large body of Churchmen believe, whether rightly or wrongly, to be obligatory upon them as laws of the Church. The difficulty exists already, and it is likely to be accentuated rather than diminished as time goes on. I have had the opportunity of talking, not only to most of our Bishops, but also to other men conversant with these matters, notably with Sir Francis Jeune, and there is a large, though not an absolute, consensus of opinion in favour of our now asking that a Royal Commission may be appointed to consider the subject.

It may be said that there is very little information available on such a subject which is not already in our possession; but I think this is a misapprehension. I believe that both from America and from the Colonies,—or, rather, from those who are able to speak

[1] *Life of Archbishop Benson*, ii. 12.

with authority about Marriage Laws and usages in those regions, —a great many facts might be obtained which would be valuable to us. Personally I cannot help thinking that out of a Royal Commission might issue recommendations (not upon these fundamental principles, but upon the mode of their operation) which would reduce very greatly the risk of harmful conflict between Church and State. There was of course a Royal Commission in 1868, but its terms of reference were very wide, and it practically broke down over an impossible endeavour to harmonise the Marriage Laws of England, Scotland, and Ireland. I would suggest—though this of course is a matter for you rather than for me—that such a Commission, if appointed, should deal only with England, and I venture with all diffidence, and merely for the elucidation of my meaning, to suggest terms of reference which would seem to be not inappropriate. I think there are some among those desirous of changes in our existing Marriage Laws who would like to see such changes brought about with the minimum of friction and difficulty; and those of us who deprecate such changes, while fearing that they may be inevitable, would agree in desiring that they should come into operation, if come they must, as peaceably as possible.

I am well aware that the course I suggest has dangers of its own, and that a Royal Commission might conceivably make recommendations or express opinions which would inflame the minds of certain controversialists, but I think the probable gain preponderates over the possible harm, and I now write with the entire approval of much the larger number of my episcopal brethren to ask you to consider the question of the appointment of such a Commission. I am ready to ask for it in a more formal way if you so desire. I could do so in the House of Lords next Session, if you think that course more expedient, but I should not wish to make the request publicly if it was to be refused, and personally I should be inclined to think that it would be better, if the Commission be appointed, that it should have a quieter origin than the birth-throes of a Parliamentary debate. About this however you are better able to judge than I.

Suggested Terms of Reference

To consider the laws regulating the solemnization and registration of marriages in England, and the validity in England of marriages wherever contracted, and to advise as to the amendment and consolidation of the said laws.

The letter was acknowledged and considered by the Cabinet:

J. S. SANDARS, ESQ., *to the* ARCHBISHOP OF CANTERBURY

Confidential. 11 Dec. 1903.

I think you know that Mr. Balfour mentioned to his colleagues your proposal for a Royal Commission on the Marriage Laws.

Mr. Balfour now tells me that some of them were anxious to be informed to what questions the labours of a Commission, if one were appointed, would be directed: that is, they would be glad to know what are the questions of controversy with which the Commission should, in your judgment, deal.

Would you, at your convenience, let me have a line which I can give to Mr. Balfour as your answer to his inquiry?

I have had a good deal of talk with Porter about Church Legislation; and Thring has got the Rochester or rather Southwark-Birmingham Bill into a very modest compass.

I quite agree with you that, unless Roffen waives priority and is prepared to take all risks, his Bill has a claim to precedence, in my view absolutely binding on the Government.

The ARCHBISHOP OF CANTERBURY *to* J. S. SANDARS, ESQ.

16th Dec. 1903.

I enclose herewith the Memorandum for which you asked, showing the kind of matters which are at present causing us trouble and seem to call for the help or elucidation which a Royal Commission might give. The Memorandum is purposely brief and does not attempt to cover the ground, but it shows the kind of ways in which difficulties occur. I honestly think it is becoming almost intolerable that Bishops should be called upon to advise the Clergy to do things which they (the Bishops), not less than the unhappy Parish Priests, believe to be contrary to Christian law. I say 'Christian law' because it is not a fussy or fanciful introduction of Church law or Canon law as contrasted with the laws of England, but fundamental principles, such for example as this: that prayers to Christ and Christian benedictions are more than unsuitable when ministerially pronounced at a very solemn moment over those who ask to be united in Christian wedlock while avowedly non-Christians.

Memorandum

The following are some of the questions with regard to Marriage Law, which might, it is conceived, be elucidated by consideration at the hands of a Royal Commission.

(1) The marriage of divorced persons. The law gives the innocent party as complete a right of claiming to be married in

his parish Church by the incumbent or his substitute as if he had not been previously married. The law gives the guilty party a right to the use of the parish church, if he can obtain the services of a clergyman, and a right to have his banns proclaimed in the parish church. But Church law has always absolutely prohibited the marriage of the guilty party and has strongly discouraged (though it has not always decisively prohibited) the marriage of the innocent party. In consequence of the deep-seated repugnance of most of the clergy to having anything to do with these marriages, it is very frequently impracticable, notwithstanding the law, for divorced persons to be married in church.

(2) The Marriage Service in the Prayer Book is based on the assumption that the parties are Christians. The Marriage Acts and secular Law recognize no distinction between Christian and non-Christian (e.g. Jews or Mahomedans).[1] Christians and non-Christians appear to have an equal right to avail themselves of the ecclesiastical machinery of Banns and Solemnization of Marriage in Church. This point creates frequent and growing friction.

(3) The difficulties created by the Deceased Wife's Sister question are well known. The anomalies are already embarrassing. For example in one part of the Diocese of Winchester—Jersey—such marriages are valid, but in the rest of the Diocese, say, in the Isle of Wight, such unions are not marriages at all. With the increasing communications between the Colonies (where, speaking generally, marriages with D.W.S. are legal) and the mother country the anomaly is growing more acute.

(4) There are several important questions of a slighter and more technical character which seem to need consideration.

(*a*) The area within which a person must reside in order to be married at a particular church.

(*b*) The nature and extent of 'residence' for this purpose.

(*c*) The variation of fees in different parishes. The absence of satisfactory methods of defining or altering them.

J. S. SANDARS, ESQ., *to the* ARCHBISHOP OF CANTERBURY

Private. 10, Downing Street, Whitehall, S.W.

29th Jan. 1904.

I read your letter to Mr. Balfour.

He desires me to say with reference to your inquiry about the

[1] This is a more practical question than might be supposed. The Indian Bishops complain of the number of cases in which Indians, either Mahomedan or Hindoo, have, while in London (as law students or otherwise), married Christian women, and questions of a grave sort arise on their return to India. [R.T.D.]

proposed Royal Commission on the Marriage Laws that there has been such pressure of business at the recent Cabinet meetings that he has not, as yet, been able to take the decision of his colleagues upon the question of the Commission.

As soon as the opportunity can be found he will bring the matter forward for determination.

The details you furnished were duly circulated to the Cabinet.

The ARCHBISHOP OF CANTERBURY *to* J. S. SANDARS, ESQ.

30th Jan. 1904.

I thank you for your letter about the possible Royal Commission on the Marriage Laws. I can easily realise how heavy the pressure has been and how things of this sort might be crowded out. You will remember however the importance which was attached by you, and I think by Mr. Balfour, to the appointment of such Commission, if it be appointed, taking place before notices are given in either House as to the introduction of Bills, because if the Deceased Wife's Sister Bill is standing upon the notice paper when the Commission is appointed, people will say, not unnaturally, that the Commission is simply proposed in order to shelve that question. This would be quite untrue in fact but most plausible in theory. My difficulties in dealing with questions of the Marriage of Jews and the like do not diminish as the months pass.

A curious incident occurred in March with regard to the custody of the volume containing the Marriage and Baptismal Register of the Royal Family. It had been in Davidson's keeping as Clerk of the Closet and then handed by him to the Librarian of the House of Lords (Dr. S. A. Strong). The Archbishop in 1904 wished to take steps for its custody in a more suitable place, and inquired of Mr. Edmund Gosse (Dr. Strong's successor) with a view to its transfer. Mr. Gosse, after making a personal inspection of every safe and cupboard in the Library without finding any trace, found, to his inexpressible relief, that it was in Dr. Strong's house!

The ARCHBISHOP OF CANTERBURY *to* SIR H. MAXWELL LYTE

Lambeth Palace, S.E.
14th March, 1904.

You may perhaps remember my speaking to you (about a year ago) with reference to the volume containing the Marriage and Baptismal Registers of the Royal Family from the middle of the 18th to the middle of the 19th Century. It is obviously a record of the highest national importance, including, as it does, the official Marriage register of Geo iii, of the Duke of Kent, and of Queen Victoria, and it might consequently become in a technical sense the 'Court of Appeal' with regard to the legitimacy of the present Royal Family.

It *was* for a time in my custody, most unsuitably, when I was Clerk of the Closet, and the King directed me some time ago to discuss with the Lord Chancellor, and indeed to *settle* with him in what custody a volume so important should be placed. It was for the moment entrusted to the Library of the House of Lords, where it now is.

The Lord Chancellor and I are of opinion that its proper resting place is the Public Record Office, and as I know that this will meet with the approval of the King, I write to ask you to procure the volume from Mr. Gosse, the Librarian of the House of Lords, and kindly to intimate to me that you have received it and that you accept responsibility for its custody.

The Register was accordingly transferred by Mr. Gosse and accepted by Sir H. Maxwell Lyte on March 23, 1904, and, at his suggestion, a note as to what had been done was placed in the Register in current use.

II

The spring of this year was, as we shall see in subsequent chapters, much occupied with the revival of the Ritual controversy, and, to a less extent, with the beginnings of the ominous controversy on the subject of Chinese Labour. But there were also a good many other claims on Davidson's attention—and we must not forget that the agitation in the Church and in the country with regard to ritual, as well as the attacks on the Archbishop for adopting what was most cruelly described as the office of 'chaplain to the Chinese compounds', made a rather stormy background for due attention to the ordinary archiepiscopal duties, as well as to receiving new burdens. It will suffice to set out a few of the more interesting issues which it fell to his lot to handle.

In August there occurred the famous decision in the House of Lords by which the United Free Church of Scotland was judged to have no title to the property of the original Free Church, which thus passed in a sensational way to the continuing minority known as the 'Wee Frees'. A few weeks before the judgement, Dr. Rainy, the Moderator of the United Free Church, spent the evening at Lambeth. The case naturally formed the theme of conversation between the Archbishop and his fellow Scot. A day or two later Dr. Rainy followed up the talk with a letter (June 30, 1904) which began: 'You referred kindly to our "case" on Tuesday, and asked "what we could do".' Dr. Rainy answered the question by speaking of the strength of feeling in Scotland, and the precarious character of any recourse to legislation: but at the back of Dr. Davidson's mind was the question whether he, adding to his own office of Primate of All England the birthright of a Scot, and an astonishing knowledge of all the intricate history of the Disruption of the Church of Scotland in 1843, might not himself 'do' something that might be of use. It was in this sense, after the delivery of the House of Lords judgements, that the Archbishop wrote to Dr. Rainy:

The ARCHBISHOP OF CANTERBURY *to the* REV. DR. RAINY

8th August, 1904.

I thank you very cordially for your kindness in sending me the memorandum on this great and troublous case. I was present, as perhaps you know, to hear the judgements given, and have followed with unfailing interest all that I have seen since then in the way of utterance on either side. I have got the newly published volume containing the full records.

I am anxious to tell you how thankful I should myself be if it should prove possible for me in any way to be of service at this juncture. It occurs to me as not impossible that some advantage might accrue if a few of us in England who are anxious for the religious well-being of Scotland, and for keeping the unity of the spirit in the bond of peace, could intervene in any way, privately or otherwise. But I am at a loss to know how this is to be done. Should anything occur to you I should be most grateful if you would let me know. Unfortunately I sail for America on the 19th. Presumably however there is no great hurry. I am hoping to see Mr. Haldane and to talk the matter over with him.

That God may bring good out of what looks at present like evil, inasmuch as it runs contrary to a desire for greater unity and harmony, is my earnest prayer.

Correspondence followed, and interviews with Lord Balfour of Burleigh, the Prime Minister, and others—as a result of which it was agreed that he should write an identical letter to the

Moderators of the United Free Church and of the Free Church. This action (he privately informed the editor of *The Times*) 'has the entire approval of the Prime Minister, the Secretary for Scotland, Sir Robert Finlay, Mr. Asquith, Mr. Haldane and Lord Balfour of Burleigh'—a doughty team of collaborators.

The ARCHBISHOP OF CANTERBURY *to the* REV. DR. RAINY

12th August, 1904.

At the risk of seeming to be intrusive, I am impelled to write to you in connection with the Ecclesiastical difficulties which have arisen in Scotland. In common with hundreds of others who stand quite outside the area of the controversy I have from the first taken a very deep interest in it; and, although I am of course not competent to form an independent opinion upon the legal questions involved, I feel sure that you will allow me to give expression, from a religious standpoint alone, to the anxiety and distress with which we regard the possibility that what has recently happened may render more difficult the maintenance and growth of any endeavour 'to keep the unity of the Spirit in the bond of peace'. The possibility of a satisfactory solution of existing difficulties largely depends, I suppose, upon the attitude of mind with which the problem is approached. It occurs to me as just possible that when the time comes for the representatives of the two parties to discuss in detail the practical steps which should be taken, it might be of advantage if they could rely upon the presence and aid of one or more friends who, while themselves unaffected by the questions at issue, do heartily care, on religious grounds, to promote a solution which shall be honourable to both parties and conducive to the deepest and best interests of Scottish life. If, when the time for necessary action draws near, it were to be found that I, as a Scotchman and an independent student of these particular questions, could render any service whatever, pray regard me as being gladly and even gratefully ready to co-operate.

I am further able to say that I have ascertained that one or two of the most competent and clear-headed of our public men would be happy to add their assistance if it were felt to be desirable.

I of course realise that the suggestion which I have offered may, for more reasons than one, be unacceptable or unnecessary. If you tell me so, I shall perfectly understand. I am only anxious to make it clear that there are men, outside the circle which is directly affected, who at such a juncture would regard it as a sacred privilege were they able to be of service. In any case we can and will unite with you in earnest prayer to Almighty God that through all difficulties and perplexities He may point for us the way to a surer knowledge of His Will, and to the advancement of the Kingdom of our Lord and Saviour Jesus Christ.

I am myself leaving England on Friday next, to spend some weeks in the United States and in Canada. I ought therefore to mention that if you should think it well, before I return home, to say anything in reply to this letter, such communication would be forwarded to me without delay.

I am writing to the Rev. Murdo Macqueen in similar terms.

The letter was acknowledged at once in a warm personal letter by Dr. Rainy, and the following formal reply was sent a few days later:

The REV. DR. RAINY *to the* ARCHBISHOP OF CANTERBURY

17th August, 1904.

I have today had the opportunity of consulting the Advisory Committee of our Church and am now able to reply formally to your Grace's letter.

We thank you very sincerely for the interest you have been led to take in the difficulties existing here, and for your willingness to spend time and trouble in the effort to remove them. We are grateful for the concern shown by members of other Churches, and we deeply feel that aid given by men like your Grace occupying a high place in general esteem, and I may add, known to be concerned simply for the welfare of our common country, may prove to be of the highest value.

For the present we can only report to you the actual state of affairs.

On the 3rd August our Law Agents addressed to the Agents of the Free Church a request to be informed, with a view to interim arrangements, what course their clients proposed to take during the next few months in regard to the property allotted to them by the decision of the House of Lords, and the suggestion was added that a Conference might take place.

On 10th August the Free Church Committee of the Assembly agreed to resolutions embodying their views of the conditions on which a *modus vivendi* might take place, say till June next, and it was intimated that a Conference might take place 'on these lines'.

On 12th August we replied that, while still desirous of Conference, we were unable to accept as preliminaries, the conditions proposed.

On 13th August we received a letter from Messrs. Simpson and Marwick, Agents for the Free Church, commenting on our reply and offering explanations which seemed to them fitted to remove our difficulties. But they wrote, as they said, only 'on our own responsibility', and we are still awaiting the authoritative answer from their clients whom they have promised to consult.

Meanwhile we add one remark. An arrangement of an interim kind would be of some value. But its main importance would lie in its leading in due time to a permanent settlement of questions of property. This point was not raised in our letter of August 3rd, for it would have been neither becoming nor expedient to ask for a decision on so grave a matter when the judgment in favour of the Free Church was only two days old. Whether the idea can be entertained by the Free Church, we are at present necessarily ignorant. But it has been so extensively canvassed by the press that we may allude to it thus far: if it comes to be practically discussed with a view to Parliamentary action, then will be the stage at which the aid of disinterested men of parliamentary influence and commanding general confidence, will be most important.

The Moderator of the Free Church also acknowledged the letter—but with less pleasure—nor did negotiations, of any official kind, arise from the Archbishop's good offices.

III

In May, June, and July a good deal of attention was paid in Convocation and outside to proposals to make certain changes with regard to the use of the Athanasian Creed in the services of the Church. In the course of an important debate in Convocation on May 5, Dr. Davidson recalled the fact that he had ever since his ordination advocated a change 'by voice and vote'—and he contrasted the comparative quiet of the present discussion with the outcry against Archbishop Tait's 'humiliating avowal' in the famous Convocation debate of 1872, that 'not a soul in the room' or in the Church of England takes the damnatory clauses[1] 'in their plain and literal sense'.[2] He added:

My own firm, humble, and deliberate acceptance of every part of the Christian Creed, my resolve to adhere to it and to maintain

[1] The two opening clauses and the last clause of the Athanasian Creed (*Quicunque Vult*)—referred to as the damnatory or minatory clauses—are as follows:
Whosoever will be saved: before all things it is necessary that he hold the Catholick Faith.
Which Faith except every one do keep whole and undefiled: without doubt he shall perish everlastingly.
This is the Catholick Faith: which except a man believe faithfully, he cannot be saved.
[2] *Life of Archbishop Tait*, ii. 142.

> it does not prevent me from eagerly desiring to relieve from the obligation of reciting the *Quicunque Vult* those who are necessarily unable, for lack of historical or theological knowledge, to estimate, as we do, its historic value and its true significance. I desire, as Archbishop Tait desired, to see the whole document retained in our Prayer-book as it has been retained by the Irish Church.

There was, however, a considerable division of opinion in the Upper House, and the following Resolution was only carried by 9 votes to 8 (May 5, 1904):

> That this House is resolved to maintain unimpaired the Catholic Faith in the Holy Trinity and in the Incarnation, as contained in the Apostles' and Nicene Creeds and in the *Quicunque Vult*, and regards the faith thus presented both in statements of doctrine and in statements of fact as the necessary basis on which the teaching of the Church reposes; but, at the same time, believing that the present manner of reciting the *Quicunque Vult* in public worship is open to serious objection, especially on the ground of the phraseology of the minatory clauses, this House respectfully requests His Grace the President to appoint a Committee to consider in what way the present use of the *Quicunque Vult* may be modified, the document itself being retained in the formularies of the Church as an authoritative statement of the Church's faith.

Rival deputations commending rival interests waited on the Archbishop at the end of May and again in July. The Upper House considered the matter in committee again in July, and adopted an important Resolution on the minatory clauses to which His Grace called the special attention of those who suggested that the Bishops were in July receding from the position of May (July 6, 1904):

> That this House, while it recognises, as taught in Holy Scriptures, the truth, often overlooked, that every man is responsible before God for the faith which he holds, and while it believes that this Scriptural truth is what the minatory clauses of the *Quicunque Vult* were primarily intended to express, acknowledges nevertheless that in their *prima facie* meaning and in the mind of many who hear them those clauses convey a more unqualified statement than Scripture warrants, and one which is not consonant with the language of the greatest teachers of the Church.

Nevertheless, after weighing all the facts—including the wide divergence of opinion in the Church, as well as among the Bishops —it decided that 'no definite proposal for a change in the use of the *Quicunque Vult* should be made' until the deliberate opinion of the Church had been 'more clearly ascertained'.

IV

Public questions of other kinds also called for Davidson's attention during this summer. His caution in responding to the requests of enthusiastic reformers, of every kind, is illustrated by a correspondence with Mr. Broomhall, the well-known leader of the campaign against the opium traffic. In the previous October Mr. Broomhall had asked the Archbishop to sign a letter to the Press calling attention to the grave question of the opium trade, and urging 'that a trade so unjust and dishonourable should no longer be carried on in the name of our country'.

The Archbishop had replied:

The ARCHBISHOP OF CANTERBURY *to* B. BROOMHALL, ESQ.

24th October 1903.

I thank you for your letter. I am afraid I am not one of those who can appropriately sign the letter which you propose to issue. Such study as I have been able to give to the subject (and I have certainly read a great deal) has not convinced me that the Royal Commission which recently gave so much time and attention to the matter was either ill-informed or unfair. I have no wish personally to promote the continuance of a trade which is undoubtedly productive of much evil, though apparently, in the opinion of many wise observers, it is also productive of a great deal that is wholesome and good. The unsparing language however which is used in opposition to it has never commended itself to me, and while I should watch with sympathy and interest any endeavours to deal wisely with what I fully admit are difficulties of a very serious kind, I could not myself, without a deeper and more prolonged study of the question in all its bearings than is possible for me in the midst of my other work, give my name to the particular Association which you represent.

The writer of the letter had kept silence at the time for the reason given in the following letter:

B. BROOMHALL, ESQ., *to the* ARCHBISHOP OF CANTERBURY

2, Pyrland Road, London, N.
Aug. 12, 1904.

Many months ago I invited Your Grace to unite with others in signing a letter to British Editors on the Opium Question. You could not see your way to do this, but sent me a very courteous letter—which I should at once have gratefully acknowledged—but for the expression of views in the letter that surprised and troubled me not a little. I wished to write after deliberate thought and not on the spur of the moment, and so deferred writing. As often happens, the thing not done at once is unduly delayed.

If I could have felt at liberty to make public what Your Grace had said, it would have done much to stimulate the movement for the suppression of the opium traffic, but I felt this undesirable. It would have fixed upon Your Grace, and upon the high position you hold, a measure of odium that would not have been removed for many years; and throughout the civilised world it would have been regarded as nothing less than scandalous that the official head of a large section of the Christian Church had referred with implied approval to the opinion of those who considered the opium trade as 'productive of a great deal that is wholesome and good'.

I showed Your Grace's letter to one of my sons who had lived in China for a number of years, and had travelled in eight of its Provinces. After reading the letter he exclaimed with much emphasis—'Incredible, Incredible; it's heartbreaking'.

I put aside at the time a book which I purposed sending to Your Grace—'The Real Chinese Question'. I now send it. It has been out of print for some time, but the copyright has been obtained, and very soon a revised edition of 10,000 copies will be published. There are some inaccuracies in the book, which will not appear in the new edition, but they do not affect the general argument of the writer, whose book, some who are well acquainted with China consider extremely valuable.

Along with this I beg to send some other papers on the Opium question which will repay the attention of Your Grace, for upon this exceedingly important question—affecting the welfare of hundreds of millions—it is much to be desired that Your Grace should be well-informed, and judging from your letter I must—with all respect—say, that is at present far from being the case.

I will not trouble you with a long letter—but in view of the near future when more will be heard upon this question, I would respectfully and earnestly beg Your Grace's careful attention to the whole matter.

And now—leaving this opium question—may I ask you to excuse me doing a rather unusual thing. It is—in all good will—asking Your Grace to accept several little publications I send herewith. Even the horizon of an Archbishop has its limitations, and perchance these little books—each with an excellence of its own—might not come in your way. They are—'Yet Another Day'—

'Marching Orders'—'The People's Day', one of the ablest things ever written on the subject, and this I believe Lord Stanley admitted at the time, and the newly issued 'Methodist Hymn Book'. This, as showing the Hymns used and sung by between three and four millions of people, is not without interest.

I trust that in the early Autumn I may be able to send Your Grace a copy of the new edition of the Honourable Chester Holcombe's book—with supplementary matter.

The Archbishop's reply is characteristic in its modesty and its caution:

The ARCHBISHOP OF CANTERBURY *to* B. BROOMHALL, ESQ.

Private. 13th August 1904.

I thank you cordially for your kindness in sending me your packet of books. I am taking the smallest of them 'Yet Another Day' in my pocket on a railway journey to-day, so I am making a good start in their perusal.

Your letter on the Opium Question will of course receive my best consideration. But I am afraid that, notwithstanding what you say, I am not at this moment prepared to regard the thoughtful, high-principled, and careful men who devoted months of study to the whole matter before embodying their opinions in the Blue Book, as being either hopelessly wrong-headed or utterly ignorant. I fully admit the immense difficulty of the subject, and I feel as strongly as anyone how appalling are the evils which an indulgence in Opium may, and does, produce. I shall at all times be ready to do my very best to understand the question properly in all its bearings so far as this is practicable consistently with my other duties, which, as you know, are onerous and anxious.

When you deprecate as terrible or incredible my expression to the effect that there are modes of using Opium which are beneficial, you, I think, are missing the point of what I desired to say. Surely it cannot be denied that there is a use of the drug which is beneficial as well as a use which is noxious and bad.

There was also the Licensing Bill, then before Parliament. The opening days of August were devoted to its consideration by the House of Lords. The character of the Bill, to one who, like Randall Davidson, had fought for so long for a very different measure, was a great disappointment. His principal aim was to secure a time-limit for the compensation of displaced licence-holders—but in the vital amendment, which he moved after a long debate, he was defeated by the Government, 52 votes being cast for him and 126 against. No wonder that F. C. G. should devote a cartoon to the subject in the *Westminster Gazette*: depicting Mr. Bung the Brewer (labelled Licensing Bill) jauntily going up the road towards the House of Lords and finding the two Archbishops with pained expressions stopping the way (Aug. 3, 1904):

A Rejected Overture.

MR. BUNG: Good-day, my lords; I'm looking to you for your usual kind consideration.

ARCHBISHOP OF CANTERBURY: Go away, go away. You've been much too familiar for a long time. I'm going to vote against you this time.

In the debate on the Third Reading, when the Bill was passed, the Archbishop once more expressed his keen disappointment—and not for the first or last time spoke of the difficulties in which he found himself in such a matter, standing between the fire of the Conservative Government on one side, and the advanced wing of the temperance reformers on the other.

In September, the Archbishop intervened in a parliamentary election in Kent on a point of some delicacy. On the death of Mr. James Lowther, an out-and-out protectionist who had represented Thanet in the House of Commons for sixteen years, Mr. Harry Marks, an orthodox Jew, a strong tariff reformer and very rich, was nominated by the local Conservatives as his successor. *The Times* issued a protest dealing with his past financial career and showing him to be in its opinion an unfit Conservative candidate for the Thanet Division. The Archbishop wrote early in the controversy to the Vicar of Margate, who asked for counsel—and in September, during the actual election, gave leave for the publication of his letter (in *The Times*, Sept. 24, 1904):

The ARCHBISHOP OF CANTERBURY *to the* REV. C. J. M. SHAW

Old Palace, Canterbury.
23 May, 1904.

In reply to your request for counsel, I do not think that I ought to say more than that in my judgement it is of quite primary importance that we should secure as our representatives in Parliament men whose personal character stands high, and is recognised as standing high.

Of the detailed facts in this particular case I know nothing personally, and I must not be understood to be expressing my opinion about them. If I had to express such an opinion it would be essential that I should first master for myself all the particulars, and I have had no means of doing so.

But I am firmly persuaded that, if our public life is to be maintained at its high level, and our public men are to justify the confidence we have been accustomed to place in them, voters must see to it that no political or partisan enthusiasm—however keenly they may feel on the questions of the hour—leads them to record their votes for men whom they do not trust or respect.

Unless we adhere unswervingly to this principle, there will be a lowering of the tone and integrity of our public life, and no temporary victory at the polls, for one political party or the other, could compensate for such a national disaster.

In spite, however, of this strong pressure, and of the absence of any letter from the Prime Minister, and the division in Conservative ranks, Mr. Marks was returned.

A curious correspondence took place towards the end of the year about Prayers for the Dead. It appeared that a Ryde incumbent, a member of the English Church Union, said publicly that the Archbishop, in the course of a four hours' conversation with him, admitted in private that he himself said prayers for the dead with the late Queen. The statement was widely reproduced, and the Archbishop received letters from newspaper editors and protests from Protestant organizations. The Archbishop inquired of the speaker, who amplified the statement, even quoting the words alleged to have been used thus: 'I say prayers for the dead: I say them before the Queen at Windsor'—phraseology which, as the Archbishop said in reply, 'is entirely alien to any that I should have used'. To his old friend Canon Benham, who had asked what had been meant, the Archbishop wrote a letter, intended for publication, stating the actual facts on which the statement had been based, and his own views:

The Archbishop of Canterbury *to the* Rev. Canon Benham

16th Dec. 1904.

I have too long delayed my reply to your letter of November 9th, calling my attention to the published report of a speech made at Liverpool, in which the speaker was said to have stated that the present Archbishop of Canterbury, when Bishop of Winchester, had, in a private conversation with him upon the subject of Prayers for the Dead, told him that he had himself said prayers for the departed with the late Queen. I have received a large number of letters upon the subject, and I have been in communication with the clergyman whose speech was thus reported.

I think it would be in every way inappropriate, and even wrong, were I to make public any statement with regard to so sacred and private a matter as this. It is impossible that I could ever have discussed it, confidentially or otherwise, with the clergyman in question. What I think may have happened is, that in an official but private conversation with him upon certain questions with which I had to deal as Bishop, some allusion was made to a particular anthem which had been sung at the private memorial service held in the Royal Mausoleum at Windsor, particulars of which were officially published at the time. This is all that I have to say upon that particular point.

Upon the general question of Prayers for the Dead, I am constantly surprised to find how little appreciation there is of the distinction which has so long existed in the Church of England between the use of such prayers in the private devotion of a worshipper whose personal belief encourages him to use them, and the insertion of such prayers in the public Services of the Church —Services in which all, whatever the differences of individual opinion, ought to be able to take part. The Church of England has of course never declared that Prayer for the Dead is contrary to sound doctrine, but prayers distinctively offered for the dead as such have been deliberately excluded from our public and authorised Services. Contrast, for example, Bishop Andrewes' volume of private devotions with the Offices which he prepared for public use in the Consecration of Churchyards.

CHAPTER XXIV

VISIT TO CANADA AND THE UNITED STATES, 1904

Religion stands a-tiptoe in our land,
Waiting to pass to the American strand!
GEORGE HERBERT.

On Friday, August 19, 1904, the Archbishop and Mrs. Davidson sailed from Liverpool in the White Star liner *Celtic* for New York. It was the first time in English history that an Archbishop of Canterbury had set foot on the American Continent, and the event aroused the greatest interest. The visit was in answer to an invitation to attend the triennial General Convention of the Protestant Episcopal Church in the United States, in Boston. The Bishop of Rhode Island (Thomas March Clark), as Presiding Bishop of the House of Bishops, conveyed the request to the Archbishop personally by William Lawrence, Bishop of Massachusetts, an old friend who had stayed at Farnham Castle in 1897.

The BISHOP OF RHODE ISLAND *to the* ARCHBISHOP OF CANTERBURY

20 May, 1903.

It would be a great gratification to us all if you could come over to that Convention. We have gladly received from time to time English Bishops, especially Bishop Selwyn. The coming of the Archbishop, however, would do much towards bringing into closer and more sympathetic relations the two branches of the Anglican Communion.... As one who was present at the first Lambeth Conference and enjoyed the hospitality of Archbishop Sumner,[1] I am glad, not only officially but also personally, to invite to this country one who is so worthy to succeed Sumner, Tait, Benson and Temple.

There was also a further link in the fact, mentioned by the Presiding Bishop, that 'when the Convention was last held in Boston in 1877 we had a message of sympathy from Archbishop Tait, presented by his son, Craufurd Tait'.

[1] Archbishop Longley presided over the first Lambeth Conference, 1867. Archbishop Sumner died 1862.

Bishop Lawrence had various talks with the Archbishop at Lambeth in the summer of 1903. He found him keenly interested, and eager to take such an opportunity of learning about conditions in the New World at first hand. But it was only a few months since he had become Archbishop, and he was a very busy man. Nothing was settled till the following spring, when Mr. J. Pierpont Morgan clinched the proposal. He first saw Mrs. Davidson —so Mr. Morgan told Bishop Lawrence on his return from England:

> Upon inquiry I found that what Mrs. Davidson should think wise or possible the Archbishop would accede to: so I saw her first and got her support: then when the Archbishop pleaded pressure of work, engagements, reporters and other difficulties, I said 'You and Mrs. Davidson and your party will be my guests from Lambeth Gate and back: and no reporter will speak to you and no-one trouble you except by my permission'.

This is the description of the decisive interview on June 10, 1904, which the Archbishop afterwards dictated:

> Nothing could exceed his kindness, and he laid emphasis in superlative terms upon the advantage to the Nation as well as to the Church which would accrue from such a visit. He says: 'Ask whom you like on either side of the Atlantic, who knows the condition of affairs, and he will tell you that no single act which could be taken by England would do more at this moment to cement friendship than a visit by the Archbishop in the way now suggested.' Of the gain to the Church he spoke equally strongly, and obviously he really cares about the matter from that point of view....
>
> After our talk, in which he showed extraordinary kindness and real earnestness of desire and purpose, he took me aside to say: 'In this matter I am representing the Church in America, and our wish is that in making this visit you should be from first to last our guest. Please therefore understand that we are responsible for all expenses of whatever kind from the time you leave Euston Square till you get back there.' He had further said that in America he would arrange for special railway facilities, so that we could go in our own car wherever and whenever we liked, and keep it throughout all the time, living in it as much or as little as we pleased while visiting any place.

Mr. Pierpont Morgan was as good as his word, and everything was arranged as he had promised. The Archbishop and Mrs. Davidson with two chaplains (the Rev. J. H. J. Ellison and the

Rev. H. Holden) were away from England altogether just over two months. The Archbishop was himself anxious to visit the Canadian Church before doing anything of an official character in the United States, and the Canadian Bishops were very much alive to this point. Accordingly, on arriving at New York the whole party hastened in Mr. Pierpont Morgan's private train to Quebec where the Archbishop was to preach on Sunday, August 28, at the Bishop of Quebec's earnest invitation, at the centenary service of the first Anglican cathedral ever built in an English colony. From Quebec they went on to Montreal and Toronto —the guests of the Archbishop and the Bishop. Archbishop Davidson preached, gave addresses, received a degree at Toronto, took part in many official functions, garden parties, and also (not least important) got the opportunity of many private talks. At Montreal, replying to addresses of welcome from the diocese, he first gave expression to one thought in particular which was with him throughout the journey, 'The world as the field of our Church's active life is so much bigger than we used to think it of old'; and he contrasted the limited nature of the day's work of an Archbishop of Canterbury a hundred, or two hundred, or three hundred years ago, with the different atmosphere of to-day. Bundles of correspondence had been preserved at Lambeth—and the Archbishop had examined them before crossing the ocean —belonging to Laud, Wake, Manners-Sutton, and others of three successive centuries:

> Speaking generally, the work, the anxieties, the responsibilities, belong to England—home England—alone. Now dip into the corresponding bundles of Lambeth correspondence at any time you like during the last twenty years, and you find the whole business, or, rather, the whole atmosphere, different—Canada, Australia, South Africa, India, in daily—literally daily—touch with Lambeth. And then, superadded to this, all the problems and ramifications of Missionary work far beyond the boundaries of even the Empire itself. One feels at once the necessity for something of the nature of a central pivot—a pivot which takes tangible shape as a man, an Archbishop, round whom the work may spin, and who, if he be nothing more, furnishes at the least (and this perforce) a point of common touch, common information, common life. I am not speaking even indirectly of any question about jurisdiction, however shadowy. I am speaking about a pivot, not a pope.

They left Toronto on September 6, and saw the Falls of Niagara before crossing the Boundary. They had many friends in the States, all anxious to entertain them; but they had very special ties with Bishop Potter of New York (who welcomed them at Cooperstown), Bishop Doane of Albany, and Bishop Lawrence of Massachusetts. They went first to stay at Bishop Doane's cottage on North-East Harbour, Mount Desert Island, where the Archbishop preached his first sermon in the United States. As the guests of Bishop Lawrence at Bar Harbour, also on Mount Desert Island (where he celebrated for the first time)—to quote his host's words:[1]

> they had the freedom of the island. Dinners and receptions there were, of course; but they were so easy and natural that they seemed to belong in the house and hills. As they arrived, I said, 'A rest, a drive, a walk, or what?' 'Oh, a walk', was their answer. 'Mr. Morgan has carried us everywhere, and we have not felt the American soil.' As we were coming back across the golf links, I remember Ellison, who was playing, pointing up the Gorge to the mountains, and shouting to the Archbishop, Scotsman as he was, 'Scotland, Scotland.'

After spending a comparatively peaceful fortnight at Mount Desert, the Archbishop and his party went on to Washington. They arrived on September 23, after a narrow escape from a railway accident, which might have had most tragic results:

> (From Mrs. Davidson's diary.)
>
> 23 Friday. *At 7 a.m. our engine ran into the other engine on the line!* Amy thrown down. Marvellous escape of everybody. Engineer on the other line a little cut. Train drew up on Bridge. Inspector's engine took us on. View—*Cemetery* just after we started.—Albany 2–3. Cathedral. Little prayer of thanksgiving.

The next day the Archbishop and Mrs. Davidson dined at the White House with President Theodore Roosevelt. On Sunday, September 25, the Archbishop celebrated at St. John's Church, and gave a 'Salutation' at a great service on behalf of Christian Unity at Mount St. Alban, the site of the future cathedral, to a congregation of 35,000. There was a rather longer stay at New York. Here he met all sorts and conditions of men—from the President of Columbia University, Dr. N. M. Butler, Bishop Potter, and

[1] *Memories of a Happy Life*, Lawrence, pp. 201–2.

the Mayor, to the inhabitants of the slums. It was characteristic of him that he should use every opportunity that came his way for adding to his store of information; and there are special packets of letters in the American Visit files devoted to such questions as immigration and divorce; while it is clear that he made special inquiry into the educational and licensing systems, with their possible bearing on the contemporary controversies in England. He was much interested in the housing of working people; and, in driving through the country, if he saw a labourer's house being built, usually all of wood but the chimney, he and Ellison would jump out, go all over the house, up the ladder, and see everything. He had a long talk with Booker Washington, the well-known negro leader in New York, about religious instruction in public schools—especially in the Southern States—and many other matters, including lynching. Wherever he went, he impressed people by his interest, his courtesy, and his simplicity. One rather amusing incident may be quoted in illustration of this, and of the unfamiliar look of the apron and gaiters of an English Bishop on American soil. The Archbishop accepted an invitation to speak to a public meeting, organized by the Annual Convention of the Brotherhood of St. Andrew, in Philadelphia on September 30. A week or two afterwards a young member of the Brotherhood who had been present reported on the meeting with enthusiasm to a friend living on the Prairies, who subsequently wrote to the Archbishop as follows:

(Oct. 23, 1904.)

> Recently a young Yankee has been temporarily employed in the Harvest here and has attended Church. In conversation with him our converse naturally turned to your Grace's most interesting visit to the States. 'Yes', he said, 'the Archbishop attended the Convention of the Brotherhood of St. Andrew, and'—here the speaker evidently thought your Grace had acted with graceful unconventionality—'*he was dressed in Scotch clothes!*' I looked incredulous, so he produced a Chicago paper with the well-known photograph of your Grace in the company of Bishop Potter, which needless to say has no trace of kilts!

The last week of the Archbishop's visit to the States was devoted to the sittings of the General Convention in Boston, attendance at which was the real occasion of his coming. The whole party were the guests of Bishop Lawrence in Commonwealth

Avenue. Here, of course, he came as a distinguished visitor, with no jurisdiction in or over the American Episcopal Church, however much he might be the senior Bishop (by virtue of his see) of the Anglican Communion. Bishop Lawrence writes:[1]

> The Church in the United States is an independent national Church, and the Presiding Bishop is its Metropolitan, as the Archbishop is the Primate of the Church of England. Hence in this country the Archbishop took the secondary place, and his crozier, which at the request of rectors he had used at Bar Harbor and other parish churches, lay throughout these days in its long, coffin-like box on the floor of our hall.

The Archbishop followed the proceedings with the keenest interest—and with a particular regard to the method of Church government as well as debate. The two opening days are annotated in his pocket-book as follows:

October 5. Wednesday.
11. Service of Convention.
1.30. Lunch. (Lawrence's and Bishops.)
3.30. Convention. *Address* both Houses.
Dine Morgan 7.30.
Reception.

October 6. Thursday.
12. Reception in LH
2.30. Missionary meeting, women. Short speech.
7. Dine Peabody's.
9. Reception in Evening at Bishop's House.

He was officially received by both Houses, the House of Bishops (90) and the House of Deputies (consisting of both priests and lay representatives sitting together). In his reply to the Official Address of Welcome on Thursday, October 6, he recalled the visit of Craufurd Tait to Boston twenty-seven years ago, bearing Archbishop Tait's invitation to the second Lambeth Conference, and his own link with the American episcopate through the action of Benjamin Whipple, Bishop of Minnesota, who came straight from Egypt to England on purpose to be among the consecrators of Randall Davidson as Bishop of Rochester on April 25, 1891. But it was his attitude to the discussions themselves as a listener that was most significant of the man. Thus he

[1] *Memories*, &c., pp. 202, 203.

noted on a half-sheet of paper (and mark his sense of the rapidity with which important decisions were taken):

The Chair { considers / requests / is of opinion } etc.

The point of order { is / is not } well taken.

Time-limit in Committee (10 minutes)

Use of hammer.

Rapidity of possible changes—

30 Sept. New York Convention [suadente Rainsford] passes [without previous notice] a Resolution against retaining the Deaconess age limit and in favour of asking General Convention to do it.

Oct. 10. House of Bishops in General Convention agrees after a few minutes' debate.

12. House of Deputies (20 minutes' discussion) agrees.

Most characteristic of all is the following description by Bishop Lawrence (in a letter to the writer):

> I am very sure that the Archbishop whose habit, as you will know, was to mix duty and pleasure, came here especially to study our American educational methods and our General Convention's. No pleasure would draw him away from the latter. I recall the second day, before he had been introduced to the House of Deputies but had been to the House of Bishops: he asked me to take him to a point where he could see the House of Deputies organized and at work: I took him up into a small room gallery from which he could get a partial view and hear what was said: on returning an hour later I found him lying on a couch flat on his stomach with his head so turned that he could hear and see all that was possible.

While the Archbishop was at Boston, Bishop Lawrence, who was Chairman of the House of Bishops, felt that the citizens of Boston should also have an opportuntiy of meeting him in Faneuil Hall, known as the Cradle of Liberty, where the pre-Revolutionary speeches had been made:

Hence a Citizens' Committee, with Henry Higginson[1] as Chair-

[1] Major Higginson, leading citizen of Boston, carried the scar of a sabre-cut still on his cheek, given in the Civil War. Richard Olney was Secretary of State

man, arranged for a noonday reception at Faneuil Hall at which Mr. Olney and President Eliot spoke. As we two walked over Beacon Hill down to the Hall, I said, 'I have no idea what will be the response to the call for this meeting; there may be only fifty there: there may be a crowd.' The situation at the main door answered the question. We had to get in by the back platform door, and found the Hall, with the floor cleared of chairs, packed with men; and what is always interesting at a Faneuil Hall meeting, a sprinkling of butchers in their white smocks.

President Eliot in his address referred to the fact that the Puritans had fled from England to escape Archbishop Laud, and hinted at the hospitality of the sons of the Puritans in welcoming one of Laud's successors.[1]

To which the Archbishop responded:

I am, as you have been reminded, the first Archbishop of Canterbury (they have lasted for 1,300 years, these predecessors of mine) —the first Archbishop of Canterbury who has crossed the ocean. But I am not the first Archbishop of Canterbury for whom or in connection with whom such a voyage was in contemplation. There is a pathetic record known to some here, the diary which was written in the Tower by Archbishop Laud, the very man whose rigid government, whose autocratic rule had led to the coming hither of the people who were to found New England. Archbishop Laud, writing in the Tower before his trial, records in his diary how, upon one sad morning, there came to him a dreadful rumour, a rumour about which he writes in terms which I should hesitate to repeat here. The rumour was this: That there was a plan being propagated, a plot, as he calls it, to give him the worst of all penalties that he could conceive—deportation to New England. He writes about the prospect with a dread which, I am bound to say, was not unnatural. For I am afraid that if that voyage had been, indeed, carried out, whatever might have been the consequences on either side in other ways—and it would be difficult for the most ingenious conjectural historian to imagine what they might have been—this at least is certain, that the welcome he would have received would not have corresponded closely to that which has been given to his successor after 250 years have come and gone.... President Eliot, with characteristic eloquence and point, has reminded us that among the mighty strides of progress which the world has seen made on your Atlantic

in Cleveland's Cabinet and with the President was responsible for the Venezuela affair, which nearly led to war between the United States and Britain. President Eliot was President of Harvard University.

[1] *Memories*, pp. 204–5.

shore, not the least has been the object lesson given in these regions as to the true meaning and the true principles of the widest and the most universal religious toleration. That principle is now so universally accepted among ourselves that it seems almost incredible that all our forefathers, practically without exception, would have regarded it as a position untenable, almost unthinkable, by an honest Christian man. To-day we have, I am thankful to say, a constant stream of visitors from this side of the Atlantic who come to see the historic home in which it is my privilege to dwell, and as they stand in Lambeth Palace Chapel, the place which is identified with the last of the struggles, the pathetic struggles of the old man Laud before he was led forth to his death, I think I may say that no visitors look upon those historical associations, those mementoes of a day that is gone, with more tenderness and sympathy, with a truer understanding of what the relation is of this present to the old past, than do the descendants of the very men whom the rigid autocratic rule of Laud and his friends and colleagues had caused in the first instance to cross the sea. . . .

Bishop Lawrence's account then continues[1]:

Dock Square was so crowded with citizens wishing to meet the Archbishop that a line was formed after the meeting whereby they were able to enter and circle around the Hall, bowing to the Archbishop standing on the front of the stage.

In Sanders Theatre[2] he spoke to a mass meeting of students; in Park Street Church to the ministers of Boston; and on other occasions. The Art Museum was opened for a great reception to him and Mrs. Davidson. They received the members of the Convention and their friends one beautiful afternoon at our Cambridge home, between the Theological School and the Longfellow House, both of which were open to guests: seventeen hundred and fifty persons by actual count passing through my study in two hours were received by Archbishop and Mrs. Davidson.

Such a description reveals a crowded week, and still omits a sermon in Trinity Church (Phillips Brooks's church), Boston ('*no* procession')—an address to non-episcopal ministers—special missionary meetings—a committee on China and a visit to Harvard University on Friday evening ('short addresses by 3 Bishops and Archbishops').

The General Convention itself lasted three weeks, but the Archbishop and Mrs. Davidson left after a week, on October 13,

[1] *Memories*, p. 205.

[2] In Harvard University.

for New York. Before their departure, the House of Bishops gave the Archbishop a piece of plate as a memento of the visit, noting the most catholic hospitality of Lambeth Palace, with the following Resolution:

THE GENERAL CONVENTION

House of Bishops

To His Grace the Archbishop of Canterbury.

The House of Bishops, recognizing the value and helpfulness of your Grace's presence with them during this session of the General Convention, and with a keen realization of the added satisfaction which your own most gracious personality has given to its official character, asks the privilege of offering this piece of silver, which they hope will find place on the table of most catholic hospitality in the Guard Room of Lambeth Palace with the request that it may be counted as a personal gift to your Grace and Mrs. Davidson.

October 12 A.D. 1904 WM. CROSWELL DOANE, Bishop of Albany.
HENRY C. POTTER, Bishop of New York.
WILLIAM LAWRENCE, Bishop of Massachusetts and Chairman of the House of Bishops.

Committee of the House of Bishops.

Bishop Lawrence made the following entry in his Diary after the departure of his guests:

Thurs. Oct. 13, 1904. The Archbishop, Mrs. Davidson, Ellison and Holden went off from Back Bay Station in Mr. Morgan's special train at five minutes of ten. Took them to station and saw them off with great regret. Hereford to breakfast. We have had two delightful visits from them. No easier, more thoughtful or delightful guests. The strain has been heavy because of reporters, people, callers etc., but they have made things as easy as possible for Julia and myself who have been in our Boston house entertaining them while the children have been at Cambridge. Mrs. Davidson is charming, a perfect lady, informal, bright and excellent company: Ellison alert, bright and keen: Holden also excellent: even Amy the maid was much liked by all. The Archbishop, as simple, natural, frank and easy as possible: we laughed and scolded at their good nature with everyone, bores and all. He is full of tact, good sense, a persistent worker, and insistent on getting all information that will help in his work. He met every situation here in a way to gratify all: he has left with the people the idea of an Archbishop who is democratic, a worker and deeply in earnest. He cannot express deep sentiments easily, but makes one feel that he feels deeply. As I bid good bye on the train, he simply said, 'My dear good friend, I cannot tell you what you have all done for me.' His coming has done much to knit the Churches and the Nation. He had the eye of Boston, the convention and the press on him.

We have all enjoyed their visit immensely and can never hope to see them in the same intimate way again.

That evening the Archbishop was entertained to dinner by the Pilgrims in New York. At the breakfast in Boston the Archbishop, who confessed to a dislike of a rough voyage and probable seasickness, had been annoyed by the expressions of satisfaction and pleasure in the stormy seas by the Bishop of Hereford (Dr. Percival) who was to sail that day on the *Cymric*. On the next day, October 14, the Archbishop sailed for England.

It was a stormy voyage, and just as it drew to its close the Archbishop sent the following letter of heartfelt thanks to the host who had given them so noble a welcome:

The ARCHBISHOP OF CANTERBURY *to* BISHOP LAWRENCE

S.S. *Cedric*, Saturday, October 22, 1904.

We are nearing Liverpool. (We ought to be there in three hours or so), and knowing what a scurry of big and urgent work awaits me the moment I set foot in England I take advantage of this opportunity to send you a single line of affectionate gratitude. In good sooth it is beyond my power to confess to you our sense of what we owe not only to your unfailing kindness, thoughtfulness and judgment, but to the thoroughness and foresight with which you made every possible arrangement for what had to be done. And yet all these are more or less superficial things, or comparatively superficial. What really made the difference, and all the difference between what our visit to Boston was and what it might have been, was the *spirit* which you, and you pre-eminently, had thrown into it all; understanding exactly the manner as well as the matter of what should be said and done.

And further, you and Mrs. Lawrence probably do not realize what was to us the restfulness, the confidence, and the peace inspired by all the bright and happy atmosphere of your home. It is a big thing in our lives to have established so real and enduring a friendship with you all. Come soon, a big party of you, to

Lambeth to get it cemented afresh. How eagerly I shall await news of your convention doings. *The Churchman* will give it to us in due course. I am so exceedingly glad that you are the chairman on whom so much turns.

Please give our affectionate greetings to Mrs. Lawrence and the maidens big and little, whom we have come to regard as members of our family circle. And again thank you *all* for making our visit what you and yours more than anybody else did make it, a permanent memory of happiness and interest. I must stop. We have had rough experiences, very, in the Atlantic, but are well and happy. God bless you all.

We hear the *Cymric* had a fearsome time on the ocean, and Hereford must have had his powers tested.

CHAPTER XXV

THE ROYAL COMMISSION ON ECCLESIASTICAL DISCIPLINE

Sir Andrew opening the book, found it to be a collection of acts of Parliament. There was in particular the Act of Uniformity, with some passages in it marked by Sir Roger's own hand. ADDISON, *Death of Sir Roger.*

Laud . . . made a disastrous mistake in trying to use force, and especially the force of royal authority, to secure discipline in the Church. But that mistake was in that age almost universal, and in England we have only seen it vanish during the last twenty years. LEIGHTON PULLAN (*Bampton Lectures*, 1922).

I

EARLY in February 1904, there was a revival of the Ritual Question. Correspondence passed between the Archbishop and several of the Bishops; and a strong move was made in certain quarters for the appointment of a Select Committee of the House of Commons (or possibly of both Houses) to inquire into ecclesiastical disorders. To many Churchmen such a proposal would seem an ominous invasion of spiritual territory by the State, and it was certainly fraught with peril. The Archbishop sought the advice of the Bishop of Oxford (Dr. Paget), on whom he was leaning more and more for counsel in just this field:

The ARCHBISHOP OF CANTERBURY *to the* BISHOP OF OXFORD

Private. 23rd Feb. 1904.

I am afraid there is going to be trouble in Parliament on the Ritual question, and I learn unofficially (Balfour is still absent, so I cannot see him) that the Government may very likely be forced by its own supporters to consent to the appointment of a Select Committee of the House of Commons to consider the subject of clerical lawlessness. Probably this may be ostensibly based on one of the Discipline Bills. It will be a matter of very careful consideration to what extent we as Bishops ought to be willing to make any statement to such a Committee. Obviously some people would resent it extremely, but personally I think we should find ourselves unable fairly to refuse to make some general statement—say through my own mouth—reserving carefully the right to refuse to answer questions which are inappropriate when coming from such a source. I do not think we could successfully argue against the right of the House of Commons, so long as we have an Established Church, to ascertain for itself what goes on within that Church as regards the public services carried on by men who are maintained by authority of Parliament in a position of privilege. In the meantime I want to be adequately armed with knowledge as to what is actually being done in the direction of repressing excesses. It seems pretty clear that the attack is going to be levelled against myself personally, and I must therefore have the facts clearly set out in my own mind, even though I make no statement to the public respecting them. I am in communication with the Bishops of London and Rochester and Exeter, and I should greatly like to have your view, and also to have any statement which you can make, either privately for my own eye only, or in a form available for wider use by me, as to specific things which have been abandoned in response to your direction, or any other overt acts of loyalty which can be noted as indisputable facts in the direction of the amendment of excesses. I am prepared to maintain publicly as well as privately that the spirit of loyalty is on the increase among advanced men, and for our own deliberations this fact is most important, for I regard the growth of a loyal spirit as far more valuable than the mere pruning of the excesses of eccentric men. But the Prime Minister, whom I am to see as soon as ever he returns to London, will certainly say that any general statement or opinion of that kind is comparatively worthless unless it can be supported by the sort of specific facts which could if necessary be adduced in Parliament.

I regard the situation as serious, and I really want your counsel and help. What can you do for me or tell me, either as regards the Church at large or more particularly in your own Diocese? Will the facts about Headington help us?

The Bishop's answer was given with clarity and conviction:

The BISHOP OF OXFORD *to the* ARCHBISHOP OF CANTERBURY

25th Feb. 1904.

I think that I shall best tell my thanks for the trust shown me and the chance given me by your Grace's letter to-day, if I answer it quite freely.

(i) With regard to the propriety of Bishops making any statement to a Committee of the House of Commons on Clerical lawlessness.

It seems to me that Parliament has the right your Grace speaks of,—the right to ascertain for itself what is going on in the public Services of the Established Church. Whether that right belongs equally to a Committee of One House, I do not at all know. But even if it does so belong, it does not seem to me to involve any right to ascertain *through* us what the Clergy are doing: and it would be disastrous to their spirit of loyalty and our claim of Fatherhood if we could be charged with recognising in any way any such right.

I know that your Grace would be most anxious and careful to restrict any statements made by us or in our names within such limits as to leave unviolated our personal and spiritual relation to the Clergy for whom we are responsible. But not only would such limits be hard to define and maintain under the stress of unsympathetic or hostile questioning: there would also be, almost certainly, an impression of concealment or evasion when we tried to maintain them: we should probably make the Committee as angry as the Clergy.

The Services of the Church are public: and a Committee could, without seeking information from us, form, if it would, a just judgement of what is going on:—of the vast amount of loyal, hard work, as well as of the rare instances of extravagance or neglect. If such a judgement were to lead Parliament to say to us or to the Clergy,—'You are not serving faithfully the Church which we are maintaining in a position of privilege: and your unfaithfulness is altering the character of the Church';—then we should have to make our answer publicly when any measure, (for Discipline or for Disestablishment,) based on this judgement, was brought forward. It would be a perilous time: but we should go into it uncompromised: I think we should find more support than is generally expected: and I believe we might do well. . . .

On February 29, the Archbishop had an interview with the Prime Minister, of which he made a full memorandum:

Then we came to the Ritual question generally. He [Mr. Balfour] had not seen, or at all events had not studied Bowen's pamphlet, but he knew of its existence and of the effect it was producing. He asked me to give him my view of the situation as it stands. I did so pretty fully, pointing out, with his entire agreement, how much more important it is to secure loyalty on a large scale among the great body of advanced men than to prune the excesses of the eccentrics. He thought the attack would be directed largely against me, as having failed to carry out any policy of restraining excesses. I told him exactly what I believed to be the case as regards the dioceses in which extreme things are commonest. He thinks it will be almost impossible for the Government to refuse a Select Committee on the general subject of Clerical Lawlessness. His own followers are more keen in that direction than the Opposition, and undoubtedly Parliamentary Elections in the North will be influenced, and have already been influenced, by the Protestant vote. He believed without doubt that if a motion in favour of a Select Committee were made in the House, the Government would be powerless to resist it, and the only thing which prevents this is the present lack of a day for the discussion. This may be remedied by any one of the weekly ballots, and he thought on the whole it would be wiser that the Government should itself consent, in answer to a question now several times repeated, to appoint a Select Committee. I called his attention to the difficulty Bishops and Clergy would find in giving evidence before a Parliamentary Committee about matters affecting the private relationship of Bishops and Clergy. He said that no Bishop who is in the House of Lords should be compelled to give evidence unless he liked, but that he was strongly of opinion that Parliament was entitled to satisfy itself, in whatever way it thought best, as to the facts of what is happening in a Church established by law. I said that in the main I agreed with this, but that I saw grave difficulties in restraining clerical indignation against the kind of proceedings and questionings which a Select Committee might produce. He replied that this must rest largely with the Chairman, and that if a Committee were appointed they would take great pains to select suitable members from the Conservative side, though they would have no influence as to who were the members selected by the Opposition. We discussed the relative advantages of a Select Committee and a Royal Commission. On the whole he was in favour of a Select Committee, but I think he could be pressed to appoint a Royal Commission instead if we thought it well. I said the difference did not seem to me to be very material. He took kindly to my suggestion that if a Committee must be appointed it had better be a Committee of both Houses and not of the House of Commons only. He thought this would be perfectly possible, and indeed, after discussion, he distinctly preferred it. We discussed possible members—(?) Selborne, (?) Salisbury, (?) Chief Justice, (?) Lord Lindley, (?) Lord Goschen. He showed me a question which was to be asked in the House next day, and after a good deal of talk we agreed that he should reply requesting the questioner to let the answer be postponed for a week, during which time, as he told me, he would consult the Cabinet, and he hoped I would consult two or three trusted friends and communicate again with him by the end of the week.

The Archbishop next saw half a dozen trusted friends, both lay and episcopal.

Memorandum as to interviews held between Monday, Feb. 29th and Friday, March 4th, upon the question of a Parliamentary Committee or Royal Commission on Ritual matters.

My interview with Balfour on Feb. 29th is fully recorded. Next day (Tuesday, March 1st) I saw Balfour again both alone and with the Bishop of Rochester. Roffen pointed out to him very strongly the arguments in favour of a Royal Commission rather than a Parliamentary Committee, but entirely agreed that the Parliamentary Committee, if formed at all, must be a Joint Committee of Lords and Commons. Balfour told us that the Cabinet had met that day and that he had sketched the situation, and that they were to consider it again, but were, generally speaking, in favour of a Joint Committee. The Royal Commission suggestion had not, I think, been before the Cabinet at all.

On Wednesday, March 2nd, I called on Lyttelton about Chinese Labour, and spoke to him also on this question. He had not greatly considered it, but was *prima facie* in favour of a Royal Commission rather than a Parliamentary Committee, but wished so far as possible to work with Balfour in whatever way he (Balfour) thought best.

A little later I saw the Lord Chancellor[1] after the hearing of a Privy Council Appeal. I sketched the situation to him briefly. He was against any Parliamentary enquiry at all, on the ground that it was an interference with the authority of the Courts: if people were dissatisfied the Law Courts were open; not till these had failed ought Parliament to be invoked.

The same evening I saw the Bishop of Oxford. He was vehement against a Parliamentary Committee in any shape or form. He went so far as to say that he would not himself co-operate, either by answering questions or by attending as a witness, if such a Committee were appointed, and that he would not feel himself able to conceal his sympathy with the Clergy, who he thought would unanimously repudiate it and hold aloof.

Late that night I saw the Bishop of Ripon. He was not personally averse to any kind of enquiry that might be desired, but was perfectly clear as to the feelings of the Clergy on the subject and the impossibility of getting them to understand the rights, or rather the duties, of Parliament in such a matter. He therefore, while willing to acquiesce in a Joint Committee, thought it full of danger and would greatly prefer a Royal Commission.

[1] The Earl of Halsbury.

On Thursday morning, March 3rd, I had a long talk with the Bishop of London. The subject was wholly new to him, but he obviously sympathised with Oxford's views, though he rather desired an enquiry of some sort, thinking that High Churchmen would come out of it with flying colours.

In the afternoon I saw Salisbury, Selborne, and Hugh Cecil successively in my room at the House of Lords, and found them all to be in agreement as to the peril of a Parliamentary Committee in face of the opinions which they admitted the Clergy would certainly entertain. Salisbury shared these opinions. Hugh Cecil did not, though he understood them well. He believed enquiry would do almost unmixed good, and scouted the fears about actual misbehaviour on the part of Welshmen or others. His objection therefore was because of what others would feel, and not because of what he felt. Selborne had had no notion that the Clergy would draw such a distinction between a Parliamentary Committee and a Royal Commission, but, after what I told him, he was strongly against a Parliamentary Committee. He was also against a Royal Commission if it could be avoided. He believed enquiry must inevitably do harm, partly because it would raise questions some of which are at present quiet, and partly because it would prove such divergence to exist in fundamental opinions that the arguments in favour of Establishment would be weakened.

While I was talking with Salisbury, Balfour came in excitedly, full of disquiet at a memorandum or letter from Roffen [Dr. E. S. Talbot, Bishop of Rochester] which he had received: [Balfour said]

> 'It is now clear to me that all the Clergy, of whatever school, are equally stupid. I had thought the range of stupidity more limited. I cannot appoint a Royal Commission: it would not satisfy the House of Commons. They would vote against me if I urged it.' (And then, turning to Salisbury) 'You are to dine with Roffen to-night. Mind you don't commit yourself, for I do not see how I can give way.'

Then he took Salisbury off to interview the publicans, a deputation of whom were waiting for him.

I then saw the Lord Chancellor again, and told him what I had gathered as to the opinion which would be entertained by the Clergy. I added that I did not think Balfour appreciated the difference in their view between a Royal Commission and a Parliamentary Committee. The Chancellor answered,

> 'I not only understand their feeling, but I entirely share it. On consideration I think a Parliamentary Committee would be intolerable.'

The Archbishop wrote to the Prime Minister as follows:

The ARCHBISHOP OF CANTERBURY *to the* RT. HON. A. J. BALFOUR

4th March, 1904.

I promised to let you know by the end of the present week as to the outcome of such communication as I could have with a few ecclesiastical advisers and friends. I wrote fully to the Archbishop of York, but I have not heard from him. I have seen (quite privately) the Bishops of London, Oxford, Ripon, and, of course, Rochester. I am to see the Bishop of Worcester to-night: he comes to London for a few hours on purpose. I have also seen several leading clergy to whom I could speak confidentially and who are free from fancifulness and are in a position to form a sound opinion.

I confess myself surprised to find how marked and even vehement is the contrast drawn between a Parliamentary Select Committee (even if it be a Joint Committee) and a Royal Commission. What is said is roughly this. (I am not adopting the arguments, but reporting them as eminently entitled to attention.)

'We regard Parliament as acting not only within its rights but properly and usefully in a great many Church matters so long as the Church remains established, and we recognise the abstract *right* of Parliament to satisfy itself in any way that seems to it good about facts connected with the Established Church. But the position is obviously a delicate one, and anything that accentuates the fact that Parliament contains many anti-Churchmen (as well as non-Churchmen and non-Christians) is liable to cause friction. We are ready, for the National good, to put up with the difficulty where it is inevitable—e.g. in obtaining Parliamentary sanction for new Bishoprics, or in exercising control over changes in the existing law. But the strain might become intolerable and preponderate over the National gain of Establishment if Parliament were to exercise its undisputed rights to the full extent that it logically can; and we think there would be grave danger of such overstrain if a Parliamentary Committee—containing non-Churchmen, and even anti-Churchmen, perhaps an Irish Roman Catholic and a Welsh enthusiast—were to cross-examine Bishops and Clergy on matters which concern the most sacred doctrines and usages of the Church. It is, after all, on sacramental questions that the ritual difficulties ultimately turn; and even if such a Committee were to abstain in fact from this misuse of its investigatory power, the fact of its appointment through Parliamentary whips, and not by the Ministers of the Crown as representing the Royal supremacy, would create an intense prejudice against it on the part of the Clergy generally, who would urge that if such detailed cross-examination and discussion by such persons be an inevitable part of Establishment, Establishment is and ought to be imperilled.'

Observe, please, that I am trying to represent the view of the clergy generally, so far as I can estimate it, rather than expressing my own opinion. But it cannot I think be questioned that such view is both tenable and in the main true. You will know from my talks with you how I should myself personally qualify it.

I do not find that similar apprehensions would be likely to be created by a Royal Commission. Such Commission, even if it contained non-Churchmen (rather a difficult point—the Ritual Commission of 1867 and the Ecclesiastical Courts Commission of 1881 consisted of Churchmen only) would not contain Roman Catholics or virulent anti-Churchmen. The Royal Supremacy is exercised by a Royal Commission much more truly, or at all events much more obviously, than by a Parliamentary Committee, and, difficult as it would doubtless be to select the Commissioners, and impossible as it would be to so select them as to satisfy everybody, it would not I think be impossible to select such a body as would carry out a fair and adequate enquiry in a way which ought to satisfy the House of Commons as well as the public generally. I do not pretend to say that the appointment of a Royal Commission would be welcomed, or to deny that it is fraught with grave possibilities of peril and even disaster. But you assure me, and I frankly accept the assurance, that enquiry of some sort is inevitable.

It would be presumptuous of me to attempt to judge of the House of Commons difficulties which you have described. No one is more keenly conscious than I both of the reality of these difficulties and of your own desire to do what is in the large sense for the best interests of the Church and the Country. But I should not be acting fairly to you were I not to represent to you the strength of the feeling which would undoubtedly be evoked in the Church if the course were followed which you foreshadowed in our recent conversations. For myself, I am anxious to help you in every way and to reduce to a minimum the undoubted difficulties of the position. I wish I could carry a larger share of your burden.

The Prime Minister agreed, and on March 8 announced to the House of Commons that he would appoint not a Select Committee but a Royal Commission.

II

The composition of the Royal Commission involved a good deal of trouble, a large share of which fell upon Mr. J. S. Sandars, who took infinite pains. In the end, after one or two disappointments, it was announced on April 20, 1904. It was composed of fourteen members, with Sir Michael Hicks Beach, late Chancellor of the Exchequer, in the Chair; and was overwhelmingly lay. There is a note in the Archbishop's memoranda, on Downing Street paper, in which their ecclesiastical colours are pencilled in red crayon by a layman's hand against each of the first ten names finally selected—Archbishop of Canterbury (general), Bishop of Oxford (High), Sir F. H. Jeune (Low), Sir L. Dibdin (Low), Dr. Gibson (High), Mr. Drury (Low), J. G. Talbot (High), Sir John Kennaway (Low), Sir Samuel Hoare (Low), Mr. G. Harwood (Low), Mr. George Prothero (Broad). In addition to Hicks Beach (who described himself as of opposite views to the Bishop of Oxford) the following three complete the number—the Marquess of Northampton, Sir Edward Clarke, and (on the death of Sir Francis Jeune, Lord St. Helier) Lord Alverstone, Lord Chief Justice of England. The Commission was undoubtedly strong, and it took immense pains. Its reference was as follows:

> To inquire into the alleged prevalence of breaches or neglect of the Law relating to the conduct of Divine Service in the Church of England and to the ornaments and fittings of Churches; and to consider the existing powers and procedure applicable to such irregularities and to make such recommendations as may be deemed requisite for dealing with the aforesaid matters.

The first of 118 meetings was held in the Church House, Westminster, May 4, 1904. Its inquiry lasted two years, and in its course received an immense amount of evidence from the different parties in the Church, as well as from scholars and experts. The Archbishop sat throughout on the Chairman's right, and the old Lord Northampton on his left, the Archbishop taking an active part in the examination of the witnesses.

The space at our disposal will only allow us to refer to the evidence given before the Commission by the Archbishop himself—with a brief reference to certain important points which emerged from that tendered by one or two other of the 164 witnesses. The Archbishop's evidence, on February 2 and 3, 1905, was a masterly review of the history of the modern ritualist movement in three periods: (1) 1840–66, (2) 1866–92, (3) 1892–1905. That it should be historical was characteristic of Davidson; and that it should be prepared with the aid of most laborious research, and of many willing helpers at Lambeth, the British Museum, and elsewhere, was equally to be expected. He had, of course, had special opportunities, partly through his work as biographer of Archbishop Tait, of amassing the information. And beyond doubt he had every justification for his claim that the evidence he gave was not 'accessible in a consecutive or coherent form in any existing book or series of published documents'.

He began by emphasizing the fact that 'from the days at least of Queen Elizabeth to our own, notwithstanding very definite rubrics and stern Acts of Uniformity and searching Episcopal injunctions... wide varieties [prevailed] in the mode of conducting Divine service', and added: 'I put it that there has never, I think, been any period in the Church of England, when what is called uniformity had not to be interpreted by a very wide elasticity.' He then gave some etymological details (carefully garnered by Mr. G. K. Fortescue of the British Museum), showing that the word 'ritualist' was not known in English till the reign of Queen Anne, the first dictionary to mention it being the *General English Dictionary* of John Kersey in 1708, thus: 'Ritualist—one that stickles for rituals or ceremonies in religious worship.' His knowledge of the Tractarian writers was displayed by substantial quotations from the writings especially of John Keble and Dr. Pusey. He always had a special reverence for John Keble, in relation to modern ritual developments which in Davidson's judgement, and evidence, formed no part of 'the original Tractarian movement'. And he pointed out here, as often on other occasions, how Keble 'never himself adopted vestments or other ritual usages of the kind. He continued to deprecate the practice of non-communicating attendance, and he strongly disapproved of any insistence upon a rule of fasting reception. On the other hand, he was, on large principles, in favour of all that gave increased dignity to, and implied a deeper reverence for, the Holy Communion.'[1]

[1] Royal Commission on Ecclesiastical Discipline, Minutes of Evidence, 12852.

In dealing with the first of the three modern periods, 1840–66, the Archbishop began by giving some striking illustrations from Newman, Pusey, and Keble of the underlying truth in Dean Stanley's frequent declaration 'that the real author of the Oxford Movement was Sir Walter Scott'—Davidson's own favourite novelist. He traced the growth of the use of vestments, introduced in St. George's-in-the-East in 1858, though apparently used in St. Thomas's, Oxford, in the forties—and a few other practices, such as the eastward position. But more particularly he dwelt on the attitude of the Bishops to the new ritual practices as discouraging rather than denouncing as illegal; and upon the stimulus given to ritual usages by the judgement in favour of High Churchmen pronounced by the Privy Council in the case of the first lawsuit, *Westerton* v. *Liddell*, 1857, authorizing the cross on the screen, and the cross behind the Holy Table, the use of the credence table, and coloured frontals. He ended his survey of the first period by quoting a remarkable passage from a charge of Bishop Thirlwall of St. David's, in October 1866, to show the rapidity of the advance between 1854 and 1866:

> . . . this ritual movement has by no means reached its term. It is still in the full vigour of its early years. It appears to be advancing both extensively, in the work of proselytism, and intensively, in doctrinal innovation, not always distinctly enunciated but clearly intimated. Its partizans seem to vie with one another in the introduction of more and more startling novelties, both of theory and practice. The adoration of the consecrated wafer, reserved for that purpose, which is one of the most characteristic Roman rites, and a legitimate consequence of the Romish Eucharistic doctrine, is contemplated, if it has not been already adopted, in some of our churches, and the Romish festival of the *Corpus Christi* instituted for the more conspicuous exercise of that adoration has, it appears, actually begun to be observed by clergymen of our church. Already public honours are paid to the Virgin Mary, and language applied to her which can only be considered as marking the first stage of a development to which no limit short of the full Romish worship can be probably assigned.[1]

The second period, 1866–92, was a period of increasing strife. Organization of church parties for contentious purposes was now for the first time fairly complete. The English Church Union (High Church) had been founded in 1860, and the

[1] Royal Commission on Ecclesiastical Discipline, Minutes of Evidence, 12885.

Church Association (Low Church) came five years later. The Archbishop, in tracing the course of the contentions, gave a very full account of such non-official action as deputations, meetings, opinion of counsel, as well as the official action taken in Convocation by Letters of Business, the appointment of the Ritual Commission, and agitation in Parliament, notably by Lord Shaftesbury. It was, however, the action of the Courts which produced crisis after crisis—and the results of the various judgements indicate alike the growth of ritualism and the strength of the agitators. In the *Martin* v. *Mackonochie* case, 1867–8, 'elevation, genuflection, altar candles, incense . . . the ceremonial mixing of the chalice' were all declared illegal, the latter two by the Court of Arches, the three former, on appeal, by the Privy Council. This decision in a court of law (said the Archbishop) was 'a very marked set back' to the ritualistic side. But more momentous was the case of *Hebbert* v. *Purchas* (1869–71). The decision of the Judicial Committee of the Privy Council, here also on appeal, declaring the eastward position and the vestments also illegal, created consternation. The protests were expressed in various ways. But the Archbishop noted, as more important than protests:

> It is from that time that we have to date the main growth of the objection alleged against the qualifications or authority of the Judicial Committee as the Court of Appeal.[1]

Three years later followed 'the stormiest year of all, 1874, the year of the so-called Public Worship Regulation Act'. This Act dealt with ritual questions, and, to put the matter very summarily, (1) added a new Court to those already in existence, by the creation of a new lay Ecclesiastical Judge; (2) directed that a monition should take the place of a penalty in the first instance, followed by suspension or deprivation in case of contumacy and, when there was contempt of court, allowing the possibility (quite unintended by those who framed the Act) of imprisonment; and (3) allowed the Bishop at his discretion to veto any prosecution. The Act was denounced by the Clergy in Convocation and outside, some antagonists going so far as to describe it as the introduction of Seven and twenty Star Chambers into the Church of England! The first case under the Act was the *Ridsdale* case, in which on appeal the Judicial Committee of the Privy Council,

[1] *Report,* Minutes of Evidence, 12918.

May 1877, condemned vestments as illegal, but legalized the eastward position. The Archbishop went on to deal with the imprisonment of four clergy who, between 1878 and 1881, were thrown into prison, as being 'never contemplated' when Parliament passed the Public Worship Regulation Act—and he added:

> It is impossible in my judgment to exaggerate the importance of those imprisonments. I believe that they did more than any single thing that has occurred in the ritual controversy to change public opinion upon the whole question of litigation of this sort; it may have been changed for good or evil, but that the change was largely due to those imprisonments I personally have no doubt.[1]

The Archbishop then went on to describe the move made by Archbishop Tait, at the end of his primacy, to secure a reform of ecclesiastical courts—leading up to the Royal Commission of 1881–3. He ended the survey of this second period by describing the *Bishop of Lincoln's* case,[2] and the judgement of Archbishop Benson, confirmed by the Privy Council in 1892—an epoch-making judgement in the Archbishop's Court, already described earlier in this book. It declared, in Dr. Davidson's words, 'that the chalice, if not ceremonially mixed, may be used with wine and water; that the Eastward position is legal throughout the service; that the *Agnus Dei* may, like other hymns, be sung; that the ablutions, as lying outside the service, and being a mode of complying with the rubric, are not illegal or wrong; that two lights are legal if the lighting of them is not made a ceremony; and that the signing of the Cross in Absolution and Benediction is illegal and must not be done.'[3]

The Archbishop then turned to the third period (1892–1905), and said that during these years there had been 'no great ritual incident, with possibly two exceptions', but 'a consolidation' of High Churchmen in certain directions, which he described as (1) 'a more solid and deliberate disallowance or distrust of the Privy Council as the ultimate court in ritual matters', and (2) the basing of the ritual advance 'on principle rather than on the usages, sometimes eccentric, of individuals'. He added two other points, of which (3) is of special importance:

> I personally attach great importance to the growth and consolidation in recent years of the opinion respecting the obligatory

[1] *Report*, Minutes of Evidence, 12943.

[2] See ch. vi *supra*.

[3] *Report*, Minutes of Evidence, 12944.

> character of what is called the rule of fasting reception of Holy Communion. . . . It is undoubtedly, I think, due to the growth of that opinion, that many of the difficulties connected both with Reservation and with high Celebrations without communicants, are really to be ascribed.[1]

The last point (4), to which the Archbishop called attention as illustrating the consolidation of High Churchmen, was the introduction of special services, 'in many cases most undesirable', without authority. And he gave as an instance the service of the Veneration of the Cross on Good Friday in 1898 in a London church, which Mr. Kensit interrupted, adding that 'the excitement within the Church generally, about unauthorized and inadmissible Services dates largely, I think, from that incident'. The Archbishop then gave a full account of the Lambeth Hearings by the two Archbishops on Incense, Processional Lights (1899), and Reservation (1900)—a step in which he himself, as he said, had some responsibility, for, he said:

> I believe I am right in saying that the matter began by a private letter from Archbishop Temple to myself, in December, 1898, in which he stated that this idea had occurred to him, and asked my advice about it. I recognised what seemed to me the wisdom of his suggestion, and respectfully urged him to go forward with the plan.[2]

He noted that the Opinion given on each occasion had been against the legality of these practices.

The Archbishop concluded his evidence by referring to certain matters of special importance. One dealt with the growth and character of the distrust of the Judicial Committee of the Privy Council as the Court of Appeal. With regard to the Privy Council, Davidson expressed his own regret that legislation had not been introduced to give effect to the Recommendation of the Royal Commission on Ecclesiastical Courts for a new final court. Of outstanding interest, however, is the summary of the peculiar difficulties of Bishops throughout the three periods. Dr. Davidson said that the answer to the question why the Bishops did not initiate prosecutions against offenders themselves was simply this:

> that after the incidents of the imprisonments which took place between the years 1876 and 1881, public opinion went right round upon the subject of the legal prosecution of ritualists.[3]

[1] *Report*, Minutes of Evidence, 12947. [2] Ibid., 12951. [3] Ibid., 12961.

And he gave abundant references from the *Record* and elsewhere to prove his point. With regard to the similar question—why the Bishops did not deal with the whole matter on wise legislative lines in Parliament and in Convocation—he stated:

> The simple answer is: Lord Shaftesbury. He was in my opinion one of the greatest and best of modern Englishmen. . . . But none the less it is true to say that what he did, with the best possible intention, contributed as a matter of fact to increase the difficulties, just as the riots in quite a different way had increased the difficulties ten years before. . . . When he endeavoured year after year to get a short and Summary Act, which should say 'All vestments are illegal except' so and so, carried through Parliament without consulting Convocation and whether the Bishops liked it or not . . . he hampered the administrative authorities in their endeavour to deal with the matter at that particular juncture.[1]

It was again a similar vehement antagonism which had a similar result in the latest period surveyed:

> Twenty years later in the last stage of our experience, when, in a position of extraordinary complexity and difficulty, Bishop Creighton and others, including to some extent Archbishop Temple himself, were trying to deal with these subjects, the incursion of Mr. Kensit and the letters of Sir William Harcourt rendered practically impossible the kind of line that the Bishops were trying to take.[2]

In the following week (February 10, 1905) the Archbishop appeared as witness again, and the whole of one day was occupied with a statement of his own personal experience as a diocesan Bishop, especially in the diocese of Winchester, in dealing with ritual difficulties. Here he went over ground already covered in an earlier part of this work, going into the case of Father Dolling, his own Charge of 1899 (at considerable length), and other matters. Incidentally he also called special attention to the terms of the new Declaration of Assent enacted by Parliament in the Clerical Subscription Act of 1865, in which the final words are: 'In public prayer and administration of the Sacraments I will use the form in the said Book [Book of Common Prayer] prescribed and none other, except so far as shall be ordered by lawful authority.' And it is worth noting a point on which the Archbishop was accustomed to lay some stress, about the intro-

[1] *Report*, Minutes of Evidence, 12962. [2] Ibid., 12962.

duction for the first time in 1865 of the words 'except so far as shall be ordered by lawful authority'. He said that, in the debates on the subject:

> The reason given for its insertion was chiefly to protect a clergyman in the case of a Service ordered by the Privy Council; such, for example, as was ordered at that time in connexion with the cattle plague. But that the words as they stand now, part of the Act of Parliament, are capable of giving to the Episcopate some larger authority than existed before, seems to me hardly to admit of a doubt.[1]

The Archbishop gave evidence on one further occasion, July 13, 1905, on the special point of the composition and possible powers of a Representative Church Council, and the steps being taken to secure a reform of Convocation.

Seventeen English diocesan Bishops, besides the Archbishop of Canterbury, gave their evidence—so that the Commission had every opportunity for hearing a first-hand account of the administrators' difficulties, as well as of the services of which complaint had been made. The fullness and variety of the evidence did not make the drafting of the Report an easier task. Sir Michael Hicks Beach had only consented to take the chair on the condition that he should not be draftsman; and the work fell to the able hands of Sir Lewis Dibdin. When the first draft was completed, Sir Lewis gave it to the Archbishop and the Bishop of Oxford. It was, of course, altered very considerably at the discussions of the Commission: as the author prophesied at the start, 'They'll knock this about a good deal, I'm afraid.' But its principles and structure remained unimpaired. What the Bishop of Oxford said, in reply to Sir Lewis's complaint, was true enough: 'If you've ever tried to skin a hare you'll find it is uncommonly difficult to get the backbone out of it.' The Bishop of Oxford had a very great deal to do with the phrasing of the Report, and the Archbishop himself depended upon him very much for the wording as for other things. At times the Bishop's scholarly style seemed involved to the laymen—and on one occasion the Chairman asked what a particular sentence meant. When he was told, he said with some heat, 'Then, why the devil can't they express it properly?' The unparliamentary remark shocked the old

[1] Ibid., 13230.

evangelical peer, Lord Northampton, on the Chairman's left hand, profoundly. He became red, and looked much upset. The Archbishop cocked his head and looked up to the cornice, as he often would on embarrassing occasions; and the incident passed. The Report[1] was a masterly statement of the actual legal situation —of the contemporary breaches and neglect of the law—emphasizing the omission to fulfil Prayer Book requirements as well as the breaches of special gravity and significance, the principal of which it enumerated as follows:

Practices of special gravity and significance

The interpolation of the prayers and ceremonies belonging to the Canon of the Mass.

The use of the words 'Behold the Lamb of God', accompanied by the exhibition of a consecrated wafer or bread.

Reservation of the Sacrament under conditions which lead to its adoration.

Mass of the Prae-sanctified.

Corpus Christi processions with the Sacrament.

Benediction with the Sacrament.

Celebration of the Holy Eucharist with the intent that there shall be no communicant except the celebrant.

Hymns, prayers, and devotions involving invocation of or confession to the Blessed Virgin Mary or the Saints.

The observance of the festivals of the Assumption of the Blessed Virgin Mary, and of the Sacred Heart.

The veneration of images and roods [2]

There was a historical survey, which dealt with the causes of failures to check irregularities, amongst which it was noted that:

> The inclination, characteristic of the temper of the sixteenth century, to ignore all varieties of feeling and opinion existing among men of the same generation, and to make no provision for changes of feeling and opinion as one age succeeded another, is one far-reaching cause of irregularity. . . . It has proved impracticable to obtain complete obedience to the Acts of Uniformity in one particular direction, partly because it is not now, and never has been, demanded in other directions.

The Report also went fully into the question of a reform of the

[1] *Signed* June 21, 1906, Cd. 3040, 1906.

[2] *Report*, § 397.

Ecclesiastical Courts. Of the Judicial Committee of the Privy Council, the Report observed:

Bishops and others have been naturally slow to appeal to a court the jurisdiction of which was so widely challenged; clergymen have claimed the liberty, and even asserted the duty, of disobedience to the decisions of a tribunal the authority of which they repudiate; and judgements of the Judicial Committee, though at least the reasoned statements of very eminent judges, are treated as valueless because they are Privy Council judgements. A Court dealing with matters of conscience and religion must, above all others, rest on moral authority if its judgements are to be effective. As thousands of clergy, with strong lay support, refuse to recognise the jurisdiction of the Judicial Committee, its judgements cannot practically be enforced.[1]

The 'two main Conclusions' to which the Commission was led were as follows:

First, the law of public worship in the Church of England is too narrow for the religious life of the present generation. It needlessly condemns much which a great section of Church people, including many of her most devoted members, value; and modern thought and feeling are characterised by a care for ceremonial, a sense of dignity in worship, and an appreciation of the continuity of the Church, which were not similarly felt at the time when the law took its present shape. In an age which has witnessed an extraordinary revival of spiritual life and activity, the Church has had to work under regulations fitted for a different condition of things, without that power of self-adjustment which is inherent in the conception of a living Church, and is, as a matter of fact, possessed by the Established Church of Scotland. . . . With an adequate power of self-adjustment, we might reasonably expect that revision of the strict letter of the law would be undertaken with such due regard for the living mind of the Church as would secure the obedience of many, now dissatisfied, who desire to be loyal, and would justify the Church as a whole in insisting on the obedience of all.[2]

Secondly, the machinery for discipline has broken down. The means of enforcing the law in the Ecclesiastical Courts, even in matters which touch the Church's faith and teaching, are defective and in some respects unsuitable. . . .[3]

The Report added:

It is important that the law should be reformed, that it should admit of reasonable elasticity, and that the means of enforcing it

[1] Ibid., § 363. [2] Ibid., § 399. [3] Ibid., § 400.

should be improved; but above all it is necessary that it should be obeyed.[1]

While the Report was, in the main, the work of Sir Lewis Dibdin, the principal Recommendations were of Dr. Davidson's shaping. They were ten. The first asked that certain specific practices (those named above as practices of special gravity and significance) 'should be promptly made to cease by the exercise of the authority belonging to the Bishops and, if necessary, by proceedings in the Ecclesiastical Courts'. The second—which was the fundamental Recommendation, and for which a very special responsibility rested with Archbishop Davidson—was that which set on foot the whole legislative process of Prayer Book Revision. It ran as follows:

2. Letters of Business should be issued to the Convocations with instructions: (*a*) to consider the preparation of a new rubric regulating the ornaments (that is to say, the vesture) of the ministers of the Church, at the times of their ministrations, with a view to its enactment by Parliament; and (*b*) to frame, with a view to their enactment by Parliament, such modifications in the existing law relating to the conduct of Divine Service and to the ornaments and fittings of churches as may tend to secure the greater elasticity which a reasonable recognition of the comprehensiveness of the Church of England and of its present needs seems to demand.

It would be most desirable for the early dealing with these important subjects that the Convocations should sit together, and we assume that they would take counsel with the Houses of Laymen.

The third Recommendation was also of considerable importance, though in the practical consideration of the series as a whole it would appear to have received too little attention:

3. In regard to the sanction to be given for the use of additional and special services, collects and hymns, the law should be so amended as to give wider scope for the exercise of a regulative authority.

This authority should be exercised within prescribed limits by the Archbishops and Bishops of both Provinces acting together for the sanction and regulation of additional and special services and collects in accordance with the teaching of the Holy Scriptures and the Book of Common Prayer, and for the forbidding of the use of hymns or anthems not in accordance with such teaching.

[1] Ibid., § 401.

The administrative discretion of individual Bishops within the several dioceses should be used in conformity with such sanction and regulation.

Other Recommendations proposed new Ecclesiastical Courts and a new Court of Final Appeal, as proposed by the Royal Commission of 1883, with the following difference:

5. . . . Where, in an appeal before the Final Court which involves charges of heresy or breach of ritual, any question touching the doctrine or use of the Church of England shall be in controversy, which question is not in the opinion of the Court governed by the plain language of documents having the force of Acts of Parliament, and involves the doctrine or use of the Church of England proper to be applied to the facts found by the Court, such question shall be referred to an assembly of the Archbishops and Bishops of both Provinces, who shall be entitled to call in such advice as they may think fit; and the opinion of the majority of such assembly of the Archbishops and Bishops with regard to any question so submitted to them shall be binding on the Court for the purposes of the said appeal.

The remaining Recommendations included the repeal of the Public Worship Regulation Act, the abolition of the Bishops' veto (subject to safeguards), and certain other disciplinary and administrative measures. It must also be noted that the Commission declared that 'those of our recommendations which will require legislation are framed as a complete scheme and must be considered mutually dependent'.

The Report was unanimous; even Sir Edward Clarke, who had been an uncertain quantity, appending his signature. On the last day the Chairman broke down with emotion, and brought the proceedings to an end by asking the Archbishop to give thanks to God, which he did with the following extempore prayer:

Almighty God, Who art the Author of Peace and Lover of Concord, we thank Thee that Thou hast given us health and strength for the task committed to us, and grace to work together in mutual trust, desiring to know Thy Truth, and to do justly. We pray Thee to pardon all that Thou hast seen to be amiss in us and in our work; and to grant that by Thy Blessing the outcome of our labours may be used for the welfare of Thy Church: that those who bear Thy Name may, without strife or discord, simply seek to advance in this land the purpose of Thy Love towards all men: through Jesus Christ our Lord. Amen.

CHAPTER XXVI

CHINESE LABOUR, 1904–6

We sail a changeful sea through halcyon days and storm
And when the ship laboureth, our stedfast purpose
Trembles like as the compass in a binnacle.
Our stability is but balance, and wisdom lies
In masterful administration of the unforeseen.

ROBERT BRIDGES, *Testament of Beauty.*

THIS chapter, like the last, though largely concerned with the second year of the Primacy, will take us a little farther forward, for the sake of completeness, before it is finished.

In the early part of 1904, the Archbishop became involved in a controversy which stirred public opinion all over the country and had far-reaching results. After the South African War the gold-mines in the Transvaal were greatly crippled for want of labour. Various expedients had been tried and had failed. In the end the choice lay between the introduction of unskilled White labour to take the place of the Kaffir, and the importation of Asiatics. Opinion in the Transvaal decided in favour of the latter, and in February 1904, with the backing of Lord Milner, the Governor-General, the Ordinance allowing the importation of Chinese under special conditions was finally passed.

The agitation against the whole plan of Chinese labour had already commenced in England. Letters appeared in *The Times* from Major J. E. B. Seely[1] and the Bishop of Worcester,[2] denouncing the unnatural and demoralizing conditions under which (it was said) the Chinese labourers were to be confined in large compounds. The Government was pressed on many sides to refuse its sanction to the Ordinance. An important debate took place in the House of Lords on February 11 and 12, at the instance of Lord Portsmouth and the Marquis of Ripon, who were opposed to the Government. The Archbishop spoke at the end of the first day. He had already made close inquiries of his own, and had had interviews and correspondence with those who had been out in South Africa. He began characteristically by emphasizing the complexity of the subject. Whatever might be said about the urgency of the problem, no one who had studied

[1] Now Lord Mottistone. [2] Dr. Gore.

the Blue Books could fail to realize the immense difficulty which surrounded it. He said he was not dealing with the economic or political aspects but simply with the moral aspect—a matter which had received little attention but 'lies at the root of the question before us'. He referred to the moral question which had arisen in connexion with the introduction of Chinese labour from 1852 to 1858 in the West Indies, Trinidad, British Guiana, and Mauritius, and the care taken with regard to the regulations. He did not think that the same careful consideration had been given on the present occasion, and he asked for more informaton, especially with regard to the possibility of wives and families accompanying or following the labourers:

> We want to know not necessarily in detail but in the roughest outline what the conditions are. We want to be assured that this system of indentured immigration will not be introducing a poison of a terrible kind into the community where the Chinese may be settled. If it is said that this poison cannot be introduced because of the restraints put upon the immigrants and that the evil cannot become rampant because the Chinamen will be deprived of all liberty of action or locomotion or intercourse with other people, such a line of defence strikes one as in itself difficult to justify. At all events it is certainly a form of administration a little difficult to reconcile with the liberties and freedom which should exist in a British Colony.

The speech made a deep impression, and Lord Carrington on the following day said, 'I think the whole of Christendom must thank him for having made the speech which he delivered last night'. But his words were received with very much less favour by the friends of the Government. He was still new to the office of Primate, and his critics commented on his assumption of the role of 'political *censor morum* when both prudence and fact should advise silence'. And his next intervention gave colour to the charge not only of imprudence but of trimming, 'not the trimming that Lord Halifax illustrated, the philosopher's repugnance to the violence of extremes, but the timid, hair-splitting type of trimming'.[1]

Three weeks later a further debate took place in the House of Lords on the question of how it was proposed to regulate the introduction of the wives and families of Chinese immigrants in

[1] *Memoirs* of Sir Almeric Fitzroy, i. 206.

the Transvaal. The Archbishop had, in the interval, pursued his inquiries, and was to some extent reassured by what he learned, notably perhaps by the receipt of a cable from Archdeacon Furse from Johannesburg (16 February), saying that he was 'personally fully convinced after discussion that Government and importers [were] entirely alive to moral and social dangers of non-importation of women'. The Archbishop was not (as Mr. Alfred Lyttelton, the Colonial Secretary, had suggested in the House of Commons) 'fully satisfied' with the assurances that he had received, but his natural honesty led him to admit that *if the proposed immigration was to take place at all* it did not seem to be clear what more the Government could have done on the moral question and all it involved. It was, however, the conclusion of this speech (on March 4, 1904) which provided his critics and the enemies of Chinese labour with the weapon which they were swift to use:

> I feel [he said] that if indeed the necessity be real it is one of the most regrettable necessities that has ever arisen in the history of our Colonial Government—that it should be found necessary under the British flag and under Christian civilisation to arrange for the importation of labour where conditions are laid down that the labourers imported shall not be permitted to utilise any exceptional powers they may have, or fulfil the desire to rise above the conditions of the merest drudges, doing the lowest kind of work whatever their qualifications for some higher kind of labour may be . . . Certainly, if it be a necessity, it is one which I personally feel to be of a very lamentable kind and one which is not without its elements of humiliation.

It was the Archbishop's fate on not a few occasions in his life to disappoint those who were hot on one side or other of the debate. He sought to be fair, and even though it caused serious misunderstanding and 'almost despair' on the part of Lord Carrington and others, who had acclaimed his former speech, he would not say less or more than he felt was warranted by the evidence. He certainly exposed himself to the reproach that he had gone back on his former condemnation. On March 12, 1904, the Government sanctioned the Ordinance.

A fresh debate took place in the House of Lords a few days later, March 21, 1904, and the Archbishop made a third speech, perhaps a little more favourable to Chinese labour, but expressing his own belief that had he been living in the Transvaal he would probably have been found in the small minority which objected to the introduction of Chinese labour. He spoke in strong disapproval of those who used lightly the word 'slavery'. He said he was still not easy as to the working of the safeguards about the moral question, but he admitted that when confronted with the fact that other men as high-minded and public-spirited as they could be, with the overwhelming advantage of detailed local knowledge, had found it impossible to do other than this, then in the end, with no small anxiety of heart, he could but leave the responsibility with those into whose hands the Government had entrusted it.

The first Chinese immigrants arrived in the Transvaal in June 1904. By the end of the year there were two thousand, and thousands more poured in during the first six months of 1905. The system was soon put to the test. A sharp attack was made on the Government by Lord Coleridge on May 16, 1905. He gave pointed expression to what was undoubtedly a growing feeling of anxiety as to the whole compound method, including the non-importation of women and the restrictions on the liberty of the Chinese. He made a particular appeal to the Archbishop to say whether official reports did not in fact show that the system had led to immorality. The Archbishop made a full speech in which he expressed himself satisfied with the information which he had been able to acquire from trustworthy sources as to the material comfort and voluntary enlistment of the Chinese. But he expressed his disquiet with regard to the moral conditions, and pressed again for fuller information thereon.

There is a good deal of correspondence in the files of these months, and especially in the latter part of 1905, which shows that the Archbishop's anxiety did not diminish, though he was most unwilling to embarrass those with whom the real responsibility, as well as, he would say, the fullest knowledge, lay; especially when they were men of the undoubted integrity and public spirit of Alfred Lyttelton, Lord Milner, and Lord Selborne, who went out to South Africa in February 1905 as Lord Milner's successor. But he was, as always, instinctively repelled by rhetoric, and by those who sought to make emotional or political capital out of a situation which seemed to him as a practical man beset with difficulties.

The correspondence and the newspapers and cartoons of the day also show that the Archbishop's attitude exposed him to a great deal of unfriendly criticism and attack. To many like Major Seely his attitude seemed 'half-hearted and disappointing'. The phrase 'regrettable necessity' proved a fatal phrase, and, torn from its context, was constantly brought up against him. To one of those who reproached him he replied thus:

9th October 1905.

I fear it is in vain for me to reiterate the facts of my attitude when the question of Chinese labour was before Parliament. It is absurdly and often maliciously travestied so as to make me appear to have said the very contrary to what I really did say, as anyone will ascertain who cares to read in their entirety the speeches which I made in the matter. My efforts have been consistently continued from the first to ensure if possible such arrangements as shall prevent the mischiefs which are apt to accompany indentured labour in all parts of our Empire. . . . You are of course aware how deliberately this particular controversy has been stimulated for political purposes and that the genuine and wholesome enthusiasm of working men and others for what is right and free and pure have been utilised for mere partisan ends.

There is no doubt that the Archbishop believed that he could help the cause he cared for most, that of religion and humanity, by the policy which he pursued, far better than by mere denunciation. Certainly his attitude was appreciated by the responsible authorities themselves, not the less because, as is shown by the following letter in answer to a question about desertions, the authorities understood the difficulties, and were perplexed to know where to find an alternative scheme:

The RT. HON. ALFRED LYTTELTON *to the* ARCHBISHOP OF CANTERBURY

Private. Colonial Office. October 29, 1905.

I arrived late yesterday. I am sincerely sorry not to have been able to write before. But the enclosed despatch which I will send in strict confidence for your personal use to-morrow will I think shew you into what an impossible position anyone must be led who advocates the veto of the Chinese Ordinances and is not prepared to embark on a crusade against all indentured labour throughout the empire. The subject does not become easier and two years' constant worry has not made the burdens of life very easy to carry. But I am consoled when I think of the extraordinary difficulties of any other course of action—above all the loss of life among the tropical natives which would I believe ensue if they replaced the tougher Chinese and which at least has been in part averted.

In December 1905 the Unionist Government resigned. A general election took place in January 1906, and there can be no doubt that Chinese labour as well as the tariff question played a vital part in the landslide which brought the Liberals (377) a clear majority of 84 over Unionists (157), Labour (53), and Irish (83).

In the autumn of 1906, sinister reports were heard with regard to most of the Chinese compounds. An official inquiry revealed a situation justifying all but the gloomiest warnings as to the perils of the compound system. The Archbishop of Canterbury called attention to the subject on November 15 in the House of Lords. He said:

> I hope at last we are in a position to get some trustworthy information upon a matter so grave, not merely in its direct and immediate effect upon the surroundings in which the mischief takes place, but also in its possible indirect effects upon other populations than those of the Chinamen, a very terrible effect which would tarnish the honour and good name not only of England but of her Colonies.

Lord Coleridge, in following, regretted that he and his friends had not been openly supported by the Archbishop in the controversy waged against the Ordinance for the last two years, and that the Archbishop had not spoken out in bold, clear, and unqualified terms of denunciation in regard to this traffic. He said, and, it must be confessed, not without justification:

> I believe that such is the recognised weight which the most reverend Primate deservedly holds in the councils of the country that if he had spoken the right word and spoken it in time the Chinese would never have been imported and these evils would never have arisen.

Lord Elgin, for the Government, whilst declaring that the grossest charges had not been substantiated, thought that the official report 'does in my judgment strengthen the view that the permanent adoption of this system is not possible, and perhaps we are justified in calling upon the most reverend Primate and those who think with him to join us in that declaration'.

These revelations, following upon the strong opposition now developing both in South Africa and England, settled the fate of Chinese labour. The system was doomed. In June 1907, General Botha as Prime Minister told the Transvaal Assembly that the Labour Ordinance would not be re-enacted, and that the Chinese would be sent home at the expiry of their contracts.

CHAPTER XXVII

FOREIGN, SOCIAL, AND CHURCH QUESTIONS

To sequester out of the world into *Atlantick* and *Eutopian* politics, which never can be drawn into use, will not mend our condition; but to ordain wisely as in this world of evil, in the midst whereof God hath placed us unavoidably. MILTON, *Areopagitica.*

THROUGHOUT his long life, as a Churchman intimately concerned with public affairs, it was Dr. Davidson's destiny to watch the development of Russian history from various angles. At the beginning of 1905, he was called upon to express his mind about Russia at war, and Russia threatened with revolution; and before the year ended it was his lot to address words of appeal to the Russian Church, begging that its influence might be powerfully used against a terrible persecution of the Jews.

I

On January 1, the fall of Port Arthur before the military and naval forces of Japan, marked a new stage in the tragic Russo-Japanese war of which the reactions were to be so far-reaching. At once the Archbishop wrote to the Prime Minister to see if any way could be found to bring the conflict to an end by mediation:

The ARCHBISHOP OF CANTERBURY *to the* RIGHT HON. A. J. BALFOUR

Old Palace, Canterbury.
3 Jan. 1905.

I venture to write to you with reference to the new position created by the surrender of Port Arthur. I am not a diplomatist and my knowledge about what is happening and about its possible consequences is no greater than that of other observers living outside the circle of special information. But I am naturally the recipient and the mouth-piece of a large body of opinion—the opinion of thousands of thoughtful and religious men, Churchmen and Nonconformists—the intensity of whose feeling of horror evoked by the carnage of this war it is impossible to exaggerate. I am quite certain that I express the opinion of an unlimited number of such persons when I say that they would hail with profound satisfaction any action which might be taken by the responsible Executive of our Country, to promote at this juncture some plan or offer of mediation, should such be possible. Those who know the international facts in a way that I of course do not may have reason to believe that such action on the part of England would at this moment be harmful or inexpedient. I recognise so fully the responsibility and the difficulty of situations such as this that I am prepared to bow to the deliberate judgment of yourself and your colleagues, well knowing that your anxious desire to bring this fearful war to an end is as keen as that of any of us..

But I should not be doing justice to those whose representations and appeals to me have been, as I think you know, both frequent and urgent, or to my own sentiments and anxieties did I not at this moment assure you that to the best of my belief the whole country would be with you or behind you if you found it possible to let England now take some overt step in the direction of bringing about the restoration of peace. Details are entirely beyond my province. But that the English people, irrespective of political party or religious creed, would welcome some such action I have no doubt whatever.

But the time was not yet. Attempts at intervention, wrote the Prime Minister in reply on January 6, were:

likely to be not only useless but worse than useless, unless and until the combatants are willing to take advantage of it. Of such a willingness we have not received from either party the faintest suggestion up to the present moment. Indeed, the only communication which has so far reached His Majesty's Government on the subject is a warning from the Government of Russia that no intervention by a neutral Power would be tolerated by them.

Later in the same month a revolutionary movement began, and January 22 was known as 'Bloody Sunday' in St. Petersburg. Although the Archbishop took no action then, the reasons which he gave for taking none are significant not only of his attitude on the point at issue but also of the volume of his work. An indignant correspondent who set himself 'the task of securing as fast as one might united prayer throughout Great Britain and America', in view of the crisis, had rushed to Lambeth and there, he thought, been received with little sympathy by a resident chaplain. This is the Archbishop's letter:

Windsor Castle.
Private. 24 Jan. 1905.

I have today received your letter and I should like to thank you myself for having written to me frankly about your recent interview with my Chaplain at Lambeth. I must not perhaps expect you quite to appreciate the impossibility of the Archbishop—if he is to do his work properly—giving immediate interviews to those who may unexpectedly call upon him with reference even to very important matters. I have known the Lambeth work now for some 28 years and I am very certain that if it is to be rightly done the Archbishop must arrange beforehand as to those whom he is to see personally in the busy round of each day's work. I write to you about it because I appreciate with keen sympathy and fellowship your desire that when it is possible we should make our prayers more keen and united in regard to the world's life and the life of nations. You may be assured how steadily and constantly I have tried to keep in touch with those at home and abroad who can best inform me on events such as those now occurring in the distracted Russian Empire, and how gladly I have taken and do take opportunity from time to time of stimulating such united prayer as you suggest. But it is another thing to say that the Archbishop should be ready at a moment's notice to put forth a request or direction (to be telegraphed as you suggest throughout the world that very hour) when he knows how liable such directions or requests are to be misinterpreted and twisted (in countries unlike our own) into a political manifesto which may do harm instead of good and hamper those who have the responsibility of delicate and anxious diplomatic representations. Day by day in these anxious times am I trying by the help of God, for whose guidance I pray, to do and say both privately and publicly what may be helpful and right. But you probably do not at all realise how requests pour in every week that the Archbishop will direct public and general prayer for some great cause or perplexity, and how these things are distorted into political and partisan channels. In the last few weeks I have been bombarded as usual with such requests—say in connection with the Japanese War, or Macedonia, or Armenia, or Chinese Labour, or Welsh Education, or the Revival Movement, or many more. Hence my caution as to issuing fresh requests—suddenly and without consultation—at a delicate and critical juncture—in addition or supplement to the requests and directions which I have already given. You will probably not realise the difficulties, but they are there all the same. I should prefer to say nothing about your insinuation that I was simply careless, and that you were put off with trivial excuses. You even suggest that because a gong sounded while you were in the house I must have been at luncheon!! and therefore did not see you!! As a matter of fact I was not. I had been at work on all kinds of important matters for many hours (8.30–1.30) and from 2.–4.30

I had another series of big duties, many of them with reference to the very sort of questions on which you supposed me to be careless, and at 4.30 I had to leave London. When you called therefore I was obliged to follow my rule and to ask Mr. Holden to see you and talk over the matter, whatever it might be. It seems to offend you that he did so, but I am always anxious that no one should leave the house without receiving all possible courtesy.

I have written all this on receiving your letter because I share so fully your eager desire that in such matters we all of us should join more than we do in constant prayer to Him who heareth prayer, and because you seem to have so strangely misunderstood my way of looking at these momentous questions.

I need hardly point out to you that this letter is altogether private. No one but myself has seen it.

P.S. I did not understand that you expected, after what had passed, to receive a letter from me. But if you did expect one I am sorry it was not sent.

In November a new calamity descended on the Russian Empire in a terrible onslaught upon the Jews. Immediately we find the Archbishop in communication with the Chief Rabbi, expressing his profound sympathy; and by telegram and letter also with the Metropolitan Anthony of St. Petersburg, whom he knew personally, having met him when he visited England. The letters were published at the time:

The ARCHBISHOP OF CANTERBURY *to the* METROPOLITAN OF ST. PETERSBURG

Lambeth Palace, S.E. 10th November, 1905.

Moved to the deepest distress in common with all who at this time have before them the accounts of what is happening in Russia, I have today sent to Your Holiness a telegram to express our eager hope that while the beneficent reforms, now happily inaugurated, are being carried into effect, there may, by the mercy of GOD, be no further scenes of so fearful a kind as those which must be causing to Your Holiness, and to thoughtful Christian men in Russia, the same sorrow as they have brought to us all.

The whole English Church would be eager, in the Name of our blessed Lord and Saviour to participate in such endeavour as Christian men can properly make to render for ever impossible hereafter in any part of the world the horrors which have lately occurred.

I do not doubt that Your Holiness, whose knowledge of England

and of English thought is so highly appreciated by us all, will realise my motive in thus writing to you an assurance of our desire to co-operate in any such task.

It is as Christians that we long for common endeavour against the unChristian spirit wherever it may be found or whoever be its victims. We pray GOD that the great Church in which Your Holiness holds so exalted a position may be guided by GOD the Holy Spirit, in days of difficulty, to stand firm on behalf of the suffering and the oppressed, and to promote in every way what is Christ-like and pure and true.

The Metropolitan replied within a week, thanking the Anglican Church for its prayers and sympathy, and adding:

The METROPOLITAN OF ST. PETERSBURG *to the* ARCHBISHOP OF CANTERBURY

14th November 1905.

Your Christian sympathy with the sorrows of our Fatherland has filled my heart with deep gratitude to you. We hope in the Lord that by His grace the State reforms which have now been inspired and begun will bring into our common life the spirit of peace and love; and we believe that by the power of the Holy Ghost and the prayers of the Church the Christian brotherly love in the hearts of our countrymen will be strengthened.

The Russian Church mourns over her children, in whom civil strife has darkened the commandment of Christ regarding love and goodwill towards our neighbours, whoever they may be, whether our fellow-believers or Hebrews of another religion, all violence against whom it has always condemned, and condemns with unalterable steadfastness, as opposed to law, piety, and the duties of civil life.

In his letter to the Chief Rabbi (Dr. Adler)—published in the press—the Archbishop said:

The ARCHBISHOP OF CANTERBURY *to the* CHIEF RABBI

November 13, 1905.

We had hoped that iniquities of this particular kind were now becoming impossible in any Christian lands, although I suppose that the records of former centuries show no country to have been free from the stain of such cruelty; and that recollection ought in my judgement to temper our indignation with humility. I am persuaded that we may now rely upon Christian earnestness and fellowship in different lands to protect Christendom from the recurrence of a like disgrace. But we cannot omit, while looking prayerfully to the future, to put on record also our abhorrence of the blind and cruel spirit which has led excited mobs to such acts of outrage, and our profound sympathy with the sufferers and victims, whatever their nationality or their creed.

The Chief Rabbi replied:

The CHIEF RABBI *to the* ARCHBISHOP OF CANTERBURY

22 Finsbury Square, London.
November 14th, 1905.

I beg to thank your Grace sincerely for your favour of the 13th inst. It greatly adds to the kindness you have already shown us in these dark days of stress and sorrow. This championship of true religion and humanity cannot fail to produce a deep impression throughout the civilized world.

Utterances such as these will, I hope, prevent a recurrence of the tragedy we all deplore, and hasten the realization of our hopes for the day when everywhere equal rights and equal justice will be dealt to all God's children as a common heritage of humanity without distinction of race and creed.[1]

II

Church questions at home were also, throughout this year, very much to the fore, and a background to the whole was provided by the Royal Commission on Ecclesiastical Discipline, the regular sittings of which, week in and week out, aroused an interest and an anxiety both tense and widespread. In February a strong deputation visited Lambeth Palace, headed by Dr. Wace, Dean of Canterbury, one of the staunchest of Protestants, who yet believed that peace could be won in the Church if every one would agree to the following principle:

That nothing can be accepted as truly Catholic which cannot claim the general assent and observance of the Christian Church before the end of the 6th Century.

The Archbishop, in replying, noted that the Dean was supported by scholars and clergy of all the great schools of thought in the Church of England (amongst them Professor W. Sanday and the Rev. T. A. Lacey)[2]; and, assuring them of his warm sympathy,

[1] *The Jewish World* for November 17, 1905, comments thus: 'The action of Dr. Randall Davidson at this crisis has shown that he knows his duty to the teachings of the great Church of which he is head. All the same, the spontaneous step was his own, prompted by the heart, and will not be forgotten by the Jewish people.'

[2] Dr. Wace, Evangelical; Dr. Sanday, Liberal; Mr. Lacey, Anglo-Catholic.

advised them to set their case in a deliberate way before the Royal Commission itself. He added, with special reference to the Royal Commission, in a characteristic spirit, of the office he himself held:

> It is at all times necessary for one who occupies the position to which in the providence of God I have been called, to be on his guard, and not to speak, on occasions such as this, incautiously or inconsiderately. But at present, at this moment, that responsibility rests upon me in an even exceptional degree.

But even though he did not commit himself on this or similar occasions, the Archbishop gave the impression of complete accessibility, and as *The Times* remarked, when commenting on the frequent pilgrimages to Lambeth Palace in these early days of the Primacy, the chief reason for these constant deputations was that 'people have confidence in Dr. Davidson's judgement and experience'.

There was a good deal of correspondence during these months about Church constitutional questions, such as the character of the Representative Church Council, and the basis of the franchise for lay electors, but progress was slow. On July 14, a debate took place in the House of Lords on the Convocation Bill, introduced afresh by the Archbishop. It was designed to declare the law as to the power of the Convocations to reform their Lower Houses, and to enable them on occasion to hold joint sittings. But to Dr. Davidson's surprise as well as chagrin, the debate was adjourned, and the Bill was eventually allowed to perish. The discussions on the Athanasian Creed, in and outside Convocation, were continued from the previous year. In February the Archbishop explained to the Upper House the steps he had taken to discover the opinions of other Provinces of the Anglican Communion, and gave ample evidence of the strength of opinion both for and against any change. But a final judgement was, by consent, deferred until after the Lambeth Conference of 1908.

III

On May 9, the Archbishop made an important speech in the House of Lords, calling attention to the treatment of the aborigines in Western Australia. It was one of many speeches made during his Primacy on behalf of native races. It was, as usual, based on a very careful inquiry, and with chapter and verse, quoted from official documents; and also, as usual, expressed in a courteous and unsensational way, but with most damaging facts. Employment was usually given to the native (he said) in order to secure control rather than for the sake of the work. There were no wages, and there were usually no indentures. The speech was lengthy and impressive. The Archbishop fully recognized that Australia was a self-governing Colony in which the British Government had no direct right to intervene; but he felt justified in pressing the Colonial Secretary, Mr. Alfred Lyttelton, for the sake of the credit of the whole empire, to take steps to reassure public opinion. Lord Tennyson, who had been Governor-General of Australia, followed the Archbishop in the debate, and the attached letter shows something of the impression the Archbishop's speech had made:

LORD TENNYSON *to the* ARCHBISHOP OF CANTERBURY

May 10, 1905.

. . . I would have thanked you in my few words last night—but I thought that it would appear patronizing in me. But I do thank you most sincerely for your most able, clear and above all kindly statement. It was as good as it could be. . . .

Unemployment assumed serious proportions this year, and in June a march of 450 unemployed workmen from Leicester to London was led by a Leicester incumbent, the Rev. F. Lewis Donaldson. A letter was sent to the Archbishop by Mr. Donaldson asking very respectfully that his Grace would receive a small deputation from these men at Lambeth, and adding: 'They feel keenly the immense importance of the Church sealing their cause as in itself sacred and noble, viz. their appeal to England for work.'

The Archbishop, who had an instinctive dislike of propaganda and sensation, and was, besides, intensely practical, did not see what good he could do by receiving a deputation, and did not at all wish Lambeth to be made the scene of a great demonstration. He replied as follows:

The ARCHBISHOP OF CANTERBURY *to the* REV. F. L. DONALDSON

Lambeth Palace. June 8, 1905.

I have today received your letter of yesterday. I yield to no one in my appreciation of the difficulties of present industrial conditions in many parts of England, and I have from early days done my best to understand the practical questions which have from time to time arisen. But such study as I am able to give to these questions tends to deepen my sense of their difficulty, and of the danger which is incurred by attempting rough and ready solutions of far reaching and complicated economic problems. Few things would give me more satisfaction than to be able so to devote myself to a deeper study of economics as to learn how to co-operate more adequately in promoting the amendment of present hardships where such exist. But a man who, like myself, has to work for 16 or 17 hours a day in discharging his own more immediate responsibilities cannot hope to be able to give to these studies so much time as many others can.

I need hardly tell you how deeply I sympathise with those whom you represent in their present lack of employment. But I am bound to say that I fail at present to see what good I could hope to effect by receiving such a Deputation as you suggest, and I cannot help fearing that I might really do harm by raising hopes and expectations which I should have no power whatever of satisfying. If what is desired is merely that I should be in possession of a statement of facts respecting the scarcity of employment in certain midland towns, I honestly believe that I should master those facts better were I to study them in writing than I should by listening to an oral statement. You think that I might, by receiving such a Deputation, shew that the Church (I quote your words) 'seals the cause as in itself sacred and noble'. I have no wish to throw any doubt upon what you describe as the sacredness and nobility of the cause. But in the ceaseless stress of other duties I must admit that I have not at present given to the details of this particular controversy such study as would justify me in making myself responsible for thus endorsing the representation of those who are coming to London to plead their cause, nor dare I hope to be able speedily to master the intricacies of the problem.

It is honestly because I am afraid of causing misunderstanding, and probably of even harming the cause I am invited to help, that I feel compelled to ask that anything which you want me to consider should be put before me in writing rather than by word of mouth.

It pains me even to seem to be unsympathetic. Nothing could be further from the facts. But it would be cowardly on my part were I, for fear of seeming unsympathetic, to do what might prejudice the very cause which you have taken in hand.

It is of interest to note that the letter was drafted during a sitting of the Royal Commission, and was shown in draft to the Chairman, Lord St. Aldwyn,[1] who passed the following note to the Archbishop after reading it:

Most excellent. Don't alter a word. A.

The REV. F. L. DONALDSON *to the* ARCHBISHOP OF CANTERBURY

Lodgings of the Unemployed. London, 11 June 1905.

We thank you very much indeed for your expressions of sympathy for the men. But I think your Grace somewhat misinterpreted the purport of our request that you should receive a small deputation.

We had no right to expect, and did not expect, that the Archbishop could go into any 'details of controversy'. But we thought that, after their pilgrimage to London, the privilege of a few of the men meeting your Grace in person should be asked for; and that if a few words of sympathy with their want of work, and therefore of food, could have been given them by your Grace in person, it would have done much to comfort them, and, through them, thousands of others in their condition throughout England. Also, we thought it would have done much to disabuse their minds of the idea, widely prevalent amongst them, that the tragedy and pathos of their condition is neither apprehended by the English Church, nor regarded by the Church as a matter with which she is most deeply concerned.

The correspondence was published, and caused a good deal of comment, which varied with the standpoint of the critics; for the pilgrimage of the unemployed had itself aroused considerable public attention. To one of his critics—and he never objected to criticism—the Archbishop expounded the reasons for his refusal—and his words at least show that he was not afraid of doing the unpopular thing:

The ARCHBISHOP OF CANTERBURY *to the* REV. C. L. ROBINSON

Private. 15th June 1905.

I thank you for writing to me frankly about what you feel respecting my reply to Mr. Donaldson's request. I think if you realised how constantly such action as I take is liable to be misrepresented, and consider too how probable it was that such misrepresentation would take place in this particular case, you would see that I have perhaps acted less unwisely than you think. What

[1] Formerly Sir Michael Hicks Beach.

would have been stated briefly would have been that the men had marched to London, that they had there been received by the Archbishop of Canterbury, who had blessed their endeavour, and, in short, given his full *imprimatur* to the particular mode they had adopted for bringing pressure to bear upon the public mind. Personally I am exceedingly doubtful whether a sensational march of this kind, however well intended and however admirable the conduct of the men, is calculated to advance their cause. Some of those who have alike the widest experience of and the deepest sympathy for the working men in the present industrial difficulties have told me emphatically how harmful they think a march of this kind is in its ultimate results. It would have been very easy, and obviously most popular, had I said 'come to see me, and I will at least give you all the encouragement that I can'. But, considering the manner in which this would have been reported, the ultimate result might have been exactly the contrary of what we wish. I am quite aware that I have taken the less popular and sensational attitude, but I have from my earliest days in Holy Orders been so keen and eager a sympathiser with working men and their endeavours that my action ought not to be misunderstood by people who care to look into the facts. I was one of those who organised and carried on the meetings of clergy in favour of trades unionism and the like more than 25 years ago when such movements were unpopular. I have not departed from the feelings which I then entertained, but perhaps the truest kindness sometimes is to brave a little unpopularity rather than to do a misleading act.

Of still greater interest, perhaps, is the Archbishop's reply to Canon Henson, who wrote a long letter to protest against the action of certain Church leaders who were agitating in connexion with the Government's Bill for helping the unemployed:

The ARCHBISHOP OF CANTERBURY *to* CANON H. HENSLEY HENSON

3rd August, 1905.

I thank you exceedingly for your very clear and most interesting letter upon the public correspondence which has taken place about the present Bill for relieving the unemployed. With much of what you say I entirely agree. I see most clearly the dangers which underlie a good deal of what is constantly being said on these matters by Christian leaders. The one point which I desired to emphasize was this: That a Bishop ought not, because he is a Bishop, to be debarred from the right which any public-spirited Christian man has of ventilating in the Press his opinions on such a question as this. If the Bishop were in any way to seem to be using the Press for directing his clergy *ex cathedra* as to what they ought to say upon a matter of this kind, I should object to it most determinedly, unless the issue were one totally different from what is now before the public. But I cannot find in the letters of the Bishops of Southwark or of Stepney, to which you seemed to be specially alluding, anything of the sort. They seem to me to write exactly as they might write if they were not Bishops, and I confess that I am surprised that you should find a difficulty in distinguishing between what a man writes as Bishop and what he writes as an individual whose position gives him means of knowledge. Were consecration to the Episcopate to deprive a man thenceforward of the right to speak out in the Press upon such subjects, it would be a most serious matter. I had not in my mind, when you spoke to me, the Bishop of Birmingham's letter, nor have I it now before me, so that I cannot check by reference to the text what you have said about it. Any attempt on the part of Bishops of our Church to tune the pulpits in the way that is undoubtedly done by Roman Catholic Bishops in some parts of the world, I should strongly object to. I confess that personally I have not seen any widespread evidence of a tendency on the part of the clergy of the Church to deal from the pulpit with matters of political controversy. Of course it is occasionally done, but the peril of doing it is, I think, great. Can anyone fairly say that anything occurs ordinarily in our churches which corresponds with the use made of Nonconformist Chapels in this respect? On the other hand you would not, I think, desire to dissociate our Christian teaching from our social life in such a manner as to make a preacher shun the application of Christian principles to the larger social issues which the community has to deal with.

IV

Two events of different character concerning the Diocese and the Cathedral Church of Canterbury took place this summer, and may be briefly recorded. On the constitution of the new Diocese of Southwark, by the Southwark and Birmingham Bishoprics Act, 1904, the parent bishopric of Rochester was left with a much diminished area. The question arose whether some rearrangement might not therefore be made in the boundaries of the two Kent dioceses of Canterbury and Rochester. In that part of West Kent belonging to Canterbury, there was a very strong desire on the part of many to remain where they were. The Dean and Chapter of Canterbury, the Bishops of Dover and Croydon, and the Archdeacon of Maidstone were all opposed to any substantial alteration. The Archbishop was therefore placed in a difficult position.

Here are two letters of successive years to the Bishop of Rochester (Dr. Talbot) dealing with different aspects of the situation:

The ARCHBISHOP OF CANTERBURY *to the* BISHOP OF ROCHESTER

17th August 1904.

As to the new Bishopric I should like to contribute £1000 please. But as I am at present deeply in debt for the money I required on 'coming in' I can't pay it all down this year. I think I can promise to pay it all without fail on or before Oct. 1. 1905.

I should like to give a bigger sum. But I can't see my way at present. It may and will be said that as I am giving up part of the Diocese I ought to contribute permanently a part of the income. But I dare not try for this. [It would I suppose need, by the way, another Act of Parliament!]

The truth is that, so far as I can see, the cost of being Archbishop will *increase* as the years go on and more and more require paid helpers and staff. The cost of Lambeth and its life is huger than I had dreamed of, *much* more than in Archbishop Tait's days.

Of course, I who do so little purely *Diocesan* work, don't really save any money at all (except in donations) by getting rid of the Dartford Deaneries. So please don't think me very shabby. If I am in a position to give better help at a later stage, I *will*.

The ARCHBISHOP OF CANTERBURY *to the* BISHOP OF ROCHESTER

3rd May 1905.

I find myself at Canterbury in the midst of a storm on the subject of the division of the Diocese. The Chapter, which has hitherto remained silent as you know, regards itself as having been treated with scant courtesy, as its members think they ought to have been given an opportunity of formal utterance before an endeavour was made 'to change the whole character of the Diocese by taking away what is now its only wealthy portion'. In old days East Kent was prosperous: extraordinary tithe made the clergy rich, the land was well let, and the squires were practically all resident. Now there are very few of the squires resident, the clergy are as poor as the farmers, or poorer, and many of the places are unlet. The members of the Chapter do not urge that this is conclusive against the change, but they think they ought to have had a say at an earlier date, and I am inclined to believe that they are right. They are now memorialising the Ecclesiastical Commission. I am of course personally abused by both parties. *Your* people all think that I ought to have *urged* the handing over of these Deaneries; and the Canterbury people feel that I have deserted them in their difficulties. But that is not the point. There is of course still a strong feeling about the prayer to which I called your attention. I have pointed out that you were asking others to join with you in praying for what you believed to be the right decision; but I own that I cannot well answer when I am asked whether they might appropriately have had prayers in the Cathedral the other way. I hope to see Dibdin to-night in London. Have you any correspondence with Archbishop Temple which refers to the four Deaneries which are in dispute? They contend here that he repeatedly said that he would never consent to part with them, and I think it not improbable that he may have said so, though I never heard him mention the subject. The obvious feeling at the Canterbury end of the county is: If Archbishop Temple had been alive we should never have been thus treated—for they are taking it for granted that the decision is going against them. Perhaps you may know more than I do how the matter now stands.

Addressing the Canterbury Diocesan Conference at Lambeth, June 26, 1905, he said:

When Parliament decided last year that the whole question of the Diocesan boundary line between the Kentish dioceses was to be settled by the Church itself and not by Parliament, I was immediately face to face with a perplexity of the gravest kind . . . I had and have every possible bias in favour of keeping in Canterbury Diocese the region into which I was myself ordained, in which a great number of my own nearest friends are working, and which has in recent years been the source in no inconsiderable measure of the supply of our diocesan funds. To pretend to be impartial about it would be absurd . . . I resolved to stand aside and to let the boundary line be settled by a Committee of men accustomed to such duties—seven men perhaps as capable of dealing with it as any men in England—three Bishops and four laymen.

The result was that the Committee recommended that the six Rural Deaneries of East and West Dartford, North and South Malling, Shoreham, and Tonbridge should be transferred from Canterbury to Rochester, and this was done.

The Archbishop always took a deep interest in everything that concerned the cathedral at Canterbury. On the south side of the choir stands the tomb of John de Stratford. He was Archbishop of Canterbury from 1333 to 1348, and Davidson's own immediate predecessor in moving from Winchester to Canterbury. For 'strange to say, no subsequent Bishop of Winchester became Archbishop, although the Pilgrims' Way from Winchester to Canterbury lay open'. The monument, with its splendid canopy, was one of the glories of the Cathedral, but had been somewhat mutilated. By good fortune a considerable number of loose parts belonging to the canopy had survived and lay in a heap together, hidden away. The Archbishop proposed that he should restore the tomb in a conservative way, and his proposal was accepted by the Dean and Chapter, with the result that before another year was out the work was happily done. Many years later, the following Latin inscription was placed on a small tablet to record the good deed and its reason:

Sexcentis annis confracta est tumba Johannis;
  Tandem Randallus sic reparavit opus,
Venta prius sedes, nunc Christi copulat aedes,
  In caelo praesul regnet uterque simul.

V

The summer holidays were spent, as usual, in Scotland. There had been a political crisis at the end of July, when Mr. Balfour had been defeated on a secondary Irish question. Davidson stayed on two successive nights at Whittingehame with Mr. Balfour and at Dalmeny with Lord Rosebery. With each he had long talks, and of each a full note was taken at the time.

Whittingehame.
Sunday night, 1st October, 1905.

Long talks yesterday and to-day with A. J. B. He was most frank both about reasons for *not* resigning when defeated in Summer... and about intentions now. He wants to have opportunity of resigning very soon after Parliament meets—preferably on defeat on some minor (not major) point in the debate on Address. Thus he would hope to be out of office by end of February. Absolutely clear of course for resignation rather than dissolution. No real doubt about Liberal victory at the polls. *How* great a victory 'nobody can guess'. He thinks his resignation may be hereafter looked back to in history as the end of the present Parliamentary and Constitutional position and that the advent of a Labour Party in force to House of Commons may split the whole into groups with infinite peril of log rolling and even corruption. He expanded all this most interestingly. But notwithstanding this he thinks it good for country that Liberals should now come into office and have the sobering and steadying influence of responsibility, and be compelled to 'possess their souls' and find out what their real position towards public questions actually is.

As regards Church questions, he is very pessimistic. Sees no real hope of anything except chaos: thinks the facts disclosed before the Royal Commission will be an incentive to actively aggressive anti-Church tirades and pledges, and is therefore most anxious that we should if possible delay the publication of Report until after the general election. He is indignant at the pledges which are now being exacted against any kind of delegation on Church questions. This is the worst and most indefensible sort of Erastianism. He is of course himself in favour of some system of delegation.

I discussed the perplexities surrounding our preparation of a Report which shall avoid giving cause for inflammatory speeches and probable schism of one kind or another. He entirely approves and agrees with my personal plans and hopes as to form of Report —i.e. (1) a definite expression of wish that Convocation and Parliament should legislate for new courts especially Court of Appeal, (on the lines of, but more Churchy than, the Report of 1883)— and (2) Request to the Crown for Letters of Business authorising Convocation to redraft the Rubrics relating to Holy Communion.

He is intensely indignant against those who are now proclaiming that if *any*body is allowed to wear vestments *they* will themselves secede.

He approves of my plan for a personal appeal *from myself* to Churchmen at large, in favour of a free hand to Convocation to deal with Ornaments Rubric. In the meantime he would personally be in favour of my Convocations Bill, and is angry with the lawyers for making difficulties about it.

He is clear that the Liberals, if in office, will do nothing legislatively on Church questions, and they by no means want to bring Disestablishment to the front otherwise than *gradually*.

Hence he thinks there would be *time* for our action in Convocation about Courts and Rubrics, provided we can get the initial sanctions.

Dalmeny House, Edinburgh. 2 Oct. 1905.
7 p.m.

Private.

Have just come in from a two hours walk and talk with Rosebery. What a strange contrast to A. J. Balfour, with whom I was walking yesterday. The self-consciousness and self-thought and lack of simplicity which characterise Rosebery even when at his best, make him a very different man to deal with. We ranged in talk over all sorts of subjects, personal, historical, political and religious.

On the political situation he is decidedly of opinion that Balfour will not resign or dissolve until the *expiration* of next session. 'Is he not likely to be beaten on the Address?' 'No, certainly not, unless he makes a strong effort so to be, and that he won't make, for he loves being in power. Of course he will resign, not dissolve. He is perfectly right in so deciding. I should do the same were I in his place. He will be tremendously beaten. The Liberals will have a majority over Tories and Irish combined. The Japanese treaty, which is absolutely right and indeed was inevitable, will strengthen the Tories a little but won't really go far. The pity, for Balfour's own reputation, is that he did not resign when his Government had its schism two years ago. He could have done it then with dignity and propriety and might quite possibly have carried the country with him and come back to power, or at all events he would have been again in power by this time.'

I said that surely a dissolution *then* might have meant a great strength for Chamberlain and protection. He thought there was something in that but not very much. He then went on to discuss different resignations and dissolutions and their respective circumstances and environment, and, returning to the Japanese Treaty, he expanded on the present importance of Foreign politics. 'Never so important as they are today—when the resentment which some nations and peoples must feel against the detriment which this treaty will bring to them, is bound to make itself felt and heard. The average British citizen is not alive to these questions, but they are the biggest for all that.'. . . We discussed in connexion with the King, the question of the Spanish marriage. He wholly agrees with me as to its inexpediency and unpopularity. . . .

We passed on, *inter alia multissima*, to discuss the lack of 'serious' men like Gladstone and Peel in political life. 'Why is it that W. E. G. did not leave a school of such?' Morley, he agreed has some of the 'serious' characteristics, though of his own peculiar sort. Rosebery assures me that Morley has still a most fervent admiration for Chamberlain—indeed 'idolises' him, and he pointed out a curious fact that, in Gladstone's *Life*, Morley wholly omits to notice the 'shameful conduct' of Chamberlain when in 1885 he took advantage of W. E. G.'s absence from England to propound his unauthorised programme, thus angering Gladstone and sowing the discord which led to their schism.

The foreign situation was increasing in importance. The Anglo-French Entente of 1904 had led to an estrangement with Germany. The Archbishop was invited by an Anglo-German Conciliation Committee to sign an address to the people of both nations protesting with emphasis against the mere thought of any conflict (of which the danger was acknowledged) between Great Britain and Germany, and urging co-operation in friendship for their common interests and the peace of the world. The Archbishop wrote at once to Lord Lansdowne for his advice. He, as Foreign Secretary, did not think that such signature could do any harm, but was doubtful of its good. The Archbishop accordingly replied as follows:

The ARCHBISHOP OF CANTERBURY *to* FRANCIS W. FOX, ESQ.

Private. 28th October 1905.

I have carefully considered your letter and the draft address which you enclose. I should not have the smallest objection to append my name to such an address, for I agree with every word of it. But I think that for the Archbishop of Canterbury to append his name might lead to a misunderstanding which we should all deprecate. In the first place it might give colour to the quite untrue supposition that there are at present strained relations between the Governments of the two countries. Such to the best of my belief is in no sense whatever true. Certain German newspapers are at strife with certain English newspapers, and each has doubtless a following. But the Governments are absolutely at one, and the very notion of any contemplated aggression on our part is absurd.

Further, there are mischievous people who might twist an address of this kind into something which could weaken the strength of our entente with France. Such a conclusion or inference would be absurd, but it is none the less possible.

On the whole therefore I think I had better not give my name. . . .

For the present, therefore, the question of Anglo-German friendship was allowed to rest. A few years later other possibilities were to be explored, and the Archbishop was to give a lead, so far as the Churches were concerned, of a more encouraging character.

VI

Two important instances of the Archbishop's keen interest in education may be set down, belonging to this year and the opening months of 1906. The first was an interview with Dr. John R. Mott, Secretary of the World's Student Federation. He was taken to see the Archbishop by the Rev. Tissington Tatlow on the introduction of Bishop Montgomery. He was a graduate of Yale, and had travelled much over the world addressing students in all sorts of universities and colleges. His addresses were partly evangelistic, partly missionary, and, perhaps most of all, sought to promote a manly, useful Christian life. Personally, he was a remarkable combination of intellectual, practical, and spiritual power. The subject then upon his mind, and upon which he wished to see the Archbishop, was the paucity of candidates for the Ministry—a subject of which the Archbishop was himself thinking a good deal. He wished to address himself very particularly to the claims of the Christian Ministry upon university students. The Archbishop saw him on February 4, 1905, and, writing afterwards to the Chairman of a new Committee which he had appointed with regard to the Ministry, described the occasion as an important and exceedingly interesting interview with a remarkable man, who 'seems to move about over the entire surface of the globe advocating the cause of Christian Union and the enlistment of officers for the Ministry. He is in touch with all denominations, from the Greeks and Roumanians to the Baptists and Methodists of to-day. He has a striking personality, and I was greatly interested in all that he had to say.' From that time on, Dr. Mott kept in close touch with the Archbishop and was always a welcome visitor to Lambeth Palace. The Archbishop's own interest in the work of the Student Christian Movement steadily increased.

The development of a scheme for the training and testing of women teachers of theology was also set forward this year. There had been a rapid advance in the education of women in the end of the last, and the opening years of the present, century. It had come to be expected of those who wished to teach in schools and colleges that they should equip themselves for their work by definite training, and possess an adequate knowledge of their subjects. But there was one exception.

> It was too commonly assumed [writes Miss G. M. Bevan] both in Church work and in schools that for the teaching of Divinity, the most vital and the most difficult of all subjects of instruction, little or no preparation need be required of the women to whom it was committed. So the question came to be asked: Could not the Church give more careful consideration to the work of teachers of Divinity, according it definite recognition as a most important department of Church service, a work of great and sacred responsibility, and one demanding the best gifts of spirit, of mind, and of heart which women could offer? Could not some provision be made by which those who felt called to this service might, after careful preparation and testing, be given a recognized place in the organization of the Church, and be duly accredited as Church teachers by receiving a direct commission and authorization from the one set in the highest office in the Church? Were there not many women who would then come forward gladly to offer their powers, their knowledge and their devotion to this ministry of teaching?

To form such a body of well-qualified and accredited teachers of theology was the purpose of the Archbishop's Licence to teach Theology, which thus came into being. And, as a preparation for the office of a teacher of Theology, the training and the examination for the Lambeth Diploma were instituted. The idea originated with Margaret Benson, daughter of Archbishop Benson, and her friend Miss G. M. Bevan. It was clear that a high standard of scholarship must be required if a Licence to teach Theology were to be issued. The Archbishop was able to secure the help of Dr. W. E. Collins, Bishop of Gibraltar, who threw himself into the task of providing a scheme of training, and became the first Director of Studies. Side by side with him were Bishop Chase of Ely and Bishop Chavasse of Liverpool, and there was a committee of women to assist. The purpose of the scheme, as stated by Bishop Collins with the Archbishop's approval, was 'the providing of a body of competent and well-instructed women as teachers of Theology having a Diploma from the Archbishop'. The candidates had to satisfy a threefold test of (*a*) systematic study; (*b*) proficiency, including knowledge of New Testament Greek on a standard approximating to that of the Honours School of Theology at a university; and (*c*) teaching capacity. The study was to be done under direction. For the Diploma, academic knowledge was required. The Archbishop's Licence to teach

Theology was given to those who did teaching work and had teaching ability.

On October 11, 1906, the first five women received the diploma from the Archbishop in Lambeth Palace Chapel, and six months later the same five received his 'Licence and Authority to teach sacred Theology'. These services were the first of a series of annual services conducted by the Archbishop in that Chapel.[1]

[1] By April 1935, 170 women had received the Diploma, of whom 153 were living; and of these 115 were licensed teachers, of whom 11 had died and 5 had surrendered their Licence, as no longer teaching divinity. Some were working in England and some abroad.

CHAPTER XXVIII

THE NEW PARLIAMENT. A CHAPTER OF CHANGES

Patience, hard thing! the hard thing but to pray,
But bid for, Patience is! Patience who asks
Wants war, wants wounds; weary his times, his tasks;
To do without, take tosses, and obey.

GERARD MANLEY HOPKINS (*Poem 46*).

ON December 4, 1905, Mr. Balfour resigned the office of Prime Minister as the result of the crisis in the Unionist party over Tariff Reform. The King invited Sir Henry Campbell-Bannerman to form a new administration. When, a week later, the names of those composing the Liberal Cabinet were announced, the Archbishop found that nearly every one of the members was a personal friend—so large was his acquaintance with the leaders of public life, whatever their politics.

He wrote thus to the Prime Minister:

The ARCHBISHOP OF CANTERBURY *to the* RT. HON. SIR HENRY CAMPBELL-BANNERMAN

Old Palace, Canterbury.
11th December, 1905.

I venture, even in the midst of all your overwhelming work this week, to intrude upon you with a few lines of warm good wishes, and (if the word be not inappropriate in so high a matter) of congratulation upon your accession to the greatest office open to a subject of the Crown. I think you will not object to my saying that I do from my heart pray God to give you strength, courage and wisdom for its tremendous responsibilities.

It has been my high privilege to be on terms of confidential friendship with your *four* immediate predecessors in that office, and with the two younger of them my intimacy has been close and real, although upon a good many public questions I differ pretty widely from the opinions of either.

Should the new Prime Minister allow me to stand in a friendly personal relation to himself I shall appreciate it on every ground, and occasions may possibly arise when the maintenance of the confidential intercourse which it has for more than 20 years been my privilege to hold with Downing Street would on public grounds have its advantages. Whether this be so or not, I hope you will let me assure you of my absolute readiness at any moment to place at your disposal, should you desire it, such information as I may be able to furnish upon any of the Ecclesiastical matters, either personal or general, which of necessity claim so frequently the attention of the Prime Minister.

It is I hope needless for me to add that I shall perfectly understand it if for any reason you would prefer to rely wholly upon others for such information with regard to Ecclesiastical facts or folk as you may from time to time require.

My sole anxiety is to make it clear to you from the outset of what will I hope be a great and memorable Premiership, that I am at your service to the best of my power, if and only if, such service be at any time desired.

The Rt. Hon. Sir Henry Campbell-Bannerman *to the* Archbishop of Canterbury

29 Belgrave Square, S.W.
13th December, 1905.

Private.

I cannot fully express to you the pleasure with which I received your very kind letter, and the comfort and satisfaction which I derive from its contents.

I hardly realize yet the position in which I find myself, and it is at least in no spirit of pride and self-confidence that I contemplate undertaking its vast duties.

I assure you that nothing would at once please and assist me more than if you were good enough to continue in my case the friendly and confidential relations which existed between you and my predecessors. I am accustomed to treat those about me with perfect frankness, and I believe in a straight course being the best and safest. I am sure you will find no difficulty with me, whether we differ on individual points or entirely agree.

This applies to every public question: and as to the Ecclesiastical matters, in which I have so heavy a responsibility, your advice would greatly ease the burden, and would be in fact indispensable.

I am therefore extremely indebted to you for your promise of assistance, and will gladly avail myself of it.

I

The general election took place in the following month, after an exciting contest. Fierce words were spoken in the heat of battle. In Canterbury itself, while the Archbishop was in residence, very bitter things were said by Nonconformist ministers about the Anglican Church, about priestcraft and Church schools, as well as slavery, militarism, and tariffs. On the other side a well-known paper even spoke of the general regret amongst Churchmen that the Archbishop of Canterbury had not felt it his duty to issue a spirited letter to his followers on the subject of Disestablishment.

The Liberals were returned with a sensational majority.[1] The striking feature of the new Parliament was the presence of a large body of 157 English Nonconformists, the largest number in any House of Commons since the time of Oliver Cromwell.

Three principal matters with which the new Government was obliged to deal were Chinese labour, Education, and the Welsh Church, which all in different ways involved the Archbishop. Each has its place in this book; but it is interesting to note the tentative way in which the disestablishment of the Welsh Church was mooted at the start:

Most Private and Confidential. Memorandum of a conversation on Feb. 21st, 1906, with the Bishop of St. Asaph.[2]

> Mr. Lloyd George had been in private communication with the Bishop, and had asked him whether if the Government were to introduce a very mild and kindly Welsh Disestablishment Bill the Welsh Church would modify its opposition and practically allow the matter to go forward even if outwardly opposing. Mr. Lloyd George promised at a later date to show the Bishop in black and white what he would himself suggest, but, roughly, it amounted to something like an arrangement that the Church should retain everything—buildings, houses, glebes, etc.—but not the tithes. These terms are of course very much more favourable than Mr. Asquith's former Bill, and the Bishop believes that Lloyd George would rather like to get Disestablishment carried with a minimum of friction.

The Archbishop talked the matter over fully with the Bishop

[1] Liberals 377, Labour 53, Nationalists 83, Total 513; Opposition, Conservatives and Unionists, 157.

[2] Dr. A. G. Edwards.

of St. Asaph, and urged great caution. 'I warned the Bishop against leaving Lloyd George in a position which could enable him to say that the Bishop had been "negotiating" with him on the subject.'

Next day the Archbishop and the Bishop saw Mr. Lloyd George in the Bishops' Robing Room in the House of Lords.

> Mr. Lloyd George told us that he had been discussing with the Prime Minister, who approved of the suggestion, a plan of now appointing a Royal Commission of (say) six persons, besides a Chairman, to consider the origin, the history, the character, and the value of the provision for spiritual needs in Wales, showing what has been done or is now being done in each parish, both by the Church and by Nonconformists. And he wanted to know whether we as Churchmen would make difficulties as to co-operating in such enquiry, or whether we would be ready to suggest names of persons who might in our judgment be appropriate members of such a Commission. I replied that my view always is that it is wrong to conceal from responsible authorities facts material to the public consideration of big questions, and that I could not prima facie see any reason why we should make any difficulties about, or show any unfriendliness to, such an enquiry. Further, that I thought it lay within the province of responsible Governments to make enquiries into existing facts in such way as they think best. But I added that I should like to see the Reference to such a Commission before expressing even a preliminary opinion about it. . . .
>
> The Bishop and I took the greatest care not to commit ourselves in any way to any co-operation or anything else: we could neither judge about it nor act about it until we knew more definitely what the Reference and plan were to be.

A fortnight later the Cabinet met to appoint a Royal Commission, Mr. Lloyd George telling the Archbishop that he hoped that a Bill of a moderate kind might be the outcome.

II

In the spring of 1906, a great stir was caused by the marriage of the young Princess Victoria Eugenie, the only daughter of Princess Beatrice of Battenburg, to Alphonso XIII, King of Spain. The Princess was only eighteen years old when, in the previous summer, she first met her future husband, himself but a year older. But she was a member of the Church of England

and he a Roman Catholic brought up in the Spanish Court and under influences of the most ultra-montane kind. The idea of such a marriage, with the change of faith which it involved, would have been unwelcome in the country at most times; but it was particularly difficult to accept at a moment when there was such hot debate between Nonconformists and Anglicans on religious allegiance in connexion with the schools.

In a matter so closely affecting the religion of Englishmen, the Archbishop of Canterbury was bound to be particularly concerned; and not less when he himself stood on such friendly terms with the Royal Family and with the mother of the intended Queen, herself the daughter of Queen Victoria. He played a striking part in the whole proceedings, both by appeal and protest in the highest quarters. The character of his intervention has never been revealed to the public, and he had, therefore, to suffer the harsh censure of innumerable Churchmen for his supposed acquiescence and cowardice. It is not even yet possible to break the silence which he so characteristically imposed upon himself. But when the full story of the betrothal, the baptism, or rebaptism, and the marriage, can be told, it will be very clear that Archbishop Davidson displayed to the full the same qualities of courage and courtesy in relation to an issue so closely affecting the Royal Family as he was accustomed to bring to the negotiation of delicate and important issues, and had already exercised in the past with regard to Queen Victoria herself.

III

In a year marked in a painful degree by religious controversy, it is worthy of notice that the Archbishop, more than once, took occasion to promote co-operation with Free Church ministers. This was especially the case with regard to Sunday observance.

In March Dr. Scott Lidgett, President of the Free Church Council, wrote expressing his pleasure at the Archbishop's desire that Free Churchmen and Anglicans should unite in this movement. The Archbishop replied:

The ARCHBISHOP OF CANTERBURY *to the* REV. J. SCOTT LIDGETT

10th March, 1906.

I am most grateful to you for your kind letter. It is to me a source of genuine satisfaction that you should be thus ready to co-operate with us in the endeavour to secure a more true and wise use of the Lord's Day, and I pray God that our joint efforts may be fruitful of good, not only in the matter of Sunday Observance but in affording evidence of the possibility and the advantage of all such co-operation when it can be undertaken without sacrifice of any fundamental or distinctive principle. To me personally it has always seemed that that area is a very wide one and I have been sorely disappointed (as I think you know) during the last three years by the ill success which has attended some of the efforts which I tried to make. I therefore welcome the more cordially the assurance which you have given me. It is just what I should have hoped for from yourself.

A great conference on Sunday observance was accordingly held two months later in the Caxton Hall, and proved a notable evidence of Christian co-operation. The Archbishop of Canterbury presided, with Dr. Scott Lidgett on his left and the Duke of Norfolk, the leading Roman Catholic layman in England, on his right. Anglican Bishops sat side by side with the Roman Catholic Prelate who represented Archbishop Bourne, and with Free Church leaders. The Archbishop of Canterbury himself said, in opening, that he doubted whether either he or any of his predecessors for a thousand years had ever taken part in a public meeting more remarkable in its component elements.

IV

One further incident deserves recording—as it gave the Archbishop an opportunity for emphasizing the sacrosanct character of the private and informal Bishops' Meetings held three times a year at Lambeth for mutual counsel.

A new hymn book, the *English Hymnal*, had been issued by high musical and literary authorities belonging to the Anglo-Catholic school.[1] Unfortunately certain of the hymns included appeared to embody teaching about the invocation of the Blessed Virgin Mary and the Saints which was not consistent with the formularies of the Church of England.

The Archbishop in his *Diocesan Gazette* expressed 'the strong

[1] The names of those concerned in the original production of the *English Hymnal* in 1906 are: W. J. Birkbeck, A. Hanbury-Tracy, W. H. H. Jervois, T. A. Lacey, D. C. Lathbury, Arthur Reynolds, Athelstan Riley, Percy Dearmer (general editor), and R. Vaughan Williams (musical editor).

wish that it should not be adopted in any Church in the diocese'—a recommendation which brought an emphatic protest from the editors of the hymnal. The whole matter had been talked over confidentially and informally at a Bishops' Meeting; and the Bishop of Durham, in writing on the subject to *The Times*, referred to this in a manner which gave the Bishops' Meetings both a much more public and a much more formal character than the Archbishop approved. Hence this letter:

The ARCHBISHOP OF CANTERBURY *to the* BISHOP OF DURHAM[1]

10th November, 1906.

We are, as you know, in the thick of difficulties respecting the English Hymnal. I have received a formal protest from the compilers of the Hymnal, and the Bishop of London has received a formal request from one of them that he may be prosecuted for heresy. All this is, I think, very foolish: None of us has charged the compilers with heresy or anything like it. We have simply recommended that the book they have compiled be not introduced into our churches. But the very essence of this has been that our action has been individual and not collective, and I am now a good deal perplexed and distressed at receiving from different quarters copies of a letter which you have written to your clergy in which you refer to the Bishops' Meeting, or at least to what you describe as 'their unanimous conviction'. And, again, you say 'I feel, *as my Episcopal brethren all feel*, that the Hymnal' etc.

We have always, as you know, regarded our meetings as in the strictest possible sense confidential, and, even if it were not so, no resolution whatever on the subject was arrived at at our recent meeting: we merely had a general conversation and then left each Bishop to act individually as he thought best. Most of us have written to our Dioceses, or to the individual clergy therein, but, except for your letter, there has, so far as I am aware, been no reference whatever to collective action or even to the fact that we had thus privately discussed the matter. I am perplexed now what to say if questions are asked me upon what you have written. I think my answer had better be that whatever you have said about the conviction of the Bishops generally can only be an impression on your part, as there has been no collective utterance or decision of the Bishops in the matter. Of course it might be possible for you to write something to the same effect. But this on other grounds might be very undesirable, as it might appear as though you had

[1] Dr. Handley Moule.

been told by other Bishops that they disagreed with your view about the Hymnal, and I do not imagine that you have heard of any such disagreement except in so far as it came out in our recent very private discussion. What troubles me most is the precedent thus set as regards a Bishops' Meeting. If it came to be thought by individual Bishops that because in our private conversation at Lambeth a general view had been expressed on some matter, each Bishop was therefore 'entitled to say' that the Bishops 'are unanimous in the conviction' etc., the whole character of our meetings would be changed, and I have been trying almost *ad nauseam* to reiterate the necessity of our observing as absolutely confidential everything that passes within these walls on such occasions. I write in some distress about it, because no less than five different Bishops have now approached me with reference to your letter and the embarrassing position in which they are placed thereby. I had hoped that we were on the highway to getting the objectionable Hymns withdrawn from the compilation, but I greatly fear that this will throw us back. If you do think of writing anything further on the subject (which I do not at all recommend) I have no doubt you will very kindly let me know beforehand what you are going to say.

I am sorry to trouble you just now when, as I learn, you are not very well, but I hope the illness is not such as to lay you aside in any way.

The Bishop, with his unfailing courtesy, agreed, and wrote a further, and guarded, explanatory letter to *The Times*. A revised edition of the *English Hymnal* was shortly published, omitting the phrases to which exception had been taken. But though both the revised and the original editions were on sale, it is the original edition which has prevailed.

CHAPTER XXIX

THE EDUCATION CONTROVERSY, 1906–1908

These Mistakes are to be lamented, tho' not easily cured, being suitable enough to the corrupted Nature of Mankind; but 'tis hard, that Men will not only invent ill Names, but they will wrest and misinterpret good ones; so afraid some are even of a reconciling sound, that they raise another noise to keep it from being heard, lest it should set up and encourage a dangerous sort of Men, who prefer Peace and Agreement, before Violence and Confusion. MARQUESS OF HALIFAX, *The Character of a Trimmer*.

IT is difficult, after the passage of a whole generation, with all the changes that have taken place in men's temper and attitude, to appreciate the violence of the agitation on the schools question in the decade before the War. The old battle-cries sound strange to-day, as well as harsh; and those who have most to do with education now look at the problem of religion in education with different eyes; while those who are thinking what the aims of education should be in modern life, will also see the whole issue in a different perspective. But while the battle raged it was both prolonged and fierce, and tested the character of the combatants on both sides in all sorts of ways. And this must explain the need for this particular chapter on a subject which has a larger array of boxes and files with more memoranda of interviews and correspondence, than any other single subject (save the Prayer Book) during the whole of the Archbishop's life. There is also the fact, not altogether to be ignored, that from the political point of view the failure of the crucial measures of Mr. Birrell was the first step in the great conflict, under a Liberal Government, between the House of Commons and the House of Lords, in which the Archbishop also played his part.

I

We propose to begin our narrative with a sketch of the issue at stake, and also of the man who faced it, drawn by one who first came to know the Archbishop in the troublesome days of 1906—through this very schools' question—and gave him more help than anybody else in tackling the problem. The artist is Sir Michael Sadler, a great educationalist who, at the time of which we write, had just been appointed Professor of the History and Administration of Education in Victoria University, Manchester. The confidence which the Archbishop placed in his judgement may be seen from the note he wrote to him on Christmas Eve 1906, just at the end of the most bitter stage in the conflict:

The ARCHBISHOP OF CANTERBURY *to* M. E. SADLER, ESQ.

I will not try to say what I feel as to the service which you have rendered to Church and Realm by your constant quiet presentation to us of the larger issues at stake, and by the guidance you have, with such extraordinary kindness, rendered to myself. I have, in my varied responsibilities for many years past, had such help from friends and counsellors and staff as makes me often blush for shame, but never have I experienced this support and guidance more helpfully than during the last two months at your hand. To say that I am 'grateful' is to fall quite short of what I feel.

I cannot but believe that words and thoughts of yours, spoken and written at this time, may prove hereafter to be fruitful a thousandfold. Not often, even in *your* life, have the expert knowledge and the mature thought had so full and varied an opportunity of service to the cause of Christian Education.

Sir Michael Sadler's sketch (prepared for this biography) is as follows:

Thory Gardiner it must have been who had spoken about me to the Archbishop in 1906. This led His Grace to ask me to Lambeth, where he admitted me to the privilege of intimate consultation. At that time, as those who followed these matters will remember, controversy about Church schools and training colleges was becoming acute. The issue at stake was the part which the modern State—the Liberal State, as the Fascists call it—should allow schools with a denominational tradition and allegiance to play in what is called the national system of education—a phrase which often veils a bleak view of education and confuses the administrative framework of school organization with the varied and subtle harmonies of our national life.

The French Revolution tried to stamp the State as secular. Some of its philosophers scorned Christianity as a superstition. Others, less thoroughgoing in scepticism, but with influence in French politics, deemed the Roman Catholic Church reactionary and the implacable foe of the Revolution. They tried therefore to clip its wings in the sphere of education. But even in France the extremists failed to get the whole of their way. In England also we have thought about the same problems and have taken action in regard to them. But French thought only seeps into England and becomes mixed with other streams of opinion. Thus with us the outcome has been a turbid though fertilising flood in which different doctrines (Jeremy Bentham's, Robert Owen's, John Stuart Mill's, John Henry Newman's, F. D. Maurice's, Dean Church's, H. G. Wells', Bertrand Russell's, and D. H. Lawrence's) are blended in a solution not easy to analyse.

Every now and again, however, the issue becomes sharp and clear, even in England which instinctively shrinks from precise definitions when compelled to handle a problem so nervous as that of national education. Thus in 1906 one heard a revolutionary note in the roar of cheers which went up from the crowded Government benches in the House of Commons when Mr. Birrell rose to speak. But the cardinal points at issue were soon blanketed. It could not be otherwise, because neither side in the controversy was homogeneous. Eager agnostics and pious nonconformists got out of step within the Liberal ranks. And, in the Opposition, backwoodsmen, who imagined the Church of England to be still the unique organ of the national will in faith and morals, went into the lobby with colleagues who pinned their educational policy to the principle of parental rights and were prepared to cut away as dead wood the Anglican predominance in hundreds of village schools. Amid treacherous currents the Archbishop proved himself a wise and cautious pilot. No chemist could analyse a broth with more scrupulous exactitude than His Grace employed in disentangling the factors which were knotted together in the English educational problem. He was determined not to be deceived by presuppositions, however dearly cherished, or to accept without firm use of the probe generalisations which were part of the worn currency of debate. But he never leapt to a conclusion until he had made sure of his ground. He never allowed himself to speak without first measuring his words and judging their public repercussions. Heavy strain on his strength and temper never broke his self-command. He had inexhaustible patience; a bridle on his tongue; courage and a noble tact in withholding assent to views which he thought exaggerated, impracticable or delusively logical. Through the dense brushwood which impeded his progress he saw shining the light towards which his course was set. But he had no formula to cover all he hoped to save or win. He moved forward with a firm hold on realities and with an unflinching faith in the truth which was to him the way of life. With the caution of the Scot, he had the Englishman's awareness of the complexity of human affairs—a complexity which often forbids a scientifically honest mind to accept in theology or in politics some clear-cut and logically immaculate conclusion.

II

It was a foregone conclusion that a Liberal Government would put the amendment of the Education Act, 1902, in the very forefront of its programme. Ever since that Act had received the Royal Assent, it had been the target for violent attack, and the special ground of that attack had been that the denominational elementary schools which were 'non-provided' (i.e. not provided by the local authority) were placed upon the rates. The secular curriculum within these schools was just the same as that within the schools owned by the State. But in schools 'provided' by the local authority, the religious instruction (where given) was bound to be undenominational; in 'non-provided' schools, it was definite and distinctive, in accordance with the Trust deeds. In 'provided' schools again, the appointment of the teachers was in the hands of the local education authority. In 'non-provided' schools it rested with the managers of the particular school, a majority of whom were appointed by the denomination to which the school belonged. There were therefore two kinds of control and two kinds of public elementary school—a system generally known as 'the dual system': and it was this division of authority over the schools, all maintained by public funds, that aroused the active indignation and the passive resistance of Nonconformists.

The new President of the Board of Education was Mr. Augustine Birrell, K.C., Honorary Fellow of Trinity Hall, Cambridge, and a distinguished writer. He was fifty-five years old, the son of a Nonconformist minister of Liverpool. He had already shown a considerable interest in the problems of elementary education—and he was known to be both a convinced Nonconformist himself and, while demanding complete popular control for all State-supported schools, including the appointment of teachers, to be in favour of attempting a reasonable compromise with regard to religious instruction. In fact he so declared himself in his own election campaign at Bristol when, speaking personally, he stated his desire to be that of the great majority of the parents of children who went to public elementary schools—'that children should be taught the simple elementary religious truths of the Fatherhood of God, the responsibilities of man, and a future State: while children whose parents desired definite religious teaching should receive it, not indeed as part of the public school curriculum, but nevertheless on school premises, if need be, though out of school hours' (*The Times*, January 3, 1906). There were, however, others, like the famous Baptist leader, Dr. John Clifford, very powerfully represented among the Liberal majority in the House of Commons, who added to their demand for (1) genuine popular control of all State-supported schools, and (2) the abolition of sectarian tests for all teachers in such schools, a further point which Sir Henry Campbell-Bannerman described as (3) 'no statutory foothold for sectarian privilege in the State school system'—and were prepared to press that third point to the limit.

The Archbishop of Canterbury knew Mr. Birrell, and on his appointment as President of the Board of Education had immediately sent him a letter expressing his satisfaction:

The Archbishop of Canterbury *to the* Right Hon. Augustine Birrell.

Lambeth Palace, S.E.

Private 15th December, 1905.

Though I know what your influx of letters must at present be, I give myself the pleasure of sending you a single line, to express the satisfaction which I, in common with the vast number of friends of Education, feel in your accession to one of the most difficult and at the same time one of the most interesting of the recently vacated posts.

From the first I hoped that it might be so, for I feel that in you the country has a man who is able to take a large and reasonable view of a difficult situation—and although I cannot expect that you and I should be in full agreement at the present juncture, I have no fears at all that the cause for which I mainly care (the efficiency of secular teaching combined with genuine and thorough grounding in scriptural knowledge and the broad elements of the Christian religion) will suffer unfairly at your hands.

I am also sure that you are one of those who realise what have been the continuous sacrifices made by generations of poor men, especially clergy, to whom these principles are sacredly dear, and that you are not likely to disregard historic facts when dealing with contemporary perplexities. You have given us good assurances of all this and therefore, in addition to all personal considerations, I rejoice that it is to you that the perplexing task has been assigned.

I am not, of course, so foolish or so unfair as to want to elicit from you at present a single syllable on these controversial questions. Nothing could be more unreasonable; only I want you to know that I, for one, can look forward with genuine hopefulness to your accomplishment of a task of supremest delicacy and difficulty. From my heart I wish you God speed in the attempt.

Can there, one asks oneself, be any adequate reason why 'men of goodwill' approaching the problem from different sides, should not be able, without sacrifice of principle on either side, to co-operate in attaining what is, I am certain, your own desire, a reasonable as well as a peaceful solution of existing perplexities, and an ending of existing strifes?

The Right Hon. Augustine Birrell *to the* Archbishop of Canterbury

70 Elm Park Road, Chelsea, S.W.
17th December, 1905.

Private. Sunday.

It was very kind of you to write to me as you have done. I cordially concur in all you say. Were we alone in the world without Parents, Children, Ratepayers, Clergy or Ministers of Religion, we could frame in a few minutes an ideal system of Education—and even as it is, and with a world full of disagreeable things—there is not much real difference between us. But I'm only a very new and humble Minister—not of Religion but of the Crown, and hardly know yet what power or influence I may possess, or what capacity either, I might add. Saturated though I am with the traditions, the noble traditions, of English religious Nonconformity—I have yet read enough in other directions to recognise the force and permanence of the Church Tradition. In an Age like ours we need all the things Spiritual we can muster without scanning them too closely. I hope from the bottom of my heart a settlement may be arrived at which will leave small room for bitterness, but it is a job.

During the general election the Archbishop had carefully refrained from contentious language on the subject of schools; and when the result was announced he publicly expressed his belief in a letter to the Secretary of the National Society (February 2, 1906) that the Government, 'as distinguished from some of its more vociferous supporters', desired to act with fairness all round. He added:

> I may be over sanguine, but I cannot believe that the problem of reconciling the results of the recent election with the maintenance of the principles for which Churchmen have contended, is really insoluble. Certainly every power which I possess is at the service of those who take such a task fairly and considerately in hand.

The Archbishop's mild attitude was not, however, popular with those in Lancashire and elsewhere, who (as some of them proclaimed) were looking to the Primate 'for a battle cry which will rally all our forces in defence of our principles', and vainly pressed him to support a deputation of agitated churchmen to Whitehall before the proposals of the Government were made known. He took care, however, to convey both to the Prime Minister and to Mr. Birrell the authoritative unanimous statement of the Church's views made by the Upper House of Canterbury Convocation on February 22, that 'no scheme of national education can be established with justice, or accepted as permanent, unless full recognition is given to the right of parents to obtain for their children, so far as is possible, instruction in their own faith; that such instruction must, if it is to serve its purpose, be given within school hours, and that it is a moral necessity that all religious instruction should be given by those who can give it with genuine belief'.

A month later (on March 20) the Archbishop saw Mr. Birrell and Lord Crewe by appointment in the House of Lords, and was told the outline of the Bill which was to be considered by the Cabinet on the following day. It was significant of the attitude of Mr. Birrell, as contrasted with that of the hot and strong Radicals, that this outline actually contained a provision for possible denominational teaching as an addition to undenominational or 'syllabus' teaching, in the ordinary provided (i.e. not the transferred) schools. The Archbishop's note on this point is as follows:

> In Provided Schools the normal teaching shall be as under the present law, the L.E.A. being allowed to arrange for anything

> between pure secularism and e.g. the London School Board Syllabus. But the L.E.A. shall have power, if it likes, to allow denominational facilities, paid for by the denomination, on two days in the week.

This provision, however, was rejected by the Cabinet on the following day and was never heard of again. The Archbishop was at once informed by Lord Crewe, and expressed his keen disappointment. During the next few days he had many interviews with Campbell-Bannerman, Asquith, Birrell, and others, and wrote a drastic criticism of the main proposal of the Bill which made a considerable stir in the Cabinet. And he notes this, after a conversation with Mr. R. L. Morant, the Permanent Secretary of the Board of Education (April 4, 1906):

> Some of the members [of the Cabinet] are indignant at the line the majority has taken, and Asquith for one wished the whole matter to be reconsidered *ab initio* but was over-ruled. The matter is not to go before the Cabinet again, and Birrell is cross and despondent, saying that the Bill will be thrown out in the Lords. . . . I told him that I had no wish to make Conservative capital, but that I regarded the attitude of the Government as disastrous in the public interest.

III

On April 9, Mr. Birrell introduced the Education Bill to the House of Commons. He had an immense and an excited audience. The Archbishops of Canterbury and York sat over the clock in the Peers' Gallery. 'Were they' (a newspaper asked) 'the Apollyons straddled across his path' to whom Mr. Birrell later referred? Archbishop Bourne was in the Distinguished Strangers' Gallery, and Dr. Clifford sat behind, 'like some alert schoolmaster who had come to listen, fearful perhaps that *his* teaching might have been ignored'. Mr. Birrell's speech was marked by wit and lucidity, and secured him a great personal success. But the Bill, for the very reasons which made it so welcome to Dr. Clifford and his friends, became at once the centre of the strongest opposition on the part of Churchmen.

Put very briefly, its main provisions were as follows:

A. As regards control:

(1) From January 1, 1908, no schools would be recognized as public elementary schools except those provided by the L.E.A.

(2) The L.E.A. may arrange to take over such existing voluntary schools as it approves for public elementary education by agreement with the Managers, and may obtain schemes for compulsory transfer in certain circumstances.

B. As regards teachers:

(1) All teachers are to be appointed by the L.E.A.

(2) No teacher employed in a public elementary school shall be required as part of his duties as teacher to give any religious instruction.

C. As regards religious instruction:

(1) Undenominational teaching may be given in all schools by members of the existing staff, who may or may not be qualified to give it, at the discretion of the L.E.A.

(2) Denominational teaching may be given on two days a week in transferred schools if this is made a condition of the transfer, but not by regular members of the teaching staff.

(3) Extended facilities for denominational teaching may be given in transferred voluntary schools in Urban areas with a population of over five thousand under certain conditions if the parents of at least four-fifths of the children attending the school desire it. In the case of these 'Four-fifths Schools' the regular teachers are allowed to give this denominational teaching, but not at the expense of the Authority.

The Archbishop the next day (April 10), in a public letter to the Secretary of the National Society, denounced the Bill as in principle unjust, and referred with special emphasis to the compulsory silencing of thousands of trained, qualified, and devoted teachers in Church schools so far as Church teaching was concerned if such a Bill became law. On the following day the Bishops met and declared their opposition as a body.

The question, however, which the Archbishop had to face was the method by which the opposition to the Bill should be directed. There were some, both among the Conservative party (a very small minority in the House of Commons) and among the leaders of the Church, who wished to adopt the most firm and uncompromising tactics and kill the Bill altogether. And during the rest of April and the summer months a violent agitation was conducted on these lines. Fierce things were said, and the controversy raged in a spirit which was little in keeping either with the interests of the children or the cause of religion.

The most outspoken champion of the 'No Surrender' policy

was the Bishop of Manchester, Dr. Knox, once his Grace's coach at Oxford and a man of remarkable force and vocabulary. He at once issued a manifesto denouncing the Bill in unmeasured terms —'it imposes religious tyranny . . . it is nothing but a very thinly-veiled Bill for secularism in the schools . . . it is a Bill of pure robbery and confiscation . . . your tea, your sugar, your tobacco, your beer and your incomes are to be taxed that the children of the Church may be robbed of their Church education and that your schools, built by your own free contributions, may be made useless for your own requirements!' In addition he took steps to organize a Churchmen's demonstration, which was to travel by thirty-two special trains from Manchester to London, on Thursday in Whitsun week, against Mr. Birrell's Bill. When, however, it was suggested that room might be made for such a united demonstration in the Lambeth grounds, the Archbishop demurred:

The ARCHBISHOP OF CANTERBURY *to the* BISHOP OF MANCHESTER

24th April, 1906.

Personally I doubt whether that mode of demonstration is the most effective, but I am old-fashioned in such things and may quite possibly be wrong. We could not have a camp at Lambeth.

It will be understood that under such vehement leadership on the part of Bishop Knox, to say nothing of the vigorous cannonade in the opposite direction on Dr. Clifford's side, in the press and on the platform, the position of the Archbishop with his conciliatory temper was by no means easy.

In May the Bill occupied the Upper House of Canterbury Convocation for three days, mostly in Committee. The Archbishop made a long speech reporting the general attitude, and no public debate took place upon it. He reiterated his desire to be conciliatory, but said that the Bill was such that Churchmen had no other course but to oppose it. Still, he deliberately left open the question whether the Bill should be opposed altogether or amended. And Campbell-Bannerman, in acknowledging the copy of the Resolution adopted, said (May 7, 1906):

Perhaps you will allow me to say that I recognize fully the temperate and reasonable, although firm and decided, tone in which this statement of view treats this difficult and important question, and you may be sure that it will receive careful consideration.

The Bill took its normal course in the House of Commons to the accompaniment of protests and demonstrations and letters of all sorts outside. From April to the end of July there were fourteen hundred meetings all over the country, sometimes thirty or forty a day, against the Bill, and petitions were signed in the same period by more than three-quarters of a million people.

In the meantime the Archbishop had many interviews with members of the Government and others. Thus, on May 25, he saw Mr. Birrell:

> He asked me whether I attached great importance to Catechism teaching as such, and I told him I felt it to be of the very first-grade of importance if Biblical teaching was to be helpfully and pointedly applied to the rules of daily life. He seemed to attach importance to what I said on the subject. He went on to say 'I do not suppose you can have a revolution based on the question of whether or not the teachers are allowed to give denominational instruction—I mean it is not the kind of subject about which you could pull down Park railings or have mobs in the streets'. I said that it probably was not, but that it raised very big questions indeed, and that personally I attach to it supreme importance. I think he had hardly realised the feeling about teachers in country parishes being silenced. I did my best to set it before him.

The following is an interesting note of a later talk with Viscount Goschen (June 25):

> Goschen emphatically supported my view that the House of Lords, speaking roughly, is never anti-Church but always anti-clerical, and that leadership by the clergy is the last thing they will like. For this reason he (Goschen) is very anxious that I should speak immediately after the Government in the debate, for he thinks that I shall not be likely to irritate by a too clerical attitude, whereas many of the Bishops would, he thought, set the Peers against the Episcopal view at the outset, and this would do real harm.

On August 1, the Education Bill came up for second reading in the House of Lords, and was expounded in a careful and moderate speech by Lord Crewe. He was followed by the Archbishop, in a full House, with some twenty Bishops supporting him, Mr. Birrell and Mr. Asquith standing on the steps of the Throne, and Dr. Clifford eagerly watching from the Gallery. The Archbishop delivered a vigorous speech which made a great impression at the time. 'Nothing better has been done from *any* of our benches for many a long year', wrote Lord Lansdowne to him that same night. But it is sufficient, at this distance from the battle, to call attention simply to a few outstanding points. The speech was historical, expository, and critical. The Archbishop agreed that the Nation had declared in favour of popular control and against 'tests'—but he urged that the control given in the Bill was very one-sided, and that at least a teacher ought to show that he was duly qualified for the work he had to undertake—including the work of religious instruction. He submitted the main object of the Bill to a devastating criticism:

> What does the Bill do? It takes 14,000 existing schools, with their trusts, and demolishes, not the mere wording of the trusts, but the very essence and pith of them. The characteristics that make a denominational school different from others are abolished, and the school is handed over to a local authority, which may, if it likes, refuse to take it; or, if it does take it, may practically secularise it save for some two hours in the week, and may appoint teachers who are unwilling to give, or untrained to give, religious teaching; and if religious teaching is given, and the teachers are willing to give it, no child need go to school until the religious lesson is over. ... We are told that local authorities will not on any large scale destroy or even impair the system of religious teaching, but are we quite sure that that can be counted upon everywhere? Of course, no man will allege it of England as a whole. I am quite prepared to say that local authorities in the main will try to act fairly, and I would trust them generally, but the Bill binds them in one direction to allow no denominational teaching, and leaves them free in another to go as far in the secular direction as they like.

He then added:

> If I am right, if it is really possible that these things can come about, surely it is childish to tell us, 'Yes, they can do all that if they like; but Mr. Birrell hopes they won't.' Does the security come to anything else?

He concluded by expressing his desire not to throw out but to amend the Bill where amendment was vital. And he named the following six points which involved 'changes which are pretty far-reaching':

(1) Religious teaching in all schools, subject to a conscience clause.

(2) Religious teaching to be given by teachers who mean what they say.
(3) Definite religious teaching for children whose parents desire it, subject to reasonable limitations by the L.E.A.
(4) Teachers to be allowed to continue to give definite religious teaching.
(5) The principle underlying the 'Four-fifths Schools', i.e. existing denominational schools in large urban areas with other schools in the area, to be enlarged.
(6) Some voice for those who have directly to do with the school in the appointment of the teacher.

The second reading was carried on August 3, and the House shortly after adjourned, the Archbishop going off to Courmayeur, where he took his ease on the Italian slopes of Mont Blanc. From Courmayeur he went to Scotland. He stayed at Belmont with Campbell-Bannerman, and at Whittingehame with Balfour, to talk about the Bill. He was disappointed with both, and was 'amazed' by the former's 'real ignorance of the question'.

IV

The debate was resumed in the House of Lords on October 25. In Committee, the number and the character of the amendments produced by the Archbishop and the Bishops on the one hand, and Lord Lansdowne and the Conservatives on the other, coupled with the weakness of the Government Bench, soon revealed that a crisis of an acute kind would have to be faced. The House of Commons, and the Liberals and Nonconformists in the country, were angered by what they deemed the wrecking character of the amendments which, while nominally accepting the principles of public control and no tests for teachers, imposed so many restrictions on their application as to make them (so it was claimed) practically unrecognizable to their authors. And the anti-Church feeling, whether widespread or not, was certainly vociferous and bitter. As the Committee stage proceeded the situation worsened. To add to the difficulties, the Lord Chancellor, Lord Loreburn, was ill, and the whole brunt of the defence fell on a single Liberal peer, Lord Crewe, who was practically unsupported and had very little independent authority himself.

Westminster Gazette, Nov. 7, 1907

SUAVITER IN MODO

The Archbishop: Dilly-dilly-dear: *do please* come and be reconstituted!

On November 16, the Archbishop had a private talk with John Morley. He pressed the extraordinary unfairness of the position:

> We were trying in the House of Lords, or at all events I was trying, to suggest in the Bill amendments which should be reasonable and consistent with the large principles on which I believed the country to have expressed itself. They were in no sense, so far as I was concerned, wrecking amendments. But our position is one almost of helplessness as regards commending what we say to the men on whom real responsibility rests. I pointed out that there are five members of the Cabinet in the House of Lords, and that four of these take absolutely no part, and, as far as I am aware, know nothing as to the details of the Bill. Three of them (Elgin, Tweedmouth, and Carrington) have never opened their lips on the subject; Lord Ripon has only spoken as a sort of figure-head, without pretending to take any lift of the matter; and everything has rested on the shoulders of Crewe, who quite obviously has had no authority given him to speak or act in a responsible or independent manner. The result is that what we say might as well be spoken to the wind.

He spent the week-end (Nov. 17–19) at Windsor, where he had a long talk with Campbell-Bannerman:

> He [Campbell-Bannerman] began by saying: 'This is a very bad business. Nothing can, so far as I see, be done with your House of Lords work. I should not be able, even if I tried, to restrain my people at all from making sharp work of what you have been doing.'

The Archbishop repudiated this interpretation and explained:

> (1) Our difficulty in having no hearers there whose position is responsible or whose ultimate judgement matters.
> (2) The way in which we are driven to amend every Clause separately by knowing nothing about what will happen to our other amendments.
> (3) The character of our amendments themselves.

But the Prime Minister—whom he saw again later on the same day about the possibility of a conference—was depressed and unhappy, and the Archbishop concluded:

> I left him with the impression on my mind that he is terribly in the hands of the more popular force among his followers and that he greatly underrates its anti-Church character.

The next days were full of anxiety. Morley himself told the Archbishop that he had been bombarded by men who said that this was an opportunity for the House of Commons to assert its position, which had been lowered under the Balfour *régime*. 'Let the House of Lords understand that England is governed by the House of Commons, and never was a better chance than now, by doing this.'

Three important conferences took place at Lansdowne's house, November 23, 26, and 27, attended by Conservative leaders and also by the Archbishop, to consider amendments on Report. Some of the more extreme points it was agreed to give up, but 'from the first it became apparent that there is a good deal of difference of opinion as to the comparative harmfulness of (1) the rejection or death of the Bill, and (2) the continuance of the existing strife'. Balfour was the leader of those who thought that any compromise on important points was undesirable.

Throughout the conferences the Archbishop (who was in favour of a settlement if it could be obtained without sacrifice of fundamental principles) was very unwell, and only got out of bed to attend them and then return to his bed. On Sunday night, November 25, the King sent the following letter to the Prime Minister:

King Edward VII *to the* Rt. Hon. Sir Henry Campbell-Bannerman

Buckingham Palace. Nov. 25, 1906.

In view of the serious state of affairs which would arise were a conflict to take place between the House of Lords and the House of Commons on the amendments passed by the former House on the Education Bill, the King feels certain that Sir H. C. Bannerman will agree with him in thinking it most important that there should, if possible, be a compromise in respect of these amendments.

The King would therefore ask Sir Henry to consider whether it would not be highly desirable that Sir Henry should discuss the matter with the Archbishop of Canterbury in the hope that some *modus vivendi*, on the line of mutual concessions, could be found to avoid the threatened collision between the two Houses.

For the King thinks it would be deplorable from a constitutional as well as from every point of view, were such a conflict to occur.

The King would wish to call Sir Henry's attention to pages 7 to 43 in the second volume of Archbishop Tait's *Life*, when a contest was on the eve of taking place between the two Houses on the Irish Church question in 1869.

The King proposes to send a copy of this letter to the Archbishop of Canterbury.

The interview accordingly took place next day at Lambeth, and Campbell-Bannerman saw the Archbishop in bed:

He had really nothing to say, and did not appear to me to be more familiar with the Bill than he was when I talked to him at Windsor. In some respects he had forgotten what I then tried to teach him as to what his Bill contained. He showed no kind of wish of his own for an uncompromising or anti-Church school attitude, but simply kept referring again to his own majority and the need of satisfying it. Pleasant as he was I felt this to be rather humiliating at such a juncture on the part of the Prime Minister of the country. When I suggested particular points—e.g. the right of the teacher to teach, and the need of discovering the qualifications of a religious teacher, and the necessity that the ballot among parents should be genuine, and that absentees shall not be reckoned against us, he at once personally acquiesced, but kept saying 'These are points on which my people are very hot'.

It is interesting to note the reference to Archbishop Tait's intervention at the time of the disestablishment of the Irish Church in 1869,[1] but the two matters, as the Archbishop pointed out, were very different, for the question at issue in the Irish Church was one of finance, and the problem here was one of deep religious convictions. Campbell-Bannerman's report to the King indicates the nature of the difference:

The RT. HON. SIR HENRY CAMPBELL-BANNERMAN *to* KING EDWARD VII

10 Downing St. 27th Nov. 1906.

. . . The Archbishop shewed, as usual, the most fair and conciliatory spirit. Practically, the principal point on which His Grace insisted as all-important was that the ordinary teacher should not be prevented from giving, if he were willing to do so, the special and distinctive religious teaching.

Your Majesty's Government, on the other part, think that this would be inadmissible, in its full extent, because it would leave the voluntary denominational schools practically as they now are in this respect, with all their powers and privileges, notwithstanding

[1] See *Life of Archbishop Tait*, vol. ii, ch. xix.

their being nominally under the control of the local authority, who would pay rent to the Church for the schools. Sir Henry Campbell-Bannerman gathers that with the Archbishop this is the main point of difference.

During the next critical days the Archbishop was bedridden with gastric influenza. Interviews, however, were possible, as well as correspondence. On December 3, the last day of the Report stage, he wrote a letter to Lord Lansdowne, of which the main part is as follows:

The ARCHBISHOP OF CANTERBURY *to the* MARQUESS OF LANSDOWNE

3rd December, 1906.

I have of course no means of gauging independently what is likely to happen to the Bill, but I have absolute knowledge as to the fact that there is a strong section in the Cabinet genuinely anxious to make some real concessions to us with a view to passing the Measure. Upon the whole, after weighing pros and cons with every care, I am I think quite definitely convinced that it would on the highest public grounds be better that the Bill should pass, if we can by our amendments secure in some reasonable form:

(*a*) Religious education in all schools within school hours, with full protection of conscience;
(*b*) A reasonable expectation that our schools will (where fit) be taken over by the L.E.A.;
(*c*) The reasonable use of teachers (if the teacher and the denomination desire it) for 'facilities' children under Clause 3;
(*d*) Practicable and effective conditions for retaining as 'extended facilities' schools the existing denominational schools in areas where the children have access to an alternative school of a non-denominational type.

All these things are not only compatible with Clause 1 as introduced, but were (except the use of the teacher) implicitly declared by the Government in many speeches to be what they wished to see; and the liberty to the teacher is essential to making ordinary facilities a reality on a large scale. In making these demands, therefore, we stand on exceedingly strong ground, and no subsequent breakdown on these points could be ascribed to 'wrecking' action on our part.

We are also in our amendments demanding two things which the Government has never in any way assented to. I allude to (1) the opportunity for denominational teaching in Council Schools, and

> (2) the acquisition of extended facilities even where there is no alternative *school*. Both of these demands can, I think, be reasonably justified in the abstract. The *principle* of general facilities has been defended by Birrell himself, and in the limited degree and form in which we ask for it we have a strong case. . . . But it is distinctly a different sort of demand from those which are really within the four corners of the Government Bill and are a mere strengthening of its weak and unreal provisions.
>
> About the other demand I feel more hesitation and difficulty than I did at first. We ask that extended facilities schools, or 'atmosphere' schools, may be claimed and secured in single school areas if satisfactory provision is somehow forthcoming for the minority. This sounds at first sight fair, and I think I have myself supported the idea before it had been worked out in black and white. I do not remember whether in our conference at Lansdowne House last week the actual words were before us, and if they were I was not physically fit to weigh them and their consequences. But I have tried to weigh them now to the best of a sick man's power, and my conclusion is that we could not, if we pass the proposed amendment, deny that we are 'turning the Bill round' and transforming into the *rule* or *norm* of many rural areas what was always and avowedly put forward by the Government as an exceptional provision to meet particular cases.

This letter alarmed the Conservatives, and Lord Salisbury came to express the fears which he and others felt, and, though referring in terms to an indiscreet remark of the Bishop of Wakefield's to Morant, he gave vent to 'a characteristic outburst as to how he wished the Bishops would leave politics to politicians'.

More conversations followed. Lord Crewe again saw the Archbishop, still in bed at Lambeth, on December 5. It became clear that the position narrowed itself down to the crucial difficulty of the teacher being free to give denominational instruction, as to which Lord Crewe made certain suggestions which were also communicated to Lansdowne.

V

Meantime Birrell made a bellicose speech in the House of Commons on a motion to reject the Lords' amendments *en bloc* on December 10. This called forth a strong protest from the Archbishop to the Prime Minister:

The Archbishop of Canterbury *to the* Rt. Hon. Sir Henry Campbell-Bannerman

December 11, 1906.

I need not tell you how keenly, in the light of my recent conversations with you, I have this morning read Birrell's speech of yesterday. I confess to a keen feeling of depression as to the prospects of such a solution as you and I agree in desiring in the interests of peace. Although Birrell foreshadows the possible acceptance by the Government of important amendments, the general tone of his utterance was, as I think you must feel, of a sort to make it extraordinarily difficult for the House of Lords to propose them. There is throughout the speech, whether intentionally or not, a sort of demand that the House of Lords shall come almost apologetically, or hat in hand, to ask the Government to listen to its proposals, and that it shall begin by practically withdrawing what is now suggested and substituting something quite different in its place.

But he got little comfort from the reply:

The Rt. Hon. Sir Henry Campbell-Bannerman *to the* Archbishop of Canterbury

10 Downing Street. 11 Dec. 06.

The course we have taken has good authority behind it, and is I firmly believe the only course which would not have extinguished or at least gravely endangered the chance of peaceful solution. As to the language used and the tone employed, it was not one whit overstrained when the general effect of all that has been done in the House of Lords is considered. You cannot expect people to be quite mealy mouthed in the circumstances. . . .

The House of Commons resolved to disagree with the Lords' amendments, after an excited debate, by 306 to 104 votes, on December 11. An important conference took place at Lansdowne House the next day, this being the first time since November 27 that the Archbishop had been able to leave the Palace. It revealed a strong difference of opinion between those who wanted the Bill to go through with reasonable amendments, and those who wanted a conflict. The Archbishop was with the former. But as Lord St. Aldwyn said to him, 'our real difficulty lies in the fact that the leader of the Party does not want a peaceable solution'; and Mr. Balfour was supported by the Duke of Norfolk.

An interview took place on December 14 between the Archbishop and Mr. Birrell and Lord Crewe:

> They made no secret of the fact that they had both of them been averse to the action of the House of Commons in sending to the House of Lords the general *en bloc* resolution. Birrell said he had fully contemplated and desired the discussion of the amendments seriatim, and evidently he did not think there would have been any impossibility in doing this. They both admitted that the House of Lords had received a rebuff or insult which no such body could be expected to accept tamely.

The Archbishop, however, was getting into very difficult waters by holding any discussions at all. Lord Crewe had hardly left the Palace when the National Society telephoned to say that they were sitting in Committee and were 'trembling at the news circulated by the *Standard* to the effect that I had seen the Prime Minister and was arranging with him a compromise'.

On December 17, Lord Lansdowne moved a Resolution in the House of Lords protesting against the rejection *en bloc* by the Commons as an innovation in constitutional procedure, and invited the Government to state their attitude in detail. Lord Crewe, after defending the Government's action by precedents, intimated that the assistant teacher (not the head teacher) might be permitted to give denominational teaching in the large Clause 3 schools, and that further provision might be made against capricious refusal by a local education authority to take over the schools, and that a four-fifths majority would not be insisted upon for Clause 4 schools.

On December 18, by the King's wish, the Archbishop was present at a private meeting at Crewe House of Mr. Balfour, Lord Lansdowne, and Lord Cawdor, with Lord Crewe, Mr. Birrell, and Mr. Asquith, at which the proposed amendments were explained. But though accommodation seemed possible on other points, the position of the teacher remained the crucial issue. The Conservative leaders had a conference in Mr. Balfour's room, and insisted that all teachers in all transferred schools ought to be allowed to volunteer their services. When the meeting was resumed in the evening, Mr. Birrell said, in reply to the Archbishop, that, whatever minor modifications the Government might accept, it could not abandon the absolute right of the local education authority to refuse leave to all teachers if they so desired. And it was this absolute supremacy of the local education authority in a matter so vital which it was impossible to concede.

The breach was complete, and though the Archbishop made another attempt to find a way across, in a conversation with Lord Crewe at Lambeth next morning, the fate of the Bill was clear. In the House of Lords, on December 19, Lord Lansdowne moved that the Lords 'do insist upon their amendments'. Lord Crewe charged the House with choosing war rather than peace, and said that the Government must refuse responsibility for the consequences which must rest upon the shoulders of the 'noble Lords opposite and the Right Reverend Bench who have chosen to wreck the Bill'. The Archbishop followed, and expressed his intense feeling of disappointment. He had done his best, but he acknowledged that, unless the Government could meet them on the question of the teachers, it was better that the Bill should disappear. Lord Lansdowne's motion was carried by 132 votes to 52, the Archbishop voting with the majority. The last scene took place in the House of Commons when Campbell-Bannerman, amidst a tumult of cheering from his followers, justified the attitude of the Government, and declared it to be intolerable that the House of Lords, while one Party in the State was in power, should be its willing servant, and when that Party had received unmistakable and emphatic condemnation by the country, should be able itself to neutralize and thwart and distort the policy which the electors had shown they approved. He added, in language ominous for the future, that the resources of the House of Commons were not exhausted, and that 'a way must be found, a way will be found, by which the will of the people, expressed through their elected representatives in this House, will be made to prevail'.[1]

V

During the next two years further efforts were made to secure a settlement of the schools question; and the failure of the last effort—Mr. Runciman's Bill—was a peculiar disappointment to the Archbishop.

In February 1908, Mr. McKenna, who had succeeded Mr.

[1] *Life of Sir Henry Campbell-Bannerman*, J. A. Spender, ii. 311–12.

Birrell as President of the Board of Education, introduced a Bill which was designed to deal comprehensively with the school question generally, though on different lines from Mr. Birrell. It would, like that Bill, only recognize one type of elementary school, that provided by the local education authority, but voluntary schools could continue as such, receiving Parliamentary grants by a system of contracting out. In particular it introduced the system of contracting out of the national system for denominational schools which would receive not rate aid but Parliamentary grants; with the proviso, however, that no denominational school in single school parishes would be allowed to contract out. It was read a second time in May 1908.

In between the first and second readings of the McKenna Bill, however, an interesting intervention was made in the House of Lords by the Bishop of St. Asaph,[1] with the marked encouragement of Mr. Lloyd George and others. He drafted a Bill, with an eye to incorporating as much of Mr. McKenna's Bill as was applicable, and at the same time made a quite new departure. It involved:

(1) the transfer of all schools to the local education authority;
(2) undenominational religious teaching in all schools at the expense of the local education authority;
(3) facilities for denominational teaching in all schools during school hours on three days a week to children whose parents desire it;
(4) complete freedom for the teachers to give either undenominational or denominational religious teaching.

The Government, it appeared from private conversations between the Archbishop and Asquith and others, were sympathetic, but cautious, and doubtful of persuading the rank and file of their followers. The Conservatives, interpreted by Mr. Balfour, were much more critical of the Bill, which seemed to be a move by the Church, and therefore seemed likely to lead to concessions from the Church rather than to the Church, and made no provision for Roman Catholics. On the other hand, both the Government and the rank and file of the opposition were anxious for a settlement of such a perplexing controversy. Church opinion was not particularly sympathetic, though some of the

[1] Dr. Edwards.

Bishops (not, however, the Bishops of Birmingham[1] or Manchester) were in favour of a second reading.

When the Bishop of St. Asaph moved the second reading on March 30, the Archbishop made a strong plea for a settlement of the education controversy and expressed himself as sympathetic with the general idea of the Bill, though he pointed out that it did not cover all cases.

On the motion of Lord Lansdowne the debate was subsequently adjourned, to give an opportunity for conference, if desired, between the promoters and the Government.

On April 5, Campbell-Bannerman resigned the Premiership, and died before the end of the month.

This involved various important political changes. Mr. Asquith became Prime Minister, and Mr. Walter Runciman succeeded Mr. McKenna as President of the Board of Education.

With the advent of Mr. Runciman a new and vigorous attempt was begun to secure a real and lasting settlement of the question. The files at Lambeth are crowded with letters and notes of interviews from May onwards between the Archbishop and the new President and many others. At the first interview, while making certain proposals of a kind more favourable to voluntary schools, Mr. Runciman made it clear that Mr. McKenna's Bill must be taken as a basis of any settlement.

During the summer the discussions continued in private and were resumed in the autumn. As an example of the amount of time and thought expended on the subject, it may suffice to note that between October 15 and December 3 there are ninety typewritten quarto pages, reporting interviews between the Archbishop and members of the Government and others, with regard to the Bill, quite apart from boxes of correspondence of all sorts and conditions, and dossiers of the critical letters to and from Mr. Runciman and the Prime Minister and other protagonists.

All the time the Archbishop kept in touch with the Bishops of London,[2] Southwark,[3] Stepney,[4] and St. Asaph—and got much assistance from Professor Michael Sadler. He also saw others who were less favourable to such a settlement. Once at least he 'kept the Bishop of Stepney and Sadler for an interview with the stiff men whom I had summoned by telegraph—Salisbury, Robert Cecil, Athelstan Riley, Brooke of Kennington'. Nor did

[1] Dr. Gore. [2] Dr. Ingram. [3] Dr. Talbot. [4] Dr. Lang.

he neglect to inform Lansdowne and the Conservative leaders in the House of Lords. But all through he deprecated haste. As he wrote in a private memorandum on October 19:

> It will take a little time to get people to examine the plan fairly, not in a spirit of mere criticism, but with an honest desire to effect an agreement. Extreme hurry will render negotiations impossible and hope of a settlement will disappear.

VII

The main elements of the proposals put forward by Mr. Runciman after their prolonged discussion were as follows:

(1) All schools receiving rate aid to be under the control and management of the local education authority.

(2) Voluntary schools in single school parishes to be transferred to the local education authority subject to an obligation on the part of the authority to give facilities for denominational instruction to those children whose parents require it on two mornings in the week, such instruction to be paid for from other than public funds.

(3) Voluntary schools in other than single area parishes may be transferred and the obligation to give facilities for denominational teaching in such schools on two mornings in the week shall be similarly imposed.

(4) Voluntary schools in other than single school parishes may contract out and will receive not rate aid but the Parliamentary grant, so being given a reasonable chance of existence, leaving, however, a substantial burden to be borne by the denomination.

(5) The local education authority shall provide Cowper-Temple instruction in all of their schools for any children whose parents demand it.

(6) Assistant teachers may volunteer to give denominational instruction subject to the consent of the local education authority, but the local education authority shall not refuse consent except on the ground that they themselves simultaneously require the teachers' services. A right of appeal is allowed to the Board of Education.

(7) The owners of transferred voluntary schools may transfer the buildings absolutely or loan them to the local education authority.

While these proposals from the Archbishop's point of view went a considerable distance and in particular contained the satisfactory provision which obliged the local education authority to provide Cowper-Temple instruction in all schools and to give facilities for denominational instruction in transferred voluntary schools, the Archbishop, and still more his advisers, wished to go further. He asked especially for:

(*a*) Statutory facilities for denominational instruction in Council schools.
(*b*) Leave to head teachers to give denominational instruction.
(*c*) Power to build new contract-out denominational schools, and
(*d*) Parents' committees for religious instruction.

Some impression of the difficulties with which he had to contend is given by the following account of the Standing Committee of the National Society on November 4:

> Rather trying meeting of National Society Standing Committee. I stated in outline what had passed, and told them plainly that I was prepared to agree to a settlement if the lines I had laid down could be genuinely followed. Speeches of mingled remonstrance, indignation, and despair were made by Hugh Cecil, Canon Cleworth, the Dean of Canterbury (who was specially wrathful), and John Talbot (sad rather than wrathful). The Bishop of Southwark spoke admirably on my side, though confining himself rightly to general terms. Brooke was less hostile than might have been expected, and indeed went a long way towards actually supporting me. Athelstan Riley did not speak. Salisbury was not wholly Cecilian, or at least not so uncompromising as Hugh.

Mr. Runciman's difficulties were not dissimilar, for when the Archbishop told him of the National Society's Meeting:

> He said it was quite as bad on the other side, and that Dr. Clifford is at present almost tearfully complaining of the position in which he finds himself, of being bombarded as a weak-kneed Moderate.

By the middle of November, after many comings and goings, interviews and conferences, including a long conference with a deputation from the National Union of Teachers, which strongly objected to contracting out, and made it clear that they would officially discourage volunteering for denominational teaching, a provisional agreement seemed to have been reached between the Archbishop and the Government. And so the

Archbishop informed Mr. Asquith on November 17; asking (among other things) for a clear statement as to the liberty of the head teacher in a transferred school to give denominational teaching; and adding at the end of his letter:

The ARCHBISHOP OF CANTERBURY *to the* RT. HON. H. H. ASQUITH

17 Nov. 1908.

In expressing assent to the provisions as they stand, I must of course reserve the right, which I presume you would also claim, to reconsider such assent in the event of amendments being carried which affect the general structure and balance of the measure. And, lastly, I must again ask that it be clearly understood that the assent which I am able to give to the Government's proposals expresses, not the claim which the Church of England is in my judgment reasonably entitled to make, but the sacrifice in which I can, speaking for myself, recommend my fellow Churchmen to acquiesce in the interests of religious and educational peace.

Mr. Asquith replied asking for a little more precision with regard to the Archbishop's demands as affecting head teachers.

On the same evening, November 18, the Archbishop was at the Bishop's house, Kennington, consulting with the Bishop of Southwark.

By a most unfortunate accident he had a very bad fall, which caused him great pain and forced him to lie up for some days. He was carried from Kennington to Lambeth. The crucial letter, replying to the Government, was written for him by the Bishop of Southwark.

The BISHOP OF SOUTHWARK *to the* RT. HON. W. RUNCIMAN

18th November, 1908.

Bishop's House, Kennington Park, S.E.

The Archbishop has had a nasty fall here, and injured his leg badly, causing him great pain.

He had just spoken to me about the last communication to him from Mr. Asquith.

He wishes me to say that, if you are able to allow the following points, that is to say:—

(i) The power of building new contracting-out schools;

(ii) The right of the existing Head Teacher in transferred Voluntary Schools to give denominational instruction during the full tenure, however long, of his existing Headmastership; and, further, to give it for a period of five years from now in any Headmastership in any transferred Voluntary School to which he may be moved; and

(iii) If you will give a clause permitting Local Education Authorities to form Committees of Advice in the way that has been suggested for matters connected with the religious teaching—

he will not himself press further for the right of the future Head Teacher, though on this point he cannot answer for others.

I hope this letter will meet the needs of the moment. It is written in circumstances of great difficulty, and not as he would have written it; that is only because I can simply put the points nakedly.

It has his authority.

The Rt. Hon. W. Runciman *to the* Bishop of Southwark

19th November, 1908.
15 Great College Street, Westminster.

In reply to your letter of yesterday, I am authorized to say that, for the sake of securing a balanced settlement, we acquiesce in:—

(i) The power to provide from private sources a new 'contracted-out' school where the money is forthcoming and a sufficient number of parents desire it.

(ii) The right of the existing Head Teacher to volunteer as described in your letter, and with a five years' time limit.

(iii) And we raise no objection to the Local Education Authorities setting up religious instruction Committees similar to those set up by the old London School Board and other School Boards for the purpose of agreeing on Syllabuses, etc. But as I often stated, it must be clearly understood that we could not concur in any arrangement which might lead to the employment of direct or indirect tests on the teachers.

We are greatly obliged to you and the Archbishop of Canterbury for your kindness in disposing of these outstanding points to-day. I hope to present the Bill, embodying the agreement arrived at, when the House meets to-morrow.

The same day, November 19, the Prime Minister announced in the House of Commons that a Concordat had been reached on the schools question; that the McKenna Bill would be withdrawn, and a new Bill, embodying the Concordat, would be introduced with the general approval of the Archbishop of Canterbury, and the leading Nonconformists, who had both promised that so far as their authority and influence go they would *ex animo* acquiesce in the settlement embodied in the Bill and give it their support.

A sudden difficulty, however, arose on the financial side. On November 20, for the first time, the money proposals embodied in the Bill were shown to the Archbishop. At once he saw that they were unsatisfactory. Mr. Runciman had assured him and the Bishop of Stepney, who was in close touch with the Archbishop all through, that 'Money can be discussed immediately we have the other two matters out of the way—and we can be generous'. The Archbishop felt obliged to write at once to the Prime Minister about the terms offered both for contracting out and for transfer.

In a letter sent simultaneously to Mr. Runciman he said, writing from his bed:

The ARCHBISHOP OF CANTERBURY *to the* RT. HON. W. RUNCIMAN

Private. November 21, 1908.

You probably scarcely realise how vehement has been the criticism of my action in having abstained from insisting upon seeing the proposed figures before allowing my assent to the settlement plan to be quoted. In answer to such protest I have said, not once but a dozen times, that I had your assurance that we need not worry about the financial part of it provided the rest was satisfactorily settled, that you saw your way to devising a plan which would be generous and that, though you could not then tell me what it was, I had implicit trust in what you had said. That trust I still retain and do not believe now that, if it can be shown that the plan in the Bill would mean a general impossibility of contracting out (except perhaps in well-to-do neighbourhoods), you would wish to hold to it as it stands. I ought not perhaps to shrink from telling you that I have been laughed at by more than one friend for this confidence—'a simple Simon negotiating with people who are not simple Simons at all'—and so forth. I have simply reiterated, that, foolish or not, I had complete confidence in what you had said.

A conference of experts was arranged. The Archbishop was supplied with the proposed figures for a number of schools which might contract out, and there was a full discussion between his representatives and the representatives of the Board.

In the meantime opposition to the Concordat had been

growing from another quarter. The Bishop of Manchester wrote an Open Letter to the Bishops of England denouncing it. The *School Guardian*, the organ of the National Society, declared that acceptance of the Bill by the Church would be a 'colossal surrender'. Mr. Athelstan Riley and other lay members had signed a petition to the Archbishop asking for a meeting of the Representative Church Council, and in accordance with their request a special meeting of that Council was summoned for December 3rd.

At the Representative Church Council meeting it was clear that feelings ran high. The Archbishop compressed the realities of the situation in a pertinent paragraph:

> Do all those who speak so vehemently, and with such obvious truth, about the value of our Church Schools realise what has been the transfer taking place in recent years? Some 550 Church of England Schools closed in the last three years, with accommodation for more than 160,000 children; while in the same three years there has been an increase of 1,056 Council Schools with accommodation for 478,000 children. What about the Church's care for those children? Such transfer of children will, for obvious reasons, be greatly accelerated in the next few years. And at such a moment we are offered the opportunity—an opportunity which may never recur—of securing by law that in every elementary school in the country—present and future—the right to give denominational teaching shall have a permanent place.

The forces against him were too strong. Sir Alfred Cripps, Lord Halifax, the Bishops of Manchester and Birmingham, and the Dean of Canterbury all spoke against the Bill. And when Sir Alfred Cripps's resolution was put, refusing to accept the terms of compromise embodied in the Education Bill, the cleavage between the Bishops and the rest of the Representative Church Council was painfully apparent. The House of Bishops alone of the three Houses had a majority against Cripps and for the Bill, the total voting being as follows:

	Ayes	*Noes*
Bishops	3	18
Clergy	73	35
Laity	113	46

The attitude of the Representative Church Council altered the whole situation. The Prime Minister on December 7 announced in the House of Commons that the Bill was withdrawn, as it could no longer be called an agreed measure. He paid a warm tribute 'first and foremost' to the patient, considerate, and indomitable efforts of Mr. Runciman, and added:

> A like tribute is due and ought to be paid to the great Archbishop, who, in the face of obstacles and difficulties which would have daunted any man of less courage, has shown himself worthy of the title of Pastor Pastorum Ecclesiae.

He thanked also the leaders of the Free Churches who, for the sake of a national settlement, had shown themselves ready to lay aside cherished ideas. And he concluded with the admission that, after a public life now prolonged for many years and spent for the most part in acute and uncompromising controversy, with a fair share both of the smiles and of the frowns of fortune:

> I am not ashamed to confess that I have never experienced a more heavy and thorough disappointment. I say again I do not regret the attempt that has been made, and I would far rather have made that attempt, so far as my part is concerned, than for fear of failure not to have made the attempt at all.

The Archbishop and Mr. Runciman, as the leaders in conciliation, were drawn close to one another, as many letters reveal: and there was a real body of opinion expressed by men of all sections, creeds, and parties, in favour of agreement. The Bill failed, and to the Archbishop then and for many years to come it remained one of the grievous disappointments of his life. But the courage with which he discharged his task and faced the failure were an example to all. The chapter shall end with the testimony of Mr. Alfred Lyttelton, who had been associated with the Archbishop on the Conservative side, and wrote to him immediately after the withdrawal of the Bill:

The RT. HON. A. LYTTELTON *to the* ARCHBISHOP OF CANTERBURY

7th December, 1908.
16 Great College Street, Westminster.

I secured the publication of the correspondence to-day as you will have seen, and feel a satisfaction to have even that small connection with labours so distinguished alike in spirit and mind. Whatever happens—and I do not in the least despair, your splendid courage and persistency have permanently and irrevocably moved this controversy out of the trough of bitterness into which it had sunk. We have almost all got too close to regard each other again as real foes. This indeed is noble work.

CHAPTER XXX

THE ARCHBISHOP, PARLIAMENT, AND SOCIAL QUESTIONS, 1906–1908

Sir Adam was unlucky in his topicks; for he suggested a doubt of the propriety of Bishops having seats in the House of Lords. *Johnson.* 'How so, Sir? Who is more proper for having the dignity of a peer, than a Bishop, provided a Bishop be what he ought to be; and if improper Bishops be made, that is not the fault of the Bishops, but of those who make them.' BOSWELL's *Life of Dr. Johnson* (1772).

IN the first bitterness of disappointment at the rejection of his Bill, Mr. Birrell had attacked the Bishops—and by implication the Archbishop—for their general attitude to social questions. His speech, and the Archbishop's reply, provide a fitting opportunity for calling attention to the Archbishop's own interest in social reform, and certain legislative measures in which he took an active part at this time. The charge was one which the Archbishop felt keenly; and of his own work in Winchester days regarding such so-called secular subjects something has already been said.

I

At a complimentary dinner, following the failure of the Education Bill, at the National Liberal Club on February 18, 1907, Mr. Birrell went out of his way to attack the Bishops. He said that he had no wish to bear grudges in politics, and went on:

> I can even contemplate the action of the Bishops with forbearance. I own freely that I have never been a great admirer of the action of these prelates in times past. I cannot remember a single great cause they ever advocated. I cannot recall a single victory they ever won; hardly a word they ever said in the cause of humanity.

He quoted Sir Samuel Romilly's Diary as comment on the past, and declared that, in acting as they had with regard to the Education Bill, the Bishops only added to their already black list.

Such an attack wounded the Archbishop deeply. He had taken his cue from his father-in-law, Tait, and he had always been at pains to show an active interest in humane causes, taking special care to represent the Church on this side in a conspicuous way in the House of Lords. He at once wrote to Birrell:

The ARCHBISHOP OF CANTERBURY *to the* RT. HON. AUGUSTINE BIRRELL

Lambeth Palace, S.E.
20th February, 1907.

In *The Times* of yesterday I read a speech of yours which, if it be correctly reported, contains and elaborates one of the gravest indictments which could be brought against a body of public men in a Christian country.

England is well accustomed to read, and adequately to appraise, the facile and wholesale denunciations of Bishops which are characteristic features of a certain kind of irresponsible oratory. It is a different thing altogether when a Cabinet Minister of the first rank, not in the heat of debate but in a deliberate speech, formulates against those who, as you truly say, ought to make it their endeavour to represent some of the Christian ideals of a Christian nation, the grave charge that in their public action they have systematically and continuously disregarded the better aspirations, convictions and feelings of the people at large.

I am not concerned to deal with your reference—possibly fair, possibly unfair—to what was said or left unsaid by Peers and Bishops in the days of Sir Samuel Romilly. He died I think in 1818. But I am closely concerned with the responsible action or inaction of the Bishops of to-day. When a statesman, whose work has required from him a special familiarity with contemporary facts, tells the world that, in what he calls the cause of humanity, the Bishops have usually kept silence in Parliament, I feel the charge to be one which I personally regard as of the utmost possible gravity.

This however is no personal matter. I sit in the House of Lords in a public capacity, and on reading your words I asked myself what correspondence they have with my recollection of the work which we have there tried to do. Will you pardon the appearance of egotism if, taking myself as a specimen, I mention some of the subjects with which one Bishop out of many has endeavoured, however inadequately, to deal by voice and vote.

I have been for twelve years a member of the House of Lords. Looking back along those years, and omitting all reference to ecclesiastical and educational debates, I recall the following as among the matters in the discussion of which I have been allowed to bear a somewhat responsible part: In 1896–7 I had the privilege of taking a labouring oar, both in the House and in the Select Committee, in framing the Infant Life Protection Act, and of supporting the Workmen's Compensation Bill of the latter year. In 1898 a great deal of my time was occupied with the details of what became, with my cordial support, the Prisons Act of that year. In 1899 I advocated the Prevention of Corruption Bill as cordially as I did in 1905 and 1906, when, in an altered shape, it became law; and I spent much time in promoting, both outside and inside the House, the unpretentious but useful Bill for compelling the provision of seats for shop assistants. In 1900 and 1901 the Bill for promoting the earlier closing of shops was under discussion both in the House and in the Select Committee, of which I was a member, and every Bishop present voted for the measure. We continued to advocate it during the subsequent years. In 1900 it fell to me to introduce, in favour of a reform of the liquor licensing laws, a resolution which gave rise to a memorable debate, all the Bishops present voting with me in the minority (42 to 45). In 1901 I introduced three separate Bills in furtherance of temperance reform, and two of these were virtually incorporated in the Act of 1902, after debates in which I had to bear a special burden of the responsibility. Similarly, in the discussions on the Government Bill of 1904 all the Bishops present supported my motion (unhappily defeated) in favour of a time limit to the compensation clause. In 1905 I introduced a Bill to regulate the hours of closing of public-houses. It was lost by six votes only, all the Bishops present voting in the minority.

In addition to these problems of Temperance legislation, I remember the importance attached during those years to the discussions, in which I was able to take part, on the Factory and Workshop Acts Amendment Bill, on the Youthful Offenders Bill, on the Employment of Children Bill, on the Outdoor Relief and Friendly Societies Bill, and especially on the very important subjects dealt with in the Midwives Bill and in the Street Betting Bill, and in the successive Bills and Committees on the difficult question of Sunday trading.

With respect to our responsibilities in matters outside the British Isles, it has fallen to me to initiate discussions in the House of Lords on the West African liquor traffic and on the treatment of the aborigines of Western Australia, and to take part in the debates on the administration of the Congo, on the treatment of the Jews in Russia, on the disorders in Macedonia, and on the introduction of Chinese labour into South Africa. On the last-named subject I was, I believe, the first to call attention to the moral dangers attending the importation, dangers which I thought, and still think, to be even graver than the other perils to which attention has been more prominently directed.

On the various Bills which have been introduced during the last decade for removing from those outside the Church of England any remaining vestige of disability or disadvantage, I have felt it to be a privilege to support by voice and vote such measures as the Nonconformist Marriages Bill of 1898, the Burial Grounds Bill of 1900, and the Public Meetings Facilities Bill of 1905 and 1906.

I enumerate these measures (and the list could be easily prolonged) not as taking credit in the smallest degree for such share as I have borne in the discussion of them. It seems to me to be a simple and obvious part of a Bishop's duty. My sole wish is to show that the Bishops have not, as a matter of fact, kept silence in the way your speech seems to suggest. I have perforce referred to my personal action because I can speak of it with fullest knowledge. The fact of my residing in or near London, and of my occupying latterly a central position, has led to my being often the spokesman of my brother Bishops. But my experience is merely a specimen of the experience of many, and in almost all the matters to which I have alluded the Bishops have acted throughout in fullest concord with one another.

The letter was published and caused some stir; and that the Archbishop himself attached importance to the record it contained is shown by the fact that he reprinted it as an appendix to his charge on 'The Call and Character of the Church of England'.

Mr. Birrell repeated his attack in a different form during the Disestablishment Debate in the House of Commons. But, for the reason given below, he did not pursue the controversy in the Press:

The RT. HON. A. BIRRELL *to the* ARCHBISHOP OF CANTERBURY

21st February, 1907.

I'm sorry you think my history all wrong. I can't pretend to be impartial but I cannot remember any historian of our Social or Political progress whose estimate of the work done by the Bishops in the House of Lords differs materially from mine. Nor am I disposed to admit that 100 years is a long time in the History of the Church. Everybody has improved *a little* during the last fifteen years, and the Bishops as might be expected have improved with them. I was thinking of Pioneers—of Unpopular Causes, Unjust Wars, Contagious Diseases Acts and things of that kind. I own I trace Episcopal shortcomings to

(1) Mode of *Election.*

(2) Supposed obligation to support the Throne—the Crest of the State.

But it is not for me to argue with you, and I am sick of controversy and very much overworked.

But though Mr. Birrell did not write to the Press, a good deal was written by others about 'Episcopal Politicians'. And when the Archbishop, in debate on the reform of the House of Lords, strongly asserted the non-party character of the Bench of Bishops and its concern for social legislation, harsh things continued to be said, the harsher, we may be certain, by reason of the still recent educational controversy.

II

That an Archbishop should be cautious, he certainly would not deny. And Archbishop Davidson's caution is illustrated by a letter on the subject of Old Age Pensions, to a correspondent who had contrasted Nonconformist fervour with the non-committal attitude of the Bishops.

His reply shows his distrust of the general and the vague, and his reluctance to commit himself in advance to things which did not seem to him at the moment to be really practical.

The ARCHBISHOP OF CANTERBURY *to the* REV. M. V. O. BRIDGEMAN

16th February, 1907.

I thank you for your further letter. The distinction you draw between the readiness of some of our Nonconformist friends to give their names to general schemes of amelioration, and the supposed unreadiness of Bishops to do the like, does I think mark a contrast of attitude in these matters. Speaking for myself at least I can say that I prefer to rest under the imputation of callousness, trying though it be, to vaguely and unprofitably giving my name to mere abstract suggestions for reform before these have been reduced to prosaic black and white and adopted or recommended by competent public men. It happens every day with regard to such things as Armenian outrages, Macedonian strife, treatment of Native Races, and other kindred things. I go so far as to say that to give our names readily to schemes which are not formulated, and which we are not competent ourselves to formulate, is a sort of selfishness, as it gains us some cheap credit with the unthinking, while it really does little or nothing to advance the good cause.

Where practical efforts can be made, I am most keen to make them. You may remember that I took upon me the responsibility of introducing in the House of Lords the question of the West African Liquor Trade, and, again the question of the treatment of Australian Natives, and in each case I think the result was advantageous. These are mere specimens: they could easily be multiplied. On a matter like Old Age Pensions I have been frequently—indeed almost continuously—in communication with responsible people, and have failed to find any scheme which is put forward in a manner rendering it practicable for me definitely to endorse it. To endorse the abstract principle is to my mind almost a mockery: it is like signing a paper to say that we want everybody to be prosperous, or that we want nobody to be overworked, or the like. You may remember my published communications on this subject of Old Age Pensions 18 months ago. In case you have forgotten it (which is improbable as you are studying the subject) I enclose a copy of a letter of mine which was widely circulated at that time. Please return it to me.

Mr. Asquith's speech a few days ago seems to hold out hopes of a definite scheme ere long, but it may turn out to be like many of its predecessors and to be rather a demonstration of goodwill than a practical endeavour to mend things. I hope to speak to him fully upon the subject within the next few days. He knows how much I am interested in it.

I trouble you with all this because your letters seem to show that you hardly realise the position I take in these matters.

This very caution, however, with regard to issues which were not yet practical politics, gave great additional weight to the utterances the Archbishop deliberately made on other large questions of public and international morality. An excellent instance of this is afforded by his action with regard to the Congo Free State. Charges of a grave character were being made both in England and in Belgium against an administration for which the Belgian King Leopold II was responsible.

On July 3, 1906, Lord Reay raised the question in the House of Lords and referred to a particularly searching report by a British Consul, Mr. Roger Casement, in 1904.[1] The Archbishop, who joined in the debate, expressed his bewilderment and distress at the revelations. He said:

Wise men always shrink from being ready to lend themselves too

[1] Africa, No. 1, 1904: Cd. 1933.

> readily to some obvious popular outcry about something which may be only imperfectly understood. . . . Cautious as we ought to be not to join too readily in an outcry which may often prove to be exaggerated or baseless, we ought on the other hand to be cautious lest we too readily put down to fanaticism or prejudice the protests which we sometimes treat too lightly because we think the facts alleged are too bad to be true.

In May 1907, he returned to the charge, when Convocation, on the motion of the Bishop of Southwark, passed a strong protest against the administration of the Congo Free State. The Archbishop said:

> On the whole, the relation of England to Africa during the last century had been not only practically, but deliberately and of set purpose, a beneficent and hopeful one. Now, however, during the last decade or more we seemed to have drifted into something which would rival, if it did not exceed, the horror of the old slave-trade, and, if the members of the House were to be silent with regard to what was taking place, they would be false to obligations which were strong for every member of a Christian State, but were strongest of all for those on whom rested the responsibility, the privilege, and the trust of Church government. . . . If this wrong went on, they must go on trying to say what was to be said on the subject until the wrong was righted.

On July 29, when Lord Monkswell made a strong attack in the House of Lords on the Congo scandal, the Archbishop gave expression to the public horror at the continuing of the cruelties to the natives—for the sake of obtaining the utmost amount of indiarubber (*Red Rubber*, Mr. E. D. Morel called it) through their labour. He described the atrocities as 'the natural and inevitable outcome of a system which is fundamentally bad', and urged 'that it ought to be possible now in some practical and real sense to take some steps forward in regard to this terrible matter'. The whole speech was one which the radical *Daily Chronicle* itself admitted, July 30, 1907, 'did something to justify the presence of Bishops in the Legislature'. And Sir Charles Dilke (no mean judge) described it as 'a marvellous performance, nothing said which should not have been said, everything said which required saying; the speech of a great statesman'.[1]

[1] Gwynn and Tuckwell, *Life of Sir Charles Dilke*, ii. 549–50.

III

This summer the Archbishop's interest was again invoked with regard to the Bulgarian atrocities in Macedonia, about which he received a letter from the Patriarch of Constantinople, through the Archimandrite Pagonis, whom he saw in his room at the House of Lords, June 27, 1907:

> I told him to thank the Patriarch for his message, and to say that I am always anxious to do anything in my power to promote the peace of any region in which troubles exist, but that I have no official status whatever which entitles me to intervene in matters of political difference even when the differences are of an ecclesiastical rather than of a political sort. I pressed upon him more than once the necessity of his making this clear to the Patriarch, while thanking him for having made a communication to me. I told the Archimandrite that I am to take part in a Deputation to the Foreign Office on Tuesday, July 9th, with reference to Macedonia, but that my voice there should be raised simply to the effect that the people of England would be thankful to know that the Government is doing its best to assist in bringing misrule and misgovernment to an end, and that I must not be supposed to be taking any side in the controversy.

Nevertheless, when, on July 9, he led a deputation to Sir Edward Grey at the Foreign Office, he pressed strongly for Government intervention, though in no way underrating the enormous difficulties of the conflict between Greek and Bulgarian:

> I do want to press this point, that the greatest evil, in my judgement, of all would be, that we should know the evils that are going on, and that we should be content to do nothing. Nothing—absolutely nothing—is more likely to sap the moral sense of our own people than that we should be aware of ghastly deeds taking place, that we should be able in some degree to diminish them, and that for one reason or another we should not be doing so.

It was an instance of the Archbishop being, in such matters, very often rather better than his word to the particular petitioners for his aid.

The second Hague Peace Conference was held in Holland from June to October 1907. Mr. W. T. Stead and others tried to secure the Archbishop's signature to a Joint Manifesto by the leaders of the Christian Church, and also his support for a Conference, representing various religions of the world, in Paris, to demonstrate the practical unity of all religious faiths in the cause of peace. The conference did not in fact come off, but in any case the Archbishop had grave doubts as to whether that was the right way of setting about it. The contrast between his point of view and that of Mr. Stead is succinctly stated in part of a note which the Archbishop took of a conversation between them, March 20, 1907:

> He [Mr. Stead] referred to the Lambeth Conference Report and Resolutions, and said they were excellent; but so was the XIII Chapter of 1 Corinthians, and that the one was as far off from practical politics as the other. I told him that for that very reason it was the kind of document the Church could appropriately put forth provided it would follow up its principles in practical action when opportunity offered, but that such practical action must be guided by what statesmen declare to be possible for the nation's life, and the Church as represented by the clergy cannot take the place which ought to be occupied by statesmen.

The Archbishop added that he did not feel inclined to sign an Appeal from the Churches for Peace, which contained the following paragraph:

> We approach the Conference with this earnest appeal, because we believe that the depth and prevalence of the movement against war, with all its accompanying calamities and miseries, is very imperfectly realised or understood by many of those who live and act in the more immediate circles of sovereigns, statesmen and diplomatists.

The Archbishop's own experience (he pointed out) was different; for he found 'the people who surround statesmen and diplomats' in fact to be 'the strongest and most outspoken of my friends', and (getting back on Mr. Stead) he was quite sure that the danger of war arises 'far more from newspapers' than from diplomatists.

In Convocation, again, he emphatically asserted the responsibility of the Press, and the duty of thoughtfulness and deliberation at times of popular excitement. And in a careful speech on the relation of the Church to the Hague Conference, while urging the 'systematic and recognized adoption of arbitration', he said, with some emphasis, that it was for the Church to inculcate large principles—but not to take the place of statesmen as regards their practical working out (April 30, 1901):

> To say, for example, that we, or the Church as such, summoned together either in mighty masses of men or in little coteries of students or theologians, ought to express an opinion as to what the size or number of our ships should be, or what sort of ships ought to be multiplied and what ought not; or how many Army corps we ought to maintain, or what—for the world's good and for the promotion of peace—ought to be enjoined as the period or interval between the inception or declaration of war and the beginning of hostilities—all that seems to me to be literally harmful on our part to attempt, because we at once discredit what we are doing within our own province by the evidence which we give of our desire to go outside that province and deal with what we do not adequately understand.

Such opinions disappointed the organizers of movements, and many others, but they were the result of mature deliberation; and no one who heard him could doubt the Archbishop's own fundamental conviction as to the duty and the possibility of preserving the peace of the world.

There were many other matters of social and international interest which engaged the Archbishop's attention during these years—in and out of Parliament. And we note, for example, that among the subjects not already mentioned, on which he made speeches in the House of Lords in 1906–7, were: Colonial Marriages Bill; Compounding for Rates; Elections (Meetings in School rooms) Bill; Inspection of Laundries; Prevention of Corruption Bill; Outrages on Jews in Russia; Shops, Restriction on Sunday Trading; Services rendered by Lord Milner in South Africa; Factory and Workshops Bill; House of Lords Reform; Housing of Working Classes; Licensing Bill; Merchant Vessels and First Aid; Liquor Traffic in Nigeria; Women and County and Borough Councils; Small Holdings and Allotments Bill; Street Traffic in London; Training Colleges.

IV

There was one important measure before Parliament in 1907, which raised ecclesiastical as well as social issues, and therefore had a double claim on the Archbishop's attention. It was the Bill ultimately passed as the Deceased Wife's Sister's Marriage

Act 1907. We propose, therefore, to devote most of the remainder of this chapter to a more particular treatment of that measure.

A Bill to allow the marriage of a man with his deceased wife's sister had been before Parliament on many occasions in the last half-century. Such a marriage was directly inconsistent with the Table of prohibited degrees drawn up by Archbishop Parker and set forth by authority in 1563, commonly printed at the end of the Book of Common Prayer.

This Table was based on very definite rules with regard to consanguinity and affinity, among them being the rules:

(1) that as husband and wife are one flesh he who is related to the one by consanguinity, is related to the other by affinity in the same degree, and further

(2) that consanguinity and affinity alike bar marriage to the third degree collaterally but no further.

Thus—in the first degree—a father cannot marry his daughter (consanguinity) or his stepdaughter (affinity); in the second degree, a brother cannot marry his sister (consanguinity) or his sister-in-law (affinity); in the third degree, an uncle cannot marry his niece (consanguinity) or his wife's niece (affinity). All such marriages were unlawful according to the law of the Church expressed in the 99th Canon of the Canons of 1604, which ran as follows:

NONE TO MARRY WITHIN THE DEGREES PROHIBITED

No person shall marry within the degrees prohibited by the laws of God and expressed in a table set forth by authority in the year of Our Lord God 1563. And all marriages so made and contracted shall be adjudged incestuous and unlawful and consequently shall be dissolved as void from the beginning, and the parties so married shall by course of law be separated. And the aforesaid table shall be in every church publicly set up and fixed at the charge of the parish.

They were also unlawful by Statute Law. A change of the Statute Law was now being sought, but no such change can be made by Parliament without repercussions on the law or authority of the Church. Previous measures had been repeatedly rejected in Parliament, though one such measure had been read a second time (1883), and one (1896) passed in the House of Lords to be defeated in the Commons. The House of Commons in 1907 carried the second reading of this new Bill by 263 votes to 34. In August it was made a Government measure, and as such it was passed. On its introduction to the Lords, August 20, the Archbishop of Canterbury made a strong speech against it, based both on social and on religious grounds. He dwelt on the coherent and consistent character of the table of affinity as it stood. He declared: 'If you wrench a stone from the carefully built and balanced structure it will be vain to expect that it can continue to stand as now it stands.'

Many Bishops spoke to the same effect, but the second reading was carried by 111 votes to 79. In committee Davidson endeavoured to secure an amendment which would leave the clergy of the Church of England outside the Bill altogether.

In this he failed, but Lord Tweedmouth on behalf of the Government said he would agree to an amendment making it absolutely optional for a clergyman either to celebrate such a marriage himself or not, and either to permit, or to refuse, the use of his church for these marriages. This, it must be noted, was a very marked advance on the provisions of the Divorce Law of 1857, according to which a clergyman, while free to refuse to celebrate the marriage of a 'guilty' party in a divorce suit, may be required to lend his church for such celebration; and may also be required himself to solemnize the marriage of the 'innocent' party.

When the Bill was finally passed in the Lords, August 26, the Archbishop emphasized the extreme difficulty and delicacy of the position, and declared:

> For the first time in the history of the Church of England, has the law of the State been brought on one specific point into direct open, overt contrast with, and contradiction of, the specific and divine law laid down in the authoritative regulations of the national church.

This was a strong statement, when we remember the passing of the Divorce Act exactly 50 years before; but although the divorce issue would seem, in the judgement of many, far graver than the issue of marriage with a deceased wife's sister, the Archbishop would certainly maintain not only that the sense of cleavage was much keener in 1907 than it had been in 1857, but that the words he used on this occasion, carefully scrutinized, were in fact just.

All through the debate in Parliament churchmen conducted a considerable agitation against the Bill, and the Archbishop received and wrote a great many letters. No formal action, however, was taken by Convocation as a result of the Act. It was nevertheless urged that guidance of some kind should be given as to the position both of the clergy in officiating at such marriages and of lay persons who might contract them. The Archbishop decided to supply this guidance in the form of a *Letter to the Diocese of Canterbury* (October 1907). In this *Letter* he gave a very careful statement of the origin and basis of the English marriage law, with quotations and references set out with characteristic thoroughness. And, on this basis, he led up to the practical question of the position of the clergy in regard to the new Act. He pointed out that the marriage of a man with his deceased wife's sister:

> 'expressly forbidden hitherto both by Statute Law and by Canon, is now by Statute Law made permissible as a civil contract. On the other hand the Canon which has been judicially declared to bind the Clergy remains unrepealed.'

Parliament had left a clear discretion to the clergy. Therefore the Archbishop gave this as his advice:

> Personally I believe that they will act wisely and rightly in saying that such marriages, when they take place, ought to take place elsewhere than in Church.

He added that it could not be fairly argued that the taking of such a line involved any real hardship on those who wished to contract a marriage which was 'at the least, "ecclesiastically irregular"'. And he considered that, if the opposite course were generally taken, it would open the door to very grave difficulties. But the 'advice' was:

> advice only, and not a formal direction or injunction. The law has given a discretion to the incumbent. If, after carefully weighing the whole circumstances, he decides that he ought to perform the marriage, or to allow it to take place in the church whereof he is the responsible minister, I shall in no way regard him as disloyal or disrespectful, because of the decision to which he has come.

Another point, however, had to be considered:

> Many who so marry will claim the ordinary privileges and ministrations of the Church. Are these to be withheld?

The Lower House of the Canterbury Convocation, when discussing the Bill, while still before the House of Commons, had passed a resolution in the most formal manner asking 'that the Bill should include a proviso that nothing contained in the Act [after the Bill should become law] shall . . . subject a clergyman to penalties for refusing the privileges of church membership to persons who contract these unions'. The Archbishop, however, while quoting the section in the Act, with a creditable desire to respect conscientious scruples of every sort, said categorically:

> I have no hesitation in saying that from men and women who are otherwise entitled to receive these privileges, they ought not in my judgment to be withheld on the mere ground of such a marriage.

He added, with regard to Holy Communion:

> If justification were to be pleaded for such refusal of Holy Communion it must presumably be based upon the Rubric which allows or enjoins the exclusion of 'an open and notorious evil liver'. It is in my judgment impossible rightly to apply these words on account of their marriage to a man and wife who have contracted as a civil contract a marriage expressly sanctioned by English law. Marriage after all is in the view of the Church itself initially and fundamentally a civil contract. We may, and most of us will, disapprove of what such persons have done. We may, and probably most of us will, discourage these marriages in every reasonable way. But this is a very different thing from imposing upon persons who have contracted such a marriage the gravest censure which we can legally lay upon an evil-doer.

The Archbishop did not deal with the question whether the Canon should be altered, nor with the desirability of giving dispensations in proper cases, nor did he treat of the sacramental side of Christian marriage. He took the view that persons who had availed themselves of the Act could not properly be comprehended under the 26th and 27th Canons which deal with grounds of refusal of Communion, and exclude 'common and notorious depravers of the Book of Common Prayer'.[1]

[1] Compare the Report of the Committee on Marriage Problems of the Lambeth Conference, 1908, which said: 'We are of opinion that marriage with a deceased wife's sister, where permitted by the law of the land, and at the same time prohibited by the Canons of the Church, is to be regarded not as a non-marital union, but as a marriage ecclesiastically irregular while not constituting the parties "open and notorious evil livers".' (*Report of the Lambeth Conference*, 1908, p. 143.)

The same principle he also applied to Christian burial. It could not, he maintained, be seriously contended by responsible men that on account of such a marriage the refusal of the rites of the Church would be right or even possible.

V

The meaning of the proviso in the Act, and incidentally the advice contained in the Archbishop's letter, was very soon to be tested in the diocese of Norwich.

Mr. A. N. Banister, a parishioner of Eaton and a frequent communicant in Eaton parish church, had married his deceased wife's sister in Canada. His marriage, lawful in Canada, was rendered valid as a civil contract in England by the 'Deceased Wife's Sister's Marriage Act' which came into operation, with retrospective effect, August 28, 1907.

Returning to Eaton, he reported his marriage to his vicar, Canon Thompson (who had previously warned him against contracting such a marriage). Mr. Banister asked Canon Thompson whether he adhered to his intention of refusing to give him Communion. Canon Thompson replied that, acting on his Bishop's instructions, he must refuse. Proceedings were taken by Mr. and Mrs. Banister against Canon Thompson, and the case was heard by Letters of Request from the Bishop of Norwich in the Court of Arches by Sir Lewis Dibdin. It was argued on behalf of Canon Thompson that:

> By reason of the affinity existing between them, such affinity being open and notorious, and of their open and notorious cohabitation as husband and wife, they were and are open and notorious evil livers, so that the congregation were and are thereby offended within the meaning of the Rubric prefixed to the Order of Administration of the Lord's Supper or Holy Communion in the Book of Common Prayer.

It was maintained therefore that Canon Thompson was fully protected by the following proviso in Clause I of the Deceased Wife's Sister's Marriage Act:

> Provided always that no clergyman in Holy Orders of the Church of England shall be liable to any suit, penalty, or censure, whether Civil or Ecclesiastical, for anything done or omitted to be done by him in the performance of the duties of his office to

which suit, penalty, or censure he would not have been liable if this Act had not been passed.

Sir Lewis Dibdin delivered judgement, July 23, 1908, and found that the defendant was not entitled to repel Mr. and Mrs. Banister from Holy Communion on the ground that they were notorious and open evil livers. He said:

> Taking the fullest account of the limiting words of the statute and putting at its highest the divergence which the Act may have created between the action of the State and the rule of the Church of England, I find it impossible to say that these persons, lawfully married according to the law of the land, can by any reasonable use of language be so described merely because they are living together as man and wife.

He also held that the proviso in Clause I:

> must be interpreted so as to restrict it to matters concerning the solemnization of marriage between a man and his deceased wife's sister, and to those only; and that consequently it did not protect the defendant.

Appeal lies from the Court of Arches to the Judicial Committee of the Privy Council. Canon Thompson, however, preferred not to appeal to the Judicial Committee. Instead he turned to the King's Bench and sought a 'prohibition' of the Court of Arches. The construing of Acts of Parliament is a matter for the King's judges; and the object of the 'prohibition' was to prevent the Ecclesiastical Court from exceeding its jurisdiction, and from giving an erroneous interpretation to the proviso in the recent statute. Canon Thompson, however, went farther; and invited the King's Bench and its Court of Appeal to deal with the whole question of the interpretation and scope of the rubric in the Office of Holy Communion. In the result the Divisional Court by a majority, and the Court of Appeal unanimously, refused to grant a writ of prohibition. The Archbishop, in a public letter to Professor W. R. Inge (February 4, 1910) after the judgement, regretted the 'innovation' introduced by Canon Thompson in going to the King's Bench on the scope of the rubric in the Office of Holy Communion, which he described as an 'endeavour to make the secular court, to all intents and purposes a tribunal of appeal from the ecclesiastical court'. Two years later, on June 20, 1912, the House of Lords unanimously upheld the decision of the Court of

Appeal, thereby affirming the jurisdiction of the Court of Arches, and concurring generally in the Dean's judgement in the case, besides authoritatively construing the proviso in Clause I of the Deceased Wife's Sister's Marriage Act.[1]

A NOTE ON PRAYERS IN THE HOUSE OF LORDS

It may be of interest to insert as a note to this chapter a letter concerning a little-known duty of the spiritual peers. It describes how the present practice of a *Rota* among the twenty-four Bishops who, in addition to the two Archbishops, have seats in the House of Lords began, and the Archbishop's own share in the plan. The letter is written to Lady Laura Ridding, wife of Bishop Ridding of Southwell, and daughter of the first Earl of Selborne (the Lord Chancellor):

The ARCHBISHOP OF CANTERBURY *to* LADY LAURA RIDDING

24th October, 1907.

I well remember the occasion to which you refer when your Bishop made a proposal in the Bishops' Meeting respecting the reading of Prayers in the House of Lords. I was not yet a Bishop but I was acting as Secretary to the Meeting. This I did ever since 1877. Difficulty had for some time been felt as to the junior Bishop giving up so much time to House of Lords work, and, as a matter of fact, I used to arrange for his relief by other Bishops voluntarily taking his place. What your Bishop proposed was that the Bishops should altogether cease to read Prayers and that a Chaplain should be appointed for the House of Lords as for the House of Commons. He said that he had broached this to Lord Selborne (at that time Chancellor) who was in general agreement. Most of the Bishops greatly disliked the proposal and thought that to abandon the immemorial custom of a Bishop's reading Prayers as a member of the House would be to pave the way for their leaving the House altogether. Archbishop Benson was very strong about this: so were Bishop Magee and Bishop Temple. Thereupon your Bishop said that it was simply impossible for him to be responsible for a whole Session's Prayers even with such help as I have referred to, as he must by so doing neglect his Diocese. Bishop Temple[2] then offered, to the surprise of everybody, to take your Bishop's place and to read regularly throughout the Session when he could get help. This was felt to be an impossible plan, and, after much discussion, it was decided that for the next

[1] See *Convocation of Canterbury Report*, No. 471, *Marriage Laws*, 1912.
[2] Then Bishop of London.

Session the experiment should be made of the Bishops dividing the work between them. I undertook the management of this and it was carried through and grew into the present plan. This was in the Autumn of 1884 or the Spring of 1885.

I do not think we have any means of knowing when the Bishops began to read Prayers. I remember the matter being enquired into some time ago, and no one was then able to discover the origin. When Parliament meets I will gladly talk it over with some of the Officers of the House who know its work best, but I do not think much new light will be thrown upon the subject. If anything I have said does not correspond with your recollection I will gladly look into it to the best of my power, but I do not think that I am wrong in the details, and I am certainly not wrong in the general facts.

CHAPTER XXXI

THE LAMBETH CONFERENCE. THE CHURCH OVERSEAS

Our Sea captain is likewise ambitious to perfect what the other began. He counts it a disgrace, seeing all mankind is one family, sundry countries but several rooms, that we who dwell in the parlour (so he counts Europe) should not know the outlodgings of the same house, and the world be scarce acquainted with itself before it be dissolved from itself at the day of judgement. He daily sees and duly considers God's wonders in the deep.

THOMAS FULLER, *The Holy State.*

THE holding of the Fifth Lambeth Conference in July 1908, and of the Pan-Anglican Congress immediately before it, provides an opportunity for observing the very close relationship between Randall Davidson, as Archbishop of Canterbury, and the various portions of the Anglican Communion.

We have already remarked on the steady development of the connexion between the see of St. Augustine and all other branches of the Anglican Church overseas. It would be difficult to exaggerate the difference which Archbishop Davidson's tenure of the Primacy made, not only because it was a long tenure but also because of the extraordinary personal knowledge he already possessed of the Provinces and Dioceses overseas, the deep interest he took in all their problems, and the eagerness with which he welcomed news and personal visits from the Bishops themselves. As we shall see, it was necessary for the Archbishop of Canterbury to be scrupulously careful not to claim even the appearance of authority over other Provinces or self-governing Churches. The secret of his remarkable influence is found in his personality, his straightforwardness and simplicity, and his obvious desire to know and to help. To give anything like a full record of his dealings with the overseas Bishops would require a separate volume, which would indeed be rich in interest. But it may be well, nevertheless, at this stage in the Primacy to bring together, almost haphazard, a few illustrations of the kind of problems on which he was consulted.

I

We will take first one or two instances of the Archbishop's relation to the Churches in the Dominions. The very difficult question of the precise meaning of the 'Legal Nexus' between the Anglican Church in Australia and the Church of England has been the subject of discussion for a great number of years and is still unsettled, largely because of a strong difference of opinion between the Diocese of Sydney and the rest of Australia. It was natural that recourse should be had to Archbishop Davidson very early in the proceedings. The Archbishop of Sydney (Saumarez Smith) therefore sought an interview with him on behalf of a Select Committee of the General Synod of the Church of England in Australia and Tasmania. He put a whole series of questions, some relating to the doctrinal formularies, e.g. the use of the Athanasian Creed, others relating to the Nexus. We set out here the question and the reply on the legal Nexus, in the form of a memorandum by the Archbishop of Sydney, embodying the substance of the Archbishop of Canterbury's replies in a form approved by the latter:

Memorandum, 2 June 1906

The Archbishop of Sydney's Question:

Legal Nexus (obligatory relations between the Home Church and the Church of England in Australia).

(i) Can we be furnished with an opinion from your legal advisers on the subject?

(ii) How far is the 'autonomy' of the Church in the Colonies an ideal to be sought for? What amount of 'centralization' in England is desirable? *Aliter*, what should be 'the range and nature of our independent legislation' in our Synods?

(iii) Exercise of *jus liturgicum* by Bishops. Modification of rules for Divine Service necessary, as regards abbreviation and elasticity, in some Colonial conditions.

(iv) Confirmation of Adults not brought up in Church of England. Any regard to be paid to 'Roman' confirmation?

The Archbishop of Canterbury's Reply:

(i) The Archbishop does not think that the lawyers would commit themselves to any *formal* opinion about the 'legal nexus'. A request emanating from the Committee appointed by the G.S. [General Synod] asking legal experts to advise concerning Constitutions, etc., might be entertained.

(ii) Some 'centralization' in England for decision of important points, and for prevention of too wide divergence in liturgical and ritual custom is desirable. The Archbishop of Canterbury himself could not, and should not, be sole Referee. But some development of the 'Committee of Reference' principle might be agreed upon by the next Lambeth Conference. 'Autonomy' in the Colonial Church is an ideal to be gradually worked out, but there should be some check on too hasty or too wide divergence from the Mother Church.

(iii) The Archbishop agrees that the two principles must have due weight, yet precaution should be taken against vagaries of an individual Bishop, and no important change should be made without reference to the body of the Bishops in the Province. The forthcoming Report of the Royal Commission will throw some further light on the subject.

(iv) The Archbishop does not himself in ordinary circumstances require that those temporarily resident in England, who belong, say, to the Established Church of Scotland, or to the Lutheran Communion in Germany or Switzerland, and who have there been communicants, should offer themselves for Confirmation as absolutely necessary before admission to Holy Communion, but he strongly advises those who desire definitely to join themselves to the Church of England to be confirmed.

The Archbishop, personally, is not in favour of 're-confirming' those who have been confirmed in the Roman Church, but he admits that as Confirmation in the Church of England occupies a somewhat different status from that in the Church of Rome, Bishops may possibly be justified in allowing applicants who have joined the Church of England to be confirmed with our Service if they themselves desire it.[1]

The inner meaning of this movement for independence, and an illustration of the dangers of an aggressive or nationalist assertion,

[1] Archbishop Davidson's own view (from a note of 1911) appears to have been similar to that of Archbishop Benson in answer to a question as to those who had 'received the Greek Chrism at their baptism': 'I have advised him to regard them as confirmed, but to have a service with them of "Admission to Holy Communion" and to give them his blessing, distinctly informing them that this is not confirmation.' (*Life of Archbishop Benson*, ii. 224.)

are put in a letter of a more personal character to the Archbishop of Brisbane (Dr. Donaldson), who had written in advance of the interview, just recorded, on the same general theme.

The ARCHBISHOP OF CANTERBURY *to the* ARCHBISHOP OF BRISBANE

Private and Confidential. 28th November, 1905.

I think I fully appreciate the importance and the bigness, and possibly the urgency, of the question of nomenclature—as regards especially your Antipodean relation to the Mother Church at home. The problem is perhaps less simple than it looks, for it is impossible to deny that an emphatic and in some mouths aggressive assertion of independence of the home Church and its name may tend to weaken somewhat the *home* sense of responsibility for helping (with men if not with money) a Church which some will say is eagerly claiming to set aside the old nomenclature and so to weaken the old nexus.

But though that feeling of almost irritation on the part of the Mother Church cannot be ignored, and may produce results which we should deplore (e.g. in a greater reluctance of men to go to Australia) I think it is not really based on a wise or wide or far-seeing view of the nature and prospects of the Anglican Communion as a whole. I will not conceal from you that some things are at present making me uncomfortable as I look *forward.* For example, the Primate of New Zealand seems to be moving towards an even active and vociferous repudiation of any nexus with the home Church except the most shadowy. And if (as seems not to be unlikely) he now acts in a way directly contrary to all home advice and conventional rule and relies upon his Primatial position as enabling him even to defy his own Bishops, and to *denounce* Lambeth, and London, and S.P.G., we have no check or hold whatever upon him.

It need only be added that Archbishop Davidson, though desirous of strengthening the fellowship of the different Churches in the Anglican Communion as self-governing Churches in communion with one another, was utterly opposed to anything in the nature of a Patriarch with powers of government over provinces outside his own. It is of interest, in the light of the reference in the above letter to the attitude of the Bishop of Dunedin (Dr. Nevill), Primate of New Zealand, to quote the Archbishop's express disclaimer of any papal authority, such as Bishop Nevill had supposed to have been asserted on behalf of the see of Canterbury:

The Archbishop of Canterbury *to the* Bishop of Dunedin, N.Z.

Private. 17th December, 1907.

You are reported as giving some details about an incident in the Lambeth Conference of 1878, with reference specially to the question which you believe to have been then discussed as to a possible Patriarchate of an official sort in the See of Canterbury. I am in full accord with the views you express as to the unwisdom of our taking any step whatever which could result in Papalizing the Anglican Church. History affords us abundant reasons to the contrary.[1]

II

Another kind of question which not seldom came Dr. Davidson's way was the linguistic problem. An interesting example is found in the difficulty which arose as to the proper translation of 'Jesus Christ' into Swahili, for use in those parts of East Africa where Swahili was spoken. The translation customary hitherto had been 'Isa Masiya', but Bishop Hine of Zanzibar wished the Society for Promoting Christian Knowledge to print another version, namely 'Yesu Kristo', and the question was referred to the Archbishop, who has the duty of approving all translations made for the S.P.C.K. The Bishop of Zanzibar wrote to the Archbishop explaining that the alteration had already been made locally ten years before:

The Bishop of Zanzibar *to the* Archbishop of Canterbury

12th December, 1905.

We made the alteration some ten years ago (i) because the word 'Isa' is a common name in use among Mohammedans here in Zanzibar. One often hears of 'Isa bin Abdallah' or 'Isa bin Mohammad'—and we felt that the Sacred Name ought not to be one in popular use among the followers of an alien religion. In the Mombasa diocese for the same reason they have changed 'Isa' into 'Yesu', though 'Isa' is still used in Uganda. (ii) 'Kristo' was

[1] The Report of the Committee of the Lambeth Conference, 1908, on Organization within the Anglican Communion, contains the following paragraph: 'Your Committee record their conviction that no supremacy of the See of Canterbury over Primatial or Metropolitan Sees outside England is either practicable or desirable. In stating this your Committee do not forget the peculiar circumstances which determine the relation of the Metropolitan See of India to the See of Canterbury. The Committee further bear witness to the universal recognition in the Anglican Communion of the ancient precedence of the See of Canterbury.'

substituted at the same time for Masiha because I found it was the form used by *all* the different Christian Missions in East and Central Africa with the single exception of C.M.S. Thus Kristo (or Kristu) is used by the various Roman Missions here in Zanzibar and on the adjacent mainland whether in British or German or Portuguese East Africa and Central Africa. It is used also by the different Nonconformist Missions, the Scotch Presbyterians in Central Africa at Blantyre and Baudawi and Koudoi: also by the Dutch Reformed Mission in Nyasaland—by the Lutheran Missions in German East Africa—by the Moravians near Tanganyika—by the Friends in Pemba—and I believe by all Missions 'of all denominations' except C.M.S. in Mombasa and Uganda.

The only objection to the form *Kristo* is that the adult African has a difficulty in pronouncing the 'Kr' sound at the beginning of a word: but this applies only to the older generation. The younger ones, boys and girls in schools and colleges, can be taught to say it quite well.

The form 'Masiha' was apparently invented by Bishop Steere (C.M.S. generally *now* writes Masihi, except in Uganda): and the rather awkward words 'Wa Masihiya', 'Ki Masihiya' were coined by Bishop Steere to represent 'Christians' and 'Christianity' respectively.

We (U.M.C.A.) dropped all these forms years ago and it would be a serious matter now to restore them again. It is C.M.S. (who have their own publication N.T. etc.) who are the only adherents of the older forms.

The Archbishop, feeling, as he told the S.P.C.K., that 'the matter seems to me to be one of the most important that can come before us, in view of the hope we entertain that 100 years hence there may be flourishing native churches throughout East Africa', wrote thus to the Bishop of Zanzibar:

The ARCHBISHOP OF CANTERBURY *to the* BISHOP OF ZANZIBAR

19th January, 1906.

I thank you cordially for the trouble you have taken in writing to me so fully upon the linguistic question, and indeed it is a matter of vital importance. My sole wish of course is to further what is best in the general interests of the Church Catholic, but I confess to feeling some anxiety at present lest we drift into an established usage of accepting a variety of names for our Blessed Lord in the different Missions of Eastern Africa. I am hoping within the next few days to see some of those who are interested in the several Missions and Societies—S.P.G., U.M.C.A., C.M.S., S.P.C.K., and Bible Society—and it would appear to me that it may be wise to have a conference upon the whole question. You will remember that some twenty-five years ago Missionary work in China was greatly hindered by the variety then existing as to the word used for God in the various Missions, and it was always said that, if the matter had been properly attended to a hundred years before, the complications which ensued might have been avoided. I presume that the rule requiring the Archbishop of Canterbury to approve the translations paid for by S.P.C.K. carries with it some measure of responsibility, and that the Archbishop is not intended simply to endorse the requests which reach him. But I should be grieved indeed were I to do anything which hindered your work. I wonder whether any co-operation was attempted, or any central sanction obtained, when the different Societies and Missions adopted different words a generation ago. I hope to communicate with you further upon the subject before long and you may rely upon my earnest desire to meet your wishes if possible.

In due course, after consultation between representatives of the different Missionary Societies, S.P.C.K., the Bible Society, the Church Missionary Society, the Universities Mission to Central Africa, and the S.P.G. (Society for the Propagation of the Gospel in Foreign Parts), a conference was held at Lambeth attended by the Bishops of Uganda and Zanzibar, Bishop Montgomery, and others. The following resolution was passed, July 2, 1906:

That this Committee make the following recommendations to the Archbishop of Canterbury:

(i) That the S.P.C.K. should proceed with the printing of the Swahili Prayer Book, retaining the form Yesu Christo but adding a note to the effect that this is the same as Isa Masiyah.

(ii) That the Bishop of Uganda should approach the Roman Missions in Uganda with a view to the adoption of the form Yesu Christo by both Roman and Anglican Missions in that area.

(iii) That the Lambeth Conference should be asked to consider the question of the translation of Our Lord's Name into languages which are subject to Semitic or Mahommedan influence.

Resolution passed by a Committee meeting at Lambeth on July 2nd under the Chairmanship of Bishop Montgomery.

Members of Committee.

Bishop Montgomery.
Bishop of Uganda.
Bishop of Zanzibar.
The Rev. E. McClure.
" J. Sharp.
" D. Craven.
" G. R. Blackledge.
" Rafaelle Scott (of Scotch Presbyterian Mission at Blantyre).

On October 15 the Bishop of Uganda (Dr. Tucker) wrote to the Archbishop as follows:

The Bishop of Uganda *to the* Archbishop of Canterbury

15th October, 1906.

At the Conference of Bishops from East Africa held at Lambeth in June last I was asked to approach the Roman Missions in Uganda with a view to their adoption of Yesu Kristo instead of Isa Masiya as the name of Our Lord.

Your Grace will be glad to hear that both Missions are willing to adopt our suggestion. This will remove my chief difficulty with regard to the matter, and will lead, I do not doubt, to the general use throughout East Africa of the Greek in place of the Semitic form.

The Archbishop's careful consideration thus brought about a singular unity on a point of vital importance for the future of Missions in East Africa. Bishop Hine of Zanzibar, who had been responsible for the change, in sending the writer a packet of the Archbishop's letters to himself for the purpose of this biography (including some quoted above), makes the following comment (June 15, 1931) on the Archbishop's extraordinary personal trouble with all his correspondence, quite apart from that of an official character.

What struck me as so wonderful about him was the trouble he took to answer letters (in earlier years always in his own handwriting) and often long ones—in answer to matters I brought before him. He was good enough to say he found my letters 'interesting' and that he gave up Sunday afternoons to replying himself to letters which were of a personal rather than an official nature.

III

Besides his constant communications with Bishops and Missionary leaders Overseas, the Archbishop also took care to use any opportunities afforded for knowledge and help of any character through the presence of Governors or High Commissioners in England on leave, especially where questions of education arose. Among the most interesting of such interviews was one with Lord Cromer about the educational problems in Egypt. Before seeing him, he had asked for and received a full account from the missionary point of view from the Rev. Douglas Thornton, one of the very best missionaries of his day, who had written to the Archbishop, on July 5, 1906:

> If Lord Cromer still refuses to give a *right of entry* to Christian teachers for Christian pupils in primary schools, it would be possible, would it not, to press strongly the justice of giving grants-in-aid to both Moslem and Christian primary and secondary schools, ready to come under government inspection in secular education, even where some foreign language (like English) is taught? Hitherto such grants have only been offered in purely vernacular schools.

Lord Cromer called at Lambeth on July 13, and here is the Archbishop's memorandum of what happened:

> He gave me a most interesting account of the educational problems in Egypt and of the need of careful and delicate steering if difficulties on the religious question are to be avoided. He thinks Gairdner and Thornton excellent fellows, but that they a little exaggerate the effectiveness of their own work and are not always very discreet. He fully agrees with them that as a matter of simple fairness the Bible might be taught to Christian children, Copts or others, in Government Schools alongside of the teaching of the Koran to Mohammedans. But, though perfectly reasonable and logically fair, this would be unworkable in practice. He said in effect 'If I were to introduce that plan, I should need 10,000 more troops in Egypt. It would be the way to raise a religious war. The children would begin by throwing the slates at one another's heads, and it would spread to outside rioting. If we had good buildings with class rooms so that the children could be separated in different rooms for their teaching, it might possibly be managed, though it would not be easy even then; but, as it is, with our big single-room schools, it is absolutely out of the question.' He does not

greatly believe in the possibility of converting Mohammedans to Christianity; nor, I think, though he did not say so, does he greatly believe in its usefulness in the present state of Egypt. But he is wholly friendly to Missionary work in the impartial way, and gave me an interesting account of his having had an interview in his own house with the son of a Syrian Sheik whom (?) Thornton had converted to Christianity, and whose father, a Moslem, was furious. He got the father and the son, together with the Missionaries and a leading Mohammedan layman, all to his house. He then closeted the father and the son together, the son being 22 years old and able to judge for himself, and when they had had their private interview he asked the son in the presence of all these people, including the father, what he wished to do, and he replied that he wished to be a Christian and to go to England with Mr. Thornton. Whereupon Cromer took down in writing the statement that he did this of his own free will, that he (Cromer) had in no kind of way advocated it or expressed approval or disapproval; and the father, though he lamented the change, was perfectly satisfied and agreed that all had been absolutely fair. . . .

He spoke with warmth of the good work being done by the missionaries to the heathen south of the Soudan. C.M.S. is much to be commended for what they are doing there. But he laughed greatly at Bishop Blyth's eager anxiety as to how the converts there were to be confirmed. He said that when men and women have been running about for centuries without a stitch of clothing, the question of their confirmation can quite well be postponed until they have learned more elementary things.

Lord Cromer's view was perhaps natural in a somewhat Olympian statesman resident in an Eastern land, but was hardly likely to appeal to a missionary of the Christian faith.

Many other illustrations could be given of Davidson's knowledge and interest, as well as of the trust placed in his judgement by the most different kinds of people. But enough has been said to give an impression, at least, of the richness of his experience and his wisdom, and to explain why so many roads led from so many provinces to Lambeth.

IV

The two great Anglican gatherings in the summer of 1908 to which we have already referred were the Pan-Anglican Congress and the Lambeth Conference. The first, held in June, was a congress attended by representatives, clerical and lay, from different parts of the Anglican Communion all over the world. It was an unofficial assembly intended to stir the imagination of the Anglican Communion, and to give the rank and file a new sense of unity, besides leading to fresh offers of service by clergy at home to the Church Overseas. The idea was due to Bishop Montgomery, the Secretary of the S.P.G., and had been set out by him in a sermon in St. Paul's Cathedral in 1902. The organization of the plan, which took five years to complete, was entrusted to the Central Board of Missions and a full-time Secretary, Rev. A. B. Mynors. A list of subjects was sent out to all Anglican Bishops and, when their answers had been received, the results were tabulated and forwarded to them for their final opinion. Preliminary papers on the topics selected were prepared in advance by leading scholars, and were also sent round the world. During the eight days in which the Congress took place, it was calculated that each day 17,000 people attended the different meetings in the different sections in the Albert Hall, the Church House, and other halls in London. A large Thank-offering Fund was raised and spent on Overseas work. The Pan-Anglican Congress was an immense achievement and kindled the enthusiasm of Churchmen all over the world. It was educational in character, the meetings were held in public, papers were read and discussion followed, but no resolutions were passed expressing any judgement of the Congress on the topic handled. The Archbishop presided over some of the meetings, and received the representatives at Lambeth Palace: but the strain was very great, and he was clear that it would never again be right for two such vast efforts as the Pan-Anglican Congress and the Lambeth Conference to be held so close together.

The Lambeth Conference itself followed the Pan-Anglican Congress. It was the regular decennial Conference of Anglican Bishops meeting in private for common counsel, and was presided over from first to last by the Archbishop of Canterbury. No account is ever issued of the speeches and debates, but the Resolution, Encyclical letters, and Reports of the Committees were published at the time, and are accessible in the official Report.[1] It is therefore unnecessary to give space to its proceedings here. It was attended by 242 Anglican Bishops from all parts of the world, and dealt with a large and varied agenda. Resolutions were

[1] *Report of the Lambeth Conference*, 1908. S.P.C.K.

passed on definitive subjects, after they had been considered by special committees of the Conference, which sat for a fortnight in between the weeks opening the session of the full Conference (July 6 to July 11) and the closing session (July 27 to August 5). The following table of the Reports of the Committees indicates the subjects discussed:

(i) The Faith and Modern Thought.
(ii) Supply and Training of Clergy.
(iii) Religious Education.
(iv) Foreign Missions.
(v) The Book of Common Prayer.
(vi) Administration of Holy Communion.
(vii) Ministries of Healing.
(viii) Marriage Problems.
(ix) Moral Witness of the Church.
(x) Organization in the Anglican Communion.
(xi) Reunion and Intercommunion.

The Encyclical letter was prepared by the Archbishop himself with assistance especially from the Bishops of Oxford (Paget), Salisbury (Wordsworth), and Bombay (Palmer). The manuscript has been preserved, in which the piecing together of the various hands is shown in a most interesting way. The leading idea of the Encyclical was 'service', and round this the general findings of the Conference were effectively grouped. There were one or two additional subjects upon which single resolutions were adopted.

A word may be added about one or two unrecorded aspects of the Conference—and especially the hospitality of Lambeth Palace, and the Chairmanship of the Archbishop. All through the summer a succession of Overseas Bishops and their wives spent two nights each at the Palace in groups of six to twelve. This gave every one of the visiting Bishops a feeling of friendship and a sense of home. Mrs. Davidson was a most generous hostess at all times; and in welcoming Bishops from overseas she excelled. 'It is a wonderful experience to stay at Lambeth,' wrote a Bishop's daughter to Mrs. Davidson afterwards, 'and I think you make it home for all those who are with you.' Moreover, the Archbishop himself used the opportunity which the visits gave him to add to his knowledge of each Bishop's problems. And he often gave the impression of knowing more about a particular diocese and its needs and difficulties than the Bishop himself. In addition to this, the Archbishop was accustomed to gather groups of Bishops from China, Japan, or East Africa respectively for special occasions, during the weeks of the Conference, in order to talk to them, and to hear them talk to one another, about the problems and possibilities of their particular part of the world.

As the Chairman of the Conference, the Archbishop used to say that the interest and responsibility of Chairmanship were enhanced by the fact that he knew himself to be presiding over professional Presidents. Every one of the Bishops attending was accustomed in his own territory to be sitting in the Chair. But Archbishop Davidson was, it was generally agreed, a masterly Chairman. Some thought him at times too patient, and one of the American Bishops was heard to 'guess' that 'that Archbishop of yours has taken a return ticket on the line of least resistance'!

At the end of the Conference the closing speech was made by the Bishop of Albany (W. C. Doane), who spoke 'not as an American Bishop but as the Bishop oldest but one in consecration and longest in attendance at these Lambeth Conferences'. This was the tribute he paid to the Chairman:

> There is nobody here in this Conference who has not been more or less occupied with the duties of presiding over public bodies; there is nobody here, I am sure, who does not realise how often that position is a difficult one, and there is none of us who has not been presided over again and again by presidents whose chief function seems to have been to prolong and to hinder the progress of business. In this instance we have a man who, in my judgment, combines a sort of concentrated extract and essence of archi-episcopal qualities: the shrewd and statesmanlike political insight of Archbishop Tait, the gracious and courteous considerateness of Archbishop Benson, and the strength and power of Archbishop Temple. I want to bear my witness to the fact that he has been over and over again in this Conference what I believe the chemical people call the solvent: that some words coming from him, often after the beginnings of such mild differences and divisions as have appeared from time to time among us, have reduced all the elements into one single and perfect condition of harmony and unity. I have been constantly convinced for many a day that the second of those beautiful prayers which I believe his Grace prepared for us has been abundantly answered by Almighty God,

in that He has given us the grace and guidance of His Holy Spirit in what we have conferred about; but above all I am perfectly clear that that petition in the Litany that we have said here every morning, namely that God would give the special gifts of wisdom and counsel to him who was called upon to preside over this Conference, has been richly and abundantly and fully granted and permitted.

So, my dear Archbishop, if you will let me, as one who has loved you for many years, one who feels that he expresses simply in his old age a feeling of infinite confidence in you in the position that you occupy officially as *primus inter pares*—personally, I believe, in the admiration and affection of all your brethren as *supremus supra pares*,—I desire merely to say that no words of mine, and I think no words of ours, can be sufficiently warm and strong to express what, under God, we owe to you for the happy conclusions to which this Conference has come.

V

The missionary interest of the Archbishop found another illustration in a wider field, which yet has a link with the Lambeth Conference of 1908. In July of that year, at the very time the Lambeth Conference was meeting, the Archbishop was invited to give his support to a great World Missionary Conference to be held in Edinburgh in 1910. The purpose of the World Conference was officially defined as 'research and conference regarding missionary work and problems'. It was to be attended by representatives of the missionary societies of the principal Protestant Churches throughout the world. And it had been formally decided that 'no resolution shall be allowed to be presented at all which involves questions of doctrine or church policy with regard to which the Churches or Societies taking part in the Conference differ among themselves'. There was, however, some nervousness in Anglican circles when the Missionary Societies of the Church of England were invited to co-operate. In the Committee on Foreign Missions of the Lambeth Conference, under the chairmanship of the Bishop of St. Albans (Jacob), the question of co-operation between Anglican and non-Anglican missions caused much discussion. In its Report printed as an appendix to the official Report of the Lambeth Conference[1] (together with the Reports of the other Committees)

[1] *The Six Lambeth Conferences, 1867–1920*, pp. 380–1, and p. 331.

the Committee emphasized the importance of 'a grateful recognition of the real unity, despite all divisions, of the Christian Society in the face of all other (non-Christian) religions'; and side by side with 'a frank recognition of denominational differences in matters of importance', the Committee expressed the desire that there should be 'an understanding between Christian bodies engaged in evangelising the non-Christian world'. The Lambeth Conference as a whole, however, expressed the general attitude of the Anglican episcopate in more guarded terms, laying special stress on the duty of prayer for Reunion:

> 58. This Conference reaffirms the resolution of the Conference of 1897 that 'Every opportunity should be taken to emphasise the Divine purpose of visible unity amongst Christians as a fact of revelation'. It desires further to affirm that in all partial projects of reunion and inter-communion the final attainment of the divine purpose should be kept in view as our object; and that care should be taken to do what will advance the reunion of the whole of Christendom, and to abstain from doing anything that will retard or prevent it.
>
> 59. The Conference recognises with thankfulness the manifold signs of the increase of the desire for unity among all Christian bodies; and, with a deep sense of the call to follow the manifest guiding of the Holy Spirit, solemnly urges the duty of special intercession for the unity of the Church, in accordance with our Lord's own prayer.

Six months later, in December 1908, the S.P.G. Standing Committee declined an invitation to be officially represented, in spite of the friendly attitude of its secretary, Bishop Montgomery. The opposition of the more rigid churchmen was therefore somewhat pronounced. What line would the Archbishop take? On July 5, 1909, he received a deputation consisting of Mr. J. R. Mott, Mr. J. H. Oldham, Mr. Tissington Tatlow, and Prebendary Fox (Secretary of the C.M.S.), together with (but not as a member of the deputation) Bishop Montgomery (Secretary of the S.P.G.). The Archbishop was formally invited to address the opening meeting on June 14, 1910. He expressed his interest —but indicated his difficulties:

> I pointed out to them the difficulties of my position: how my going thither might compromise some people who are quite willing to keep silence, although they disapprove of the joint action, but

who would not keep silence if they thought that by the Archbishop's presence the whole Church was committed. I told them that I must think the whole matter over and take counsel with those who can advise me best.

Eight months passed, and a letter to Mr. Oldham showed that he was still uncertain. But in the end, two months before the Conference took place, he decided to go. He gave an admirable address at the first public meeting of the Conference, attended by some 1,200 delegates from all over the world, in the Assembly Hall at Edinburgh on June 14, 1910—emphasizing the central place which missionary work should hold in the Church of Christ. He spoke of his own experience:

> It is perhaps not presumptuous to say that probably to the desk of no other man in the British Isles does there flow in weekly, daily, almost hourly, so varied a stream of communications about the Church's activities and problems, its mistakes and its failures, and its victories, as flows in steady volume from the whole circumference of the earth to my room, not, of course, as to a place of authority or governance—pray understand that—but as to a central pivot or exchange. And happily it is not letters only that flow in; it is also men and women.

He told of the immense opportunity which such a Conference must reveal:

> We meet, as has been well said, for the most serious attempt which the Church has yet made to look steadily at the whole fact of the non-Christian world, and to understand its meaning and its challenge. We look at it from standpoints not by any means the same, geographical, racial, or denominational. No one of us bates a jot of the distinctive convictions which he deliberately holds. Therein lies in part the value of the several contributions which will be made to our debates. But we are absolutely one in our allegiance to our living Lord.

And it was with deep religious conviction that he closed, as he began:

> Be quite sure—it is my single thought tonight that the place of missions in the life of the Church must be the central place and none other.

Thus the Archbishop had given a conspicuous witness not only to his convictions on the central place of missions in the life of the Church; but to the whole scope of Christianity in the mission field.

VI

This chapter shall end with an account of the launching of the Archbishops' Western Canada Fund in the same year as the World Missionary Conference. It was the largest missionary effort with which Archbishop Davidson was personally and directly associated. It had its origin in the rapid development of Western Canada, with its immense resources, at the beginning of the twentieth century. There had been a great inrush of settlers from the British Isles, from the Continent of Europe, and from the United States of America, and in a comparatively few years Western Canada had become a great and swiftly growing nation. The Church of England in Canada and other religious bodies had made valiant efforts to provide for the spiritual interests of this vast influx of immigrants. But the task was beyond the powers of the Canadian Churches and the various agencies in England and Scotland which had endeavoured to support them. Much greater help from outside Canada was urgently required. As the Archbishop of Rupertsland[1] wrote:

> It is to supplement the efforts of the Canadian Church, and to fill up what is lacking in its power to help at this crisis in the history of the Canadian West, that I desire to see the Church in the Mother Land make a supreme endeavour just now.

The Church in Eastern Canada, with the exception of the diocese of Algoma, no longer needed or asked for assistance from England: indeed, it gave large help to the Church in the West. Again, British Columbia, beyond the Rocky Mountains, had already received substantial aid from agencies in England, although the inrush of settlers into that territory had not as yet been so overwhelming as it had become in the Prairie Provinces. It was, then, for the Prairie Provinces of Manitoba, Saskatchewan, and Alberta that the Archbishops of Canterbury and York, after forming an influential Council to support them, on February 26, 1910, issued an earnest appeal. And the object of their appeal was to ask the Home Church to do its utmost to supply the Canadian Church with workers, and the means to support them, and

[1] Dr. S. P. Matheson.

to help to establish churches and schools, and other agencies for spiritual work, among the settlers. In making this appeal they counted upon the active co-operation of the societies in England (S.P.C.K., S.P.G., the Colonial and Continental Church Society, the Qu'Appelle Association, the Algoma Association, the Navvy Mission, etc.) which had already done much to support the Canadian Church in the past. There was at first some idea of merging these older efforts in the Archbishops' Fund; but it was ultimately decided that the new appeal should be made independently.

Within a few months the two Archbishops were able to report that the amount received in answer to their appeal was approaching £35,000; that the Rev. W. G. Boyd (Archbishop Davidson's Resident Chaplain), with eight other clergymen and several laymen, had gone to Canada and had established themselves at Edmonton as a missionary centre; and that the Rev. Douglas Ellison, formerly head of the Railway Mission in South Africa, had undertaken to organize work on the Canadian railways. The Fund was strongly supported by the Governor-General of Canada, Earl Grey, an old friend of the Archbishop ever since their time together at Harrow. In due course three centres were founded in the then dioceses of Edmonton, Qu'Appelle, and Calgary.

The Fund (with Canon T. G. Beal as Secretary) lasted ten years, in the midst of which came the War, resulting in a sad shortage of clergy. As time went on other difficulties appeared. But by 1920, when the Fund was closed, the sum of £180,000 had been raised, 138 workers had been sent out, seventy churches had been built and missions established, and 168 sites for churches had been bought. And from start to close the personal sympathy and attention of Archbishop Davidson never failed.

R. T. D. DOCTOR OF DIVINITY
ABERDEEN UNIVERSITY
(1906)

CHAPTER XXXII

INTERLUDE

The proposition which I have now endeavoured to illustrate was, at a subsequent period of his life, the opinion of Johnson himself. He said to Sir Joshua Reynolds, 'If a man does not make new acquaintance as he advances through life, he will soon find himself left alone. A man, Sir, should keep his friendship *in constant repair*.'
BOSWELL, *Life of Dr. Johnson* (1755).

I

IT is one of the penalties of such an office as that of Archbishop of Canterbury that public business tends to be so exacting as to leave all too little space for the happiness of intimate friendships. Yet Archbishop Davidson, in spite of all the pressure upon him, never let the personal element go: and never failed to reveal a deep human interest in all his dealings with other people, old or young. An acquaintance which began over political business very frequently grew into a firm friendship, quite independent of politics. We have seen that his intimacy with Mr. Balfour began with meetings about the Education Act of 1902; and we have seen also that his relations with Mr. Runciman were strengthened into a fine mutual trust through all the changes and chances of the Education Bill in 1908. Nor did a sharp difference of opinion over great public issues weaken the personal intimacy or confidence which bound him in other matters to such formidable ecclesiastical critics as Lord Halifax and Sir Alfred Cripps. The latter, indeed, had felt bound to offer resignation of his post as Vicar-General just because of his difference with Davidson over the educational issue in 1908: and an admirable instance of the Archbishop's largeness of mind and of his trust in his counsellors is seen in the reply which he sent dissuading him from such a course:

The ARCHBISHOP OF CANTERBURY *to* SIR ALFRED CRIPPS

Lambeth Palace, S.E. 25th November, 1908.

My dear Vicar General,

Pray do not take this grave step without our having a talk. I do think you misunderstand my position and attitude in this matter.

I have the gravest conceivable responsibility at a critical juncture in our history, and I *must* be guided by the dictates of conscience as in the sight of God. But I want to have the help and counsel, however widely you and others differ from me, of friends and advisers, or even 'protesters' like yourself, and it would, I honestly think, be a serious disaster were difference of opinion upon a great question of Educational policy to lead to the severance of ties of an official kind, wherewith that question—momentous as it is—has nothing to do.

So pray let us talk it over, and *then* if you decide that you must resign, I of course will not try to press you unfairly. But surely the time has not yet come at any rate?

Whatever happens I am not going to let our *friendship* be broken —so far as I am concerned—and I honestly think you may suppose my position to be a different one from what it is.

The talk followed, and, after the failure of the Bill, the offer of resignation was withdrawn.

In a similar spirit of generous friendship about the same time he wrote to congratulate his doughty antagonist, Dr. Clifford, on the completion of a pastorate of fifty years at the Westbourne Chapel: and the letters of both may be placed side by side to their mutual credit.

The Archbishop of Canterbury *to the* Rev. Dr. Clifford

Old Palace, Canterbury.
17th October, 1908.

I see that during the last ten days your friends—the circle is, I know, a wide one—have been most appropriately commemorating your pastoral jubilee.

I should like to be allowed to add, for myself, a word of fraternal greeting to a Christian teacher who has for so many years fought with strenuousness and perseverance on behalf of purity and temperance and moral earnestness and many another principle which should be dear to the followers of our Lord and Saviour Jesus Christ.

There are big and important matters upon which you and I profoundly differ—there are some, wherein you regard me, I believe, as in a high degree mischievous and wrong-headed, both in policy and action. But you will at least let me assure you of my respectful and sympathetic appreciation of such effort as you have continuously devoted, for half a century of London life, to the furtherance of civic righteousness and Christian citizenship and progress. After all, the things wherein we differ bulk very small in comparison with those wherein, in our Master's service, we are at one.

The REV. DR. CLIFFORD *to the* ARCHBISHOP OF CANTERBURY

Westbourne Park Chapel, Porchester Road,
London, W.
20. 10. 1908.

I am deeply indebted to Your Grace for your most kind and fraternal letter, so full of cordial appreciation and good wishes. It is most welcome; and with all my heart I completely reciprocate the fine Christian feeling it expresses.

We stand at different angles of the Christian life; but there are large breadths of Christian thought and faith and work in which we are agreed. Our judgements on some matters that go down to the very roots of the life and well-being of the nation and of the Christian Church differ; but we are one in whole-hearted allegiance to the Lord Jesus Christ as our Saviour and Master, in desire for the triumph of the Redeemer's Kingdom, in the honesty with which we have reached our conclusions and in the sincerity with which we defend them; and these are the things of supreme importance.

For all your kind congratulations on my fifty years pastorate in this City I offer my heartiest thanks.

A more personal ministry was that which the Archbishop gave to Sir Henry Campbell-Bannerman in the weeks before his death.[1] Many a day, as Campbell-Bannerman lay conscious that the end was approaching, Randall Davidson would walk to the house and sit by his bedside and speak to him, and listen as well. He often used to remark on the frankness with which Campbell-Bannerman, during these days, criticized his own colleagues; and the Archbishop's own comfort and ministry, as a brother Scot and a Christian minister, did much to lighten and cheer his last weeks. The following letter, written by Mr. Vaughan Nash[2] just after Campbell-Bannerman's death, is a testimony to this:

VAUGHAN NASH, ESQ., *to the* ARCHBISHOP OF CANTERBURY

10 Downing Street, Whitehall, S.W.
22nd April, 1908.

Mrs. Campbell does not feel equal to writing to-day, and she has asked me to thank you for your kind telegram and for all your

[1] *Life of Sir Henry Campbell-Bannerman*, J. A. Spender, ii. 385–6.
[2] Private Secretary to Sir Henry Campbell-Bannerman.

affectionate and helpful ministrations, which did so much to brighten Sir Henry's last days. I cannot tell you how much difference your visits made to him.

The end was rather unexpected—quite painless and no distress. He had been unconscious for some time.

The first part of the funeral service will be at Westminster Abbey on Monday, and the burial will be at Meigle the following day.

The Archbishop was one of the pall-bearers at the first part of the funeral in Westminster Abbey.

Another instance of deep personal consideration, side by side with a sense of high public duty, was found this same year in his tender co-operation with Mrs. Maclagan in persuading the old Archbishop of York to resign. It was not easy; for the Archbishop of York did not at first perceive the necessity of departure. There was no precedent for such resignation of either the Northern or the Southern Primacy; and it was strange that Archbishop Davidson should join in the making of such precedent, first, in 1908, for Dr. Maclagan, and then, in 1928, in his own case. Mrs. Maclagan by herself was not sure of bringing her husband to the point, and turned to Randall Davidson both for practical help and for comfort. No letter of Archbishop Davidson's own has been preserved, but his power and his wisdom may both be seen in the following letter:

MRS. MACLAGAN *to the* ARCHBISHOP OF CANTERBURY

Bishopthorpe, York.
2nd October, 1908.

Very Private.

I trust your holiday has been a real success, and that you will come back as a giant refreshed.

Important events have marched quickly since we returned here, and my dear husband has now quite made up his mind to resign. Moreover he has entirely forgotten all our attempts to persuade him to this decision, and, as far as I can judge, I think he believes he is acting entirely on his own initiative. He will do nothing till he has seen you, and I need hardly tell you how patient and gentle you must be with him. . . . His mental powers are very much weaker than they were in London, and my children and I feel the great importance of getting the question settled as soon as possible. He talks of resigning on the 1st January. I expect it will take a long time to arrange the legal business—pension, etc., as there are no precedents to guide us. . . .

Forgive this long, rambling letter, you have brought it on yourself by your more than brotherly kindness to a sorrowful woman.

My dear love to Edith.

The Archbishop of York duly came to Lambeth, and signed his deed of resignation. As the Archbishop and Mrs. Maclagan left the house, Mrs. Davidson was heard to remark: 'I hope that when our time comes we shall go with such dignity.'

As a pendant, however, to these illustrations of the Archbishop's constant readiness to help those in positions of great responsibility in Church or State, in these human ways, we may add a story of Sir Thomas Barlow's which shows a readiness just as great to help all sorts of people.

When in the zenith of their powers and activities the Archbishop and Mrs. Davidson made themselves accessible to all sorts and conditions of men out of all reasonable bounds, 'beyond all common sense'. That at least was Sir Thomas's view, and so he gave the Archbishop a little homily. He said: 'You know you are not only Archbishop of Canterbury but have got a very prominent place in the government of the country. However much you are bored by it you are bound to be consulted in vastly important matters. There are only twenty-four hours in the day. If you are so ready to help Tom, Dick, and Harry in their small matters it will be physically impossible for you to attend to the weightier matters of the law.' The Archbishop simply replied: 'Well, I can only tell you that such help as I could give to Tom, Dick, and Harry, as you call them, has helped me to give counsel in the weightier matters of the law.' In telling this story to the writer, Sir Thomas described the Archbishop's answer as 'the very finest thing I ever heard him say'.[1]

II

We have already shown more than once how keen was the Archbishop's enjoyment of a holiday. One of the best he ever had was this year at Courmayeur, after the toils of the Lambeth Conference and before the educational trials of the autumn. A

[1] Sir Thomas, in telling the same story to another friend, added, 'And I said to myself, "He's right. T. B., be quiet!"'

picture of him taken at the time, with the Bishop of Oxford (Dr. Paget) and others, shows him enjoying his ease. Here is a letter in reply to one from Mrs. Creighton, the widow of Bishop Mandell Creighton, describing both his pleasure and his reflections:

The ARCHBISHOP OF CANTERBURY *to* MRS. CREIGHTON

Alagna. September 10, 1908.

You know, I think, all the places we have been seeing. We came out via Martigny and Aosta to Courmayeur, stayed there a fortnight. Then by Châtillon and Issogne to Gressoney. Stayed there a week. Then over the Col d'Olen to this quiet village. Again and again in long walks of glorious sunshine and fresh air I have thought about your 'feel' as to mountains. I think on the whole I agree with you as to our love of them growing keener as one grows old. At all events it is a different sort of love. But my own caring for mountains always depends greatly on the conditions. A big blaring Hotel full of English (even when they are of the best sort) takes away from the mountains half their charm. We have been lucky enough to have no English at all in these inns—save here and there a climber—and our walks have been in keeping with the quiet rests of the long evenings. The Bishop of Oxford has been with us all through—until today when he has gone off for England—and we have the hotel to ourselves. Tomorrow we hope the Bishop of Southwark will bring Winny to join us and leave her to go with us to Varallo and then to the lakes—getting back to Lambeth we hope by Oct. 1. with all the prospect of a big busy bustling striving session before Christmas.

What a year it has been. I don't need to tell you how keenly I, of all men, have longed to have had your husband with us in the talkings and doings which have filled our hours. People no doubt must be saying that all our Conferences don't issue in very much that is practical, but I think they mistake the real gist and intent and working-gain of the Conferences. To me the good that has come from the intercourse with the far-off workers has been immeasurable—both spiritually and in other widening ways. How we can make it all fruitful is a different and I think a most puzzling problem. I shall ask for your help in trying to solve it. You are one of the very few who seem to me to combine the power of vision with the power of action in our present-day Church life. Scores of helpful folk have one or the other—but I find it hard to make the visions of the thinkers bear fruit in the actions of the others.

Surely there ought to be, in some way or other, a large quiet practical new start, with a fuller knowledge of what ought to be our purpose—and a wider application of experience from many lands.

My fear is that we on whom so much responsibility must rest for central work will get plunged forthwith into the cauldron of Parliamentary strife—Education—Licensing—and so on—and miss the bigger opportunity until the chance of using it has gone by. Please help us to keep clear of that. If this time of glorious rest and sunshine and fresh air has not fitted us (I mean Edith and me) better for what lies ahead—we must be wretches indeed.

God bless and keep you dear friend. You—(with all that you think and say) *matter* to me more than most people!

The Bishop of Oxford (Dr. Francis Paget), looking back at Christmas on their happiness together, wrote the following verses:

Christmas Day, 1908. With grateful and affectionate obedience.

F.O., Cuddesdon,
Wheatley, S.O., Oxon.

But, is there really such a place
Within this realm of time and space?
And can it really ever be
That I shall go to Innisfree?

And shall I never hear again,
In weariness that's worse than pain,
The Minutes of last Meeting read,
The 'few words'—sad and countless—said?

And is the air quite clear and still?
Have they no Education Bill?
Do points of order never rise?
Are there no Rubrics to revise?

Does Convocation never sit?
(Does no one feel the need of it?)
And have they there no R.C.C.,
No E.C.U., no Q.A.B.?

Your Grace, let's go! our places book,
Our luggage register with Cook.
Arise, let's go!—just you and me,—
With just two more,—to Innisfree!

III

Randall Davidson and Mrs. Davidson often took their own nieces or the daughters of old friends to enjoy their holidays with them. One of the members of the party in 1908 was Miss L. C. (Winnie) Talbot, daughter of the Bishop of Southwark, then in the twenties.

She has written the following note of her friendship, which began when she first met him at Farnham in 1898, as a girl of sixteen:

> I rode once with him in London and had tea with him afterwards, and put milk by mistake into the teapot, and hoped and prayed he wouldn't find out. I remember so well the rather nervous moment of setting out over Lambeth Bridge, on a rather fresh horse, and the feeling of elation at going with him.
>
> It was during a formidable visit to Whittingehame that I made friends with him. I was alone there—September or October, 1906, when I was 24—and in that terrifying milieu I drew to him and he fathered me. I don't remember being frightened of him. I remember walking up and down the lawn with him discussing whether or not we ought to go to kirk in Scotland, and being rather shocked at his saying that as Archbishop he wouldn't go for fear of giving offence, but obviously not with any strong principle about *not* going! Later in the afternoon we said Evensong together in his room, and afterwards he began to ask me searching questions about my Bible reading. I remember trying to hedge behind some copying or something I had done for Mr. Holland, through which flimsy screen he pierced at once. It was from that time that I felt the great tie with him, which has lasted ever since for 24 years. Up till the time I went to South Africa in 1921, I stayed often at Lambeth, and went abroad with the Davidsons three times, to Alagna, Varallo, Varese, Menaggio, to Generoso, Lanzo d'Intelvi, Simplon, Milan.
>
> Across those years there are many memories grave and gay. We had many jokes abroad, and I finally and for ever lost all shyness of him as he knelt in his shirt-sleeves on my box to make it shut. He was an affairé traveller—he could never conceive how Father fitted in plans abroad and at home. He liked having plenty of time and to know exactly what was happening and where he was going. I can well see his anxious face at the booking-office at some small Italian station. On the other hand he was very equable. I remember a maddening Customs Official at Isella or Domo,

throwing the contents of a suitcase on the platform, and though we raged, the Archbishop only raised his eyebrows in patient and ironic submission. I don't think in all my knowledge of him I ever saw him *cross*. He enjoyed the times to the full and was a delightful companion. He was amused at my pleasure at doing things *de luxe* compared to our own economical ways of travelling. We had delightful readings aloud. I remember best Lindsay's *History of the Reformation*, which occasioned many an argument. In those days I was more of a rigid Tractarian! I remember well outside the Hotel at Menaggio his taking me gravely aside and saying that he should like to show me the spiritual aspect of Mattins! We also read Macaulay's *History*; especially the trial of the Seven Bishops. He was shocked at my abyssmal ignorance. I remember also he asked me what the National Debt was, and when I had to cry ignorance—'You old donkey, don't you know *that*?' He was a delightful expounder of things and never minded explaining anything, and didn't make you feel a fool. I used abroad to help him with his letters and had a glimpse of his wonderful thoroughness and method. We had a great 'travailing' over his Church Congress sermon in 1911, reading it over and re-writing. He always wanted to know how his writings struck someone else. . . .

Lambeth has played so much part all through. I know the feel of the weight of the big front door, and the steps up, and the long passage. It seemed an empty place when he wasn't there. I can see his figure emerging out of his room or the study, often affairé with some impending function or appointment, or moments of warm welcome either in drawing-room or passage. . . . I know the feel so well of knocking at his door and hearing his rather loud 'Come in' and the sight of him writing at his table, saying—'Come in, my child.' He had a way of sitting with his leg somehow tucked under him in his leather chair. . . . There was a wonderful sense of strength in his touch, and in his firm, strong, gentle hand. I can feel it on my shoulder, or stretching out to grasp my hand, or in blessing on my head. And as host at his own table he had a characteristic way of stretching out his hand to beckon one to sit next him. Meals could sometimes be rather shy occasions, if he was cumbered or in a silent mood, and somehow asking him to pass the butter made me shy! He didn't like general talk much. He was too discreet for it! and the meals were sometimes heavy. I used to welcome the pushing back of his chair and withdrawing to the fireplace, or a little talk along the big corridor. . . .

He had a beautiful quiet voice. I can hear him calling, 'Lavinia Caroline'—a foolish joke of his. But also I loved his reading the Bible in Chapel and his reading of the prayers, a particular inflection of 'through Jesus Christ our Lord'. He read aloud very well.

There was a rare magnanimity about him, and he had to a greater degree than anyone I have known the quality of patience. This was shown towards others' actions with which he didn't agree. But it came out mostly in regard to the many wearisome little checks of ill-health and malaise which were so constantly his. He fell down our badly lighted front steps at Kennington and broke a tendon in his thigh. He had come to discuss some point in the Education crisis—was it in 1907 or 1908? The doctor was amazed at his courage. While in great pain he drafted a letter to the Prime Minister. He called himself 'Little Johnnie Head in Air' when I saw him next day.

This quality of a strong patience was what helped to give him that rock-like quality of friendship and help and counsel. That, and his horror of exaggeration and excess, and also the wonderful way he gave one the whole of his attention, as if you were the one person and problem in the world. He wrote to me in his own hand when he did write,—'I like to write to my friends in my own hand'.

I wish I had penetrated more into his own religion so far as might be, but I do know his was that deep, simple, pious godliness, depending on Prayer and devout reception of the Sacrament. One could not quite call him a Sacramentalist in the sense one would, say, Bishop Gore, for instance. . . . And his whole life was shot through by prayer. I remember a cousin of ours being amazed at his telling her he remembered her in his prayers, and he often told me he prayed for me every day. I suppose his religion was eminently sane and strong and sensible and unmystical. 'Godliness' is the word which seemed to apply to him rather than 'holiness'. I remembered his saying that if he had had Bishop Awdry's[1] beauty of face he could have done anything with the Church of England!

[1] William Awdry, Bishop of Southampton, 1895–6; Bishop of Osaka, 1896–8; Bishop of South Tokyo, 1898–1908.

CHAPTER XXXIII

FOREIGN AFFAIRS. THE PEOPLE'S BUDGET

'Lydgate has lots of ideas, quite new, about ventilation and that sort of thing', resumed Mr. Brooke, after he had handed out Lady Chettam, and had returned to be civil to a group of Middlemarchers. 'Hang it, do you think that is quite sound?—upsetting the old treatment, which has made Englishmen what they are?' said Mr. Standish. GEORGE ELIOT, *Middlemarch*.

AN increasing amount of the Archbishop's correspondence during these years came from abroad. Some of the letters were appeals for help to relieve material distress. Others were addressed to him with the hardly disguised hope that he might use some supposed political influence with the British Government to secure redress for an oppressed or suffering nation.

I

In each case care had to be exercised to prevent extravagant hopes or groundless expectations. Thus, when in February 1909 a Deputation of Armenians wished to wait upon him publicly, to solicit his aid in obtaining help for the sufferers from famine in Cilicia, he felt obliged to point out the danger of a misapprehension with regard to his powers:

The ARCHBISHOP'S PRIVATE SECRETARY *to* PROFESSOR HAGOPIAN

Private. 27th February, 1909.

If you or other gentlemen who know the details of this appalling distress like to wait upon the Archbishop in order that he may understand the circumstances, he will be willing to arrange to receive them, but it would he thinks be most misleading were he to receive a Deputation publicly, as it would probably raise hopes the realisation of which would be entirely outside his powers. You probably know how wide is the misapprehension prevailing in Eastern Europe and in Western Asia as regards the powers of the Archbishop in such matters. Letters constantly reach Lambeth showing that the writers imagine that the Archbishop is a sort of philanthropic centre whose word is law with the generous and who can elicit subscriptions for all and every purpose. Such a misapprehension would be encouraged were a Deputation of the kind you suggest to be received in a way that would become publicly known. It will be obvious to you, and to others who know London and the facts of English life, that it is from such persons as the Lord Mayor of London that an appeal to the sympathies of the public more properly emanates. Further, the Archbishop has during the last six months had several other requests similar to that which you transmit. He has been asked to put himself at the head of an organization for raising funds for the suffering Jacobite Christians in Eastern Turkey, and also for the Nestorian Christians in Western Persia, all of whom are suffering, as your countrymen are, from the results of severe famine. The Archbishop thinks you will understand the difficulty, and will let me know for His Grace's information whether you, with the other gentlemen named, would desire to see him privately, or whether you think that a written communication which can be made public would be more desirable.

In this instance he saw the Deputation privately, and wrote a letter which was used to obtain help, though the results of the Appeal were less satisfactory than he had hoped.

An Appeal of a different kind was made by the Archbishop of Belgrade, Metropolitan of Serbia (Dimitri), whose country had been shocked by the abrupt annexation of the Slav provinces of Herzgovinia and Bosnia by the Austrian-Hungarian Empire in October 1908:

The ARCHBISHOP OF BELGRADE *to the* ARCHBISHOP OF CANTERBURY

2nd January, 1909.

A fatal blow has been struck at the Serbian race and its unity by the annexation of Bosnia and Herzgovinia, and the whole Serbian nation has been deeply stirred by it, especially the independent States, Serbia and Montenegro. Following the advice of powerful friends the Serbian peoples were tranquillized, feeling convinced that the Powers will take their cause into their hands. But it appears that their steps in this direction will remain without any result and the Serbian peoples have again to face a desperate look out for which there seems no help but to trust in God and in their own strength. In consequence of this I venture to write to your Grace and lay the grievances of my Flock before you in these difficult times and to ask your brotherly assistance and consolation.

After dwelling on the injuries of the Serbian people who have been 'stirred to the very bottom of their hearts' and also to 'the two most terrible powers directed against the Serbian fatherland, "the police and the executioner" on the one hand, and "dark Jesuitism" on the other', the Serbian Archbishop ended his letter thus:

> I beg to request Your Grace to be good enough to communicate the misfortune of my Flock to your people, to whom may God grant to continue to live in peace and spiritual satisfaction, and to call upon them that they might, in the spirit of mutual Christian love, unite their prayers with ours to Our Saviour The Lord Jesus Christ, to help the Serbian nation in this difficult hour of trial and to avert from them the fatal blow which threatens them.
>
> I on my part will not cease to offer hearty prayers to God for the mighty and noble English nation, whose sympathies are giving us strength not to succumb but to trust in the eternal justice of God, which upholds and can save the feeble.

The Archbishop's answer was as follows:

The ARCHBISHOP OF CANTERBURY *to the* ARCHBISHOP OF BELGRADE

30th January, 1909.

I have the honour to acknowledge the receipt of Your Grace's letter of December 20th (January 2nd) and to thank you for the assurance you give of the prayers which you are offering on behalf of our Church and Nation.

With regard to the anxieties and fears to which Your Grace refers, it is my duty to point out that the Bishops of the Church of England abstain carefully from intervention in the anxious and difficult political questions which press at present upon the people of Eastern Europe, feeling that their knowledge of the problems is not sufficient to justify them in expressing opinions upon the subject. I can, however, assure Your Grace of our continuous prayers that to those troubled regions, and especially to the Christian populations therein, our Heavenly Father may in His own good time vouchsafe the blessings of peace. We pray too that all things which tend to disturbance and discord may, by the working of His Divine Providence, be steadily brought to an end, so that His Church in all lands may be permitted to work for the advancement of His Kingdom among men and for the promotion of whatsoever things are just and pure and lovely and of good report.

II

During February and March the Archbishop's influence was also being solicited at home in connexion with the Navy Scare and the talk of a war with Germany. The Mayor of Canterbury invited him to attend a meeting at the Canterbury Guild Hall, which had been called in order to pass a Resolution 'that the present superiority of the Navy should be maintained'. This invitation he refused. He received an appeal of a different kind from the President of the Free Church Council:

The REV. J. SCOTT LIDGETT *to the* ARCHBISHOP OF CANTERBURY

21st March 1909.
Bermondsey Settlement, S.E.

It has been suggested to me that in the present excited state of public feeling with the talk of an 'inevitable war' between this country and Germany, it might be possible and would be well for the two Archbishops and the Heads of the other Churches in this country to issue a message to the nation. It would naturally avoid the material and party issues, but state the importance of maintaining the peace-loving spirit, seeking harmonious relations with the whole world, and endeavouring to facilitate a speedy arrangement as to armaments.

It seems to me that the suggestion is a good one. We should discharge our responsibility and it might be of practical service if a declaration were carefully worded. May I ask Your Grace whether you think so, and if so, whether you would undertake the preparation of such a document, which should be signed by the Scottish Moderators as well as by the others I have named.

The following was his answer:

The ARCHBISHOP OF CANTERBURY *to the* REV. J. SCOTT LIDGETT

Private. 23rd March, 1909.

I thank you cordially for a very interesting and important letter received this morning. I think you and I are probably in full agreement as to what we want at present to impress upon the public mind, but I am afraid I cannot think that we could effectively or usefully put out at this particular moment such a manifesto as you refer to. If such a document is to have the character of a public pronouncement no amount of precaution on our part, or of protestation that we are not acting politically, would prevent the utterance from being twisted into a political declaration. On the other hand I think we ought as individuals holding responsible positions to be speaking strongly as to the need of such an attitude of mind as you describe. I shall certainly take opportunities of doing this myself, and I have no doubt that you can do it also. After a little time, when the feverishness of to-day has calmed, we may perhaps find means of speaking together in some weighty way on the lines you advocate; but to do it at this moment would in my judgement be a blunder. The 'plain man' would say, 'This tall talk or pious injunction is all very well, but do you mean that we are to have new Dreadnoughts or not? That is the point at the moment. How am I as a rank-and-file Member of Parliament or a common-place citizen to vote?' Of course such a comment on a joint utterance of ours would be quite unfair, but I think it would be inevitable, and therefore I think we should act wisely in not at this moment putting ourselves in that position. I have just been speaking to the Bishop of Southwark on the subject of your letter, and he entirely agrees with me, while he shares my sense of the obligation resting upon us to try individually in our own circles to do everything we possibly can to inculcate an attitude of mind more consistent with the principles which should actuate a Christian nation.

III

A step towards international friendship was taken this year through the visit of leaders of different Churches in England to Germany in return for a similar visit of German Ministers the previous year, in which the Archbishop had shown his interest.

He wrote as follows to the Bishop of Ripon (Dr. Boyd Carpenter):

The ARCHBISHOP OF CANTERBURY *to the* BISHOP OF RIPON

12th April, 1909.

I write this letter with reference to the endeavour which is being made to get together an adequately representative body of leading Churchmen to go to Germany in response to the visit of the German Pastors to England last year. I learn that there is some chance that you may be able to go, and I write to say how very earnestly I hope that this is true. Nobody would be so acceptable to Germany, and nobody would do so well what is wanted. I know that some other Bishops are trying to arrange matters so as if possible to go, but I do not feel sure of their succeeding. Hereford and Welldon are I believe secured. The Dean of Westminster is trying to manage it, and London and Southwark would both like to go, but their difficulties seem immense, owing to the rush of engagements at that time including the great Church Pageant at Fulham, which needs the Bishop of London's presence. I merely write because I feel so strongly that it would be disastrous were it to appear as if the Nonconformists were anxious for friendliness with Germany, while we Churchmen were only anxious to build more Dreadnoughts. Such a notion is ludicrous, but it would probably not be easy for Germans to understand the difficulties of English Bishops in getting away from England during the Summer, even for a few days, and misrepresentations might arise. So, if you can make it practicable to go, you will, I am sure, be doing a service both to Nation and Church, and to the cause of International Peace as well. Only of course you must do nothing that is wrong as regards your own health.

The Bishop of Ripon was unable to go. But four English Diocesan Bishops and a number of Anglican, Roman Catholic, and Nonconformist representatives, both clerical and lay, went out, together with several Members of Parliament. They were cordially welcomed. The German Emperor himself received them at Potsdam, and expressed the hope that the visit would tend to promote good feeling between two great kindred nations. A provisional Committee was formed to promote the good cause led by three M.P.s, Mr. J. Allen Baker, Mr. W. H. Dickinson, and Mr. J. E. Ellis. This also had the support of the Archbishop, though he pointed out that a good cause may itself be injured by those who 'do protest too much'.

The ARCHBISHOP OF CANTERBURY *to* J. E. ELLIS, ESQ.

24th June, 1909.

I thank you cordially for a very interesting letter giving me your impression of the value of the recent visit paid to Germany by English representatives of Christian teaching and thought who received so warm a welcome. I have had the advantage of hearing also from other friends who were privileged to be of the party. Their general view as to the outcome corresponds pretty closely with your own, and there cannot I think be any real doubt as to the value of such intercourse in general or of this visit in particular. It is in this kind of way, I believe, that public opinion, or rather public sentiment, on both sides will be best elicited, consolidated, and made effective. Personally I do not think it well that we should keep on reiterating mere statements that we are friendly with one another. Of course we are; and the reiteration may even suggest the very thing that we deny. I am also in full accord with your view that our common action for strengthening the basis of friendliness and good-will gains by being quiet and unemotional. It is harmed when it loses itself in shouting. What we want is a simple deliberate recognition of common interests, common aims, and unifying forces and facts; and this is just what has I believe been helpfully furthered by the recent visit. I feel very thankful about it all.

IV

Meantime a new crisis was rapidly developing in Parliament. And it was a crisis so serious that its issue affected the whole future relations of the two Houses to each other. Mr. Lloyd George had introduced his Budget, known as the People's Budget, on April 29. It introduced a tax on land, proposed super-taxation, higher death duties, and new taxes on licence holders. It was hailed by the Liberals as the first democratic Budget. It was denounced by Lord Lansdowne at a meeting of Unionists as 'a monument of reckless and improvident finance'.

It soon became clear that, while its course through the Commons was secure, it was bound to arouse the deepest hostility in the Lords. And here a very interesting question arose as to the attitude which the Bishops ought to adopt in a conflict of an acute character between the two Houses. Were they to vote for the Bill, on the ground that it was a finance Bill, for which on constitutional grounds the House of Commons must be held responsible, or on the ground that it was a great measure of Social Reform? Were they to vote against it, as a Bill full of dangers? Or were they to stand aside on the ground that the issue had, in fact, become an issue between the two chief political parties?

We have already seen that Archbishop Davidson was accustomed to take an active and also an independent part in the discussion of large public questions in the House of Lords. Thus on July 20, 1908, he took an unpopular line on the Old Age Pension Bill—when he urged that the time for action had arrived and that the question of the cost was one for the House of Commons. This Bill was passed. Again in the Autumn session of the same year he had vigorously supported the Government's Licensing Bill in the House of Lords, to the displeasure of the Unionist Opposition. Indeed Balfour, who never disguised his dislike of episcopal excursions into these fields, said once in the House of Commons, amidst laughter and cheers, 'There is no use in quoting Bishops to me on a question of this kind!' The Archbishop was also one of the minority when the Licensing Bill was rejected for a second reading on November 27, 1908, in the House of Lords to the great indignation of the Commons. Once more, in September 1909, he made a long and careful speech on the Report of the Royal Commission on the Poor Law. The subject had not become controversial so far as Parliament was concerned. But since the two Reports—Majority and Minority—had been published at the beginning of the year, neither of the two political parties had shown any particular disposition to treat the question of Poor Law Reform with the seriousness it demanded. The Archbishop made what Lord Crewe described as a very clear and masterly statement, to a somewhat unsympathetic audience. He showed a thoroughness and a zeal which gave evidence of an intense interest in the details of social conditions and an unmistakable sense of the 'need of action in a matter vitally affecting the credit and the well-being of a Christian country'. The Lords were unsympathetic because they were at that very moment oppressed with the Budget.

V

The Budget was the Government's Budget. Would the Archbishop oppose the Government, or would he oppose the majority in the House of Lords? From the first the Archbishop's own inclination was to abstain from voting, if the issue could be kept within strictly financial limits. But from the first he also feared the possibility of a transformation into a constitutional crisis. The following is the reply which he sent to an inquiry from the Bishop of Wakefield (Dr. Eden):

The ARCHBISHOP OF CANTERBURY *to the* BISHOP OF WAKEFIELD

Private. 16th September, 1909.

Personally I have no present intention of speaking on the Finance Bill. But if there is a serious and really formidable endeavour to throw the Bill out, the discussion may easily get shifted from financial to constitutional lines, and in that case I might feel forced to say a word. I understand from you that Crewe definitely

> wants you to support the Finance Bill *as such*. That is of course another question. I am very far from saying or thinking that Bishops ought necessarily to abstain from such speech. In old days —say 50 years ago—they constantly intervened in partisan political debate of that kind. It has been less common recently, and I have myself endeavoured to keep clear of that sort of controversy, where no moral question seems to be directly and obviously involved. But that is a matter of personal behaviour rather than of principle, and I should be very sorry to seem to urge silence upon any of our body if they have psalm or prophecy to utter, and think it really expedient to say their say. Hereford has I think done so more than once, but your intervention would be regarded as more important.

All through the next few weeks the Archbishop was in constant attendance at the House of Lords, and the recipient of a great many confidences. The elder Unionist statesmen, like Cromer and St. Aldwyn, however much they shook their heads over the merits of the Budget, disliked the idea of rejection, with all that it involved. The younger members of the same party had no such qualms about throwing it out. The Archbishop saw both, and made it clear to Lord Lansdowne, the Leader of the Unionist Opposition (on October 26, 1909), that he thought rejection would be a tactical blunder, not only because he believed that the Budget was popular (barring the Landlord classes and the keen Tariff Reformers), but also because he was afraid of the constitutional issue being raised if the Budget were thrown out. Lord Lansdowne disagreed, favouring rejection on the grounds of the dignity of the House of Lords. He did not think that 'the Radicals could effectively mix up the Budget question and the House of Lords Question. They would have to be brought before the constituencies separately.'

The Archbishop's view was not popular with the Unionists. Mr. Balfour's private secretary (J. S. Sandars) saw him next day (October 27) and pointed out how much the Unionist leaders:

> were impressed by the danger that, if such a Bill as this were allowed to go through, similar tactics might hereafter be employed for advancing political objects independently of their financial bearing. He instanced (doubtless for my benefit) the possibility, for example, of disestablishing the Church of England by putting into what purposed to be a mere Money Bill a clause saying that the endowments of the Church should be taxed say 50 per cent.

of their value. I thought this argument was a little polished up for my special digestion, and I told him that of course it was very familiar to me, but that none the less I felt on the whole unshaken.

Everthing now pointed to a definite partisan fight: and in this the Archbishop refused to be involved. He and most of the Bishops decided on a course of abstention, but he made it clear to Bishops asking his advice that he hoped 'that every Bishop would as a matter of course preserve his absolute independence of action and take the line which seems to him right'.

VI

The Bill came before the House of Lords on November 23. The line which the Archbishop had dreaded was followed.

It was a partisan fight. Between November 23 and November 30, amongst a large number of other speakers, the new Archbishop of York (Dr. Lang), in a maiden speech, and the Bishop of Birmingham (Dr. Gore) supported the Bill, while the Bishop of Bristol (Dr. Browne) opposed it.

The majority of the Bishops, however, after consideration, resolved to stand on one side.

The Archbishop of Canterbury spoke on November 24 and stated the decision to which he and the majority of the Bishops had come. He had taken great pains in clearing his mind, and his speech, instead of being delivered, as was his custom, from very full notes, was written out in his own hand complete. It was quite short. He said that he did not propose to enter into the merits of the controversy either in its financial or its constitutional aspects. He believed that the Bishops had peculiar opportunities for knowing about and handling the moral, religious, educational, and social questions with which the House had constantly to deal. Such questions:

> range from Poor Law Reform and Prison Reform to University or Ecclesiastical Reform, from sweating and overcrowding at home to the treatment of Aborigines in Australia or West Africa and elsewhere. While in such matters as Temperance or Education it goes without saying that the Bishops are expected to be the mouthpiece of many thousands of people outside.

Then he added:

> I am satisfied as to the usefulness of that function, but I believe that its usefulness is enhanced, and that the weight attached to

what is said from these Benches is augmented by the fact that, speaking generally, the Bishops have, in recent years at least, held themselves free from the ties of what is ordinarily known as party allegiance.

I am very far from denying that questions of a distinctly political character may arise and do arise, in the treatment of which all the Bishops may rightly and consistently take full part—and I think it would be affectation to pretend that we are not, as citizens, quite as well qualified as the average Members of this House to form and express opinions on those questions. But I believe that, ordinarily speaking at any rate, the Bishops act wisely in—as I have said—sitting loose to party ties.

In the present instance it was abundantly clear that the division was to have a strictly party character, a fact which he personally much regretted. Therefore, in his judgement and in that of the majority of the Bishops, this was one of the occasions in which they were right in standing aside, though individual Bishops might quite rightly use their individual liberty.

The direct issue [he said] is the question whether or not the money which is required for the expenditure—the increasing expenditure of the country—can or cannot be rightly raised in a particular way without a further appeal to the constituents. The other grave issues—which are not obscurely involved—are indirect issues or consequences after all. . . . It is not because I and those who think with me are indifferent to the great social questions which are astir in England in connection with the life of the poor that we are taking the line we do take. I have tried to shew that what we are doing, we are doing deliberately, in the genuine belief that—by adhering to an independent standpoint—we increase our power of contributing usefully to the solution of some of the greatest, deepest, and most urgent problems which Parliament has continuously to consider and to decide.

In the division the Archbishop of Canterbury and the majority of Bishops abstained from voting. The Bill was defeated by 350 votes to 75.

On December 2, Mr. Asquith carried a Resolution in the House of Commons 'that the action of the House of Lords in refusing to pass into Law the financial provision made by the House for the Services of the year is a breach of the Constitution and an usurpation of the rights of the Commons'.

On December 3, Parliament was dissolved.

CHAPTER XXXIV

THE CONSTITUTIONAL CRISIS, 1910

From the Reform Act the function of the House of Lords has been altered in English history. Before that Act it was, if not a directing Chamber, at least a Chamber of Directors. . . . Since the Reform Act the House of Lords has become a revising and suspending House. It can alter Bills; it can reject Bills on which the House of Commons is not yet thoroughly in earnest—upon which the nation is not yet determined. Their veto is a sort of hypothetical veto. They say, We reject your Bill for this once, or these twice, or even these thrice; but if you keep on sending it up, at last we won't reject it. The House has ceased to be one of latent directors, and has become one of temporary rejectors and palpable alterers. BAGEHOT, *The English Constitution*, ch. iv.

IN the crisis of the Finance Bill in the House of Lords, the Archbishop had deliberately asserted his independence and the independence of the Bishops as a Bench from party conflicts. By refusing to take sides he had indeed laid himself open to criticism from many, both Unionists and Radicals; though the confidence of more thoughtful statesmen was not shaken by his abstention from the division.

I

The path of moderation is not easy. It has special difficulties when party spirit is running high. And when that party spirit found an additional outlet in the stirring up of religious animosities, in the throes of a General Election, the Archbishop's heart might well be sore. Thus he wrote as follows, on reading the report of an inflammatory speech of the Chancellor of the Exchequer, Mr. Lloyd George himself, to a great rally of Free Churchmen in the Queen's Hall on December 16, 1909:

The ARCHBISHOP OF CANTERBURY *to the* REV. J. SCOTT LIDGETT

Private. 18th December, 1909.

My heart is very sore and I feel constrained to write to you about it. You and I have prayed and spoken and worked together for peace at home, for justice and Christianity of spirit abroad, and I have learned to look on you as a trusted friend. You probably know my position in the present controversy. I am in no sense acting or feeling with the Tory and Tariff Reforms party or policy.

I opposed privately to the utmost of my power the line of action which I found was going to be taken. But I am so certain of the detriment which ensues to the cause of spiritual religion when the ministers of religion don this partisan armour and rush into the political fray, that I with most of the Bishops deliberately took no part in the House of Lords battle. I did this after full consultation with—*inter alios*—men like the Lord Chancellor—John Morley and others.

But now! Here is a foremost Member of the Government gathering round him a great cohort of Ministers of Religion *as such* accompanied by their lay friends—again there in *their religious capacity*, and he delivers an oration appealing to every passion that can be inflamed by the recollection of past controversy and to every prejudice which can be utilised to excite hatred, envy, malice and all uncharitableness, and this in the name of religion, and under the auspices of ministers of Christ, and then those ministers of Christ speak in gratitude and support, and the party organs peal out triumphant paeans over a 'noble speech' and so on.

And alongside of this, I am being asked in connection with the great Edinburgh Missionary Conference of next year to invite the co-operation of yourself and others in again calling for joint prayer for the drawing together of Christian folk, and for the healing of our divisions, and I long—as I always have longed and striven—to move on those lines. Dare I do it now? Shall I be repulsed by those whom (e.g. yourself) I should be eager to invite to join with us in such prayer? I had hoped that Whitsuntide might again see us on our knees together in the name of the Prince of Peace, and in honest prayer that God the Holy Spirit would draw us into one. I don't want to make a mockery of such prayers, and I feel rebuffed as to any such plan.

Of course I am not in the smallest degree criticising or objecting to any vigorous political speeches, even on the part of ministers of religion, if they deem that to be right—though I hope to be able to restrain *our own* people, those who must be sorely tempted to reply to such utterances—those whom I have a right to counsel or help—from doing anything of the sort.

But what does really upset all one's highest plans and hopes and endeavours and aspirations, is to find this spirit of sheer unmitigated scornful *hatred* encouraged, inflamed and proclaimed as that which Nonconformists should adopt.

I can't believe that those who listened to the oration I speak of can have felt that what was said corresponded to the prayers they came to offer or betokened the spirit in which they want a grave responsibility to be discharged. Come what may, you may rely upon my doing all that in me lies, God helping me, to encourage the opposite spirit and to strive to hinder the upgrowth of those hateful passions which are now being fostered as an asset in the party fight. Such fostering seems to me to be in the most literal sense the work of the Devil. Yet I see no single word of the vigorous protest from those quarters where I should have thought we might have really counted on it. Hence my heart's sadness and bewilderment, and a wondering sense of whether I shall simply be upsetting my friends among the ministers of Nonconformist Churches by inviting them to pray with us at Whitsuntide for the grace of God to draw us really together in connection with our spiritual work at home and abroad.

I know you will pardon me for this private letter, and will give me your fraternal counsel—a counsel which I have found so valuable before now not once or twice.

P.S. Of course, I am profoundly and thankfully aware that the widest differences of political opinion or of lines of social policy are compatible with absolute unity in prayer and purpose upon things spiritual. What I am referring to is in no way the political differences (between yourself and myself these would be slight) but the spirit which is being proclaimed and fostered and utilised—the spirit of *what*?

The REV. J. SCOTT LIDGETT *to the* ARCHBISHOP OF CANTERBURY

Private. 19th December, 1909.

Your letter reached me last night and I hasten to reply to it in all frankness and sincerity: with cordial thanks to you for having written, and especially in such terms of friendship and confidence to me personally.

Perhaps I may be allowed to invert the order of your letter and to deal with the most important and practical part first.

I most earnestly trust that you will not turn aside for a moment from your intention to invite us all to prayer next Whitsuntide. There is not the slightest possibility of such an invitation being received less warmly than, I know, it will be given. The World Missionary Conference will be of unique importance and its success ought to react upon all the relations between the Reformed Churches throughout the world. Free Churchmen will rejoice to take part—not only in the Conference, but in all the Spiritual preparation for it. Moreover, should a period of intense political controversy be before the Nation, it becomes all the more necessary that, on all sides, we should show our power, by God's help, to transcend our lower differences by means of our spiritual agreements. There will be the less difficulty about this because controversy will be almost entirely *political*, dealing with the powers of the House of Lords. *Ecclesiastical* differences will not be in the forefront, so that strong feeling on both sides will, I should suppose, be concentrated largely outside the sphere where denominational divergences spring up.

Let me next speak of the general position of Free Churchmen at the coming Election. Speaking broadly—and leaving out the question whether we have been right or wrong—our course is marked out for us by our past action. Had the Education question been settled and the Licensing Bill passed our position would have been very different. It is true that if the Constitutional question had arisen under such conditions, Free Churchmen would have been greatly exercised in mind. Our history, our principles and our needs make us extremely tenacious of the privileges of the House of Commons. It is this that is making 'the quiet men' as they are called—like Jowett, Munro Gibson and a host more that I could name—rally at the present time as they have never done before. It is fashionable in some quarters to suppose that inertia or desire for Tariff Reform will make the country indifferent to a Constitutional encroachment, only thinly disguised, by the House of Lords. Those who argue like this forget that the spirit of the Revolution of 1688 still lives in the Nonconformists and will drive them to equivalent action in 1910, that is to say to apply their old principles and ideals to the new situation. However, had the Constitutional question stood alone, I think it would have been left to ordinary political action. But there is the Educational difficulty which, we recognise, would have been settled so far as your lead and influence are concerned. Then there was the contemptuous rejection of the Licensing Bill. I own that that is the determining motive of my own action. I have regarded the action of the House of Lords as 'the unpardonable sin' so far as that institution is concerned. I should not have said so had an attempt been made to reach a settlement, even though it had failed. But the way in which the subject was treated constituted to my mind a scandal that must not be repeated if those who desire to prevent it can succeed. These two Causes have brought the Free Churchmen into action, and have freed them to include the position of the House of Lords in their resolutions. . . . But I must conclude by saying, once more, that the general effect of the Meeting was not to sow discord between Churches, but to strengthen the determination to remove a hindrance to justice and progress. The belief being there, I think the action necessarily follows.

In conclusion, I feel very deeply the risks to which the present situation and prospects expose Churches. I would that warning voices had checked the House of Lords before it was too late, and especially in their past dealing with such subjects as the Licensing Bill. But the struggle has to come. Speaking for multitudes of Free Churchmen, I can truly say that we shall pray and work for righteousness and goodwill, appreciating our friends of the Established Church even when we differ from them. We shall realise the difficulties of their position, as I hope they will those of ours. Above all, we will seek for compensations for differences in wider agreements.

I pray your Grace therefore not to be distressed and not to turn aside from the path you have hitherto taken with such advantage to us all, and to great ends we all hold sacred.

II

Another letter, received through Lord Salisbury, shows another side of the difficulties with which the Archbishop's road was strewn. In his New Year's letter to the Diocese, the Archbishop had naturally spoken of the perplexities and anxieties of a General Election; and of the need of calm and of a sense of grave personal responsibility.

He deliberately refrained from dealing with controversial issues. He asked for prayer:

> a prayer, for 'unity, peace and concord' among the Nations and for what shall tend thereto; a prayer for the relief of human loneliness and suffering and for the rightful sharing of our burdens; a prayer for the stability and balance of the best and sanest forces in our public life; a prayer for the security and adequacy of our provision for due ministry of word and sacrament throughout the land; a prayer for truer unity and harmony among Christian men; a prayer for whatsoever shall safeguard and deepen the purity of home-life and the sanctity of the marriage bond; a prayer for the better upbringing of our little children in the faith and fear of God.

Sir Alfred Cripps, the Archbishop's Vicar-General and a Conservative candidate, on January 8, 1910, wrote a strong letter of protest to Lord Salisbury, as Chairman of the House of Laymen. The very silence of the Archbishop on controversial issues seemed to him as good as supporting the Liberal party. In his judgement the Archbishop ought to have declared himself in the most vigorous terms against Disestablishment and the Destruction of Church Schools, two of the planks in the Liberal programme.

Lord Salisbury sent the letter on with a covering note to the Archbishop, adding:

Of course I am in no way responsible for what Sir Alfred says in the enclosure but I can hardly treat an official communication of this character in any other way than by sending it to you.

The Archbishop replied as follows:

The Archbishop of Canterbury *to the* Marquess of Salisbury

12th January, 1910.

I have received your letter enclosing Sir Alfred Cripps'. I return it herewith.

I am exceedingly sorry that he should feel as he does about my own action, or, as he thinks, my own harmful inaction, at the present juncture. He is so good a friend that I should always value and respect his criticism, however vigorously he expresses it. He says he would rather have Disestablishment than 'political Prelates', but I cannot help thinking that his real objection is that the Prelates he censures are not political enough. My conscience certainly does not accuse me of having (to use his word) 'betrayed' him and others. I do deliberately think that we should make a grave tactical blunder were we at this moment to throw our strength into an appeal against Welsh Disestablishment. Important as that issue is, it is surely not the really dominant issue throughout Great Britain in this Election. Were we now to fire our last cartridge, or even to beat our loudest drum upon that subject, we should, I venture to believe, come to regret it a little while hence when those efforts may be more immediately needed and when we ought to be able to make them with an effectiveness due in part to the greater freshness of the fray. It is certainly new to me to find myself supposed to be lukewarm on the subject of Disestablishment. Surely I have spoken on this subject with no uncertain voice at Swansea last October as well as many times before. If he or you or anyone desires to quote my words there is no lack of material.

With regard to the Schools Question, I can better understand Sir Alfred's fears or reproaches. I have never concealed my opinion that the line of mere insistence on the maintenance of our Denominational Schools as they are was a short-sighted policy, and upon that point I fancy that you and I are fairly in agreement, although we should not see eye to eye as to the amount of possible concession which might in the last resort be expedient. Sir Alfred may very possibly find that some of his supporters share my opinions as to the wisest mode of really securing definite religious teaching for the largest number of Church children in Elementary Schools; but here again my conscience gives me no pricks as to any lukewarmness about the cause we have at heart. It is a mere question as to the wisest mode of securing what we all desire.

On the general question of the attitude of Bishops at a time like this, I honestly believe that we best serve the interests both of Church and Nation by abstaining from identifying ourselves vociferously with one side or other in an acute political conflict wherein Church questions occupy really a subordinate place.

My behaviour at this moment may be right or wrong (it must always be a matter of opinion), but I find it difficult to feel that it is properly described as the behaviour of a 'political Prelate'.

I have read your letter in to-day's *Times* with interest and admiration. It puts the point admirably, and I think with perfect fairness, and with a courtesy which some of our public men might emulate with advantage.

The result of the General Election was indecisive. The Liberals (274) had lost, and the Unionists (272) had gained, about 100 seats each. Thus the Liberals depended for a working majority on the Irish and Labour votes.

The crucial issue with which the new Cabinet had to deal was the power of the House of Lords. And the King's Speech referred to proposals to be laid before both Houses:

With all convenient speed to define the relations between the Houses of Parliament so as to secure the undivided authority of the House of Commons over Finance and its predominance in Legislation.

Even as early as February 28, ominous references were made in the Commons to the possibility of the Prime Minister asking the Crown to create 500 peers, if all other means failed to restrict the veto of the Lords on legislation, with a view to securing the predominance of the deliberate will of the Commons within the lifetime of a single Parliament. There were debates during March in the House of Lords, when Lord Rosebery moved three Resolutions for the reform and reconstitution of the Second Chamber; and these were supported by the Archbishop.

By April 14 the three Veto Resolutions had all been adopted by the House of Commons. They had the object respectively of (1) disabling the Lords from rejecting a Money Bill, (2) securing that any other public Bill, which had passed the Commons in three successive sessions and had three times been rejected by the Lords in a period of not less than two years, should become Law without the consent of the Lords, on the Royal Assent being declared; (3) limiting the duration of Parliament to five years. And besides this, Mr. Asquith as Prime Minister declared that, if the Lords rejected this policy, the Government intended to advise the Crown as to the steps necessary if that policy were to receive statutory effect. He said:

> What the precise terms of that advice will be, it will, of course, not be right for me to say now, but if we do not find ourselves in a position to ensure that statutory effect will be given to that policy in this Parliament, we shall then either resign our offices or recommend the dissolution of Parliament. Let me add this: that in no case will we recommend Dissolution except under such conditions as will secure that in the new Parliament the judgement of the people as expressed at the elections will be carried into law. (House of Commons, 14th April, 1910.)

The allusion as to the steps which will have to be taken 'included not only the use of the Royal Prerogative, but the possibility of a Referendum'.[1] The statement was denounced by Mr. Balfour, and there was great excitement in the House.

All through these weeks the Archbishop had been following the course of events with the keenest interest. The King was abroad during most of March and April at Biarritz, but he was due to return before the end of May. His Majesty himself thought that the Government's policy was 'the destruction of the House of Lords';[2] and the question of the use of the Royal prerogative was beset with difficulties. What was the King to do? Various views have been expressed as to the policy which King Edward would in fact have decided to adopt had he lived to make the decision. Asquith's biographer clearly states that in his opinion the King, after an election had taken place definitely on that policy 'must necessarily have led Asquith to suppose that . . . he would accept the result and if need be exercise the Royal prerogative to give effect to it'.[3] It will be observed that the words 'must necessarily',

[1] *Life of Lord Oxford*, i. 279. [2] Ibid. [3] Ibid., pp. 279–80.

strong as they are, allow for the existence, at least in theory, of an alternative course or alternative courses. It was to the problem of such an alternative course that the Archbishop, as a matter of deep personal interest, gave his attention during these days. Other leading public men were similarly canvassing possibilities and expressing various views. The problem which had to be faced presented itself thus to the Archbishop's mind. Suppose that Parliament were dissolved, and the Prime Minister came to the King and demanded the creation of 400 Peers in order to secure the passing of the Government Bill, the situation would be one of an unprecedented character. In a memorandum which he has left of his own views on the matter, written in his own hand at this very time, the Archbishop states clearly that he was not prepared to agree that 'schemes of this absolutely novel and, in the quiet sense, revolutionary character ought to be acquiesced in by the King on the mere ground that the Prime Minister proposing them has, for the moment, a small or even a large Parliamentary majority'. Indeed, he clearly thought that some means ought to be found, and could be found, for enabling the King to show the country that, while of course willing to give effect to the decided and deliberate opinion of the electors, he required that it should be clear that the country realized the bigness of the contemplated change and decisively and deliberately sent a genuine majority of members to enact it. And with a view to this, or at least as a possible method of assuring himself as to the real wishes of the public on so drastic a step, the Archbishop turned over in his own mind 'the possibility, and very likely the expediency, of the King taking the public into his confidence as regards the exercise of his own responsibility'. The Memorandum, thus simply written at the time for the clearing of his own mind, adds:

> If it be said, and said with perfect truth, that for the King to make public some statement of his own position at so critical a moment is unconstitutional and unprecedented, the explanation is obvious, that no such occasion has ever before arisen. If the King is asked, by creating 400 peers, to take a wholly unconstitutional and unexampled step, he must be allowed to speak also in an unprecedented statement.
>
> 'The King has been advised to create peers with a view to reversing the present balance of party in the House of Lords.

> The King is ready to act in accordance with the expressed wish of his people. But as the course he is advised to follow, whether it be desirable or not, would be contrary to all precedent, he feels justified in asking in an exceptional way for the opinion of the country respecting it.'

Of course such words would have to be most carefully weighed. Perhaps they might even be submitted to the leaders of the two political parties for criticism. But they could be so drafted as to be absolutely free from political partisanship. Very likely no occasion requiring their use may arise, but I am clear that the possibility of the King so acting ought not—at so unique a juncture—to be lightly dismissed.

On Monday, April 25, he discussed with Lord Rosebery the possibility of the King thus speaking to the country:

I drove with Rosebery from Grillions' dinner to Lambeth and had a good deal of talk both at dinner and afterwards. He is full of the King saying what he has to say *himself*.

Mr. Balfour was also impressed with the Archbishop's idea, and thought that, though its preparation would require care, a satisfactory document could be framed setting out the King's view, and that, if successfully framed, it would add much lustre to the position of the Sovereign. The Archbishop had many conversations with public men of different points of view, and a good deal was said for the plan of a Referendum, of which Mr. J. St. Loe Strachey, the editor of *The Spectator*, was a strong advocate.

Nothing, however, had been as yet settled as to the actual procedure which the Government should adopt. It appeared that Asquith would rely on the precedents of 1832, when Lord Grey secured the passing of the Reform Bill by obtaining the reluctant consent of William IV to create a sufficient number of Peers, after the King had first refused to do so, and Lord Grey had resigned. But the future was still obscure when the King returned to Buckingham Palace on April 26. On Tuesday, May 2, he was taken ill, and by Friday, May 6, he was dead.

CHAPTER XXXV

DEATH OF KING EDWARD

'The deaths of Kings travel so much faster than any post, that I cannot expect to tell you news, when I say your old master is dead.' HORACE WALPOLE *to* SIR HORACE MANN, *Oct. 28, 1760.*

ON Friday morning, May 6, the Archbishop read in the press the news of the King's illness. By some accident he had missed the newspaper bulletin of the previous evening. He hastened immediately to Buckingham Palace, where Lord Knollys, whom he found in keen distress, welcomed him most warmly. The doctors were at that moment in consultation, and a bulletin was drawn up showing the serious character of the illness. The Archbishop spent the morning at the Palace. The King, though very ill, insisted on being up and dressed, and, though the doctors did their best to prevent him seeing anybody outside the family and the household, they could not succeed entirely.

The Archbishop had two long interviews with the Prince of Wales during the morning, and 'was struck by his self-possessed dignity, along with the extremest affection and anxiety about the King'. He went back to Lambeth for luncheon and important business, and returned to Buckingham Palace in the afternoon, and stayed there for several hours, sitting in Lord Knollys' room:

> I again saw the Prince of Wales, as matters grew graver and graver and had some quiet and, I hope, helpful talk both with him and with poor Knollys, whose grief was most touching.

At 7.30 the Archbishop left the Palace, to preside over a great meeting to promote legislation on the Poor Law Report. He returned immediately after making his speech and found the situation as dark as possible:

> For more than an hour I remained there, saying what I could at intervals, and finally, as the breath grew weaker and the end was evidently come, I said the Commendatory Prayer, and a few moments afterwards he simply ceased to breathe. I have seldom or never seen a quieter passing of the river.

It was now just before midnight. The memorandum continues:

> The family remained alone for a few minutes, then the Prince of Wales, now King, came out, and I was the first person to greet him as Sovereign. This was exactly what had happened with his father at the bedroom door at Osborne when Queen Victoria died.

The Archbishop's memorandum goes on to give a very full account of all that followed with regard to preparations for the funeral, the meeting of the Privy Council, his own sermon in the Abbey on Sunday, May 8, the alterations in the Prayer Book, a special service in the King's bedroom at Buckingham Palace, the Lying-in-State at Westminster Hall, the Service in St. George's Chapel. A few extracts may be given:

> A summons had reached me to attend the Privy Council at 4 p.m. for the formal declarations etc. of the new King . . .
>
> I was one of three or four who had officially to go and fetch the King from another room and usher him into the Council. He read his speech with a simplicity and dignity and earnestness which impressed everybody. I was very much struck too by the tact and graciousness with which he acted in receiving the Oath of Allegiance from the Privy Councillors. All the older men, and some of those who had special links with him, he treated with marked respect and some symptom of peculiar regard, and yet all was quiet and perfectly dignified. I saw him for a moment after the Council, when he spoke about the help, such as it was, that I had given him as to the speech. While the proceedings went on, after the King had left—e.g. signing the roll etc., I had some talk with leading men about my wish (which turned out afterwards to be historically accurate) that Queen Alexandra should in official designations and in the Prayer Book, etc. be called Queen Mother and not Queen Dowager. Balfour, Halsbury, Loreburn, and many more cordially approved; the only person who objected was Rosebery, but it was so settled. He also wanted the Queen to be called Queen May, not Queen Mary, but no-one agreed with him. . . .
>
> Much other work had accumulated in these days, and my hands were full. I had a long sitting to Sargent[1] for my picture, on Wednesday the 11th, which was a relief from the stress. . . .
>
> At 7 o'clock on that day, Wednesday May 11th, I went by request to Buckingham Palace to hold a little service over the

[1] Portrait by J. S. Sargent, R.A., now at Lambeth Palace.

dead King. Queen Alexandra specially wished for it, and before the service she went with me to the room. . . .

On Tuesday the 17th the transfer from Buckingham Palace to Westminster Hall was admirably carried out, and the whole proceedings were, by universal consent, regarded as dignified, simple, devotional and impressive. The Dean of Westminster read the lesson, and I took the rest of the service and gave the address, and the Abbey choir sang the hymn from the steps at the end of the Hall. Unfortunately their voices were quite overpowered by the strong band standing behind them, and the Houses of Parliament did not as we had hoped take up the hymn. Hertslet carried my primatial cross, and stood below the rostrum. . . .

There is nothing special to recount about the service in St. George's Chapel. . . .

The service was conducted entirely from the Sacrarium, the two Archbishops, the Bishop of Winchester, and the Dean of Windsor standing in front of the altar. I thought it best however, and this ought to be noted in view of some future occasion, to go down to the head, or rather foot, of the grave in order to pronounce the actual sentences of committal.

In the Castle, after the well-managed luncheon arrangements, I had interviews with the King, the German Emperor, President Roosevelt, the Queen of Norway, and some others, and also a few words with Queen Mary.

The Archbishop's address, in Westminster Hall, one of the most difficult ordeals of the kind he ever had to face, in the presence both of the Royal mourners and the two Houses of Parliament, was as follows:

Brothers, the Sovereign whom his Empire and the World delighted to honour is suddenly taken from our head, and perhaps we find it difficult to fix in our thoughts the significance of these memorable days, the lesson of this scene for us and for the multitudes who will throng to look upon it. Here in the great Hall of English history we stand in the presence of Death. But Death is, to us Christians, swallowed up in a larger Life. Our common sorrow reminds us of our common hope. Rise from sorrow to thanksgiving and prayer. We give thanks. We thank God for a Ruler devoted to the service of his people; we thank God for the peace and prosperity which have marked King Edward's reign; we thank God for teaching us still to see His hand in the story of our Nation's well-being. And we pray: we pray God that as we are united by this great sorrow we may be united for the tasks which lie before us, for the fight against all that is unworthy of our calling—as the Christian inheritors of a great Empire—the fight against selfishness and impurity and greed, the fight against the spirit that is callous or profane. Let us pledge ourselves afresh from this solemn hour to a deliberate and unswerving effort, as Christian folk, to set forward what is true and just, what is lovely and of good report, in the daily life, both public and private, of a people to whom much is given and of whom much will be required.

CHAPTER XXXVI

THE ACCESSION OF KING GEORGE

In a limited Monarchy, Prerogative and Liberty are as jealous of one another as any two neighbouring States can be of their respective Incroachments.

MARQUESS OF HALIFAX, *Political Thoughts and Reflections.*

WHEN Parliament met on June 8, it met under totally new conditions. The political crisis was perforce postponed. There was a general desire to avoid embarrassing the new King, and there was even reason to believe[1] that the new King himself had let it be known that he welcomed conversations between representatives of the two parties with a view to a compromise. In the event a Constitutional Conference of four Liberals and four Unionists was summoned by agreement between the leaders of both sides, and held its first meeting on June 17.

While the Conference lasted a truce was observed. There was, however, one matter, unconnected with the crisis yet of considerable constitutional importance, which demanded a settlement. This was the question of the Declaration required to be made by every Sovereign on succeeding to the throne 'on the day of the meeting of the first Parliament after his accession or at his coronation'. Its history is curious. It came into existence in 1678 when the country was in a fever after the Popish Plot. It had then to be made by all members of both Houses of Parliament and by sworn servants of the Sovereign, and the Act embodying it is described as an Act 'for the more effectual preserving the King's person and Government by disabling Papists from sitting in either House of Parliament'. It was not, however, extended to the Crown until 1689, after the accession of William and Mary, by the 'Act declaring the Rights and Liberties of the Subject and Settling the Succession of the Crowne' (commonly known as the Declaration of Rights);[2] and this was due to the fact, recited in the Preamble to the Statute, that 'the late King James II by the assistance of diverse evil counsellors, judges and minis-

[1] *Annual Register*, 1910, p. 130.

[2] 1 Will. and Mar., c. 2, s. 2, 1689.

ters did endeavour . . . to subvert and extirpate the Protestant religion and laws and liberties of the Kingdom'.

The Declaration ran as follows:

> I, A. B., do solemnly and sincerely, in the presence of God, profess, testify, and declare that I do believe that in the Sacrament of the Lord's Supper there is not any Transubstantiation of the Elements of Bread and Wine into the Body and Blood of Christ, at or after the consecration thereof by any person whatsoever; and that the Invocation or Adoration of the Virgin Mary or any other Saint, and the Sacrifice of the Mass, as they are now used in the Church of Rome, are superstitious and idolatrous. And I do solemnly, in the presence of God, profess, testify, and declare, that I do make this declaration and every part thereof in the plain and ordinary sense of the words read unto me, as they are commonly understood by *English Protestants*, without any Evasion, Equivocation, or mental Reservation whatsoever, and without any dispensation already granted me for this purpose by the Pope, or any other authority or person whatsoever, or without any hope of any such dispensation from any person or authority whatsoever, or without thinking that I am or can be acquitted before God or man, or absolved of this declaration or any part thereof, although the Pope or any other person or persons or power whatsoever should dispense with or annul the same or declare that it was null and void from the beginning.

No candid person would deny, as the Prime Minister said, that circumstances had been totally changed since 1689. The Declaration was gravely resented by Roman Catholics. The King himself, when Prince of Wales, had been anxious for its amendment, and had discussed the matter informally both with Ministers and with the Archbishop. From time to time the question had been raised in the House of Lords. It had been mentioned soon after the accession of King Edward, but had then been dropped. The Archbishop had himself been approached on the subject by some Roman Catholic Peers. There was, however, a difficulty, for the very idea of mitigating the anti-Roman character of the Declaration was exceedingly objectionable to many staunch Protestants. Thus a considerable literature had sprung up opposing the change. Moreover, there was the further difficulty that while many of a more tolerant frame of mind might object to the harsh terms of the existing Declaration there was no guarantee that they would be united in an alternative form. As the Archbishop had written to Lord Crewe:

The ARCHBISHOP OF CANTERBURY *to the* MARQUESS OF CREWE

Confidential. 25th May 1908.

The difficulty consists in finding the right form of words, which must be, so far as possible, inoffensive to the Roman Catholic body, and yet must be strong enough to be *indisputably* effective. I say 'indisputably' because, as you will remember, the question of 'effectiveness' was vehemently disputed in the former discussions. My fear is that some of those (belonging to no fanatical section) who were dissatisfied before will be even less easy to satisfy now, arguing, as they certainly will, that the Spanish Marriage has shown their apprehensions to possess a more solid basis than their opponents used to admit.

The form agreed also had to satisfy both Anglicans and Nonconformists. After various attempts—following the efforts of earlier years—a new form was proposed by the Prime Minister to Parliament on June 28, 1910, as follows:

I (*George*) do solemnly and sincerely in the presence of God profess, testify, and declare that I am a faithful member of the Protestant Reformed Church by law established in England, and that I will, according to the true intent of the enactments which secure the Protestant succession to the Throne of my Realm, uphold and maintain the said enactments to the best of my powers according to law.

But this form at once aroused objections on behalf of the Church of England. The Archbishop told the Prime Minister that the term 'Protestant Reformed Church by law established in England' would be greatly resented. He stated his objections in an interview and left a Memorandum, making one or two alternative suggestions; and afterwards wrote the following letter:

The ARCHBISHOP OF CANTERBURY *to the* RT. HON. H. H. ASQUITH

9th July, 1910.

I have been thinking over the question you unexpectedly asked me in our interview this morning—viz—How would those whom I represented view such an expression as 'Protestant Reformed Church of England'? It would so far be to the good that it brings in the words 'Church of England'—a familiar and unambiguous legal designation. But do we not by prefacing these epithets qualify the familiar term in a misleading way? There was—I rather think there still is—a body calling itself 'The Reformed Church of England', and I am not quite sure whether there is not also a body calling itself 'The Protestant Church of England'. These epithets therefore, as qualifying or limiting the term 'Church of England', might in that place be really misleading, and I certainly should not regard such a term as 'Protestant Reformed Church of England' as one which I could advocate. On the other hand, if the term 'Church of England' is used minus these qualifying epithets, it involves no ambiguity, and the words 'established by law' might I think be omitted without disadvantage if their omission, as you indicated, gives satisfaction to a large section of your supporters. I take no kind of exception to the words 'Protestant and Reformed' in their proper places, but the *onus probandi* surely rests upon those who want the term 'Protestant Reformed Church by law established in England' instead of the simpler and quite unambiguous words 'Church of England', and the words 'Protestant and Reformed' are introduced quite simply and effectively two lines lower down in the Memorandum I left with you.

In my Memorandum and in this letter, I have put before you, as in duty bound, a view which will I know be taken by a vast number of Churchmen of a reasonable and moderate sort, and there for the moment I must leave it. No one realises more clearly than I the difficulties which surround you in dealing with this matter wherein a movement in any direction brings you up against a wall of opposition.

In describing the situation to the Bishop of Southwark, the Archbishop said on the same day:

The ARCHBISHOP OF CANTERBURY *to the* BISHOP OF SOUTHWARK

9th July, 1910.

I did not find him very amenable. He was in a condition of extreme irritation against the ecclesiastical mind generally, including in the field of his scorn his Nonconformist supporters quite as much as the Church of England or the Roman Catholics. He says it is like the quibbles of the schoolmen, and I scarcely think that I succeeded in persuading him as to the difference which we, I think, see very clearly.

The *impasse* continued. But the Archbishop did his best to find a way out, and, after consulting a number of Bishops, wrote a further letter to the Prime Minister.

The Archbishop of Canterbury *to the* Rt. Hon. H. H. Asquith

27th July, 1910.

I am in bed with influenza, but am mending fast and hope to be about again, without peril to myself or others, in a very few days. Had I been well, I should have asked leave to see you this morning about the present phase of the Royal Declaration controversy.

I gather that in some quarters it is supposed that those who, as Bishops or otherwise, claim to speak for the Church of England are all bent upon securing that the King shall in his Declaration proclaim himself a member of the Church of England. To the best of my belief this is far from being the fact. Doubtless some Churchmen would attach great importance to the King's so declaring himself, but I think that the wiser and weightier men are satisfied with the terms used in the Act of Settlement. What we do object to is some new designation or attempted definition of the Church of England—e.g. 'The Protestant Reformed Church by law established in England', or other similar terms. Such circumlocutory designation of the National Church raises (needlessly as it seems to me) controversial questions both historical and practical. The first of the possible alternative forms suggested in the Memorandum which I left with you on July 9th could be simplified without, as I think, any serious detriment by omitting the phrase 'and that I am a faithful member of the same'. And the words would then run—

> I do solemnly and sincerely in the presence of God profess, testify, and declare that I am not a Roman Catholic, and that I join in communion with the Church of England as by law established. And I will uphold and maintain the Protestant reformed religion established by law, and the Protestant succession to the Throne of this Realm according to the true intent of the enactments which secure the same.

But I am prepared to go further, and, so far as I can at present see, and subject to anything which may unexpectedly arise in debate, I should be quite ready to agree to the words which, as I gather, commend themselves in Nonconformist circles, viz:—

> I . . . declare that I am a faithful Protestant, and that I will, according to the true intent of the enactments which secure the Protestant succession to the Throne of my Realm, uphold and

maintain the said enactments to the best of my powers according to law.

It is obvious that such a form of Declaration avoids most of the difficulties surrounding other forms, and uses the word 'Protestant' in its true and effective sense. Though I am not in a position to speak authoritatively on behalf of the Bishops or others, I cannot help hoping that the adoption of that simpler form might meet with very general acceptance, and in what I am here saying I have the concurrence of the Archbishop of York, who is here to-day and who has seen and approved of this letter.

The Prime Minister replied:

The RT. HON. H. H. ASQUITH *to the* ARCHBISHOP OF CANTERBURY

27th July, 1910.

I am very much obliged to you for your letter of to-day.

I at once accepted—gladly and with gratitude—the second of your suggestions, which I am pleased to learn has the assent of the Archbishop of York.

I gather, from the course of the debate this evening, that this form of Declaration is generally acknowledged in all quarters—by Anglicans, Scottish Presbyterians, and English Nonconformists—as the best solution of the problem.

So I think the way is now clear to a final settlement of this troublesome matter.

I hope that you are making real progress, and that you may be able to say a word in the House of Lords next week.

The Bill with the new Declaration was brought before Parliament, passed the House of Commons without difficulty, was supported in the House of Lords by the Archbishop in a speech on August 1, received the Royal Assent on August 3, and the Prime Minister wrote to the Archbishop expressing his satisfaction that the Bill had got safely to port, adding, 'I renew my expressions of gratitude for your help'.

Between June and November, the Constitutional Conference proceeded in the utmost secrecy, though it is clear from a private inquiry by Mr. Lloyd George of the Bishop of St. Asaph, and through him of the Archbishop, that it was dealing not only with the Constitutional question but with political controversies of other kinds, amongst them Welsh Disestablishment.

But on November 10, the Conference broke down. The situation was most serious. And when, two days later, the Archbishop had a talk with John Morley just before the regular meeting of British Museum Trustees:

> Morley spoke very gravely of the whole situation, and said, 'I think we must face the fact that we are entering upon a revolutionary period. I do not mean guillotines, but revolution can be carried on without that.' I thought him sad and rather depressed, but this was in part due to the trouble which, as he told me, he felt in passing from the busy scene of work and responsibility at the India Office to a room, solemn and silent, at the Privy Council, where nothing happens and there is no work to do. He said that Lord Wolverhampton had always prided himself on having no arrears in that office. Morley added, 'There may easily be no arrears, because nothing comes in'.

After the meeting the Archbishop walked home with Esher, to whom Morley also had been talking:

> Esher agreed with me in deep sympathy for the difficulties of the King's position. His father's opinion would have been so weighty that the Government could hardly have disregarded it without greatly losing popularity in the country by so doing if it came out that they were going against the King's wishes. (This Morley had frankly admitted in conversation with me.)

A few days later the Prime Minister announced that Parliament would be dissolved.

The Dissolution took place on November 28, and was followed by an energetic campaign in the country.

By December 20, a new Parliament was returned. There was, however, very little alteration in the strength of the rival parties; and the Liberals depended, as before, for a working majority on the Irish and Labour votes. No one could doubt that the future was perilous. At the end of the year, the Archbishop wrote in his annual message to the Diocese:

> Twice within the twelve months a new Parliament has come into life. New questions, or new aspects of old questions, political, social, imperial, racial, industrial, mechanical, are to the fore. The issues of these changes and chances may be vaster than we know. The more need that, as the new year opens, we should find ourselves again and again upon our knees. Ask Him Who is the same and Whose years shall not fail to inspire and strengthen our common life, and to shew us as a people, as a Church, as households and citizens whose interests which must be manifold can

yet be one, how to use aright the unborn days of the year of Our Lord 1911. 'The year of our Lord.' The words are no mere index of the lapse of time. They remind us of a living fact, a living Captain and King.

If ever in the unfolding of our people's life it was at once a duty and a possibility for thoughtful men and women, as individuals and not mere partisans, to face our larger problems, secular and sacred, with deliberateness and hope, that time is now.

CHAPTER XXXVII

THE PARLIAMENT ACT

To state the matter shortly, the Sovereign has, under a constitutional monarchy such as ours, three rights—the right to be consulted, the right to encourage, the right to warn. And a King of great sense and sagacity would want no others. He would find that his having no others would enable him to use these with singular effect. He would say to his minister: 'The responsibility of these measures is upon you. Whatever you think best must be done. Whatever you think best shall have my full and effectual support. *But* you will observe that for this reason and that reason what you propose to do is bad; for this reason and that reason what you do not propose is better. I do not oppose, it is my duty not to oppose; but observe that I *warn*.' Supposing the King to be right, and to have what Kings often have, the gift of effectual expression, he could not help moving his minister. He might not always turn his course, but he would always trouble his mind.

BAGEHOT, *The English Constitution*, ch. iii.

THE preliminaries to the passing of the Parliament Act, 1911, as well as that Act itself, will continue to interest students of the English Constitution for many years to come. Some of the politicians who played a prominent part in the proceedings have given their version of the events in their own words; and the attitude of others is described in their biographies. The historian of the future will take account of them all, and of whatever subsequent material later memoirs may disclose. It is safe to say that in any account written from a distance, allowance must also be made for the attitude of Archbishop Davidson as revealed in his various notes and records of the passing events on different critical days, written at the very time.

Something has already been said of a possible alternative course which had presented itself to the Archbishop's mind in the last few days of King Edward's reign. He was the least likely person to imagine that the Sovereign could act in any way which might be justly described as unconstitutional. But he held, and held strongly, that the situation with which King George was faced was without a precedent of any adequate kind in the history of the British Constitution, and that if the King were to be asked by the Prime Minister of the day to take the really unexampled step of creating 400 peers, he must be allowed also to speak in an unprecedented way to the public. In the Archbishop's journal already described, there are various memoranda made at different times during the first seven months of 1911; but the main idea—that the Sovereign should speak himself to the people—comes out plainly in all; and it is set out most fully and plainly in a memorandum written by the Archbishop as a review of the actual situation at the opening of the New Year. The memorandum is dated January 11, 1911. It runs as follows:

All sorts of people are ventilating their opinions, whether sapient or the reverse, about the Constitutional problem which confronts us. I think that this is well, for it is one of the occasions upon which ventilation is useful, both in making the public realize the difficulties of the situation and in emphasizing to the responsible leaders on either side the need of caution and patience.

But in none of the articles and letters that I have seen has adequate importance been attached to a point which seems to me to be both practical and urgent.

In coming to that conclusion, I take as a basis a few facts which will hardly be challenged by reasonable men on either side.

(1) The confirmation in December of the verdict given in January in favour of the present Government strengthens materially their claim to possess the confidence and to be executing the wishes of the majority of the people at large.

(2) In estimating the nature of, and the weight belonging to, the Parliamentary majority in favour of the proposed change in the Constitution, the Nationalist members must not be counted *simpliciter* or *sans phrase* as members of the Government majority. Their spokesmen have repeatedly avowed their absolute indifference to the well-being of the British Constitution, or even their contempt for it. They swell the actual majority in favour of curtailing the powers of the House of Lords, not because they are in a large sense in favour of an amended Constitution, but merely because they want Home Rule. Home Rule once granted, they might, so far as we have evidence, vote either way about such Constitutional changes. This greatly reduces the majority which can claim to be deliberately of opinion that, for the common good of the whole country, the proposed change ought to be made.

(3) The Minority which has voted at the polls against the Government and its proposals is so large, that it may be called almost half the Nation. Taking into account the uncontested Seats, there is a question whether it is not an actual majority of the voters in England itself. Anyhow, it is so large as to make it unreasonable and even intolerable to merely ignore or despise its opinion upon the gravest proposal in Constitutional change which has come before Parliament since the Revolution. To effect such

a change by the sheer numerical strength of a heterogeneous majority would be to ensure mischievous and even disastrous consequences for the Country when the time for reaction comes.

(4) These facts render it pre-eminently desirable that every effort should be made to secure some degree of consent before Constitutional changes so important to the whole Country are decided upon. . . .

It is clear that the Minority has shown no spirit of obstinate objection to changes in the existing Constitution. On one great department of the controversy (the intervention of the House of Lords in matters of Finance) the disputed point has been already ceded by the Minority, and the area of controversy is thus materially narrowed. The Minority, by its very readiness to make modifications, has increased its claim to reasonable consideration and share in the deliberations which will lead to the fashioning of the ultimate conclusion.

It is in these circumstances that we arrive at a stage in the controversy when the Prime Minister, in accordance with the pledges he has given, may possibly endeavour, before initiating a great Parliamentary debate, to secure from the Sovereign a promise that such debating in the House of Commons shall not be in vain; that there shall be no 'ploughing of the sands'; that a prolonged discussion shall not result in the contemptuous rejection by the House of Lords of the Parliament Bill which may be carried through the Commons.

The question must obviously be considered, what kind of undertaking, if any, ought the King to be willing to give to the Prime Minister in response to such a request.

And it is with reference to that point that people seem to me to overlook a fundamentally important consideration. It is this: There is all the difference in the world between (1) a promise or quasi-promise given by the King now, before the actual Bill has even been debated, far less amended, in either House of Parliament, and (2) such promise or undertaking of co-operation, given by the King hereafter, when the specific point of difference has come formally before the Sovereign and his advisers in black and white.

Such stage would have been reached if the House of Commons had passed its Bill and sent it to the Lords, and the Lords had amended it and sent it back, and the Commons had dealt with the Lords' amendments. Then, and not till then, would the actual stile be reached. Then, and not till then, does the question practically arise how to cross the stile. People talk and write as if the King were bound now to declare what he may ultimately deem it

> to be right to do, if it appears that the deliberate and ascertained will of the Nation is going to be flouted or disregarded by the Lords.
>
> How can it possibly be the King's duty to make such declaration or promise now, while all is necessarily hypothetical?
>
> I regard His Majesty as being more than entitled—as being almost bound—to refuse to give any such declaration whatever at the present stage, and this on the simple and intelligible ground that the actual crisis has not yet practically arisen and is not even, with any certainty, within sight.
>
> It may be said that if the King were now to decline to give to the Prime Minister the guarantees for which he may ask, His Majesty's refusal might be met by the resignation of the Government.
>
> I can hardly conceive it to be possible that such a course could be taken if the words used by the King in conveying his refusal are carefully chosen, and are put in such shape as to be capable of being quoted should necessity require it.

As will be seen from the last sentences, the memorandum at this point almost takes the form of a soliloquy.

The Archbishop was of course perfectly clear from the start that if in the end the request were made for the creation of 400 peers, after the opinion of the country had been fully ascertained, it would be impossible to resist it. But what he regarded as really vital was that, when the time came, some State paper should be available, and if need be produced, describing the actual situation at a particular date and 'the actual point at which the divergence between the two Houses seemed to the Government to be so important as to call for an act on the part of the Crown, which is not only without precedent in the history of England but tramples upon constitutional usage, if not upon the Constitution itself'.

We have set out the Archbishop's views fully, as we believe that they have a considerable intrinsic interest, even though, for reasons which will appear, it was already too late to give effect to such a proposal. And attention may be drawn to the strong sense of constitutional form which the Archbishop showed, even while emphasizing the value of a personal appeal on the part of the Sovereign in the unprecedented conditions with which the country was faced. But it has to be recognized that, like everybody else at the time, the Archbishop was entirely in the dark as to what had already occurred between the King and the Government, and the Archbishop's views as to the desirability of personal action on the part of the King within the limits of the Constitution, no less than the views of Mr. Strachey and others as to the desirability of a Referendum, had therefore by then been put outside the range of practical politics. The very situation which the Archbishop had been most anxious to see avoided had already been faced, and the pledge in advance, to which he was so strenuously opposed, had already been given. The facts are as follows.

Mr. Asquith saw the King at Sandringham, November 11, 1910, and:

> pointed out that this would be [the] second time in the course of twelve months that the question of the relations between the two Houses had been submitted to the electorate. It was necessary, therefore, that in the event of the Government obtaining an adequate majority in the New House of Commons, the matter should be put in train for final settlement. This could only be brought about (if the Lords were not ready to give way) by the willingness of the Crown to exercise its prerogative to give effect to the will of the nation.[1]

On November 15, the Cabinet adopted a memorandum advising an immediate dissolution, and adding:

> H.M. Ministers cannot, however, take the responsibility of advising a dissolution, unless they may understand that in the event of the policy of the Government being approved by an adequate majority in the new House of Commons, H.M. will be ready to exercise his constitutional powers (which may involve the prerogative of creating Peers) if needed, to secure that effect shall be given to the decision of the country.[2]

On November 16, Mr. Asquith with Lord Crewe saw the King at Buckingham Palace, and, after discussion, so Mr. Asquith informed the House of Commons later on (August 7, 1911):

> His Majesty, after careful consideration of all the circumstances past and present, and after discussing the matter in all its bearings with myself and with my noble friend and colleague, Lord Crewe, felt that he had no alternative but to assent to the advice of the Cabinet.[3]

[1] *Life of Lord Oxford and Asquith*, J. A. Spender and Cyril Asquith, i. 296.
[2] Ibid., p. 297.
[3] Ibid., p. 298.

Lord Oxford's biographer remarks that the words just quoted from Mr. Asquith's speech of August 7, describing the King's assent, were 'carefully chosen'. To the Archbishop, however, at the time they were uttered, they seemed lamentably insufficient. But even in the story as Mr. Spender tells it, a careful reader can detect signs that the King's consent had not by any means been easily given. The biographer allows that the presence of Lord Crewe at the audience with the King was criticized at the time (though in his view unjustly) as unusual. He quotes a letter from Mr. Asquith which, while praising the King, permits some echo of the arguing to be heard; and he acknowledges that 'there were moments when the result seemed in doubt'.[1] Still more important was the admission of Lord Crewe in the House of Lords, although conveyed, as the Archbishop described it at the time, in rather halting phrases. Lord Crewe acknowledged the 'natural and ... legitimate reluctance' with which His Majesty faced the contingency and entertained the suggestion, and his words also suggest, if they do not actually say, that Mr. Asquith and Lord Crewe threatened the resignation of the Government if their advice were not taken, with the result of an immediate dissolution and the consequent mixing up of the Crown in a most unfortunate political controversy.[2]

To the end of his life the Archbishop maintained, and, as his papers amply show, had good reason for maintaining, that undue pressure had been brought to bear on the King in order to gain his assent. He was only newly come to the throne. He had not had time to master all the material to which his father had access, nor was he prepared for Ministers coming to their Sovereign, asking for an immediate answer, and announcing the course which they would take if they failed to get their way. And one particular point the Archbishop always regarded as the key to the situation. The precise request made *viva voce* by Mr. Asquith to the King, with the consequences of refusal on the King's part,

[1] Ibid., p. 297. 'I have never seen the King to better advantage', Asquith wrote the same evening; 'he argued well and showed no obstinacy.'

[2] Lord Crewe in the House of Lords, August 8, 1911: 'His Majesty, however, naturally entertained the feeling—a feeling which we entirely shared—that if we resigned our offices, having as we had a large majority in the House of Commons, the only result could be an immediate dissolution in which it would practically be impossible, however anxious we naturally should be, to keep the Crown out of the controversy. The mixing up of the Crown in a controversy such as that was naturally most distasteful to its illustrious wearer. . . .'

should have been put in writing, and time allowed for an answer also to be given in writing. It is true that a Memorandum had been sent to the King on the previous day, but the interview with Mr. Asquith ranged far beyond the Memorandum. Had that precaution been taken, and Mr. Asquith been asked that the Government's request should be put into writing in detail, the Government would, in the Archbishop's view, have been nonplussed, for Mr. Asquith would not have dared to put on paper what he had said by word of mouth.

A further element in the whole transaction, which the Archbishop regarded as unjust, was the pledge of secrecy imposed upon the Crown in the Cabinet Memorandum of November 15, 1910:

> 'H.M. will doubtless agree that it would be inadvisable in the interests of the State that any communication of the intentions of the Crown should be made public unless and until the actual occasion should arise.'[1]

The fact of this assent having been given had, however, been kept entirely secret until July 18, 1911, when Mr. Lloyd George met Mr. Balfour and Lord Lansdowne and stated that a pledge to create peers had been obtained from the King as far back as November.[2] Thus the Archbishop made the following note of part of a conversation between himself and Lord Lansdowne on June 20, 1911:

> [Lansdowne] rather pressed me as to whether I knew anything about what had passed between the King and the Government about the creation of Peers, and whether I knew what the King would do.... Lansdowne said 'Suppose he were instead to send for Balfour, and Balfour were to be willing to form a Government'. I replied that I... personally should do everything in my power to prevent such shaping of events as would result in a General Election which could be represented as King and Peers *versus* People of England. I thought this would be disastrous in many ways and certainly ineffectual. The so-called popular cause would inevitably win, and the Monarchy would have suffered irremediably in popular estimation when such defeat took place. I regarded it as gambling in the most dangerous manner, with the

[1] *Life of Lord Oxford and Asquith*, J. A. Spender and Cyril Asquith, i. 297.

[2] *Lord Lansdowne: A Biography*, Lord Newton, p. 417. See also Memorandum of Lord Lansdowne's interview with Lord Knollys, July 19 (ibid., p. 418).

King as stakes. We discussed this somewhat fully, and I pressed my view, and Lansdowne evidently attached importance to what I said. He gave me no hint as to whether Balfour himself would like to take office in such conditions.

On July 20 Mr. Asquith wrote to Lord Lansdowne and Mr. Balfour informing them that the King had agreed to exercise his prerogative to secure the passing into law of the Parliament Bill. Five days later the Archbishop reports another conversation with Lord Lansdowne on July 25:

[Lansdowne] spoke frankly of the difficulties of the situation, and especially of the wrong which, as he thinks, was done when the King was virtually coerced into making the promise that he did make. He draws the widest possible distinction between such a promise being given now (this he thinks inevitable and even right constitutionally) and its having been given seven months ago.

We turn now to the Archbishop's action in the House of Lords. Twice he publicly appealed, in vain, for negotiation and mutual concession. The first time was in the debates of May 24; the second time on July 20. As July drew to a close, the question arose as to the line which he and the Bishops would take about voting. He was himself at this stage (the end of July) in favour of abstaining. On August 1, Lord Crewe and Lord Salisbury each independently approached the Archbishop with the same question. Lord Crewe (for the Government) said, 'We are now calculating numbers. What will the Bishops do?'—but he did not urge the Archbishop at all. Lord Salisbury brought the following letter in his hand, and pressed its assertions and questions with much vigour:

The MARQUESS OF SALISBURY *to the* ARCHBISHOP OF CANTERBURY

Private. 1st August, 1911.

Selborne tells me that he hears that the large majority of the Bishops are going to vote *for* the Government when the Parliament Bill returns to the House of Lords. We have both been much shocked and we hope it is not true. I need not say I do not suggest that the Bishops should as a body vote *against* the Government. They are men of peace who ought to be far removed from Party conflict, and there can be no doubt that apart from strong convictions in particular cases they might be expected to take no part.

But to vote *for* the Government!! Please reflect what this means. It means to become responsible in a measure for the Parliament Bill which is designed to destroy the Establishment in Wales. It means bitterly to offend the most fighting elements in the Unionist Party—in Parliament but far more outside. What will be the good next year attempting to spread abroad the bitter cry of the Church in Wales, when staunch worker after staunch worker will say 'But the Bishops voted against Lord Halsbury and in favour of the Parliament Bill'. And for what reason should the Bishops vote against us? To save the House of Lords from being swamped? There is evidently no danger of it. To restore discipline in the Unionist Party? They have nothing to do with this. To avoid the creation of a batch of unconstitutional peers? The breach of the constitution, the straining of the prerogative, has already been committed. What is the good of pretending? The House of Lords is to be coerced by the creation of peers. That is certain. Nothing can alter it. It is true the actual creation can be avoided. But that is only ordinary British dislike of the truth. The essential fact is unalterable I am afraid.

Depend upon it, to offend men like . . . and the electoral strength they possess, to estrange some of the best Conservatives in the Country, is a heavy price to pay for helping to pass the Parliament Bill. And if the result is to conceal from the people the identity between a threat and its performance where both are equally successful there will be an added evil of great magnitude. Please consider these points.

The Archbishop adds (of the same day, August 1):

Later in the afternoon, after some of the other interviews described below, I spoke to Salisbury and asked him what had led him or Selborne to suppose that the Bishops generally were going to vote with the Government. He replied that they had been given to understand that the Bishops had met and decided to do this as a body. I told him that the story was baseless, that nothing of the kind had happened, and that while I thought it not impossible that some Bishops might so vote, I was not definitely aware of any except the three who had promised to support the Government. I further pressed upon him that I absolutely declined to be in any sense a whip in this matter or to bring pressure, direct or indirect, to bear upon the Bishops. Each one of them is quite as well able as I to judge of a political matter of this sort. I reiterated this in the hope that he would repeat it to his friends. He professed himself quite satisfied, but adhered to all the strong things he had said in his letter. He was himself of opinion that if any Peers were created it would be the merest handful.

On my saying that I thought he was mistaken, and that if they created any they might have to create hundreds, he replied sharply, 'No, the King has definitely said that he will only consent to create as many as are actually required.'

I replied, 'Yes, but how many may be required who can say, if those who have now promised abstention are turned into supporters of yours by the fact that some Peers are created'.

He replied airily, 'Oh, that comes to nothing: there are some people who try to make your flesh creep.'

I said that I thought those gentlemen were not found on one side only.

The whole of the same afternoon (August 1) was one of successive political discussions 'wholly unsought by me; every interview being asked for by others and not on my own initiative'.

In the censure debate in the House of Commons on August 7, Asquith announced categorically and bluntly that the King had consented to the creation of peers as might be necessary to secure the passing of the Bill.

The next few days were crowded and anxious. Till almost the very end the Archbishop was uncertain whether to vote or not. It seemed that most of the Bishops would abstain, two or three only being decidedly for, or decidedly against, the Bill. But let the conclusion of the final debate on August 10 be told in the Archbishop's own words (August 13):

In the afternoon we were more anxious, as it became clear that Halsbury and Co. were going to muster in fuller strength than had been supposed, and that—to say the least—the division would be very close, and every vote might count. When Norfolk and Halifax before dinner on Thursday announced their adhesion to Halsbury's group, matters became even more serious, as it was thought that they would influence a good many.

Rosebery came to me in the House about 7 o'clock and discussed the situation. He did not think he could himself vote—'It would be crucifixion to do so'—but he implied a courteous hope that I might see my way to voting. I told him that I thought *not*, but could not say decidedly.

I came back to a quick dinner at Lambeth in the garden, and (after dismissing Ernest and Co. to Aix) returned to the House of Lords at 9 o'clock with Edith (whose quiet counsel was a real help) and on getting there found everybody very gloomy in expectation of a Halsbury victory. . . . I . . . ascertained . . . that the very grave and deliberate announcement read out by Morley in the afternoon as to the King's assent to the creation of an ample number of Peers (see its wording in the papers) had been drafted . . . by the King's desire, in order to meet the Selborne-Salisbury fable that the King would certainly *not* create more than a few Peers. It was therefore now evident that the Bill would in any case be certainly carried, and that the question was merely whether it should be carried *at once* by the vote given to-night, or carried a few weeks or months hence by the addition of, say, 500 Peers. . . .

That being so, I was now inclining to vote. . . . Seeing Sir William Anson in the crowd of Privy Councillors packed on the steps of the Throne, I got hold of him and found him very helpful, sagacious, constitutional, well-informed. He made little of the threats which were pouring in as to the harm which it would do to the Church were Bishops' votes to defeat Halsbury and Co. He was quietly and clearly in favour of my voting.

Finally, after ten minutes quiet in my room, I decided that it would on the whole be right to vote, and I at once had an opportunity of saying so in the House. Rosebery was not in the House when I spoke, so when he came in just afterwards I sent him a note telling him what I had done. My few words had, I believe, a marked effect on the House, but of course made the Halsburians angrier than ever.

After Rosebery had intervened and in vigorous terms promised to vote, Curzon made a good speech of a grave sort, followed by a wonderfully brisk 'last ditch' speech from Halsbury, and a strangely violent anti-Rosebery utterance (of no special point) from Selborne. Then came the division. The scene has been abundantly described in the papers. The thing which separated it off as regards 'excitement' from any other similar occasion within our memory was the absolute uncertainty as to the issue, an uncertainty which lasted far on into the actual taking of the division. My number was I think 67, and when I got to my place those about me believed that Halsbury had won. By that time I felt no sort of doubt that I had decided and acted rightly. Probably if I could have known beforehand that the majority would be as large as it was, I might have abstained, but *no one* expected that, and if I had held my peace and abstained, it would quite possibly have gone otherwise than it did. At all events a good many men—Loreburn, Lytton, St. Asaph, Cadogan, etc.—thought so. Cadogan told me that my action and words had brought him into the Government Lobby instead of *the other*

Lobby (!) and Kinnaird implied that he would have abstained but for my 'lead'.

I went home satisfied at having had a share in averting a veritable calamity to the Nation.

In the division, there voted for the Government 131, against 114. It was a narrow majority indeed. Of the Bishops the two Archbishops and eleven Bishops voted with the majority and two against.[1] The influence exercised by the Archbishop's speech was freely acknowledged.

Let us hear the two leaders. Lord Lansdowne told Archbishop Davidson on August 16 that in his judgement Lord Morley's announcement had made the whole situation far more alarming, that he appreciated the courage the Archbishop had shown, and added: 'I consider that he, Morley, was saved by the action of those who voted like yourself, and I think you ought to know this.'

Lord Morley's own testimony is even stronger. In his published account of the debate he writes as follows:

> The speeches that followed [Morley's] though some were made by leading men, went in the strain of altercation, hot or cold rather than serious contribution. The one most reassuring for Ministers of them all took no more than three or four minutes. It fell from the Primate,—the head of the hierarchy who have their seats in the House not by descent and birth, nor by election from Scotland or Ireland, nor by political or secular service, a man of broad mind, sagacious temper, steady and careful judgment, good knowledge of the workable strength of rival sections. While those who were for conciliation and those who resisted smote one another the Archbishop recalled both to the gravity of the issue. He admitted the course of the debate had made him change his mind. And what was it in the course of the debate that had produced an effect so rare? It was the callousness—he had almost said levity—with which some noble Lords seemed to contemplate the creation of 500 new peers; a course of action that would make this House, and indeed the country, the laughing stock of the British Dominions beyond the sea, and of those foreign countries whose constitutional life and progress had been largely modelled on our own. Nothing could have been either more true or more apt.[2]

[1] Bishops for: Canterbury, York, Bath and Wells, Birmingham, Carlisle, Chester, Hereford, Lichfield, Ripon, St. Asaph, Southwell, Wakefield, Winchester. Bishops against: Bangor, Worcester.

[2] *Recollections, Viscount Morley,* ii. 353–4.

But the Archbishop's speech and action had caused great indignation amongst the Halsburians inside the House and their admirers outside. Letters of abuse came pouring in. He was called a trimmer, a traitor, a stifler of his conscience, a politician, and an ally of revolutionary radicals. And he was told by many furious correspondents that after such conduct it was impossible for them to continue to seek for the maintenance of the establishment! To one of these who expressed his distress in more moderate terms, the Archbishop thought it right to send a reply for publication. As it was his own explanation of the grounds on which he thought it his duty to record his vote, we quote the central paragraphs:

The ARCHBISHOP OF CANTERBURY *to a* CHICHESTER CHURCHMAN

Lambeth Palace, S.E. August 18th, 1911.

The question which had to be then decided was not whether the Parliament Bill should pass, but whether it should pass immediately or pass a few weeks hence, after the House had been flooded with new Peers for the purpose.

To be more exact: The motion on which we voted was that the Lords 'do not insist upon their amendment'. In the course of the debate the Government made a definite announcement that they had the King's assent to the creation of whatever number of Peers might be necessary to pass the Parliament Bill. This would probably have been from 450 to 500. Had the motion that the Lords 'do not insist' been lost, these Peers would forthwith have been created. About this fact there is no question whatever. I had hoped, as a Bishop, to be able to abstain from voting on the subject, but it became clear that the issue was going to turn upon a very few votes, and that it was only by voting against insistence that we could prevent the influx of a swamping majority of Peers, prepared to pass speedily the threatened legislation affecting Ireland and Wales before the country had time to understand the proposals better, and possibly to reject them. By not insisting on the amendment we prevented the creation of these Peers, and therefore interposed a period of delay before such proposals could become law.

I had hoped that this was obvious to most people. But clearly a great number of good men misunderstood it; hence, I imagine, letters such as yours. I explained my position to the House in a single sentence, but most people do not read carefully any full report of the debates. You, for example, are of opinion that the vote which we gave will promote speedy Disestablishment. I believe the exact contrary to be true. No one feels more strongly than I the mischief which Disestablishment would bring to the country, especially to the poor, and it was this, among other reasons, which led me quite deliberately to act as I did. It is worth while to make some sacrifice to prevent an ignominious 'ending' of the oldest legislative Chamber in the world by a process which would be ludicrous if it were not, as it would be, a national disaster—a process, too, which would have hastened and not retarded the mischiefs which you agree with me in desiring to avert.

CHAPTER XXXVIII

GENERAL WORK AND CHURCH QUESTIONS 1911–1912

Though I have a dull head yet I see, partly by myself and partly by others, how the game goeth. *The* ARCHBISHOP OF CANTERBURY *to* LORD BURGHLEY, *Feb. 18, 1574–5* (*Correspondence of Archbishop Parker*).

THE claims of the Parliament crisis in the summer of 1911 were so absorbing in their character that the Coronation of King George and Queen Mary finds a much smaller place in the Archbishop's papers than it would have received in any ordinary year. Indeed it is surprising that, so far as we can trace, the Archbishop never wrote or dictated any personal record of the day or its happenings; though allusions to the preparations for the Coronation are sprinkled through the very full memoranda on the Parliamentary crisis quoted in the last chapter. But those who were nearest to him at the time knew how much it weighed on his mind; and how anxious he was that its solemnity and significance should be recognized by all. One interesting point in connexion with the service was raised by the suggestion that the Archbishop of York should crown the Queen. The suggestion was disallowed; though the Archbishop of York was invited to preach the sermon.[1]

A problem outside the Abbey service itself was caused by the Bishop of Hereford's[2] invitation to Nonconformists to join with members of the Church of England at Holy Communion in Hereford Cathedral on the occasion of the Coronation. This led to indignant protests from many Churchmen, including a strong letter from Lord Halifax and the Council of the English Church Union to the Archbishop himself. The letter followed upon a discussion in the Upper House of Convocation, where both the Archbishop and the Bishop of Winchester[3] had criticized Dr. Percival's action.

[1] Further material having come to light since the publication of the first edition of this work, a more detailed account of the Archbishop's part in the Coronation will be found in Appendix IV, p. 1390.

[2] Dr. Percival.

[3] Dr. Talbot.

The Bishop of Hereford *to the* Archbishop of Canterbury

Private. The Palace, Hereford.
13th May, 1911.

I have just observed that Lord Halifax is attacking me through a protest addressed to you, and he and his aggressive and insolent faction will no doubt do their worst. My purpose has been to take no notice of the attacks of sacerdotalists and mediaevalists; but I think perhaps I ought to inform you before you reply to him that I may possibly have to defend myself by some public utterance, though I think it most likely that I shall rest content with the manifold expressions of approval and support I have received from Church people of all sorts except the High Sacerdotal party. These expressions have been beyond anything I could have anticipated; and I feel sorry you joined Winchester in expressing disapproval.

This, I confess, disappointed me, as I had expected you to reply to his attack as Archbishop Tait replied to his predecessors, or at least to have given a neutral utterance, as there was to be no discussion by the House. Your siding with him seemed in fact to give his attack a weight it did not deserve on its merits.

Please do not trouble to acknowledge this. I merely wished you to have it before you write to Lord Halifax.

The Archbishop of Canterbury *to the* Bishop of Hereford

Private. 15th May, 1911.

I am not surprised to learn that you are receiving such letters as you describe: that was to be reckoned as a certainty. But you would be utterly mistaken in the facts if you supposed that these letters cover the ground save for the opinions of those whom you describe as 'sacerdotalists and mediaevalists'. One friend after another of most moderate opinions who has been working hard for bringing about a better spirit of unity has spoken to me almost in despair as to the result which must ensue from the matter having been, so to speak, crystallised and forced into formal shape at this moment by what you have felt it to be right to do. I have throughout tried to show that those who attack you are often unfair and are forgetful of a good deal of Church history. I tried to do this in the speech in Convocation which you condemn. My whole endeavour so long as I have had to do with public affairs has been in the direction of promoting the sort of unity and fellowship which you and I alike desire to further. But, as was said to me yesterday by a prominent man, a member of the Edinburgh Conference Continuation Committee, and not at all a High Churchman, 'you can in no way destroy the *spirit* of unity so effectively as by trying to crystallise it *in action* at times of difficulty'. This in one form or another has been said to me from every side. The men with whom I have worked in the endeavour to draw, say, Presbyterians and Anglicans nearer together feel that what has now happened will probably throw our endeavours back for years. Of course I am perfectly familiar with the fact that men like, say, Bishop Cosin, might perhaps have acted just as you have acted, and that their action was in those days useful and helpful. But the conditions of our day are different, and if we are really to promote the unity of those who love our Lord Jesus Christ in sincerity, we must bear in mind the position and the difficulties not only of those who belong to the liberal side in theology, but of those who do not. . . . You mention Archbishop Tait, and there I am upon familiar ground. This question came up again and again while I was working with him. He never swerved from the position that while we may rightly throw the responsibility for seeking to communicate in our Church upon the individual Presbyterian or Nonconformist who desires to communicate, it would defeat our end absolutely were we to issue formal invitations to Nonconformists as such to come. I have written many letters for him to that effect, and what I said in Convocation was exactly upon the lines which he throughout followed. . . . Surely in common fairness we must admit that there is a very wide difference between our letting it quietly be known that we have no desire to repel any good Christian man and that the responsibility rests mainly with the individual communicant, and on the other hand a formal Episcopal utterance specifically inviting to Communion those who, according to strict technicality, are not qualified to communicate. Perhaps this distinction does not seem to you to be a real one, but it certainly seems to be real to a great many whose opinions in most matters you would I think respect.

I

After the Coronation on June 22, the King and Queen proposed to hold a grand Durbar at Delhi by way of personally celebrating the great solemnity in the King Emperor's Indian Dominions. There is some interesting correspondence between the Archbishop and Lord Stamfordham, following representations made to the Archbishop by the Bishop of Lahore[1] and others, on the

[1] Dr. Lefroy.

religious side of the celebrations, and the Archbishop urged with success that a great State service with the King present should be held in the open air at Delhi under the direction of the Metropolitan of India,[1] in addition to the regular services in Cathedral or camp which the King had proposed to attend. It is also of interest to note that the Archbishop's office and his personal devotion to the King were recognized this year by his inclusion among the four 'Counsellors of State' appointed to transact the necessary business of the Crown in the King's absence. The others were Prince Arthur of Connaught, the Lord Chancellor (Loreburn), and the Lord President of the Council (Morley). They held office from November 11 to the end of January, when the King returned to England.

II

A religious question of another kind is illustrated by an account of an interview with Mrs. Besant, President of the Theosophical Society. She had written to the Archbishop to say it was her earnest desire to 'subserve Christianity'.

In the course of a discussion between them on the differences which marked off Theosophy from Christianity, the Archbishop wrote down the following words in her presence as representing the Theosophical position, and Mrs. Besant agreed that they were in her judgement 'absolutely accurate':

> 28th June, 1911.
>
> The Christian Church speaks of Christ as the second Person of the Trinity. We should say that Christ is only so in the same way as many others are and have been. The Christian says: God was incarnate in Jesus Christ. We say Yes, but in all men the human spirit is an incarnation of the Divine, though supremely so in Christ. Only the Christ Incarnation was not unique in history: there have been many others besides.

They then spoke of the Atonement, and Mrs. Besant at once admitted that the Theosophical view was entirely different from what was known as the orthodox Church doctrine:

> Having expanded all this we returned to the point with which she started, 'What is the attitude of Church authorities towards

[1] Dr. Copleston.

clergy who join the Theosophical Society?' I pointed out to her the difference between the position of clergy who are accredited as teachers and guides on the strength of their adherence to certain specific doctrines, and the position of other Christian folk who are not so accredited. The difference appeared never to have struck her, and to my surprise she said, 'If you put it like that I do not wonder at the difficulty you find'. She went on to admit that a full member of her Society like—e.g. Mr. Scott-Moncrieff, whom she frequently named, would necessarily hold that there was nothing unique in the Incarnation of Christ, although He was a supreme teacher, that the whole doctrine of the Atonement must be re-set as meaning nothing more than a closer union between God and man as shown in Christ, and so on. And when I said, 'Do you think I could rightly accredit as a Christian teacher to whom—e.g. Christian parents may send their children, a man who can only say the Creed with such expansion or modification as that?' she replied, 'Well, now you put it so, I do not think you could.' Yet, so far as I understand, she came here in order to get me to say that there was nothing in the position she inculcates inconsistent with the holding of the Christian faith even by a teacher thereof.

III

The tercentenary of the Authorized Version of the Bible was celebrated in 1911, when the Archbishop and Mr. Asquith spoke at a great commemorative meeting organized by the Bible Society in the Albert Hall. This caused some interesting questions to be put to the Archbishop. The first concerned the copyright of the Bible. The Archbishop was approached by the Home Secretary, Mr. Winston Churchill, for advice as to whether a request of the Bible Society to be allowed to print the Authorized Version might be granted by the Crown: the privilege being at present restricted in England and Wales to the King's Printers and the University Presses of Oxford and Cambridge. The Archbishop was at first inclined to favour 'free trade in Bibles', and doubted whether the existing restrictions were quite consonant with the spirit of our time. But on going into the matter with great care, and hearing all that was to be said upon the subject by the King's Printers and by the University Presses of Oxford and Cambridge, he came to the conclusion expressed in the following letter to the Home Secretary:

The Archbishop of Canterbury *to the* Rt. Hon. Winston Churchill

1st August, 1912.

On the whole I am clearly of opinion that no adequate case has been made out for any change in the existing rules. The Bible Society does not in my judgement show that there is any real grievance as things now stand, and the Syndics of the University Presses have presented the case both of themselves and of the King's Printers with a backing of cogent argument which it would be difficult to upset. Certainly if a change were to be made it could not be made without adequate notice to those who have, on the strength of the existing rules, invested very large sums of money for carrying out a system of printing and publishing which seems to me to be conducive beyond all doubt to the public interest and advantage.

I do not think it would be possible to restrict to the British and Foreign Bible Society the privilege of such printing if it be extended beyond the present limits, and I could if necessary support from independent knowledge the contention of the Syndics of the University Presses as to the confusion and mischief which might arise if existing restrictions were altogether broken down.

Mr. Churchill agreed with this advice and the application was refused.

Other questions referred to the desirability of a fresh revision of the New Testament. A Memorial presented in May 1911 by a number of scholars and public men of great distinction, including Arthur Balfour, A. C. Bradley, Robert Bridges, H. C. Beeching, Lord Curzon, Dr. Inge, M. R. James, Andrew Lang, Walter Raleigh, Henry Jackson, and the Professors of English Literature of most of the Universities (though, curiously, very few Biblical scholars), asked for an emendation of the Authorized Version in those places, and in those places only, where its meaning was misleading or obscure. The Memorialists were critical of the Revised Version of the New Testament, but satisfied with that of the Old. The Archbishop, however, in replying, said that from the point of view of scholarship the time was not, in his judgement, opportune, and that it would be better to wait a few years. He suggested that in the meanwhile a number of scholars might be privately invited to undertake an experimental work voluntarily, and that, if they were successful on such a task as the Epistle to the Hebrews, a new enterprise might be launched by authority. The reply disappointed the deputation, though it was entirely endorsed by public opinion outside.

IV

A more serious, and far more agitating, question with which the Archbishop had to contend was that involved in the Bill to disestablish the Welsh Church, introduced in April 1912. The Prime Minister's action carried with it the practical certainty that, under the Parliament Act, it would in time receive the Royal Assent, despite its rejection by the Lords. During the whole of the long agitation which had led up to the Bill, as well as during the proceedings in Parliament, the Archbishop had been in the closest touch with the Bishops of the four Welsh dioceses which it was proposed to sunder from the Province of Canterbury. And be it remembered that all four Bishops were Welsh patriots, and two at least very eloquent patriots, with a gift of fervid oratory, namely St. Asaph (Edwards) and St. David's (Owen). They were not likely, therefore, to undervalue the special genius of the Welsh nation, or to discourage what in their judgement might serve to make the Welsh Church more and more the Church of the Welsh people. Nor did they forget that Christianity had flourished in Wales before it had flourished in Canterbury, and that their Welsh dioceses had a more ancient title than any diocese in England. But, while perfectly well able to take care of the Welsh Church and Welsh interests, they valued with an equal affection the very old connexion between their four dioceses and the rest of the dioceses of England and Wales. Their relationship to the Province of Canterbury was a living relationship: and their share in the councils of the Convocation of Canterbury of a vital character. Their violent sundering from those councils and that life they therefore indignantly resented. It was natural for them to look for leadership and help to the Archbishop of Canterbury, the head of the Province and the President of the Convocation. It was also natural for the Archbishop to give all the help in his power; since the body over which he ruled was to receive a grievous wound; and an attack on any portion of the Church which looked to him as Primate seemed to him to be an attack on the whole. Nor was this the only or the chief reason why he felt bound to lend his strength to the champion defenders of the Church in Wales. He was well aware of the material disadvantages which would be bound to come to the temporalities of the Church through the disendowment. But grievous as that loss might be, a more important principle still than disendowment was at stake. He was a profound and convinced believer in the whole principle of establishment. The national recognition of religion was to him of inestimable importance. And above all incidental features of establishment he put the existence of the parochial system:

> We have at present [he said, in his Charge[1]], such a rule, supported by both Church and State—a rule which requires the continuous residence and the personal service of a duly appointed and qualified officer who has a recognised status and a defined authority in matters ecclesiastical within an accurately prescribed area, surrounded on every side by other areas prescribed with equal accuracy, each of them served by a religious officer with status and responsibilities corresponding to his own.
>
> Let anyone familiar with our common English life in any thickly populated area of, say, half a dozen parishes, contrast the position held therein by a devoted and capable Nonconformist minister with the position held by the *personae* or 'parsons' of the National Church in those parishes, and he will begin perhaps to realise what the change would mean when the legal obligations and local responsibilities with which we are familiar had ceased. The ministers of all the various denominations, the Church of England being one of them, would then have a status identical in character, each of them ministering to his own congregation or adherents, with no responsibility resting upon one of them more than upon another to care for those who lie outside all 'congregations'. Probably every parish priest here to-day could point to many such people who, with little profession of caring for religion, and certainly no membership in any congregation, make constant and almost automatic claims upon the man whom immemorial usage, as well as technical rule, has taught everyone, whatever his belief or non-belief, to regard and to use as the parish 'minister'—the accredited servant, that is, of all the people.

What, we may ask, was the reason why the Prime Minister should desire this disestablishment of the Welsh Church? It was in the main because it was now, he maintained, the Church of a minority. It was not in fact the national Church, and therefore

[1] *Character and Call of the Church of England*, p. 93 f. (February 1912).

ought not to be given the privileges over other churches which a national Church might claim. The Royal Commission[1] had conclusively shown that its adherents were less numerous than those of the Nonconforming churches, and a great sense of injury was burning in the hearts of the Welsh people. Nor could it be denied that 31 of 34 Welsh M.P.s had been returned, in each of the two General Elections since 1909, with the very definite expectation that they would work for the disestablishment of the Church.

The provisions of the Bill,[2] as introduced in the Commons in April 1912, may be briefly outlined. After the passing of the Act, the four Welsh dioceses[3] would cease to be dioceses of the Province of Canterbury; the ecclesiastical corporations in them (sole or otherwise) would be dissolved, and the ecclesiastical jurisdiction abolished. The organization, however, was to be kept in being, as the subject of an implied contract between its members, and power was given to hold synods for the future government of the Church.

All the cathedrals and parish churches, ecclesiastical residences and closed burial grounds, together with the income from endowments which should pass to the disendowed Church, were to be vested in three Welsh Commissioners with instructions to transfer the whole property to a Representative Body, which was to be constituted by the Church itself.

The income to be left to the Church was calculated in the following way.[4] The Church's income from endowments in 1910 was £268,558. The date which should determine the difference between the ancient endowments and the endowments specifically intended for the Church was fixed as 1662, this being the date of the Book of Common Prayer, and of the founding of

[1] The Warrant setting up the Royal Commission was dated May 1, 1907. Its Report was dated November 1, 1910.

[2] A previous Bill had been introduced in the Commons in 1909.

[3] Actually seven dioceses were affected by the Bill. One whole Deanery of St. Asaph, viz. Oswestry, was not disestablished.

[4] Mr. Frank Morgan, Secretary of the Representative Body of the Church in Wales, states in a letter to the writer (June 5, 1935) that at the time when the Royal Commission was appointed the date for the division between ancient and modern was 1703, and, taking that date, the Memorandum of Archdeacon Evans and Lord Hugh Cecil, attached to the Report of the Commission, put the amount of endowments at £116,287, and the total at £215,507. But by the time the Commission reported, the endowments had risen to £268,558.

Nonconformity. The ancient endowments, it was argued, might properly be regarded as national property, and amounted to more than half the total. This sum was to be alienated for the University of Wales and the County Councils. Life interests were, however, to be preserved and commuted.

On the eve of the introduction of the Bill, the Archbishop of Canterbury addressed a meeting of 10,000 Churchmen at Carnarvon, on April 22, 1912. He declared that he had come officially to Carnarvon in order to show the support given by the English Church to their Welsh brethren. On April 30 there was a vigorous debate in Convocation when the Archbishop and Bishops (the Bishops of Oxford,[1] Hereford,[2] and Lincoln[3] dissenting) called upon Churchmen and Churchwomen and other Christian people to offer the most strenuous opposition.

The second reading of the Bill was carried in May in spite of violent attacks in and out of the House; and had passed through its various stages in the House of Commons by February 1913. In the Lords the Bill was thrown out, a second reading being refused on February 13, after three days' debate, by 252 votes to 51. The Archbishop made a long speech, stating the facts and the history. He took care to emphasize the point that disestablishment would not touch the spiritual life of the Church, though it would cripple its work.

A new session began in March. The Welsh Church Bill had passed a second time through the House of Commons by the beginning of July 1913. Once again it came to the Lords, and again, after two days' debate, the second reading was refused (July 22) by 243 votes to 48.

Demonstrations continued in the country, and the Archbishop made a strong speech against the Bill in a meeting in the Albert Hall on November 20. In April 1914, the Bill was re-introduced into the House of Commons, and passed the Commons a third time on May 19.

Two new points were now taken up—or at least pressed with new vigour. It was urged that Parliament was acting in a harsh and violent way against Convocation by the forcible separation of the four Welsh dioceses from the Canterbury Synod. It was also urged that a great deal of Nonconformist feeling had lately been aroused against the Bill. Accordingly, on June 25 the

[1] Dr. Gore. [2] Dr. Percival. [3] Dr. E. L. Hicks.

Government agreed to appoint a Select Committee before the second reading was again taken in the House of Lords in order to inquire (1) whether the constitution of the Convocations of the Church of England had ever been altered by Act of Parliament without the assent and against the protest of the Convocations, and (2) whether the memorials attributed to Welsh Nonconformists against disendowment represented a real and increasing objection to it among them.

The War broke out before the Committee could report. And, though not without a vigorous protest from the Archbishop, the Welsh Church Act was 'duly passed under the provisions of the Parliament Act 1911'.

A Suspensory Act was carried at the same time, postponing the operation of the Act for twelve months, or to a further date not later than the termination of the War, to be fixed by order in Council. The rest of the story will be told in a subsequent chapter.

V

The account of an Act of disestablishment may be followed by an illustration of the grave difficulties under which the Church of England laboured as an Established Church in securing even moderate administrative reforms before the passing of the Enabling Act of 1919. It had been agreed, the money had been found, and all the necessary steps had been taken so far as the Church could go, to create three new dioceses, Sheffield, Chelmsford, and St. Edmundsbury and Ipswich; thus giving considerable relief to the three large dioceses from which they were to be carved. But, on the Bill being introduced into the House of Commons, it was met with obstruction. The Prime Minister, on January 14, 1913, wrote to the Archbishop pointing out the strength of the obstruction and regretting that he saw no chance of the Bill getting through. To everybody's surprise, including the Archbishop's, the Bill was suddenly passed in August. The Archbishop, hearing the good news, wrote at once to Lord Hugh Cecil:

The ARCHBISHOP OF CANTERBURY *to the* RT. HON. LORD HUGH CECIL

16th August, 1913.

One line I must send you from the Alps to express the supreme satisfaction with which I learn—though without any particulars—

of the passage of the three Bishoprics' Bill. It is a huge cause of thankfulness, not least because of what it may mean as regards the life of the Bishop of St. Albans[1]—on whom we lean so much.

I wonder how it came about. Was it a *coup* of yours in the *absence* of our obstinate friends? Or was it a Parliamentary *deal*? Or what is the explanation? One word of explication (addressed to Lambeth) would be very acceptable.

We are revelling in Alpine sunlight on the ridge 'twixt Switzerland and Italy—an old and favourite haunt of ours.

The RT. HON. LORD HUGH CECIL *to the* ARCHBISHOP OF CANTERBURY

19th August, 1913.

The passage of the Bishoprics Bill resulted, like other great events, from the concatenation of circumstances. My nephew, Wolmer, on the Friday before the Prorogation, suggested that we might oppose, and so prevent the passage of, a number of Nonconformist Charity Bills unless we got the Bishoprics Bill through. At first I thought this would hardly work, but, when he pressed his plan, it seemed to me that it would be worth trying. Accordingly we revived the Bishoprics Bill, which was dropped, and put it down again for Monday; and I spoke to the Prime Minister and asked his assistance. He said he would be delighted to do what he could if we could square the opposition to the Bill. This seemed possible because the Nonconformist opponents might be bought off by allowing their Charity Bills to pass, and the Liverpool opponents, I hoped, would all be away. Monday and Tuesday were spent in animated negotiations between Wolmer and myself on one side and the Government Whip, Illingworth, and some of the Ministerial opponents of the Bill on the other. In the end the Bill was starred, and, after much hesitation, its Second Reading was taken at the end of the Tuesday sitting on Wednesday morning. We had gained this concession by promising to let through no fewer than sixteen Charity Bills, of which fourteen related to Nonconformist Charities.

The opposition of Colonel Challoner to the Second Reading greatly alarmed Illingworth and imperilled the Bill; and on Wednesday afternoon we were still very anxious. But we got my brother Robert and the Bishop of Oxford to see the Prime Minister, who supported us admirably, as indeed he had done all through. Finally, the Bill passed easily through Committee, the Liverpool people not turning up, and the rest of the opposition

[1] Dr. Jacob (the diocese of Chelmsford being taken out of the diocese of St. Albans).

being either bought off or overawed by Asquith's influence. By dinner time on Wednesday the Bill had been read a third time.

So you see that the passage of the Bill resulted partly from a Parliamentary deal, partly from the good-will of the Prime Minister, partly from the absence of the Liverpool Members and of some strong Radical opponents who were abroad. Asquith thought that we had been unwise in leaving the matter till the last moment. That we did so was an accident; but the cunningest calculation would not have led us to any other course because, if we had not had all the advantage of surprise, the Protestant drum would have been beaten and the opposition to the Bill brought together again. What we did was the best possible way of carrying the Bill, although the suddenness of it was an accident; for we did not think of attempting to pass the Bill till the Friday afternoon and it was read a third time the following Wednesday by dinner time. We were a good deal pressed to accept the Bishopric of Sheffield alone, but we thought, first, that the Chelmsford case was the strongest and most urgent, and, secondly, that if there was to be a scandal, it would answer to us better that the scandal should be a big one, as more likely to lead us to a general Enabling Bill. We also resisted a suggestion that the Places of Worship Enfranchisement Bill should be passed in consideration of the passage of this Bill. We kept that to barter against a general Enabling Bill.

This, I think, answers Your Grace's question. Credit is chiefly due to Wolmer for the bold plan which ultimately succeeded and to the Prime Minister for his invaluable help.

The secrecy required to achieve success showed, perhaps even more than any failure would have done, the grave disadvantages with which the promoters of Church legislation had to contend.

CHAPTER XXXIX

PRAYER BOOK REVISION BEFORE THE WAR, 1906–1914

Matter grows under our hands. Let no man say, 'Come, I'll write a *duodecimo.*'
LAURENCE STERNE, *Tristram Shandy*, vol. v, ch. xvi.

IN one form or another, the problem of the Prayer Book stayed with the Archbishop from the beginning to the end of his Primacy. The first three years (1903–6) form the opening act of the drama—for, following the stormy Prologue in Temple's rule, they set out the demand for a solution of the ritual difficulties as they existed at that time—beginning with a public agitation and a deputation to Lambeth (1903), and continuing with the labours of the Royal Commission on Ecclesiastical Discipline (1904–6). The second act is occupied with the initiation of the revision of the Prayer Book through Convocation in the eight years leading up to the War (1906–14). The War—with its revelation of new needs, outdistancing the old—provides the stage for the third act. The fourth act is the long process of legislation through the Church Assembly, with its waxing intensity. The fifth act takes place in the House of Commons. It may be well in a few pages, before the crisis of the War, to give a summary account of the procedure between the publication of the unanimous Report of the Royal Commission in 1906, and August 1914.

It would be far too long a story to describe the various stages even of the progress to and in Convocation. But certain outstanding facts and features must be brought out. In the first place the procedure by Letters of Business had itself to be commended both to the Government of the day and also to the Church at large. The Prime Minister in 1906, Sir Henry Campbell-Bannerman, when approached by the Archbishop, replied:

The RT. HON. SIR HENRY CAMPBELL-BANNERMAN *to the* ARCHBISHOP OF CANTERBURY

4 August, 1906.

His Majesty's Government have fully considered your Grace's suggestion that Letters of Business should be issued to the Convocations as recommended in the report of the Royal Commission on Ecclesiastical Discipline. Custom undoubtedly warrants the grant of Letters in such cases in order that Convocation may be free to deliberate and express its opinion.

But His Majesty's Government believe that very far-reaching consequences may follow, and they do not think it would be right to set on foot a proceeding which may lead to such serious issues in the Church of England, except upon the initiative of the Church itself acting through its recognized authorities.

If therefore either your Grace and the Archbishop of York think fit to submit a request to the Crown for Letters of Business, or the Convocations present a petition to the same effect, I shall advise His Majesty to issue Letters.

The two Archbishops accordingly wrote:

The ARCHBISHOPS OF CANTERBURY AND YORK[1] *to the* RT. HON. SIR HENRY CAMPBELL-BANNERMAN

Lambeth Palace, S.E. 7 August 1906.

It will be within your knowledge that the recently presented Report of the Royal Commission on Ecclesiastical Discipline contained, among other recommendations, the following:

'We recommend that—

'Letters of Business should be issued to the Convocations with instructions—(a) to consider the preparation of a new rubric regulating the ornaments (that is to say, the vesture) of the ministers of the Church at the times of their ministrations, with a view to its enactment by Parliament; and (b) to frame, with a view to their enactment by Parliament, such modifications in the existing law relating to the conduct of Divine Service and to the ornaments and fittings of churches as may tend to secure the greater elasticity which a reasonable recognition of the comprehensiveness of the Church of England and of its present needs seems to demand.'

We think that in all the circumstances it is desirable in the interests of the Church of England, that this recommendation should be adopted, and accordingly we venture, as those on whom central responsibility rests in Church affairs, to express our hope that you may see your way to advise His Majesty the King to direct that Letters of Business be issued.

[1] Dr. Maclagan.

The Rt. Hon. Sir Henry Campbell-Bannerman *to the* Archbishop of Canterbury

10, Downing Street, Whitehall, S.W.
August 18th, 1906.

I have received the letter of yourself and the Archbishop of York of the 7th instant, requesting me to move His Majesty to grant Letters of Business to the Convocations in accordance with the recommendation of the Royal Commission. In view of this request it will be my duty to lay the matter before the King in time for the meeting of Convocation. Your Grace will of course understand that though I have thought myself bound to comply in such a matter with the request of the two Archbishops, His Majesty's Government must hold themselves entirely free to judge for themselves the course that they ought to adopt both in regard to the Royal Commissioners' proposals for legislation and in other respects, whatever view may be taken by the Convocations.

The following is the Letter of Business to the Convocation of Canterbury, under the Royal Sign Manual, issued from the Home Office, November 10, 1906:

Edward R. and I.

Edward the Seventh, by the Grace of God, of the United Kingdom of Great Britain and Ireland and of the British Dominions beyond the Seas, King, Defender of the Faith, To Our Right Trusty and Right Entirely Beloved Councillor, Randall Thomas, Archbishop of Canterbury, Knight Grand Cross of Our Royal Victorian Order, Primate of all England and Metropolitan, to the Right Reverend the Bishops, the Very Reverend the Deans, the Venerable the Archdeacons, and to the Reverend the Proctors representing the Cathedral and Collegiate Chapters and Clergy of the Province of Canterbury,

Greeting!

Whereas Our Commissioners appointed to inquire into the alleged prevalence of breaches or neglect of the law relating to the conduct of Divine Service in the Church of England have submitted to Us their report:

And whereas We deem it expedient that certain recommendations of Our said Commissioners should be by you discussed:

Our Will and Pleasure therefore is, and We do hereby authorize you, the said Randall Thomas, Archbishop of Canterbury, President of the said Convocation, and the Bishops of your said Province, and the Deans of the Cathedral Churches and also the

Archdeacons, and the Proctors representing the Chapters and Colleges and the whole Clergy of every Diocese of your said Province, that you do debate, consider, consult, and agree upon the following points, matters, and things contained in the recommendations of the said Report, *videlicet*, the desirability and the form and contents of a new Rubric regulating the ornaments (that is to say the vesture) of the Ministers of the Church at the times of their ministrations, and also of any modifications of the existing law relating to the conduct of Divine Service and to the ornaments and fittings of Churches; and, after mature debate, consideration, consultations, and agreement that you do present to Us a Report or Reports thereon in writing.

Given at Our Court at Sandringham, the tenth day of November, 1906, in the Sixth year of Our Reign.

By His Majesty's Command,

H. J. Gladstone.

Letter of Business authorizing the Convocation of the Province of Canterbury to discuss and report upon certain recommendations contained in the Report of the Royal Commission on Ecclesiastical Discipline.

In commending the procedure to the Church, the Archbishop of Canterbury, first in a letter of June 1906 to the Members of Convocation and of the House of Laymen, said:

I realise as clearly as any man the great difficulties and dangers which will attend our course after the Letters of Business have been issued. I can enter into the thoughts of those who on that ground will be ready to censure the above recommendation as rash and ill-advised. But every student of history knows how often the courageous line of action has proved to be the most prudent; and when it is also the most obviously straightforward, the probability that it ought to be chosen is raised almost to certainty. What I venture with some confidence to ask is, that I may, as President of our Convocation, be supported on all sides in the endeavour which must now be made to bring to an end a situation which, for those at least who are in the front rank of administrative responsibility, has become well-nigh intolerable. It has become abundantly clear that to secure the exact observance, in the twentieth century, of detailed rubrics drawn up in the sixteenth and seventeenth centuries, is neither possible nor, from any point of view, desirable. Rules clear in principle and yet elastic in detail we do absolutely require, if the Church, in its manifold activities, is to be abreast of modern needs and yet loyal to ancient order.

> Are we always to shrink back affrighted from the task of trying to decide what, in such matters as our rubrics deal with, the living Church of England desires?

In his address to the Full Synod on November 13, 1906, he repeated this appeal. Two things in particular are significant. It is significant that in 1906 (and for some years later) it is the question of vestments, the Ornaments Rubric, which is the predominant issue; the question, namely, whether the chasuble and the other Eucharistic vestments are or are not lawful—whether they were or were not in use '*in this Church of England by the authority of Parliament in the second year of the reign of King Edward the Sixth*'—and whether in any case they may be lawfully used now The Archbishop said (November 13, 1906):

> In the forefront of the direction or request which has been given to us stands that much-enduring document, the Ornaments Rubric —that document which is unlike, as I imagine, any other document in history, appealed to on either side in the controversy as conclusive, but appealed to with interpretations attached which on the two sides are diametrically opposite. I doubt whether the same number of words in English or in any other tongue have ever stood in quite the same relation as these words stand to a great controversy or to a great epoch in Church life. There would, to my mind, be something almost verging on the absurd in the position of that document were it not that the matter is so intensely grave and momentous to our common life. My own belief, quite unswerving, after abundant thought and abundant prayer—my own personal belief—is that we ought to go forward and deal with, I do not say that document necessarily, but with the controversies in which that document holds so prominent a place—that we ought to go forward and to deal with it now in our Convocations.

The Ornaments Rubric was fated to pass into the background of the discussion before many years had passed. Not so the other significant point on which the Archbishop dwelt, the relation to Parliament:

> The moment this question is raised people are apt to say, 'Have you forgotten that in the long run any change of rubric or other document which has statutory force would require Parliamentary sanction?' Does anybody forget that for an hour who thinks about these subjects? It is the very crux of our difficulties. But we have to remember this—as far as I am aware, no responsible people in

public life want that the rubrical details of the Book of Common Prayer shall be discussed in Parliament. Certainly no political party desires that that should take place, and I doubt whether any ecclesiastical party, even the smallest, entertains that desire to-day. And, therefore, the thought should be borne in mind, when we are considering whether that perfectly plain and obvious difficulty across the path of our action is really a fatal bar or no. The task before us ultimately will be how to find a mode of securing the Parliamentary sanction which will be necessary if, and only if, the change of any rubric is recommended—how to secure that without involving discussions which would be quite obviously and manifestly unsuited to Parliament if they necessitated discussions there upon the details either of worship or of doctrine. Personally, I do not believe a solution of that problem to be impossible which should retain the full privileges alike of the National Church, and of what our Bidding Prayer calls the 'great Council of the nation assembled in Parliament'.

Convocation, on the Archbishop's advice, decided to prepare a full Reply to the Royal Letter of Business. But the Reply was bound to take time—not least on account of the large amount of hesitation and lukewarmness, as well as opposition for different reasons, among Church people generally. A certain amount of interest was taken in the proposal to modify the rule which required the *Quicunque Vult* to be recited on the great festivals of the Church. But quite clearly, the chief matter of public interest was the use of vestments. In 1908 a most valuable Historical Report (120 pp.) on Ornaments (No. 416) was presented to the Upper House of Convocation by a subcommittee of five Bishops, of whom Bishop John Wordsworth was the leader. Bishop Wordsworth's words, accounting for the passion[1] which the controversy aroused, are worth quoting. Speaking in the Upper House on February 5, 1908, he said:

I have come to the conclusion that it is because our countrymen have largely mistaken irrational instincts for religious inspirations. Extreme partisans on one side shrink from a ritualist as they would from a snake, or dismiss him contemptuously as possessed by the idle vanity of a peacock. Those on the other side

[1] In a Protest organized by the Church Association in 1906, signed by 118,624 lay members of the Church of England, against the legalization of mass vestments, it was stated that they were worn by 'upwards of 2,300 clergy of the Church of England'. The total number of clergy in the Church of England is about 25,000.

regard Puritans as 'wild boars out of the wood', bent on rooting up all that is decent and beautiful.

The Report, which brought forward a great deal of evidence in favour of the legality of vestments, even though it contained no recommendation as to present policy, called forth a shower of memorials and protests. The Upper House declared its own attitude three years later in the following Resolution (July 7, 1911):

> That this House, holding that in the present circumstances of the Church of England it is not desirable (1) that any alteration should be made in the terms of the Ornaments Rubric, and (2) that either of the two existing usages as regards the vesture of the minister at the Holy Communion (other than the use of the cope as ordered by Canon 24) should in all cases be excluded from the public worship of the Church—declares its opinion that, by whatsoever process may be hereafter recommended by this House, provision shall be made to authorize, under specified conditions and with due safeguards, a diversity of use. And it is hereby explicitly declared that by this Resolution no sanction is intended to be given to any doctrine other than what is set forth in the Prayer Book and Articles of the Church of England.

With regard to the remainder of the Prayer Book, the policy at this time was to do as little as possible—not least on account of the misconceptions and suspicions of which the Archbishop was fully conscious, as he told the Upper House in November 1910, when he said:

> No thoughtful man can fail to think that such changes as are made in the Rubrics should be reduced sternly to the smallest possible dimensions.

The procedure, it must be remembered, was liable to be cumbersome and complicated; because, as the Archbishop made plain from the beginning, each of the two Houses in Canterbury Convocation, and each of the two Houses in York Convocation were dealing with the same matters—in 'independent deliberation with occasional conference':[1] and the Archbishop had also promised that the outcome of Convocation's deliberations was 'sooner or later to be communicated to the House of Laymen'.[2] In 1911, the provisional result of the Upper House's work in

[1] Letter to Prolocutor, May 4, 1909. [2] Ibid.

Committee was a quite slight leaflet, dealing with what then seemed necessary (No. 427; 19 pp.). There was a bare allowance of Reservation for 'the sick person' only. But there was no change of importance in the Order of Holy Communion. The Archbishop, writing this year to a correspondent, said:

> Yes, I am keen about Prayer Book Revision *now*. In my own belief the changes likely to be adopted are for the most part quite uncontroversial, but there are two or three which will be subjects of keen debate.

Between 1911 and 1914, the movement in favour of revision had grown, and much work was done in both Houses of Convocation, with some assistance from an advisory committee of liturgical scholars, appointed July 1912. A larger Report, No. 481 (40 pp.),[1] embodied the results of the Upper House's work—but it was still comparatively small; and, while including provision for Reservation for 'the sick person', it still made no change of any importance connected with the Prayer of Consecration in Holy Communion. The increase in the number of Recommendations was simply due to an increasing demand for enrichment. The work of Prayer Book revision had begun (said the Bishop of Bristol,[2] February 18, 1914, in reporting the results of six years' labour) with two main desires:

> First, that there should be a minimum of change, and next, that there should be no change that in any sort of way could honestly be said to touch doctrine at all. As time went on, the question of enrichment came up, and that had grown to very considerable dimensions. Whether it had grown to overburdening dimensions, would be a matter for careful consideration.

In April 1914, at the Archbishop's suggestion, a joint committee of both Houses of Canterbury Convocation was appointed to harmonize their material, with a view also to agreement, if possible, with York. A Committee of the Upper House was appointed to consider procedure by canon, 'the necessary Parliamentary sanction being subsequently sought'.

Thus, in the summer of 1914, it seemed that the main part of the Reply to the Royal Letters of Business had been completed.

[1] February 1914.

[2] Dr. G. F. Browne.

CHAPTER XL

MARCHES AND COUNTERMARCHES

'Tis a church militant week with me, full of marches and counter marches.
LAURENCE STERNE (Letter to J. Hall-Stevenson, 1764).

IN the years which immediately preceded the outbreak of the Great War, there were many signs of impending calamity, both at home and abroad. The Archbishop himself, though very well aware of the state of crisis at home, did not believe in the likelihood of a great conflict in Europe. And his desire for peace and for friendly relations with Germany in particular is shown in a whole series of communications with the Church leaders in Germany.

I

In February 1911, occurred a notable visit to England of representatives of the German Churches Committee for fostering friendly relations between Great Britain and Germany. Professor Harnack of Berlin, the famous New Testament scholar, came with Dr. Spiecker. They visited Buckingham Palace on Sunday (February 5) with the Archbishop, and attended Divine Service in the private Chapel, the King and Queen both being present. And afterwards they were presented by the Archbishop to Their Majesties. On the following day, February 6, the day of the opening of Parliament, the Archbishop presided at a meeting held in the Queen's Hall, for the purpose of forming the British section of the 'Associated Council of the Churches of the British and German Empires for fostering friendly relations'.

Both the Archbishop and Dr. Harnack declared that their nations wished for peace. And both spoke of the danger which came from *provocateurs*, and similar 'noxious creatures', which had the power of causing irritation and inflammation in the body politic, and traded on ignorance. The Archbishop spoke of their Association of British and German Churches:

> They wanted each of the two great nations to have at its centre a solid corps of men and women thus vivified [by the power of the Holy Spirit, and the spirit of Christian brotherhood], and they

believed that in that way they would bring about what would make the bare possibility of war, or the spirit and tone which gave rise to war, first unlikely, then difficult, ultimately quite impossible.[1]

Dr. Harnack on his side described the Association as 'A Regiment of Peace'; and, referring to the ideal of human brotherhood proclaimed by Christ, added:

> We dare not cast forth this ideal from the realm of politics, we are bound to recognise its validity even there. We ought not to act as if our Christianity bound us only in the home and in the Church, whilst elsewhere its authority failed; as if the sword of the barbarian maintained a lawful place among us![2]

At the moment, in spite of the *provocateurs* on either side, there was apparent quiet. But a few weeks after the meeting, a fresh crisis in Morocco led to a French occupation of the Moroccan capital Fez. The German Government resented this action, and suddenly, on July 1, sent a gunboat to Agadir, on the western coast of Morocco, to protect German subjects in that disorderly country. This in turn alarmed British statesmen, and Mr. Lloyd George made a speech in the Mansion House, with the full authority of the Government, which was immediately taken as a grave warning to German aims. England was at once attacked as the real enemy of Germany. German pastors and professors, who had been in the forefront of the movement for friendship between the Churches of the two countries, feared a violent set-back.

Letters were received by various members of the British Council of the Churches for fostering friendly relations between the two peoples, definitely expressing the writers' belief that the British fleet had twice in recent months been ready to throw itself upon Germany. The Archbishop took up the matter with the Prime Minister. The whole idea of a raid in the autumn was incredible to him. But he wished to be able to deny such a charge in the most authoritative fashion:

The ARCHBISHOP OF CANTERBURY *to the* RT. HON. H. H. ASQUITH

5th January, 1912.

I have been seeing the letters written by Ministers of Religion and others in Germany who have been strong friends of England, and I am rather aghast to find how deeply rooted among these friendly folk is the belief that England contemplated last Summer

[1] *The Times*, February 7, 1911. [2] *Christian World*, February 9, 1911.

a raid upon Germany without notice, and had actually made preparations for it. I have again and again said that I am persuaded not only that this is untrue, but that it has no foundation. Such assurances seem to be in vain. People think I am merely ignorant.

The RT. HON. H. H. ASQUITH *to the* ARCHBISHOP OF CANTERBURY

Private. 8th January, 1912.

Many thanks for your letter of the 5th, which I showed to Sir Edward Grey this morning.

We both think that nothing good could result from any declaration prior to the German elections, which begin at the end of this week. Any such declaration would be sure to be misunderstood and distorted, and exploited for party purposes.

But there is no reason why you should not know, and let it be known to all whom it may concern, that the story that last summer—or at any time—this country contemplated a raid upon Germany, is a ridiculous fiction. It is totally without any kind of foundation in fact.

The movements and operations of our Fleet this summer and autumn were perfectly normal, which (*between you and me*) is more than could be said of the German Fleet.

I return your enclosures.

The Archbishop at once wrote a letter to Mr. Allen Baker, the Chairman of the British Executive Committee, for communication to Dr. Spiecker, the Chairman of the German Executive Committee. He also wrote as follows to Dr. Harnack:

The ARCHBISHOP OF CANTERBURY *to* PROFESSOR ADOLF HARNACK

11th January, 1912.

I believe I am right in thinking that you have been asked to write a short article for the English Magazine *The Peacemaker*, an organ which is devoted to the cause of promoting International Peace, and especially at present of furthering good-will and close friendship between Germany and England. I have no personal connexion with *The Peacemaker*, and I only heard incidentally of this request having been made to you. But when I remember the weight which was rightly attached to your notable speech last year, and when I bear in mind the weight of influence which you exercise, not in Germany only but among thoughtful and educated people in England, I cannot but feel that any word from Your Excellency at this juncture would be of even more than usual service to the cause which we have at heart. It is to me a matter of deep distress to learn that there are at this moment in Germany many people, hitherto quite friendly to England, who have been led to attach credence to the story, absolutely without foundation, that there was last Autumn a design entertained in England to make some kind of naval attack or raid upon Germany. I am able to say with absolute knowledge that such story has no foundation whatever, and yet I imagine that the circulation of this fable has had an influence prejudicial to the cause of friendliness between the two countries. If Your Excellency should find it to be possible to send either to *The Peacemaker*, or to some other journal, any assurance of your own maintenance of the noble friendliness towards England to which you have given expression, I believe that the advantage might be great; but of course Your Excellency will judge whether or not this is a step which you can rightly and appropriately take.

With the assurance of my profound respect and with grateful recollections of Your Excellency's visit last year to England.

PROFESSOR ADOLF HARNACK *to the* ARCHBISHOP OF CANTERBURY

14th January, 1912.

I express my hearty thanks for the friendly lines which you have addressed to me. So far as I remember I have not yet received any invitation to write an article for the Magazine *The Peacemaker*. It would be difficult for me *at present* to write any such article, for the English Government has not denied the assertion that last Autumn it was nearly on the point of suddenly surprising us with war. To me personally, it is of the highest value that Your Grace writes that this assertion is absolutely without foundation, but I am unfortunately not in the position to convince my fellow-countrymen of this, so long as the English Government is silent, or at least so long as it does not prove to Germany that it cherishes friendly dispositions. I have never doubted that Your Grace and all the distinguished men who of late years have promoted friendly relations between England and Germany, stand true to the dispositions of Peace, and I can also on my side give the assurance that I hold firmly to them; but it does not stand in my power, nor in the power of my Fatherland, to disperse the gloomy cloud which has come to us across the Channel, and even if there were, as Your Grace asserts, no cloud, yet at least it was a shadow, which it lies with England alone, not with us to disperse. Until then, we who are the friends of Peace in Germany, must impose upon ourselves a certain reserve—not in our dispositions, nor in our activity in favour of Peace in our own Country—but certainly in our external relations.

I remember gratefully and gladly my visit to England.

P.S. N.B.

I beg Your Grace to consider whether a publication of our correspondence would be in the interests of the matter, and whether it would be most appropriately done through Your Grace or through myself.

The Archbishop replied, after consulting Sir Edward Grey at the Foreign Office:

The ARCHBISHOP OF CANTERBURY *to* PROFESSOR ADOLF HARNACK

24th January, 1912.

I must apologise for my delay in thanking you for your very important letter which I received a few days ago. I have considered most carefully all that Your Excellency has said, and I have also had further opportunity of communication with those who are, in this great matter, entitled to speak with absolute knowledge and authority. In the postscript of your letter you refer to the question of the possible publication of our correspondence. I am sure you will allow me to tell you frankly that, in view of what you have said in your letter, it seems to me that its publication would certainly not have any beneficial influence on the public opinion of the two countries. In any case I had not regarded my correspondence with you as being other than a private communication passing between one friend of peace and another. Your letter leads me to fear that you still attach some credence to the entirely false reports which appear to have gained, I know not how, some currency to the effect that England had unfriendly intentions towards Germany. These reports are really unjust to us, for I have placed myself in a position to be again able to assure you from absolute personal knowledge that it has, during recent events, been the firm intention of England not to be the first to break the peace, and not to encourage any one else to do so.

So far as I understand the matter, the anxiety which was felt by the public in England, (although a great many of us did not share it) was on account of their doubt as to the ultimate intention of the German Government. My own belief that there was no ground for alarm on that score may now, I hope, be corroborated by what you have said in your letter to me, a letter which clearly implies that there has been no unfriendly intent whatever on the part of Germany.

I need not again assure Your Excellency how thankful I shall feel if in any way you and I are able quietly to co-operate by the help of God, in establishing upon an impregnable basis those relations of perfect amity and mutual respect which ought always to subsist between our two countries, and which England, I assure you, desires to strengthen in every reasonable way.

PROFESSOR ADOLF HARNACK *to the* ARCHBISHOP OF CANTERBURY

29th January 1912.

I thank you sincerely for your friendly letter of Jan. 24. I have brought to the knowledge of a good number of people the communication of Your Grace that the wide-spread opinion in Germany that England intended to attack us in the Summer is 'absolutely without foundation', and I promise myself a good effect from this.

I must for the rest observe that the opinion did not arise in Germany, but came to us from England, and became current with us because it was not denied for a long time. The opinion has played *no* role in our elections so far as I can definitely assure myself.

I have, at the wish of English and German friends, written a short article upon the state of feeling in Germany. This I could not and ought not to represent as other than it is. The article will appear in a few days and immediately be translated into English.

Just as the sentiments of Your Grace and our English friends in regard to peace have not altered, so may you be sure that we also wish nothing more earnestly than that we may soon be able to say:—

'*Nubicula fuit; transiit.*'

I hope definitely that it will come to that, and I see in the work for the brightening up of our relations an important pledge for it, and one for which we may be thankful.

The situation was greatly eased. And it was therefore an indication of a better atmosphere when Lord Haldane went on an embassy to Berlin in the hope of clearing up political misunderstandings. Mr. Asquith made a reassuring declaration in the House of Commons on February 14; and the German Chancellor, Bethmann von Hollweg, made a similar statement in the Reichstag on February 15.

On March 25, the first Annual Meeting of the British Council of the Associated Churches for fostering friendly relations between the British and German peoples was held in London. It was reported that there were already 7,000 members in Britain and the Colonies. The Archbishop made a long speech strongly emphasizing the spiritual links between Germany and England, and the overwhelming mass of British public opinion in favour of friendship, and he also said:

> When people talk lightly of inevitable war, they are creating the mischief which they profess to deplore. It is a notion absolutely untrue. We believe the thing to be morally impossible in view of our home responsibilities both in England and Germany. We are representative for the inculcation of that right spirit of dealing with those who in national life as in private life are our neighbours and our friends. Then we feel it to be impossible in view of our world-wide responsibilities to other peoples.

Dr. Spiecker and Dr. Adolf Deissmann also spoke. The latter dwelt on the importance of each of the two nations being strong, and of the Committee's task being that of destroying the tares of mistrust which were constantly springing up among the wheat of British and German hopes.

In the following year the Archbishop had himself hoped to visit Berlin to congratulate the German Emperor upon the completion of twenty-five years of his reign. But illness of a rather serious kind prevented his going, and Bishop Boyd Carpenter took his place. He wrote to Dr. Dryander, the Kaiser's senior Court Chaplain:

The ARCHBISHOP OF CANTERBURY *to* DR. DRYANDER

11 June 1913.

> It is a matter of profound disappointment to me that I am in consequence of recent illness unable to have the privilege of being one of the Deputation which is next week to have the honour of presenting congratulations to His Majesty the Emperor...
>
> The occasion gives a noteworthy opportunity of expressing our sense of the great service which His Majesty has rendered to the cause of International Peace. At this moment everything is happily tending to a truer understanding of the essential brotherhood of Germany and Great Britain.

II

A large part of 1912 was marked by great industrial unrest. In the early spring there was a coal strike of unprecedented magnitude. In the summer another great strike took place in the Transport Trade, and in December there was a strike on the North Eastern Railway. Many were the appeals made to Lambeth that the Archbishops should intervene. But however great an Archbishop's sympathy may be, or however strong his wish to help, the problem of helping with effect is less simply solved than the eager petitioners usually understand; while these eager petitioners sometimes think that they have taken effective action themselves by their appeals to him!

Archbishop Davidson's general attitude of goodwill and desire to help, coupled with a consciousness of the limitations which lack of peculiar expert authority imposed, is set forth at the end of a speech which he made in Convocation on February 17, 1912 on a resolution about the coal strike:

> Therefore I, with all my heart, support what has been proposed, and I will put it to the House as something which it is particularly suitable that we should join in. When each one of your Lordships was consecrated to the Episcopate, one of the questions asked of you was 'Will you maintain and set forth, as much as shall lie in you, quietness, peace, and love among all men?' That is one of the duties laid in our Ordinal on every Bishop at the moment of his consecration. The particular thought that was in the minds of those who compiled the Ordinal and used those words was probably not that which is specially in our minds at this moment. They were speaking rather of peace and love among those whose quarrels we have some special power of helping to reconcile. I imagine that the personal power of Bishops to intervene, after the fashion in which our great Prophet-Bishop, Dr. Westcott, intervened years ago, has a little passed out of our hands and hardly exists to-day; but I know that every one of us would be anxious to do anything in his power. That it would be useful, I need not say. I believe that I am right in thinking that those who can judge best, feel that the attempt at personal intervention must be left in the hands of experts, although a noble example has been set by the late Bishop of Durham. The Government has now practically taken the matter in hand with high expert knowledge, and entrusted it to men with particular power to deal with it. I think that for us to intervene at this moment would probably be an anachronism, but none the less we wish to show that we agree about this matter with our whole heart. This Resolution will show our interest, and we bid our people fall to prayer to get help in the very best possible way.

In a burning social question of another kind the Archbishop did intervene, with considerable vigour. This was the nefarious White Slave Traffic; and the occasion was the introduction of the Criminal Law Amendment Bill. He made this attack both in public meetings and in Parliament. It was not often that he expressed himself with passion, but he never found it 'easy to keep cool' in face of 'the nefarious and well-established trade of the Procurer and the Procuress'. It is another aspect of him perhaps than that with which those who only knew him on the outside were familiar that finds vent in the words:

> And then the other objection; you must not increase the punishment—above all you must never use the lash—lest you degrade either the criminal or the man who flogs. Degrade whom? Degrade the villain who has sunk to the cowardly devilry of battening on the craftily-contrived ruin of innocent girls? I defy you, do what you will, to degrade that man. Will you degrade the man who wields the lash? A most unwelcome duty—but who would not honourably fulfil it if thereby he helps, as he will, to render less likely the ruin of one innocent girl? (Nov. 12th, 1912.)

Many of those, however, who welcomed his efforts to save innocent girls from such terrible exploitation, found him far too cool and rational in the movement to give women the vote. He was greatly disturbed by the violent courses and indignant language of the advocates of Women's Suffrage. One of the most prominent of these was Dr. Ethel Smyth, the well-known composer, a connexion of his by marriage. Here is a portion of the correspondence which took place:

DR. ETHEL SMYTH *to the* ARCHBISHOP OF CANTERBURY

[Undated. June 1913?]

With reference to the regrets recently expressed by Your Grace at the Church Congress that the women's movement should have become practically a struggle for the vote, may I point out that there is no reason for believing that the serious and gifted women who all the world over are heading in the same direction are by nature less capable and desirous than Your Grace of taking the wider views you advocate.

If these women have abandoned special fields of activity, such as municipal, rescue, missionary and other work in order to concentrate upon the vote, I submit it is because their woman's experience, as opposed to the theories of your Grace and other men about women, has shewn them that attempts to better woman's lot are worse than futile as long as we are without the direct leverage on Governments which the vote alone provides.

The effect of generalities being to paralyse action, I fancy Your Grace's exhortation will win more applause among politicians than among women.

There is one subject to which it is impossible not to refer, the death of Miss Davison.[1] I understand that last year Your Grace was privately approached with a request to invite prayer in our Churches for guidance on the woman's question, as was done in the case of the industrial unrest; that the request was refused; and that the result of that refusal has been the formation of the Church Protest Committee.

It comes then to this; that after persistently ignoring for years, from motives it is impossible to regard as spiritual, the greatest moral revolution the world has ever seen, the Church actually refused to women, who are her mainstay, what was conceded to outsiders, such as nonconformist and socialist voters, and foreigners, such as the revolutionary Chinese Government![2]

These things being so, is it surprising that one of our members has herself gone to plead our Cause before the Great Judge, and that we women bring to-day the grave charge, not only against the Government but against the Church, of responsibility for the tragic situation in which women find themselves, and more particularly for the death of Emily Wilding Davison?

I am forwarding copies of the above to several newspapers who probably will not print it; in that case it will appear in the weekly column to be started (owing to the rigid suppression of similar communications) in one of the Suffrage papers, entitled: 'Letters refused by the Daily Press.'

The ARCHBISHOP OF CANTERBURY *to* DR. ETHEL SMYTH

21st June, 1913.

Stress of work during this week, while I am only slowly regaining strength after illness, has delayed my reply to an important letter which I received from you a few days ago.

It would not, I imagine, be of any practical use were I to try to discuss with you by letter the question upon which you have so

[1] Miss Davison threw herself under the King's horse at the Derby and was killed.

[2] In April 1913, the Archbishop in Convocation had asked for the prayers of the Church for the Chinese Government on April 27, in response to an appeal for a day of prayer for the nation addressed by that Government to the Christian Churches in China, 'for the National Assembly now in session, for the newly established Government, for the President yet to be elected, for the constitution of the Republic'.

clearly made up your mind, namely the right manner of handling this large subject, and of meeting the difficulties which attend its settlement. It is a genuine help to me that those who feel strongly and even vehemently in the matter should write to me, as so many on either side do, without any reserve.

There is however one point in your letter—a simple matter of fact—about which I ought not to let you remain, as now, under a misapprehension.

It is a total mistake to imagine that I, or other Bishops, have, as you put it, 'refused' to enjoin or encourage the prayers of the Church that guidance may be given for the solution of these difficulties. On the contrary I and, to the best of my belief, all the other Bishops have reiterated again and again with all the weight at our command, a request that such prayers may be offered by all Christian people who think about the well-being of our Nation. I myself took opportunity at the opening of this year to urge upon all whom my words could reach, the duty of such prayer upon what I described as 'the huge and far-reaching question of the right share of Christian womanhood in the duties and responsibilities of the community'. I called attention to 'the sacred character of the question' and urged that it should be made the subject of constant and steady prayer.

That is merely one instance of what we have been saying and urging throughout the controversy. I have before me, for example, at this moment, the formal and authoritative direction of the Bishop of one of our most important Dioceses, issued a few weeks ago. He directs that, in the usual parochial intercessions, there should be incorporated a prayer 'that whatever should be given to women of fuller life, of greater honour, of worthier treatment by men, may be granted to the faith and prayer of Thy people' and that 'the hearts of men and women, especially of those who bear the Name of Christ, may be turned from the ways of violence and lawlessness'.

These quotations—and they could be indefinitely multiplied—will, I hope, show you that, as a simple matter of fact, you have been entirely mistaken as to the attitude and utterances of the Bishops, and that instead of refusing requests that prayer should be offered, we have everywhere inculcated it.

The comparison or contrast which you draw between what was done during the days or weeks of an acute industrial dispute, in directing at that particular time the use of a specific collect or prayer for the success of those who were endeavouring to effect a settlement satisfactory to both groups of disputants, and the different procedure followed in the case of this long-standing, complicated, and in the main 'political' controversy, is surely due to a forgetfulness of the contrast between the conditions of that controversy and the conditions of this.

I need not, I think, say more, except to assure you that nothing was further from my thought than to draw, as you suggest, a comparison between the weight belonging to other people's opinions, and the weight belonging to my own. We must in each case say what we believe to be true and right, as God shall show us how, in answer to our earnest prayers.

DR. ETHEL SMYTH *to the* ARCHBISHOP OF CANTERBURY

17th October, 1913.

I have been asked to let you know what perhaps you guess, that the interruption of the Church Services is to be a policy.

At this moment the Government of this country is deliberately trying to kill Annie Kenney (who is said to be dying, and will nevertheless be dragged back to prison) and to either kill or render insane other women, some of whom are absolutely blameless—and known to be so.

With all my heart I hope that the faithless, cowardly ministers of Christ, who let these things be done without protest, will reap their reward.

The ARCHBISHOP OF CANTERBURY *to* DR. ETHEL SMYTH

18th October, 1913.

I have received your letter of yesterday in which you tell me that what you describe as 'the interruption of the Church Services' is now to be 'a policy'.

I have, I think, done my best to understand and adequately to appreciate the meaning and intent of what is now going on. Nothing would be gained, I know, by my trying to discuss with you what is right or what is wrong in the arrangements made by those who, as administrators of existing law, are responsible for preventing, so far as they can do so, both crime and suicide.

But I should like to say to you that I simply cannot understand at all how thoughtful, intelligent, and in some cases I suppose religious-minded women can think that they will either do good to the community or advance the cause of what they believe to be right by going to Church in order to interrupt by disorder the prayers which are there being offered to God.

In the early part of 1914 fresh efforts were made by the leaders of the Women's Suffrage Movement to secure the Archbishop's support. Deputations visited Lambeth Palace from time to time, with a view, so their leaders said, to ascertain his mind about the forcible feeding of women in prison. Mrs. Pankhurst on one occasion sent a message asking him to visit her on her coming out of Holloway Prison. He expressed his readiness to pay the visit in the following letter:

The ARCHBISHOP OF CANTERBURY *to* MRS. PANKHURST

Private. 17th March, 1914.

I have received an intimation, but not from yourself, that you are seriously ill and that you desire to see me. You will, I am sure, realise that with every desire to be helpful to those who are in sickness and trouble, it is impossible for me, in view of my other work, to pay such visits on any extensive scale. I should, however, be exceedingly sorry to refuse as a clergyman to see anyone who in sickness or trouble desired on special grounds to speak to me on personal and private matters. If, therefore, you tell me yourself that such is your wish, and that it is on personal and spiritual matters that you desire to speak to me, I will do my best to arrange privately to pay a visit to you at the earliest possible date. I must ask, however, that, if I pay such a visit, it should be clearly understood that it is on these private matters and not on public questions that you wish to speak to me; and further that the visit should be altogether private, and that to the best of your power you will prevent any notice as to this visit appearing in the Public Press. Such notice might lead to the misunderstanding that I had called to see you in relation to public or controversial matters.

Her reply was as follows:

MRS. PANKHURST *to the* ARCHBISHOP OF CANTERBURY

18th March, 1914.

I do not wish to see you on personal and private matters.

I desire to have an interview with you so that I may try to make you realise the serious responsibility of the Church towards women at the present time.

Perhaps Your Grace may remember that some time ago we discussed the militant movement for the enfranchisement of women. I came away from that interview profoundly saddened by Your Grace's failure to understand the great need for the reform, and the gravity of the situation.

Since then, in common with many other women, I have been subjected to treatment by the Government that has brought me several times to the point of death. At such times one loses sight of worldly considerations, and many things become clear that ordinarily are hidden or obscure.

I come out of prison again feeling I have a message and a warning to give to those who, by their position, should be the spiritual guides of the nation. Your Grace should be the chief of these.

We have both of us grave responsibility in this matter; you as head of the Church, which has duties towards women; I as one whom many women accept as their representative in the Woman's Movement.

I again ask you to see me and hear what I have to say.

P.S. Since you wish it, your visit would be kept strictly private.

The Archbishop replied that he would make an appointment for a private talk. But the talk never came off, as Mrs. Pankhurst suddenly left London to take part in a Bye-Election in East Fife. In informing the Archbishop of her departure, she wrote (March 31, 1914):

MRS. PANKHURST *to the* ARCHBISHOP OF CANTERBURY

As long as I have life I shall call upon women to refuse to obey, and men to vote against, a Government which, while professing the principles of representative Government, refuses to apply them to women, and coerces, imprisons and tortures those women who revolt against the oppression of their sex.

Again I regret that you have failed to realise how urgent and important was my request that you should see me. An opportunity for the Church to help women to obtain justice has been lost.

Another incident concerned a certain Miss Annie Kenney, introduced by an acquaintance of the Archbishop, who had been put in prison as a militant suffragette and then been released. She called at Lambeth in a taxi at 9.30 a.m. on May 22. She was with a friend who sent in her card, with Miss Kenney's name in the corner, and then left her. The Archbishop found her sitting on the top of the stairs when he came out from breakfast. He listened to what she had to say, and told her that he must make quite clear his complete disapproval of militant methods both as wrong in themselves, and as injurious to a cause which he himself believed in. Miss Kenney then announced her intention of staying at Lambeth till the Bill was passed. She said this might be a matter of months, but need only be a matter of weeks, if the Archbishop and others would do their duty.

She stayed on through the morning, was given her meals, and sat in a room reading the papers. An Inspector of Police called in the afternoon, as the news had got abroad. Detectives were posted outside the different gates, and sent in a note to the Archbishop, saying that he and the household were placing themselves in a very difficult position by harbouring a woman who was wanted by the police.

Miss Kenney still refused to go, and the police came in about 6 o'clock on their own responsibility. Miss Kenney, after a little expostulation, went away quietly with them.

The Archbishop received a great many letters after this incident. In reply he used to tell his correspondents, after pointing out the misrepresentations to which he was subject, that it was foolish to suppose that any personal action on his part could bring about the great legislative change they desired. To one of these critics he said (June 27, 1914):

> I have for years taken keen interest in the whole subject and I know intimately some of those who have been foremost in the controversy. I have voted in favour of women's suffrage on the only occasion when I had an opportunity of doing so. I have been again and again in personal communication with the authorities, political and administrative. To pass to what is more sacred, and specially concerns the Church, I have continually published my directions or requests that prayer should be offered to Almighty God for wisdom and guidance in the matter, and have dwelt again and again in published sermons and speeches upon the need and duty of a larger view than that which is sometimes taken of a question which has proved to be so difficult and complex both in legislation and administration.
>
> These efforts I shall not relax, but it would be misleading if I did not add that while I am still not unhopeful of the conversion of English public opinion to the side of those who believe that a reasonable extension of the suffrage to women would be for the common good, the difficulty of bringing about the change is being steadily increased by the fact of these outrages taking place, by their strange condonation by some supporters of the movement, who do not themselves advocate them, and by the misrepresentations which are published as to the action of the prison authorities.

There were, of course, many (including one or two Bishops)

who desired a more aggressive action. It was even suggested by the Bishop of London that a Deputation of Bishops should go to the Home Office. But, with his customary shrewdness, the Archbishop pointed out that such a deputation must not only call attention to the gravity of the subject but suggest a positive line:

The ARCHBISHOP OF CANTERBURY *to the* BISHOP OF LONDON

17th June, 1914.

I return these interesting letters. By all means take a Deputation of Bishops to the Home Office if you have something to say. You will feel I imagine that there is no use in taking them there to tell the Home Secretary that the matter is very grave: you must have a constructive policy, and I presume that you have this as you think the Deputation worth while. I am myself in the thick of the general question, as these ladies do not leave me alone, but I do not find myself equipped with suggestions so definite that I could myself ask the Home Office to consider them. I rejoice that others see a way more clearly.

CHAPTER XLI

CLERICAL ORTHODOXY

'I tell you frankly that the Review . . . will be conducted on Oxford principles.'
'Orthodox principles, I suppose you mean, sir?'
'I do, sir; I am no linguist, but I believe the words are synonymous.'

GEORGE BORROW, *Lavengro*, ch. xxx.

ONE of the most anxious questions with which the Church had to deal at the beginning of the present century was the question of modern criticism and the Creeds. For the Roman Catholic Church, Pope Pius X in 1907 issued his Encyclical *Pascendi* and his decree *Lamentabili*, condemning in the most uncompromising terms what was popularly called Modernism. Not a few Roman Catholic priests came under the ban and suffered severely, especially after the new oath against the errors of Modernism had been imposed by an order of the Pope on all candidates for Holy Orders, confessors, parish priests, canons, and other ecclesiastics.

In this country, where a similar anxiety existed, there were many who wished the Bishops to give the same relentless reply as the Pope of Rome, and to mete out the same treatment to the troubles disturbing men's minds in the Church of England. The moment for decision arrived in the spring of 1914, a few months before the European War began. On the nature of that decision, and on the lead given by the Archbishop of Canterbury, very much was to depend.

For some three years before the crucial discussion took place in the Upper House of Canterbury Convocation, powerful efforts had been made to secure a Declaration by the Bishops on Clerical Orthodoxy. The leader of that movement, so far as the Bishops were concerned, was Charles Gore, Bishop of Birmingham, afterwards Bishop of Oxford, whom we have already seen as the head of that *Lux Mundi* group which had caused Dr. Liddon such pain twenty years before. He was a man who desired the Church to say in terms of unmistakable clarity exactly what it held on the whole question of modern criticism, and to denounce those clergy who held what he conceived to be wrong views with regard to the miracles of the New Testament, and especially the

Virgin Birth and the Resurrection of Christ. It was with him that the Archbishop had in some way or other to solve the question at issue.

The decision taken in 1914 was led up to by stages. In 1911 a book was published by J. M. Thompson, Fellow and Dean of Divinity at Magdalen College, Oxford, called *The Miracles of the New Testament*. This book was an examination of the miracles in considerable detail, which came to very radical and negative conclusions. It caused no small stir. The Bishop of Winchester (Dr. Talbot) who was Visitor and had episcopal jurisdiction in the College, withdrew Mr. Thompson's licence, though not without protests from many who took Mr. Thompson's side. Bishop Gore informed the Archbishop that he desired to bring the whole subject up before Convocation at the beginning of July; and accordingly drafted Resolutions of a most clear-cut character, with a preamble beginning:

> That in view of the fact that ordained ministers of the Church of England in recent years have published works, in which the actual occurrence of the miraculous events recorded in the Creeds —Our Lord's birth of a virgin mother and His resurrection on the third day from the dead—is either brought into doubt or positively denied. . . .

The Archbishop at once called for the help of the Bishops of Winchester and Ely (Dr. Chase), who agreed that precipitate action would be most unwise. The Bishop of Ely in particular protested against such a statement as that contained in the preamble, and stated that such books as Dr. Gore had in mind had been few and far between. Dr. Gore, in a generous letter, agreed to content himself with a private discussion when Convocation met, instead of a public debate.

Dr. Paget, Bishop of Oxford, died in August 1911, and was succeeded by Dr. Gore. The matter rested for a while, but at the end of 1912 Bishop Gore returned to the charge. Two new books of a disturbing character had appeared. One was *Foundations*, a book of essays edited by Canon Streeter, with a contribution by the editor on the Historic Christ. The other was Canon Henson's *The Creed in the Pulpit*. Dr. Gore wrote to the Archbishop, asking for leave to discuss the whole subject at the private meeting of Bishops in January 1913, with special reference to these two books. The Archbishop agreed. But some Bishops certainly objected in private, and told the Archbishop their views. Thus Bishop Jayne of Chester complained:

The BISHOP OF CHESTER *to the* ARCHBISHOP OF CANTERBURY

19th December, 1912.

Are Bishops' meetings to become largely gatherings at which the Bishop of Oxford delivers constant, copious and highly impassioned, if not minatory, allocutions to his brethren? This may be a hygienic safety-valve for him, but he has, I think, done something to change the atmosphere of the meetings. I raise these points with very genuine admiration for his many high qualities, and not without a readiness to be convinced that his *modus operandi* is valuable, if it does not become dominant. I am bound to say that, *at first sight*, his latest subject for discussion opens up a vista of awkward possibilities of other subjects.

The private meeting was held, but was profoundly unsatisfactory to Bishop Gore, if we may judge from the correspondence. He talked of resignation, but with the knowledge that he was not at all well; and as he 'again reached a good conscience about resignation' he decided to postpone the whole question for some months. The Archbishop's reply came from his heart:

The ARCHBISHOP OF CANTERBURY *to the* BISHOP OF OXFORD

25th February, 1913.

Private.

You and your anxieties have been seldom outside the range of my thoughts and prayers in these last weeks. I have re-read, and tried to weigh aright as in the sight of God, a good many things which seem to bear on the vital questions which we have been discussing. I am not going to try to argue afresh for what seems to me the right line for us Bishops to take. I feel (*most* honestly) that there is something which verges on impertinence in my bandying argument with you, whose theology, in the strict sense, is so incomparably deeper than mine is—upon the definitely theological side of the question. But when one comes to the practical thought of what your resignation would be taken, just now, to mean (however unreasonably or exaggeratedly),—I feel that I am better justified in giving expression to a strong judgement. If it were to bring about a great schism in the Church, with a big lurch or exodus Romeward—and a yet bigger movement into a *crystallised* Harnackism, I should feel that nothing but real necessity could have justified it, and that those of your friends who 'kept silence even from good words' had not been the truest friends to you or to the Church. Of course I am the last man who would try to press you to a placid acquiescence in what you feel to be vitally wrong. But the resignation of your See would, whatever you might say, be *taken* to mean very much more than this—a sense of the Anglican position as now interpreted having become untenable—a sort of move to 'Littlemore' with a consequent unsettlement (and not a wholesome kind of unsettlement) of quantities of our best Clergy. Therefore I am absolutely sure that such a step, if it is ever to come, ought not to come without much more ample thought, i.e. not just at present, and I do on my knees thank God that you have decided at all events to do nothing during the next few months. It would be to me a very real gain to secure an opportunity, some day before very long, of a quiet unhurried talk with you. I can say honestly that I never think over a talk with you without finding cause to thank God for something which you have taught or are teaching me; even when, as often happens, I cannot follow with you quite completely. You have been and are 'a succourer of many and of myself also'.

A year later the storm burst in full force. Bishop Frank Weston of Zanzibar had written his famous letter to the Bishop of St. Albans, in which he raised the whole question of what it is for which the Ecclesia Anglicana stands; and called attention in forcible terms to the disorders (as he judged them) of a Church which allowed inter-communion with Nonconformists at Kikuyu in East Africa, and tolerated Canon Streeter's views on the Incarnation. Controversy flared up. The Bishop of London was formally approached by a number of his clergy, mainly of the Anglo-Catholic school, who addressed a Memorial to Convocation asking their spiritual fathers (*inter alia*) 'to repudiate the claim of some clergy to reject the miracles of Our Lord's birth of a Virgin and the actual resurrection of His body from the tomb, because we believe that these truths lie at the very centre of the faith, and that the statements of the Bible and the Creeds with regard to them are perfectly plain and unambiguous'.

The Bishop of London presented the Memorial to Convocation on February 17, 1914, and announced, with the Archbishop's agreement, that he would move a resolution on the whole subject at the next group of sessions. The announcement had been preceded by private discussion, and a good deal of further conversation took place between the Archbishop and Gore. Thus the Archbishop noted at the time:

On Tuesday night, 17th February, 1914, I had some grave talk with Gore about Church affairs. I spoke of the possibility that I am myself growing to be out of touch with the strongest advances in the Church, or rather that these are growing to be out of touch with me. And I said that I should not remain at the helm if I found myself trying to steer a course clearly contrary to the best Church of England feeling and spirit. We talked about it gravely, and he said little. Next morning, Wednesday, the 18th, he talked to me very earnestly of his own accord—'I have been thinking over what you said, and I want to make my opinion clear to you. I know that I differ from you in many things. But I am profoundly convinced, with a certainty that is unshakable, that the very greatest disaster that could at this time befall the Church would be the loss of you from Lambeth. I have said this times without number to people who differ widely from you and perhaps from me. I am more and more sure of it, and I am bound to tell you so with all the gravity and earnestness that I can. There lives on earth no other man at present who could possibly do what you are doing for the Church of England. I say this very deliberately, and I think you ought to know it.'

He was moved a good deal, and obviously was tremendously in earnest. I have thought it well to set this down in view of questions and perplexities which seem to lie ahead for a good many of us.

At the end of March, a Resolution drafted by Gore, for the Bishop of London to move, was forwarded by the latter to the Archbishop. His Grace was in Bath, where Mrs. Davidson was recovering from a long and troublesome illness. The resolution ran as follows:

That 'in view of tendencies widely shown in the writings of the present day', this House, following the resolution of the Lambeth Conference of 1908, 'hereby places on record its conviction that the historical facts stated in the Apostles' and Nicene Creeds', and in particular our Lord's birth of a Virgin Mother and His resurrection on the third day from the dead, 'are essential parts of the faith of the Church'.

And further, inasmuch as the claim has been widely made that these Creeds can legitimately be recited by Clergymen in their public ministry when they have themselves deliberately ceased to believe that our Lord was in fact born of a Virgin or did (in the sense of the New Testament) rise again the third day from the dead, and inasmuch as the public opinion of the Church has been repeatedly challenged to allow this claim, we feel it to be our duty solemnly to affirm that we can give no countenance to what we cannot but regard as seriously contrary to that sincerity of profession which is specially necessary for the Christian Ministry.

On receiving the draft Resolution, the Archbishop replied to the Bishop of London that he could not possibly support the issue by the Bishops of any declaration in those terms:

The ARCHBISHOP OF CANTERBURY *to the* BISHOP OF LONDON

31st March, 1914.

I have of course known for a long time that the Bishop of Oxford was in favour of the issue of some declaration, whatever its cost, but I did not know that you agreed with him on the point. Anything that Gore says is entitled to far more than ordinary respect, and my deep personal affection for him and regard for his opinions make me always anxious to support him when I can. But, so far as I can at present see, I could not, even at your and his request, join in the issue of a declaration the outcome of which would, I honestly believe, be that we should render intolerable the position of quite a large group of our best and most thoughtful clergy, not because they themselves differ from you or me in their beliefs, but because they could not stand the issue of a new and authoritative declaration which, unless it be a mere truism, is intended to have the effect of pronouncing loyal churchmanship to be incompatible with a readiness to allow any 'reserve' or 'suspended judgment' as to the manner of receiving and holding certain credal clauses which the impugned men willingly, habitually and reverently use.

And he added:

To myself, if it really comes to this, it will be a matter so grave that I hardly like to contemplate what it might mean. Have you considered how you could practically *act* on it, if it were adopted by the House? I earnestly trust that you will let me have some talk with you about it, before you make this matter public, though I am sure you are not acting lightly.

The Bishop of London replied:

The BISHOP OF LONDON *to the* ARCHBISHOP OF CANTERBURY

April 3, 1914.

I need not say how appalled I was at the prospect you opened out before me yesterday. To lose *you* would be 'unthinkable' but do strengthen up all that you conscientiously can the declaration you are framing. I am very much afraid of losing Gore—the next greatest calamity to losing you. . . .

But surely it does not pass the wit of man to say what is *strong* enough without hurting the good people you mentioned. Will you send me also the Charge in which you declared your own personal belief. That will be a great help to me in dealing with others.

Meantime there was a warfare of pamphlets in which Drs. Gore, Gwatkin, Bethune-Baker, Strong, Sanday, Streeter, and others took part. The most trenchant was by Gore, and the central paragraph in his Open Letter[1] follows:

I believe these narratives to be really true and trustworthy. But that is not now the question. The question is, Is it consistent with the sincerity which ought to attach to public office, and especially to public office in the Christian Church, that a man should pledge himself to the constant recitation of these creeds, as an officer of the society which so strenuously holds them, if he personally does not believe that these miraculous events occurred, if he believes that our Lord was born as other men, or that His dead body did in fact 'see corruption' . . .?

Now our Church has been, over a considerable period of years, publicly and repeatedly challenged by some very distinguished men to allow the recitation of the creeds by those who do not believe the miraculous events, and who in their books give their reasons for dissenting in mind from what they must affirm with their lips. The challenge has been so steadily and repeatedly made, without any formal expression of the Church's dissent, that we are as near as possible to official complicity. Under these circumstances I feel certain that, unless without delay, we as the Church, through our Bishops declare that we cannot regard as tolerable the proposed licence, we must be regarded as corporately committed to allow what we refuse explicitly to disown.

On the other side we may quote Dr. Sanday:[2]

I would make bold to claim that our critical English scholars of the left wing, including especially those named by the Bishop of Oxford, are not less deserving of the respect and gratitude of their countrymen. There is nothing wanton about them, nothing supercilious, nothing cynical; they obey their conscience, and go where their conscience leads them; they are evidently, all of them,

[1] *The Basis of Anglican Fellowship*, C. Gore, pp. 13, 14.

[2] *Bishop Gore's Challenge to Criticism*, W. Sanday, pp. 30–1.

genuinely religious men and good Christians. I would say of all but one (so far as I know) of those who have written on these subjects that they show an anxious desire to conserve all that can be rightly conserved of the old beliefs. And so much at least I would claim for myself.

If it is said that what I have written is Modernism, I would reply that I believe—I emphatically and hopefully believe—that a sound and right Modernism is really possible; that the Saviour of mankind extends His arms towards the cultivated modern man just as much as He does towards the simple believer. I believe that the cultivated modern man may enter the Church of Christ with his head erect—with some change of language due to differences of times, but all of the nature of re-interpretation of old truths, and without any real equivocation at his heart. I believe that he can afford to say what he really thinks—provided only that his fellow Christians of more traditional types are willing to greet him with the sympathetic intelligence which he deserves, and do not turn towards him the cold shoulder of suspicion and denunciation.

Less than a month now remained before the meeting of Convocation. The Archbishop bent his whole strength to secure a Declaration which he could himself *ex animo* accept. Of those whose help he sought, the Bishop of Ely gave the greatest service. Bishop Chase was a scholar himself, had been President of Queens' College, Cambridge, and was an authority on New Testament criticism, besides being a man of great wisdom and prudence; and had recently published a valuable essay on *The Gospels in the Light of Historical Research*. He at once demurred to the draft proposed by the Bishop of London and Bishop Gore, and prepared a reply to the Memorial of a more positive character (April 6, 1914):

Inasmuch as there is reason to believe that the minds of many members of the Church of England are perplexed and disquieted at the present time in regard to questions of Faith and of Order, this House feels it to be its duty to put forth the following Resolutions:

This House desires to adopt the words of the Second Resolution of the Lambeth Conference in 1908 and, 'in view of tendencies widely shown in the writings of the present day, hereby' to place 'on record its conviction that the historical facts stated in the Creeds are an essential part of the Faith of the Church'.

And further this House, while ready to accept the well established results of Biblical criticism, solemnly affirms that in its judgement the denial of any of 'the historical facts stated in the Creeds' is not compatible with that sincerity of profession which it holds to be necessary in the Ministers of the Word and Sacraments.

The BISHOP OF OXFORD *to the* ARCHBISHOP OF CANTERBURY

Private. 7th April, 1914.

You will get, perhaps have already received, an 'open letter' of mine. I don't feel sure how much you will disapprove of it. But, as you will see, if you are good enough to read it, it involves certain consequences. Especially that I must put down on the *Agenda* paper for the next Convocation this resolution. (I shall be sending it up on Thursday or to-morrow.)

'That inasmuch as the claim has been widely made that the Apostles' and Nicene Creeds can legitimately be recited by clergymen in their public ministry when they have themselves deliberately ceased to believe that our Lord was in fact born of a virgin or did (in the sense of the New Testament) rise again the third day from the dead, and inasmuch as the public opinion of the church has been repeatedly challenged to allow this claim, we feel it to be our duty as bishops solemnly to affirm that we can give no countenance to what we cannot but regard as seriously contrary to that sincerity of profession which is specially necessary for the Christian ministry.'

I *hope* the Bishop of London will make this (or the like) one of *his* resolutions, and if so, of course, mine must be withdrawn. But otherwise (and no declaration of *our own belief merely* would satisfy me), I must press this declaration to a public discussion, and I should feel that a refusal to repudiate the 'Liberal' claim—being really the same thing as conniving at it—carried with it for me the last consequences.

I think I had better tell you this quite simply. But I do not want to say anything of this kind about consequences to the public.

But I do mean to press this particular matter to a public discussion or public vote.

The ARCHBISHOP OF CANTERBURY *to the* BISHOP OF OXFORD

Private. 9th April, 1914.

I have received your two letters and the copies most thoughtfully sent of your pamphlet, which, like the letters, I have read with earnest care. I note too that you have sent to Lee, for the Convocation *Agenda*, the Resolution whereof you have given me a copy. Now, I cannot help thinking from the letters, sent to me by the Bishop of London, from Ely and Winton as well as from his (London's) letters that we shall find ourselves less widely sundered than you suppose. *Ely*, on the lines of his recent preface, which you commend in your pamphlet, has drafted a Resolution (perhaps you have seen it) which goes very far with you as pronouncing the denial of credal statements to be incompatible with the sincerity we must require. How far we could all sign what he has written I am not at present sure, but its phraseology relieves me of some of the difficulty I feel about your own wording, and I can't help thinking that, with a little care, we might arrive at a statement which could be accepted by us all. The Bishop of London agreed with my suggestion that, for the Agenda paper which is published before we meet, it would suffice that he should say,

'The Bishop of London to call attention to the recent Memorial presented etc., and to move a Resolution.'

The Resolution itself, which he means to propose, would be printed and circulated privately for the *Bishops* to consider before the Convocation meets—but we want to avoid if possible the circulation to the outside public of rival Resolutions, for them to discuss in any inflammatory way before Convocation meets, and therefore before they have heard your own weighty words with which you would accompany the actual *moving*. Surely the notice, as given by London, will suffice *beforehand* for the public, and would deprive you of no right or advantage as to the wording you prefer. For I can quite definitely promise you that you shall have opportunity, in public debate, of moving the exact words you yourself like best—and there would therefore be no difficulty in everybody knowing exactly what you want us to accept and say.

I earnestly trust you will regard this as adequate, for I think you will share my apprehensions as to the mischief of an outside discussion of rival Resolutions prior to the speeches of the Bishops who explain and expound them. Pray tell me that the process I have suggested commends itself to you; or, if it seems to deprive you of any rightful opportunity, tell me how it does so and I will do my utmost to prevent it. Personally I should like a fuller reference to the weighty and well hammered-out words we used in the Encyclical of the Lambeth Conference, and I have drafted something to that effect. But I am not very determinedly bent on this, if the Bishops prefer other wording which I could conscientiously accept.

You a little misunderstand me about 'Ministering discipline'. I quite realise that you don't invite us to enter upon *prosecutions*. But all sorts of questions about Licence etc. may arise wherein each case has to be judged on its own merits, and I fear greatly what we might do in hampering ourselves by using words difficult of interpretation and practice in particular cases. But all this we can discuss privately, before the public debate—and in that public debate, I promise you, that, so far as I can ensure it, you shall be absolutely unhampered.

May God the Holy Spirit guide us to a right judgment both as to what to say and *how* to say it.

The next few days produced various alternative drafts from the Archbishop himself and the Bishop of Winchester. The Archbishop's own draft was long, and full of quotations from the Lambeth Conference of 1908, and contained nothing corresponding to the vital paragraph quoted in Gore's letter. Gore felt bound to insist that some of those whose views he condemned 'are in no tentative position. They have all come *not to believe* that certain alleged events occurred.' He added, April 12, 1914:

The Bishop of Oxford *to the* Archbishop of Canterbury

I can't tell you how I feel for you if not with you. But I feel no doubt that it will not be you who will be found on May 2nd in an impossible position. I feel a troubled sinking at the heart: but no quivering of conscience.

In a letter to the Bishop of London, Gore showed how deeply he was distressed by the possibility of resignation of which the Archbishop had spoken:

April 11, 1914.

I would naturally do anything my ultimate conscience would allow to avoid such a catastrophe. But I am sure no mere declaration of *our belief* will suffice. It is *their challenge* we have to meet.

Meanwhile the Bishop of Ely drafted his proposal. But how far was the Bishop of Ely prepared to include in his draft 'the substantial repudiation of an intolerable claim'?

The following letter from the Bishop of Ely to Gore brings out very clearly the difference between actual denial and suspension of belief:

The Bishop of Ely *to the* Bishop of Oxford

15th April, 1914.

The words 'the denial of any of the historical facts stated in the Creeds' were very deliberate. It seems to me—and I can hardly say how strongly I feel it—that the position at the present time is a very complex one and a very delicate one. We Bishops have many kinds of persons to consider in any declaration we put forward. We must allow that e.g. the Virgin Birth is not a matter so clear and beyond question as it used to be to our Fathers and our Grandfathers with their old view of the Bible. I am sure that there are many men who do not deny and do not expect that they will ever deny—certainly are as far as possible from wishing to deny—who are perplexed and wait for the Spirit of God to teach them. There are an infinite number of stages between belief and disbelief, and apparent disbelief at the moment is very often temporary and passes away. Some of us—certainly I myself—have in past days gone through experiences of this kind when we have been overdone or disappointed or out of health bodily or spiritual. Then the light of God's countenance has again been manifested; and the difficulty has passed away. This is much more likely to be the case now than when we were younger men. Now, at times like that a rough challenge from authority may well make a scrupulous man *decide* on the negative side, as he never would otherwise have done. I greatly fear that a resolution of the kind you, I think, would desire might do infinite harm among those—specially younger men—for whom we all have a tender regard. Hence *I* could not touch in the Resolution what is subjective—the subtle inner processes of belief. If we condemn, let us condemn denial—disbelief which is so assured that it expresses itself. That, as I understand matters, saves us from what you fear—our silently acquiescing in the challenge put forth by some.

I have written with great frankness. I know that you will regard this letter as in confidence.

On April 17, Gore went to Bath to see the Archbishop. They were together over two hours. In the end agreement was reached, and a resolution satisfactory to both was achieved. Writing to the Archbishop that evening Gore said, 'I feel as if what we did to-day we did really under the leading of the Holy Spirit.'

The following is the form of the Resolutions as finally proposed by the Bishop of London in Convocation, April 29, 1914:

Inasmuch as there is reason to believe that the minds of many Members of the Church of England are perplexed and disquieted at the present time in regard to certain questions of Faith and of Church Order, the Bishops of the Upper House of the Province of Canterbury feel it to be their duty to put forth the following Resolutions:

1. We call attention to the Resolution which was passed in this House on May 10, 1905, as follows:

'That this House is resolved to maintain unimpaired the Catholic Faith in the Holy Trinity and the Incarnation as contained in the Apostles' and Nicene Creeds, and in the *Quicunque Vult*, and regards the Faith there presented, both in statements of doctrine and in statements of fact, as the necessary basis on which the teaching of the Church reposes.'

We further desire to direct attention afresh to the following Resolution, which was unanimously agreed to by the Bishops of the Anglican Communion attending the Lambeth Conference of 1908:

'This Conference, in view of tendencies widely shown in the writings of the present day, hereby places on record its conviction that the historical facts stated in the Creeds are an essential part of the Faith of the Church.'

2. These Resolutions we desire solemnly to re-affirm, and in accordance therewith to express our deliberate judgement that the denial of any of the historical facts stated in the Creeds goes beyond the limits of legitimate interpretation, and gravely imperils that sincerity of profession which is plainly incumbent on the ministers of the Word and Sacraments. At the same time, recognising that our generation is called to face new problems raised by historical criticism, we are anxious not to lay unnecessary burdens upon consciences, nor unduly to limit freedom of thought and inquiry, whether among clergy or among laity. We desire, therefore, to lay stress on the need of considerateness in dealing with that which is tentative and provisional in the thought and work of earnest and reverent students.

Before the actual debate began, petitions were presented to the House from a very large number of persons, including 45,000 Evangelicals, a number of Members of Parliament, and Clergy and Communicants from various Dioceses. On the other side were petitions from the Council of the Churchmen's Union, a large number of University Professors and others, headed by the Dean of St. Paul's.[1] The central paragraph in the last petition is as follows:

While asserting without reserve our belief in the Incarnation and Resurrection of our Lord Jesus Christ, we submit that a wide liberty of belief should be allowed with regard to the mode and attendant circumstances of both.

We believe that real study, thought, and discussion will be discouraged if clergymen, who, in matters not affecting the essential truth of Christianity, arrive at conclusions which are opposed to traditional or momentarily dominant opinions, are to

[1] Dr. W. R. Inge.

> be removed from their offices or denounced as dishonest for retaining them. We venture to recall to your lordships the dictum of Archbishop Temple, 'If the conclusions are prescribed, the study is precluded'.

The debate which followed was on a high level, and lasted two days. Gore expressed his own thankfulness for 'the solemn and measured' Resolution. He did not pretend that every word in it was such as he would have wished it to be, but he thought that it did precisely hit the point, and that what it said was satisfactory, serious, and sufficient. He accepted, the more he thought about it, the word 'denial'. He appreciated the note of tenderness with all trials of doubt, all tentative positions: and agreed that they were rightly tolerant until a man reached the stage of denial. And if unhappily men finally made up their minds that they must deny, and not affirm, the occurrence of the miracles, then they could no longer legitimately recite the Creeds as Ministers of the Church.

The Archbishop summed up the discussion on April 30. He referred to the variety of the memorials, and his own instinctive distrust of episcopal declarations, but he agreed that a general answer was called for, and this 'though not with a very glad mind' he was prepared to give, in the form proposed by the Bishop of London. He continued:

> Some of you know how great have been my own difficulties in regard to shaping the sentences which may effect what we want to effect without doing what I think mischievous and harmful. Its original form or forms suggested in the wording of the memorials or otherwise did not commend themselves to me. I did not wish to speak of those who had in their own hearts, which God alone can read, 'come to disbelieve' in this or that. Nor again did I wish to single out and specify particular clauses in the Creed. Our words ought, I thought, to be not less grave, but to be more general, and I desire, here and now, to make it quite clear what, as I understand it, we are doing, and what we are not doing, when we pass this Resolution. We do not, as I understand our words, say to students or seekers after truth, as such, 'Stop; that path is barred, that conclusion is forbidden; you must not go there.'
>
> If we did, we should be open to the taunt conveyed in the phrase which has been quoted more than once as used by Dr. Temple in his Rugby days, 'If the conclusions are prescribed, the study is precluded'. So much attention has been called to that phrase

that I should just like to remind you that it occurs almost incidentally in the course of a long letter written by Dr. Temple in the days of his Rugby Headmastership. When the time came, about thirty years afterwards, for the biography of Archbishop Tait to be published, I went to Dr. Temple and asked him what he would like me to do about that correspondence. Characteristically he said, 'I see you must for the story's sake publish some of it; you had better publish it all.' I replied that it seemed to me that there were many things in the letters on either side that might, without the slightest detriment to the narrative, be omitted. 'No,' he said, 'you had better publish it all. I was a young man, and I said things I would not say now; but I was mightily angry.' One loved him for saying it; it was splendid; but it would be a simple blunder of fact were we to take the phrase as a deliberate Episcopal dictum governing our action in such a matter as this.

If we were by this Resolution saying to students as students, 'We prescribe conclusions beyond which you must not go', I should agree that it would be a mockery to tell them to study, and then to arrest them in such a manner. I do not say anything of the kind. Rather I would say to every honest student of these matters, 'Follow the truth; do your utmost to find it, and let it be your guide, whithersoever it may lead you.' Such study, fearless and free, is the strength of the Church's progress. We owe much at all periods of our Church's life to the fearless student and thinker and teacher. Therefore I should say to every conscientious student, as student, 'Do not let your study be hampered by a single thought about what the consequences of this or that conclusion may be to you or to others. If it is true, go forward for that truth, go forward bravely. Even if it should come about (though why should it?) that you find yourself led far from the beaten path, the path you used to tread, the path that your friends tread still, do not imagine that therefore God has deserted you. If you can still call yourself and feel yourself a Christian, thank God for that. Come and be nourished by the Sacrament of His love, if you can honestly take it and hold yourself in any real sense a Christian.' My lords, I find it hard to conceive of any case in which I should, on the mere ground of his opinions, refuse Communion to an honest man, an honest student as such, if he called himself a Christian and asked for the Sacramental gift, whatever I thought about the opinions he had formed. Therefore never let it be said that we are checking or hindering the search for truth. It is not so. Our whole attitude as guides and teachers would, in my opinion, be set wrong and put out of its course if we were to take the line of discouraging among students and scholars an honest and fearless search for truth.

He then emphasized the responsibility of the teacher, and the distinction between accredited Clergy, and students and inquirers:

Our Church of England spirit has, for centuries, been a spirit of comprehension. She has asserted large principles of liberty. Men have braved the fires of Smithfield in face of authority which would bid them make their reason blind and simply obey. The Reformation, with its fresh air, sunlight, and freedom, is not for nothing in Church history. Therefore I, for one, would beware of taking any step which, to a reasonable observer, could even seem to be stopping freedom of inquiry and hampering freedom of thought. If I considered that our Resolution did that, I would vote against it with all the strength in my power. But does our Resolution do anything of the kind? It does nothing of the sort. Those whom we warn here are 'the ministers of the Word and Sacraments'. We do not warn them in their capacity as students and inquirers, but as accredited clergy, who are entitled, on the strength of the authority given by the Bishops, to stand up as the Church's chosen spokesmen and teachers, and what we say to them is clearly different from what we should say to the mere student and inquirer who had no such trust and no such responsibility. Here are the words. 'We express our deliberate judgement that a denial of any of the historical facts stated in the Creeds goes beyond the limits of legitimate interpretation, and gravely imperils that sincerity of profession which is plainly incumbent on the ministers of the Word and Sacraments.' In speaking of 'sincerity of profession' we are not referring merely to a man's assent to the prescribed formula, but rather to the whole setting of his ministerial work, and the presentment of the Creeds to the people. When a child is brought to be baptized, the minister is called upon to ask the godparents clause by clause to go over the Creed, and to ask them whether they steadfastly believe it. For such ministering it is surely essential on his part that he should believe it himself and boldly stand by it. But even towards men who do hold that trust and responsibility, who are among the clergy and who are students of these subjects, we desire with earnestness beyond words to show to them throughout their investigations and inquiries a considerateness, a respect, a patience, a hopefulness, and an encouragement to the utmost of our power. We are bound to do so on the ground of our fatherly relation to those whom we want to help and stimulate as fellow-students, and whose difficulties we are eager to smooth, and whose path we want to guide aright where we may. We value with them the love of truth, and the liberty of thought; we value the close friendship which links them and us. Some of us have our own ample personal experience of such difficulties, and therefore we should extend a sympathetic and considerate hand to them. To such men we are not inquisitorial. The Resolution does not say 'If you feel that at present you do not steadfastly believe this or that'. The man's present position may be anxious, unhappy, hesitating, and for that very reason temporary. What do we say to a man who distinctly maintains, 'I recognise that the Faith of the Church of which I am a minister rests on a great basis of historic as well as doctrinal statement, and part of that historic statement I deny'? To him we deliberately say, 'Hold; consider your position as an accredited spokesman claiming the Church's authority to teach.'

He ended with a reference to the petition presented by the Bishop of Southwark[1] on behalf of certain University Professors of Theology and others:

We may be making a mistake in any set declaration for which we vote, but we do it with the humble thought that if, trusting to the guidance of God the Holy Spirit, we do our best, we shall receive such aid from on high as to secure that we shall not be doing harm, but good, in the long run. I do not wish to be too dogmatic about it, but I do not myself see anything in the actual wording of what is obviously the weightiest of the memorials that were presented to us, that to which the Bishop of Southwark yesterday called attention, which is necessarily inconsistent with what we are now declaring. Put the two documents, the Petition and our Resolution, side by side, dismissing all thought of who are the men who are supporting either of them, and I confess that I find nothing in the two that is radically or essentially inconsistent. They ask for reasonable liberty, and we propose that they shall have that liberty, but there are limits to that liberty, and we have tried in some measure to define it. Our words are carefully drawn. I can accept them. They are grave; they are honest; and in my heart I believe they are true.

An amendment by the Bishop of Hereford, deprecating the issue of any fresh declaration at the present time, having been defeated, the Bishop of London's Resolutions were carried *nem con.*

Certain words in the Archbishop's speech, particularly his reference to the petition presented by the Bishop of Southwark,

[1] Dr. Burge.

had made Gore uneasy, and he both spoke and wrote to the Archbishop about it. The following letters passed:

The BISHOP OF OXFORD *to the* ARCHBISHOP OF CANTERBURY

House of Lords. April 30, '14.

Private.

May I put on paper as shortly as possible the drift of what I said just now in the motor?

I understood that we had agreed upon a form of words which substantially said *no* to a specific claim of Rashdall and his friends: viz. that a man might (deliberately and finally) deny that our Lord was born of a virgin or that he rose again from the grave in his body, and still remain an acting clergyman, reciting the Creeds. I thought we had agreed to mention 'any of the historical facts in the Creeds' without further specification, and to emphasize *denial* and not any less decided or emphatic state of mind. I thought the compromise lay in those two points. But granted these I thought our declaration was intended to say *no* to a specific proposal. I cannot therefore accept as fair your statement (as I understood it) that we are not by our declaration rejecting the petition of the Liberal Council *if we have regard to its known meaning.* And such a statement if made public would be *disastrous.* If we have not done this we have done nothing. At the last analysis it is precisely that only that was in question. Of course you can say 'We have not, *as far as their words* go, rejected their petition?' But that I think is quite unreal. Precisely what we have done is to say no to their petition as it is meant. If we are not understood to have done this, the whole weary matter will begin again. I did feel your speech as it was spoken seemed to imperil what I hope and trust has been the real gain.

Forgive me.

The ARCHBISHOP OF CANTERBURY *to the* BISHOP OF OXFORD

Lambeth Palace. 1 May, 1914.

I am most grateful to you for your letter, following upon our talk in the car yesterday.

I am often a clumsy speaker, and I must have been even exceptionally clumsy yesterday if I so spoke as to leave any doubt as to the position I had reached, after my conversation with you at Bath, viz: that we ought in present circumstances formally to declare that a man who denies 'any of the historical facts stated in the Creeds' is, if he continues to minister, violating the conditions which are incumbent upon such ministry.

I will endeavour, in correcting the proofs of my speech, to secure that this is made absolutely clear and indisputable.

Further I will be on the watch for any clumsy or ill-considered word which could lead to the impression that I either share (or condone in ministers) certain opinions said to be entertained and published by some of those who signed the petition read by the Bishop of Southwark.

All I meant to say is that the *ipsissima verba* of that petition and the *ipsissima verba* of our Resolution are not incompatible with one another, when taken as they stand, (quite apart from the known personal opinions of those who have supported either document).

I hope this will show you that I am in no way whatever departing from, or whittling down, the undertaking I gave you at Bath, as to my attitude.

The BISHOP OF OXFORD *to the* ARCHBISHOP OF CANTERBURY

Cuddesdon, Wheatley, Oxon. May 2, '14.

Thank you indeed for your very kind and satisfying letter. I have ventured to send it to London in confidence.

On the opposite side came a letter from Dr. Sanday whom the Archbishop had seen, and with whom he had also been in correspondence about his own pamphlet in answer to Bishop Gore. He wrote:

The REV. DR. W. SANDAY *to the* ARCHBISHOP OF CANTERBURY

Christ Church, Oxford, May 10, 1914.

My first duty is to thank your Grace very sincerely for your kindness in sending me your Charge, which I am extremely glad to possess. If I may be allowed to say so, I read with the greatest interest your Grace's speech on the Resolutions. Nothing could be weightier or more really judicial.

CHAPTER XLII

KIKUYU, 1913–1914

A Church of England man hath a true veneration for the scheme established among us of ecclesiastic government; and though he will not determine whether Episcopacy be of divine right, he is sure it is most agreeable to primitive institution, fittest of all others for preserving order and purity; and under its present regulations best calculated for our civil State.

SWIFT, *The Sentiments of a Church of England Man.*

ON August 9, 1913, there appeared in *The Scotsman* a vivid report of a Missionary gathering in the heart of British East Africa at Kikuyu. It was written by an eyewitness, the Rev. Norman Maclean, a Presbyterian minister on a visit to the Missions of his Church in that area. He described it as 'The most wonderful gathering I ever saw'; for in it were represented all the 'Protestant Missions in the Protectorate'. The Church of Scotland was there, the Africa Inland Mission (American), the Friends, the United Methodists, the Lutherans, the Seventh Day Adventists, all these were present. Most surprising of all, here was the Church of England, represented by the Bishop of Mombasa (Peel) and the Bishop of Uganda (Willis), from two neighbouring Anglican dioceses, with a body of Anglican clergy. Some sixty missionaries of different Societies were present and Bishop Willis was in the Chair.

I

The business before the meeting was the consideration of a Scheme of Federation between the different missionary bodies working in British East Africa. No difficulty confronting Christian Missions in Africa is greater than that which is created by the riven and divided state of Christendom in their battle with Heathenism. Here was an attempt, among the leaders of a number of Missionary Societies, to take a step towards uniting by agreement upon a common basis, leading on to an African Church, and the effective presentation of the Christian faith to the Africans.

The proposed Scheme of Federation, as Mr. Maclean reported it, had as its basis:

1. The loyal acceptance of the Holy Scriptures as the supreme rule of faith and practice; of the Apostles' and Nicene Creeds as a general expression of fundamental Christian belief; and, in particular, belief in the absolute authority of Holy Scripture as the Word of God; in the Deity of Jesus Christ; and in the atoning death of Our Lord as the ground of our forgiveness.

2. Recognition of common membership between the societies in the federation.

3. Regular administration of the two sacraments by outward signs.

4. A common form of Church organization.

Mr. Maclean added: 'The Missions in British East Africa have solved the problem of how to coalesce Episcopacy and Presbyterianism.' And his report ended with the account of a service of Holy Communion held on the evening of the closing day, in the Scottish Church. Bishop Peel had celebrated in the form from the Anglican Prayer Book, a Presbyterian had preached the sermon, and all the Mission delegates, except the Friends, had received the Sacrament from the Bishop's hands.

The report aroused much interest in Church circles at home.

It should be added, so as to make the outline of the Scheme of Federation quite clear, (*a*) that each Society joining the Federation was to be autonomous within its own sphere, and each was bound to respect the others' spheres; (*b*) that recognized church members of the different Societies would be allowed to communicate in the churches of other Societies when residing temporarily in other districts; (*c*) that recognized ministers of each Society would be welcomed to preach in other federated churches; (*d*) that a common or public worship should be used with sufficient frequency to enable the members of all the churches to become familiar with a common order. The suggested common organization was that of parishes or small subdistricts, with Parochial Church Councils, leading on to District Church Councils, and a Representative Church Council linking them together. Members of the Parochial and District Church Councils would be members only of the Church occupying the district for which that Council is responsible. Further, it was the aim of the proposed Federation to keep steadily in view the ultimate ideal, the United Native Church.

The two Anglican dioceses concerned were closely connected

with the Church Missionary Society, and were of the evangelical school. Of the Bishops, Bishop Peel was the senior by some years, Bishop Willis being only in the early forties.

There was, however, another Anglican Bishop on the borders of Mombasa, besides Bishop Willis. The third Bishop, who felt himself very nearly affected by the action of his brethren, was Frank Weston, Bishop of Zanzibar in German East Africa. He was forty-three, had gone to Zanzibar in 1898, and had been consecrated as bishop ten years later. He was a brilliant speaker and teacher, the author of a striking study of the Incarnation which had won Dr. Sanday's praise, and was passionately devoted to the Africans. He was also an Anglo-Catholic—the Diocese of Zanzibar being supported by the Universities Mission to Central Africa.

On August 5, 1913, four days before the article had been printed in *The Scotsman*, the Bishop of Zanzibar wrote to the Archbishop of Canterbury, to whom, since there was no province of East Africa, he owed canonical obedience. He stated that, on his return from the mainland, he had found his staff much upset by the reports of the recent action of the two Bishops 'in federating the Protestant Sects with their Churches'. He said that he would wait for a copy of the document of federation, but, if he found it confirmed the reports, 'There is no shadow of doubt that this Diocese will refuse communion with the dioceses of Mombasa and Uganda.'

This letter, acknowledged by the Archbishop on September 6th, was followed by a more formidable pronouncement. The Bishop of Zanzibar wrote on September 30:

The Bishop of Zanzibar *to the* Archbishop of Canterbury

30 September 1913.

I feel intensely my position; your junior in years, in rank, your inferior in every way by many degrees; and yet speaking boldly to you! You must forgive me! And *please* don't think I am affected by the climate, as Winchester thinks and says of me!

I believe in Episcopacy, not in the Papacy of Rome, or in any system that ignores the equal *responsibility* of every Bishop for the witness that his Communion gives to the world.

Therefore, after a day of prayer with my local staff, I am risking my place in the respect of all the Bishops at home by acting in what may seem a most aggressive way. God will judge, Who knows our hearts.

I am the nearest Bishop to Mombasa and Uganda, and I tell you, my leader and Father in God, that the remedy which alone will touch the disease is a public admission on their part that they have not faithfully emphasized:

(1) The Athanasian Creed
(2) Confirmation
(3) Absolution
(4) Infant Baptism
(5) Holy Communion as different from Communion administered in Protestant Bodies
(6) The broad difference between Church Doctrine and that of the Protestant Bodies, so that it is impossible
(*a*) to communicate at one another's Altars
(*b*) to preach in one another's pulpits
(*c*) to prepare men of all these bodies with Church candidates either for Baptism or Ordination
and (7) the need of Episcopacy in the Church.

So that unless they will so 'recant', I must most humbly and respectfully urge my plea for a 'Synodical' Court, or, so far as I see to-day, resign my See on the ground that heresy has been condoned in the sight of the Missionary Churches in East Africa, who do not see things as we Englishmen see them.

I am at your feet in shame at seeming to interfere; yet I am a Bishop, and must answer to my Master. Please try to understand me.

And I am in sore distress; and my staff in real danger, and my people also.

Hence my prayer for as little delay as possible.

Will you of your kindness to me communicate with my representatives at home? They can give you all my mind and will send to me by cable messages from your Grace.

They are W. B. Trevelyan, of Liddon House, and R. E. Giraud, of Munster Square, and H. E. Simpson, Warden of the House of Charity, 1 Greek Street, Soho. He it is whom Your Grace should send to: he will call the others. I hope to come home immediately after Christmas—unless Your Grace *needs* me before. This will suit the diocese best; it will probably fit in with the general movement of the case.

I beg Your Grace's forbearance and forgiveness if I have erred in phrase or tone. The situation is intolerable: and I am more than usually human!

Accompanying this, was an indictment of the two Bishops, framed in the most official style, setting out the charges, including the charge that, on the closing day of the Conference Holy Communion was celebrated in a Presbyterian Church by the Bishop of Mombasa, 'the sacrament being given to many members of Protestant Bodies whose very existence is hostile to Christ's Holy Church.'

The indictment continued:

> Therefore We, Frank, by Divine Permission Lord Bishop of Zanzibar and East Africa, do by these presents accuse and charge the Right Reverend Father in God William, Lord Bishop of Mombasa, and the Right Reverend Father in God John Jameson, Lord Bishop of Uganda, with the grievous faults of propagating heresy and committing schism:
>
> And We do hereby most humbly implore Your Grace to obtain from them for publication in East Africa and Zanzibar a complete and categorical recantation of the errors which they have taught in word and action:
>
> Or failing that We do hereby request Your Grace to appoint us a day and place in which, conformably with Catholic precedent, We may appear before You and not less than twelve of Your Grace's comprovincial Bishops sitting with Your Grace as Judges of this cause, and to permit us there and then to meet the aforesaid Lord Bishop of Mombasa and Lord Bishop of Uganda, and in open Assembly to allow us to make and sustain our charges and accusations against them.

From this indictment by the Bishop of Zanzibar, a public controversy on an astonishing scale started in the English Press, and continued for a long while throughout the Churches. To some, the scheme of Kikuyu seemed a magnificent move forward to Christian reunion. To others, it appeared to be 'a certain step to the disruption of the Anglican Communion'.

'I doubt', wrote Bishop Gore to *The Times*, 29 December, 1913, 'if the cohesion of the Church of England was ever more seriously threatened than it is now.' It is well to note that both to Gore and to Weston this modernizing of the ministry, and looseness of view about the Church, was part of a wider modernist movement which seemed to threaten the foundations of the Faith.

II

The Archbishop of Canterbury was very well aware of the dangers to cohesion which the controversy and its settlement involved. But he was not disposed to be unduly alarmed. He replied as follows:

The ARCHBISHOP OF CANTERBURY *to the* BISHOP OF ZANZIBAR

22nd October, 1913.

I have received your very important letter of September 30th, together with the formal enclosure therein of the same date duly signed and sealed. It has reached me at a moment of special pressure, and in any case you will realise that so grave a matter requires quiet consideration with regard to the manner of dealing with it, as well as with regard to the merits of the questions raised. To the best of my belief there exists no precedent which would give clear guidance on procedure such as you suggest, but you will not understand me to mean that for that reason no such action could possibly be taken or a proper tribunal constituted to handle it. I will give quiet consideration to the matter next week. I imagine that in any circumstances there would rest with me some initial responsibility as to whether or not the suit (if that word may be used) which you desire to promote should or should not go forward—responsibility, I mean, corresponding to what is known in England as the Bishop's power of veto. I shall therefore have to consider preliminarily what are the indisputable facts of the matter apart from the question of the character attaching to what was done. It may, for example, turn out that the action of the two Bishops was not what you suppose it to have been. I find that Bishop Willis is expected in England almost immediately. This may enable me, without going into the merits of the case, to ascertain elementary facts about which I am at present in some uncertainty.

Should it appear to me to be necessary that you should come to England at an early date, I shall not scruple to tell you so. Matters of this kind are too important to be treated otherwise than with the utmost exactitude and care.

I am sending a copy of this letter to Mr. Simpson, with whom you ask me to communicate.

In a later letter (29 October) Weston told the Archbishop that Bishop Willis was staying with him in Zanzibar; and that he had explained certain points which would make it necessary for

Weston to amend his original appeal. But he said that he could not be satisfied that Episcopacy had been taught in the Kikuyu Conference as the vital foundation of the Church, or that the sacramental system had been given its right place; and he added that, as to Nonconformist celebrations of the Communion, 'We are bound to declare them null and void except as spiritual communion.' 'The Bishop is quite delightful, but, believe me, it is no use our going on side by side on the present lines. . . . He is sure all is well because he thinks it well.'

On receiving this letter (November 18) the Archbishop telegraphed to Bishop Weston to come home immediately for a Conference. Meantime Bishop Willis had written from Uganda on September 22 to tell the Archbishop that he also was coming home, in accordance with his Grace's advice. He reached London at the end of November and at once saw the Archbishop at Canterbury. After seeing him, Dr. Davidson told the Archbishop of York: 'The thing dwindles greatly as regards what is open to criticism when the facts are fairly told, apart from the question of the joint communion services held in the Presbyterian Church. The actual conference was wholly and avowedly subject to having all its resolutions submitted to the authorities in England.' And Bishop Willis wrote to Mrs. Davidson that he would never forget the Archbishop's kindness and sympathy. Bishop Willis also published a full statement of the facts with the text of the Scheme, in which he made it clear that 'no church and no society stands committed: the whole Scheme is still *sub judice*'. In a subsequent interview Bishop Willis agreed 'that the charges made against the Kikuyu Conference are two, more or less distinct, (1) based on the character of the scheme, (2) based on the character of the United Communion Service at the close of the Conference, which, it is agreed by Bishop Willis, was of a very exceptional character'. Bishop Willis, however, demurred when it was suggested that he should pledge himself in advance never under *any* circumstances to invite members of non-Episcopal churches to attend an Anglican celebration of the Holy Communion.

Bishop Weston reached London on February 6, 1914, and saw the Archbishop the following day. The Bishop asked very definitely for a formal handling of the charge, and expressed his own strong view, which he reiterated several times, that the case ought to be tried, and by the Bishops of the Province; not that he claimed with certainty to be one of those Bishops, but because the Archbishop of Canterbury was his Metropolitan, and as such could not try a case except with his comprovincial Bishops.

The Archbishop's memorandum of the interview ends:

> I could not help thinking, however, that he is really open to wiser opinions than those he has in the isolation of Zanzibar[1] given utterance to. He said, for example, that he had been a good deal puzzled by finding, as he now found, that Bishop Hine had given Communion to Non-Episcopal Missionaries, and again he said that Gore's opinions on *Kenosis* were to his mind as bad as the things said in *Foundations*, and yet Gore was his friend and guide in all these matters of Modernism. He was delightfully loyal, friendly, and frank, and I was much touched by his whole attitude and behaviour.

On February 9 the Archbishop published a full statement in which, after giving a narrative of the events, he announced his decision as to procedure. He refused to allow a trial of the Bishops of Mombasa and Uganda for heresy and schism, as the facts before him afforded no grounds for such proceedings; but he held that inquiry was essential, and proposed to summon the Consultative Body of the Lambeth Conference, an elected body of fourteen Bishops from different Provinces of the Anglican Communion. The Consultative Body would meet in July, and the Archbishop added:

> I shall submit my questions in the following form, and I shall be prepared to accompany my own statement by any written or printed communication which may, for that purpose, be placed in my hands by any of the three Bishops concerned:
>
> 1. In June 1913 a Conference of Missionaries working in British East Africa was held at Kikuyu, and the Resolutions of the Conference embodied a 'Proposed Scheme of Federation of Missionary Societies' with a view to ultimate Union of the Native Churches. The Bishop of Uganda, as Chairman of the Conference, has explained in a published Pamphlet that 'nothing has as yet been settled'. 'From the first', he says, 'it has been clearly understood that none of the signatories (of the proposed Scheme) claimed any power to decide. The utmost that has been done has been to submit to the authorities concerned what have seemed to the Missionaries in Conference to be feasible

[1] Bishop Weston had published *Ecclesia Anglicana: For what does she stand?* dated Zanzibar, 11 October 1913, dealing with Dr. Streeter's theology in *Foundations* as well as Kikuyu.

proposals in the direction of united action. No Church and no Society stands committed: the whole Scheme is still *sub judice.*' In accordance with this, the Bishop has formally submitted to me, as his Metropolitan, the draft Scheme. Some of its administrative provisions relate specially to the work of Missionary Societies as such, and have a technical character, necessitating their careful consideration by the authorities of the different Missionary Societies to which the signatories belong, as well as by others.

I desire to obtain the advice of the Consultative Body upon a larger question, namely: Do the provisions of the proposed Scheme contravene any principles of Church Order, the observance of which is obligatory upon the Bishops, the Clergy, and the layworkers of the Church of England at home and abroad? If so, in what particulars?

2. At the close of the Conference, the Bishop of Mombasa, assisted by the Bishop of Uganda, celebrated the Holy Communion according to the Order prescribed in the Book of Common Prayer. The Service was attended by a large number of the Missionaries who had taken part in the Conference, and many of those who communicated were not members of the Church of England and had not been episcopally confirmed. All, however, had taken as the basis of possible federation 'the loyal acceptance of the Holy Scriptures as our supreme rule of Faith and practice, and of the Apostles' and Nicene Creeds as a general expression of fundamental Christian belief.'

I desire to ask whether, due consideration being given to precedent and to all the circumstances of the case, the action of the Bishops who arranged and conducted the admittedly abnormal Service in question was, in the opinion of the Consultative Body, consistent or inconsistent with principles accepted by the Church of England.

Bishop Weston, in a long public reply, dissented from the Archbishop's answer, expressing his dissatisfaction with the Consultative Body, as a 'prejudiced commission of enquiry', and his regret at the Archbishop's ruling that he could not hear the Bishop of Zanzibar's appeal, as Metropolitan acting judicially with his comprovincial Bishops. After some further public correspondence on points of detail, the more satisfactory process of private conversation was resumed. And Dr. Weston was clearly a much more reasonable man in private than his letters alone would reveal. The talks, lasting sometimes for hours, covered various subjects. It became clear that, while opposed to the scheme, there was a good deal that might be accepted cordially by him and his friends. He promised, therefore, to draw up his own proposals for co-operation between Missionary Societies. It would be difficult to find a greater contrast than that between the mental methods of the two men. The Archbishop pressed hard upon the facts, while Bishop Weston spoke as impulse led him.

The Archbishop noted, after a talk on February 25 of nearly three hours:

> What struck me repeatedly in the conversation was that he does not think out his problems before coming to his conclusions. Several times, after he had been emphatic in saying that something or other was impossible to accept, he was ready, when I had pointed out the difficulties of the situation, to say, 'Perhaps I am wrong: I think after all I could consent to that', and so on. This was disappointing in a man who has had such opportunity during recent months of quietly thinking over everything.

A little later, after some very careful negotiations (for Weston could not see how hurt a brother Bishop might be by the charge of heresy and schism still not withdrawn) the Archbishop arranged for a talk between the two Bishops in his presence at Lambeth. It was a very private and friendly affair, after the first soothing words of the Archbishop; and it was concerned mostly with Bishop Weston's proposals for co-operation, which Bishop Willis urged should be published. Then the two Bishops were left alone to have tea together. After the talk Bishop Willis wrote as follows to the Archbishop:

The Bishop of Uganda *to the* Archbishop of Canterbury

Private. 18th March, 1914.

I write to thank you for arranging in spite of myself the interview this afternoon with Zanzibar. If it has done nothing else, it has served to renew the personal link between us, which, in a matter like this, is of supreme importance. We knelt down in prayer together, and parted, as we had parted at Zanzibar, on the best terms. Such a coming together will not have been in vain.

III

Bishop Willis returned to his diocese for a month, and Bishop Peel of Mombasa came next upon the scene. The Archbishop found him, to his surprise, quite as liberal-minded as the Bishop of Uganda. Amongst other things Bishop Peel was able to refute some of the specific personal charges which had been made against him by the Bishop of Zanzibar, regarding his attitude to the Zanzibar clergy and communicants.

After the last public letter of Bishop Weston to the Archbishop popular interest a little subsided, pending the meeting of the Consultative Body in July, though a very large correspondence continued to pour in on the Archbishop and each of the three Bishops. The Archbishop characteristically mobilized his forces, getting information and counsel from all manner of sources, the Metropolitans of other Provinces, Missionary Bishops, English diocesans as different as Jayne and Gore, and from scholars. An especially valuable piece of work was done by Dr. A. J. Mason, in the shape of an elaborate Catena of extracts from the ancient and the English Fathers on Episcopacy.[1]

The Bishop of Zanzibar, and the Bishops of Mombasa and Uganda, also prepared their respective cases. These subsequently appeared in print. It will assist the understanding of the issues, if we attempt briefly to state their points of view.

The approach of the two sides to the matter at stake was as different as could be. The very titles tell their tale. Bishop Willis's title is *Steps towards Re-union*; Bishop Weston's is *The Case against Kikuyu, a Study in Vital Principles*.

Bishops Willis and Peel offered a careful well-documented account of the whole proceedings, their history from 1908 to 1913, their relation to the resolutions of the Lambeth Conferences from 1888 onwards, and the peculiar difficulties of a policy of mere isolation. The writing was deliberate, solid, and even dull.

Bishop Weston was only concerned with ultimate questions, went to the root of churchmanship, and asked the meaning of the Church of England and the Church of Africa. His writing was that of a man on fire, brilliant, passionate, swift, very moving.

The Bishops of Mombasa and Uganda pointed out that the Lambeth Conference had for many years recommended Conferences with other Churches, preparing the way for reunion or relations shaping towards it. They took four points known as the Lambeth Quadrilateral, which, in the opinion of the Lambeth Conference, supplied a basis for reunion (*a*) the Holy Scriptures, (*b*) the Apostles' and Nicene Creed, (*c*) the Sacraments of Baptism

[1] *The Church of England and Episcopacy*, A. J. Mason, 1914

and Holy Communion, (*d*) the historic Episcopate. They urged that the Kikuyu proposals were a serious attempt to solve an actual and urgent problem; and further that the Societies proposing to federate accepted all the first three points of the Lambeth Quadrilateral. With regard to Episcopacy, they pointed out that it was not rejected nor was its power curtailed, though they admitted that it was not specifically mentioned. They claimed further that, with regard to Inter-communion between the federated Societies, Anglican precedents justified the attendance of Nonconformists at Anglican celebrations. With regard to the attendance of Anglicans at a non-Episcopal communion, when no church of their own was available, they argued that, when the Lambeth Conference Committee of 1908 had carefully refused to 'pronounce negatively upon the value in God's sight of the ministry in other communions', they, as Bishops, could not forbid their converts to communicate in non-Episcopal churches, as that would in effect be to pronounce positively against the validity of the non-Episcopal ministry.

The Bishop of Zanzibar, in his *Case against Kikuyu* followed a very different course. He presented a theological treatise, clearly and logically written. He studied vital principles, and he did not attempt to examine the scheme, as it stood, point by point. For him the omission of the Episcopate from the Kikuyu proposals was not simply a failure to accept just one condition out of the four of the Lambeth Quadrilateral, but the contravention of 'the fundamental principle of Church order, which is, that every Christian depends for his full membership in the Catholic Church of Christ upon his loyal fellowship in faith and worship with his own local Bishop'. As he wrote in the Preface:

> We must then concentrate our power upon winning from all Christians, catholic and non-catholic, an acknowledgment that in the local Bishop is the Christ-given centre of union here on earth, and in the universal College of Bishops is the permanent bond of union between all members of the Church, of every nation and tongue, on earth and beyond the veil.

The Anglican Bishops were (he claimed) the English section of the Universal College of Bishops, and 'a Bishop sent from England to Africa goes out, not as a Bishop of the English Church, but simply as a Catholic Bishop, who owes his consecration to the universal Episcopate represented to him by prelates of the

Church in England'. The underlying principle of the Kikuyu Conference, on the other hand, was that of 'practical equality of all religious bodies and their ministries'. He maintained that non-Episcopal churches could not be 'branches of the Catholic Church' (as the Archbishop himself had implied in his formal answer); for though the members of these churches, as individuals, are by baptism members of the Kingdom, they have omitted to enlist themselves under the authority of the Bishops, who hold the King's Commission; and so lack the *corporate* relation to the Kingdom which can justify the term 'part or branch'.

IV

The Consultative Body met at Lambeth at the end of July. The following were present: the Archbishops of York, Armagh, the West Indies, Rupertsland, and the Bishop of Brechin; the Bishops of Winchester, Exeter, and Gibraltar, Bishops Copleston, Wallis, and Ryle. They had prolonged interviews both with the Bishops of Mombasa and Uganda, and with the Bishop of Zanzibar; who had seen one another's statements before meeting the Consultative Body. The Archbishop of Canterbury was present at the interviews and during the preliminary investigations, but he was not present during the preparation of the reply, the Archbishop of York then taking his place. The anxiety of their deliberations was deepened by the greater crisis of the outbreak of the European War. The meeting lasted from July 27 to July 31, 1914.

On the final day the Prime Minister warned the country of the imminence of a catastrophe of which it was impossible to measure either the dimensions or the effects. The Consultative Body parted. They had come to an unanimous agreement, and made their report in writing to the Archbishop of Canterbury.

On August 4 War was declared. The Archbishop was at once plunged into the very different work and thoughts which that involved. The Bishops of Uganda and Zanzibar made haste to get back to their African flocks. What could they say when they arrived, about the problems which had brought them home? The Archbishop was clear that he could not publish the Consultative Body's reply, except simultaneously with his own reply.

But this would take time, for his words needed most careful weighing and deliberation, for which the outbreak of War could give no space.

He had a last talk with the Bishop of Zanzibar on August 26th. The Bishop pointed out how difficult it would be if he reached his Diocese and had to tell the people that he knew no more than they did of what the Archbishop was likely to say. The Archbishop accordingly promised to write him 'a confidential letter *for himself only*, giving such general indication of the position I must take up in my published letter as would enable him to form at the least some opinion as to what his course may have to be':

> We then discussed a little his own position. I said that I did not want to ask unfair questions, but that if he liked to tell me what he felt he should be bound to do if I were to say something which seemed to him wholly wrong, it would interest me to hear it. He said, 'If you do that, there are only three alternatives before me. One is to join the Church of Rome. I do not think I could ever do it. I am anti-Roman to the core as regards the Papacy, and if I were driven for lack of any other port of refuge to become a Roman, I should not seek Ordination but live as a layman. I cannot think that will ever come. The second would be to make myself unpleasant, to point out that the excellent gentlemen (i.e. of the Consultative Body) had spoken with no authority, and to sever communion with the two neighbouring Dioceses, and put you in a constant difficulty by insisting upon knowing whether or not you were in communion with me if I was not in communion with them. I think I could make things unpleasant for a long time. But I do not want to do it at all.' I asked whether he might take the same attitude towards the Lambeth Conference as he spoke of possibly taking towards the Consultative Body. He said he thought it was possible, but he had not considered that point. We expanded on this a little, and he was clever and humorous, but I thought quite unconvincing and rather unthoughtful. His third course would be to retire into lay communion in our own Church, lamenting the behaviour of the ecclesiastical authorities and ceasing to be one of them. He then sketched another position that he might take, although he had at first said there were only three. He thought he might form a little alliance with a few men like the Bishops of Oxford (if he could get him), Corea, and a few others, who might in the Lambeth Conference protest against the action of the others, and make a clique of their own. He thought

the second of these four courses would be for us, or for me, the most difficult, because he would have considerable support.

All was very pleasant and friendly, though he was speaking with his usual uncompromisingness. He ended by saying that, if I could say that the Federation was wrong and that the admission of unconfirmed folk to Communion must in those Dioceses be against the 'rule', even if it were allowed by dispensation, and further that the Open Communion at Kikuyu had been—I do not think he used the term but he meant—'scandalous', the controversy would be at an end so far as he is concerned until at least the Lambeth Conference time, when some of the points would presumably have to be considered.

The next day the Archbishop had a similar last talk with the Bishop of Uganda, who was also very anxious not to arrive in his Diocese in complete darkness. The Archbishop promised in the same way to send him a strictly confidential letter for himself:

> I told him that the Consultative Body had given unanimous advice, and that that ought to show him that he ought not to be in a state of trepidation that something terrible was likely to happen.

The private letters were sent, as promised, being timed to reach each Bishop just on the eve of sailing. The Bishop of Uganda sailed first, and the letter to him with a covering personal note is dated 2nd September. The Archbishop felt obliged to tell him '(1) that the scheme in its present shape is not one I could rightly sanction as it stands, and (2) that with regard to the joint communion service you will not be surprised if I am bound to call attention to principles which you did not to the best of my belief intend in any permanent or far-reaching way to contravene'.

The Bishop of Uganda, in a letter on September 5, expressed his disappointment, though confessing that his knowledge must be imperfect until a full answer was made; and adding a hint of how keenly he had felt being placarded as a heretic and schismatic, and his regret, therefore, that no more had been said by the Archbishop to relieve his mind on that point.

To the Bishop of Zanzibar the Archbishop wrote on September 14 to a similar effect and with a similar covering note. The Bishop replied:

The Bishop of Zanzibar *to the* Archbishop of Canterbury

15th September, 1914.

I thank you very much for your kind letter which accompanies your official communication. The outlook in East Africa is certainly not encouraging. But the rumour that all our staff has been removed and interned I do not accept, and in any case I should not allow it to be 'accepted' officially by the Mission. I have begged the office not to let it become public, for I think it untrue. At least, I hope so!

I do not propose to offer any remarks upon your official communication. It is enough that I acknowledge its receipt with sincere thanks for your Grace's courtesy.

V

The Archbishop had to wait some months, with all the War's pressing duties, before he could find time for quietness of thought to publish his own answer to the question raised by the Kikuyu Conference. But he issued it at Easter 1915. It may be summarized as follows:

The Answer begins with a careful account of the problems before him, and points out that the Kikuyu problem was not peculiar to East Africa; it was the problem of the growing Native Church, which ought not to 'be hampered in its young life by schisms and divergences whose origin and meaning are due to what may almost be called the accidental happenings of English or Scottish life—political, social, and ecclesiastical—150 or 250 years ago'.

After quoting the recommendations of the Lambeth Conferences from 1888 to 1908, he then passed to the two questions.

1. The Scheme of Federation.

His opinion is given thus:

The details of the Scheme of Federation may be fairly open to criticism or even to repudiation. Not so, by members of the Lambeth Conferences, the principle which actuated its promoters.

With regard to the details:

It is in the working out of details, and not in the main idea of co-operation, that difficulties and differences present themselves. They turn partly on the question whether the Church of England, in addition to the emphasis she deliberately sets upon our Episcopal system, has laid down a rule which marks all non-Episcopalians as *extra Ecclesiam*. The threefold ministry comes down to us from Apostolic times, and we reverently maintain it as an essential element in our own historic system, and as a part of our Church's witness to 'the laws of ecclesiastical polity'. We believe it to be the right method of Church government, a method which no new generation in the Church of England would be at liberty to get rid of, or to treat as indifferent. We believe further that the proper method of Ordination is by duly consecrated Bishops, as those who, in the words of the Article, 'have publick authority given to them in the Congregation to call and send ministers into the Lord's Vineyard'. But to maintain that witness with all steadfastness is not the same thing as to place of necessity *extra Ecclesiam* every system and every body of men who follow a different use, however careful, strict and orderly their plan. The words and acts of many leading High Churchmen in Caroline days, as well as the carefully chosen sentences and, it may perhaps be added, the significant silences in some of our formularies, throw a grave *onus probandi* upon those who contend for the rigid and uncompromising maintenance of the absolutely exclusive rule. On the other hand, the difficulty of showing that such a rule has ever been explicitly laid down, by no means involves an approbation *en bloc* of the Federation Scheme drawn up at Kikuyu, and the Consultative Body has pointed out with perfect clearness three items of special difficulty which arise under that Scheme:

(1) The admission to our pulpits of men who have not been episcopally ordained;
(2) The admission to Holy Communion of Christians who have not been episcopally confirmed; and
(3) The sanction directly or by implication given to members of our Church to receive the Holy Communion at the hands of Ministers not episcopally ordained.

Then, after expressing his view that Federation, while falling short of corporate reunion, was something more than co-operation, he indicated that the whole question of a 'formal and quasi-constitutional Federation in British East Africa of different denominations whereof our Church is one, requires, as it seems to me, a sanction which must be more than local. The matter is exactly one of those which the Lambeth Conference of Bishops can appropriately discuss.'

With regard to the three points of difficulty:

(1) the admission to our pulpits of men who have not been episcopally ordained:

I see no reason to restrict the freedom of a Bishop in the Mission

Field as to those whom he may invite to address his people, or as to the sanction which may be given to a Priest or Deacon of his Diocese to address in their own buildings, on due invitation given, Christians who belong to other denominations. No fundamental principle seems to me to be involved. It is a matter of local, and primarily of Diocesan, administration.

(2) The admission to Holy Communion of Christians who have not been episcopally confirmed:

Looking carefully at present-day facts and conditions, I have no hesitation in saying that in my opinion a Diocesan Bishop acts rightly in sanctioning, when circumstances seem to call for it, the admission to Holy Communion of a devout Christian man to whom the ministrations of his own Church are for the time inaccessible, and who, as a baptised person, desires to avail himself of the opportunity of communicating at one of our Altars.

(3) The sanction directly or by implication given to members of our Church to receive the Holy Communion at the hands of ministers not episcopally ordained:

To imagine that the occasional admission of non-episcopalians who in special circumstances seek the Holy Communion at our hands carries or implies a corresponding readiness to bid the members of our Church, when temporarily isolated, seek the Holy Communion at the hands of any Christian Minister though not Episcopally ordained, who may be within reach, to whatsoever denomination or system he belongs, is gravely to misapprehend the position and to run the risk of creating serious confusion.... If such a principle were once laid down it would be impossible to limit its operation to British East Africa. ... It is a satisfaction to me to point out that the question is at present of an academic rather than a practical kind, for it became apparent in our personal communications with the Bishops of Mombasa and Uganda that they are so conscious of the difficulties and perplexities which might arise that they have no wish or intention to give that advice to African Christians belonging to their Dioceses.

2. The Holding of the Joint Communion Service.

The Archbishop noted that this was a single spontaneous act of devotion on the part of a group of keen Christian Missionaries in a vast heathen country. There was no question of inaugurating a new policy or initiating a new plan of inter-communion. It was also:

far from being the first time that, in the Mission Fields of Africa or of the Far East, non-Episcopal Missionaries have participated in such a Service, when the celebrant was a Missionary Bishop or a leading Presbyter of our own Church, and in commenting upon the action of the Bishops and Clergy at Kikuyu it is unfair to forget that fact.

At the same time, as the stir of the controversy which had arisen had proved, there was the danger that a Joint Communion Service of the kind described 'admittedly abnormal, admittedly irregular' might be acclaimed as a 'demonstration'.

I need hardly add that the question of such open Communion on special occasions is of course entirely independent of the question which I have discussed earlier as to the exercise of temporary or occasional 'hospitality' towards individuals deprived for a time of the ministrations of their own Church, be they French Protestants in the seventeenth century or Scotch Presbyterians in the twentieth. To mix the two questions is only to confuse matters. I believe that we shall act rightly, and that the wisest and strongest Missionaries believe that we shall act rightly, in abstaining at present from such Services as the closing Service held at Kikuyu, now that in a world of quick tidings and of ample talk they are shown to be open to the kind of misunderstandings which have arisen.

Such was the Archbishop's opinion or answer to the two questions. It was longer than the answer of the Central Consultative Body, which was a clear, concise statement to the same general effect, though with the definition which greater brevity exacted.[1] It was in a way less official, and more personal and pastoral in character, and the Archbishop deliberately refrained from giving it any other title than *Kikuyu. The Archbishop of Canterbury*.

The statement pleased neither side, and was blamed both by the friends of Zanzibar and by the friends of Uganda, for what it said or did not say. But the Archbishop was not perturbed, and held that this mixture of abuse was far more satisfactory than if he had been praised by one party, and been by the other denounced.

[1] Of the Consultative Body's reply on the Joint Communion Service it was wittily said at the time, 'The Commission comes to the conclusion that the Service at Kikuyu was eminently pleasing to God, and must on no account be repeated.'

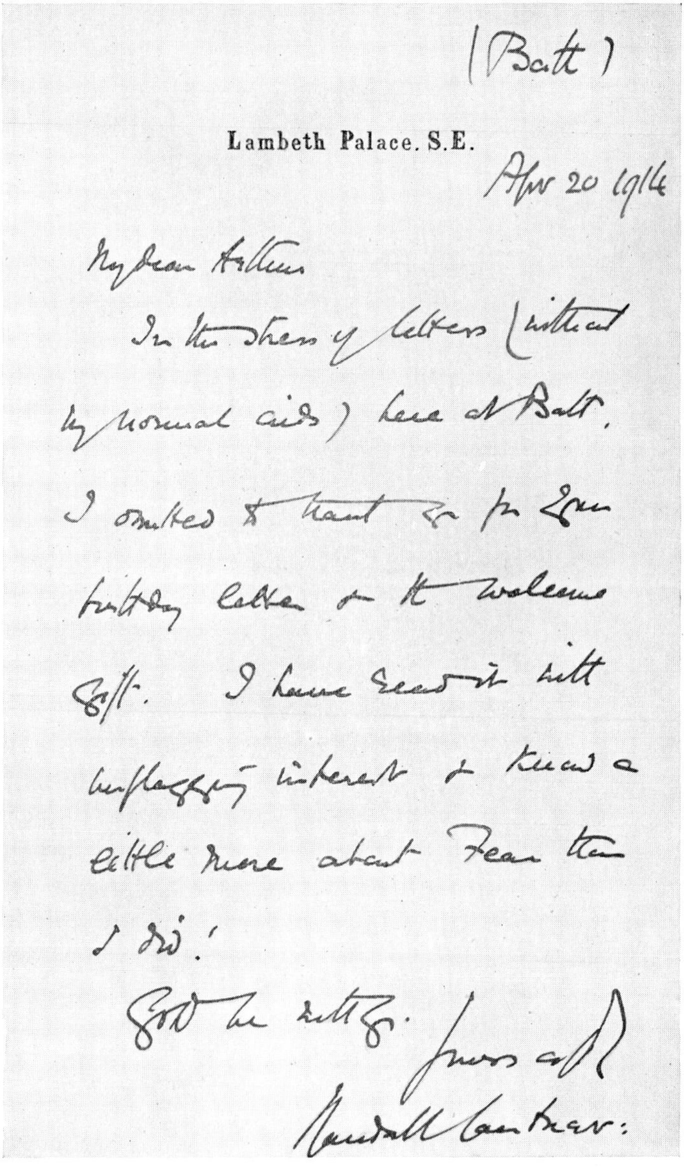

(Bath)

Lambeth Palace. S.E.

Apr 20 1914

My dear Arthur

In the stress of letters (without my normal aids) here at Bath, I omitted to thank you for your birthday letter and the welcome gift. I have read it with unflagging interest and know a little more about Fear than I did!

God be with you. Yours aff.

Randall Cantuar:

Facsimile of a letter to Arthur Christopher Benson written by Randall Davidson a few days after his 66th birthday

CHAPTER XLIII

A LOOK BACK: 1903–1914

Though with a strong dash of the sanguine, without which, indeed, there can be no great projector in any walk of life, Archibald Constable was one of the most sagacious persons that ever followed his profession. LOCKHART, *Life of Scott*, ch. xviii.

IN this chapter we propose to make a pause in order to take stock of the manner of man the Archbishop was at this time of his life, and of his relation to his friends. The moment is apt for more reasons than one.

I

By the beginning of 1914 Randall Davidson had been Archbishop of Canterbury for eleven years. He was sixty-five years old, and the great dividing line of the War was only six months distant.

During the time of his Archbishopric, he had kept in good health on the whole. He still suffered from the results of the old shooting accident at Harrow, one of which was a serious rupture and another a liability to attacks of lumbago, partly caused by the damage to the muscles of the hips. The terrible first illness and its two successors, which afflicted him at Rochester, left their traces behind, and sometimes took the form of bad attacks of pain of a gastric character, but the fresh air of Farnham had made him a stronger man altogether. He was also liable to attacks of influenza, and in April 1913 he lay in the study for some weeks, as a consequence of a chill involving other troubles which had to be carefully guarded against till the end of his life. But he was a model patient. Sir Thomas Barlow, who was a model doctor, has told the writer that he never had to do with anybody more rational, loyal, intelligent, and willing to obey. The Archbishop, Sir Thomas said, liked to know everything, and never cherished up any symptom privately, and thus the doctor was able to allow his patient liberties. He had the reward of his sanity. None of his attacks of illness was brought on by himself.

> I cannot [said Sir Thomas] use language strong enough to describe his satisfactoriness. He was not only loyal but grateful, and the nurses would do any mortal thing for him. The lessons of his illness have a real spiritual value. His was a very fine life.

What enormous things could be done if people would only have patience, and learn to cut their coat according to their cloth and wait till the storm goes by!

It is only right to add that the Archbishop owed a very great deal also to the strong common sense of Mrs. Davidson, who knew exactly when to put him to bed and keep him there, as a precautionary measure, thus securing rest of body and mind, but a rest in which he never allowed himself (as he put it) to 'waste his time'. So his illnesses, formidable handicaps though they were during the whole of his life, were nevertheless means of recuperation in all sorts of ways, and, treated as he treated them, strengthened his character and prolonged his life.

II

We may also note that the Archbishop won an unusual affection from those with whom he had to do, as we have often seen already. It was not only that he knew the men of influence, but he became their close and valued friend. Up to the time of the War he had known six Prime Ministers, and with four of these—Rosebery, Balfour, Campbell-Bannerman, and Asquith—he was intimate; and there were many other statesmen and men engaged in public life, with whom he established really close relations. In a memorandum of 1913 about his friendships he writes:

This kind of wide intimacy has certainly not been equalled in regard to any of the Archbishops during the last 70 or 80 years. Archbishops Tait and Benson were both of them members of Grillions, but they did not use those opportunities nearly so often as I have used them. The thing sounds a small one, but experience has taught me that it is not slight in the occasions it offers. I doubt if I should have known Grey, or Sir John Simon, or Cromer, or a good many others so well as I do, had it not been for those dinners. It means a good deal in my judgement for the Church's good that the man who holds the Archbishop's position should have this kind of natural and friendly access to the men to whom is given the responsibility for the nation's affairs. It places, not the Archbishop only, but the Church, in quite a different relation to public life in its religious and secular aspects. I do not mean to imply that I have used these continuous opportunities with adequate wisdom or effectiveness, but it cannot fail to have done a great deal for the bridging of difficulties.

Such personal relations with Cabinet Ministers, and others, also revealed a certain quality in the actual method of his working. He had what may be called a hidden personal influence. It was not until much later in his life that he became in any way a popular figure. He had not the popular gift, nor, skilful and persuasive as he was, would he have ever been acclaimed as a great orator. His influence was of an extraordinarily individual quality, difficult to analyse, but certainly including in a happy composition goodness, simplicity, wisdom, and a deep interest in other people and the world. Again, it was the intimate entering into the other man's point of view, and the identification of himself with the other's interests at that particular moment, that won him the affection and confidence of many an ecclesiastical and educational opponent. It might almost have been said that his closest friendships were with those with whom he in opinion disagreed, not least Charles Gore. 'The Archbishop is a broad gauge man, I love him', was the verdict of Dr. J. R. Mott, the American missionary leader, very early in his acquaintance in 1910.

III

Similarly, in the actual government of the Church, his methods were largely personal and, so to speak, private, as he trusted in human contacts and the help of proved counsellors rather than in any formal organization like a Curia. It is interesting to read what he says about the desirability of a Curia—such as was much more in accordance with Archbishop Benson's desires—in his Charge on *The Character and Call of the Church of England*, given at his second Visitation of the Diocese of Canterbury in February 1912:

> To anyone who sets himself to consider what the Cathedral and See of Canterbury now connote, popularly as well as officially, as the historic centre of a great constitutional system, the enquiry naturally suggests itself: Should there not, for dealing with these larger matters, be a group of officially appointed men, call it by what name you will—Council, Curia, Cabinet, Board, Committee—who might jointly bear the burden, and, speaking with collective voice, increase immensely the weight of what is said, and ensure for it a hearing to which no one man's voice, in a system such as ours, can possibly be entitled? The answer lies in the facts of the case. Such Council or Curia, if formed, would necessarily

be an official body for doing official work. But then no technically official position, bearing relation to the whole Anglican Communion, belongs of right to, or is to-day claimed by, the Archbishop of Canterbury. To speak of it as his by right, or to claim for him any authoritative voice, beyond the quite limited range of the fifty-seven dioceses subject to his metropolitical jurisdiction, would be a new departure of the gravest and, in my judgement, of the most perilous kind. Nay, even to define in any formal manner a relation, other than such as I have described as subsisting between the Archbishop of Canterbury and the Bishops or Dioceses of other Provinces, would be to twist and tangle, and perhaps to break, a bond of fellowship which has grown stronger with our Church's growth, and which is real and practical and useful just because it is informal and undefined. And the moment you bring into being a body of men who are to share, as of right, the daily responsibilities of what I have called a 'pivotship', which has come into existence, so to speak, 'of itself', and by no fiat or ordinance, the whole position is immediately changed by the necessity of definition and of rules, and 'the mutual society help and comfort' become ready to vanish away. I say nothing of the practical difficulty which would beset the actual formation or selection of such a Council or Curia, which must outlast, presumably, the tenure of the individual Archbishop under whom or by whom it was created. Nothing again need I say of the problem how to secure the retention by its members, as their years advance, of the alertness and promptitude or the range of knowledge which led to their nomination at the outset. Difficulties of that sort, grave as they would be, need not prove insuperable if, on general grounds, the plan were found to be a right one. I say nothing again of the warnings which are furnished, in this particular field, by even a little knowledge of modern Roman history.* It is unnecessary to dwell upon these points because the reason which I have already given is for my purpose adequate and indeed conclusive.[1]

Chief among these personal counsellors were Bishop John Wordsworth, Bishop Francis Paget, Bishop Edward Talbot, and, to an ever-increasing extent, the Archbishop of York, Dr. Lang. Bishop Wordsworth was a man of extraordinary learning, with 'stores of solid knowledge, marvellously ready at call, and given out ungrudgingly in his unselfish service to the Church of God',[2] though he was, critics used to say, constantly expecting that two

* In support of this, to which there is ample independent testimony, see e.g. *Pan-Anglican Congress Report*, 1908, vol. vii, p. 220.

[1] *Character and Call of the Church of England*, pp. 8–10.

[2] Ibid. p. 12.

and two would make five. Francis Paget, Bishop of Oxford, was a scholar and theologian, but especially 'the quiet, wise counsellor and Christian friend to whom, in periods of closest intercourse at home and abroad, one never turned in vain for inspiration or guidance; and whose grace of literary touch gave a peculiar dignity, if one may use the phrase, to the ready and tender flow of personal sympathy on which his friends had come so confidently to rely'.[1] Both Bishop Wordsworth and Bishop Paget died in 1911. Bishop Talbot, first at Southwark and then at Winchester, was one of the Archbishop's staunchest supporters. He had a gift of deep understanding, and a great sense of fairness, and was a valuable interpreter of the Tractarian point of view. Archbishop Lang, who had gone from Stepney to York in 1909, was a tower of strength, and the unity in counsel and constant contact between the two Archbishops was something new in the relations of the two Primates. It was characteristic of Archbishop Davidson that immediately Dr. Lang (some fifteen years his junior) was appointed to York, he should invite him to make Lambeth his London home, in order to get his counsel and aid. The Archbishop of York thus always made Lambeth his headquarters whenever he came to London, and had two rooms of his own in the Palace. Chief of all Randall Davidson's friends was Lord Stamfordham, with whom he had been intimate from Windsor days. Hardly a week passed without a talk or talks between these two, and it was a Sunday treat to both of them when Stamfordham walked over to Lambeth Palace in the afternoon for a quiet talk between lunch and tea.

We must not forget, when speaking of the personal side of the Archbishop's life-work, how much it was helped by the home quality of Lambeth and the sense that here was the centre of a family rather than of an ecclesiastic organization, with Mrs. Davidson always in the midst welcoming, entertaining, recreating. Here is a letter from Bishop Francis Paget to his son Bernard written from Lambeth Palace:

The BISHOP OF OXFORD *to* BERNARD PAGET

February 2, 1911.

This week's letter comes, you see, from the busiest and kindest of homes. . . . I never come here without feeling afresh the height

[1] Ibid., p. 13.

of the example which the Archbishop and Mrs. Davidson set us. There is so much hard and heavy work always in hand. And yet it never be-glooms life, or hinders them from entering into all that is pleasant and humorous, and all the cares and joys of other people's lives. They really are gallant workers, and true, generous friends.

A similar tribute to the quality of the life at Lambeth is paid by Sir Michael Sadler, whose particular and intimate acquaintance with the Archbishop at the time of the Education controversy (1906–8) we have already noted:

The days were filled with his labours. However late he had to work, he rarely missed the service in Chapel early in the morning. Letters, great numbers of them written with his own hand, were promptly sent in reply to every kind of correspondent. 'In his busy and weighty employment', like Izaac Walton's honoured friend, Dr. Robert Sanderson, Archbishop Davidson 'practised obligingness to all men of what degree so ever'. His insight into the true value of a man's service was regardless of social standing. In hospitality, in generous private gifts, he was cordial, simple, spontaneous. He was never shaken out of composure, cheerfulness, and courteous consideration for others by fatigue, indisposition, or the pressure of public affairs.

Others, who knew him far longer and far better than I, will say more fitly from what deep source he drew the strength which made him so wise, so resilient, so much beloved. But no one who has had the almost inestimable privilege of living, even for a short time, with the Archbishop and Mrs. Davidson at Lambeth, can think of either without thinking of the two together and of the calm which fell upon them and us through the services in Chapel.

IV

In tackling the hard and heavy work which had to be done at Lambeth, the Archbishop had also a great gift for getting the best out of the members of his staff. He was such a gallant worker himself that Chaplains and secretaries delighted in their labours under him. They knew that he trusted them and they quickly responded. Most faithful of all, and longest in his service, was Arthur Sheppard, whom he had engaged at first as a half-time private secretary, at Windsor in 1889, as a young man of twenty-seven, and had taken with him first to Rochester, then to Farnham, and last to Lambeth. He was with the Archbishop altogether for thirty-four years, 1889 to 1923. No man was more careful or devoted, and the Archbishop's confidence in his ability and loyalty was unceasing. To his two Chaplains, one for Diocesan work, the other for the more general departments, the Archbishop also gave his complete trust. Remembering his own apprenticeship with Tait, he enjoyed training them and explaining the various problems, and discovering how far they had taken in the points at issue. And at times, especially in driving about the Diocese, or on rare occasions when he took a Chaplain away on a brief holiday at Christmas, he would tell him of men he had known, and of the difficulties in Church and State with which he had had to deal. Like Tait, he had an invariable wish for a second pair of eyes or ears in judging an important letter, or the text of an important message or speech. Like Tait too, he would go right through the baskets of letters which the Chaplain brought up, and insist on taking them as they came, down to the last σπλάγχνα, as he called them.

V

Perhaps there is another point which ought to be mentioned as a very considerable assistance to the Archbishop in the discharge of his duties. Circumstances undoubtedly led him to know more about the previous half-century of the Church's life than any other living man. Not merely had he already enjoyed thirty years of daily acquaintance with Lambeth and its life, but he had had to master the preceding history, beginning in the fifties, when writing the *Life of Archbishop Tait*. It is certain that nobody prior to Randall Davidson had attempted any such coherent, consecutive, and detailed story of central Church affairs during a very eventful time. He used to say how invaluable he found this knowledge in estimating aright the origins and meanings of contemporary movements in the Church.

Again, an immense amount of work was, as we have already seen, connected with the Church overseas.

> As soon as he came to Lambeth [wrote Bishop Montgomery] he instituted the Thursday Celebration in the Chapel on purpose for Bishops. He told me always to be present, and to see that any Bishop from abroad who was in London should be warmly in-

vited. And such Bishop should sit next to him at breakfast. The result was that the Bishop became an intimate friend of his, and was asked to correspond with Lambeth as often as he wished. So his correspondence grew as the years passed.

He took the greatest pains over his correspondence with Bishops abroad, and gave them always the very best help that he could. He was not only accessible to the Secretaries of the great Missionary Societies, but called for their aid, and the aid of any others able to give the special help needed for the special problem, so that he might give the best and most fully-informed advice that he could. To his more personal letters he devoted many a Sunday afternoon. For other letters dealing with official problems, he would often set apart a particular day or morning from time to time. The variety and range of his correspondence is indicated in the following note, which appears in the files of 1912, entitled 'A Day's Work':

Notes of the subjects upon which the Archbishop wrote important letters on August 5, 1912.

To Archbishop Donaldson of Brisbane on the whole question of the Australian Church and its connexion with the Church of England.

To Bishop King of Madagascar, discussing the problem of French government in Madagascar in its relation to Missions and to Christianity generally.

To Bishop Price of Fuhkien, China, with regard to the suggestion that the Church in Ireland might nominate and support a Bishop in China.

To the Bishop of Madras upon the suggested re-arrangement of Dioceses and Provinces in India, and the bearing of this upon Disestablishment in India, the Archbishop's advice having been definitely asked.

To Bishop Cecil [Boutflower] of South Tokyo on the proposed new Theological College in Japan, and upon the question of Church Unity among Missionaries in the Japanese Empire.

To Dr. J. R. Mott, in New York, giving him formal letters of introduction to Bishops in the Far East, and discussing the value of the Student Christian Federation Movement and the Missionary Continuation Committee.

To the Bishop of Lahore about the idea of a great Cathedral in Delhi as the new Capital, and the problem of how far it would be possible to enlist the King's support.

To the Bishop of Gibraltar upon the relation the Bishop bears to Continental Chaplaincies under Societies, and the respective rights of each party.

To Archdeacon Moule of China on Missionary methods of work, and on the form which the Appeal for Missions should take.

These were in addition to a large number of other subjects such as the Divorce question (Mr. Gamble of Sloane Street); Irvingism and its position in relation to the Church of England (a Mr. Royle Shore); the Duke of Connaught (about Army patronage and nominations); St. Katharine's Hospital in Regent's Park and its re-arrangement; Deceased Wife's Sister question and his Pastoral (Bishop of Worcester). All these were in one morning.

No matter how busy he was, the Archbishop took great trouble with his sermons. They were always thoughtful and well planned, like all his public utterances; but he sometimes became depressed and wondered how far anything had got home. The following is an exchange of letters after a sermon preached at the Church Congress at Swansea in 1909:

Mrs. Creighton *to the* Archbishop of Canterbury

Hampton Court Palace, 10 October 1909.

May I just say that I have read your Congress sermon and liked it very much and altogether agreed with it. Do you remember that I wrote to you about Mr. Figgis' sermons, and one on 'Other-worldliness' which had specially struck me and set me thinking? In a way it raised in the crude way natural to a younger man the same thoughts as your much saner and riper sermon. We try and do without the vision sometimes, and at other times we are half ashamed of owning that we have it, and instead of trying to lift others to see it, go down and meet them in their grey world.

I have had an interesting though hard week, all day at the missionary commission, planning out our report, and am now left with a bit of it to write. Our chairman is a very able and agreeable man, not an American but a Scotch Presbyterian who has been 14 years in America and is head of Hartford College. He managed us all with great skill and delicacy, and we were all in consequence most obedient and amenable.

I hope you are less burdened. Since I came back from the peace of the country, it has seemed to me that all the people I have met are burdened and I feel there must be something wrong about it. It is the vision that will help these too, will it not?

The ARCHBISHOP OF CANTERBURY *to* MRS. CREIGHTON

Lambeth, 12 October 1909.

Your letter about the Swansea sermon is a very real cheer to me. I sometimes think that nobody cares a rap what I say about anything in heaven or earth, and though that may be the fault of what is said or of the manner of saying it, it is not the less disheartening. I am going to read to-night Mr. Figgis' sermon on Other-worldliness to which you have sent me.

I believe—and especially from what you say—that this Edinburgh Conference may be the beginning of a new era for our Foreign Missions. The wretched drawback is that just as we are beginning to understand better how to spend Missionary money, the sources of supply seem to be drying up, or at the best to be stagnant. God bless you, my dear Friend.

VI

Readers of this book may have been surprised at the large amount of space given to the political interests of the Archbishop, especially in relation to the various episodes in the crisis between the two Houses of Parliament. These were a prominent part of the life of England during the years preceding the War. But it is to be observed that, during the next fifteen years of the Archbishopric, political crises as such take a much smaller place in the general picture. This is partly because the House of Lords was now deprived of a great part of its powers. But it was partly also due to the increasing opportunities, of which the Archbishop made increasing use, for giving a strong Christian witness in larger questions still, concerning Europe and the world. It was also partly due to the growing needs of the Church, and the claims which the government of the Church, and its problems, made upon his time, and the opportunities for setting forward the life and work of the Church which the next fifteen years were to yield in abundant measure.

It may perhaps be well to end this chapter with another quotation from the Charge[1] describing his view of the distinctive character of the Church of England:

> I am not referring now to the fundamentals of the Faith, the great truths common to Christianity throughout the world, but only to those traits which when taken together (and that is essential) give

[1] *Character and Call of the Church of England*, pp. 46–7.

its distinctive character to our Anglican Communion. I am attempting no technical definitions or demarcations. That, so far as it is done at all, has been done for us in accepted formularies. But, expressing the matter in common non-technical phraseology, I should myself describe our distinctive characteristics somewhat as follows. We lay emphasis upon the historic continuity of the Church's corporate and organic life. We stand accordingly for a sacramental, governmental, ministerial, and even ritual system which, with adaptation to local requirements, has come down to us from Apostolic days. We stand for the unfettered study of Holy Scripture and for its circulation in the vernacular tongue, whatever it be. We stand for the liberty of private judgement in the interpretation of Holy Scripture and in matters of faith, combined, as regards our own members, with the definiteness of such actual *credenda* as are set forth in our Formularies. We stand for the right of National Churches to a wide elasticity and variety in system, in ritual and in worship, combined with a general loyalty to the principles and usages which have come down from the past, and especially from the first six centuries. And lastly we stand for the principle of plainness, openness and simplicity in all formularies, usages and services, so that every word of each may, so far as possible, be understanded and followed by even the unlearned among our people.

It was to guard and establish this Church that his labour was to be more and more applied, in difficult days, for the rest of his primacy.

CHAPTER XLIV

THE IRISH CRISIS: 1914

BOSWELL. 'Pray, Mr. Dilly, how does Dr. Leland's "History of Ireland" sell?'

JOHNSON (bursting forth with a generous indignation). 'The Irish are in a most unnatural state; for we see there the minority prevailing over the majority. There is no instance, even in the ten persecutions, of such severity as that which the protestants of Ireland have exercised against the Catholicks. Did we tell them we have conquered them, it would be above board: to punish them by confiscation and other penalties, as rebels, was monstrous injustice. King William was not their lawful sovereign: he had not been acknowledged by the Parliament of Ireland, when they appeared in arms against him.' BOSWELL, *Life of Dr. Johnson* (1773).

IN the long history of Lambeth Palace there is no record of any visit by a reigning King and Queen together, until King George and Queen Mary went to dinner with the Archbishop of Canterbury and Mrs. Randall Davidson on February 23, 1914. The party consisted of thirty persons altogether, including the Lansdownes, the Loreburns, the Archbishop of Brisbane[1] from Australia, the Bishop of Yukon from Canada, Lord Balfour of Burleigh, the Editor of *The Times*,[2] Charles Booth, Sidney Colvin, and Mrs. Benson, who had in her husband's Primacy welcomed the Royal guests at Lambeth, when Duke and Duchess of York. The Archbishop showed the King and Queen over the Palace after dinner, and the evening ended with a short service in the Chapel.

We note the event rather for the interest of the actual visit than for any special incident of the evening. This visit of the King to Lambeth took place when the public mind was absorbed with the Irish question, and there was an unsuspected fitness in its happening at that time.

No man could hold the office of Archbishop of Canterbury, least of all Randall Davidson, and fail to feel a grave anxiety at the course of events in Ireland. Throughout the previous months he had taken care to inform himself as completely as he could of the difficulties and the dangers. The memoranda which he has left show that in the autumn of 1913 he was in touch with various people at the centre, and also with Lord Rosebery, about

[1] Dr. Donaldson, afterwards Bishop of Salisbury.

[2] Mr. Geoffrey Robinson (later Dawson).

political eventualities. He was gravely disturbed by the formation of the Ulster Provisional Government. He was also well aware of the course suggested by leading Unionists of petitioning the King before the Royal Assent to the Home Rule Bill, with a view to obtaining Dissolution; and he undoubtedly held, apart from any such drastic policy as this, that the passing of the Parliament Act had so altered the Constitution, as to place a greater responsibility upon the Sovereign than he could have exercised while the House of Lords retained a veto on the legislation of the Commons.

On January 21, 1914, on his way to a Privy Council at Windsor, to authorize the scheme for the three new Sees,[1] he had a long talk with Lord Morley.

> Morley asked specially for some quiet talk, and I had a good deal both on the journey and in the Castle. He is terribly distraught about the situation, and seemed to me in rather a pitiably helpless condition. He feels intensely for the King, dreads Civil War beyond words, does not see how to avert it, and thinks (though he puts it guardedly) that the King has a stronger position than the Prime Minister and others have admitted, inasmuch as there is only one House of Parliament at present, and the King's responsibility is therefore increased. He did not see, he said, any answer to the contention made on behalf of the King by some of his friends, though not by the King himself, that His Majesty has to take up personal responsibilities because so much turns on his individual action. Morley put it quite bluntly: If the King dismisses us by insisting on a Dissolution, he may be acting unwisely, but he is certainly not exceeding his legal rights or, what is arguable, his right course. The public will hold him responsible if there is Civil War. 'He is the one man who (they will say) could have stopped it. He did not so act. Civil War came. The King must bear the responsibility for it.' If, on the other hand, he does order a Dissolution, it is indisputable that he will be regarded as taking sides, and will discredit himself in the eyes of those who think he is siding against them. Even if the Unionists win, the other side will bitterly resent the supposed throwing of the King's weight into the scale against them. I suggested in addition that, if this was true in England, it would be more true still in the Colonies, where the people, largely owing to ignorance of the facts, are blindly Home Rulers, and their now strong trust in the King might be

[1] The new Bishoprics of Sheffield, Chelmsford, and St. Edmundsbury and Ipswich. See pp. 644–6.

upset if they thought he had become a partisan on the other side. So, too, would the working classes, with whom he is at present popular, who are not keen politicians always, and who would be taught by orators to think the King was acting one-sidedly. When I pressed Morley for anything constructive as to what the King, in his judgment, ought to do, he was pitiably devoid of suggestions. He was to dine that night privately with Asquith, Grey, and Haldane to talk over the situation. He had a talk to the King after the Privy Council, and the King (as His Majesty subsequently told me) gave him a peremptory message for Asquith, to say that he adhered to every word that he had said about his primary duty being to prevent Civil War, whatever the consequences to his own reputation or the reputation of the Government.

The situation grew more anxious in the next few weeks. On March 3, a National Appeal was published, with such signatories as Lords Roberts, Milner, Halifax, Balfour of Burleigh, Professor A. V. Dicey, Rudyard Kipling, and (of all men) the Dean of Canterbury (Dr. Wace), demanding Dissolution and declaring that if the Home Rule Bill were passed without being submitted to the country, the signatories would hold themselves justified in taking any steps or supporting any action that might be effective to prevent its being put into operation, including the preventing of the use of the armed forces of the Crown to coerce Ulster. The same evening Mr. Bonar Law came, at his own request, to see the Archbishop. He had a long talk about the whole Irish question and also the King's position:

> Then we turned to the Irish question. He said he would be quite frank with me and tell me how things stand. It would be strictly confidential, but he added a reserve that it need not be secret from. . . . He then developed his statement as follows. These are not his words, but the outcome of long talk.
>
> There will be no settlement about Ulster. When I [i.e. Bonar Law] first saw Asquith some months ago I told him: There are only two possibilities of peace—(1) a General Election or Referendum; (2) the exclusion of Ulster. At the next interview he told me that he had decided to submit to the Cabinet a definite proposal for the Exclusion of Ulster. Then came his public speech (? Ladybank) wherein he withdrew from the exclusion policy. Since then he has shifted backwards and forwards, and I am certain that he has found Redmond implacable and that he (Asquith) is therefore helpless; for Redmond, actively disliking both Exclusion and a General Election, finds that the second would be the less intoler-

able to him, for he would retain his own position in Ireland, whereas if he consented to Exclusion he would be kicked out of leadership by his own people. Devlin would feel this even more strongly, as his strength lies among the Roman Catholics of Belfast, and if Belfast were excluded Devlin would be nowhere. Therefore the Irishmen will decline the Exclusion policy and the only alternative will be to coerce Ulster or to have a General Election. Asquith cannot in the last resort adopt the Civil War policy, and will therefore be forced to a General Election or a Referendum. He will resist and proclaim it to be impossible, but he will give way in the end. This will be ensured by the evidence, which will now be forthcoming, that England is waking up to the reality of the Civil War peril, and the Government will have to admit it and give way. The expected Irish debate for to-night, Tuesday March 3rd, will not come off, for Asquith, in answer to a question from me, will tell us that he is going to make his statement of policy next Monday, and I shall therefore ask my friends to have no discussion to-day. Next Monday I expect Asquith to offer the 'Home Rule within Home Rule' plan for Ulster—not Exclusion in the larger sense, but internal Home Rule subject to a Dublin Parliament. This we shall not accept. I shall on that day declare plainly that we offer the Government peace on one of two lines and those only —(*a*) a General Election or Referendum; (*b*) complete Exclusion of Ulster. To that we shall stand firm. But I shall go on to say that if a General Election or Referendum shows a majority for Home Rule we shall accept the verdict and shall not avail ourselves of the Parliament Act delay, but agree, immediately on the meeting of Parliament, to the Home Rule policy which the people by that time have endorsed. I have not yet got Lansdowne's promise to agree to this, but I have no doubt about securing it. We could make a plausible case for starting the Parliament Act process again and thus postponing things for three years. But we shall not do so: we think the more honest, simple and straightforward policy is to accept the verdict of the Nation forthwith, and we should promise to do so. I believe that Asquith will find himself forced to acquiesce, and that there will be either a General Election or a Referendum quite soon.

All this came out by degrees in conversation. I think I have summarised it correctly.

Then we had some talk about the King's position. I asked simply for information and as one knowing nothing. He did not ask me how much or how little I knew. He thinks Asquith has placed the King in an intolerable position, not from evil intent, but from the exigencies of his own policy. 'Supposing things to go forward without an Election, the King must either sign the Bill or refuse. It is difficult to say which would be the more disastrous position for him. Asquith will say to him 'You may safely sign it, for as soon as it is signed there will be a General Election and therefore no need for bloodshed'. But this is most untrue. The moment the Bill is passed, there will be fighting long before a General Election takes place, and the King will be held responsible for this and will incur the hatred of Ulster. If, on the other hand, he refuses to sign, the cry of Liberals, led by the voices of demagogues, both in England and Ireland, will be unbounded. I hope, however, that it will never come to this, for I think the General Election far more probable. Indeed there is another possibility. Some Ulstermen urge that the moment the Home Rule Bill passes the House of Commons, before it reaches the Lords, the Provisional Government in Ulster should be set up. This will force the Government's hands. The procedure will be that the Ulster Police will be told 'We have no need of you. Go away. You are private citizens. We will police ourselves.' No Government can tolerate this, and fighting must begin forthwith. Thus the King's position might be saved, for the Bill would not yet have come to him for signature. But it would mean Civil War. . . .

Then we passed to another branch of the question. I asked him what he thought about the suggestion now current, that the King ought to insist upon a Dissolution. He replied that on the whole he thought it not impossible that the position might arise when this would be the King's duty, but he was not clear about the form which such insistence should take, or the exact stage at which it would be most appropriate. I said it had occurred to me as conceivable that the King might send the Government a formal Memorandum to the effect that a Dissolution ought in his judgment to take place immediately; and that he hoped the Government would, owing to the gravity of the situation, agree with him. He had as King no wish either way about Home Rule, but he had a strong wish to do what his people honestly desired, and he felt it essential that this should be ascertained. Such Memorandum would not have the form of an Ultimatum, but it could be so worded as to throw upon the Government the onus of resigning, and avoid the slightest appearance of dismissing them. It might be sent to them as a help upon which they might fall back, by stating to the country that they were only so acting by desire of the King. But in that case the King ought to insist that his actual Memorandum should be made public and not merely alluded to. Would this in B.L's judgment be unconstitutional as making a statement independent of Ministers? He replied that it would be, he thought, unusual, but in no sense wrong. It would be unusual because the situation is unusual, and a strong man must take an unusual step when something unprecedented happens. He instanced the Speaker in the early days of obstruction taking the high hand and stopping the debate. Such act had no authority, but was justified by public opinion. B. Law added that of course if such a Memorandum were sent, and Asquith declined to use it after he had been told that he was entitled to use it, and also declined to resign, the King would be justified in taking a firmer course and insisting on its being made public, and it would be impossible for Asquith in that case to avoid resignation. If he had resigned without using it, it would be open to his successors in office to use it afterwards, so as to show what were the real conditions in which the Government had resigned. Of course if Asquith preferred to dissolve Parliament without using the Memorandum, no harm would be done, for the result would have been attained. What he would not be entitled to do would be to resign with the belief that the Memorandum would never be made public.

The Archbishop kept in touch with all that went forward during the next few critical days. On March 9 the Prime Minister announced the concessions which the Government were then preparing to make to Ulster. The same day the Archbishop wrote the following letter to *The Times*:

The ARCHBISHOP OF CANTERBURY *to the* EDITOR *of the Times*

Lambeth Palace, March 9.

Now and then in a nation's story there comes a crisis hour. Great issues turn upon whether it is used or missed. It passes quickly, and there is no sounder test of greatness in the leadership of men than the power to know the time and to 'redeem' it.

When this year began we prayed that, by the help of God, our statesmen might have that vision, and that among the men and women of the land a resolute public spirit might replace what seemed to be a pervading apathy. Has the hour come to-night in which to look for an answer to that prayer? Have not statesmen, in this afternoon's debate, trod ground the very treading of which makes possible a solution of what seemed insoluble?

It depends upon what they learn to be the force behind them making for peace, not strife. It is an hour for steady thought, for broad resolve, for expectant prayer.

The scene then shifted to Ulster. A grave crisis occurred at the

Curragh, and a conflict seemed imminent between the Army and the Government. The wildest rumours were abroad in London on March 21 and 22, and on Sunday, March 22, the Prime Minister authorized a statement that it was untrue that the Government contemplated instituting a General Enquiry into the intentions of Army Officers if asked to take up arms against Ulster.

The Archbishop returned from Bath (where Mrs. Davidson was recovering from an illness) late on the Saturday night, March 21:

> I had been at Bath on Saturday, and only got back to London quite late that night. So I had heard nothing of the details about Army resignations, etc., until this (Sunday) morning when G. Robinson (editor[1]) rang up to ask for an interview. This was after early service which I had celebrated in the Parish Church. Robinson came at 11.0. and gave me all the facts he knew about resignation and political suggestions—regarding the matter as intensely grave and urgent. With the Army question I did not feel that I could deal in any way, but I came to the conclusion that with respect to the political deadlock I ought to attempt something more than I had yet done.

After arranging for the Bishop of Croydon to take a confirmation for him that afternoon in Croydon Parish Church, he had successive interviews with Bonar Law and Asquith.

After a talk with Bonar Law at his house for nearly an hour, in which he found him in not a very sanguine mood and busy with a draft letter to the Prime Minister, the Archbishop went on to Asquith at Downing Street:

> I said that I had come in case I could in any practical form be of service at a moment of crisis. The man in the street, whom I might be taken to represent, regards the position as complex and does not follow the arguments and interchanged challenges of recent debates. He sees or thinks he sees that both sides have during the last fortnight been drawn more closely together, but the present exact points of outstanding difference seemed to him small and not very clear. Is there nothing which I as a non-partisan intermediary can do to elucidate things or to diminish the remaining differences?

Asquith heard the Archbishop out, and after a long conversation went on to say what was the direction in which he thought a

[1] Editor of *The Times*.

via salutis, or, as he preferred to call it, a *via solvendi* might be found.

He could not answer for his colleagues, far less for his party, for *at present* he didn't think he could get them to go so far by any persuasion—but, speaking for himself personally, he would be prepared to agree to either of two possible compromises.

(*a*) Let the proposed plebiscite take place as suggested by Government in all the nine counties, with a proviso that those who stand out shall have a second plebiscite at the expiration of [*x*] years. (Nothing sacrosanct about the *number* of years.)

(*b*) Have no plebiscite now, but let the Bill definitely exclude six counties, i.e. the Protestant four—plus Tyrone and Fermanagh and let those counties have a plebiscite at the end of [*x*] years, and abide by it.

To either of these proposals *if suggested by the opposition* he would personally be prepared to agree, so far as he himself is concerned —but he said this suggestion was not only 'without prejudice', but without any certainty that he could get his people, or the Irish, to agree to it. He was doubtful, or more than doubtful, about some of his own colleagues. But at all events it would receive *his own* favourable consideration.

I asked whether I might state to Mr. Bonar Law what he had said. He answered yes, he thought it might be useful if I did, provided I made it quite clear that he was making no 'firm offer' to that effect, and making no *promise* that he would accept it. But he thought it to be the line upon which a solution might perhaps be reached.

With this in his hand, the Archbishop went to Bonar Law, who went over the ground carefully, and expressed himself as in full agreement with Asquith as to the real *via solvendi*. He thought Asquith's move through the Archbishop of great importance, and the Archbishop took down the following Memorandum in Bonar Law's presence with his authority to tell Asquith the result:

Bonar Law agrees that the second of the two alternatives named by Asquith (see Memorandum) is the only possible line of solution. [It would require to be accompanied by, or] include some such modification in the details of the Bill (e.g. Post Office and Customs and perhaps judiciary) as would make it possible to fit it in with some definite scheme of devolution. [But he did not anticipate difficulty with Asquith over this.]

If the Prime Minister would ask for a further [private] conversation or Conference with a view to making *that* his proposal and taking the risks involved, Bonar Law would on his part take the risks involved for himself in accepting it.

'He recognises that before proposing this *publicly* the Prime Minister has a right to ask Bonar Law to shew him that if it is publicly made he can secure the acquiescence of the Unionists party in such a plan.'

Those are (with the exception of what is in square brackets) Bonar Law's own words, and he strongly encouraged me to put the suggestion in that form, before Asquith. I promised to do so.

On Monday evening the Archbishop was sent for by the King and reported what had passed. On Tuesday, March 24, he again saw Mr. Asquith, and was struck by his testimony to Mr. Bonar Law's straightforwardness. He still thought it afforded a basis for discussion between them and expressed his gratitude to the Archbishop for his help. The same afternoon the Archbishop saw Mr. Bonar Law and told him Mr. Asquith's views.

The next few days the Archbishop listened to the debates in the House of Commons. He also saw other important people, and there was a great deal of comment in the Radical Press as to how it was that the Archbishop came to be mixed up in these political affairs.

On Friday evening, March 27, the Archbishop met Asquith in the Athenaeum and asked him if he (Davidson) was *functus officio*. 'He answered, "for the moment, yes, but I am very far from saying that there is no *officium* for you still, and it may arise in a few days. I am very grateful to you for what you have done. Your work has been very far from fruitless and we may want more of it." I do not say that these are his precise phrases, but this was the substance.'

The general anxiety was deepened by the news that Sir Edward Carson had landed 35,000 rifles in Ulster on April 25. An Amending Bill was introduced into the House of Lords by Lord Crewe on June 23, offering exclusion for six years to any Ulster county that expressed its desire through a poll. This was five days before the murder of Archduke Ferdinand at Sarajevo. The Archbishop was still in close touch with events and had a long talk with the Speaker on June 27, who told him of his own vain attempt to get Carson and Redmond to meet in his presence without impossible preliminary conditions. He also had an interview on June 29 with twelve M.P.s who had asked to see him and begged him to secure a Conference between Lord Lansdowne and Mr. Asquith. This led to interviews with Lord Lansdowne on June 30, and Mr. Asquith later the same day. Neither, however, thought there would be any gain in a Conference at the moment. Mr. Asquith said, as recorded in Archbishop Davidson's memorandum:

'The real issue is not between us at all, but between Redmond and Carson. They are the two who matter. If anyone could suggest a reasonable and far-seeing policy as to the area of exclusion the thing could be settled without any difficulty at all. It entirely turns upon this single question of the area. The time-limit I do not set any store by. We can easily allow another plebiscite at the end of any period, but the area question at the moment seems to present insuperable difficulties. Nobody either in England or Ireland actually wants the Exclusion policy, but we have reached a point where it is the only solution to avoid strife. It is quite easy to say what Counties *must* be excluded, but, the moment that is said, we get into the area of the remaining Counties whose exclusion is either difficult or (in two cases) practically impossible. Keep your mind to the thought that this Area question is the only thing that matters. All the rest is "leather and prunella".'

The Archbishop saw Lord Morley and a few others during the first part of July and spoke in the House of Lords on the Amending Bill on July 8, when he urged that the dividing line for the Area to be excluded should be chosen geographically, and not as distinguishing Protestants from Catholics. His notes show that he was fully abreast of affairs—the summoning of the Buckingham Palace Conference by the King (at Mr. Asquith's suggestion as the only way of getting Irishmen to attend); the King's speech drafted under the King's personal direction, but approved by Asquith with its appeal for generous compromise, and the warning sentence:

To-day the cry of Civil War is on the lips of the most responsible and soberminded of my people.

His notes add:

Stamfordham further told me how friendly the Conference had been, and how ready the men were to interchange talk with one another. He had not himself been present in the Room during the Conference but had been there when they met and had himself had talk with several. He had been agreeably impressed by Craig, whom he did not before know.

But though the opening of the Conference was friendly, it collapsed on July 24, no agreement being possible on the Area for exclusion from the Home Rule Bill. But by the end of the following week, everything gave way to a new crisis of a graver kind, and all men's minds were turned to the issues of Peace and War in Europe.

VOLUME II

RANDALL DAVIDSON AGE 75

CHAPTER XLV

THE OUTBREAK OF WAR

NORTHUMBERLAND. Alas! sweet wife, my honour is at pawn;
And, but my going, nothing can redeem it.
LADY PERCY. O! yet for God's sake, go not to these wars.
SHAKESPEARE, *2 King Henry IV*, II. iii.

IT is for the historian, and not for the biographer, to analyse the causes of the world crisis and record the successive shocks which led to the outbreak of war in August 1914. Certainly there were few leaders in English public life to whom the tragic event was more unexpected than Randall Davidson. As we have seen, he had friends in Germany, and on more than one occasion in recent years he had expressed the view that war between his country and theirs was unbelievable.

I

The thought of Christians in Germany and England being at war was peculiarly hard to entertain: and it so happens that the very last letter the Archbishop wrote to a German Churchman before war began dealt with this very point. It was in reply to Dr. Ernst Dryander—one of the most eminent Lutherans in Germany and chief Court Chaplain to the Kaiser. Dr. Dryander had written on July 17, 1914, in a personal way, inquiring whether the Anglican Church would be likely to accept an invitation to take part in the Jubilee of the four-hundredth year of the Reformation in 1917.[1] He was anxious not to embarrass the Archbishop by later making an official request which might be difficult to grant. So he asked:

DR. ERNST DRYANDER *to the* ARCHBISHOP OF CANTERBURY

17 July 1914.

Before, however, we take any further steps for the working out of the idea, it lies on our hearts that we should know, in quite a personal and absolutely confidential way, whether such a proposition would be able to reckon on a favourable reception and friendly treatment on the part of those Evangelical Churches outside Ger-

[1] Its beginning was reckoned as October 31, 1517.

many which have relations with us. Before all, we must learn whether we can have the sympathy and participation of the Anglican Church with its world-wide influence.

The Archbishop replied, on August 1, 1914, expressing his sense 'of the great value of your courteous considerateness in writing to me thus privately beforehand', and he explained the grave difficulty which he foresaw in official participation by the Anglican Church:

The ARCHBISHOP OF CANTERBURY *to* DR. ERNST DRYANDER

Private. 1 August, 1914.

In accordance with your wish therefore I will tell you frankly and without reserve that there would in my opinion be very grave difficulty in arranging that the Anglican Church should officially and corporately identify itself with the movement for commemorating the words and acts of Martin Luther in the dawn of Protestantism. To one who has studied our history, and who understands our theological and ecclesiastical position so clearly as you do, I need not explain the significance of the double relation which our Church holds, both historically and actually, to European Christianity. We have, and I rejoice in it, a firm and assured hold upon the principles of the Reformation, and therefore a very definite and brotherly relation to the Reformed Churches of the Continent, especially to their Teutonic and Scandinavian branches. On the other hand we have, both historically and practically, a relation to the historic doctrine and system of the Western Church, a relation which is rightly valued intensely by great sections of English Churchmen. Your knowledge of England will enable you to appreciate the consequent difficulty which would arise were it proposed that we should corporately throw ourselves into a commemoration which might, however unintentionally, take the form, or at least bear some appearance, of a declaration of a coherent and solidly united Protestantism against a coherent and solidly united Catholicism. I do not think that such would be your endeavour or your wish, but I feel so certain that misunderstandings on the subject would arise in England that I am sure it would be on public grounds wisest that the Church of England should not officially or formally identify itself with your proposed celebration. Hence the very great value of your courteous considerateness in writing to me thus privately before-hand. My reply is, like your letter, personal and confidential. That there are important teachers and leaders within the Church of England who would rejoice personally to show sympathy with what you propose to do, I do not doubt. But this, as you will be the first to recognise, is a different thing from the kind of corporate and official co-operation about which you make enquiry.

The inquiry which Dr. Dryander made, thus received a full and courteous answer, but it was prefaced with the following pregnant sentences:

. . . The present condition of public affairs is such as to cause all of us the keenest anxiety and to absorb our daily interest. You are, I am very sure, joining together with us in daily prayer to Almighty God that by His mercy the possibility of international conflict may be removed far from us. War between two great Christian nations of kindred race and sympathies is, or ought to be, unthinkable in the twentieth century of the Gospel of the Prince of Peace.

The day on which Archbishop Davidson wrote this letter, and the days immediately before and after, were days of keen anxiety to him and to others. At the very moment when statesmen were striving for peace in the capitals of Europe, a conference of Churchmen of the different countries was assembling at Lake Constance—the fruit of the Anglo-German Society for Friendship between the Churches—and actually met to found, on August 4, the World Alliance for Promoting International Friendship through the Churches, a body which was not to meet a second time till July 1919, when the War was over, at the Hague.

Mr. Allen Baker, M.P., one of the leaders of the movement, on his way to Lake Constance, came to see the Archbishop on July 30, on behalf of a House of Commons Committee which was preparing a memorial to Asquith in favour of England's non-intervention in the war. The Archbishop notes:

I objected to much of its phraseology and also said that I could not possibly sign it without an assurance that it was on lines which the Government would find helpful and not harmful.

The Archbishop saw Asquith on July 31:

Asquith was absolutely clear that for the next few days at least anything of the sort would be actively harmful. The position is this: That England is the one Power in Europe which has diplomatic weight at present, inasmuch as it has neither any axe to grind or any Treaty Alliances to hamper it, or any standing quarrel with any one of the great Powers. As a matter of fact the position, were it not so tragic, is almost ludicrous. The credit of Europe has collapsed. Our Stock Exchange is to-day closed; the Bank of England is going to make an order which has not been made for half-a-century about paper currency, etc.; and all for what? Because of the vagaries of a wild little State like Serbia, for which nobody has a good word, so badly has it behaved. But though France and Russia, and still more Germany, are averse to going to War—and Germany is actively eager to the contrary—they are all more or less depending on one another. Russia dare not, in view of popular sentiment, let the Serbians be completely smashed. France dare not, if it can help it, leave Russia unhelped; and Germany dare not let Russia and France join to smash Austria without German intervention. All turns on what England may do, and the object of our Foreign Office at present is to keep Europe in suspense on that point. So long as Europe does not know what England is likely to do, there is a great steadying influence upon both France and Russia, for they both feel that Germany might be difficult to tackle unless the other Powers had us supporting them. Germany in the meantime shrinks from aggressive action—e.g. through Belgium, because it does not know whether or not we should vehemently oppose; and, if we did, their task would be doubled in difficulty. Hence the expediency of our not saying at present what we will or will not do. We virtually hold the balance. For these reasons it would be most mischievous were the military party in Germany to be able to point out that England had shown such an expression of public opinion against intervention that it would clearly stand aloof, and therefore Germany need have no fear that its shipping would be interfered with in the North Sea. Sir Edward Grey is doing all that he can to utilize this strong position of ours in favour of peace, and during the last few hours the horizon has grown a little lighter, inasmuch as Vienna is now talking to St. Petersburg, whereas communications had been interrupted.

All this being so, Asquith begged me to use my influence to prevent any demonstrations or memorials in favour of our non-intervention finding expression at present in a manner which might mislead the Continent into thinking that England had popularly made up its mind to have nothing to do with the matter. He thought that the next few days would show what chance there is of localising the conflict and preventing any spread. He thought Serbia deserved a thorough thrashing, but he feared that Russia dare not stand up and see the Serbs completely humiliated. If only Austria would consent to declare that she has no ambitions beyond proving to the Serbians that they cannot flout her with impunity, all might be well. But Austria at present is disinclined to say anything of the sort. Austria is thus, among the great Powers, the chief obstacle to a speedy settlement. Asquith highly approved of my preaching if possible in the Abbey, with a view to saying something against the panic, and preventing a general sense of confusion and even panic.

That night one of the Royal Princesses was staying at Lambeth, and spoke of the seriousness of the situation, with the remark: 'Now we are all in it.' And the Archbishop replied, gravely: 'Princess, you must not say that. That must not be.'

The following are notes given as they were written in Mrs. Davidson's diary of those days. It will be remembered that the Lambeth Conference Consultative Body all this week had been considering the issues of Kikuyu:

Meeting of Lambeth Conference Consultative Committee on the Friday, July 31.

At Early service there seemed a sound in one's ears like a Bugle call—

Then at breakfast *telephone message from Craufurd*—he and Marjorie *must* be married at once, *as war was certain* and he would be ordered out.

Arranged for marriage on Sunday in Lambeth Chapel.

The Consultative Committee ended—all left with heavy hearts.

Sunday, Aug. 2. Randall *thinking*—THINKING. In early morning, sent off message should he go to Buckingham Palace to preach to the King? *Answer yes—Went off. 10.30 service* and sermon: *at* 12 marriage of Craufurd and Marjorie which he took. *About 2 lunch.* The young couple went off at once to Camberley to join regiment. At 3 *Westminster Abbey. Randall preached*—TEXT 'OUR FATHER'. Just as he began—cries arose from transept seats 'Votes for women'. The Suffragettes had chained themselves to their seats! Randall waited *quite quietly* till they had gone out. Then preached—OUR FATHER.

The Archbishop preached in the Abbey on the text 'After this manner therefore pray ye: Our Father which art in Heaven' (Matt. vi. 9). His opening words showed what was in his heart—'What is happening is fearful beyond all words, both in actual fact and in the thought of what it may come to be. . . . This thing which is now astir in Europe is not the work of God but the work of the devil.'

He was present next day at the Debate in the House of Commons, and heard Sir Edward Grey's speech. When he came back to Lambeth, sad though he was that such a tragedy should be, he was convinced that no other course was possible than that taken by the Government.

The Archbishop's own first words in the House of Lords on August 5 included an appeal to the public to abstain from acts of individual selfishness or gain, which made it harder for others to meet the difficulties 'which we should all try to face as well as may be, standing shoulder to shoulder'.

II

Throughout the afternoon of August 3 and the whole of August 4, on the Archbishop's summons to Lambeth, the Bishop of Ely (Dr. Chase), the Dean of Wells (Dr. Armitage Robinson), and Canon Bullock Webster were busy preparing special prayers; and these were issued in accordance with an order of the Privy Council of August 4, and were used all over England on the following Sunday, on the special Day of Prayer and Intercession on Friday, August 21, and continuously. They were grave, serious prayers, breathing trust and asking for guidance for the removal of 'arrogance and feebleness' as well as for the gift of 'courage and loyalty, tranquillity and self-control'. Some wished a sharper note to be struck, and the Archbishop was reproached by more than one correspondent for the want of a direct prayer for victory. To a peer who complained of this omission he replied:

The ARCHBISHOP OF CANTERBURY *to* LORD G——.

27 August, 1914.

I thank you for your letter. Such criticisms are always useful, but I think I ought to tell you that, if there was one request which poured in more strenuously upon me than others from all quarters when we were compiling these prayers, it was that we should abstain from identifying ourselves with the Divine Will to such an extent as to claim that God is simply on our side, and that this is a matter of course. Surely our ordinary prayers in daily use—e.g. what is called the Second Collect at Morning Prayer ('O God who art the author of peace', etc.), the Prayer for the King's Majesty, and, in the Litany, the third of the petitions for the King, and many others express a definite petition for victory. Then with regard to the new Prayers, will you look at page 10 on the small Form I enclose, and at pages 8, 9, 18, 23 on the gray-covered

Form enclosed? I think it possible that you have overlooked these. I am very grateful to you for sending me a copy of your own which I have added to others which we have in frequent use, for of course what we have suggested is only meant for a nucleus around which people will add such prayers as they individually feel to be appropriate and right.

Many strange suggestions as to the manner and the form of prayer flowed in to Lambeth, of which one may be quoted here from R. W. Raper, a Senior Fellow of the Archbishop's own College of Trinity, Oxford:

R. W. RAPER, ESQ., *to the* ARCHBISHOP OF CANTERBURY

Hoe Court, Colwall, Malvern. Sept. 5, 1914.

Many thanks for sending me your rules for conferring degrees. I would not have troubled you if I had known of them, but nevertheless I am grateful. In proof whereof I trouble you again in a matter which does not seem at first sight to be my special province and does seem to be yours. It is for another national prayer to be used at the same hour on the same day (Sunday) in every Church in the land: very short and intense and to the point, and may be repeated with or without music, many times.

My point is that one of the greatest powers of prayer is that of the mind of man over the mind of man: be it direct or goeth it round by heaven, it is spiritual and from mind to mind through whatever medium;—it would be no use praying for a 16 inch gun to be an 18 inch gun—but most efficacious would be a prayer to confound the gunner: and I suggest something like this

> 'Strike the fear of God (at last) into the heart of the Kaiser (or our Enemy) so that he depart and go back whence he came: strike the fear of God into his hosts so that what is left of them may make haste to return with him' (even as Sennacherib, King of Assyria, and his remnant arose early in the morning and made haste to go back and dwell in Nineveh).

To achieve this end concentration of force and numbers of those praying are likely to be most effective, but the gift of concentration is limited, and therefore there is need of brevity to meet human nature while the numbers swell the mass and volume of spiritual power sent forth.

Please don't regard this as anything but the highest trust worthy of your high position. I have only expressed myself in chance and unprepared words but they are absolutely true, as you are sure to see. A wonder may be more easily wrought on William than on most, because he believes in such things in a way—a perverted way—and is even at this moment impelled by a prophecy which rightly interpreted means his doom. Be our Isaiah and help to send him home.

The Archbishop replied:

The ARCHBISHOP OF CANTERBURY *to* R. W. RAPER, ESQ.

[September 1914.]

I thank you for your letter. The subject of the prayers to be used in our Churches is occupying a great deal of my time. I take due note of what you have suggested, but I do not, I think, share altogether the view to which you give expression as to the form which our prayers for the ending of this terrible time of warfare ought to take.

But other duties thronged the Archbishop of Canterbury, and his guidance and help were sought in all kinds of ways. He was very depressed at the tragedy and waste of it all—and hated the war. But there was little time for personal questions. Lambeth Palace was even more of a workshop than ever. At the very beginning of the war, the Archbishop offered it to the authorities for use as a hospital. The offer was considered but refused, most fortunately, as it would have been hard to know what the Archbishop could have done if he had left his house. There was no chance of a visit to Canterbury, where Cricket Week had begun and ended in a single day—Bank Holiday, August 4; but he was kept in touch with events there by letter, about the troops pouring into the place, about the soldiers having their sing-songs on the Green Court in the evening, and the extra hospital accommodation at St. Augustine's, and the recreation rooms in St. George's Hall and St. Peter's Parish Room. And for some weeks in the autumn the Archbishop lent the Old Palace as the head-quarters of the local military command.

III

So far as the Church was concerned, the immediate question was the duty of the Clergy, as a whole, in time of war, and the supply of Chaplains to the Army. Both questions were to cause a good deal of agitation in very different ways during the next few years. The Archbishop was in touch with the Chaplain-

General (Bishop Taylor-Smith) about the Army's needs; and the number of offers already made for service as chaplains was far beyond the number that could be used (900 beyond the requirements on September 1). On September 2, he wrote as follows to the Diocesan Bishops:

> I have been receiving, like many other Bishops, enquiries both from clergy and laity as to whether it is legitimate and reasonable that clergy should now volunteer for service as combatants. I recognise the *prima facie* arguments which can be used by the younger clergy, or by others on their behalf, in support of such action at a moment like the present, and I have given careful attention to a question which some people feel to be a very difficult one. By every line of thought which I have pursued, I am led to the conclusion that I have been right in maintaining from the first that the position of an actual combatant in our Army is incompatible with the position of one who has sought and received Holy Orders. The whole idea which underlies and surrounds Ordination implies this. We have a calling of our own of a quite specific kind, and throughout the whole history of the Church, authoritative expression has been given to the paramount obligation of that calling. Under this obligation those who have been ordained to the Ministry of Word and Sacrament ought, even in time of actual warfare, to regard that Ministry, whether at home or in the field, as their special contribution to the country's service.

This ruling with regard to combatant service gave rise to a certain amount of criticism, but was generally regarded at the time as both 'authoritative and conspicuously sensible'. With regard to non-combatant service, for example with the R.A.M.C., the Archbishop gave no such injunction, and he thus expressed his views in a letter dated September 22, to Surgeon-General Macpherson:

> Provided a man can rightly leave his home work, I do not think that the fact of his being in Holy Orders ought in itself to be a bar to his undertaking work which is explicitly that of caring for the sick and wounded, and is distinctly non-combatant.

The Archbishop's assistance was, however, asked in the general appeal for recruits. He had no desire to refuse any help he could properly give, but when he was invited on September 4, by the Parliamentary Recruiting Committee to say something in an 'Appeal for Recruits from Religious Leaders' he expressed some hesitation. Lord Esher, in writing to Davidson about a British Museum matter, after a talk with Lord Kitchener, used these words:

VISCOUNT ESHER *to the* ARCHBISHOP OF CANTERBURY

Sept. 10, 1914.

Lord K. does not wish for any 'Campaign' on behalf of recruiting under the auspices of the Church. He would 'intensely dislike it'—his words.

The Archbishop had some correspondence with Mr. Percy Illingworth, M.P., Chairman of the Recruiting Committee, saying he was puzzled. The following was the explanation provided by Sir George Arthur, Lord Kitchener's private secretary:

SIR GEORGE ARTHUR, BT., *to* PERCY ILLINGWORTH, ESQ.

War Office, Whitehall, S.W. 1 Oct. 1914.

Regarding the 'Parliamentary Recruiting', I think I may assure you that a letter from the Archbishop of Canterbury on the same encouraging lines observed by the Archbishop of York would in no way conflict with the remarks made by Lord Esher. I think these referred to the Church—as such—being made a vehicle for military purposes and especially to pulpit pronouncements.

One may be quite certain that the Archbishop—if he writes—will use words as felicitous as they will be useful.

IV

While this correspondence was proceeding, a manifesto of a very different kind had reached Lambeth Palace. Early in September a very earnest 'Appeal to Evangelical Christians abroad' from German theologians reached England through American channels. It had been drawn up in August by some of those who had been most active in the Anglo-German friendship movement, and especially in the World Missionary Conference at Edinburgh, 1910. Amongst its supporters were: Professors Harnack, Herrmann, Eucken, Wundt, Deissmann, Loofs, Julius Richter, Dr. Spiecker, Mission Director Axenfeld, Dr. Dryander, Pastor Bodelschwingh, and General Superintendents Kaftan and Lahusen.

The Appeal began by denouncing the network of lies which had endeavoured to cast on the German people and its Government the guilt for the outbreak of this war, and maintained that only under the compulsion to repel a wanton attack had Germany now drawn the sword. It reminded 'Christian friends abroad' of the joyfulness with which 'we German Christians greeted the fellowship in faith and service which the Edinburgh World Missionary Conference left as a sacred legacy to Protestant Christendom'. If the fellowship with the Christians of other lands in obedience to the Universal Mission of Jesus were now irreparably destroyed, 'the guilt of this rests, this we hereby declare before our Christian brethren of other lands with calm certainty, not on our people':

> We know full well that through this sanguinary judgment God is also calling our nation to repentance, and we rejoice that she is hearing His holy voice and turning to Him. But in this we know that we are at one with all the Christians among our people, that we can and must repudiate on their behalf and on behalf of their Government the responsibility for the terrible crime of this war and all its consequences for the development of the Kingdom of God on earth. With the deepest conviction we must attribute it to those who have long secretly and cunningly been spinning a web of conspiracy against Germany, which now they have flung over us in order to strangle us therein.

As soon as the Archbishop saw the manifesto he felt that an answer should be made. He consulted some friends, especially the Dean of Wells, Dr. Scott Lidgett, Mr. W. H. Dickinson, and Sir Claud Schuster, who met him on September 11. He himself drafted what became the beginning and end of a long and careful reply, the middle portion of which consisted of two considered statements about (1) the Course of the Negotiations, (2) the Neutrality of Belgium.

After referring to the brothers and friends of our own in the Church of Christ, the reply expressed the 'amazement' of the Archbishop and his co-signatories:

> That those who occupy the positions held by the signatories of this appeal should commit themselves to a statement of the political causes of the War, which departs so strangely from what seem to us to be the plain facts of this grave hour in European history.

It continued (and these are the Archbishop's own words):

> It has not been a light thing for us to give our assent to the action of the Government of our country in this matter. But the

> facts of the case as we know them have made it impossible for us to do otherwise. Of these facts we offer here a brief but a careful summary, derived from the official papers, the accuracy of which cannot be challenged. It is upon these facts that we rest our assured conviction that, for men who desire to maintain the paramount obligation of fidelity to plighted word, and the duty of defending weaker nations against violence and wrong, no possible course was open but that which our country has taken.

Then followed a statement of Sir Edward Grey's efforts for peace, from the White Book, and the obligations regarding the neutrality of Belgium. The reply continued (and here again the words are the Archbishop's):

> God knows what it means to us to be separated for a time by this great War from many with whom it has been our privilege—with whom we hope it will be our privilege again—to work for the setting forward of the Christian message among men. We unite whole-heartedly with our German brethren in deploring the disastrous consequences of the War, and in particular its effect in diverting the energies and resources of the Christian nations from the great constructive tasks to which they were providentially called on behalf of the peoples of Asia and Africa.
>
> But there must be no mistake about our own position. Eagerly desirous of peace, foremost to the best of our power in furthering it, keen especially to promote the close fellowship of Germany and England, we have nevertheless been driven to declare that, dear to us as peace is, the principles of truth and honour are yet more dear.

There is one phrase in the Archbishop's pencil draft which does not appear in the final version (the work of the little Drafting Committee already mentioned) but is important, especially as we look back from a long distance. It is this, which forms his conclusion:

> While we must perforce leave to the future the disentanglement of these diplomatic controversies, the palpable facts are neither obscure nor difficult. They mean our adherence to an engagement to which we have solemnly been party, and the upholding of the essential condition of brotherhood among the nations of the world.

The Archbishop's reference to the need of 'disentanglement' at such a date is especially significant. It was, however, altered by the Drafting Committee and the final paragraph ran in the complete text as follows:

> To have acted otherwise than we have acted would have meant deliberate unfaithfulness to an engagement by which we had solemnly bound ourselves, and a refusal of our responsibilities and duties in regard to the maintenance of the public law of Europe. We have taken our stand for international good faith, for the safeguarding of smaller nationalities, and for the upholding of the essential conditions of brotherhood among the nations of the world.

The reply was signed by the Archbishops of Canterbury, York, and Armagh; the Bishops of London, Winchester, Brechin, Dean Inge, Dr. Scott Lidgett, Dr. T. M. Lindsay, Dr. J. Hope Moulton, Sir William Ramsay, Dr. John Clifford, Dr. W. P. Paterson, Dr. W. Sanday, Dr. G. Adam Smith, Dr. H. Scott Holland, Dr. H. B. Swete, Dean Armitage Robinson, Bishop Hassé, Lord Balfour of Burleigh, Dr. F. L. Wiseman, Eugene Stock, and many others, and was dated September 23, 1914. It was translated into many languages, and had a very wide circulation. The Archbishop also sent the answer to Dr. Nathan Söderblom, the newly-elected Archbishop of Upsala, who had written to him and other Church leaders in Europe and America asking them to sign an appeal 'to all those who have power or influence in the matter . . . seriously to keep peace before their eyes in order that bloodshed soon may cease'. The Appeal drafted by Dr. Söderblom stated:

> Our Faith perceives what the eye cannot always see. . . . The strife of nations must finally serve the dispensation of the Almighty, and all the Faithful in Christ are one.

In refusing to sign the Appeal, Archbishop Davidson said:

The Archbishop of Canterbury *to the* Archbishop of Upsala

Oct. 9, 1914.

You may be certain, however, that at the first moment when it seems to me that an opening is presented for securing a righteous and enduring peace, I shall do my utmost to urge it, but I am clear that that moment, greatly as we long for it, has not yet come.

The conflict which has been forced upon Europe (I impute no motive but merely state a fact) must I fear, now that it has begun, proceed for the bringing to an issue the fundamental moral principle of faithfulness to a Nation's obligation to its solemnly plighted word. The recognition of the moral validity of such an obligation is fundamental to the maintenance of peace and progress among the Nations of the World.

War was, beyond a doubt, to deepen the mutual understanding of members of different Christian Churches in England. And it is interesting to note that, early in the autumn, on October 9, the Archbishop summoned a Conference of Christian Ministers and Laymen to the Guard Room at Lambeth Palace, 'to study the deeper bearings upon our own country, Europe, and the world of this great war and convulsion of the nations'. Besides the two Archbishops and the Bishops of Winchester, Oxford, and London and other representative Anglicans, were Dr. Clifford, Dr. Shakespeare, Dr. Scott-Lidgett, T. E. Harvey, Arnold Rowntree, and other Free Churchmen and members of the Society of Friends. The Conference was followed by prayer in the Chapel. But the Conference revealed a good deal of difference, explicit or implicit, on the rightfulness of war.

V

In France also, there were tokens of kindly feeling between the authorities of the Roman Catholic Church and Anglican Chaplains to the Forces and the soldiers to whom they ministered. The Archbishop of Rouen[1] showed much personal courtesy, and also in the early months of the war gave his sanction for Church of England Services (including Holy Communion) in the Roman Catholic chapels attached to two buildings then being used as Military Hospitals.[2]

The following correspondence passed:

The ARCHBISHOP OF CANTERBURY *to the* ARCHBISHOP OF ROUEN

Monseigneur, Lambeth Palace, 3rd November 1914.

I hope you will not think it intrusive on my part if I send you a few words of grateful acknowledgment and thanks for your abundant courtesy and kindness to our English soldiers who have been in Rouen during these eventful months. I have heard from several different quarters of the kindness of your action and the

[1] Mgr. Fuzet.

[2] The first was in peace time a Home of Rest for working girls from Paris: the second (used as a Red Cross Hospital for officers only) Le Séminaire, a theological college, attached to the Archbishop's Palace.

helpfulness of your spoken words, and I am sure that the facilities which you were good enough to offer have been greatly valued by those who have been ministering spiritually to our men. We are passing through a time of profound solemnity, and the stress of bereavement and anxiety is pressing upon all our homes. It is well that at such a time we, to whom is entrusted the privilege of ministry, should everywhere be doing what we can to brighten and strengthen the lives of those on whose courage and high spirit so much depends for both our countries.

With the assurance of my high respect and grateful regard

I remain, Monseigneur,

Your faithful brother and servant

in our Lord Jesus Christ,

RANDALL CANTUAR:

The ARCHBISHOP OF ROUEN *to the* ARCHBISHOP OF CANTERBURY

My Lord, Rouen, 15th November, 1914.

Your thanks are very precious to me. They are more than I deserve for what I have been able to do for the soldiers, your countrymen, stationed in Rouen. It is nevertheless sweet to me to be assured on such high authority that the modest tokens of goodwill which I have shewn to the sons of England, at the hour when our two nations are suffering in like manner, have been welcome. We look to the bravery of our soldiers for the success of our arms; we look still more to heaven. That is why each one of us prays fervently, in perfect integrity of faith [en toute droiture de foi]; that is why also we seek to bring all those who are fighting to God, as often as we may, in religious worship. In lifting our souls towards God, we exalt our courage also. How much more ready we are to do and to die like heroes when we have just worshipped the All-Mighty, and when our consciences are pure. Let us do what we can to keep our dear soldiers always thus! And may our common prayer also avail to bring about a speedy end to this terrible calamity! And may the victory of England, of Russia, of Belgium, and of France be complete and swift. Their cause is that of justice and of true civilisation; it is the cause, we do not doubt, that Providence has taken in hand.

I offer to Your Grace,

My Lord,

the assurance of my feelings of high esteem and of religious devotion in Our Saviour Jesus Christ

✠ FREDERIC, Archbishop of Rouen.

VI

In view of subsequent developments it is also worth noting the first occasion of the Archbishop's contact with Russia during the war. It has a curious significance to-day. A certain Mrs. Sonia Howe, the Russian wife of a Finchley vicar, begged the Archbishop for an interview in October 1914, and implored him to get English influence exerted to persuade the Russian Government to give some relief as regards their political prisoners. She was herself, she said, in touch with Prince Kropotkin—and was obviously a woman of sense and ability. The Archbishop passed the request on to Sir Edward Grey, who sent a somewhat chilling reply (November 10, 1914) to the effect that the British were always on the side of liberty, 'but to demand from His Majesty's Government promises to interfere in the internal affairs of another country is both futile and mischievous'.

VII

Other problems connected with the camps also engaged the Archbishop's attention. Within ten days of the declaration of war, disquieting accounts reached him from different places, in his own diocese and elsewhere, about the temptations to which the soldiers of the new Army were subject by the exuberant hospitality of their friends who offered them drink. He knew that the same thing was happening in almost every place in which troops were quartered; and he wrote to the Home Secretary (Mr. R. McKenna) on August 13, 1914, begging him to secure means for the earlier closing of public houses. 'So much interference', he said, 'with ordinary law and regulations has been apparently found possible at present, that I have thought it may be practicable in this matter also. It will indeed be a disastrous thing if, during the period when these lads are thus absent from their homes, they should get into disorderly ways, and one would like to reduce the temptations to a minimum.'

The Home Secretary replied that he entirely sympathized with the Archbishop's views, and that the matter was under consideration. The Archbishop also had a long interview with Lord Kitchener at the War Office on the subject—which he followed up with a letter:

The Archbishop of Canterbury *to* Earl Kitchener of Khartoum

23rd October, 1914.

I undertook at your kind request to send you a note to-day about what I meant as to the appeal which as it seems to us might at this juncture be made by you to the public with reference to the terrible mischief which is going on as regards Drink in the neighbourhood of our Camps, and indeed elsewhere.

With regard to the Women, among whom the new wave of Drink is most serious, we must ourselves fight the mischief as well as we can. It sounds horrid to say it, but the fact is that the women dependents of our soldiers are getting more money than they can wisely handle, accustomed as they are to dealing with shillings where they now have in some cases pounds at a time. However, this mischief we will do our best to combat.

There is a more general mischief which I believe no one in the land can stay or stem except yourself: I refer to the universal treating of men in uniform which is going on to a degree almost incredible and producing scenes about which I hear from almost every town with which I have to deal. And not towns only. It is rampant in some country places. A man told me last night of his having seen eight men in uniform lying in a ditch within one mile of road in a country place in Surrey. Waterloo Station has become proverbial, and I have seen a letter to-day from a young officer in one of the South Coast Camps (it would perhaps be unfair to mention the regiments or the place) who describes the terrible difficulties that he and other Subalterns are having in regard to the drunkenness among recruits and some of the Territorials. I believe the fault to rest largely with the public whose stupid and mischievous friendliness takes the form of making these poor fellows drink. On the top of this, especially at night, comes the moral question. I have direct statements as to soldiers being taken from the public houses to brothels, when they are too drunk to walk, and to this our young men are liable, many of whom have been steady and respectable fellows until now. What is wanted so far as I can judge is a stirring, sharp appeal, not from parsons or social reformers as such, but from those responsible for the conduct of the War, and above all and pre-eminently from yourself. I believe honestly that a published note from you to the effect:

> We have to see this War through. We can do it provided our men remain fit. They cannot remain fit if they get into bad ways at the start; and the public helps to this by the stupid mischievous habit of treating them to Drink. If we are to do

> aright what is now before us, we need fit men, and the public is doing its best to make them unfit. For Heaven's sake mind what you are about.

Of course you will put this in your own way ten times better than I can put it; but I honestly believe that that kind of utterance, coming from you at this moment, would go far to bring the mischief to an end. And probably you would add a word to the men themselves about self-control and right behaviour quite apart from treating.

Do not suppose that I am making any wholesale accusation against either the Territorials or the New Army, far less against our regiments generally. I have plenty of evidence as to places in which things have gone thoroughly well and drunkenness has been markedly absent. . . . A word from you to the effect I have suggested, that if the War is to be carried through this thing must stop, would I believe have untold effect. I should feel presumptuous in writing this to you but for the encouragement you gave me yesterday that I should send you such a letter for your private eye. Of course it would spoil it all if it were supposed to be suggested by men like me.

Lord Kitchener did not, however, feel inclined at the moment himself to write such a letter, having already written in general terms. But he encouraged the Archbishop to do so. The Archbishop issued an appeal in *The Times* for abstinence during the war. He repeated Lord Kitchener's warning to help men to keep clear of temptations, and he urged that as many citizens as could should undertake to be abstainers during the continuance of the war. He said:

The ARCHBISHOP OF CANTERBURY *to the* EDITOR *of 'The Times'*

Oct. 27, 1914.

By doing so they would strengthen the hands of those soldiers—the large majority of our troops—who are manfully resisting such temptation. They would be seizing the opportunity to bear a deliberate part in the self-denial and discipline of the hour. Their example would make the rough roadway a little easier for those wives and mothers to whom unusual circumstances and anxiety are, with sad effectiveness, bringing unusual temptation.

A few months later he joined in a further appeal to a similar effect, with the civilian population even more markedly in view. Drink was having disastrous results, not only in camps but in factories and docks. In March 1915, Mr. Lloyd George received an important Deputation from Shipbuilders lamenting the deplorable results of the increase of wages on the amount of work done and the vast quantities of drink consumed. Many members of the Deputation stated that the only remedy was total prohibition. Lloyd George got into touch with the Archbishop and told him of his anxiety to rouse public opinion in favour of total abstinence. Could the Church give a lead? And he similarly asked the leaders of the various professions whether they could give a lead. The King announced on March 30 his intention to 'set the example by giving up all alcoholic liquor himself and issued orders against its consumption in the Royal household' during the War. The Archbishop, after a great number of interviews and communications, secured the publication of the following statement on April 6:

> In view of all that is now happening, and following the unprecedented lead of His Majesty the King, we desire to press seriously upon the minds of those whom we can influence the duty and privilege of bearing voluntary part in the Nation's self-discipline and self-sacrifice by abstaining from all alcoholic drink during the continuance of the War. Some definite act on the part of us all is due to our brave men, to the Nation at large, and to God.
>
> RANDALL CANTUAR:
> COSMO EBOR:
> FRANCIS, CARDINAL BOURNE.
> JOSEPH COMPTON-RICKETT.
> (*President of the Free Church Council.*)

VIII

A problem of a different kind but, as the Archbishop pressed upon politicians, social rather than military, was that of the unmarried mother. To the wives and dependants of the sailors and soldiers serving, separation allowances were given. It was clear that dependants, who had been in fact living with men as their partners, though not married to them, ought not to suffer extra hardship through those men's patriotism. But it was also clear that unmarried mothers could not be treated as in all respects on a par with the married. Extremists on one side pressed for great generosity, and no over-strictness about technicalities like marriage lines. Extremists on the other side declaimed against the breaking down of the sacredness of marriage. And, an extra complication, there was a multiplicity of authorities, local and central, statutory and voluntary, eager to help, but sometimes most unscientific in their activities. The Archbishops and Bishops, at their Meeting in October 1914, pressed for a real consideration of the problem. The Archbishop had interviewed Asquith, Bonar Law, and others, and took an immense amount of pains in getting to the bottom of the matter by seeing not only statesmen but many social workers. The magnitude of the problem was not recognized at the outset. A preliminary Committee was appointed in December, and the strength of its membership shows the importance attached to the subject. It consisted of Lloyd George, McKenna, Bonar Law, Austen Chamberlain, T. P. O'Connor, and G. N. Barnes. The Archbishop himself appeared before it on March 4, 1915, and gave his evidence with a great amount of care, information, and persuasiveness. The Archbishop made the point throughout that 'in acting generously to those dependants of soldiers, who had the place of wives without being wives, there must be the utmost care taken not to break down the distinction between the married and the not married'. And in the end he claimed that the distinction drawn in the official paper subsequently issued, and the procedure followed, were due to the efforts he and others had made. By these arrangements, the married woman with her children came as a matter of right to claim her allowance, while other allowances would be given by the War Office to *other dependants* 'only after considering the recommendations made by the local Old Age Pension Committee', and on the distinct condition that the dependant must also be receiving a definite proportion of the soldier's pay assigned voluntarily by himself.

The relief of dependants was but one, though the most exhausting one, of the many domestic war questions which claimed the Archbishop's attention. He had also to do, and often in considerable detail, with recreation rooms, the moral safeguarding of camp surroundings, the concentration camps of interned Germans, and the safety of East Kent in case of invasion.

CHAPTER XLVI

THE FIRST YEAR OF THE WAR

He this day again defended duelling, and put his argument upon what I have ever thought the most solid basis; that if publick war be allowed to be consistent with morality, private war must be equally so. Indeed we may observe what strained arguments are used to reconcile war with the Christian religion. But, in my opinion, it is exceedingly clear that duelling having better reasons for its barbarous violence, is more justifiable than war in which thousands go forth without any cause of personal quarrel, and massacre each other. BOSWELL, *Life of Dr. Johnson* (1773).

THE first Christmas of the war was spent at the Old Palace, Canterbury. As he looked back in December, the Archbishop's general impression of the course of events was that 'the Government has done exceedingly well considering the extraordinary difficulties due to the suddenness with which the whole catastrophe came upon the world'. What he did criticize at the end of four and a half months was 'the readiness of some Government departments to shelter themselves against severe criticism by pleading the hurry and confusion of the first weeks', and he complained that some subjects like the relief of the dependants of soldiers and the appointment of chaplains, which ought to have received much more quiet consideration, were still 'chaotically unsolved'. (Memorandum dictated December 13, 1914.)

The Archbishop and Mrs. Davidson kept open house at the Old Palace for friends, new and old, for soldiers of different regiments, and for young officers fresh from the University. Here too they offered sympathy and a welcome for more than one of those who had lost a husband or a son; and sometimes, in the evening, a chaplain would read *John Inglesant*, or Tolstoy's tale 'God sees but waits'.

I

On New Year's Day 1915, Mr. Asquith, his wife and their daughter, Elizabeth, came to lunch at the Old Palace. At lunch Mr. Asquith spoke of Oxford, and painted pictures of the horrors of the War for the Germans in Poland—the snow covering those that fall and the wolves coming by night to devour them. Afterwards the Archbishop took the party round the Cathedral, where the Prime Minister showed a keen interest in Heraldry. The first Sunday in the year, January 3, was observed all over England, not, as some had desired, as a day of national humiliation, but as a day of humble prayer and intercession. It had been settled after communications between the Archbishop and the King, and with the full support of the Roman Catholic authorities and of the Free Churches. Indeed the observance, partly through the help of Cardinal Bourne, partly by direct communication from the Archbishop to the authorities of other Churches, was extended to the Church in France, Belgium, and Russia, and even to neutral countries, especially America. The Archbishop preached in St. Paul's Cathedral on the Peace of God which was to guard ('garrison') men's hearts from unworthy fear, from depression, the love of ease, and (he added this at the end) 'against the peril of letting anger—even if it be righteous anger—be fanned and cherished into something like an un-Christian hate'. It was a sermon nobly thought and built up, nobly spoken, and heard with absorbed attention by the vast congregation.

On January 5, the Archbishop married the Dean of Wells and Miss Amy Faithfull in Lambeth Palace Chapel. Miss Faithfull for many years had been a most intimate friend and helper, both at Farnham and Lambeth, living with the Davidsons as Mrs. Davidson's secretary. Then—the first break since war had been declared—he and Mrs. Davidson went off for a fortnight's rest to Sidmouth. Here he played golf, went to see friends and did, to a certain extent, take a little ease from the pressure of Lambeth. It was characteristic, however, that when he learnt that Stephen Reynolds, author of various books, half literary, half sociological, lived in the town, he got him to breakfast and had a good talk with him. But though he was much attracted by Reynolds personally, the Archbishop was not impressed by his thinking power or his preparedness to defend the views he had expressed in *Seems So*, which the Archbishop had read the previous night. He besides had a full talk with the local Excise Officer, whose various duties as Secretary to the Old Age Pensions Committee, and to the Soldiers' and Sailors' Families Association, enabled him to give the Archbishop most useful information about the problems of unmarried mothers and soldiers' dependants, of which the Archbishop's mind was then full. He also worked at the draft of his statement on Kikuyu.

II

In February, the Archbishop took the opportunity of a talk with Asquith about the Welsh Church, to discuss the question which he had already raised in a previous conversation before Christmas, as to the publication of untrue statements under Government authority. His note is as follows (Feb. 4, 1915):

> I brought before him the disquiet which many of us are feeling about the publication of untrue statements under Government authority. He was taken aback by the bluntness of the form in which I put it. When I mentioned the 'Audacious' he gave me once more the explanation that the facts about the loss of the ship had not been made public because no lives were lost, and it was certain the Germans were themselves puzzled as to what had happened with regard to the actual sinking or non-sinking of the ship. He went on to say that he had himself wished from the first to make everything public, but that he had been over-ruled in the Cabinet and, to some extent, convinced. I answered that I had no wish to re-open that question, although I have my own opinion, but that I regarded the publication in the Navy List of the account of the 'Audacious', with her armament and her crew, as a definitely untrue statement put under the Royal authority by the King on the 1st January. He said 'Are you sure it is in the Navy List?' I assured him that it was so, and begged him to send for a copy. He said he would take my word for it, but he was unaware of it and thought it open to criticism. I was very frank about it and said that criticism was not the word: it meant direct condonation on the part of all of us of a statement which could only be regarded as a deliberate untruth—deliberate because it must have been carefully thought out whether it should appear or not, and untrue because the book has the definite imprint that it is corrected up to Dec. 31st, 1914, and is published under authority of the Government. I asked what reply I should give to American friends who said that they had hitherto believed English official documents to be absolutely trustworthy and were confronted now with the Navy List for January. He said he would think it over and consult Winston Churchill. I said that I wanted an answer which I could give to critical friends, and he replied that he was afraid he could not help me. He made some lame explanation that in war-time facts about ships and guns were often concealed in order not to inform the enemy, and that this was so in the history of all our wars. I said I should be interested, perhaps relieved, if he could show me examples of the publication in past years of

Navy Lists or Army Lists giving definite statements which were untrue, though I should be surprised to learn that these had been accepted by public opinion as justifiable. He said he was not prepared with any such. As a matter of fact he offered no defence and was obviously uncomfortable.

The Archbishop had a special object in desiring an answer to his criticisms (and he instanced another at the time), as he had recently seen two extremely intelligent Americans who were passing between Germany, England, and the United States during the war months, on disinterested philanthropic or missionary errands, and were in touch with important leaders of religious thought in Germany.

Convocation met, for the first time since the war, in February, and the Agenda paper contained as its first item, repeated session after session for four years, 'The Church and the War'. There were various questions, of the relief of dependants, army chaplains, prayer—all came up; and the Archbishop explained the action he was taking or had taken. And there were other general subjects, such as Prayer Book revision, the care of ancient churches, and training for the Ministry.

On March 4, John Parker died, after thirty years' service as porter at Lambeth Palace. He was one of the inner circle of the Archbishop's domestic staff, a charming character, willing, and not without humour. When he took Americans round Lambeth Palace he often stood before Morton's Tower and said 'This tower, ladies and gentlemen, was built about 1486—six years before America was discovered.' He was greatly appreciated by the large number of visitors both from home and abroad, who came to see the Palace, and had some awkward moments, for example with the suffragettes, in which his good sense and humour were of great service to the Archbishop. A tablet to his memory was placed on the ante-chapel wall in Lambeth Palace with the following inscription:

In Loving Memory of
JOHN PARKER,
Born 29 *August*, 1845. *Died* 4 *March*, 1915.
Porter and Custodian of Lambeth Palace, 1883–1915.

He threw into the performance of his duties such real readiness and good humour that he enjoyed the confidence and affectionate regard of the three Archbishops under whom he served; while all alike, whether household or visitors, valued and remembered his courteous and cheerful welcome, his exact and eager knowledge of the antiquities and traditions of the Palace, and his friendly and faithful good-will.

Erected by Friends at home and abroad, 1916.

III

The Archbishop had already seen signs of an 'un-Christian hate' when he preached at St. Paul's. As the War went on, the difficulty of distinguishing righteous indignation from hatred increased a hundred-fold. It was not the men at the Front who were haters. The Christmas fraternizing between British and German soldiers hardly suggested that. But there was often great bitterness at home, in quarters where it might have been least expected. To a Worcestershire clergyman, who sent a violent and cruel letter to an English Princess, the Archbishop wrote as follows:

The ARCHBISHOP OF CANTERBURY *to the* REV. N— F—

26th April 1915.

You are I believe aware of the fact that Princess ——, feeling deeply the character of the letter which you wrote to her a few weeks ago, sent it to me. Not having the advantage of knowing you personally, I informed the Bishop of Worcester, sending him a copy of the letter and asking him for some information. He told me that he thought the letter must be a malicious forgery on the part of someone who wished to misrepresent your character. He now tells me that he finds on enquiry that this is not so. I confess I had thought with him that it was almost incredible that a letter so coarse and even brutal in its rudeness could have been addressed by a clergyman or a gentleman to a lady who from her position is absolutely helpless to reply or to protect herself from that kind of insult—a lady, too, who has during a rather long life been an active leader in untiring effort of every kind for the benefit of her English fellow countrymen and countrywomen—a lady, further, whose dearly-loved son laid down his life in the service of our country.

I shall be obliged if you will kindly acknowledge the receipt of this letter, adding anything that you may desire to say. I will then consider what further step, if any, I ought to take, either by the publication of the letters or otherwise. My hope is that you may be able to say that you wrote that intolerable letter when in a condition of overstrain or excitement and that you have since realised its actual character. You will notice that I have said nothing whatever to suggest any restriction as to opinions which a thoughtful man may entertain on public questions. Such opinions ought of course to be based on adequate knowledge of details, but the responsibility rests simply with the man himself. I have referred solely to the character of the letter which you allowed yourself to write.

The clergyman was impenitent. He replied that 'you must remember that in this matter you are writing as man to man, there being no question of ecclesiastical law or discipline in the case': and 'the fact remains that she is a Princess of Germany, having a son serving in that army of savages'. One or two more letters passed. The Archbishop saw the Princess again, and they decided 'to leave the man to his own reflections'.

During the opening months of 1915 the War spirit grew fiercer. The Archbishop from the first took an active interest in the condition of prisoners of war, whether in England or in Germany—and set his face firmly against retaliation. In a debate in the House of Lords on March 15, 1915, on British Prisoners in Germany, he said:

There are many ways in which this war may possibly do harm to England and the English people, but one disaster would be greater than any other that I can imagine. I mean this and I say it with my whole heart. If once we became infected with a lower spirit and adopted a lower ideal in this matter by imitating bad habits and bad ways of which we might hear elsewhere, it would be the worst misfortune that the war could bring upon us.

The first Zeppelin air raids on the east coast in April and May, the sinking of the *Lusitania* with the loss of 1,189 lives, the publication of the Bryce report on German atrocities in the same month—all had their influence. There was a deepening of resolve, but also a hardening of temper. We find a growing evidence of the increasing determination, in the language used by the Archbishop and his brother Bishops at Whitsuntide. In the Homily which had been read all over the country on January 3, there were words of self-examination, humility, repentence; and side by side with prayer for a speedy and decisive victory this paragraph stood:

We shall have no desire to see our enemies crushed merely for the sake of their humiliation. We shall wish for them as for ourselves that their eyes may be opened to know what is true; and we shall pray that the day may come, by the mercy of God, when we may learn to understand and respect one another, and may be united as friends to pursue the common good.

At Whitsuntide the note of determination was far more strongly struck. It is the severity of the national ordeal that is most emphasized in the Pastoral Letter issued by the whole diocesan episcopate:

> After 10 months of war we see more clearly than at first the greatness and the severity of the ordeal which is putting the spirit of our nation to the test. . . . The spirit arrayed against us threatens the very foundations of civilized order in Christendom. . . . It can only be decisively rolled back if we, for our part, concentrate the whole strength of body, mind, and soul which our nation, our Empire, holds.

But we also find, though less conspicuous in the same Pastoral, and little quoted, a warning against reaction in spiritual things:

> We have more to say, and it matters most of all. It is the office of the Church of Christ to quicken and to guide the spiritual forces on which the strength, the stedfastness, and the nobility of the national spirit depend. Are these forces as alert, as watchful, as persistent now as they ought to be? We have cause to fear that they have languished a little since the earlier weeks of the war. A reaction comes. . . .

It was at this time that the Government's policy against aliens increased in its severity. Many pathetic instances came to the Archbishop's notice of hardship to aliens, and he did his best to secure consideration and mercy, in many cases by personal communication with the Aliens Department at the Home Office, both now and later. It was also at this time that the use of poison gas was first foreshadowed and then determined; and the first signs appeared of that reprisal policy against which Dr. Davidson was to protest, quietly but firmly, every year the war continued.

IV

On May 6, having heard of the proposal to adopt asphyxiating gas, in reply to the German use of it, he wrote a strong letter to Lord Stamfordham. He urged that it would have been regarded a few weeks ago as altogether out of the question 'a barbaric act, impossible for English soldiers', and that 'the fact that our barbarian-like opponents have sunk to that level' was no reason why we should sink with them. Lord Stamfordham replied sympathetically but not holding out much hope. 'I have read letters from General Officers', he replied on May 6, 'who say, for the first time in the War, the men are getting impatient and cross at being thus sacrificed while we do nothing to retaliate.'

The Archbishop then wrote to the Prime Minister:

The ARCHBISHOP OF CANTERBURY *to the* RT. HON. H. H. ASQUITH

May 7, 1915.

May I write to you with frankness about a matter which is causing me the gravest concern. From what has been said, both in Parliament and outside, I gather that our authorities, military and civil, who have the responsibility for the conduct of the War, are at present contemplating as a practical matter the question whether the conduct of our enemies in the barbarous employment of poisonous gas as a means of warfare ought to be met by corresponding action on the part of our own Army. I have not seen any official statement to the effect that this is definitely intended, but the words used both in Parliament and outside seem to show that it is at all events not out of the question. The infamous conduct of the German military authorities in deliberately organising this mode of warfare, and the fact that it has been put into effective operation in defiance of every principle of international ethics, have aroused a burning sense of indignation among all reasonable men. I am no soldier, but as a Christian citizen I try to understand the situation as it exists, and I confess that I am profoundly disquieted by the indications that our own Army may be bidden to meet the new situation by itself adopting these inhuman tactics. I suppose that if anyone had suggested a few months ago that the British Army would use poisonous gases for creating fatal disease among its enemies, the notion would have been scouted as preposterous. What has happened to change our view? Nothing, so far as I know, except that our opponents have sunk to that level of misconduct in defiance of International Conventions and of the dictates of common humanity. Is the reason adequate? They have degraded the traditions of military honour and the good name of the German Army by adopting these vile practices. We can no doubt follow their example if we choose. If we adopt that line of reprisal (and this is a really important point) how far will the principle carry us? If they are poisoning the wells in South Africa, and perhaps ultimately in Belgium, are we forthwith to do the like? If so, can we retain self-respect on the part either of the Army or the Nation? It seems to me that international agreements for securing the honourable conduct of war would then be obliterated in a brutal rivalry as to the horrors which can be perpetrated by both sides. The result would be such a tangle, that the world will soon be saying, and history will say hereafter, that there was nothing to choose between the nations who were at War, and it would become a matter of small importance, and probably of disputed fact, who it was who began the general course of adopting these vile usages. That is how the matter strikes me. I have, as I say, no knowledge whatever of military matters and I may be making some blunder of thought, but I try as a Christian man to look fairly at these things, and I own that the vision of what may be about to happen disquiets me profoundly. I wonder what the real effect would be were our Sovereign through the proper channel to make it known that he was so horrified by these barbarities that he desired definitely that his Army should—do what?—resolutely abstain from any such foul conduct, and, while taking every precaution possible to secure our soldiers from the effects of this infamous weapon, leave the indelible disgrace of its adoption upon the Germans alone?

You may say that I am an ignoramus and that this is a matter for experts. But is it not really the sort of question on which the average intelligent citizen of a Christian country is entitled to have an opinion? Do you think we should be satisfied ten years hence as a people if we had to look back upon having done these things ourselves?

The letter was acknowledged, and was followed by an interview between the Archbishop and Asquith, and by a letter which dealt in a broader and milder way with the same situation, giving the protest a general framework of assurance that the Government had behind it a united people, unhesitatingly sure of the rightness of their cause, and their conviction of the true nature 'of the fight we have to wage against the unbridled forces of cruelty and wrong'. The milder letter was published, together with Asquith's reply, which appreciated the assurance but said little about poison gas. On May 18, Lord Kitchener spoke of the use of poison gas as 'diabolical', and in the next sentence said: 'His Majesty's Government feel that our troops must be adequately protected by the employment of similar methods'. The Archbishop was seriously disturbed, and wrote to beg the Prime Minister for a definite assurance that the 'diabolical' method would not be used by British soldiers. But the battle was lost. On May 24, the Prime Minister's Private Secretary wrote:

MAURICE BONHAM CARTER, ESQ., *to the* ARCHBISHOP OF CANTERBURY

10 Downing Street, Whitehall, S.W. 24 May 1915.

I showed the Prime Minister your letter with regard to the use by our army of poisonous gases.

Leave has been given to Sir John French to make use of gases, for urgent military reasons, the French having already taken this decision.

It is one which on humanitarian grounds cannot but be regretted, but we cannot deny to our soldiers the use in self defence of a weapon which has proved *effective* in the hands of our enemy.

We are ready at the earliest moment to agree to the abandonment by both sides of their use, and steps are now being considered to secure this.

More than this cannot at the moment be said, but you may rest assured that no-one is more aware than the Prime Minister of the objections to their use and no-one more anxious to bring to an end or at least to limit such hideous methods of warfare.

On May 27 the *Princess Irene*, an auxiliary ship, was blown up in Sheerness Harbour. It was a calamity without an explanation. Only one man was saved. The Archbishop with unfailing sympathy went off to Sheerness and conducted a memorial service on June 1. He preached on a favourite text, 'A Faithful Creator'. It was a fine, simple sermon, much read and full of comfort at the time, and a few sentences may be given here:

Faithful Creator! We hold our service to-night at a time of national strain and stress and widespread sorrow. In the height of a great war every day's news, whether its prevailing note be of anxiety or of good cheer, every day's news when we at last get it in full, must carry grief to many homes; for it is certain to be weighted with tidings of the earthly close of dearly loved lives—lives of buoyant sunshine, lives valorous and full of hope.

The mass of human sorrow thus accumulated is almost incalculable. Usually the sorrow is distributed widely over many places; now and then the day comes when the sorrow is concentrated in great volume in one place. Last Thursday night, after the thunderous roll of a great explosion, that dark pall of sorrow fell in Sheerness. I have been anxious, as the chief pastor in this part of

England, in our own historic Kent, to come here to-night and join my prayers with yours, that we may together face the calamity in the right way and not in the wrong way.

V

There had been a great deal of dissatisfaction with the supply of Army chaplains during the first months of the War. It came to a head in June and July 1915.

The Archbishop had asked a question in the House of Lords on June 16 about the number of chaplains—more as a signal than as a criticism. The Bishop of London followed with a long, critical speech in Convocation on July 6 and 7. He had himself visited the troops in France in the Spring, and was in close touch with much that was felt and said. He asked for a private conference between the War Office authorities and certain of the Bishops upon the whole question of religious ministrations to the army. Without doubt the most important outcome of the discussion, and of the conference which resulted, was the appointment of a Bishop for the Troops in France. Bishop Llewellyn H. Gwynne, Bishop in Egypt and the Soudan, was made Deputy Chaplain-General, and at once took up his office with the British Expeditionary Forces—an office which he discharged with conspicuous sympathy, courage, and ability. Hardly any man in the Army was more welcome than he, wherever he went, and no priest or bishop in the whole Chaplains Department was more appreciated in his pastoral ministry. Through him, from the date of his appointment to the end, the Archbishop, as we shall see, was kept in the closest touch with the religious and moral needs of the Army.

In July the first step was taken towards compulsory service, by the passing of the National Registration Act. Under this Act the following question was asked of every person, other than sailors and soldiers, between the ages of 15 and 65: 'whether he is skilled in, and able and willing to perform, any work other than the work (if any) at which he is at the time employed, and, if so, the nature thereof.' During its passage through Parliament two suggestions were made to the Archbishop: (1) That the Church might undertake through the Clergy the whole of the analysing, tabulating, and indexing of the returns made under the National Registration Scheme. (2) That as it had been decided that the

Clergy should be exempt from military service, they should have authoritative guidance as to what service they ought to perform.

As to (1) the Archbishop did not feel that he could encourage the clergy to undertake that particular task. Such work, he argued, required skilled knowledge, and an offer from the clergy to do it could only be justifiably made if there were the certainty that they had, as a body, both the ability and the time to do it thoroughly. He feared that many clergy in country parishes, who might have the time, would not be able to tackle the work successfully; and clergy with large parishes, either in town or country, had their hands full with all the work that was peculiarly their own in that grave and anxious time.

As to (2), the two Archbishops gave the following guidance to the Bishops for their clergy. Premising that 'the work of the clergy amongst the people in their parishes is national service in the highest sense of the word', the Archbishops said that (*a*) the clergy might offer any special skill or experience outside their pastoral work, in their own neighbourhood, and especially help in dealing with the needs of sailors, soldiers and their dependants, and encouraging thrift: (*b*) the clergy might serve as chaplains in the Navy and Army with the Bishop's approval; or volunteer—again with the Bishop's approval—for *non-combatant* service with the R.A.M.C. or the Red Cross. But in answer to the plea, continually repeated, that the young clergy might join the fighting lines, the Archbishops said (Aug. 6, 1915):

> We still hold that it is unsuitable for the Clergy to serve as combatants, and we believe that, at the present juncture, the work of the Clergy in their parishes is certainly as necessary as other kinds of 'necessary work' which exempt from Army service those who are so employed. The task of the Clergy is a task which no other man can discharge. Let this be rightly understood, and we are sure that many of the perplexities which have been felt will disappear.

At the end of August (the 23rd) the Archbishop had a long private talk with Lord Curzon. Of recent months he had not been able to get in close touch with all the actual facts about public affairs for various reasons. Asquith, for some reason, had not been either very responsive or very illuminating. Curzon welcomed the talk, and gave the Archbishop frank and confidential information on the situation as a whole. He told him about the different fronts, and also about the division in the Cabinet upon compulsory national service, as to which he said 'Kitchener is cryptic and does nothing to commit himself'. While Asquith was strongly opposed to conscription, Lloyd George was in favour, and Balfour insisted on handling the question philosophically! There followed some criticism of the colossal blunders made by the War Office, of which, however, 'we are not allowed to say that this can be in any degree Kitchener's fault. He is sacrosanct, and I am not dwelling on that point now.'

Then came a question and answer:

Archbishop: 'What do you personally feel as to the certainty of our ultimate success?'

Lord Curzon: 'I have never regarded as impossible the idea of our failure to conquer Germany in the sterner sense of conquering, but our resources against Germany's conquest of us are very great and far-reaching.'

VI

Almost immediately after this interview, the Archbishop was taken ill. The strain of the past twelve months had told upon him. It was a serious illness—a recurrence of the trouble which had attacked him in 1913—and for some weeks he had to be nursed most carefully at 'Tremans' in Horsted Keynes—the home of Mrs. Benson. His friends were alarmed, and there was at one time grave cause for anxiety. A note or two written to Mrs. Davidson will show the affection in which he was held:

The BISHOP OF OXFORD *to* MRS. DAVIDSON

August 31, 1915.

There is no man more necessary to England—of that I feel sure.

M. E. SADLER, Esq. *to* MRS. DAVIDSON

Sept. 2, 1915.

One feels that through him one is in the presence of such accumulated stores of wisdom in Government—with Queen Victoria's judgment immediately behind his, and layer after layer of personal tradition lying behind that again. But all this knowledge is, with him, deepened into wisdom by the presence of some more sacred influence, and one learns from him the infinite depth of simple things.

There is no doubt that Dr. Davidson, patient as he was, felt his illness acutely. He did not like being laid aside, away from affairs and the possibility of intimate knowledge of what was going on. And when the War news was bad, he took a rather unusually gloomy view and seemed prepared for all eventualities. Indeed one of those who knew him best remarked at the time that he was sure the Archbishop had thought out exactly what he would do if the Kaiser came to England after a decisive march, and went to Buckingham Palace!

In October he published a small collection of War sermons—*Quit you like Men* (S.P.C.K.) They are mentioned here because, though they had no large sale, they were greatly appreciated by some of those who knew good literature when they saw it. Much treasured was a letter from his old friend and teacher, Dr. Montagu Butler, Master of Trinity:

The MASTER OF TRINITY *to the* ARCHBISHOP OF CANTERBURY

October 27, 1915. Trinity Lodge, Cambridge.

The 'Quit you like Men' series has, if possible, knit me to you more closely than ever, and made me feel how exactly—how loftily and how tenderly—you have struck just the right chord, Christian and patriotic, that we all needed for our Country, for our Families, and for ourselves. I thank God that you have been able to employ your great office for this priceless service. . . .

With the winter, the second stage was taken on the road to Conscription. Lord Derby was put in charge of a new Recruiting Scheme which began in October and lasted for two months. It was frankly the last attempt to see whether the necessary number of troops could be raised without Conscription. Everybody of military age was to be asked whether he would enlist, except the men whose names had been starred by the local officers. The clergy were also amongst those who received the appeal from Lord Derby. But the Archbishop held to the line he had already followed, and, even when asked to write something for the Recruiting Supplement of *The Times*, he made a special point of the 'task of the Clergy' as a separate task, outside the combatant ranks. Nor was he willing, in spite of Lord Derby's request, to ask the clergy to make an appeal from their pulpits on the last Sunday in November, begging men to enlist. The Archbishop saw Lord Derby on several occasions, and found him most considerate throughout. In a letter meant for publication, he assured the Archbishop that in his view the clergy, 'however much they may wish to enlist, equally do their duty when obeying the directions of those who are set in authority over them': though he thought—and the Archbishop agreed—that candidates for Ordination ought to be encouraged to enlist. He could not, he said, go further than this, and did not know what the House of Commons might later decide in case of Conscription. The Archbishop's view did not pass without criticism. There was restiveness on the part of certain Clergy, and some Bishops were more favourable than others to the idea of combatant service. It was indeed sometimes suggested by laymen that the Bishops were hindering recruiting. Mr. Snowden asked in the House of Commons whether the provisions of the Defence of the Realm Act might not be put in motion against them (November 30, 1915); and Lord Derby himself privately asked the Archbishop whether 'you do not think it would be a good thing to allow all Curates, if they so wish, to be attested under the Scheme'; and added, on November 22, 'I find there is a very strong feeling growing up on this subject, not only amongst those who are opposed to our Church, but also amongst those who are its chief supporters. They feel the Church is being very much weakened by this exceptional treatment that is being meted out to the Clergy.' A conversation took place, and the following correspondence was made public, and settled the question:

The ARCHBISHOP OF CANTERBURY *to the* EARL OF DERBY

Lambeth Palace, S.E. 3 Dec. 1915.

I am sorry to trouble you again upon the subject of the enlistment of clergy as combatants. But there is clearly so much confusion of thought and variety of action among many local recruiting authorities that I feel compelled to re-state the matter.

In accordance with your published letter to me of 29th October and your conversation with me on November 17th I and other Bishops have instructed clergy who have sought our advice that they are following a perfectly legitimate course if, in reply to recruiting officers, they say that acting under the instruction of their Bishops, they are unable to offer themselves for combatant service. I now learn that clergy who have so acted are in some cases informed that their names, not having been starred by the local tribunals, will be placed on the list of those who while at liberty to offer themselves for service have declined to do so—in other words among those who are popularly described as 'shirkers'. This seems to be an intolerable position in which to place men who are eager and willing in whatever way is fitting to serve their country at this time. It is obvious that Parliament alone can ultimately decide on the terms of any Compulsion Act, should such an Act become necessary. Meantime are we at liberty to state that in your judgment the men who have followed the instruction of their Bishops and relied upon your own words ought not to be discredited either by being placed upon any such list as I have indicated, or by being classed among those who have without due reason refused to offer themselves for combatant service? We have repeatedly drawn the distinction between such combatant service and the non-combatant branches of Army work. In such work clergy who can rightly be spared from their parishes may, in our judgment, most properly take their part.

The EARL OF DERBY *to the* ARCHBISHOP OF CANTERBURY

War Office. 3 December, 1915.

In answer to your letter of the 3rd December, I would repeat what I said to you in my letter of October 29th, namely that 'I am strongly of the opinion that Ministers of all denominations, however much they may wish to enlist, are equally doing their duty when obeying the orders of those set in authority over them'. That was my personal opinion then; it is my personal opinion now, and no slur can possibly be attached to any individual Minister who, acting under your Grace's instructions, declines to join the Army. He is only doing what I, in my letter, said I thought it was his duty to do—obey the orders of those who are set in authority over him in the Church to which he belongs.

I gladly recognise your Grace's statement that where it is possible to spare men in Orders to join non-combatant branches of His Majesty's Forces, you will be prepared to sanction, and indeed will welcome their doing so.

CHAPTER XLVII

THE NATIONAL MISSION

The Church of England is a fine church,' said I; 'I would not advise any one to speak ill of the Church of England before me.'

'I have nothing to say against the church,' said Peter; 'all I wish is that it would fling itself a little more open, and that its priests would a little more bestir themselves; in a word, that it would shoulder the cross and become a missionary church.'

GEORGE BORROW, *Lavengro*, ch. lxxix.

I

THE first year of the War had revealed, in some measure at home, and in a far greater degree abroad, an unsuspected capacity for religious faith and devotion. On many sides men asked, though too lightly, 'Is there a religious revival?' and here and there efforts were made to deepen the response to the religious spirit, for example by pilgrimages of prayer, started by women in the villages, or through the newly formed 'League of the Spiritual War'. The Archbishop decided to invite twelve priests of different schools of thought to report to him on 'The Spiritual Call to the Nation and the Church—what is being done by the War and what should be done'. Four of the priests afterwards became Bishops[1] (W. Temple, W. H. Frere, E. A. Burroughs, G. C. Joyce), and others were Canon Peter Green and Canon V. F. Storr. The Chairman was Dr. A. W. Robinson. The outstanding recommendation of this Committee in October 1915 was 'a National Mission led by the Archbishops . . . through all the cities and towns and villages of the land'. Such an effort is much more easily recommended than accomplished, but the Archbishop decided to do what in him lay to carry it out, after it had been approved by the Bishops as a body. It cannot be said that it was started with overwhelming enthusiasm, and very early in the preparation Dr. A. W. Robinson reported:

The REV. A. W. ROBINSON *to the* ARCHBISHOP OF CANTERBURY

24 Nov. 1915.

It was extremely difficult to make any progress in face of the determined pessimism of the Bishop of Oxford and Peter Green.

[1] Archbishop of York: Bishop of Truro: Bishop of Ripon: Bishop of Monmouth.

The Bishop maintained that there was 'a rot amongst the clergy', who chiefly desired to flee from their spiritual duties; and that the Church was in such a state that any talk of a Mission to the Nation was quite out of the question. Peter Green was sure that the influence of the clergy in the community was nil.

The Bishop of London directed us most patiently and sympathetically, and the results arrived at were better than could at one moment have been expected. . . .

It was a Mission of an unusual kind, to the Nation, undertaken by the Church of England, though the Archbishop informed both Cardinal Bourne and the Heads of the Free Churches of what was planned, in the hope (not altogether realized) that the authorities of those Churches might see their way to take some corresponding action. It was a Mission of Witness by the Church of England. It was carefully distinguished from anything like Parochial Missions. Its aim was 'the removal, if it may be, of popular misconception as to the character of the Gospel Message and its relation to the daily life of ordinary men and women', and especially 'to call the men and women of England to earnest and honest repentance of our sins and shortcomings as a nation and to claim that in the Living Christ, in the loyal acceptance of him as the Lord of all life, individual and social—lies the one sure hope'.

An immense organization was set on foot, and a large volume of literature was poured out, the Bishop of London throwing himself with unselfish enthusiasm into the task of Chairman of the Central Council. There was also a special Panel of Archbishop's Messengers. The date of the Mission itself was fixed for October and November 1916, each diocese making its own arrangements, the preparation of the clergy coming first. And, after the special effort had been made, it was agreed that the Mission should go on in a less intensive form with the help of five Archbishops' Committees of Enquiry which were set up, and a general Consultative Committee with the Bishop of Lichfield in charge.

II

There were naturally difficulties in the course of the Mission, and to one objection, expressed with some violence at the time, we ought perhaps to refer. A Resolution had been carried by the Central Council, urging upon the Bishops 'the importance of giving definite directions as to the best ways of using the services and receiving the message of women speakers, whether in church or elsewhere.' Miss Maude Royden, a prominent speaker and writer on the Women's Movement, was a member of the Council, and naturally interested in the Resolution. Mr. Athelstan Riley, another member of the Council, protested vigorously to the Archbishop that this Resolution was 'the first recognized step in an organized movement to claim the priesthood for women'. In the same letter he objected to the interest taken in the Labour Movement by the Council. Mr. Riley was supported by a large number of Church people, especially by prominent members of the English Church Union, and (at the opposite end) Dean Wace. The Archbishop replied:

The ARCHBISHOP OF CANTERBURY *to* ATHELSTAN RILEY, ESQ.

Lambeth Palace. 22nd July 1916.

I thank you for your letter received two days ago. I think that your summary of what has passed in the Council and its Committees would convey to readers a somewhat different impression from that which was left upon the minds of some at least of those who took part in the discussions. But, what is more important, you take exception, if I rightly interpret your words, to the action of the Council in requesting the Bishops to give definite direction as to the best ways of using the services and receiving the message of women speakers, many of whom are, in the Pilgrimage of Prayer and otherwise, giving such real and acceptable help in our little rural parishes. To me it seems very desirable that the Bishops should thus direct what is being attempted. For example, I have observed with much appreciation what is being done both in England and in France by women who have quietly gathered a few girls and children in church and helped to guide their prayers, and I think it is on the Bishops that the responsibility rightly devolves for seeing that such endeavours are duly regulated. It does not seem to me that the apprehensions you entertain as to what may ensue are based upon adequate grounds.

Again, you criticise, if I do not misunderstand you, the invitation we extended to some of those who know and understand labour movements, to take part in the Council's deliberations as to how the Church can best promote the common good of the English people. I welcome their aid and I believe it may prove helpful to us in all ways.

But to discuss these questions would lead us into wide fields, and

I will only add that I welcome the assurance you give me of your feeling that the two Archbishops will, to the best of their power, 'guard the Apostolic Faith and Discipline' in the protection of which they have, as you remind us, a grave responsibility.

And writing a few days later to the Archbishop of York, he expressed himself as follows:

The ARCHBISHOP OF CANTERBURY *to the* ARCHBISHOP OF YORK

8 Aug. 1916.

I have just been reading the reports in my own Diocese from the parishes in which the Pilgrimage of Prayer has been taking place. The good that is done is beyond all question, and the welcome it has met with from unexpected people is remarkable. In not one single instance has there been any attempt or desire on the part of any of the women to give the sort of general Address in Church which Riley imagines to be part of what is contemplated if women are allowed to help their younger or simpler sisters and children. When I was in France, there was scarcely a single Church without women in little groups praying together, one of them leading the others, and the Roman Bishop of Southwark, speaking to Burge the other day, said 'Your people seem afraid of the very thing which we are trying to encourage as much as we can'. I certainly should feel it to be wrong to restrain this simple mode of teaching people in little country villages to use their own churches for prayers, and I do not believe that it is going to lead to what Riley and his friends suppose. But he has whipped up a mischievous agitation about it and men like Lord Victor Seymour and George Russell and others are trying to beat a big drum about it.

III

A very particular illustration of the Archbishop's own share in the National Mission was shown in his determination to meet the clergy of his own diocese face to face. It is never easy for one with all the cares of the Primacy upon him to be in constant personal touch with his parish priests. Of necessity he left much of the individual visitation and counsel to his Suffragan Bishops, of Croydon[1] and Dover. He had just secured a new Bishop of Dover

[1] Dr. H. H. Pereira had been consecrated Bishop of Croydon in 1904: and was in 1916, 72 years old. Dr. Bilbrough was 49.

in Harold Ernest Bilbrough, Rector of Liverpool, who, for the next eleven years, served him and the diocese with an affectionate and unselfish enthusiasm which would be difficult to over-value. Personal touch with the majority of the clergy was harder than ever in the war years, when public affairs claimed every moment of Davidson's time and thought. But now the need of seeing his clergy and speaking to them as a father to his sons came to the Archbishop with special force. How were these men who were receiving exemption from combatant service discharging their own special task? Were they rising to their trust? In what way could he help them to do their peculiar service with a greater seriousness of purpose and a greater readiness for sacrifices?

Accordingly from January 11–14 all the clergy of the diocese were summoned to Canterbury Cathedral, meeting separately in the two archdeaconries for the better part of two days and a night. The gathering, as the Archbishop told them, was unique. The Cathedral itself was strangely altered from days of peace. The lovely ancient glass had, for safety's sake, been taken from the windows, and was buried. The Black Prince's monument and all the beautiful tombs were surrounded with sandbags, a protection against attack from the air. And right down the Nave a huge Velarium was hung for the better hearing of lesson and sermon at the vast Soldiers' Parades held every Sunday morning. Never before in the thousand years of their history had the walls of the Cathedral Church looked down on quite such a gathering. *Totus Clerus*—the whole clergy of the diocese met, not for conference, not for visitation, not for synod, but to draw nearer to God in prayer and thought and penitence, and go back to their work with a deeper inspiration, a clearer hope, a firmer and less faltering tread.

It is not possible to repeat the whole series of the three addresses which the Archbishop gave. They were very solemn, very moving, and piercing too. And, as so often with him, a deep note of personal sympathy was struck from the start, with peculiar effect. He felt much—perhaps most of all—for the clergy in the remotest country parishes who found it specially difficult to let the new thoughts, the new conditions, in. 'These parishes make, *me judice*, a more anxious, if not a heavier, call on a man's *spiritual* resources than the busiest town parish makes. The plea of such a vicar is one of the most pathetic, when he says like the old monk in the rural monastery in Tennyson's *Holy Grail*:

I trust
We are green in Heaven's eyes: but here too much
We moulder.'

He spoke of the *pathos* of the trust on the Nation's part, which had led to the exemption from military service, in the Bill that week before Parliament, of men who 'at the date of the passing of the Act are in holy orders, or regular ministers of any religious denomination'. Why had it happened? 'Because of the general sense on the Nation's part (1) that there is a higher side of life, whether in war or peace, than the material; (2) that therein a greater thing has been given *us* to do; (3) that the call on its officers in their own department is supreme and paramount, for the good of all.' He begged his hearers to take quiet, deep, detailed, most solemn thought, prayer, counsel, as to how far they were answering the trust reposed in them. And speaking very simply, and with pauses for silence, and with prayer, he said 'Thou, Lord, who livest and wast dead—Make us feel and know Thy Presence with us now.' 'Speak, Lord, for Thy servant heareth.' In a second address he brought his clergy face to face with their Ordination vows, and bade them examine themselves as to how far they were faithful messengers—watchmen—stewards in their own immediate work. Looking at the manhood of England, 'What is the proportion of those who feel *active* responsibility as Christians? as Churchmen? When we face these facts, these proportions, is it not a cause of thankfulness, an avoidance of despair, to feel that we can say "No, no". It is not that these men are all inaccessible to the stir, enthusiasm, of God's message, or hardened against the Saviour's love, or deliberately deaf to His call. That would be desperate indeed. But it is not so. It is *we*. It is *I* and *I* and *I* who have failed, been inadequate, in our part as *messengers, watchmen*. Give me, by thy grace, O God, power to make a new, redoubled, quadrupled, endeavour in Thy strength, and then the Gospel message *can, will*, win its way.' In a third address he spoke of the wartime and its opportunity 'almost impossible to overstate' with the manhood, the womanhood, and the children. 'For all these things our inadequacy, our weakness, is known to *Pastor Pastorum*—He knows. . . . But see for your cheer what the old Apostle who knew man's weakness says.

"God did the most wonderful thing in the world's life when he raised Christ from the dead. Well, that is the power, the same power, which he wants to wield, use, for you."'

Perhaps the reader may catch some shadow of the profound impression which the Archbishop, now in his sixty-eighth year, made as he spoke from the great throne in the Cathedral choir to his sons in the Church, from the sentences quoted above. And another piece of evidence from a former chaplain, then Vicar of Ramsgate, may, from a different angle, bring the same thought home:

REV. E. L. A. HERTSLET *to* MRS. BENSON

The Vicarage, Ramsgate. 13 January, 1916.

You took, I know, so great an interest in the Archbishop's gathering of Clergy, and in the message which was thought out under your roof, that I think you may like to have an impression of the Days from one of the insignificant Clergy who went to Canterbury this week.

Well—the first impression one got of *him*—and it remained strong to the end—was *Power*: he seemed to have regained completely mental and physical strength, and sureness of grip. He was quite certain of his message. There was no hesitation or parenthetical insertion. It was all very deliberate, very simple, very grave. He managed to convey to us straight away on the first evening his own sense of the almost overpowering opportunity of such a moment.

His division of the message, was, I think, exactly right,—putting the 'war-time' to the forefront in the first and last address, and concentrating the whole of the centre one on the individual personal life of the Clergy. He spoke entirely from his heart, with extraordinary gentleness and frankness, and one felt very close to him indeed. A large gathering of Clergy is always a bizarre and somewhat depressing sight, and yesterday's was no exception. They ranged through every type—the decrepit, the rugged, the bulgy, the hearty, the suave, and the grim; the grubby scholar, the gray saint, the young spike, the hairy protestant—they were all there with their very different views and standpoints and problems,—but they all melted into a very real and touching unity as soon as they got settled down to listen; all seemed to be fused into one body of hushed and reverent hearers, and I really think before the end—of touched and penitent men. There was a *really* spiritual atmosphere about the whole thing, and to my mind the Devotional time, with the Archbishop leading the prayers with intervals of silence, was the finest bit of all. For many of the men there, it was probably the first experience they had ever had of any sort of 'Retreat',—and it was more that than anything else. And I am certain it was exactly what everyone wanted. From the men's attitude in betweenwhiles, and their remarks, I know that they were really impressed and grateful. Even such trifling things as 'He got in there'—'He had us all round'—'There was no getting away from *that*' etc. mean a great deal when one knows the men who say them. From all this you will see that I am quite enthusiastic over this great experiment: you would have thought that the Archbishop had been taking Quiet Days for Clergy all his life. Nothing could have been better. I wish all the Bishops would do it—or better still—that he were able to get at *Totum Clerum* himself. I know you will be glad to know how once again the Peace of Tremans has been the prelude to the putting forth of Power from on high. I think of it—and you—very often.

CHAPTER XLVIII

THE WORK OF THE CLERGY. THE ARCHBISHOP VISITS FRANCE

I wish, quoth my uncle Toby, you had seen what prodigious armies we had in Flanders. LAURENCE STERNE, *Tristram Shandy*, Bk. II, ch. xviii.

I

A FEW days after the gathering of the clergy in Canterbury Cathedral the Military Service Bill, No. 2, which called unattached single men and childless widowers, from the age of 18 to 40, to the colours, came before the House of Lords. The clergy and all regular ministers of a religious denomination were in the schedule of exemptions. There was some criticism at the time—and the Archbishop felt it right to speak on the subject. He said that the Bishops' approval of the exemption was not due to any desire that the clergy should 'evade the obligation of bearing their part and doing their share in this mighty national effort to roll back a great wrong'. He referred in passing to the canon[1] law of the Church which forbids the shedding of blood by those who are in Orders, but 'it is not upon that that I, and those who think with me, rest our concurrence in the provision which this Bill makes'. He preferred to state his reason thus:

> The nation at this moment has, I believe, recognized to the full that there is something other than physical force required for the

[1] Sir Lewis Dibdin writing in the *Guardian*, February 24, 1916, supplements the Archbishop's remarks with reference to Church Law thus: 'The general Canon Law again and again forbade Clerks to bear arms. In England the prohibition is to be found so early as Archbishop Theodore's Penitential (668–90) and is formally laid down in Provincial and Legatine Canons by Archbishop Lanfranc (1070), by the Legate Alberic at Westminster (1138), by Archbishop Richard (1175), and by the Legate Othobon (1268).

'That the rule was frequently broken is as true of this as of other laws, but its existence was never open to doubt. That it was not abrogated at the Reformation as "contrarient or repugnant to the laws, statutes, and customs of this realm" we have the authority of Coke himself, who, writing in the seventeenth century, lays it down as clear law that clergymen "ought not in person to serve in war". Thus whether you inquire as to English ecclesiastical law (for instance, the constitutional conditions under which the Established Church enjoys its status and property), or as to English Canon Law pure and simple, or as to the general Canon Law of the West, the answer is the same.'

> successful conduct of this war—moral earnestness in our corporate life, deliberate self-denial and self-discipline in our homes, quiet and buoyant courage in hours of stress, anxiety, and sorrow, and an eager and high resolve on the part of a united people on behalf of what is just, righteous, and true. These, it goes without saying, in this House at least, are assets not less important to our cause than even ships and guns, and every whit as vital to our securing the right kind of victory and the right kind of peace. I venture to say, my Lords, that if these assets are to be safeguarded they need to have a religious basis behind them, and if that basis or background is to be unimpaired at such a time as this, we must have men in the field of war, in the preparation for the field of war, and in the home life of the country, whose special business, or I would rather say whose special privilege, it is to help to make those principles a reality and to further and strengthen them in every possible way. The clergy are such men. They have that special duty, that special privilege, assigned to them. They may have inadequately discharged it many a time. But they have that obligation upon them, and the nation, quite rightly in my view, declines to relieve them of it.

Here was the main argument advanced by the Archbishop. He spoke of the work to be done by the clergy as chaplains in the Navy and the Army—in camps and hospitals—and in the parishes which indeed, in the anxiety and sorrow pressing so heavily on so many homes, called out to the parish priest for his help, which no other could give, in a special way. He said that for the religious ministry to the troops, in the field and at home, the Bishops would eagerly and gladly continue to send all that were wanted. He would not hold men back from non-combatant service if really wanted ('it has not been clearly shown'), and if their places could be adequately filled at home. His speech ended thus:

> We are bound to remember that, to their calling, these men have been solemnly set apart on the greatest day of their lives—set apart in a sacred fashion to which no other profession or calling offers any parallel. I wish our critics, and our people generally, would read afresh the Ordination Service in our Book of Common Prayer. To take wholesale from those duties at the very moment when they are more urgently needed than ever they were before the men who have been thus solemnly set apart, would be to misunderstand or miss one great part of the meaning and character of a time of war, one great part of the nation's need, one great secret of what will be the nation's path to victory.

II

While the Military Service Bill was passing through Parliament—and indeed earlier—an agitation was going forward in the press 'to urge upon the Government a declared policy of air reprisals for Zeppelin raids on London and other open cities'. Mr. Joynson Hicks,[1] for example, urged: 'If our airmen dropped bombs upon the open towns of Germany, and insisted upon an eye for an eye, and a tooth for a tooth, the Zeppelin raids would soon cease.' Sir Arthur Conan Doyle was equally violent, though he could 'well imagine that our airmen would find such work repugnant'. There were others, like Lord Bryce and Sir Edward Clarke, who took a very different view. On February 17, the Archbishop felt it right to raise the question in Convocation. He proposed the following motion which was carried unanimously:

> That this House, while fully recognizing that it does not lie within its province to express any opinion on matters purely military, desires to record its conviction that the principles of morality forbid a policy of reprisal which has, as a deliberate object, the killing and wounding of non-combatants, and believes that the adoption of such a mode of retaliation, even for barbarous outrages, would permanently lower the standard of honourable conduct between nation and nation.

The Archbishop, in a long speech, was careful to emphasize the limiting clause with which the Resolution opened. He did not underestimate the difficulties, but he felt it to be the duty of the Church to give guidance as to the moral and ethical considerations involved. He referred to the extreme forms of advice recently given in the public press: and he uttered a grave warning against a gradual debasing of our moral currency:

> We can imagine even lower levels of degradation of honourable rules of warfare than we have yet seen. Poisoned wells, deliberate ill-treatment of prisoners, and the like, were not unknown in certain kinds of warfare in ancient days, but such things were long banished, as we had hoped, from the standards possible for Christian nations of to-day. Can it be said that, if—God avert such a thing occurring—such things were adopted by those opposed to us, we should in retaliation adopt like measures? If not, let us take care that at an early stage of the wrong doing we stand across

[1] Afterwards Viscount Brentford.

the path and warn people that there are ethical as well as military considerations which attach to action such as is now being suggested—not adopted—in our own land.

The Archbishop's words—and the Debate in Convocation—were effective at the time, though bitterly resented by large numbers of his fellow citizens. There was one message from an unknown correspondent in the Midlands, which he specially treasured. It ran thus (Feb. 18, 1916):

The German View

Frau Schmidt: Another Zeppelin raid over England, Gretchen! Isn't it lovely to think of those hideous English women and children being killed and tortured by our patriotic airmen?

Frau Schwarz: Yes, but suppose that the wicked English should make reprisals on us!

Frau Schmidt: Ach! that's all right. Gott sei Dankt! Our Kaiser's God has raised up fool-friends for us amongst the English themselves. They have two old women, the Archbishops of Canterbury and York, who have ordered that their young men shall stay in safety at home and that their Government shall make no reprisals.

III

In May 1916, the Archbishop, by special invitation, spent eight days with the troops in Belgium and France. He had been asked to go the previous year, but his serious illness had made it impossible. But now, at a comparatively quiet time, before the June offensive on the Somme, he went, at the urgent request of the Deputy Chaplain-General, with the warm concurrence of the Commander-in-Chief, for the visit which he always regarded as 'very memorable in my own life'. He has left a vivid account of his time, in a sort of diary of 100 pages, with maps and photographs of the different places seen. And his interest and keen sympathy with all he saw is clear in every line. His passport caused 'some amusement at the different places of examination and check, as my portrait, which had to be stuck in it, was a post-card portraying me with cope and crozier—not quite usual in a passport office'. Bishop Gwynne, the Deputy Chaplain-General, was with him most of the time, and his old chaplain, J. V. Macmillan,[1] C.F., throughout. He worked very hard. He saw 'more or less the whole front line held by the English from north of

[1] Bishop of Guildford, 1935.

Ypres to the Somme', and much of the hinterland twenty or thirty miles back. It was right that he should spend some time in seeing the men who occupied the positions of greatest responsibility, and he was the guest in one form or another, at their headquarters, of all four Army Commanders, and at G.H.Q. of the Commander-in-Chief.

But the Archbishop's visit [J. V. Macmillan writes] was, to borrow a phrase from the language of the country where it was paid, something quite different from a 'visite de cérémonie'. He had come for two quite definite objects. The first was to do what he could to cheer and encourage the Chaplains—his own clergy—to let them feel that he was anxious to understand their problems and their difficulties and their opportunities; and the second was, so far as opportunities could be given, to let the men of the Armies themselves see that the Archbishop of Canterbury, leader of the Church of England, wanted to see something of what they were going through.

At four different centres, one in each of the four Armies which then made up the B.E.F.—at Poperinghe, at Corbie (on the Somme), at S. Pol, and at Bethune—the A.C.G. of the Army concerned had got together as many of the C. of E. Chaplains as could be got together for conferences with the Archbishop. There were also present, to the Archbishop's own delight, Chaplains of other Denominations—of the Church of Scotland and of the English Free Churches. At each of these centres there was a short Service at which the Archbishop himself spoke, but the central feature was the conference itself in which he drew out what the Chaplains had to say about the attitude of the men to religion and to the Church. To one who listened to those conferences, what remains most vivid is the impression made by the simplicity and real anxiety to learn of the Archbishop himself. It has been said of him again and again and in many connections, that it was his power of being completely at the disposal of those to whom he was talking and his obvious readiness to hear and weigh what anyone had to say to him, that were no small part of the real greatness of the man. I doubt if that ever came out so clearly as in those conferences with the Chaplains in France, and, as has been said at the beginning of these notes, there must have been many a man amongst those who afterwards came home, as well as others who did not, who then first learnt to love the man Randall Davidson and to trust the Archbishop of Canterbury as they had never dreamed of doing.

One of the conferences of chaplains took place in the garden of Talbot House, Poperinghe; and after it in 'an exceedingly upper room' in the house, a long garret transformed into a chapel, the Archbishop took a Service for the Chaplains, and then confirmed about 36 or 40 men presented by P. B. Clayton. J. V. Macmillan says:

> That place is a place of many memories, and among them both here on earth, and beyond, there must surely remain that of the old Archbishop sitting in his chair, with the lighted candles behind him as the darkness came on, and the candidates kneeling before him, while outside in the street there was the ceaseless rumble of troops moving up to the Salient and the intermittent sound of firing.

A few notes from the Archbishop's Diary follow:

> We walked about Poperinghe and found Norman Davidson[1] at Headquarters office, and *his* car then took us, i.e. Norman, Mac, Neville Talbot and myself, to Ypres. It is an absolutely straight road of about nine miles, and we were now within the near sound of the constant guns, and as we approached Ypres the road grew more and more war-strewn, the trees all broken, every house smashed and uninhabited—the road itself ploughed up by shell marks everywhere and being constantly repaired. It is the only road into Ypres this way and consequently has at night to be used for all the road transport, and the Germans therefore shell it continuously. Before getting near Ypres we had to put on steel helmets, furnished to us at Poperinghe, and each to carry the gas mask in a bag ready for use at a moment's notice. The shelling at Ypres was still going on, but was quiet at the time we were there, or at least not severe enough to make General Fielding prohibit our going about the shattered streets. I afterwards learned from General Plumer, in command of the Second Army, that if he had been in France he would have forbidden my going to Ypres. Fortunately he was not. . . . (May 17).
>
> I think I had talk with every man, and some of them were full of interest. I was very much struck with the quiet simplicity, and even the unconscious dignity of the chaplains, some of whom I had known quite well; and all of them seemed to me to have 'grown' in the best sense. . . . (May 17).
>
> I had rather a wakeful night, meditating upon all the new things I had seen that day, and listening to the artillery at inter-

[1] The Archbishop's nephew; he fell in action.

vals! One felt more and more the fearsomeness of all this going on between Christian peoples, and the helplessness of religious leadership to intervene, and *per contra* the gain and opportunity which is coming to the manhood of England and of France, and our obligation to use it. . . . (May 18).

I also got a good deal of talk with the Tommies who were billeted in the village where we broke down. One of them a very interesting quite young soldier from Tooting, who had got some keen and rather original thoughts about the war and its lessons for him and others. I felt when I got to bed that the day had been a fruitful one. . . . (May 19).

At 4.45 the Generals of the Army, whom Blackburne[1] had invited from all the region round, began to arrive and soon we had in the garden about 40 Generals. I managed to get a short conversation—sometimes quite short—with nearly everyone of them, and in the majority of cases I got to the point about which I greatly cared, the work of our chaplains, their fitness for it, any suggestions which could make matters better, and the help the Generals are giving and can give. As before I was immensely struck with the keen appreciation shown by everyone of these leading officers as to the first-rate character, capacity, courage and perseverance of the chaplains and how very much has now come to turn on their work. Nearly every General spoke of them as being just the men who ought to be there and of having got a real grip upon their troops and cheering them in every way. The gathering in the garden was a striking instance of the pulling together of padres and officers and their mutual appreciation of one another. . . . (May 20, at Béthune).

Tea was over at 5.40, and Sir Henry Wilson had arranged to have a strong rapid car waiting in which he whirled off Mac and me, together with his own aide-de-camp, Locker-Lampson, who had been at Eton with Mac. We drove to the ridge of Notre Dame de Lorette, some miles off. It is a long ridge which Wilson compared to the Hog's Back, but it is not so steep or high. As we went up the side road near Bovigny, through villages greatly broken by shell fire and among the dug-outs of the wayside, a shell of the smaller sort, which Lampson called a 'pipsqueak', burst not far behind us, to the surprise and, I think, a little to the disquiet of our military hosts. Locker-Lampson tried hard to find out where it fell, but it was not clear, only it was not far away. I was glad to have the experience. It was an isolated spot with no special

[1] H. W. Blackburne, afterwards Dean of Bristol.

reason for being shelled. We got to some open ground on the top of the hill, with a French cemetery of rows and rows of little graves, many hundreds with little crosses, about half the crosses having names. They are some of those who fell in the gaining of the ridge by the French. It is said to have cost them 150,000 casualties. We walked along the ridge near the edge of the Bois de Bovigny, and there Sir H. Wilson pointed out the whole lie of the land—with Loos in the distance on the North-East, down towards Arras South-East on the right, and the Vimy ridge in the left foreground, a little south of east, and the shattered village of Souchez, between the Lorette and Vimy ridges, corresponding, as Wilson pointed out, to the position of Guildford on the Hog's Back. We were standing just above a farm called Marqueffles, in which, as Sir H. Wilson explained, he had three 9·2 guns concealed, which the Germans were always trying to find. 'Now and then they have shelled the neighbouring fields, but they have never found the exact place of the guns which are there in those buildings, just below us'—say 250 yards. He had hardly said this when Locker-Lampson called out 'I hear a German shell whistling,' and the great shell came with a scream and whistling sound and landed plump among the buildings which we were looking at, with an earth-shaking explosion. The General was much excited—'The brutes! They have got us. What splendid shooting! They have the very spot.' Then came another shell almost on the same spot. We went a little nearer after this so as to observe better, and two more shells came. It was all as if it had been got up as an exhibition for us, and nothing could have been clearer or more absorbingly interesting. There was nothing to show us the exact effect of the shooting upon the hidden guns. We could only see the considerable smashing of earth and buildings, and the General said he would not know till later on at night when a report would come in to him. Then we went on examining the English and German trenches through our glasses and could watch the rifle fire going on between them, and occasional guns, ours and theirs, further off, but well within sight. Meanwhile a very plucky airman of ours was circling just overhead and the Germans kept firing shells at him, all of which we could watch quite close. It was a wonderful object lesson of a varied sort, and, as Locker-Lampson said afterwards—'You had simply an extraordinary exhibition because of your higher standpoint and the visibleness of everything.' . . . (May 20, Béthune).

I never saw so many partridges—we were putting up pairs of them everywhere along the road. They were basking in the dust, and the outcome of so many pairs must be prodigious. . . . (May 21, a drive from St. Omer to Hesdin).

I found Haig rather shy and difficult to talk to at first, but when he thawed he was delightful in his quiet, earnest frankness of conversation. I pressed him for criticism about the work of the chaplains, but I could not elicit anything except laudation. He was strong on the great value of the changed administrative order which now encourages the chaplains to go forward into the trenches, if they will do so, instead of being, as formerly, kept behind at the casualty clearing stations, or even further back. Haig was enthusiastic about the fine type of young Padre now at work in all parts of the line. There was hardly one whom he knew whom he would wish changed. He has himself a great affection for the Presbyterian Chaplain, Duncan, who is attached to Headquarters, and whose ministry Haig himself, who is I suppose a semi-Presbyterian, often attends. Both Haig and Fowke spoke in terms of real affection about Bishop Gwynne, and the tact and vigour of his administrative work. It is remarkable how Gwynne's simple goodness has evidently been his passport to the affection of these people, while his efficiency wins their respect. . . . (May 21, near Montreuil).

We discussed the question of visits of Bishops. He was very emphatic and spoke with a quiet gravity about it. 'We don't want books written about visits to the Front. We don't want our men and their ways exploited, and we certainly don't want men of a different type to come out for joy rides about the country.' [This referred, not obscurely, to * * *.] But he went on—'Visits like yours for quiet consultation with us and for giving stimulus to officers and chaplains, and speaking to the gatherings of men which you come across naturally, are of very real good.' . . . (May 21, continued, conversation with Haig).

[In the ruined convent chapel at Arras.] The whole scene was striking—the service so perilously surrounded, so noisily accompanied, the soldiers growing quite used to it, and Bailey, the Chaplain, one of our Edmonton men, under Boyd, arranging all quite simply and happily. When they sang 'There is a green hill far away' I found it difficult to restrain myself. . . . (May 21).

So ends, as I rough-hew it in the train which is crawling into London, the record of a journey unique in my own experience as a man, and I think unique historically in the experience of an Archbishop. I have seen more or less the whole front line held by the English from north of Ypres to the Somme, and much of the hinterland twenty or thirty miles back. I have not seen the great Bases at Rouen and Havre, and this is a distinct loss, but it was impossible to do everything. We have been blessed throughout by splendid weather, by the extreme kindness of everybody without exception, and by the smooth working of the carefully made arrangements. To Bishop Gwynne I owe more than I can easily express. Unfailing in kindness, inspiring in work and good spirits, and, above all, continuing instant in prayer, he has impressed me more and more each day. I thank God for all the lessons of these nine days, and I trust I may find it possible to do my work a little less inadequately in consequence. *Quod faxit Deus.*

CHAPTER XLIX

POLITICAL PROBLEMS. THE FALL OF ASQUITH

There is an idea among some of your acquaintances which I partly acquiesce in, that you are in general somewhat of a procrastinator. I believe I have noticed the same thing myself. LOCKHART's *Life of Scott*, ch. xlii.

THE summer of 1916 confronted the Archbishop with grave questions of a very different kind.

I

On the Irish question, for example, he was very unexpectedly asked to advise Lord Curzon, on June 27, whether or not he should resign from the Cabinet on the ground that Lloyd George had exceeded his commission as negotiator with Sinn Fein:

> He began by saying that, strange to tell, the fate of the Government and possibly of national affairs seemed to turn upon a decision which he must make within the next two hours. The person whose advice he wanted was myself.

A full story of the crisis followed—and of the division in the Cabinet. Of the nine Unionist members of the Cabinet, four had decided to resign, and four were against resignation, including Balfour and Bonar Law. Curzon therefore held the balance:

> Such was Curzon's statement, and he then said 'I have put the facts fairly before you. I want your definite judgment as to what I ought to do.' I replied that it was a fearfully grave thing to be asked to give such an opinion the moment one had heard the case stated, without any time for reflection. My clear feeling, however, as he had told his story, was that Arthur Balfour is right: the War is what matters just now, and almost anything is preferable to the wild confusion which might ensue if the Lloyd George settlement were now thrown to the winds by the action of the Unionists and our hands therefore paralysed in the War. I could not think it likely that the House of Lords would force an Election in September, unless indeed the War conditions had vastly changed for the better. And if that risk be removed, a temporary settlement of the Irish affairs seems to me at all costs to be expedient, one might almost say necessary, to success.

We discussed several points in detail, but 4.30 arrived, and Selborne was actually on his legs in the House. Curzon thought I had said enough to give him real help, and he left me, saying that his judgment on the whole coincided with mine and that he thought he would certainly act upon it.

II

There was also the very painful case of Sir Roger Casement, sentenced to death for high treason in connexion with the Irish rebellion of Easter 1916. The Archbishop had known Casement's work in connexion with the Congo atrocities a few years before, had seen something of him then, and been much impressed. When, therefore, an appeal was made for a reprieve on account of his great services in the past to the subject races of South America and Central Africa, the Archbishop, while declining to join in a petition, wrote a personal letter to the Home Secretary:

The ARCHBISHOP OF CANTERBURY *to the* RT. HON. HERBERT SAMUEL

Private. 14th July, 1916.

Like other people I am receiving a good many requests from different quarters that I should sign some document or protest or petition in favour of a mitigation of the capital sentence passed on Roger Casement. I am refusing to do this, feeling that the matter is safe in the hands of the legal authorities and yourself, and that the relation of his criminality, about which there can be no doubt, to the political situation is one which you are well qualified to settle. At the same time I think perhaps I ought to write a few lines to you on account of the relation I formerly had to Casement when I was promoting the protests or agitation about the Congo, and subsequently when the Putumayo atrocities were being investigated. At each of these times I saw something of Casement and was always impressed by his capacity, his enthusiasm, and his apparent straightforwardness. I find it difficult not to think that he has been mentally affected, for the man now revealed to us, in the evidence which has been made public, seems a different creature from the man whose actions I knew and watched. . . .

He went on to say that he knew of certain other charges made against Casement's moral character which, if proved, might be taken as further evidence of his having become mentally unhinged, and begged that Mr. J. H. Harris, a close friend and collaborator of Casement in the Congo days, might be consulted.

Mr. Harris was sent for, and the details of a very sad story were made known to him. The Archbishop, who had also seen Mr. Justice Darling who tried the case, as well as the niece and secretary of Casement, after a further talk with Mr. Samuel, saw the Lord Chancellor, and followed up his conversation with a letter:

The ARCHBISHOP OF CANTERBURY *to the* RT. HON. LORD BUCKMASTER

Lambeth Palace. 1st August, 1916. 11.30 p.m.

I have been thinking over the conversation I had with you a few hours ago upon this wretchedly distressing and perplexing business of Sir Roger Casement.

I think that perhaps, in my talk with you, I overmuch concealed the strength of the *instinct* I find stirring within me to the effect that the really *courageous* course for the Government to adopt would be the commutation of the death sentence. The case presents itself to me somewhat thus:

As a question of *policy* there can, I suppose, be no doubt that a reprieve would be wiser than an execution. Ireland, America, and possibly other countries would find people to make mischievous capital of the execution, and far more so if they could (as they would) spin a tale to the effect that after hanging a 'political prisoner' the authorities had been privy to the trumping up of an infamous story about the man's immorality, an accusation with which he had never even been confronted—far less had the accusation been proved after proper investigation. Such would be the shape the accusation against the Government would take.

Of course you can, in one sense, afford to ignore all such attacks. But they will, none the less, be mischievous, and in America especially they will do real harm. As a question of pure *policy* therefore, the avoidance of an execution is to be desired.

In the present circumstances of the world it savours, I think, of pedantry to contend that 'policy' has nothing to do with the decision you should, as a Government, come to, and that 'justice' only has to be considered. The thing is not so simple as that. The object of an execution is to deter offenders. Whom would this execution, as a matter of fact, deter? Whom would a commutation of the sentence encourage in evil deeds? No one.

What would doubtless happen would be an outcry on the part

of a good many people who would say 'It is sheer cowardice which has let this man off, after the shooting of weaker or less important rebels. If ever a man deserved hanging it is this man.'

The other rebels were shot, so to speak, red-handed after court-martial. This man was not red-handed in that sense, though no doubt, as the wire-puller, he may be regarded as more guilty than any. I certainly do not attempt to deny that he *deserves* hanging. But when we think of the results which would almost certainly follow, we ought, I believe, to have the courage to be apparently inconsistent and to send him to Broadmoor instead. The sound argument would, I think, be 'Here is a rebel who has done things worthy of death. But his case is peculiar. For many years beyond all possibility of doubt, he battled nobly on behalf of the oppressed native folk. He had infinite difficulties to contend with, but, at the cost of his health, he fought on. He succeeded, and his name will always, and rightly, be held in honour for what he there did, whatever may have happened afterwards. All sorts of complications as to the rebel's real life came subsequently to light. Investigation showed perplexing contradictions in his behaviour, and though not technically (according to the experts) a man out of his mind, he is shown to have been mentally and morally unhinged. In these complicated circumstances we believe that the more sane and fair course is to choose the less irreparable of two acts, and to commute the sentence, and we accordingly do so.'

Of course the more *obvious* course would be to send him to the gallows. But is it not really the less courageous line to follow? It is followed 'lest we seem inconsistent'. I should brave *that*, and do what is really in the truest interest of the country and the Empire. 'Policy' in the largest sense of the word *can't* be excluded, if those on whose shoulders the responsibility rests are facing their duty from the highest standpoint. After all, the whole thing concerns the well-being and safety of the Empire and nothing less or lower, or more merely *technical*. I have purposely not dwelt upon all the complexities of immoral morbidities, about which I have so much unpleasing experience every month of my life. Though my experience is abundant and varied, we must *in the main* be guided, in that field, by professional mental experts. '*In the main*', but not to the exclusion of the unprofessional but solid experience of actual facts which is possessed by some of us, and forms an element, no more, in our consideration of the question.

I feel that I owe you an apology for this intrusion into the field of jurisprudence. But I must plead in defence your own encouragement, and your express wish that I should tell you how it all presents itself to me. And 'jurisprudence' after all when widely interpreted, shades off into political ethics wherein the most amateurish of us may have a voice.

The reprieve, however, was not granted. The Archbishop saw the Lord Chancellor on August 2 in the House of Lords:

He told me that the matter had then been settled by the Cabinet. He had been impressed by my letter. He did not say whether he agreed with my conclusions or not, but he had felt the letter to be so important that he had laid it before the Cabinet that morning, and they therefore had my views in full before they reached their decision. He did not say or imply that the decision had been easy or unanimous: he rather implied, though he did not say, the contrary. He was specially full of the fact of certain Irish prisoners in Germany, some of whom had now returned to England invalided, their illness being due to German ill-treatment consequent on their refusal to listen to Casement's treasonable blandishments. This he thought had weighed strongly in favour of the execution taking place.

III

The summer holiday of 1916 was spent by the Archbishop in Scotland. In accordance with his habit, he and Mrs. Davidson visited various friends in their homes, spending a week or so with each. One old friend, who particularly valued his sympathy at this time, was Lord Haldane, who, in the shuffle of the Cabinet in the spring of 1915, had lost his place owing to unfair attacks on his supposed pro-Germanism. They had many talks together, and Haldane showed the Archbishop the Memorandum which he had drawn up, on his part in policy and preparations before the War. The Archbishop took care to let his own appreciation of Haldane and his work be known in quarters where a word was likely to be useful. There is an interesting letter after the holidays from Edmund Gosse, following upon an article by St. Loe Strachey in *The Spectator*, which shows the value attached by intimate friends to Dr. Davidson's sympathy:

EDMUND GOSSE, ESQ., *to the* ARCHBISHOP OF CANTERBURY

17, Hanover Terrace, Regent's Park, N.W.
6 November, 1916.

When I saw the *Spectator* on Saturday, my first thought was that your benevolence had operated with miraculous celerity—

and then I realised that St. Loe S. had acted 'on his own'! I am greatly pleased with the article, and so will Haldane be. I am to see Haldane alone this afternoon, and we shall go over the whole situation. But I must repeat, what I said to you on Wednesday, that I regard you at this moment as the most useful friend he has, and that I hope you will see him as often as you can.

There were many other calls for the Archbishop's sympathy in the tragic losses of the War, and he never failed in speaking words of comfort and healing. Two letters may be quoted. One was to a vicar in his own diocese who had just lost a son; and the other is from Mr. Asquith, who lost his son at the same time:

The ARCHBISHOP OF CANTERBURY *to the* REV. H. E.——

Lambeth Palace, S.E. 26 Sept., 1916.

We were absent yesterday. Hence the delay.

You will know how our hearts go out to you in this hour of cloud.

May Our Lord in His love have you and G. in His keeping.

These are the times which test the fibre whereof we are made. What must it mean to those who in S. Paul's words are οἱ λοιποὶ οἱ μὴ ἔχοντες ἐλπίδα?

We shall remember you steadily in our prayers.

I have just come from sitting with Asquith, whose frame is sore stricken, for he was wrapped up in Raymond.

Tonight I go to see ——, whose son and heir, intensely loved, was killed yesterday—and so it is, day by day. The sense of life being a larger thing than we can see must surely be burning itself in upon great circles who have thought less of its meaning hitherto.

τίς οἶδεν εἰ τὸ ζῆν μέν ἐστι κατθανεῖν, τὸ κατθανεῖν δὲ ζῆν;

Give my love and paternal blessing to G. My wife has, I hope, by this time written to her. She is at both Canterbury and Sheerness today, and I am not sure of her possibilities. Her special link with J. brings it home to us both.

The RT. HON. H. H. ASQUITH *to the* ARCHBISHOP OF CANTERBURY

Personal.

The Wharf, Sutton Courtney, Berks. 22 Sept 1916.

I cannot thank you sufficiently for your letter which was a real help.

Apparent waste is the real tragedy, and one is bound to cling to and cherish the larger hope.

Anyway it is not they—the young, who lived well, and, with

promise still unfulfilled, died nobly—who are to be pitied, but we who remain and wait.

I hope to be back on the quarter deck on Monday, and we can then talk of business.

Another letter written by a Bishop at the same time, whose daughters were nursing at St. Thomas' Hospital and formed two of the contingent of nurses for whom the Archbishop and Mrs. Davidson made special sleeping provision at Lambeth, shows an appreciation of another kind:

The BISHOP OF WAKEFIELD *to* MRS. DAVIDSON

Bishopgarth, Wakefield. Sept. 24, 1916.

. . . I cannot tell you how deeply I have appreciated and felt the altogether unusual hospitality you have shown to my two children —Margaret and Dorothy. It seemed stupid to keep on writing, and I am slow to express the things that go deepest. But I have often wanted to tell the Archbishop and yourself all that Lambeth has been to me and mine for so long. It is a unique place—a huge business establishment with resident clerks and secretaries, telephones and offices, and a constant tide of Church affairs surging through it. And yet you both manage to make your guests feel that they are in a home, where they are welcome, where all their wants are studied, and where the whole household is striving to make them comfortable and happy. Many people, even strangers, have said the same thing to me. It is a very rare kind of grace . . .

IV

In December the Archbishop was in close touch with some of those who were most deeply concerned in the ministerial crisis. On December 4, after reading the newspaper tales of Cabinet disputations, he went to dine quietly and alone with a friend who knew the latest news:

A more tangled situation can hardly be conceived. Meanwhile some members of the Cabinet seem to be wholly disloyal to the Army . . . Poor —— is having a tempestuous time—but he seems to me to be doing it all extremely well, and the King is behaving with wisdom and circumspection—and with complete fairness for Asquith, who is evidently touched thereby.

He saw a good many others, anxious to hear all that was passing, but purely spectatorwise, between December 4 and 10. Lord

Buckmaster told him that Lord Reading was likely to succeed him as Lord Chancellor and that if he were appointed, by the law with regard to Jews, all the Patronage of the Lord Chancellor would have to be exercised by the Archbishop of Canterbury. This increase of Lambeth labours, however, did not come to pass. He saw a former Lord Chancellor, Lord Loreburn, in the House of Lords on December 5:

> I saw, in the Princes Chamber Loreburn in a great state of excitement, denouncing the Liberal Cabinet men for not offering their services to Lloyd George—not that Loreburn had a good word to say for Lloyd George. His line was (and it was emphasised by violent walking up and down the room)—'These fellows who dragged us into this war ought to be thankful to be allowed now to serve as bottle-washers or bootblacks, if they are wanted. The country has a right to keep them to see the thing through. Asquith naturally enough could not serve under Lloyd George, but why not these men? Every one of them is guilty of mere selfish cowardice if he declines to bear his part, supposing the new Prime Minister wants him', and so on and so on in anything but a judicial vein. . . .

On December 9 he lunched with Asquith at 10 Downing Street:

> It struck me as interesting, though I did not have an opportunity of referring to the matter with him, that I had been in Downing Street when he came back from Biarritz, and was the first to greet him there, and now I was present on his farewell day in the house, for he is leaving it 48 hours hence, or at latest on Wednesday morning . . .

He had a good deal of private talk with Asquith:

> The strain has been in every way so great for him that the personal relief at being, by no fault of his own, relieved, is incalculable. 'I have not', he said, 'had one single day, literally not one single day, since Whitsuntide 1914, without the burden pressing ceaselessly upon me, and I have found, especially since Raymond's death, a lack of resilience (that was his exact phrase) which makes everything terribly trying.' He went on to say that he intends to go to the House of Commons regularly, and to bear his part in supporting Lloyd George. It would be quite easy for him, and I gather that some of his friends had advised it, to abstain largely from the Commons, and let the new Government wrestle with its own difficulties. But he does not think that this would be patriotic, and I very warmly commended his resolve

to go to the House regularly to bear his part in the way that he will as a supporter of the Government of the hour. I told him that I had had a good deal of thought about whether he ought to resign, but that I had come to the conclusion that he was right, and that I thought his conduct in the matter, so far as the facts are revealed, correct and honourable in every way. I think he was glad that I should say this, and we had some rather earnest private talk in which he showed genuine feeling and, I think, warm personal regard. He agrees with me in discrediting any prophecies that Lloyd George would try to use his opportunity as Prime Minister to harm the Church of England. . . .

The only word of sarcasm or taunt which he used was that he said that 'Lloyd George felt he must turn me out in order to have a Cabinet of three people, the Prime Minister not being a member of it. He has now got a Cabinet of six people with the Prime Minister as chairman.' . . . He spoke with grave regret, rather than anger, about newspaper domination and a country ruled by Northcliffe. . . .

The following day, Sunday, December 10, the Archbishop wrote a letter to the new First Minister of the Crown:

The ARCHBISHOP OF CANTERBURY *to the* RT. HON. DAVID LLOYD GEORGE.

Private. 10 Dec. 1916. *Lambeth Palace,* S.E.

It is not fair to write to you at this moment, and yet I want to speak out at once.

Your call, at perhaps the most critical hour in English History, to the place you hold is an event which would be *solemn* to any man, and to a man of your temperament and 'make' must be, in the most literal sense, almost overwhelming. May God endue you with such a 'spirit of wisdom and understanding, of counsel and strength' as may enable you to rise to so mighty an opportunity and to utilise it to the full. I suppose there is no instance in English public life commensurate with this in some at least of its characteristics.

It would be of course unreal were I to pretend to see eye to eye with you in regard to *some* of the affairs and 'policies' of our country in its home life, either civil or religious. But I am eager that you should realise that in any way in which I can at this juncture give you support, I shall be most anxious so to do. The offices of high trust which we respectively hold have many points of contact, direct or indirect—and I have had the privilege, ever since I came to Lambeth nearly 14 years ago, of being on terms of active and sometimes close friendship with your four predecessors. I do not ask more than that you should count upon my willingness to be helpful, at such a time as this, wheresoever I rightly can.

Again assuring you that I do not forget you and your literally 'tremendous' burden when I say my prayers.

The RT. HON. DAVID LLOYD GEORGE, *to the* ARCHBISHOP OF CANTERBURY

10, Downing Street, Whitehall, S.W.
December 14th, 1916

I was deeply touched by your letter and the kindly message which you sent me at such a difficult time, I assure you, will not be forgotten. Your warm sympathy and encouragement will be a source of strength and inspiration in the difficult task which I have been called upon to undertake.

CHAPTER L

THE ARCHBISHOP'S POLICY. RESERVATION

I will not enter into the question, how much truth is preferable to peace. Perhaps truth may be far better. But as we have scarcely ever the same certainty in the one that we have in the other, I would, unless truth were evident indeed, hold fast to peace, which has in her company charity, the highest of the virtues. EDMUND BURKE, *Speech on the Act of Uniformity.*

ON Christmas Day, 1916, the Archbishop fell ill. He was laid up in his bedroom for over three weeks. He did not really get back to work till the end of January, and it was not till February 18 that he was again attending Prayers in the Chapel.

I

While he was ill, he dictated some notes about the aims he had set himself as Archbishop during the fourteen years of his Primacy (January 1917):

Suppose someone were to ask me what, if expressed in a summary way, had, while Archbishop, been my aim as regards Church administration, I should find it a little difficult to answer categorically. I do not think that either at the start, or since, I have had before me a clearly defined purpose intended to be pursued *coûte que coûte* in face of opposition. On the other hand, I have had an underlying and, I think, continuous policy, the outcome partly of my general way of looking at things, partly perhaps of my upbringing, and partly of my sense of what is needed in the Church of England to-day, and of the opposite things which offend my sense of what is the will of God for us and for our Church.

If I were forced to put it in a single phrase, I suppose it might be described as a desire to assert in practice the thoughtful and deliberate comprehensiveness of the Church of England, as contrasted with the clear-cut lines and fences of demarcation which mark the rulings of the Church of Rome, and the corresponding, though quite different, rulings of protesting sects in England, Scotland, America, and presumably Germany in the 17th century and since.

This comprehensiveness, as I understand and value it, is assertable in three directions, affecting severally our boundaries of legitimate doctrinal belief, our boundaries of would-be denominational differences, our boundaries of legitimate ritual and devotional variety—this last including what become very nearly credal differences.

In all these fields it has, I think, been my earnest endeavour to cast the net wide, and to be slow to draw its boundary line very rigidly. I venture to think that in the first two of these three my fourteen years of Archiepiscopate have been useful, and that I have personally contributed a good deal of the usefulness.

In the course of his reflections on the first head, Dr. Davidson refers to the critical discussions on the Creed in 1914, which might have issued in the resignation either of himself or of Bishop Gore. And he sums up:

This specific instance is only an example of what has been a continuous and deliberate endeavour on my own part to avert putting forth by authority 'cocksure' definitions and boundary lines at a time when scientific thought and the growth of historical criticism render such action not dangerous only, but unreasonable. Under this head, therefore, I believe that I have contributed something to the maintenance and assertion of what I believe to be the true principles of thought within the Church of England and English Christianity generally.

Dealing next with the question of denominational differences, he speaks in a general way of the Lambeth Conference of 1908. Of Kikuyu he says:

I do not defend what was done at Kikuyu. I think it was rash and that it lacked appreciation of large principles which cannot be put out of sight. But to denounce it in the way that it was denounced by the Bishop of Zanzibar, and those who followed him, was preposterous.

But the important note upon this is as follows:

All this, however, was simply one incidental object lesson in a wide field of controversy. It is not easy at present to formulate exactly what are the two sides of the controversy about our relation to fellow-workers in the Christian field who do not belong to our Communion. On the one hand there has been in S.P.G. circles and elsewhere a growing nervousness about our relation to, or our conference with, Nonconformists. Or perhaps it may be more true to say that the greater life and vigour of the missionary societies has brought into prominence the feelings of ring-fence exclusiveness and Anglican self-containedness which were there

> all along, but had less scope in the quieter days a generation ago. My own feelings have always been strongly in sympathy with a desire, not only to confer with, but, so far as possible, to work with, Christians outside our own Church, and this, as I have always contended, can be done without any compromise of our own distinctive principles, if the difference between undenominationalism and interdenominationalism, is kept prominent and clear. The Missionary Conference in Edinburgh was a notable example. It was to my mind simply lamentable that S.P.G. was not officially represented there. True, Bishop Montgomery, Mrs. Creighton, and others were present, but they did not go as formally representing the Society, which thus seemed to be holding aloof from a Conference on which so much turned. My own action in going was widely criticized, but I am certain that I was right.

He refers to 'the question (not alien from the Kikuyu debates) of the sanction we give to the admission of, e.g., an isolated Presbyterian or Lutheran who desires to communicate with us'; the controversy about the use of Anglican Churches in India and England for Presbyterian regiments, and he sums up:

> Summing it up, I feel pretty clear that I have, during my Archiepiscopate, contributed steadily and with considerable effect to the maintenance of a reasonably comprehensive spirit in our Church's polity. Bishop Gore of Oxford regards me as perilously lax in what I teach and practise as regards the National character of the Church of England, a phrase to which he has a special antipathy. I am increasingly certain that the rigorist attitude is a mistaken one, and that we rightly inculcate and use an elasticity in these matters—an elasticity which I have sought not only to condone, but even to encourage in certain credal matters referred to above, wherein I have stood upon one side, and the rigorist Bishops on the other.
>
> In this department, therefore, of my general Episcopal purpose and practice, I think I have to a large extent succeeded in what I have tried to do and say.

On the Ritualistic issue, however, he is unable to give so satisfactory a report:

> I come to the question of boundaries of legitimate ritual variety, and here I must sadly confess to myself that, whether it be my misfortune or my fault, I have been quite unsuccessful in introducing a comprehensiveness of a reasonable and, in a large sense, law-abiding kind. At this moment, January 1917, there is I think

a larger body of clergy than there has ever been before who quite deliberately resent, and even defy, the exercise of episcopal authority for inculcating, or, if need be, enforcing compliance with what may be largely called Prayer Book rules. The contrast between that school to-day and the corresponding school in Tractarian days is not merely wide, but the two things are almost contradictory, and the very men who attach the most vital importance to episcopal succession and the episcopal system, are those who in practice are now turning to scorn episcopal direction or rule which they dislike. At this moment, January 28th, 1917, I am awaiting with genuine alarm discussions which may take place in Convocation ten days hence about Reservation, which would give evidence of a defiance of episcopal authority on the part of many hundreds of clergy who mean to insist on the right of priests and congregations to insist on the use of the Reserved Sacrament for purposes of devotion (as contrasted with Communion) in a way which would have been not only surprising, but repellent, to Lancelot Andrewes, or William Laud, or E. B. Pusey, or John Keble. What exactly is going to happen I do not know, but the controversy of these weeks gives good exemplification of our failure, I must certainly say my failure, to keep within bounds the vagaries of men who are, I honestly think, inculcating doctrines and usages distinctly repudiated by the Church of England in practically, with the tiniest exceptions, all its schools from the days of Cranmer and Parker to our own. I think the matter is stated with reasonable fairness in the Report of the Royal Commission on Ecclesiastical Discipline in 1906. Of course the phraseology of that Report is the result of some measure of compromise. The legal spirits would have liked it to be much more rigid and less sympathetic, and some of the clerical spirits would have softened some of the criticisms as to ritual extremes. But speaking generally, it is, I think, a fair statement, and, if so, our failure to gain general support among High Church clergy for the verdict it pronounces, and perhaps even for the recommendations it contains, is both obvious and melancholy. I do not think it is so much due to a widespread spirit of lawlessness among otherwise sober men, for I doubt whether there is such, as to a wisely manœuvred accentuation of the difficulties about Ecclesiastical Courts etc. which has been cleverly used by E.C.U. officers and the like to discredit the duty of obedience to authority exercised by the Bishops in any formal manner. Things are likely to develop quickly now, and there are undoubted elements of danger which may even lead to schism. All that I am here concerned to say about it, is that I can claim no success in any endeavours that

I have made to produce a truer spirit of loyalty and harmony in these matters among the extremer Church partisans on the High Church side.

II

From these reflections in his illness, and especially his own sense of his lack of success with regard to ritual questions, it is natural to pass to Prayer Book Revision, and especially to the issue of Reservation, at that very time in his mind, which was to form the topic of an important debate in the following month.

In the first two years after the outbreak of War, the Convocations had continued their work of preparing an answer to the Royal Letters of Business dealing with Prayer Book Revision. In 1915, the Report of the Joint Committee of Convocation of Canterbury, which had been appointed in April 1914 to harmonize the material of the two Houses, was published. It was entitled '1915. Royal Letters of Business. No. 487' and consisted of forty-eight pages. It included the Upper House's proposal for 'a diversity of use' in the matter of vestments; and a proposal (agreed to by the Lower House only, in February 1914) for a rearrangement of the Prayer of Consecration in the Order of Holy Communion, as follows:

> Permission shall be given for the rearrangement of the Canon as follows: The Prayer of Consecration shall be said immediately after the Sanctus, the *Amen* at the end being omitted; the Prayer of Oblation shall follow at once (prefaced by the word *Wherefore*) and the Lord's Prayer; then shall be said the Prayer of Humble Access, followed by the Communion of Priest and People; after the Communion shall follow the Thanksgiving, the Gloria, and the Blessing.

These, and certain other proposals, aroused alarm among Evangelical Churchmen. A memorial was presented to the Archbishop by Sir Edward Clarke (a signatory of the Royal Commission's Report) signed by many members of the House of Laymen and others, begging the Archbishop 'to postpone until after the war any further action or discussion in Convocation respecting the Revision of the Prayer Book'. A counter-memorial, signed by a number of fellows of Cambridge Colleges and others, begged the Archbishop to go forward notwithstanding the war. The Archbishop replied to Sir E. Clarke that nothing should be settled without the House of Laymen—and agreed that the

House of Laymen, many of whom were on active service, could not take part in Prayer Book discussions while the War was still in progress. But he went on (23 April 1915):

The ARCHBISHOP OF CANTERBURY *to* SIR EDWARD CLARKE

I do not think that this difficulty is operative within the Convocation itself. We are approaching the close of deliberations which have occupied an inordinately long time. Very few members of Convocation are prevented by duties connected with the War from giving us their help in completing, so far as Convocation itself is concerned, the task assigned to us.

Obviously and rightly our thoughts and energies are concentrated at present on problems and anxieties very far removed from things liturgical, and it would be wholly out of place for us to inaugurate just now the handling of Prayer Book questions as though these were in the foreground of our thoughts. For example, our Convocation Agenda Paper for next week directs us primarily to matters connected with the War. But that is not to say that in the further time at our disposal we clergy should refuse to carry forward to its provisional conclusion the consideration of questions with which we have so long been dealing. We want Convocation to be ready, by the time the War is over, to submit its suggestions for the consideration of Churchmen generally, and it would I think be detrimental to our doing this effectively were we altogether to set aside, for perhaps a considerable time, our unfinished task.

It may be added that on April 28, 1915, the Upper House rejected, by 15 votes to 5, the proposal for a rearrangement of the Prayer of Consecration (as set out above), the Archbishop himself taking no part in the debate.

A year later (April 1916) Lord Halifax visited the Archbishop at Lambeth, with a special proposal about the Order of Holy Communion. He had for a great many years (he said) used the Liturgy of the First Prayer Book of Edward VI (1549) in his private chapel at Hickleton, with the sanction of successive Archbishops of York.

His communication is summarized by the Archbishop as follows:

April 1st, 1916.

His real point is a definite suggestion.

'Will you intimate to me, tacitly if not openly, that you would not regard it as disloyal were a priest to use what is practically the Communion Office of Edward VI's First Book in lieu of the Prayer Book use? We do it at Hickleton with the sanction of successive Archbishops. I have had three conferences of the extreme men there, purposely inviting those who are accustomed, as I know, to interpolate (*secreto*) the Latin Canon in order to supply the defects of our Canon. I have allowed them to celebrate with our use, which is carefully arranged, and they have practically all of them told me that it satisfies their aspirations, and that if they were to use that they would cease to wish for interpolations from the Roman Canon. I do not expect you to tell me that you could authorise such use of the First Prayer Book. Of course it would be irregular, and if you authorised it you would be open to all kinds of accusations. But if I knew in my heart that you would not regard such conduct on these men's part as disloyal, I think I could bring it about that the Romanising system I have referred to should be dropped in almost every parish where it is now usual, and that they would be satisfied with the other. . . .'

The Archbishop told Halifax that he had 'learned by experience the danger of allowing even apparently insignificant changes in exceptional cases because they are instantly taken advantage of as a starting point for something fresh, the contention being "This much we have now definitely gained for good. We start afresh for our further enterprise".' But he asked him why he and his friends desired the change:

> He [Halifax] said that they have now to use the Roman parts secretly not openly, and that the Service is very much spoiled by this process, the Prayer Book words being audible, the rest inaudible, to bring them into the category of private devotions, though they are not really private at all. I cordially agreed with him about this, and spoke of the intolerableness in my view of men adopting such use when they have solemnly declared as a condition of Institution or Ordination that they will 'use the form in the said Book prescribed and none other', etc. He had no answer to this and hardly attempted it. . . .

All that the Archbishop felt able to say in reply was that in Scotland he had used the Scottish Office and in the United States the American Office, both being based on the Order of 1549; that he 'had no kind of objection' to either Office, as he 'found nothing in that Office which jars upon me as unorthodox or wrong, but it is not the Office which I have said that I will observe and enjoin upon others for use', and went on to say that

> personally if we were starting afresh in this whole matter and could legislate in the Church without the difficulties due to party conflict, I should personally prefer an enactment of a new Office compiled by the re-handling of our existing Prayer Book Office. But my personal preference for what would be desirable is one thing; my feeling of what is practicable or expedient is quite another; and he must not take it that I am giving him either tacitly or otherwise any other assurance beyond what I have stated, namely that personally I take no exception to the Scotch or American Office where it can be used in accordance with the due order of the Church.

III

It has already appeared that the problems connected with the Reservation of the Sacrament had occupied the thoughts of Churchmen long before the War. The increasing frequency of celebrations of Holy Communion during the past fifty years was itself a sign of the increase of reverence with which that Sacrament was regarded. 'Early celebrations of the Holy Communion were, I suppose, almost unknown in the first quarter of the nineteenth century.'[1] And when those who were well came more often to Holy Communion, it was not surprising either that the sick should desire more frequent opportunities of coming themselves, or that recognition should be given to the need of special arrangements for giving them their Communion privately after the celebration in church. The Book of Common Prayer provides a shortened form of the Order of Holy Communion for sick persons, in the sick person's chamber, with others receiving at the time. The practice of Reservation, which had ancient authority, though not mentioned in the Prayer Book, made it possible for the sick person to receive the Sacrament, reserved from the public service, without a fresh celebration. After a long period, some 300 years of almost unbroken desuetude since the first Reformation Prayer Book of 1549, where provision was made,[2]

[1] R. T. C. before the Royal Commission on Ecclesiastical Discipline, 12855 A (b).

[2] The rubric in 'The Communion of the Sick' in the Prayer Book of 1549 ran thus: 'If the same day there be a celebration of the Holy Communion in the church, then shall the priest reserve (at the open Communion) so much of the sacrament of the Body and Blood, as shall serve the sick person, and so many as shall communi-

the practice was revived in the middle of the nineteenth century. It was at first exceedingly rare, but developed by degrees. And with the revival of the practice a problem was raised, viz. the proper treatment of the consecrated elements thus reserved, outside the actual communion. In the Eastern Church the Reserved Sacrament is put in a place apart, in or near the sanctuary, without a light, and receives no special reverence at all. But in the Roman Church, for a long time (though not in the first 1,000 years of the Church's history) the Reserved Sacrament was made the object of a *cultus*, the focus of a devotion. And the reason was doctrinal—the Roman dogma of Transubstantiation. Thus, to quote the concluding words of the standard book on the history of *The Sacrament Reserved* by W. H. Freestone, 'the original purpose of official Reservation (i.e. Reservation in Church) was purely practical (for communion). The development of any *cultus* of the Reserved Eucharist was the direct outcome of the acceptance of the doctrine of transubstantiation as the orthodox belief.' The problems connected with Reservation in the Church of England arose from the perils of an extra-liturgical *cultus*.

The Archbishop, in his evidence before the Royal Commission on Ecclesiastical Discipline in 1906, and in a very important speech in the Upper House of Convocation in February 1917, has given a summary history of the development from 1856 to 1917 of the problem in the Provinces of Canterbury and York. In 1856, following a lawsuit, a Memorial on Eucharistic Adoration had been drawn up by Dr. Pusey, Mr. Keble, Mr. Carter of Clewer, and Dr. Neale—in language very different from that of those who claimed to be the inheritors of their opinions. In 1866, Bishop Thirlwall declared:[1]

> But this ritual movement has by no means reached its term. It is still in the full vigour of its early years. It appears to be advancing both extensively, in the work of proselytism, and intensively, in doctrinal innovation, not always distinctly enunciated but clearly intimated. Its partisans seem to vie with one another in the introduction of more and more startling novelties, both of theory and practice. The adoration of the consecrated wafer, reserved for that purpose, which is one of the most characteristic Roman rites, and a legitimate consequence of the Romish Eucharistic

cate with him (if there be any). And so soon as he conveniently may, after the open Communion ended in the church, shall go and minister the same.'

[1] Royal Commission on Ecclesiastical Discipline, 12885.

> doctrine, is contemplated, if it has not been already adopted, in some of our churches, and the Romish festival of the *Corpus Christi* instituted for the more conspicuous exercise of that adoration, has, it appears, actually begun to be observed by clergymen of our church.

In 1868 and 1876, the subject of Reservation was very briefly discussed in Convocation, as the result of memorials or petitions put before the Upper House, the request being markedly limited to making provision for the sick. There was a fuller discussion in 1885, when the Bishops unanimously declined to sanction Reservation as a law or usage: but the speeches showed that there might be possible exceptions, especially in hospitals, and in times of epidemics, and even in the particularly difficult circumstances of some parishes. Discussion continued in the Church, but without any special notice of an official character until 1899–1900, when Archbishops Temple and Maclagan, in the Lambeth Hearing, forbade Reservation absolutely. In 1905–6 came the Royal Commission. In the evidence it was clear that the Reserved Sacrament was in several churches made the centre of a *cultus*. Exposition, Benediction, Processions of the Reserved Sacrament, and Devotions with Adoration of the Sacrament were in use in some London churches and in a few churches outside London. At the same time, in his own evidence, the Bishop of London thought 'that a perfectly clear distinction could be drawn between Reservation for the purposes of the sick alone, and Reservation under conditions which rendered it possible that it should be used for purposes of devotion', though he subsequently saw reason to change his view of the possibilities in some of the instances he then adduced.

IV

To summarize the general result of this slow but steady movement in a portion of the Church: (1) it was coming to be seen that some relaxation of the ordinarily accepted law forbidding Reservation was desirable for the Communion of the sick, subject to the Bishop's regulation; (2) there was no sort of claim or request on the part of those pressing the need of Reservation that sanction should be given for the use of the Reserved Sacrament for any other purpose whatever; (3) in a few churches a use of the

Reserved Sacrament for purposes of adoration was practised. Accordingly, when, in the revision of the Book of Common Prayer, the Order for the Communion of the Sick came up for consideration, the Bishops added a proviso allowing Reservation under certain limited conditions—which they recognized to be a departure from the usage allowed in the Prayer Book but to be a legitimate requirement of the circumstances of the time. The permission was contained in a Draft Rubric, which set out, not what was allowable, but what they hoped would be allowable if the revision of the Prayer Book received full canonical and legal sanction. It ran as follows, being drafted in this form by the Upper House of Convocation in 1911:[1]

THE COMMUNION OF THE SICK

When the Holy Communion may not by reason of grave difficulty be celebrated at the sick person's house, the Priest may (with the consent of the sick person) on any day when there is a celebration of the Holy Communion in the Church set apart at the open Communion so much of the consecrated Bread and Wine as shall serve for the sick person, and so many as shall communicate with him (if there be any), and, the open Communion being ended, he shall, on the same day and with as little delay as may be, go and minister the same. And, except where extreme sickness shall otherwise require, before he administer the consecrated Bread and Wine, at least the parts of the appointed office here named shall be used, namely, the *General Confession*, the *Absolution*, and the *Prayer of Humble Access*, and after the delivery of the Bread and Wine the *Lord's Prayer* and the *Blessing*. And immediately thereafter any of the Bread and Wine that remains over shall reverently be consumed.

If the consecrated Bread and Wine be from any urgent cause not taken immediately to the sick person, they shall be kept in such place and after such manner as the Ordinary shall direct, so that they be not used for any other purpose whatsoever.

The consecrated Bread and Wine shall be taken to the sick person in such simple and reverent manner as the Ordinary may direct.

If any question arise as to the manner of doing anything that is here enjoined or allowed it shall be reported to the Ordinary for his decision.

[1] See *Report* No. 427 (1911), p. 17. The Draft Rubric remains unaltered in *Report* No. 481 (1914), p. 32. Certain slight changes appear in the form given in *Report* No. 504 (1917), p. 54.

The vital paragraph is the second—and the vital words in that paragraph, designed to limit the use of the Reserved Sacrament unconditionally to the Communion of the sick, are: 'so that they be not used for any other purpose whatsoever'.

By general agreement this Draft Rubric was accepted by the Bishops as giving them guidance in their administrative capacity for dealing with particular questions of Reservation. And it must be specially observed that it contemplated Reservation for a sick person or sick persons who desire to receive the Communion on the same day as the day of the particular celebration—and was not intended to allow anything like general, permanent, or continuous Reservation for such people.

Such was the rule which the Bishops bound themselves to administer to the best of their power, three years before the War. There were difficulties and irregularities, especially in the dioceses of London, Chichester, and Birmingham—but these were not sufficient to make the rule impossibly hard for other Bishops, especially the Bishop of Oxford, to enforce. There were a few churches in London, particularly, where continuous Reservation was practised—on the strict condition that the Reserved Sacrament was there kept in a secluded chapel, inaccessible for purposes of worship.

V

With the War, however, the difficulty grew in acuteness. The emotions of the time—the tide of human grief and anxiety—made it very hard for some to observe the regulations of the Draft Rubric in all their strictness. It was a stern test of episcopal unity. The Bishop of Oxford had been foremost in insisting upon it. But as the months passed the strictness was little by little relaxed by the Bishop of London, and at last to such an extent that the Bishop of Oxford felt his own further insistence impossible. It was in the summer of 1915, when the war situation was grave, and the general tension already sufficiently severe, that the Bishop of Oxford announced his intention of abandoning his stand. He reminded the Archbishop of a Conference held at Lambeth attended by the Bishops of London and Winchester and himself at which, he said (8th June, 1915), 'I understood that there was a sort of informal agreement that where Permanent Reservation of the Blessed Sacrament was allowed, it should be allowed only in a secluded chapel not accessible for worship.' He claimed that the crucial phrase in the Draft Rubric of 1911, 'so that they be not used for any other purpose whatsoever', meant Reservation only in a secluded chapel; and he added:

The BISHOP OF OXFORD *to the* ARCHBISHOP OF CANTERBURY

Cuddesdon, Wheatley, Oxon. 8th June, 1915.

I have felt myself obliged to resist pressure of the strongest kind which has been put on me to allow Reservation in the open Church. I have only succeeded in maintaining this resistance by the strongest exercise of Episcopal Authority—first at Birmingham and now at Oxford—but it is constantly represented to me that no such requirement is made at Birmingham[1] since I left it, and in other dioceses, notably London and Chichester.[2] In these dioceses Reservation is allowed in the open Church, and the Blessed Sacrament so Reserved becomes at once an occasion and centre of worship.

The Archbishop sent a long letter in reply pointing out the far-reaching consequences of such a step on Gore's part. In particular he spoke thus of the general policy foreshadowed:

The ARCHBISHOP OF CANTERBURY *to the* BISHOP OF OXFORD

Lambeth Palace, S.E. 10th June, 1915.

. . . Then I should like to say a word about the policy generally which you foreshadow as now necessary. The argument I suppose would be this: Some Dioceses (exceptionally circumstanced) have not held to the rule repeatedly set forth that Reservation should be for the sick only, and if some Dioceses fail to enforce it the rest of us Bishops must give up what we have repeatedly said is the right principle. In other words we Bishops should be abandoning any attempt at discipline in this matter because the Episcopate has not succeeded in maintaining and enforcing a uniformity of Episcopal action. I wonder myself how far there ever has been such complete uniformity of Episcopal action. Has it not been an ideal rather than a fact? And may not the difficulty or impossibility of attaining it be an example of those characteristics of the English Church upon which Dean Church so often dwelt?

On the other hand should you feel it to be possible to back up now the line which I and those who will go with me must certainly take, of adhering to what we have said and doing our very utmost to prevent the misuse for other purposes of Reservation allowed for the Sick, you would strengthen our hands more than any other men could, and would help immeasurably the Bishop of London

[1] Bishop Russell Wakefield. [2] Bishop C. J. Ridgeway.

and other Bishops, whose difficulties are exceptional, to maintain true principles. Such action on your part would be worthy of you and would in my judgment have an immense effect for good throughout the whole Church of England.

If the other line be taken and the use of Reservation for other purposes than the Communion of the Sick be encouraged, and indeed proclaimed, by the abandonment or proposed abandonment of the safeguarding words, it is to me quite obvious that we should have encouraged, perhaps even fostered, the growth of the usages we deplore—Monstrance, Exposition, Benediction. So far as I know my own mind, and I think I do, I could never under any pressure tolerate these things, believing them as I do to be perilous in the highest and deepest sense.

The matter is so sacred that I should like to have much time for thought before writing about it. But I have not got that time at the present moment, and this particular juncture in National life is quite extraordinarily unfortunate as a moment for our launching upon the Church what would probably be the gravest controversy of our generation. Must it be pressed forward now?

Further correspondence followed. Bishop Gore agreed to further talk before action. He said:

The BISHOP OF OXFORD *to the* ARCHBISHOP OF CANTERBURY

Private. Cuddesdon, Wheatley, Oxon. June 12, 1915.

Yes indeed, I am more than ready for talk before action. I am still anxious to maintain the rule I have maintained that reservation should be in a secluded place. It is I think only this year that the Bishop of London has surrendered. What needs to be impressed on him is that it is not enough to secure or think he secures 'no public devotions before the Blessed Sacrament'. Nothing effective will be done unless he insists that reservation must be in a chapel to which there is no access.

He begged the Archbishop to press the Bishop of London not to commit himself at a conference which he was about to hold with certain Anglo-Catholic clergy. The Archbishop also got into communication with the Bishop of London explaining his perplexity:

The ARCHBISHOP OF CANTERBURY *to the* BISHOP OF LONDON

16th June, 1915.

I remember well your own account to me of the care you had taken in some of the Churches—I think St. Mary's, Paddington, was one—to go yourself over the building so as to secure that the Reservation should not be in a place accessible for devotional intent. I gather that by degrees this has been completely altered and that although you forbid Reservation in a tabernacle over the Altar it is quite well-known now that Reservation takes place in certain Chapels at or near side Altars, and that as a regular system people pray there in consequence; and this not incidentally but avowedly. This undoubtedly means a very marked change from what we planned a few years ago. . . .

You mentioned to me last night the suggestion that we might cease to allow Reservation at all, or rather might cease to avow that we are allowing it. I do not understand how this suggestion could be made effective. If we cut out what has been agreed upon by both Houses we shall seem to tell everyone that Reservation for the Sick is not after all to be sanctioned. But as a fact it will be just the other way. We shall be cutting it out because some of us find it necessary to sanction that which the suggested Rubric would forbid—i.e. the use of the Reserved Elements for Devotion. I do not understand that you would suggest that we could do this without explaining what we are doing, for if not we should mislead everybody. I am therefore simply bewildered as to what is intended. The mere fact that the men with whom you have been conferring are (1) prepared to repudiate the action of Mr. Kilburn, and (2) to state formally that they accept the Bishop's directions about how Reservation is to be arranged, does not seem to me to cover the ground, if in making this declaration they do it on the tacit understanding that the Bishop has so far modified his original direction as to sanction the use of the Reserved Elements for Devotion as a part of the arrangements of the Church. . . .

The Archbishop spoke again of his distress that the matter should be forced forward at such an hour:

I can hardly find words to say how sad I think it to be that men like those advanced skirmishers of yours should force this matter forward at the present moment when our thoughts and prayers are concentrated on other things. But the issues are so large and so grave, and for some of us perhaps so absolutely vital, that it is clearly impossible to let things drift until after the War.

In a note to the Archbishop, the Bishop of London said that there were eighteen churches (but 'the list has been drawn up rapidly and is not meant to be complete') in which he sanctioned Reservation—in a secluded place; that in three of these the Sacrament was reserved in a side chapel or other chapel, and that in four others the devout were allowed to enter the chapel and say their private prayers, and might kneel *outside* the chapel in other churches for the same purpose (22 June 1915). The following is a Memorandum of an Interview on July 5:

Memorandum.

Interview at Lambeth on Monday, July 5th, 1915, with the Bishops of London, Winchester, Oxford, and Chichester, about Reservation and the use now sanctioned or tolerated in London. The Bishop of Oxford reiterated strongly his view that he could not be party to a declaration by Convocation that Reservation was for the Sick and no other purpose whatsoever, unless this was being reasonably observed by the Bishops generally, and he regarded the action of the Bishop of London in the tolerance he exercises as being sufficient to make his (Oxon's) support of the Convocation words impossible. As the matter was not coming up during the ensuing meeting of Convocation the discussion was rather academic, but both London and Chichester took the line that it was no longer possible for them strictly to follow the rules which Oxon and Winchester had followed, of forbidding Reservation within the Church in a place known, and therefore used for devotion. The Bishop of Oxford pressed strongly that more was being done in London than the Bishop of London realised, and the Bishop of Winchester made a great deal of the point that in the Roman Catholic Church Veneration of the Reserved Sacrament cannot be recognized if there be a wall between the person praying and the Reserved Sacrament—i.e. that the mere knowledge that there is the Sacrament reserved in a Chapel on the other side of a wall would not suffice to justify acts of veneration. I think the Bishop of London practically admitted, though he did not say so in terms, that he had now departed widely from what he laid down when he described his action to the Bishops a couple of years ago.

The Bishop of Chichester pressed the point that all we could rightly insist upon now is the absence of actual Services formally conducted under the direction of the Clergy in connexion with the Reserved Sacrament, but he said that the difficulty only arose in three or four churches at the most in his Diocese.

The Bishop of Oxford said that he adheres distinctly to what he has written on the subject in *The Body of Christ*, but he admitted that that writing was rather what he felt to be theologically true than what he found to accord with his private feelings, or, as Winton called them, temptations.

R. T. C.

VI

The Archbishop had thus got the subject postponed for that year. Bishop Gore, however, returned to the charge in May 1916 and desired to bring the matter before Convocation. The campaign for an extra-liturgical *cultus* had grown, and pamphlets were published by an Anglo-Catholic Society[1] strongly advocating both Exposition and Benediction. But after some talk with the Archbishop, Gore was persuaded to drop his request for an open discussion, on account of the National Mission then in progress under the leadership of the Bishop of London. Instead a special private meeting of the Bishops was held. There was a great and very grave division, and a clear recognition of the possibility of a schism from the Church, which yet might be preferable to disintegration within it. The Archbishop promised that, in the next group of Sessions, the whole subject should be publicly brought before the Church in Convocation. The Bishop of Oxford had by this time been persuaded, by the Archbishop's persistence, to maintain his original position and to give up his proposal to omit from the Draft Rubric the vital words 'and for no other purpose whatsoever'. He proposed the following Resolution in the Upper House of Canterbury Convocation on February 9, 1917:

> In view of misunderstandings which appear to have arisen, the Bishops desire to call attention to the terms of the Rubric[2] in the Order for the Communion of the Sick proposed for adoption (see Report No. 481, p. 32) as part of the answer to be returned to the Royal Letters of Business, and to declare that they adhere to the Recommendations there made.

Seven bishops spoke, in addition to the Archbishop, in the debate, which lasted a whole day and attracted a great deal of public attention—all the more on account of a Memorial signed by nearly 1,000 priests opposing the policy expressed in the Draft Rubric and declaring that compliance with the restriction proposed, i.e. refusal of access to the place of Reservation, 'cannot rightly be demanded and will not be given'. The Bishop of Oxford spoke very strongly—emphatically reasserting his own whole-hearted belief in the ancient Catholic doctrine of the Real Presence of Christ in the Holy Sacrament, which he believed to

[1] The Society of St. Peter and St. Paul. [2] See p. 805.

have been seriously impaired by the later Western doctrine of Transubstantiation, with all its consequences such as leading the faithful to seek 'nearness to Jesus' by an external visit to the Blessed Sacrament as reserved in the tabernacle, or monstrance, instead of finding Him spiritually present within themselves through the communion of His Body and Blood. And he asked that the Upper House should reaffirm their deliberate decision taken in 1911 to allow, when circumstances required it, Reservation for the purpose of communicating the sick and for no other purpose whatsoever.

Bishop Gore was followed by the Bishop of London, who was in charge of the diocese which was the storm centre of the dispute. He spoke very fully. He said that he had never allowed, and would never allow, unless convocation allowed, Benediction or Exposition. He admitted that it had proved impossible for him to refuse all access to the Blessed Sacrament, when and where it was reserved for the sick. He had succeeded when there were only about eighteen chapels in the diocese in which the Sacrament was reserved. But 'He frankly admitted now that the plan had broken down: it began to break down before the war, and the war had finished it; the tide of human grief and anxiety had been too great, the longing to get as near as possible to the Sacramental Presence of our Lord had been too urgent'. He therefore 'found it impossible to promise to-day that every one of the forty-two chapels where the Sacrament was at present reserved in London should be locked and barred'. Nor was he sure that such a policy was a desirable policy.

The Archbishop summed up at the end. He spoke of the danger lest older men should belittle the views of the younger.

> Those opinions of younger men are derived from premises different perhaps from the premises which were current in our youth, and upon which we learned long ago to base the conclusions we have reached to-day. We have to recollect, it is those younger men who will some day have to bear the burden of administration, in the Church or Realm, of that which issues from what we are doing or leaving undone just now. I try always and increasingly to be on my own guard against that peril, for I am certain it is often a real one, and this may possibly be an occasion in which we ought to be in an exceptional sense alert.

But at the same time there was the duty attaching to long experience; and the speaker gave an account, with arresting illustrations, of the development of the practice of Reservation during the past sixty years—and its dangers. Nor did he omit to answer certain of the points, both in diocesan administration and existing American and Scottish practice, which the Bishop of London had brought up. And he noted by the way that it was not always possible to share 'the characteristically sanguine and trustful view which the Bishop of London took'. Before he finished his speech, he referred in stern terms to the Memorial of the nearly 1,000 priests—an important document from the mere fact that it carried that number of signatures. To him the Memorial appeared simply deplorable—'alike as to the manner in which it must have been devised and framed, as to the policy which it appears to advocate, and, above all, perhaps, as to the unseemly threats which it contains'.

The Resolution was then put and carried *nem. con.* The meaning of the Resolution to adhere to the Draft Rubric was still far from clear. The Bishop of Oxford knew what he intended—but it was surely a very different intention from that of the Bishop of London, who voted for it on the distinct understanding that 'he did not commit himself to refusing to the faithful access to the Blessed Sacrament where it was reserved for the sick'.[1]

VII

In the following July, at a special meeting of the Bishops, a Memorandum was accepted which removed the main ambiguity, for it explicitly stated that Permanent Reservation was not covered by the terms of the Draft Rubric, and that, if any Bishop gave sanction for such, his action 'will be individual and exceptional, and will lie outside what the episcopate has assented to'. The Memorandum, which was simply a document for the guidance of the Bishops, and at first kept private, was published in 1918.

MEMORANDUM ACCEPTED BY THE BISHOPS' MEETING, *6th July*, 1917.

I

Under the present directions of the Book of Common Prayer we cannot admit any claim on the part of the parish priest or any

[1] See *Chronicle of Canterbury Convocation*, February 1917, pp. 81–126.

other minister of the Church to reserve the Blessed Sacrament, apart from the sanction of the Ordinary, for any purpose or in any manner.

II

We decline to go beyond the limitations with respect to Reservation to which the two Convocations in their Upper Houses have respectively agreed, and cannot recognise permanent Reservation as covered by the terms of either resolution.

III

If the Rubrics on the Reservation of the Sacrament for the Sick proposed by the Upper Houses of Convocation of Canterbury and York were duly authorised, they would lay down what would be permissible in all Churches in all circumstances, without the special consent of the Ordinary or reference to him, save as is expressly provided in those Rubrics.

IV

If a Bishop believes that owing to special conditions it is desirable that a parish priest or other minister should be allowed by him to go beyond what would, if the Rubrics became law, be set forth as the permissible rule or custom in the Church, his action in giving such sanction will be individual and exceptional, and will lie outside what the episcopate has assented to. Should a Bishop so exercise his administrative responsibility, any instruction that he gives either as to the place or manner of such Reservation should be in accordance with the principle that the Reserved Sacrament is to be used for the Communion of the Sick and for no other purpose whatsoever.

July 1917 R. T. C.
C. E.

VIII

Some of the Bishops—and a great many others as well—would have been glad if the Archbishop himself could have given a definite lead in this and other questions of worship and ritual. An evangelical bishop, for example, before the Convocation debate, in discussing the issues with a friend, spoke of his own readiness to accept practices such as incense, or the use of the Scottish Office of Communion as a permissible alternative, if the Bishops would agree to act together. He also admitted the principle of perpetual Reservation in hospitals and similar places. But he longed for a lead from the Archbishop on some of the vexed points, and he believed that the Bishops would thankfully accept it.

Why was such a lead not given? It is not easy to answer. It may have been because the problem of Reservation as a theological problem did not in itself make a strong appeal to Randall Davidson. Indeed it was a perplexing problem—and he knew that it was the sort of issue which might lead to most divisive results. He wished to avoid such calamities; and he certainly would do his best to keep the ship steady. But, though he was not ignorant of the dogmatic implications, and had a genuine anxiety about the perils of a *cultus*, the issue did not stir his soul. Perhaps a note of a talk at this very time between the Archbishop and a friend may throw a little light on the temper of his mind. It was a few days after the Convocation debate on Reservation. A letter from Mr. Hanbury Tracey in the *Church Times*,[1] stating that the Bishops had originally intended to pass a Resolution forbidding access to the Blessed Sacrament but had quailed before the Memorial of the 1,000 priests, had made the Archbishop very indignant. And on Sunday, in the drawing-room at Lambeth at tea, the Dean of Wells's review of Sparrow Simpson's *Prayer of Consecration* was mentioned. This started the Archbishop on a very interesting statement as to the important and the unimportant things just then occupying religious minds. He said he could not bring himself to stress the points of liturgical reform and a change in the Canon of Holy Communion as comparable with the fight against evil.

[1] February 16, 1917.

CHAPTER LI

CONSCIENTIOUS OBJECTORS, REPRISALS, AND OTHER WAR QUESTIONS

Wise men patience never want,
    Good men pity cannot hide;
Feeble spirits only vaunt
    Of revenge, the poorest pride:
He alone forgive that can
Bears the true soul of a man.

THOMAS CAMPION.

THE work with which the third year of the War began was very varied in its character. On New Year's Day, the Bishop of Zanzibar's Commissary called about his Bishop's proposal to take over German Missions provisionally during the War. There was a talk on the telephone about the vacant Deanery of York, Lloyd George's first ecclesiastical appointment ('he mustn't act without consulting the Archbishop'). The same night the Archbishop of York came to stay, and conferred about National Mission Committees and other affairs. On January 4, the Chaplain-General came to discuss the needs of soldier Confirmation candidates in Mesopotamia. Another day, January 5, the Archbishop was busy supervising the starting of religious and social work amongst women and girls in munition factories. A telegram came on January 8 from the Holy Synod of Athens begging him to persuade the British Government to stop the blockade of Greece. On January 16, the Deputy Chaplain-General reported from the Front, with a plan for what he called a 'Bombing School for Chaplains'—that is, a school of instruction and prayer to help the chaplains in France to do their religious work more effectively, with the Rev. B. K. Cunningham in charge. Bishop Gore arrived on January 17 to discuss Reservation and other things, and when some one asked him at breakfast, apropos of the School for Chaplains, 'What would *you* do if you had charge of a school?' he replied, with a rueful shake of the head and twinkle of the eye, 'I should retire to my tomb.... I do not think I am cut out for a schoolmaster!'

I

A good deal of time in the first weeks of this year was taken up with the making of plans for additional national service for the clergy. Mr. Neville Chamberlain, the Director-General of National Service, came to see the Archbishop to discuss the question at large. It was, however, the Archbishop of York who took the main burden of this off the Archbishop of Canterbury's shoulders and worked out a careful scheme in conjunction with Mr. Neville Chamberlain, allowing for suitable branches of national service other than those which the clergy were already fulfilling through the ordinary duties of their calling. The plan gave some satisfaction to chaplains in France, for, as the Deputy Chaplain-General wrote:

Bishop Gwynne *to the* Archbishop of Canterbury

10 February, 1917.

. . . We are all more than pleased with the scheme of conscripting the Clergy for national service, and feel that we are now free from the carping criticism of those who shouted against us when the Clergy were exempted from the Conscription Bill.

It was varied enough in its range, but Archbishop Davidson warned the Archbishop of York against too great precision. 'It is', he said (February 5), 'a little dangerous to be too categorical, for the Clergy as well as other people might say "Why should the Bishops lock us up in this cupboard they have made? We are quite game to take an independent line of our own." ' At the same time when, at the request of Convocation, the Ecclesiastical Services (Omission on account of War) Act, 1917, received a Second Reading in the House of Lords on February 20, the Archbishop was able to give remarkable details as to the very varied special and general service which the clergy were in fact rendering to the nation.

II

A subject which caused the Archbishop keen anxiety, and came up this Spring, was the case of the Conscientious Objector. A large correspondence followed the passing of the Military Service Act, and letters from conscientious objectors, interviews with them or their friends, and representations to the Government on their behalf, took up much of the Archbishop's time during 1916 and 1917 as well as later. He never disguised his own disagreement with their convictions, which he yet completely respected so far as the objection to actual military service was concerned. But he found it difficult to acquiesce in the refusal by the 'absolutists' of an exemption conditional on the applicant's undertaking work of national importance. 'One of the chief difficulties', so he stated to an intimate friend of several objectors (September 26, 1916), 'relates to the refusal of so many men to do any work whatever for the nation, however far removed from military service. It is this abnegation of the ordinary obligations of citizenship which renders reasonable treatment of these men so extraordinarily difficult.' To another correspondent—who reported that a young man whose plea was dismissed by the South Staffordshire Appeal Tribunal on the ground that, as he was a member of the Church of England, and that Church was praying for victory, it was hypocrisy for one of its members to claim a conscientious objection—the Archbishop caused the following letter to be sent by his Private Secretary:

A. SHEPPARD, ESQ., *to the* HON. G. COLLIER

4 April, 1916.

The Archbishop of Canterbury has received your letter of April 2nd with reference to a recent application made for exemption from Military Service on the plea of conscientious objection to such service. The Archbishop can express no opinion with regard to the merits of a particular application which has been considered by the duly appointed Tribunal. You ask as a general question whether conscientious objection to Military Service is in the Archbishop's judgement incompatible with membership in the Church of England. As to this the Archbishop directs me to say that, while he cannot himself regard as reasonable or consistent with Christian common-sense the position of those who claim for themselves and their property the protection of a civilised order of society while repudiating its corresponding claim upon their service, he has learned by experience that membership of a religious community is not found to be incompatible with even the extreme vagaries of individual opinion.

It was, however, not only the problem of the relation of the conscientious objector to the Church, but that of the relation of the Church to the conscientious objector, which found a frequent place in the letters sent to Lambeth. And there was no criticism more likely to touch Archbishop Davidson than that of lack of consideration on his part for those who had a claim to expect it. Dr. Alfred Salter, of Bermondsey, a Friend and a Socialist, at the end of 1916 wrote a long letter on this very point to the Archbishop, in the course of which he said:

DR. ALFRED SALTER *to the* ARCHBISHOP OF CANTERBURY

Nov. 27, 1916.

> . . . I cannot believe that Your Grace can approve of this set and deliberate persecution of men on account of their religious faith, and yet I cannot learn that you have used your powerful position to put an end to it. It is a fact that, at the present minute in England, there are more men in prison for the sake of their religious convictions than at any time for centuries past. Surely this is an extraordinary comment on the attitude of organised Christianity in this country! Cannot Your Grace take steps to impress on the Government the wickedness, and at the same time the uselessness, of attempting to force men to do that which they believe to be wrong?

The Archbishop did not send a long argumentative letter in reply. He sent for the writer, and they talked for an hour. In describing the interview the Archbishop wrote to a friend: 'I tried a little to corner him as to the length to which his opinions would carry him, but he practically shrunk from nothing. I wrote down the following and read it to him and he said it expressed his views—though of course he would add other things:

> If the Government were acting properly now, according to my view it would allow any man who objects to enlistment for whatever reason to go freely on his way without restraint or internment. I say this even if such freedom involve (1) his effective efforts being used to dissuade other men who feel any qualms on the subject from taking their part in carrying out the Nation's purpose in this War; (2) his competing successfully if he can (like the men who are over military age) with the trade or occupation of those who are at a disadvantage because they have accepted service in the Army or munition works.'

At the same time, in spite of this 'cornering', the Archbishop was a good deal moved by a particularly bad story Dr. Salter told him of a young Bermondsey man who, after his plea as a conscientious objector had failed, was arrested, taken to a depot, ordered to wear khaki—and on his refusal stripped, and had khaki put on him by force. The young man was at the moment awaiting court martial:

The ARCHBISHOP OF CANTERBURY *to the* RT. HON. W. H. LONG

1st December, 1916.

I am not sure whether you are the person to whom I ought to write about Conscientious Objectors. I am not proposing to raise a discussion on the whole question, but from the many interviews I have had with members of the Government, and from what was said in the House of Lords on two or three different occasions, I had thought that we had now done with the question of sending these hopelessly unreasonable people to a Camp to be put under military authorities and forced into khaki and so on. I have repeatedly stated this, and yesterday I was nonplussed by receiving at the hands of Dr. Salter, the well-known Socialist doctor in South London, a man of high character who is over military age and is a pacifist, a statement which I took down from him and which I enclose. Please observe that my point is not the imprisonment of these men but the placing of them under military rule. This seems to me to be as irrational as it is cruel.

Memorandum.

The following statement was made to me on November 30th, 1916, by Dr. Salter, J.P., of 5 Storks Road, Bermondsey:

S. N., —— Street, Bermondsey, is the third son of a widow. His two elder brothers are in prison for refusal to serve. He is not a Quaker but he is a Pacifist. He was brought before a Tribunal and raised on religious grounds objection to serve. His plea was rejected. He appealed to the Higher Tribunal which also rejected it. No offer of alternative service was made to him, though Dr. Salter thinks that if it had been made he would have rejected it. He was arrested and taken to a depot on Monday, November 27th. He was there ordered to wear khaki; he refused; he was stripped and the clothing forced upon him; he is now awaiting court martial.

Mr. Long in reply wrote a general statement of the position under the Military Service Acts, not very sympathetic—and the conclusion of his letter is a sufficient indication of ordinary public opinion at the time:

The RT. HON. W. H. LONG *to the* ARCHBISHOP OF CANTERBURY

Local Government Board, Whitehall. 4th December, 1916.

. . . If the matter had to be discussed again, I do not think the House of Commons, or the Country, would regard as tolerable the degree of latitude which we have allowed to all who allege a conscientious objection to military service. I am pretty sure that public opinion would demand much more drastic treatment of these people than the Government have been willing to mete out to them, and that in their own interest it is not desirable to disturb the present practice.

The Archbishop wrote a few months later to Lord Milner, asking more for arbitrarily exercised common sense than for a change of the law:

The ARCHBISHOP OF CANTERBURY *to* VISCOUNT MILNER

21 May, 1917.

I understand (rightly or wrongly) that you are grappling with the question of the conscientious objector—one of the most difficult of present problems—and that some official discussion on the whole matter is imminent in Government circles.

I hope you will not deem me intrusive if I write to you to say that my view, often expressed in the House of Lords in favour of a large commonsense attitude towards these men, as being politic and desirable, has been greatly strengthened of late by what I have been learning about the men in question.

Stephen Hobhouse is of course the most conspicuous instance of a really fine fellow, who is, or has been, suffering in mind and body on account of 'crankiness' which is in no sense mischievous in itself. But there are a good many more, who could not be ranked alongside of him with respect to their nobility of service in days gone by, but who are really as conscientious as he is and are certainly not to be 'tamed' or converted by mere severity. I do honestly think that the matter is one for the exercise of a rather arbitrary discretion in favour of men whose supposed 'persecution' is doing far more mischief than would be done by the relaxation of logical, and technically defensible, sternness, and the granting of release on condition that it is not used for promoting anti-war policy.

No mere insistence on a logical application of military law will, so far as I can judge, *ever* meet these cases, and I have now a rather extensive knowledge of them.

Of course this is only my own opinion, and I have no right to speak as a representative of others, but I am constantly surprised to find how many 'stiffish' men are being led to the same conclusion.

I hold no brief for the men in question. I regard them as utterly misguided and unreasonable in the riding of their hobby. But sometimes a little arbitrarily exercised commonsense will solve a problem insoluble by either law or logic.

III

The Archbishop's 'common-sense' way of looking at things was also called into play this year on the Sunday question. Early in 1917 a considerable anxiety arose as to the food supply of the country.

There was a late frost, and it was urged by agriculturalists that Sundays as well as week-days should be used for tilling. Mr. Bonar Law came to see the Archbishop on February 26. The Prime Minister had, it appeared, promised Mr. Prothero, the Minister of Agriculture, to make a speech in the House of Commons urging the necessity of sowing during the coming season with the greatest possible zeal both on week-days and Sundays. But Bonar Law was asked to find out from Dr. J. H. Shakespeare, the President of the Free Church Council, whether Nonconformists would resent Sunday sowing. He said that he ought also in that case to ask the Archbishop. Dr. Shakespeare had replied that many Nonconformists would resent Sunday sowing. Bonar Law asked the Archbishop what he thought, and whether he would be inclined to stimulate Sunday sowing himself. He replied that it was outside his sphere to do this, but, if he were asked for his opinion on the subject, he would gladly give it, and that he certainly approved of Sunday sowing in this emergency. Bonar Law thereupon said that he would get a question asked in the House of Commons, the form of the question being agreed with the Archbishop, and went away happy. It may be added that the Archbishop's advice had already been asked by various Bishops, as Sunday labour on the farm had become an immediate practical problem. After further communication with Mr. Prothero, the following correspondence appeared in the Press:

The RT. HON. R. PROTHERO *to the* ARCHBISHOP OF CANTERBURY

14th March, 1917.

The delay which has been caused by the frost in ploughing land for the harvest of 1917 makes every day of the utmost importance to the food supply of the country. In these circumstances of great urgency and national necessity, I should be very much obliged if you would give me your opinion on the question of tilling soil for food on Sundays.

The ARCHBISHOP OF CANTERBURY *to the* RT. HON. R. PROTHERO

14th March, 1917.

I thank you for your letter about Sunday labour in the fields during these vitally important weeks. Our inheritance of the English Sunday, with its privilege of abstention from all ordinary work, is a God-given boon of inestimable value, and I desire to maintain and safeguard it in every reasonable way; but occasions may arise when, for the well-being of the people of our land, exceptional obligations are laid upon us. As Minister of Agriculture, you assure us that such an emergency has now arisen, and that the security of the nation's food supply may largely depend upon the labour which can be devoted to the land in the next few weeks. This being so, we are, I think, following the guidance given in the Gospel if, in such a case, we make a temporary departure from our rule. I have no hesitation in saying that, in the need which these weeks present, men and women may with a clear conscience do field work on Sundays. Care would of course, be taken to safeguard from compulsion those who would feel such action on their part to be wrong, or whose health would be seriously endangered by the extra strain.

The incident is worthy of notice, as showing the strength of the public opinion in favour of Sunday rest, and the need which the civil power felt for assistance from the highest ecclesiastical authority in countenancing a departure even for a season from its observance.[1]

The Archbishop's attitude was approved by the main body of Christian opinion, but there were some notable protests and a very large number of letters and resolutions found their way

[1] The Roman Catholic Church through Cardinal Bourne, in *The Times* on March 22, advised 'That all the while the present national emergency lasts Catholics may lawfully engage in necessary agricultural work on Sundays provided they do not on this account neglect their essential religious duties'.

to Lambeth, while some very strange comments were made on both sides of the controversy by the Press. Thus the *Evening Standard and St. James' Gazette*[1] said:

> The Archbishop of Canterbury has taken the first definite step to put the Church in line with the people as regards the practical side of the war. He expresses the view that with a clear conscience Church people, men and women, can do field work on Sundays.
>
> We welcome this decision, not only because it has both common sense and Christianity on its side, but because it goes some way towards breaking down the aloofness of the Church on the great question of the day.

The Archbishop did not publicly notice the various remonstrances and complaints, except in one instance when a letter appeared in *The Times* of April 20 from Dr. R. F. Horton, an eminent Nonconformist minister in Hampstead, who had co-operated with the Archbishop in many departments of social service.

The REV. DR. R. F. HORTON *to the* EDITOR *of* '*The Times*'

20 April, 1917.

May I through your columns address a question to his Grace the Archbishop of Canterbury: When and how is the suspended Fourth Commandment to come again into operation? It was wonderful to see how swiftly and effectively his Grace's dispensation worked. At once the churches were half-emptied and the fields were filled with toilers on the day of rest. But when and how will the old sanction be restored? It is easier to shatter than to restore those 'unwritten and unfailing ordinances of the Gods', as Sophocles called them, which men cherish by an instinct and surrender only by the sophistication of an earthly authority.

The Bishop of my own district told Churchmen to 'do their religious duties' on Sunday morning and then go into the fields to dig and to sow for the rest of the day. Unfortunately, one of those religious duties is to receive the Holy Communion; and that service begins with the recitation of the Ten Commandments and the humble prayer after each for an inclination to keep it. The men, therefore, of my neighbourhood have been called on to listen to this Fourth Commandment: 'Six days shalt thou labour; the seventh is the Sabbath of the Lord thy God, in it thou shalt do no work.' Their attention may even have been called to the commandment in Ex. xxxiv. 21, that the law is to apply even in the

[1] March 15, 1917.

times of sowing and harvest. Then, having humbly asked God for mercy and an inclination to keep the commandment, they are to go out and—break it.

The Archbishop replied as follows in a letter to Dr. Horton (published in *The Times* on April 28):

The ARCHBISHOP OF CANTERBURY *to the* REV. DR. R. F. HORTON

21 April, 1917.

I read with great interest, and, I confess, with some bewilderment, your letter in *The Times* of yesterday, noting especially what it leaves unsaid. You and I are ministers of the Gospel of Jesus Christ. Yet in your handling of a subject with which Our Lord dealt so often, I find no reference to His teaching or example. Our thoughts are directed by you, most rightly, to Sinai—they are even directed to Sophocles—but not to the Son of Man, Who, as Lord of the Sabbath, taught His disciples to use that day, should special need require, for acts of beneficent service.

Your letter refers to the Sabbath, which I gather that you would bid us observe in literal and exact compliance with the directions of the Pentateuch. With regard to the kindred, but not identical, subject of Sunday observance, I am surprised that anyone—least of all a friend like yourself, with whom I have worked in this matter—should suppose me to be among those who regard it lightly. For many years I have been strenuous—and perforce prominent—in the endeavour to safeguard the Lord's Day. I hope to be strenuous to the end.

The Archbishop then reproduced the correspondence which had taken place five weeks previously between himself and Mr. Prothero, as quoted above, and continued:

This counsel I believe to be in full accord with what Our Lord taught us by word and act. Does the 'withered hand' differ in principle from the field rendered useless for lack of vitalizing seed? I have tried, throughout my ministry, to teach what I believe my Divine Master would have me teach. Far back in the dawn of Israel's history the people were Divinely taught that, if the life was to be maintained at its best, there must be some part of it kept free from the dust and the toil of ordinary days; and Israel grew to a mighty tree, and to a place among the world's peoples, with Sabbath observance at the very heart of its corporate life. Sunday, it has been well said, 'is no mere revival of the Jewish Sabbath upon a different day. It commemorates a different fact. It is permeated by a different idea.' Its primary and characteristic observance is worship. The privilege, the duty, of rest, vitally important as it is, came in separately. It is impossible to exaggerate the responsibility resting upon every man and woman in the Church of Christ for making right use of the Lord's Day, for safeguarding so inestimable a thing from being lightly tampered with, for cherishing and honouring it for everybody's good. The Lord's Day is no mere accidental observance, which might be dropped without interfering with the Christian system. It has been inwrought in the life of the Church of Christ from Apostolic days, and the principle which it enshrines, the principle of rest as well as worship, goes back and back into the very origins of God's revelation and God's word. And Our Lord trusts us to use it reverently as a possession majestical in its history, and practical in its effective power over the working days of our whole life—trusts us to use it unselfishly, as something which belongs equally to us all, as Christians, and must be so handled by us as to keep it safe for those who shall come after, and for those among us who, in our complex social life, may be least able, by independent action, to keep their treasure unharmed. That is how the Sunday, God's gift, presents itself to my mind.

The circumstances to-day are unique. By those who have a right to speak, we are assured that we are standing at an hour of tremendous emergency, and at such a time it may be right to sacrifice for a while a portion of our privilege, and to ask God's blessing on the sacrifice. Take it in this spirit, and I fear no ill result.

You tell us that the publication of my letter to Mr. Prothero had the result that 'at once the churches were half-emptied and the fields were filled with toilers'. It may be so in Hampstead. I have not heard of similar experience elsewhere. But I believe that, when, as a minister of Christ, I answered to the best of my power the question legitimately asked of me, I was helping to bring wholesome relief to some, perhaps to many, honest Christian people who were perplexed as to their duty in these weeks of stress and might welcome an expression of opinion from myself.

Dr. Horton, in thanking the Archbishop for his letter, in a private note said:

The REV. DR. R. F. HORTON *to the* ARCHBISHOP OF CANTERBURY

April 23, 1917.

What I wanted to elicit from you was the authoritative judgment that the Fourth Commandment holds, and that its suspension was only for a definite time, viz. six weeks.

He had hoped that the Archbishop would have seen his way 'to doing something more decisive and effective'. But he said that he would send the Archbishop's letter to *The Times*, and added, 'as a personal vindication it is absolutely effective'.

IV

The demand made on previous occasions for a Day of National Humiliation and Prayer by Royal Proclamation, was pressed again with extraordinary emphasis in 1917. It was not enough, declared the World's Evangelical Alliance and its friends, that the Churches should call to prayer; the State itself must act. The Archbishop gave many interviews on the subject to Mr. H. M. Gooch, its Secretary, and others, and was at great pains to represent their views to the King and to the Prime Minister. He appreciated the earnestness of the wish, even while hardly himself convinced that the proposal was desirable; and he went out of his way to try to learn the views not only of religious leaders but of serious statesmen. In the end the Archbishop succeeded in buttonholing Lloyd George on June 20, who gave his decision and refused to advise any intervention by the State:

> I had button-holed him firmly at the Luncheon to Balfour and insisted on an interview if possible to-day. Accordingly I went to Downing Street half an hour later, and he was perfectly friendly and gave a full hearing. He is evidently puzzled, but he has in his own mind resolved not to ask for a Day of Prayer by Royal Proclamation or to advise the King to ask for it. He is quite clear that it would be misunderstood both by our enemies and by our Allies. The anxieties are very great both in the East—Mesopotamia, Syria, etc.—and with regard to Submarines. Russia is collapsing, he thinks hopelessly, though, as he added, 'They are a very unexpected people, and something may occur, and I believe they are going to put up a fight next week'. In view of all these things he is distinctly of opinion that it would be unwise for the State to take the line suggested, and he is vehemently supported in this view by Bonar Law.
>
> 'What then', I asked, 'about the Deputation? Mr. Gooch wants me to head a Deputation to you and is awaiting my reply before asking you to receive it. The point of the Deputation will be this: We want you to bring about on State authority the observance, not of a new day, but of the first Sunday in August, the third anniversary of the War. Of course we shall observe it, but

what we want is that the observance shall be of a State initiative and of a State character. Whether it is the Government, or the King, or the Privy Council, is a small matter provided it is the State. But we should further regard it as essential that the authorities who thus permit it, should themselves play the game—i.e. show that they care about it by themselves attending, etc., and making it really the act of the State or country as such. This is what I should say if I came on the Deputation.'

Lloyd George answered 'I earnestly hope you will not come. I do not think I could refuse to receive a Deputation from the Alliance, but I shall certainly not grant their request. In these circumstances, it would put me in an almost intolerable position if you came and pressed me to do it and I had to decline. You see my difficulties, and I hope you will help me. I do not ask you to promise that no Bishop would come (that would not be fair), but if you or the Archbishop of York came, my position would be extraordinarily difficult.' I replied to the effect 'That is all very well, but as I think that some "day" of the kind is desirable I do not want to be left under the imputation that the lack of it is due to my having failed the Deputation, and that had I been there it would have been granted'. He answered 'I will take care of that. I should tell the Deputation that I have been in communication with you, and that you have put the wish before me which they express, but that I have explained to you, as I will explain to them, that I think it undesirable'. He then repeated again his strong feeling about the certainty of misunderstanding, and his hope that the Day would be observed on the initiative of the Churches as in former years. He added further 'It would be quite different if the State had asked for this each year from the beginning. Then there would be nothing exceptional about our doing it just now. But at a time when our anxieties are so grave, and when our enemies are trying to exaggerate them and make out that things are worse for us than they are, they would leap at the opportunity of saying: "See the plight to which they are reduced. We told you so." For these reasons I am quite clear that we ought not to do it.'

V

This year the Forms of Prayer issued by authority for use, where the Ordinary permits, on August 4 and 5, contained for the first time a prayer for the Departed. It ran as follows:

Almighty and Everlasting God, unto whom no prayer is ever made without hope of thy compassion: We remember before thee our brethren who have laid down their lives in the cause wherein their King and country sent them. Grant that they, who have readily obeyed the call of those to whom thou hast given authority on earth, may be accounted worthy of a place among thy faithful servants in the kingdom of heaven; and give both to them and to us forgiveness of all our sins, and an ever increasing understanding of thy will; for his sake who loved us and gave himself for us, thy Son our Saviour Jesus Christ. *Amen.*

The following letters passed:

The BISHOP OF LIVERPOOL[1] *to the* ARCHBISHOP OF CANTERBURY

Leighton Vicarage, Welshport.
July 17, 1917.

I have received, this morning, the Forms of Prayer for use on August 4 and 5. On page 11, at the foot, appears a Prayer for the Dead more definite and precise than any that has yet appeared.

I know how pressed and harassed your Grace is, and I am exceedingly unwilling to add to your burden and worry at such a time as this. But I think that your Grace can hardly be aware of the strong feeling of distress and resentment which the insertion of such Prayers is arousing in the minds of a large number of Church people, and those not the least loyal. May I venture to suggest that an alternative Form be issued by authority with a *Thanks*giving for the Dead, as in the Prayer for the Church Militant.

Your Grace is so just and reasonable that I am sure you will try to meet the need and anxiety of those who have always believed that the Church of England does not authorize the public use of Prayers for the Dead, and that there is no authority for their use in Holy Scriptures.

Forgive me, your Grace, for writing so frankly. We are drawing too near the rocks for me to keep silent.

The ARCHBISHOP OF CANTERBURY *to the* BISHOP OF LIVERPOOL

18th July 1917.

I am grateful to you for writing to me frankly about the difficulty you feel respecting the Service authorized for use on August 5th 'where the Ordinary permits'. I was keenly awake to the point of the difficulty which you feel about the mention of those departed, and I took special pains that nothing which goes a hair's breadth beyond what is clearly furnished in the Prayer Book should appear in the Office for Holy Communion, which will presumably be used

[1] Dr. F. J. Chavasse.

in most churches. I did not feel that in all the circumstances a quite similar difficulty need be felt with regard to the Supplementary Prayers to be used, as is specially stated, 'at the discretion of the Minister' as well as being subject to the permission of the Ordinary. Even here I was very anxious not to go beyond what has, I think, become very usual in churches of all schools of thought, including very markedly some of the most Evangelical of our brethren. I do not think that the particular prayer to which you call attention ought to present difficulties to anybody. It might have been better had the comma after the word 'they', in the penultimate line of page 11, not been there, and I am a little inclined to doubt whether it would be found in the original manuscript. My own feeling was that we were really suggesting a prayer which would meet the wishes of almost everybody, for it must be remembered that there are hundreds of thousands who are eagerly anxious for some prayer which can to them, as they use it, convey the idea of intercession with Our Heavenly Father on behalf of those whose life is now going on beyond our sight. I have passionate appeals to that effect, and it goes to my heart not to be able to meet their wishes more fully, believing as I do that such prayers are not forbidden by any doctrine of the Church of England, although their use liturgically was for very obvious reasons practically abolished. Surely, with the Rubric which stands at the top of page 9,[1] we may leave it to the discretion of the Minister to use or not to use the particular prayer you mention. Those who feel as you do about it would obviously not use it. Others, including as I know a great many men of marked Evangelical opinion, would thankfully use it; and of course if any Bishop feels that he would desire that it should not be used, it is easy for him to say that he authorises the use of the Form *with the exception of that prayer*, which he thinks undesirable. Have we not thus really done our best to meet the varying wishes of devout people? The criticisms which I receive are much more frequently directed against our Forms on account of the absence of the sort of Prayers for the Dead which I have declined to sanction for liturgical use. I greatly hope that what I have said may to some extent meet your wishes.

The Bishop of Manchester (Dr. Knox), alone of the Bishops, joined his brother of Liverpool in the protest. The Archbishop had already, at the end of 1914,[2] stated his own views on the

[1] 'Here may be added, at the discretion of the Minister, any of the Prayers which follow, or any other of the special Prayers already issued by authority.'

[2] The following is an extract from a sermon preached by the Archbishop at All

permissibility of Prayers for the Departed, but it was not till 1917 that the official forms included such prayer.

VI

In the spring of 1917 a new and more violent agitation for reprisals was started in the Press and continued till the end of the year. Public indignation had been stirred by a succession of attacks aimed, it was held, simply at the civilian population or those unable to protect themselves in the Channel or on the high seas. Thus, at the beginning of February, the Anchor liner *California* was torpedoed without warning, on a voyage from New York to Glasgow, with 43 lives lost; the White Star liner *Afric* a few days later, with 25 lives lost; and the Cunard liner *Laconia* at the end of the month. Bombs were also dropped from the air on the Kent coast towns and elsewhere, in March; but it was not till two British hospital ships were torpedoed without warning during the same month that a deliberate retaliation took place. On April 14 a large squadron of British and French aeroplanes bombarded Freiburg, and the attack was stated to be by way of reprisal for that outrage. The Archbishop's aid was at once invoked to protest. He made a speech in the House of Lords on May 2, asking His Majesty's Government whether it was possible, without detriment to public interests, to make any statement

Hallows, Barking by the Tower, November 2, 1914. It was much quoted at the time: '. . . And surely we are right to be on our guard lest in one who thus reverently, trustfully, thinks and prays and wonders, we discourage the upraising of the devout soul in prayer for the loved one out of sight. We are not forgetful of the long and mischievous abuse of that devotion in the later mediaeval days until, as your first Warden-Vicar has written, "It might almost be said that the main object of religion in the fifteenth century had been to deliver souls out of the ever-heightening horrors of Purgatory and to ensure the living against incurring them". Nay, we have not forgotten or ignored the same abuses still alive, still in some fields prevalent—the dogmatism about things we cannot know, and the perils which such abuse involves. . . . But surely now there is place for a gentler recognition of the instinctive, the natural, the loyal craving of the bereaved, and the abuses of the chantry system and the extravagances of Tetzel need not now, nearly four centuries afterwards, thwart or hinder the reverent, the absolutely trustful prayer of a wounded spirit who feels it natural and helpful to pray for him whom we shall not greet on earth again, but who, in his Father's loving keeping, still lives, and, as we may surely believe, still grows from strength to strength in truer purity and in deepened reverence and love.' Few things of the kind were more remarkable than the great change effected during the first year of the war in popular opinion, and church practice, with regard to Prayer for the Dead. In 1914 such Prayers were most uncommon: by 1918 their use was widespread.

respecting the adoption of a policy of reprisal, at Freiburg or elsewhere, in retaliation for the outrages perpetrated by the German fleet. He spoke of his personal interest, since 'no corner of England has suffered in its open towns and innocent populations so severely as the Isle of Thanet' in his own diocese. But he maintained:

> I do know that the Christian judgement of England—and I do not shrink from using that term in its fullest sense—is that when we come out of this war (scarred and wounded, yes; bereft of some of our best and noblest and most hopeful, yes), we mean to come out with clean hands and with the right to feel sure that in the coming years, whatever record leaps to light, we never shall be ashamed.

On the previous day the Upper House of Canterbury Convocation had reaffirmed the Resolution adopted on February 17, 1916; and the Archbishop was also able to quote the Free Church Council as opposed to any such measure of reprisal. The Archbishop was heard with respect by the Lords, and Lord Curzon in replying for the Government was more half-hearted than some of the supporters of retaliation approved. A long correspondence with all sorts of people followed. Letters reached him from a supporter of reprisals like Hall Caine, who argued that 'to justify war and to condemn its natural if tragical developments is to strain at the gnat and swallow the camel'; as well as from General Bramwell Booth, Dr. Scott Lidgett, Dr. Horton, and very many besides. In addition he and his friends were the object of violent attack in the Press from the Duke of Argyll, who said: 'The war is not going to be won by going back to coracles and arrows', and bade 'the bishops stick to their belfries, and cobblers to their lasts'; from Sir Arthur Conan Doyle, who wrote a series of eloquent letters on 'The uses of hatred'; from Sir Henry T. Eve, Eden Philpotts, and a host of minor but impassioned antagonists. The following letters may be quoted as showing the Archbishop's own view:

SIR THOMAS BARLOW *to the* ARCHBISHOP OF CANTERBURY

20 June, 1917.

Comments in the Press and elsewhere show, I think, imperfect apprehension of your attitude towards 'reprisals'. Are you willing to tell me what is the fundamental principle which you maintain ought to be considered? Such a statement, if published, would, I believe, help many people in the formation of a reasoned judgment on a very difficult question.

The ARCHBISHOP OF CANTERBURY *to* SIR THOMAS BARLOW

Lambeth Palace, 21st June, 1917.

You are right, I think, in believing that what I have said and written in regard to Reprisals has been curiously and even persistently misunderstood. The question of our moral duty in the matter is admittedly a difficult one, and it has a margin line which may easily be blurred. The foundation principle, however, does not seem to me to be obscure. My own point is best expressed in the words of a Resolution[1] passed, on my motion, by the Bishops of the Province of Canterbury. We there, 'while fully recognising that it does not lie within the province of Bishops to express any opinion upon matters purely military', recorded our conviction 'that the principles of morality forbid a policy of reprisal which has, as a deliberate object, the killing and wounding of non-combatants, and [this House] believes that the adoption of such a mode of retaliation, even for barbarous outrages, would permanently lower the standard of honourable conduct between nation and nation'.

The key of the situation lies in the intention of the act—not an uncertain hope of ultimate consequence, but its immediate practical intention.

Of course in one sense 'reprisal' is of the essence of war. But what kind of reprisal? We bombard a fortified town. This must often involve risk to innocent non-combatants. But that is not its object. Its object is to harm the enemy's combatant forces. The incidental harming of non-combatants is lamentable, and it will, so far as military conditions permit, be avoided. But it is sometimes inevitable.

Quite different from this, is an attack the direct object of which is to harm or kill non-combatants, either for reasons of vengeance, or in order to promote terror, or in the hope of deterring the enemy from perpetrating outrages. That is the kind of 'reprisal' in which some people wish us in England to indulge.

Its advocates speak sometimes in general terms which disguise or evade the ultimate meaning. Others are more explicit. In the natural, the inevitable, strain of these sorrows, sorrows whose depth baffles expression, men and women write excitedly. But it is well to try to realise what their words mean. I am urged, for

[1] February 17, 1916. See p. 777.

example, to see to it that we insist upon 'reprisals, swift, bloody and unrelenting. Let gutters run with German blood. Let us smash to pulp the German old men, women, and children', and so on. Do those who describe the terrible sight of little London children lying dead really want to see little German children lying slaughtered in like manner by us?

In my belief such action on our part, if we were so mistaken as to adopt it, would be altogether futile as a deterrent: the Germans would always out-distance us in ruthlessness. But my belief or conjecture on that question is valueless: nor can the opinion of anyone about it be more than surmise. Of this I am quite certain: many thousands of the best and most thoughtful people in this country are resolved that, so far as we civilians are allowed any say in the matter, we mean to support the prosecution of the war with every power we have and every sacrifice that we can make, but we mean to come out of it with untainted honour and with clean hands. We are determined to leave to the Germans the unenviable monopoly of an infamous disregard of what is honourable and decent in warfare. We absolutely decline to degrade ourselves to that level. Suppose we were to act otherwise; suppose our righteous wrath against these outrages were to provoke us to retaliating in kind either on prisoners or on the harmless inhabitants of unfortified towns and villages. Two results would follow. In the first place, history would draw no difference between the nations which had acted thus alike and had placed themselves on one level. In the next place, if another war should come (God forbid it), it would doubtless begin by outrages of this sort, as the perpetration of them could no longer be regarded as outside the pale. The whole moral currency of international life would have been debased. I am persuaded that the Christian judgement and purpose of England is that when we come out of this appalling war we must come out of it unstained by these atrocities.

That is my position. I believe it to be the position of the best and most thoughtful of our fellow-countrymen—sailors, soldiers, and civilians alike.

The ARCHBISHOP OF CANTERBURY *to* HALL CAINE, ESQ.

12th July 1917.

I thank you for your courtesy in sending me a copy of your appeal to German Mothers. I hope it may do great good, if it ever reaches them, but my fear would be that that is unlikely. I note with great interest what you say about Reprisals and about the opinion of most good and reasonable people. I am, I confess, somewhat appalled by the letters which pour in upon me in quite extraordinary numbers, breathing blood and slaughter, not against combatants but against the people of Germany if only they can be got at, with a special wish for the destruction of women and children. Of course, as you know, I have never said a syllable against Reprisals in the sense of our retaliating upon combatants. Unhappily war consists, and necessarily consists, of such retaliation. I have chosen my words carefully throughout, deprecating simply such kind of reprisals as have for their deliberate object the killing of non-combatants, not incidentally but of set purpose. I trust that you will take any step that may be possible to get your appeal to German women made known in Germany.

HALL CAINE, ESQ., *to the* ARCHBISHOP OF CANTERBURY

Heath Brow, Hampstead Heath, N.W. 3. July 16, 1917.

I thank you very warmly for your kind letter. The Foreign Office undertook the distribution of my letter to the Mothers of Germany, and it went out in about half a dozen languages (German among them) to all the neutral countries, and particularly the cantons of Switzerland, which are in closest touch with Germany, and have newspapers in the German language crossing the frontier. In addition to this they have adopted other measures for the distribution of the letter from the air, over nearly all the territory that lies within easy reach. Therefore, there is perhaps some reason to think that the letter will reach its destination. Whether the German mother is open to approach on the side of her purely human emotions, when they are opposed to what appears to be the political interests of her country, remains to be seen. I have, however, immense faith in the power of the human instincts, and the response which has already reached me from women of many nationalities seems to justify it.

I am interested, but not surprised, to gather that you have had a flood of correspondence on the subject of reprisals, and that much of this has taken the form of a passionate cry for revenge. I have, on my part, received a vast number of letters, some of them denunciatory of my own views, some intelligently appreciative, but many breathing evil passions which certainly never entered into my calculation as the natural sequel to my teaching. I confess to feeling a certain alarm at the spirit of revenge which has been awakened in our people, particularly among the women of the humbler and less educated classes.

If you could have gone down to the districts of Hoxton and Stoke Newington within a few hours of the last raid on London, you would have been able to realise, as no letters, however vehement, could show, how intense is the desire on the part of the humbler mother to revenge herself for the loss of her children by these brutal methods of warfare. I would almost suggest to you, if I may, that in the event (which God forbid) of another such air raid occurring, you should drive down to the densely populated districts in which the worst slaughter has more than once occurred. I feel quite certain that you would be treated with the utmost respect. It is conceivable that some of the more passionate in the dense crowds of women might shriek and yell and curse, but they are, after all, a very simple-hearted and almost child-like race under their ugly outer cloak of blasphemy. I am sure it would interest and move you to realise how deep and true is the human feeling that lies beneath.

More than once I have felt the impulse to speak to the crowds down there, and I feel certain that if you were to do so, saying just the right word at the hot moment, it would have an immensely beneficial effect.

I trust you will not think it presumptuous if I say that again and again at such moments of great national emotion, I have told myself that the Head of a great Church is in the position of wielding power immeasurably greater than that of any statesman or other public person whatsoever. Perhaps you will remember what a tremendous effect was produced by Cardinal Manning when he went down to the Docks at a moment of great excitement and public danger.

The ARCHBISHOP OF CANTERBURY *to* HALL CAINE, ESQ.

Private. 17th July 1917.

I thank you much for your full and courteous letter. It interests me, and indeed it is a satisfaction also to me, to learn that you share my feeling of alarm at the spirit of revenge which has been awakened in our people by the German outrages. I am certain that it is our duty to allay this so far as possible, even while we encourage to the utmost of our power the due use of military reprisal on military objectives. The more vigorously such reprisal, in the true sense of the word, can be carried on, the better ground we shall have for making appeal against what I at least think to be the wholly mischievous form of reprisal which has as its deliberate object the killing or maiming of non-combatants.

With regard to what you say about our acquainting ourselves on the spot with the feelings of those who are subjected to this suffering, I have made this from the first my endeavour. In each raid with which I have had anything to do—e.g. at Folkestone, at Ramsgate, at Croydon, and elsewhere—I have tried to get as quickly as possible into touch with the sufferers and with their homes. In some of these places I think I saw everyone who had been wounded, and a great proportion of those who had been bereaved, visiting their houses and cheering and encouraging them to the best of my power. I am not certain that it would clearly be best that I should do this in East London, far from my own house and outside the area of my own immediate jurisdiction, if (or I fear I must say when) another raid of a like sort occurs. My relation to South London is a little different, and it would be my hope that I might be on the spot as speedily as possible should such incidents occur in this part of London. I am of course very familiar with its poorest regions and with the homes of the people there.

To Dr. Horton, with whom he had engaged in an earlier correspondence on the Sunday question, he also wrote in October, in response to his appeal for an authoritative lead 'against this vindictive passion of our political leaders':

The ARCHBISHOP OF CANTERBURY *to* DR. R. F. HORTON

11th October 1917.

I am exceedingly glad to receive your letter of yesterday. I share to a great extent your feelings on the question of Reprisals. But it seems to me that it would be superfluous at this moment for me to speak again unless someone else raises a point calling for my answer in Parliament or elsewhere. I am regarded apparently as the representative mouthpiece of those who object to reprisals undertaken with the deliberate object of injuring non-combatants, and I am in consequence the recipient of a continuous shower of protests, denunciations, and often virulent abuse, from every part of England, especially from London. I am said to be the cause of the Air Raids, to be in league with the Germans, and to be responsible for the death of those who have suffered, and so on. Devout prayers are expressed that I (and occasionally my wife, to whom they sometimes write) may be the next person to be blown to pieces. It is all coupled, strangely enough, with my action in approving a certain amount of agricultural work on Sundays as an emergency measure. In short, it is now taken as a recognized fact, both by friends and opponents, that I represent in the fullest degree that school of protesters: indeed even Government authorities and other public men speak to me as the representative who has (as one of them put it to me) burned his boats upon this question. I think therefore that I have said my say and, so to speak, nailed my colours both adequately and with sufficient publicity. Another protest by me would have no fresh weight at all: whatever I could say I have said, and everybody knows it. If independent testimony is now borne backing up what I have said it may be most valuable. My letter to Sir Thomas Barlow (in *The Times* of June 22nd) expresses my opinion exactly, and I have repeatedly referred my correspondents to that letter.

CHAPTER LII

THE RUSSIAN COLLAPSE

When a world, not yet doomed for death, is rushing down to ever-deeper Baseness and Confusion, it is a dire necessity of Nature's to bring in her ARISTOCRACIES, her BEST, even by forcible methods. When their descendants or representatives cease entirely to *be* the Best, Nature's poor world will very soon rush down again to Baseness; and it becomes a dire Necessity of Nature's to cast them out. Hence French Revolutions, Five-point Charters, Democracies, and a mournful list of *Etceteras*, in these our afflicted times. THOMAS CARLYLE, *Past and Present*, III. xiii.

IN preaching at Westminster Abbey on Sunday, August 5, 1917, the third anniversary of the War, in the presence of the King, the Prime Minister, and most members of the Government, the Archbishop spoke of the need of patience. His text was Hebrews xii. 1: 'Let us run with patience the race that is set before us.' After the service he had a long talk with Lloyd George, and was with him over an hour. Lloyd George spoke about many things: the vacant Bishopric of Hereford; the Archbishop's sermon; the situation in Russia; the dangerous discontent of the French army; the impossibility of effective American help before next year; and the possibility of years of war, a new Napoleonic war, with England as the only people who really were fighting consistently and bravely. He was especially full of Russia, and when the Archbishop asked him whether the warning in his speech the previous day meant that Russia might collapse altogether and leave the Allies without her aid—the Archbishop's note proceeds:

> He turned round in his walk about the room, and standing still and lifting up his hand said, 'If Russia collapses completely, the entire world situation is changed and we must make new arrangements altogether'. I think these were his words. I pressed, as to what these new arrangements might be, and he said, 'I think we should have to make peace forthwith with Austria and Turkey on any obtainable terms.'

What was the Archbishop's own attitude to the Russian Revolution, and to Peace during these months? For answer we can give one or two significant illustrations.

I

The Tsar was deposed on March 15, 1917. These two letters to Miss Blanche Sitwell, one of the Archbishop's oldest friends, show one side of the picture:

The ARCHBISHOP OF CANTERBURY *to* MISS BLANCHE SITWELL

Tremans, Horsted Keynes, Sussex.
7 April 1917.

I wish I could feel quite as hopeful as you do about the doings in Russia. One can't help recalling the way in which the French Revolution—with which you contrast it—began, as people all pointed out, with an absence of bloodshed and an apparent sobriety of Liberal purpose. God grant that Russia may be enabled to escape, or that she has even now escaped, the blood-thirstiness which is apt to enthuse Revolutionaries. I feel a bit anxious about Fleet and Army, though one mustn't be led to look too *sombrely* at what ought clearly to be so glorious and glad an emancipation from archaic ways, and from *misrulers*. I am in fullest sympathy with the averred aims of those who have now risen, and I hope it may turn out that to those aims and that line of action they adhere.

I have read these *Nation* letters and I return them. Surely it is hardly necessary for Jack Hutchinson to bid us eschew the bad and foolish drivel of the few old ex-officers, etc., who look on the war as a sort of game played for our country's, and other countries' amusement.

But there is much in these letters with which I agree very fully. We have certainly managed to *muddle* the question of the conscientious objector. But he does make our helping of him nearly impossible. When a man (one of those these letters mention) won't help to make bandages for the sick, or food for the hungry, or relief packets for the destitute, and then refuses to let the doctor examine him even superficially, and yet claims the rights and properties of a *citizen*, for whom the State is responsible, he puts despair into the hearts of those who want to help him, and have spent day after day trying to do it. But enough of that.

The ARCHBISHOP OF CANTERBURY *to* MISS BLANCHE SITWELL

Old Palace, Canterbury.
May 28, 1917.

I entirely share the opinions expressed by (? Miss) Leigh if she has really been so unlucky in the Churches she has attended. It is *monstrous* how stupid and unimaginative a good many of the clergy are, and how they are missing great opportunities of being helpful at this time. But surely, surely there are scores or hundreds of parishes everywhere where that is not so. I have any amount of abusive letters and critical letters about it all, and that is right, for I am fair game, and the right target for folk to shoot at. But I have the other side too in abundance. Of course it would be splendid if the clergy were all able to be pointed, suggestive, eloquent, up to date, kindly and profound; but how are we to expect to get that sort of man everywhere as a parson when 'we have only got the laity to draw upon'! I don't excuse it a bit. It is heart breaking. But it is only a very limited number of men, *of any sort of class or profession*, who would be fit at such a juncture to do all that is needed, and possibly what (Miss?) Leigh calls a 'pro German' service, which sends her out of the Church, would be regarded by *you* as the sort of fair-minded unbigoted thing you specially liked! Well, we must wrestle on and do our best. (I like Miss Leigh's letter very much indeed; it says what wants saying.)

You ask about Smuts. I have been seeing a good deal of him. He dined quietly with us one night, and another evening I had him and Page, and (whom do you think?) *Milner*, together at a very interesting quiet talk about it all for nearly three hours. Milner is less pessimistic about Russia than Smuts is. Smuts thinks Russia has simply gone to bits, not being equal (i.e. the people's grasp and grit) for such a time, and he thinks the outlook in Russia is black. Milner, though he sees all the mischief of what is happening both in Army and Navy, takes a more (at least *rather* more) hopeful view. The murder of Officers has been very bad, especially in the Navy where ALL the leading men have been killed. But he believes more than Smuts does in the coming forward of good men among the Revolutionaries. Only it will take time, and meanwhile mischief, and especially *desertion*, are rife. Probably the best line for your young friend to take, in her Russian advocacy, is just what you tell me she *does* take, namely to say it isn't true and that these murders and desertions etc. are lies concocted by the European Governments (and I suppose Lord Northcliffe!). Unhappily that won't do. Jellicoe has been giving me the very ghastly facts. The wretched part of it is that, unless we can somehow get Germany more beaten within the next few months, the Russian collapse will mean the going *on and on* of the War.

All this sounds rather 'grousy' but I don't mean it to be. We are going to get through these troubles, and better things will be the outgrowth.

Two other messages, the fruit of his anxiety, show his sympathy with the Russian Church. The first, an Easter greeting, April 15, being the Russian Easter Day, was published in the Russian press and received a cordial welcome:

The ARCHBISHOP OF CANTERBURY *to the* HOLY SYNOD OF RUSSIA

April 15, 1917.

On behalf of the Church of England, I exchange with you, at this sacred season, the fraternal greeting of thanksgiving and hope. Christos voskress.[1]

May the blessing of the risen Lord 'fill you with joy and peace in believing', even amidst the anxiety and strain of this eventful year.

May the strife and confusion issue in a righteous victory over the high-handed wrong of our enemy, and in abiding peace and freedom for the peoples of Europe.

May the Russian people, in its newborn strength, be guided by the Holy Spirit of God to bear therein a worthy part. The Easter benediction rests to-day upon our great peoples, united under new conditions by bonds of ever-deepening sympathy and friendship.

Christos voskress.

The second was dated September 11, 1917, while the Russian Holy Synod was deliberating on church reforms:

The ARCHBISHOP OF CANTERBURY *to the* HOLY SYNOD OF RUSSIA

September 11, 1917.

I desire on behalf of the Church of England to convey to the Holy Synod of the Russian Church, and to its responsible authorities throughout the land, the assurance of our deep fraternal interest in the efforts which are now being made by the Bishops, Clergy, and laity of the Russian Church to use for the good of the whole people the new opportunities which—even in the present turmoil—have arisen: and to express our firm hope and the promise of our confident prayer that it may please God Almighty, through our Lord and Saviour Jesus Christ, to grant to the whole Church in Russia the spirit of wisdom and strength at this time of crisis and difficulty and hope.

In December the Archbishop sent a further message, following the decision of the Russian Church to revive the Patriarchate of

[1] i.e. Christ is risen—the Russian Easter greeting.

Moscow (after a suppression of nearly 250 years, due to Peter the Great) and have one supreme spiritual leader in the Patriarch of All Russia. The man chosen for the great office was Tykhon,[1] who had been elected Metropolitan of Moscow by popular vote in June 1917:

The ARCHBISHOP OF CANTERBURY *to* HIS HOLINESS TYKHON, PATRIARCH OF ALL RUSSIA

Lambeth Palace, December 17, 1917.

I desire in the name of the Church of England to send to your Holiness our respectful and fraternal greeting on your election to the ancient Patriarchate of Russia. It is to the Christian Church united throughout the world in the bonds of our Holy Faith that mankind must look in hours of darkness and confusion for light and healing. We assure your Holiness of our unfailing prayer that the hand of our living Lord may rest upon you in blessing, that the Holy Spirit may guide you in thought and word and act, and that you may be strengthened to discharge to the glory of God and to the good of His people the high and sacred duties in the Church of our Lord and Saviour Jesus Christ, to which in the revival of the Holy Patriarchate you have at a time of difficulty and anxiety been solemnly called.

This message was duly handed to His Holiness, at a special audience, by the British Representative at Moscow, with as much ceremony as the circumstances permitted. The Patriarch immediately sent the following reply, in English, written with his own hand, and with the signature in purple ink.

†

2 Cor. i. 3–5.

TO HIS GRACE RANDALL CANTUAR, ARCHBISHOP OF CANTERBURY, ETC.

Your Grace,

We beg to acknowledge the receipt of your kind message with the greetings in the name of the Church of England on our election to the Patriarchate of Russia.

[1] The Patriarch was 52 years of age. He was the son of a priest in the Diocese of Pskov. He had worked on the staff in the Ecclesiastical Academies of St. Petersburg and Kazan. He then became Bishop, first of Liublin, and then for the Aleutian Islands, with his residence at San Francisco. After some years in America he returned to Russia, becoming Archbishop in 1905 and holding the sees of Yaroslev and Lithuania from 1913 to 1917. He was regarded as cordially interested in the Church of England.

Permit us to express our sincere gratitude for your fraternal feelings, and our profound wish that your prayers, which are of great value and moral comfort to us at this hour of general anti-Christian spirit in the world, may fulfil, and all Christians unite in strong fight for the glorious banner of our Faith—Holy Cross of our Saviour.

It makes us happy to know that the Church of England keeps the Russian Church close to her heart, and in the name of the Holy Orthodox Russian Church we ask you to accept our warm appreciation of your belief, which we here fully share, that 'it is to the Christian Church united throughout the world in the bonds of our Holy Faith that mankind must look in this hour of darkness and confusion for light and health'.

Therefore, let us pray that the vial of wrath of God may yet spare humanity, and that 'for the elect's sake' these days of tribulation may be shortened, and general misfortunes of nowadays may teach all branches of Christianity to approach nearer one another in the Spirit of love and unity.

Our blessings to all. With the best wishes and cordiality, we are, Sir, faithfully yours,

† TYKHON, Patriarch of All Russia.

Moscow.

January 12/25, 1918.

The next communication to the Church of England from the Church of Russia was a bitter cry from Odessa in December, for help in the midst of cruel persecution.

II

An interesting plan for helping the Serbian Church took shape this year, after considerable discussion. It sprang out of the terrible needs of a stricken country from which multitudes had been driven by the invading troops. The Archbishop of Belgrade (Dimitri) was himself an exile, with large numbers of priests. One of these, Fr. Nicholai Velimirovic, a very remarkable man, proposed that the Church of England should help selected Serbian students, most of them young seminarists whose theological work had been interrupted by the war, to complete their training in certain English colleges under the supervision of Serbian priests.

The plan (which it was understood that the Archbishop of

Belgrade blessed) was put to the Archbishop. But it seemed to him that a good deal of caution was needed. On the one hand, he wished to know what exactly the plan involved. On the other hand, he saw the risk that in later days it might be said that the Church of England for its own purposes had been proselytizing young Serbs, and teaching them unorthodox Anglican ways! His Grace was therefore reluctant to give the plan his official sanction without a clear authorization from the Serbian Archbishop. Many piteous letters, with sad stories of his Church's sufferings, reached Lambeth Palace from Archbishop Dimitri, now a refugee at Corfu, but neither they, nor a telegram which followed, seemed to Archbishop Davidson to be precise enough to justify him in giving his official approval to the scheme. The following letter from Fr. Nicholai to his Grace's chaplain, indicates the difficulty sometimes felt by the more impetuous souls in understanding the Archbishop of Canterbury's caution:

FR. NICHOLAI VELIMIROVIC *to the* REV. G. K. A. BELL

Serbian Information Bureau, 9, King Street, St. James'.
June 15, 1917.

Many thanks for your kind note. Nothing is so very precise in this time of the universal chaos. And I am afraid our poor Archbishop of Serbia is not speaking very clearly and precisely as to the Serbian theological students.

I think you have to deal with the Serbian students as with the refugees who ask your help, the material and spiritual. The letter of the Archbishop asking for the help of the Serbian church includes the spiritual help of the Serbian candidates for priesthood. The Roman Catholics would not ask for an absolute clearness and preciseness. His Grace the Archbishop of Canterbury has enough ground to help Serbia in any way he wishes. As to the details I am here in London to explain. The general idea and apply is given already by the Archbishop of Serbia.

We have got now 11 Serbian students of theology. They are a very good material. All the responsibility for any action I will take myself. Don't be afraid of anything. Either the church will awake during this war or never. It is an exceptional time. The people of Serbia are asking for material and spiritual help. Just as you do not ask anybody in the world whether to help materially the Serbians, so why should you ask anybody to help them spiritually? Yet, our Archbishop agrees quite. But he can't tell it quite clearly, as His Grace can't tell everything quite clearly as he desires.

The letter of the Archbishop concerns a Committee in Serbia, of which he is the Chairman, with purpose to help the suffering people from war. Well, it suggests the idea that a Committee may be formed in the Church of England to help the Church of Serbia in her distress, i.e.

(*a*) to help the Serbian clergy (700 are now been interned, starving in Austria and Bulgaria),

(*b*) to help the Serbian students of theology, who are asking for spiritual help (it is now impossible for them to go to Russia and study there),

(*c*) to publish a Prayer Book for the Serbian soldiers at the front, who are longing to have a spiritual book in Serbian language to read.

I think it is clear now. But if you think anything to be unclear still, I will explain to you *in extenso*. I will not be here during 3 next days, because I am going to Peterboro to preach there. But I would be glad to meet you on Thursday next to tell you the rest that you wish to know.

The Archbishop saw Fr. Nicholai,[1] who called himself 'Your Grace's minor brother in Christ', and accepted a clear written statement from him as the Archbishop of Belgrade's accredited representative. The scheme with his *imprimatur* was started, and Canon Carnegie, the Rector of St. Margaret's, Westminster, became Chairman of a Serbian Church Students Aid Council. In a period of two years, some sixty Serbian students were trained in Cuddesdon and Oxford. The Archbishop's hesitations were shown to be not unjustified. There was great delay between his approval of the scheme and the arrival of the first students in April, 1918, for there were obstacles at home in the Serbian Church. There were also greater financial difficulties about continuing the scheme than were originally expected. More serious was the eventual leakage, to lay posts in the Serbian State, of men trained in England for ordination in the Serbian Church. But the real value of the step thus taken was beyond doubt. It lay in the precedent set for the coming of other theological students for study in England, from other Orthodox countries—and the understanding established between many individual clergy of the two Churches.

[1] Fr. Nicholai subsequently became Bishop of Ochrida.

III

The Archbishop's attitude to peace was tested by the publication of Lord Lansdowne's Peace Letter in the *Daily Telegraph* on November 29, 1917. There is an interesting note of the way in which it came to be composed:

On Thursday, November 29th, Lansdowne's long letter appeared in the *Daily Telegraph*, having been, on public grounds, rejected by *The Times*. His argument is—we must go on fighting strenuously and win, but to do this intelligently we, and as many as possible of our people, must know definitely what we are fighting for. He dwells on two points—reparation and security, and deprecates the vague and rather windy shoutings which are taken advantage of by Germans as betokening a blind fury on our part which will be satisfied with nothing less than their virtual extinction as a nation. Of course no one has said that, but we do not adequately, he thinks, insist the contrary. His letter is a reasonable plea for a quiet re-statement, which he thinks would be useful, both to our home public, our American Allies, our French Allies, and, in its own way, to the reasonable folk in Germany. It has created a storm of abuse, most of it, as it seems to me, monstrously unfair, misrepresenting Lansdowne's position, and belittling his authority and experience. But many reasonable people are carried away by this abuse, and some of them, I am certain, have shouted against Lansdowne as a pacifist, and so on, without having read his letter—a letter which is about as anti-pacifist as it could be. The present popular theory is that Lansdowne evolved this out of his own mind and launched it on the public without regard to the harm he might do to the Government, and therefore to the country. As a matter of fact, I know privately that the facts were very different. I have talked to Lansdowne about it. He welcomed the opportunity of most confidentially telling me the true facts. He desired to raise the question of a fuller declaration of our policy, and told Arthur Balfour that he would like to do so in the Lords, if Balfour saw no objection. Balfour deprecated this as likely to do harm, but he considered Lansdowne's memorandum, and conferred with him on the points at issue. Lansdowne thereupon told Balfour that he would write to the newspapers instead, and to this Balfour took no exception. Two days before the letter was published, Lansdowne and Balfour met, I know not where, and Lansdowne asked him (Balfour) to read the letter he had drafted. Balfour felt he could not at the moment do this, basing his refusal on the fact that he was just starting for France, for the

> Paris Conference. Balfour and Lansdowne agreed, however, that Lansdowne should show the letter to Lord Hardinge, Balfour's second in command. 'He', said Balfour, 'knew his (Balfour's) opinions and would give the soundest possible counsel.' Lansdowne took the letter to Hardinge, discussed it with him in detail and Hardinge approved it highly, and even suggested the altering of one or two words. Thereupon Lansdowne sent it to *The Times*, and on its being there declined to the *Daily Telegraph*. How Balfour and Hardinge can now rest quiet, under the accusations brought against Lansdowne, amazes me. . . . I believe Balfour has made a memorandum for the Cabinet of what passed, so that they at least may know that Lansdowne did not act as supposed.

In the *Life of Lord Lansdowne*,[1] the Archbishop is counted by Lord Lansdowne as on his side—but no public sign was given. The Peace question was, however, to be raised again in the New Year in connexion with a fresh invitation from the Archbishop of Upsala.[2]

IV

A matter which caused the Archbishop much thought and anxiety at the end of 1917, was the provision of an adequate number of chaplains for the Front. The leakage in the B.E.F. area, from one cause or another, was in October nine per week, and for the supply of these places, and places in other stations at home and abroad, the Chaplain-General got a total call of not less than twelve each week.

The Chaplain-General's office had long been strengthened—and there was an Advisory Committee presided over by Lord Salisbury, as well as a most efficient Assistant Chaplain-General at Whitehall, in Canon E. H. Pearce. But unfortunately the records of applications and service according to dioceses—the crucial thing in such an organization—were incompletely kept. The Deputy Chaplain-General wrote home from France pressing that clergy (like doctors) should be conscripted for service as chaplains wherever required, by means of a short Bill passed through Parliament. The Archbishop did not think that such a drastic course was required, the failure in supply being due to gaps in the organization rather than to any unreadiness of the clergy to volunteer. With the Archbishop of York's help, he

[1] Lord Newton, *Lord Lansdowne: A Biography*, p. 472.

[2] See p. 885.

simply set to work in December and January. The result was a system which met the need admirably, but really meant the taking over by Lambeth of the main responsibility for communicating with the Diocesan Bishops, and securing a steady flow of the right men into the Chaplains' Department. By this means not only were the vacancies filled as they occurred, but there were a large number of men whose names were kept at Lambeth waiting to be sent up to the Chaplain-General by relays as required. The following letter, written on the last day of 1917 to the Bishop of Winchester, shows something of the pressure upon the Archbishop, and the spirit with which he faced his duties:

The ARCHBISHOP OF CANTERBURY *to the* BISHOP OF WINCHESTER

Old Palace, Canterbury.
December 31st, 1917.

I thank you for writing to me about Chaplains. Your letter arrived after I had spent most of the day in arranging with the Archbishop of York, who came here for the purpose, a long letter to all the Bishops, laying down a scheme for their sending to me from every diocese, North and South, a list of men whose names they submit for chaplaincies, and I will then send on the list to the Chaplain-General, and hold myself responsible for understanding why any of them are rejected. It does not work the thing out quite as completely as your plan for your diocese does, but it makes what I think will be a workable arrangement for England as a whole. I have asked to have the replies before the Bishops' Meeting, so that we may then be able to deal with the thing afresh if the replies are inadequate, or the supply of men seems too small. It is all being most difficult, but I think we are on the right tack. I think your own plans very good, but I doubt whether they would be applicable in all dioceses. . . .

We have had a heavy Christmas week, for my perplexities are rather numerous. I have troubles both in Canada and in India in regard to the consecration of Bishops, and they have involved much cabling and immense correspondence with Government offices. We want to get men consecrated over-seas, if possible, instead of bringing them back through all the perils to England, only to face them again a few weeks later after consecration. The Sees in question are Newfoundland and Mombasa.

The Henson business is also of necessity bringing much correspondence from Bishops and others.

I own to feeling the general situation as regards the war to be exceedingly anxious. Reading between the lines it seems to me clear that our leading men think so too. I suppose that if the Germans can bring literally overwhelming forces from the Eastern front, they may be able to do what would otherwise be impossible in the West. I find the officers, there are many, who are here, are all a bit grave about it.

Pardon brevity. I am over-crowded to-night. The year closes rather cloudily, but I see no real signs of a deep-down failure of heart or spirit either in England or in the Army. I was preaching last night in the Cathedral, trying to say what is needed. Unfortunately I have to preach in the Abbey on Sunday at the National Service, and I seem to have no upspringing thoughts. But I must say my prayers.

NOTE

1. The total number of chaplains of all denominations on the pre-war establishment in 1914 was 113.

2. The total number serving with the Forces at the armistice, 1918, was 3,480.

3. The total number serving with the Forces in January 1919 was 3,463.

4. The total number of Church of England chaplains in January 1919 was 1,973.

5. The total number of clergy of the *Church of England* commissioned as chaplains during the war was 3,030; killed or died on service, 88.

CHAPTER LIII

THE HEREFORD BISHOPRIC

My Lord of Hereford and I be neighbours, and we often meet and confer by reason of council-matters here, and commissions directed unto us. I have brotherly monished him of such things as I saw in him, or heard of him; he hath promised, when occasion shall serve, to do the like to me. 24th Oct. 1560. *The* BISHOP OF WORCESTER (SANDYS) *to the* ARCHBISHOP OF CANTERBURY. (*Correspondence of Archbishop Parker.*)

IN the summer of 1917, Dr. Percival announced his intention of resigning the see of Hereford on account of old age. Mr. Lloyd George was Prime Minister, and it so happened that this was the first episcopal vacancy which it fell to his lot to fill. That fact, in itself, gave an interest to the appointment. He very early got into communication with the Archbishop on the subject; and they had a long talk, as we have seen, after the Abbey Service of August 5. At this interview Mr. Lloyd George, after referring to the Diocese of Hereford as predominantly rural, discussed various names. Mr. Lloyd George was emphatic about the need of a good preacher:

> He pressed with a good deal of fervour, and even pathos, the need of having good preachers among the Bishops. He seemed to have a sound idea of the Archbishop of York as a preacher who deservedly carried weight, but he did not speak with equal respect of some other of our Episcopal brethren, though how far he had actually heard them, or how far he was speaking of popular rumour, I do not know.

At the moment Mr. Lloyd George seemed to contemplate an appointment to Hereford by translation:

> He seemed as he went along to make up his mind that Hereford had better be filled by translation from another see, where some young and fresh man is needed.

And he suggested that the vacancy thus created should be filled by a new man.

I

Three names were before him, Dr. Furse of Pretoria, Dr. David of Rugby, and 'very markedly Hensley Henson'. The third of these, Dr. Herbert Hensley Henson, had been Rector of St.

Margaret's and Canon of Westminster for twelve years; and Dean of Durham[1] since 1912. In April 1917, he was just under fifty-four years old, a remarkable orator, with a fine literary style—and a man of high intellectual ability. No one could deny that he was one of the half-dozen greatest preachers in the Church of England of the day. He was also a scholar—for he had been elected to a Fellowship of All Souls, in October 1884, before he was twenty-one, after matriculating as an unattached student while under eighteen. He had had great experience in the industrial parish of Barking, after a short tenure of the Headship of the Oxford House, Bethnal Green, in which he was succeeded by Dr. Winnington Ingram. And he was a brilliant controversialist both by speech and by pen. He had been a strong High Churchman—but had long since abandoned their ranks, and was liberal or broad, both in matters of Church Order and in matters of doctrine. He had great charm, though to some his brilliant wit and obvious delight in debate seemed to suggest over-confidence: and with not a few of those, like Dr. Charles Gore, whom he opposed and embarrassed by his ecclesiastical activities, he was yet on terms of the closest personal friendship. He had published books in defence of a liberal interpretation of the Creeds which had aroused a good deal of criticism—notably *The Creed in the Pulpit*, which contained a preface dealing with the liberty of the preacher, and criticizing, in the case of the Rev. J. M. Thompson, Fellow of Magdalen College, the actions of the Bishops of Winchester and Oxford, the former of whom had withdrawn his licence, as Visitor, and the latter of whom had refused him permission to officiate in the diocese of Oxford. In this preface he had said:

> One thing is unquestionable. In setting a ring-fence about the narratives of Christ's birth and resurrection, and exempting them from the operation of critical methods allowed to control the rest of the New Testament, Mr. Thompson's opponents have taken up a position which it is really impossible to justify on any other principles than those which direct the policy of the Vatican.[2]

[1] Mr. Asquith, who appointed Dr. Henson to Durham, had a high opinion of his preaching powers, as well as his vitality. Writing to the Archbishop (Aug. 30, 1910) with reference to the Deanery of Lincoln, then vacant, he said: 'If, as you say, they need a preacher, one might try Henson. It would be rather like sending a torpedo destroyer into a land locked pool, and his place at Westminster would be a difficult one to fill.'

[2] *The Creed in the Pulpit*, p. xvii.

The Archbishop told Mr. Lloyd George that he would greatly prefer Dr. David to either Dr. Henson or Dr. Furse, and Lloyd George took note of the preference, and said he would inquire further. The Archbishop noted after the interview:

> It is a curious experience handling these matters with a man who has so very little knowledge either of the conditions of Church life, the nature of different regions (ecclesiastically), or the men who might be appointed to them. He takes in good part all that I say, and I pressed with no uncertainty the difficulties and perhaps the public protests which would arise if he nominated Henson. I said this would be more so than after his nomination of Rashdall to the deanery of Carlisle. He replied with some vigour and amusement that I warned him of the difficulties which would arise in regard to Rashdall, but that he had had nothing but praise from all who had spoken to him about it, including Lord Robert Cecil. I told him he need have no anticipations of an equally smooth course if he nominated Henson to a bishopric.

II

There was no immediate action, but in the early autumn there were clear signs that the appointment of Dr. Henson to a Bishopric was very much in the Prime Minister's mind. Archdeacon Pearce, who had stepped into the position of unofficial ecclesiastical adviser to the Prime Minister, was very much in favour, while Bishop Burge and others also supported his claims. Suggestions of various translations came to nothing, and at the end of November the Prime Minister wrote to the Archbishop to suggest definitely that the see should be offered to the Dean of Durham. He said:

The RT. HON. DAVID LLOYD GEORGE *to the* ARCHBISHOP OF CANTERBURY

10 Downing Street, Whitehall, S.W. 1. 26 November, 1917.

You will readily understand that the complexities of public business have caused delay in communicating with you further about the vacant See of Hereford.

What I want now to suggest is that it should be offered to the Dean of Durham. It is true that I should have preferred to propose him for a more urban and industrial diocese; but I believe he has never yet failed to devote himself eagerly to whatever work lay before him.

Moreover, Hereford has this advantage that, as I understand, the ritual problems of the diocese are not serious, and so the Dean would be little troubled by internal controversies.

On the other hand, I deem it to be of great advantage that the opportunity should be given to him to utilise his power to express logically, opinions that are largely held outside, rather in the Councils of the Southern Episcopate than in the public press.

I have one or two other men in my mind,—Archdeacon Lisle Carr of Norfolk, Archdeacon Gresford Jones of Sheffield; and Prebendary Swayne. But, as you know, none of these is of equal calibre to the Dean either as preacher or as thinker. . . .

The Archbishop replied:

The ARCHBISHOP OF CANTERBURY *to the* RT. HON. DAVID LLOYD GEORGE

28th November 1917.

I have given much anxious thought to your letter. The Dean of Durham is a personal friend of mine, and I think it is natural and right that his friends (and they are legion) should desire him to hold Episcopal office. It is not therefore at all with the desire to prevent this (and I am anxious to make that point quite clear) that I ask you to consider afresh whether the sending of him to such a Diocese as Hereford is really best. A large rural Diocese, calling for the plodding work of a man who has experience of varied parochial life, does not seem to me quite the place for a preacher and speaker with the particular sort of popular gifts which Dr. Henson possesses. You may consider it so desirable to nominate him for Consecration to the Episcopate that these objections ought to be swept aside. Personally, however, I am persuaded that it would be much better to wait for some future opening more appropriate. There must be such before long. I do not consider that the absence of ritual difficulties in Hereford Diocese is an argument in favour of sending Dr. Henson there. On the contrary, I think that what he rather needs for the exercise of his powers is the steadying which responsibility gives when a man has to deal with the kind of problems, the management of which by others, he has been accustomed to criticise. I feel the less scruple in asking you to consider afresh the question, because you have named as the next possible man one who is eminently qualified for such a See as Hereford. Archdeacon Lisle Carr is universally acceptable, and is possessed of very many of the sort of gifts a Diocese like Hereford calls for. He is active, popular, liberal-minded, and an admirable preacher. I do not claim that he possesses the same remarkable intellectual gifts as the Dean of Durham, but he is a man far above the average both intellectually and in practical experience and capacity.

I feel bound to put before you my view of the situation, since you have asked for my opinion. At the same time I am particularly anxious not to seem to be derogating from the merits and powers of Dr. Hensley Henson. That his appointment would cause something of a storm is undoubted, and this would have to be faced whenever and wherever he was nominated a Bishop. I confess that I should prefer in the interests of the Church of England that your own first nomination to the Episcopate should be of a less controversial kind. But this is a matter on which perhaps I have no right to express to you my opinion. It is not that which chiefly influences me in putting before you for consideration the points I have mentioned. I repeat that Dr. Henson is a personal friend of mine for whom, though differing from him on many points, I have the warmest affection and regard. His powers are of course beyond question.

The Prime Minister replied:

The RT. HON. D. LLOYD GEORGE *to the* ARCHBISHOP OF CANTERBURY

6th December, 1917.

I have very carefully weighed your valuable letter of November 28, about the See of Hereford.

I entirely agree with you that the Dean of Durham is in the end more suited to a large industrial sphere, and, as you know, I have tried so to arrange. But I believe he has powers of adaptability which will stand him in good stead at Hereford, and, if it turns out that I am right, I shall be only too glad to suggest his later transference to some more urban Diocese.

Meanwhile, he will be learning his job in what ought not to be a very hard school, and I am sure you will feel the advantage of his bringing a vigorous mind to bear on the many difficulties which beset a Bishop's office at this time.

I am therefore writing to him to this effect.

The Archbishop's own view of Henson's orthodoxy is given in a Memorandum on the situation which he made on Christmas Day 1917:

The knowledge that [Henson's nomination to a Bishopric] was in contemplation made me read again some of Henson's writings, or rather utterances, and I confess to having found them far less heterodox than I had expected. It is true that he throws his shield over men like Thompson of Magdalen, and others who go very much further than he does, and, further, it is true that he avoids handling the precise points of acutest controversy, e.g. the articles in the Creed relating to the Virgin Birth and physical Resurrection of Our Lord. But he shows repeatedly in his sermons a firm, and even enthusiastic, belief in the Incarnation of Our Lord. When Lloyd George a few weeks ago intimated to me that he had offered the See of Hereford to Henson, I wrote to Henson and had from him a rather characteristic reply. He referred me to a sermon he had preached on leaving St. Margaret's. It is the first sermon in his little book *Notes of my Ministry*, and in it he summarises his doctrinal teaching. He certainly avoids the kind of controversial points I have alluded to, and he uses phrases like 'Mankind, stricken, distracted, and undone, finds in the Birth at Bethlehem the re-Birth of Humanity. Thus, it has seemed to me, the Christian belief in Jesus Christ as the Incarnate Creator compels an attitude of sympathy towards every expression of the religious instinct' etc.

III

The announcement of Dr. Henson's nomination appeared in the Press on December 11. Immediately the storm anticipated by Dr. Davidson broke out. Resolutions and protests came pouring into Lambeth, and a fierce controversy started in the Press. The *Church Times*, whose editor, the Rev. E. Hermitage Day, had lately come to live in Hereford, sharpened its weapons; and protagonists on one side or another declared their various views in the columns of *The Times*. The leader of the attack was the Bishop of Oxford. Three days after the announcement in *The Times*, he sent to all Bishops of the Province a private and confidential notice to the effect that he proposed to make a Formal Protest to the Archbishop of Canterbury against the consecration of Dr. Hensley Henson, and inviting them, if they saw fit, to join him. In this letter he called special attention to the books: *Sincerity and Subscription* (1903), *The Liberty of Prophesying* (1909), *The Creed in the Pulpit* (1912); and said that, failing a retractation by Dr. Henson, if the consecration was to proceed and his protest was unavailing, 'I see no course *practicable* but to resign from the episcopate'.

On December 17, Gore spent the night with the Archbishop at Lambeth:

> Gore admitted frankly that Henson is a firm believer in the Incarnation, but that Henson's belief in that great doctrine is accompanied by a disbelief in those miraculous events of the Human Ministry which Gore regards as essential to the Incarnation doctrine in its entirety. He was somewhat excited, though not to the degree I have often seen, but he passionately exclaimed—'it all turns, though you won't see it, on his disbelief in miracles as such. He believes Our Lord had a human father, and that His Body rotted in the tomb. A man who believes that cannot, with my consent, be made a Bishop of the Province.' This he expanded in many ways. I argued quietly with him to the best of my power, on the lines familiar to him and me in the controversy between us a few years ago respecting the declaration in Convocation on which he makes so much to turn.

The Archbishop saw Dr. Henson on December 19, at Lambeth, and gave him the impression of being depressed and morose. Dr. Henson himself says in a Diary written at the time:

> He told me that he was receiving numerous letters calling upon him to see the King and insist upon this scandalous nomination being cancelled and that he should refuse to consecrate!

He adds:

> I came away from the Palace with an uncomfortable suspicion that the Archbishop would like to throw me over if he decently could.

Dr. Davidson's own note is:

> On Wednesday, the 19th, Henson came to breakfast, and I had full talk with him. He was pleasant and friendly, but he disappointed me by his self-satisfaction, and his rather venomous denunciation of those who were opposing his appointment.

The English Church Union was meantime engaged in marshalling all its forces to prevent Dr. Henson's consecration. Their reports were, perhaps, assisted by the fact that the late Bishop of Hereford (Dr. Percival) had not been popular in the Diocese, owing partly to his radicalism in politics, partly to his liberalism in doctrine; while the Cathedral Chapter, composed in the main of learned scholars, had not been itself in close touch with the exceedingly rural County. As Dr. Henson wrote to the Archbishop on December 22 with regard to the pressure of the English Church Union on the local clergy:

The DEAN OF DURHAM *to the* ARCHBISHOP OF CANTERBURY

December 22, 1917.

The material on which these conspirators work is the great volume of discontent and resentment, more political than religious, which has undoubtedly accumulated against the late Bishop. The Dean and Canons do not appear to have much relation with the diocese, but formed a flatterous clique round the old Bishop, and brought him no popularity on their own behalf. Nevertheless, I doubt whether there is any genuine substance in the agitation: and, though it may carry as far as refusing to elect by influencing the Prebendaries, I doubt if it will survive save as a memory to blush for.

That the E.C.U. is a powerful organisation is unfortunately true: but we have hardly yet reached the point when the King's nominations must be approved by that body before they can count on being effective. For myself, I have to say this. As I was led by long and anxious thought to the conclusion that it was my plain *duty* to accept a place on the Episcopal Bench if it were offered me, so I am not likely to be deflected from my course by *clamour*. Nor will I yield one inch to a Society with the principles and methods of the E.C.U.

It grieves me deeply that you should have worry on my account, but in this matter I am absolutely guiltless. . . .

The agitation of the E.C.U., both in the town and in the diocese of Hereford, failed of its object. The Mayor of Hereford refused the use of the Town Hall for a meeting, and repudiated the agitation. Nor did the efforts of the propagandists in the Press to persuade the Hereford Chapter to risk the penalties which might fall on their heads by refusing to elect, meet with better success. The Chapter met on January 4. Nineteen Prebendaries (residentiary and non-residentiary) were present, and elected Dr. Henson with a dissentient minority of four. Meanwhile the Bishop of Oxford had sent his Formal Protest to the Archbishop with a personal note, 'I never wrote anything with such loathing as I have written this':

FORMAL PROTEST

The Bishop of Oxford *to the* Archbishop of Canterbury

Cuddesdon, Wheatley, Oxon.
Jan. 3rd, 1918.

I am compelled, under an overwhelming sense of responsibility, to address to you a solemn protest against the nomination of Dr. Hensley Henson, Dean of Durham, to the Bishopric of Hereford.

I am not taking this action because of anything which he has said about the ministry of the Church, or any other matter of Church polity or policy, with regard to which he and I have publicly differed in the past, for in respect of these things his views are shared substantially by many Evangelical and other members of the Church, with whom I am quite conscientiously able to live in unity of fellowship. I am driven to act as I am doing solely because his expressed beliefs touching the fundamental matters of faith seem to me incompatible with the sincere profession of the Creeds.

In more than one book he has argued that, though a man has been led to believe that our Lord was not born of a virgin mother, he should still be free to exercise his ministry in the Church and to recite the services of the Church in which the miracle is unmistakably and repeatedly affirmed: and even if he believe that 'no miracles accompanied His entrance into, or presence in, or departure from the world' he should still hold this 'freedom' to make public profession to the contrary.* But may I think that the Dean is simply pleading for freedom for others? I am led reluctantly to conclude that I cannot. His treatment of the Virgin Birth seems to me incompatible with personal belief in its occurrence.† Again, he expressly repudiates belief in the 'nature-miracles'‡ recorded in the Gospels as wrought by our Lord. He writes explicitly, 'From the standpoint of historical science they must be held to be incredible.'§ But the birth of a virgin mother, and the bodily resurrection of our Lord—that His body did not 'see corruption' but was raised again the third day to a new and wonderful life—are similar 'nature-miracles' ascribed in the Gospels to the same power and Spirit of the Father as the miracles upon

* *The Creed in the Pulpit* (Hodder and Stoughton), pp. xiv ff.

† See *Sincerity and Subscription* (Macmillan), pp. 43 ff. *The Creed*, &c., p. xxiv, pp. 18–22, 49.

‡ Physical miracles which the 'normal' order of nature cannot account for; Dr. Henson distinguished such 'nature-miracles' from the miracles of healing which he thinks may 'be fairly called normal'.

§ *The Creed*, &c., pp. 88–9.

nature worked by our Lord during His ministry. I can conceive no rational ground for repudiating the latter as incredible and believing the former. The Dean himself seems incidentally to include both classes of miracles in the same category.|| He does indeed confidently and constantly affirm the truth of the Resurrection of Christ; but he seems to me by 'resurrection' to mean no more than personal survival.** He repudiates again and again any insistence upon the 'empty tomb', and declares it to have no significance.†† But the empty tomb was an absolutely necessary condition of any such resurrection as the New Testament postulates. If the tomb was not empty, Christ was not, in the New Testament sense, risen again. On the whole I am led irresistibly to the conclusion that, though he nowhere explicitly expresses in so many words his personal disbelief in the physical miracles affirmed in the Creeds, he does in fact regard them as incredible.

I am amazed by what seems to me the one-sidedness and unsatisfactoriness of the Dean of Durham's presentation of the evidence. But that is not my point at present. Again, I am amazed at the naïve confidence with which he assumes that the theological ideas of the Creed and the New Testament, to which he gives noble expression, can survive unimpaired when the miraculous facts have been repudiated—an assumption which the history of recent criticism in Europe generally seems to me to negative. But that again is not my point at present. I am now concerned only with the conditions on which a man can sincerely profess the Creeds and exercise his ministry in the Church of England. And here I will recall the terms of a solemn declaration which the Bishops of our Province recently affirmed:

> 'Inasmuch as there is reason to believe that the minds of many members of the Church of England are perplexed and disquieted at the present time in regard to certain questions of Faith [and of Church order], the Bishops of the Upper House of the Province of Canterbury feel it to be their duty to put forth the following resolutions:
>
> 1. We call attention to the resolution which was passed in this House on May 10, 1905, as follows:—
>
> "That this House is resolved to maintain unimpaired the

|| *The Creed*, &c., pp. 90–1 (at the bottom).

** e.g. he speaks of Christ returning to the Church in 'the fullness' or 'plenitude of personal life' (p. 211). But he speaks also of all the dead as 'persisting' in the plenitude of individual being'.

†† *The Creed*, &c., pp. 199, 208, 211.

Catholic Faith in the Holy Trinity and the Incarnation as contained in the Apostles' and Nicene Creeds, and in the Quicunque Vult, and regards the Faith there presented, both in statements of doctrine and in statements of fact, as the necessary basis on which the teaching of the Church reposes."

We further desire to direct attention afresh to the following resolution which was unanimously agreed to by the Bishops of the Anglican Communion attending the Lambeth Conference of 1908:—

"The Conference, in view of tendencies widely shown in the writings of the present day, hereby places on record its conviction that the historical facts stated in the Creeds are an essential part of the Faith of the Church."

2. These resolutions we desire solemnly to re-affirm, and in accordance therewith we express our deliberate judgemen that the denial of any of the historical facts stated in the Creeds goes beyond the limits of legitimate interpretation, and gravely imperils that sincerity of profession which is plainly incumbent on the ministers of the Word and Sacraments. At the same time, recognizing that our generation is called to face new problems raised by historical criticism, we are anxious not to lay unnecessary burdens upon consciences, nor unduly to limit freedom of thought and enquiry whether among clergy or among laity. We desire, therefore, to lay stress on the need of considerateness in dealing with that which is tentative and provisional in the thought and work of earnest and reverent students.'

Of course if, in order to be affected by this declaration, a man must explicitly and in so many words have denied the particular miraculous facts recorded in the Creeds, the Dean of Durham is not affected by it. But then I think the declaration is nugatory. A man can express a negative intention without any such express verbal denial. I think the declaration must be supposed to take into account the whole effect of a man's language. And taking this into account, apart from any fresh declaration of his belief which he may think fit to make, I can only draw the conclusion that the Dean's language falls outside the limits of 'legitimate interpretation' of the statements of the Creeds which according to our declaration must be observed by the clergy and, most of all I suppose, by the bishops. As things stand, that is judging only from his published writings, if Dr. Henson were to take his place among the bishops, I think three results would follow:

1. It would be impossible to deny that the Bishops—not all of

them individually, but the bishops as a body—are prepared to admit to the episcopate, and therefore to the other orders of the ministry, one who does not believe in the miracles of the Creed, supposing he unfeignedly believes (as Dr. Henson does) in the doctrine of the person of Christ. And this, it appears to me, is to abandon the standing ground of the Catholic Church from the beginning, which has insisted on holding together the ideas and the miraculous facts. I do not mean that the action of the bishops would commit the Church of England. I think the mind of the Church of England would be opposed to their action. But I think it would commit the bishops corporately.

2. An atmosphere of suspicion will increasingly attach itself in the mind of the nation to the most solemn public assertions of the clergy, in the matter of religion, just at the time when we are constantly hearing that the awful experiences of the war have forced us back upon realities.

3. An effective (though not, I think, a legitimate) excuse will be afforded to all officers of the Church to treat their solemn declarations on other subjects as 'scraps of paper'. Any discipline on the basis of official declarations will become more and more difficult; and the authority of the episcopate will be quite undermined.

In order that such disastrous consequences may be avoided, I feel myself constrained to intreat your Grace and my brother bishops, in the event of the Dean of Durham being elected to the see of Hereford by the chapter, to refuse him consecration.

I need not say with what profound sorrow I have written this protest and appeal. Dr. Henson and I have always been friends, and, though we have often differed in public, I believe no angry word has ever passed between us or marred our friendship: and I believe him to be personally among the most honourable and courageous of men. Nevertheless I have been obliged to write it.

With the humble prayer that God will cleanse and defend the distracted part of the Church to which we belong and will guide your Grace and the Bishops with the spirit of wisdom.

The Protest was published in *The Times* on January 10. But meanwhile, the gravity of the doctrinal conflict was emphasized by a letter to *The Times* from Dr. Darwell Stone, on January 1, giving a catena of quotations from Dr. Henson's books, by way of specific accusations against the Bishop-designate's orthodoxy:

The Rev. Dr. Stone *to the Editor of 'The Times'*[1]

Pusey House, Oxford. December 29.

The Dean of Canterbury writes with reference to the appointment of Dr. Henson to the Bishopric of Hereford:—'If the opponents could allege any definite disqualification, either in doctrine or life against a nominee of the Crown, they would be within their rights or perhaps their duty in urging it.' The definite disqualification in doctrine in the case of Dr. Henson is his attitude in regard to miracles, and especially to the Virgin Birth and the Resurrection of our Lord. In his *Creed in the Pulpit*, page 89, he wrote of the 'nature miracles' recorded in the Gospels that 'from the standpoint of historical science, they must be held to be incredible'. In the same book, on pages xxiv, 18, 37, he spoke of 'Biblical Sciences' 'disallowing the belief in an incarnation effected by miracles', of our Lord's nature as being 'a severely normal humanity', of the narratives of our Lord's birth being 'generally assumed by the learned to belong less to history than to poetry', of the Incarnation being 'effected in the normal working of the Divine Providence'; and on page 211 he says that the doctrine of the Resurrection taught by S. Paul 'definitely disallows the theory on which alone "the empty tomb" can have any vital relation to Christian faith'. Many similar statements may be found in Dr. Henson's writings, notably, for instance, in *Sincerity and Subscription* pages 43–46, and *The Liberty of Prophesying* pages 86–89. The opinions thus expressed in regard to truths affirmed in the Creeds are the cause of the present grave anxiety. And I, for one, had hoped that the doctrines involved were as clear to the Dean of Canterbury as they are to myself.'

On the other side, a long letter from Dr. Sanday, defending Dr. Henson, had the formidable effect of uniting Dean Wace and Darwell Stone against Dr. Henson. Dr. Sanday's letter in *The Times* on January 5 stated:

The Rev. Dr. Sanday *to the Editor of 'The Times'*

My own general position is so similar to Dr. Henson's that I believe he will accept me as an advocate.

And he went on to quote the following sentences from his own contributions to a recent book, *Form and Content in the Christian Tradition* (pp. xii–xiii):

The Virgin Birth, the physical Resurrection, and physical Ascension,

[1] January 1, 1918.

are all realistic expressions adapted to the thought of the time, of ineffable truths which the thought of the time could not express in any other way. To conceive of them realistically was natural and right in the age in which they took shape. Speaking for myself and for those who agree with me, I should say that it was no longer natural and therefore no longer to be enforced as right—to be taken if we please as a human symbol for *x* but not to be identified in any hard and fast manner with it.

He then added:

By every word of this statement I am prepared to stand and I believe that Dr. Henson would take his stand with me.

Dr. Henson was very far from desiring such an advocate. It was no wonder that Dean Wace should write to *The Times* of January 9:

The DEAN OF CANTERBURY *to the Editor of* '*The Times*'

I feel bound to acknowledge that the letters of Dr. Darwell Stone and Dr. Sanday, especially the latter, afford abundant justification for opposition to Dr. Henson's appointment, and I feel reluctantly obliged to join in the appeal which is being made to the Archbishop and the Bishops not to proceed to this consecration.

It was not surprising that the Archbishop should thus express his own disquiet:

The ARCHBISHOP OF CANTERBURY *to the* DEAN OF CANTERBURY

9 January, 1918.

I am a little disquieted on reading your letter in *The Times* to-day. The letter you showed me last week seemed so very much more like yourself and your calm judgment than the letter which appears to-day. What occurred to that first letter I do not know. As you had kindly shown it to me and told me that it was going an hour later to *The Times* by rail, I ventured (of course quite privately) to mention to more than one friend that you had written such a letter characterised by your robust commonsense as to the misuse of isolated extracts. It is fair to you that I should say that I had done this (of course confidentially) with no idea at all that you had changed your mind.

With regard to Dr. Sanday's letter it is a case of 'save me from my friends', for the position of Sanday and Henson are very widely apart. About this I have no doubt at all. Henson is taking the

> line taken by Temple those many years ago that to make a public statement or apologia now would be out of place and open to grave misunderstanding. This may be right or wrong, but he seems clear about it.
>
> I need not descant upon the position that would be created if I were now to say 'I decline to obey the King's Mandate and to proceed to Confirmation and Consecration'. We talked it over together so fully that you know my position and what that decision on my part would apparently involve. I should not on that account be deterred if I felt the decision to be a right one.
>
> I send you this letter because of my having mentioned the fact of your having shown me at the moment of its departure the letter you were sending to *The Times*.

So, just as Lord Shaftesbury and Dr. Pusey made their famous alliance in their day against Old Testament criticism, the Principal of Pusey House and Dr. Wace stood up together in 1918 against the criticism of the New Testament in *The Creed and the Pulpit.*

IV

As the days wore on, the anxiety of the Archbishop deepened. Letters continued to pour in, and not a few of them were from Bishops. He decided to ask Henson to come and see him. Henson came on January 7 (two days before Dean Wace's letter in *The Times*) from Durham, and the Archbishop notes as follows:

> I was with him from six to eight in close converse. I found him entirely pleasant to deal with, though self-conscious and cocksure in a way that is always to me a little trying. He is also strangely sensitive to criticism, while he proclaims his complete indifference to it. He told me that he was determined to make no declaration which could be regarded as an admission to the rights of others other than the legal authorities acting in Court to question him as to his beliefs. If he were questioned, say in connexion with his Confirmation, or otherwise, he would simply present in reply a copy of his books, and say that the answer lay there. At the same time he would declare his perfect readiness to be tried in an Ecclesiastical Court for heresy, if anyone chose to indict him. He would neither resent such indictment, nor rebel against its decision, or sentence, whatever it might be. 'What I will not stand is that this party, led by Gore and his friends, should first repudiate all existing Courts and then try to set up another Court which they

manipulate for trying heresy.' He then went on to say that to me, as an individual, he, as an individual and a friend, was quite ready to state his credal position, provided I would regard his statement as wholly confidential. It must not be quoted in any way, nor the fact made public that he had made any such statement to me. I replied that I had no wish to draw a statement from him, but that if he had anything to say, that he would like to say, for the relief of his mind, in view of the present controversy, it was of course open to him to say it, and I should make no public use of the fact that he had so spoken to me. He then proceeded to tell me under this confidential bond that I am absolutely right in regarding his position with respect to the Virgin Birth as practically the same as that of Armitage Robinson, in his preface to the little book *Some Thoughts on the Incarnation.* He in no sense denies the truth of that narrative, as traditionally interpreted, or of the narrative of the Resurrection. But with regard to the details, he adopts a position of what he calls Christian Agnosticism, considering it to be true to say that progress of human knowledge forces us to state historic facts in a different way at different epochs. The facts remain throughout what they were at first. We should not nowadays narrate what occurred in Gospel days as the same facts were narrated by the original writers. Science, criticism, historical knowledge, and general mental advance, with a wider outlook on life as a whole, necessitates our being ready to admit a restatement to-day of what was stated in quite different words long ago. I referred him to his note in the little book '*Sincerity and Subscription* written in 1903, pp. 43–46. He said emphatically that note is to justify us in not regarding the opinions of men who go much further than I go as placing them outside the Church's pale. I asked him whether it is not true to say that a reader of these pages would rise from them with the feeling, if not the evidence, that the writer does, as a matter of fact, think that Our Lord had a human father? He said emphatically that he had no such intention; that it would not fairly present his position, and that he had entirely declined to formulate with certainty a judgment upon what had happened. He must, I think, have seen that I regarded his answer as not very satisfactory. He went on to press the point that it had somehow fallen to him to be the champion of the principle that wide toleration of modernism is now the duty of honest men within the Church, and so on. Our talk was long, and it left me with the impression that, while his ideas are not very clear and definite, he quite distinctly and definitely does not deny the truths of the Creed as traditionally interpreted. We discussed what might happen as to the position which would be reached if

I were to decline to consecrate him and to resign my office. He said that if I declined to consecrate him he would have no course open to him but to retire from the Ministry of the Church, as he could not possibly return e.g. to the Deanery of Durham as a man unfit for consecration as a Bishop. But he foresaw what distraction that would cause, and practically foretold schism. With regard to my own possible resignation, he thought that would be equally, or rather much more disastrous, and would place him in exactly the same position as if I retained office while refusing to consecrate him.

The Bishop of Ely (Dr. Chase) had begged the Archbishop to summon the Bishops of the Province to take counsel together. The Archbishop's Memorandum continues:

> On receiving the letter yesterday morning (January 7) I telegraphed to him to come at once to London. He came, while Henson was with me, and, after dinner, he and I had a very long talk. I think I convinced him that the summoning of the Bishops of the Province, in the way he suggested, would be unworkable, misleading, and ineffective. Should they discuss matters and vote, what would their vote mean? If it was in favour of consecration, it would mean an imprimatur of a certain sort given provincially to opinions like Henson's. If it were against consecration, it would rather add to my difficulties than remove them, for the refusal to consecrate would not be less grave in its character and results than it would be if I decided upon it of my own accord. We then discussed Henson's writings and opinions as gathered therefrom. He was, as always, reasonable, tolerant, and yet somewhat rigidly orthodox. We went over the whole ground afresh, and, though we did not attempt a formal decision as to what is right, I think he was of opinion when he left me that I should do rightly if I proceeded to the consecration in the ordinary way.

The next day was a very heavy one. It included taking a marriage in Chelsea in the morning, followed by a meeting with the War Cabinet in Downing Street about the proposal that the British Museum should be taken over to house the Air Board:

> After the briefest peep at the house gathering of the Bride's friends in Tite Street, I had to go off to Downing Street for the War Cabinet, picking up Sir Frederic Kenyon at the Athenaeum on the way, to talk over the Museum position with him. He and I were shown into the Cabinet Room, where those present consisted of Lloyd George, Curzon, Milner, Carson, Bonar Law, Barnes, Smuts, and, outside the Cabinet, Sir Alfred Mond, Sir Lionel

Earle, Sir Maurice Hankey, and one or two others whom I did not know. Before the discussion was over, Lord Derby, and Lord Robert Cecil, and one or two others arrived for the meeting which was to follow the Museum discussion. I said my say, and was rather examined as a hostile witness by the Prime Minister. Sir Frederic Kenyon gave a clear statement in support of my deprecation of taking over the Museum, and during the discussion I felt the position changing. When we began, Carson, Bonar Law, and Barnes, and to some extent Milner, were evidently strongly against the Trustees' opinion. They wanted the Museum, and meant to have it. Curzon was vehemently the other way, and had prepared a memorandum which he began to read, but Lloyd George stopped him and requested that it should be not read while outsiders were present. Rather an absurd position, as we had already seen it! Curzon behaved very well. We left with the sense that we had made a good case and had impressed the Cabinet with the untenableness of the position they had taken up. I may add that in the evening I saw Curzon and learned from him that he would the next day make a public statement that the matter had been reconsidered—so our arguments had prevailed.

The day also included a visit to Rosebery, whom the Archbishop had not seen since Neil Primrose's death. The conversation was a most interesting personal one about Neil, and religion. Then it turned to political matters:

> We talked a good deal about Asquith. He thinks Asquith the greatest Parliamentarian that ever lived. Much greater than Gladstone or Dizzy, or Palmerston, or Peel. A cultured scholar of amazing power of Parliamentary speech; never a word wrong, and never a word too much; wholly unlike Gladstone whose exuberance of oratory marred its effectiveness. He thought Asquith had never been so great as since Lloyd George came into power.

The Archbishop's own comment on Rosebery, at the end of the talk, must be added:

> He was much keener and livelier than I have generally seen him of late, and less cynically morose. But I could not help feeling all the while the strangeness of his isolated position at such a time of crisis as the present. A man who has been Foreign Secretary and Prime Minister; intimate with Gladstone; a friend of Bismarck; friend of successive sovereigns; the darling of the public in his oratory; the foremost figure in the House of Lords; the first Chair-

man of the London County Council; and so on: that such a man, with such a record, should, while still amply fit for a great deal of work, be a complete outsider in national affairs, and apparently doing hardly anything for anybody, and living in his own shell, is both mysterious, and deeply disappointing. He knows what I feel about this, and I only hinted at it again to-day. It is not very easy to say what he could do to get back into public affairs, as I sometimes think he would half like to do, if he could do it with dignity. He and I walked from his house to Lambeth together, or at least to Lambeth Bridge, where his brougham met him and took him back, for he is not fit for long walks.

There was still more work to be done that day before turning again to Henson:

I was back at Lambeth soon after three, and had an hour there before going to the House of Lords. During it I had business with Hugh Lee about the consecration of the Bishop of Mombasa in India, and the consecration of the Bishop of Newfoundland in Nova Scotia, both new problems which nobody quite understands except, I think, myself.

Then the House of Lords, where the Representation of the People Bill, the biggest Reform Bill in our history, came up for discussion in Committee. . . .

After the Reform Bill debate, I got through the Committee stage of the Bill for the Bishoprics of Coventry and Bradford—the time occupied being perhaps three and a half minutes! Then back to Lambeth with Edith, who had been in the House of Lords, to find the Bishop of Gloucester—Gibson—who was dining quietly with us to talk over the Henson difficulty.

Such were the events of a single day—the background against which the Archbishop had to determine the battle of the Creed and the Pulpit.

V

Dr. Henson himself was pressed by some of his comrades to withdraw his acceptance of the bishopric, and by others to make some sort of an explanation or apology. He refused to do either, justly claiming that his books and writings were well known and had been before the public for a long while, and that if he was to be accused as a heretic the charge should be made in the regular Courts. Sunday, January 13, was spent by the Archbishop at Tremans, Horsted Keynes, where he drafted a long letter to

Bishop Gore. He left on the Monday, in deep snow, and had further talks with Sir Lewis Dibdin and Professor Jenkins. There were some who wished to persuade him to use the Confirmation of the Bishop-elect for the purpose of examining Dr. Henson's orthodoxy. The Vicar-General, Lord Parmoor, was clear that such a course was out of the question, nor was the Archbishop likely to take it. If he believed that there was a case for accusing Dr. Henson of heresy, his remedy was to resign rather than issue the fiat. At the same time the Archbishop knew well that if he resigned rather than consecrate Dr. Henson, it would be impossible for the latter himself to retain office in the Church of England, and a schism was probable.

The Archbishop went to the House of Lords at 3.30 on the Monday, January 14:

> Found Halifax awaiting me, excited and eager; beseeching me to refuse consecration to a man who will, whatever his own beliesf, ordain unbelievers. He saw, however, the difficulty of the situation. Then a very full talk with Parmoor, as Vicar-General. He is evidently very uneasy about the Confirmation, and, after much talk, advised me to see Gore and Henson with a view to more fully satisfying my own mind prior to signing the *fiat* for Confirmation, which ends my personal discretion, the subsequent stage being Ministerial. He is clear that I have some discretion as to issuing the *fiat*; if no discretion in law, certainly some in conscience, when the sacredness of the issue is remembered. Then a full talk for another hour with the Lord Chancellor, Finlay, in his room. He had forgotten the particulars in these matters, though he appeared for the Crown in the Gore case. He was very anxious, and was terrified at the thought of my possibly resigning. He did not disapprove absolutely of my seeing either Gore or Henson privately, provided it was wholly private, and not so conducted as to have in any way the character of a Court of Inquiry, or capable of being represented as such. Specially he deprecated my getting into the position that I was refusing consecration because Henson refused to answer questions asked by me. He thought I should have no case, and could not allege such silence as ground for refusing consecration. He realised, however, (for I pressed it upon him) the sacred and solemn character of my responsibilities in their religious aspect.

He had further talks with Archdeacon Holmes about a draft letter from the Bishop of London, on which he refused to comment beyond saying that he thought a short letter better than a long one. He saw the Bishop of Peterborough, Woods, who also had drafted a letter; then Lord Selborne, who poured out earnestly his grave fears and personal horror; and he was immediately followed by Lord Salisbury, who took the same view but much more calmly. He then returned to Lambeth to find Sir Lewis Dibdin who had come by appointment to dine and sleep and talk afresh over the situation:

> I settled with him that I should not be wrong in summoning Henson and asking him quite definitely the simple question whether, or not, he believed that Our Lord had a human father. He thought this quite different from a general inquiry into his opinions. This last he would strongly deprecate, supporting Henson's contention that he, Henson, could only be so questioned in a duly constituted Court.

The situation was extraordinarily difficult—and Dr. Davidson's ability to keep both parties abiding in the ship of the Church was seldom more sharply tested. He had no doubt that Dr. Henson's beliefs were fundamentally orthodox, and were compatible with his being a Bishop in the English Church; and yet he could perfectly understand the alarm which Dr. Henson's combination of a championship for liberty with a delight in strong and unguarded statements aroused in multitudes of Churchmen. After much thought he decided to summon Dr. Henson from Durham to Lambeth for a long and private conversation on January 15. Dr. Henson came; and after making it plain that the conversation was that of friend with friend, and not an examination, the Archbishop showed him a portion of the Reply he was preparing for Bishop Gore, and especially the paragraph where he said he had found nothing 'which, when it is fairly weighed in its true setting, I can regard as inconsistent with the belief which he firmly asserts in the facts and doctrines of the faith as set forth in the Creeds'. The Archbishop notes as follows:

> Henson arrived from Durham in time for dinner in response to a telegram from me. From nine p.m. to midnight I was steadily at talk with him. We went into matters unreservedly. I read him part of my draft letter to Gore, in order to reassure him as to my wish to defend him from unjust criticism. And I called upon him to facilitate my task by letting me understand clearly what his true attitude to credal questions is. We referred, of course, specially

to the Virgin Birth and the Resurrection. He talked at great length, and I took down bits of what he said, and then wove these into a memorandum, expressive of his position and belief, and read it over to him more than once. He agreed that it correctly stated his position. This was a great relief to my mind, and made me feel justified in arranging to let the Confirmation and Consecration go forward unless new pitfalls should open. He behaved well, having been, I think, helped by finding that I was endeavouring to treat him with scrupulous fairness. I do not think at first he realised the difficulty of my own position, but he came to do so, hence the memorandum and assent to it. I told him that I should not make any use of it in a public way unless I obtained his leave hereafter for doing so. But I reserved the right to make such statement as to my belief about him as might be necessary in my intercourse with responsible counsellors. The memorandum was as follows:—

> I repeat and accept the words of the Creed *ex animo*. I use them without any sense of incongruity, and with no desire to change them. With me it is a question of emphasis. I desire that the emphasis of the Apostolic teaching should be preserved in the teaching of the Church. No man who believes in the Incarnation could postulate for Our Saviour an ordinary Birth. I believe that in the Birth of Jesus Christ, Whom I worship, as in the fullest sense Divine, there was special action of the Holy Spirit. But when in the Creed I affirm, as I readily do, the traditional belief of the Church in the Birth of Jesus Christ without a human father, I am bound to add that the belief in the Incarnation may be consistent now, as it was consistent in Apostolic days, with other notions or explanations of the mode of what happened therein. I have never seen any satisfying alternative to the dogma of the Virgin Birth.

There can be little doubt that Dr. Henson disliked making such informal special statement of his belief. And he made it, as he recorded it at the time, simply because 'the Archbishop appealed to me for the relief of his own conscience in performing a very difficult act'.

VI

The next crucial stage must be described in the Archbishop's own words:

During the evening of Wednesday (Jan. 16th), I felt rather overweighted with the perplexities arising from the situation. It was clear that Henson's complete silence gave a handle to those who declared that he was obviously unable to express a definite belief in the credal articles on which he is unsound. On the other hand, one felt the difficulty of his seeming to be trimming a statement of belief in order to enter the port of Episcopacy, and his vehement and rather irritable spirit would lead him to listen greedily to those who urge him to leave the onus on his opponents, and to preserve a dignified silence. While this might be well enough for him, it did not go far to relieve me of the charge that I was carelessly ordaining an unbelieving man because the Crown bade me do so. Past midnight, just when going to bed, it occurred to me that possibly I might write something to which he might assent. I scribbled down a draft letter, abbreviating it to the narrowest compass, and a yet briefer draft reply. I slept over these, so far as I did sleep, and in the morning showed them to Dibdin, who had come to breakfast at my request. He was very much against my asking Henson to fall in with such a plan. He was sure to refuse, and then I should be in a most undignified position, having apparently gone begging to him to get us out of a morass, and having failed in the attempt. While Dibdin and I were talking, the servant announced that the Dean of Durham was in the next room. I bundled Dibdin into another room, and brought Henson in. He showed me a telephone message which had come to him through the porter of his hotel, saying 'The Archbishop of Westminster wishes to see you at once'. He was amused at the suggestion that he had been summoned by Cardinal Bourne, but had interpreted it as meaning me, and had at once obeyed what he thought was my call. I explained that I had not sent any message, and we agreed that it must mean the Archdeacon of Westminster, Henson's friend, Pearce. However, he was glad to have a few minutes' talk, as he wished to tell me that he had, at my request, decided to stay away from the City Temple meeting, at which he had been announced to speak that Thursday evening. I thanked him cordially for this, and we went on to a little general talk. I tentatively suggested the possibility of some such letter as I had drafted, but said I was by no means certain that it would be best, and was merely thinking aloud. I showed him the rough draft I had made, and he at once replied 'I should have no objection at all to write you such a note of reply to an enquiry, but I should wish to add another sentence'. I took down the sentence as he said it. I append the letter here, with Henson's additional words so marked. He signed the rough paper. I have preserved it, and then I asked him to let me decide whether to send the two letters to the press, or not. He gladly left it in my hands, and went away.

Then I saw Dibdin again, and he, Dibdin, at once withdrew the objections he had raised, and thought that, since Henson welcomed the opportunity, the whole position was changed, and the two letters might usefully be published.

The following are the letters:

The ARCHBISHOP OF CANTERBURY *to the* DEAN OF DURHAM

Lambeth Palace, 16th January 1918.

I am receiving communications from many earnest men of different schools who are disquieted by what they have been led to suppose to be your disbelief in the Apostles' Creed, and especially in the clauses relating to Our Lord's Birth and Resurrection. I reply to them that they are misinformed, and that I am persuaded that when you repeat the words of the Creed you do so *ex animo* and without any desire to change them. I think I understand your reluctance to make at this moment a statement the motives of which might be misconstrued, and it is only because you would relieve many good people from real distress that I ask you to let me publish this letter with a word of reassurance from yourself.

The DEAN OF DURHAM *to the* ARCHBISHOP OF CANTERBURY

17th January 1918.

I do not like to leave any letter of yours unanswered. It is strange that it should be thought by anyone to be necessary that I should give such an assurance as you mention, but of course what you say is absolutely true. I am indeed astonished that any candid reader of my published books, or anyone acquainted with my public Ministry of thirty years, could entertain a suggestion so dishonourable to me as a man and as a clergyman.

The last sentence of the letter just printed ('I am indeed astonished . . .') gives the additional words which the Archbishop took down at Dr. Henson's dictation. His Grace's personal appeal to Dr. Henson for some means of reassuring the panic-stricken, was very strong. Dr. Henson responded. But, in giving such response, Dr. Henson desired to make it plain that, if he answered such a letter as the Archbishop wrote, the essential thing was explicitly to stand to his ministry, written and spoken.

On January 18 the two letters quoted above were published in *The Times*, together with the Archbishop's full answer to Bishop Gore:

The Archbishop of Canterbury *to the* Bishop of Oxford

Lambeth Palace. 16th January 1918.

You need no assurance from me as to the grave and sedulous care with which I have weighed all that you say in your published letter of Protest respecting the Crown's nomination of Dr. Hensley Henson to the See of Hereford.

I have, as you know, always maintained that in the last resort a large measure of responsibility must belong to the Ecclesiastical authorities, and especially to the Archbishop of the Province, in regard to the filling of a vacant See by the consecration thereto of a priest duly nominated by the Crown. It is therefore appropriate that you should write to me as you have written on a matter about which you feel so strongly. No constitutional rule or usage can force the Archbishop to the solemn act of Consecration, if he be prepared, by resignation or otherwise, to abide the consequences of declaring himself *in foro conscientiae* unable to proceed. I should be deliberately prepared to take that course if I found myself called upon at any time to consecrate to the Episcopate a man who, in my judgment, is clearly unworthy of that Office or false to the Christian Faith as taught by the Church of England.

Dr. Hensley Henson has now, on the nomination of the Crown, been duly elected by the Chapter of Hereford. I have personal knowledge of the care taken by some at least of the prebendaries who voted for him to satisfy themselves as to his teaching, and I am informed that of the nineteen members of the Chapter who took part in the proceedings, all but four voted in his favour. I do not say that the fact of his formal election finally disposes of all question as to his consecration: I mention it because it is an important step in the procedure. I have now, by the help of God, to exercise my own responsibility to the best of my power.

You call upon me to refuse consecration to Dr. Henson. You rest your protest simply on his published writings. These extend over many years, during which he has held positions of considerable importance in the Church of England, and has there been liable to formal proceedings in case of heresy or false teaching. To the best of my belief, no such accusation has ever been formulated against him in such manner as to enable it to be authoritatively tested.

During the last few weeks I have read with care most of Dr. Henson's published books, and since receiving your Protest I have re-read with close attention all the passages to which your Protest refers. Taking them, as in fairness they must be taken, with their full context, I find opinions expressed with which I definitely disagree: I find in some pages a want of balance, and a crudity of abrupt statement, which may give satisfaction or even help to certain minds or temperaments, but must inevitably be painful and possibly even dangerous to others: I find what seem to me to be almost irreconcilable inconsistencies: I find much that seems to me to need explanation, qualification or re-statement. But the result of my consideration of the whole matter—and it has not been slight or hurried—is that, neither in Dr. Henson's books nor in the careful communications which have taken place between him and myself on the subject, have I found anything which, when it is fairly weighed in its true setting, I can regard as inconsistent with the belief which he firmly asserts in the facts and doctrines of the Faith as set forth in the Creeds. Some of the collections of isolated extracts from his writings, as sent to me by correspondents, are even more than usually unfair. And, as you say in your letter, 'he gives noble expression' to what you have called 'the Theological ideas of the Creed and the New Testament'.

We are familiar with the danger, common in ecclesiastical controversy, that a critic, taking his opponent's premisses, may base on them what seems to him to be an obvious conclusion, and then describe, or perhaps denounce, that conclusion as the opinion of the man whom he is criticising, when, as a matter of fact, whether logically or illogically, the writer commits himself to no such opinion. This danger is very real in the case of a writer so exuberant as Dr. Henson. It is a satisfaction to me to note your explicit statement that the 'denial' which you attribute to him, is your inference from what he has written and is not found in the words themselves.

I am bold to say that no fair-minded man can read consecutively a series of Dr. Henson's sermons without feeling that we have in him a brilliant and powerful teacher of the Christian faith, who regards the Incarnation of the Son of God as the central fact of human history, who accepts without qualification the Divinity of our Blessed Lord, and who brings these supreme realities to bear with persuasive force upon the daily problems and perplexities of human life. That he has also a singular power of effectively presenting the Gospel message to the hearts of a congregation of quite ordinary and untheological people, is a fact of which I have personal knowledge and experience.

You have legitimately directed attention to a Resolution which was adopted *nemine contradicente* by the Bishops of the Province of Canterbury on April 30, 1914, in reply to certain Memorials which had been presented to us. I do not myself find in that Resolution, interpreted either literally as it stands, or in the light of the ample and weighty debate which introduced it, anything which leads me, as one of those who voted for it, to feel that I should be acting inconsistently in proceeding in due course to the consecration of Dr. Henson.

I am acting, in a difficult matter, with a sense of high and sacred responsibility towards God and man, after giving weight to the theological, the ecclesiastical, the constitutional, the practical, and the personal issues involved.

I think it right to add that, while my conclusion is, in all the circumstances, clear, I do not regard without appreciation and even sympathy the anxieties to which expression has been given by yourself, and by others who have, in a less formal and responsible way, addressed me. Yet I believe that, under the good Hand of God, the outcome of these anxious days will be to His glory, and to the well being of the Church of His Son, Jesus Christ our Lord.

Every controversy must be decided on its own merits, and, in such a connection, precedents and analogies are dangerous, but it cannot be quite out of place that I should add a brief reference to some historical precedents within our own life-time. You are familiar with the remarkable Chapter written by Dean Church at the very close of his life, in which he looks back upon the Hampden controversies of half a century before, and in language of characteristic force and moderation shows how easily in such controversies unfairness may be shown and serious misunderstandings may arise. 'A manifold and varied experience', he says, 'has taught most of us some lessons against impatience and violent measures.'[1]

Not dissimilarly, in the course of a Debate in which I was myself concerned, in the Lower House of Canterbury Convocation on February 4th 1891, Archdeacon Denison, the protagonist in the denunciation of *Essays and Reviews* thirty years before, and in the subsequent and consequent opposition to Dr. Temple's consecration to the See of Exeter, confessed that he would not, after the lapse of years, endorse the protest which he had himself drawn up and presented to Convocation in 1861.[2]

That incident occurred in the Convocation Debate upon the volume called *Lux Mundi*. It is my unhesitating belief that, if the life of the great teacher and divine, Henry Parry Liddon, had been, to our great gain, prolonged for twenty or even for ten years, his view of that volume would have been very different from what it was when he wrote of it, in the last year of his life,

[1] *The Oxford Movement, 1833–1845*, by Dean Church, chapter ix.

[2] *Chronicle of Convocation*, February 4, 1891, p. 60. See p. 109, *supra*.

as a book with 'a materialistic and Pelagianising tone, the writers (of which) seem to think it a gain when they can prune away or economise the supernatural'.[1] To myself, as one who owes much to that volume, those words seem almost incredibly unfair.

I thank you, as an old and tried friend, for having written to me so frankly in this grave matter. May God the Holy Spirit guide us both in discharging to the best of our power the great trust which He has laid upon us.

VII

The effect was remarkable. The Bishop of Oxford at once wrote privately to the Archbishop that his idea was to take Dr. Henson's reply at its full value and withdraw his protest—but that he would write formally after consulting Dr. Stone and other friends. He wrote shortly after as follows:

The BISHOP OF OXFORD *to the* ARCHBISHOP OF CANTERBURY

Cuddesdon, Wheatley, Oxon. 22nd January, 1918.

In the protest which I thought it my duty to address to you against the consecration of the Dean of Durham to the see of Hereford, I wrote that I was 'judging only from his published writings', and 'apart from any fresh declaration of his belief which he may think fit to make'.

In your letter to him of Jan. 16th, your Grace expressed your conviction that those who had been led to suppose that he disbelieved 'in the Apostles' Creed, and especially in the clauses relating to Our Lord's Birth and Resurrection', were misinformed. You added—'I am persuaded that when you repeat the words of the Creed, you do so *ex animo* and without any desire to change them'.

To this the Dean replied on Jan. 17th, 'What you say is absolutely true'. I observe that your Grace's question is explicit, and that Dr. Henson's reply is given without reservation. I own that I am still profoundly surprised that he should profess astonishment at the fact that opposite conclusions about his personal beliefs should have been drawn from his published writings. But I joyfully accept his present assurance.

I consider myself now entitled to declare that Dr. Henson believes what I thought he disbelieved, and affirms *ex animo* what I thought he did not affirm. I am also entitled to declare that the declaration of the bishops in Convocation would stand unim-

[1] *Life of Liddon*, Johnston, p. 372.

paired by Dr. Henson's consecration: and with this twofold assurance I beg respectfully to withdraw my protest against his consecration.

Just before getting this formal letter the Archbishop had seen the Bishop of Winchester, and noted as follows (January 22):

After luncheon I saw the Bishop of Winchester, in Lollards Tower, as he was passing through London, and he was rejoiced to hear of Gore's change of attitude, though he apparently felt that it somewhat stultified something he had himself written for publication. 'At all events', he said most earnestly, 'we shall not now have Gore resigning.' I joined with him in thankfulness that that was so.

Other objectors were not so ready to accept Dr. Henson's statement. The E.C.U. continued its opposition. Its Secretary (H. W. Hill) declared that the words in Dr. Henson's letter to the Archbishop, to have been of any value, should have been accompanied by a retractation of what he had published in his books. If the words had been accompanied by such a retractation, they might be sufficient. And Lord Halifax, writing on behalf of the Council of the E.C.U., felt compelled to inform his Grace that they were 'constrained to reconsider our whole position in regard to the conditions under which the Church of England is now governed'.

The confirmation took place in Bow Church on January 23. Two objections, one from Dr. Hermitage Day, and another from a layman in the Hereford diocese, alleged Dr. Henson's heresy and general unfitness for episcopal office. They were ruled out as inadmissible, and the Bishop-elect was duly confirmed. The Archbishop invited Dr. Henson to stay at Lambeth for the day of consecration and the following week. The future Bishop's feelings of grief and injustice are clear from the following letter:

The DEAN OF DURHAM *to the* ARCHBISHOP OF CANTERBURY

Deanery, Durham. January 30th, 1918.

You are very good, and your kind letter is welcome. My wife and I will be pleased to accept your invitation to stay at Lambeth from Monday till Friday next week. There can be no question that I shall stand in great need of counsel on many matters, and I am grateful for the assurance that I can draw on your Grace's resources.

The behaviour of the Bishops has certainly made a deep and painful impression on my mind. Obsessed with the ambition of securing a 'clean bill of orthodoxy' from the English Church Union, they seem never to have given a thought to the inevitable, or probable, consequences of their action. My personal relation with the Bishops who have announced to the world that they cannot assist in my Consecration, must needs be very difficult. To forgive an injury of that kind is a duty which I shall endeavour to fulfil, but to forget is hardly in my power. I shall, however, try to content myself with leaving their Lordships to the comfort of their consciences, and the lasting satisfaction of their memory.

Ordinarily some measure of devotional retirement is permitted to a man on the verge of so momentous a new departure. That has been denied to me, and I have instead to carry to my Consecration a mind harassed and fatigued, and a wounded heart. Were it not that Consecration carries me into a Presence where a Higher Equity and a more Generous Charity than that of the Bishops may be counted upon, I could hardly stand it all.

The Archbishop wrote a long and tender letter after the consecration:

The ARCHBISHOP OF CANTERBURY *to the* BISHOP OF HEREFORD

Private. Lambeth Palace. Feb. 10, 1918.

I value very much your letter, and the assurance of your affection gives me real pleasure. It has meant a great deal to us having you here this last week, and I have been and am remembering you steadily when I say my prayers and think of your difficulties and obstacles and of the strain which these weeks of controversy have involved both for you and me. On Tuesday when you are being enthroned we shall have you in special remembrance.

I confess to being a little taken aback by what you told me as we walked through Little Smith Street on Friday about your not preaching in the Diocese just yet, and taking very few Confirmations during the Spring. I will tell you how it strikes me as I think it over. You have at this moment an opportunity the like of which may never come to you again—an opportunity of shewing what are and what are not to you the great realities, and what is the *proportion* of things in our Faith and Life. I rejoice in the glowing accounts I have had of your sermon in the Temple Church this morning—where you shewed the truest wisdom in dwelling upon the eternal realities in Christ which illuminate and steady our life, and in eschewing the perhaps expected reference to these controversial weeks of misunderstanding and criticism.

What I long for beyond easy expression, is that in the immediately coming weeks you should stand before and among your new folk as the shepherd conscious of his trust and his message, and bent on being the *friend* and *warden* and *father* both of clergy and people. Few men could do this so effectively as you, and it may make all the difference to the coming years, for the fruit will abide. No such opportunity may ever be so decisively yours again of shewing by living example as well as spoken word (if I may quote the Consecration Service) 'how ye be minded to behave yourself in the Church of God'.

I think I should, if I were in your place, take quick opportunity of some quiet, simple confirmation, and should try my best to give the *simplest* message in the Master's name. And I am very sure that I should watch eagerly for any who among clergy or laity are in sorrow or sickness and go quietly and unobtrusively to see them—say parents whose son has been killed—or clergy who are ill, and if they happen to be among those whose criticism of your appointment, or whose protest against it, is known to you I should be doubly anxious—in absolute simplicity and privacy and without fuss—to tell them now of Christian comfort. I believe that to do this would be in accord with the dictates of your own heart, even though the 'natural man' in any of us might give a pull the other way! It is an hour when the 'natural man' has to be pushed behind us, and the servant of Christ to do his true part. A few simple, straight sermons, translating into elementary words, the sort of teaching you gave in the Temple to-day, may lead more who have been in trouble and fear, to see their mistake and to become your yokefellows in the work—and it is big—which lies ahead for exploring the waste places and making Christ's message tell. I write unreservedly, not for any eye but yours, but I do feel sure of my ground. Believe me, my dear friend, silence 'even from good words' at this critical time may be not only misunderstood—that is a small matter—but may be harmful. I don't want to bore you by referring again to Temple's advent into Exeter Diocese. But I happen to know the facts intimately (Courtenay, one of his chief opponents, was my valued friend at Windsor and spoke of it often). He simply killed the opposition by words of quiet, steady, Christian messages spoken in and around Exeter *during his first few weeks*, without even a reference to the organised opposition which had been aglow among the clergy. (It was far more intense than in your case. Every Rural Deanery had its spokesman, and Lord Shaftesbury and Dr. Pusey were organisers at Headquarters.) The cases are not identical, but they are similar. He was a strong man—but so are you—and I believe that our prayers for you are going to be answered, and that you are going to be the truest of Bishops to those rather hungry souls in Herefordshire. Pardon me for writing all this with a full heart.

Dr. Henson took his advice; and an episcopate began which, though destined to last only two years before his translation to Durham, was very happy, truly pastoral, and was rewarded with the affection and trust of the clergy and laity of the diocese alike.

For the Archbishop himself, these weeks had been, as he told the Bishops at the private meeting just prior to the consecration, the most anxious and harassing in the whole of his life.

CHAPTER LIV

THE CLERGY AND CONSCRIPTION

'How came priests and Bishops, an please your Honour, to trouble their heads about gunpowder?'

'God knows, said my uncle Toby—his providence brings good out of everything.'

LAURENCE STERNE, *Tristram Shandy*, VIII. xix.

FOR a few days towards the end of the Hereford crisis, the Archbishop and Mrs. Davidson were able to escape for a brief rest at Tremans, the home of Mrs. Benson and Miss Tait. But when he returned to Lambeth just before Dr. Henson's consecration, he had his hands 'singularly overfull' of other matters of quite first-rate importance.

I

In 1917 he had been appointed a member of the Speaker's Conference on the Reform of the Second Chamber. Hitherto, though a regular attendant at the meetings, he had spoken little. But, by the end of January 1918, the Conference had come to the voting stage upon the preliminary draft report. Accordingly on January 29 he spoke rather fully on the question of the retention of Bishops in the House of Lords. In his speech he proposed that six Bishops should remain members, but expressed a readiness to accept any mode of choosing the six that the Conference should recommend. On January 31, when the discussion was resumed, there was some rather excited opposition, on the part of a few liberals, to any inclusion of Bishops.

> But the real heat was imparted by Sir Thomas Whittaker, who denounced the proposal in a violent way as perfectly monstrous and intolerable, and altogether made an exhibition of sectarian heat for which I was quite unprepared.

After others had spoken, a motion by Lord Burnham was carried: that it be a definite direction that five Bishops should be chosen, together with the hereditary peers chosen by the Standing Joint Committee of the two Houses.

> Thereupon Whittaker rose in white heat, and moved that the Conference adjourn immediately. 'Such a decision made the continuance of discussion impossible', and so on. Different members

who had voted with him appealed one after another to him to withdraw such a proposal, Chamberlain, Crewe, Hudson, and, I think, Sir Charles Hobhouse. Finally he did so, but with very bad grace, and it was obvious that the matter would come up again, and I think it may turn out in the end a point of controversy so acute as to imperil the unanimity, if that be attainable, of the Report.

II

There were, of course, in addition a good many war questions causing Dr. Davidson anxiety, and involving a good deal of trouble throughout this time. The problems likely to arise both before and after demobilization, had been much in his mind, and with the Archbishop of York he had decided to appoint a Church Council on War Problems, under their joint presidency, of over a hundred members, naval, military, and ecclesiastical. He had besides been considering the method of dealing with candidates for Ordination from the Navy and Army, and he told Convocation on February 8 of his official assurance through the Chaplain-General to 'all really suitable and qualified men who desire to be candidates for Orders, and who are chosen as suitable for it, that the financial difficulties shall not be allowed to stand in the way'. There was also the moral and spiritual welfare of women workers: both those working in munition factories, to deal with which the Archbishops had set up an Archbishops' Committee, with an office at Lambeth Palace, from which, under the guidance of the Bishop of Dover, over fifty paid and unpaid workers had been sent to different centres by the beginning of February; and the members of the Women's Auxiliary Corps, in which the Archbishop and Mrs. Davidson interested themselves deeply. And there were moral problems which will claim our full attention a little later.

There was, however, another question, affecting not so much the continuance of the War as the means of bringing it to an end, which troubled the Archbishop's thoughts a good deal at this time. We have already seen how, on the outbreak of the War, the Archbishop of Upsala begged Davidson, with other Church leaders in the combatant and neutral countries, to issue a general appeal in the interests of peace. In December 1917, Dr. Söderblom had called together an important conference of neutral Churchmen at Upsala, to deal with questions of practical Christian unity, and the Church's task in the settlement of international controversies and the support of international justice. It issued a statement, over the signature of the Primates of the Churches of Sweden, Norway, and Denmark. In February 1918, the Archbishop of Canterbury received from Archbishop Söderblom an official invitation to send representatives to an Oecumenical Conference of all the Churches at Upsala. The object of the Conference was to proclaim to mankind the uniting power of the Cross, and to call the Churches themselves to labour together in the application of Christian principles in the relation of the nations to one another, and the regeneration of society. The Archbishop saw both the importance, and even more clearly the difficulties, of the Upsala proposal. And it is very interesting to observe the way in which the receiving of such an invitation at this critical stage in the World War set his mind to work. He was concerned not only with the answer which he should give to the immediate proposal, but also with the deeper question whether the Church, in England, was doing enough in the direction of peace. One of the first of those whom he consulted was Lord Lansdowne, who was himself at that very moment taking his own peace movement a step farther. Lord Lansdowne agreed that the acceptance or non-acceptance of the Upsala invitation was one that the Church ought to consider on its own merits. But (the Archbishop writes) 'I pointed out at the same time the difficulty I felt about the Conference from its almost platitudinous character if it did not talk about actual terms of peace, and its very dangerous character if it did, without having the Government and country behind it.' He also saw Arthur Balfour and Robert Cecil together. The former:

> took a characteristically philosophical line about the whole situation—Christian spokesmen have always weighted themselves with the thought that they were not adequately asserting the Christian position in the World's life; they have tried to remedy the mischief in different ways; the Papacy . . . by making itself political; Puritans . . . in another way, and so on. All this is a blunder. The men deceive themselves. They think they are following Christ, and they are not; they are trying to be politicians rather than Christians, whereas they ought to be making people everywhere Christian, and then the political lines will be automatically sound.

Robert Cecil disagreed, and maintained that 'as Christians we want to affect politics by making Christianity permeate the whole body' (January 30). On February 8 the Archbishop had a talk with Asquith of which he made the following note:

I spoke first of the Upsala Conference, and found him entirely in accord with me in the reply we are making, namely that we could only send delegates to such a conference if the other great organised Churches, the Roman and the Eastern, were doing the like.

Then we passed to a larger question. I asked him, did he think that the Church, using that word in its widest sense, was fairly chargeable with having failed to find and use its opportunities during the war. He replied that, on the whole, he did think so, though it was difficult to speak positively, and he admitted that everyone is apt to criticise everyone else at such a time. I asked him to put his finger, if he could, on any special lack of duty on our part, or to name any time during the war when it had been specific and definite. He could not do so, and I pressed him as to whether the dissatisfaction in the matter, which undoubtedly exists, is not the rather fretful criticism of other people which is the outcome of general dissatisfaction with the condition of things. It would be different if he could name anything specific, but he certainly could not.

Then, leaving the past, I asked him about the present. Is there opening now for an utterance on the part of the representatives of the Christian Church on behalf of the fundamental principles of peace and goodwill for which Christianity exists? If so, on what lines ought a wise Christian teacher to proceed? What kind of appeal can he effectively make in England or Europe just now, and, so far as England is concerned, from what platform? Sermons are constant, but produce small effect, and yet, so far as our foremost teachers go, I did, and do think, that men in posts of responsibility had done their best. I named my own case, and the utterances I had tried to make on the different anniversaries in St. Paul's, the Abbey, and elsewhere. He said he had no exception to take to my own part which had seemed to him useful and appropriate, and if the effect was small he did not think it was my fault. He did not feel the same about ***, who preached what he regarded as sheer jingoism of the shallowest kind. He thought his utterances deplorable. 'Well, if that be so, is there anything more', I asked, 'just now open to us? I am in favour of the position taken by e.g. Lansdowne, and I think by yourself in these later months—namely that peace by sheer victory is unobtainable; peace due to revolutions in the different countries is uncertain, and certainly not what I would advocate; and there seems to remain only the peace by some sort of negotiation. Shall we be better able thus to negotiate a year hence than we are now, supposing things to go on in their stalemate condition?' He replied decidedly that he did not think they could go on. He thought a break-up must come on one side or the other from popular discontent and war weariness. No chance of a smashing victory. No satisfaction from a prolongation of an indecisive trench warfare to which we have become used. 'If so', I answered, 'what then? Is there anything that either you or I can do? If you see anything I ought to do, or any direction in which I should be moving, tell me frankly.' He confessed himself unable to make any suggestion.

Such consultations certainly show some of the thoughts then stirring in the Archbishop's mind: but so far as the immediate question went of sending representatives to Upsala, a temporizing answer was sent, leaving room for the further soundings which took place later on in the year.

III

On February 12, he was taken ill—with a recurrence of his old trouble, and spent some time in bed. But he was not idle. The memoranda which are preserved show the deep interest he took in Lloyd George's difficulties with the military chiefs or vice versa: and most other public affairs, including the sad outlook in Ireland.

On April 7 Dr. Davidson kept his seventieth birthday. He was at Canterbury at the time, and a large number of letters reached him, but there was little time for birthday festivities at so grave a crisis in the War. It came only a few days before Haig's famous order to the troops: 'With our backs to the wall, and believing in the justice of our cause, each one of us must fight on to the end' (April 13). The immediate task to be grappled was the position of the Clergy under the new Man Power Bill which raised the military age for compulsory service from 41 to 50 and in some cases 55. In the form in which it was introduced to the House of Commons the clergy were no longer exempted from compulsory military service. Their inclusion was approved by the Archbishop. The new Bill was introduced on April 9, but six days later the decision was reversed. The Archbishop reported the change, in the following letter to the Bishops of London, Winchester, and Southwark:

The ARCHBISHOP OF CANTERBURY *to the* BISHOPS OF LONDON, WINCHESTER, *and* SOUTHWARK

April 15th, 1918.

The situation is changed about the clergy exemptions. I have been with Cave[1] this afternoon, and find that the Government, frightened by Ireland's refusal to let the priests serve in the Army, and the impossibility of doing in England what cannot be done in Ireland, are likely to withdraw the clause conscripting the clergy. I do not think the House of Lords will take this peaceably, and I myself should feel bound, I think, to make it very clear that it was not being done by our wish, and possibly should feel bound to say that we ought to bid the clergy, who are willing to do so, volunteer for service, preferably non-combatant, but not exclusively so. Further, it may pass the Commons under the guillotine, and, therefore, without any discussion or explanation at all. This would reserve the discussion for the House of Lords. If that happens in the Commons to-morrow, Wednesday and Thursday may be important in the Lords. This is private, but you may be glad to have it.

When the Second Reading of the Military Service Bill was moved in the House of Lords on April 17, 1918, the Archbishop made his own position plain. He said that the exemption of the clergy in the original Military Service Act of 1916 had not been asked for by the Bishops and clergy of the Church of England; though he had approved of it as wiser 'as things then stood', and Lord Kitchener had emphatically assured him of his own agreement with his view. And he gave an account of the way in which the clergy and ministers of religion in their parishes, and as chaplains, and in war work of all kinds, had risen to the occasion and met needs which perhaps they alone could adequately fill. He went on:

Now came the change. A few weeks ago a new emergency arose. . . . The call took a new and more vibrant sound, and we all felt that it concerned not those who were fighting only, but ourselves who were at home. In those circumstances, before the Prime Minister made his speech in the House of Commons, I took upon myself to write a letter to him with regard to the particular point that I am dwelling upon. I was obliged to write on my own responsibility; the matter was sudden, and it was impossible to take counsel with my brother Bishops or others. . . . I wrote to him

[1] Home Secretary.

> 'My dear Prime Minister,
>
> In confronting your task of summoning the manhood of England even more urgently than before to rally to the conflict on behalf of righteousness and freedom, you may possibly be uncertain as to how your appeal will be met.
>
> I should like, so far as I am entitled to do so without formal consultation, to reassure you with regard at least to one section of the people. We clergy, in face of an emergency so great, are ready, I firmly believe, to answer with whole-hearted loyalty to any new call that the nation through its responsible spokesmen makes upon us. The hour is too grave for any reply but one, and the very sacredness of our distinctive trust deepens our sense of responsibility for seeing that no detriment or lack accrue by any default on our part, or on the part of those whom we can influence' . . .

> It is not for me to say why the change was made. The noble Viscount (Lord Peel) . . . stated that it was due merely to the fact that the numbers who would be available in any circumstances from the ranks of the clergy and ministers would at best be small. I agree that it would be far smaller than people suppose. . . . But there would have been a considerable number still remaining. . . . It is not for me to say what reasons may have induced the Government to come to the conclusion at which they have arrived. But I wish to make one thing clear—namely, that it was in no sense at our request . . . let no man say hereafter that the clergy of the Church of England have asked for exemption at this hour. . . . In my judgment the very contrary is the case.

The Archbishop ended his speech by a promise 'to see what we can do voluntarily under conditions so different—and this is the real point—from those of 1915–16 as to justify a different attitude on our part from that which we took up at that time'.

Five days later, a special meeting of Diocesan Bishops was held at Lambeth. The seventeen Bishops present agreed unanimously that they would endeavour by diocesan arrangement to give to the clergy, under a voluntary system, facilities for putting themselves in the same position as that which would have been theirs under conscription. Effective provision was made for non-combatant service, but combatant service was allowed. Some Bishops found it more difficult than others to distinguish between the facilitating of what was really voluntary action, and the maintenance of an atmosphere which ceased to make it voluntary. The Bishop of

London, in a summons to his diocese dated 'St. George's Day', offered 'special dispensations' to clergy undertaking combatant service, 'now that the lives and honour of women and children depend upon the courage and skill of their menfolk'. Tribunals were appointed in the different dioceses to decide whether offers should be accepted or refused; and the working out of the system was everywhere helped by the Ministry of National Service. In some dioceses, a number of clergy were in fact released, but it was found on the whole that, so far as the younger men were concerned, allowing for chaplaincy needs, the combing had already been fairly complete.[1] In reporting to the Upper House oı Convocation, July 9, 1918, the Archbishop said of the general outcome of the diocesan efforts: 'What, I think, is coming out, as far as I can judge, is that the demand for men for quite inevitable and indispensable work in our parishes has been, by the public outside, though not by us, underrated.'

[1] The Bishop of Bristol, May 11, 1918, sent the Archbishop the following summary: Total number of clergy in Bristol Diocese, August 4, 1914, 310. Of these 71 had been commissioned as Chaplains in the Navy or Army, 4 were serving as combatants, 4 working in Church Army Huts. Of the 124 of military age (May 1918), 41 alone were immediately available; and of these 19 would become Army Chaplains, 10 have volunteered for non-combatant service, 4 for combatant, 8 for work in Church Army Huts abroad.

CHAPTER LV

THE CRISIS OF THE WAR

For what is war? what is it, Yorick, when fought as ours has been, upon principles of *liberty*, and upon principles of *honour*? what is it, but the getting together of quiet and harmless people, with their swords in their hands, to keep the ambitious and the turbulent within bounds? LAURENCE STERNE, *Tristram Shandy*, VII. xxxii.

IN the last ten months of the war, there were many other cares which pressed upon the Archbishop. Some were cares for promoting peace. Thus, in February 1918, the Upper House of Canterbury Convocation passed a Resolution welcoming the proposal of a League of Nations:

> That this House notes with especial satisfaction the prominent place recently given by prominent statesmen among the Allies to the proposal of a League of Nations. We desire to welcome in the name of the Prince of Peace the idea of such a League as shall promote the brotherhood of man, and shall have power at the last resort to constrain by economic pressure or armed force any nation which should refuse to submit to an international tribunal any dispute with another nation. Further, we desire that such a League of Nations should not merely be regarded as a more or less remote consequence of peace, but that provision for its organisation should be included in the conditions of a settlement. (February 7th, 1918.)

The Archbishop, in a full speech, gave it strong support, and took pains to indicate that there had been brave men before Agamemnon; successive British Prime Ministers, for example, and General Smuts, having spoken up for the principle of a League earlier than Woodrow Wilson. Later in the month, he headed a manifesto by the leaders of many Churches, including the Church of Scotland, the Free Churches, and the Roman Catholic Church, to a similar effect, urging again that the League 'should be put in the very forefront of the peace terms as their presupposition and guarantee'.

I

The spring of 1918 was the most critical period of the War; and the Archbishop's anxiety was great. One particular trouble, which caused him special concern in these months, was the question of morals and health among soldiers of the Expeditionary Force in France. From the beginning of the War, he had kept a watch on the subject, not least in connexion with the troops quartered in Folkestone, in his own Diocese; and he had remained in close touch both with the chaplains to the Forces, and social workers, and with the Home Office and the military authorities. In February 1918, a good deal of public indignation was stirred at what seemed the *nonchalance* of the responsible people both in France and at home, with regard to some particularly bad cases of *maisons tolerées* in Havre and Cayeux, and also to the considerable prevalence of disease. With the arrival of the American troops, Bishop Brent, acting as their unofficial Chaplain-General, pressed hard for joint action between the British and American armies, and also between chaplains, doctors, and officers. The Archbishop went thoroughly into the whole question with Bishop Gwynne, the Deputy Chaplain-General of the British Expeditionary Force; and had many communications with Lord Derby, the Secretary of State for War. Various Resolutions were passed by the Bishops in Convocation, and a good deal of indignation was expressed all over the country. The Archbishop told Lord Derby that he was not surprised at the agitation, 'for the reputation of the Army is supposed to be distinctly lowered by such incidents' (February 9, 1918). A fortnight later he asked Lord Derby for a further interview, and, after saying that he was laid up in bed at the time, added:

The ARCHBISHOP OF CANTERBURY *to the* EARL OF DERBY

25th February 1918.

I have however had full conversation with Bishop Gwynne, the Deputy Chaplain-General who is now in England, and have arranged with him that he should send me a report from the Chaplains' standpoint with regard to the problem both at Cayeux and at other like places.

The idea of a report from the Chaplains' standpoint caused something of a stir in high military circles; and the Chaplain-General sent the Archbishop a copy of a letter from the Adjutant-General (Sir Nevil Macready) to Bishop Gwynne as follows:

The ADJUTANT-GENERAL *to the* DEPUTY CHAPLAIN-GENERAL

27th February 1918.

Lord Derby has received a letter from the Archbishop of Canterbury to the effect that he has arranged with you to send a report from the Chaplains' standpoint, in regard to the problem of venereal disease and French brothels.

You will no doubt appreciate that any report you may send, or, indeed, conversation you may have with an official unconnected with the Army, must be rendered through and with the consent of your immediate superior, who of course is the Adjutant-General in France.

I do not, of course, refer to the purely spiritual side of the position you hold, nor would I suggest that this should not be a matter of discussion with the high authorities of your Church, although even here it may be questionable whether reference before doing so should not be made to the Chaplain-General.

This roused the Archbishop:

The ARCHBISHOP OF CANTERBURY *to the* CHAPLAIN-GENERAL

1 March, 1918.

I return the letter which the Adjutant-General has written to Bishop Gwynne. I cannot conceive that the Adjutant-General would contend that men in the position of yourself and the Deputy Chaplain-General cannot talk over with me the moral problems of the Army with a view to the removal and resistance of temptation. If he were to say so, the country would not support him in demanding it. Nor, I am sure, would the Secretary of State support him in endeavouring to restrict intercourse among us Bishops upon the moral question which is stirring the hearts of the whole people. Of course formal letters prescribing policy to be followed by the Army authorities in connexion with Brothels and the like are not in contemplation between us, and neither you nor I would think of acting in such a matter formally and publicly without communicating with the highest military authorities. But our whole *raison d'être* is that we should try to promote the moral and spiritual well-being of the manhood of England now serving in the Army; and to say that we must not take counsel on this subject with a view to ascertaining the facts, or that what the Adjutant-General calls 'purely spiritual' questions can be separated off from moral questions, is surely out of the question. I am quite prepared to face the public on that subject if necessary, and I am ready at any moment to see the Secretary of State on the subject. The immediate occasion of my letter to Lord Derby was a request from him that we should give him counsel and information about these very questions. Nothing could have been more frank and encouraging than his wish that we should help him if possible to get to the roots of a problem of intense difficulty. He knew and desired that we should try to put before him all the information available.

Pray show this letter to Bishop Gwynne. I am certain that you are yourself whole-heartedly with me in the determination to know all that we need to know about the morality and the temptations of our men and to consider in what way we can best help them.

It also roused Bishop Gwynne, who said in a letter to the Archbishop's Chaplain (March 4): 'Macready's letter to me is rather an insult to my chief—the Archbishop—which I ought not to take sitting down. I do not mean to answer the A. G. until I have seen his Grace.' The Archbishop saw Lord Derby on March 7 at the House of Lords, and notes: 'He entirely agreed in scouting the idea that there was anything inappropriate in my communicating as fully as possible with the Chaplain-General, or with the Deputy Chaplain-General, upon all that belongs to our relation with soldiers on moral as well as on spiritual questions. He thought the Adjutant-General had pictured to himself some kind of formal report. . . .'

A few days later, the Archbishop gave notice of his intention to raise the general question in the House of Lords, putting a motion on the paper in the following form:

To call attention to conditions affecting morals and health among soldiers of the Expeditionary Force in France.

The Archbishop had already acquired an immense amount of information, and, between the sending in of his motion in the middle of March and the actual debate, he gained still more from both British and American sources.

The expected debate took place on April 11. The Archbishop was well aware of the delicate character of his task; and he discharged it with no less consideration than courage. He reminded the House that this was not a new question. He spoke of his own experience 'for more than three years now', during which he had been in constant touch, especially on the conditions of camps on the south coast, with military, medical, magisterial, and municipal authorities, and testified that alike from them and from the Home Office under successive Home Secretaries, and other Government departments, he had received much more than courtesy. He paid a great tribute to the young men serving in the British Army. Then he went on: 'We owe everything to these men. Are we doing everything for them that we can possibly do?' He spoke of his own very close touch with men on leave, officers, intimate friends, medical men of the highest knowledge and character and experience, and not least with the chaplains:

> And from all these we learn a very great deal which cheers and inspires, a very great deal which evokes our admiration, our gratitude, and our sympathy, and we learn something, too, that gives us disquiet. To take an example. There are special hospitals on a huge scale—I need not name them or their character—where groups of lads can be seen by any one of us who will go to see them, lads who a little time ago were, many of them, clean and healthy, and who are not clean and healthy now. And we older men, we men who are perforce stay-at-homes, ask ourselves, 'Have we, as representatives of British citizenship and British affairs at home, done all that in the country lies to prevent, or to render unlikely, the kind of charge which object-lessons like that present to us?

There were, he suggested, always three groups of men who had a responsibility for action and administration in these matters—the military authorities, the medical authorities, and 'a body of men whose business lies with moral questions, religious questions, and with keeping up . . . the spirit and the tone', the padres and their fellows. Were they co-ordinated, or were they even acting in rivalry with one another? 'We are told that that co-ordination is found, but it does not always seem so to the young officer who talks to us about these things, who speaks about France and its temptations, about the Paris leave, about the streets of the great base cities—perhaps above all about the condition of England itself, and of London itself, to those who are on leave.'

Then he referred to the American forces, and the great difference their incoming made; the methods they had adopted, with the greatest possible encouragement from their highest naval and military authorities; and he begged for an adequate co-ordination of the work the Americans were taking in hand with the work of the English. And he spoke of the home region, for which civilians had a special responsibility, as affording a very large part of the source of the moral mischief affecting the tone and health of the Army. There were branches of this question which he and his friends were bound to leave to the military authorities—such as the penal consequence of a soldier's wrongdoing, or the rules and methods of early treatment, and medical inspection. But on one department in particular he did claim a right to speak as a matter of principle—the whole system of *maisons tolerées*. This he attacked root and branch. The Archbishop, at the close of his speech, pleaded once again for the co-ordination of English and American efforts, and ended thus:

> . . . if the Government can give us encouragement we believe that by such co-ordination of effort and unity of action by ourselves and our brothers from other lands, we can produce something more effective than we have at present on the preventive, educative, and recreative side, we shall not merely bring strength to a great many of those to whom we owe everything for what they are doing in the field, but comfort and encouragement to thousands of English homes.

The speech made a great impression. Lord Derby, after speaking of his own difficulties, and appreciating the Archbishop's clear recognition of some of the brutal facts in the whole matter, said from his own different standpoint he was 'in entire agreement with what the Archbishop of Canterbury had said', and would do his best to help him. One point he had already anticipated. He had seen Bishop Brent, whose presence in France had made so great a difference, and had taken steps to arrange a conference between the American and British representatives, including the Archbishop of Canterbury, on the whole question.

A month after the debate, on May 10, the first conference was held under the chairmanship of Mr. Ian Macpherson, the Under-Secretary. The Archbishop was present, and representatives of the Army, Navy, New Zealand, Canada, and the American Army (including Bishop Brent), the Chaplains' Department, and the Medical Services, as well as Lord Sydenham, the Chairman of the Royal Commission on Venereal Diseases. One result of the Conference was the issue of a revised official War Office circular on early treatment in which, at the Archbishop's special request, in addition to the medical remedies, words[1] were included to emphasize the authorities' desire that the men 'should keep themselves in all respects fit and clean'. A second conference was held

[1] The words (they did not go as far as the Archbishop wished) were as follows [24/Gen. No./6398 (AMD2) 25 May 1918]: 'The first duty of a soldier is to keep himself fit and to avoid any risk of incapacitating himself from the performance of his duty. One of the greatest risks is that of venereal disease against which continence and self-control prove the only real safeguard.'

on July 11—when a distinguished French doctor attended (Dr. Gougenot), as well as the other representatives. The difficulties were not small. On August 4, 1918, when the Archbishop dictated his reflections on some of the points which had been most in his mind during the past few months, he wrote as follows:

> There have been other things connected especially with the Army's morals and health, both physical and other, which have been a ceaseless cause of anxious consultations, cross-currents of half-informed enthusiasms and wrath. On the whole, I think we have perhaps done as much as was practicable, but it is disappointing. Bishop Brent, whose presence in France at the head of the Chaplains, is an immense boon, has discussed it with me time after time, and we are working well together. It is a miserable subject, and one which inflames people almost beyond any other. . . .

II

There were other anxieties to which the Archbishop had to attend, concerning the special duties of the Church in the reconstruction of social life when hostilities were over. And there were some, most urgent of all, which arose out of the gravity of the military situation. He followed the fortunes of Navy and Army alike with the closest attention. After the fall of Zeebrugge, he wrote to Admiral Roger Keyes, whose reply shows how much his sympathy was appreciated by brave men on a dangerous venture:

The Archbishop of Canterbury *to* Vice-Admiral Keyes

Lambeth Palace. S.E.
S. George's Day. Apr. 23, 1918.

The news which tonight's paper gives us is of the sort which makes a man 'hold his breath' in admiration of the magnificent courage and skill involved in such an enterprise.

As one to whom our Kentish shores mean much—for they lie within Canterbury Diocese—I should like (on St. George's Day) to say to you and to your brave men how intensely we appreciate the heroism of such deeds, and how proud we are of those who are thus adding lustre to the long and varied records of English seamanship and naval prowess.

We know nothing yet, save the brief news in tonight's papers, but I am sure you will not mind my sending you this appreciative word.

VICE-ADMIRAL KEYES *to the* ARCHBISHOP OF CANTERBURY

Admiral's Office, Dover. 25th April /18.

It was a very kind thought of yours to write to me and to send such an inspiriting message to the gallant force I am so very proud to have commanded on St. George's Day. It will interest you to know that, just before we went into action, I signalled 'St. George for England'! I felt we had at last struck the right day—after two great disappointments, in one of which we—108 vessels of sorts, having come over 100 miles, were within gun range of our objective when the wind changed to a direction which would have brought disaster had we not turned back before we were committed—horribly afraid that we might be discovered by aircraft at dawn before we could get back to our hiding places. The disappointments were most trying to the men cooped up in ships for 17 days almost out of sight of land, but their cheery patience and confidence that they would be 'put there' in time thrilled me with admiration and pride—and later, the way in which they took their heavy losses, at a moment when I was feeling desperately sad, touched me more than I can say.

Thank you, Sir, on their behalf and mine, for writing.

Two days later the Archbishop had lunch with the Asquiths. The following extract is from a memorandum made at the time:

Lunched with the Asquiths Saturday April 27th. After luncheon I had a full talk with him in his study. The loss of Mont Kemmel had been announced the night before, and I naturally tried to draw from him his view of the whole situation resultant therefrom. He was naturally cautious from lack of detailed personal knowledge, but his acquaintance with the war problems generally, and with the locality, and with the leading Generals, gives weight, of course, to what he thinks and says at such an hour. The situation, he says, is the gravest we have yet had to face; matters are darker than they have been at any time during the war. Nobody is to blame, on a great scale, at least. It is due to the collapse of Russia. The pity is that the public are allowed by Lloyd George to suppose that we are secure against German attacks by the numbers of our men and the solidity of our positions. . . . I reminded Asquith of his original Guildhall speech, 'Never sheathing the sword until German militarism was destroyed', etc. 'I suppose you would say that the conditions have so completely changed that those words could no longer be expected to hold good?' He answered 'Certainly. No one at the moment I spoke had the vestige of an idea of the collapse of Russia, which really governs the whole situation. I should be quite ready to say so. . . .'

His friendliness to myself was very warm. He gave me a copy of his book *Occasional Addresses*, and said warm words about our friendship. I thought him at his best—healthy-looking, not excited, large minded, full of knowledge, and expressing himself with the force and weight which are always his in such talks.

III

The summer of 1918 was unusually strenuous, even for the Archbishop. He was plunged, as ever, into all manner of public affairs. He took the deepest interest in the affairs of General Maurice, whom he saw on several occasions after his famous letter to *The Times*,[1] and admired his great dignity and courage. The diocese, Convocation, Parliament all had their absorbing claims. In Convocation, echoes of the Hereford controversy made themselves heard. It was not to be wondered that Dr. Henson should have resented the agitation opened by Gore with regard to Crown Nominations to ecclesiastical offices 'in view of the anxiety widely felt in many quarters with regard to the present method'—and a speech made at a Life and Liberty Meeting by the same Bishop, containing the words 'Another appointment like that to Hereford would bring the whole system tumbling to the ground'. Nor can we be surprised that Dr. Henson should object to a petition, presented to the Upper House by another Bishop of the Province, with regard to the maintenance of the Christian faith, as part of 'the long tissue of insult which had misrepresented everything that he accepted'.

In Parliament the Archbishop renewed appeals he had made in 1915, 1916, and 1917 in the House of Lords on behalf of prisoners of war. He asked on March 7, 1918, for an *en bloc* exchange of prisoners. Again on July 24, he protested about the difficulty of obtaining any direct answers from the Government, and on October 16, spoke of the widespread indignation at their slowness. At the same time he gave his full support to the Education Act which Mr. Fisher piloted through the Commons. There was no religious controversy; and when the Act took its place on the

[1] *The Times*, May 7, 1918. Major-General Sir Frederick Maurice, Director of Military Operations, Imperial General Staff (1915–18), charged Ministers with a series of misstatements on the military situation.

Statute Book in August the following letter reached him from its author:

RT. HON. H. A. L. FISHER *to the* ARCHBISHOP OF CANTERBURY

Board of Education, Whitehall, London, S.W. 8.8.18.

Now that the Education Bill has been placed on the Statute Book, will you allow me to tender you my most sincere and heartfelt thanks for the invaluable help which you have given me at every stage of the Bill, and more especially during its passage through the House of Lords.

I feel that I should also like to tell you how very much I appreciate the wise and broad-minded attitude which Mr. Holland of the National Society has adopted throughout. He has kept us in touch with the body of opinion which he represents, but has always stood for moderate and sensible counsels, and I feel that we have indeed been fortunate in finding in the Secretary of the National Society a man of so balanced and generous a temper.

I hope that the Act will be found to be as fair in its working as it is in its intention. That it will be a means of raising the education of our people on to an altogether higher level, I have no doubt whatever.

The Archbishop's own summary of these months, as he looked back upon them (Aug. 4), was as follows:

I think I have written nothing since the first week in May, and yet these three months have been in some respects the most important months of our common life, as regards the things which have been happening. One wonders intensely what people will think who, with competent knowledge and pains, are fifty years hence discussing what we have now been doing, saying, or leaving unsaid. I have been in pretty close touch with prominent actors and thinkers who have been handling English affairs and policy. Abundant talks with men like Curzon, Bryce, Crewe, sometimes Asquith, occasionally Arthur Balfour, and occasionally Lloyd George. Also with men of a different group or grade, Sanderson, Newton, Kenyon of the British Museum, the Speaker, the Lord Chancellor, and military men like Maurice, occasionally Robertson, and the War Office administrators, and so on. Besides this, I have been in close and constant touch with Stamfordham, who has kept me abreast of many things, and prevented my ever being quite out of touch with any important things which were happening, or under debate. I have also had my ears open in the House of Lords, where I have attended with great regularity, and in the House of Commons when important things were under debate.

All this results in my finding myself abreast of conversations among public men, when I am present at such, and on a good many points I think I have perhaps a wider knowledge than many with whom I converse, even though they be officials with access to Government information. And yet there is no outstanding controversial matter in which I find myself brimming or effervescing with thought, or controverting vehemently a current view. Perhaps the most outstanding is what people are learning to call the 'Lansdowne' controversy. . . . A few days ago appeared his second letter to the press. Whether its publication was wisely handled by him or his friends, I doubt. I think he allowed himself to be exploited by men whose pacifist views he entirely repudiates. . . . Our distinct view is that whether Lansdowne's wording is well chosen, or his modes of making his views public fortunate, he is to this extent right—no defeat we have at present inflicted on the Germans in France, or Africa, goes far enough to ensure German anti-militarism in finding a voice, and backward and forward battlings on the Western Front might apparently go on interminably, unless there be economic or food questions forcing an issue, and this seems exceedingly doubtful. In these circumstances, we do need, as Lansdowne says, to be feeling our way, not towards peace terms, but towards the bringing about a discussion as to whether peace terms are obtainable. Lansdowne's quotation from Smuts' speech in Glasgow, May 17th, is to my mind of supreme importance, and that speech goes quite as far as anything Lansdowne has said. . . .

Another matter, in which Lord Lansdowne and the Archbishop were both interested, was the question of a Tombola. A proposal was made that a Tombola should be promoted for the funds of the Red Cross, with a prize of a magnificent pearl necklace made up of single pearls; it being calculated that the result of such a Tombola or Lottery would realize well over one million pounds. The Archbishop had some correspondence and interviews with Mr. Geoffrey Dawson, editor of *The Times*, and Lord Lansdowne on the subject, especially with the former, who had been sent to him by the Prime Minister to ask him what line he would take if the Government were to promote the Tombola. His view was stated in the following letter to Mr. Geoffrey Dawson:

The ARCHBISHOP OF CANTERBURY *to* GEOFFREY DAWSON, ESQ.

2nd July, 1918.

I have given careful consideration to what you told me about the plan of raising money for the Red Cross by means of a Lottery or Tombola of the Pearls collected for Necklaces. I have taken counsel with one or two friends interested in social life and progress, and experienced in the conditions which confronted us before the War, as regards the mischievous growth of a gambling spirit among the lads. I was necessarily in constant touch with these difficulties, which were I think almost universally felt to be very grave. The War has of necessity operated to check the opportunities, and therefore the temptations, and our hope is that in after-War conditions we shall be able to grapple more effectively with what was a growing danger. I am not I think a fanatic on that subject: many of my friends use more vehement language than I do: but the man must be blind indeed who is unaware of what was, and will again be, the rampant peril among both boys and girls, including specially the factory workers of both sexes. In these circumstances I have no doubt at all that an imprimatur given by the Government, for the first time in recent years, to a general Lottery on a huge scale, would be intensely harmful to any efforts which we may hereafter have to renew for combating the mischief. I have no right to press on you other considerations such as the pain which would undoubtedly be given to many donors of Pearls, sometimes given in memory of those who have fallen, were their gifts to be thus utilised for what they would believe to be a mischievous mode of raising money. And you are as well able to judge as I whether the Red Cross cause would be permanently helped by such action. You asked me whether I should feel bound to denounce this lottery plan if it be undertaken under Government authority. I do not know exactly what kind of denunciation you were forecasting. I have no wish to threaten a public outcry, but an outcry is I think inevitable, whether I speak or hold my tongue; and if people were to be ranged on two sides as regards the expediency and rightness of such procedure, I should have no doubt on which side I should be bound to stand. Nor can I suppose for a moment that appeal would not be made to me for some utterance on the subject.

I do not like saying all this, for it may seem discouraging to the splendid effort which has been and is being made for the Red Cross. There is no worthier object for our gifts.

A Bill was nevertheless promoted in the House of Lords:

Lansdowne was somehow got to be the spokesman of this measure in the House of Lords, and his advocacy had the result of silencing what would have been the hostile voices of many of his friends and long admirers. More than one Peer told me that he thought there was a great deal in what I said, but he could not vote against Lansdowne (*Memorandum, 4 Aug. 1918*).

The Bill was carried in the Lords on August 2—in spite of the Archbishop's opposition—but it failed to pass the Commons.

IV

A change of a different kind, in the temper of the people, was shown in the renewal of the agitation against enemy aliens, and a demand was made for a drastic review of all cases in which exemption from internment had been given. There can be little doubt that this, as well as other questions more political in colour, were in Dr. Davidson's mind when he preached at St. Margaret's, Westminster, on the fourth anniversary of the Declaration of War, Sunday, August 4, 1918, in the presence of the King and Queen and the two Houses of Parliament. His text was 'Thou shalt not take the name of the Lord thy God in vain' (Exod. xx. 7). He spoke of the loftiness of the nation's trust, and the three special perils which may mar its nobility at a crisis hour: that its pure ideal may be weakened, or may be coarsened by selfishness and greed of gain, or crossed with temper of another kind:

> And again: the high ideals and aims to which we proclaimed our fealty at the start may, in the dust and distraction of the long-drawn strife, with its confusions and perplexities, its passions and its devilries, come to be crossed and seamed and transfused with temper of another kind. There is a righteous wrath, which is not only compatible with the noblest of God-given impulses, but may even be of their essence. Yes, but there is also a form of wrath which may degenerate into a poisonous hatred, running right counter to the principles of a Christian's creed, right counter to what was taught us by the Lord Christ, and which, once its roots get a firm place in our lives, may do worse than weaken, worse than coarsen and lower our high aims: it may corrupt and defile them with a horrid miasma, transforming what was a righteous—yes, a wholesome—wrath against wrong into a sour and envenomed hatred of whole sections of our fellow-men. That peril is no mere vague possibility. It exists. Such a spirit has, here and there, found voice among the sons of men in these years of strain and sorrow. As pledged disciples of a living Lord and Master who died upon the Cross for those who hated Him, we have to see to it that the spirit of hate find no nurture in our hearts.

His own account written immediately after the sermon was:

> This morning I had to preach at the unique service of the fourth anniversary of the war, when the King and the two Houses attended St. Margaret's. I felt the occasion to be an important one, but it would have been, I think, an abuse of the pulpit had one tried to outline questions of policy, even in the largest way. It was not an easy sermon to preach, for the very reason that political questions in the controversial sense had to be avoided, and, on the other hand, one wished to avoid, and I think I did avoid, the comparatively easy and certainly popular course of beating the big drum, and simply belauding ourselves and our cause. I tried to say some things which are not politically controversial, but which cut at the root of our religious attitude and temptations. I was listened to with unbroken attention. It remains to be seen whether I have so trodden on susceptible toes as to produce protest or attack. Whether my words do so or not, I am at present sure that I was right in saying them.

V

The summer holiday was spent as usual in Scotland, and almost entirely in the neighbourhood of Perth, Crieff and Gask, Aberuchill and Cloan. Everywhere he and Mrs. Davidson stayed with friends. At Gask, Bryce was a fellow visitor:

> He was rather eager that the Church as such should put out something which should smooth the road to peace—only he is vehemently hostile to negotiations being opened with the Germans at present. He thinks Lansdowne had gone too far in that direction.

The Archbishop was laid up at Gask for a few days with his old illness, but not seriously, and talked a good deal, as well as reading, amongst other literature, a very interesting memorandum which the Colonial Office had sent him on African questions, by Dr. Norman Leys, the future author of *Kenya*.

> At Aberuchill I revived the memories of boyhood at Dunira and elsewhere, and revelled in the glory of the hills. I still think it the most beautiful part of Scotland, and our hosts were kindness itself. I hope to be allowed future visits there. I preached in Comrie.
>
> Then we had a week with Haldane at Cloan. I preached at Auchterarder on the Sunday. Every day I had abundant walking and talking with Haldane. I had one adventure with him. He took me for a walk along a ravine where he had not been for a long time. The path disappeared, the sides were precipitous, loose

earth, and many of the little trees, which were abundant, were decayed and gave no hold, and the earth slithered away. Haldane, who is most inagile, would not go further, and I think he was right, but when we tried to get up the bank on our return, he stuck, and for some minutes I was seriously alarmed that he would slip into the ravine below—a really serious matter. However, I got above him and hauled him up with my stick. He is not a good climbing companion. He recognised it to the full and even exaggerated the perils in which he had been. We felt it would have been an odd incident if the Archbishop and a Lord Chancellor had together tumbled down a valley into a burn and been killed! But the thing was really not impossible.

On our walks we had abundant confidential talk. I still think he makes good his contention that he was after all in the right as regards his endeavours to establish friendship between England and Germany in 1911, 1912, 1913, 1914. . . . It is an extraordinary fact that he should be regarded as pro-German in policy. He is one of the most determined patriots in regard to the war policy etc. that England possesses. He does believe in the greatness of German intellect, the thoroughness of German work, and the usefulness of German education in the world's life, and he believes, as I do, that any attempt to rule Germany outside the pale of civilised nations after the war, is as impolitic as it is unworkable.

He had many interesting walks and talks with Haldane while at Cloan—dwelling on the future more than on the past—on subjects as varied as the question of producing centres of electric power for English industries, Haldane's friendship with the first Mrs. Asquith, contemporary politicians, the need of preparing people's minds about peace terms, and Haldane's own educational theories:

I think that he believes that England cares much more than England does about his opinion on educational subjects. He does really know a great deal, but it is of a very academic and unattractive sort, a complete contrast e.g. to Fisher. He intends, however, to make speeches about it, and he gave me notes to read which I have not yet opened.

I greatly enjoyed my walks and talks with him, and I was touched by his unstinted confidence, and I think genuine caring for my opinion.

In the evenings he read and recited Browning and some of the Brontë poems, which he has at his fingers' ends.

VI

On his return to England, on September 9, the Archbishop found himself immersed in work, and had to grapple with the accumulation of arrears:

> I have written a long letter about this to the Bishop of Winchester, which is preserved with this memorandum, as it gives a good specimen of the duties devolving upon the Archbishop of Canterbury of the 20th Century.

Here is the letter. Certainly it would be hard to provide a better picture of the amount and variety of the work in which a modern Primate, with Dr. Davidson's range of interests as well as responsibilities, was absorbed:

The Archbishop of Canterbury *to the* Bishop of Winchester

September 15th, 1918.

This is going to be rather a long letter, but I shall relieve my mind by writing it, and you will think it over, and we can talk about it when the opportunity comes.

Each time that I return, as I am now returning, to my work after a little holiday, the thought comes over me that it may be the last time one is grappling with these problems in the sort of way one does when they have accumulated for a fortnight or so, and I want to face up to them and to look at the whole wood, and not only at the trees, and to view the position and its responsibilities in the sort of way in which one would like to commend it and describe it in handing it on to a successor.

The real difficulty is to keep a reasonable proportion between the great things of first rate importance, and the small things, quite necessary and important, but apt to multiply to the obscuring of the bigger. I suppose my 'make' has always been to look at things in the concrete, and not abstractively. Part of the glamour and mystery and inspiration to me of a teacher like Westcott, was that he looked at everything with a certain abstractness, seeing the principles rather than worrying about the practical details, when he was writing, though in action he was pretty good in details also.

I myself see few things clearly except in the concrete—that is what makes me a bad metaphysician, and perhaps a bad, and certainly an indifferent, Archbishop. Therefore let me come to the concrete. I this week have had to face a pile of things most of which belong to the last six or seven days only, for I attended to a good many while I was absent. When I look at this mass of subjects and feel, as one must, how much really depends on what I, individually, do and say about each, I am faced by the thought that we are trying to do an impossibility in leaving on the Archbishop's shoulders the responsibility for so many things which seem to be nobody else's business, except his; and yet when we consider how to contrive conciliar aid one is baffled as to how it can be done, or what sort of council would be workable and reasonably permanent and tolerably acceptable to Bishops at home and abroad, and to Church folk generally.

This is Sunday afternoon—let me give you a list of the questions I have been trying to deal with since Friday morning—two days and a half.

1. The Bishop of Zanzibar's repudiation of Canterbury, and the duty of Canterbury in relation thereto, remembering our general organisation of Lambeth Conferences etc.

2. The Charge of the Bishop of Korea, dealing with the same kind of questions—the relation of Bishops on the circumference and in missionary fields to us at the centre.

3. A very practical question pressing for attention as to the Australian dioceses and their relation to the home Church. Ought they to be doing without home aid; or is such aid still as necessary as the Colonial and Continental Church Society, which is organising a big campaign on the matter, thinks?

4. The strange diocese of Polynesia, and the qualifications, or disqualifications, needed in its Bishop.

5. The varied and far reaching problems raised by Bishop Cecil of South Tokyo, about the Japanese Episcopate, and Nippon Sei Kokwai.

6. The North China dioceses, with a corresponding problem to that of Japan, and the subsidiary question whether a Church officer in England can do certain work consistently with the principle of a native Chinese Church.

7. Bishop MacInnes of Cairo and Jerusalem, and the questions about his diocese which are made burning by the war, but are really permanent.

8. The Mission to Western Canada, and the winding up of it. Ought we to endow the Mission we have founded, or ought Canada to do it? A most delicate matter.

9. The Bishops needed for the troops in Mesopotamia. Are they to go from England, or from India, and, if the former, how am I to furnish them?

10. The proposed visit of Swedish clergy to England, and the relation of their Church to our own, especially in connexion with the recently proposed Upsala Conference.

11. The visit of clergy from the United States to England—is it now desirable or inexpedient, in regard both to war policy and ecclesiastical questions?

12. The fearful needs of the Assyrian Christians in Persia, and the action of the Foreign Office in relation thereto.

13. The impending arrival of the Archbishop of Belgrade in England to deal with Serbian questions, and the alleged possible consecration in England of a Serbian Bishop—query, with or without Anglican co-operation.

14. The visit of the Greek Archbishop of Athens to England to organise what looks very like opposition to some portions of the Eastern Church, and to obtain England's support.

15. The diocese of Bermuda and its proper relation to the Canadian Church or the home Church, the decision being thrown upon me.

The foregoing 15 subjects all need practical attention forthwith. Besides all these there come the questions like:

16. The League of Nations and the part we ought to take—a matter about which Bryce and others are very anxious, and Dickinson and Co. very eager, while the critics are also hard at work.

17. The request made by Chaplains at the Front, through the D.C.G., that we should, forthwith, re-establish Minor Orders in England for ex-soldiers who want to be Ministers, but are unfit to be Priests. They seem to think it can be done almost offhand.

18. The problem of what is called 'International Insurance', as raised by Principal Jacks and others on moral and almost religious grounds, though really an international question.

On all these later heads, 16, 17, 18, I have no difficulty in getting home counsel, but the others are difficult. There is scarcely one of them that can adequately be handled without several Episcopal heads being put together over it, but whose heads are they to be? And we want different people's heads for the different numerals in my list.

You will see, I think, how very practical is the question I am giving you to think about, in view of the fact that the present Archbishop is past three score and ten, and a new one will soon be needed. Meantime the unhappy man who has to handle these subjects finds also a daily pile of the usual things about dilapidations and stable roofs, or the salary of a curate-in-charge, or a churchwarden's objection to a processional hymn, or the publication of Banns by laymen, and far smaller things than these. I have the best and most admirable of Suffragans to help me, but I do not see clearly what ought to be the policy of the future. I am honestly anxious not to be fainthearted, or to croak lugubriously, but the outlook is to me a most difficult one for the Church.

You will, of course, realise that I have not picked out a special time of unique aggregation of problems. It is a normal condition of things, only I do not usually formulate lists of the subjects of each week's correspondence. I do not think that the list I have given above is markedly exceptional, though undoubtedly it is rather a high temperature of feverish work. I wonder what Moore or Manners Sutton would have said about it.

You have yourself recently raised to me several questions which are in your view looming ominously, and they lie outside the little list I have given above. Anyhow I have offered you some material for your meditations and your counsel, and, having dictated this, I must have some tea.

The letter was written from Canterbury where the Archbishop spent the best part of a month. His eager interest in all that went on was evident in all sorts of ways:

While there we went (Edith and I) for two nights to Sheerness, (Sept. 16–18) staying with Admiral and Mrs. Hyde Smith, delightful people. We visited Faversham, Friday Sept. 20th, and inspected the powder factories etc. On Thursday the 26th I spent a day with General Dallas in manœuvres of immense interest in the Canterbury, Ashford, Stone Street, Waltham region. On Friday the 27th Bell and I spent a day at Lympne, inspecting aerodromes and learning a great deal about flying.

All this was, of course, in addition to innumerable diocesan engagements and interviews, meetings with the Archdeacons and Rural Deans, sermons in the Cathedral (to the troops as well as to the evening congregation) and at Margate. Certainly here was a crowded life such as few men could manage in their prime—and the Archbishop was now past seventy.

CHAPTER LVI

THE COMING OF PEACE

> Let it not disgrace me,
> If I demand, before this royal view,
> What rub or what impediment there is,
> Why that the naked, poor, and mangled Peace,
> Dear nurse of arts, plenties and joyful births,
> Should not in this best garden of the world,
> Our fertile France, put up her lovely visage?
> Alas! she hath from France too long been chased.
>
> SHAKESPEARE, *King Henry V*, v. 2.

ON Sunday, September 29, 1918, there were Services of Thanksgiving all over England—for the delivery of Palestine: and the Archbishop made this the theme of his own two sermons in Canterbury Cathedral. The following day saw the publication of a letter from his pen in *The Times*, on the League of Nations. It was written at the express suggestion of Lord Robert Cecil, prompted by President Wilson's speech reported in the press on September 28.

LORD ROBERT CECIL *to the* ARCHBISHOP OF CANTERBURY

Confidential. Foreign Office. 28 Sept. 1918.

I am venturing to send this note to you by the hands of Wolmer. President Wilson's speech last night is of the utmost importance as it seems to me. It lays down with vigour the true principles of peace and brings into proper perspective the League of Nations. You have probably noticed symptoms here of a cooling off in some important quarters of the feeling in favour of a League. That is inevitable. There are so many people who will never be really enthusiastic for it—the militarists, the bureaucrats and all the conservative forces who disapprove of change. As victory comes nearer, the conquerors will see less reason for it. It is therefore specially important that at this juncture the President should have spoken out so unmistakably, and should have directly challenged the opinion of the Allied Governments on his utterance. May I venture to say that it seems to me that this gives a special opportunity for the Church? If the President's words are allowed to fall flat and if in consequence this Government returns the ordinary kind of non-committal reply, a priceless opportunity will have been lost. Now is the time for a real lead from the Church. If your Grace could see your way to write a stirring letter to appear in *The Times*, and/or other papers on Monday morning, warmly endorsing the President's utterance, the effect would be very great. It might make all the difference to the official attitude.

Wolmer will be able to tell you more in detail what I have tried to say in this hasty scrawl.

The Archbishop's response was instantaneous:

The ARCHBISHOP OF CANTERBURY *to the* EDITOR *of 'The Times'*

Canterbury, 28th September, 1918.

With the straightness and force which we have learned to expect from him, President Wilson, in his speech of yesterday, describes the character and the vastness of the issues which are at stake. He appeals to the Governments of the Allied Nations to say plainly whether or no, in the plan now being shaped for a League of Nations, their vision and their purpose correspond with his. I can speak for no Government, but I am convinced that the mass of thoughtful Christian folk in England feel with an earnestness beyond words the force of his contention that for reasons not of policy but of principle, not of national interest but of righteousness and justice and enduring peace, we want a League of Nations on the very lines which he has drawn. Details there may be in his description which need elucidation or development, but his outline has our unhesitating support. We are not afraid of such items of self-surrender as may here and there be involved for this nation or that. The issues are world-wide. Our vision and our purpose must be world-wide too. Let Mr. Wilson rest assured of the vivid and eager response which his appeal awakens in the minds of tens of thousands of the Christian men and women upon whose will, in the long run, the effective decision must turn. The Churches in our land have spoken with no uncertain voice. The responsible vote of our Bishops, given eight months ago, was deliberate and unanimous. We not merely welcomed in the Name of the Prince of Peace the idea of such a League, but we desired that provision for it should be included in the conditions of settlement when it comes. Other Churches agreed or followed suit. We have not spoken lightly or without assurance of the width and warmth of the support on which we count. We give no mere lip-adherence to a great ideal. We mean that the thing shall come to pass.

The letter met with very wide approval and comment. And a few days later the Archbishop attended the meeting addressed by Lord Grey in the Central Hall, Westminster, on the League of Nations—and moved a vote of thanks to him. 'I think', notes the Archbishop, 'this committed the Church, so far as I by any means can, to the project, though I am painfully conscious of its somewhat general and even vague character.'

Peace was now coming in sight—but there were still some weeks before the end was quite decided. And much happened in between. A Conference of representatives of all four Houses of the two Convocations on the possibility of presenting an agreed reply to the Royal Letters of Business for Prayer Book Revision was held from October 8 to 15. At dinner on October 9, the Archbishop of York, who had come to the Conference, repeated a remarkable story about Professor Harnack which he had been told by President Hadley during his visit to America:

> Hadley and Delbrück (Harnack's brother-in-law) were great friends, and Hadley asked him one day if he might ask him a personal question about Harnack which Delbrück need not answer: 'How is it that Harnack is such a blind follower and flatterer of the Kaiser?' 'I can tell you that,' said Delbrück. 'Harnack believes there are two sources of Divine Revelation, one in the Bible, the Old Testament and the New Testament, of spiritual truths; the other through great men of action like the Kaiser, of political truths: the Kaiser to Harnack is divinely inspired, his words are true.' 'But he doesn't really believe that?' 'Yes, he does: and I'm going to tell you another thing. Two-thirds of me refuses to believe it, thinks it nonsense; but there's another third, the Prussian part, which thinks that after all it may be true!'

On October 12, the Archbishop dined as the guest of M. Paschitch, Prime Minister of Serbia, at Claridge's Hotel. It was a dinner to a group of Anglican clergy, in recognition of the help given by the Church of England to the Serbian Church during the War. At the end of dinner, to the Archbishop's infinite surprise, M. Paschitch rose by his side and publicly decorated the Archbishop with the sash and brooch of the 1st-class grade of the Serbian Order of St. Sava—all resplendent blue and white—on behalf of the King of Serbia. The rest of the guests were informed that they would be similarly decorated later on, with suitably lower grades, but might wear their rosettes at once!

On October 14, the King returned to London. The Archbishop notes:

On Monday last the King returned to London and I went to Buckingham Palace and there met Stamfordham, Lloyd George and Sir Henry Wilson. Wilson was furious with the American President[1], who had written his first letter of October 8, but not then his subsequent letter of October 14. He, Sir Henry Wilson, said: 'My cousin Woodrow (so he always calls the President) has simply bungled as a civilian would. He has mixed up armistice and peace. The making of an armistice is not his business at all, and he had no right to have alluded to it. It is a purely military matter. The making of ultimate peace is another question, which does belong to frock coats, not khaki tunics. But we in khaki mean to have a great deal to say before we leave the frock coats to go into council. We are not such fools as to fall into the trap into which Cousin Woodrow has nearly fallen, and telegrams have gone pretty stiffly from Versailles to Washington telling the President to hurry up with a second letter, getting himself out of the hole.' With all this, Lloyd George was in full agreement. What has exactly happened in these private circles since, I do not know, but I shall probably learn ere long.

On Tuesday I again saw Stamfordham at the House of Lords, and on Wednesday I dined at Grillions where we had abundant talk—Haldane, Sumner, Desart, Neville Lyttelton, Bryce, Sir G. Murray, with Selborne and Crewe in the background, though I had no talk with them. I have never known any occasion on which the front rank experts were so wildly contrary in expectation one with another as in this matter. Haldane thinks Germany is on the eve of collapse, and that fighting will be over in a week or two. He believes their home affairs to be in such a state as to make it impossible to have a coherent policy supported by public opinion. Some of the others, on the contrary, are convinced that Germany would resist to the last ditch the kind of humiliation which we should be obliged to impose as part of the terms of a peace, and that she must be much more soundly beaten before she will take the attitude rendering peace negotiations thinkable by us.

On October 16, the Archbishop attended the funeral of Sir Hubert Parry, the great composer, in St. Paul's Cathedral. There had been some hesitation on the part of the Dean and Chapter as to allowing him to be buried in the Cathedral, and

[1] On October 4, Germany addressed through Switzerland a Note to President Wilson inviting the opening of Peace negotiations and asking for the immediate conclusion of an armistice. On October 8, President Wilson replied to Germany requiring the Germans' retreat to their own territory before the question of an armistice could be considered.

the Archbishop's letter recommending it had decided in Parry's favour. The Archbishop told Canon Alexander that the immense congregation was itself a justification, not to mention the musical participation in the service of such eminent musicians as W. G. Alcock, Hugh Allen, Walford Davies, Walter Parratt, and H. G. Ley.

On Saturday, October 19, the Archbishop issued a message to the press, calling the whole nation to prayer for the nation's statesmen at this crisis. He also issued invitations to a large number of Church and Free Church leaders to a conference at Lambeth (duly held on October 29) to promote the Churches' co-operation on behalf of the League of Nations.

During the next few days we find Dr. Davidson preaching at Lambeth Parish Church, and at Sevenoaks (for the C.E.T.S.); discussing West Indies questions with Archbishop Parry; and consulting about the League of Nations and Germany, and the African colonies, with General Smuts. Two old friends passed away in Bishop Boyd Carpenter and Bishop Walsh of Dover, and the Archbishop ministered at their burial. He received a deputation of 'unredeemed Greeks'. He learned the latest news about T. E. Lawrence and the Arab situation:

> A man called Lawrence, an officer in the British Army, who has been living with the Arabs, an extremely intelligent man, has been with Bigge about it, and also with the Government. He thinks that we shall produce quite disastrous results if we do not cancel the French agreement and adhere to what we promised the Arabs.

Preparations were also on hand for the peace demonstrations —whenever they should be due. The two Archbishops also prepared an Address to the newly enfranchised Electors, to be issued simultaneously with the announcement of the Dissolution.

On November 6, the Archbishop visited Bristol and spoke to a great meeting of men under the Chairmanship of a Labour Lord Mayor (Sheppard). On November 7, he dined with the Asquiths—one of those mixed dinners, he said, where husbands are invited without their wives, and wives without their husbands. He fell a victim to lumbago on November 8—when he offered nevertheless to preach in the Abbey on Sunday, November 10; and thanks to massage by a sister from St. Thomas's, got steady relief. The rest must be told in the Archbishop's own words:

> The next day, Saturday, I was able to attend the British Museum

meeting in the morning, when we began the plans for bringing back from underground the buried treasures, and settled also some other questions. I drove Fisher back with me from the Museum, making a circuit to avoid the Lord Mayor's procession. At night, I attended the great Guildhall Banquet, driven thither by Bigge in a royal carriage. It was a memorable scene, and I was glad to have been there, though the proceedings were of interminable length. I thought the Prime Minister's speech excellent, and the reception which greeted him was without parallel in my experience. As he came up the Hall, and the whole company stood on chairs and shouted and waved, I was standing by Arthur Balfour, near the Lord Mayor, and I remarked with amusement on this demonstration to a man who, ten years before, was regarded in the City as unutterable, and Balfour's reply in the din was shouted into my ear, 'Well, the little beggar deserves it all'. As to the speech, he was, I thought, quite justified in scoring heavily against his opponents in reference to side-shows, and 'knock-out blow'—the two things for which he was always criticised. Where were the critics now? The speech exists on record, so I need not try to summarise it. The whole scene in the Banquet-Hall was extraordinary. There was a sense of elation and enthusiasm which burst out into shouts at some points in the speech, and was buoyant all through. Lloyd George announced the abdication of the Kaiser, which some of the audience had heard an hour or two before, but some had not, and there were shouts of joy. Cambon also spoke well. Arthur Balfour had plenty to say, but was as usual unprepared and very ineffective. Geddes had too much to say, but said it well; some of the others were most needlessly lengthy, and we did not rise from table till past 11.[1]

Sunday November 10th. The morning I spent in bed, working at my sermon for the Abbey in the evening, which, thanks to Mary in the morning, and Clements in the afternoon, was admirably ready in time, and was sent also to the press. The scene in the Abbey was to me intensely moving. The analogy was striking between my sermon on the Sunday before the declaration of war, and this Sunday before the peace armistice. It had been half

[1] On returning home that night, the Archbishop remarked that Lloyd George had told him that the signing of the Armistice was constantly expected—though the German envoy had been delayed en route for Spa, owing to the German barrage. Lloyd George told the Archbishop that the difficulty was due to the fact that the Germans were flying so fast that the envoy could not catch them up. The Archbishop said, 'You are not going to say that in your speech?' 'Do you think not?' 'Most certainly, keep a high tone.' 'You are right.' The Archbishop said he saved him from that error of taste.

hoped that the signing of the armistice might have taken place, but it had not. We supped with the Ryles; the Archbishop of York was with us.

On the next morning, the armistice was signed. Bigge telephoned to me soon after nine, and the public knew it by about ten-thirty or earlier. Maroons were exploded in the air, and London was in hubbub within half an hour. St. Paul's and the Abbey were crowded with people almost immediately, and a series of services were held throughout the day, and in some places far into the night. St. Martin's in the Fields was crowded at 11.30 p.m., services having been held on and off for about 12 hours. We had a service in Chapel at one, and in the evening I preached in the Parish Church to a congregation of Lambeth people, who were not merely attentive, but visibly moved. The attendance was remarkable.

But before that service, we had an eventful afternoon. I went to the House of Commons and heard Lloyd George announce the signing of the Armistice and recount the terms it contained. After reading them, he moved that the House should adjourn to St. Margaret's to pray. This Asquith seconded, and they went forth. They were joined on the way by the House of Lords walking in procession with the Lord Chancellor. I myself went across before them, and robed in St. Margaret's, and took part in the service—simple, solemn, and intensely moving. To say it was managed well, is not at all the right way to put it. It managed itself because everybody was in earnest, and to tell the truth the least effective part of it was * * *'s reading of the prayers and thanksgiving. I do not suppose there has ever been in our history a more significant recognition of the Divine Presence and aid than in this sudden attendance of the Houses at Divine Service in lieu of a Commons debate. The House of Lords presented a curious and, some would say, a characteristic spectacle. Curzon was absent in Belgium with the King and Queen of the Belgians, and his place was taken by Crawford who read the Armistice terms with exceeding dullness and with difficulty from a badly written typed paper, which turned out afterwards to be an uncorrected draft, and not the paper which he ought to have read. After this most ineffective performance, not a word was spoken by anybody, but the House proceeded to some prosaic business, including a Tithe Bill, and a Teachers' Superannuation Bill, on both of which I had to speak—the debates being of the dullest and most prosaic, carried on by a mere handful of peers. For good or for ill, the House of Lords is a queer place!'

CHAPTER LVII

THE ARCHBISHOP AND GERMAN CHURCHMEN

They stood aloof, the scars remaining,
Like cliffs which had been rent asunder;
A dreary sea now flows between;
But neither heat, nor frost, nor thunder
Shall wholly do away, I ween,
The marks of that which once hath been.

COLERIDGE, *Christabel.*

WE have already seen how, on the very eve of the War, Dr. Davidson was in correspondence with Dr. Ernst Dryander about the great Lutheran celebrations proposed for 1917.[1] We also observed the action which he took in reply to the Appeal of the Evangelical Churches in Germany to their Brethren abroad on the issues of the War. The severance of his relations with German Churchmen was no ordinary sorrow to the Archbishop. He had striven for friendship and mutual understanding, and he felt the ruin of his efforts and hopes most keenly. In war time, the severance was inevitably almost complete: but throughout the four long years he both maintained the hope of renewing his friendship and did what he could to keep alive the spirit of charity. Moreover, certain written communications, additional to those mentioned above, passed from Archbishop Davidson in England to Professor Adolf Deissmann in Germany, which are of high importance: and certain action was taken by the Archbishop (with Mr. J. H. Oldham and others) in relation to German Missions, which no just account of the attitude of the leaders of the Churches in war time could omit.

I

Direct communication of a personal character, it goes without saying, was impossible. Nevertheless, the Archbishop, from quite early days in the War, was able to learn, through American friends who had missionary or philanthropic errands both in England and Germany, something of the attitude of individual German Church people, as well as of the general atmosphere of the nation. His principal informants were Dr. John R. Mott,

[1] See p. 731.

without a doubt the most distinguished missionary statesman in the English-speaking world; and Dr. Battin, a Professor of German in an American University who was spending a year's holiday in Europe when the War broke out. Dr. Mott, after a long evening at Lambeth, took the following letter with him, from England to Berlin for a Missionary Conference in October:

The Archbishop of Canterbury *to* Dr. J. R. Mott

13th October, 1914.

Your visit yesterday was a great gain and solace to me. God grant you guidance, strength, judgement, and quietness of soul in your busy days in Europe at this time. In case you may be able to use the German version of the paper I gave you yesterday, some copies of that translation are being posted to you to-day. Of course in the present confusion of boats and mails you may never receive such letters or packets.

You will judge for yourself how far it is well that, in your conversations with German friends, you should make reference to myself or to what I have said to you. It is possible that in the present strain, and while the spirit which has found voice in Germany is prevalent, any reference to myself might be harmful to the cause of 'quiet understanding', rather than helpful. But if you feel otherwise and care, in conversation with my honoured friend, Dr. Spiecker, or others, to make reference to myself, pray let it be made clear to them that I, for my part, am resolved not to let these terrible international strifes impair a friendship and a community of thought and prayer which I have valued beyond words. That our German brothers and friends in the Faith of our Lord Jesus Christ desire simply to be loyal to the cause of Our Master and of truth, I do not doubt for an hour. The incomprehensible thing to me is how it can come about that our views of plain historic facts and of prevalent teaching can differ so widely. I literally have no notion at all, for example, of how Dr. Spiecker interprets Treitschke and his teaching.

But I retain, through thick and thin, my belief in the honesty of those German friends, and my trust that they will join their prayers with ours, that Our Father may find for us a way out of all this fearful strife, and bring us outwardly as well as inwardly to the peace which passeth understanding.

And on Dr. Mott's return to England, the Archbishop wrote again to Dr. Dryander, who had told Dr. Mott that he had not received the Archbishop's reply to his letter of July.[1] He sent

[1] *Supra*, p. 732.

him a copy of that reply through the American Ambassador, Mr. Walter Page. The Archbishop wrote:

The ARCHBISHOP OF CANTERBURY *to* DR. DRYANDER

27th October, 1914.

. . . It would at all times be to me a matter of extreme regret were I to seem to treat discourteously or carelessly any communication from you. But above all should I feel this at a time like the present. It is my earnest hope and prayer that, notwithstanding differences and misunderstandings which are inevitably keeping us apart, or interfering with our usual freedom of communication and friendship, we shall allow nothing to interrupt the Christian fellowship of thought and hope and prayer which ought to be holding us together in spite of every difficulty. I am certain that you join your prayers with ours that it may please God to again make possible before long the relation of friendly brotherhood between Germany and England, which you and I, together with so many friends in both countries, have for years been earnestly striving to foster and maintain. If there are misunderstandings which I can help to remove, I shall be profoundly grateful if you will communicate with me on the subject, supposing that you can find means of doing so. . . .

During his visit, Dr. Mott saw Harnack, Spiecker, Siegmund-Schultze, and many others—reporting his experiences to Dr. Davidson on November 10, before going back to America. Dr. Battin, whom the Archbishop first saw at the end of 1914, was less intimate with religious leaders, and had a somewhat unusual access to politicians; but nevertheless made the acquaintance of certain Churchmen. At the end of 1916, he not only showed the Archbishop the whole series of Dr. Deissmann's printed Letters to American Protestants for the year, but brought from Harnack (hitherto the most bitter of anti-English spokesmen) 'courteous messages of friendship' to the Archbishop.

II

The first direct written communication from a German Churchman to Lambeth came from Dr. Adolf Deissmann in 1915:

DR. ADOLF DEISSMANN *to the* ARCHBISHOP OF CANTERBURY

Berlin-Wilmersdorf, Prinzregentenstr. 6. 26 April, 1915.

I have the honour to communicate most humbly the following information to Your Grace. I have learnt that a pamphlet is being prepared on the fortunes of the German Evangelical Mission of 1914 in the Cameroons. In this pamphlet will be communicated, based on the testimony of witnesses, the methods practised by organs of the British government against German missionaries. Now from the personal knowledge of your Christian character which I have gained from frequent meetings and also from having been your guest at Lambeth in 1912, I have a confidence in Your Grace's unqualified *bona fides* and *bona voluntas* which remains undestroyed even in the present situation. I am, therefore, convinced that Your Grace, when you have been satisfied of the actuality of these incidents, will not approve them, but on the contrary will now and subsequently do everything to remedy them so far as possible. Although those concerned with publication of the work in Germany consider its appearance to be absolutely necessary, it seems to me desirable that Your Grace should not learn first of the work (*perhaps in a garbled form*) through discussion of it in the Press, but should be in possession of the documents even before publication. It will perhaps then be the more possible for Your Grace to do something to ensure that incidents of the kind are not repeated.

I have accordingly asked the Editor, Pastor W. Stark, to let me have, before printing, a copy of the final proof which I transmit herewith to Your Grace.

I gladly take the opportunity of thanking Your Grace most heartily for the successful efforts to mitigate the lot of the German prisoners in Great Britain. The care of prisoners is a common meeting ground, even in the present situation, for Christians of all countries, following in the steps of their common Master, Jesus Christ.

Accompanying the letter, was a pamphlet by a German, Pastor Stark, containing allegations of the ill-treatment of German missionaries in the Cameroons by British soldiers and native troops under British officials, on the surrender of Duala, the capital of the German Protectorate, September 27, 1914. The charges were curiously varied: that a price was set upon the head of every German, and the natives incited to murder; that a reward was given for severed hands; that they were robbed, starved, deprived of clean water, made to stand out in a blazing sun, insulted, maltreated, made to carry their own luggage, and so on. But the main grounds of complaint were that they were not allowed to take all their personal belongings away with them into captivity, that they were put under guard by native soldiers, and that they were in great discomfort on board the ships which brought them to England. In particular, two white women were said to have died through lack of proper care and treatment. The Archbishop immediately communicated with the Colonial Office and other Government authorities. The charges were already known, and had been investigated. The evidence which he saw completely satisfied the Archbishop that they were unfounded. Later, in November 1915, both the accusations and the answers were published as a Blue Book.[1] The Archbishop, however, did not reply at once. And in September he received from Dr. Deissmann a bundle of typewritten copies of a series of Weekly Letters which he had circulated among American Protestants, and which dealt with the religious attitude of Germany in connexion with the War. The Archbishop regarded this action of his as constituting 'virtually a sort of challenge to me to send some comment'. He at once drafted an answer to Dr. Deissmann, which should also be an answer to his earlier letter about the alleged cruelties in the Cameroons. This letter was dispatched by the Foreign Office to Berlin via the Consul-General at Rotterdam:

The ARCHBISHOP OF CANTERBURY *to* DR. ADOLF DEISSMANN

Lambeth Palace, S.E. 22nd September, 1915.

You may sometimes have wondered why I have not written in reply to a letter about the Kamaroons which I received from you in May, or, again, in reply to your kindness in sending to me last month by the hands of a friend a typewritten copy of your series of weekly letters (Dec. 6 to June 26) addressed to Protestant friends in the United States.

Assuredly my silence has not been due to any unreadiness on my part to welcome and reciprocate your kindly words of Christian confidence with regard to myself personally. I thank God for the assurance which, among all this confusion, I hold without wavering, that behind and below the appalling international strife there still endures among men of goodwill in Germany and in England a bond of fellowship—strained but not severed—a bond which finds its meaning in the loyalty which we unite in cherishing towards the Divine Lord and Saviour whom you and I alike adore. God speed the return of days when we may again be able to strive unitedly to give effect to the words of brotherly fellowship which have been spoken in successive years by the German and the

[1] *Correspondence relative to the alleged ill-treatment of German subjects captured in the Cameroons*, 1915, Cd. 7974.

English representatives in the memorable gatherings of the Associated Councils of the Churches of the British and German Empires for fostering friendly relations between the two peoples.

But, my dear Doctor Deissmann, it would be vain to deny that the path towards the active renewal of that Christian fellowship is at present so darkened and broken as to be almost impassable. If we seek, as I have honestly sought, to believe that the words of hatred towards the English people which ring through Germany are the voice only of a limited military group of men over-mastered by war fever, we find ourselves confronted everywhere by the assurance that it is the German people as a whole who wish us to hear their sentiments expressed in the 'Hymn of Hate' and in the malediction which is being deliberately taught even to little children in the homes and schools of Germany. Personally I still desire to disbelieve this, and to retain my ancient confidence in the Christian spirit and goodwill of the mass of intelligent and religiously minded German citizens: but I seek in vain for any assurance on the part of German friends that my hope is justified. With the single exception of the sermon by Pastor F. Lahusen, a copy of which you have kindly sent to me, everything which I see and read points lamentably the other way. It is for this reason that in sheer sorrow of heart I have (like the author of Psalm xxxix) 'kept silence even from good words', lest I should do more harm than good.

With regard to the pamphlet on the Kamaroons, written by Pastor W. Stark, which formed the subject of your letter of April 26, I have made all the enquiry in my power, and from the very full official papers and reports which I have before me it appears that the allegations of ill-treatment of a grave sort can be definitely shown to be untrue, and that the minor accusations of what is described as rough and inconsiderate treatment relate either to the inevitable discomforts of a rather crowded steamer or to rudeness on the part of native Africans at a moment of great excitement and confusion when it is presumably difficult for European officers, whether German or English, to secure the decorum and courtesy which are desirable. I have seen within the last few days accounts from the same region of an incident of much graver character, including the expression of regret by a German officer in the Kamaroons that he had been unable to prevent his men from entering a hospital and shooting some of the patients in their beds. I can hardly doubt that there must be exaggeration or misstatement, but the possibility of such a story being current shows the difficulties of the situation where, in an uncivilised country, native troops are concerned.

I turn to the European picture. In face of all the incidents of this ghastly war, and in face of one's feeling of personal helplessness, I should find it, as I have said, much easier and less painful to say nothing. During the last few weeks however I have been seriously ill, and have perforce had much time for quiet thought, and it seems to me on the whole that the genuine respect which I feel for yourself, as a Christian teacher and friend, to whose words, spoken and written, I owe much, justifies or even requires me to tell you simply and with fraternal openness how the situation now presents itself to my view. Though I dare not hope to secure your full agreement, you will, I confidently believe, pardon and even welcome my openness of speech. You have indeed by sending me your American letters invited me to tell you what is the impression they leave upon my mind.

Let me say then that the first impression left is one of sheer bewilderment as to how I am to reconcile what you write about the origin of the war with my knowledge of your well established usage in the handling of documents and in the compilation of evidence therefrom. You have been accustomed to treat documents sacred or secular with fearless frankness, taking obvious care not to keep back evidence of importance. We may agree or disagree with your conclusions, but we have recognised the value of your method. Hence our bewildered surprise in finding that when you put before your American readers, as in letter 26 (May 29, 1915), a summary statement on the matter, to the effect that Germany throughout strove for peace and England insisted upon war, you ignore the existence of the chief documents which have led reasonable and impartial men to a conclusion opposite to your own. I cannot of course in this letter handle the complicated details of that controversy, but I know that my surprise with regard to your own statement is felt also by others of your friends. The mere fact of England's unpreparedness for war seems to us to prove incontestably what we know, by other evidence, to be true. I must not expect you, however, to share my convictions. Nor will you perhaps attach importance to my statement that my intimate personal knowledge of the English statesmen on whom chief responsibility rested enables me to speak with absolute assurance as to their wholehearted and unwavering efforts during that momentous week and in all that had preceded it, to avert from Europe the unspeakable calamity of this war.

In the next place I am even more perplexed at finding in your long series of papers no reference to the terrible evidence which has now been formally produced and marshalled relating to the conduct of the German soldiery in Belgium and in France during the earlier months of the war. We have to deal in that matter not with unsifted accusations or hearsay reports emanating from anonymous or unknown sources. The statements made have been investigated with scrupulous care by seven public men of the highest possible authority, experienced in the sifting of evidence, biassed, if they were biassed at all, against giving credence to stories of outrage and wrong, and incapable, as the whole world knows, of deviating in the least degree from the fairness of balanced and well-considered statement. This weighty committee, under the chairmanship of Lord Bryce, whose name has for many years been almost as well known and honoured in Germany as in America and England, presented a unanimous Report, based wholly upon first-hand evidence, including, and I lay special stress upon this, the autograph diaries of German officers and the officially published proclamations of German Generals. The facts authoritatively brought to light in the Report are of so terrible a character and affect so gravely the reputation of the responsible officers of the German Army that I find it simply impossible to understand the absence of any reference to them in the long series of your letters. The Report may be said to defy criticism as to the truth of what it sets forth, and the terrible deeds it recounts must, I am quite certain, be as detestable to you as they are to English readers. Their gravity as an element in men's appreciation of the whole story of the war is surely indisputable. How then are we to understand your silence respecting them? I simply do not know.

The same difficulty confronts me with regard to such acts as the deliberate sinking of the Lusitania with its hapless population of non-combatants, largely women and little children. I am not referring to the crime itself but to the silent condonation or apparent approval of it by the spokesmen of a Christian people. Once more, how to explain it I simply do not know.

I have written to you, my dear Doctor Deissmann, without reserve, because I understand you, by sending me your series of letters, to invite my frank remarks upon them. If my letter reaches you, and if you deem it right to send me any reply, I need hardly assure you with what respect and attention I shall read anything that you say. For I should like to end, as I began, with an expression of my unshaken belief in the *bona voluntas* of friends like yourself, and of my earnest hope and prayer for the return of happier days when the fraternal Christian intercourse, which has meant so much to the great central group of Christian thinkers and teachers in Germany and England may again prevail among us, for the good of both our peoples and for the furtherance of the Kingdom of Our Lord among men.

The Archbishop's original intention was to give sufficient time for a reply to reach him from Dr. Deissmann, and then to publish the letter. One or two friends who had seen the letter were very anxious that it should be sent to the Press. But the Archbishop was determined not to publish until he heard for certain that the letter had reached Dr. Deissmann. On November 24, the Archbishop was ready to publish, but was not quite sure of the form of publication. There was a little delay owing to the Archbishop's absence from London. And on November 30, the Archbishop received a letter, dated November 11, from Dr. Siegmund-Schultze in Berlin, telling him that Dr. Deissmann had received his letter a few days before and was replying to it. He also received a message from Dr. Siegmund-Schultze through Mr. W. H. Dickinson to say that Dr. Deissmann had replied to it. He therefore decided to wait until the reply came before publishing his letter. But Dr. Deissmann's reply was never sent; and instead he only referred to the Archbishop's letter in one or two of his Weekly Letters to American Protestants. So the Archbishop's Letter was never published in the English Press. Dr. Deissmann's own reference to the letter is, however, worthy of reproduction:

Letter 83. Berlin, June 21, 1916.

Among these men of good will I count the Archbishop of Canterbury. I am in possession of a long letter from him as answer to mine, to which I already referred in 'Letter' No. 49 (November 6, 1915). In it he dwells at length and in detail upon the war, its causes, and present methods. His point of view is widely variant from mine, and I believe, because England is almost hermetically sealed against any reports from Germany, during the war a really fruitful discussion is practically impossible. For the time being, at least, I have given up my first intention of answering at full length, but regard the letter of the Archbishop as a sign that, as soon as God grants us the possibility of an open discussion with English Christians, the noble Christian spirit of the Archbishop will be a guarantee for the helpfulness of such a discussion.

III

Two great centres of German missionary work lay in India and Africa—on the east coast as well as on the west. Each centre, as the War went on, had to be closed: and there is no doubt that the German Church leaders in Berlin felt the suppression of the work, as well as the internment of their own missionaries as aliens, very keenly. The Archbishop was, naturally, chiefly concerned with this problem as it affected Anglican missions or dioceses; but he was also kept in close and constant touch with the whole international mission problem, both by the Anglican societies, and especially by Mr. J. H. Oldham, the secretary of the Conference of Missionary Societies in Great Britain and Ireland. It is impossible to chronicle the whole of the work which he did in this field. But we may illustrate his interest and influence by taking two examples, the first concerning the actual closing during the War of a particular German mission in India, the second his treatment of the highly perilous question of the future status of ex-enemy missionary work after the War. On July 2, 1915, the Society for the Propagation of the Gospel received a telegram from the Bishop of Chota Nagpur (Dr. Foss Westcott) containing these words:

> Germans interned. How many men can you possibly send, and when?

A letter warning the S.P.G. of such a possibility had explained that the Germans of the important and prosperous Gossner Mission in Chota Nagpur would be placed in a concentration camp till the end of the War. The Archbishop was at once informed by Bishop Montgomery, Secretary of the S.P.G., and in July received a full account of the whole situation from the Metropolitan of India (Dr. Lefroy), enclosing correspondence with the Bishop of Chota Nagpur (Dr. Westcott). The Metropolitan said:

The BISHOP OF CALCUTTA *to the* ARCHBISHOP OF CANTERBURY

23 June, 1915.

> The accompanying correspondence deals with so grave a matter that I believe you will feel that I am justified in troubling you upon it. . . . It seems to me that it will be disastrous if the Government attempt just at this time, when feeling is running so very high, to settle the supremely difficult question of what our relations to Germans in general, and German missionaries in particular, are to be after the war. At the same time, I need scarcely say that great pressure is being brought to bear upon them to do this very thing, and, if the information which has reached Bishop Westcott is correct, there seems too much reason to fear that they are giving in to the outcry. The matter is, however, of course one

> which must be dealt with by the Government at home, and I am sending you the papers in the hope that you may find it possible to bring influence to bear in some form.

It was a large and difficult problem, for in that district alone—an area as big as England—there were over 300 German schools, and some 400 teachers in them, besides 42 German Pastors and nearly 500 Catechists. It involved the temporary oversight of nearly 100,000 Indian Christians who were not in communion with the Church of England. The Archbishop wrote back to the Metropolitan:

The ARCHBISHOP OF CANTERBURY *to the* BISHOP OF CALCUTTA

16 July, 1915.

> I need hardly tell you with what intense interest I have been considering the strangely difficult question which has arisen about the action which we ought to take in consequence of the interning of the German Missionaries. I do not think I have ever known a more perplexing condition of things. It has its wholesome side as showing the critics at home—young Curates and others—that it is not so easy as they think to lay down universally applicable rules off-hand as regards our relation to non-Anglicans. But it is surrounded with perplexities, and I am glad it is in such wise hands as those of yourself and Foss Westcott. I have had some talk with Montgomery about it, but he rightly shrinks, as representing the Society, from saying more than that the Society ought to aid the Bishops with men and money in what they desire to do. I do not think anything would at this moment be gained by my own intervention, and probably I shall hear further from you, or from Bishop Westcott, before long. You may rely upon my using any influence that I can in the whole matter. Sir Arthur Hirtzel will obviously be a very helpful counsellor. At present I am not clear as to what is Bishop Westcott's plan, even supposing he had the men and the money.
>
> Meantime, I wish you were able to give a better account of your own health. I should like to hear of you as being really robust again. God be with you day by day.

Bishop Westcott, with the help of the Metropolitan, took the matter in hand at once, and made wise and statesmanlike arrangements for dealing with the situation. He had always been on the most friendly terms with the German Mission and Pastors, and there was now no friction. On the contrary, he received the warm thanks of the interned Missionaries for the delicate and sympathetic manner in which he faced the crisis. With what help he could obtain from England, and from other dioceses in India, he took over the administration of the Mission. But it was made quite clear that there was to be no attempt whatever to proselytize or to influence in any way the religious convictions of these Lutheran Christians. The Anglican administrators would take no Service, nor would they give religious instruction in the schools. All such matters would be left to the Indian pastors, catechists, and school teachers. Behind them, in all their duties and responsibilities, would stand certain Anglican clergy for the purpose of administration. The workers of all kinds would have to be paid, and all accounts accurately kept. Further, Indian pastors and workers would have to be supported in their duties of discipline and control, and buildings kept in repair. If the pastors and other workers needed advice, the Anglican superintendents would be at hand sympathetically to advise them, and would do so in full accordance with the regulations and principles of the Mission.

The Archbishop warmly commended the steps that were taken, and wrote to the Bishop of Chota Nagpur on September 4:

The ARCHBISHOP OF CANTERBURY *to the* BISHOP OF CHOTA NAGPUR

4 September, 1915.

Your letter of August 13 gives me just the information I wanted, and I thank GOD for all the wisdom, courage and judgment which has been shown by you and by the Metropolitan in dealing with this large, anxious and possibly complex problem. I am certain that what has been done is absolutely right and we shall have guidance given us for what is needed as the time runs on.

I have been seriously ill, and this is one of the earliest letters I have dictated. May GOD bless and help you in all these complexities.

In November, a fresh complication was added, when the Archbishop received a letter, dated November 12, from Archbishop Söderblom of Upsala, in which he said:

The ARCHBISHOP OF UPSALA *to the* ARCHBISHOP OF CANTERBURY

12 November, 1915.

. . . The mutual position, in which the present war has placed the greater nations of Europe, has unfortunately had a disastrous effect also on the international work for spreading the Gospel to non-Christian peoples, which has in our days gained a more vigorous development than ever. Mission work within the Colonies of the powers at war, has of course been most deeply and heavily affected. The undoubted desire and the efforts of their respective Governments to keep Missions outside the strife of nations, have from political reasons not sufficed to protect the Mission work from serious derangements.

Thus the German Missionaries, who work in British India, have, especially during the last months, been placed in a more and more difficult position, and the whole of their work will apparently have to be given up, unless it can be taken over by Missionary organisations belonging to England, her allies, or some neutral nation.

The so called Basel Missionary Society, whose German Missionaries were all interned during the earliest stage of the war, has already had recourse to this latter expedient. This mission, which has been carried on by Germans and Swiss jointly, has with the consent of the Government been committed to its Swiss elements, who have altogether undertaken the work.

The Mission in South India, carried on by German and Russian subjects, with which the Church of Sweden Mission has for decenniums worked together, has appealed to the said Mission to undertake the direction and management of its Mission field among the Tamil people, at the same time becoming the possessors of their property. This step has been taken in consequence of the decision of Government to withdraw its grants to their schools, and of its proclamation that all German Missionaries liable to military service should shortly be interned, while those of advanced age, and also women and children, should be sent home.

The Committee of the Church of Sweden Mission feel their responsibility no less strongly than do their workers out in the field—who have declared themselves willing, in addition to their previous duties, to take upon them this enormous burden of work—to rescue if possible, from deep injury, nay perhaps destruction, this venerable Evangelical Mission, which has for two centuries been of the greatest importance to the natives of South India. After earnest consideration the Committee made an agreement with the Kollegium of Leipzig to the effect that the Church of Sweden Mission should, from the time of the impending internment, take the direction and management of the whole Evangelical Lutheran Mission in India, with all its stations, congregations, schools and other places of instruction, and with full proprietary rights to all the property of the Mission, both real and movable.

An essential condition to such an agreement is, of course, the

Consent of the British Government in India. An application to that effect has, however, not yet led to any official reply. Not until such sanction be given, can the agreement come into force, and the Committee have carefully pointed out to those in charge in India the importance of acting with perfect openness and loyalty to the Authorities of the country. . . .

The Archbishop, in acknowledging this letter (Nov. 22, 1915) assured the Archbishop of Upsala that 'you may rely upon my anxiety to be helpful in every way that I rightly can', and promised to send him a fuller report as to what was being done in this 'most difficult' matter. Meanwhile, the Archbishop sent on Archbishop Söderblom's letter to Bishop Montgomery, with the request that he would prepare a Memorandum on the subject, and added: 'It is important on all grounds that we should keep in with Söderblom, who is a strong friend of England, though a neutral, and probably a friend also to Germany. It would be disastrous to push him on to the German side.' Accordingly Bishop Montgomery drafted a statement on the arrangements already made for German Missions in India which was sent to Archbishop Söderblom. The Archbishop also communicated with the India Office with regard to the specific point of the management of the Leipzig Mission in South India, and wrote as follows to Upsala:

The ARCHBISHOP OF CANTERBURY *to the* ARCHBISHOP OF UPSALA

Old Palace, Canterbury. 23 December, 1915.

. . . I have made enquiry with regard to the matter about which you write in your letter of Dec. 11th. So far as I can ascertain, the India Office in England has no information at all as to the facts mentioned in your Grace's letter, but I am quite sure that I may say without hesitation that the Government of Madras, to whom, as I understand, the German Mission has already addressed communication, will give all possible assistance in arriving at a workable arrangement consistent with the public interest. . . .

The Permanent Under-Secretary at the India Office, however, had added a note of warning in a letter written earlier in December on the general subject:

SIR ARTHUR HIRTZEL *to the* ARCHBISHOP OF CANTERBURY

It is quite true that the Bishop of Chota Nagpur undertook charge of the Gossner Mission in Chota Nagpur as a temporary measure

> for the duration of the war. But a good deal has happened since July, and you must now reckon with the possibility—amounting perhaps to a probability—that, after the war, German Missionaries will be permanently excluded from India. You may like to know of this possibility in order to be considering in good time the problem which will arise if it becomes a fact.

It is to this latter possibility, and the action taken by the Archbishop, in conjunction with J. H. Oldham and others, that we must now turn.

IV

The question of the future operations of German Missions in British territory was described by Dr. Davidson, in May 1919, as 'one of the most difficult questions of modern Christianity and International relations'. As soon as the first German missionary was interned as a war measure, it was bound to arise: and the best that could be hoped was that any permanent decision about a particular mission might be postponed till the War was over. At the same time, preliminary thinking had to be done, and all through 1917 the Archbishop was in close touch with the War and Missions Committee and the various Government departments. The point to be decided was not simple. On the one hand, there was the principle, repeatedly affirmed by British and German missionaries alike, of 'the supra-national character of Christian missions', due to the fact that they represent the first and highest allegiance of Christian men to the King of all the earth, in whom His disciples of every race are one. On the other hand, as citizens of particular countries, missionaries did in fact owe a particular political allegiance which, in time of war, with the best will in the world, they found exceedingly difficult to conceal; and, in the case therefore of missionaries of 'enemy nationality' it sometimes led, or was supposed to lead, to action which, in the interests of public safety, the Government was compelled to restrain. Before the War, freedom had been accorded to missions of all nationalities in every part of the British Empire. To deny that freedom after the War, would be likely to have very unfortunate effects. For example, the imposition of unnecessary restrictions on American missionaries would make a bad impression on public opinion in America, in face of the policy of the American Government as declared officially in various Treaties and Documents.[1] It might also be used as an argument for retaining, and even increasing, such restrictions by other Governments, like France, China, and Japan. The problem was an African problem, and an Indian problem—but Indian most of all. It was therefore in communication, in the main, with the India Office that the whole future policy of the Government had to be discussed and determined.

A conference was arranged between the missionary representatives and the representatives of the various Government departments, in which the Archbishop was to be the missionary societies' spokesman. Before attending it, Dr. Davidson took the precaution of writing to Mr. Balfour, the Foreign Secretary, to press upon him its great importance, and urging full attention by the Foreign Office to the issues involved—in view of 'the magnitude of the interests, religious, educational and civilizing which are affected'. It was also deemed best by the Archbishop that the non-Roman representatives of the non-Roman missions should meet the Joint Conference by themselves, as the relations of the Roman missions to the Vatican opened up a different set of considerations.

The conference took place on December 12, 1917, at the India Office. The proposals made on behalf of the Government, for discussion, were of a very drastic character. Briefly they involved (1) the exclusion from certain prescribed parts of the Empire of all 'enemy' organizations and individuals engaged in philanthropic, educational, or medical work; (2) the adoption of a system of licences, in certain prescribed parts of the Empire, for all foreigners engaged in such work; (3) in the event of (2) being considered invidious, the extension of the system of licences to British organizations as well. The severity of this plan was no doubt due in part to the peculiarly anxious situation at the Front, and the strained condition of public opinion. But the Archbishop had to point out, on behalf of the missionary repre-

[1] From a Statement made by the Solicitor for the Department of State at Washington to the Commission on Missions and Governments, World Missionary Conference, Edinburgh 1910: 'The policy of the United States is to regard the missionary as a citizen, and, in the absence of specific treaties granting exceptional rights and privileges, to extend to him the protection ordinarily granted to American citizens in foreign parts; to advance missionary enterprise in so far as it does not raise political questions and interfere with the orderly and constitutional development of the country in which the mission is located: to favour the mission in all proper ways . . . to secure for them the right to hold property.'

sentatives, that it was a plan likely to be viewed with great dissatisfaction. He appreciated the difficulty which the Government had to meet, but he pointed out the misapprehension inevitable both among civilized and uncivilized peoples (and not least in U.S.A.) if the British Government were to impose restrictions and disabilities on missionary, philanthropic, and educational agencies which were not to be imposed upon traders! He pleaded for a definite assertion of religious liberty in any official document dealing with this question; he said that the missionaries would help the government in working out a plan for securing loyalty on the part of the foreign missionary to the government of the country. He asked at the least for delay before any drastic or novel steps were taken: and he begged the Government to do nothing by their attitude to discourage the men and women who were giving their lives unreservedly for the bettering of the Empire and the world. 'We don't apologize for our missionary work, it is one of *your* greatest assets if you knew it.'

The representations of the Archbishop and the deputation (including Mr. Oldham) had considerable effect; and the final memorandum of Government policy embodied the following principles: (1) A declaration of welcome and appreciation of missionary work, irrespective of nationality; (2) the placing of no restrictions on American missionaries, the door being left open for similar treatment to be accorded later to missionaries of other nationalities; (3) an undertaking to use the national organizations of missionary societies in Great Britain, U.S.A., and India as intermediaries in all questions relating to the admission of missionary societies and agents of alien nationality for work in India and other parts of the Empire. Subsequently, by the terms of the Treaty of Versailles, the property of German missionary societies was transferred to boards of trustees composed of persons holding the faith of the mission whose property was involved; and the Allied and associated governments undertook to safeguard the interests of such missions. The effect of the action then taken is that all the German missions which have desired to do so have now returned to their old fields in the British Empire, excluding India, West Africa, East Africa, and Hong Kong, and have had restored to them in all cases the full use and, except in a few instances where the necessary legislation has still to be passed, the full ownership of their former property.

There were other particular problems relating to the work of German missionary societies in the British Empire with which Davidson had to deal. But the case of the future status of German missions generally after the War has been treated with some fullness as of special importance, and as an illustration of the way in which Archbishop Davidson's help was sought by the missionary societies, and his word carried weight with the Government authorities, where questions of high policy were raised.

V

While the War lasted, direct correspondence between the Archbishop and friends of old days in Germany was impossible. We have spoken already of certain letters exchanged on one or two occasions in the early part of the War. But between September 1915 and the Armistice, there was silence, only broken by a verbal message now and then borne by Dr. Battin or Dr. Mott on their travels. This did not mean that there was lack of thought, or of remembrance, or of hope for the re-knitting of the bonds that had been so cruelly broken: and we have seen how Davidson, throughout these years, did what he could to stem the spirit of vengeance and hatred at home. With the signing of the Armistice, new possibilities arose. And when an appeal, couched in urgent tones, reached him from his former correspondent, Dr. Deissmann, he was quick to reply.

It was in Upsala, the ancient University and Cathedral city in Sweden, that Dr. Deissmann first heard the news of the catastrophe which had overwhelmed alike Kaiser, Army, and people. The Archbishop of Upsala was his host—and Dr. Söderblom has more than once recalled the consternation and deep gloom with which the news was received. Dr. Deissmann returned to Berlin, and thence addressed a telegram to his host in Sweden, which he begged him to transmit to the Archbishop of Canterbury:

PROFESSOR ADOLF DEISSMANN *to the* ARCHBISHOP OF UPSALA

Berlin, Nov. 15, 1918.

Christian circles of all belligerent nations desire, after the agonies of the struggle, an age of mutual forgiveness and conciliation, in order to fight in unison against the terrible consequences of the war, and to serve the moral improvement of the nations and of mankind. The German people having declared its readiness to make extensive sacrifices, and to make good again (Wiedergutmachung)[1] sees, however, in the conditions of the truce now imposed a presage of a peace which would not mean reconciliation, but an aggravation of the misery.

After a four years' war of starvation, millions of the weakest and innocent would once more be endangered for incalculable time, and the deep bitterness thereof would prevent for generations the fulfilment of all ideals about Christian and human solidarity. But the state of mind among us has never been more favourable for a conciliation between the peoples than now. Armistice being concluded, a democratic[2] movement, pouring forth with elemental power, began to give political foundations to our country. The endeavours of this movement for social improvement and the strengthening of the spirit of fraternal solidarity among all fellow-citizens and between all nations find an answer to ardent collaboration in the hearts of innumerable German Christians. To disturb this hopeful situation, by ruthlessly exercising the idea of brute force, would mean an unpardonable sin against the new spirit passing through mankind, and in its noblest motive powers closely akin to the Gospel. Manifestations from earnest Christian leaders, especially in the Anglo-Saxon communities, above all the manifesto from the Federal Council of the Churches of Christ in America, in May, 1917, have proved that this spirit is also to be found amongst our antagonists.

Standing from the beginning of the war in the work for international Christian understanding, I now find it my duty at the end of the war to make an appeal to the Christian leaders, whom I know in the belligerent countries to use all their influence so that the approaching peace may not contain the seed of new universal catastrophes, but instead release all available conciliatory and rebuilding powers between the nations. I beg you to forward this telegram to the Archbishop of Canterbury and the Federal Council in America.

This telegram, sent from Berlin on November 15, reached Lambeth by way of Upsala on November 21. The Archbishop realized its importance at once, and discussed it fully with Lord Robert Cecil. The Archbishop would not accept Dr. Deissmann's presentation of the situation. He had never wavered in his view

[1] This was the English translation published at the time. But Dr. Deissmann has pointed out to the biographer that the correct translation for *Wiedergutmachung* is 'reparations'.

[2] The proper translation for *Volksbewegung* should be 'popular movement', but 'democratic movement' was that published at the time.

that Germany had committed a great crime in letting war loose on Europe: and he had condemned her actual conduct of the War. 'When once Peace terms have been decided upon and accepted by Germany', he wrote to a friend, 'the whole situation will in my opinion be changed. But until that time I cannot confabulate with Germany on mere terms of Christian amity.'

He accordingly wrote the following letter to the Archbishop of Upsala:

The ARCHBISHOP OF CANTERBURY *to the* ARCHBISHOP OF UPSALA

Lambeth Palace, S.E. 1. Nov. 25. 1918.

I have received your telegram embodying the full message which Professor Adolf Deissmann asks you to convey to me in relation to the approaching Conference about a Peace Settlement. It would not be easy to answer such a message by telegram, as I find myself under the necessity of explaining my position rather fully. I can do this better in the form of a letter, and, as Professor Deissmann invites you to be the intermediary, I hope that you may be able to communicate to him what I desire to say.

Professor Deissmann's statement as to the present situation is not one which I can accept as correct. He speaks of the European situation as though all that is needed, on the part of Christian circles in the belligerent nations, were 'mutual forgiveness and conciliation in order to fight in unison against the terrible consequences of the war and to serve the moral improvement of the nations and of mankind'. This form of statement ignores, as it seems to me, both the historic origin of the war and the manner in which Germany has conducted it. I called attention to those essential matters in a long letter which I wrote to Professor Deissmann on September 22, 1915. To that letter he sent no reply except a verbal acknowledgment. We in England did not choose this war. On the contrary, every possible endeavour to prevent it was made by our statesmen up to the very latest moment. Upon that subject no fair-minded or impartial man can entertain any doubt. We were forced into the war, though unprepared for it, because a grave wrong had been done, which cut at the very root of international honour and of faith to plighted word, and ran counter to the principles which must regulate the conduct of Christian nations. Our object was the vindication of freedom and justice, and the ultimate securing of a righteous peace, which should make war with all its horrors impossible of recurrence.

We have fought without hatred, and, so far as possible, without passion; and now that victory crowns the cause for which we fought, we desire to be equally free from hatred and passion in the course which we follow as victors. But we cannot forget the terrible crime wrought against humanity and civilization when this stupendous war, with its irreparable agony and cruelty, was let loose in Europe. Nor can we possibly ignore the savagery which the German High Command has displayed in carrying on the war. The outrages in Belgium in the early months, and indeed ever since; the character of the devastation wrought in France, including the inhuman deportation of innocent citizens; the submarine warfare against passenger ships like the Lusitania and the rejoicings which ensued in Germany; the unspeakable cruelties exercised on defenceless prisoners down to the very end, including even the last few weeks; all these things compel the authorities of the Allied Powers to take security against the repetition of such a crime. The position would be different had there been on the part of Christian circles in Germany any public protest against these gross wrongs, or any repudiation of their perpetrators.

The conditions of the armistice offer the best preliminary guarantees against a renewal of hostilities and a consequent postponement of peace. There is, I firmly believe, no spirit of mere bitterness or vindictiveness in the hearts of those who are imposing these conditions. The peace we hope to achieve must be a peace, not of hate or revenge, the fruits of which might be further and even more terrible strife. We wish by every means to avert that possibility. But righteousness must be vindicated, even although the vindication involves sternness. And the making good (Wiedergutmachung), to which Professor Deissmann refers, must be genuine, and, so far as is possible, complete. There is, however, as I need hardly say, no wish on the part of the Allied nations to crush or destroy the peoples of Germany. Evidence to the contrary is happily abundant. I thankfully repeat to Professor Deissmann what I wrote to him in September, 1915, my firm assurance that, in spite even of the horrors of this world war, we recognize the sacred ties which bind together in ultimate unity the children of Our Father who is in Heaven, the deep and enduring ties of Christian fellowship. That fellowship may be broken or impaired, but it cannot perish, and it is my hope and prayer, that when the right and necessary reparation has been made, we may be enabled once more to lay hold of that fellowship, and to make it mutually operative anew. It is in proportion as that Christian fellowship is sincerely maintained among the Christian people of all lands that the sorrows of the world can be healed, and true peace and good will established unbreakably among men. To that sacred end you are yourself, my dear Archbishop and brother, labouring, and I therein join you with my whole heart. Pray let Professor Deissmann be assured that that is not only my hope and prayer, but that it will be the ultimate object of my untiring effort.

The Archbishop's letter was a bitter disappointment to Dr. Deissmann. It was a moment when an added word of kindness might have done inestimable good. He did not reply direct, but in the Evangelical Weekly Letter dated December 20, 1918, he dealt fully with the points which it contained. While expressing his conviction of the Archbishop's bona fides Professor Deissmann was equally sure that the information on which his Grace relied was fragmentary and defective. He demurred to the Archbishop's account both of the origin and of the conduct of the War by Germany; he spoke of the credulity of the public in wartime and also of a table of parallel atrocities for which the Allies were responsible 'not less frightful' than those attributed to German arms. But the principal point which he made concerned the blockade, begun in the autumn of 1914 and, at the very moment of the Armistice in November 1918, made more stringent. 'Everything is thrown into the shade by the great action of England beginning in the autumn of 1914, which was the real cause of the German submarine warfare, because, under the innocent name of blockade it has been a war of extermination against the German civil population, especially against the weak, the women, the children and the old people. On this point I miss so far any explanation by the Archbishop.' And then by way of preface to some pages of statistics dealing with the increase of mortality and sickness which it caused, Dr. Deissmann uses these mordant words to describe 'the most brutal and inhuman way of annihilating innocent people':

> One thing must be admitted. The blockade does not look as brutal as it is. It has a certain appearance of '*Eleganz*', and avoids blood, bomb and 'brand'. It works in the world as a gentleman criminal, quiet and unobtrusive, and decks its visiting card with the doctorate of international law. In contrast with the dramatic scenes on sea and land, it cannot be worked into the atrocity film; its victims do not fly into the air or into the deep mutilated by explosions, but are extinguished unheeded and noiseless in some miserable garret in a crowded town. They do not even die of 'Blockade'. That illness is not on the register. Modestly the Blockade yields the *pas* to her murderers, decline, tuberculosis, pneumonia.

There is much besides, sharply critical in character, which Deissmann's bitter disappointment drove him to set down. Certainly the Archbishop himself would be the last to deny that 'war as such is the atrocity of atrocities and you cannot pick individual actions out of the hideous chain'. But it is needless to say more. To the Archbishop it was 'obviously clear' that Deissmann's original appeal through Upsala was 'political rather than ecclesiastical, though I do not question the sincerity of Deissmann's desires for religious intervention in favour of gentleness and peace'. And there was something in the Archbishop's mind which was outside Deissmann's comprehension. For Deissmann himself confessed, before the end of his letter: 'In any case, from my personal knowledge of the man, I wish to utter a warning against rash judgement of him'; and again, 'From the answer from Lambeth discussed in this letter, one does not get quite a correct picture of the Archbishop, because it is incomplete'. Before the War they had been friends. Then came the madness and the poison. After the War, so both might hope, some substance or some shadow of the former friendship would, in time, return.[1]

[1] For the next meeting, over four years later, between the Archbishop and Dr. Deissmann at Lambeth Palace on March 9, 1923, see p. 1170.

CHAPTER LVIII

AFTER THE ARMISTICE

It is not our business to collect trophies, but to bring back the world to peaceful habits. VISCOUNT CASTLEREAGH (1769–1822), *Memoirs and Correspondence*, x. 486.

THE days and weeks which followed the signing of the Armistice were crowded with work of all kinds. Peace questions, League of Nations questions, problems relating to the Christians of the East, as well as the urgent need of action by the Representative Church Council on Church and State, constantly claimed the Archbishop's attention. An illustration of his own frame of mind is to be found in the perplexity by which he was troubled about being fit to tackle the next Lambeth Conference. According to precedent, the sixth Conference should have taken place in 1918—ten years after the last. But that was impossible. On November 18, the two Archbishops discussed whether the date should be 1920 or 1921. Archbishop Davidson said: 'I don't want to be on stilts at all, or talk affectedly, but I don't think I shall preside over the next Lambeth Conference.' The Archbishop of York protested with some vigour that his weight and his moral influence were greatly needed, and asked who but he could restrain those who might easily prove its wreckers, like the Bishop of Zanzibar. The protest visibly impressed the Archbishop, even though he urged characteristically the precedent that the same Archbishop never had presided over two Lambeth Conferences.

I

Archbishop Davidson's attitude to Germany and to possible conditions of peace, we have already seen in his reply to Professor Deissmann's telegram, forwarded through Archbishop Söderblom. In answer to a formal invitation from Archbishop Söderblom himself to a Conference at Upsala, respecting the holding of an International Church Conference at Upsala or elsewhere, he wrote:

The ARCHBISHOP OF CANTERBURY *to the* ARCHBISHOP OF UPSALA

25 November, 1918

In your letter you write that you and others are strongly of opinion 'as to the necessity of such a Conference when Peace is in sight or after Peace has been concluded'. I am sure that the second of these two alternatives which you suggest is the right one. Such Conference, if it took place at all, should be held after Peace had been concluded and not during the discussions and deliberations preceding the conclusion of Peace. A Conference held during these diplomatic and international negotiations would undoubtedly be regarded, however mistakenly, as an attempt to intervene in the negotiations themselves. To this I could not be party, for I am sure that the position of those who represent Christian Churches and religious influences would be misunderstood were such Christian Conference held concurrently with the State negotiations. Christian Churches and Communities will be able to speak both more freely and with greater weight after the conclusion of Peace, when the process of reconstruction under new conditions is going on. . . . Mr. Hellerstrom told me that there is some possibility that you may yourself be paying a visit to England before long. If so, it would be most important and most agreeable to me that we should have full conversation upon the subject. But in any case this letter will I hope make my own position clear—namely, that Christian conference of any formal kind wherein the belligerents on both sides are represented can only take place advantageously after Peace has been concluded.

On November 25, Archbishop Meletios Metaxakis, Metropolitan of Athens, dined at Lambeth. It was the first of many occasions on which he was to have dealings with the Archbishop of Canterbury. He was a tall, vigorous man of forty-seven—with bright eyes, a black beard streaked with grey, and possessed of a strong voice. He was an ardent church reformer, and a great champion of the Reunion of Christendom. He was also a staunch supporter of M. Venizelos. He expressed himself with vehemence as to the infamy it would be if the Allies failed to restore S. Sophia, Constantinople, to the Christian Church. The conversation was followed by a dinner at the Athenaeum given by Mr. Riley—at which the Metropolitan of Athens, the Greek and Serbian Ministers, and many more were present, and a meeting on December 4, in the Central Hall, Westminster, about the persecution of the Eastern Christians, at which the Metropolitan again spoke. The

Archbishop of Canterbury also wrote to Mr. Balfour on December 4, pressing for the transfer of S. Sophia from the Turks, but received a guarded reply. And, in spite of an influentially signed Memorial, the danger of violent Moslem resentment effectively prevented such a transfer into Christian hands. So early in the post-Armistice months did the Eastern question knock at the doors of Lambeth.

A few days later, while President Wilson was crossing the Atlantic on his way to Europe for the Peace Conference, the Archbishop sent him a telegram inviting his presence at a special meeting representing the Churches in London. But, though he saw the President later, it was not possible for any such meeting to be arranged.

II

The General Election took place on December 14. The Archbishop could not approve of the flood of hatred and passion let loose on the hustings; but he kept silence. There were some who wished him to raise his voice in protest against the loud cries for the hanging of the Kaiser and the crushing of the German nation; and he was urged to denounce what was described as 'Lloyd George's infamous breach of faith in declaring himself, and almost declaring England, to be in favour of demanding indemnities from Germany independently of what is called reparation for wrongs done to civil property'. The Archbishop thought the charge of a definite breach of faith a little over-rated, though he agreed that the indemnity claim was wholly novel when compared with the popular speeches of Lloyd George himself, not to say President Wilson. He noted (December 8):

> Every day has added, in my judgement, to the evidence that the holding of a General Election is in the highest degree harmful, for the heckling of candidates for Parliament about indemnities, expulsion of aliens, trial of the Kaiser, and many other things, is beyond measure mischievous, as those who have to make answer have given no study whatever to those exceedingly difficult subjects, and yet may be committed to making promises for votes. And all this before the Peace Conference has begun to sit.

But it was a misfortune that the Archbishop, though entertaining these opinions, did not proclaim them to the world.

On January 4, he left for his second visit to the Front. This time (for he had been ill in December, and there were many qualms about his wisdom in going) he was accompanied by his friend Sir Alfred Pearce Gould, the distinguished surgeon. Together with Bishop Gwynne they visited all the Army Head-quarters, including the Second Army at Cologne. Conferences were held everywhere with the chaplains and with the officers. The subjects were this time far more concerned with the future than with immediate needs. The Reports given at Lambeth afterwards show the variety of the themes—Church Unity, Reform, Demobilization, Church and Labour, Y.M.C.A., Permanent Diaconate, etc. There was a good deal of criticism of the rather sensational appeals then appearing in the press for the Central Church Fund, and a good deal of interest in the Enabling Bill, and impatience at its apparently slow progress. The Archbishop also had the opportunity of testing on the spot the unrest among chaplains, and the discontent of some of their number with the 'official' Church of England. This unrest had been reported to him before by Bishop Gwynne, who took such notable care to keep Lambeth *au courant* with what was passing in the chaplains' minds. There was a plan of equalizing stipends in the benefices and curacies to which the chaplains would return—called the *plus* and *minus* scheme, meaning that each would be told what was fair for him to receive, and would surrender any superfluity. Another was a scheme of 'rovers' in each diocese—a kind of Flying Squadron of special missioners under authority. A third plan was for clergy to go and work as artisans in factories, and do their spiritual work in a voluntary way without benefice or licence. Indeed, one leading chaplain urged that all chaplains should strike when the War was over, and refuse to come back save on their own terms. The Archbishop knew all this—and sympathized, though he did not find the chaplains very constructive in their views. Some of the unrest, the rebellion (in mid-war, before the armistice), was, he thought, due consciously or unconsciously, to an unwillingness to face the old parochial grind. Possessing so much freedom, how should they ever be bond servants again?

Very good it was, then, to have the old Archbishop out in the midst of men with such experiences as theirs! good for them to see him with his humanity, simplicity, and utter lack of pride, and to know that they were understood, and had his sympathy.

He returned from his visit on January 24, much cheered, and in excellent health.

It will not be out of place here to say something of a very practical scheme, with which Randall Davidson was intimately concerned, born of the brains of chaplains and of the needs of the War. At least as early as the spring of 1916, the thought of a special call to the ministry for soldiers and sailors then on active service was brought up at Lambeth. Young officers and N.C.O.s who entertained the hope of being ordained were known to several chaplains—and their numbers grew with the progress of the War, though they were sometimes exaggerated. There were two problems in particular, after a reasonable sifting of the men: finance and training. The Archbishops, with no little courage, guaranteed the first, giving the pledge that no soldier otherwise fit should be denied ordination for lack of money. The pledge was honoured, and altogether £378,000 was spent on the training of 1,039 Service candidates. The Central Board of Finance of the Church of England, with Canon Frank Partridge as Secretary, raised the necessary funds, and also found the persons to administer them; thus rendering a great service to the Church. The other question was the place and manner of their training, especially a training of a pre-university type. With astonishing ingenuity P. B. Clayton found a disused jail at Knutsford, which, with the Archbishop's unstinted backing, was converted (in 1919) into an Ordination Test School. Here for three years a total of 675 candidates were trained (of whom 435 were eventually ordained) with F. R. Barry as their Principal, and a first-rate staff. Both Clayton (founder of Toc H) and Barry (each of them Army Chaplains through the War), were altogether uncommon men—vigorous, brave, and full of imagination. There could not have been better men for the task in hand. But they themselves would be the first to confess that, had they been without Randall Davidson as their Chief, their whole work might have been unattempted, or attempted in vain.

III

In the New Year the statesmen were busy in Paris with the Covenant of the League of Nations. Late on February 3, the Archbishop heard from Mr. J. H. Oldham that there was a real risk of the accidental omission of any provision, such as appeared in the Berlin Treaty, for freedom of conscience or religion. He wrote post-haste to Lord Robert Cecil in Paris, and had the satisfaction of receiving the following reply:

LORD ROBERT CECIL *to the* ARCHBISHOP OF CANTERBURY.

British Delegation, Paris.
February 7, 1919.

Many thanks for your Grace's letter of the 3rd which I have just got. It arrived in the nick of time, and I will see whether I can safeguard the point you mention. Of course I fully recognise the immense importance of the point.

It was just in time, as the draft agreement for a League of Nations was presented to the Plenary Inter-Allied Conference on February 14, 1919, and the Archbishop thus had the satisfaction of contributing both a principle and a phrase to the Covenant. The phrase (freedom of conscience or religion) appeared in what subsequently became Article 22, as follows:

> Other peoples, especially those of Central Africa, are at such a stage that the Mandatory must be responsible for the administration of the territory under conditions which will guarantee freedom of conscience or religion, subject only to the maintenance of public order and morals....

The Covenant was accepted, and, with the rest of the draft Treaty, was presented to the German delegation on May 7. The following correspondence took place:

LORD ROBERT CECIL *to the* ARCHBISHOP OF CANTERBURY.

Private. British Delegation, Paris. 4 May, 1919.

Now that the Covenant has been accepted, I venture to write to you to suggest that some action should be taken to ask God's blessing upon it. That has, of course, been necessary in all its stages. But it is daily brought home to me here that there is on the Continent, and especially among the Governments, very little appreciation or even understanding of the conceptions upon which it rests. Machinery—and the Covenant is nothing more—has no value of itself unless it is put in motion by some power. Humanly speaking that power can only come from the peoples of the world, and especially the English-speaking peoples. Unless, therefore, they are inspired to make a real attempt to improve international life, no covenants or Leagues will be of the slightest use. Indeed there is to me something approaching to blasphemy to expect anything from mere machinery. I express myself badly, but doubtless you will understand. It is not for me to suggest what should be done—but it should be something as solemn and as little splashy as possible. Perhaps a Special Communion Service in all the Cathedrals and in as many churches as possible?

Would this not be an opportunity for the C.E.M.S.?

Could you speak to the Archbishop of York about it?

I am trying to communicate with the Pope.

The ARCHBISHOP OF CANTERBURY *to* LORD ROBERT CECIL

12th May 1919.

I agree with every word that you say about the League of Nations and the need of our securing a spiritual basis for all our action instead of trusting to machinery, however good. I believe the machinery to be good, but we must see more emphatically to the spirit that is to lie behind and below. I am going to Scotland next week to speak to the General Assemblies, both Established and Free, on the subject of the League of Nations and the Restoration of Peace, and I shall express myself emphatically in the direction you indicate: indeed it would be the substance of what I have to say. I have already spoken of it in Convocation, and I am in communication with the Archbishop of York about it. I am sure that we do not want a great splash in our religious recognition of the League of Nations. We need quiet inculcation of prayer, not now only but for some time to come, and this I am setting myself to promote in every way that I can. Possibly we may put forth, as you have suggested, some unsensational injunction as to special celebrations of Holy Communion in Cathedrals and Parish Churches.

More serious anxieties about the whole Treaty of Peace disturbed the Archbishop as they disturbed others. Speaking in Convocation on May 6 he said:

It is an important thing that in a great document like this, agreed to by the representatives of all the prominent nations of the earth, there should be recognition given to the fact that, in the administration of territory occupied by uncivilised and semi-civilised nations, we should insist on conditions giving freedom of conscience and religion, prohibition of abuses such as the slave trade, arms traffic, and liquor traffic, and so on, and that there should be a recognition of the high purpose underlying that combination of the national powers. That seems to me to be essential with regard to all that the Peace Conference has done. We have been disappointed at the dragging of it on from week to week—perhaps unfairly, but we have been disappointed. We have been disappointed a little at the absence of that kind of glad unanimity which we should have liked to see, but which I am afraid history has shewn us is very difficult to obtain when allied nations are agreeing upon excessively complicated subjects. But whatever disappointments we may have had, we do at least thank God always that the Covenant has been signed, that the peace arrangements outside the Covenant of the League of Nations are in prospect of something like settlement, and that we have no clear evidence at present of wide division of policy and purpose among the nations. That is something for which we can be profoundly thankful.

He knew only too well how much 'screwing up' of terms there had been, and privately deplored the false promises and ruinous threats which had been so freely uttered. He recorded his own feeling 'that we have no statesman big enough to handle these problems . . . certainly not Lloyd George'. He discussed with some of his friends the difficulties of speaking out. Should he, for example, attack the proposed Peace Terms, so far known, at Edinburgh when he was speaking at the General Assembly on the League of Nations? His friends advised against—on the ground (as Lord Robert Cecil put it to him) that nothing should be done to give the Germans a handle for not signing—with the consequent horrible continuance of the Blockade. Instead the Archbishop wrote as follows to the Prime Minister:

The Archbishop of Canterbury *to the* Rt. Hon. D. Lloyd George

Private. 24th May, 1919.

I venture to write to you on a very important matter. It is one which must be constantly before your own mind, and you will not suppose that I underrate the gravity and difficulty of your position at this juncture. We think of it constantly, and we remember you steadily in our prayers.

I have thought that it may be not unprofitable that I should tell you how many communications are reaching me from people who to a large degree eschew ordinary politics, and who are as conscious as I am of the inability of us folk who are outside the central diplomatic and international circle to see the case all round, to the effect that they are anxious and disquieted about the terms of Peace. I have said, and shall continue to say, that we must trust you, and those who are working with you, to secure what is both just in its bearing on the wrong-doers, and righteous and Christian in its fundamental character. I have absolutely declined to be led off myself into discussions by people who, without adequate technical knowledge, insist on trying to handle such questions as the amount and nature of reparation, the boundary lines of the new States, the transference of Silesia, and so on. What my friends to whom I refer keep saying is, that while presumably each item may be plausibly justified, the cumulative effect is to ask impossibilities. It is perfectly certain that this view is entertained with almost trembling earnestness by a great many people who have no sort of wish to minimise German wrong-doing and its necessary outcome, and who are patriotic to their own land and absolutely loyal to the victorious Allied cause and its necessary expression in action.

I am myself going to-night to Scotland, in order next week to speak in the General Assemblies of the Established Church and of the United Free Church—a curious incident in ecclesiastical history. They want me to speak about the Peace and the League of Nations. I shall be very careful in what I say, but my point will be that we trust you and your colleagues to succeed in securing a Peace which shall correspond with our purposes in entering the War, which shall be such that we can ask God's blessing upon it, and which shall be of the kind that will be lasting and not the beginning of new strife. You must, of course, be receiving abundant communications both from those who may be roughly called pacificists and from those who have no other thought than the humiliation of Germany. I am not thinking of either of these parties. I am thinking of, and indirectly voicing, a great central body which is ordinarily silent and which has no adequate representation in the ordinary channels of the Press.

You will not, I think, mind my having said all this to you. I am anxious to deliver my soul because of the number of communications which are reaching me from really weighty and trustworthy people. But of course this letter is in the fullest sense private.

The letter was shown to the Council of Four.[1] It elicited the following friendly reply:

The RT. HON. D. LLOYD GEORGE *to the* ARCHBISHOP OF CANTERBURY

Personal. British Delegation, Paris. 30th May 1919.

Thank you very much for writing to me in regard to the pro-

[1] These were M. Clemenceau (France), Mr. Lloyd George, President Wilson (U.S.A.), and Signor Orlando (Italy).

posed terms of peace with Germany. I can assure you that we have given most careful consideration to every aspect of the proposed peace, in fact the Peace Conference was assailed for weeks for its delay and procrastination simply because it felt that it could not hurry or scamp its work in so all-important a matter.

We shall certainly give the fullest and most impartial consideration to the German reply. We have given them an extension of time, in order to make sure that they had time in which to marshal their case. If they can establish a just case for modification, I am sure modifications will be made. We shall not be influenced by public clamour if we think that we ought to make concessions to meet the German point of view.

At the same time, I am certain that what is most important is that we should not weaken the fundamental principles which underlie the peace. It is always difficult in human affairs to adjust mercy and justice, and, if it is important that we should remember mercy, it is not less important that we should remember justice. No nation has ever committed such a crime against its neighbours as have the German people, under the instigation of Prussian Kultur. It will not make for lasting peace, for early appeasement, nor even for the future well-being of the German people themselves and their future position in the world, should we refrain from imposing on their country the conditions which justice demands.

I have just perused the German reply. It seems to establish a strong *prima facie* case for reconsideration of the Eastern boundary.

The Treaty was signed on June 28. On July 6, the Archbishop preached at the great Thanksgiving Service in St. Paul's, in the presence of the King and Queen, the Ambassadors, members of the Government, and an immense congregation. He spoke of the events of the four previous Julys, when in Italy and the East the banks and plains of the Piave and the Jordan and the Tigris were still alive with war (1918), when there was a great daylight raid on London (1917), when woods and villages in what were once the lovely valleys of the Somme won imperishable fame (1916), when the world's records of heroism were being enacted by what Gallipoli can tell (1915). He dwelt on the horribleness of war, the need of peace, the significance of the League, the peoples' part—of 'the rugged pathway' which 'may want, I think it will want, consideration and adjustment here and there as the months or years run on'—the need of stern discipline and of the tasks immediately ahead:

> Outstanding surely among these is the staying, throughout Europe if we may, of one of the darkest ravages of war, the scourge of impending famine.

IV

Two other memories mingling war and peace may be quoted. The first is connected with chaplains. There was a Memorial Service for Chaplains in the Abbey on June 27. Sir Douglas Haig came to the Vestry when all was over, and, in answer to Bishop Ryle who thanked him for coming, simply said 'I could not do less'. It is significant of Randall Davidson's own close sympathy and comradeship with the chaplains as a body and their chief out in France that Bishop Gwynne, D.C.G., sent him the following letter, just as he was leaving to return to Khartoum:

BISHOP GWYNNE *to the* ARCHBISHOP OF CANTERBURY

P. & O.S.N.Co. S.S. Assaye. July 30, 1919.

> I am writing, on my first day out, to some of my friends who have been an inspiration and support to me during these five years of war, and your name has come first on my list. Never before have I had any conception of the vastness of your responsibilities and problems, until I took over a tiny corner of the whole. I have often spoken unwisely and unadvisedly with my lips, as if we of a younger generation were the only people who knew. I know now that the very power to make any forward move towards a new development came from the work and life of those who had gone before. God let me see how exceedingly small was that which we had not received from God through the labours of our forbears. I want to thank you Sir, for all that you have been to me—your humility, your generosity, and your great faith will be a great inspiration to me in days to come. My tongue was tied because of the knowledge of my own unworthiness when you spoke so generously of what I tried to do in France.
>
> I go back with my heart full of gratitude to God for all the experiences of the last five years. There are about 20 of my own Khartoum flock on board this boat, and you can imagine the real joy and happiness of being with them again.

The other memory is more painful, and concerns the statesmen. On August 13, the Archbishop and Lord Stamfordham had breakfast with Lloyd George; the Archbishop for the purpose of talking on episcopal vacancies. At the table Lloyd George was in characteristic form—full of conversation about Clemenceau and Wilson. Clemenceau disliked 'the President Wilson' (as he always called him) very keenly. On one occasion Wilson had spoken for three-quarters of an hour about moral principles being greater than force. All the time Clemenceau had listened with bowed head. Then he lifted himself up, and crushed Wilson's arguments completely. He talked to Lloyd George about 'force'. The President had said that Napoleon had put force below moral principles on his death-bed. Clemenceau's comment was, 'It took him a long time to find out, and then he was wrong.' Force made America. Force kept America together in the Civil War, and has kept it going since. As to himself, Clemenceau said he had had a tempestuous life, was deserted by his mother, betrayed by his wife, disappointed by his children. Now he was an old man—'But I've got my teeth left and I mean to use them!'

V

Throughout the year there had been a good deal of unrest in the industrial world, both above and under ground. At the end of September, a very serious railway strike commenced. It was suggested that, possibly, J. H. Thomas, the Railwaymen's leader, would not be sorry to find some channel for negotiation with the Government. The Archbishop offered his services, and wrote both to Mr. Thomas and Lloyd George. Each replied in a friendly way—and the Archbishop was given to understand, before the strike ended, that his offer of mediation, merely as an offer, had done good. The incident is mentioned, in view of the action taken, some years later, on the occasion of the General Strike. And it is interesting for the same reason to note that in 1919 a joint appeal to the nation was issued in the name of the Archbishop of Canterbury, the Bishop of London, Dr. F. B. Meyer, and the Rev. J. Scott-Lidgett, and also in that of Cardinal Bourne. The appeal included the following words (*The Times*, Oct. 2, 1919):

> We frankly deplore the strike, the suffering it entails, and the precipitancy with which so grave a step was taken. But we deplore still more the currently expressed opinion that such a struggle was inevitable and must be fought out. We believe this to be one of

those 'strong delusions' with which from time to time the powers of evil distract the world.

Never was there a time in England when the whole community was so resolutely set upon securing really worthy conditions of life for all grades of industrial workers. The comradeship of the war has quickened the public conscience, and we do mean, please God, that all who work for the community should be able to live as men and women ought to live. Upon that vital issue an appeal to our fellow-citizens will be more successful than ever before. But to be effective the appeal must be made to reason, and not enforced by coercion. Coercion which threatens to paralyse the life of the community alienates the very sympathies which are everywhere awake, and, by the general suffering which is involved, engenders passion instead of fellowship.

In November an attempt was made, like that of two years before, to raise money for the State by the issue of premium bonds. The Archbishop again published a strong protest against it; and the attempt again collapsed.

More difficult, in view of the state of public opinion, was the task he set himself to secure justice for the conscientious objectors who were returning to civil service after the War during which they had done work of national importance. He had to deal with the question as it concerned the British Museum, and was told that the present House of Commons would not approve of reinstatement. He wrote as follows to the Chancellor of the Exchequer:

The ARCHBISHOP OF CANTERBURY *to the* RT. HON. AUSTEN CHAMBERLAIN

19 November 1919.

Last week I discussed with you not only Premium Bonds about which I have already written, but the matter of Conscientious Objectors and their return to Civil Service employment. I find that Sir Frederic Kenyon, as Director of the British Museum, has had an interview with Sir Malcolm Ramsay. Sir Frederic learns that the position the Government takes is that these men, when they were suspended from their employment in the Civil Service and sent to take up work of National importance in lieu of Military Service, ceased thereby to be permanent Civil Servants, and that they are now taken back, if the Heads of the Departments so choose, on a purely temporary basis, and that it is not yet determined whether they shall be permanently reinstated in their former positions. To me it seems that this is an indefensible position in the case of a man who acted in strict accordance with what the law allowed—i.e. declined to fight, but undertook other work of National importance assigned to him instead. We may, if we will, condemn or dislike or despise him and his works, but surely a man, when external work of National importance done in lieu of fighting is over, goes back to his former position unless Parliament has decided that he is to be permanently degraded and lose the right of pension belonging to Civil Servants. I cannot find that Parliament has ever so decided, or that it could so decide without a formal Act. I do not want to raise a disturbance on the matter if it can be avoided, but I find myself, as a Trustee of the British Museum, implicated in what seems to me an act of real unfairness, and the very feelings of hostility which I entertain towards these men make me anxious to guard myself from the bias towards unfairness. You kindly undertook to look into the question and, I suppose, to let me know the result. May I hear what the facts are as they now present themselves to you?

Mr. Chamberlain replied that the matter was to be left open until the bulk of the civil servants who had fought had been demobilized. But the Archbishop's letter stated a claim which had to be admitted in the end.

VI

Reference has already been made to appeals which the Archbishop received from time to time from Germany for interests of various kinds. One or two more instances may be given, as indicating the reliance placed at least on the Archbishop's sincerity and friendliness.

In December 1919, Prince Max von Baden appealed to the Archbishop on behalf of the 400,000 German prisoners still kept as hostages in France. After describing how his other attempts to remedy the position had failed, he continued:

PRINCE MAX VON BADEN *to the* ARCHBISHOP OF CANTERBURY

Salem.
1 December 1919.

. . . I have turned to your Grace, remembering that, when war passions ran high, you, as did the Bishops of North and Central Europe[1] and of Winchester,[2] have taken a strong stand against

[1] Dr. Herbert Bury.

[2] Dr. E. S. Talbot.

reprisals being inflicted on innocents. The ugly usages of war become fiendish crimes when maintained after there is an end of war and war-necessities, and the coarse war-spirit should have gone too.

I am told the conscience of the British people is to-day denouncing the Blockade which was maintained against the German people after the close of hostilities. The prisoners languishing in France to-day are as helpless and innocent as were the German women and children killed during the Armistice-period.

In addressing you, my Lord, I should like to appeal at the same time to British soldiers who have returned from German captivity. I am thinking particularly of those who were exchanged during the war, and whose joy I was able to witness.

The Archbishop replied:

The ARCHBISHOP OF CANTERBURY *to* PRINCE MAX VON BADEN

Old Palace, Canterbury. December 23, 1919.

I have received Your Highness' important letter on the anxious and difficult subject of the position of German prisoners who are still in France. Indeed I have received one copy from yourself, and another sent to me through H.R.H. the Crown Princess of Sweden. On receiving these letters I communicated with Earl Curzon, as Secretary of State for Foreign Affairs, and I have seen him upon the subject. Lord Curzon points out what is indeed evident that the matter is one falling under the responsibility of the French Government, and he obviously feels that it would be in a high degree inappropriate were the British Government to intervene or attempt to intervene in a matter wherein it has no real status. If that be true of His Majesty's Government, it is not less markedly true of the Ecclesiastical authorities in this country. Advice from such Ecclesiastical quarters tendered to the French Government would, I am afraid, be regarded as somewhat unwarrantable.

We know so well in England how kind and how persevering have been the efforts made by Your Highness on behalf of prisoners belonging to different countries, and on behalf of those subjected to suffering, that it would at all times be to me a special privilege to be able to associate myself with Your Highness in the beneficent work with which you have been identified in relief of distress or hardship. Your Highness may rely on my being at all times watchful and ready to be useful in those directions when suitable opportunity is given me, and I feel keenly the importance of everything which may help to reduce to a minimum the suffering and trials incidental to a great war, not only during its continuance but after the actual warfare has come to an end.

A final work of mercy, in which all Christians took part, may be mentioned. In view of the suffering of children, from famine and disease in many countries, an appeal was made by the Save the Children Fund (founded by Miss Eglantyne Jebb) for a collection in all places of worship, on the last Sunday of the year, a very appropriate day for the purpose, being the Feast of the Massacre of the Innocents. The Archbishop took an active part in promoting this, and largely by his efforts, and through the kindly offices of Count de Salis (the British representative at the Vatican), the Pope, as well as the leaders of the Reformed Churches, the Patriarchs and Archbishops of the Orthodox Churches, and the Primates of the Anglican Communion, all appealed to their flock to offer their alms.

Fitly enough, at the end of the year the Archbishop published a selection of the addresses he had given during wartime. They bore the title *The Testing of a Nation*, and were recognized at once as veritable sections cut from the atmosphere of thought and feeling in which our world moved in the several crises of the war. Lord Haldane, on receiving a copy, wrote (December 29):

The VISCOUNT HALDANE *to the* ARCHBISHOP OF CANTERBURY

These sermons and the addresses you delivered through the War are part of the history of the time. I only wish that some of your speeches in Parliament had been included, and even more that the standard of the Government in action had been like that laid down by the leader of the Church of England in the deliverances in this volume.

CHAPTER LIX

THE ENABLING ACT

Yet still there is reason that propositions for such laws should sometimes come from the Church; which we must suppose well skilled (or in her proper business) in forming and digesting such new regulations, before they come before the consideration of the Legislature. . . . For to have laws framed and modelled solely by the State and (without previous communication) imposed upon the Church, is making of it the meanest and most abject of the State's creatures.

WARBURTON, *The Alliance between Church and State*, Part II, Section 3.

A REMARKABLE change in the relations of Church and State was effected by the Enabling Bill of 1919. The immediate origin of the change is to be found in a Resolution adopted by the Representative Church Council in July 1913. For some considerable while, there had been a growing dissatisfaction with the difficulties which stood in the way of legislation for the Church through Parliament. The position of the Church of Scotland was quoted, and Lord Halifax wrote to the Archbishop:

The VISCOUNT HALIFAX *to the* ARCHBISHOP OF CANTERBURY

June 24, 1913.

. . . I have been in communication with Lord Balfour of Burleigh in regard to what has been happening in Scotland, and Lord Wolmer and others in the House of Commons who, as your Grace knows, go by the name of 'The Church Lads' Brigade', are anxious to utilize the opportunity for setting on foot a movement which should enable the Church here to deal with its own affairs without discussion of them in detail in Parliament, and without the chance of such Bills as the 'Sheffield Bishopric Bill' being blocked as they now are. If something in this direction could be done, it would not only get rid of all these questions of Disestablishment and Disendowment, but it would unite all Churchmen in a common object about which, I should imagine, there could be but little difference of opinion.

The dissatisfaction was specially acute for those who were foremost in their resistance to the Disestablishment of the Church of Wales. As Lord Wolmer, who was destined to play a highly influential part in securing the change, wrote to the Archbishop:

The Viscount Wolmer *to the* Archbishop of Canterbury

June 25, 1913.

Lord Halifax tells me that he has mentioned to you the idea which has been occupying the thoughts of several keen Churchmen besides ourselves, that the time has come when there might be some devolution of ecclesiastical legislation from Parliament to a Body strictly representative of the Church.

Those of us who have been engaged in the work of Church Defence have been taunted by the promoters of Disestablishment with the fact that it is, under the present conditions, quite impossible to carry legislation that is necessary for the full development of the Church's work, and that the present state of affairs deprives the Church of all real liberty.

The force of this argument cannot be denied, but it seems to us that the answer should be that we should claim for the Established Church in England the same liberty of self-government as is enjoyed by the Established Church of Scotland.

Sir Alfred Cripps, in the Representative Church Council in July 1913, by way of answer (so it was understood) to Mr. C. F. G. Masterman's speech in Parliament in favour of Disestablishment, moved the Resolution which started the new system, having Lord Wolmer as his seconder. It was carried in the following form:

That there is in principle no inconsistency between a national recognition of religion and the spiritual independence of the Church, and this Council requests the Archbishops of Canterbury and York to consider the advisability of appointing a Committee to inquire what changes are advisable in order to secure in the relations of Church and State a fuller expression of the spiritual independence of the Church as well as of the national recognition of religion.

I

The Archbishops' Committee on Church and State was duly appointed, with Lord Selborne as its Chairman, and a very representative and influential set of members. The Archbishop was well aware of the difficulties which the appointment of a Committee on such a subject was bound to raise. They were admirably and, in view of the Prayer Book controversy thirteen years later, prophetically described, in a letter from Mr. Arthur Balfour who wrote:

The Rt. Hon. A. J. Balfour *to the* Archbishop of Canterbury

Whittingehame, Prestonkirk, Scotland. Jan. 9th, 1914.
Private.

I am strongly in favour of the principle of spiritual independence, and have never admitted any fundamental inconsistency between this and the principle of establishment. As evidence of this I may point to the part I took in giving the Church of Scotland control over its own symbols. Control over its own ritual it already possessed.

I wish something similar could be done for the Church of England; but I confess to being anxious on the subject. The Church of Scotland had in its origin not a trace of compromise, and, if it is now in practice one of the most liberal of churches (in the good sense of the word liberal), this has been entirely due to a process of internal evolution. The 'Wee Frees' in the Highlands really represent the original tradition!

Now the case of the English Church is entirely different. It has been from the start a comprehensive Body, and this great merit was attained at the beginning by compromise, and, amid all the changes of centuries, the original marks of the compromise have never been obliterated.

All this is commonplace; but it leads up to my point, which is this. Increased autonomy means increased strain within the organisation and between its parts. Do you think the fabric, weakened by these immemorial lines of cleavage, is sufficiently strong to stand it? If not, I would rather rub along as we are than risk a change which may lead to schism.

What makes the case of the Church of England more difficult than the case of the Church of Scotland, under modern conditions, is the fact that so many of its differences centre in ritual; and where ritual is concerned, mankind seem more than usually incapable of retaining any sense of proportion. I greatly fear, therefore, that autonomy may mean serious disturbances in an important percentage of Parishes, especially rural Parishes. Will the parson consent to allowing his parishioners, or even the communicants in his Parish, to determine the question of vestments and other matters on which the ritualistic section of the High Church Party feels strongly? What powers is a High Churchman prepared to give to the laity? Can you deal with the question of autonomy without settling these preliminary questions of principle? And is there on this question of principle the least chance of coming to a working agreement? If not, will not the attempt to increase

> the autonomy of the Church increase and emphasise its one weak point?
>
> These are the questions which I anxiously ask myself, and which, before joining your Committee, I should like to talk over with you. I certainly cannot unconditionally refuse your invitation, for that would look as if I do not desire the object which the Committee is intended to attain. As a matter of fact, I desire it passionately. My only fear is lest in our attempt to fly from ills which we know only too well, yet worse ills, which we can easily foresee, may come upon us.

The Archbishop discussed the difficulties with Mr. Balfour, who agreed to serve, having great confidence in Lord Selborne as Chairman; and he accepted the Archbishop's points that some risks must be faced, and that the harmfulness of refusing to appoint such a Committee, when it had been asked for *nem. con.* by the Representative Church Council would be greater than the harmfulness of running the risk of these difficulties with their eyes open to them.

The Committee, which had hardly started its work when the War broke out, nevertheless, thanks to the admirable leadership of Lord Selborne, published a unanimous Report in July 1916. It was a first-rate piece of work, with invaluable appendices, both historical and constitutional; and the principle on which its recommendations were based was clear. The Committee did not set forth, as some had expected, a whole series of measures. Instead it proposed that the Representative Church Council, composed of Bishops, Clergy, and Laity, after certain reforms, should receive statutory recognition, and be given real legislative powers in Church matters, subject to a Parliamentary veto.

The Representative Church Council was itself a youthful body. It had started in 1903, the same year as Randall Davidson became Primate. It consisted of three Houses, the House of Bishops, i.e. the Upper Houses of the Convocations of Canterbury and York sitting together; the House of Clergy, i.e. the Lower Houses of the two Convocations sitting together; the House of Laymen, i.e. the Houses of Laymen of the two Provinces sitting together—a body of seven hundred persons all told. The reforms which the Archbishops' Committee proposed gave the Parochial Clergy a majority in the House of Clergy and provided *inter alia* for the special representation of wage-earners and students and teachers in the Diocesan Conferences through which the members of the House of Laity were elected. The electors to the Diocesan Conferences and the Parochial Church Councils had to be either actual communicants or persons who had been baptized and confirmed. The Parochial Church Councils themselves were to be endowed with new powers after the Representative Church Council had obtained its own constitution and powers.

The method of legislation proposed may be summarized as follows:

> A measure shall not be deemed to be passed by the Church Council unless it secures a majority of votes in each House.
>
> Special provision is recommended to protect the powers of the Episcopate in regard to all questions of doctrine.
>
> Any measure that is passed by the Church Council shall lie upon the tables of both Houses of Parliament for forty days. To assist Parliament in the exercise of its powers over ecclesiastical legislation, the constitution of a Special Committee of the Privy Council (to be known as the Ecclesiastical Committee) is recommended. This Committee, after consultation, if necessary, with a Committee of the Church Council (called the 'Legislative Committee'), is to draft an advisory report to the Crown on the measure, such report to be laid before Parliament with the measure.
>
> This report is intended to show the effect of the measure in question, what alterations in existing Acts of Parliament its enactment would entail, and whether there is any objection from the point of view of the State to its passage. If the report is favourable to the measure, it shall automatically be presented for the Royal Assent on the expiry of forty days, unless either House of Parliament by resolution direct to the contrary.
>
> If the report is not favourable, it shall not be presented for the Royal Assent unless both Houses of Parliament by resolution order that it shall be so presented.
>
> Any measure on receiving the Royal Assent shall acquire the force of an Act of Parliament.

The Report was, on the whole, very cordially received. A special meeting of Bishops was held in May 1917, and announced their general assent to the principles underlying the proposals of the Committee. The Upper House of Canterbury Convocation welcomed the Report in July 1917; but the Archbishop warned the over ardent—

> It is obvious to anyone that it is impossible to make this a *fait accompli* during the war.

II

In addition, an official Church Self-Government Association was formed to promote the plan. And another movement of a more vehement kind was created. It so happened that 1916 was the year of the National Mission which, amongst other events, brought large numbers of enthusiastic Churchmen together all over the country. It was followed by the nomination of special Committees dealing with special departments of the Church's task. The Rev. W. Temple[1] (who had been on the Archbishops' Committee), the Rev. H. R. L. Sheppard[2] (who had not), and a number of other friends got together. The former wrote to the Archbishop on February 4, 1917, with special reference to his fellow enthusiasts:

> The War and the Mission have brought them to boiling point. It is a psychological necessity that they should explode.

It was vital, he said, that the more ardent members of the company should be prevented from breaking off and giving up in despair of the Church, and that there should be 'some recognized expression of the desire for a forward move'. At first the 'forward move' was not precisely described, and the Archbishop remarked to Mr. Temple as its sponsor that he had 'not the least idea' what 'a forward move' in those general terms covered. But in the early summer the forward move assumed the name of the Life and Liberty Movement, which had as its object: 'To win for the Church the liberty essential to fullness of life.'

An enthusiastic meeting was held by this group in the Queen's Hall, London, on July 16, 1917. It passed the following Resolution, with the Dean of Durham (Dr. Hensley Henson) as the only dissentient:

> That whereas the present conditions under which the Church lives and works constitute an intolerable hindrance to its spiritual activity, this Meeting instructs the Council, as a first step, to approach the Archbishops, in order to urge upon them that they should ascertain without delay, and make known to the Church at large, whether and on what terms Parliament is prepared to give freedom to the Church in the sense of full power to manage its own

[1] Afterwards Archbishop of York.
[2] Afterwards Dean of Canterbury; later Canon of St. Paul's.

life, that so it may the better fulfil its duty to God and to the nation and its mission to the world.

The Archbishop received a deputation from the Life and Liberty Council, and the deputation went away contented. But he was not specially pleased with the Queen's Hall Meeting, or the Chairman's speech:

The ARCHBISHOP OF CANTERBURY *to the* REV. W. TEMPLE

Private. 17 July, 1917.

You will just let me say this: While you say nothing, barring a question of the possibilities of the present hour in Parliament, to which I could take the slightest exception, I confess that, if I had read the speech knowing nothing about the circumstances, the impression left upon my mind would have differed a good deal from what are the familiar facts as I know them. I try to picture, if it were conceivable, someone reading that speech 50 years hence, without any knowledge at all of what were the contemporary happenings in England. Would such a reader conjecture that there had, during the last year been a National Mission inaugurated by the Archbishops 'off their own bat', and that the Committees appointed, as a result, for dealing with the practical questions of the hour were now vigorously in session, and that the Secretary of some of these was the Chairman of this meeting? On the contrary, I should have pictured Bishops of the order of Lucretian divinities, or say like the 18th century Archbishops (Cornwallis or Moore) bewigged and besleeved, who might doubtless pass placid Resolutions in Convocation, but had no thought of putting them into action. I know that this is not the sort of picture you meant to draw. Probably you take for granted that nobody would suppose such to be the facts. Here I think you are mistaken. However, that matters comparatively little, except that it obviously makes what the Bishops are trying to do a good deal more difficult. The point of practical importance which emerges is that which I spoke of to you before I saw the Resolution. You are going to ask us, as Archbishops, to go to Lloyd George and his War Cabinet—men who are over head and ears in affairs of hourly pressure as to the Nation's existence, and cannot be even got at for five minutes' conversation—and to bid them forthwith 'make known to the Church at large on what terms Parliament is prepared to give freedom to the Church' etc. We are to do this at a time when such representative laymen as the Church possesses in the Representative Church Council have stated by an overwhelming majority that even the Council, full as it is of Church interest, cannot meet at present because all men are absorbed in War thoughts. The Prime Minister is then to say what Parliament will do. Presumably he can only do this by asking Parliament, and how he is supposed to do this I cannot even dimly conjecture. That is the practical difficulty which strikes me in the matter. Perhaps you will say it does not affect the purport of the speeches of yesterday, and I daresay this is so as regards their large motive and principle. But what does it really come to in practical possibility, while we are at death-grips with the Germans? Could I really insist on an interview at Downing Street, which generally means calling the Prime Minister out from a Cabinet meeting, to speak standing up in the ante-room, and ask him what conditions of Church life he would regard as the right ones for the future?

The single dissentient gave his view of the meeting as follows:

The DEAN OF DURHAM *to the* ARCHBISHOP OF CANTERBURY

The Athenaeum, Pall Mall, S.W. 1. July 17, 1917.

It occurs to me that you might care to have a record of the impression which last night's meeting of the 'Life and Liberty' agitators made on an unsympathetic but never deliberately unfair observer. So far as numbers went, it was a good meeting; indeed, there was an overflow. The audience was three-parts composed of women, and the remaining part was mainly made up of youngish parsons. Socially, I conjectured that the meeting consisted of upper middle-class people, who form the congregations of West-end Churches. There was no trace of the working classes perceptible. The ecclesiastical type of the audience was, perhaps, disclosed by the circumstance that, when the Apostles' Creed was repeated, the crowded platform *seemed* to make the sign of the Cross unanimously. I was quite startled by so unusual a phenomenon. This petty incident was significant because ordinary English Churchmen are not accustomed to the practice of signing themselves with the Cross. The Headmasters seem to be deep in the movement. David of Rugby read prayers, and the Headmasters of Eton and Harrow were on the platform. Of course family reasons may have led the latter, rather than personal conviction: but this display of pedagogues set me thinking. The academic, the feminist, the Socialist, the clericalist—these are not the constituents of an ecclesiastical policy which is likely to be tolerant, or virile, or just, or large. Temple's speech was well-phrased and well-delivered. He has an admirable voice, and, though his manner is a little too dogmatic and professional, he is in the succession of orators. There was not much stuff in the speech, perhaps, because he had 'said his say' in a pamphlet which had been distributed in the seats: but he made it very plain that the 'Life and Liberty' movement intends the *present* Parliament to pass the requisite legislation, either to grant autonomy, or to disestablish. The duration of the War was spoken of as an 'accepted hour', in which the Church of England must 'find salvation' or for ever fall! None of the other speakers were adequate. Miss Maude Royden was confused, incoherent, and, when intelligible, irrelevant. 'Father' Carey adopted a jocose manner, unworthy of the occasion, and seemed to blame the Church for the defects of the individual clergy. A returned Chaplain in khaki assured us that great numbers of officers and men were eagerly longing for the prompt and drastic handling of the Church: and Mr. 'Dick' Sheppard concluded with an ecstatic appeal for enthusiasm. *Voilà tout!*

I cannot say that the meeting seemed to me in any marked degree enthusiastic. Partly this may have been due to the great predominance of women: but mostly, I suspect, it arose from the fact that neither the Catholic, nor the national note was sounded, but only the 'denominational', and you can't get up much enthusiasm over sectarianizing a national Church. I do not doubt that both the E.C.U. and the Church Defence Institution could get together more enthusiastic meetings. The Bishop of Oxford's name was greeted with applause, but then the meeting was 'Gore's Crowd'.

I held up my hand against a resolution that said what my experience for 30 years past proves to me is untrue, that the present conditions of the Church's life constitute 'an intolerable hindrance to her spiritual work'. No clergyman who speaks the truth can really say *that* of his personal knowledge. But I will not embark on a discussion, where I only designed a description.

A considerable controversy followed, in the next few months, in *The Times* and elsewhere. Nevertheless William Temple and his Life and Liberty men pressed vigorously forward, and tried to get the Archbishop to act with far greater speed than His Grace thought was fair or likely to produce the desired result. When, for example, the Representative Church Council met, after an interval of two years, in November 1917, and, at the end of two days' debate upon the recommendations of the Archbishops' Committee, decided to appoint a Grand Committee 'to prepare a Report thereon and if they think it desirable to prepare a scheme to be presented to the Council at its next Meeting', the

Life and Liberty Council instructed Mr. Temple as its Chairman to express in a letter to *The Times* 'our great disappointment that no direct vote was taken on the broad issues of self-government for the Church . . . the procedure adopted certainly does not suggest urgency' (December 7, 1917). The Archbishop wrote a personal letter to Mr. Temple:

The ARCHBISHOP OF CANTERBURY *to the* REV. W. TEMPLE

7th December 1917.

I am not, I think, apt to be over-sensitive or thin-skinned in matters of this sort, or to seek to evade a criticism which, however rough, may be most useful. But of course you are right when you say, or imply in your private letter that, by what is now published, my own personal difficulties are greatly augmented. This is a comparatively small matter unless it hinders the cause which I, like you, have at heart. This I fear it may do, but I shall endeavour to prevent it as far as possible. There is nothing in the letter which could be called violent or rude. Pray feel quite relieved on that score.

I am looking forward keenly to the outcome of your Missionary effort to awaken the sense of Churchmen generally to the need of changes. I am certain that in that policy you are right. It is what specially needs doing at present, and it is just what can at present be done. Where I think that you and others are mistaken is in your belief that we could, with advantage to the cause of wise reform, take steps at the present moment for propounding schemes in Parliament, or committing thoughtful people who care about the Church's life to a particular and detailed policy. I am mixing for hours on most days in the week with the men prominent in our public life, on whose aid we should have to rely if the changes we want were to be made, and I do not literally know one of them who would share your view as to the practicability of the forward push in an official way at the present moment, when every thought and every ounce of energy is absorbed in England's struggle for its very life. This makes me absolutely certain that I have been right in advocating or insisting upon the necessity of our eschewing a policy of hustle and push in matters ecclesiastical, during these months of daily and nightly strain upon the thoughts and time of every public man who is worthy of the name.

The Archbishop knew the world better than his correspondent. He was perhaps a little hurt, but went calmly forward. A Grand Committee was duly appointed under the chairmanship of

Bishop Ryle. The first few months of 1918 were heavy with anxiety, due to the Spring offensive in France. But the Grand Committee went on with its task, and the Report, which included a Scheme, was signed on October 3, 1918. Peace drew near, but with peace came the practical certainty of a General Election. This meant not only that it would be impossible to hold a meeting of the Representative Church Council at the end of November, but 'that unless other steps are taken the Church would have no clear policy in regard to self-government to lay before the country at this crucial moment'. The Life and Liberty Movement and the Church Self-Government Council therefore asked that 'a small deputation' might wait on the Archbishops to express that view. The 'small deputation' came, eighty strong, on October 24. In the dining-room at Lambeth Palace the Archbishops faced a company of whom some at least were very ready to explode. Six speeches were made before the Archbishops replied, all asking that a definite lead should be given to the Church. One of the speakers, claiming to represent the younger 'impetuous and unreasonable people', expressed his regret that 'no leadership had been given in the last four or five years'. Another warned the Archbishop before the meeting: 'We want you to scream.' All were passionately convinced of the necessity of dramatic public action being taken at once. The Archbishop was fully aware of the critical character of his audience, but he refused to be rushed. He pointed out what had already been done to promote the consideration of the Report in the official assemblies. He said that the Archbishops had a tremendous responsibility; they were not individuals, but Heads of the Church which spoke in its representative bodies. He did not think that 'going over the top' really applied either in Church or War to those who had to think the matter out. 'In Church History the best things have not been done by spasm or scream, but by determination.' He was prepared with all his heart to advocate the proposals of the Church and State Committee as urgently necessary for the life of the Church to-day, but while Life and Liberty might shout or cry on the house-tops, the Archbishops must go forward 'reasonably, progressively, constitutionally', and the need of sureness was all the greater now in view of the feverish excitement all round. Yet, though the Archbishop's words had a somewhat chilling effect, and the deputation went away discouraged, the

Archbishop was more impressed as to the need of a definite pronouncement than he showed at the time. Parliament was dissolved. The Report of the Grand Committee of the Representative Church Council was published. On December 2, the Archbishop wrote a letter to Lord Selborne, which was issued to the Press, in the course of which he said:

The ARCHBISHOP OF CANTERBURY *to the* EARL OF SELBORNE

2 December 1918.

. . . I gladly reiterate my own deliberate opinion that the proposals thus commended to us are sound in principle, and that if they can be adopted and made operative in something like the form now proposed, it will be to the great practical advantage of all our work. In such a matter criticism is of course easy, and it may be very helpful to us in matters of detail. Difficulties there must inevitably be. But a full discussion will shew, I think, that they can be satisfactorily overcome. It is my earnest hope that the Representative Church Council will give so marked a support to the new scheme as to strengthen our hands immeasurably in the endeavour to secure its constitutional adoption.

Both the Church and the Nation will, I am convinced, have cause for gratitude if, by God's blessing, our efforts are successful.

III

The scene of the next act in the drama was laid in the Representative Church Council on February 25–8, 1919. It met in the Hoare Memorial Hall, as the Australians were still in occupation of the Great Hall of the Church House. The main points in which the scheme presented by the Grand Committee differed from that of the Selborne Committee were: (1) The body on which legislative powers were to be conferred was called the National Assembly of the Church of England; (2) the omission of proposals for the reform of the Lower Houses of Convocation which were deliberately left for these Houses themselves; and (3) the alteration of the franchise from Confirmation to Baptism, with a declaration that the elector was a member of the Church of England and did not belong to any religious body which is not in communion with the Church of England. On the third point, a vigorous controversy took place in the Press.

There were nineteen pages of amendments on the Order paper,

and the opposition, some of it from convinced champions of the *status quo*, like the Bishop of Hereford (Dr. Henson), some from High Churchmen, like Mr. Athelstan Riley and Major Edward Wood,[1] was very strong. The occasion was critical and needed consummate powers of chairmanship. The Archbishop, who presided, left the Chair on the afternoon of the first day, and made a speech which produced a profound effect. It was based on his forty years' experience of the need of reform, and the impossibility of getting adequate Parliamentary time for considering Church Measures. He spoke strongly of the tradition and spirit of the National Church, and said:

> If I thought, with the Bishop of Hereford, that by passing this scheme we were in actual peril of losing that which I for one value so much, namely, the maintenance of those traditions and that spirit, very real though very indefinable, I should feel bound to support him in opposing the scheme as it stands. But I think nothing of the kind.

But he had a word also for some of the enthusiastic supporters:

> On the other hand, I am bound in fairness to say that a great many enthusiastic supporters of this scheme seem to me to expect from its adoption much more inevitable results, much more far-reaching results, and much more immediate results than I believe would follow if the change were made. 'Life' and 'Liberty' are large and splendid words. I believe in both. I believe that by what we are now doing, if we go on with our plan, we shall gain more of both of them, and that they will increase and grow. But it will not be by the waving of a wand or by the mere adoption of a scheme.

The main bulk of his argument was to show, and he gave example after example, that not from opposition, but sheer inability, Parliament could not add this to all its other work:

> Not once or twice, or five times or perhaps ten times, have I brought before the Ministers in power during the last quarter of a century matters which, big or little, I thought needed attention at the time in the Church's life, and the answer has been again and again the same, 'Probably you are quite right; but with the present pressure upon the time of Parliament and the present atti-

[1] Subsequently Viceroy of India, with the title Lord Irwin; afterwards Viscount Halifax.

> tude of the House of Commons towards the varied work that lies urgently before it, we never could ask the House to give up the days or the weeks that would be necessary'. They did not say, 'We are opposed to it', or 'We are objecting to what you do', but rather 'You are asking a machine to do it, which is already so clogged with work, and work of a different kind, that you are asking an impossibility'.

The Archbishop made it clear that this 'quite dully, quite prosaically' was the real position. He said that the work of the Church was hampered just as a man who had important work to do was hampered by a broken finger-nail or a bad toothache. His health was not permanently injured, he was not going to die! He could not subscribe to the large statements as to an intolerable hindrance:

> We find ourselves prevented from doing it better by things which it is in our power to get removed. Therefore we want to get them removed, not necessarily to satisfy any large and far-reaching theory, but for the practical doing better of the work with which we are entrusted as administrators for the sake of all.

The speech was an immense success, and was praised enthusiastically, even by Lord Wolmer and Mr. Temple, in spite of its minimizing tendency. When the Archbishop sat down he received an ovation. The hostile amendment moved by Mr. Riley was immediately withdrawn, and the Report was 'received for consideration'. During the next four days, the Representative Church Council considered the constitution of the new Church Assembly, and the provisions of the Enabling Bill itself. The main division concerned the franchise. After a long debate, an amendment in favour of a Confirmation franchise instead of the Baptismal with a declaration, was defeated, the figures being as follows:

	For	*Against*
Bishops . . .	7	17
Clergy . . .	37	62
Laity . . .	65	80

On February 28, the scheme and the Enabling Bill were adopted by the Council, almost *nem. con.* It had been a remarkable week, and the Archbishop's powers of chairmanship were seldom seen to greater effect. The following letter came from Bishop Gore who had been defeated on what he conceived the crucial question of the franchise:

The Bishop of Oxford *to the* Archbishop of Canterbury

Cuddesdon, Wheatley, Oxon. March 1st, 1919.

I am going to write to you—less agreeably—about *the R.C.C.* Now I will only say that I hope you were not over-tired. You have not my cause of dis-satisfaction and, eliminating that, I should think the whole meeting was an almost brilliant success—thanks to you.

IV

This letter was followed by another letter, disagreeable but decided, declaring that he (Dr. Gore) had decided to resign.

Bishop Gore had threatened resignation on other occasions, but this time there was no going back. In reply to his first letter of March 4, the Archbishop begged him to come for a talk, though not for reconsideration, and wrote:

The Archbishop of Canterbury *to the* Bishop of Oxford

Private. Lambeth Palace, 4 March 1919.

. . . There is perhaps no change which could come about in the 'College' of Bishops which would affect me so deeply and bewilder me so much, for (what must be at most) the few remaining years of my tenure of this appallingly difficult office. I can only 'fall to prayer' and ask for guidance and strength in a veritable bereavement.

As a result of the talk, on March 10, the Archbishop persuaded Gore to modify some parts of his official letter of resignation—altering *established* to *national*, and adding certain words:

The Bishop of Oxford *to the* Archbishop of Canterbury

Cuddesdon, March 15, 1919.

I am writing to tell you that I have decided to resign the see of Oxford. My main motive is the conviction, which has been growing in me for some time, that the best way in which I can use the rest of my life, for the Church and other causes in which I am deeply interested, is by seeking such leisure as would enable me to do serious study and to write something better than 'little books', and I hope to have the opportunity of more continuous preaching and speaking than my present position makes possible. As you know very well, being bishop of such a see as this leaves one no chance of such leisure. I have had 17½ years of being a bishop, and for me at least that is enough. I used to discuss the matter with my predecessor Francis Paget. We agreed that there was no obligation upon us to continue being bishops till we were decrepit. His life was cut short alas! But I hope he approves what I am doing.

I know I shall be told that it is wrong to resign in such critical times for the Church: and I can quite believe that when some anxious debate is taking place in Convocation or the Lambeth Conference, I shall have a 'bad moment' of doubt whether I am justified in being absent by my own act. But I have faced the question as well as I can, and very often: and I am convinced that I am right on the whole. The crisis, I feel sure, in the Church will continue, and indeed, perhaps become more acute for years to come: and I believe that I can serve the causes of reconstruction best by getting time for thinking, studying, writing and preaching. I am not, of course, in any sense resigning my ministry, but only one kind of administrative office which, in our enormous dioceses, with all the attendant work on central committees, gives no opportunity for these things. Moreover my resignation does not imply any kind of weakening in my allegiance to Anglican principles, but only the choice of what is, I think, the better way for serving them.

I must add that, while the main motive for resigning my bishopric is what I have described, the choice of the moment is partly due to the decision of the Representative Church Council a few days ago about the future franchise. I am convinced that, in abandoning the present basis of franchise which includes confirmation, we have sacrificed principle to the desire for larger numbers on our rolls, and that largely for the sake of maintaining the 'national' position of the Church. I know this does not represent your point of view, or that of others of my friends who gave their vote for the baptismal franchise. But it represents, I think, the effect of the vote on the whole. And it leaves me in a very embarrassing position. I cannot fight against a movement towards autonomy for the Church to which for many years past I have largely devoted my life: but I cannot any longer co-operate cordially with the movement now that it has placed itself on what I think is so false a basis. However, as I say, this is not my main motive.

I do not want to lay any share of responsibility on you. I know you have formally to consent by accepting the document of resignation. But you cannot force a man to continue in any office he is determined to resign. I propose to sign the document as soon as I have heard from you, and to announce the fact in the diocesan magazine for April: but to ask you to accept it and make it effective on July 1st, after which date I desire to be free. Perhaps I need not say that I do not propose to ask for or take any pension.

You know how grateful I feel to you for all your kindness and generosity to me over so many years.

The ARCHBISHOP OF CANTERBURY *to the* BISHOP OF OXFORD

Lambeth Palace. March 17th, 1919.

You will know of the distress with which I received your letter of March 15th. From many talks about such matters during recent years I have been aware of your personal feeling that it is as a teacher and writer rather than as the administrator of a Diocese that you can most effectively serve Church and people, and it would therefore be unfair to yourself were I to say that your letter takes me altogether by surprise. I agree with you that a man cannot rightly be pressed to retain an office which he deliberately thinks it to be his duty to resign. I must not therefore oppose your decision, deeply as I regret it. In the intimacy of our close friendship during so many strenuous years, I have gained from you more than I can here express in words, and on the aid which comes from such fraternal counsel I know that I can still confidently rely. Its usefulness to me has often been greatest on occasions when our difference in opinion or conclusions has been, and has remained, most wide. What I chiefly deplore, for the whole Church's sake, is the loss of your constant and faithful contribution to our united Episcopal discussions, formal and informal, upon the problems and issues which we have daily to handle in matters both sacred and secular. You have unfailingly put before us with wide knowledge, large thoughtfulness, and fervid conviction that aspect of each question which is most vivid to yourself, and I do not exaggerate when I say that the loss of that contribution seems to me at present to be almost irreparable. But we have work to do, and we must go forward to the doing of it, each in his own way.

Of the particular occasion or incident which has given point to your final decision, I will only say what you already know, that I cannot regard as you do either its character or its consequence. To discuss these in this letter would be useless and out of place.

I pray God that for many years to come, and long after my own working days are over, your learning, your devotion, and your personality may be as heretofore at the service of the Church and people of England.

The parting was a real distress to Randall Davidson, and caused anxiety in other quarters lest, without responsibility and the need of consultation with other Bishops, Dr. Charles Gore might become an added element of peril. A proposal for making him a Bishop *in partibus* was half-seriously proposed—but did not seem practicable to the Archbishop. So the Bishop retired to write books, and deliver lectures on theology in King's College, London; and he took great pains to avoid being a cause of embarrassment to his former colleagues. There was no doubt about his own personal feeling of relief, as he wrote just before his resignation took effect:

May 10, 1919.

> I feel selfishly radiant at the prospect before me, and 'full of beans' as the boys say. . . .

V

The next step was the introduction of the Enabling Bill into Parliament. It is important to observe that, while the constitution of the Church Assembly was the subject of prolonged debate by the Representative Church Council, while the Enabling Bill was passed with little discussion, it was the Enabling Bill alone which formed the subject of debate in Parliament. The constitution of the Church Assembly was withdrawn, and intentionally withdrawn, from Parliamentary enactment. It was not made a schedule to the Bill, but was referred to in the title, which was as follows:

> An Act to confer powers on the National Assembly of the Church of England constituted in accordance with the constitution attached as an Appendix to the Addresses presented to His Majesty by the Convocations of Canterbury and York on the tenth day of May, nineteen hundred and nineteen, and for other purposes connected therewith.

The reason (to which strong exception was taken by Lord Haldane in the House of Lords) is given in the Report of the Archbishops' Committee on Church and State (p. 61):

> The Bill might also contain in a schedule the constitution of the Church Council and its legislative procedure. But this would be objectionable both on theoretical and on practical grounds. For it would mean that the constitution of the Church would be fixed by Parliament; and though Parliament might use its opportunity of framing a Church constitution very sparingly, or might even acquiesce silently in whatever scheme was propounded by the authorities of the Church, it might on the other hand make important modifications in the constitution which could only be rejected by the Church at the price of wrecking the whole scheme, and

> might under this pressure be accepted by the Church. But such acceptance would be a sacrifice of spiritual independence indefensible and offensive to the sentiments of Churchmen.

The distinction was fundamental, and accordingly the Constitution was embodied in an address laying before His Majesty:

> A recommendation agreed to by both Houses of this Convocation on the 8th day of May 1919, that, subject to the control and authority of Your Majesty and of the two Houses of Parliament, powers in regard to legislation touching matters concerning the Church of England shall be conferred on the National Assembly of the Church of England constituted in the manner set forth in the Appendix attached to this Address.

From the middle of April to the beginning of July, a controversy raged in the Press on the whole question of Church and State, led by the Bishops of Hereford (Dr. Henson) and Manchester (Dr. Knox), with the help of a few Broad Churchmen. Some Nonconformists were favourable, like Dr. Scott Lidgett and Dr. Selbie. Others were opposed, like Dr. Clifford and Dr. Forsyth. The Enabling Bill was variously described as 'a blank cheque for absolutism', or 'a masked revolution'. By some it was thought to be certain to precipitate a cleavage between Clergy and Laity, to give more power to the Ritualists, to make reunion more difficult, and orthodoxy more rigid. By others it was charged with being an attack on the constitutional rights of the Englishman. The Bishop of Hereford put this objection succinctly thus in a letter to *The Times*:

The BISHOP OF HEREFORD *to the* EDITOR *of* '*The Times*'

May 17. 1919.

> Before the Reformation, the Church of England was the local branch of the Holy Roman Church, two provinces of the Latin obedience. Since the Reformation, the Church of England has been the Church of the English nation, in which every Englishman has rights, and for which every Englishman has responsibility. Henceforward, if the Enabling Bill passes into law, the Church of England will be a denomination, one among many, though still suffered to possess the ancient religious endowments of the nation. . . . The Enabling Bill implies the total, if gradual, destruction of the Establishment.

The opposition, especially that which appealed to the interests of the Establishment and the dread of Ritualism, was of a powerful character. It was supported, incidentally, by *The Times*. 'It is because the Bill if passed must destroy some of the most valuable elements in the life of the Church of England that we hope it will not become law.'[1] It is not too much to say that a championship of the Enabling Bill based on the theoretical idea of spiritual independence, and merely denouncing the intolerable hindrance to spiritual activity of the present conditions in which the Church of England lived, would have tumbled to ruin. It was accordingly once more as a practical statesman that the Archbishop of Canterbury expounded the merits of the Enabling Bill, when he moved the Second Reading in the House of Lords on June 3. He spoke for over an hour to an attentive and well-filled House. His opening words were characteristic: 'My Lords, I ask your Lordships to give a Second Reading to a Bill to enable the Church of England to do its work properly.' He added that the proposals in the Bill had been widely discussed and criticized, and went on, with a disarming simplicity:

> Its opponents—and there may be some of them in this House—descry in it perils, which I think are either quite imaginary or are no greater than those which attend all brave and adventurous legislation. Those fears I altogether repudiate. As to its friends, I find a little difficulty in making my own all the hopes and ambitions which have found eloquent expression in the fine body of men and women who have advocated it.

He begged the House to remember that they were not dealing at all with deeper spiritual things but only with the framework, 'the outer secular rules within which our work has to be done'. He spoke of the growth in population of the last two hundred years, yet with little change in the system of Church machinery. In 1700, there were just over 5,000,000 people in England and Wales, 'and now we have to apply the same machinery, roughly speaking, as was applied in the old days, to 36,000,000 people, and infinite complications and difficulties have arisen, largely from that cause'. He asked their Lordships to look at Stephens's Ecclesiastical Statutes, the second volume of which, containing 1,106 pages, was devoted exclusively to the annotated Statutes between 1828 and 1844:

> The Pluralities Act, the great Act, which may want amending but which we have to act upon to-day, is one of 133 sections, and the

[1] *The Times*, May 30, 1919 (leading article).

> foolscap edition covers fifty-four pages. Imagine attempting to-day to get an Ecclesiastical Bill of that size through Parliament!

He gave instances of the changes which had come over the whole scene since 1845, due to the altered conditions of English public life, and of the difficulties, of which he had first-hand knowledge during the past forty years of intimate connexion with central Church affairs. He dealt not at all with theory but showed how impossible it had been to get things done, even after Royal Commissions had recommended specific reforms. He claimed that the Bill was desired by the Church as a whole, by diocese after diocese, and by many Low Churchmen as well as High Churchmen; and with one strong word about the Establishment ('I would rather go on as we are, if disestablishment were the only alternative'), he again begged Parliament to help the Church to do its work better.

The Archbishop was followed by Lord Haldane, who moved the following amendment:

> That this House is unwilling, especially in the absence of independent inquiry, to assent to legislation which would exclude the greater part of the people of England from effective influence in the affairs of the National Church as established by the Constitution, and which is so framed as to enable members of that Church to pass laws that may wholly change its character without adequate supervision by Parliament.

He offered uncompromising opposition on Parliamentary and constitutional grounds, attacking the whole doctrine on which the Bill was based as rank treason to the doctrine of the Constitution. It was an able speech, and travelled across a very different territory from that of the Archbishop, suggesting before the end that the practical difficulties which the Archbishop had emphasized might be met through Orders in Council. Church and State, he said, were conterminous, the rule was conterminous. He claimed that the Judicial Committee of the Privy Council had saved each great party in the Church in succession, and that it was by Parliament that the Church must have its limits of powers over others prescribed. If the Enabling Bill were passed, it would convert the Church from being an organization representative of the nation at large into a denomination, and substitute the influence of episcopacy for public opinion.

Other speakers followed, but the Archbishop's speech once

again, by its attention to practical considerations, had cleared the ground. Next day was Derby Day, and the House of Lords did not meet. Between then and the division, conversations were started by Sir Lewis Dibdin, who had written to Lord Haldane admiring his speech, and asking him to explore the possibility of procedure by Provisional Orders. He suggested that such Orders might be made by a Secretary of State, for examination by an Ecclesiastical Committee of the Privy Council. The Archbishops would have to satisfy themselves that the particular reform had the Church's approval. They would, he said, probably use the Church Assembly for the purpose. But Parliament would not have recognized the Assembly. Lord Haldane generally agreed with this plan—not so Lord Selborne, who objected to these conspiracies behind the scenes. The Archbishop, to whom Sir Lewis had written, was not so determinedly opposed, but in the end the idea was dropped. The division was taken on July 2, and Lord Haldane's amendment was rejected by 130 votes to 33.

The Committee stage was fixed for July 10. The Archbishop was conciliatory. Lord Haldane's amendment to delete the Ecclesiastical Committee of the Privy Council was lost by 78 votes to 17, and his other amendment to include the constitution of the Church Assembly in a Schedule to the Bill was lost without a division.

There was also an important amendment moved by Lord Willoughby de Broke, with regard to the Book of Common Prayer. He moved the insertion of the following proviso:

> Provided that no measure shall be submitted to the Ecclesiastical Committee which would make any alteration in the Book of Common Prayer as by law prescribed to be used in Churches at the passing of this Act.

The Archbishop, in his reply, said that he had listened to the noble Lord's speech with the greatest possible pleasure, but added some sentences, which ought perhaps to be recorded here in view of later events:

> At the same time I should be deceiving the House if I were to accept for a moment the proposition that we do not intend in any case to touch anything connected with the rubrics of Common Prayer. One of the very reasons why we find the present position difficult is that in small matters, but matters which are nevertheless of practical importance, we want to facilitate sometimes an

abbreviation, sometimes an adaptation of the existing form to slightly different circumstances, sometimes even the addition of extra Collects on particular occasions, such as the noble Lord has taken exception to. It is with the object of doing those things legally, instead of illegally, and being relieved from the responsibility of having done things for which the law gives us no sanction at present, and for which we could not get sanction without an elaborate process of going to Parliament, that we want to use—though we shall certainly use them most sparingly—the powers which this Bill would give us of altering, where the need requires, some things in the rubrics of the Prayer Book.

There was a further question, which the Archbishop answered, from Lord Chaplin:

Viscount Chaplin: What I want to ascertain from the promoters of the Bill is whether it would be necessary as the Bill now stands, for the permission of Parliament to be obtained in any circumstances before anything of that kind is done.

The Lord Archbishop of Canterbury: Yes.

Viscount Chaplin: If that is so, I think it is quite satisfactory.

Lord Parmoor: There is no doubt that the permission of Parliament will be required.

The amendment was then withdrawn.

The Archbishop accepted two amendments moved by the Lord Chancellor (Lord Finlay). It had been originally proposed that 'after considering the Measure the Ecclesiastical Committee shall draft a Report thereon to His Majesty, advising that the Royal Assent ought or ought not to be given to it, and stating the reasons for such advice'. Lord Finlay's amendment, accepted by the Archbishop, made the paragraph run:

After considering the Measure the Ecclesiastical Committee shall draft a Report thereon to His Majesty, stating the nature and legal effect of the Measure, and their views as to its expediency, especially with relation to the constitutional rights of all His Majesty's subjects.

It had also been proposed originally that:

If the Ecclesiastical Committee shall have advised His Majesty to give His Royal Assent to the measure, then, unless within forty days either House of Parliament shall direct to the contrary, such measure shall be presented to His Majesty, and shall have the force and effect of an Act of Parliament on the Royal Assent being signified thereto.

The second amendment moved by Lord Finlay altered the whole character of the Bill. It provided that only 'on address from each House of Parliament asking that such Measure should be presented to His Majesty, such Measure shall be presented to His Majesty, and shall have the force and effect of an Act of Parliament on the Royal Assent being signified thereto'. This was a very different thing from allowing Measures to pass unless either House directed to the contrary. Nevertheless, the Archbishop accepted the amendment, thus making, as Lord Finlay said, what was a very substantial concession. The passing of the Bill through the Committee stage was thus secured without further difficulty.

Next morning, when Dr. Jenkins, the Lambeth Librarian, congratulated the Archbishop on the result, he said: 'My dear Jenkins, if people would only let me do things in my own way, the Church of England would get on all right!' He had gone through most of his life, he added, on the policy that half a loaf was better than no bread.

When the Third Reading was carried on July 21, Lord Wolmer, who had watched from the steps of the throne, congratulated the Archbishop, apologized for his former doubts and rudeness, and said that he was prepared to follow the Archbishop in the whole question of strategy in the House of Commons. This pleased the Archbishop much.

In the House of Commons, the main work was done by Lord Wolmer. He had been unflagging in his explanations, conferences, and correspondence. He had got together a large committee of supporters and had done first-class work. The Second Reading was carried by 304 votes to 16 on November 7. For three days the Bill was considered in Standing Committee E. On December 5, the Third Reading was carried with cheers. A number of small amendments were inserted. There was one amendment of substance, which did away with the Ecclesiastical Committee of the Privy Council and put in its place an Ecclesiastical Committee of both Houses of Parliament, consisting of fifteen Peers nominated by the Lord Chancellor and fifteen Members of the House of Commons nominated by the Speaker. The House of Lords accepted the amendments on December 15. On December 23 the Bill received the Royal Assent.

Thus a very notable change in the constitution of the Church of England was accomplished, and with a speed that is startling to those who look back. Its achievement was due to Randall Davidson more than to any other single person. Without him it could not have happened when it did. The qualities which secured its success have been sufficiently indicated, it is to be hoped, in the course of this record. But at the same time, while Randall Davidson was the leader and accomplisher, it is right to acknowledge that it was also the enthusiasm of the younger men—even, it may be, their pressure upon the Archbishop and the driving force which they applied—that made the achievement possible. And among the younger men stand, on an eminence of their own, William Temple, the son of a former Archbishop of Canterbury, and Viscount Wolmer, the son of the main sponsor and author of the original Report of the Archbishops' Committee on Church and State, Lord Selborne.

CHAPTER LX

THE WELSH CHURCH

As I returned to the inn I had a good deal of conversation with the landlord on religious subjects. He told me that the Church of England, which for a long time had been a down-trodden Church in Wales, had of late begun to raise its head, and chiefly owing to the zeal and activity of its present ministers. . . . He seemed to think that the time was not far distant when the Anglican Church would be the popular as well as the established Church of Wales.

GEORGE BORROW, *Wild Wales*, ch. lxxii.

THE position of the Welsh Church after 'the date of Disestablishment' was left uncertain when the War began. As the War continued, steps were taken to elect a Representative Body and a (larger) Governing Body, with a view to the general management and government of the Church in Wales and its property. The first meeting of the Governing Body was held in London in January 1918. At the end of the War, two principal questions had to be solved. The first was what may be described as the political, including the financial, question. The second was the ecclesiastical, that is the relation of the four Welsh dioceses after Disestablishment to the Province of Canterbury.

I

In his letter of November 2, 1918, to Mr. Bonar Law, outlining the future policy of the Coalition Government, Mr. Lloyd George wrote:

The RT. HON. D. LLOYD GEORGE *to the* RT. HON. A. BONAR LAW

The Welsh Church Act is on the Statute Book, and I do not think that there is any desire, even on the part of the Welsh Church itself, that the Act should be repealed. But I recognize that the long continuance of the War has created financial problems which must be taken into account.

Writing to the Archbishop on November 18, the date of this letter's publication, the Bishop of St. David's,[1] who had seen Mr. Bonar Law, said:

The BISHOP OF ST. DAVID'S *to the* ARCHBISHOP OF CANTERBURY

I attribute the inclusion of the Welsh Church question side by side with the Fiscal question and the Irish question in the Prime

[1] Dr. John Owen.

Minister's letter, to the effect of the Memorial on the subject presented to Mr. Bonar Law with the signature of 182 members of the House of Commons, and to the strong resolution on the subject unanimously passed on Lord Selborne's motion by the National Unionist Association in the beginning of last October.

But though the Bishop of St. David's was ready to make the best of the position, there were others who took a very different view. Lord Robert Cecil, in particular, decided to leave the Government. He resigned, and announced as his reason the fact that he was deeply pledged by word and conduct to the defence of the Church in Wales. He told the Archbishop, in conversation at the Foreign Office, where the Archbishop had gone to consult him about Professor Deissmann's telegram,[1] that Bonar Law had 'betrayed the Welsh Church, and he would not, by remaining in the Government, delude his friends into thinking that all was well'. Lord Robert added that the Bishop of St. David's had been deluded, 'poor innocent little man'. During the next few months a good deal of pressure was brought to bear upon the Government to reimburse the Church in Wales fully for the loss of its endowments. The necessity of revising the financial terms was generally admitted. No one worked harder, or understood the realities of the situation better, than the Bishop of St. David's, and he, as well as the Bishop of St. Asaph,[2] was in constant communication with the Archbishop of Canterbury. A special Welsh Church Parliamentary Committee was appointed by the Governing Body of the Church in Wales at Easter 1919, to deal on its behalf with any offer of settlement that might come from the Government.

In July 1919, when the Enabling Bill was going through the House of Lords, a draft of the Welsh Church Temporalities Bill began to emerge. The two senior Welsh Bishops had interviews respectively with the Prime Minister and Bonar Law. The Bishop of St. David's was a good deal ruffled after his interview with the latter, to whom, he said, he had to speak 'very plainly'. He was sore with the Archbishop himself for not seeing him at once when he sent a message to Lambeth, on July 22 or 23, when he said Welsh Church matters were very critical. 'The Archbishop has never failed me before—he has now.' But next time (July 31) he was in high feather. The Archbishop saw the two

[1] See p. 935.

[2] Dr. A. G. Edwards.

Welsh Bishops and Lord Robert Cecil together, and separately, that day in the House of Lords:

> It seemed that the two Bishops had agreed with Lloyd George and Bonar Law upon the terms of a Bill re-adjusting the Welsh Disestablishment Act of 1914, and they were privately of opinion that the terms offered by the Government were much better than they had anticipated. Robert Cecil was of opinion, however, that he must adhere to the line he had taken throughout of persistent opposition to any secularisation of Church funds, even if secularisation be much less than we had all feared. I may be mistaken, but it did not seem to me that Robert Cecil thought that the Bishops ought certainly to oppose the Government plan. It was only that he could not himself abandon his personal position, and this seemed to me a reasonable attitude on his part.

The Bishop of St. Asaph reported the interview with the Archbishop to Bonar Law and Lloyd George. In the evening of the same day, he and the Bishop of St. David's came to Lambeth at 9.15, when the Archbishop and Mrs. Davidson were entertaining the American Ambassador and his wife to dinner. They now asked the Archbishop for a definite letter stating his approval of the Bill, which, if necessary, Bonar Law could quote publicly. The Archbishop complied with their request, after studying the Bill and the actuaries' memorandum. Under the Bill, the Church in Wales was to lose £48,000 a year in income from its ancient endowments. But without the Bill, the corresponding loss would have been £102,000 a year. The Bill, therefore, restored to the Church £54,000 a year of its lost property. This was possible principally through the allowance of £22,500 for the lapsed vested interests of incumbents who had vacated their benefices in Wales between September 1914 and the date of Disestablishment, and the allowance of £30,000 a year from the commutation of vested interests in tithe. The Ecclesiastical Commissioners were also empowered by the Bill to make an equitable compensation to the Church in Wales for its loss during the past five years in respect of capital and other augmentation grants which would have been made to the Welsh Benefices but for the passing of the Welsh Church Act —a compensation which, in fact, resulted in a substantial sum being transferred to the Welsh Church. The following letters passed:

The ARCHBISHOP OF CANTERBURY *to the* BISHOP OF ST. ASAPH

July 31st, 1919.

I have read with care and interest the draft which has been shown to me of the Welsh Church Temporalities Bill, which is now, as I understand, to be introduced. The circumstances are difficult, and I appreciate your wish to have my counsel in the matter.

Taking everything into consideration, it seems to me that we should act rightly in accepting the Bill as now drafted. Nothing would, I think, be gained by delaying a final settlement, and I am of opinion that, in all the circumstances, the Church ought for the sake of peace to agree to the proposals now made. I have not in the least changed my view upon the general question of Welsh Church Disestablishment, but we must recognize facts as they are, and the prolongation of strife upon this subject would not, I think, be to the advantage of the cause of religion in Wales and in England.

I am not myself an expert in these financial readjustments, and it is possible that there may be some points which I have not accurately understood in detail, but the general position is clear, and, taking it as a whole, I consider that you and we will act rightly in accepting the proposals now made, and in setting ourselves to make the best of the inevitable difficulties, and to throw our strength into setting forward the Church's work in the new conditions which we are called to face.

The BISHOP OF ST. ASAPH *to the* ARCHBISHOP OF CANTERBURY

The Athenaeum, Pall Mall, S.W. 1. 1st August, 1919.

I took your letter this morning, and the Prime Minister and Mr. Bonar Law read it carefully. Notice of the introduction of the Bill (on Monday) is to be given this afternoon.

The next few days, however, witnessed an indignant opposition to the Bill on the part of Lord Salisbury, Lord Robert Cecil, and others, who were angry both with Bonar Law and the Bishops. For a moment it looked as if the Bill would fail. The Archbishop supported the Bill in the House of Lords, but two wrecking amendments were carried under the leadership of Lord Salisbury, who complained that he and his brother had not been consulted —one amendment giving the disused graveyards back to the Church, and the other making the withdrawal of the Welsh Dioceses from Convocation optional. On August 15, the Archbishop was sent for by Bonar Law and Lloyd George, who told him excitedly that if the Lords persisted in their amendments the Bill would be wrecked. The Lords did not persist, though Lord Salisbury, writing to the Archbishop, expressed a strong sense of grievance:

The Marquess of Salisbury *to the* Archbishop of Canterbury

22nd August, 1919.

. . . I cannot think it good tactics to allow your protagonist to resign office on your behalf, and then to settle matters—to settle the very matter upon which he resigned, behind his back or at any rate over his head. This is however precisely what the two Welsh Bishops have done. I was therefore not sorry to see them sitting absolutely alone as the end was reached. As I stood by the Throne I noted that there was not a single peer on our Bench, and only two independent Unionist peers all told in the House. To do him justice I thought St. David's looked very unhappy.

The Archbishop replied as follows:

The Archbishop of Canterbury *to the* Marquess of Salisbury

As from Lambeth Palace, S.E. 1. 26 August, 1919.

I have received in Argyllshire your letter about the final stage of the Welsh Church Bill.

I am honestly most thankful that the Bill has become an Act, and that the episode is closed. The story is not, I think, a creditable one either to the Asquith Government which passed the original Bill, or to the Coalition Government of to-day, but I do not believe that by prolonging the controversy we should in the end have secured a fairer arrangement, or that we could have avoided a mischievous exacerbation of Welsh opinion with consequent damage to the cause of religion both in England and in Wales.

I hold no special brief for the Welsh Bishops, who were forced into the arcana of the final negotiations, but I realize that their position was an intensely difficult one, dragging political considerations into the religious field where their own obligations markedly lie. After all, they do know and understand better than we (or at all events better than *I*) do the cross-currents of Welsh religious opinion, and it was for them, far more than for us, to judge what the controversy meant in Wales in its bearing upon the really paramount matter, the religious well-being of their people.

They apparently had the practically unanimous opinion of their Welsh Councillors, including the three Judges as well as other laymen, with them in favour of the settlement, and, so far as I can judge, I should myself in like circumstances, and with like religious responsibilities, have acted as they did. They had throughout to look beyond the 'tactics' to which you refer, but their appreciation of your brother's action and your own has been enthusiastic, so far at least as I have seen and heard them. I do not know all the details of Lord Robert's original action, and I was not even aware (till this letter of yours) that he had consulted the Bishops about his resignation. Nothing could be more bravely consistent than his action throughout. It is characteristic of the man.[1]

We have all tried to do our best in an exceedingly difficult matter, and we have a right to expect that the following of a straightforward and high-minded course will meet with the benediction which will make it fruitful of good. It will be a matter of extraordinary interest, as well as of no small anxiety, to see what are the religious results of the change in Wales.

I think that with regard to the making of a Welsh Province, it will be well for us to act rather speedily so as to anticipate the coming into force of the 'impertinent' Parliamentary enactment.

II

There was another question of great importance which had to be solved. It was the question of the Province. The Welsh Church Act of 1914 had in the most high-handed way ordered that:

> As from the date of disestablishment the bishops and clergy of the Church in Wales shall cease to be members of, or be represented in, the Houses of Convocation of the Province of Canterbury, but nothing in this Act shall affect the powers of those Houses so far as they relate to matters outside Wales and Monmouthshire.

[1] The Bishop of St. David's, in a statement to St. David's Diocese on the acceptance of the Welsh Church Temporalities Act 1919, writing after its passage, said: 'Lord Robert Cecil, to whom the Church in Wales owes a greater debt of gratitude than it can ever repay, true to the noblest traditions of British public life, resigned high office rather than accept any responsibility for the indefiniteness of the Government's policy upon a question of principle, and with honourable consistency felt bound to condemn very strongly the inadequacy, in point of principle, of the Act of 1919. It is not surprising that so just a man, under all the circumstances, failed to appreciate justly the position which compelled the Welsh Bishops to believe it to be their clear duty with great sorrow to accept the Bill.'

But whatever their feelings of protest against such an outrageous dealing with a constitutional body which was older than Parliament, the question had to be faced: Shall the Welsh dioceses still cling to the Church of England and try to remain, in whatever way possible, a part of the Province, or shall they form a Province of their own? The Archbishop was consulted and saw the Welsh Bishops. The following letters passed:

The Bishop of St. Asaph *to the* Archbishop of Canterbury

The Palace, St. Asaph. 23rd May, 1919.

The time has come when, as Chairman of the Governing Body, I venture respectfully to ask you for your Grace's guidance in reference to the provision in the Welsh Church Bill which excludes from the Convocation of Canterbury the representatives of the Church in Wales.

Would your Grace advise us as to the possibility and the wisdom of our attempting to retain our place in the Convocations of Canterbury, on, of course, the same terms of equality as heretofore?

Or would your Grace advise the Church in Wales to accept the new conditions and to form its own Welsh province?

The Archbishop of Canterbury *to the* Bishop of St. Asaph

24th May, 1919.

I have received your very important letter in which, as Chairman of the Governing Body of the Church of England in Wales, you ask for my counsel respecting the future relation of the four Welsh Dioceses to the rest of our present Province of Canterbury. You are aware that I have continuously, on behalf of our English Bishops, pressed upon you and your Welsh brethren in the Episcopate the assurance of our simple wish to be guided by your wishes and the wishes of the Church in Wales as regards the relation of the Church in Wales after Disestablishment to the Province of Canterbury and its Convocation. We have learnt to value the presence of our four Welsh brethren so highly that the loss to us would be very great if, or when, they leave our Convocation House, and I am certain that the same feeling is entertained in the Lower House. I have protested publicly and privately against the proposed statutory enactment interfering, without any consultation with us, with the existing Constitution of Convocation. I have pointed out, in my evidence before the Select Committee of 1914 and elsewhere, the wrongness of such Parliamentary action and its unconstitutional character.

On the other hand, if, as seems now to be the case, the disestablishment of the four Dioceses must unhappily be regarded as a *fait accompli* to take effect after the War, we have to consider what ought in future to be the position of your four Dioceses. I have, as I think you know, taken counsel on the subject with most of our English Bishops, as well as with all the Welsh Bishops, and I am prepared to say that I have the support of, at the very least, the great majority of them in expressing my deliberate opinion that it will conduce to the happy and orderly working of the whole Church in England and Wales if by our own joint action a separate Province be formed for Wales: indeed, I cannot help fearing that unless this be done there is some danger of confusion and even chaos in the arrangements for the future. We shall hope in every possible way to retain the close fellowship in thought and action which has subsisted between the Bishops in the English and the Welsh Dioceses: but constitutionally the formation of a new Province will, as I believe, be essential to due orderliness and smoothness of working. If I had reason to believe that this advice ran counter to the deliberate opinion of the bishops, clergy, and laymen who have been devising a new Constitution for the Church in Wales, I should feel more hesitation than I do in giving you the advice which I here tender. Most gladly will I confer further with you and with your colleagues in the Welsh Sees, if you so desire. But the power and the resources which have been shown by the Welsh Church in the construction of its new arrangements, seem to make it improbable that if once your decision be adopted, you will be in need of any help at our hands. Whatever we can do with you and for you, at this juncture in our history, is wholly at your service, and I repeat that we are not going to allow the legal severance of some of the formal bonds which at present unite us to impair in the smallest degree the fellowship of the deeper kind which will continue to unite us in things spiritual.

The Governing Body of the Church in Wales passed the following Resolution, in June 1919, which was confirmed at Rhyl on January 6, 1920 (the Bishop of Bangor[1] and the Bangor Diocesan Registrar alone dissenting):

That the Governing Body respectfully requests the President to invite the Archbishop of Canterbury to take such steps as may be necessary to constitute the four Dioceses of Wales into an Ecclesiastical Province.

The Archbishop responded to their request by two successive acts.

[1] Dr. Watkin Williams.

He first sent each of the four Welsh Bishops the following release from their Oaths of Due Obedience to himself as Metropolitan:

The ARCHBISHOP OF CANTERBURY *to the* BISHOP OF ST. ASAPH

24th January, 1920.

I have given full consideration to the Resolution transmitted to me from the Governing Body of the Church in Wales, as passed at Rhyl, January 6th, 1920, on the subject of the formation of an Ecclesiastical Province for Wales. I believe the decision arrived at to be eminently wise, and, with a view to effect being given to it, I write this formal letter to intimate to you that I regard you as being from the ensuing thirty-first day of March released from any obligation under which you lie by reason of the Oath of Due Obedience to the See of Canterbury, which was taken by you at your Consecration to your present See.

When our Convocation meets on February 10th, I hope to make a full and formal statement in public on the whole subject.

He then, in full Synod of the two Houses of the Convocation of Canterbury, on February 10, 1920, but without any Resolution being adopted in either House, made a formal announcement of the facts, and then declared the four Dioceses of Wales to be from the 31st Day of March, 1920, separate from the Province of Canterbury, and free to form themselves, should they so desire, into an Ecclesiastical Province.

The roadway to the new Provincial life is therefore clear, and it will be my desire to co-operate, by counsel or otherwise, in every way that can be helpful, towards the due formation of the new Province and the clothing of its Metropolitan, when elected, with every necessary power and dignity. By my formal utterance from this chair to-day, following upon what has already been written, my brothers, by me and by you, we are performing ecclesiastically what must needs be done on our side, in conjunction with the action of the civil power, that all may be duly in order by the appointed day. Though our Convocation will be the poorer, the new little Province will, we hope and believe, be strong—strong in the memories of a richly-storied past, a past older than ours—strong, too, in the peculiar vigour which belongs to an old life's renewal of its youth. We shall have the Church of Wales entering upon its old new life, not without mark of storm and loss, but under a glow of sunrise, a glow which is to abide and to lighten into its perfect day. Brothers, solemnly, affectionately, hopefully, we who remain in these Convocation halls will wish you Godspeed.

It was not wonderful, when the Archbishop's patience and kindness is remembered, in difficult times and dealing with men of much sensibility, that the Bishop of St. Asaph, in acknowledging the formal parchment certificate setting out what had occurred, should exclaim (February 25, 1920):

> A thousand thanks for all your goodness and kindness to the Church in Wales!

The new Province was inaugurated at St. Asaph, on June 1, 1920, when the Archbishop of Canterbury enthroned the Bishop of St. Asaph in the midst of a great assembly, as first Archbishop of Wales. It was an historic occasion such as the Archbishop loved. Prince Arthur of Connaught was there, representing the King, the Prime Minister was there, the Archbishop of York and the Archbishop of Dublin were present. Not least remarkable was the attendance of official representatives of the Nonconformist Churches. The Archbishop wrote (June 27, 1920):

> The month began by the inauguration of the Welsh Province, the enthronement of St. Asaph as Archbishop in the movable wooden chair, a facsimile of St. Augustine's Canterbury *sedes*. The weather was propitious, and the whole proceedings were extraordinarily well arranged, and, so far as I can judge, every one, both Churchmen and Nonconformists, was well pleased with the doings of the day. The Prime Minister arrived at St. Asaph Palace the previous evening, a few hours after us, and I had abundant talk with him next morning before the Cathedral function. To our surprise, he and his wife appeared at the Early Service in the Cathedral. This has created a teapot storm in ecclesiastical circles of the *Church Times* sort, but in my judgement the net outcome will be entirely good. He did not come there to triumph, or to belittle what was happening, or to curry favour. He came as a religious man, who, I imagine, had no conception that any one would do other than welcome him. Nor did the new Archbishop.

When all was over after the enthronement, Archbishop Davidson went to spend a few days of friendship and peace with the Bishop of Bangor, the one Bishop who, though with complete loyalty and affection and taking his full share in the constitution of the new Province, had voted, and in his last session of the Upper House of Canterbury Convocation lifted up his voice, against the parting of the four Welsh Dioceses from the Province of Canterbury.

CHAPTER LXI

MARRIAGE AND DIVORCE

I repeated to him an argument of a lady of my acquaintance, who maintained, that her husband's having been guilty of numberless infidelities, released her from conjugal obligations because they were reciprocal. JOHNSON. 'This is miserable stuff, Sir. To the contract of marriage, besides the man and wife, there is a third party—Society; and if it be considered as a vow—GOD: and, therefore, it cannot be dissolved by their consent alone. Laws are not made for particular cases, but for men in general. A woman may be unhappy with her husband; but she cannot be freed from him without the approbation of the civil and ecclesiastical power.'

BOSWELL, *Life of Dr. Johnson* (1776).

A GRAVE social and religious issue was raised in the spring of 1920 by the introduction of a Bill in the House of Lords to extend the grounds on which a married person might apply for a divorce. The Bill, under the name of the Matrimonial Causes Bill, was promoted by Lord Buckmaster. It was based on the recommendations contained in the Majority Report of the Royal Commission on Divorce and Matrimonial Causes, over which the first Lord Gorell had presided. It proposed to repeal the existing Acts, including the Act of 1857, which allowed a marriage to be dissolved, but for only one cause, namely adultery; and to restate the law in a form embodying all the principal recommendations of the Royal Commission. It was not the first time since the publication of the Report in 1912 that legislation had been attempted. In August 1917, a strong Parliamentary movement was set on foot to press the Government to undertake legislation to give liberty to marry to persons who had been separated. This had been countered by a Memorial organized by the Archbishop of Canterbury, and signed by the two Archbishops, Cardinal Bourne, three Bishops, five Free Church leaders and a number of others, men and women, influential in public life. In November 1918, Lord Buckmaster himself introduced a short Bill to enable divorce to be obtained for desertion, and to give poor people access to the County Courts for the purpose of obtaining divorce; but it had been lost upon a Division by 39 votes to 29.

I

The present Bill was a much more serious affair. It was very comprehensive, and it was wholly based upon the Royal

Commission and its Report. It contained the provisions on which both the Minority and the Majority Reports of the Royal Commission were agreed, notably for the placing of men and women on an equal footing with regard to divorce, the decentralization of the sittings of the Court so as to help the poorer applicants, and for the giving of new grounds for obtaining decrees of nullity. But in the centre of the Bill five new grounds for divorce were added to the existing ground of adultery—according to the recommendations of the Majority of the Royal Commission. These five new grounds were: (1) desertion for three years; (2) cruelty; (3) incurable insanity after five years confinement; (4) habitual drunkenness found incurable after three years from the first order of separation; and (5) imprisonment under a commuted death sentence. The protagonists for the Bill were Lord Buckmaster and Lord Birkenhead, then Lord Chancellor—a formidable combination. The leaders of the opposition were the Archbishop of Canterbury, the Archbishop of York (who with Sir Lewis Dibdin and Sir William Anson had signed the original Minority Report), and certain lay peers, among them Lord Selborne, Lord Phillimore, and the Duke of Northumberland. The contest was a sharp one—and the deepest interest was taken in every stage of the debate by the Press and by the public at large. In order to understand the gravity of the issue from the Church's point of view, it should be remembered that, while without doubt the Divorce Act of 1857 had changed the laws of the State, the law of the Church itself had not been changed. That law was declared by the Canons of 1604, which dealt only with divorce *a thoro et mensa* (separation) and cases of Nullity of Marriage, and not with divorce *a vinculo* (dissolution of a valid marriage). In other words, marriage was still treated as indissoluble, and divorce *a vinculo* of a valid marriage was unknown. To use Sir Lewis Dibdin's words, in an article in the *Quarterly Review*, October 1911, 'As Church law stood before the Reformation... so it stood under the Canons of 1604, so it stood after the Divorce Act of 1857, and so it stands to-day.' There was beyond doubt a difference of opinion, in the first fifty years after the Reformation, as to whether the 'law of God' recognized the entire dissolution of marriages when one of the partners was guilty of adultery, with or without the sentence of the Court. But no one doubted that the ecclesiastical law in England in those years forbade a divorce *a vinculo* of a marriage validly contracted. At the same time, the fact that the Divorce Act of 1857 had been passed, allowing adultery as a cause, had beyond dispute affected the application of the Church's law. Many Churchmen still insisted on the complete indissolubility of the marriage bond,[1] save by death. But there were others—and the Archbishop of Canterbury was among them—who admitted that the bond might be broken by adultery; on the ground that in St. Matthew's version of our Lord's words, adultery was acknowledged as a reason for dissolving marriage.[2] It was a breach of the canon law of the Anglican (as well as the Roman) Church to acquiesce even so far. How, then, could the addition of new causes of dissolution be tolerable? Such was the problem.

Lord Buckmaster, in moving the Second Reading of the Bill on March 10, 1920, admitted that no argument and no persuasion could avail against those who regarded the marriage tie as so permeated and interpenetrated with divine sanction and authority, that to dissolve it under any circumstances was to cause offence against something higher than earthly laws. He did not attempt such argument, but based his appeal on the undoubted sufferings and difficulties of innumerable human lives. He laid great stress on the fact, brought out by the Majority Report of the Royal Commission, that 'experience teaches that causes other than death do in fact intervene to make continuous married life practically impossible and to frustrate the objects for which the union was formed'. And he quoted the Royal Commissioners' words, which were almost an epitome of his whole argument:

> We have to deal with human nature as it has always been, and as it is: and it is established beyond all question that for various reasons, amongst others improvident, reckless, and early marriages, drunkenness, sensuality, brutality, immorality, lunacy, and crime, many marriages become absolute failures, and married life becomes either morally or physically, or both morally and physically, impossible.

[1] Canon 107 (of 1604) said: In all sentences pronounced only for divorce and separation *a thoro et mensa*, there shall be a caution and restraint inserted in the act of the said sentence, That the parties so separated shall live chastely and continently; neither shall they, during each other's life, contract matrimony with any other person.

[2] St. Matt. v. 32 and xix. 9.

No one who heard Lord Buckmaster could doubt how deeply he himself was moved by the hardships of those whose marriage for any of the causes named had been frustrated of its object. And he quoted instances in which cruelty, and especially desertion (not least in war time), had left poor women derelict and desolate, sometimes with one child and sometimes with more: women who often and often had the opportunity of remarriage, and yet were barred by the law, and often in consequence fell victims to the temptations of irregular unions. In the name of justice and humanity he pleaded for relief.

The principal speech against the Bill on the first day was made by the Archbishop of York, who affirmed the Church's view of marriage as dissoluble only by death, though recognizing the difficulty caused by the exception of adultery, which some believed on the authority of St. Matthew's Gospel to have been 'authorized by Christ himself'. The Archbishop, however, deliberately rested his arguments not upon the ground of religious authority but upon that of public welfare. On that ground he resisted the plea made by the accumulation of individual cases of hardship, and claimed that the general good of the community, and the interests of the institution of matrimony, made it most undesirable to add any of the proposed new grounds to the admitted ground of adultery, which was an offence 'constituting a breach in the marriage tie wholly unique in its character'.

The debate, after further speeches, was resumed on March 24 by the Lord Chancellor (Birkenhead) in a speech of great brilliance, though delivered in a manner which had something repelling rather than persuasive about it. He went through the new grounds for divorce in detail, and laid great emphasis on the experience of Scotland, where desertion was allowed, and where no ill effects followed: and, especially in dealing with the case of an innocent wife forced to separate from her husband by the latter's cruelty, he poured a great deal of scorn on the whole notion of judicial separation. He quoted with approval words which appeared in the Majority Report of the Royal Commission, describing it as 'this proceeding [which,] neither dissolving the marriage nor reconciling the parties, nor yet changing their natures' was 'one of the most corrupting devices ever imposed by serious natures on blindness and credulity . . . tolerated only because men believed as a part of their religion that dissolution would be an offence against God'. But before taking the detailed points, the Lord Chancellor enlarged upon two principles of the greatest importance, not hitherto clearly brought out. First he claimed that the only real controversy—the only controversy on principle—was that between those who believed that marriage ought to be indissoluble for any reason, and those who did not hold that belief. But the principle that marriage was, and ought to be, indissoluble was 'excised with almost universal approval from our institutions 350 years ago', when it was first recognized that by the procedure of a private Act of Parliament, divorce ought to be obtainable on the ground of adultery.[1] The second main point of principle which the Lord Chancellor made was that 'the spiritual and moral sides of marriage are incomparably more important than the physical side', that 'a breach of that which is highest must be treated by the State as not less grave than a breach of that which is lower', and that the ecclesiastical case that, although marriage is not otherwise dissoluble, it may nevertheless be dissolved in cases where adultery has been committed, was a case adopted under the influence of an almost unconscious opportunism.

The Archbishop of Canterbury, who followed Lord Birkenhead, was well aware of the difficulties he had to face in reply. It was, he said, 'a formidable task' for a simple man who claimed no power of fervent eloquence. And he was not at his best. He did not deal at all with the question of principle—a failure which exposed him to a good deal of criticism outside. He contented himself with a careful dealing with the argument that the number of applications for separation orders was evidence of the number of cases in which people who ought to be divorced were not at present able to get divorce, and applied for separation orders instead. The practical argument, the handling of actual facts as opposed to theories, was characteristic of the Archbishop, and he had taken very great pains to obtain from the associated societies for the protection of women and children, from the Charity Organization Society, those who had had to do with Canadian soldiers in

[1] The reference is to the Act of Parliament of 1551–2, which declared the second marriage of William Parr, Marquis of Northampton, good, notwithstanding the first marriage and any canon or ecclesiastical law to the contrary. Parr had in 1542 obtained a sentence of divorce *a thoro et mensa* against Anne Bourchier, on the ground of her adultery. In 1547 (?) Parr married Elizabeth Brooke. See *English Church Law and Divorce*, Dibdin and Chadwyck Healey, 1912, pp. 62–9.

war-time, and many others, all the facts they could supply about the numbers of deserted wives. In the previous speeches, statements had been made about thousands, even tens of thousands, of desertions, and he was able to show very clearly that when the actual facts were examined, such large statements did not find support. For example, there were 412,000 Canadian soldiers in England during the War, but, in spite of all that had been said or implied, the number of deserted wives had been only 200. He further argued—and with this he closed his speech—that a Bill which contented itself with indicating the points on which the minority and majority of the Royal Commission were agreed—cheaper divorce, equality of sex conditions, and increased grounds for declaring marriages null—would do all that was needed, while to go farther was to set their feet upon a slippery slope.

After a few further speeches, the Second Reading was carried by 93 votes to 45.

II

Next time the Bill came before the House, on April 20, when the Committee stage began, the Archbishop of Canterbury took the opportunity to reply to Lord Birkenhead's charge that the Church attached chief importance to the lower or physical side of marriage, and that Churchmen like himself were committed to 'this monstrous and medieval paradox that they assent to divorce for a breach of the less important obligation, and they deny divorce for a breach of the more important obligations of marriage'. The Archbishop's answer was twofold. First he accepted all that the Lord Chancellor had said about the high and ennobling intercourse of soul with soul—memory, fellowship, hope, etc.—but he refused to isolate the spiritual from the physical. 'It is', he said, 'because these elevate and uplift and sanctify what he most inadequately called the purely physical or carnal side, that I am unable to follow him in the wide dissociation which he seemed to advocate between the different obligations of married life.' But next he pointed out that the allowance of adultery as the only justifiable ground for breaking the marriage tie, was not a medieval paradox, but 'the words are given in the Gospel as spoken by Our Lord himself' as quoted by St. Matthew—'I say unto you that every one that putteth away his wife saving for the cause of fornication, maketh her an adulteress, and whosoever shall marry her when she is put away committeth adultery'; and the Lord Chancellor himself had taken the trouble 'to assure the House that he agreed with St. Matthew'! The Archbishop added:

> We live in a free country, and as individuals we may repudiate these words—that teaching, that guidance. Those sanctions are sacred to most of us, but not to all. But whatever else may be said of them it is not a medieval paradox. It is not something which has grown up in corrupt ages of the Church, but which goes back to the Founder of our faith. If we make that guidance ours, and hold to these words, which I do, there is nothing more to say.

The Committee stage proceeded with successive victories for the upholders of the Bill. But it was still necessary to make plain, if the Bill became an Act of Parliament, how the Church would regard the subsequent marriages of persons who had been divorced under its provisions. Bishop Gore wrote to the Archbishop as follows:

BISHOP GORE *to the* ARCHBISHOP OF CANTERBURY

April 25, 1920.

> I know how ill you were on the occasion of the 2nd Reading Debate on the Divorce Bill in the Lords. But I think I must tell you that on the whole, as far as my limited means of information suggest, a painful impression was created by both debates, among other than extreme churchmen, that the position had not been made clear that, whatever Bill might be passed and put upon the Statute Book, the Church could not recognize marriages, which lie outside what on any interpretation is the will of Christ, either in respect of the use of its churches or ministers or in respect of subsequent Communion.

The Archbishop determined to put an end to any doubt as to the Church's position. On May 4, he moved the insertion of a new clause:

> The marriage of a person whose previous marriage has been dissolved under the provisions of this act, and whose former husband or wife is still living, shall not be solemnized in any Church or Chapel of the Church of England.

As the law stood under the Act of 1857, an incumbent was not entitled to refuse to solemnize a marriage in his church of 'the innocent party' in a divorce suit; and, though he might refuse to solemnize the marriage of 'the guilty party', he was bound to allow the use of his Church for the solemnization of such a marriage by any other clergyman, 'entitled to officiate within the Diocese, who is willing to perform the ceremony'. Lord Buckmaster, under his Bill, was proposing to leave the discretion with the individual clergyman as to whether or no he would solemnize the marriage of *any* divorced person whose former spouse is still living. The Archbishop's amendment declared in a clear and challenging form that in his view no marriages of divorced persons should be allowed to take place in church in any circumstances whatever.

There was a good and attentive House. The Archbishop spoke admirably, with great force, simplicity, and earnestness. It was a grave and weighty appeal to the House and to Lord Buckmaster for fair play, and a cogent statement of the intolerable position in which the Church would be placed if an indiscriminate practice prevailed as a result of this Bill. He quoted again the text from St. Matthew, and pointed out that those who accepted the theory of divorce which the Bill embodied must disregard these words:

> If the Bill becomes law, the State will allow divorce for causes which the whole Church of the West has quite invariably repudiated.

To expect the Church of England to give up its rule and put a Parliamentary rule in its place, was a quite impossible position for him to accept:

> If any of your Lordships think that the mere connection of the Church and the State, or the application of the system which we call 'establishment' carries with it that, I utterly and entirely repudiate it.

It was one of the Archbishop's best speeches, crisp and vigorous, and was received with much sympathy, the House cheering loudly and generally when he resumed his seat. Lord Buckmaster could not accept the amendment as it stood, but offered the forbidding of the marriage of the guilty person in Church. Lord Birkenhead said that, if the Archbishop held to his view about the threat to the Establishment, he for one among many 'profound believers and supporters of the policy of Establishment' would find it necessary to reconsider the basis upon which his belief depended. When the division was called the amendment was lost by one vote (50 to 51). The two Archbishops and eleven Bishops were in the minority. The Archbishop did not conceal his regret that more Bishops had not been in their places, for, as Sir Lewis Dibdin said privately afterwards, it was the only occasion that he remembered when there was a straight issue on the laws of the Church *versus* the laws of the State.[1]

Another example of the cleavage between the law of the Church and the law of the State arose with regard to the admission to Communion of persons who had been divorced. Lord Selborne moved an amendment to secure 'that no clergyman should be penalized for refusing to admit [such persons] to Communion'. The Archbishop was not best pleased with the amendment, as he did not think that the question of admission to Communion was suitably discussed in Parliament. But he could not decline to support an amendment when put forward. The justification for the amendment was due to a ruling by Sir Lewis Dibdin as Dean of the Arches in the case of *Banister* v. *Thomson* (1908). Sir Lewis had there held that a man who had contracted a marriage which the law of the State allowed, though it was condemned by the law of the Church, did not become thereby a notorious evil liver, and that therefore the clergyman was bound to admit him to Communion. Unless something more

[1] The form in which the Clause 34, 'Saving for rights of clergymen of the Church of England', was ultimately passed on report with the amendment offered and moved by Lord Buckmaster, was as follows:

(1) 'A clergyman in holy orders of the Church of England shall not be compelled to publish the banns of marriage of or to solemnise the marriage of any person whose previous marriage has been dissolved either in the United Kingdom or elsewhere, and whose former husband or wife is still living, and shall not be liable to any suit, penalty or censure for publishing the banns of marriage, or for refusing to publish the banns of marriage of, or for solemnising or refusing to solemnise the marriage of any such person.'

(2) 'If any minister of any church or chapel of the Church of England refuses to publish the banns of marriage of, or to solemnise the marriage of any persons who but for such refusal would have been entitled to have their banns published or their marriage solemnised in the church or chapel, the minister may permit any other clergyman in holy orders of the Church of England entitled to publish the banns of marriage, or to officiate within the diocese within which the church or chapel is situate to solemnise the marriage in the church or chapel: Provided that the marriage of a person who as a defendant has been divorced under the provisions of this Act and whose former husband or wife is still living, shall not be solemnised in any church or chapel of the Church of England.'

direct and special than appeared in the Deceased Wife's Sister's Act were put into the proposed Matrimonial Causes Act, the result, it was feared, would be the same. The Archbishop of Canterbury spoke on lines similar to those on which he had supported his own previous amendment. The State might indeed make new marriage laws, but 'you must not go on to say that therefore and thereby the Church must change its rules and accept for full Church privilege any one who is conforming to the State law, even if the Church believes these new enactments to be contrary to God's law'. Marriages made under the Act would be legal marriages—he did not dispute that: but the men and women who would have contracted them, while 'perfectly good, honest, straightforward citizens', would have 'placed themselves outside the rules of the Church of England, and the Church must retain its power to deal with each case on its merits as it arises'. And as to the Establishment:

> I yield to none in my sense of the value to the nation of the Establishment, for which I care with my whole heart; but there are higher considerations even than that, if you do force us into the position of loyalty to the one thing or of loyalty to the other thing. I cannot believe that your Lordships, when the facts are fully before you, desire to place us Bishops as well as the clergy—perhaps more than the clergy—in that intolerable position. Most seriously do I protest against it, and tell you that from this protest I cannot conscientiously depart.

The point was further emphasized in the question and answer which took place immediately before the division:

> *The Lord Archbishop of Canterbury*: I want to be quite clear whether I have misinterpreted the noble and learned Lord. As I understood him, the position is this. Let Parliament pass a law giving any conditions you like for divorce and re-marriage, the Church is powerless and must follow suit and regard such people as capable of taking part in the highest and most spiritual functions. I want to know whether that is really so or not. The noble and learned Lord told us early in the debate that although the Bill went quite far he would like to go further, and therefore we were left with the expectation of possible further advance. Are we to understand that whatever happens we shall be expected simply to follow suit and to make our rules correspond?

> *Lord Buckmaster*: What may happen at other times I cannot tell you, but unless a person is an open and notorious evil liver, or a

depraver of the book of Common Prayer, as the law stands to-day he is entitled to have access to Holy Communion.

No wonder that the Archbishop should protest against such a position. But Lord Selborne's amendment was lost by 61 votes to 87.

The final scene in the drama took place in the House of Lords on June 22. The first two speakers moved and seconded the rejection of the Bill, but hardly did justice to the opposition, Lord Braye, a Roman Catholic peer, being indistinctly heard, and Lord Halifax, though pathetic in his appeal, forgetting himself in the middle of his speech and, after long pauses, sitting down. The Archbishop followed, and by arrangement was the only episcopal spokesman. He said that he knew, and had great sympathy with, hard cases, but hard though they were they were capable of being enormously exaggerated by comparison with the homes of England as a whole, and many hard cases would remain untouched by this Bill. He repeated his acceptance of the one exception of adultery for which marriage might be dissolved—and, in answer to a direct question by Lord Birkenhead, acknowledged that he did not consider the innocent party who remarried to be guilty of adultery. He spoke of the extraordinary unsettlement of the times, the absence of any mass of popular demand, and the impossibility of ever going back from such a change if it were to be made. Four more speeches followed from the Lord Chancellor, Lord Selborne, Lord Buckmaster, and Lord Finlay, after which the Third Reading of the Bill was carried by 154 votes to 107.

So much space has been given to the deliberations on this Bill, because it was by far the most serious debate on marriage and divorce which took place in Parliament during the episcopate of Archbishop Davidson, and also because the whole question clearly brings out the Archbishop's own view of a subject of the gravest importance. He stood firm on the ground which he believed to be the right ground—making admissions with regard to the consequences of the excepting clause in St. Matthew's Gospel which were very unwelcome to some of his allies. And he also insisted, in the most unmistakable way, that the Church had its own rules, and that those rules were not to be changed at the will of the State. To the proposals for cheaper divorce, equality of the sexes, and the increasing of the grounds of nullity, he was ready to assent, and he supported a Bill to enact these proposals, introduced in 1921 by Lord Gorell.[1] The Matrimonial Causes Bill itself, however, in spite of the support received in the House of Lords, did not proceed further and, though it was re-introduced in later years by Lord Buckmaster, without being debated upon the same ample scale, it still failed to win the approval of Parliament.[2]

[1] This Bill was, however, altered during its progress through the House of Lords, through the making of desertion for three years a cause for divorce, and the Archbishop therefore withdrew his support, as also did Lord Gorell.

[2] Seven years after Archbishop Davidson's death, on the initiative of Mr. A. P. Herbert, *The Matrimonial Causes Act, 1937*, received the Royal Assent. It included the first three of the new grounds enumerated on p. 992, *supra*, but omitted (4) and (5). The following Clause was also incorporated under the title 'Relief for Clergy of Church of England and of Church in Wales'.

'12. The following subsection shall be substituted for subsections (2) and (3) of section one hundred and eighty four of the principal Act:—

"(2) No clergyman of the Church of England or of the Church in Wales shall be compelled to solemnize the marriage of any person whose former marriage has been dissolved on any ground and whose former husband or wife is still living or to permit the marriage of any such person to be solemnized in the Church or Chapel of which he is the minister".'

CHAPTER LXII

THE SIXTH LAMBETH CONFERENCE

Il faut compter parmi les plus grands maux de notre temps le fait que les Églises soient si disunies. Pour ce qui me concerne, si l'on a besoin de moi, je n'hésiterai pas à traverser dix océans pour ce but. JEAN CALVIN, *Lettre à Cranmer*, 1552.

THERE can be no doubt that the decision to hold the sixth Lambeth Conference so soon after the War was very wise. As far as the Bishops themselves were concerned, the idea of a coming home from the ends of the earth, after the years of strain and suffering and isolation, was most welcome. There were, besides, all sorts of questions, just emerging in the post-war world, which demanded counsel and answer. And in the different provinces of the Anglican Communion, indeed among the English-speaking peoples as a whole, men desired illumination. A conference, with a history behind it, composed of Bishops of an ancient Church now widespread in the new world and the old, all with very definite duties and responsibilities of their own, was better adapted to leadership, on some at least of the issues, than any new and untried conference on Faith and Order, or any special congress born merely of the needs of the time. Moreover, the general trust in the judgement of Randall Davidson, and the affection for his personality, which the Anglican episcopacy entertained, gave an added weight to the influence which he would naturally exercise as Archbishop of Canterbury.

I

Yet the difficulties in the way of a successful accomplishment of the Conference's aims were of a serious character. Some of the subjects calling for attention were unusually contentious. There were the various questions concerning marriage, there were the racial problems, the controversy raised by the ministry of women, and the challenges flung out by theosophy, spiritualism, and their like. Would there be a split between the stricter and the more liberal Bishops on some of these? Or would the Bishops utter 'mere platitudinous statements that this or that heresy (spiritualism, Christian Science, etc.) has a basis of truth, but that one must safeguard Catholic Order?' As the Archbishop shrewdly noted, 'Any of us could say that, and we should be a laughing-stock if we bring people from the ends of the earth to put that on paper.'

There were two questions which the Archbishop judged to be specially acute, Modernism and Reunion. As Bishop Gore put it from his point of view:

BISHOP GORE *to the* ARCHBISHOP OF CANTERBURY

Private. Jan. 13, 1920.

I hope that Divine Providence intends the Church of England to exist over the next year or two without a schism which would separate off the Catholic section, but I dread the Lambeth Conference and its consequences. It seems to me that the whole hope of the Church of England is in danger of being sacrificed (i) to the Modernists, who are daily becoming more and more conscious that their objections to the Creed are fundamental both as to ideas and to miracles, i.e. that the Sanday-Henson position is impossible. (ii) to Reunionists who yield themselves to their amiable impulses and do no clear thinking. There is no doubt always a crisis: but this is unique. But I know how much and deeply I differ from you, and I ask no answer.

And, as the Archbishop himself wrote in a private Memorandum, looking back when all was over (15 August):

> We had to deal for the first time, as frequently pointed out in conversation, with the probability that we should find a minority in the Conference who would not be content to be an acquiescent minority, but might march out denouncing us, or raise cohorts outside.

Of the two issues, Modernism seemed the more dangerous; and certainly public sympathy, and general Church sympathy, would be far more readily extended to a schism or revolt which had credal questions as its cause than to one due to questions of order. It must be admitted that the Archbishop was often a little inclined to over-estimate perils, and that the alarms sounded by Dr. Gore were not so substantial in fact as they seemed to be in his imagination. But at least the anticipation of dangers caused him to be singularly well prepared to meet them should they come. And Randall Davidson was determined to do everything he could to prevent the creeds forming a subject of discussion.

These found no place on the Agenda prepared in July 1919; the Bishops interested contented themselves with the assurance that they would try to introduce something strong in the Encyclical Letter. In May, there was what the Archbishop playfully called Lollards' Revolt—in the shape of a letter from the Bishop of Gloucester (Dr. Gibson), with the support of the Bishops of Ely (Dr. Chase) and Chichester (Dr. Burrows), who had rooms in the Lollards' Tower. This letter expressed the view that the Creed and its interpretation could 'hardly be altogether excluded from consideration when we come to the Resolutions', and went on:

The Bishop of Gloucester *to the* Archbishop of Canterbury

Private. 12 May 1920.

Though we realize fully the difficulty of saying *any*thing, yet we are agreed that *some*thing ought to be said, though *what* this should be requires most careful consideration. We cannot but feel that there is grave danger of some unguarded and perhaps exaggerated resolution being suggested if we do nothing.

The Bishop added that he was in consultation with a number of other Bishops on the subject.

The Archbishop's attitude is clearly stated in his reply:

The Archbishop of Canterbury *to the* Bishop of Gloucester

15th May, 1920.

Your exceedingly important letter of May 12th has given me abundant food for thought.

I gather that you and other Diocesans, whom you have consulted, think that we have done wrong in not giving, through the Agenda Paper of the Lambeth Conference, an opportunity to the Bishops to discuss the need of our urging a stricter adherence on the part of the clergy generally to the credal obligations which they have undertaken, and that you would like still to endeavour to get emphasis laid upon these obligations by resolutions of the Conference or by the encyclical letter.

No one, I think, can feel more strongly than I do the gravity, at this moment, of our right handling of the whole question of what is meant by 'Credal Loyalty', but I do quite distinctly feel that we run a very grave risk of alienating some of the best and most devout among the younger men and women of to-day, who are intellectually keen, religiously earnest, and wholesomely progressive in thought, if we try to stiffen the obligations incumbent on a Christian believer, and encourage the clergy to such action and influence. I quite see that there is another side to all this, but, to my mind, the danger is infinitely greater in the direction I have indicated than in the opposite direction. You will remember the labour that was devoted to this subject by the best brains among us at the Conference twelve years ago, and, as at present advised, I remain distinctly of opinion that we should be more likely to do harm than good were we to attempt a general revision of these questions with a view to—what would be regarded as—a 'warning off' of men and women who are feeling their way towards a firmer Faith at a time of profound unrest and of much experimental and provisional thought.

I should not be honest with you if I did not say this frankly in reply to your letter, but of course I have no right to be dogmatic or autocratic on the subject, and it is quite obvious that, in an encyclical letter or in other ways, opportunity may be found of giving expression to our position and its obligations, without incurring dangers which seem to me to be very real.

You know that forces are to be brought into play, immediately before the Conference, with a view to bringing pressure upon the Bishops in the direction, I will not say which you have indicated, but which the promoters indicate in no uncertain way. You may feel that for that very reason it is desirable that what you think is needed should be said wisely instead of being said in a truculent and minatory way. Personally, unless the phrases chosen be of so mild a sort as would not satisfy you, I should rather prefer a truculent and minatory attitude to have its free expression, and produce its appropriate result. My own belief is that our best line of advance is the firm adherence to our quiet and steady assurance of the truth of what is committed to our keeping, and that we serve this best by shewing, rather than proclaiming, our allegiance to it. But here again, I am expressing what, obviously, is a matter of opinion only.

Till the very end of the Conference, the Archbishop was 'in daily anticipation' of receiving a request for some strong statement, on the Bishop of Gloucester's lines, in the Encyclical Letter. But none came. One precaution the Archbishop had taken. In the Address, at the opening of the Conference, from St. Augustine's Chair in Canterbury Cathedral, he spoke strongly and firmly about the vital significance of the old Creed:

The phrases though cast in other days, other surroundings than ours, and retaining their birthmarks, are no empty survival of effete or dying things. They live. They have hands and feet. . . . To this chair cling varied memories. An Anselm, a Langton, a Cranmer, a Secker, a Benson, had each of them a revelation to understand and to assimilate, a message to carry to his contemporaries, an interpretation to offer. So have we. But for us, as for them, it is the old Creed which stands.

In addition the Archbishop noted in his private Memorandum:

For the drafting of the Encyclical Letter, I invited the help of Ely among others, partly to occupy him on the lines we had laid down, and partly because I felt that, if the question of credal obligation were raised, he would be the most helpful representative of that school.

II

The second critical issue had the principal place on the Agenda of the Conference as 'Relation to and Reunion with other Churches'. In each of the last three Conferences, it had been the subject of a Report and Regulations, and the War had given the whole movement towards Church Unity an additional impetus. The East African Bishops would certainly want to say something more about Kikuyu.[1] A union scheme had just been started in South India, in which the Anglican Church was very much concerned. The Bishop of London had discussed reunion with a group of Wesleyan ministers, on the basis of episcopacy. The American Episcopal Church was considering a proposal whereby any congregationalist minister who desired it might be confirmed and episcopally ordained without giving up his Congregational membership and ministry. There had also been conferences at Mansfield College, Oxford, between Anglicans and Nonconformists, which appeared to go a long way in the direction of intercommunion and mutual recognition. And there was the well-known project of a World Conference on Faith and Order initiated in 1910. No wonder then that alike the fears and the hopes which such prospects aroused should make a clamour at Lambeth. One group said—to quote the Archbishop's words:

If you yield one jot to these would-be reformers who are trying to validate non-Episcopal Eucharists and non-Episcopal Orders, we must reconsider our position in the Church of England, and we warn you also to beware how you move an inch towards releasing

[1] See ch. xlii.

> the obligation of a plain interpretation of the Creeds. We regard the Bishop of Norwich and Tissington Tatlow as leading us into harmful comprehensiveness, and Henson and Rashdall as leading us, if they only could, into perilous unorthodoxy. Beware what you do, for we do not mean to keep silent if you thus offend.

On the other side there were earnest people who pressed 'almost tearfully':

> It is simply impossible for us to go on in friendly relation to these Nonconformists whom we reverence and trust, and with whom you bid us take counsel on missionary and other similar matters, and then to be barred from preaching to them, or they to us, in a regular way, or from an occasional fellowship in Eucharistic worship and Communion. We mean indeed to use what we believe to be our true liberty, and not to wait for Episcopal authority before reverently joining them in things sacramental.

Each side turned to Randall Davidson for protection and encouragement—not for advice, as their minds were fully made up—and the outlook was neither bright nor simple. And yet, as we shall see, out of this real conflict there came the greatest achievement, the resounding success, of the whole Conference, the Appeal to all Christian People.

III

The published Report gives the conclusions to which the Conference came on the various topics. But it should be stated that no small part of its success was due to the trouble taken in planning it beforehand. By the time the Conference met, there was in existence a mass of material[1] quite different from anything that previous Conferences had had, and to this the Archbishop personally attributed a good deal of the smoothness with which the Conference worked. For the first time, a whole series of papers on the points to be raised was circulated to the members; and also for the first time episcopal secretaries, in addition to the main secretary, the Bishop of Peterborough,[2] were booked in advance for the several committees, the Archbishop thinking it best to

[1] A bibliography giving some recent books on subjects to be considered in the Lambeth Conference in 1920, and various printed memoranda, were circulated by the Archbishop to the Bishops well in advance of the Conference.

[2] Dr. F. T. Woods, subsequently Bishop of Winchester.

leave the election of chairmen to the committees when chosen. There was an even more abundant atmosphere of hospitality than in 1908, less stiffness (it was noticed) between the English Bishops and those from overseas. There were many stories and not a few amusing incidents. The American Bishops in particular regaled one another with stories in the off hours. Thus Dr. Gailor, Bishop of Tennessee, who was their Presiding Bishop, told how a man had come up to him and said in the free American way, 'I reckon you're a Preacher.' 'Yes', said the Bishop. 'What Church?' 'Episcopal.' 'Ah, that's an old historic steady institution, had time for its religion to calm down. My religion is a new religion—we have to make plenty of noise as we're just blasting the foundations.' 'What religion is that?' asked Bishop Gailor. The other replied, 'The True Seed in the Spirit' (which turned out to be a very particular form of the Baptist belief). On another occasion the Archbishop was very much troubled with lumbago. One of the English Suffragans ran after him to suggest an infallible cure, 'Tie a fiddle string round your waist'; to which the Archbishop mildly replied, 'You are always very kind.' The devotional arrangements were all admirably planned by the Bishop of Dover (Dr. Bilbrough).[1] There was one difference in the composition of the Conference from that of former years. Before 1920, all the members were Bishops in active work, with responsibilities of a diocesan character. Thus, in the Encyclical Letter of 1908, they were described as 'All having superintendence over dioceses or lawfully commissioned to exercise episcopal functions therein'. On this occasion (though the Archbishop did not personally favour the plan) invitations were extended by Resolution of the Conference on the first day, to certain retired Bishops, among them Bishops Bernard, Gore, and Ryle. These three Bishops, however, refused on the ground that they no longer had responsibility, and therefore that their counsel would not be appropriate. As, however, three other retired Bishops accepted the invitation, the Encyclical Letter described the assembly as simply 'Archbishops and Bishops in full communion with the Church of England'.

The personnel of the Conference was strangely mixed. Almost all schools of thought and many types of character were represented among the 252 members. There was the American

[1] Bishop of Newcastle, 1927.

Bishop who delivered a wonderful speech about women, to which the Bishop of Durham assured the Conference that he listened with enjoyment and agreement 'but my enjoyment was greater than my agreement'; the Canadian Archbishop who announced with what dazed bewilderment he listened to the expression of advanced liberal sentiments in an assembly which he had every reason to expect would be staunchly conservative; a Bishop from India—a busy figure pressing his way through to the Library, with his smoked glasses, his patent leather satchels with steel handles, sometimes stamping his feet with indignation, sometimes bursting into tumultuous stammering speech on Church Unity; a Bishop from China speaking in gentle and persuasive tones of provincial organization and the Chung hua Sheng Kung hui, a name greeted at first by a surprised conference with a ripple of mild laughter. Most striking of all was Frank Weston, Bishop of Zanzibar, with his extraordinary mixture of generosity and menace—the latter revealed, for example, when, just as a mediating Resolution on a marriage question was about to be put at the end of a prolonged debate, he strode to the rostrum and said ominously that he would not like to determine his relation to the Lambeth Conference by a vote on such a Resolution in a House of such a size! There was also an Orthodox Bishop present for the first time at any Lambeth Conference. He came to confer with the Committee on Reunion as a delegate from the Patriarchate of Constantinople. He was Philaretos, Metropolitan of Demotica, but he stood outside the Conference proper. He was a gentle old man with a quaint humour. 'Ah, c'est terrible, notre histoire!' said he once, as he told of the fearful indignities which the Patriarch used to endure in old days when visiting the Grand Vizier at Constantinople, kneeling and grovelling on the floor like a dog. He spoke also of the Patriarch's lodgings in a monastery at Constantinople, contrasting their narrow range with the splendour of Lambeth. Then, when he finally came to bid the Archbishop good-bye, after friendly talk and expressions of hope on either side for closer relationship between the two Churches leading to union, the Archbishop of Canterbury said 'Mais pas trop vite', and the words were echoed with gusto by the Metropolitan of Demotica, 'Pas trop vite'.

In such an assembly, the Archbishop's considered policy was not to act as the ordinary chairman but to treat every Bishop with the utmost deference, so that none might say hereafter that the view of any Bishop of the Church had not had a fair hearing. 'The Archbishop of Canterbury is a wonderfully wise man', said the Primate of All Ireland, and in speaking of his patience, open-mindedness, and fairness, he spoke for every one. The first week, and the two closing weeks, the Conference sat together, and the Archbishop presided all the while—though for the first few days he was sorely crippled with lumbago, sitting in his chair with rugs over his knees and (to his disgust) a hot-water apparatus beneath. He attended most of the Committees at one time or another—hearing the debates or the evidence, and once at least giving evidence himself.

IV

The large Reunion Committee was the one which the Archbishop most frequented—and it was here that the Appeal was worked out. Of this Committee the Archbishop of York was Chairman. At first, as the various local schemes of federation or union were presented, progress was extraordinarily slow. Nobody seemed able to go further than envisaging such a plan as that put out in 1888 and known as the Lambeth Quadrilateral: (1) the Bible; (2) the Creeds; (3) the two Sacraments of Baptism and the Supper of the Lord, and (4) 'The Historic Episcopate, locally adapted in the methods of its administration to the varying needs of the nation and peoples called of God into the Unity of His Church'. And there seemed very little chance of any favour for anything in the nature of immediate action. For many days the Committee sat in perplexity, and no progress was made. Then the Chairman, the Archbishop of York, conceived the plan of a Letter to Christian People, which might be warmer and more persuasive than any mere restatement of conditions of union. This plan seemed to fit in with an idea, which had been sketched in the opening week by the Bishop of Zanzibar, of a Great Church in which the denominations of non-episcopal origin might be groups: it had been taken up by one or two others, like Bishop Brent; and, with the Archbishop of Canterbury's connivance, a group of kindred episcopal souls met by themselves in Lollards' Tower to see whether anything might come from that. A new and hopeful 'statement on reunion' was prepared, with some of the younger Bishops such as the Bishops of Bombay (Dr. Palmer), Pretoria (Dr. Neville Talbot), and Pennsylvania (Dr. Rhinelander) as its draftsmen. The Archbishop describes how on the Sunday (July 18) between the two Committee weeks:

> a little group sat all the afternoon under the tree on the lawn. It consisted of the two Archbishops, Bishop Rhinelander of Pennsylvania, Bishop Brent, the Bishop of Peterborough. . . . We went through the various drafts, Resolutions etc. which had been suggested, but on the whole decided to transpose it into an Appeal of a consecutive sort.

The Archbishop of York had an immense influence in the shaping of the Appeal, and in its presentation to, and acceptance by, the Conference—but it was without doubt the eloquent and unexpected championship by the Bishop of Zanzibar of the position the Appeal contained that proved the decisive factor:

> The surprise of the Conference was the line taken by the Bishop of Zanzibar (Weston). Had he been an unknown person who made his début at this Conference, it would have been said what a wonderful thing it is for the present time to have a Bishop of real learning and eloquence, who is a strong High Churchman, and yet holds such liberal, tolerant, kindly views and shows such readiness to see and appreciate the views of those who differ from him. He and Henson became personal friends, and Uganda and Mombasa were constantly by his side, and he and they desired that I should be photographed with them as a group. This was done. Whether his strange temperament will show itself by some outbreak of another kind now that the Conference is over, I cannot tell. I feel a little uneasy sometimes. I hope this is not faithless.

The great principles of the Appeal were these. It was an Appeal to all Christian people (not 'churches')—and the Bishops who sent it forth acknowledged 'all those who believe in our Lord Jesus Christ and have been baptized into the Name of the Holy Trinity as sharing with us membership in the universal Church of Christ which is His Body'. It recognized the grounds of disunity, the relationship of Anglican Churches to both the ancient episcopal communions of East and West, and the non-episcopal. 'We acknowledge this condition of broken fellowship to be contrary to God's will, and we desire frankly to confess our share in the guilt of thus crippling the Body of Christ and hindering the activity of His Spirit.' The Appeal called for a new and wide vision of a united Catholic Church, within which 'Christian communions now separated from one another would retain much that has long been distinctive in their methods of worship and service'. Such a visible unity would, the Bishops believed, involve the whole-hearted acceptance of the Holy Scripture, the Nicene Creed, the Sacraments of Baptism and the Holy Communion, and:

> A ministry acknowledged by every part of the Church as possessing not only the inward call of the Spirit, but also the commission of Christ and the authority of the whole body.

The Bishops went on to ask in the following paragraph:

> May we not reasonably claim that the Episcopate is the one means of providing such a ministry? It is not that we call in question for a moment the spiritual reality of the ministries of those Communions which do not possess the Episcopate. On the contrary we thankfully acknowledge that these ministries have been manifestly blessed and owned by the Holy Spirit as effective means of grace. But we submit that considerations alike of history and of present experience justify the claim which we make on behalf of the Episcopate.

The Appeal also expressed the desire that 'the office of a Bishop should be everywhere exercised in a representative and constitutional manner'. To the crucial question, what was to be done in the meantime, the Bishops replied by asking for 'mutual deference to one another's consciences'. They declared their belief that 'terms of union having been otherwise satisfactorily adjusted', Anglican Bishops and clergy would willingly accept from the authorities of other Communions:

> a form of commission or recognition which would commend our ministry to their congregations, as having its place in the one family life:

and hoped that ministers of non-episcopal Communions would accept:

> a commission through episcopal ordination, as obtaining for them a ministry throughout the whole fellowship.

The Appeal concluded with these words:

> We do not ask that any one Communion should consent to be absorbed in another. We do ask that all should unite in a new

> and great endeavour to recover and to manifest to the world the unity of the Body of Christ for which He prayed.

It was a fine and moving document: it was magnificently presented by the Archbishop of York, and enthusiastically adopted, with only four dissentients.

There was, however, a very notable addition to the Appeal, in the shape of a substantial Resolution dealing with the vexed problems of intercommunion and exchange of pulpits. The Bishop of Zanzibar and others made it plain that it would make a great difference to their attitude if the non-episcopal ministers and laymen concerned were agreed upon, and waiting for, a basis of Reunion. After a great deal of framing, and with one moment when the Bishop of Zanzibar said that he had felt that 'to-day might be the last day on which he could attend the Committee'—so great a line of cleavage had been shown—a Resolution was passed, explicitly disapproving, 'general schemes of intercommunion or exchange of pulpits', but stating that, '*in view of prospects and projects of reunion*:

> A Bishop is justified in giving occasional authorization to ministers, not episcopally ordained, who in his judgement are working towards an ideal of union such as is described in our Appeal, to preach in churches within his Diocese, and to clergy of the Diocese to preach in the churches of such ministers.

and also declaring that:

> Nothing in these Resolutions is intended to indicate that the rule of Confirmation as conditioning admission to the Holy Communion must necessarily apply to the case of baptized persons who seek Communion under conditions which in the Bishop's judgement justify their admission thereto.

The Appeal and the Resolution were almost unbelievable after everything that had been said before the Conference began. Not only were the lions in the path overcome, but something new and creative had been done, and a great blow struck for the Reunion of Christendom. With a very full heart did the Archbishop of Canterbury join in the Doxology which the brethren lifted up! The Archbishop did not minimize the difficulties in the way of working out the Appeal. He had too shrewd a sense of reality for that. He knew that the non-Episcopalians would urge that, important as episcopacy might be for future ordinations, it was not important enough to render it necessary for Anglicans to ask those who were already Ministers to receive episcopal ordination: and that the non-Episcopalians would almost certainly propose that Anglicans should 'simply recognize their Ministry as it is, in the hope and expectation that they will gradually transform it into an Episcopal system for the future'. The Archbishop's private comment on any such proposal as he thus anticipated was as follows:

> This I am quite sure we cannot say (apart from the question of whether it is fundamentally sound) without creating at once and irrevocably a deep schism among our own people and giving triumph to the Romans and others who would laugh such a Conference to scorn—also to Easterns. Thus the difficulty really consists in our finding a mode of getting over the intervening period without either evoking defiance from non-Episcopals, or creating among ourselves an incurable schism.

The Appeal, and the whole Report of the Conference were received with general admiration. The Appeal itself was translated and on sale in six languages. The Encyclical Letter, largely the work of the Bishop of Bombay, summed up the general judgements of the Conference, and laid a very special emphasis upon the idea of Fellowship, in accordance with the Archbishop's own deliberate plan.

The Conference closed on August 7, with overflowing gratitude to the Archbishop and Mrs. Davidson; and a beautiful ebony crozier was chosen for a gift to the President.

A Note on Relations with the Church of Sweden.

The Lambeth Conference of 1920 was also notable for a considerable step forward in fraternal relations between the Anglican Communion and the Church of Sweden. A Commission appointed by Archbishop Davidson visited Sweden in 1909 and conferred with a Swedish committee appointed by the Archbishop of Upsala (Dr. Ekman). As a result of its Report published in 1911 the Lambeth Conference accepted the conclusions of the Commission 'on the succession of the Bishops of the Church of Sweden and the conception of the priesthood set forth in its standards' and recommended 'that members of that Church [of Sweden], qualified to receive the Sacrament in their own Church should be admitted to Holy Communion in ours'. Further, also following a Resolution of the Lambeth Conference, on the invitation of the Archbishop of Upsala (Dr. Söderblom) the Bishops of Durham (Dr. Henson), and Peterborough (Dr. Woods), took part in the consecration of the Bishops of Västerås (Dr. Billing) and Visby (Dr. Rundgren) in Upsala Cathedral on September 19th, 1920. The Bishop of Härnösand (Dr. Lönegren) took part in the consecration of the Bishop of Dover (Dr. Macmillan) in Canterbury Cathedral on November 1st 1927.

CHAPTER LXIII

THE CASE OF BISHOP MATHEW

Likewise Bishops, being principal pastors, are either at large or else with restraint; at large, when the subject of their regiment is indefinite and not tied to any certain place; Bishops with restraint are they whose regiment over the Church is contained within some definite local compass, beyond which compass their jurisdiction reacheth not. HOOKER, *Ecclesiastical Polity*, Bk. VII, Sect. II.

ONE of the most curious figures whom the Archbishop met in the ecclesiastical sphere was a certain Bishop Arnold H. Mathew. He was, the Archbishop believed, personally virtuous, but partly through vanity, partly through an ill-considered enthusiasm for a special kind of reunion, he succeeded in doing a most embarrassing amount of havoc to the cause he professed to serve. To anticipate the Archbishop's words in his letter of September 12, 1917, to the Bishop of London, Bishop Mathew 'played fast and loose with great questions of Church order, and thus set going in different ways and in different lands schisms which it may take many years to heal'. The Archbishop first heard from the Rev. A. H. Mathew in July 1907, when Mr. Mathew, who was then fifty-four years of age and described himself as *de jure* Earl of Landaff, asked whether he could be given some ministerial charge in the Church of England, the Church of his baptism and boyhood. He recounted his preparation in youth for the Anglican Ministry, his Ordination to the Priesthood in the Church of Rome (1878), his marriage in 1892, his readmission to the Church of England, and his temporary service, under the name (it would seem) of Count Pavoleri, in a London curacy with the sanction of Bishop Temple. He had subsequently, he said, lived quietly in the country, discarding clerical dress and doing no ministerial work. He desired to assure the Archbishop that he repudiated Papal claims, that he entertained no doubt about Anglican Orders, and that his wish would be to hold an incumbency in the Church of England. He had been a friend of Père Hyacinth Loyson[1] at Paris in 1889; and became later a friend of Father George Tyrrell, the Jesuit; and it was on the latter's advice that he desired to take up work with the Church of Eng-

[1] For Archbishop Tait's interest in Père Hyacinth see his *Life*, ii. 527, 547.

land. These connexions were of interest; but the project was not quite as simple as Mr. Mathew expected. When the Archbishop explained that, in addition to adequate testimony to personal character, about which there would obviously be no difficulty, there must be some period of probationary and subordinate work before the question of such nomination as had been suggested could be even considered, Mr. Mathew replied, not unnaturally, that he preferred to abandon the project and to remain as he was. The Archbishop accepted this conclusion, assuring Mr. Mathew that he was not precluded from reopening the question at a future date should he so desire. Mr. Mathew took occasion to reiterate his conviction about the Church of Rome:

> The Papacy itself [he wrote (August 12, 1907)] instead of being the 'visible centre of unity', I regard as the centre and origin of ecclesiastical discord and disunion, the fomenter of schisms, and the seat of ecclesiastical despotism and tyranny.

Disappointed in his first wish, a few months later he made a fresh and more ambitious proposal, giving the first indication of his association with the Old Catholics. On December 19, 1907, he wrote to the Archbishop as follows:

The Rev. A. H. Mathew *to the* Archbishop of Canterbury

> I think that a way to serve the Church of England as *une église amie* may be open to me, which will also, I hope, help forward the movement of Re-union of those Churches which reject the modern Papal pretensions. I have been approached within the past few days by several Roman Catholics who wish to embrace the tenets of the Old Catholic Communities of Germany and Switzerland and have implored me to assist them. If this can be done in harmony and friendship with the Established Church I think a sphere of very useful labour is thus unexpectedly presenting itself, one also which it may be my duty to enter upon. Should this prove to be so the enquiries which will have been made will have been very advantageous to our movement. I have long thought that if it were possible for a Bishop of the Church of England to accept the services of an Old Catholic Coadjutor, or Assistant, who could take part in Ordinations, the Roman Catholic and Oriental objections to Anglican Orders would be effectually silenced without any sacrifice of principle whatever. Such an arrangement might be difficult. I do not know.

On December 30 he wrote again, and stated definitely that he had decided to join the Old Catholics:

The REV. A. H. MATHEW *to the* ARCHBISHOP'S CHAPLAIN

In view of the difficulty of arrangements for entering the Ministry of the Church of England, I have at length definitely decided to abandon the idea and to throw in my lot with the Old Catholics. We shall open a Mission in this country for the benefit of those Roman Catholics who are unable to continue conscientious adhesion to the Vatican, and this we shall do in a spirit of perfect and cordial amity for the Church of England and in no spirit of aggression, still less of proselytism . . . I am now in correspondence with the Archbishop of Utrecht, who will formally authorise the formation of a branch of the Church in Great Britain on the lines I have indicated.

In his reply the Archbishop wrote:

The ARCHBISHOP OF CANTERBURY *to the* REV. A. H. MATHEW

Jan. 20. 1908.

I do not gather that there is any step which you now desire me to take in the matter. I am, of course, at all times glad to learn of any movement within the Church of Rome in the direction of sounder principles of doctrine and usage. But, believing as I do that the Church of England is in this country the true representative of the Catholic Church as it comes down to us from the past, I can hardly be expected to look favourably upon the establishment in England of another society claiming that position, even though it does so in a less exclusive and arrogant spirit than that which finds its centre and expression in the Vatican.

Other letters followed, but no intimation was given of any proposed episcopal consecration until, on April 8, 1908, the Archbishop received, presumably from Mr. Mathew, a lithographed card stating that on that very day his 'Episcopal Consecration' would take place at Utrecht. It did not at once take place, for the reason, as was stated on behalf of the Old Catholic Bishops, that they had unexpectedly become aware of the fact that Mr. Mathew was a married man. A vigorous protest against such an action on the part of the Old Catholics of Holland was also immediately made (April 9) by Bishop Wordsworth of Salisbury to Bishop Van Thiel of Haarlem. The Consecration, however, took place at Utrecht on April 28, 1908. It appeared later that Bishop Mathew himself was deceived by an ex-Roman priest, who brought him Arthur Galton's article in *The Fortnightly Review* about the Romanists in England who did not accept Vaticanism, and assured him, quite falsely, that there were some 250 priests who would like to be led by a bishop on the lines of Old Catholicism. But the harm was done, and Bishop Mathew claimed to be a regionary Catholic Bishop in the British Isles, with special supervision over foreign Old Catholics resident in England. The step was bound to lead to extraordinary confusions. The Lambeth Conference of 1908 passed a Resolution earnestly deprecating 'the setting up of a new organized body in regions where a Church with apostolic ministry and Catholic doctrine offers religious privileges without the imposition of uncatholic terms of communion, more especially in cases where no difference of language or nationality exists'. There really were no genuine Old Catholics in England to whom a special Old Catholic Bishop could minister. The idea of creating an Old Catholic Church in England for Englishmen, with English ministers ordained by an Old Catholic Bishop and receiving 'valid orders', was utterly repugnant to the Archbishop. 'I believe', he wrote in a private letter to Mr. Brodhurst, the Editor of *The Guardian*, February 22, 1909, 'that for Englishmen in England the Church of England covers the ground which Old Catholics occupy in such Continental countries'; and he objected strongly to what he described as 'the unnecessary multiplication of independent sections of validly ordained clergy in England ministering to Englishmen'. The confusion was still further increased by Bishop Mathew's preposterous proposal to get some kind of working alliance with the High Church party in the Church of England, and to secure by degrees the recognition of Anglican orders by Rome through the intervention of a new line of succession through himself. He began ordaining men to the diaconate and the priesthood. He actually gave conditional ordination to four Anglican priests who were uncertain about their orders, and he later consecrated some seven or eight men (including disaffected Roman priests) to the Episcopate.

In 1910, the Old Catholics of Holland, who found that they had been grossly deceived, broke with him. And he then described himself in various ways. Sometimes he was 'Catholic Bishop': sometimes 'Bishop in England and Ireland' of 'the English Catholic Church in communion with the Archiepiscopal See of Utrecht', later 'The Western Orthodox Catholic Church in

Great Britain and Ireland'. Next he became 'Archbishop of London and Metropolitan'. In March 1911, the title was 'Archbishop and Metropolitan of the English Catholic Church'. This became 'The Catholic Church in England, Latin Uniate Branch', and, two months later, 'The Catholic Church in England, Latin and Orthodox United,' under a leader described as 'Archbishop of England', and subsequently as 'Sa Grandeur Mgr A. H. Mathieu, Archevêque de Londres, Comte de Landave, Métropolitain de Grande-Bretagne et d'Irlande, Évêque provisoire de l'Église Catholique Française'. As time went on, and his position became less and less favourable, his claims became more and more high sounding. In 1911, he petitioned the Eastern Orthodox Church for reunion, and, while refused by Russia, was apparently accepted by Antioch.

Accounts of his relations to the Roman Catholic Church were given in documents produced in the course of the unsuccessful libel action brought by Bishop Mathew against *The Times* newspaper in April 1913, the grounds of action being the publication by *The Times* on February 28, 1911, of the following words, used in a Papal document connected with the excommunication of two priests who had claimed to have received Episcopal consecration from Bishop Mathew:

> Nor was this information left without authentic testimony, for the person who was the chief author of this sacrilegious misdeed —a certain pseudo-Bishop named Arnold Harris Mathew—was not ashamed to confirm the fact in letters, full of self-assumption, which he has addressed to us. This person has, moreover, thought fit to bestow upon himself the title of Anglo-Catholic Archbishop of London.

In the early part of 1915, Bishop Mathew wrote to the Bishop of London, alleging that he had re-ordained 300[1] of the Anglican clergy, and inviting him to submit himself for re-ordination— an offer which the Archbishop ironically mentioned in a Memorandum about Bishop Mathew which he published in May 1915. Bishop Mathew's movement became weaker and weaker; and while he himself remained orthodox, though more and more solitary, at least half a dozen of his clergy became Theosophists. On April 15, 1916, the Archbishop gave him a personal inter-

[1] Bishop Mathew later denied that he made this statement, and said that he had in fact only given conditional ordination to three or four Anglican clergy.

view at Canterbury. Bishop Mathew described the history of his 'little movement', and told a curious story about his recent effort to be received back by Rome. The Archbishop was personally friendly, but could not disguise his condemnation of the position Bishop Mathew had adopted. In the course of the interview, of which he made a full Memorandum at the time, the Archbishop expressed himself 'almost exactly as follows', after thanking Bishop Mathew for putting the facts before him from his point of view:

> 'It will be honest that I should tell you plainly how the situation presents itself to me. I have never challenged your loyalty to the Christian faith, but I do challenge your loyalty to elementary principles of Church Order. You have handled—I incline to say trifled with,—the great questions of the sort which give force to our prayers against schism. Your relation successively to the Church of England, then to the Church of Rome, then to the Church of England again, then to the Old Catholics, then to the Eastern Church, then to the independent organisation under your headship, then to the Church of Rome again, and now, as you suggest, to the Church of England again, give a story of loyalties and disloyalties which seems to me incompatible with any adequate sense of the responsibilities belonging to membership in an organised body which has Christ as its Head.
>
> 'I cannot in honesty refrain from pointing out to you the position in which the men are placed who have been by you ordained or consecrated, whether validly or invalidly, and whose position now is—what? There are, I think, some seven or eight men, perhaps more, whom you have purported to consecrate to the Episcopate —Bacon, Scott-Hall, Hinton, Egerton, de Landes, Beale, Howarth, Willoughby, and there are many more to whom you have given, regularly or irregularly, validly or invalidly, the priesthood, and now you write to me that you have decided to "terminate the organisation". Is this a tolerable position to maintain?'

There was a good deal of correspondence afterwards. The Archbishop said that he could not authorize Bishop Mathew to officiate as a minister in the Church of England—he would only sanction his admission to Holy Communion in the Church of England as a layman. To this attitude, in spite of many representations, the Archbishop adhered to the end; and his view is stated in kindly terms in the following letter to the Bishop of London, after hearing of Bishop Mathew's sad domestic and financial circumstances:

The Archbishop of Canterbury *to the* Bishop of London

September 12th, 1917.

I have read with attention and with great interest the letters you send me from Mr. Hay to yourself, and from Bishop Mathew to Mr. Hay. Of course I regard them as private documents, but I can write to you frankly on the subject, and I have no objection at all to Mr. Hay seeing my letter if you so desire. The story has now become a pathetic one. It is pitiable to think of Bishop Mathew's desertion by the lady whom he wrote about as Countess of Landaff, and whose picture he sent to us with pride. What is meant by her being able to claim the control of her children if she deserts her husband, I do not the least understand. The pamphlet about his earldom, and the pictures of his countess, look strangely now. It is also pathetic that he should now find himself in financial straits, if that is indeed so. I fear that the fomenting of schisms, and the founding of Churches, have involved much expenditure on some one's part, both in East and West, and it is possible that this has hit him hard. I feel intensely sorry for him, foolish and harmful as his doings have been. To those who only know bits of the long story, it no doubt looks as if we, and especially I myself, were harsh towards him. Very likely it is best that this should be the popular view, and that I should bear the blame. I have no objection at all to that. Our duty to the Church in the matter is, as you well know, not doubtful; and if I chose to make everything public it would be easy to justify all that we have done, or refused to do. But the publication, or republication, of these strange doings would, I think, only increase the mischief, such as it is. Bishop Mathew is, to the best of my belief (though of course I speak without knowledge of what is said by his wife or any one else against him), a virtuous old fellow, with a delightfully attractive manner, a fine appearance, a certain amount of ecclesiastical learning, and a strange lack of balance. His harmfulness has lain in the real lightness (strenuously as he denies it) with which he played fast and loose with great questions of Church Order, and thus set going, in different ways and in different lands, schisms which it may take many years to heal. He has given to ecclesiastical adventurers less honest than himself, an example fraught with abundant peril. None the less, I have a personal regard for him, and, although he has only himself to thank for his present position, I should like to be able to help him, in some way which did not do harm to the Church wherein I am set to be a responsible custodian of what is right. I should certainly fail as such a custodian if I were to say now, what neither you nor any other

Bishop whom I have met would wish me to say, that, after all that has passed, we propose to recognise him as one who might rightly hold the trust of ministry in the Church of England.

Mr. Hay, I see, suggests that some work as a librarian, or some secretarial office might be found for him, or an extra-parochial chaplain, to some Hospital or Home. I cannot conceive how such a post could be found for him. He is not the sort of man to fit in appropriately to work of a secretarial sort, and to place him as a duly accredited priest of the Church of England in charge of the religious life of a public institution would, so far as I can judge, be wholly wrong. I must, as I have said, continue to bear the brunt of such criticism as his friends will quite naturally continue to make, but I am glad to know that, in what I have said and done, I have had the support, not only of yourself, but of the other Bishops, a limited number, but our wisest, who are conversant with the facts.

At the end of 1919, Bishop Mathew was still trying to get recognition for some sort of ministerial work. He begged, through the vicar of South Mymms, where he was residing, that he might at least be allowed to sit in the choir of South Mymms Church, robed as a Bishop or as a Priest, and read the lessons. And there is something pathetic in the fact that, while this last request was under consideration, the poor would-be 'Metropolitan of the English Catholic Church' died suddenly in the village, at the age of sixty-seven, during the week before Christmas (December 19, 1919).

The story closes with the Lambeth Conference of 1920, when a letter was received from the Old Catholic Bishops of Holland stating that the episcopal consecration of the Rev. A. H. Mathew in 1908 had been 'surreptitiously secured by the production of false testimony', and that the Old Catholics had no ecclesiastical relation with him or with those ordained by him. The following is the Resolution adopted by the Lambeth Conference:

27. We regret that on a review of all the facts we are unable to regard the so-called Old Catholic Church in Great Britain (under the late Bishop Mathew and his successors), and its extensions overseas, as a properly constituted Church, or to recognize the orders of its ministers, and we recommend that, in the event of any of its ministers desiring to join our communion, who are in other respects duly qualified, they should be ordained *sub conditione* in accordance with the provisions suggested in the Report of our Committee.

CHAPTER LXIV

COLLATERAL ILLUSTRATIONS

I interrupt, for a moment, Sir Walter's diary, to introduce a few collateral illustrations. LOCKHART, *Life of Scott*, ch. lxvii.

THE year of the sixth Lambeth Conference was more crowded than usual with affairs of high importance. The two other principal events in the Church's history were the enthronement of the first Archbishop of Wales, and the first meeting of the new National Assembly of the Church of England. The latter took place for two days just before the Lambeth Conference began, and set the machinery in motion. It was satisfactory to hear it described by the chief ecclesiastical critic of the Enabling Act (Dr. Henson) as, in spite of all, 'the most representative body of Church people that can as yet be devised'. In this chapter we propose to give examples of some of the lesser incidents, and also of some of the more personal relationships, in which the Archbishop was concerned.

On January 6, Dr. Davidson was talking of the anxieties which lay ahead, and of his own old age. He was now seventy-one. He went on to explain why he went so constantly to the House of Lords. The Bishop of London had told him he thought it was waste of time, but the Archbishop did not think so at all. It enabled him, he said, to be in touch and in close personal relations with many influential and important people. Besides, it was half a rest, though not entirely so; it was a rest which partook of the nature of work. Similarly, he felt it was a great gain to the Church of England that he should go to Grillions and 'The Club', meeting statesmen and other prominent persons as friends. Once more, other Archbishops of Canterbury had been on ceremonial terms with the King and the Royal Family, but he was on terms of personal friendship—quite a new thing. All this was for the advantage of the Church of England, and in all this he was quite unlike other Archbishops who had been before him.

I

On February 26, Archbishop Davidson and the Archbishop of York received a deputation from the Federation of Catholic

Priests about Reservation. Dr. Darwell Stone and Father H. P. Bull, S.S.J.E., who led it, reported the alarm felt by their friends lest the recent case in which the Bishop of Truro (Dr. Burrows) had prosecuted the vicar of Cury, and another case at Taunton in which the Bishop of Bath and Wells (Dr. Kennion) was prosecutor, were introducing a new era of appeal to the Courts. After Dr. Darwell Stone had stated his position, and declared: 'If Bishops pursue the Cury policy, I cannot see any other upshot than a series of bitter conflicts', the following conversation took place:

The Archbishop: What do you think should be done?

Dr. Stone: First of all, personal influence, discussion, reasoned argument. Suppose, however, after this the Bishop failed, I should like to see the Bishop prepared to bear some defiance rather than go to a Court of law. When argument and influence have come to an end, then he must bear defiance as something that must be borne.

The Archbishop: I have looked up the Cury case. I do not want to go over the story of that to show whether or not Bishop Burrows was right. I do not want to go into the theory of Benediction. I have, however, looked in vain in your statements for an expression of view as to the manner in which the Bishop should persuade the Parish Priest to follow the right course. The Bishop has promised to exercise discipline—an awful responsibility—as he, as well as the incumbent, has charge of the parish. Do you tell me there does not exist on earth any mode for dealing with such a man as Wason? You say the institution of legal procedure is unjust. Do you mean that the Bishop must retire and give up the matter when the Priest persists in defiance? You say 'In the last resort I should accept defiance', but it is not the Bishop who accepts defiance. It is the people, his charge.

Father Bull: The Church of England has one hand tied behind it in the system of Ecclesiastical Courts.

The Archbishop: I agree that the Courts must be changed. I have done all I could to do this. Yet here are the Courts under which we were ordained in the meanwhile.

Dr. Stone: I did say that in the last resort the Bishop must accept defiance. But the cases would be fewer if Synodical judgement were exercised, the Bishop sitting with his Clergy.

The Archbishop: Conceivably. But we have not got it at present. Legal enactment would be necessary to get this through. In the meantime we have our present system. Sometimes—very occasionally—a man does stand out against everything. Take the Cury case as given in the published open letter. Bishop Stubbs drew a ring round him. Bishop Burrows withdrew it in 1912, held a Synod in 1914, interviewed him, formally enjoined him, visited the parish, pronounced his formal judgement in the church, waited, asked Wason to advise on the Court, and at last was driven to the Court in 1919. The petition which you bring says 'No opportunity given for obedience to formal admonition'. Do you really hold this?

Dr. Stone: Yes, this gives our view.

The Archbishop: If this is so, we must accept it. You wish us to give an undertaking that we shall refuse to have authoritative regulation?

Father Bull: We object to ecclesiastical authority going to the Courts.

The Archbishop: At no time have Bishops been less willing to go to the Courts than now. I speak after 44 years' experience. Do you mean that when we have exhausted every other means we can do nothing?

Father Bull: Our position is that Church and State are so entangled that there is nothing that can be done.

The Archbishop: Since Constantine's time?

Father Bull: Yes.

The Archbishop: I have never had a case before the Court, but I could not undertake not to do it if I am to be faithful and loyal to my conception of duty. Does this Federation stand for obedience?

Father Bull: We have recommended all our Clergy to refrain from extra-liturgical Services till the Bishop gives sanction.

The Archbishop: Do you wish us to say 'Let a man be defiant enough and nothing will happen'?

Father Bull: No. Let the Bishop inhibit a man, showing that the Church does not authorise him, where the Creed is concerned.

The Archbishop: If I were in your place I should take the line that this is a matter for the Bishop's responsibility—lay it on him—and acquiesce in his ruling, however much under protest.

Dr. Stone: This is the attitude the Federation recommends. If *your* attitude could be, by your influence, that of all other Bishops, we should feel that the object of our deputation had been achieved.

II

On March 1, the Archbishop drove out to see Lord Rosebery:

I had a real interest yesterday. I spent three hours with Rosebery, talking right on end from the first minute to the last. I had offered to go to Epsom to see him, and he welcomed it so cordially that I rejoiced to go. A glorious spring day. I drove from London, and got to him at the Durdans at 12.30. I found him much less ill than I had anticipated. He has largely lost the use of one side and completely of his left arm, but, barring this, one would have thought him very much as of old, only looking unkempt and as if he needed somebody to tidy him up—a rather melancholy condition. He wants a wife, or a sister, or a daughter.

But he was full of freshness and talk, and as keen as ever about all that is happening. He discussed rather eagerly the Peace Treaty, the mess that the Government have, he thinks, made of foreign affairs, the return of Asquith two days before for Paisley, and he poured out comparisons of all these with the days of Pitt, of Dizzy, and Gladstone, and his own experiences. One felt that he would be so much the better for having more people to see him and talk about things, for, solitary as his life has been for many years, it is more solitary than ever now that he complains that he cannot read the paper properly because he cannot turn it over with one hand, and that his books tumble down when he tries to turn up things.

We walked about the garden, where he was proud of his crocuses and things in a rather pathetic way. But he was full of vivid reminiscences of past days, and of our friendship. He asked rather earnestly if he might have a photograph of Edith, for her face had always given him some special thoughts, and so on. I promised him this. He was very shrewd and wise about political affairs, as it seemed to me, and his whole talk brought home to one intensely the pathos of the country having had throughout the War this man with all his gifts and powers and knowledge and memories, and no hand's turn help given to the country thereby. It is largely, yes, almost entirely, his own fault, but it is the fault of former years rather than of now. A man who has been Prime Minister, and was one of the very best of Foreign Secretaries; a man who knew Bismarck intimately, and the French statesmen, and had been the trusted confidant of Gladstone, and Granville, and, on the other side, the friend of Dizzy, and intimate confidant of Queen Victoria, and still more of King Edward, and so on—and all this wasted. For he really does nothing with it now, save when now and then he pours out to a friend as he did to me.

He also talked about the higher side of things, and I tried to get in some helpful prods, for he is quite amenable to them for all his religious reserve. All the beauty of his quiet surroundings, among yew hedges and lawns, made one long that somebody were sharing it with him, or that he were giving out from what is really the deep well of his knowledge and thoughtfulness. He did not, through our three hours of talk, say one bitter word about anybody, and he had abundant appreciation of all sorts of people, and was kindlier than of old, with less cynicism. He talked a good deal about ecclesiastical appointments and the responsibility of it and the care he had tried to take, and his affection for Kennion, and his belief in and interest in things I had tried to do. I thought I traced a sort of yearning after untouched, or at least unaccomplished, plans of his own, if plans be not too strong a word.

When I left him I had rather a lump in my throat, and wondered whether I should get such a chance again. I suppose he might have another stroke at any time. Or again one might fail to find him alone and so communicative.

Here is a reminiscence of a dinner at 'The Club' (March 2):

To-night I have had a singularly interesting dinner at 'The Club'—one of the best gatherings I have ever known in the way of interest and vivacity and range of talk. Arthur Eliot in the chair, and the following present—Prothero, Lord Sumner, Admiral Sturdee, Sir Henry Newbolt, Stamfordham, Kenyon, Bishop Gore, Pember of All Souls, Murray, Hugh Cecil, Sir Maurice Hankey, and myself. The talk was very general, and most brilliantly kept up, especially by Murray, Lord Hugh, and Arthur Eliot, with Gore and Pember taking part, and Hankey present for the first time on election, brimful of knowledge of the doings of every day in the Peace Conference and elsewhere. I thought Hugh Cecil at his very best, epigrammatic and thoughtful, but not cynical. We discussed Gladstone and Dizzy and Rosebery[1]—all this of special interest to me after my talks with Rosebery yesterday—also Queen Victoria and the Prince Consort, and, oddly enough, Hymns Ancient and Modern, about which Pember and Hugh Cecil and Prothero had things to say. Hankey I found intensely interesting in less general talk. I told him how we had this morning been rather sparring with the Foreign Office about the telegram to America—the American Bishops having telegraphed to me bidding us take heed to preserve the rights of the Christian

[1] In a conversation afterwards (June 2) the Archbishop noted one of the points made on a similar occasion about Lord Rosebery. The question had been raised, said the Archbishop, at 'The Club', 'What makes the difference between a first-rate statesman and others?' The names of Palmerston, Disraeli, Lord John Russell, and others came up, but Mr. Balfour replied, 'Being ready to go out in rough weather.' 'Well,' said Rosebery, 'you have done that more than most.' 'I have done my best,' said Balfour. But, said the Archbishop, Balfour did not return the compliment, as it was just this which Rosebery never could do. A sort of self-indulgence was his besetting sin.

folk under the Turks, and my draft reply sent to the Foreign Office, with a somewhat pointed retort that we should continue to do our best, but relied on America taking its share. These words had been cut out from our draft by Curzon, who thought America had had enough of it. So I sent Bell back again to the Foreign Office this morning to insist that I was not going to send the telegram without these words, else it would seem as if I accepted their criticism or condescending counsel to us. Bell had been quite successful, and the Foreign Office had sent off the telegram with my words in full. Hankey was specially pleased with this, as he thought America needed to have the truth rather more plainly spoken to her, and that this could be excellently done in my non-political way. Also he and I discussed the Easterns now in England—the Armenian Patriarch, and Bishop Severus, and Surma Khanim and her capacity. He knew all about it. I wonder whether any man had quite his experience before. A retired young naval officer becoming secretary of the Defence Committee, and then of the Cabinet, and then of the Peace Conference, with intimate personal knowledge of all that had passed and is passing—a great power of memory and of keeping his head, and a wonderful absence of self-consciousness or swagger, or affectation of humility. As one knows him better, he is really a striking contemporary.

On May 16 he wrote:

I feel like the May Queen, who passed from autumn to winter, and winter to spring, and heard the bleating of the lamb, for I have been silent since Easter, and it is now Ascension. . . . I have been feeling the burden of things rather heavily during the last six weeks, but there has been nothing gravely amiss, only a most uncomfortable form of indigestion which makes one feel like a collapsed India rubber ball. . . . As to America, I know nothing, nor, I think, does Stamfordham, of the communications which have passed unofficially between Lloyd George and the Wilson Group since Wilson's illness. There again I think while the American attitude is in the highest degree disappointing, inasmuch as they are failing to accept any part of the International burden which belongs to post-war settlement, especially in Turkey, and the East, I yet think that many English critics are very unfair to Americans in failing to realise how immensely the policy we want them to adopt differs from what was their immemorial principle and custom as regards non-intervention in far-away troubles of an international kind. I think they have failed to realise that the request we make to them is of necessity without precedent, because the conditions are without precedent, and that, this being so, they ought to be prepared to go much further than they have gone in helping us through the Mesopotamian, Armenian, and even Balkan troubles. . . . Another thing which is causing me great anxiety in our ecclesiastical world is the practical failure of the Central Church Fund. At present I understand that our liabilities may amount to about £350,000, for which the Archbishop of York and I have made ourselves responsible, on the assurance by these leading laymen, Brassey, Selborne, Salisbury, Midleton, Grey, Kindersley, and many more, that there was no doubt about the money coming in. Selborne still thinks it will, and anyhow a great deal will, but the outlook is in a high degree alarming, and I am taking the strong measure of allowing a few spokesmen, Selborne, Partridge, and Dibdin (who is giving immense help) to come to a Bishops' meeting this week, and see a group of Bishops, and state the case bluntly and strenuously.

III

In May and June of this year, the Archbishop had to consider an application that he would confer a medical degree in peculiar circumstances. The general right which he was asked to exercise was obtained as a result of the Act of 1534 (25 Henry VIII, c. 21, forbidding Papal Dispensations and the payment of Peter's Pence), by which the Archbishop of Canterbury was given power to grant 'all manner such Licences, Dispensations, Compositions, Faculties, Grants, Rescripts, Delegacies, Instruments, and all other Writings . . . as heretofore has been used and accustomed to be had and obtained . . . at the see of Rome'. These Faculties included degrees. The degree most commonly given by the Archbishop was a Degree in Divinity, but Degrees in Music and in Civil Law were also given from time to time, and, up to the War, ordinary M.A. Degrees were given after examination. The last-named degree, however, was discontinued by Archbishop Davidson, as he considered that, with the growth of modern universities, the justification for granting it had been considerably diminished; though he allowed two priests to take the degree after the war who had begun to study before the new rule was in force.

The Archbishop always gave sparingly,[1] remembering that a

[1] In the twenty-five years, 1903 to 1928, Archbishop Davidson conferred the following degrees: 55 D.D.; 8 B.D.; 1 D.C.L.; 14 Mus.Doc.; 8 M.A.; Total, 86.

lavish use of his power would produce legitimate criticism and diminish the honour. When he conferred a Lambeth Degree, he did so either to enable a man to hold some ecclesiastical office, for which a B.D. or D.D. was required by statute as a qualification, or on appointment to a bishopric, or as a recognition of distinguished service. In the last case he granted the degree only after receiving independent testimony from men of the highest eminence in the musical or other department, or, in the case of a Divinity Degree, from those who had indubitable right to speak for educational or missionary work.

The most notable instance of a petition to the Archbishop was that made on behalf of a distinguished manipulative surgeon, Mr. H. A. Barker. In twenty-five years, Mr. Barker had made an extraordinary reputation for his ability. In 1912, a leading article in *The Times* described him as 'a master of manipulative surgery, who relieves suffering for which no relief can be found elsewhere' (December 7, 1912). During the War and after, his reputation had grown even greater, but he was not a qualified physician or surgeon, and the General Medical Council had actually, in May 1911, removed the name of a qualified medical practitioner, Dr. Axham, from the medical register, as he had been 'adjudged guilty of infamous conduct in a professional respect, for having assisted Herbert Atkinson Barker, an unregistered person practising in a department of surgery, in carrying on such practice by administering anaesthetics on his behalf'.

In 1920, 307 Members of Parliament and ex-Members of Parliament prayed the Archbishop of Canterbury to confer upon Mr. H. A. Barker a Lambeth Degree, *honoris causa*. Among the petitioners were the Lord Chancellor (Lord Birkenhead), the Attorney-General (Sir Gordon Hewart), the Solicitor-General (Sir Ernest Pollock), Viscount Cave, formerly Home Secretary, and Sir Edward Carson. It was clear that the Archbishop technically had the power of acceding to the request by conferring a Medical Degree. In the previous century, thirty-one persons had been made Doctors of Medicine by an Archbishop. But the Medical Act of 1858 (21 & 22 Vict. c. 90) had prescribed that the degree could not give any qualification to practise. The Archbishop was therefore fully aware that the conferring, by him, of a Lambeth Degree might unintentionally have the effect of deceiving the public, for even though Mr. Barker, after receiving such a degree, had the right to describe himself as H. A. Barker, M.D., he would not thereby be any the more qualified in law to practise, and he would be subject, by section 40 of the Medical Act, to a penalty of £20 if he were wilfully or falsely to use the name or title of Doctor of Medicine, or any other description implying that he had been registered under the Act, or was recognized by law as a medical practitioner. The Archbishop consulted both legal and medical friends, amongst the latter, Sir Rickman Godlee, Sir Thomas Barlow, and Sir Alfred Pearce Gould. The doctors themselves were not prepared heartily to defend the General Medical Council's action with regard to Mr. Barker, especially in the case of the anaesthetist, and the Archbishop himself said, in writing to Sir Lewis Dibdin (May 27, 1920):

The ARCHBISHOP OF CANTERBURY *to* SIR LEWIS DIBDIN

I feel bound to have a fling at the medical men who have, as it seems to me, acted in a rather intolerable way towards a man of genius who has got a knack denied to them. They might easily have safeguarded their professional rules while generously recognising his quite undisputed skill and gift.

He thought, however, that some other distinction, such as a title, would be a more appropriate method of recognition of the service of Mr. Barker, than a Lambeth Degree with the possible misrepresentation to which that might lead. He accordingly wrote the following letter:

The ARCHBISHOP OF CANTERBURY *to the* REV. J. L. WALTON

21st June, 1920.

I have for some time had under consideration the Petition which you have transmitted to me, with the appended signatures of a very large number of distinguished men, including the Lord Chancellor, the Attorney General, the Solicitor General, Sir Edward Carson, and many other eminent lawyers, public servants, Members of Parliament, and men of political and literary distinction. They unite in asking me to confer a Medical Degree upon Mr. Herbert Atkinson Barker. The petitioners urge that the Medical Degree should be given to Mr. Barker, 'in order that his assistance may be more generally available for injured soldiers and sailors at the present time'. I have, as you will remember, enquired from you in what way Mr. Barker's possession of the title in question would render his assistance more generally available. From letters which have reached me, I gather that some at least of those who have signed the Petition are, or were, under the impression that by holding a Lambeth Medical Degree *honoris causa* Mr. Barker would become qualified to undertake medical or surgical practice, from which as an unregistered practitioner he is at present debarred. This impression, as you fully realise, is a mistaken one. The legislation which limits registration to men qualified by the ordinary professional training expressly, and I think rightly, provides that the status acquired by registration is not given by the Degree which the petitioners invite me to confer on Mr. Barker. In your reply to my enquiry, you dwell upon the remarkable character and proved success of Mr. Barker's methods, and upon his desire 'to demonstrate his system before the medical authorities with a view to its adoption in the Medical Schools'. You point out, justly as I think, that Mr. Barker could not reasonably be expected at his age to enter upon the course of study necessary for obtaining a Medical Degree in the ordinary way. But, this being so, I am at a loss to know in what way Mr. Barker's assistance would be made more generally available by his holding a Lambeth Medical Degree, unless it were by leading the public to suppose that he possesses the technical qualifications of a registered practitioner. The popular use of the title 'Doctor' in connection with his name would, I imagine, have this probable result, but the supposition would not be in accordance with facts. On these grounds I come distinctly to the conclusion that I should not be acting in the public interest were I to accede to the prayer of the Petition. I should feel more at liberty to grant the request if the Degree were being sought simply as a public recognition of Mr. Barker's beneficial work in the past, and were being given, for example, on his retirement from practice, so that it could not have the misleading result which I have indicated. Indeed, I cannot help hoping that some means may be found of marking the public appreciation of what I cannot but call Mr. Barker's eminent service to sufferers, to whom his manipulative method has proved beneficial when other efforts of a more normal sort had failed. No one can read the published accounts—the general veracity of which is unchallenged—of what Mr. Barker has been enabled to do, or give attention to the individual testimony abundantly furnished to me by letter and by word of mouth, without reaching the conviction that he possesses some manipulative gift of a most unusual kind, and has the knowledge and skill necessary for applying that gift to the benefit of patients who place themselves under his treatment. I am myself, however, concerned simply with the request that I should grant to Mr. Barker the Degree of Doctor of Medicine. I cannot do this without grave danger of misleading the public as to the exact character of the qualifications possessed by a remarkable man, who has, in the face of many difficulties, achieved a reputation for manipulative surgery which no one who looks into the facts can doubt that he has deserved.

The fitness of the reply was generally recognized. Mr. Barker himself, in a personal letter, expressed his gratitude to the Archbishop, and the Archbishop and the petitioners had the satisfaction a little later, as the result of an approach to the Prime Minister by some of the most eminent of his friends, of seeing Mr. Barker honoured by the receipt of a Knighthood from the King.

IV

At the end of June, just before the beginning of the Lambeth Conference, the Archbishop received a letter 'greatly perplexed and pained' from Prebendary F. L. Boyd, about his supposed attitude to the Anglo-Catholic Congress, the Congress which, he said, was first contemplated before the War, and was now being held for the first time in order to exhibit 'with all the weight of authority that we could gather together, the true content and proportion of Catholic faith and practice in the Church of England'. The Archbishop replied:

The ARCHBISHOP OF CANTERBURY *to the* REV. PREBENDARY F. L. BOYD

29 June 1920.

I have received your letter of June 26th. I am grateful to you for writing to me fully and frankly, but I own to being simply amazed by the things which your letter contains. First you tell me that you hear it constantly said, with reference to the coming Anglo-Catholic Congress, that the Archbishop is 'rocking with laughter at it'; or, again, that I am 'deeply annoyed'; and so on. What these statements made to you are based upon, beyond wild conjecture, I have not the slightest idea. I never to my knowledge gave the slightest shadow of ground for either statement, and neither amusement nor annoyance could possibly be suggested by the meeting so far as I know about it. To tell the truth, I have spoken very little to people about it. It has not come prominently before me in any way, nor, of course, was I approached about it either in its inception or afterwards. I have received a certain number of unimportant letters of protest against it, and a few quite insignificant and effervescent letters saying how the Congress will in its power show up the feebleness of the Bishops. But these are quite unimportant things in the ordinary day's correspondence, and I repeat that I literally cannot conjecture upon what the statements you refer to are supposed to rest. I think it possible that some people have been rather irritated with me that I have not given more time or attention to the fact that such a Congress is being held, but I have never had to do so, and yours is, so far as I remember, the first statement I have seen or heard from any of my friends about its beginning. I am much interested to learn from you how it originated, and what you and some others of its promoters have felt to be its true and useful purpose. I shall join with you in thankfulness if, as I hope, your expectations and intentions should be abundantly fulfilled. I have, I think, been quite casually asked by a few people during recent weeks as to whether they should take part in it, and to the best of my recollection I encouraged them in every case to do so. But I cannot be quite sure about this, as I may have felt that some particular man had better keep aloof from this kind of necessarily sectional gathering.

More serious, however, than that part of your letter, important as it is, is the statement you make to me that, after conversation with me some time ago, you went away with the impression that I 'regarded High Churchmen as pariahs—a real nuisance to the Church, to be repressed, and if possible extruded'. I own this to be amazing indeed. I should have thought that my whole public life had given abundant evidence of the utter baselessness of such a supposition. Not a few of my most intimate friends, men with whom I have for years taken counsel, belong indisputably to the section which I am supposed to regard as pariahs. Talbot and Gore are two of the most intimate friends and counsellors that I have, though I am glad to say that I have others belonging to different groups of religious thought to whose friendship I owe equal gratitude. If, however, a man with your knowledge of the Church and its life thinks that to be my attitude, I can only say that it makes one despair of getting people to understand anything. Ask Bishop Gore among the older men; or, say, Edward Talbot of Mirfield, or Father Kelly, or almost any other typical men of that school with whom I have been intimate; and you will see how strange has been your misapprehension. It is so fundamental that I feel it impossible to argue about it. Certainly as one grows older one learns how odd are the misconceptions which arise. Sometimes I have had to defend High Church principles from opinions expressed even by men like yourself. For example, when in your pamphlet about Kikuyu you contended that Communion as administered in the Roman Catholic Church is invalid, I felt I had to stand up among my friends against such a theory. Probably you would say that that was not quite what your words meant. I instance it merely as an example of my desire to be honestly fair all round, in a Church which I believe to be comprehensive enough to include rightly men of widely varied opinions. I should greatly like a further talk with you some day soon. But unhappily the stress in these actual days is so terrific that quiet interviews are nearly impracticable, except upon matters of urgent public business which I cannot escape.

I have dictated this off-hand on receiving your letter. If anything else occurs to me on re-reading what you have said, I may perhaps write again.

After the Lambeth Conference, the Archbishop and Mrs. Davidson took their holiday as usual in Scotland. They visited amongst others (the Archbishop noted at the time) 'the Haldanes at Cloan, the Burghcleres at Finavon, Annie Jones at Aberuchill, the Gordon Duffs at Drummuir (recalling vividly the old visits in my sporting years, say '69 to '85)'.

In September, there was a meeting of the International Committee of the World Alliance for promoting friendship through the Churches at St. Beatenberg. The World Alliance had been born at the very outbreak of the War, in August 1914, at Lake Constance, the fruit of the former Anglo-German Friendship Committee. But it had hardly been formed before its members had to disperse. It had met again in 1919 at The Hague, but the French had refused to attend because the Germans were present. It met again in September 1920, and had to appoint a President. The Archbishop of Canterbury was proposed, the representatives of the different Churches desiring to do honour to a great Churchman who had tried to stand above the battle during the War. The leader of the German delegation, Dr. Spiecker, in a courteous spirit protested against the election as premature. He said that much as the Germans respected Archbishop Davidson, yet he was the chief ecclesiastic of a great hostile power. A representative of the Serbian Church, Father Janic, at once rose to say that all the Orthodox representatives present asked him to declare that they wanted the Archbishop of Canterbury as President, and were unanimous that he was the greatest man they could have. Then, turning to the German delegation, the Serb delegate said: 'And as for you, you ought to be thankful that the Archbishop of Canterbury should be President. He has been a true friend to you. All through the War, though English, he has taken a more than English view of the War. He is the most internationally minded man in Europe. When I was in London he made two great speeches, all in support of you.[1] You ought to be glad of him.' This speech was received with great applause. The election was carried without dissent, as the Germans did not vote against the Archbishop.

At the end of October, the Archbishop spoke in St. Martin's-in-the-Fields, on the Lambeth Conference, and took some delight in glancing at certain members of the congregation, such as William Temple and Dick Sheppard, as he said, 'Half the people in this church' (indicating Sheppard himself with a gesture) 'accuse the Bishops of being asleep, never giving a lead—and now they have given a lead.'

At the beginning of November, he was very unwell, but:

> On Thursday the 11th I was well enough to take part in the Cenotaph unveiling, and the burial of the Unknown Warrior in the Abbey. It was important on all accounts that I should be there. I had had some keen controversy with the Prime Minister and the Cabinet, especially Curzon, about the proceedings at the Cenotaph. They had wished, or the Prime Minister had wished, that the proceedings should be wholly secular, alleging as reason that Mohammedans and Hindus were among those to whose memory it stood. . . . But I prevailed, and we had prayer and 'O God our help,' (Lord's Prayer and Big Ben).[2] Instead of anybody disapproving, there was unanimous expression of thankfulness that we had thus marked our Christian fellowship. The scene in the Abbey, at the grave of the Unknown Warrior, was one of the most stirring in English history, but all this is recounted publicly, and I have no special facts to add.

In November, the Church Assembly, at its second session, passed the first Measure which dealt with the Convocations of Canterbury and York:

> In the November session we passed the measure declaring Convocation's power to reform itself by Canon, and it passed with

[1] Father Janic, the speaker, was probably referring to the Archbishop's speeches in the House of Lords about Reprisals.

[2] The bracketed words are a reference to the interesting fact noted in a letter to the Archbishop afterwards. The writer of the letter said that he had been at the top of Big Ben at the time and heard the words of the Lord's Prayer ascending.

amazing smoothness through its preliminary stages, Legislative Committee of the Assembly, Ecclesiastical Committee of Parliament, resolutions in both Houses of Parliament, and Royal Assent. All was over before Christmas, and the measure became law. Of course it was an unopposed measure, no one being able legitimately to criticise it, but there might easily have been some awkward hitch in the official arrangements, and the absence of any such obstacle has been an encouragement as to the soundness of our plan.

In commenting on the procedure which followed on the reform of Convocation by itself, the Archbishop made this interesting note:

With regard to Convocation reform, a curious technicality has been, I think, overcome more easily than I expected. Convocation has from time immemorial been dissolved only when Parliament is dissolved. We have now been told that we may reform Convocation by Canon when we will, but it would be rather a farce to reform it and then leave it sitting in its unreformed condition till the next dissolution. To meet this, I privately got hold of Sir Almeric FitzRoy, and through him Sir Claud Schuster, and the Home Secretary, and the President of the Council, A. J. Balfour, and they have consented to advise the Crown to dissolve Convocation as soon as the Canon has been enacted. If this enactment takes place, as I hope it will, in the April session of Convocation (after being discussed and agreed to in the February session of Convocation), the dissolution might take place about the end of April, so that the reformed Convocation could meet in the first week of July as originally intended. All these negotiations have involved a great deal of individual work on my part, and I think I am not wrong in saying that my personal influence with those in authority has been of real value, and that this is appreciated by the large circle which is cognisant of the difficulties and of our apparent conquest of them. Altogether it would be affectation to ignore that people are pleased with my own conducting of the business in the three sessions of the Assembly which have already been held, as well as in the original business of the Enabling Bill. I believe that as leader I have now the confidence of a great many people belonging to the progressive schools, who had been fretful about what they thought my lack of push, activity, and vociferousness in carrying things forward. The vociferousness which they wanted would have been the very thing to wreck either the Enabling Bill in its cradle, or the Convocational reform at the stage which it has at present reached.

In December the first Conference took place between the Archbishops and Bishops and the Nonconformists on the Lambeth Appeal, in response to formal letters from the Archbishop of Canterbury to the Heads of each Church, sending them copies of the Appeal. The Archbishop noted:

> We cannot estimate what is going to be the help or hindrance we get from the non-episcopal rank and file. My personal belief has always been that our danger would lie in trying to go too fast. We cannot get Reunion by a short cut. Lambeth Conferences lie ten years apart from one another, and the conditions in England and America differ very widely. It will take years to get our principles rightly understood and assimilated, and any attempt to press hurriedly forward is bound to defeat itself. But it is very difficult to persuade eager men and women, whose interest in these subjects is recent and crude, that we must go step by step, and steadily avoid even the appearance of hurry. This delay is always distasteful to the enthusiasts, especially the young enthusiasts, and I have to fulfil the unpleasant rôle of curbing the sort of buoyant and sanguine expectations that the work can be accomplished forthwith offhand, so sound are its principles, so Christian its aim.

At the end of the year, the Archbishop was rather concerned at the way in which such an immense burden fell on his shoulders, almost unshared by any Bishop save the Archbishop of York who had come to Canterbury, as often before, to spend the last days of the old year with him. He spoke very seriously to the Archbishop of York on the whole question. A record of the main matters discussed between the two Archbishops will show the range of the Archbishop of Canterbury's regular programme:

Membership of the Archbishops' Committee on the property and revenues of the Church.
How to make the Canon for the reform of Convocation.
Relations of the National Assembly to Convocation.
Action on the Lambeth Appeal Resolutions.
Action on the Resolutions about the Ministry of women.
The question of a Sub-Committee of Bishops for the Lambeth Appeal.
Lay Readers.
National Assembly business—standing orders.
Parochial Church Councils.
Resolution on Unemployment.
Ecclesiastical Courts.

Committee on Spiritual Healing.
Committee on Liturgies.
Committee on Moral Theology.
Councils of Social Welfare.
Gorell's Divorce Bill.
League of Nations.
Etc.

Both Archbishops enjoyed such talks; and there was an occasional lightening of the atmosphere as well. Thus Archbishop Davidson told Archbishop Lang of Dean Wace's disgust with the Bishop of Chelmsford (Dr. Watts Ditchfield)—whom he (Wace) had pressed for a bishopric—partly because he had included a friendly reference to Anglo-Catholics in his Church Congress speech! Dean Wace, in expressing his disgust, had said to the Archbishop: 'If I were a young man I should join the Wesleyans, but I am too old now!'

A HOLIDAY AT ABERUCHILL
(1920)

THE ARCHBISHOP OF YORK (COSMO GORDON LANG) — THE ARCHBISHOP OF CANTERBURY (R. T. D.)

CHAPTER LXV

AN UNSETTLED YEAR

Wellington was victorious, the great conqueror was overthrown, England stood the most triumphant nation of the world. But with an enormous debt, a dissatisfied people, gaining peace without tranquillity, greatness without intrinsic strength, the present time uneasy, the future dark and threatening.

NAPIER, *History of the War in the Peninsula*, Book XXIV, ch. vi.

THE conditions of the country, the Church, and the world in the years immediately following the War were strangely unsettled. 'There can be no question at all', wrote the Archbishop in February 1921, 'that we are passing through a time of immense uncertainty as regards the larger polity of the Church.' The rapid enactment of the Enabling Bill was evidence at least of great vitality, though the direction in which the new Assembly would move was still to be seen. Certainly, so far as its early proceedings were concerned, there was no need for any qualms in the Archbishop's mind as to his ability to keep his hand on the helm; and, thanks to his patient guidance, the new Measure, giving powers to the Parochial Church Councils, emerged, after a week's ceaseless debate, in a coherent and intelligible shape. But Parochial Church Councils themselves might well be unsettling institutions.[1]

I

A personal anxiety which weighed heavily on the Archbishop's mind was caused by the trial of Archdeacon Wakeford and another public discipline case affecting a priest, and the thoughts which they stirred. Were such lapses due to the prevailing nervousness and psychical upset of post-War days, with conse-

[1] The Archbishop, writing February 6, 1921, said: 'I doubt whether any event in the constitutional history of Church and State has ever been wrought out with so little friction, and on so smooth a current as this great change. Even now it is difficult to realise that fifteen months ago we were constitutionally in the same position as we had been for centuries, so firmly has the new system fashioned its foothold and made good its powers. I think it is indisputable that if we had failed in December 1919 to get through Parliament what is popularly called the Enabling Bill, we might have waited for it for many a long year with increasing and most harmful loss of enthusiasm, and growth of irritation among the progressive groups. Instead of this we have had a continuous stream of praise and thankful gratulation at the way in which the new system has begun to work.'

quent loosening of fibre and lack of self-control, or was there really a loss of grip on moral orderliness and elemental right or wrong?

All through the year the crisis in Ireland continued, and the Archbishop had his full share in its tragic perplexities. There was the coal strike, with the threatened sympathetic action of the industrial Triple Alliance. There was the appalling suffering caused by the famine in Russia under a Bolshevik régime. There was the grave unrest in the East, the danger to the Christian races in the old Ottoman Empire, as well as the growing Arab protest against the Jewish settlement in Palestine. There was also the problem regarding the condition of the natives in East Africa. In every one of these events or crises the Archbishop perforce had a share, while all the time carrying on his immediate duties in the Diocese and the Province.

II

Early this year the Student Christian Movement was pressing the Bishop of Southwell (Dr. Hoskyns), in whose diocese lay Swanwick, the great centre for interdenominational conferences of students, on the subject of intercommunion. The Bishop asked the Archbishop's advice:

The BISHOP OF SOUTHWELL *to the* ARCHBISHOP OF CANTERBURY

Bishop's Manor, Southwell. Feb. 26/21.

. . . I am now in this letter pressed much further and asked to adopt definitely a plan of Intercommunion.

Remembering the extreme youthfulness, and ignorance of the students as to the faith and order of the Church, and remembering also that the students are rather kicking at all the restraints of Institutional Religion, I shrink from coming to a judgement on my own responsibility.

If this crowd of young students go back to their various schools and colleges with the message that Church Order and Confirmation goes for nothing, what will be the result?

The Archbishop replied:

The ARCHBISHOP OF CANTERBURY *to the* BISHOP OF SOUTHWELL

4th March 1921.

You are indeed confronted by a practical question of no small importance and difficulty in regard to these good enthusiasts at

Swanwick. We have always to remember with regard to them, when inclined to harsh judgement, that most of them are quite young and inexperienced, and that they rather incite one another into a sort of free lance attitude towards men and things, both sacred and secular. We must not therefore treat them as though it were deliberate conciliar action on their part which reached conclusions which we regard as dangerous. I do not think I differ at all from what you have said. It appears to me that you must take the responsibility of telling them definitely that we have reiterated our intention of awaiting Provincial authority before ourselves making operative the counsels given in the Lambeth Conference, and that any action by an individual Bishop or an individual group of would-be loyal Church people is fraught with peril if it anticipates the ultimate conclusion and thus gives a handle to those who deem us rash and inconsiderate in our operations. The Church of England is not a young body and does not—and ought not to—move with over-rapid steps in effecting changes. So much for the large principle. Then we come to the working out of the details. They ought to see that what they propose may be easy enough for them in their gathering, but if it becomes a precedent would be by no means so easy on other occasions and in other surroundings. I am not myself one of those who want to be meticulously rigid about enquiring into the antecedents or sentiments of those who, as responsible Christian men and women, present themselves for Holy Communion in our churches. I think the responsibility rests with the individual who thus comes, but I am sure you are right in feeling that we go far beyond this if we deliberately say that the non-Anglican members of a great conference, in a formal or quasi-formal way, be invited to come to our Communion, notwithstanding the fact that no decision to that effect has yet been adopted by our Province. The case would of course be still stronger with regard to the attendance of our Church folk deliberately and corporately at a Communion Service conducted by others than our ordained Ministry.[1]

[1] In June 1921 the organ of the Student Movement had an article by Tissington Tatlow, the General Secretary, containing this official ruling: 'The General Committee [of the Student Christian Movement] does not feel that to take to itself the functions of a Church and to arrange a united Communion Service at Swanwick would be of any real service to the cause of unity; and it further recognises that to take this step would be to turn its back upon the inter-denominational policy upon which it has built up its work and its relation to the Churches during the last twenty years. . . . The end [intercommunion at Swanwick] is to be achieved not by asking the General Committee of the Student Movement to take action outside its province, but by seeking to move the Churches.'

III

At the beginning of March, the Archbishop's counsel was asked privately by the Lord Chamberlain, as often before, with regard to a religious play. He replied:

The ARCHBISHOP OF CANTERBURY *to* VISCOUNT SANDHURST

3 March 1921.

I have read carefully the little sacred drama which you send me —*The Upper Room.* It is, as the memorandum in your envelope puts it, a devotional exercise rather than a play in the ordinary sense. I do not know what are the conditions under which it is intended to produce it. I note that it is said that the profits are to go to a charity, but is it to be open to the public in the ordinary way for ordinary payment, and is it proposed to allow it not merely in the Philbeach Hall, as named but also in a theatre? And, if the latter, what precautions can possibly be taken as regards the manner of its production? It is so intensely sacred, and once this were licensed for ordinary theatrical exhibition or performance I do not see where any line could, on religious grounds, be ultimately drawn with regard to religious drama unless it were because the writing was irreverent. This is the reverse of irreverent. Some would call it superstitiously devotional. I should not myself use that word, though of course the whole details are drawn out on sacramental lines of the most pronounced kind—Roman rather than Anglican, though there is nothing so far as I can see that is contrary to sound Christian teaching of the sacramental sort. In my view the performance of this in a hall and with precautions against interruption or applause of any sort might be for those who attend it a religious exercise of a profitable kind. But is it for the Lord Chamberlain to license such religious exercise in King's Theatre, Hammersmith, on Good Friday? About this I do not know, for I am ignorant as to the limits of your authority and the manner of its exercise. What I can definitely say is that the drama is solemnly devotional and Christian and certainly could not be objected to on the ground of lowering the dignity of the sacred story of the Passion. It has also adequate reticence. For example, though Our Lord's voice is once heard He never appears.

My difficulty in giving advice is that I do not quite know what limitations you have power to make as to the manner of its presentation or the rough and ready way in which it might be handled. At this moment presentations of Mystery Plays are taking place in Church Halls in more than one part of London—

> notably, in the Church House, where *Everyman* is being performed and money is being paid for admission. But that is being done by religious people, mainly clergy, on quite definitely religious lines. Once guarantee this, and I see no harm in such presentations, even to the extent of allowing *The Upper Room*, which I gather has already been performed. Given adequate guarantees, I could not myself object to the performance of this, but can you secure that it is not mixed up with other things in some such way, for example, as a performance of the ballet of *The Foolish Virgins* which is now being presented in London Music Halls? If this were degraded in that manner it would be terrible indeed.

The Lord Chamberlain decided to issue his licence with the proviso that 'this play shall not be produced anywhere in Great Britain except under such conditions as shall be approved by the Lord Chamberlain'.

On April 7, the Archbishop's seventy-third birthday, Lytton Strachey's *Life of Queen Victoria* was published. The Archbishop talked about it at dinner and was relieved that the book was not sarcastic. Indeed, he said that he would like to review the book if he had time, and show that Queen Victoria was a great person. In judging her, he said, 'you must always remember she never had any companions of her own age to play with, or knock any nonsense out of her'. She had told him once that she was the only person alive probably who had outlived four generations of her contemporaries; meaning the generations represented by Lord Melbourne, Lord Palmerston, Lord John Russell and Sir Robert Peel, Mr. Gladstone and Lord Beaconsfield. She had, he said, a perfectly marvellous memory. She was not bookish, but she had read good books. He agreed with Strachey that the Prince Consort was very clever, but he did not agree with the prophecy that, had he lived, he might have altered the whole constitutional history of England. Many at Windsor who had known the Prince Consort when he (the Archbishop) had gone there as Dean, had had the feeling that he was growing less popular and was *felix opportunitate mortis*.

IV

There was a coal strike in April, in which the Archbishop sent an identical telegram offering his services to Frank Hodges

(Miners' Federation), Evan Williams (Mining Association), and J. H. Thomas (National Union of Railwaymen), while at the same time making a public appeal for prayer:

Telegram.

Private. April 9, 1921.

If my services can be of any value towards composing the industrial quarrel which is a wound alike to our common Christianity and the prosperity of the country, I am ready to do anything in my power.

ARCHBISHOP OF CANTERBURY.

At the same time he wrote to the Prime Minister (9 April 1921):

The ARCHBISHOP OF CANTERBURY *to the* RT. HON. D. LLOYD GEORGE

At a time like this, I am of necessity kept in touch every hour with all sorts and conditions of men, and the fact that they turn towards a religious centre is, I would fain hope, of good omen. May I add my voice to others which must at this moment be making appeal to you that you should not allow technicalities of procedure and of logical fairness to stand in the way of a straight, open, unconditional discussion with those whose temper or whose suspicion seems sometimes to get the better of their patriotism and their commonsense.

Nothing material occurred as a result. When, however, a debate in the Upper House of Convocation led to strong speeches on the part of some of the Bishops, Mr. Bridgeman, Secretary of Mines and well known to the Archbishop, wrote a letter expressing his grave disappointment:

The RT. HON. W. C. BRIDGEMAN *to the* ARCHBISHOP OF CANTERBURY

April 30th, 1921.

Of course no one can complain of Bishops or any one else taking a sentimental view rather than an economic one of a great question like this. But it was singularly unfortunate that at the most critical days of the Conference men of influence should have dashed in with speeches obviously ill-informed on a subject as complicated and difficult as can be found, and created an impression of being partisans rather than mediators.

The Archbishop replied in a letter which he himself described later as 'rather a hurried one', while the Bishop of Winchester, to whom he sent copies of the correspondence, felt 'a little bit given away'. The Archbishop had, however, said in the Upper House, that he was 'not in the least prepared to express an opinion upon the details of the plans of pooling and the rest. . . . Some Bishops to-day have done so. Their knowledge may justify them—mine certainly does not.' He agreed with the Resolution, but he differentiated definitely between the Resolution and the speeches in support of it. The final form of the Resolution (April 27) was as follows:

That this House, believing that moral no less than economic issues are involved in the present dispute in the coal industry—

(1) Welcomes, on the part of the miners, the desire that the strong should help to bear the burdens of the weak, and, on the part of the mine-owners, a frank recognition that the living wage should be regarded as the first charge on the industry, and also their willingness to forgo profits during the present period of stress.

(2) Recognises as the root of the present trouble the neglect to prepare for the critical moment of Decontrol by any constructive changes in the organisation of the industry.

(3) Affirms its conviction that only on the lines suggested in the Resolution 74, passed by the Lambeth Conference, can a lasting settlement be hoped for in this or other industrial dispute: 'An outstanding and pressing duty of the Church is to convince its members of the necessity of nothing less than a fundamental change in the spirit and working of our economic life. This change can only be effected by accepting as the basis of industrial relations the principle of co-operation in service for the common good in place of unrestricted competition for private or sectional advantage. All Christian people ought to take an active part in bringing about this change, by which alone we can hope to remove class dissensions and resolve industrial discords.'

(4) Calls on all members of the Church to do all in their power to spread a spirit of fellowship by personal example, by a consistent advocacy of justice and good faith between man and man, and not least by doing all in their power to relieve the distress caused by the widespread unemployment at the present time.

The letter written to Mr. Bridgeman ran as follows:

The ARCHBISHOP OF CANTERBURY *to the* RT. HON. W. C. BRIDGEMAN

Lambeth Palace, S.E. 1. May 2, 1921.

I am not surprised to receive your letter. Our session of Convocation last week was a poor one in more ways than one. The attendance was small and the speaking was inadequate and rather onesided and unbalanced—though there was more said of a 'steadying' kind than the newspapers, to whom quiet speeches are bad 'copy', told the world. I have not read carefully the reports which did appear, but they seemed to me on quick reading to be neither clear nor fair.

But I own I was greatly disappointed at the attitude taken—strangely onesidedly—by some of my brethren—and in my own few words I tried to counteract this if I could, and I deprecated our being supposed to be experts in these extraordinarily difficult matters.

A Bishop, who is in touch with a mining population, is apt to be stirred by all that is good in the men who trust him, and the former tradition of Episcopal words and acts in industrial controversies has been so markedly on the other side that the pendulum when it swings is apt to swing far. And, I repeat, the newspapers, in what they reproduce out of a long debate, are apt to give simply what they regard as spicey and arresting. But I share, on the whole, your disappointment.

V

During the coal crisis a visit was paid to Lambeth by the Archbishop of Upsala, Dr. Nathan Söderblom, and his wife. He was one of the most famous churchmen of his day, with a great desire that the Church should rise to the opportunities of the time. Once when the Archbishop (at a private meeting in the House of Lords) chaffed him on his conviction that Upsala was the most natural place in the world for Englishmen to visit, Dr. Söderblom replied that he had been much struck with the order of words in the General Confession in the English Book of Common Prayer, where the confession 'We have left undone those things that we ought to have done' preceded the confession that 'we have done those things that we ought not to have done'; and, adding that this order was very true to the New Testament spirit, he said

'Let that be my excuse!' His special wish in visiting Lambeth on this occasion was to engage the Archbishop of Canterbury's support for a World Conference of the Churches on Practical Christianity at Stockholm. The Archbishop named an hour on April 15 for the talk. It was a busy day. After his correspondence in the morning Dr. Davidson had to go to the Law Courts to give judgement with Lord Coleridge in a case of clergy discipline. Later in the day, he and a few others were engaged in an interview with the Lord Chancellor on Ireland; and that very afternoon the threat of a general strike was declared cancelled; so that there was much for the Archbishop to think of. The chaplain, after a conversation with Dr. Söderblom, had prepared a number of subjects as the material for the conversation, and had jotted them down on a half-sheet of paper. Dr. Söderblom came into his study to wait, and while the chaplain was out of the room Dr. Söderblom, wandering about and looking at the desk, saw this half-sheet, sat down, added a subject or two, and numbered them all in quite a new order of his own. Notably he put 'Universal Conference on Life and Work', which was third, up to the first place. When the chaplain returned to the study, Archbishop Söderblom said, 'These are the things which the Archbishop would like to discuss with me? I think this would be a better order.' The chaplain accordingly wrote them out afresh in this order, and on another sheet of paper. Then the bell rang and the chaplain entered the Archbishop's study with the half-sheet. The Archbishop asked, 'Has he seen this?' The chaplain replied: 'Yes, and altered their order and re-arranged them thus.' The Archbishop smiled and said, 'He is a dangerous man.'

The Archbishop of Upsala then entered, and sat by the fireplace in a low chair opposite the desk. It was half-past twelve. Sitting down did not suit his vivacity nearly as much as standing or moving about, with the freedom which that gave for gesture. The Archbishop of Canterbury at once opened the conversation by talking about the Lambeth Conference Appeal—which was the second item on the half-sheet. Dr. Söderblom, always ready to talk freely and interestingly once a subject was started, expatiated on this. From that the passage was easy to the other Scandinavian Churches, including the Church of Esthonia for which Archbishop Söderblom was shortly to consecrate a Bishop. His flow of speech had hardly ceased when Archbishop Davidson turned him on to questions of Indian Missions. Archbishop Söderblom observed that the minutes were flying, and became a little anxious lest the Universal Conference should fail to get its due attention. But the Archbishop of Canterbury, surprised to find how many things he had to talk about to the Archbishop of Upsala, switched on to the question of the fixed Easter. Dr. Söderblom explained his personal disinclination for a fixed Easter, and then skilfully referred to the raising of this question in the Encyclical Letter from the Patriarchate of Constantinople 'Unto all the Churches'[1] (1920), and suggested that the Oecumenical Council, which would result from the Universal Conference, would be just the body to discuss such a question. The Archbishop of Canterbury smiled, but refused to be drawn. He turned to the German Archaeological Institute at Jerusalem and read a letter from the Governor of Jerusalem. Dr. Söderblom once more ended this discussion by expressing a hope that the Archaeological Institute might prove a home for the Oecumenical Council. The Archbishop again laughed, but went forward to another item on the programme, 'Occupied districts in Germany'. The Archbishop of Upsala was now a little restless, but with excellent courtesy and vigour explained his views of French cruelty and vindictiveness. It had now struck one, and still the relentless Archbishop of Canterbury refused to touch the main subject, and went on to discuss Posen and the future of the German Church there. Dr. Söderblom (who, when Jerusalem had first been mentioned, had tried to stop the discussion, in a way, by saying that he had explained the situation fully to the chaplain) made as though all the main facts were sufficiently stated in documents which he had previously presented to the Archbishop. But the discussion was successfully curtailed and Posen (as Dr. Söderblom had stated before) was an instance of the useful work which an Oecumenical Council could do. So at last the Universal Conference was reached, and the Archbishop of Canterbury, laughing and well aware of the game he had been playing and that he had brought down the first item on the Agenda to be the last for discussion, said 'All roads lead to the Oecumenical Council!'

The Archbishop of Upsala then, in the poor ten minutes left him before lunch, expatiated on the Conference and his hopes

[1] Bell's *Documents on Christian Unity*, p. 44.

that it might take place in 1923 at Upsala, or Stockholm, or the Hague, and elaborated on his statistics of religious strength, its relation to British organizations and upon the best methods to be adopted for inviting the Church of England and other Churches to be represented officially. Even so, he did not obtain a clear opinion about the Conference from the Archbishop of Canterbury, who was unwilling to give himself away, either for or against, and had previously told his chaplain that he hoped he would not be asked for a definite answer, but if he were asked he would say that he would consult the Archbishop of York.[1]

VI

The Archbishop went to Edinburgh in June, and expounded the Lambeth Appeal to the General Assemblies of the Church of Scotland and the United Free Church. He was most cordially received in both places. Of his visit to the General Assembly of the Church of Scotland he said:

> I took the line of avoiding almost entirely the distinctly controversial questions about re-ordination, or new commission etc., suggested in our Appeal, and dwelling simply on the weight attaching to the Lambeth Conference, and the earnestness with which we made our Appeal, and the impossibility of localizing the matter to the British Isles, or the English-speaking race, forgetful of both Eastern and Western Churches.
>
> After I had spoken, Dr. Wallace Williamson in a very formal way, after saying nice things about me and my speech, launched a kind of ultimatum by giving me then and there, on behalf of the Church of Scotland, a formal invitation to preach in St. Giles, implying, though he did not say it, that upon it would depend their sense of the reality of our desire for better relations. I did not myself think his speech discourteous or markedly unfair, but I find that many others did. Dr. Cooper, I believe, writes indignant letters about it to the Primus and others, and several people when the Assembly was breaking up came up to me in the Lobby and introduced themselves and said 'do not suppose we agree with Williamson. We are much more with you than you suppose. You must not take his position as meaning too much', and so on. I had

[1] The 'Universal Christian Conference on Life and Work' took place at Stockholm in 1925; with the Patriarch of Constantinople (represented by the Metropolitan of Thyateira), the Archbishop of Canterbury (represented by the Bishop of Winchester), the Archbishop of Upsala, and Dr. A. J. Brown (U.S.A.), as joint presidents. The Stockholm Conference appointed a Continuation Committee, which in 1930 became 'The Universal Christian Council for Life and Work'.

> not regarded it as opposition, and to tell the honest truth I am inclined to think that he can make a very good case against me if, after all I have said, I distinctly refused his invitation. He did not expect an answer then and there, and I have plenty of time to think about it.

Nothing came of the invitation, as it happened, but the Archbishop did not dismiss its acceptance as quite out of the question, for accepting an invitation to St. Giles's pulpit seemed to him something 'quite different from going for a Gospel sermon as though we were in a general way interchanging pulpits'. During the spring the Archbishop did a certain amount of preaching, but not very much. He notes especially a visit to the cadets at Sandhurst to dedicate their Chapel—'A fine gathering with considerable interest and pathos, for the Sandhurst lads gave their lives for their country literally in hundreds and thousands.' Later in June (17th) he dined at Lord Haldane's to meet Einstein. He says:

> I have never seen a more typical scientific lion in appearance—he might have been prepared for that rôle on the stage—a mass of long black hair tossed back, and a general appearance of scientific untidiness, but he was modest and quiet to talk to, and disclaimed a great deal of what is attributed to him.

One of his disclaimers was in reply to the Archbishop's inquiry, 'Lord Haldane tells us that your theory ought to make a great difference to our morals.' Einstein replied, 'Do not believe a word of it. It makes no difference. It is purely abstract—science.' Mrs. Einstein, talking to Mrs. Davidson after dinner, was full of amusement because some lady had expressed her interest in Einstein's theory 'especially in its mystical aspect'. Mrs. Einstein exclaimed: 'Mystical! Mystical! My Husband mystical!' as though it were the greatest possible joke.

There was a happy interlude on a Saturday afternoon when the Archbishop watched a game of polo:

> Yesterday, Saturday the 18th, Edith and I saw for the first time a really great polo match, England v. America. We lunched with Annie Jones at Hurlingham and saw the game in luxury afterwards—complimentary tickets costing £25 had been sent to us by the Committee—Heaven knows why! America triumphed overwhelmingly, largely owing to the wonders of their horseflesh, but partly to what even an ignoramus could see to be superior skill. It is a rare thing in my life to have spent two Saturdays running looking on at games, and that in the middle of a very busy summer,

It was still Ireland, however, that was the most absorbing interest in his mind. His memoranda show him to have been deeply stirred by the King's visit to Belfast and the great good it did, while he notes with some indignation the extraordinary shifting of ground in the Cabinet, and the conflict between the advocates of force and the advocates of conciliation. Bishop Nicholai Velimirovic, the Serbian Bishop, who was in London at this time, pressed him to pay a visit to Palestine, and take Serbia and Greece on the way, and was very disappointed because the Archbishop expressed the fear that he could not get away from his work to take such a journey. 'But his work', said the Bishop, 'seems primarily to be Ireland, the House of Lords, and other affairs of a public character which could get on without him. The Archbishop should remember that he stands for the eternal.' The criticism is worth setting down, though the Archbishop would himself have strongly maintained that the Eternal God acted in history, and thus have abundantly justified his concern for temporal things.

On July 20 came the news of the sudden death of his childhood's friend, Kate Swinton, at the age of seventy-five at Doune. She had been present at his christening. She had travelled in the old days with him and his father on the Continent, and was a real companion, and her death meant much.

VII

Throughout the autumn the Irish question still clouded everything else, and the sense of strain was intense. The Archbishop himself was tired and unhappy, with many things to add to his anxieties: difficult debates in the Church Assembly about the Parochial Church Councils; meetings of a Royal Chapels Committee to decide upon a successor to Subdean Edgar Sheppard, who had died; the beginnings of an inquiry about Conversations at Malines; telegrams from the Armenian Archbishop of Cilicia and the Armenian Patriarch of Constantinople protesting against the Franco-Kemalist agreement and the abandonment of Cilicia and the Christians to the Turk; also deputations from America about the World Conference on Faith and Order; and an important meeting between Nonconformists and the Archbishops and Bishops to clear up ambiguous expressions in the Lambeth Appeal.

At the end of the year, just before the Ordination, he was suddenly taken ill with the old glandular trouble of six years before. He had already had an attack twice, and each time seriously. The doctors came and he was miserable all day, and the Ordination was taken for him by the Bishop of Dover. He asked Sir Thomas Barlow whether he ought to resign, but there was no question of that, though the illness must not be treated lightly. Later on the Archbishop improved, but he was not really well again till towards the end of January.

CHAPTER LXVI

IRELAND, 1920–1921

Whether England doth not really love us and wish well to us, as bone of her bone, and flesh of her flesh? And whether it be not our part to cultivate this love and affection all manner of ways? RT. REV. DR. GEORGE BERKELEY, LORD BISHOP OF CLOYNE, *The Querist*, No. 323, 1750.

NO one in a position of central responsibility in Great Britain could remain unmoved by the deplorable events taking place across St. George's Channel in 1920–1. It would have been very unlike Archbishop Davidson to have stood aloof. This does not mean that he took sides or wished to make any kind of political intervention. That would equally have been very unlike him. But if, as Archbishop of Canterbury, he conceived it important to understand, as a matter of history happening in his own time, a dispute about a patriarchal election in a foreign Church[1] and the troubles in the Near East, much more would he deem it his duty, as Primate of the National Church, to be in the closest touch with a crisis in Ireland fraught with grave issues for the nation and the empire as a whole. And certainly the quantity of letters which he received, and the appeals which reached Lambeth from all sorts of quarters, showed that there were many intimately involved in the struggle who felt this too.

I

But what, it may be asked, could the Archbishop actually do? First of all he made it his business (as always) to keep himself fully informed. He never missed an opportunity of getting any news he could from people in authority, and people on the spot who visited London. He had, of course, plenty of correspondents and visitors with views of their own, and ideas which they were anxious that the Archbishop should adopt—and he listened patiently, though his own information often enabled him to check (and disprove) what they proposed. Further, where, as he considered, a moral issue was raised, he could make that moral issue plain.

[1] See ch. lxviii.

In May 1920, at a time when he was pretty well absorbed in preparing for the Lambeth Conference, the starting of the Welsh Church on its new voyage, the beginning of the Church Assembly, and Lord Buckmaster's Bill on Divorce, altogether apart from diocesan and foreign affairs, he wrote an important letter to the Prime Minister.

A debate took place in the House of Lords, on May 6, on the terrorism in Ireland, and in its course reference was made to the attitude of the Roman Catholic Bishops. The Bishop of Killaloe had described the conduct of the police as 'a mad riot of raids, arrests and organised assassination', while the Bishop of Cork had adopted a totally different line and said openly 'the killing of policemen is murder'. The Roman hierarchy was a very powerful body in Ireland, with very great responsibilities—so the Archbishop argued in his own mind, and privately with some of the Peers. Could not the Bishops be challenged to declare their mind? This therefore was his letter to Lloyd George:

The ARCHBISHOP OF CANTERBURY *to the* RT. HON. D. LLOYD GEORGE

May 9th, 1920.

I feel presumptuous in writing to you about a matter on which I have no special knowledge whatever—the fearful perplexities of the Irish problem. My excuse is that while I have no knowledge of Ireland I have a long experience of holding high ecclesiastical office with its great responsibilities. These responsibilities have always seemed to me to involve this, that we ecclesiastics should abstain from political controversy except where some fundamental moral principle is involved. And when we do say anything we ought always to be prepared to be not merely critical, but to have something constructive to contribute.

Now in Ireland there are men—the Irish Roman Catholic hierarchy—occupying a corresponding position with in some sense an even larger responsibility, because of the allegiance they claim, or enforce, among the Irish people in at least three provinces. At this moment the Irish Bishops seem to me to be evading a responsibility, the discharge of which ought to be forced upon them. I am sure that if I were one of them I should feel it so and should be amazed if I were allowed to evade that responsibility. Month after month the Irish hierarchy is quoted in Ireland as giving its support to the anti-English movement, even if it abstains from throwing its shield over outrages. I suppose it is indisputable that masses of the less educated Irish folk believe that the Bishops and priests are in sympathy with full Sinn Fein aspirations. The published letters and speeches by the Bishops leave them with this impression, and markedly shun any disavowal of the policy of bringing about an independent Irish Republic. Yet it is impossible to believe that most of these great ecclesiastics are so fatuous as really to imagine that that Republic can be attained, or that its promotion would be desirable even if obtainable.

Has not the time come when something should be publicly done by the Government to force these ecclesiastics into the open? I do not suppose that they would easily be so forced, or would consent to give a categorical reply stating in outspoken truth what is their real opinion and desire. But to me it seems clear that they ought to be confronted with a formal request or demand that they state unequivocally what it is they want. If they evade the reply, which is, I suppose, probable, let the evasion be made clear, and be openly and officially commented upon as evidence that they dare not express their real opinion, and that they are not in truth the Sinn Feiners people believe them to be. As I try to put myself in their place, the kind of appeal I should expect to receive from the Government is something like this:

> 'You hold a great and responsible position in the country; you are responsible to God and man for promoting its religious and moral well-being, and to that end its political stability and peace. We recognise your responsibility and we deliberately desire a statement of your views as a contribution to our deliberations and policy at a very grave hour. Do you, or do you not, back the loudly proclaimed desire and intention to secure an independent Irish republic? We have a right to seek your counsel, for you are recognised by the people as leaders, and you, therefore, share our answerableness, and we have a right to know your views. If you deliberately wish success to the Sinn Fein Republic policy, we want to know it. If you believe that policy to be mistaken, we want to know it, and we consider that the people of Ireland has a right to know it. We gravely ask you for an answer, and we ask it with a sense of responsibility attaching both to the question and to the reply.'

All this could be far more weightily and pointedly put than I have put it. No one would do that so well as you. But I think the thing needs doing before the eyes of all men. I do not mean that the request should be made public before the reply is received, but it should be so written as to be suited for publication whatever the issue. I am quite sure that if I were in the position of the Irish

Roman Catholic Archbishops, I should expect to be thus formally brought into the open. I cannot but believe that to ask the question thus, whether the answer be given or evaded—and I presume it would be evaded—is in every sense right.

I repeat that I feel presumptuously out of place in writing all this, for you and your colleagues must have faced the problem many a time, and I have no Irish knowledge whatever. But I do not like to leave unsaid what is constantly in my mind, and I think that my own ecclesiastical position, with my constant sense of its grave responsibilities, justifies me in at least putting before you what I feel. If this is useless, you have only to throw it aside, but at least I shall have said what I think and suggestions at an hour so fearfully perplexing and anxious may have some value, even if in the form they are put they must be cast aside.

The Archbishop talked over his letter with the Prime Minister at St. Asaph on June 1. It had apparently been circulated to the Cabinet and been considered by them, and the Cabinet had been grateful. But the prevailing view was that the Irish Bishops would get out of the question by saying 'It is not our business'—while one of the most eminent members of the hierarchy was known to be strongly in favour of a Republic.

The Archbishop's watchfulness was undoubtedly of value. People wanted his help, but they also wanted to know what he thought. He kept an even keel. He refused to join Lord Henry Bentinck's 'Peace with Ireland' Committee. Again, when asked by the Editor of the *New York Nation* to give his blessing to an American investigation into atrocities, he took strong exception to the Editor's telegram and pointed out—his reply being published at the time—that the real controversy was not between Ireland and England, but in the main between the two great sections of the Irish people themselves. He refused to intervene in what he conceived the rash and misguided policy of the friends of the Lord Mayor of Cork (McSwiney), who tried to secure a change in the Government's attitude by starving himself to death in Brixton jail. Nevertheless, when ugly stories were published about reprisals by the Black and Tans in the autumn of 1920, he was a good deal disturbed. After checking the accuracy of some of the accounts, he decided to make a firm speech against reprisals in the House of Lords, on November 2, 1920. He spoke guardedly, and denounced the outrages committed against the police and the loyalists as 'unutterably horrible', and used strong words to express his sympathy with those who had to face the forces of rebellion, and with those whose homes had been darkened by the outrages which had taken place. But the point of his speech was a plain and severe remonstrance against the reprisals inflicted by the Black and Tans against persons and property as facts beyond dispute. He distinguished between reprisals under orderly authority, definitely taken in hand as a conceivable course if conditions became so bad (against which he would not feel it his duty to protest), and the present reprisals which had occurred 'where the disciplined forces of the Crown, appointed to suppress disorder, have themselves, though without definite superior authority and command, given terrible examples of the very kind of disorder which they are sent there to suppress'; and he begged the Government, for the credit of the public life of England, to bring such reprisals to an end.

It was a brave speech, and exposed him to a great deal of criticism from quarters with which he was usually found in agreement. 'The present campaign of murder', said an Irish correspondent, 'must be ended at all costs, and I beseech Your Grace to pause before using your great influence to hamper the Government in their difficult and dangerous task.' The Archbishop's words of condemnation of the Sinn Fein outrages were, as he had frequent occasion to point out, seldom given the same prominence, though they were strong enough when read in the official report.

As Lord Curzon, leader of the House of Lords, privately admitted after his speech, there was no answer to the Archbishop's charge; but the reprisals went on. The Archbishop made a longer and more deliberate speech to the same effect on February 22, 1921. He defended himself against the accusation of political partisanship, and spoke again with even greater severity of the insane wickedness of the murderous gangs which the Government forces had to put down. But he maintained that the question with which he was concerned was a question of ethics in politics. He gave detailed examples of the reprisals. He agreed that the Sinn Fein outrages were ten times worse than the Black and Tan, but 'you cannot justifiably punish wrongdoing by lawlessly doing the like. Not by calling in the Devil will you cast out devils or punish devilry.' The Lord Chancellor (Birkenhead), who replied, after some heated exchanges between himself and

Lord Buckmaster, paid a tribute to the unexceptionable character of the Archbishop's manner of criticizing the Government, and told him afterwards that his speech could do nothing but good. It certainly was not a speech on the popular side, and before delivering it he said it was one of the most difficult he had ever had to make in the House of Lords. But there was good reason to believe it had a valuable influence on public opinion and policy.

II

The weeks which followed saw the Archbishop 'in the thick of many debates and controversies about the horribleness of the Irish situation'. He was in touch with several independent political leaders on the look-out for light, and attended private deputations to the Lord Chancellor. Various suggestions were made for a manifesto on the part of the Churches of England and Scotland, and even for a combined visit to Ireland of himself, Cardinal Bourne, and some others. But the Archbishop did not favour such proposals.

On more than one occasion he was asked to take the chair at a big public meeting on Ireland, with a view, as it was put, to coercing the conscience of Churchmen. To an enthusiastic advocate of this proposal, the Archbishop propounded a series of questions with admirable patience:

> *Archbishop*: What do you want your meeting to do?
> *Enthusiastic Clergyman*: To arouse public opinion.
> *Archbishop*: To ——?
> *E.C.*: To arouse public opinion.
> *Archbishop*: Yes, but *what* to?
> *E.C.*: To realize their responsibilities.
> *Archbishop*: To do *what*?
> *E.C.*: Here opinions might differ, but I should like a truce.
> *Archbishop*: To do *what*?

There was no reply. Clearly such enthusiasts as this had not thought the matter out, and the Archbishop said that a great many people wanted to ease their consciences, and therefore made such proposals without any plans at all, or any considered purpose.

He was conscious of the general dissatisfaction with the handling of the situation by the politicians. He did not, however, feel that it was for him to take part in purely political debate. On June 12, 1921, he wrote in a private memorandum:

> To-day we are again on the eve of discussion in the House of Lords, about which Lord Buxton has been telephoning to me frequently during the last forty-eight hours. They want me to take some part in it, but at present I do not see that I can contribute anything. Much has been said about the speech I delivered in the House of Lords some months ago against government reprisals. This has defined my own position, and I am inclined to think I had better stand aside and not try to contribute to a debate wherein I shall be over-weighted by men who have more practical knowledge of Ireland.

He added:

> I doubt whether there has ever been anything more discreditable in modern politics than the present condition of Ireland, for it is impossible to suppose that wise statesmanship and consistent policy could have got into the really anarchic condition in which they stand.

He was warmly in favour of the King's visit to Belfast, and his memoranda tell a curious story of the way in which the famous appeal for conciliation took final shape. It is curious also to notice, as a sign of the impression his independent attitude had made upon Ireland, that on at least two occasions mysterious messages reached him about or from De Valera. One of the messengers, Mr. Barry Egan, Deputy-Mayor of Cork, introduced by Monsignor W. F. Brown,[1] a well-known Roman Catholic priest, had come over from Dublin to London on June 28 to see the new Viceroy, Lord FitzAlan, but found him ill in bed. 'As he must return instantly to Dublin and wanted to see somebody,' wrote the Archbishop, 'he had thought that I would be the right person!' Mr. Egan wanted the Archbishop's opinion as to what they ought to do about the proposed interview between Lloyd George and De Valera. The Archbishop told him that in his personal judgement the one chance of an interview or conference succeeding would be if the Prime Minister and De Valera entered into it wholly untrammelled, i.e. without conditions laid down beforehand; that each should behave in a trustful and generous manner towards the other. The Archbishop's statement was

[1] Mgr. Brown lived in Vauxhall, and saw the Archbishop occasionally on educational and social questions. He later became Bishop of Pella.

eagerly welcomed by Mr. Egan, who said he would tell De Valera, while the Archbishop promised to let the Prime Minister know, the next day, what had happened. The end of the interview is thus described by Monsignor Brown:

> The Archbishop . . . asked Mr. Egan what Irishmen thought of the British troops. The Deputy-Mayor replied that their 'Boys', as he put it, liked the Regulars of the British Army well enough and regarded them as pleasant and somewhat harmless fellows. 'But', he went on, 'the men they admire are the Black and Tans.' This came as a profound surprise to the Archbishop, who exclaimed, 'Oh, really! Why so?' in that pleasant, melodious voice of his. A short and swift reply completely disconcerted him. It was this—'Because they are such devils to fight.' The Archbishop cast a glance at me, as much as to say, what can you make of such people? However, I thought after that it was time for us to come away.

How far the Archbishop's expression of his personal opinion helped is not easy to say—but it may have contributed its own share in hastening the truce which began on July 11, and in promoting the conversations between De Valera and Lloyd George. On July 8, the Archbishop issued the following statement:

> Lambeth, 8th July 1921.
>
> Urgent and acute anxiety about Ireland has many a time in the last few years clouded our days or marred our nights. But never was the anxiety so urgent, so acute, as it is this week. The outlook is not all dark. The streak of dawn is broadening. God give us clearness of vision, largeness of soul, and competence of resolve to seize the hour and to redeem it.
>
> Natural to shew that bitter memories, distant or near, bar the way to reconciliation. Natural, yes. But, I dare to ask, would Christ have it so?
>
> Let those who meet in conference behind closed doors know of a certainty that the English people outside, alert to the new-born possibilities, are eager to let nothing that is removable stand in the way of winning peace. Let the men on either side look with eyes of new and generous trust upon those with whom they are conferring. Such trust, courageous and reciprocal, may, and I believe will, win the day. But those with whom rest the responsibilities of proposal or of action must be able to feel that the people for whom they speak are behind them in generous, resolute, and brave-

hearted hope, and that Christian folk are everywhere upholding them in the best of all ways by quiet and persistent prayer.

I would enjoin all to whom my words may carry any weight to set themselves to such prayer with the assurance that it is not going to be in vain.

III

There were a good many anxieties to be met, and difficulties to be solved, on all sides during the next few months. But at last, on December 6, the Articles of Agreement between the Irish and the British delegations were signed at half-past two in the morning. The Archbishop had a long talk at the Athenaeum with the Provost of Trinity, Bishop J. H. Bernard, who had been summoned by the Prime Minister from Ireland to confer on the position of the Southern Unionists. The Archbishop issued the following message of thanksgiving for the nearer approach of peace:

Lambeth, December 7th, 1921.

Tens of thousands of Christian folk are to-day thanking God for the nearer approach of peace and goodwill among the people of Ireland.

For months past in Church and at home we have steadily invoked for our counsellors perseverance and wisdom and courage. To-day we can add thanksgiving to our prayers. Not to do so would be graceless indeed. Much has still to be examined and tested ere we reach firm ground, and we ask with deliberate thoughtfulness for the spirit of wise counsel and of strength. But to-day the note is one of thanksgiving, and it should ring out publicly and privately as opportunity may be given. For, though the end be not yet, it hath surely pleased God thus far 'to guide our feet into the way of peace'.

The Archbishop's relief was profound, but men's feelings were very tense and often bitter. 'I have read your message', wrote one, 'with the greatest sorrow and disappointment. How can you, Sir, reconcile it with your conscience as the Primate of the English Church, as a man and as a Christian, to ask for a blessing on the most abject and ignominious surrender to organized crime, the condonation of murder, which is involved, the acquiescence in the robbery of the loyal and faithful people of Southern Ireland who have stood by the Empire?' More bitter still was the following comment, quoted from the *Morning Post*, December 8, 1921:

PRIMATE'S THANKSGIVING

. . . to-day the note is one of thanksgiving (for Peace in Ireland).

RANDALL CANTUAR.

For the success of the Devil's work in Ireland, for the murder of hundreds of Loyalists, for the Betrayal of all the Loyalists remaining, for the sorrows of widows and orphans, for the suffering of the homeless and bereaved, for treachery to God, King and Country,

We thank Thee, O God.

There were many other letters of protest. But, amongst the letters of gratitude which gave him most satisfaction, was one from the prominent Roman Catholic priest who had introduced the messenger from De Valera the previous June:

MONSIGNOR W. F. BROWN *to the* ARCHBISHOP OF CANTERBURY

St. Anne's, Vauxhall, S.E. 11. 11 Dec. 1921.

Writing to-day to the Bishop of Killaloe, who will no doubt read my letter to the Irish Hierarchy at the Maynooth Meeting on Tuesday, I have recalled how you spoke out boldly against outrages in Ireland when few voices were raised in defence of the suffering people in the affected districts. Now the Irish question is fashionable, and many who reproached people like your Grace some months ago are only too anxious to be in the fashion and on the side of Royalty. I have never hesitated to point out the value of your timely intervention—at a time when prominent persons in our own Church here were silent about the excesses, and now that Peace has come I gladly congratulate your Grace on the part you played so manfully in the dark hours of irregular warfare.

On December 15 he spoke on the Irish settlement in the House of Lords. One of the peers present, whom the Archbishop had long known, and a loyal Churchman, wrote to express his grief at the Archbishop's attitude and his apparent condoning of the inconsistencies of politicians. He said (December 18):

The EARL OF *** *to the* ARCHBISHOP OF CANTERBURY

I wondered also, as I listened yesterday to the singing of the 94th Psalm and recalled your Grace's speech on behalf of the settlement, whether it now really is the policy of the Church of England to overlook wrong when right ensues—granted that the Agreement, won as it has been by murder and outrage, is right.

The Archbishop's reply gives, as well as any of his letters or statements at the time, the principles by which he had tried to act:

The ARCHBISHOP OF CANTERBURY *to the* EARL OF ***

Private. December 26th, 1921.

Illness, for I have been pretty bad, and am still absolutely laid up and prohibited from letter-writing, has delayed my replying to your letter, which reached me a few days ago.

I thank you for writing. It is always a satisfaction to me when friends who feel strongly about my doings or sayings and care to write, do so frankly and without reserve. This is not the first time you have thus acted, and I appreciate it.

At the same time I must say at once that I did not act lightly, and I do not think that I am wrong. In one's 74th year, after some forty years of intimate knowledge of the inside of public affairs, and of the principles governing them, one gains a certain sureness of foothold as to what one ought to do and say at crisis times when large issues have to be faced. This Irish negotiation question has been such an issue. I have never spared my criticism of the vacillation, ineptitude, and mismanagement which each Government has shown, and the last thing I have thought of doing was to say that inconsistencies do not matter. What seemed to me absurd was the tit for tat attitude of the two Front Benches, charging one another with changeableness. But a new condition arose when the King's speech in Belfast inaugurated a new idea—the idea of substituting conference for guns, and making a clear new start. Of course it is inconsistent, and the change was like many great changes made abruptly. I both appreciate and respect the position of those who, like yourself, as I gather, think it was all wrong, and that instead of Downing Street conferences we ought by this time to have machine guns and aeroplanes dealing death in Southern Ireland, as the consistent adherence to the principle of enforcing law and order. I appreciate that view, but I do not share it. Immeasurably difficult as the alternative policy is, it is at least a policy which, if it answers, will lead to peace. The other policy, witness the outcome of Cromwell's régime, might produce enforced quiet, but would be the seed plot of worse strife and hatred for ever. Hence my encouragement of the alternative plan with all its difficulties which grow greater as day follows day. It may completely fail, but at least we shall have tried.

That is my view, and I hold it without any doubt or qualms, nor do I think it inconsistent with my position, or with the truths I try to teach, that I should say so. That is all.

Again I thank you for writing, and I always welcome such inquiry or criticism.

He wrote a rather longer letter to Lord Salisbury, who had sent him an equally strong remonstrance. It was on similar lines and ended thus:

The ARCHBISHOP OF CANTERBURY *to the* MARQUESS OF SALISBURY

Private. 10 December, 1921.

... In short, I should like to adopt the first sentence of your letter to me:—'I suppose we have all prayed for peace in Ireland, and when peace is assured we ought to thank God for it. But that is a very different thing from approving the policy of the Government.' You mean, if I understand you, that the time may come when these efforts for peace have proved successful, and that then we should have thanksgivings. But meantime it was obviously necessary that I should say something to guide people who sought guidance.

I hope I have at least explained my position, however unsatisfactory that position may seem to you to be. At least I have not been thoughtless on the subject.

I have been reading with very keen interest the first volume of your father's life: 'England', he says, 'has committed many mistakes as a nation in the course of her history, but the mischief has been more than corrected by the heartiness with which, after each great struggle, victors and vanquished have forgotten their former battles and have combined together to lead the new policy to its best results.'

Of course those words apply to quite other sets of circumstances from those of to-day. It is not here a mere difference of policy, but I think the words have a permanent bearing, which your sister well brings out in the comment she makes as to your father's acceptance of things he had disliked and his subsequent desire to make the best of them.

I have run on longer than I intended, and this letter is dictated rather hurriedly at the close of a heavy day. But I do honestly thank you for writing, and I hope you will always do so when you feel impelled thereto.

CHAPTER LXVII
THE RUSSIAN CHURCH

They that deny a God destroy a man's nobility; for certainly man is kin to the beasts by his body; and, if he be not of kin to God by his spirit, he is a base and ignoble creature. It destroys likewise magnanimity, and the raising of human nature. FRANCIS BACON, *Essay on Atheism.*

THE months which followed the first interchange of messages, December 1917 to January 1918, between the Archbishop of Canterbury and the newly elected Patriarch of Moscow, as described in a previous chapter, were fateful for Russia and the Russian Church. The effect of the Bolshevik Revolution soon made itself felt. One of the first acts of the new Government was to disestablish and disendow the Church. All Church property was nationalized, and all connexion between Church and State brought to an end. In answer to these decrees, the Patriarch appealed to all Christians to oppose the Bolsheviks with might and main, and formally excommunicated the entire Bolshevik Party. The position of the Patriarch, although apparently exposed to every sort of danger during the succeeding months, was nevertheless extraordinarily strong. He denounced the execution of the deposed Tsar as 'a crime without a name'. In October 1918, on the first anniversary of the Revolution, he issued his famous denunciation, which began and ended with the text, 'They that take the sword shall perish by the sword.'

The persecution of the Russian Church developed on a great scale. And immediately piteous appeals for aid were addressed to the Archbishop of Canterbury. The first was from Odessa, and arrived at a time when any communication at all from that town was almost a miracle. It was dated December 30, 1918, and ran as follows:

PLATON, METROPOLITAN OF ODESSA, *to the* ARCHBISHOP OF CANTERBURY

I fervently beg your Eminence to protect the Orthodox Russian Church. The Revolutionary Government is subjecting it to cruelties by the side of which the persecutions of the Christians in the first three centuries pale. Many Archbishops, hundreds of priests, have been martyred and shot. The Churches are profaned and pillaged. On December 18, Antony, Metropolitan of Kiev, was arrested without reasons and taken we know not whither. All my efforts to liberate this innocent martyr led to nothing. I implore your Eminence and your body of Bishops to save the Metropolitan from the hands of his persecutors and the Church from the frightful agonies [*angoisses effroyables*] which she is enduring.

The Archbishop replied:

The ARCHBISHOP OF CANTERBURY *to* PLATON, METROPOLITAN OF ODESSA

8 January 1919.

The Church of England sends her deep sympathy to the Russian Orthodox Church in the trials and dangers through which she is passing. The terrible persecutions and martyrdoms detailed by your Eminence awake profound emotions in the hearts of the Christian people in this country. I am doing all I can, and meanwhile assure you of the prayers of our Bishops and people.

Other tragic appeals came from Omsk, Archangel, and Odessa again, all telling of trials and tribulations and imploring the Archbishop to come to their rescue. When he was urged to prevent the withdrawal of British troops, or to assist a famous British Field-Marshal (who appealed to him personally) to raise an army of 5,000 men paid out of private funds to replace those troops, he could only courteously explain the impossibility of such action. When he was asked to secure the release of three Russian Bishops[1] from their strict confinement in a Roman Catholic monastery in Cracow, he could only bring the facts to the notice of the authorities. When he was implored to come to the aid of the suffering by 'organizing for their benefit collections of money, underlinen, boots, and all kinds of wearing apparel', he called a meeting at Lambeth Palace[2] to launch the Imperial War Relief Fund with a view to a combined effort for the relief of distress in the famine-stricken areas, not least in Southern Russia.

[1] Antonius, Metropolitan of Kieff; Eulogius, Archbishop of Volhynia; Nikodimus, Suffragan Bishop. After inquiry the Archbishop informed the members of the Russian colony in Belgrade, who had approached him, that they were released (September 1919).

[2] March 12, 1920.

Then came the great Russian famine. Its main scene was the Volga basin, an area at least of a thousand miles from north to south of which the southern region was the finest wheat-producing country in the world, with some millions of inhabitants, of whom it was calculated that about fifteen or sixteen millions were literally starving to death. The main cause of the famine was the system of requisition adopted by the Soviet Government, which year by year took half the produce of the fields for public service or supposed public service, with the result that year by year the farmer or peasant grew half what he had grown the previous year, expecting to be left with that half. But every year half of that was again taken until the drought came and the crops went to nothing at all.

The famine proved the occasion of a fresh contact between the Patriarch of All Russia and the Archbishop of Canterbury, and provided an excuse for a fresh attack by the Bolsheviks on the Orthodox Church.

Two urgent appeals were issued from Moscow for help from Europe and America. One came from Maxim Gorki addressed to 'All Honest People'. The other was sent by the Patriarch Tikhon to the Archbishop of Canterbury. It was dated July 5, 1921, and reached the Archbishop some three weeks later through the Esthonian legation in London:

TIKHON, PATRIARCH OF MOSCOW, *to the* ARCHBISHOP OF CANTERBURY

Moscow, Russia, July 5, 1921.

Most Reverend and Dear Sir,—I call through you to the English people: our country is famishing. The bulk of her people is doomed to starve. The corn-crops are destroyed with drought in those districts which used to victual the whole country. The famine is causing dreadful epidemics. The help on the largest possible scale is urgently required—immediately.

All considerations of other character must be laid aside, as the people are perishing, and all its future is threatened with ruin, for the population leave their homes, farms, and fields, running eastward and crying for bread. Send us bread and medicaments without delay. The retardation would cause calamities unheard hitherto.

I am sending an identical appeal to the people of the United

States of America through the Right Reverend Bishop of New York.

Pray our Lord that His holy ire against us may be appeased.

The Archbishop at once telegraphed to express his profound distress at the famine reports, together with his sense of the immense difficulties attending any measure of adequate relief, and stating his anxiety to promote all such help as might be possible. A Russian Famine Relief Fund was started, and the Archbishop joined in promoting a national appeal. The Archbishop kept himself constantly informed as to the scale of the famine and of the work of relief. He knew the difficulties and did not disguise the fact, sometimes no doubt to the dissatisfaction of the more crusading spirits. He saw Dr. Nansen, who had been appointed High Commissioner by the League of Nations, and Sir Benjamin Robertson, who had been sent out to report by the Russian Famine Relief Fund, with the direct encouragement of the Foreign Office, and kept touch with Miss Ruth Fry of the Friends, and other British and American Famine Relief workers. On February 23, 1922, he spoke at length in the House of Lords, surveying the whole field in a masterly manner, but failing to extract any help from the Government.

In May 1922, a fresh crisis arose. The Patriarch, at the very outbreak of the famine, had expressed his wish to help to the utmost. In the autumn of 1921 he had founded a Church Relief Committee, and collected money for the sufferers; but by order of the Soviets the Committee had been disbanded and the funds handed over to the Government. He had then been asked by the Soviets to order the Churches to give their treasures to the Famine Fund. In reply he agreed in principle to the handing over of unconsecrated objects, i.e. ornamental jewels and such things as were not used for the holy rites. But he pointed out that to hand over consecrated objects to lay persons would be sacrilege. Nor indeed was there any guarantee how the treasures would be used. At the same time he proposed another method by which he would raise the same amount of money as the sale of the Church treasures would bring in, if those treasures were left unharmed. The request was refused. The surrender of the unconsecrated objects, though conceded by the Patriarch, was soon pronounced to be insufficient, and on February 23, 1922, the Soviets issued a decree to the effect that within one month all valuable objects made of gold or silver or containing precious stones should be removed from ecclesiastical establishments and churches of all religions and presented to a special Famine Fund. It was stipulated that the decree should not apply in the case of objects the removal of which would essentially affect the interests of the cult. The Patriarch published an Epistle to the Faithful declaring that such action with regard to consecrated objects was sacrilege. But the decree was swiftly enforced, and a violent campaign was started in the press accusing the hierarchy of the Church of counter-revolution and treachery towards the starving population of Russia.

The wholesale confiscations were bitterly resented. In many cases there was strong resistance and sometimes bloodshed. The Patriarch was summoned before the Cheka and told to pacify the people, but he replied that he could not consent to the surrender of the treasures against the canons of the Church. He was again summoned and urged to leave the country, ostensibly in order to raise money for famine relief. He refused, saying that he would stay with his people and share their sufferings.[1]

News of these events first reached the Archbishop of Canterbury from a private source. It was natural to ask 'Is there not something which Christians outside can do to help?', and his first response to the melancholy tale was to write a letter to inform and warn the Prime Minister, at that time in daily touch with the Russian delegation at Genoa (May 3, 1922):

The ARCHBISHOP OF CANTERBURY *to the* RT. HON. D. LLOYD GEORGE

I am led to understand that the Russian delegates attending at Genoa are likely to represent, or are actually representing, the Church in Russia as being hostile to the endeavour to raise funds by self-sacrificing effort on behalf of the sufferers from famine. It is said that allegations are made to the effect that the Church in Russia is refusing to co-operate, and will neither raise money itself nor allow any part of the Church properties to be sold for meeting these urgent distresses. I am in a position to assure you that these allegations, if they are made, misrepresent the facts very gravely.

[1] It is said on good authority that the entire yield from the sale of the Church treasures was only about £500,000—a very small sum in comparison with the value of the Crown jewels held by the Government for other uses. Many of the treasures simply found their way to museums.

He then set out the facts, as described above, and continued:

> It is, I think, of very great importance that those who are dealing with this subject at Genoa or elsewhere, should themselves be aware that these statements as to the Church's unhelpfulness are altogether untrue. It is said that they are simply circulated with a view to damaging the Church in the eyes of the world.

In May, the Patriarch was arrested by the Soviet Government. The following appeal was addressed to the Archbishop by the Metropolitan Eulogius (whose release from prison the Archbishop had helped to secure) now resident at Berlin:

The METROPOLITAN EULOGIUS *to the* ARCHBISHOP OF CANTERBURY

Alexanderheim, Borsegnalde, Berlin.
May 11th, 1922.

To-day's paper brought us the sad news of All Russia's Patriarch Tikhon's arrest by the Moscow Soviet authorities, who will not fail undoubtedly to inflict on him the severest penalty. The only accusation brought against him is his obedience to a sense of duty in refusing to submit to the theft of Church property, of sacred vessels, and relics and all needed for holy services.

In the name of Our Lord Jesus Christ we appeal to you and to all the Episcopalian members of the Church of England to lift your voice in protest of this act of unheard of violence and illegality, directed against the highest representative of the Russian clergy. We implore you to use your influence to alleviate as much as possible Patriarch Tikhon's undeserved chastisement.

On May 25, 1922, the Archbishop raised the question in the House of Lords; he described what the Patriarch had done and wished to do for the relief of the famine-stricken, and spoke of his arrest, in such circumstances, as a very grave outrage in Christendom. At the same time he decided to address a protest direct to the Soviet Government in Moscow. The Vatican had just concluded an agreement at Genoa about its own mission in Russia. Would the Pope join in the protest? The Archbishop telegraphed to the British Minister at the Vatican on May 26, and the reply came at once that the Holy See had already made representations and was prepared to repeat them. The Archbishop also communicated with the Archbishop of York, the two Scottish

Moderators, and the Heads of the Free Churches. On May 31, he sent the following telegram to Lenin:

The ARCHBISHOP OF CANTERBURY (*and others*) *to* PRESIDENT LENIN

President of the Council of the People's Commissars,
Kremlin, Moscow.

Lambeth Palace,
31st May, 1922.

In the name of the Christian Communions which we represent we desire to protest most earnestly against the attack on the Russian Church in the person of its Patriarch Tikhon. The public mind and conscience of Christendom, and indeed of the whole civilized world, cannot tolerate silently so great a wrong.

RANDALL CANTUAR: (Archbishop of Canterbury).
COSMO EBOR: (Archbishop of York).
JOHN SMITH (Moderator of the General Assembly of the Church of Scotland).
DONALD FRASER (Moderator of the General Assembly of the United Free Church of Scotland).
JOHN CHOWN (President of the Baptist Union of Great Britain and Ireland).
THOMAS YATES (Chairman of the Congregational Union of England and Wales).
HERBERT R. MUMFORD (President of the British Provincial Board of the Moravian Church).
IVOR J. ROBERTSON (Moderator of the General Assembly of the Presbyterian Church of England).
SAMUEL HORTON (President of the Primitive Methodist Conference).
W. TREFFRY (President of the United Methodist Conference).
J. ALFRED SHARP (President of the Wesleyan Methodist Conference).

The protest made a profound impression. In Russia itself, so the Archbishop heard, its joint character surprised the Bolshevik chiefs. 'It appears', said his informant, 'that the Bolsheviks regard the Anglican Church as hopelessly counter-revolutionary, but they expected more sympathy from the Nonconformist bodies . . . and were quite unprepared for the joint note.' The

Bolsheviks, at any rate, decided to reply, and the following answer was sent:

The RUSSIAN SOVIET GOVERNMENT *to the* ARCHBISHOP OF CANTERBURY

128, New Bond-street, W. 1, June 6, 1922.

Mr. Krassin, the Official Agent of the Russian Soviet Government in Great Britain, presents his compliments to his Grace the Archbishop of Canterbury, and, in accordance with instructions received from his Government, begs to enclose a copy of the reply (in Russian and English text) to the protest addressed by his Grace to the Soviet Government on June 1:

'The protest addressed to the Soviet Government by a number of Churchmen of Great Britain in connection with the proceedings instituted against Patriarch Tikhon calls for the following elucidation:

'1. In spite of the statement contained in the protest there has been no attack on the Church. Only proceedings have been instituted against individual representatives of the Church, including its former Patriarch, in connection with the resistance organised by them against measures of the Soviet authorities, which measures were taken in order to save the lives of tens of millions of human beings, including children.

'2. In the conflict between Patriarch Tikhon and the Soviet Powers, the vast majority of the clergy sides with the Soviet Power and the labouring masses it represents. Only an insignificant number of the clergy—those who were the most privileged and demoralised through their connection with the Tsarist nobility and with capital—form the group of the Patriarch Tikhon. Public opinion in Russia takes note that the protesting English Churchmen express their solidarity not with the starving labouring masses of Russia, nor even with the majority of the clergy, but with an insignificant number of Churchmen who have always been working hand in hand with the Tsars, with the bureaucracy, and with the nobility, and who have now entered into an open opposition to the power of the workers and peasants.

'3. Public opinion in Russia also notes that at the most inhuman period of the blockade, in which blockade the British Government took part, the authors of the protest did not raise their voices against the strangling of Russian workers, peasants, and children. The people of Russia have not heard that the signatories of the appeal protested against the attempts to strangle with the noose of usury the labouring masses of Russia.

'4. The Soviet Power, as well as the labouring masses, consider the above protest of the hierarchy of the various churches of Great Britain to be dictated by a narrow caste solidarity because it is entirely directed against the real interests of the people, and against the elementary demands of humanity.

'774, June 3, 1922, Moscow, Kremlin, Administration manager of the Council of People's Commissaries. 'SMOLANINOFF.'

The Archbishop sent an immediate rejoinder, with the suggestion that a small delegation from the Churches should proceed to Moscow to investigate:

The REV. G. K. A. BELL *to* MR. KRASSIN

Lambeth Palace, S.E., June 7, 1922.

In reply to your communication of June 6 on behalf of the Russian Soviet Government, the Archbishop of Canterbury cannot withdraw any of the statements already made by him in the House of Lords on May 25, statements which were based on first-hand information from Russia. The first-hand information in the Archbishop's possession particularly emphasises the fact that the Patriarch of the Russian Church has repeatedly offered the help of the Church for the relief of the famine, and that his offers have been consistently refused by the Soviet Government. But, in view of the explicit démenti issued by the Soviet Government, the Archbishop feels it incumbent upon him to request that permission be given to a small body of representatives of the various Churches in this country to go to Russia to examine the situation on the spot in order to avoid future misunderstandings.

This message, the Archbishop heard some months afterwards, made a sensation in Russia. It was printed in the Bolshevik press. The Bolsheviks were very angry at the excitement caused, while members of the Church were greatly encouraged. There were all sorts of rumours to the effect that the Archbishop of Canterbury had arrived in Russia, that he had been seen by many people, and again that he had arrived, but in disguise. After a month's delay the following communication from the Assistant Commissar for Foreign Affairs, M. Karakhan, was forwarded to Lambeth, on July 8, 1922:

MR. KLISHKO, ASSISTANT OFFICIAL AGENT, *to the* REV. G. K. A. BELL

128 New Bond Street, London, W. 1, July 8, 1922.

I beg to enclose herewith copy of the communication from the Assistant Commissar for Foreign Affairs, M. Karakhan, in reply to your letter of June 7 on behalf of the Archbishop of Canterbury.

'July 1, 1922.

'In reply to your communication of June 7 on behalf of the Archbishop of Canterbury, I beg to inform you that my Government does not see any grounds for insisting upon the withdrawal of the statements made by the Archbishop of Canterbury in the House of Lords on May 25, since these statements clearly emanate from sources which, in the eyes of the labouring masses of Russia and the whole world, do not merit any confidence. They merely serve to illustrate the class solidarity of the "princes" of the various Churches, which solidarity is known to be directed against the labouring masses. The suggestion made by the Archbishop of Canterbury to send to Russia a body of "representatives of the various churches" in order to investigate the situation on the spot constitutes a claim even less justifiable than would be a suggestion made by the Soviet Government to send to England a small commission to investigate to what extent the labouring masses are exploited materially and spiritually by the hierarchy of the various English Churches in order to maintain the domination of the exploiting classes.'

The following memorandum from the Archbishop ended the correspondence:

The REV. G. K. A. BELL *to* MR. KLISHKO

Lambeth Palace, S.E. 1. July 10, 1922.

I beg leave to acknowledge the receipt of your letter of July 8. I have submitted its enclosure to the Archbishop of Canterbury, and I am directed to send you the enclosed memorandum in reply.

'The Archbishop of Canterbury has considered carefully the communication transmitted to him in reply to his request made on June 7 that a small body of representatives of the various Churches responsible for the remonstrance of May 31 might be permitted by the Soviet Government to visit Russia. The purpose of such delegation would be to ascertain the particulars of the reported action by the Soviet Government which gave rise to the remonstrance. The reply now received refusing this request, does not, as the Archbishop notes, challenge the statement made as to the arrest and prosecution of leading clergy of the Russian Church, nor does it elucidate the obvious contradiction between the detailed account of these arrests and prosecutions given at first hand to the Archbishop of Canterbury, and the account given on behalf of the Soviet Government.

'The allegation that the representatives of the Church of England and of the other Christian denominations who signed the protest were actuated by political or class considerations is devoid of foundation. They were actuated simply by elementary considerations of humanity and of Christian feeling.

'The Archbishop deplores the refusal of the Soviet Government to allow this information to be obtained. Very many people in Great Britain are anxious to promote the friendliest relation between the Russian people at large and the peoples of the English-speaking countries, and the letters which the Archbishop received from America show a similar desire. The present action of the Soviet Government is calculated to retard or prevent the realisation of such a hope. If the announcement published during the last few days respecting the death sentence passed upon religious leaders in Russia proves to be well founded, the effect will be one of indignation and horror among civilised people of all classes.

'Lambeth Palace, July 10, 1922.'

The Patriarch remained a prisoner, and was now at the Donskoi Monastery; while a group of clergy under a certain Metropolitan Antonine, and known as 'the Living Church', with the help of the Soviet Government usurped the administration, and made their head-quarters at the Patriarchal Palace.

Meantime other prominent clergy were put on trial, and among them Benjamin, Metropolitan of Petrograd, and the Bishop of Kronstadt. Benjamin was the successor of Pitirim and of a very different kind from that friend of Rasputin. The charges brought against him were that he had resisted the confiscation of Church treasures and was guilty of counter-revolutionary conspiracy, apparently with the Metropolitan Eulogius and the Metropolitan Antony of Kieff, who had in a moment of extraordinary rashness, at the so-called All-Russian Assembly at Karlowitz, in December 1921, proclaimed the re-establishment of the monarchy and the restoration of the Romanoff dynasty in Russia, an act which the Patriarch, on hearing the news, immediately peremptorily denounced. Benjamin denied the charges. He said: 'I was elected by the people. The people depose me. I bless the people. I thank God for everything. But I do not consider myself guilty. My policy has always been one of mutual forgiveness and love. I will take your sentence quietly. I am not afraid of death.' The death sentence was passed. The Archbishop's help was eagerly sought, and appeals came from many quarters outside Russia. But the Archbishop could only make representations to the Foreign Office, which was in entire agreement with himself as to the horror of such executions. He wrote also to the Labour leader, Mr. George Lansbury, himself a Churchman and personally known to the Archbishop, and found that he and his friends were likewise doing everything in their power to prevent the death penalty from being imposed. But all was in vain. Nevertheless the trial of the Patriarch was still delayed.

The next blow to be struck at the Church, upon which the Archbishop was approached, fell in March 1923. His help was now implored for the Roman Catholic Archbishop of Petrograd, Monsignor Cieplak, and certain Roman Catholic priests, also accused of counter-revolutionary activity and opposition to the confiscation of Church ornaments. On the same day, March 14, 1923, the First Secretary of the Polish Legation called at Lambeth to ask for the Archbishop of Canterbury's help; and the following telegram came from Cardinal Mercier, Archbishop of Malines:

CARDINAL MERCIER *to the* ARCHBISHOP OF CANTERBURY

Malines, 14 March, 1923.

Have received by telegram Monsignor Cieplak Catholic Metropolitan of Petrograd and thirteen priests arrested and threatened with immediate death. Am appealing to Curzon. Can you support?

It was thought that the condemnation of Monsignor Cieplak was intended to lead up to a great anti-Christian demonstration at Easter, and so to the trial of the Patriarch. The Archbishop of Canterbury immediately made his sympathy known, and on March 20, 1923, in the House of Lords, asked for information from the Government both as to the arrest of Archbishop Cieplak and as to the present position of the Patriarch Tikhon. By the Pope's desire, in making his speech, he informed the House that His Holiness had himself just made an urgent appeal on behalf of the Patriarch, when appealing for the Roman Catholic Archbishop and priests. Lord Curzon said, in reply:

No one, as I know very well from long experience of the interventions of the Most Reverend Primate, takes greater trouble than he does to acquaint himself with every possible source of information

> before he addresses your Lordships, and sometimes in answering him I find that he has greater information than the Government have at their disposal. I am not certain that this is not the case in the present instance.

But nothing could be done. The trial proceeded, and Archbishop Cieplak and Constantine Boutkevitch were condemned to death on March 26. The sentence on the Archbishop was commuted to one of ten years' solitary confinement. The death sentence on Monsignor Boutkevitch was confirmed.

The war against religion was now at its height. It was not only the lives of religious leaders that were at stake, though they were ready to be martyrs. It was not only Christianity which was the object of the attack, but religion of any kind. Clause 121 of the new Criminal Code ran as follows:

> The teaching of religious beliefs in State or private educational establishments and schools to children of tender age and minors, is punishable by forced labour for a period not exceeding one year.

In the trial of the Roman Catholic clergy, March 1923, this clause was interpreted as forbidding religious instruction at all to children in groups; nor did the Jews speak too strongly when, in a protest of September 11, 1922, the Joint Foreign Committee of the Board of Deputies of the British Jews and the Anglo-Jewish Association thus described these laws so far as their religion was concerned:

> They imperil the very existence of the Jewish Church, and they condemn the rising generation of Jews not merely to religious indifferentism but, as they are convinced, to moral depravity.

It was significant that the Chief Rabbi should let the Archbishop of Canterbury know, on April 4, 1923, that he would be 'ready to co-operate' in any measure which the heads of the Christian Churches might deem it necessary to take for the vindication of religion and religious principles in face of the persecuting atheism of the Government of Soviet Russia.

The Archbishop of Canterbury decided that the hour had come for the most weighty protest that religious leaders in England could then devise. On April 13, 1923, the following declaration appeared:

> To all men and women of goodwill,
>
> The last few weeks have witnessed a portent which has filled all generous-hearted men and women with horror. The ruthless

warfare which the Soviet Government of Russia has long carried on against all forms of religious belief has come to a head. During the period of the Soviet rule, hundreds of thousands of religious people, and Ministers of Religion of all ranks and creeds, have been subjected to a savage persecution, the express object of which has been to root religion out of the land. The central facts for which religion stands have been systematically outraged and insulted. The most sacred of religious festivals have been made the occasion for blasphemous travesty, and at this moment the attack upon religion itself finds fresh illustration in the trial for their lives of the chief leaders of religion in Russia.

The Bolsheviks themselves have not disguised the purpose which they have in view. In their own journal only three weeks ago they confessed both their aim and their difficulty. To quote their words: 'We must carry on our agitation against religion just as systematically as we do in political questions, but with even more determination. . . . Although we have declared war on the denizens of Heaven, it is by no means easy to sweep them from the households of the workmen.' (See *The Times*, March 29.)

It is for the sake of those workmen and of the whole people of Russia, and for the preservation in their hearts of faith in God, and the maintenance of religious liberty that we appeal. We represent many religious communions and many political opinions, but we are united in the indignation and horror with which we regard the present policy of systematic persecution of religion in all its forms. Such a policy cannot be tolerated in silence by those who value religion or liberty. Our protest will, we are confident, evoke a response everywhere on the part of those who have at heart the well-being of the world.

RANDALL CANTUAR:

COSMO EBOR:

FRANCIS, CARDINAL BOURNE.

JOHN SMITH, Moderator of the General Assembly of the Church of Scotland.

J. D. JONES (Congregationalist), Moderator of the Federal Council of the Evangelical Free Churches of England.

J. H. SHAKESPEARE (Baptist), ex-Moderator of the Federal Council of the Evangelical Free Churches of England.

W. LEWIS ROBERTSON (Presbyterian),

W. H. ARMSTRONG (Wesleyan),
Secretaries of the Federal Council of the Evangelical Free Churches of England.

F. C. SPURR (Baptist), President of the National Free Church Council.

THOS. NIGHTINGALE (United Methodist), Secretary of the National Free Church Council.

J. SCOTT LIDGETT (Wesleyan), Hon. Secretary of the National Free Church Council.

JOHN CLIFFORD, ex-President of the Baptist World Alliance.

A. E. GARVIE, ex-Chairman of the Congregational Union.

R. F. HORTON, Minister of Lyndhurst-road, Hampstead, Congregational Church.

J. H. JOWETT, formerly Minister, Westminster Chapel.

W. BRAMWELL BOOTH, General of the Salvation Army.

J. H. HERTZ, Chief Rabbi.

The effect was electric. There were, of course, attacks on the protest on political grounds, with the suggestion that it was another move in the anti-Russian campaign intended to pave the way for the denunciation of the trade agreement between Britain and Russia. Some play was also made with the fact that *The Times*'s quotation given in the protest, by a sub-editorial slip, attributed to a single issue of *Pravda* the two sentences divided by the separating dots, which actually appeared in separate numbers of *Pravda* for March 18 and March 16, as the Archbishop's Chaplain pointed out in a published reply to Mr. H. N. Brailsford in the *Daily Herald*. There were also critics in England who disliked any protest on the grounds that, as one of them wrote in *The Nation and the Athenaeum*, April 21, 1923:

> Through all the long dark years of bloody tyranny which preceded the Revolution, the Church in Russia lent its countenance to the unspeakable horrors of wholesale deportation and private execution of persons suspected of holding enlightened political opinions. . . . Thanks largely to the Church, 90 per cent. of the population in Russia can neither read nor write; and the priesthood are reaping to-day the fruits of their lack of foresight in having neglected to educate those who were one day to become their masters.

The following personal letter from Mr. Asquith takes the same view:

The RIGHT HON. H. H. ASQUITH *to the* ARCHBISHOP OF CANTERBURY

Personal. 22nd April, 1923.

One of the reasons why I have felt estopped (as the lawyers say) from taking part in the protests against the flagrant iniquities of the Bolshevist government in these matters, is that I see no answer to the question 'Where was the conscience of the Churches in

England, when for the lifetime of two generations the Church in Russia was a mere annexe to the bureaucracy, and not only connived at, but inspired and inflamed campaigns, and indeed orgies, of persecution, proscription and assassination, against both the Roman Catholics and the Jews?' Few Churches have in this regard a blacker record than the Orthodox Church in Russia, or less reason for sympathy when, in the revolution of time, they find they have to reap what they have sown.

Such criticisms of the pre-revolutionary Orthodox Church cannot be simply brushed aside; but they lose much of their value when it is remembered, as it must be remembered, that the Jews and the Old Believers and the Baptists and the Roman Catholics were all involved in the systematic anti-religious policy of the Soviet Government. Nor must Archbishop Davidson's personal intervention, both public and private, in earlier days, be forgotten.[1]

The Government at Moscow still maintained its negative attitude. In one of the series of notes between the Soviet Government and the British Government, upon the relations between them, the Soviet Government felt constrained to declare (May 13, 1923):

> Although the question of status of Churches in Soviet Republics does not come in slightest degree into region of mutual relations of these Republics with Great Britain, none the less, in the interests of correctly informing public opinion, Russian Government considers it necessary in most categorical manner to deny baseless charge that it is persecuting any religion of any sort. Soviet justice falls only on such of clergy as utilise their position as servitors in one of the Churches for political activity directed against internal or external safety of Soviet republics.[2]

And the Supreme Church Council under Bishop Antonine and other clergy of the 'Living Church', who had broken with the Patriarch and claimed to be the Russian Orthodox Church, in a telegram to the Archbishop on May 14, made the following statement:

> *The* SUPREME CHURCH COUNCIL UNDER THE METROPOLITAN ANTONINE *to the* ARCHBISHOP OF CANTERBURY
>
> Moscow, May 14, 1923.
>
> Your Eminence, the Supreme Church Council of the Russian Orthodox Church acquainting itself with the memorandum of the

[1] See pp. 484–6, 746. [2] Russia, No. 3 (1923). Cmd. 1874. H.M. Stationery Office.

Government of Great Britain handed on the 8th of May of this year to the Soviet Russian Government in that part of it which concerns the position of religion in Russia, and perceiving in it a threat directed against the children of our Fatherland, considers that it is its Christian duty, in the Name of the love and teachings of Our Master and Lord Jesus Christ, to give enlightenment as to the actual state of the things.

The memorandum of your Government is in essence a hidden patronage of the manifested enemies of our country, an attempt against the peaceful life of our people.

In concluding its labours the Sacred Assembly[1] of the Russian Orthodox Church of the year 1923 recognized the contemporary position of the Church in the Soviet Republic as fully satisfactory, differing advantageously from its servile position in the period of the autocracy of the Tsars, wherefore the references of your Government are entirely without foundation. The Supreme Church Council with a feeling of profound spiritual satisfaction considers it necessary to bring it to the knowledge of Your Eminence that religious life at the present time enjoys such freedom as it has never had under any of the former Governments of our Fatherland.

It should already be known to Your Eminence that the Sacred Assembly expressed its decisive condemnation of the ex-Patriarch Tikhon and together with him of the counter-revolution beyond the borders.

With regard to the condemnation by the secular authorities of ecclesiastics for contraventions of the existing laws of the Soviet Republic the moral responsibility for their fate and unhappy situation is wholly their own and that of the secret instigators of their criminal deeds.

We are convinced that if the aforesaid persons had committed their criminal deeds on English territory in England also heavy punishment would have been inflicted upon them.

The Russian Orthodox Church true to the everlasting Counsels of the evangel ceaselessly prays and enjoins upon its children peaceful and brotherly unity with all peoples. But in the case of an attempt on the honour and dignity of their country it has given and will give its blessing to those who stand in its defence and sacrifice themselves for the salvation and freedom of their state.

The telegram was signed by Antonine, as Metropolitan of Moscow and President of the Supreme Church Council; the Vice-President, Vladimir Krasnitzky; Peter, as Metropolitan of all Siberia; Alexander Vvedensky, as Archbishop of Krutitzi;

[1] The Sacred Assembly had deposed and unfrocked the Patriarch.

Evdokim, as Metropolitan of Odessa; and six others, four arch-priests, one archdeacon, and a layman, A. Novikoff, administrator of the Supreme Church Council.

The Archbishop made no answer to this telegram.

Then suddenly, on June 27, the Patriarch Tikhon was released, after signing the following recantation:

DECLARATION OF PATRIARCH TIKHON

In appealing with the present declaration to the Supreme Court of the R.S.F.S.R., I hold it to be my duty to my conscience as a Priest to state the following:—

Having been brought up in monarchist society and having been up to the time of my arrest under the influence of anti-Soviet persons, I was indeed hostilely disposed towards the Soviet power and my hostility at times passed from a passive state to one of acts, such as my proclamation regarding the Bolsheviks in 1918, the anathema I pronounced against the Soviet power in the same year, and, finally, my appeal against the decree regarding the confiscation of church treasures in 1922. All of my anti-Soviet acts, with a few inaccuracies, are laid out in the indictment of the Supreme Court. Recognising the justice of the decision of the court to take proceedings against me for anti-Soviet activity under the clause of the Criminal Code mentioned in the indictment, I repent of these actions against the State, and request the Supreme Court to remove the measures of repression taken against me, that is, to set me at liberty.

And I hereby declare to the Tribunal that I, from now on, am no enemy to the Soviet power. I finally and decisively dissociate myself both from foreign and from internal monarchist-white guard counter-revolution.

PATRIARCH TIKHON.

June 16th, 1923.

The surprise with which this event was received was profound. On leaving prison, the Patriarch, who had never resigned, resumed full authority. The great majority of the Orthodox rallied round him. The leaders of the 'Living Church' collapsed, and the acts of the recent Sacred Assembly which had purported to depose him were annulled as illegal. The document of recantation, it is true, caused mixed feelings. To some it seemed an act of madness or shame. But others claimed that it was the only way of saving the Church, just as the Patriarch Hermogen[1] had made his peace with the Poles to save the Church in the seven-

[1] Patriarch of Moscow, 1606–12.

teenth century. On the latter view the declaration was a bridge to enable the Soviet Government to abandon its policy of hostility, and also a means of uniting the members of the Orthodox Church once more. The Patriarch himself said later that he was not now struggling against the Soviets but against the 'Living Church':

> I have never sought to overthrow the Government. I am not a counter-revolutionary, for all that some of my appeals have an anti-Soviet character. The power of the Soviet Government has greatly increased in Russia; and it has undergone various developments. We, the members of the old Clergy, are not now struggling against the Soviets but against the 'Living Church' . . . I am persuaded that having studied my case the Government has convinced itself that I am no counter-revolutionary. It was suggested that I should make a public declaration of the fact and I wrote a letter to say so.[1]

The document itself was no doubt in part the cause as well as the occasion of the Patriarch's release. But the release was also due to the great volume of foreign protest which the recent executions had created, and to the belief that if the trial of the Patriarch were to proceed and the supreme penalty to be imposed, the Soviet régime would be still further discredited abroad. It was also due, and perhaps in no small degree, to the strength of the British protests and the powerful and sustained advocacy of Archbishop Davidson.

The Archbishop kept himself abreast of the later developments and followed the news from Russia with deep interest, not unmixed with anxiety, as letters intimating other dangers reached him from different quarters, sometimes from Russia, sometimes from Russian Bishops in different parts of Europe.

Twice again he was brought into personal touch with the Patriarch. On one occasion he received an Ikon from the Patriarch through Bishop Bury, Bishop of Northern and Central Europe, when visiting Moscow—an Ikon which he acknowledged in the following letter:

The ARCHBISHOP OF CANTERBURY *to* HIS HOLINESS TIKHON, PATRIARCH OF ALL RUSSIA

12th December, 1923.

I have received through Bishop Bury the gift which Your Holiness has been good enough to send to me. I value it very

[1] Interview published in *Manchester Guardian*, September 28, 1923.

highly. Such a gift coming from yourself is of deep historic interest and will continue as a reminder to us all of the pathetic story of what you have suffered in health during these anxious and difficult years.

I do not enter upon the public affairs of your Church or of our own because you and I have throughout abstained from corresponding on these very difficult matters. We know, however, that your perils and trials have been great, and it would be a joy to us to think that we have been enabled by the representations which we made to alleviate in any way the long strain and the frequent suffering.

We unite our prayers with those of Your Holiness that God in His mercy may vouchsafe to our two Churches the light of His Presence to guide our feet into the way of peace.

We shall continue to watch eagerly for tidings of your welfare and to pray to Our Heavenly Father on your behalf.

The last occasion was at the Patriarch's death, on April 8, 1925, after some months of illness. The only tribute sent by a religious body outside Russia for the funeral was a wreath placed by the coffin of the Patriarch, bearing the name, and witnessing to the sympathy, of the Archbishop of Canterbury.

CHAPTER LXVIII

THE ARCHBISHOP AND CONSTANTINOPLE

'And who,' quoth the Patriarch of Constantinople, the supreme head and primate of the Greek Church of Asia, 'who is the Archbishop of Canterbury?'
'What?' said I, a little astonished at the question.
'Who,' said he, 'is this Archbishop?'
'Why, the Archbishop of Canterbury.'
'Archbishop of *what*?' said the Patriarch.
'*Canterbury*,' said I.
'Oh,' said the Patriarch. 'Ah yes! and who is he?'

R. CURZON, *Monasteries in the Near East*, ch. xxii.

THE dialogue placed at the head of this chapter significantly shows the greatness of the distance travelled in 100 years in the mutual relations of the Primate of All England and the Oecumenical Patriarch of the Eastern Orthodox Church. In 1837, on the eve of Queen Victoria's coronation, when a scion of the House of Curzon presented a letter of introduction from Archbishop Howley to the Patriarch Gregory, that worthy prelate betrayed a complete ignorance of the very existence of such a person as the Archbishop of Canterbury. And even though, as the Honourable Robert Curzon who relates this experience confesses, the Patriarch of that day may have been a man of straw—still it was a little daunting to discover that 'the Patriarch of the Greek Church, the successor of Gregory Nazienzen, John Chrysostom, and the heresiarch Nestorius', seemed to be quite unaware that there was such a thing as a Church of England.

It is curious to reflect how, especially in the years which immediately followed the War, and at a moment when the foreign policy of the British Empire was largely under the care of another member of the same family of Curzon, not only was the office of the Archbishop of Canterbury universally honoured, but successive occupants of the Patriarchal See of Constantinople, as well as Armenian Patriarchs, Assyrian Patriarchs, Syrian Archbishops, and many Eastern prelates besides from Serbia, Rumania, and elsewhere, came expressly to Lambeth Palace to invoke his help.

There were many reasons why this should be the case. Not

least, of course, is the fact that the British nation had a paramount political influence in the counsels of the Allies, and that the Archbishop of Canterbury was conceived to possess a very great official influence of his own, as Primate of the National Church. But there were other reasons besides. For without a doubt all through the past half-century mutual knowledge and interest had grown between the two Churches. Long before Queen Victoria's accession there had been occasional contacts, and since that date the communications had been steadily increasing. But it was the War itself, or rather the long-drawn process of negotiating peace between the Allies and the Turks in the five years which followed the War, which made the whole difference to the strengthening of the links between the Eastern and the Anglican Churches, coupled with the general trust in the character and wisdom of Randall, by Divine Providence, Archbishop of Canterbury, during this critical time.

We have already recounted the first visit to Lambeth of Meletios, the Metropolitan of Athens, in November 1918,[1] and the disappointment which attended the move for the restoration to the Orthodox Communion of the Church of St. Sophia in Constantinople. The years which followed were to witness failures of a still more serious kind, all of them reflected in the mass of the Archbishop's correspondence. Indeed, throughout this whole period the misfortunes of the Near East occupied a quite extraordinary place in his letters and in his interest, and form the subject of many representations to successive Ministers and their departments in Whitehall. The lamentable delay in the completion of the Turkish Peace Settlement was responsible for much of the trouble. But it was only itself the result of more lamentable causes—the absorption of the Powers, great and small, with their nationalist policies, the disagreement of the Allies, and the failure of the United States of America to take its share in the protection of the Christian populations.

With the purely military or the purely political aspects of the general problem the Archbishop had no concern. But the issues of religion were often mixed with other large questions, and though, as we shall see, his help was often claimed for the constitutional questions which affected the future of the Orthodox Church, it was chiefly sought and most eagerly given when

[1] See p. 941.

their very survival, the very existence of Christian people, was at stake.

Amongst the communications received in the early stages was a letter from Dorotheos, the locum tenens of the Oecumenical Patriarchate, who came to Paris in connexion with the Peace Conference. His letter sufficiently declared the general sense of all those others who made their appeal to Lambeth, reminding him (May 28, 1919) of the massacres and crimes which the Turks had committed, declaring, 'There can be only one safeguard for us; it is the dislodgement of the Sultan from Constantinople' and begging 'our sister church in England' to join her efforts to theirs. The Archbishop replied in friendly terms, encouraging Dorotheos to press the gravity of the issue upon the members of the Peace Conference. But the attention of the Delegates at Paris was unhappily difficult to secure—so engrossed were they with the more urgent issues of the Treaty of Versailles. And meantime, delay helped the Turks, and deepened the anxiety of those who had suffered under their yoke as subject races—especially the Armenians and the Assyrians, whose cause the Archbishop in turn pressed most earnestly upon Lord Curzon in the following August, with special reference to the withdrawal of British troops from the Caucasus. Lord Curzon replied that the British were doing their best, but that the fault really lay with America, who could not make up her mind whether she wanted to look after Armenia or not. On December 17, 1919, the Archbishop raised the whole question of the sufferings of the Christian populations, in the House of Lords, and called attention to the promises of His Majesty's Government that they should be set free from the dominion of the Turk. In his speech he gave a clear and damning account of the atrocities perpetrated during the War on the helpless races, as recorded in Lord Bryce's official Report. But while Lord Curzon admitted the responsibility of the Allies, and spoke of his disappointment with regard to American aid in the permanent building up of a great Armenian State, no definite and clear-cut policy emerged.

The Archbishop also, like Lord Curzon, was deeply distressed by the failure of America. He had many American friends, and he was not a little provoked by what he considered the lack of perception of the need of practical action on America's part, which their utterances showed.

The following exchange of telegrams makes this clear:

The BISHOP OF NEW YORK[1] *to the* ARCHBISHOP OF CANTERBURY

New York. Feb. 26, 1920.

One hundred Bishops of the American Church join me in the following message:

We are grateful for your leadership in crusade against proposed retention of Turks in Constantinople and spoliation of Armenia. Any compromise with Turks will be condonation of crime and will outrage conscience of Christendom. We believe Armenia landlocked and robbed of her fairest portions cannot achieve real independence or self-support. We respectfully but energetically protest against proposed measures and appeal to people of Great Britain to prevent the perpetuation of a fresh act of injustice against Martyr Armenia. American people have always placed implicit faith in the pledges of Great Britain. We cannot believe Great Britain will disappoint us by failing to do full justice to Armenia.

The ARCHBISHOP OF CANTERBURY *to the* BISHOP OF NEW YORK

2 March, 1920.

Am glad to assure American Bishops of my continued and cordial sympathy in measures to secure safety, independence and freedom of worship to all Christian races hitherto subjected to Turkey. Question of best means to attain this object is receiving most careful consideration of British Government in concert with their Allies. We have counted on America's co-operation in this matter, and hope we may feel assured that she will bear her part in protection of oppressed Eastern nationalities.

The Archbishop's own public championship of the cause of oppressed Christians aroused deep gratitude in Constantinople and elsewhere. The acting Orthodox Patriarch telegraphed to tell him how deeply the bleeding hearts of enslaved Christians had been stirred by the voice he had raised for their liberation from bondage. The Armenian Patriarch of Constantinople, Zaven, came to see him at Lambeth. And telegrams and letters poured in, when a new massacre began in Cilicia, in March 1920, and a new Anatolian war broke out in the autumn of the same year. The Archbishop felt the tragedy of the situation acutely. He spoke in the House of Lords on March 11. He wrote to the Foreign Office. He pressed his views in private on members of the Cabinet. But he was baffled by the apparent impossibility

[1] Charles Sumner Burch.

of effective action. Three months later Dorotheos, the locum tenens of the Oecumenical Patriarchate, came a second time to Paris, and from Paris to London. He was the first occupant of the Patriarchal See of Constantinople to come to the West since the Patriarch Joseph attended the Council of Florence in 1439. He was a sick man when he arrived, old and terribly depressed by the condition of Christians under the Turk. And he came to invoke the Archbishop's aid in a most touching way and to thank him for his unfailing sympathy. He twice visited Lambeth, and on the second occasion (March 10, 1921) formally presented the Archbishop with a gift from the Holy Synod of Constantinople, as an earnest of the brotherly feeling of the Orthodox Church for the Anglican. It was an *enkolpion*, i.e. an ecclesiastical emblem of great beauty bearing the crowned or double-headed eagle of the Patriarchate, which had been originally made for Patriarch Joachim III and had been worn by five successive Patriarchs in virtue of their office. The next day Dorotheos had an audience with the King; and a day or two later saw Lord Curzon at the Foreign Office. But the visit ended in tragedy. The strain proved too great. He fell suddenly ill, and on March 18, 1921, died in London—paying, so many of the Orthodox believed, the same price for his visit to the West as the Patriarch Joseph who had died in Florence in 1439.

The Archbishop attended the funeral service in the Greek Church in Moscow Road, and (to quote his own words):

> For the first time in history the Archbishop of Canterbury officiated by reading the Gospel in English at funeral rites in the Greek Church in Bayswater.

The situation went from bad to worse during the next twelve months; and all the time telegrams and letters poured into Lambeth, from Smyrna, Cilicia, and elsewhere. The Archbishop replied with sympathy, and at the same time made it plain that in denouncing the cruelty of Turkish rule he was not attacking the Faith of Islam. In the course of a long letter to Lord Curzon on November 23, 1921, on the proposal of the French Government to withdraw its troops from Cilicia he said:

The ARCHBISHOP OF CANTERBURY *to the* MARQUESS CURZON

> I am quite certain that there is a steadily growing sense of resentment against the very idea of our acquiescing in what is

apparently French policy, the abandonment of these Christian populations to the very foes who have been most ruthless hitherto in their cruelty, mis-government, and massacres.

Lord Curzon replied that he also was greatly distressed, and would spare no effort for the safety of these unhappy people.

In the beginning of 1922, the Archbishop received one of the most extraordinary ecclesiastical appeals which can ever have come to an Archbishop of Canterbury. It concerned the Oecumenical Patriarchate of Constantinople, the centre of the Orthodox world. By virtue of his office the Patriarch was both the head of a religious community and a civil official. And apart from his local ecclesiastical jurisdiction, his throne was honoured by a hundred and fifty million Orthodox believers.

The last Patriarch, Germanos V (1913–18), had resigned just before the Armistice. The election of a successor had been postponed owing to the hopes of the Greek Church that a Treaty would be signed between Turkey and the Allies which would define the boundaries and also the rights of both Turk and Greek. But, as three years passed and no Treaty emerged, the desire grew that the vacant throne should be filled. There was opposition from Turkey to such a proposal. But there was also opposition from a section of the Greeks. The Greeks of Constantinople were strongly pro-Ally and Venizelist. The Greeks of Athens, however, at the end of 1921, were strongly anti-Venizelist, and unfriendly to the Allies, and Meletios, the former Metropolitan, who had been expelled, was an exile in New York, where he was known as an ardent Venizelist. Nevertheless, despite all obstacles, the Greeks in Constantinople resolved that the election should go forward. It is unnecessary here to recount the complicated details and all the comings and goings of Bishops on this side or that. The choice fell on Meletios, who immediately telegraphed his acceptance from New York. But the validity of the election was challenged by the faction which sided with the anti-Venizelists at Athens: and especially on the ground that seven leading Bishops had withdrawn at the last moment. The election of Meletios was also cabled to the Archbishop—then on his sick-bed at Canterbury—together with an intimation that Meletios wished to come to England. It was indeed an extraordinary thing that it was to the Archbishop of Canterbury that the Patriarch-designate of Constantinople desired to state the

Canonical and regular character of his election. But such was the fact. It was equally extraordinary that just about the same time that Meletios arrived in England, Chrysanthos of Trebizond, the representative of the dissenting Bishops, also arrived, for the very purpose of stating in the same quarter the reasons why the election was uncanonical and therefore void.

The Archbishop, being ill, deputed Bishop Gore, as Chairman of the Archbishops' Eastern Churches Committee, to pay his respects to each Archbishop in turn. The Archbishop's own natural reluctance to intervene was confirmed by the cautious advice of the Foreign Office. And yet he enjoyed the singularity of the event. To Bishop Gore he wrote:

The ARCHBISHOP OF CANTERBURY *to* BISHOP GORE

January 6, 1922.

. . . It is the unexpected that happens in modern history. Do you realise that Meletios, elected Patriarch of Constantinople, and Chrysanthos, Metropolitan of Trebizond, head of the anti-Meletios party in the Holy Synod, are both in London in order to seek the support of the Archbishop of Canterbury to one side or other of the rival groups, pro-Meletios or pro-Chrysanthos? Meantime the Archbishop whom they seek as patron or arbiter is laid up and cannot see either.

While most anxious not to intervene in a situation 'capable of raising political as well as ecclesiastical considerations', the Archbishop would be sorry to miss the experience of seeing and hearing, could that experience be one without too great peril. Therefore his letter ended:

If, having seen Meletios and Chrysanthos, you thought it necessary or highly desirable, I could no doubt arrange to see Meletios and Chrysanthos, even if it were in bed. But in no case should I think it right to say anything betokening partisanship in so delicate a situation.

Both Meletios and Chrysanthos were staying in London, one at the Ritz and the other at the Curzon hotel. When it was explained to Meletios that the Archbishop's illness was genuine and not diplomatic, though deeply disappointed he told his story at length, that it might be reported to the Archbishop. Meletios's main difficulty was how to get to Constantinople, for the Greek Government would give him no facilities through their territory, and the Turks would equally resist. Would a British gun-boat be available to convey him? Could the Archbishop help him to see the King or the Prime Minister and Lord Curzon? Could the British High Commissioner at Constantinople be urged to realize the high public importance of the matter?

All this, as well as Meletios's account of the election, was passed on to the Archbishop. And an account from the opposite point of view was also passed on after another interview with the Metropolitan of Trebizond the same day.

Meletios was, however, particularly desirous to see the Archbishop himself, and his Grace received the following telegram which in later days he sometimes recollected with a smile:

The PATRIARCH MELETIOS *to the* ARCHBISHOP OF CANTERBURY

London, W. January 9.

Am happy to receive your Grace's brotherly greeting but feel deeply sorry to hear you lie sick at bed. Am mentally standing beside your bed praying for rapid recovery of health so valuable for work of Gospel. I wish to say Jesus Christ maketh thee whole, coming in person near your bed.

Ten days later the Archbishop was sufficiently recovered to receive Meletios in person at a house which had been lent him for convalescence at St. Margaret's Bay. He came on January 19, and in the highest spirits; for, the day before, he had seen Lloyd George, to whom Venizelos had cabled urgently from California pressing him to do everything he could for the new Patriarch. The Archbishop's own account of the interview is as follows:

I had invited him with caution, meaning to be very reticent, and merely let him talk about the controversy. I had already written strongly to him to the effect that I must stand entirely outside it, and express no opinions. I found myself, however, relieved of political responsibility (about which the Foreign Office had been very emphatic—see the letters) by the fact that, on the day before coming to see me, Meletios had spent a long time with Mr. Lloyd George, who had emphatically assured him of friendliness, and invoked his aid to get the Venizelist cause promoted to the utmost of his power. After this I felt myself free to converse without restraint on the question, though, of course, I expressed no sort of opinion about the technical validity of Meletios' election. He, Meletios, and his friends, had brought papers with them in addition to those they had already sent to me, giving statistical figures and comparisons with previous elections to the effect that Meletios' election had been as fully supported numerically as previous Patriarchs, and that his opponents had absolutely no case against it. . . . I showed to Meletios the utmost friendliness, and maintained the same affectionate relation which we had adopted when he was in England before. . . . He spoke very interestingly about his election, professing to be genuinely surprised that he should have been elected, especially when he was absent in America, and attributed it to two causes—first that he had been a sufferer for the cause of freedom, and of all that Venizelos represented during the war, and had thus a claim on recognition as a sort of martyr; and secondly, because the wrongs of the Greeks who were friendly to the Allies, were widely and deeply felt, and that he was known to represent with Venizelos the cause of those who had thus suffered. This had made his election popular, and would continue to do so. He appeared to entertain no doubt that if once he could get to Constantinople and assume the throne to which he had been duly elected, he would be able to carry on the work of the Patriarchate in the ordinary way, with general, though not universal support. He said emphatically to me that one of his first duties as Patriarch would be to promote in every possible manner friendliness with the Anglican Church, and to recognise our position. He did not actually speak of the validity of our Orders, but I understood him to imply it. I ought to add that exactly the same argument is being used by Chrysanthos of Trebizond, though he has not used it to me. . . . I discount this assurance on both sides. I think it rather significant of the sort of way in which these ecclesiastics mix up policy and principle in their declarations and procedure.

According to Meletios, Lloyd George had poured out his enthusiasm for the cause of Venizelos. He had declared that the return of the Royalists to Athens was the worst misfortune for that part of the world since the fall of Constantinople in 1453. Meletios believed that Lloyd George was likely to send him in an English gunboat from Marseilles to Constantinople, which would get rid of all passport difficulties. . . .

He was with us at St. Margaret's Bay for three hours, and talked for a great deal of the time. Should he be formally established as Patriarch, there must be a very great gain in our having secured so completely a fraternal and friendly relationship as now subsists between us.

The Archbishop of Canterbury also saw the Metropolitan of Trebizond, on January 26, for an hour, and listened to his suggestion that a special Synod of Orthodox Bishops should be held at Jerusalem (where there was a British administration) to determine the question of the election. But he made it plain that he could not in any way intervene; and as to the propriety or sufficiency of the voting at the time of the election the Archbishop said:

> It is quite clear that these are such technical points that even if those belonging to the Church of England were qualified to express an opinion, it is undesirable that they should do so. I have asked these questions because I desired to understand, and I think that I do now understand.

To the Archbishop it was a matter of history, happening in our own time, which he desired to understand—that was all, though there was an added interest in the fact that at the very moment the Cardinals at Rome were about to elect a Pope, in the place of Benedict XV, who had died on January 22. The Metropolitan said that they did not want the Church of England to intervene, but their two Churches were so close to one another that they wished the Archbishop to be fully informed. The Archbishop agreed. He said that the interest of the Anglican Church in the question of the Patriarchate was of a much closer kind than it could be in the election of the Pope. They were too far apart from Rome—but they were not so far apart from the Eastern Church. And the Metropolitan ended with the assurance that, whatever their internal controversies, all were unanimous in their feelings for the Anglican Church. When peace came, they would do all on their part to make the connexion closer.

A few days later the difficulties in the way of Meletios's journey to Constantinople were removed. He sailed up the Golden Horn in a French launch, and was immediately enthroned as Meletios IV, on the very same day that Cardinal Achille Ratti was elected Pope as Pius XI. The following telegrams were exchanged:

The PATRIARCH OF CONSTANTINOPLE *to the* ARCHBISHOP OF CANTERBURY

Constantinople. 11th February, 1922.

In public ecclesiastical ceremony enthroned since yesterday on Holy Apostolical and Patriarchal Throne of Constantinople am sending from it brotherly in Christ the Chief Pastor embrace to your Grace the Head of Anglican Church in confirmation of most excellent relations existing by divine favour between the two churches and of positive hopes of their further by heavenly aid advancement to a complete sacred communion of faith and grace am gladly remembering marks of true love which I obtained from your Grace while passing through England and am seizing the opportunity to assure you that the crew of my church also shares my feeling of deepest gratitude.

The ARCHBISHOP OF CANTERBURY *to the* PATRIARCH OF CONSTANTINOPLE.

I thank Your Holiness for courteous intimation of your enthronement. I rejoice in the happy relations already existing, and pray that they may lead to even closer fellowship between the Anglican Communion and the whole Eastern Orthodox Communion. And may the peace of God be secured and maintained.

In the following March, the Archbishop had important interviews with both Armenian and Kemalist delegates, and did not hesitate to confront the latter with the Bryce Report on Armenian atrocities of 1915, which was lying on the table, by way of quietly showing them 'the monstrous inconsistency between his view of the matter and the account therein given'. It was just before the meeting of the Supreme Council in Paris.

The Archbishop again spoke in the House of Lords on March 30, expressing a certain uneasiness about some of the particulars in the Paris proposals. A month later in Convocation (May 2), he secured the adoption of a resolution pressing upon the Government 'the vital importance in the interests of civilization of giving full effect, in the international arrangements now under consideration, to the promises which have repeatedly been made as to the protection of Christian minorities within the Turkish Empire'. He wrote also both to Mr. Lloyd George and to M. Poincaré pressing the claims of the Armenians.

In October, after the occupation and burning of Smyrna by the Turks, M. Venizelos asked to see the Archbishop, and spent an hour in his study at Lambeth on October 17, 1922:

His object in coming to see me was to pour out his soul about the magnitude of the present Greek distress. He thinks that neither in England nor in America is the scale of it all recognised. Many hundreds of thousands (he gave me the figures, but I cannot remember them) are absolutely homeless in their expulsion or flight from Asia Minor or from Eastern Thrace, and the fearful problem is: How can Greece, a little poor country with no room to spare, find a place of refuge for a million people, and, when it is found, support them there? It needs gigantic help, and no other Powers than England or America can be looked to for much practical aid. France will do scarcely anything. Italy will do nothing. Scandinavia may do a little, but the real help must come from England and America. In America they are beginning to realise the situation. Make them realise it, if you can, in England.

Venizelos spoke with great emotion, raising his voice while he talked, so that it seemed to the chaplain in the next room that the Archbishop was very quiet and silent, while Venizelos was storming. The Archbishop's memorandum continues:

Dr. Nansen, in whom I have the most absolute confidence as an administrative genius with the unique power of managing these huge things, has got the matter in hand. But he must have the backing of the Christian Powers who are willing to help and he must be known to have it. All this Venizelos reiterated again and again, his voice growing louder and louder. He asked me if there was anything I wished to know from him. I said I should like to ask first: What are we entitled to say about Greek outrages on Turks? He replied 'You may say without the slightest fear of contradiction that in Thrace and in Greece there is no such thing. Some particular group in some village may have done a violent act, but I challenge fullest enquiry into the treatment of the Turkish population under Greek rule. I am certain no wrong-doing can be found. Let any emissary be sent to examine the facts and he will find that I am absolutely right. See what General Harington says in *The Times* of to-day'. 'I am not speaking', he added, 'of what happened during the Greek Retreat in Asia Minor. I do believe that villages were there set on fire by the retreating Greeks. It was deplorable and unjustifiable, but I do not deny it. All I object to is the describing of it as corresponding to the Turkish outrages upon Christians. These incidents were the lawless excess of a terrified and retreating army or groups of it. The Turkish massacres of Christians were a deliberate policy definitely avowed. The Turks have declared that there are to be no Christians in Asia Minor. They have formally stated through the Foreign Minister that no Christians will be allowed to return to Asia Minor in any circumstances. If your Government, as is possible, doubts whether this is their distinct policy, let them ask the question and the Turks will be bound to answer—We do not mean to let Christians return. This being so, place must be found somewhere for

> those, say, two million people who can no longer find homes anywhere in Asia Minor or in Eastern Thrace.

Venizelos went on:

> 'Do not let,' he exclaimed louder and louder, 'Do not let political circumstances come into the thing at all. Here are a million or a million and a half of people absolutely destitute and homeless. They are barred from forming homes for themselves in any part of the Turkish possessions. We have got to find first homes, and then maintenance, for them somewhere. We cannot do it. You must carry the burden. It is a purely humanitarian question. . . . I assured Venizelos that I would not forget what he had said, and that every influence I possessed would be used in the direction of obtaining such help as is possible, but I felt bound to remind him of the immense difficulties. . . .

The Archbishop did all he could to encourage public generosity and consistently supported the All British Appeal launched by the Lord Mayor of London, and kept in close touch with the agents of relief and reconstruction.

The same month, October 1922, saw the end of the Coalition Government under Mr. Lloyd George, and the appointment of Mr. Bonar Law as Prime Minister. With the change, a campaign was started in certain quarters, mainly on grounds of economy, to set the British Government free of its commitments in the Near East. It was a dangerous moment. The Archbishop deemed it wise to inform Mr. Bonar Law of his own views and those of his brother Bishops, before the agitation went farther:

The Archbishop of Canterbury *to the* Rt. Hon. A. Bonar Law

October 24, 1922.

> I am painfully conscious of the inconvenience to yourself, I may almost say audacity, on my part of writing to you at this moment upon public affairs affecting National policy, but I feel bound to do so with reference to one point which indirectly I suppose may affect the plans or programme which you are presumably going to adumbrate forthwith. I refer to the Near Eastern question with reference specially to the position of the Christian populations. Circumstances have led me, as you can easily understand, to be in close touch with those who represent the great Orthodox Church of the East and the Armenian Church, and in addition I have for years been in close touch with the Assyrian Church. . . . At present comparatively few people in this country realise the

extent, and I may say the solemnity, of the promises we have made. But they are bound to know about it soon, and in view of the extraordinary difficulty of what you have to say you ought to be aware of the strength of religious opinion which will be behind you and supporting you if you make it clear that whatever else happens our pledged word cannot be broken or ignored. Such breach would be regarded by tens of thousands of religious people when informed of the facts as nothing short of infamous.

I could easily say more or give you ample details, but I have already written enough for the moment. My only desire has been that feeling what we do we should say it now and not in any circumstances be told afterwards—You ought to have spoken in time.

Mr. Bonar Law replied as follows:

The RT. HON. A. BONAR LAW *to the* ARCHBISHOP OF CANTERBURY

10, Downing Street, Whitehall, S.W. 1.
31st October 1922.

I thank you for your letter of the 24th October, which I have read, I need not say, with the utmost care. It is a subject on which as I know you have already had some communication with Lord Curzon. At present in the very act of undertaking my new responsibilities I cannot say more than that the most earnest attention will be given to the views which you put before me. You will also, I am sure, realise that in this matter the British Government can never be entirely free agents but any successful work would be impossible unless we could carry our Allies with us.

The Lausanne Conference to negotiate peace with Turkey began on November 20, 1922, under the presidency of Lord Curzon. The Turkish delegation demanded with great stubbornness that the Oecumenical Patriarchate itself should be removed from Constantinople; and made the conclusion of the convention for the exchange of populations conditional on such removal. But with the disappearance of the Patriarchate the end of Constantinople as in any sense a Christian city would be near at hand. The following telegram reached the Archbishop from Meletios:

The PATRIARCH OF CONSTANTINOPLE *to the* ARCHBISHOP OF CANTERBURY

Constantinople, 20 December 1922.

The first conqueror cast the most holy apostolic oecumenical throne out of the Church of St. Sophia. The second conqueror is now attempting to drive the throne out of the very borders of Constantinople, and is seeking to make the representatives of the Christian Powers also partners of this crime.

Join with us, O brother beloved, and with all the Orthodox Bishops, together with your own brethren, both in prayer to God and in protest to the Conference for the averting of the wrong which is being wrought against the whole Orthodox Church.

The Archbishop sent the telegram to Lord Curzon at Lausanne, and in his letter accompanying it he pointed out the new danger of the creation of a Turkish Orthodox Church through the machinations of a certain Papa Eftim, who had begun to be active on behalf of the Kemalists. Others also wrote imploring intervention.

After weighing his words well and choosing the moment, the Archbishop decided to send the following telegram:

The ARCHBISHOP OF CANTERBURY *to the* PATRIARCH OF CONSTANTINOPLE

December 22, 1922.

I have throughout continued to press upon the Conference at Lausanne our earnest hope and desire that no breach should take place in the maintenance of the historic Oecumenical Patriarchate in Constantinople. The continuity of the Patriarchate in Constantinople is profoundly important to the whole Christian Church.

This telegram when made public produced a profound effect and gave a powerful weight to the representations then being made by Lord Curzon at Lausanne. A great volume of public opinion found expression, and Lord Curzon himself took a very strong line from the start. On December 26, a compromise was suggested by a French delegate and supported by a British, that the Oecumenical Patriarchate should be allowed to remain in Constantinople but 'should exercise no political or spiritual jurisdiction in Turkey'. Such a proposal would have been fatal to the whole idea of the Patriarchate, and the Archbishop wrote a strong protest to Lord Curzon (December 29, 1922):

The ARCHBISHOP OF CANTERBURY *to the* MARQUESS CURZON

I can hardly suppose that this means that the great Orthodox population in Constantinople would have another ecclesiastical head independent of the nominal Patriarch. If that were so, the peril and wrong would be grave indeed. We might then have what they call the Papa Eftim Church, which would mean the merest travesty of regular Christian authority, but even if that danger be avoided by the Patriarch's retaining jurisdiction in Constantinople itself, what about the other Dioceses—say, in Macedonia and elsewhere?

Lord Curzon replied reassuringly, and by his directions the British delegate made the following declaration on January 2, 1923:

DECLARATION *by the* BRITISH DELEGATE

Having acquainted Lord Curzon with what passed at the last meeting, I have received his Lordship's express instructions to state once more that he cannot see his way to acquiesce in any proposal for the removal of the Oecumenical Patriarch from Constantinople. Lord Curzon considers that whatever may be the solution of the question of the civil and the political rights of the Greek community it would be unjust to infringe the purely spiritual rights and jurisdiction which belonged to the Oecumenical Patriarch as Primate of the Orthodox Churches, and as head of the Greek Orthodox Church in Turkey.

The Greek delegate read a similar statement.

The Turkish delegates bowed to the ultimatum. On January 10, Ismet Pasha 'took note before the Commission of the solemn declarations and assurances which had just been delivered by the Allied and Greek delegations, whereby the Patriarchate was no longer to take any part whatever in affairs of a political or administrative character, and was to confine itself within the limits of purely religious matters', and withdrew the Turkish demand for its removal. Lord Curzon and the Archbishop had won.

Telegrams of congratulation and gratitude reached Lambeth from many Eastern Bishops. The following was the message from Meletios:

The PATRIARCH OF CONSTANTINOPLE *to the* ARCHBISHOP OF CANTERBURY

January 13, 1923.

It is announced to us from Lausanne that the demand for the expulsion of the Oecumenical Patriarchate has been defeated. Giving thanks to God the fountain of good we acknowledge also the debt which we owe to your Grace for the help which you afforded us in the establishing of justice. Receive our warm thanks.

The Treaty of Lausanne was at last signed, on July 24, 1923. But though the Oecumenical Patriarchate was saved, it was recognized that Meletios could not remain. M. Venizelos himself urged him to resign as the only sure way of improving the position of the Greeks in Constantinople and Turkey. Even before the evacuation of the Allied troops, he was roughly handled. On July 10, he left Constantinople and went to Mount Athos, and in November his formal abdication was announced.[1]

[1] 'By abdicating Mgr. Meletios IV. has followed the example of a large number of his predecessors on the Oecumenical Throne since Sultan Mohamed Fatih took Constantinople in 1453 and re-established the Orthodox character of the Patriarchate of Constantinople. Since then the Oecumenical Patriarchate has been vacated during the centuries in the following manner:

Century:—	*15th.*	*16th.*	*17th.*	*18th.*	*19th.*	*20th.*
Violent death . . .	..	1	3	..	2	..
Deposition . . .	10	13	39	24	18	1
Abdication . . .	2	1	12	4	6	2
Natural death . . .	2	8	1	5	4	1

Thus the Turks have on 105 occasions driven Patriarchs from their Throne; there have been 27 abdications, often involuntary, six Patriarchs have suffered violent death by hanging, poisoning, or drowning, and 21 have died natural deaths while in office.' (*The Times*, Nov. 10, 1923.)

CHAPTER LXIX

THE ORTHODOX CHURCH

The Greek Patriarch, the better to express his desire of communion with our old Church of England, by mee declared unto him, gave me his Bull or Patriarchal Seal, in a Blank (which is their way of credence), besides many other respects.

A letter written by the REV. DR. BASIRE *to* SIR RICHARD BROWN, *relating his Travel and Endeavour to propagate the knowledge of the Doctrine and Discipline established in the Britannick Church among the Greeks, Arabians, &c., 1661.*

DURING all the years which had passed since Randall Davidson first went as resident chaplain to Lambeth, there had been a steady development in the relationship between the Church of England and the Orthodox Church. Bishops John Wordsworth and William Collins, in particular, together with Mr. W. J. Birkbeck, had prepared the Church of England for the next advance. And good work had been done at the Lambeth Conferences of 1897 and 1908. But nothing that had happened hitherto could compare with the immense move forward which had been brought about by the event of the War. So the Archbishop declared in the speech which he made to the Full Synod of Canterbury Convocation, February 16, 1923. In 1919, the Eastern Churches Committee was appointed under the chairmanship of Bishop Gore. In 1920, a delegation came from Constantinople to confer with the Committee of the sixth Lambeth Conference. In 1921, a careful study on Anglican Ordinations by Professor Komnenos, one of the delegates, saw the light. In the same year there also appeared a semi-official Anglican statement on 'Suggested Terms of Intercommunion',[1] drawn up at the request of the Eastern Churches Committee. In May 1922 the Patriarch of Constantinople, Meletios, nominated Archbishop Germanos to be Metropolitan of Thyateira and his representative, or *apokrisiarios*, to the Archbishop of Canterbury, resident in London, as a special sign of 'our desire for a firmer complete communion of the Orthodox and English Churches which the Lord is plainly leading to union with each other'. In August 1922, the famous Declaration on the Validity of Anglican Orders was officially communicated by the Patriarch to the Archbishop of Canterbury.

[1] See Bell, *Documents on Christian Unity*, p. 77.

I

The story of the circumstances in which the Declaration was made has its own interest. The hope of such a Declaration had been entertained for some while by a few ardent Anglican friends of the Orthodox Church, of whom the chief was the Rev. J. A. Douglas, author of *The Relations of the Anglican Churches with the Eastern Orthodox* (1921). It was well known to them that the Orthodox Church would be more ready to acknowledge the validity of Anglican Orders if they could be sure that a considerable body of Anglicans held a doctrine of Ordination approximating to that of the Orthodox. On Mr. Douglas's initiative, therefore, a Declaration of Faith was prepared and widely signed, dealing with that and other topics from a strong Anglo-Catholic standpoint. It was intended to present it to the Patriarch of Constantinople. The Declaration at once became the centre of a controversy. It was signed, amongst others, by Bishop Gore, Chairman of the Eastern Churches Committee—a fact which called forth a strong remonstrance from Dr. A. C. Headlam, a main author of the much more conservative 'Suggested Terms of Intercommunion'. It was condemned by some as entirely incompatible with the statement of doctrine representing the points of agreement reached at a Joint Conference at Lambeth Palace between Nonconformists and Anglicans which was almost simultaneously issued.[1] Its reference to the Thirty-nine Articles was denounced by others as unjust and untruthful,[2] and when the Bishop of Durham preached against it in Westminster Abbey, from the text 'Let love be without hypocrisy', the Orthodox advocates of Reunion in Constantinople wrote to their English friends that the Declaration was dead so far as presenting it to the Patriarch was concerned.[3] It nevertheless reached the Patriarch, and was not without effect.

No doubt the knowledge that the doctrines contained in the

[1] 'Church Unity, May 1922'. See Bell, *Documents on Christian Unity*, p. 143.

[2] 'We account the Thirty-nine Articles of Religion as a document of secondary importance concerned with local controversies of the sixteenth century, and to be interpreted in accordance with the faith of that Universal Church of which the English Church is but a part.'

[3] The Declaration, reprinted in Bell's *Documents*, p. 90, originally had 56 signatures in May, 1922, which was increased to 3,715 before the list was complete. It was prepared by a Committee of the English Church Union, and approved by the President and Council of that Body.

proposed Declaration were held by many members of the Anglican Church had its weight with the Holy Synod. It was actually a pastoral need that brought matters to a head. As a result of the theological study of Professor Komnenos and others before and since the Lambeth Conference, the conclusion had been reached at Constantinople, with a view to its communication to the other Orthodox Churches, that Anglican Orders were valid. The importance of such a conclusion in view of the possible regularization of Anglican ministrations is obvious. The publication of the Declaration was in fact determined on the occasion of a visit to Constantinople by an American priest, the Rev. W. C. Emhardt, who was travelling in the Near East with a mission from the American Episcopal Church to take up the case of Orthodox subjects who found themselves in different parts of the United States, far removed from any Orthodox Bishop or Priest. The urgency of the need was emphasized, and in the end the Holy Synod adopted the conclusion, which the Patriarch communicated, in the following letter, to the Archbishop of Canterbury:

The PATRIARCH OF CONSTANTINOPLE *to the* ARCHBISHOP OF CANTERBURY

July 28, 1922.

Most Reverend Archbishop of Canterbury and Chief Hierarch of all England, Brother, beloved and yearned for in Christ our God, Lord Randall, greetings; your Reverence well beloved by us, fraternally in the Lord, we address you with gladness.

Our special committee dealing with the Union of the Churches has drawn our attention and that of our Holy Synod to the question of the validity of Anglican ordinations from the Orthodox point of view, for that it would be profitable in regard to the whole question of union that the opinion of the Holy Orthodox Church should be known upon this matter.

Accordingly the Holy Synod on this opportunity taking under our presidency the matter under consideration, and, having examined it from every point of view, has concluded that, as before the Orthodox Church, the ordinations of the Anglican Episcopal Confession of bishops, priests, and deacons, possesses the same validity as those of the Roman, Old Catholic, and Armenian Churches possess, inasmuch as all essentials are found in them which are held indispensable from the Orthodox point of view for the recognition of the 'Charisma' of the priesthood derived from Apostolic Succession.

Indeed, on the one hand, it is plain that there is as yet no matter here of a decree by the whole Orthodox Church. For it is necessary that the rest of the Orthodox Churches should be found to be of the same opinion (in the matter) as the Most Holy Church of Constantinople.

But even so it is an event not without significance that the Synod of one, and that the Primatial Throne of the Orthodox Churches, when taking the matter into consideration, has come to this conclusion.

Therefore with great joy we communicate the matter to Your beloved Grace as the Chief Hierarch of the whole Anglican Church, being sure that your Grace will be equally favourably disposed towards this conclusion, as recognizing in it a step forward in that work of general union which is dear to God.

May the Heavenly Father grant unto us to be of the same mind, through the grace of our Lord Jesus Christ, who is blessed for ever and ever.

It was a notable act, and caused much satisfaction amongst large numbers of Churchmen. The Archbishop of Canterbury accepted it with courtesy, but took care to show, in any allusion or letter he wrote about it, that it was no matter of surprise, nor was he specially concerned to rejoice because other Churches were led to acknowledge what had always been true. As he wrote to Bishop McInnes, with reference to the Patriarch of Jerusalem, who had expressed his agreement with the Patriarch of Constantinople:

The ARCHBISHOP OF CANTERBURY *to the* BISHOP IN JERUSALEM

24 March, 1923.

We are glad to receive any information as to what the Patriarchate has decided, but we do not ask for it in such a manner as to suggest that there is any hesitation on our part, or that we are dependent on the opinions which are expressed respecting our position and Orders.

There was on the Archbishop's side no invitation of any expression of opinion from any Orthodox Prelate. He had never requested Meletios or anybody else to express an opinion on the matter, and his policy with regard to the East was identical with his policy in regard to Rome many years before, when he had counselled Archbishop Benson to refrain from asking the Pope whether or no Rome recognized Anglican Orders.[1]

The Archbishop communicated the Declaration to Convocation in full Synod on February 16, 1923. He there again made it plain that, while he welcomed the Declaration, he did not exaggerate its importance. In particular he was careful to point out the limitations involved. Before it could become an oecumenical act, binding all the Orthodox Churches, the formal acceptance of Anglican Ordinations, he said, would have to be accepted by all severally, or approved in a General Council. It did not in itself lead to intercommunion. Its importance lay in preparing the way for future advance; though of course it was an admission of real importance for the future relations of the two Churches, as having been made by the Oecumenical Patriarchate of Constantinople.[2]

II

The Archbishop's care in relation to the general attitude of the Eastern Orthodox Communion to the Anglican Communion is abundantly clear. He was not less careful when dealing with particular problems, or particular requests. Two examples will suffice.

In 1924, a Rumanian priest, M. Popescu, was condemned by the authorities of the Rumanian Church for heresy. He had in fact been converted to a more evangelical view of religion, and the chief charge brought against him related to the omission of a sentence in the Liturgy which seemed to involve the thought of salvation being dependent upon the Blessed Virgin Mary. For this he had been deprived of his church in Bucharest and excommunicated. As he could not get any other building in which to preach, and many desired to hear him preach the simple gospel of salvation through faith in a personal Saviour, the agent of the London Society for Promoting Christianity amongst the Jews (an Anglican mission), the Rev. J. H. Adeney, lent him his

[1] See p. 229 f.

[2] The Patriarchate of Jerusalem and the Church of Cyprus expressed their agreement with the Patriarch of Constantinople, in February and March, 1923, and the Patriarchate of Alexandria in 1931; but no opinion has been expressed (1935) by the remaining Patriarchates of Antioch and Russia, or the remaining autocephalous Churches of Greece, Jugoslavia, Rumania, and Poland, or by the Church of Bulgaria.

Hall and he preached there. This at once gave rise to a difficulty, as appearing to show that the Church of England was willing to harbour and encourage a schismatic priest whom the Orthodox Church had expelled. The Bishop of Gibraltar (Dr. Greig), who was eager for closer relations between the Rumanian and the Anglican Churches, felt the problem keenly, and disapproved of Mr. Adeney's action. In writing to the Archbishop he expressed his disapproval. He pointed out how disastrous it would be if no notice were taken of Mr. Adeney's patronage of Popescu, as the present position involved a clashing with, and upsetting of, the aims and settled policy of the Church of England towards the Orthodox East. He added in his memorandum of November 1, 1924:

The BISHOP OF GIBRALTAR *to the* ARCHBISHOP OF CANTERBURY

November 1, 1924.

I ought perhaps to add that I am not judging, still less condemning, Popescu. I am prepared to believe that he is a God-fearing Christian man, and that envy and mere ignorant dislike of any change have much the biggest part in his suspension. I daresay, though I do not know, that this is true. But the rights or wrongs of his case are not relevant. The broad fact is that we have a wonderful chance during the next few years of helping forward a real religious revival in the National Church of Rumania by strengthening and supporting it.

The Archbishop wrote in reply:

The ARCHBISHOP OF CANTERBURY *to the* BISHOP OF GIBRALTAR

Old Palace, Canterbury. 13th November, 1924.

Private.

I have read with close attention your Memorandum of November 1st about the Rumanian Position with respect especially to Adeney and Popescu. The matter appears to me to be one in which very great care is necessary. I hope to see the Secretary of the Jews' Society a few days hence, when I can be in London. I shall certainly want to get all the facts that he can give me.

At present I confess that I am anxious for a clearer knowledge than I now have of the ground upon which Popescu was suspended or placed under discipline. I understand you to say that this point is irrelevant to the present question. But is it irrelevant? Gore, with whom I have had some conversation, has an idea that

Popescu's condemnation was because he declined to address the Blessed Virgin as Saviour, while he was ready to use the lesser forms of veneration. If that be so he, Gore, feels rather strongly the need of care on our part lest we identify ourselves too readily with the denunciation of Popescu. We should be in a strange position if it were to come about that he is really standing for what is more or less fundamental in our view of true teaching on this subject and has consequently been excommunicated. I wonder whether you could write to the Metropolitan asking, without saying why, for a statement as to the nature of Popescu's offence? What was the doctrine which he taught or the fault which he committed?

Of course I entirely share your view that we must take care not to let the Jews' Society, or its agent, involve us as a Church in difficulties. But on the other hand we must be very sure of our ground in the matter.

The Archbishop took endless pains, saw the Secretary of the London Jews' Society, as well as Bishop Gore, the Bishop of Gibraltar, and Mr. Adeney himself. He agreed that it might probably be right to bring about the ending of Popescu's sermons in a building belonging to an Anglican society, however admirable and even uncontroversial the sermons. But he added (November 29, 1924):

The ARCHBISHOP OF CANTERBURY *to the* BISHOP OF GIBRALTAR

I do think, and Bishop Gore is very strong about this, that when a man is excommunicated and they tell us so, we ought to be told exactly what is the offence he has committed. I do not think the Metropolitan can resent that question being asked if it is done in courteous terms—not with a view to our saying that Popescu is to go on with his preaching, but with a view to our acting with our eyes open to all the facts.

In the end the Archbishop counselled Mr. Adeney, and the counsel commended itself both to Mr. Adeney and to the Bishop of Gibraltar, that the Hall might still be used by M. Popescu while he was taking steps to build another Hall as soon as possible, on condition that M. Popescu should not, in his teaching, attack the Rumanian Church as such, or try to win people from it, and also that if it should be found in England that mischief was being done, and the relations of the Church of England to the other Churches were gravely compromised, he would have to ask Popescu to terminate his use of the Hall.

III

The second example arises from the requests which sometimes reached the Archbishop from different countries that he should consecrate a Bishop.[1] An interesting one came from Albania in 1922.

The Orthodox Christians of the South desired an autonomous Church like other Balkan peoples, and the desire had been agreed to by the Albanian Government. The head of the Orthodox Albanians in the South was Monsignor Noli. It was proposed that he should be consecrated by the Russian Patriarch at Moscow, but he would gladly take consecration at the hands of the Church of England. The matter was pressed upon the Archbishop by Mr. Aubrey Herbert and Lord Robert Cecil. The Archbishop however saw difficulties of a rather important kind, and he was supported in feeling these difficulties by some members of the Lambeth Conference Consultative Body, who happened to be at Lambeth in July. He expressed his inability to take the step proposed. The idea put forward was simply that 'Theophan Noli should be consecrated as an Anglican Bishop in the ordinary form and with the ordinary permission from the Crown, just as if he were going to be a Bishop ministering to an Anglican Community in Albania!' The Archbishop wrote an official reply as follows:

The ARCHBISHOP OF CANTERBURY *to* LORD ROBERT CECIL

25th July, 1922.

I have given very careful attention to the letter you wrote to me about the possibility of my consecrating in England a Bishop for the Albanian Church. Mr. Aubrey Herbert has also written

[1] In this connexion it may be of interest to note a not dissimilar reply from the Archbishop to a certain Russian Bishop, rather far away from Russian influence, that he might be made a Bishop of the Anglican Communion. The Archbishop's reply, on February 23, 1920, was as follows: 'I have given careful consideration to your request for admission into the membership of the Church of England. I fear, however, that Your Lordship is under a misconception as to the position and function of the English Church. We make no claim to a universal mission. We do not maintain a Bishop or Missionary of our Communion anywhere except (1) to look after our own people: (2) for the conversion of the non-Christian world: (3) where we are, as at Jerusalem or among the Assyrians, acting in agreement with the local ecclesiastical authorities.

'Under these circumstances, I fear, therefore, that it is not possible for the Church of England to accept Your Lordship as a Bishop or Missionary of the Anglican Communion. . . .'

to me making the same request. I consulted several of our leading Bishops who are familiar with the ecclesiastical laws and usages in these matters and I find them all to be in agreement with me in thinking that we should complicate rather than simplify matters were we to grant the request which you have transmitted. I should not be acting legally were I in England to consecrate a Bishop otherwise than according to the Anglican Rite and with the Anglican Oath of Allegiance taken either to the Archbishop of Canterbury or to some other Metropolitan of our Church. This would be impossible in the case of an Albanian Bishop; and glad as I should be to do anything helpful to the Albanian Church, for whose members I entertain profound respect and warm sympathy, I am sure that I should not be advancing the real interests either of the Church at large, or of the local Church in Albania, were I to do something which would create an entirely new precedent and one which would certainly cause wide comment, and perhaps offence, among the Bishops of other Churches in Eastern Europe in addition to the more direct difficulties I have pointed out. It is disappointing to me to be obliged to write thus, but I feel sure that I am right, and I venture to think that the facts as to our laws, usages, and restrictions were perhaps not adequately realised by those on whose behalf you kindly put the matter before me.

Perhaps you will be good enough to take the necessary steps for communicating this to those who approached you in the matter. They have not written direct to myself, feeling most wisely that their cause would be safe in your hands.

IV

There was a remarkable demonstration of the growing *rapprochement* between the Orthodox and Anglican Churches when the 1,600th anniversary of the Council of Nicaea was celebrated at Westminster Abbey on June 29, 1925. Had the conditions either of Russia or of Constantinople allowed, there would, in all probability, have been a great celebration, on Orthodox soil, of the holding of the first Oecumenical Council of 325, to which delegates of all the Orthodox Churches would have been summoned in the most solemn way. But such a pan-Orthodox assembly was impossible in the political circumstances of 1925. The idea was therefore conceived of a special celebration in London. The necessary soundings were taken in different Orthodox centres by the Rev. J. A. Douglas, who once again played a prominent part in the drawing together of the Orthodox and Anglican Churches.

Official invitations were dispatched by the Bishop of London to the authorities of each of the ten autocephalous Churches, nearly all of which sent delegations. The most notable delegates were the Patriarchs Photios of Alexandria and Damianos of Jerusalem, besides the Russian Metropolitans (outside Russia) Eulogius, and Antony of Kieff; and there were also representatives of the Rumanian and the Greek Churches. The Service of Commemoration took place in Westminster Abbey on St. Peter's Day. In addition to the Orthodox representatives twenty Anglican Archbishops and Bishops were present as well as Mar Shimun, the young Assyrian Patriarch, an Armenian representative, and an eminent representative of the Lutheran Church in Dr. Söderblom, the Archbishop of Upsala. The Archbishop of Canterbury preached the sermon. He called attention to the changes wrought in London and Nicaea in 1,600 years: the former then 'a little Roman-British citadel protecting the roadway on the north bank of the Thames, with, for Westminster, a broad stretch of sandy shore with a few Roman villas and some fishermen's huts among the osier-beds, and an outlook across the wooded slopes into the forest of Middlesex'; while the latter had been chosen for the place of the Nicene Council in 325 'for its dignity, its salubrity, its accessibleness, and the appropriateness of its name, the "City of Victory", connected in our minds with Constantine's title and vision and watchword.' Alas, Nicaea was in 1925 a 'deserted and poverty-stricken hamlet in a swamp'! The Archbishop spoke of the issues which the first Oecumenical Council had had to face, and then of the fellowship of the Church represented by that gathering:

'It is no ordinary congregation which is gathered in this hallowed place, surrounded by the memorials of those who, in storm and sunshine, have in their varied ways taken the lead in making history—the history of a people which has stood and stands for truth and freedom in the ordered public life of a Christian country. Yes. *Circumspice*. These chairs and stalls have many unaccustomed occupants. Some of them are the lineal successors of the very men who met in conclave at Nicaea from the dioceses and cities of the East sixteen centuries ago. They are here to join with our own their prayers, their thanksgivings, their credal testimony of loyalty to our living Lord. It is well that they should be here. It touches us profoundly that, when we resolved to commemorate the far-off Council to which we owe, in one of its several varieties of phrase, the actual Creed or symbol which forms the basis of our own, they should have expressed a desire to join with us here to pray, to stand with us here to join in our solemn declaration of Faith in Him.'

At the end of his sermon, the Nicene Creed having already been recited in English in its Western form, Archbishop Davidson asked the Patriarch of Alexandria to recite the Creed in Greek according to the Orthodox use, without the *filioque* clause. That day's celebration, as the Archbishop said, when the Service was over, was rendered unique by the presence in England for the first time in history of the two ruling Patriarchs of Alexandria and Jerusalem. It was unique, not only in the history of the Anglican Communion, but in the story of the whole Church of Christ.

CHAPTER LXX

THE ARCHBISHOP AND THE FREE CHURCHES

I am deeplier afflicted for the disagreements of Christians than I was when I was a younger Christian. Except the case of the infidel world, nothing is so sad and grievous to my thoughts, as the case of the divided Churches.

RICHARD BAXTER, *Reliquiae Baxterianae.*

IN the first few years which followed the War, a new desire for the Reunion of Christendom was kindled in many Christian Communions and seemed to quicken the hearts of Christian leaders. The Appeal to All Christian People was everywhere regarded as most significant evidence of the longing for unity which inspired the Anglican Church. And, as was natural, it made a deep impression upon many members of the non-Episcopal Churches in Great Britain.

I

We turn therefore to the Evangelical Free Churches of England.[1] The Appeal to All Christian People was issued in August 1920. There was an immediate and friendly response on the side of the Free Churches. In September 1920, a Provisional Statement was published under the joint authority of the Federal Council of the Evangelical Free Churches of England and of the National Free Church Council. A private and informal conversation took place at Lambeth Palace on December 8, 1920, between the two Archbishops with six diocesan bishops and a special committee of Free Churchmen. In the following spring an important Report, *The Free Churches and the Lambeth Appeal*, was published under the joint authority of the same two Free Church Councils. It was transmitted to the authorities of the Free Churches. The Archbishop of Canterbury on receiving the Report suggested both central and local conferences between representatives of Episcopal and non-Episcopal Communions upon the Appeal and its possibilities. The suggestion was

[1] For the relevant documents of the Joint Conference see Bell, *Documents on Christian Unity* (1920–30).

welcomed by the Federal Council. The Baptists, the Presbyterians, the Methodists, the Congregationalists, and the Moravians, expressed their sympathy with the general spirit of the Appeal at their annual assemblies. But more information was required before a further advance could be made. Accordingly the Federal Council, with the approval of the different Free Churches, appointed twenty-five leading Free Churchmen with a view to conferring with the two Archbishops and with other members of the Church of England whom they might appoint. So on November 30, 1921, these Free Church delegates came to Lambeth to confer on the Appeal with the two Archbishops and nine diocesan bishops, their purpose being not to negotiate but to explore. A tenth Bishop and two priests were added later.

More than three hundred years had passed since the first Nonconformists had broken away from the Church of England. The causes of each separation from that Church were very mixed, partly political and social as well as religious. And it was not to be expected that they could be swiftly removed. Certainly Archbishop Davidson himself was under no illusion in that matter. A very real peril lay, he said, in overspeed. Yet none was more convinced than he of the necessity of making a beginning. The Appeal was the ground for such a beginning, and systematic conference between Bishops and Free Churchmen was beyond doubt an admirable way of making the start. The holding, therefore, of the Joint Conferences which began in 1921 and were suspended in 1925 after twenty-two meetings, was a very important event in the history of Christianity in England. And although groups of interested theologians had met for such discussion at intervals before, in an informal way, this was an altogether new event, the like of which had not been seen since the break-down of the Savoy Conference of twelve Bishops and twelve Presbyterians in 1661, which was followed the next year by the ejection of at least twelve hundred (traditionally two thousand) Puritan clergy as a result of the passing of the Act of Uniformity. Nor was its significance diminished by the Archbishop's declaration, when the Joint Conferences began, that he would strive for the movement now commenced so long as the breath was in his body.

The main work of the Joint Conferences was done in a Sub-Committee of which the Archbishop of York was Chairman. It was carefully composed so as to represent on the Anglican side the different schools within the Church of England, and on the Free Church side the strong Church principles of the Presbyterian Church, the Baptists' and Congregationalists' distrust of Creeds and dislike of ecclesiasticism, the Methodists with their traditional feeling for order and their use of Lay Evangelists. The Free Church members were also at one in their dislike of sacerdotalism and establishment. The outstanding personality all through was the Archbishop of York, whose conciliatory spirit came as a surprise to some who had supposed him to be the most rigid of orthodox ecclesiastics; while on the Free Church side the main part was taken by Dr. P. Carnegie Simpson (Presbyterian), Dr. Scott Lidgett (Wesleyan), and Dr. Garvie (Congregationalist). Archbishop Davidson all through was a sympathetic observer, attending the sub-committees occasionally, but leaving the general direction to his brother of York.

II

At the very first session, November 30, 1921, after a striking tribute to the generous spirit of the Lambeth Appeal, the two points emerged for which Free Churchmen contended all through as of chief importance: (1) the claim that the non-episcopal communions to which the delegates belonged should be recognized as 'Churches' and as themselves corporate parts of the Church of Christ; (2) the refusal of the Free Church ministers to submit to 're-Ordination'. But there also emerged the outstanding points by which the Bishops held: (1) the need of organic unity on the basis of episcopacy; (2) the impossibility of acquiescing in the continuation of 'Churches' as independent organized bodies, out of communion with one another within the Catholic Church; and (3) the necessity of making distinctions between 'existing Churches' as to their Church standing, i.e. according to their acceptance or not of certain postulates, the community of faith, Sacrament, order, which were of the first importance.

It was therefore resolved that the first thing for the Joint Conference to do was to draw up Points of Agreement and on that basis tackle the issues on which they were opposed. The result was remarkable. At the end of a year, a Report was adopted consisting of three parts with eight or ten brief propositions each, and dealing with the nature of the Church, the Ministry, and the place of the Creed in a united Church. The agreement was surprising, and it was recognized far and wide that the principles to which Free Church leaders in common with the Bishops had set their signatures represented a great advance on anything hitherto conceived as likely to be jointly accepted in respect of the three fundamental subjects. But the proposals on which most interest was focused related to the Ministry. The Joint Conference accepted the episcopate (without implying the acceptance of any particular theory as to its origin or character) 'for the united Church of the future' as the means of giving the authority of the whole body to its ministers; and 'similarly'—a great stress was laid by the Free Churchmen on this word, placed at the beginning of the crucial proposition:

> Similarly, in view of the place which the Council of Presbyters and the Congregation of the faithful had in the constitution of the early Church, and the preservation of these elements of presbyteral and congregational order in large sections of Christendom, we agree that they should be maintained with a representative and constitutional Episcopate as permanent elements in the order and life of the United Church.

The successful association of the very things for which Presbyterians and Congregationalists stood with Episcopacy, was important. Some of the members of the Federal Council on receiving the Report were certainly doubtful about some of its features, and when the Council met there was a motion to let the whole thing lie on the table. But this point, and the harmonious character of the proceedings thus far, secured a mandate to continue the conversations. At the same time certain questions were set out by the Federal Council to which a reply was sought. It was also urged that discussion should be accompanied by acts of unity between the Churches in Conference.

III

So far, however, the discussion had been theoretical in character. It was concerned with the Church and its ministry, especially from the point of view of the Church of the future. The Report laid out a number of postulates which were capable of inclusion in a Constitution for uniting Communions. Amongst other things, that Constitution would provide for a definite place for the Council of Presbyters and the Congregation of the laity, as well as episcopal ordination for all new ministers. But there was a vital practical problem which also raised questions of principle. What was to be the place of the Presbyterian, Wesleyan, Congregationalist, and other ministers who had not been episcopally ordained, after the date of union, in the united Church? The period in view was, it is true, a transitional period, but there would be thousands of ministers affected. What was to happen to them? Would they officiate in the new united Church without further ceremony? Would they receive an additional commission? Or would they be ordained, or 're-ordained'? That was the practical problem, and the character of the answer depended in part at least on the view taken of non-episcopal ministers as such. So the Bishops were asked to expound their view of the status of the existing Free Church Ministry.

Had the Archbishop of Canterbury been asked to give the answer by himself alone, it is doubtful whether he would have replied in any very categorical form. A story is told by Dr. Berry,[1] Secretary of the Congregational Union, that he once asked His Grace, 'Do you not think that union is coming along the lines rather of mutual recognition than of re-ordination?' The Archbishop had replied, turning to him with a look he would never forget, 'Berry, I am an old man, and old men do not prophesy!' The actual answer finally given by the Anglican representatives and accepted by Archbishop Davidson was framed by the Archbishop of York. It made an admission which was warmly welcomed by Free Churchmen, but it did not cover the whole ground. In the process of reaching that answer a good many difficulties had to be overcome, and there were moments of acute strain when it looked as though a complete impasse had been reached. The old and the new Bishops of Gloucester, for example, took almost opposite lines. Dr. Gibson (the old) was emphatic for episcopal ordination for all ministers officiating fully in the United Church. Dr. Headlam (the new) wished for mutual

[1] Dr. S. M. Berry was at the time minister of Carr's Lane Church, Birmingham. Bishop Hamilton Baynes, then at the Cathedral Church, discussed with him the possibility of union between the Church of England and the Free Churches 'on the basis of their ministries being mutually recommissioned or reordained'. And a particular project was put forward by Bishop Baynes for his own recommissioning for service in Carr's Lane Church, and the recommissioning or reordination of Dr. Berry for any service in the Cathedral. The matter was referred to Archbishop Davidson, who said he did not think that union was coming in that way.

recognition of ministers and Sacraments but with the proviso that only episcopally ordained ministers should officiate in Churches accustomed to an episcopal ministry. Against this some of the Anglicans suggested that a solution might be found if it could be agreed that ministers episcopally ordained were 'Priests' while non-episcopal ministers were 'Prophets'—a suggestion that was rejected with decision by the Free Churchmen. On the other hand, it was agreed that only those ministers who were ordained to a ministry that was Christ's, i.e. universal, not sectional, and for lifelong service and in a regular way for a regular purpose, need be considered for the present discussion.

IV

In the end the crucial statement was first verbally made by the Archbishop of York, on April 25, 1923:

> We must regard these ministries as ministries of Christ's Word and Sacraments within the Universal Church of Christ which is His Body.

This statement was welcomed with profound appreciation by Dr. Carnegie Simpson and Dr. Scott Lidgett. Subsequently, after not a few struggles behind the scenes in which Archbishop Davidson effectively influenced the minority of Dr. Gibson and Dr. Chase, it was embodied in the following form in the Report to the Federal Council:

> We consider that we are entitled, by manifest tokens of Divine blessing which these ministries possess, and also by the spirit and the terms of the Lambeth Appeal about them, to go further, and to say that we regard them as being within their several spheres real ministries in the Universal Church.

The acknowledgement was rightly felt to go a definite step beyond the words of the Lambeth Appeal. That had spoken of 'the spiritual reality of non-episcopal ministries' and owned them as effective means of Grace, but now the Archbishops and ten Bishops declared:

> It seems to us to be in accordance with the Lambeth Appeal to say, as we are prepared to say, that the ministries which we have in view in this memorandum, ministries which imply a sincere intention to preach Christ's Word and administer the Sacraments as Christ has ordained, and to which authority so to do has been solemnly given by the Church concerned, are real ministries of Christ's Word and Sacraments in the Universal Church.

The memorandum containing the acknowledgement made a profound impression on the Free Church members, and as one of them said (Dr. A. S. Peake): 'I cannot see how the Anglicans can go further'; while Dr. Simpson, speaking in 1926 to the General Assembly of the Presbyterian Church of England, described it as 'the most notable thing which Lambeth has said to any non-episcopal Church since the time of, say, Bancroft or Laud'. The admission was confessedly great, but at the very moment he made it, April 25, 1923, the Archbishop of York had added that the question how these different ministries were to be admitted in the united Church was another matter. And the memorandum on the status of the existing Free Church Ministry also made it perfectly plain that ministries, even when regarded as real, may be in varying degrees irregular or defective, and that the Anglican Church must require episcopal Ordination for the Ministers of its congregations.

V

The Federal Council further, while welcoming the crucial declaration, quoted above, expressed its regret that the Bishops still required, in the case of Free Church ministers desiring to exercise a full ministry within the Anglican Church, the same plan as that followed in the case of persons claiming no kind of ministry, viz. Episcopal Ordination. The vital question had therefore now to be faced: Must all existing Free Church Ministers be Episcopally Ordained if they are to become full Ministers of the United Church? The reply took a couple of years to make. It may be summarized thus.

The question is not one of spiritual efficacy—that is conceded to the non-Episcopal ministers—but of due authority. Episcopal Ordination is the means of bestowing the authority of the whole body to the Ministry, and the Anglican Church has a special trust with regard to it. The Free Church delegates have accepted the principle for all future ministers. To the question whether there would be any way of modifying the application of that principle in the case of existing ministers, the Bishops very tentatively made two suggestions:

(1) They suggested in lieu of Ordination a solemn authorization by the laying-on-of-hands by a Bishop, with the invocation of the Holy Spirit in some such form as this: 'Take thou Authority,

now committed unto thee by the Imposition of our hands, for the Office and work of a Priest (or presbyter). And be thou a faithful Dispenser of the Word of God, and of his holy Sacraments; In the Name of the Father, and of the Son, and of the Holy Ghost. Amen.' But they made this suggestion with hesitation on account of the ambiguity lurking within it. Was it in fact a conferring of order or only of jurisdiction? And they made it plain that while they did not rule this method out they preferred:

(2) The plan of Ordination *sub conditione*. According to this method Episcopal Ordination would be given to all such Ministers, but the act of such Ordination would be prefaced by such words as 'If thou art not already Ordained'—expressing the fact that a doubt did exist on one side, and by Ordaining the Minister 'if not already Ordained', removing that doubt from the Ordainer's mind while not committing the person conditionally Ordained to accepting that doubt.

VI

Here the conversations stayed.[1] The proposal of Ordination *sub conditione* was condemned by the Federal Council as unconvincing and unpromising, and both the Bishops and the Free Churchmen felt that for the moment it was impossible to get further. By common consent therefore the deliberations were suspended in order that full opportunity might be given to the Churches concerned to try and understand the issues at stake, and the agreement as well as the disagreement which had been revealed. The Annual Assemblies of the Churches themselves, on the suspension of the Conferences, took much the same line as the Federal Council; and some of them definitely emphasized their opposition to any form of re-Ordination or Ordination. Only one Church dismissed the whole proposal contained in the Appeal. This was the Baptist Union, which in 1926 stated positively that 'union of such a kind as the Bishops have contemplated is not possible for us'.

There were many who were disappointed that a pause had to be made. Not so the Archbishop. He knew the need of deliberation and of the education of the rank and file. He also knew the gains that had been made. The leaders of the Churches had got

[1] The Lambeth Conference 1930 led to further joint conferences, still proceeding (1938).

to know one another and understand their respective points of view. Through their being brought together at Lambeth, in social intercourse, in study, and in worship in the Chapel, on so many occasions, a spirit of amity had grown, a spirit all important to the progress of Christian unity; and besides this, a quite unexpected amount of agreement was reached on the fundamental doctrines of the Faith. It was to this friendship, and to the working out of this agreement, that Archbishop Davidson made so signal a contribution himself that it is no exaggeration to say that no Archbishop has ever been so respected and revered by the whole Nonconformist world. For in truth no Archbishop of Canterbury had the opportunity to do so much as he, but none having such an opportunity could have used it to greater effect.

VII

A remarkable instance of Dr. Davidson's personal interest in Reunion with the Free Churches, was his visit to the Conference of the Wesleyan Methodists at Bristol, on July 21, 1923. The connexion between the Church of England and the Methodists was closer than that with any other of the Free Churches, and their reception of the Lambeth Appeal had been more than usually cordial. Besides which, the Archbishop had some very good friends among the Methodist leaders, notably the Rev. J. Scott Lidgett, D.D., Warden of Bermondsey Settlement, and the Rt Hon. Walter Runciman. When he entered the Hall, the Conference received him upstanding, and the President (the Rev. T. Ferrier Hulme) in a happy address spoke of the occasion as the first in the whole series of 180 Annual Conferences at which the successors of St. Augustine and Wesley had stood side by side. The Archbishop delivered his address, reading it, very quietly and impressively, to a most attentive audience who were pleased that he did not play down to them in any way. His subject was Christian Reunion, and he reminded them of how they, as Christian ministers and Christian laymen, were 'just now standing together at a juncture in human history, so vast in its import, so measureless in its possibilities'. And after describing the work of the English theologians in the nineteenth century, stirred by the publication of Darwin's *Origin of Species*, he spoke of the sheer necessity that they should draw together and stay together now as 'joint inheritors of what has been wrought and taught for 200 years since John Wesley took his place in the ranks of the Church's ministry'. He did not discuss the details of how a new comradeship among Christians could come about—or its range or its credentials: he only pressed its necessity. And in another informal speech a little later in the day, he quoted the advice of a Scotch uncle that 'if you want your roads to last they must be made slowly'. There were many comments in the press, and one of the most interesting was that made by Mr. Arthur Porritt, the Editor of the *Christian World*, in an American journal:

> The Archbishop's speech delighted the Conference. One might almost say that Dr. Randall Davidson is the first Archbishop of Canterbury for whom the English Nonconformists have a real affection. . . . It can assuredly be said that more Nonconformists have found a welcome at Lambeth Palace in the last twenty years than in the preceding two hundred years. . . . Not tolerance but good will has been ushered into ecclesiastical relationships during Dr. Davidson's régime at Canterbury. (*The Congregationalist*, U.S.A., August 30, 1923.)

In May 1928 the Archbishop paid a similar visit to the General Assembly of the Presbyterian Church of England, the Moderator of which that year was Dr. Carnegie Simpson. In his reply to the Moderator's welcome, he spoke of his 'eager desire to recognize, both publicly and privately, how comparatively transitory are the feuds which, in earlier days, used to sunder the branches of the Church of Christ in this country, and how eternal and unbreakable are the bonds which unite us when viewed in the light of God's revelation in history, and as before the judgement of the higher world'.

THE ARCHBISHOP and MRS. DAVIDSON
(1920)

CHAPTER LXXI
RELIGION AND THE SCHOOLS

On the plausible . . . pretext of the multitude and variety of religions, and for the suppression of bigotry and negative persecution, national education is to be finally sundered from all religion, but speedily and decisively emancipated from the superintendence of the national clergy. Education is to be reformed, and defined as synonymous with instruction.

S. T. COLERIDGE, *On the Constitution of Church and State*, ch. vii.

AMONG the many fields in which the moderating influence of Archbishop Davidson was at work in the years after the War was that of the religious question in the schools. The whole situation had changed since the days of Mr. Birrell's Education Bill. There was a far more cordial feeling between the representatives of the different Churches, and this grew still stronger in the course of the conversations on Christian Unity which followed the Appeal to All Christian People issued by the Lambeth Conference of 1920. And besides this, there was an increasing sense of the widespread ignorance of the Christian religion among the younger generation, as revealed in the evidence from the Army. Various informal conferences took place at Lambeth Palace and elsewhere, in which the different interests were represented. But the outstanding contribution was made in what came to be known as the Fisher Proposals. It is to them and their sequel that we will therefore turn.

I

The Education Act of 1918 left the religious difficulty untouched, but not therefore forgotten. Mr. H. A. L. Fisher, the Minister responsible for the Act, was one of those most anxious to solve it. He therefore wrote to invite the Archbishop of Canterbury, on one side, and Dr. Scott Lidgett representing the Free Churches, each to nominate six persons who could take part in a conference at the Board of Education under his presidency. In the course of his letter he said:

The RT. HON. H. A. L. FISHER *to the* ARCHBISHOP OF CANTERBURY

19th June, 1919.

I am aware that discussions have taken place between representatives of different parties with a great deal of friendly feeling and a sincere desire to meet difficulties, and though those discussions have not led to any definite conclusions, it has been suggested to me that I might render good service to the cause of national education by intervening at this juncture.

I have a most earnest desire to contribute, if I possibly can, to the solution of the denominational problem in English education; and I feel that until that problem is solved the public system of education will be embarrassed and will not attain that full and harmonious development which the Education Act of 1918 was designed to promote. I am quite aware that my intervention, even in the most modest form, involves certain risks and may give rise to misunderstanding, and if it is not successful may possibly check that approximation between the two sides which appears to me so hopeful. I feel, however, that I should be failing in my duty if I did not take those risks. . . .

The Archbishop replied:

The ARCHBISHOP OF CANTERBURY *to the* RT. HON. H. A. L. FISHER

21st June, 1919.

I thank you for your important letter of June 19th, suggesting a private conference at the Education Office under your presidency, to be attended by six Churchmen and six Nonconformists. The difficulties of the subject are very great, and anticipations of a ready solution of the questions at issue may be doomed to disappointment. But I am quite sure that the effort ought to be made, and I welcome your kind proposal. . . .

The promotion of such a Conference, though private, was recognized to be of first-rate importance. Indeed, it was a new thing in educational procedure, and it made a special appeal to the Archbishop because he felt that much the best hope of settling a controversy, with such a history behind it, lay precisely in independent action by the President of the Board, who could bring the parties together and persuade them to agree.

The first meeting was held on July 31, 1919. It was attended by stalwarts from the old debates, like the Bishop of Manchester[1] and Dr. Clifford, and also included Dr. Scott Lidgett, Dr. Selbie, Mr. Holland, and Mr. Riley. There were no Roman Catholics, and the Archbishop noted their absence with regret. Mr. Fisher expressed the desire that the Conference should tackle

[1] Dr. E. A. Knox.

at once the two very difficult questions of the new Central Schools and the Single School Area. The Archbishop, however, urged that before getting down to these details it was vital to see where all stood on the larger and more fundamental questions. As these fundamentals determined the general policy of the Church in later discussions in other assemblies, it is well to give them in the exact formula adopted on this occasion by the Archbishop:

> I would say the fundamentals of our position are these: we regard religious teaching as an essential element in right education; next we regard it as essential that that religious teaching, if it is to be worth having, should be given by competent men, and given genuinely by men who do it both because they are properly qualified and because they can do it conscientiously. Thirdly it is in our view almost axiomatic that if religious teaching is to be effective it cannot rest content with indefiniteness, but must have some specific statement of doctrine, especially as the children grow a little older.

The Archbishop's contention was accepted, and the Conference generally determined to see—and in the course of five meetings did see—what could be done to move towards a national system in which those three essential principles were secured. In the end a general agreement was reached on proposals for a national system of education which did in fact conserve all three of the Archbishop's conditions. These proposals involved the ending of the existing dual system[1] and the placing of the appointment and dismissal of all teachers in the hands of the local education authorities. But they also included statutory provision for

[1] 'The dual system as we have it under the present Education Law has two primary bases, which involve fundamental differences of outlook. These fundamental differences are expressed in certain sections of the Consolidated Education Act, 1921, which give respectively the rules for the conduct of provided and non-provided schools. Put shortly, the position is this: In the provided schools religious instruction is not an essential. To a greater or less extent it may, or may not, form part of the school course. To a greater or less extent it may be looked after or neglected. In the non-provided schools, on the other hand, religious instruction is an integral and necessary part of the school curriculum. The only *positive* and binding statutory provision made by the Education Acts with respect to religious instruction or observance in elementary schools is that which requires, as one of the conditions of annual grants, that the religious instruction in voluntary schools shall be in accordance with the provisions of the School Trust Deeds.' (From a *Memorandum on the Problem of the Abolition of Dual Control in Elementary Education*, issued on the joint authority of the Education Committee of the National Assembly of the Church of England and the Standing Committee of the National Society, Oct. 5, 1922.)

religious instruction in all elementary schools, which instruction might be, as in Scotland, either denominational or general. They included also a condition that the teachers giving that instruction must be suitable from the point of view both of sincerity and competence to give it, and willing, thus involving a provision of adequate facilities in the Training College system for making teachers competent. It was recognized that some schools would prefer to stand out of the national system under whatever conditions, but the Archbishop insisted that all denominations should be dealt with alike in this, and that the Roman Catholics, for example, should not have preferential treatment. Unfortunately, before the last session was concluded, Dr. Clifford had withdrawn, as he could not support denominational instruction in a Council School, and the Roman Catholics, who had been separately consulted, refused their approval on the ground, apparently, that the definite instruction given by Roman Catholic teachers in Roman Catholic schools could not be exchanged for such precarious arrangements as local authorities might be willing to provide or sanction, and that the proposed control of religious instruction was inadequate and illusory.

The Archbishop felt that he had gone a long way himself, but was prepared to stand by the proposals, and urged their publication. He wrote (February 18, 1920):

The ARCHBISHOP OF CANTERBURY *to the* RT. HON. H. A. L. FISHER

Of course arguments in favour of delaying publication are quite easy on the part of those who have conferences to hold publicly or privately, and who are a little timid about the way their old followers may view their action. No one has more reason to apprehend criticism in this matter than I have. . . . I knew, when I consented to come with my friends to your Council Room, that I had irrevocably committed myself to a strong line of action. You would be the last man to place me in the position of having to confess failure and lie open to the charge of having bungled the whole matter. You have, in what you have said, shewn that you appreciate the length to which we Churchmen *have now committed ourselves*, and, of course, we have done this simply on the basis of the Memorandum being published *as the proposal of the President of the Board of Education*, after such communications as he thought right with parties chiefly concerned. . . .

Accordingly Mr. Fisher published the proposals in outline, in a speech at the Kingsway Hall, March 27, 1920, intended for L.C.C. teachers, but as the L.C.C. teachers refused to listen, owing to a quarrel on an entirely different matter, the speech had to be circulated to the Press. In the course of his speech Mr. Fisher expressed his belief that 'a purely secular system of instruction in public Elementary Schools would not, at present at all events, be in accordance with the national wishes, and that the broadest way of dealing with the problem which has suggested itself to me is to put denominational and undenominational religious instruction on an equal footing in the public system of elementary education'; and he set out the following four principles of an agreed settlement, which he would be prepared, if there were such general agreement, to submit for the consideration of the Government:

(1) That the appointment, promotion, and dismissal of all teachers in public elementary schools should be in the hands of the local education authority, and that no teacher in an ordinary public elementary school should be obliged to give religious instruction unless specially appointed for that purpose only, or be in a better or worse position by reason of giving or not giving religious instruction.

(2) That the local education authority should have the free use of the premises of existing non-provided schools for any educational purpose for which they are competent to provide, and that the local education authority should be under the obligation to maintain the premises and have the right to alter them for school purposes.

(3) That the local education authority should be under an obligation to make adequate provision in all public elementary schools for religious observance and instruction, differentiated so far as practicable in relation to religious tenets, to be given in school hours by teachers suitable and willing to give it, subject to a conscience clause and provision for withdrawal for religious observance or instruction elsewhere.

(4) That no privilege of 'standing out' of the system should be conceded to one denomination which is not open to other denominations.

The proposals were widely discussed at the time. On the whole they were welcomed by Churchmen, and they had the advantage of warning Churchmen against the danger of their putting forward schemes for local agreement of a much less satisfactory character. The National Society, at its Annual Meeting in June 1920, unanimously passed a favourable resolution. Nonconformists were divided, but the old war-cries were sounded somewhat ominously by Dr. Clifford and a few others. To the teachers, the idea of a national service, which the Fisher proposals with regard to appointment and 'no tests for teachers' involved, was naturally attractive. But the Government were unwilling to embark upon anything in the nature of controversial legislation; and this was sufficient to prevent any new Government Measure.

II

In the following year, a Private Member's Bill embodying the Fisher proposals was introduced into the House of Commons by Mr. Thomas Davies, M.P., and in addition two other schemes were published known as 'the Welsh Scheme'[1] and the Leslie Scheme,[2] which were much less satisfactory than Mr. Fisher's proposals on the side of denominational instruction. There was also an important move made on behalf of the Congregational Union, for a conference 'for the purpose of considering how the present dual system of elementary schools may be modified so as to secure economy, efficiency, and religious equality in elementary education, and an equitable system for the promotion of teachers'. The Archbishop of Canterbury, with the unanimous approval of the National Society's Consultative Committee, accepted the Congregational Union's invitation, and at a preliminary meeting, on December 9, 1921, between the parties to the Conference, laid down three essential principles as regards religious instruction. These principles were adopted by the meeting, and the reference to the Conference then became the following:

> To consider how the present dual system of elementary schools may be modified so as to secure economy, efficiency, and religious equality in elementary education and an equitable system for the promotion of teachers, with observance of the three following principles:—
>
> (1) That in all schools supported or subsidised by the State

[1] Formulated by a Joint Committee of thirty-three representatives appointed by the Governing Body of the Church in Wales and by the Council of Evangelical Churches in Wales.

[2] Formulated by Mr. Alderman Leslie of Liverpool.

religious instruction should form an integral part of the education given, and that religious observance and instruction should have a place in the regular curriculum, and be available, subject to conscience clause, for all children. The proper authority should be in a position to ascertain from time to time that such instruction is regularly and efficiently given.

(2) That religious teaching, if it is to be worth having, must be given by men and women who are qualified to give it and can give it conscientiously.

(3) That religious teaching must not be of a vague or indefinite character, but must mean for Christian children the definite teaching of the elements of the Christian Faith.

In explaining the situation to the National Assembly, the following February (February 9, 1922), the Archbishop stated why he pressed these three principles so firmly:

> I did not find anybody in that room who said that they doubted any one of those three principles: the need of religion as part of education; the need that the instruction shall be given genuinely and competently if it is given at all; and that it shall not be a vague or windy or washy thing, but that it shall be the grounding of children in the elements of the Christian faith. Of course, each of these principles leads off into a great many questions upon which those who talk of this matter always want to dwell. I want to get back to those three principles, and to ask those who want to get a unified system applied throughout England at the expense of the sacrifice, as many would regard it, of our present Church Schools, whether they are prepared to stand by those three principles? If not, which of them do they challenge? Do they challenge the need of religion? Do they challenge the principle that it must be given genuinely and competently? Do they challenge what we mean by it—namely, the grounding of the children in the elements of the Christian faith? Then, having got those principles, I would throw upon others, rather than only on ourselves, the responsibility of formulating a way of getting out of the difficulty, if our way of trying to get out of it is not regarded as quite meeting the case. That, I am quite sure, is the right method of doing it.

The Conference, however—known as the Memorial Hall Conference—failed to reach agreement. Three different schemes were presented. The Anglicans presented their scheme, on the authority of the Education Committee of the National Assembly, and of the Standing Committee of the National Society; a scheme in which 'the Church of England has thus officially proclaimed its readiness to accept a settlement on the lines of Mr. Fisher's proposals'. But the Anglican scheme was rejected by the other members of a special sub-committee who produced majority and minority proposals of their own, generally based on the Welsh concordat; a scheme which implicitly recognized the existence of a demand for instruction in the principles of particular denominations, but in practice limited the satisfaction of any such demand to those neighbourhoods where voluntary schools happened to exist, and to those particular school buildings which were owned by the various denominational bodies.

III

So far—with the warm encouragement of the Archbishop—the educational spokesmen in the Church of England had been steady in their desire to negotiate with the representatives of the Free Churches, and the teachers, and the local educational authorities, for securing by agreement a single national organization of elementary schools in the place of the present dual arrangement of 'provided' and 'non-provided' schools. But once again the hope of agreement was dashed to the ground by the action of these same stalwart champions of the dual system who, the Archbishop felt, were so blindly devoted to the maintenance of Church schools at all costs as to forget that the majority of the total number of children attend Council schools, and that it is an increasing majority—and to fail to notice the danger, as he put it more than once, of 'drifting into secular education by a side wind'.

At the Annual Meeting of the National Society on May 30, 1923, the Archbishop made a full speech. He had the satisfaction of hearing the case for which he contended put by a strong High Churchman, Sir Frederick Holiday, who moved the official Resolution, in the following words:

> As I look back over the fifty-three years since the Education Act of 1870, during the whole of which period I have been closely and intimately associated with every phase of the subject, two questions are constantly coming into my mind.
>
> The first question is: Will it have to be said that in this matter the Church of England knew not the time of her visitation?

> As each crisis arose and passed in 1896, 1902, 1906, 1918, and 1920 without any settlement of the religious question, the Church schools have drifted on, receiving from time to time additional help from public funds to which they were fully entitled, but fewer in number and weaker *qua* Church schools.
>
> And the second question is: Will an exclusive consideration for these schools, without any due regard for the needs of the millions of children who are outside them, bring upon them the judgment: 'He that will save his life shall lose it'?

The Resolution, of which full notice had been given, was immediately moved, reaffirming the National Society's adhesion to the three essential principles laid down by the Archbishop in December 1921, and expressing its willingness to consider any proposals designed to carry those principles into effect. But then came an amendment which, as it was put afterwards, torpedoed the official policy. No notice had been given. The Archbishop himself knew nothing of it until he came into the room. It was moved by Prebendary Thicknesse, and ran as follows:

> That the National Society considers that it is urgently necessary that the authorities of the Church should be respectfully invited to abandon the policy of negotiation for the surrender of Church schools, and to aid the Society by putting forth a strong appeal to all Church people to maintain Church schools and training colleges in a condition of the greatest possible efficiency, while pressing for the definite teaching of the elements of the Christian faith to Christian children in all schools.

Whatever may be thought of the wisdom of the policy advocated, its phraseology was manifestly objectionable. But to the Archbishop's keen disappointment it was carried by 47 votes to 37.

So ended another chapter in the story of religion and the schools.

CHAPTER LXXII

TOWARDS DOCTRINAL AGREEMENT

In my youth I was quickly past my fundamentals, and was running up into a multitude of controversies, and greatly delighted with metaphysical and scholastic writings . . . but the older I grew the smaller stress I laid upon these controversies and curiosities (though still my intellect abhorreth confusion) as finding far greater uncertainties in them than I at first discerned, and finding less usefulness comparatively, even where there is the greatest certainty. And now it is the fundamental doctrines of the catechism, which I highliest value, and daily think of, and find most useful to myself and others. RICHARD BAXTER, *Reliquiae Baxterianae*.

ONE of the most important questions before the Church during Dr. Davidson's primacy was the question of unity in belief. There were many points of doctrine on which members of the Church of England were sharply divided. There was also a considerable controversy, more vehement at some times than at others, regarding the essentials of the Christian faith. The disputes between Anglo-Catholics and Evangelicals were hardly edifying. But the conflict, often bitter, between Modernist and Conservative was of a much more disturbing character. It was bad for the internal life of the Church of England. It was not less harmful for the efforts which the Church of England was making for a *rapprochement* with other Christian communions. Ought not such a Church, it was not unnaturally urged, to take special pains to know its own mind and to be at unity within itself? It is to the initiation of a very serious attempt to face this issue that the present chapter will be devoted.

I

The Archbishop, as we have already made plain in previous pages, was determined to maintain the comprehensiveness of the Church of England in matters relating to the Creeds as well as in other departments of its life. He received many appeals, addressed sometimes to him, sometimes to the Bishops as a body, that he should denounce particular writings or opinions as heretical. On three separate occasions at least, before the War, Declarations or Resolutions dealing with Modernism were in fact authoritatively published. On May 10, 1905, the Upper

House of Canterbury Convocation passed a Resolution reaffirming the Faith presented in the Apostles' and Nicene Creeds. In August 1908, the Lambeth Conference issued two Resolutions on the Faith and Modern Thought, and devoted a considerable passage in the Encyclical Letter of the Bishops to the same theme. On April 29, 1914, in the Upper House of Canterbury Convocation, the two critical Resolutions on Orthodoxy were carried in a form which just secured the agreement from different angles alike of Dr. Davidson and Dr. Gore. And towards the end of the War, in the winter of 1917–18, another fierce controversy had arisen through the nomination of Dr. Henson to the Bishopric of Hereford, which required all the Archbishop's efforts to bring to a happy conclusion.

The Resolutions just cited were in the main reassertions of the essential place of the historic facts stated by the Creeds in the structure of the Church's faith; and the utterances of 1908 and 1914 also recognized the need of considerateness, and of not unduly limiting freedom of thought and inquiry. But here they had stopped—although the Lambeth Conference Encyclical Letter called marked attention to the 'need of a far greater effort on the part of the Church to deal with the intellectual side of religion and life'. Such a persistent Reaffirmation, however, was hardly sufficient for the perplexities of the time. A much more definite and sustained theological effort was demanded.

II

It was here that a new turn of an important kind was given to the controversies so long continued. Archbishop Davidson, though in Church policy a firm opponent of all rigorism, was not himself a theologian. He was deeply interested in history and biography, but hardly in philosophy or doctrine, and it must be admitted that his own failure, as he always regarded it, in the academic field, had tended to make him somewhat shy in his attitude to the universities, and to lead to an unfortunate lack of vital contact between Lambeth on the one side and Oxford and Cambridge on the other, throughout his primacy.

The real initiative towards a sustained endeavour to find a basis of doctrinal agreement came from a group of younger theologians, notably Mr. Will Spens, Fellow (and later Master) of Corpus Christi College, Cambridge, who approached the Bishop of Oxford (Dr. Burge) after the first Anglo-Catholic Congress in 1920. A series of meetings was held, and Dr. Burge and his younger colleagues propounded a scheme for a new Doctrinal Commission to be composed of theological representatives of the Anglo-Catholic and the Liberal and the Evangelical schools, which should undertake a sincere and thorough examination of the teaching of the Church of England, in mutual conference over a considerable period. It was realized from the first that the inquiry would be protracted. But it was hoped that as a result of the long labours, in spite of the difference which existed in important matters, a fundamental agreement might be revealed which would give so clear and convincing an answer to the question 'For what does the Church of England stand?' that the present controversies would be closed, and those in authority could allow scope for differences of practice, teaching, and worship—based on principle—which at present they were thought to allow simply because they felt themselves helpless. And it was essential to the proposal that any such Doctrinal Commission should not be regarded as a mere personal venture on the part of some individuals of different schools of thought to reach a private agreement, but should be authoritatively given a corporate responsibility for reaching a common mind.

Those who urged the appointment of such a commission laid their principal emphasis on the need and importance of an effort for agreement. This rather than later procedure was the dominant interest. But it is hardly too much to say that at the back of the scheme lay a desire for something fresh in the way of exercising authority in matters of faith. It was hoped, certainly by some of its promoters, that the members of the Commission, thus authoritatively appointed, after taking long enough time to enter fully into each other's point of view and so reach a common mind, would express that common mind fully, coherently and explicitly, in the form of a book. When the book appeared, the Bishops might, if they found themselves able, make some kind of pronouncement to the effect that the doctrine therein contained was, in their view, generally agreeable to the word of God and expressive of the general mind of the Church of England, but must not be taken as binding individuals. This body of doctrine would then (it was suggested) stand as a general norm of Anglican teaching, with a general episcopal approval. Appeal could be made to it by all clergy who desired, while it would also serve to check and test the teaching of those clergy who were so fond of individual initiative that they were apt to claim the Church's sanction for what were in fact their private and quite unauthorized views. No one would be silenced or made liable to heresy hunts, but no one would be able to claim the authority of the Church of England for what was opposed and contradictory to this statement of doctrine thus generally agreed and approved.

The proposal thus sketched was first brought to the Archbishop's notice by Dr. Burge, in August 1921. He reported the conversations which had been going on during the previous twelve months; and sent the Archbishop a preliminary draft of the letter which it was proposed to send. This letter expressed the belief that men of all parties were growing weary of disputes, and were anxious to find a basis of agreement with other elements in the English Church. It also stated the conviction of the signatories that an investigation of basic principles by men of all parties would prove that all but a comparatively small number of extremists of each school could eventually reach agreement, both on the essentials of the Christian faith and on the points of controversy which had bitterly divided them in the past. It was, the proposed letter said, becoming increasingly clear that the only adequate safeguard against far more serious disruption lay not in the fact of the Establishment, but in securing genuine unity of belief. It further pleaded that the statement of the Church's faith should be given and received, not as a series of ambiguous formulae, but as a positive statement of faith. The signatories finally asked that a Doctrinal Commission should be appointed and solemnly commended by authority to the prayers of the Church, that it should be allowed ten or twenty years for its labours, and that it should be largely composed of younger men in the Church, of wide sympathies, trusted by their respective parties and representing all parties in the Church of England, however extreme in whatever direction, which were willing to seek a common basis of agreement.

The Archbishop's first reaction was somewhat critical and unwelcoming. He expressed his surprise that the question of Establishment should be regarded as so important an element in the present acceptance of, or pretension to, 'unity, such as it is':

The Archbishop of Canterbury *to the* Bishop of Oxford

September, 1921.

I believe rather that our Church, established or disestablished, has a position and status in the religious thought of the world which is wholly independent of Establishment (witness U.S.A. or S. Africa), and where *differentia* from Rome turns largely upon its comprehensiveness or its realisation of the Vincentian '*in dubiis libertas*' which no doubt means an enlargement—as compared with Rome—of what is meant by '*dubia*'. To Rome and men of the make which Rome encourages and fosters, the '*necessaria*' are more numerous by far than they are with us.

The Archbishop's main objection, if pressed, would have cut at the root of the whole proposal:

Can the task really be entrusted formally, and with the prayers of the whole Church, to a group of men, however fresh in spirit and power and learning, who are to be asked to speak directly or indirectly *ex cathedra*? Dare we give them, whoever they be, such a trust? And would not their utterance really be lacking in the sort of claim to authority which was given rightly or wrongly to Conciliar utterances?

Would it not really be more true to fact and more desirable in itself that they should—like the writers of the Tracts or of *Lux Mundi* or *Foundations*—stand on their own merits as scholars, thinkers, teachers, representative of the faith of to-day, and not be given a rather doubtful and fallacious authority by being called a Commission, or by being started on their task by the prayers (and the ? confidence) of the Church as a whole and the promised *imprimatur* of its official spokesmen?

All this sounds terribly critical and unwelcoming towards your proposal. I do not at all mean it to have a discouraging effect on your mind, for I share your view that such an endeavour as you suggest is both possible and desirable. But I think it should be quite unofficial, and should carry just the weight which legitimately belongs to it, without the adventitious and I think inappropriate and even anachronistic aid of a sort of official *imprimatur*.

If you have by you the Chronicle of Convocation, and would turn to the debates in the Lower House of Canterbury, in or about 1885 or 1886, on the proposed addenda to the Catechism, you would find what was said by men of that day. Gregory and Bright on one side, and Dean Vaughan and his friends, including my humble self, on the other; and it all bears, I think, on your proposal, not as a discouragement of the endeavour, but as criticism of the *modus operandi.*[1]

Bishop Burge replied at some length. He answered the central criticism by pointing out that *Lux Mundi* and *Foundations* were both books compiled by like-minded men, the writers of the former volume, in particular, being fully conscious that they were of one mind, and added:

The Bishop of Oxford *to the* Archbishop of Canterbury

September 24, 1921.

Now the method of approach which this Committee desire is something different: it is not a question with them of a group of 'like-minded' men, interested in investigating the subject of the supposed comprehensiveness of the C. of E., and giving the Church and others the benefit of their investigations: they want to see the Church, through its authorities, deliberately setting itself to decide, in the light of the controversies and criticisms, which distract and dishearten so many of its members, and in the light of its own development, where it now stands—and I think the Committee would say that in this way and this way alone would you be able to make the position and the policy of those in authority, what at present it is *not*, intelligible and consistent and convincing.

III

More correspondence followed, and there were further conferences under the chairmanship of the Bishop of Oxford. But in the meantime a good deal of point had been given to the need of a Doctrinal Commission which should investigate the essentials of the Christian Faith in the way proposed, by a Conference of Modern Churchmen held at Cambridge, in August 1921, the

[1] The debate was in February 1889. Dr. Davidson, as Dean of Windsor, was very fond of showing the difficulties of adding to the Church Catechism by quoting the Questions and Answers describing the Church (especially the Anglican Church) as drawn up in 1833 by 'the advance-guard of High Churchmen'. And he stated that this Catechism was 'almost the only document which received in its details the personal supervision of all' the principal Tractarian leaders.

Q. What do you mean by 'the Church'?

A. The Society belonging to the Lord Christ.

Q. What branches of the Church continue both in the doctrine and the fellowship?

A. Those called Protestant Episcopal in England, Ireland, Scotland.

papers read being subsequently published in *The Modern Churchman*, September 1921. Various statements of a highly controversial character were made at that Conference by leading spokesmen of the Modernist school, Dr. Major, Dr. Rashdall, and others, on the general subject of 'Christ and the Creeds'. These statements led to a violent discussion, in the Press and elsewhere, and Canterbury Convocation was formally approached by the President and Council of the English Church Union (the leading Anglo-Catholic organization), asking for authoritative condemnation of much of the teaching expounded at the Conference, as 'entirely subversive of the Christian Faith and the Christian Religion'. The Archbishop, in reference to the Petition presented by the Bishop of Gloucester (Dr. Gibson) in the Upper House of Canterbury Convocation, February 15, 1922, made a remark which was somewhat resented by the friends of the English Church Union. He said:

> To judge from some of the things which have been said and written, it might be supposed that there was a great phalanx of heresiarchs set in battle array against the doctrine of the Church Catholic, and that we were called upon to rally the Church in defence of the Christian Faith. I am hardly over-stating the kind of, I will not say, phrases but the kind of representations made as to what is now happening. In my belief the whole of that is grossly exaggerated.

The following correspondence passed:

BISHOP GORE *to the* ARCHBISHOP OF CANTERBURY

Private. 6, Margaret St., W. 1. February 17, 22.

I feel constrained to tell you that your speech in Convocation in reference to the E.C.U. petition etc. is to some of us a grievous affliction. I venture to say that this sort of chaff, or apparently light-hearted disparagement of the gravity of the situation tends to drive us wild. It is not a wise way of dealing with us.

I did not sign the petition, because I thought it was perhaps improper for a former member of the House, who might still have been a member if he had willed, to present petitions to it. Also I want to concentrate on the work of presenting the truth independently of authority or ecclesiastical reference. But I feel as if your speech had made it impossible.

I am at a loss to understand what you mean. Has not this Modernist Group in fact shown its hand? You wish to try and persuade me that their position (as Sanday assured us) only touched facts (miracles) and not doctrines. Now it is quite plain that the most fundamental doctrines of the faith of S. Paul and S. John and the Church are being repudiated from somewhat different points of view by Major, Rashdall and others. It appears to me that if under these circumstances the Bishops do not at the least rebuke them by a solemn reaffirmation of the basis on which the Church of England stands and the message which the ministers of the Church are commissioned to deliver, it will have assented to the idea that Major and Rashdall's teaching is legitimate—a 'school of thought' within the Church of England. They *are* heresiarchs, and very fundamentally so, and very formidable. So I think. I don't know what to do. But I think something must be done to make the Bishops alive to the situation. I never felt 'official optimism' so sickening.

THE ARCHBISHOP OF CANTERBURY *to* BISHOP GORE

Private. 18th February 1922.

I thank you cordially for your letter. It always distresses me to find that I have said or done something which afflicts you, and I am afraid the occasions have been a good many. The last thing I wanted to do in this case was to scoff in any way at the uneasiness which is felt, but I do honestly think that the matter has been exaggerated to a degree that you perhaps scarcely realise. I have had letters calling on me to see that these traducers of Our Divine Lord are instantly deprived, and desiring that public meetings should be held for declaring the truth of the Creed, and so on. Of course these are eccentricities, but I genuinely believe that we meet the difficulty best by taking the thing calmly, and, as you know, the Bishop of Gloucester is going to bring it up at the next group of sessions and make some suggestions corresponding probably more or less with what you would be likely to desire. Personally I think the real action we ought to take is exactly the action which you, and others like you, are taking in setting forth the truth in positive form and with the weight of your authority. Your last book is precisely of the sort to which we ought now to call attention, and the fact that it has gone through, as Murray tells me, some fourteen thousand copies (I think I am not mistaken) is really the best assurance that we can have that people are getting the medicine or the food which the conditions of the hour require. I shall be very glad now to get a chance of talking the thing over with you, and you may rely upon it that I am not going to belittle the difficulties of those who are distressed, even though I think their apprehensions are a little out of proportion. I do not know

Mr. Major personally, but it does seem to me that (to put it colloquially) he takes himself a little too seriously, and rather puts on the dress of a leader, which he is not. The testimony to his personal earnestness and devotion and his studious abstention from pressing his views upon those who attend his Lectures is abundant. Headlam's testimony to him is rather remarkable. Does not Headlam, in his article in the *Church Quarterly*, take what you regard as a reasonable view of the situation? But do let us get a talk about it ere long.

In the following May, when the Petition was fully discussed, the Archbishop spoke again in the same sense. His own note of the proceedings runs thus:

The Convocation debates in the first week of May were of the highest importance on the subject of Modernism. In that matter I took, behind the scenes, a leading part. The Resolution passed by Convocation was in itself largely my own work, for the really important part of it was the recognition of the need of free inquiry, and this was wholly due to me.

He made a full speech on May 2, before putting the Resolution, which was carried unanimously as follows:

This House declares its conviction that adhesion to the teaching of the Catholic Church as set forth in the 'Nicene' Creed—and in particular concerning the eternal pre-existence of the Son of God, His true Godhead, and His Incarnation—is essential to the life of the Church, and calls attention to the fact that the Church commissions as its Ministers those only who have solemnly expressed such adhesion.

Further, this House recognises the gain which arises from enquiry, at once fearless and reverent, into the meaning and expression of the Faith, and welcomes every aid which the thoughtful student finds in the results of sound historical and literary criticism, and of modern scientific investigation of the problems of human psychology; and it deprecates the mere blunt denunciation of contributions made by earnest men in their endeavour to bring new light to bear upon these difficult and anxious problems. At the same time it sees a grave and obvious danger in the publication of debateable suggestions as if they were ascertained truths, and emphasises the need of caution in this whole matter, especially on the part of responsible teachers in the Church.

The above Resolution is a further instance of that persistent

Reaffirmation which it was one of the objects of the proposal for a Doctrinal Commission to avoid. But the coincidence of this whole discussion on the Cambridge Conference, with the other discussion on the Doctrinal Commission was probably an assistance to the latter. And it is noteworthy that the Archbishop himself in speaking at the end of the debate and recalling earlier battles and disputes used such sentences as these:

> I believe that the harm which has arisen from some of the controversies in the last 50 years has been largely because of the lack of anything in the nature of mutual conference among the people ranged on particular sides.

and (with reference to a statement by Bishop Samuel Wilberforce):

> When we look back upon that now, do we not see that matters would almost certainly have been dealt with differently, had there been conference and discussion between men who varied in their way of looking at the question, and in their way of presenting it? Does not the quotation of that 'authoritative' utterance, preceded by no Conference, show us the good that may be gained from the sort of discussion that we are considering?

and again:

> One more example. Recall the pathetic divergence between Dr. Liddon and the authors of *Lux Mundi*, especially Dr. Charles Gore. No one can read the extraordinarily touching chapter of the close of Dr. Liddon's life, or refer to two of his final sermons, one on 'The Value of the Old Testament' delivered at Oxford, and one the title of which I forget, preached in St. Paul's Cathedral, without feeling that somehow or other, had the people dealing with the two sides of the question had conference together in the presence of others, the result would have been a gain. Dr. Liddon spoke of Dr. Gore's 'capitulation at the feet of the young Rationalistic Professors'. One cannot help thinking that if there had been conference that sort of thing would never have been said.

IV

The official letter to the Archbishop, suggesting the appointment of a Commission on Christian Doctrine, was presented in January 1922. It was signed by nine Diocesan Bishops, by seventeen clergy, Anglo-Catholic, Evangelical, and Modernist, and by one layman (Mr. Spens).

Memorial to the ARCHBISHOP OF CANTERBURY

January 1922.

Your Grace,

After discussing the subject at a series of Meetings, we desire to suggest to your Grace the appointment of a Commission to endeavour to find a basis of doctrinal agreement on matters which are the subject of controversy between different sections of the Church of England.

It is becoming increasingly clear that the methods of controversy traditional in ecclesiastical matters show no prospect of yielding any fruitful results. They rather tend to perpetuate the existence of hostility and suspicion, and to divert to the sphere of controversy energies which should be devoted to the edification of the faithful and to the conversion of unbelievers both at home and abroad. Moreover, the perpetuation of controversy weakens the loyalty of individuals and their sense of obligation to the Church of which they are members, and it renders the Church as a whole powerless to give her proper witness in the political and social difficulties of the present time. Consequently many men of all parties are growing weary of disputes and are anxious to find a basis of agreement with other elements in the English Church. In view of the great efforts that are being made to secure reunion with other Christian bodies it seems only reasonable that such efforts should find their necessary complement within the Church of England; indeed, reunion with other bodies without a more real unity among ourselves will at best only increase the existing confusion.

We do not disguise from ourselves the possibility that the attempt to find a basis of doctrinal agreement might reveal the existence of differences of so irremovable a character as to render impossible anything but a purely artificial and external unity based on the fact of the Establishment rather than on agreement in belief. There are, indeed, critics of the Church of England who say that, in fact, our differences are fundamental. We believe, however, agreement might be reached both on the essentials of the Christian faith, and on the more important of those points of controversy which have bitterly divided us in the past. We believe that an enquiry animated by nothing but the desire to arrive at the truth would ultimately reveal that the matters on which agreement was impossible were those on which differences of opinion are obviously legitimate and even, within certain limits, desirable. Possibly some few, as the result of such an agreement, might secede voluntarily to other bodies, though our whole purpose is not to promote but to preclude secession. But it is becoming increasingly clear that the only adequate safeguard against far more serious disruption lies not in the fact of the Establishment, but in securing a genuine unity of belief. We are convinced that in spite of her failings the Church of England stands for a certain vital aspect of Christianity, and that it should prove possible for the vast majority of her members to agree upon an unambiguous statement of her doctrines to which they could give general adherence. On the other hand, we desire to make clear that we would wish such a statement to be regarded not as a new test but as an expression of the Church's official teaching.

Whether or no the human mind is capable of attaining absolute truth, we should be disloyal to our faith if we denied that if men sincerely and prayerfully seek truth they will approach nearer to it and therefore to each other. Such a failure of faith would create a dangerous atmosphere of distrust at a time when fundamental doctrines are being brought into question.

Again, it is of almost primary importance to solve the actual pastoral problem which is presented by directly contradictory teaching in different parishes in respect of doctrines which are closely bound up with the devotional life of all Christians. Such contradictions often affect disastrously the religious life of individuals. They constitute also a graver obstacle than is ordinarily recognized to the evangelization of the nation.

People differ on particular questions because they differ as to the grounds of belief; it is through re-examination of these grounds that differences will be reconciled and agreement will be reached. Such re-examination appears to us also to be required for this other reason: our apologetic as well as our doctrinal teaching is inconsistent, and is therefore far less effective than it ought to be. We are now face to face with serious tendencies of modern thought and teaching which assail not only Christian doctrine but also Christian morality. Our apologetic therefore needs to be consistent and convincing.

We believe that a sincere attempt to surmount our differences will be fruitful of much good; that it might secure a substantial unity of doctrine in matters of importance, while neither imposing a cut-and-dried system nor creating new tests, nor ignoring the fact that different temperaments need different methods of devotion. We urge therefore that a commission should be appointed for this purpose.

At the same time, we are convinced that certain conditions are, humanly speaking, essential if any good result is to be attained by such a step; and we have in mind especially three suggestions which appear to us so important that we venture to put them before your Grace. In the first place, the work should be undertaken with a very great sense of responsibility and should be solemnly commended by authority to the prayers of the Church. Secondly, it should be recognized from the first that any such commission can only adequately achieve its purpose by systematic work extending over a long period: in short, that the work should be regarded as no less onerous and no less important than, for example, the production of the R.V. of the New Testament. On the other hand, we think it would be essential that an interim report should be presented in a year or two, in order that the committee should not be continued unless a substantial measure of success seemed likely to be secured.

We believe also that the choice of men to serve on the Commission should be determined mainly by four considerations:

(i) They must be thoroughly representative of all those parties in the Church, however extreme in whatever direction, which are willing to seek a basis of agreement.

(ii) They must be men of wide sympathies and tolerant temper, who will be able and anxious to understand each other's position.

(iii) They must be men of constructive minds. Men may have all the qualities mentioned above and yet lack the imaginative power to create a synthesis.

(iv) In order that continuity of work and thought may be secured, a large proportion of them should be comparatively young men, say under forty-five.

We desire to be always,

Your Grace's obedient and faithful servants,

H. M. Oxon:	M. E. Atlay.	O. Quick.
G. Bristol.	G. H. Clayton.	C. E. Raven.
J. E. Chelmsford.	A. S. Duncan-Jones.	T. G. Rogers.
H. L. Chester.	M. G. Glazebrook.	E. G. Selwyn.
M. L. Hereford.	H. L. Goudge.	C. J. Shebbeare.
J. Lichfield.	A. W. Greenup.	W. Spens.
W. Manchester.	G. F. Irwin.	L. S. Thornton.
T. Petriburg:	W. Knox.	F. Underhill.
M. St. Alban:	J. K. Mozley.	H. A. Wilson

The Archbishop, after consulting some of the Bishops and others, replied with friendliness but also with caution. He asked for more particulars, and was unwilling to give a *carte blanche*. Above all, any statement which such a Commission might produce must not be a new test of orthodoxy, as another Thirty-nine Articles:

The Archbishop of Canterbury *to the* Bishop of Oxford

15th February, 1922.

I do not see my way to doing exactly what your letter asks. I am profoundly conscious of the truth of your contention as to the confusion, the harmfulness, and the probable needlessness of a great deal of present-day controversy within the Church. The second paragraph of your letter has my full concurrence. I believe accordingly that endeavours may usefully be made to obtain by conferences 'a basis of doctrinal agreement on matters which are the subject of controversy between different sections of the Church of England'.

My difficulty arises when you go on to advocate the procedure which, in your judgement, might now be usefully adopted. You ask me to appoint a Commission consisting in large proportion of comparatively young men, 'thoroughly representative of all those parties in the Church, however extreme in whatever direction, which are willing to seek a basis of agreement', in order that, with a view to 'securing a genuine unity of belief', they may draw up 'an unambiguous statement of the doctrines [of the Church of England] to which they could give general adherence'; this statement 'to be regarded . . . as an expression of the Church's official teaching'.

The gravity and far-reaching character of this proposal are such as to make me wonder whether it does not say more than you actually mean. If it were laid upon me to appoint with such instruction or 'reference' a Commission to be 'solemnly commended by authority to the prayers of the Church' for a task which, in your judgment, would certainly occupy several years, I honestly confess that I do not know to what body of picked men, a large proportion of them under forty-five years of age, I could properly assign it, or what character or authority would belong to such 'expression of the Church's official teaching' when ultimately produced.

I should like to have a clearer indication of the sort of questions —theological, ecclesiastical, or practical—to which you think such a Commission might find useful answer, and in what sort of shape you suggest that such answer should be formulated. I should also like to have some indication as to the number of men, roughly speaking, whom you have in mind for the constitution of such a

Commission, and as to its relation, if any, to the existing Synodical and Constitutional bodies of the Church of England.

The Bishop and his fellow memorialists answered:

The BISHOP OF OXFORD *to the* ARCHBISHOP OF CANTERBURY

May 4, 1922.

In reply to your Grace, we would wish to make clear that we do not contemplate, and have never contemplated, authority being given to a commission to frame either a statement of doctrine which would be binding on the Church or the clergy, or even a statement of doctrine which would *ipso facto* be held to be the official teaching of the Church. In regard to the first of these possibilities, we have emphatically no desire to see new tests imposed. We believe that doctrinal agreement has a legitimate claim to be regarded as authoritative precisely in the degree in which it is a free agreement. In regard to the second possibility, any such procedure would be obviously inconsistent with due regard for the function of the Episcopate. It is for the Bishops to consider how far further action might be desirable in regard to any agreed conclusions which such a commission might reach.

What we are immediately concerned to secure is not this or that expression of closer agreement between different points of view when once this has been reached, but a step which will emphasize the importance of closer agreement and which will initiate a more systematic effort to find bases for such agreement. We have repudiated any desire to see the enforcement by authority of a series of doctrinal conclusions. But we would wish to quote and to make our own a sentence which occurs in the course of a vigorous protest against such a use of authority. In his published reply to Cardinal Mercier, Father Tyrrell wrote as follows:—

> I am not blind to the fact that variety without unity may be almost as great an evil as unity without variety; that where general agreement is not the goal of all individual effort, and where diversity is accepted as final and satisfactory, there can be no progress, but only an aimless analysis and disintegration.

With many of Father Tyrrell's conclusions and arguments we should disagree; but apart from the question of which of the two evils he mentions is the greater, we find it impossible to frame a better statement of our attitude to doctrinal unity. Both an enforced uniformity, and acquiescence, indefinitely continued, in grave doctrinal differences, which closely affect the religious life of every member of the Church, seem to us to be serious dangers to the well-being of the Church.

We are convinced that the problem is not merely to discover an agreement which already exists. On a number of important questions there is disagreement which is as real as it is disastrous. We would submit to your Grace, with all the emphasis within our power, that our present disagreements can only be overcome in any degree by a laborious and systematic effort to reconcile different points of view in a clearer apprehension of those truths of which the different points of view give a partial presentation. We are jealous for liberty of thought, but we are no less desirous that every effort should be made to reconcile disagreements by a closer approach to truth, that this goal should be steadily set before the Church by those in authority, and that those in authority should themselves initiate a more systematic effort, in this direction. Valuable and necessary as are informal conferences, in our judgement there is also required a more systematic, laborious and continued effort than can thus be secured. We are anxious to see the Bishops themselves initiate such an effort, because their action would bring before the Church the importance of finding and appreciating the real agreement that lies behind divergencies, and of diminishing as far as possible these divergencies, and would thus do much to create the right atmosphere for the enquiry; but we also desire official action, because such an effort would be so onerous, as well as so important, that men could only fairly be asked to co-operate in it in response to an authoritative appeal.

The letter concluded by suggesting a method of selecting the members of the Commission and Terms of Reference, and stated finally:

That the Report of the Commission should not be an authoritative statement, but would, we hope, be laid before the Bishops for them to consider what further action (if any) should be taken.

After further correspondence about procedure, the Archbishop of Canterbury sent the following letter to the Bishop of Oxford appointing the Commission and giving the names of the members:

The ARCHBISHOP OF CANTERBURY *to the* BISHOP OF OXFORD

Lambeth Palace, S.E. December 28, 1922.

In pursuance of my letter of September 8 and of your subsequent letter of November 29, I write on behalf of the Archbishop of York and myself to say that it is our wish to nominate those whose names

I append hereto to act as a Commission with the following Reference—

> To consider the nature and grounds of Christian Doctrine with a view to demonstrating the extent of existing agreement within the Church of England and with a view to investigating how far it is possible to remove or diminish existing differences.

We note and approve your proposal that the Report of the Commission should not be an authoritative statement, but that it should, when prepared, be laid before the Bishops for them to consider what further action (if any) should be taken.

List of those suggested as Members of the Commission on Christian Doctrine.

The Bishop of Oxford.	Professor W. Moberly.[2]
The Bishop of Manchester.	The Rev. J. K. Mozley.
The Dean of Bristol.[1]	The Rev. Canon O. C. Quick.
The Rev. F. R. Barry.	The Rev. A. E. J. Rawlinson.
The Rev. Preb. E. J. Bicknell.	The Rev. E. G. Selwyn.
The Rev. J. M. Creed.	The Rev. C. J. Shebbeare.
The Rev. Canon J. R. Darbyshire.	W. Spens, Esq.
The Rev. C. W. Emmet.	The Rev. Canon V. F. Storr.
The Rev. H. B. Gooding.	The Rev. Canon B. H. Streeter.
The Rev. L. W. Grensted.	Professor A. E. Taylor.
The Rev. W. L. Knox.	The Rev. L. S. Thornton.
The Rev. Prof. W. R. Matthews.	Professor C. C. J. Webb.

The Rev. Canon H. Albert Wilson.

It will be noted that the names represent all schools of thought, and include a large number of distinguished theologians. The first Meeting was held at University College, Oxford, in September 1923. The Bishop of Oxford served as Chairman until his death in 1925, when the Bishop of Manchester (Dr. Temple)[3] took his place.

[1] Dr. E. A. Burroughs, afterwards Bishop of Ripon.

[2] This name was not in the original letter, but was added in the published list.

[3] Afterwards Archbishop of York. The Commission published its Report (which was unanimous) in 1938, under the title *Doctrine in the Church of England.*

CHAPTER LXXIII

THE ARCHBISHOP AT SEVENTY-FIVE

Biography, the most interesting perhaps of every species of composition, loses all its interest with me, when the shades and lights of the principal character are not accurately and faithfully detailed; nor have I much patience with such exaggerated daubing as Mr. Hayley has bestowed upon poor Cowper. I can no more sympathize with a mere eulogist than I can with a ranting hero upon the stage.

LOCKHART, *Life of Scott*, ch. xi.

IN 1923 Randall Davidson completed the twentieth year of his primacy and the seventy-fifth year of his age. The double anniversary itself evoked a great warmth of feeling on all sides. His hold on the public mind had steadily grown. He was better known than he had ever been before; and his simplicity as well as his shrewdness won him a large popular regard, while his chairmanship of the Church Assembly for the past three years had made him, at the end of his life, both a familiar and a venerated figure amongst Churchmen all over England. In other Churches, too, he was regarded with deep respect, and even affection, as letters from a Cardinal, a Patriarch, and Free Church leaders abundantly testified. Indeed it is very remarkable to observe the growth of his influence as Archbishop of Canterbury.

I

When he became Primate, he was regarded at best as an ecclesiastical statesman, at worst as an opportunist and a courtier. The world at large simply did not know very much about him. In the first few years, he still seemed to the man in the street a prelate with a broad mind, but much more interested in the conduct of public affairs and political or semi-political controversies than in the intimate life of the Church. And a large portion of the memoranda covering the years before the War do in fact show his extraordinary interest, almost at times his absorption, in successive political crises. They also show the considerable personal part which he played behind the scenes as well as sometimes with decisive effect in his place in Parliament. The great business of administration, of course, went on all the time—and very efficient administration—but without any such striking events in the general stream of religious life as would impress the imagination of the outsider.

Then came the War. All political controversies were silenced —and the popular mind and the time of Parliament alike were occupied in the primary task of organizing for victory. Up to the very outbreak of the conflict, from the point of view of the ordinary man, Randall Davidson was still rather an increasingly important figure in the background than a great public character: a very cautious and a very wary man, not too anxious to commit himself. With the growing gravity of the War, he gradually emerged. His steadfastness and his devotion to the work in hand made their impression. His refusal to be carried away, whether in ultra-nationalism or ultra-pacificism, begot a confidence in his judgement. There was something massive about him, massive and true. And throughout the four and a half years of the War, on the repeated solemn occasions on which he had to address the whole people at or through special national services, he spoke the brave, strong, and heartening words of a Christian bishop. He said nothing common, or mean—nothing vindictive. On the contrary, he did not hesitate, in the very midst of the conflict, to utter his protests against actions and speeches which seemed to him unworthy of the traditions of his country. It is true that he lacked the high and imaginative ardour of a seer, and set small store by sentimental oratory, or idealistic appeals, trusting rather to the arguments of what he called common sense. But, perhaps for that very reason, people would often take much from him which they would not have taken from more prophetic and enthusiastic lips. Certainly he was far better known, and more fully respected, when the Armistice was signed than he had ever been before.

With the close of the War, he emerged still further. And we notice two facts of deep interest. He retained his old concern for political crises, and his passion for knowing as much as possible of what went forward in those circles. But there he was much more the spectator than the actor.

The first striking fact which we notice is that he tended much more to prove himself the great constructive Churchman. This revealed itself in one or two ways. Thus the holding of the Lambeth Conference, in 1920, under his presidency marked a great epoch not only in the idea of Christian unity but in the setting on foot of constructive plans towards its achievement. The appeal to All Christian People resounded through Christendom, inevitably carrying Archbishop Davidson's name whithersoever it went. Again, the passing of the Enabling Act in 1919, and still more the regular sitting of the new Church Assembly from 1920 onwards, not only showed Dr. Davidson as the prudent master builder of the Church of England, but also revealed him to the rank and file of Church people all over the country both as a most considerate and impartial Chairman and as a living human being, in a way that was impossible before.

The second fact of outstanding interest is this. During the War and the years that followed, the office of Archbishop of Canterbury gathered to itself a wholly new character in the international field. Appeals began to reach Lambeth from all over the world. Patriarchs and Metropolitans, and the various oppressed and persecuted Churches in the East, begged for and even demanded his support or intervention. This was largely due, no doubt, to the great political prestige of Great Britain, and the assumption that the Archbishop of Canterbury would be able to exercise a corresponding authority. It was owing in part to the special quality and the historic character and continuity of the Church of England and its sister Churches—a character which made the judgement of the Lambeth Conference a much wider affair than the opinions of new Assemblies on a world-wide scale meeting for the first time. But it was also due to the feeling of trust in the personality of Dr. Randall Davidson which had been tested over so many difficult years. It was not only appeals that reached Lambeth, but requests for counsel and leadership. 'What do they think of us at Lambeth?' was, said Dr. J. R. Mott, the missionary traveller and statesman, in May 1923 to the Archbishop, the sort of question which he was continually asked in his journeys up and down the world. Certain it is that during Randall Davidson's tenure of the archiepiscopal see the office of Archbishop of Canterbury acquired a commanding position in the communions of Christendom unprecedented in the previous history of the Church.

II

Dr. Davidson had a long experience of archbishops and bishops on which to look back, and used at times to speak of the difference between their duties, or their times, and his. In this very year—1923—shortly after his seventy-fifth birthday, when pondering the possibility of resigning, he spoke in a ruminating sort of way to his chaplain of the contrasts behind and of the difficulties ahead; and the following is a note which that chaplain made at the time. It was May 21, 1923, actually the day on which Bonar Law's resignation of the Premiership was announced—a fact no doubt that stirred his own thoughts. He said that he sometimes wondered whether the time had not come for him to hand over to another who was more in touch with the needs of the generation than himself. Looking at the last three Archbishops he felt that Tait was *felix opportunitate mortis*—he had done a great work placing the Church in the life of the nation—but would have had no understanding of or patience with ecclesiastical details and the disputes of Benson's time. He felt that Benson again had died *feliciter*, for the modern movement of parochial church councils &c. would have simply irritated him, but he had done great work in other more ecclesiastical fields. Temple's best work had been done before he came to Lambeth. For himself he felt that he had done good work in certain directions, in launching the new Church Assembly, in keeping the balance in favour of Liberalism and enabling both conservative and advanced thinkers to remain in post. But had the time come to end? He did not want his primacy to end in a feeble way. He wondered whether he was a drag on modern ways: there ought to be a drag—it was useful: but the drag ought not to be in the position of leader. Particularly he wondered how far he was in sympathy with the modern social interpretations of Christianity and modern modes of worship. If he resigned, no doubt his position would be a difficult one; people seeing him about would wonder why he resigned, if he kept well—and it would be difficult not to do things if he were still able to take an active part.

A month or two later, on July 13, following a tumultuous meeting of the Anglo-Catholic Congress at the Albert Hall, at which the Bishop of Zanzibar (Weston) appealed to the Congress to insist on their right to worship Christ in the Tabernacle and said that he did not ask the Clergy to obey their Bishops except when acting in accordance with Catholic tradition, the Bishop of Salisbury, who had been present, told him: 'We are in for a new Reformation', to which the Archbishop had replied: 'If it is to be a new Reformation, younger men must tackle it. I am too old for that.' And he was very much depressed, and added: 'I feel very Protestant to-day.'

The remarks thus quoted about his personal problem were more in the nature of thinking aloud than a demand for an answer; and certainly any for whose opinion he did actually ask were of one mind in bidding him stay where he was. But they throw an interesting light on his view of his predecessors and of contemporary problems.

Similarly, he used sometimes to speak of the difference between Bishops as he knew them first in Tait's day, and the modern Bench. Bishops were 'more interesting' in Tait's time, and later, than they were in his own Primacy, though the general level of present-day Bishops was higher; and in the old days there were great clashes in the Bishops' meetings.[1] He also recalled his own time as diocesan Bishop, occupying one of the four sets of episcopal lodgings in the Lollards' Tower at Lambeth Palace, where he lived for years with three great men, all very learned, who between them could answer any question you might ask.[2] Of those who had been diocesan Bishops when he was enthroned, only three—the Bishops of London (Winnington Ingram), Wakefield (Eden), and Liverpool (Chavasse) still held the same sees in the same Provinces—while Bishop Talbot had been twice translated,[3] and Dr. Edwards, Archbishop of Wales (Bishop of St. Asaph, 1889), Dr. Owen, Bishop of St. David's (consecrated 1897), and Dr. Williams, Bishop of Bangor (consecrated in 1898), had in 1920 become Bishops of the disestablished Church of Wales. Of the newer Bishops, as it seemed to him, there were few with whom he could take intimate counsel as he used to take counsel with Bishops Paget[4] and Wordsworth. It is true that Bishops felt the increasing claims of diocesan work, in modern conditions; but they were extraordinarily loyal to the Archbishop, readily responding to his special calls, as well as faithful in attendance at Bishops' meetings. The taking of counsel, in a regular way, over large questions, was a difficult thing; though sometimes Dr. Davidson was perhaps unduly despon-

[1] See *Life of Robert Gray*, ii. 33–51.

[2] Dr. Stubbs (Oxford); Dr. Westcott (Durham); Dr. John Wordsworth (Salisbury).

[3] Appointed Bishop of Rochester, 1895; Southwark, 1905; Winchester, 1911.

[4] Bishop of Oxford.

dent, feeling that Bishops could not realize how much was done by Lambeth and by Lambeth alone.

On the Archbishop of York, however, from 1909 onwards, Dr. Davidson came to lean more and more. He was the closest counsellor and most trusted of all, both most unselfish in his readiness to come from York to Lambeth to consult about the affairs of the Church, and most effective in the advice he gave. Indeed, it may be questioned whether the Archbishops of Canterbury and York were ever before in the history of the Church of England on such intimate terms of mutual trust and affection.

The Archbishop of York in 1928 became Archbishop of Canterbury, and by his kindness the biographer is able to print Dr. Lang's own view of the constant and intimate consultations:

> I have been asked to write a Note about the relationship between the Archbishops of the two Provinces during twenty years of Archbishop Davidson's tenure of his office. It may, I am sure, be confidently said that never before in history had this relation been more close and cordial. Indeed it was a co-operation so unprecedented that it seems in itself to be an event noteworthy in the long history of the Church of England. It is very difficult to compress within a few sentences any account of an intercourse so constant and so prolonged. It was an honour and a privilege for a man much younger in years to be taken from the first into the full confidence of Archbishop Davidson, to learn from him as from a Master, to watch his knowledge, wisdom, and experience at work among all the problems—national and ecclesiastical—of his time.
>
> We had, of course, our distinctive outlooks and temperaments, but I cannot remember (except perhaps once) any real difference. His calls for such help and counsel as I could give were somewhat exacting in view of my own work as Bishop of a large Diocese and Archbishop of the Province of York: but I regarded each call as an honour, and tried to obey it. Constant visits to London were made the easier by the kindness with which the Archbishop and Mrs. Davidson (as she then was) made me look upon Lambeth Palace as my London home for all these twenty years. My memory will always recall talks in the Study at Lambeth, prolonged far into the night, and Mrs. Davidson looking in to rebuke us and bidding her husband go to bed. At the beginning of almost every year, I used to spend a week at Canterbury for a more unhurried review of current and ultimate problems of the Church than was possible at Lambeth.

Let me try, though it is not easy, to summarise some of the impressions made upon my mind by these years of intimate co-operation. He carried into every detail of his work a deep, it sometimes seemed an almost burdensome, sense of his responsibility. He approached every letter he had to write, every person he had to see, with the same thoughtful care as he gave to large matters of policy. It was indeed his chief pleasure in life to talk to important persons about important affairs; but to all sorts of people, whether important or unimportant, he would give the best of his experience, judgement, and sympathy.

Again, it was most impressive to watch the exercise of his singular gift of judgement. On every matter which came before him he would ponder over every aspect of the case, every word he wrote or spoke about it, and the result always seemed to have the quality of decisiveness. Respect for and trust in his judgement was a chief cause of his ever increasing influence. It can well be imagined how deeply touched I was by the words twice repeated in the final Blessing he gave me, as recorded on another page—'Give him judgement'.

It is not for me to speak here of other elements in his character, as I am only speaking of impressions made by seeing him at work. But I cannot close without some reference to his religion. Doubtless in the overwhelming pressure of his life he had little time for private meditation or prayer; but it always seemed to me that his whole work was done in the spirit and atmosphere of prayer, in the desire to see the God-ward aspect of every matter with which he had to deal; and in constant and humble reliance on the guidance and help of God.

After watching him for twenty years in the midst of his ceaseless labours for the Church and people I feel that no words more fitly sum up my impressions than those which his wife chose for his grave in the Cloister Garth at Canterbury—'He fed them with a faithful and true heart: and ruled them prudently with all his power'.

And Archbishop Lang's judgement may fitly be followed by a long letter also specially written to the biographer by Bishop Gore (July 23, 1931):

You asked me to write some kind of 'impression' of the great Archbishop. I have been first sick, and then busy with arrears and other necessary occupations, but this letter is intended as a meagre fulfilment of what I think I promised in response to your request. You can, with my good will, either (*a*) put this letter when you have read it into the waste paper basket as not wanted for your purposes or (*b*) send it back requesting alteration or omission or expansion or (*c*) make any use of it you please as it stands.

I had very little personal contact with R. D. till I became a bishop in 1901–2. I knew how much intimate friends of mine admired him (him and Lady D.[1] taken together), but I had not much personal experience. I disliked his Erastianism (in the popular rather than the historical sense of this word) and what I dare say I should have called his 'official optimism'. While I was a diocesan bishop (1902–19), he was, as you know, very kind to me and guided me in my ignorance. But we had several collisions of a rather serious kind. This is not the place to expound my own views, except as illustrating the Archbishop's mind. I desired the C. of E. to be the home of a wide toleration: but a toleration which had declared limits. I did not want doctrinal prosecutions, in view of the unsatisfactory nature of the court and other causes, but I wanted the bishops to make evident that denial of the historical articles of the Creeds, on the part of the clergy, could not be countenanced or accepted as tolerable. I drew up a resolution which I should have wished the bishops to pass: which, he said, if it were passed, would force him to resign. I did not desire any such thing, and knew of course that the merest hint of such a consequence would prevent its passing. It was on event amended, and passed in a form which rejoiced me, and was reiterated several times. One of the bishops—Dr. Chase—took it seriously, and acted upon it. But I think the Archbishop's attitude, and that of most of the bishops, was to regard it as something done to satisfy dogmatic persons and not to be seriously acted upon. I was reminded of a saying of Dr. Jayne's, that the bishops were like the slothful man in Proverbs who fails to roast what he took in hunting. But in the Archbishop's case it was assuredly not sloth which affected him. It was a deliberate desire to avoid raising a clear issue, and to maintain a tone of official and general optimism by the avoidance of definition. We had another collision over the definition (for the purpose of the New Church Assembly) of the Churchman who should be admitted to vote—whether confirmation should be required. Here again I was struck (with his justice to me in giving me full opportunity to say what I wanted but also) with his deliberate unwillingness to bring a clear principle forward to

[1] The Bishop of Wakefield (Dr. Seaton) told the biographer that when he, as Principal of Cuddesdon, paid his first visit to Lambeth in August 1914, on the invitation of the Archbishop, Bishop Gore, as Bishop of Oxford, said to him, 'Have you never met the Archbishop before? Well, you are going to the most beautiful home in England—with not a particle of side or swagger about it, and you will meet the very wisest man in all England—and as for Mrs. Davidson, she is a pearl among women.'

determine an issue. The clearest declaration of principle I remember him making was his declaration on the essential independence of the Church in spiritual matters, which he made after the rejection of the Revised Prayer Book by the House of Commons. I never got to know him very well till I had resigned my bishopric and came to live in London. Then I used very often to sup at Lambeth on Sundays and have long talks with the Archbishop in his study, who told me everything that was going on, and wanted to hear what I had got to say. Then we became very intimate. We knew to the end that there was a difference of principle between us. But I was overwhelmed by the sense of his personal goodness: his exceedingly genuine humility and the total absence of spite or uncharitableness or injustice in his character. His deep knowledge of the evil in the world, whether the secular world or the religious, which he never attempted to minimize, never dimmed his Christian outlook or his sense of mercy. He hated the knowledge of sin, which was always being presented to him, but it never embittered him. I never saw him out of temper, even when he was confronted with some one deliberately provoking or maliciously misrepresenting him. And the depth and sincerity of his personal religious life—his life of prayer—was unmistakable. In spite of his attitude towards 'heretics', I do not think he was ever touched by 'doubts' in his own mind.

Intellectually what was most noticeable in him was his almost miraculous memory for persons and events, not only ecclesiastical persons or events. He was not a philosopher, or a man of letters, nor perhaps would you call him a theologian—though his knowledge of the theological opinions current in the Victorian Church, and in the first decade of this century, was wide and accurate—his chief interest was in persons and events. He loved his position in the House of Lords. It may be doubted whether any Archbishop during the centuries since the Reformation has held the position he did in the House of Lords: but there, I think, nothing gave him more satisfaction than to correct erroneous statements as to matters of fact. Only the future can decide whether the almost absolute mastery which he won in the counsels of the bishops—both those of the Church in England and those of other lands—was wholly good for the Anglican Communion. But I do not think any one can doubt that it was gained and deepened to the end in the main by the grand and stainless character of the man.

I am rather ashamed of sending you this. You must take it as a rough statement which must be revised, when you can give me an idea whether you want it, or what you want in it.

The letter shows in a striking way the difference in outlook between the two men. Dr. Gore delighted in opportunities for making things precise and clear, and there were many amusing friendly dialogues between them. Thus, in June 1923, when they were talking together about Cardinal Mercier, and the Archbishop had to say something somewhat careful in public to prepare people for the announcement about the Malines Conversations at the end of the year, he said to Bishop Gore, 'I don't think I gave anything away', and, when Bishop Gore replied, 'On the contrary', the Archbishop added, 'Of course people may think that I failed to seize an opportunity—yes, but I do not want to grasp an opportunity at the risk of being misunderstood.' And there is also a story told by Dr. Gore himself about his attitude when approaching the Archbishop's study for a talk on some subject of importance, and his attitude at the moment of departing when the talk was done. The Bishop is speaking to a friend:

'When I go up the stairs at Lambeth, I say, *Charles, you be very careful.*

'When I come down the stairs, I say, *Charles, you know that you never meant to agree to that.*'

It must be admitted that others besides Dr. Gore lamented what he describes as the avoidance of definition. Convinced evangelicals, for example, while very well aware that Archbishop Davidson was no ritualist, could not understand his steady persistence along a middle course, and were inclined to put it down to a want of conviction. He gave the impression not of leading the Church in a direction which he had thought out, but of being led by circumstances as they arose; and of disliking to face the ultimate consequences of each step in his policy. And so far as ritual is concerned, it must be acknowledged that there was some truth in this charge. He was, as we shall see, not really interested in the intricacies of Prayer Book Revision; and here it might be the case that those who knew their own mind were able—in a phrase sometimes used by Dr. Gore—to 'squeeze' him. But with regard to the deepest things, and what he believed to be the essentials of the Christian faith itself, and also the call and character of the Church of England, avoidance of meticulous definition was a foundation principle, because he believed that such avoidance was a part of the faith.

And more still must be said. There are two kinds of leadership.

There are those who are leaders of a cause on the success of which they stake everything they have: and all their efforts, all their acts, are devoted to the achievement of their particular plan or their particular doctrine. Such leaders will drive forward as fast as they can, and will cry aloud to their followers to make haste after them. But there is another kind of leader, who, having a charge entrusted to him and a body of people at whose head he is placed, rather seeks to act as the interpreter of the best mind that is in them and to give it expression, to discover the *communis sensus* of the society, and to use all the means in his power to give it the opportunity of expression. Such a leader will guide and will show the way, and he will teach and suggest, but he will not be likely to lift his voice from the housetops, and to cry aloud to the laggards to come on at full speed. He will realize the diversity of human nature, of the material with which he has to deal, and will give it, or lead it to, the best and the highest unity of which he believes it to be capable under the given conditions. Such a man will not be the leader of a forlorn hope. His is the leadership of the Chairman or the Moderator. He will wish to keep the boat even, without endangering the passengers. He prefers peace and agreement before violence and confusion. He runs the risk of misrepresentation, and is unlikely to win great popular applause. But he is not on that account to be dismissed as an unsuitable kind of leader in dangerous and unsettled times.

III

Although no Archbishop of Canterbury is free to give all the time he would wish to the care of his Diocese, Dr. Davidson took a very real interest in the life and work of the Church in East Kent and Croydon. He did not, at least in the years after the War, travel about in the parishes a great deal, but he was always accessible both to clergy and laity who desired his help. And he constantly surprised successive Bishops of Dover by his personal knowledge both of men and places. Again, he always endeavoured to attend the annual Meeting of the Church of England Temperance Society and preached on the Sunday in the town in which the Meetings were being held. Further, he did all he could to promote the work of moral welfare throughout the Diocese. From the very first year of their married life, he and Mrs. Davidson had felt the call of this particular need with special force, and the moral welfare workers knew that they had in both him and his wife a true friend and counsellor. Indeed, in this work he had been, from Rochester days onwards, a pioneer. So far as the general parochial work of the Diocese was concerned, he used such special opportunities for getting to know the parishes as those provided by the annual Weeks of Prayer and Preaching held in different deaneries each year in the autumn. The special missioners or preachers were commissioned by him, as a rule on the Saturday afternoon, in one of the churches in the deanery, and in addition he would take his turn as preacher on the Sunday in one or more churches in the deanery. Most of his residence was inevitably at Lambeth Palace. But the Archbishop and Mrs. Davidson used to go to Canterbury for certain special periods or events, the two Ordinations at Advent and Trinity, Whitsuntide, the weeks around Christmas, and a longer spell in the autumn, including as much as possible of the months of October and November. Each autumn too he held the Annual Meeting of Archdeacons and Rural Deans, an occasion which was thoroughly valued by both sides and gave the Archbishop an opportunity of counsel and information on both diocesan and general questions. In the summer the Diocesan Conference took place, and this gave the Archbishop an opportunity, which he used to the full, of abundant hospitality to the Diocese as a whole in the Old Palace. Many were invited to stay for a couple of nights, and there was an At Home in the evening for all members of the Conference, where there was a quite extraordinary atmosphere of affection and welcome. It has not been possible to deal in detail with the diocesan side of the Archbishop's work, in which he was most admirably served by the Suffragan Bishops of Dover and Croydon, but just so much has been said lest it should appear through omission that he was wanting in devotion to the Diocese, or in the affection and trust of his clergy and laity.

IV

The Archbishop's counsellors and friends were by no means all of them diocesan bishops; and they were extraordinarily varied in character.

One was Sir Lewis Dibdin. He was Dean of the Arches, and First Church Estates Commissioner. In 1924, on the resignation of Lord Parmoor, he succeeded also to the office of Vicar-General.

Sir Lewis was in almost daily contact with the Archbishop all the time he was at Lambeth and was consulted upon almost everything, though seldom (if ever) on ecclesiastical appointments. He was very learned and very conscientious, but somewhat impatient of criticism from those less learned than himself. He was a disciple of Archbishop Benson, but, unlike his master, an evangelical. He was also a strong Establishment man. The Archbishop owed much to his service in all sorts of ways, and no trouble was too great for Sir Lewis to take, as the countless memoranda in the files bearing his name make plain. Incidentally, he gave ungrudging help in difficult cases concerning clerical discipline. The Archbishop always attached great importance to his counsel, yet followed the wise Rule of St. Benedict where it says of the abbot: *Audiens consilium fratrum, tractet apud se.*

Another counsellor was the Bishop of Dover, Dr. Bilbrough, most cheerful and faithful of Suffragans, through whom the Archbishop kept in the closest relations with the Diocese of Canterbury, and with whom he often went fishing in Scotland in the summer. Another was Mrs. Creighton, most staunch and indomitable. And there were many besides. The Archbishop kept his mind and his affections open to old and young. Sometimes the latter regarded him as a little too inclined, as they put it, 'to take the wind out of a man'. Thus, a junior overseas Bishop once said that the Archbishop was a 'champion deflator', his policy being to stretch your proposal at once to its extremest logical conclusion, and if you suggested the desirability of having more Bishops, he would show it to be ridiculous by saying, 'I suppose you mean that every Rural Dean should be a Bishop.' But, though Randall Davidson was critical of vagueness and windiness, and liked to bring men down to the earth, their habitation, no one was more ready to listen, and to try to understand the thoughts of the younger generation. He won the friendship and the reverence of all sorts and kinds of people. Men and women, when they went to see him, got a sense of security from their talks, and even a man so utterly unlike the Archbishop as the writer Joseph Conrad said, fresh from seeing him for the first time at the Old Palace, in January 1923, 'I go back to my work sustained.'

Sometimes from the style and tone of letters addressed to him (as both Lockhart and Southey observe) a man's character may be gathered even more surely than from those written by himself.[1] The Archbishop, during his summer holidays, used to spend a few days at Cloan with the Haldanes, and he delighted not only in his friendship with the Lord Chancellor and his sister, Elizabeth Haldane, but in the wonderful charm of their mother. Two birthday letters in the two years following the Archbishop's seventy-fifth birthday, which passed between him and Mrs. Haldane, are too touching not to be reproduced. The first is a reply to the Archbishop's counsel on her entering the centenary year:

MRS. HALDANE *to the* ARCHBISHOP OF CANTERBURY

Cloan, Auchterarder, N.B. May 3rd, 1924.

I would have written immediately on the receipt of your most exquisitely beautiful letter to myself, had I been able. It was too good in you to send me such a precious message of affection and interest and wise counsel for the future. I prize and value all immensely. I need not remind you that I never cease to pray for the good of the Church and people through your means, and also for a special blessing on yourself and on dear Mrs. Davidson. I have full confidence that our prayers are heard, and rejoice in the full expectation that the blessing of God will rest and remain with you and yours.

The nearer I approach eternity, the more satisfied and happy that life seems to become. I do not know why; but I think it is owing to the greater realization of the Sovereign will of God, overruling everything and leaving us helpless in His hands.

We *rest* as little helpless infants in His arms.

May I, once more, thank you and Mrs. Davidson, and warmly welcome you home, and will you allow me to be the bearer of constant petitions on your behalf and of the church of God, always remaining a quiet unobtrusive unit in the body corporate united closely in spirit and most affectionately attached.

The second is a letter written by the Archbishop on his own seventy-seventh birthday:

The ARCHBISHOP OF CANTERBURY *to* MRS. HALDANE

Lambeth Palace, S.E. 7 April 1925.

I am painfully conscious of wrongdoing in adding this rivulet to the flood which will pour in upon Cloan this week. And to sin with one's eyes open is grave indeed. But selfishly I cannot refrain.

[1] Lockhart's *Life of Scott*, chaps. v and xvi.

This is *my* birthday. I am 77, and when I saw the light in 1848 (in a week of Continental hurly-burly and of Chartist disorder at home) you were already a well grown up lady four years past her 'teens. Yet somehow I never can get myself to regard *you* as being nearly so old as *I feel*. Whenever I talk to you I find a well-spring of buoyant thought, and an easy readiness in handling the memories of the past, which I admire but cannot rival. And will you let me say to you that your quiet gift of sure touch upon the deepest things has been to me, many a time, a spur and an inspiration. I like to thank you for it now. Sometimes when I find myself plunged perforce in the 'strife of tongues', and perhaps rather frightened and depressed by the sense of inability to guide things as one would, I have recalled simple words of yours about the Guide and Keeper of our souls, and have gratefully reminded myself of your assurance that you do not forget us in your prayers.

'What a many' people in difficult places, or with hard steering to do in rough water and rough weather, you must in these long decades have been thus uplifting though they knew it not. I should like you to know that one at least of these weather-beaten folk pays to you in his own thoughts and prayers the meed of gratitude which you have earned.

And another thing. We are in happy touch with those who, in middle life or beyond it, are now exercising from your home or its out-posts, the sort of influence which *tells* in fields social or political or scientific, and who owe their power of straightness and of forcefulness in no small part to what they learned from a Mother whom we can all of us thank for what she has done and is still doing for each. In the truest sense 'Her children arise and call her blessed'.

I trust you, my dear friend, to pardon all this, for it comes from my heart.

I am venturing to send you a little book—the 'text book' of my master and prophet and friend for nearly forty years—Dr. Westcott. I think you will find in it some thoughts which will be after your mind.

May our Lord Himself have you in His keeping now and always.

V

We end with a note on the Archbishop's religion, though with due heed to that reticence which he, above all men, would deem most necessary here. It was part and parcel of his whole being. But it had nothing emotional about it, and nothing of the peculiar ardour, or the sacramental quality, which mark the great masters of private or liturgical devotion. It was simple and straightforward, and closely bound up with the work or the needs of the day. He attended the daily services of Lambeth Palace Chapel, always adding to their peace and gravity by his reading of the Lessons and of the final prayers. Sundays he usually spent quietly at home, of set purpose, for recuperation and study and reflection. And when people came to him at some crisis in their lives, he often prayed with them in a way which gave them strength and comfort for a long while to come, as in the following prayer, much treasured by him with whom he used it:

> Grant, O LORD, that in the weariness of unceasing work our intercourse with Thee may ever be fresh.

Of himself he used to say:

> As one grows old, I find that meditation takes the place of more definite prayer; and that one thinks upon people and problems and work, as in the Presence of God.

He had a profound belief in Providence; in God's working through history. Therefore he regarded the ordered sequence of events as of the most serious import. 'The Lord reigneth', he used constantly to say. This kept him calm and firm amid the turmoil, and also made him deem those who took the second step before they were sure of the first, in some particular course of action, as not only foolish but irreverent. A favourite text was 'One generation shall praise Thy works unto another'. Once, preaching on this text about Archbishop Whitgift, he said, 'In the life of a man, from boyhood to old age, some parts may be, and certainly will be, more stirring, more eventful, than others; but each bit has to do—quite necessarily and clearly—with what went before and what comes after.... God has had a purpose in moulding that life, personal or national bit by bit, and to His all-seeing eye each little epoch, each set of years, is concerned with all the rest, both past and future.'[1] His instinctive approach to every subject was historical and evolutionary, and he saw every issue that came up as continuous with all else that had gone before it. Again and again he took the view that if people understood how a state of things had come to be, they would see what the next right step was. And when he stressed the evolutionary in history, it was always in terms rather of God's action than of mere develop-

[1] *Captains and Comrades in the Faith*, p. 38.

ment. We might not be able to see the relation between the little issues confronting each one of us and the plan of the Great Commander, but such a relation there always was. And his own sense of the importance of most of the things he was given to deal with was, at least in large measure, a sense of their ultimate importance in God's purpose. In close connexion with his conviction that God was at work in history came his sense of Man's personal responsibility—'answerableness', he would call it—for all his daily actions, the sense that eternal issues were involved in the choices and decisions of every hour. Thus at every step man might advance or hinder God's purpose. His trust in God was of a straightforward and simple kind, an almost childlike faith that light and strength would come in answer to prayer when the difficulties and hindrances seemed too great. Again and again those nearest him have seen the Archbishop fussed beyond measure at not being able to get something out before he went to bed, to see his way through some problem, and then quite obviously leaving the matter in faith and committing himself to the belief that if he awoke early and remained in bed something would be given to him in the morning—as it always was.

Very significant as to his own personal practice is the following passage from a sermon entitled 'Prayer and Business'.[1] It happens to be a sermon preached at the very beginning of his Primacy, but was characteristic of the whole attitude of his life. It is the account of a man, very busy, immersed in the duties of his office, and practising his religion in the very midst of his secular work:

> . . . the story of Daniel sets before us no picture of a mystic visionary, an ascetic thinker living outside the stream and swing of the world's life. He is set before us as a busy man of affairs, with a huge trust laid upon him for active administrative service; immersed, as we should nowadays express it, in public business. But on the life is set the stamp of faithfulness to God, whatever that faithfulness might cost. . . . This man, of quiet, unflinching, prayerful purpose, avowedly took the work which was allotted to him—the public work in a heathen capital—as of Divine appointing, to be done to the very best of his power under the all-seeing eye and the personal guidance of the Lord his God. . . . But the two sides or divisions of his life were inseparably one, and therein, in part, lies the lesson of his story. It is in the very centre of what the

[1] Ibid., pp. 329–31.

Bible tells us about his converse with God—in the midst of what we should nowadays call his 'deepest religious thoughts' and words and visions—that we find the old man immersed in the duties of his secular office. 'I rose up and did the King's business.' The vividness of his communion with God is not one whit restrained or marred by his secular work, nor must that secular work—those prosaic, responsible duties of his office and calling—be set aside or disregarded even when there has come to him the deepest, the most overwhelming of spiritual visions or messages from on high. The two 'departments' if we may use the word, were the complement each of the other. The vision might literally overpower him when it came—nay, it did so overpower him utterly—but it would send him back the stronger to his duties. 'I rose up and did the King's business, and I was astonished at the vision.'

Such was the spirit of communion with God in which Randall Davidson fulfilled the duties of his calling. His relations with his fellows were marked by a faith of a similar kind. He had a real trust in and a genuine power of evoking the great spiritual and moral possibilities of ordinary human beings. He was a man in whose presence people grew.

CHAPTER LXXIV

A YEAR OF CHANGE

Parliaments are now grown to be quite other things than they were formerly.
MARQUESS OF HALIFAX, *Some Cautions offered to the Consideration of those who are to chuse Members to serve for the Ensuing Parliament.*

THE actual date of the twentieth anniversary of Archbishop Davidson's enthronement as Primate was February 12, 1923. By a happy coincidence, on that very day a Meeting of the Privy Council was held, and King George made his Declaration of Consent under the Royal Marriages Act to the projected marriage of the Duke of York. The Archbishop of Canterbury was summoned—the Lord Chancellor and the Prime Minister, the Lord President, the Home Secretary, and the Lord Chamberlain. We may be sure that the occasion awoke many memories of the great Queen whose grandson was now on the Throne, of the old days at the Castle, and of the many changes and chances, marryings and giving in marriage, since the Archbishop himself had first gone as a young Dean to Windsor forty years before. What wonder that, as the Clerk of the Privy Council noted in his journal for the day, his Grace should be 'the modest recipient of every one's congratulations'.[1]

I

The year 1923 was a full one, and the Davidson papers show a great deal of business and a great deal of intercourse of various kinds. A few extracts will illustrate the manner of things which occupied the Archbishop's mind and time:

Dictated February 4th, 1923.

I have been in rather a crocky condition, was unable to preach as usual at the close of the year, being largely in bed during that fortnight with troublesome indigestion which refused to yield to the ordinary treatment. Then we went to Ludwell for ten days, and there I was better. . . .

The Assembly week had gone well. I sat through all the sessions except one afternoon when I purposely put Ebor in the chair,

[1] *Memoirs of Sir Almeric Fitzroy*, ii. 794.

not because I was really unwell, but because it was better to have a little elasticity. I have not had much important speaking to do during the week, but have had to be a wakeful chairman. The debating has been of a high order, admirable speeches being made by Ebor and Durham and several more. We gave general approval to the scheme for dividing the Winchester Diocese, but with a very emphatic warning to the Committee which will be formed for the revision stage that they should in their revision consider amendments, and I think they will. I do not like the scheme as it stands, but it would have disheartened the diocese too much if we had simply refused general approval, and thus postponed all action of any kind for at least a year.

Dictated March 18th, 1923.

On Friday March 9th, Dr. Deissmann of Berlin spent several hours here. I found him most friendly. We did not discuss the wartime correspondence which had passed between us, but he spoke quite freely about the present state of German feeling, which he says is not really anti-English, though it is angrily anti-French. He is very unhopeful about the future in Germany owing to financial stress. He will not admit that there is any very strong militarist group of the old fashion now remaining, though of course there are a few die-hards. He ridiculed (but seriously, not lightly) the idea that Germany could by any possibility in present conditions raise a new Army, or start a new war, but without reserve admits its helplessness. He is delivering some lectures in England, but is apparently engaged almost entirely in Nonconformist circles, and, except for his talk with me, has little or no intercourse with Church of England folk. I got Ryle and Iremonger and Mrs. Creighton to meet him, and Armitage Robinson was staying here; so he got a good dose of Anglicanism for his good.

Dictated April 22nd, 1923.

Yesterday, Saturday, I preached at St. Mary Aldermanbury, about the First Folio of Shakespeare—the sermon is being published forthwith. It may appear in Monday's press. The sermon gave wide satisfaction—Sidney Lee, Gollancz, Headlam, and many more speaking rather eagerly about its value. The service was followed by a luncheon at which there were some admirable speeches.

Dictated August 12th, 1923.

In truth, this summer has been one of the most important in my life, not because of great things happening, but because I seem to have been more in the forefront of people's minds than ever before. It is not easy to know why this has been, but so it is. I think it is partly due to a great fuss about my birthday last April, 75th, coming on the top of an earlier fuss in February about the completion of my 20th year of Archbishopric. . . . I have been very regular in House of Lords attendance, and have been considering the rights and wrongs of it. I am clear on the whole that it is best to do as I have done and go practically every day when the House sits, for my room has been to a greater degree than ever before beset with people, public men, desiring interviews. All kinds of important people, on subjects political, international, and of course ecclesiastical, have been coming thither for talks, and I think it is not without value that I should put in an appearance at the House itself whenever anything of the least importance is happening. I have not made many important speeches, but numerically I think they have been fairly frequent. I have talked about Russia; about the Eastern Church; about Divorce; about East Africa (Kenya), and rather importantly about a very local matter, the Whitgift Hospital at Croydon, which became the centre of acute controversy among historians, architects, aesthetes, though indeed the thoughtful people were all on one side and we triumphed overwhelmingly.

. . . The National Assembly meeting in July (9th–13th) was very important, but not heatedly controversial. We dealt in a businesslike way with big subjects, pensions, dilapidations, and the like, the only very controversial question being the proposed division of the diocese of Winchester. Upon that subject I was in a difficult position. It was commonly recognised, among those who knew the facts, that I could, if I liked, destroy the proposed Bill by some outspoken opposition based on my personal experience, both of that diocese, and of the Church at large. But while I disliked the Bill, I felt distinctly that if I so acted it would do real harm. I had in the previous session urged that the matter should go again before the Winchester Diocese, which should consider in Diocesan Conference the criticisms and objections, and I felt fairly sure that there would be there a large minority hostile to the Bill. I found that the minority dwindled into the merest handful, and this appeared to me to make it the duty of the Assembly to yield to the wish of the diocese, provided no really trifling proposals were made. As the Bill issued from the Assembly, it requires the raising of more than £100,000 before the desired change can be effected, and this will, in my judgement, hinder the thing indefinitely and give time for ampler consideration. If I had in the Assembly bludgeoned the Bill out of existence, its destruction would have been regarded as wholly my handiwork in the teeth of the wish of the people who understand the subject better. As it is, no one can question that the problem has been reasonably handled, and that if a mistake is made by the diocese, it is by a deliberate and democratic voice. I spent a night at Farnham three days ago—a farewell visit, I suppose, to the Talbots there, though we may visit their successor, whoever he may be. It was pathetic in the extreme, and I felt deeply for them both. I have never seen Farnham looking so beautiful, and as I told the Bishop (now that the milk is spilt and my tongue loosed) the beauty of the scene made me detest the measure more than ever! . . .

The next matter of importance which has been occupying me during recent months has been the discussion of new ecclesiastical appointments to be made by the new Prime Minister. I find Baldwin delightful to deal with. . . .

I am a little disappointed by our management of social things this year, though I cannot blame either myself or anyone else. Looking ahead in the spring it always seems that we should have more opportunity for quiet dinners of few people than practically turns out to be possible. I had looked forward to doing something of the sort this year We have failed to do so, and yet it seems inevitable. We had one very successful evening party to which all kinds of important people, diplomatic and other came. We omitted to have any notice of it in the press, and I must admit that if we had done so we should have created more soreness on the part of the uninvited! We also had . . . a large and successful party for the Stewards of the Sons of the Clergy. We have had some interesting visits from outsiders, including Söderblom from Upsala and his family. We had a quiet and successful dinner for Lloyd George, President Murray Butler being there also. We have paid visits to Norwich, to Bristol for the Wesleyan Conference, to Walmer Castle for the great Shepway Court, or demonstration by Beauchamp as Warden of the Cinque Ports on August 4th. This last was historically and picturesquely triumphant. Whether it will do much good I am not clear, but I think it can do no harm, and it gave me an opportunity of saying something guardedly, but definitely, about the appalling problem of our responsibilities in connexion with the Franco-German confusion and strife.

We have dined out rather more than usual, e.g. with Lord Newton, with the American Chargé d'Affaires, with Lord Lee, with Lord Lansdowne, and we also dined at the great banquet which the Prince of Wales gave with admirable effect in St. James's Palace. This reminds me that I have omitted to mention the marriage of the Duke of York in Westminster Abbey in April—

which again was a most successful function—the address to my great satisfaction being given by the Archbishop of York. He is less played out in the giving of these addresses than his brother Primate! . . .

II

Dictated October 28th, 1923.

We had more than six weeks in Scotland, and barring the fact that we got wet practically every day we had nothing but good to record. First there were some 15 or 16 days at Lairg with Bilbrough, father and son. . . . We caught some salmon, but there was too much water in the river, and I personally got very few. Dover fished more vigorously, and with more skill, and also had better luck. We had about 30 fish in all, the average size being some 17 lbs; a very high standard.

From Lairg we went to the Portlands at Langwell, and had a delightful week. . . . The Duchess drove us on to Stirkoke when our week was up, and there the Hornes gave us a different sort of experience in quiet local interests. . . . The great Langwell car was sent for us to bring us back there for a night on our way to Moy where we were for a few days with the Mackintosh. Wet as usual, but not uninteresting. . . .

Then a week at Aberuchill, with a day at Dunira, and the renewal of old memories, very vivid to me, of early shooting days and boyish fishing and the like. . . .

Then a week with the Haldanes at Cloan. . . . I had much interesting talk too with Haldane about the political situation. He thinks there is no political future for Lloyd George or for Asquith, or presumably for himself; but he does not anticipate a Labour Government until several years have passed by, which means he would personally be approaching the age of the 'shelf'; and anyhow, he would not, whatever he may say, be really a congenial spirit to the Labour folk who would hold the reins. It is all very well for him to theorize about his Labour principles as an abstract doctrine, but when it comes to practical politics he would be a back number.

Old Mrs. Haldane was an inspiration as always. She seems to the eye no worse than in former years, but I gather that, as a matter of fact, there are symptoms which might at any time bring her wonderful life to a close.

From Cloan we went to Dalmeny, and I very greatly enjoyed the renewal of talks, once so frequent, but latterly so rare. Rosebery is at present a pathetic figure in the country's life, though the country does not see him. It is strange to find a man with his wealth of reminiscences, political and personal, stretching back across a full half-century, and no opportunity at present, or at least no used opportunity, of saying his say, or contributing anything to the nation's life. I find him specially anxious to talk in his own quiet and reserved way about religious things and the relation of life here to the life hereafter. I think he turns to me rather more easily than to others on these matters, though perhaps he may talk to men of whom I know nothing. I do not think so. I sat with him, and drove with him, and we had abundant intercourse. . . . After we had left, he wrote to Edith about the pleasure our visit had given him—a sort of reversed Collins!

While we were at Dalmeny, we spent a full morning at Muirhouse. I was most agreeably surprised to find the small degree of interference with old things. Looking from the top of the Tower one would hardly see any difference between the scene now and the scene 50 or 60 years ago. The Wellingtonia in the flower garden was brought by me in little packets in my hand from the Pantheon in Oxford Street, where I bought it, just 60 years ago.

Mr. Sanderson showed us all over the house, and walked with us to the beach and was kindness itself. They have modernised the house with admirable taste, though, of course, the old frescoes etc. have disappeared, and everything looks much more different than it really is.

Mr. Sanderson specially wished us to open the cupboard door in my Father's old room, and showed us the marked heights of all of us back to the year 1859. There must be at least 40 entries on the door, the successive generations of ourselves, and Harry's children, and Ernest's, and some cousins. He insisted on my being measured again, and writing my name opposite the mark. He did it all with excellent taste, and I valued his appreciation of the stories of those past years.

Dictated November 18th, 1923.

On Saturday [November 3] the marriage of the Crown Prince of Sweden; strange to marry the same man a second time, but I think all promises happiness. It gave me the opportunity of paying a deserved tribute to Prince Louis, the bride's father, and I had evidence at once of how much pleasure this gave to the King and Queen, Princess Louise and others. . . .

Meantime Mr. Baldwin, as Prime Minister, had announced a new programme of Protection in a speech at Manchester on November 2; and a great struggle began on the issue of Protection versus Free Trade. Parliament was dissolved on November 16, and the General Election was fixed for December 6.

Dictated November 18th (continued).

As regards the issue of the impending conflict nobody seems able to form any estimate of a trustworthy sort. At the Parliamentary Banquet . . . which I attended last Wednesday,[1] I sat between Neville Chamberlain, Chancellor of the Exchequer, and Ramsay MacDonald and had plenty of talk with both, though of course with a certain measure of reserve in either case, and of course I had so to talk as not to be speaking to both neighbours at once.

I found Ramsay MacDonald extraordinarily interesting. He had just come back from a journey to Constantinople and Athens, Corfu and Rome, and other places—a hurried tour, but he is a man with his eyes open, and he had a great deal to say about Turkey and about Italy. He takes a pessimistic view of the European situation, and is really apprehensive of the renewal of war at no distant date.

In the early days of the New Year the Archbishop was, as his memoranda show, intimately informed of the different stages of the crisis. Indeed his interest in the successive scenes in the development of the political drama was intense. And he was in at the death, spending no less than six hours in the House of Commons listening to the speeches which wound up the Government's life before the fateful division on January 21, when the Government under Mr. Baldwin was defeated by a combination of Liberal and Labour votes. On January 22, Mr. Baldwin resigned and Mr. Ramsay MacDonald was commissioned by the King to form a Ministry. The Archbishop followed the formation of the first Labour Government with keen attention. He was much impressed by Mr. Ramsay MacDonald, and in mentioning the fact in a private letter to Bishop Talbot (January 27, 1924) he added, 'Have you read the memoir he wrote of his wife? It seems to me a really fine picture of a remarkable woman, and its pathos is deep.' To Mr. Ramsay MacDonald himself he wrote as follows:

The ARCHBISHOP OF CANTERBURY *to the* RT. HON. J. RAMSAY MACDONALD

[22 January 1924.]

This letter is not of the same sort as most of those which will be submerging you to-morrow. I want to strike a different note.

[1] November 14.

> Having a day in bed a week ago gave me the opportunity of reading from cover to cover your memoir of the earthly years of the gracious and radiant lady whose influence upon your life must have been alike an inspiration, a stimulus and an abiding force. I have seldom read a book of its kind which has moved me more deeply, and I should like to be among those who thank you for giving it to us all.
>
> At this moment what impels me to write is the thought which was mine as I listened to you yesterday in the House: the difference between what the taking of this great trust means to you now —and what it would have meant had she been here to share it with you. That such a trust is shared, and such a burden half-borne, by a true wife is a fact which no living man can realise better than I, with my experience of 45 years of what it means. How often it happens that when the biggest things, be they trust or adventure, come to a man, they come to him after those who would have cared most to see him facing them have passed beyond his ken. Whether he is outside their ken is another question. I do not dare to say that any of us is left *alone* in that sense.
>
> I hope that in entering upon the great task which is now yours in the world's life, you realise how many there are of us who do watch, who do care, who do pray, who do desire in the best way to aid, even if their judgement as to the wisest policy in any given problem among our many perplexities, may be different from your own. If such a thought can make loneliness a little less, I shall be thankful to have reminded you of it.

A few days later, on February 4, he met the new Prime Minister at dinner in Lord Parmoor's house, and immediately the two men warmed to one another. Curiously enough, they found they had a common link in John Morley:

> whom he appears to have known more intimately than anybody else did, seeing him almost every day during these last years. He rather interested me by saying that Morley had again and again talked to him about me, and about what he thought was my usefulness in the line I had taken about India and about other things.

III

On October 30, 1923, just before the political crisis, came the death of Mr. Bonar Law, who had succeeded Lloyd George as Prime Minister. Mr. Baldwin obtained the Dean's consent to his burial in Westminster Abbey, and wrote to ask the Archbishop to take part in the funeral service.

The Archbishop's views on the Dean's discretion in such cases are illuminating. In his opinion, the Dean should certainly agree to a formal request from the Government in such a case, leaving the responsibility for the decision with the Government. He thought however that, where a public man who was not a statesman—like George Meredith—was concerned, the Dean was perfectly free to form his own judgement on the rights of the case, and the strength of any popular demand. A former Dean of Westminster, Dr. Armitage Robinson, happened to be staying at Lambeth on the day of the funeral, November 5, 1923. Dean Robinson agreed that any Dean of Westminster would certainly follow the expressed wish either of the King or the House of Commons (or the Government acting on its behalf) with regard to burial in the Abbey, though adding that the Government would of course always consult the Dean before their wish was announced. Dr. Robinson recalled the great agitation that had taken place in the time of Dean Stanley over a monument which it was proposed to erect in the Abbey to Prince Louis Napoleon, the Prince Imperial, who died June 2, 1879. Queen Victoria and Dean Stanley strongly desired it. The public, however, was opposed. In the end, the House of Commons on July 16, 1880, resolved by 162 votes to 147, that 'in the opinion of this House the erection of a statue to the memory of the late Prince Louis Napoleon Bonaparte would be inconsistent with the national character of that edifice'.

Dean Robinson, it is interesting to note, had himself decided against burying George Meredith in the Abbey.[1] A leading article appeared in *The Times* urging it strongly, but the Dean was steadfast in his refusal, in spite of that and of much other pressure. His view was that George Meredith was not in the highest rank of men of letters and in a few years' time would have ceased to be a conspicuous literary figure. He had also had to settle the question of commemorating Herbert Spencer.[2] A group of admirers asked the Dean to allow a bust of Herbert Spencer to be erected in the Abbey. Dean Robinson took counsel; but of those whom he consulted, the philosophers said that Spencer was no philosopher though he might be a scientist, while the scientists said he was no scientist though he might be a philosopher. The Dean accordingly refused; and was glad to receive a word of

[1] Died May 16, 1909.

[2] Died December 8, 1903.

commendation for his refusal from Lord Kelvin, who said to him one day at a party at Buckingham Palace, 'I am glad you did not put that fellow Spencer in the Abbey!'

In 1928, the Archbishop was himself consulted with regard to Lord Oxford and Asquith. The Dean of Westminster (Dr. Norris) asked him to advise the reply to be made in case he received a request. The Archbishop took the line already described, that if the Dean were approached in any way on behalf of Parliament the request ought to be granted. In his opinion not only was Lord Oxford a much greater man than Bonar Law, but it was very proper that a great War statesman, particularly the Prime Minister who had made the decision that England should enter the conflict, should be buried in the Abbey. When, however, it was announced that Lord Oxford had left instructions that he was to be buried as privately as possible, and that therefore burial in the Abbey, which the Dean offered, must be declined, the Archbishop was not well pleased. He thought that such wishes, however much they might be inspired by modesty, ought not to be respected. In his judgement great men belonged to the nation, and in such matters the individual ought not to override the nation's wishes. He added that if a great man objected to cremation (that being the condition of burial in the Abbey) such a wish might be respected, but he could not agree that the mere wish for a private burial was in such cases a proper wish.

CHAPTER LXXV

THE ASSYRIAN CHURCH

Who can name the Catalonians without a tear? Brave, unhappy people! Drawn into the War by the encouragement of the Maritime Powers . . . now abandoned and exposed to the resentment of an enraged Prince, whose person and interest they have always opposed. . . . Poor, unhappy Catalonians, worthy of a better Fate! Good and gracious God! to whom shall be attributed the loss of this brave People? Dreadful the doom of those who shall in thy sight be esteemed their destroyers. RICHARD STEELE, *The Crisis* (1714).

AMONG all the Churches—and nations—outside England with which the Archbishop of Canterbury had to do during his primacy, none had a braver or sadder story, and none made more continuous calls on his sympathy and his thought, in the years after the War, than the Assyrian Church. The Assyrians were a primitive and agricultural people, living in clans under a Patriarch, known as Mar Shimun (the Lord Simon), and were settled in two separate districts. One section lived near Lake Urmia in north-west Persia, under Persian sovereignty; the other and larger section were highlanders, established in the mountainous country north of Mosul in Kurdistan under Turkish rule. They first came into definite and regular relations with the Church of England in 1886, when Archbishop Benson founded the Archbishop of Canterbury's Mission to the Assyrian Christians for purely educational and religious purposes, and especially 'the education of those youths who will hereafter become bishops, priests and leaders of the people'.[1]

I

The Mission lasted from 1886 to 1915; but in the last few years there had been a considerable cooling in the friendship of the Assyrians for the Anglican Church, and a strong movement towards an alliance or union with the Church of Russia. Indeed the situation had become so strained in 1913, that Archbishop Davidson (who had followed the Mission's fortunes most closely from the start) was obliged to inform the Head of the Mission (August 7, 1913) that if the ancient Assyrian Church wished to

[1] Archbishop Benson to Mar Shimun, June 2, 1886: *Life of Archbishop Benson*, ii. 184.

effect a union with the Russian Church, there was nothing to do but to accept the situation.

In September 1914, the Missioners, when compelled to leave the country on account of the War, reported to the Archbishop in a joint letter (September 18, 1914) that Mar Shimun showed no regret when bidding them good-bye, and expressed no desire to see them again:

> It appears to us, therefore, that the time has come to record our conviction, arrived at most reluctantly and after much thought and consideration, that Mar Shimun and his people definitely desire to get rid of Your Grace's Mission, in order to leave the field clear for more effective helpers.

It was not, therefore, unnatural that after the Missioners had returned to England, taking the War and everything else into account, the Archbishop's Assyrian Committee, on May 26, 1915, resolved as follows:

> That the present unhappy circumstances and the enforced withdrawal of the Mission staff make it necessary to terminate the operations of the Mission at the end of the current year.

II

The Assyrians were drawn into the War in the wake of Russia, but long before the end of 1915 they were in great distress. With the Russian collapse in 1917, they suffered disaster after disaster at the hands of the Turks, and in May 1918 their Patriarch Mar Benyamin was murdered by a Kurdish brigand acting under Persian instructions. By the end of the War, the main body of the tribes were living, as refugees from their homes, in a great camp on the plain of Baquba under British protection, reduced to some 45,000 men, women, and children.

After the War, the question of their future settlement arose. They had joined the Allies when Russia was a great Power; and the collapse of Russia had involved them in calamities which nobody could have foreseen. Where should they live, and to whom should they turn for support? The Archbishop's Mission had formally closed down, and the Archbishop had made it quite clear that, whatever happened in the War, 'the resumption[1] of our old

[1] The Archbishop of Canterbury to W. G. Langdon (U.S.A.):

12 July, 1915.

It is quite certain that after the War the conditions of that whole region must be different from what they have been before. If the Russians are in possession, I

work after the War would be impossible'. But some of the Missioners, notably Dr. W. A. Wigram and the Rev. F. N. Heazell, were far too devoted to their Assyrian friends not to wish to do everything they could to help them in their adversity. And Archbishop Davidson himself was anxious to do whatever he could. But his powers were limited. Both the Archbishops, however, and the old Missioners, and the Archbishop's Assyrian Committee which was still in existence, did their best to secure the presentation of the Assyrian case to the British Government or through them to the Allied Powers: and the files of correspondence, and memoranda of interviews, bear witness to the persistency with which that case was presented through successive years.

There were three principal moments when the Archbishop's personal assistance was most strenuously invoked—and they were marked by the arrival in England of three principal spokesmen of the Assyrian claims.

III

The first occasion was in 1920, and the spokesman was the Lady Surma d'Mar Shimun, the sister of the Assyrian Patriarch. She came, with the full sanction of the British military and civil authorities in Mesopotamia, as the official representative of the whole Assyrian nation, authorized to lay their case before the British Government, and if necessary before the Peace Conference at Paris. She at once made a deep impression on the Archbishop. She had been educated in the Mission, spoke English quite well, and was an extremely intelligent woman, about thirty-four years old, with a fine natural dignity. She had never been out of Asia before. A close friendship soon sprang up between her and the Archbishop and Mrs. Davidson. And by his

imagine that the Assyrians are almost certain to make arrangements for joining ecclesiastically with the Orthodox Church, whether or not any special conditions are allowed them. If on the other hand (which God forbid) a Germanised Turkey should be dominant in those mountains and plains the position again would be different from any that we have known. In any case therefore we feel that the resumption of our old work after the War would be impossible. I say 'the resumption of our old work', for I do not at all mean that it is our wish or intention to lose touch altogether with the Syrian folk with whom we have had this association for more than a quarter of a century. But when we start afresh hereafter it may be on larger lines enabling us to co-operate and be in touch with other bodies of Christians in those whole Eastern regions.

arrangement, she saw the Queen, Lord Curzon, the Rt. Hon. E. S. Montagu, and others.

Lady Surma stayed in England from October 1919 until August 31, 1920. During the whole of this time, the Assyrian settlement was the chief burden of her thoughts—and she often discussed it with the Archbishop, who in turn discussed it with Lord Curzon and other Government authorities. But the Government tarried. For all sorts of reasons the authorities found it hard to make up their minds. Lady Surma pressed certain pledges said to have been given to the Assyrians towards the end of the War.

In reply to the Archbishop's inquiries, these pledges were formulated as follows:

The REV. W. A. WIGRAM, D.D., *to the* REV. G. K. A. BELL

Watling House. St. Albans. July 15th. 6.30 p.m.

Your letter of July 14th has only come to hand this moment. As concerns the Assyrians and British promises. I am not aware of any definite *written* promise made by British Officials to the effect that the British Government would do its best for the Assyrians, if they supported them in the war. Verbal promises to that effect, however, were given by Captain Gracey, an officer on the staff of General Offley Shore, who was sent to Urmi at the time of the Military Mission to the Caucasus, in the Spring of 1917, to organize the nation as a British and Russian ally. These promises were given at a meeting of the 'notables' of the nation, held at Urmi, in the American Mission, under the presidency of Dr. W. A. Shedd of that Mission.

It was then, by the advice of this Captain Gracey, that the Assyrians entered into that alliance with Simko Agha, which led directly to the death of Mar Shimun.

Military difficulties (notably the Russian collapse) prevented the execution of General Shore's strategic plan, but the nation was definitely recognized as an ally of Great Britain. For the rest of the war, they acted as such, and messages were sent to them (in particular that brought by Lieutenant Pennington to Urmi in July 1918) directing them how to act in that capacity.

Further, the contingent raised from among this nation (under British Officers) has been in British employ in Mesopotamia since the close of the general war, and has been on active service, and won honorable mention, in a campaign against the Kurds.

These facts surely constitute a definite recognition as an ally, and are enough to justify the general expectation of the nation, that Great Britain would not neglect their interests and safety in the general settlement.

I have sent a copy of this letter to Surma Khanim, asking her to communicate at once with you if she has anything to add to what I have written above.

LADY SURMA *to the* REV. G. K. A. BELL

House of Retreat, Lloyd Square, W.C. July 16, 1920.

I got the copy of the letter that Dr. Wigram sent to you. I have nothing to add to the letter, except that letters too, were brought to Dr. Shedd by Lieutenant Pennington to direct us in our action. And it was in January 1918 that Captain Gracey[1] came, had the meeting in Urmi etc. also French officers of the red-cross were present. Alas! nobody should think of asking a written promise from British officials. *Their* word was a promise once in our part of the East. I am afraid we have to get used to some changes.

The Archbishop in turn made representations to the Foreign Office. But all that he could discover (so he told Dr. Wigram) was that 'during the war . . . particularly in Eastern regions, a good deal of diplomacy was conducted under the wing of the War Office, rather than the Foreign Office'. The Archbishop had many communications with the Government. But no proposal seemed to bear fruit. 'It is extraordinarily difficult', he wrote to Dr. A. J. Mason, Chairman of the Archbishop's Assyrian Committee (August 16, 1920). 'The Government, plainly enough, is at its wits' end. Unless we can send a great force of troops it is mere mockery to pretend that we could give secure protection to the Assyrians. . . . The truth is that we have had left upon our shoulders at this juncture responsibilities ranging far

[1] Mar Polus, writing to the Archbishop, thus describes the visit in January 1918 of Captain Gracey, an officer on the staff of General Offley Shore and reputed the author of the promise of help:

'January 10, 1919.

'During these days there was sent to us an ambassador, an Englishman, by name Captain Gracey who spoke in our assembly: it was at the time of the late Patriarch who preceded me: there were present also the Russian Consul, Mr. Nikitine, and the American Vice Consul, Dr. Shedd, and the Latin Bishop, Monsignor Sontag, and the Chief of the French Medical Staff, Mon. Cushwal, and all the chief men of our nation: he (Capt. Gracey) commanded us to hold out and to preserve our lives from the destroying Turks: he promised us that after three months we should be helped by the Allies, and we rejoiced greatly at his words: he remained with us for a few days and then left for Tabriz.'

beyond anything that we can discharge. The Americans have really left us in the lurch.'

Surma Khanim left England for Basra on August 31, 1920—and wrote to the Archbishop on the eve of her departure that 'your love and sympathy for me will be a sweet and sacred remembrance during my life. And what you have done for me will never be forgotten.' But there were, as she also said in her letter, many sorrows waiting for her at Baquba. There is a great sheaf of correspondence between the Archbishop and Dr. Wigram on the whole subject of the settlement, throughout 1921; and accounts of many interviews (as well as letters) between the Archbishop and the authorities at the Colonial Office. It is impossible to summarize them here. But while Lady Surma had been in England, Mar Shimun XX (Polus), who had succeeded Mar Benyamin (the murdered Patriarch) in 1918, had died of consumption in May 1920. In her absence a minority of the Assyrians had taken the rash step of consecrating a boy of thirteen, Mar Ishai, nephew of Mar Polus, as Patriarch. This caused a cleavage between the Patriarchal family and the rest. By September 1921, the refugee camp at Baquba was dispersed: and a settlement of the Mountaineer Assyrians, in the Mosul Vilayet, was achieved, at an estimated cost to the British Exchequer of £400,000. But the Mosul frontier was uncertain—and revision expected. The Assyrians themselves were not easy to deal with, after two years of life in refugee camps. The settlement was not satisfactory; and, as a high British official admitted to the Archbishop, the British had undoubtedly made promises to the Assyrians which they were bankrupt of the power to fulfil: partly owing to the American default, and partly owing to the original Russian collapse.

IV

In May 1923, a new crisis arose with the startling change of policy announced by the British Government in Baghdad, by which the period of the Treaty between Great Britain and Iraq fixed—only eight months before—in October 1922 for twenty years was reduced to four years, or till such earlier date as Iraq might be admitted to membership of the League of Nations. This produced a great revulsion of feeling among the Assyrians in Iraq. They believed that they had finally embroiled themselves with Islam by their attitude during the War, and felt therefore that it would be impossible for them to remain in Asia after the withdrawal of British troops. Their whole attention therefore became concentrated on emigration, preferably to Canada or Australia.

In this unhappy situation, a new Assyrian visitor, Mar Timotheus, kinsman of Lady Surma and Metropolitan of Malabar in India, came to England. He was about forty years old. His health was bad, and he was subject to attacks which prostrated him for long periods, and his illness without doubt affected his spirits. He had long interviews with the Archbishop and others, including Government officials. He asked that the British Government should find the Assyrians a home. But he unhappily found it difficult to convince either the Archbishop or the Colonial Office that he was a very practical ambassador. Some of his proposals would have involved a war with Turkey—though Mar Timotheus said he did not want war. The Archbishop was obliged to face him with realities—and at a special meeting the Committee of the Archbishop's Assyrian Mission put into his hands a long Memorandum (drafted by the Archbishop), which set out the position as he and the Committee saw it, for Mar Timotheus's guidance on a projected visit to America, whither he urged him to go now. After outlining the history of the Mission's beginnings, emphasizing its purely religious aim as stated at the very start, and noting that 'the official papers issued at that time (1886) make it absolutely clear that the objects of the Mission were wholly spiritual and educational, and that everything of a political kind was excluded', the Memorandum proceeds:

Nov. 7, 1923.

A new situation arose a few years before the War. Approaches were made by Russian authorities, both civil and ecclesiastical, to the then Mar Shimun with a view to Russian protection, material as well as spiritual, being extended to the sorely-pressed and poverty-stricken people, both on Persian and Turkish sides of the frontier, who owed allegiance to Mar Shimun as Patriarch. The Patriarch accordingly explained to the Archbishop of Canterbury that he and his people desired to avail themselves of Russian rather than Anglican aid, and while retaining friendly relations with those who, like the Archbishop's Mission, had given them the sort of help above indicated, proposed to place themselves rather under the guidance of the Russian Orthodox Church.

Letters to that effect passed between Mar Shimun and the Archbishop of Canterbury at that time, and by August 1914, though there was no actual breach with the Archbishop of Canterbury's Mission, the Patriarch was endeavouring to place himself definitely under the guidance and direction of the Russian authorities.

At the outbreak of War, or rather early in 1915, as a result of Russian overtures and promises of help, the Assyrian fighting men rallied to the side of the Allies and fought against the Turks. But Russia, instead of holding, as had been anticipated, the dominant position in those regions, lost even the status it had held. The whole area was ultimately plunged into utter confusion. Before the War was over, Mar Shimun wrote to the Archbishop of Canterbury stating with plaintive earnestness, that his people had been abandoned by the Russians and left to the tender mercy of the Turks, and that they must again appeal to him to use his influence for their salvation.

The Armistice was signed a few months later, and the hope was at that time widely entertained that means might be found of re-establishing the Christian communities, both Armenian and Assyrian, in regions under their own quasi-independent Government, or under some Mandatory control. There was even a high hope that a Mandatory position might be undertaken in Mesopotamia by the United States. It is unnecessary to describe the political perplexities, disappointments, and confusion which late years have seen. It is certain that the Assyrian people have suffered untold hardship, and it is in no way unnatural that they should feel bitterly disappointed in finding that active European control under Christian auspices will, so far as it exists, be withdrawn ere long from the whole area which is the historic home of these Christian peoples. Into the question of political understandings or virtual promises given, or which were understood to have been given, by the military or political authorities during the War, it would be inappropriate to enter in this Memorandum. The point is that such political and military history is wholly independent of that which belongs to the Archbishop's religious and educational Mission. Naturally the representatives of the present Patriarch turn in their distress to the source from which so much friendly aid had been given them for a great many years until the time when they decided rather to rely upon the Russian support which would, as they hoped in their poverty, be of a more material kind. No one can be surprised if they fail to distinguish clearly at this time between the responsibilities, whatever they be, attaching to the political authorities, and the supposed responsibilities of the Archbishop's Mission, a Mission which had from its very beginning repudiated any responsibility other than that of a religious and educational kind.

After the War, Surma Khanim, the remarkable lady belonging to the Patriarchal family, and chosen to be her people's spokesman and to explain their necessities, visited England in 1920, under the auspices of His Majesty's Government, and was received by the British authorities, who attached the highest importance to her very able advocacy and her lucid exposition of her people's needs. Lord Curzon bore strong testimony to this in the House of Lords. Surma Khanim, herself a pupil trained by the Archbishop's Mission, was, during her stay in England, naturally in close touch with the Archbishop of Canterbury and others connected with that Mission, but she never failed to realise the distinction between the political or material considerations and the considerations belonging to the religious authorities as such.

On the 15th May 1922, a letter was written to the Archbishop of Canterbury, to be carried as a commission by Mar Timotheus, Metropolitan of Malabar, a native of Assyria who proposed to visit England from India to plead for his suffering fellow countrymen in Mesopotamia. Owing to a local law suit and other Indian business his journey was postponed, and he laid his letter before the Archbishop of Canterbury when he reached England during the present Autumn (1923). That letter, while it deals with the necessity for new Schools and other religious and educational needs, does to some extent appeal also for what is, in this Memorandum, described as political aid; and it has been necessary to point out to Mar Timotheus the distinction which this Memorandum draws. The Archbishop of Canterbury, however, has done his best to secure for Mar Timotheus the attention of the representatives of His Majesty's Government, who have shown perfect willingness to hear all that he has to say, and who have written to the Archbishop a very important explanatory letter, a copy of which is in Mar Timotheus' hands. In that letter the extreme difficulty of the situation is set out clearly and frankly, and it would only complicate matters were this Memorandum dealing with the Archbishop's Mission to enter into these.

It will not be supposed from what is above written that the Council of the Archbishop of Canterbury's Mission is indifferent to the terrible situation of the people whom, for so many years, the Mission has endeavoured, religiously and educationally, to help. The position is deplorable. Disappointment—even indignant disappointment, is natural, especially among those who are unable to estimate adequately the great political issues which are involved, and the vast sums that would be required were the political aspirations of the Assyrian people to be adequately satisfied. Everything that the Archbishop of Canterbury and those who work with him can do to further the interests of a Nation and a Church for which they have endeavoured so much, will continue to be done, and the Archbishop will in no way relax the constant effort he has made to aid His Majesty's Government by information or advice in its endeavour to grapple with the apparently almost insoluble problem of the situation.

In regard to the kind of work for which it has in past years held responsibility, the Archbishop's Mission has repeatedly assured the representatives of the Assyrians as well as the British Government and other authorities that, as a Council, it would to the very utmost of its power promote the establishment or revival of Christian Schools. But, as has been repeatedly pointed out, this endeavour can only be made with even tolerable effectiveness when the political and social conditions are such as to give reasonable guarantee for quietness, progress, and social order. These conditions are very far from having been realised at present.

The Memorandum was a grievous blow to Mar Timotheus; but it was the only way of making him see the real situation and the limitations of the power of the Archbishop of Canterbury.

The next few months, however, brought little further light—though there are many letters showing the Archbishop's close interest in the question of the frontier. In April 1924 Mar Timotheus left England for America—a disappointed man.

V

In the summer and autumn of 1924, the question of the boundary between Iraq and Turkey became acute; and the Archbishop had a good deal of correspondence on the subject, in view of the importance of the decision on which side of the Boundary the Assyrians were to be placed. In September 1924, the Council of the League of Nations decided to send a Commission to settle the question; and the Commissioners arrived in Baghdad the following January. That very month the seventeen-year-old Patriarch, Mar Shimun, arrived in England to undertake a plan for his education that had been discussed by Mar Timotheus on his behalf. The Archbishop himself was not quite happy in his mind as to the result of a spell of ordinary education in England—as a training for his peculiar duties. But it was arranged that Mar Shimun should be received as a pupil at

St. Augustine's College, Canterbury, where he remained for about a year, entering fully into the life of the College.

In March, Lady Surma wrote to Mrs. Davidson expressing her happiness at the care taken of Mar Shimun, and also saying she had seen the League of Nations Commissioner, who could promise her nothing. She added:

LADY SURMA *to* MRS. DAVIDSON

March 31, 1925.

Of course if there is not somebody to put the Assyrian cause strongly in the 'League', I fear that, having so big and important things to settle, our poor cause will be forgotten, or more likely will be soaked in Mosul oil.

In response to a further letter from Lady Surma, suggesting that she might herself be sent to Geneva to plead for the Assyrians, the Archbishop wrote promising to do his best, but warning her against hoping for the impossible. He was in constant touch with Sir Samuel Hoare at the Air Ministry, with Sir Percy Cox[1] and Mr. Amery at the Colonial Office; and eventually it was arranged that Lady Surma should fly to Geneva. The case for a boundary which would include the villages north of Mosul was put before the League by Mr. Amery. At the same time there was an agitation in the Press, abusing the Government and clamouring for the abandonment of Britain's obligations, mainly on the ground that by so doing great economies would be secured. The Archbishop was moved to make a public appeal to the Prime Minister against any such surrender:

The ARCHBISHOP OF CANTERBURY *to the* RT. HON. STANLEY BALDWIN

Lambeth Palace, S.E. 28th September, 1925.

If I keep silence I should not be doing justice either to my own feelings, or to the representations made to me by others with regard to the plight of our fellow Christians in Mesopotamia. It seems to me that public opinion is largely failing to realise virtual pledges of honour which are ours in regard to these unhappy people In the statements, arguments and appeals, which now find currency in the papers, the main emphasis appears to be laid upon questions of finance, questions of the material resources of the country—oil

[1] Sir Percy Cox was British High Commissioner in Mesopotamia, 1920–3; and British Plenipotentiary for negotiations with Turkey regarding the Turko-Iraq frontier, 1924.

or other—and questions of military strategy. With none of these am I competent to deal. . . .

I have myself, as you probably know, been for many years in close touch with the Christians of that whole region, and especially with the Assyrian Church. It is unnecessary for me to remind you of the acute sense which those Churches entertain of Britain's moral obligation, as regards the endeavour to protect them from the possibility of hideous and irreparable cruelty and wrong. I am now in close touch with the Christian leaders who are trying to safeguard the interests of the Assyrians and others, upon whose aid in the regiments we enlisted from among them Britain relied during the war.

Uninformed newspaper writers, and perhaps some politicians who are less uninformed, may talk airily to the effect that our proper policy is simply to rid ourselves of any responsibility in those distracted regions. They base their argument on economic grounds, and of course I am profoundly conscious of the complications of this question. I do not, however, feel justified in not assuring you how widespread among earnest and thoughtful people in England and Scotland would be the sense of shame, were it to be announced that we meant simply to ignore the pledges which we practically gave, and to leave the Christian populations in a position, to say the least, of the gravest peril.

It is with a full sense of the extraordinary difficulty of the situation that I desire to assure you of the strength of religious opinion which will be behind you if you are able to make it clear that, whatever else happens, we do not forget, or ignore, the obligations which we have incurred.

The Prime Minister promised that the Government should not lose sight of 'this important aspect of the problem'.

In October, a further appeal to public opinion was made by the Archbishop in view of the large deportation of Christians from Turkish territory, and the tragic suffering caused. A special Assyrian and Iraq Christians Committee was formed under his presidency, with the energetic leadership of Sir Henry Lunn, and the support of Mr. Amery. The Archbishop spoke at public meetings, and a fair amount of money was raised. But the Assyrians were once more filled with alarm by the decision of the League, in December 1925, which gave Mosul to Iraq under the mandate of Great Britain, but left the Assyrian territory (in the Hakkiari country) on the Turkish side of the frontier—a decision which proved later to be fraught with most unhappy consequences.

Lady Surma had come to England from Geneva, and saw a good deal of the Archbishop. The Archbishop communicated his view to Mr. Amery in the following letter:

The ARCHBISHOP OF CANTERBURY *to the* RT. HON. L. S. AMERY

28th December, 1925.

> I am afraid from what [Lady Surma] tells me that there is very little prospect of these unhappy Nestorians being settled on the frontier line in any way that would seem to them satisfactory for the future. This is disappointing, but I am bound to say they make a strong case as to the difficulties. Surma says that there are not, she thinks, more than the merest handful of children, say a dozen, among all the thirty thousand of her people who are now living in the flat country south of the Brussels line—this is owing to its unhealthiness. She may be exaggerating, but she has a great many facts. This is rather a depressing result to reach after all our efforts.

Mr. Amery was most sympathetic throughout the negotiations, but he could not hold out any hope of an improvement of the boundary—and he was not specially encouraging about the alternative plan put forward to Lady Surma by a body of Assyrian petitioners, 'that we should be emigrated to one of the British colonies whose climate suits us, so that we may live in peace and find an end to all our tribulations'. It seemed that there was nothing to be done, except to arouse sympathy. And the Archbishop welcomed the proposal made by Sir Henry Lunn that Lady Surma should visit America and tell her story there. She visited the United States and Canada in the spring of 1926—but the results were disappointing. She returned to Mosul in November 1926.

VI

The settlement of the Assyrians was still a problem for the future. The truth was that a problem, which might have been solved with comparative ease in the early days after the War, had been postponed and postponed until no satisfactory solution was possible. The British statesmen at home had allowed the conclusion of peace with Turkey to wait until victory had been forgotten. The Americans (as the Archbishop always felt) had contributed to the difficulty by washing their hands of the whole

Mesopotamian question. And money spent on their maintenance, enough to have settled the nation several times over, was no more available. The Assyrians, it must also be confessed, had sometimes brought new difficulties upon themselves—e.g. in the Great Raid of 1921, when Agha Petros attempted to create an independent state in the territory from Gawar to Ushnu; or in the Kirkuk outbreak of May 1924. Yet, to balance this, the Assyrian levy had done excellent service under British officers, and was still providing an admirable defence for the ground establishments of the British Air Force in Iraq. It was a piteous tale. The Archbishop kept the needs of the unhappy people as much to the fore as he could—but important as his influence and his interest were, he was not Prime Minister, nor was he the leader of a political party. He did his best to comfort Lady Surma, and told her of the constant assurance which he had received from the British officials on the spot that they would help in any way they rightly could. But his words, though full of sympathy, could only bring cold comfort to Lady Surma and her people:

The ARCHBISHOP OF CANTERBURY *to* LADY SURMA

22 June, 1927.

The fact is that the hopes we entertained during the war, and at its close, about the settlement of your tribes in a land of their own, where they could be protected by English influence, proved impossible of full accomplishment.

In August 1927, Mar Shimun left England for Iraq, having completed two years of English education, the first year at St. Augustine's College, Canterbury, and the second at Westcott House, Cambridge. On reaching Mosul, he found new difficulties and divisions in which Mar Timotheus himself played a prominent part. He wrote and told the Archbishop of the situation: though, alas, in its material aspects that showed no change. In November 1927, Dr. Wigram went out to Iraq, and sent the Archbishop a full account of what he found. But he was only able to state problems—which were still to await solution. The main question naturally concerned the settlement of the Assyrians, and the Archbishop was not destined to live to see any real progress made in that field.

CHAPTER LXXVI
VARIOUS EMPLOYMENTS

How various his employments whom the world
Calls idle, and who justly in return
Esteems that busy world an idler too.

COWPER, *The Task.*

THIS chapter headed 'Various Employments' might be equally well entitled 'A Chapter of Illustrations'; for we propose in the main part of the chapter to give a few typical instances of the calls which were made on the Archbishop's time and counsel, in addition to the heavy routine tasks of every day and the larger subjects which demand a special and fuller treatment. The employments described will for the most part fall within the closing five years of his primacy, though not quite entirely; and their variety, which could without difficulty be considerably enhanced, will help to illustrate the many-sidedness of the life at Lambeth. But, that we may avoid giving an impression of unbroken toil as the Archbishop's immutable lot, we shall end the section with a brief note on his holidays.

I

As Archbishop of Canterbury, Dr. Davidson had a special link with the Whitgift Hospital, Croydon. This was an ancient College with its cottage homes combined into a fair court, and its old brothers and sisters, founded in 1596 by Archbishop Whitgift. In 1923, not for the first time, the Croydon Corporation promoted a road-widening scheme which would have meant the demolition of the Hospital. The first attack had been made in 1884, when the Croydon Council desired to pull it down and build a Town Hall on the site. That plan was defeated locally. There were later schemes for road widening, on which Archbishop Benson kept a watchful eye.[1] And Archbishop Davidson

[1] Describing a visit to the Hospital in January 1889, Archbishop Benson wrote this in his Diary: 'I proposed to the whole table-full that we should let the College be removed to widen the street, and rebuilt in some pretty quiet country place. They said almost in horror that not a brick of the College must be touched—dear old place—and that they much preferred Croydon to any country place.

'Then I said would it not be agreeable to them to live at their own homes with

had himself helped to defeat a scheme involving demolition in 1909. The present onslaught was even more dangerous. On February 21, the Archbishop went with a deputation to the Ministry of Transport, carrying in his hand the original Rules of the Hospital signed by Archbishop Whitgift's own hand. On April 18, he took part in a debate in the House of Lords, on a motion by the Earl of Crawford:

> That it be an instruction to the Committee on the Croydon Corporation Bill to strike out of the Bill all powers relating to the compulsory acquisition of the Hospital of the Holy Trinity (otherwise known as the Whitgift Hospital) in Croydon with its Chapel and Offices.

The Archbishop, after referring to the facts of the case, said:

> We are keeping this year [1923] in some of its forms the tercentenary of Shakespeare. There is a large demand, as booksellers will tell you, for a vision of the England of Shakespeare's days—its scenery, urban and rural; its people and its buildings. Here we have a building, beautiful in its simplicity, remarkable for its quiet dignity, in the middle of a great noisy borough, built in Shakespeare's day, opened, worked, and occupied in Shakespeare's day practically as it is now, and used from that time forward, as it was used then, with the same green sward, the same little chapel, the same little common room and hall, the same warden's chambers, and the rest, from that time down to this. It stands at the centre of the great borough. Are we to allow it to be pulled down? If so, for what? To make the motor traffic, or the tram traffic a little easier or a little speedier at that point, while at the same time preserving intact the public house which stands opposite, and the shops that might well make way for the traffic. That is what we are asked to do.

The instruction was unanimously adopted.

The Archbishop had a genuine love of historic buildings, and deplored their destruction as though it were almost a sacrilege, so deep was his care for the continuity of English life. And it was the same kind of feeling which lay behind his dislike of the division of the old diocese of Winchester into three small bishoprics, and the alienation from Winchester of the historic Farnham

their own friends, and have a weekly allowance in full for whatever they now enjoyed? There was quite a clamour in answer—"No! no!" they almost shouted; "College was the thing—we are all proud of the College."' *Life of Archbishop Benson*, ii. 254.

Castle. His words on the episcopal palaces connected with the three senior sees of London, Durham, and Winchester, in the debate in the Church Assembly on the Division of Winchester Diocese, July 12, 1923, are significant of his attitude:

> It was not for love of big houses that most people desired to maintain the great places like Fulham, Farnham and Auckland Castle, which were symbols of what happened in past history, and examples of the way in which English people regarded the peculiar responsibility for the common good that rested on the men who lived in them. It was not for their own sakes, but for the common good, that a special status of responsibility was attached to these three dioceses. . . . A Bishop of Winchester, whose income was smaller than that of most dioceses in England, who had left the ancient home at Farnham which had a place in English life for many centuries, and was living in a house within the precincts of the Cathedral City, could not necessarily and inherently retain all that the old state of things carried with it. . . . Lord Selborne had suggested that if the diocese of Canterbury were to be reduced to the City of Canterbury and very little more, there would be no real change as regards the status and prestige of the diocese. The analogy was not close, because an Archbishopric had a status of its own. But Lord Selborne ought to have gone further, and asked whether it would make any difference to the position of the Archbishop of Canterbury, not merely if the See of Canterbury were reduced, but if he vacated Lambeth, and Lambeth were transferred to a council or a committee with a power of sale or power to use it for other purposes, and the Archbishop had to live at No. 16, The Precincts, Canterbury. The position of the Archbishop would not be ruined by that; but it would certainly be a changed position and the change would affect a great many things in English life. They were dealing to-day with something that concerned many different threads of English life, and reached back along those threads into the roots of English history.

II

A department of his official activities which gave him the keenest satisfaction was his work as Principal Trustee of the British Museum. The following account is from the pen of Sir Frederic Kenyon, with whom (as Director) Dr. Davidson was in the closest association during most of his tenure of the primacy. Sir Frederic in sending it adds 'no words would be strong enough to express my sense of his services to the Museum or of his kindness to myself':

The Archbishop first became a Trustee of the British Museum in 1884, as the nominee of the Sovereign. As Archbishop of Canterbury, he became *ex officio* the senior of the three Principal Trustees, and as such presided at every meeting of the Trustees or of the Standing Committee at which he was present. Some at any rate of his predecessors had not regarded these *ex officio* responsibilities as being of prime importance, and had only attended when some special business seemed to require their presence; but Archbishop Davidson took the duty seriously, and found it a pleasure. Though one of the busiest people in the kingdom, he attended whenever he was not imperatively required elsewhere; he made himself familiar with the work of the Museum, and his interest in it was very far from being perfunctory. With his natural gifts of character in addition, he was an admirable chairman, understanding all the points that arose, and was able both to guide and support the executive officers of the Museum.

My own acquaintance with him began shortly before my appointment as Director, when he sent for me to Lambeth, no doubt to satisfy himself as to the propriety of my nomination. To an inexperienced Director his support and advice were of inestimable value. He wished to be informed in advance of any important question that was likely to come up, and to have the materials for forming his judgement put before him; and he never failed to respond to any request for advice or help. He made it his principle to support the executive officers, and he never fussed about minor details; but he required to be informed, and to satisfy himself of the reasonableness of the course proposed to be taken. If he was not satisfied, he would seek information elsewhere, but never without informing the Director that he wished to do so and asking his assent. Such occasions were rare; but I remember one in particular, when he thought a suggested appointment would have been a hardship to another deserving member of the staff, and it need hardly be said that his judgement was followed. Where he gave his confidence, he gave it fully; and the Museum under his guidance was a happy family, and was troubled by few crises.

He was, however, quite ready to fight for the Museum when it was necessary. In the time of my predecessor, there was a period of sharp controversy, involving the relations between Bloomsbury and the Natural History Museum. The Archbishop went into all the details of the case, made up his mind as to the rights of it, and thereafter supported the Director and Principal Librarian without flinching. A recrudescence of the same trouble occurred early in my time, and again the Archbishop took his full share in publicly defending what he was satisfied was right. In such cases he never spared time or trouble. He took his full responsibility as the head of the Governing Body of the Museum.

His interest in the Museum included a constant care for the interests of the staff. He was always anxious that the senior officers of the Museum should receive due public recognition of their services. It was sometimes an ungrateful task to secure this recognition from an unsympathetic Prime Minister with many claims on his consideration; but the Archbishop did not hesitate to expose himself to rebuffs on behalf of the staff for whom he felt himself responsible. I have many letters from him expressing his regret that what he thought the just claims of distinguished officials of the Museum (not put forward by themselves in any instance within my knowledge, but on their behalf) had been disregarded; and, if he had had his way, some unfortunate omissions in this respect would not have occurred. If for a time no recommendations were put forward, he would sometimes ask whether they were not due. He thought that the merits of the Museum staff were undervalued in the world at large, and he did all that he could to secure their more adequate recognition.

Another instance of his care for the interests of the staff was in connexion with the Official Guide-Lecturers, who had come into existence during his time. When all efforts to secure a moderately adequate remuneration for them through the ordinary channels had failed, he put himself at the head of a formidable deputation of Trustees to the Prime Minister, which carried too much weight to be resisted. The sum involved was insignificant, except to the recipients of it; but he thought it their due, and was ready to exert himself to secure it.

During the War, the Museum had to face two crises of first-class importance. The first was the question of the protection of the collections from the danger of attack from the air. The Archbishop, as head of the body of Trustees, was in the early days of the War the target for much ill-informed and panicky criticism. The actual danger was at that time small; indeed there was more risk of injury to the collections by hurried removal than from enemy action, while public alarm would have been increased by exaggerated precautions. The Archbishop accepted this point of view, but not without satisfying himself on the subject by personally visiting the Museum, inspecting the basements available for storage, and interviewing some of the heads of departments. At a later date, in view of increased popular fears, he represented that, in the then existing circumstances, more alarm might be caused by not taking precautions than by taking them; and while it might be true that the chances of injury were mathematically very small, if a bomb *did* drop on the Museum, the Trustees would certainly be blamed for inaction. His advice, as usual, combined a wise estimate of actual facts with a statesmanlike perception of the necessity of taking account of public opinion; and the policy of graduated protection then adopted was on the lines which he had indicated. The final removal of all the more valuable objects to places of safety in the last year of the War, necessitated by official warnings of the greatly increased air peril to be expected, was a different matter, as to which there were no two opinions. It was a matter of necessity; though, as it turned out, no bomb fell on the Museum throughout the War.

A more serious crisis was the sudden proposal in December 1917 to take over the whole Museum as head-quarters for the Air Ministry. This hastily formed and ill-considered scheme had to be resisted to the utmost by all who cared for the treasures of the Museum and the honour of the country, to say nothing of the best interests of the Air Ministry, for which the Museum buildings were very ill-adapted. The Archbishop threw himself into the front of the fray, which was sharp though fortunately short. He attended two meetings of the War Cabinet to state the case for the Trustees. At the first his plea was somewhat light-heartedly dismissed on the ground that if the Air Ministry wanted the place, the opinion of the Trustees did not much matter; but at the second, when public opinion had expressed itself with unmistakable vigour, the advocates of the scheme beat a prudent retreat, and the Archbishop returned triumphant to receive the thanks of his colleagues for his successful defence.

For twenty-five years he remained the head of the Museum, as first of the Principal Trustees; and having served under him as Director for nineteen of those years, I can testify to his deep interest in the Museum, his courtesy and efficiency as chairman at the meetings of the Board,[1] his care for all grades of the staff, his loyal support of the officers, his constant readiness to help and advise, and (I cannot help adding) his most kindly personal friendship to

[1] The business was of the most varied—and unexpected—kind; and the Archbishop on returning to Lambeth used often to remark on the surprises which he had encountered. Thus in a Memorandum of June 22, 1922, he noted: 'On Saturday 22nd a very important meeting of the Natural History Museum—an odd question arose which it seemed strange that we ecclesiastics and statesmen should have to settle—the tendency among negro boys to eat young flamingoes, or again the skin-diseases of the humpbacked whales.' (*Dictated July 25.*)

myself. I know my predecessor had the same warmly affectionate feeling for him. When the time came for his decision to resign the Archbishopric, it became evident that he would deeply regret the termination of his connexion with the Museum; for his trusteeship being *ex officio*, it would cease with his tenure of the Archbishopric. It was clear that the Museum was not to him merely one of his official responsibilities, which he had discharged just because it was his way to take his responsibilities seriously, but that it had a strong hold on his affection. Fortunately it was found possible to avoid a severance which would have been equally regretted by the other Trustees and the staff. A Trustee (Lord Kilbracken), whose age and absence from town had for some time debarred him from attendance, readily resigned his Trusteeship, to which the Archbishop was promptly elected; and a supernumerary place was created for him on the Standing Committee, so that he might continue to take an active part in the administration of the Museum. His gratitude for this arrangement was most feelingly expressed; and to those connected with the Museum it was most gratifying to have this unimpeachable evidence of his affection for it. So, when the end came, he died as a Trustee of the Museum, after forty-six years continuous service; and the Museum felt deeply honoured when Lady Davidson invited its Director to be one of the pall-bearers at his funeral.

III

The Archbishop, by virtue of his office, was the recipient of many strange requests. Few were stranger than those repeated at intervals from 1915 to 1927—that he should arrange for the opening of a box supposed to contain sealed prophetic writings by Joanna Southcott—described by some as a prophetess, by others as a fanatic, and self-designated as 'The Lamb's Wife'—a farmer's daughter born in Devonshire in 1750. She had left directions at her death in 1814, after a most remarkable career, that the box should not be opened until a hundred years had passed, and then only in the presence of twenty-four Bishops, as representing the four-and-twenty elders described in Revelation iv. 4, and with a carefully prescribed ceremonial. Many were the petitions, and many were the prophecies, that if only the Archbishop would open the box untold blessings would result for the whole world. His invariable response was that it was unsatisfactory that any box containing old papers should be kept locked up for so long, and that in his judgement it should be opened; but he was accustomed to add that to prevent erroneous reports some one should be present at the opening, accustomed to making minor legal investigations—such as taking affidavits from witnesses or the like—say 'a solicitor in the neighbourhood who was entitled to public confidence', and that the papers should be placed under proper custody and examined at leisure by some impartial and competent man. He steadily refused, however, to be in any sense a party to the opening himself. The following is a letter sent by his direction in 1922. It is not without its humour:

The ARCHBISHOP'S PRIVATE SECRETARY *to the* REV. G. C. ROBINSON

Private. November 2nd, 1922.

The Archbishop of Canterbury directs me to thank you for your letter of October 28th, about Joanna Southcott and her mysterious box. For many years past His Grace has been importuned by good and earnest (but, as he thinks, misguided) people to convene a solemn council of Bishops before whom this box may be opened. He has always been strongly against such a course, feeling, as he does, that the whole idea of the opening of the box in such circumstances is fantastic, and that the belief of Joanna's followers that it contains some wonderful revelation of the Divine purposes rests upon quite unsubstantial grounds. He has, however, said that he sees no reason why the box should not be opened by the people who have the custody of it, in the presence of some reputable person or persons, in order that those who have an interest in the matter may be satisfied as to what it contains; but he has consistently declined to be a party to any arrangement of the kind demanded by Joanna's followers. Some ten years ago Bishop Boyd Carpenter, anxious to set the minds of these worthy enthusiasts at rest, consented to be present, with a few other trustworthy persons, at an opening of the box. But the good people concerned would not accept anything short of a council of 24 Bishops (representing, it was suggested, the four-and-twenty elders of the Apocalyptic vision) and the solemn opening of the box in their presence (see PS.). The Archbishop thinks that those who, like yourself, are not followers of Joanna, and yet desire the Bishops to accede to the request, cannot fail on reflection to see in what an absurd position the Bishops would be placed if, having consented to the conditions demanded, the box were opened in their presence and found to contain nothing more than an additional collection of the strange writings of that strange woman—or, conceivably, nothing at all!

PS. The Archbishop wishes me to add that, as a matter of fact, several Bishops did undertake to be present at the opening, and the Dean of Westminster offered that it should take place in the Jerusalem Chamber. This was declined by Joanna's followers, who said (if His Grace recollects rightly) that there must be, besides the 24 Bishops, 2,000 maidens in white—a not very easy arrangement. They were to represent, he thinks, the angels. Meantime two or three people wrote to say that there were rival boxes in different parts of England, and the Dean of Westminster and the others concerned allowed the matter to come to an end. This is private, but the Archbishop thinks that you ought to know about it.

The whole proceedings struck the Archbishop as 'partly profane and partly ridiculous'. The opening of the box was at last achieved on July 11, 1927. The scene was the Church House, Westminster, under the auspices of the National Laboratory for Psychical Research. The box was opened in the presence of one Bishop alone, the Bishop of Grantham, with the help of a Professor, and of a sufficient audience. The contents of the box had been already X-rayed, but, when the bands round it had been cut, the first two objects extracted by the Bishop were a woman's night-cap and a book called 'The Surprises of Love: or An Adventure in Greenwich Park'. The remaining treasures were a little less strange, but of hardly greater importance to the destinies of the world—a lottery ticket of 1796, a calendar of the French Court in 1793, a medal of Augusta, Princess of Wales, of 1772, a pistol, a dice-box, and a few coins. It was, truly, a queer revelation![1]

IV

In the course of his life there were many occasions on which the Archbishop was asked to give his advice on marriage questions of different kinds—and the demands increased after the War. In offering his counsel, he was never doctrinaire. But, while perfectly clear in his ruling, he often appealed to what he called common sense, and sometimes founded his answer on the actual wording of the marriage vows in the Service in the Book of

[1] In view of this discomfiture, episcopal aid is now (1935) being solicited for the opening of another box, alleged also to be the true box.

Common Prayer. Thus, where one of the parties was a Quaker, and so unbaptized, he would not feel obliged, solely on the ground of lack of baptism, to advise against marriage in the parish church, if both parties so desired; but would ask rather whether both parties fully appreciated the whole solemnity and doctrine of the Service, including the significance of the lifelong vow in the Name of the Trinity. From time to time he was asked to give advice or a ruling where one of the parties was a Jew. His attitude on such occasions is well indicated in the following letter to a young woman, the grand-daughter of an archdeacon, well known in old days to the Archbishop:

The ARCHBISHOP OF CANTERBURY *to* MISS ——

November 2, 1925.

I have your important letter of October 29th. The problem you raise is one which has frequently been before me. It resolves itself practically into this: Can a parish priest be urged to marry a man who distinctly declines to call himself a Christian and who has to make a Declaration of a most solemn kind 'In the Name of the Father, and of the Son, and of the Holy Ghost'? There are many men who, though nominally Jews, are virtually Christians of a liberal sort, and I have every wish to encourage such. But it is another thing to ask a priest to put those words into the mouth of a man to whom the central phrase is not only unmeaning but untrue. I had to discuss the subject with a leading statesman not long ago whose son was in the same position as the bridegroom in this case, and after looking into it all he told me he was sure that I was right. I am very sorry but I cannot say otherwise, deeply as I sympathize with you in the circumstances.

His correspondent replied that, when her fiancé first discussed the question with her, 'he was prepared to be baptised if that was essential, but we were told it was not—for which he was glad as he did not like the idea of going through a service in which he had to make reservations'. She added:

MISS —— *to the* ARCHBISHOP OF CANTERBURY

November 4, 1925.

Another question I would ask Your Grace, if you feel that it is wrong for an unbaptised person to use the termination 'In the name of the Father, and of the Son, and of the Holy Ghost'—would it not be possible to omit that and substitute 'In the name of God the Father'?

The Archbishop replied:

The ARCHBISHOP OF CANTERBURY *to* MISS ——

9 November 1925.

I thank you for your letter of November 4th. I note what you tell me as to an interpretation which the bridegroom might, in this case, be prepared to put upon the Christian words; but in the same letter you point out to me that he is definitely not in any full sense prepared to accept the position of membership in the Christian Church as such. You tell me that he is not baptised, and that he could not in honesty be baptised because he would have to make 'reservations'. With a view to meeting the difficulties, you suggest that I should sanction the alteration in the Marriage Service of the very solemn words in which the bridegroom makes his declaration. To do this would be illegal, even if it were desirable. I am very sorry indeed that you should be confronted with difficulties so grave, but I think you hardly realize what would be the position were the Archbishop of Canterbury to declare that it is the duty of a parish priest to use this quite distinctly Christian Service with a Christian declaration of a dogmatic kind at its centre for the marriage of one who, however earnest and excellent his religious life, is not prepared to declare himself a member of the Church of Christ.

The Archbishop's general attitude towards changes in the Law regarding the dissolution of the marriage bond has been explained in some detail in connexion with Lord Buckmaster's Matrimonial Causes Bill 1920. He had, however, an increasing number of personal problems propounded to him by clergy and others. He never shirked the difficulties which particular cases only too often involved; and was always willing both in letter and in conversation to give the best help he could. But the principles which guided his advice were always the same; and are clearly stated in the following letter, written to an incumbent of the diocese regarding his son who had become engaged to a lady who, some six years previously, had divorced her husband for gross misconduct. The incumbent concerned was very unhappy and wished to do what was right. The Archbishop replied:

The ARCHBISHOP OF CANTERBURY *to the* REV. ——

July 18, 1924.

I am afraid I can never regard it as other than extremely undesirable (I could use a much stronger term) that a man should marry a lady who has passed through the Divorce Court. We may be perfectly persuaded in our own mind of the innocence of the petitioner in a Divorce Suit, and very often he or she is, as you say, much to be pitied, but undoubtedly the remarriage of such a person, be it man or woman, is contrary to the spirit and intent of our Church, if not to its positive enactments. I express the sense I entertain of disapproving of such marriages by declining to issue a Licence for their celebration. I do not say that it is impossible that such a Licence could be issued in some quite extraordinary case, but as a practice we decline to issue them.

With regard to a priest celebrating such a marriage in church after Banns, I have never forbidden him to do so if he makes up his own mind that it is right. I do not think he is guilty of an offence by so doing, and I leave the responsibility with him. I do not think, again, that it would be true to say that the priest celebrating such a marriage is condoning sin. It would be difficult to declare it so, when we remember that such men as Bishop Christopher Wordsworth of Lincoln, Bishop Edward King of Lincoln, and Canon William Bright of Christ Church, three of the staunchest Churchmen of the century, though deprecating these marriages as undesirable, believed in and advocated their legitimacy. I am not sure that Bishop Wordsworth does not draw a distinction between the husband and the wife in the matter. But anyhow none of those three regard the thing as in itself sinful. I do not consider that an innocent divorcee thus remarried is thereby excluded from Communion.

I feel deeply for you in this trial in your life, and I feel sure that you are acting wisely in taking care not to let what has occurred bring about a breach between yourself and your son. I am quite sure that you want to do what is right in the matter.

Again, as the Visitor of some schools and on the governing body of others, the Archbishop had, on more than one occasion, to consider the difficult situation caused when a schoolmaster divorced his wife and married again. These cases undoubtedly caused him a great deal of anxiety, as two separate questions were involved, one concerning the continuance of the individual master on the staff, the other, the admission of the master as a member of the Church of England to Holy Communion. Generally speaking, the Archbishop took the view that the first was a matter for the headmaster, and one in which the governing body might claim some say; while the second was a matter for the Bishop of the diocese. With regard to the latter he did not take any different line from that which he was accustomed to take in dealing with the various individual cases which came before him. Putting the matter succinctly, he wrote to a particular headmaster who had consulted him, as follows:

The ARCHBISHOP OF CANTERBURY *to the* HEADMASTER OF ——

November 20, 1922.

Personally I have never regarded the remarriage of the innocent party after divorce as disqualifying for Communion the innocent man or woman who has thus remarried; but I greatly dislike and disapprove of such remarriages. I refuse to grant Licences for them or to perform them. Somė of my Episcopal brothers go further and regard the remarriage as grossly sinful. I cannot myself take that view greatly as I disapprove of the act. I follow in this the line taken by Bishop King and Dr. William Bright.

On the general question with which the headmaster and the governing body were concerned, after a good deal of consideration he expressed his final views in a letter which was clearly intended by him to be of general application:

The ARCHBISHOP OF CANTERBURY *to the* HEADMASTER OF ——

July 27, 1923.

You will remember that in our recent conversation I told you that I should like to write you a letter indicating my personal view respecting the problem you have recently had before you at ——.

I feel strongly that a man who accepts a mastership in one of our great Public Schools places himself under limitations affecting his personal liberty of action to a degree inapplicable in the case of an ordinary man, whether he be in Orders or a layman. The life, and not least the domestic life, of a schoolmaster concerns many others besides his intimate friends or his family circle. Especially does this principle become applicable when any question of divorce and remarriage arises. There may be men who are placed in a position which, in their view, necessitates application to the Divorce Court for relief. I do not think this is certainly so, for I believe that judicial separation could practically effect in almost all cases what is obtainable by a divorce, with the single difference that remarriage is not possible. But, granted that divorce may sometimes be necessary or possibly even desirable (a large assumption), it is quite clear that a man cannot be under a corresponding obligation to effect a new marriage. I think that if any master on the staff of a great Public School decides to apply to the Divorce Court, opportunity should be taken by the Headmaster or the authorities of the School to intimate to him that, should he obtain a divorce, his remarriage after such divorce would not during the life of the divorced wife be consonant with his position as one of the School Staff of Masters. There is perhaps no subject upon which there are keener feelings aroused at present, in great sections of our population, than upon this subject, and, considering how far reaching is the trust which parents repose in the master under whom their son is placed in a Public School, they ought not, I think, to be liable to the risk of finding that the master whom they thus trusted has placed himself in a position which they regard as morally wrong. Further, if a new wife takes the position towards little boys which the wife of a good schoolmaster rightly takes, the difficulty is enhanced, and the distress to certain parents who feel keenly on such matters is necessarily great. At the same time, the parents are in present conditions precluded from removing the son, as he probably could not obtain a corresponding position in any other school.

A Headmaster ought not, I think, to find any real difficulty in putting this before any master whom he knows to be instituting divorce proceedings. But the Headmaster's action in so doing would, I suppose, be facilitated if he were able to say that he was acting upon a settled rule or custom or upon the advice of those to whom he is entitled to turn for authoritative counsel. I have, of course, no such status as entitles me to lay down such a rule with authority or to prescribe to a Headmaster the course he ought to follow, but I should not feel quite happy, in view of what has recently occurred, did I not say that such is my deliberate opinion, and place the opinion thus on record. Nor should I feel myself precluded from stating to colleagues on the Governing Body, or to Headmasters and Assistant Masters in our Public Schools, that I do formally put this opinion in writing as one by which I am prepared to stand. I would go further and say that, if a Headmaster were being appointed to a School wherein I occupied a leading position on the Governing Body, I should probably feel it to be right to make to him such a formal statement of opinion. Of course it is entirely different with regard to one who is already a Headmaster. He must judge for himself as to what is right after weighing circumstances and counsel to the best of his ability.

V

From the first moment that it even appeared to come within the range of practical politics, the Archbishop was a firm supporter of the League of Nations. It was, therefore, very fitting that Dr. Davidson should be asked to preach the sermon in St. Peter's Cathedral,[1] Geneva, on the Sunday before the opening of the Third Assembly of the League of Nations. But it was none the less very remarkable—and made a great stir at the time—that an Archbishop of Canterbury should preach in the pulpit of John Calvin. The Archbishop, describing his visit, wrote thus:

> September 12, 1922.
>
> During the last fortnight we have had an experience novel and unforgettable in attending the Assembly of the League of Nations. It was suggested by many of those prominent in the matter, notably Willoughby Dickinson and Robert Cecil, that it would be a good thing if I were to preach at Geneva before the opening of the third Assembly of the League, and after going into the matter we decided to accept. Arthur Balfour, Fisher, and Lloyd George himself expressed to me their earnest satisfaction at my resolve, and that it would make a genuine difference to the position of the League in the public eye.

He saw a great deal during the time—going over the Headquarters of the League, and of the International Labour Office, attending two meetings of the Council, besides the Assembly, and having many talks with Balfour (on the problem of the Holy Places in Palestine, and the Near East generally), Lord Robert Cecil, Mr. Herbert Fisher, and others, as well as with leading Swiss pastors and laymen:

> Sunday, September 3rd, we went to the English Church early. I celebrated, and walked home with Robert Cecil. We went to the Cathedral by 10.30 or so, and found the congregation mustering already in great force. Seats were reserved for officials of all sorts, and the whole place was crowded. Some were standing at the West End where hearing must have been difficult. Arthur Balfour came in before the service and was introduced by me to the Consistoire.

The Archbishop went to his place at the east end of the cathedral, the little silver cross on its ebony staff, which had been presented

[1] 'By courteous permission of the Consistory of the National Protestant Church at Geneva'.

to him by the Bishops of the Lambeth Conference, steering him through the people, past the pulpit, up to the stalls on the east—a rather notable and unfamiliar sight in this Protestant shrine. Mr. Balfour read the Lesson. The sermon, which 'lasted for some 50 minutes, but nobody seemed to mind', was an admirably planned and considered statement of the Christian doctrine on the obligation of a State and a group of States towards our Lord's words 'Seek ye first the Kingdom of God'; on the positive duty of the nations to seek righteousness; and on the positive constructive work done by the League itself in promoting the righteousness of God—'in its deliberate care for what is just, what is merciful, what is tender to human weakness', with special reference to the 22nd and 23rd Articles of the Covenant. And it ended with a strong, massive appeal against war:

> I have left to my last word the gravest and most urgent of our thoughts, that to which, after all, the League of Nations owes its birth—the awful, the horrible, the devil-devised barrier of war. Vain to talk of the 'righteousness of God' while that monstrous arbitrament impends. . . . We have seen with our own eyes, we have heard in our own homes and hospitals, its unspeakable, its illimitable horrors. And deliberately we say that, God helping us, there shall be no 'next time'. The foremost thinkers and statesmen and rulers now alive in Christendom have thrown their strength into devising plans—by tribunals, by delays, by pledges, by conditions, by sanctions—to make the thing impossible. And meantime we may surely say that militarism has fashioned its own coffin. We are here to clinch the nails. Every thinking man who is worthy of the name, whatever his creed, whatever his nationality, is with us in the resolve. Civilized humanity, yea, and uncivilized, is on our side. It is, or it ought to be, unthinkable that we fail. . . . We are here to-day as Christians. If only every man and woman who holds that holy faith, could realize for himself, for herself, what the love of Jesus Christ our Saviour means, would there be need for a League of Nations? Before the impact of that love, whatever is vile or cowardly or self-seeking would go down, and righteousness and peace would stand. And it is there. Use it to that great end. Concentrated here on holy ground in this nineteen hundred and twenty-second year of grace—year of Christ—we call God to witness that, as Christians, we will neither doubt nor flinch nor fail. Once let the Christian men and women upon earth, West and East, North and South, kneel to God side by side, stand shoulder to shoulder before men, to say what they mean

> shall happen, or rather, what shall not happen, in the round world again, and they are irresistible. Would to God that any words of mine to-day should help to rally that unconquerable force to pledge itself with one voice to the great emprise. Resistless, invincible, yes, because it is the Will of God, and if we answer to that Will there is none other that can stand. The Lord God Omnipotent reigneth. May the kingdoms of this world become the kingdoms of our Lord and of His Christ.

But though the Archbishop was beyond doubt a steadfast champion of peace—he was always a realist. He was not willing to commit himself to vast world conferences, with no special plan behind them—and more than once he refused to be party to a great utterance in favour of world peace 'at this very time for example [October 1922] when the Near East is hovering on the brink of war, which we are doing all that we can, God helping us, to avert, but which may become any day a reality'. The very same distrust of generalities and vagueness also made him somewhat cold to Memorials on War Guilt, or Peace Letters. Thus he wrote to the Bishop of Manchester (Dr. Temple):

The ARCHBISHOP OF CANTERBURY *to the* BISHOP OF MANCHESTER

October 9, 1924.

> I realize the importance of your suggestion that the Bishops should commit themselves to a statement about War guilt in 1914, but I own that I see the greatest difficulty or even impossibility in getting the Episcopate to sign any document of the sort you suggest. I fear I should myself feel bound to say, if the matter were discussed, that while I entirely agree in saying that a hundred years of international rivalries, commercial and other, had their natural sequence in a War it is impossible to place ourselves on a level with either Germany, Austria, Russia, or possibly France, in regard to responsibility for the 1914 War. I know too well the ceaseless endeavours which had been made by all our best leaders in this country to avert such a calamity and to quench as far as they could the inflammatory endeavours of our militant section of Englishmen. If I feel this, I am certain that many other Bishops would feel it much more strongly, and even if this were not so, can it be said that a private Meeting of Bishops is a proper place for formulating a document on that subject? I cannot think so. But I should like to talk the matter over with you.

In a similar spirit he refused to sign the following peace letter to the Prime Minister, which was forwarded to him by Mr. Arthur Ponsonby:

Proposed Letter to the PRIME MINISTER

Sir,

We the undersigned, convinced that all disputes between nations are capable of settlement either by diplomatic negotiation or by some form of International Arbitration, hereby solemnly declare that we shall refuse to support or render war service to any Government which resorts to arms.

The Archbishop replied:

The ARCHBISHOP OF CANTERBURY *to* A. PONSONBY, ESQ.

November 26, 1925.

Sheer stress of work by day and night has delayed my reply to your letter of November 19th. I am afraid I could not sign, for transmission to the Prime Minister, the blunt little letter which you enclosed. I do not think that we can thus in a sentence dogmatize in such a way as to cover all possible contingencies. Ought the Swiss in the days of William Tell to have made such a declaration? Ought Belgium to have made it in 1914? Perhaps you will say 'Yes' in both cases, but peace-lover as I am, my dogmatic instinct is not keen enough to take that view in this unhesitating way. I have never been able to support the principles which Tolstoy inculcated, and your letter to the Prime Minister seems to mean that and nothing else. The League of Nations would have to be rewritten if this were what we held.

VI

It was just in these last five years of his Archbishopric that Dr. Davidson came into touch with the great new public service of broadcasting.[1] In March 1923, he was approached by Mr. J. C. W. Reith, the General Manager of the Company, with regard to the provision of addresses at religious services on Sundays, and the formation of a small advisory committee. At that time, so Mr. Reith told the Archbishop, there were something like 100,000 listeners in London. The Archbishop was much interested in the whole idea, asked various questions, and saw at

[1] The British Broadcasting Company was formally incorporated December 15, 1922, and on January 18, 1923, received a licence to establish and work a system of broadcasting.

once the possibilities. In the course of conversation Mr. Reith suggested that the Archbishop might like to hear wireless for himself: and accordingly he and Mrs. Davidson dined with the Reiths on March 20. While they were talking together before dinner, Mr. Reith pressed the button turning on the wireless unobserved by the Archbishop and Mrs. Davidson. They were entirely amazed. The Archbishop arranged for a conference of some fourteen Churchmen and Free Churchmen on April 20, 1923—sending out the following note for agenda beforehand:

> On Friday, April 20th, at 5 p.m., I am holding at Lambeth Palace a little private meeting of some twelve or fifteen people to discuss the question laid before me by the promoters of the Broadcasting System as to the use which could rightly and profitably be made of broadcasting on Sundays and especially Sunday evenings. Ought there to be a religious element? If so, what? And by whom arranged? The officers of the Broadcasting Company, whose aim is obviously a high one, are anxious to have wise advice.
>
> RANDALL CANTUAR:

The meeting actually took place in the Archbishop's room in the House of Lords. The Archbishop warmly welcomed Mr. Reith's two principles of (1) no transmission during the hours of service, (2) a religious address every Sunday evening. An advisory committee was set up in London representing the Church of England, the Free Churches, and the Roman Catholics; and similar committees were started in connexion with the various stations. The question of broadcasting regular church services was discussed between the Archbishop and Mr. Reith; but this was postponed, and Mr. Reith himself took the view that, after the refusal of the Dean of Westminster to allow the wedding of the Duke of York to be broadcast from the Abbey, he was not ready to make any more overtures in that direction for the time. The Archbishop's own first broadcast was on the last night of the same year, December 31, 1923—and all went well.

VII

The Archbishop was not a frequenter of the theatre. He appreciated a really good production of Shakespeare's plays; and though not musical he thoroughly enjoyed Gilbert and Sullivan's operas. It was not, however, until the last years of his life that, as

Archbishop, he actually saw a modern play—the first two being Drinkwater's *Abraham Lincoln* and *Robert E. Lee.* In 1924, he saw Bernard Shaw's *St. Joan*, and the following letter from the actress who played the title part—an old friend of the Davidsons since Rochester days—reflects something at least of his interest in that drama.

DAME SYBIL THORNDIKE *to the* ARCHBISHOP OF CANTERBURY

6 Carlyle Sq. New Theatre. June 7, 1924.

I do not know how to thank you enough for writing so kindly and so helpfully in the midst of your overwhelmingly busy life. It was a great encouragement and stimulant to us both to have such a letter. When one is engrossed and absorbed, as we have necessarily to be in the technical side of one's art, one is apt to lose sight a little of the other side of it—for which of course one primarily exists—the effect on the public. This play and the Greek plays have shown us how the public do respond to something which is fundamentally great. This *St. Joan* is particularly wonderful to me because it is the first great Christian play I've ever known. The Greeks have influenced our art so much—and even Shakespeare in his greatest moments gets away from Christianity to the real tragedy of the Pagan. It was Shaw or Masefield that said to me the other day 'There is no such thing as a Christian tragedy', and *that*'s what has made 'Joan' so marvellous to me—it has shown that there *is* in people—in humans—something as profound as tragedy but transcending it. Tragedy was the expression of the highest and most moving—the deepest things that humans share; I've often wondered why there was nothing that touched the heights and depths that was of happiness instead of sorrow—but I've found out its only in Christianity one gets the bigger expression. One has known it in pictures. Christianity has produced the greatest—that's why I love *St. Joan* so—it has something of the quality of the mediaevals, only in the modern expression. But it needs great Christians to write this thing which transcends tragedy, and G.B.S. has at last shown a Faith which we who know him and love him have been sure was there—but he hides his own self so—and he is such a great deeply religious man. Please forgive this long vague answer. Your letter was so wonderful—we wish we could find more such plays—but they will come, I feel, because people *want* them. Thank you from both of us for your very kind thought—coming to the play and writing to us.

The Archbishop liked a good, simple story, well acted. Once he went to see Tchekov's *Cherry Orchard.* Miss Mary Mills, who went with him, writes:

> It was an anxious experiment, but succeeded because in every scene he felt that something must bring matters to a head; and as the curtain went up on one scene he whispered, 'I think he *must* propose now!'—but of course nothing did occur.

Dr. Davidson was on various occasions privately consulted by the Lord Chamberlain, when questions arose about plays on religious subjects. Two typical answers are given below.

The ARCHBISHOP OF CANTERBURY *to the* EARL OF CROMER

13th November 1924.

I return herewith the Play *Judas Iscariot.* I wish they did not write these Plays, for the men who write them are not men qualified to handle these great subjects greatly. This good man has handled it feebly but quite harmlessly unless we were to say that nothing of the kind could be on the Stage at all, and that position can no longer be sustained. So far therefore as I am concerned I should raise no criticism to your giving him the licence. My belief is that the Play is so thin that it would not attract great attention. One dare not, however, say this when the title is of so sensational a sort and the whole subject is so unfamiliar to quantities of our fellow countrymen that they may imagine Mr. Thurston to be an original theological thinker, which is very far from being the case. Nothing could be more reverent and proper than the style in which he writes, granted that we are to have such Plays. I am rather glad that Bernard Shaw does not take a Play of that sort in hand for he might raise for us much more perilous issues.

A more difficult issue was raised when John Masefield asked for permission to present for public performance a play in which Our Lord appeared. The play (*The Trial of Jesus*) was stated certainly to go beyond what had been previously allowed in the treatment of the subject. The Archbishop gave his opinion as follows:

The ARCHBISHOP OF CANTERBURY *to the* EARL OF CROMER

10th March 1926.

I have read the Masefield play, or nearly all of it. The problem before you is not an easy one and I am afraid it is going to be a recurrent one. In these circumstances it seems to me that the moment has come when there must be some quite definite ruling adopted for the time at least in dealing with these border-line religious questions when they arise. If so, one very simple rule would be that whatever else is sanctioned or forbidden it must be definitely forbidden that our Lord Himself should be represented on the stage as a character in a play. In this particular play the author has said nothing that is irreverent and nothing, so far as I can judge, which is necessarily inconsistent with the Gospel narrative, though I should take exception if I were a critic to some of the implications, and I think it most undesirable that the passages about our Lord's Mother which you have marked should stand in any authorised play. Of course the opinion which the speakers express in those passages is not a new or modern scoff or talk; it has occasionally found expression for many generations but it is unnecessary to the course of the narrative and I think it does harm.

The real point, however, on which I should lay emphasis is that our Lord appears as a character in the drama and although his actual spoken words are said with greater or less accuracy to be only what Scripture or ancient tradition gives us, the fact remains that the Divine Figure is placed upon the stage. Of course 'Oberammergau' would be quoted by the other side, but that stands entirely by itself. It has never been regarded as falling within the category of licensed dramatic representations. I think a quite clear rule laid down to the effect that our Lord Himself must not appear in a drama would be understood by the public generally if the question were raised. Once sanction it and I do not see where you could stop. Suppose, for example, some great drama were written on Miltonic lines introducing not our Lord only but even God the Father. Most people I think would be shocked and public opinion would certainly support the authorities in refusing licence for it. Masefield I think is a very reasonable person and I believe would understand such a prohibition as I have suggested. Its value lies in its definiteness. It is not a matter of degree alone but of positiveness, and this would make the rule easier both to understand and to apply. Probably in this case you would feel it to be right that a letter should be written to the author so as to show that you are not accusing him of irreverence or profaneness but that you simply must apply such a rule as I have suggested. Of course it would not mean that you were necessarily going to sanction every Gospel drama from which the Figure of our Lord was absent. Each case would have to be considered on its merits, but you could at least be quite definite in the particular point.

I am afraid that all this is rather unhelpful, but I find it very difficult to say more. To tighten the rein overmuch when the author is reverent in intent and phrase might I think lead to reaction and protest, whereas I do not think protest would be awakened by the definite ruling that the Figure of our Blessed Lord Himself must not be produced in any drama which you sanction.

VIII

The Archbishop was from time to time invited to write prefaces, or (in later years) tributes to his contemporaries. He often consented, and indeed liked to pay honour to those who had been his friends or fellow workers. On one particular occasion he was invited to undertake the more arduous task of writing a study of Queen Victoria in the closing years of her life. In 1925, he noted in his Papers as follows:

> I have been feeling very anxious as to what might happen when the next volume of Queen Victoria's Letters are published, as I think they may present a picture of her which would need a good deal of explanation if it is to be rightly understood. I have long had a great wish that Rosebery should write a little preface to the volumes, for it would come with quite unique weight from him, considering his detachment from partisan questions and the width of his knowledge of European as well as English statesmanship. We visited him at Dalmeny in September, and I pressed it upon him again, but I could not get him to undertake even the briefest production of the kind. I dread the growth of a totally misleading view, which may be taken by a generation of readers who never saw her, and who will probably quite underrate the magnitude of her real influence on English life, and the grounds on which it rested. Of course he and others say that I ought to write something myself, but that is quite different from anything which might emanate from a man like Rosebery. Any words of mine would be utterly discounted in a way which his could not. Bigge agrees with me about this, and the same applies, though for different reasons, to himself; what he wrote would be looked upon as belonging to the clique of her own people and not to English life as a whole. I am hoping to see Rosebery again at the Durdans, and shall return to the charge, but with very faint hope of success.

The Archbishop read some of the proofs of the new volume (Second Series, vol. i) in the summer. He tried his best to persuade Lord Rosebery to write, but with little result. 'I could no more extract from my decrepit brain a piece worthy of Queen Victoria than I could jump over the moon'—so he wrote to the

Archbishop on February 8, 1926. Mr. Geoffrey Dawson, the editor, then begged the Archbishop himself to write a short article. The Archbishop consented, and the article duly appeared in *The Times* on February 24, the day before the publication of the *Letters*. He was glad to do it, for, as he said, the general estimate of that august Lady amongst the younger generation of average Englishmen was not a true one, underrating her real greatness both as woman and as Queen. The Archbishop spoke of her unfailing memory, 'tireless diligence applied with straightforward common sense', 'lofty moral standard', 'imperative sense of duty', 'intense human sympathy', and the whole 'permeated by genuine religious earnestness'. But perhaps the most interesting paragraph in the article, from the biographer's point of view, is the following:

> What exactly it was which constituted the irresistible charm attaching to her, I have never been able quite clearly to define, but I think it was the combination of absolute truthfulness and simplicity with the instinctive recognition and quiet assertion of her position as Queen and of what belonged to it. I have known many prominent people, but with hardly one of them was it found by all and sundry so easy to speak freely and frankly after even a very long acquaintance. I have sometimes wondered whether the same combination of qualities would have been as effective in a person of stately or splendid appearance. May it have been that the very lack of those physical advantages, when combined with her undeniable dignity of word and movement, produced what was in itself a sort of charm? People were taken by surprise by the sheer force of her personality. It may seem strange, but it is true that as a woman she was both shy and humble. Abundant examples will occur to those who knew her. But as a Queen she was neither shy nor humble, and asserted her position unhesitatingly.

The tribute (which in the end had a brief note from Rosebery attached as a sort of postscript) was received with general admiration. Lord Rosebery himself described it as giving 'the fairest and most illuminating portrait of the Queen that we have'. Mr. Buckle wrote to the same effect, and with a particular appreciation of the literary expression: while the following, from Lord Esher, was a prophecy of the complete change of public opinion about Queen Victoria which in fact followed the publication of the *Letters* with an almost miraculous rapidity:

VISCOUNT ESHER *to the* ARCHBISHOP OF CANTERBURY

Roman Camp, Callander, N.B. 23 Feb. 1926.

I like your admirable paper immensely. I only wish my review was half as good. The most striking thing you say is the contrast between the shy humble woman, and the Queen, who was neither. It is so true.

The silly people, and the writers out for 'effect', who scoff at the Queen and her servants have no chance at all against the overwhelming facts and the 'documentation'—as the French say—which cannot fail to place the Queen on a par (not second) with Elizabeth. Both had their frailties. Both left a deeper mark on England than any other sovereign.

Rosebery would have been good. But *no one* carries so much conviction as you do—standing outside the political arena.

IX

There was one employment or post of honour which did not come his way, though many desired it for him, partly because of this very independence of the political arena. But the story is not without its value.

It so happened that in the spring of 1925 a new Chancellor for the University of Oxford had to be elected, in succession to Lord Curzon and Lord Milner. The President of Trinity sounded the Archbishop in the middle of May to see whether he would allow himself to be nominated. There was much talk and much correspondence. It was clear that the Archbishop had a good deal of support. It was also clear that those who, on the conservative side, had so recently secured the election of Lord Milner had no other candidate to put forward. But the Archbishop disliked the notion of any contest—and he particularly disliked the thought of a contest which would be anti-liberal, and also anti-Asquith; for Lord Grey had been dropped in favour of Lord Oxford, who had the support, outside the residents, both of Sir John Simon and of Lord Birkenhead. The Archbishop accordingly wrote the following letter to the President of Trinity (Dr. H. E. D. Blakiston):

The ARCHBISHOP OF CANTERBURY *to the* PRESIDENT OF TRINITY COLLEGE, OXFORD

Lambeth Palace. May 30, 1925.

Let me first say how gratefully I appreciate the kindness, the considerateness and the judgment which you have shown as regards myself in this rather tangled business of the Chancellorship. I have also had a quite new and unexpected revelation of friendship and confidence on the part of many of those whom I respect most cordially both in Oxford and outside. To them too I am intensely grateful. I am, of course, not so foolish as to suppose that personality has been the main factor, or even a large factor, in evoking the encouragement and support of those on whose behalf you have been writing to me. It is largely to the Office which I hold that the respect has been shown and this I most warmly appreciate on public grounds.

But in all the circumstances, as they have now developed, I do not feel that I could appropriately or with any satisfaction allow myself to be nominated with a view to a contest with Asquith, who, both in his personality and in the record of his life, has so much that marks him as a fit man for that great position. I hope that he may be elected without a contest.

He sent a copy to Lord Oxford, who replied as follows:

The EARL OF OXFORD AND ASQUITH *to the* ARCHBISHOP OF CANTERBURY

The Wharf, Sutton Courtney, Berks. 1 June, 1925.

I cannot sufficiently thank you for your own letter, and for letting me see the enclosure.

I can honestly say that I was not at all anxious to become a candidate; indeed, I was well content with the selection of Milner.

And the idea of a contest on anything like party lines was thoroughly repugnant to me; as I have no doubt it was to many of those who were wishful that you should consent to stand. It was only when I was assured that my nomination was desired by not a few who belong to the other political camps that I agreed to it.

The generosity and real friendliness which you have shown me in the matter I can never forget. They form one of those rare tributes of which a man may well be proud.

X

From these various employments Randall Davidson turned with never-failing delight to his holidays. He especially enjoyed a holiday abroad, above all in Italy, whether in Venice or Florence, or by Lake Maggiore at Baveno or Cannero, or by some of the other lakes. He loved the walks on the hills by the lakes, and the rests during which Mrs. Davidson or others might read aloud while he would sketch, thus practising what was a very real gift that in former days found expression in admirable water-colour drawings. In Florence his favourite haunt was the Spanish Chapel; and the pictures which particularly pleased him always had history in them. He had an intimate knowledge of Venice, and in September 1922 spent twelve golden days of sunshine there, enjoying the gondola as well as the long rambling walks about the streets, backwards and forwards on the bridges.

But the Italian holidays were not so usual after the War as they had been before. It was Scotland that most clearly called him. Sir Walter Scott once said to a friend, 'If I did not see the heather at least once a year, *I think I should die*.'[1] It was the same with the Archbishop. We give two pictures from those who nearly every year had the Archbishop and Mrs. Davidson with them in their homes north of the Tweed. The first is from Miss Elizabeth Haldane describing the time at Cloan:

> Once the Archbishop crossed the Border and reached his native land he seemed to us to cast off his cares of office and to become the boy he was at Muirhouse when he used to carry a sister-in-law on his shoulders. With his gaiters discarded he became what our people described as 'like ane o 'oor ain ministers', which meant that every trace of the self-consciousness which the Scot associates with high dignitaries in the Church of England disappeared. And when he took Family Prayers on Sunday evenings he adopted the Scottish fashion of doing so quite simply, knowing that this was what would appeal to the household.
>
> Then at Cloan we had such wonderful walks, for he cared for long walks just as we did, and as Mrs. Davidson did, for she and he seemed the same as far as tastes and interests were concerned. We wandered over the Ochils and negotiated dry-stone-dykes and burns successfully. So many of these walks remain in my mind because of the conversations that took place on them. My brother Richard and he discussed deep politics as well as personalities, and we every now and then joined in. . . .
>
> Then he loved fishing and the young people longed to get him to 'guddle' i.e. catch trout in a burn from under the stones by hand —he knew the pastime well—and knowing his passion for the art, they tried one Sunday afternoon to arrange to leave fishing tackle all ready close to a solitary little loch, and see, if every one discreetly disappeared, whether he would succumb to the temptation and break the Sabbath! Needless to say their efforts were in vain.

[1] Lockhart's *Life of Scott*, ch. xxxix.

The second picture is supplied by Mrs. Andrew Carnegie and shows the Archbishop and Lady Davidson on their visits to Skibo Castle:

He and Lady Davidson were always such welcome visitors, for he was so genial and took such a keen and delightful interest in all the little incidents of our home life. Every body loved him, from the oldest to the youngest member of the family. I remember, particularly, one afternoon when the grandchildren were trying to fly a large kite directed by their father on the lawn. They had some difficulty in raising it at first. The Archbishop was starting out for his walk, but everything was forgotten in his keen interest in watching every detail of the kite's raising. He was like a boy, and was as pleased as the children when they finally succeeded in raising it to a considerable height.

Often in the evenings the young people would retire to the billiard room to make fudge (an American sweet) in a chafing-dish. The Archbishop would slip away from us in the drawing room, and later we would discover him seated beside the young people, a broad smile on his face, watching the process—from the cracking of the nuts then being added to the boiling mixture of sugar and milk, and no one was more interested and pleased with the finished product than he. He also often joined the young people in playing billiards and they always enjoyed their games with him, for he was as keen as they.

. . . In every way, he joined heartily in everything that interested us. The prattle of the children interested him. He would draw them out to tell of the books they were reading and listened intently to what they told him. He always took occasion, during his visits, for a little friendly talk with each member of the family, and he showed such genuine interest, we were delighted to talk quite freely to him. During one of his early visits in my husband's lifetime, a very delightful incident occurred, and a few years ago when I told the Archbishop my husband's life was being written by Burton J. Hendrick, he asked me if I would like to have him write out the incident for Mr. Hendrick to use if he wished. Of course, I was delighted. The Life of Mr. Carnegie has just been published and Mr. Hendrick uses the incident just as the Archbishop wrote it, and I copy it for you:

'I have always been a student of birds and their ways. I mentioned to Mr. Carnegie that I had that morning watched one of the autumnal gatherings of golden crested wrens, who were about to flit, and who, before flitting, are accustomed to gather excitedly, and are strangely tame at such a time. He was interested and asked me to take him to the place. We went together, and I felt the usual trepidation one has lest an animal whose actions one has foretold should decline to "play up" when the time comes. We were standing on a little rustic bridge over a burn at the edge of a wood not far from the house. The wrens were all about us, in the trees and even on the ground. I urged Mr. Carnegie to remain absolutely still; this he did, and to my wonder and delight one of the wrens hopped up the rough fir branch which formed the railing of the bridge and on which his hand was laid. It went on, hopped up his arm and sat on his shoulder. I have never seen such a thing before or since, and I was profoundly grateful to the wren for thus endorsing the rather rash prophecy I had made as to its behaviour. Since then I have tried more than once to stand near a gathering of wrens at such a time, but the bird I have described was, so far as my experience goes, a unique personality.'

CHAPTER LXXVII

THE LAST YEARS—MISSIONARY AND RACE PROBLEMS

It is by the finest tints and most insensible gradations that Nature descends from the fairest face about St. James's to the sootiest complexion in Africa. At which tint of these is it, that the ties of blood are to cease? and how many shades must we descend lower still in the scale, ere mercy is to vanish with them?

LAURENCE STERNE to IGNATIUS SANCHO, July 27, 1766.

FEW things interested the Archbishop more than the questions so constantly referred to Lambeth by Bishops overseas. No trouble was too much, no season too busy for him to give them the very best help he could. Some of the help was given by letter, some by personal conversation—and it may be safely said that hardly any Bishop of a diocese overseas came to England on leave without a part of a day, or more often a night, at Lambeth or Canterbury. Among many questions with which he was asked to deal, some were concerned with matters of internal organization; some with problems of race; some with the development of a young self-governing Church; and some with the relation of the Anglican Churches to other Churches in their neighbourhood. He was always anxious to enlist the help of those who had a responsibility in the matter—often more for their sake than his own, though this never appeared; and constant were the visits of the Secretaries of the Missionary Societies, and the Missionary Council, and the International Missionary Council, and Commissaries of different dioceses.

We have already in an earlier chapter given instances of the problems which he handled, and the reality of his care for the work of the Church overseas will have been apparent in various other pages of this biography. It is impossible to do justice to the scope of his interest, or to the continuous exercise of an almost patriarchal solicitude for different parts of the Anglican Communion. A few incidents, however, may be quoted to give some indication of the variety of the claims upon his time and attention.

I

Our first illustration is of a personal character, and concerns one of the very few cases in which he felt obliged to tell a Bishop that he ought to resign. A clergyman of unusual evangelistic powers had been appointed before the War to the charge of an immense diocese in the Pacific. He endeavoured to raise the large sum of £100,000 to maintain religious, educational, and medical ministrations on an ample scale in every centre in his diocese in which there were British residents: and he proposed to make England his head-quarters for raising this fund during five or six years, making annual visits to his diocese. The plan was not unnaturally criticized, and the appeal failed. The Archbishop had many interviews and much correspondence with the Bishop, and persuaded him to return to his see. Unhappily, however, the Bishop did not prove a good administrator, and serious complaints of the administration of the diocese reached the Archbishop at Lambeth. He returned home, this time seriously ill; but, after a time of recuperation, the Archbishop saw him again and encouraged him—for though, as usual, very sanguine about the future, 'he seemed to have a better basis than formerly for his hopes'. The Bishop after some further delay arrived back in his diocese in July 1914. But it soon became clear that the condition of the diocese had gone from bad to worse, and had become, in the Archbishop's judgement, wellnigh hopeless.

On September 10, 1914, the Archbishop wrote to the Bishop, telling him frankly of the adverse reports about his administration (or, rather, lack of administration) of his diocese, and adding:

The ARCHBISHOP OF CANTERBURY *to the* BISHOP OF ——

10 September 1914.

I may be mistaken, but it seems to me that two alternatives only are before you. One is that you should settle down in such central place as you deem best, with a firm resolve and a published promise that you will stay there steadily for some years to come, except for visits to particular places within the Diocese, and that on these visits you will really be at the call of those who want to see you, and will stir up enthusiasm by persistent and devoted service. That is one possibility. The other is that you should resign. It goes to my heart to say this, but I think it is only honest both to you and to the Church that I should now say it. I attribute the failure—for so I must so far regard it—as having been due chiefly to your absence from the Diocese, and subsequently to your ill-health. This last was, again, responsible, by no fault of yours, for a further absence. You will judge whether you now feel strong enough and buoyant enough and hopeful enough to be able to adopt the first of the two courses I have suggested. If so, God bless you in it. If not, the other course seems to me to be inevitable. No one realises better than I the peculiar difficulties of your extraordinary Diocese. It is not merely the long-extended coast-line, the distance between the different centres, and so on: it is also the system of what one may call trustee-chaplaincies, where a church has come to be regarded as almost the private property of those who form its committee, or vestry, or trustees. All this needs for its management an extraordinary tactfulness as well as a persistent, a quiet, and a self-forgetful energy.

Well, I have said my say. This letter is entirely private, and you may feel that I am taking an unfair and discoloured view of the situation. Perhaps I am, but I have done my best, and I cannot feel that the prolongation of the present state of matters, without my saying to you what I have here said, would be wise and right either for yourself, or for the Diocese, or for the Church at large. I pray God to help and guide you to a right decision. We are at one in our desire that what we do may be to His glory and to the good of the Church wherein we are set to be Bishops and guides.

Before this letter (which the Archbishop afterwards described as 'the sternest letter I have ever written to a brother Bishop') reached its destination, the Bishop was once again on his way back to England. En route he wrote a long letter to the Archbishop, laying all the blame for all the difficulties he had encountered, partly on certain people with whom he had failed to get on, but, mainly, on a particular Missionary Society, with whom he declared that he could no longer work.

An interview with the Archbishop followed, in which the Archbishop read to him the letter from himself quoted above. The Bishop admitted that every word in it was justified, and said that he believed that resignation was the only proper course for him; although he adhered to his view that he had been the victim of circumstances rather than of his own shortcomings, and he also urged that his ill health had been largely responsible for his non-success. After much correspondence it was agreed between the Archbishop and the Bishop that the following paragraph should go to the Press:

The Right Rev. ——, on account of ill-health, placed in the hands of the Archbishop of Canterbury his resignation of the Bishopric of ——. The resignation will take effect on Dec. 31st, 1914.

The resignation took place as arranged. But the Bishop lived eleven more years, and during the whole of this time, as the voluminous correspondence makes plain, the Archbishop, with other staunch churchmen, did his best to help him through his troubles, and befriended him in various ways until the end came in November 1925.

II

Our next illustration shall be in connexion with missionary work among Moslems in Egypt. The Coptic Church is the national Christian Church of Egypt, but its missionary activities are slight, and there was said to be a leakage of not less than 400 Copts to the Mahommedan religion every year. Such staunch Anglican evangelists as Bishop Gwynne and Canon Gairdner, who desired to convert the Moslems to Christianity, were greatly concerned at such a state of affairs. They proposed therefore to take a number of native Egyptians belonging to the Coptic Church, to train them as evangelists, and ultimately ordain them in the Anglican Church. The flaw in their plan was that it savoured of proselytization by the Anglican Church, in a way likely to be resented by all Eastern Churches. The Archbishop pointed this out to Bishop Gwynne, who accordingly, with the Anglican missionaries in Egypt, composed what they called a 'Spiritual Charter' to which they asked the official assent of the Coptic Patriarch. In answer to the request, the Patriarch sent the Bishop a most flattering but non-committal letter, in which the Patriarch told him of his prayers to Almighty God 'to preserve your honourable person for ever and ever, to give you success in your beneficent deeds which bring blessing and happiness on mankind'. With the letter he sent his photograph 'as souvenir to your beloved respected person'. 'This', wrote Bishop Gwynne to the Archbishop, 'is not quite what I wanted, but as much as we are likely to get at the present time'... and he added (March 7, 1924):

The Bishop in Egypt and the Sudan *to the* Archbishop of Canterbury

I should be very grateful if Your Grace would kindly inform me whether, in your opinion, we might go forward on this declaration of friendship from the Patriarch, and whether it would satisfy that portion of our Church which might give trouble if there were found in our native congregations men and women from the Coptic Church.

The Archbishop grasped the situation at once. He pointed out the weak points in the Spiritual Charter, and asked for reconsideration of what was, he supposed, only in a very initial and draft stage:

The ARCHBISHOP OF CANTERBURY *to the* BISHOP IN EGYPT AND THE SUDAN

March 19, 1924.

I am certain that there are numbers of our own people who would be staggered to learn that we propose 'to ordain when the time came the fittest persons [we] can find and irrespective of their ecclesiastical antecedents'. Apply this in other fields—in Scotland, in the United States, in India—and we might find ourselves in strange confusion.

Explanations followed, and an interview at Lambeth, which reassured the Archbishop to some extent; but he could not (as he remarked) forget the line taken by so learned a man as Canon Liddon when Archdeacon Popham Blyth was appointed 'Bishop of the Church of England in Jerusalem'. So he promised to discuss the whole situation with Bishop Gore, who was going out to Egypt in January 1925. The result was a new document, which said what was wanted, but in a very different way, unexceptionable from the Orthodox and the Anglo-Catholic point of view. It was called 'Practical working principles of the Arabic Branch for the (Anglican) Episcopal Church in Egypt'. It stated quite clearly that the Anglican Church in Egypt had no desire to increase its membership by accession from other organizations, whether Coptic, Orthodox, Presbyterian, or otherwise; but, recognizing the fact that individuals belonging to those other organizations do sometimes on their own deliberate initiative desire to join the Anglican Church, proceeded to lay down certain conditions on which such individuals might be admitted. It received the assent of Coptic and Anglo-Catholic, of Bishop Gwynne, the Archbishop of Canterbury, and the Church Missionary Society.

III

The next illustration shall be from China. The story of the Church in China during the last few years of the Archbishop's life affords various illustrations of the deep interest which he took in the growth of the Anglican Communion overseas. There were many personal letters, some of them touching in their character. The Archbishop had a great reverence for such men as Bishop Cassels, the missionary Bishop of the vast diocese of Western China, an apostolic labourer for the Church. Another close friend was Bishop F. L. Norris of North China. During the various troubles in China, political and other, he was ever ready to show his sympathy, and cheered the Bishops by his messages from time to time. But perhaps the most important and significant instance of the help he gave, is that connected with the development over many years of the dioceses in China into an autonomous Church of the Anglican Communion. Up to 1912, the Anglican dioceses in China were a collection of dioceses unrelated to one another and owing their allegiance to three Home Churches—the Church of England, the Church of England in Canada, and the Protestant Episcopal Church in America—from which came their financial support. In that year, there was organized, for the first time, a General Synod on which all the Chinese dioceses were represented. This prelude is necessary before we turn to a group of events centring round Bishop H. J. Molony, the Anglican (and English) Bishop in Chekiang.

In 1917, with the approval of the General Synod of the Anglican Church in China (Chung Hua Sheng Kung Hui), a Chinese-born priest, Archdeacon Sing, was chosen by Bishop Molony to be his assistant Bishop. It was a new step in the history of the Church in China—as there had been no Chinese-born Bishop before. But his election raised various problems. The existing diocesan Bishops were English, American, and Canadian. They had been consecrated by Bishops of their respective Home Churches, and at their consecration had promised obedience and loyalty to the proper ecclesiastical authorities of those Home Churches. To whom should a Chinese assistant Bishop (who incidentally could speak no English) give his allegiance, pending the creation of Provincial organization in China? The Archbishop of Canterbury—when asked to approve the consecration of Archdeacon Sing, at once pointed out the importance of this question. He wrote to Bishop Molony, February 26, 1918:

The ARCHBISHOP OF CANTERBURY *to the* BISHOP IN CHEKIANG

Prior to the consecration of a Bishop by the Bishops of the Chung Hua Sheng Kung Hui it is absolutely essential that some formal regulation should be made respecting the manner in which the Chinese Church is to secure the orthodoxy and the loyalty of a man nominated for the Episcopate. . . . I am ready to agree that notwithstanding any usage to the contrary hitherto observed in regard to China a Bishop who is a native of China shall on consecration make his profession of canonical obedience to the Chung Hua Sheng Kung Hui and the laws, canons, doctrine and discipline thereof rather than to any other ecclesiastical authority.

The necessary regulation was adopted; and Archdeacon Sing was consecrated in Shanghai, in October 1918, as Assistant Bishop in Chekiang.

Ten years later, in 1928, Bishop Molony wished to resign. By that time the Anglican Church in China had become more fully organized and more nearly autonomous. And though some dependence on the Home Churches remained, owing chiefly to reliance on financial aid, the Archbishop, in July 1928, stated emphatically his individual opinion 'that the quasi-Metropolitan relationship exercised by Canterbury, Canada, and U.S.A. cannot continuously be maintained in regard to Bishops belonging to the Church in China' and added that he was 'most keen to bring this arrangement to an end'. He gave substance to his conviction in dealing with Bishop Molony's resignation—and insisted, when the Bishop wrote offering his resignation to him, that the proper authority to receive and accept the resignation of a Bishop of the Anglican Church in China was the Chairman of the House of Bishops. So it was to the Chairman of the House of Bishops of that Church that Bishop Molony resigned—and the proper precedent was set.

In the same year, 1928, a successor had to be appointed for the see of Chekiang. And the Archbishop did two things which gave the autonomy of the Church in China a deeper emphasis. He encouraged and secured the nomination of Bishop Molony's successor (Bishop Curtis) by the House of Bishops (instead of through the C.M.S. by himself); and he requested the Chairman of the

House of Bishops to arrange for the consecration of the new Bishop in China. Bishop Curtis was accordingly consecrated on January 6, 1929, in Ningpo, the first English Bishop to be consecrated in China, and the first 'foreign' Bishop to be consecrated as a Bishop of the Chung Hua Sheng Kung Hui and *not* as a Missionary Bishop of the Church of England. The importance of this event in the development of a self-governing Church in China is obvious.

IV

Our last illustration deals with a different kind of missionary problem, which received a large share of the Archbishop's attention after the War—the rights of the natives in Africa. One call for his help came in the summer of 1920, from the Rev. A. S. Cripps, a champion of the native races in Southern Rhodesia, and a poet of no mean distinction. The Archbishop listened with sympathy, and helped him to put his statement of the right of the Matabele and Mashona people to a sufficient share of land, both to Lord Milner at the Colonial Office and to the public. But the territory which in the problem of the welfare of the Africans was raised most acutely was East Africa, and here he was in the closest touch with the East African Bishops. As an evidence of the steady interest which he took in all such matters, as well as of his readiness to help, an extract from a reply to the Bishop of Zanzibar's appeal in October 1920 may be quoted:

The ARCHBISHOP OF CANTERBURY *to the* BISHOP OF ZANZIBAR

4 October 1920.

I am of course familiar with the successive Despatches of Lord Milner and have also been in correspondence with him on the question, not wholly alien from this, about Native rights etc. in Rhodesia. You may rely upon my supporting you to the best of my power in all that seems to me to concern the highest interests of the Natives. I have, as you know, fought the battles for the Native Races under the pressure of labour problems in—e.g. the South Sea Islands, Queensland, West Africa, Ceylon (imported Tamils), Nigeria, and in India itself. I think there are more, but these alone spring to my mind.

In the East Africa Protectorate, or, as it afterwards came to be known, Kenya, the matter came very much to the fore. A circular issued by the Chief Native Commissioner, in October 1919, from Nairobi appeared to introduce a new principle by which able-bodied male natives were to be induced by 'every possible lawful influence' to go into the labour field. The Bishops of Mombasa and Uganda, and Dr. Arthur of the Church of Scotland Mission, criticized the circular strongly, but, on the assumption that recourse would in any case be had to compulsory labour, urged that so long as it was clearly necessary it should be definitely legalized. The Bishop of Zanzibar took the strongest exception to any legal recognition of forced labour, and the missionary societies in Great Britain also regarded such a course as highly objectionable. An appeal was made to the Archbishop, whose response was immediate. He worked in the closest co-operation with Mr. J. H. Oldham, the able and statesmanlike Secretary of the Conference of the Missionary Societies of Great Britain and Ireland; and on his uncommon thoroughness and capacity for acquiring information and measuring its value, as well as for shaping a positive and practical policy, the Archbishop put the greatest reliance. The Archbishop studied the facts closely, and had successive interviews with missionaries and many others who had dealt with the difficulties on the spot in a civilian capacity; and he took pains to appreciate the settlers' point of view as well. When he felt himself sufficiently equipped with information he pressed the cause of the Africans in Kenya most persistently. And from the autumn of 1920 onwards we find him in constant touch with the Colonial Office and successive Secretaries of State and Under-Secretaries. In August 1920, Lord Milner issued a dispatch to the Governor of the East Africa Protectorate which said that a policy of compulsory labour for private employment 'would be absolutely opposed to the traditional policy of His Majesty's Government'. But it still allowed compulsory labour for public purposes in an unsatisfactory form. On December 14, 1920, the Archbishop led a deputation to Lord Milner (with whom he had previously had long talks), presented him with a Memorandum, signed by the leaders of the Missionary Societies and a large number of eminent men in and out of Parliament, calling attention to the grave dangers under the existing system, and appealed for the appointment of a Royal Commission. The deputation did good in showing the existence of considerable anxiety, though its request for a Royal Commission was not granted. A little later Mr. Churchill, as Secretary of State, issued a dispatch of September 5, 1921, placing it on public record that it was the declared policy of the Government to avoid recourse to compulsory labour for Government purposes except when this was absolutely necessary for essential services, and laying down that the powers conferred under the Ordinance could only be used with the previous sanction of the Secretary of State.[1]

A very important element in the whole situation was the status of Indians in Kenya, bitterness among whom had been greatly increased by the disparaging references in official reports, and proposals for strict control of immigration. The Indian cause was championed by the Government of India. Protracted discussions took place between the Secretary of State for India and the Secretary of State for the Colonies. Proposals for a new franchise giving a more favourable position to the Indians for representation on the Executive Council, caused a considerable agitation among settlers and Indians in Kenya.[2] All through the spring and summer the Archbishop was in constant communication with Indian statesmen and their friends as well as the missionaries. He saw many people closely in touch with policy in India—and many others as well: and the following note in the midst of a bundle of correspondence gives a slight idea of the range of his interviews:

Kenya. 18th May 1923.

I have now interviewed Oldham, Andrews,[3] Sastri, Ross, Bp. Willis, Lord Hardinge, the Bp. of Bombay and of course the Duke of Devonshire. I have read carefully General Stone's article in the xixth Century for May. (See Memoranda.)

In close co-operation with Mr. Oldham, the Archbishop made a strong appeal to the Duke of Devonshire, as Colonial Secretary, in a letter of May 29, 1923, accompanied by a Memorandum of

[1] Cmd. 1509. (Also compare Cmd. 2464 Kenya. Compulsory Labour for Government Purposes, July 1925.)

[2] The population in Kenya was estimated as follows (April 1923): Natives, 2,500,000 to 3,000,000; Europeans, nearly 10,000; Indians, 23,000 to 24,000. There were 300,000,000 Indians in India.

[3] The Rev. C. F. Andrews, a friend of Gandhi; Rt. Hon. Srinirasa Sastri, leader of an Indian delegation; W. Macgregor Ross, formerly Director of Public Works in Kenya; the Bishop of Uganda; a former Viceroy of India; Dr. E. J. Palmer.

policy, having assured himself that the Indians were prepared to accept the terms of the Memorandum:

Memorandum. Kenya.

(1) H.M. Government to declare that it is their policy that the East African Crown Colonies and Protectorates, including Kenya, shall be administered under the direct authority of the Imperial Government acting as trustee for the native inhabitants and for civilisation as a whole, and that as between the different communities inhabiting these territories the interests of the native population are paramount.

(2) A royal commission to be appointed to consider and report how this principle can best be applied to conditions in Kenya, with due regard to the rights and claims of each of the alien immigrant communities.

(3) No material change to be made to the disadvantage of any of the three communities until the commission has reported and H.M. Government has acted upon the report.

Much correspondence and many interviews followed—and it became clear that the official opposition to a Royal Commission was very strong, owing mainly, it appeared, to the difficulty of finding a personnel which would not be suspect by one side or the other. The Indians were gravely discouraged, fearing that nothing at all would be done. In the end, on July 23, 1923, the Duke of Devonshire issued a White Paper,[1] which made two important pronouncements:

Primarily, Kenya is an African territory, and His Majesty's Government think it necessary definitely to record their considered opinion that the interests of the African natives must be paramount, and that if, and when, those interests and the interests of the immigrant races should conflict, the former should prevail. Obviously the interests of the other communities, European, Indian or Arab, must severally be safeguarded. Whatever the circumstances in which members of these communities have entered Kenya, there will be no drastic action or reversal of measures already introduced, such as may have been contemplated in some quarters, the result of which might be to destroy or impair the existing interests of those who have already settled in Kenya. But in the administration of Kenya His Majesty's Government regard themselves as exercising a trust on behalf of the African population, and they are unable to delegate or share this trust, the object of which may be defined as the protection and advancement of the native races.

[1] *Indians in Kenya*, Cmd. 1922.

And:

> His Majesty's Government cannot but regard the grant of responsible self-government as out of the question within any period of time which need now be taken into consideration. Nor, indeed, would they contemplate yet the possibility of substituting an unofficial majority in the Council for the Government official majority.

But the request for a Royal Commission was refused. The Archbishop, speaking in the House of Lords on July 26, 1923, when the Duke of Devonshire made the announcement, welcomed the statement of principle stated above 'that the interests of the African natives must be paramount' as of the utmost importance. He knew, however, that the Indians were not satisfied and he made the following important point—'Everything must turn . . . upon the manner in which this scheme is put into practice.'

The White Paper did indeed cause dismay to Mr. C. F. Andrews, speaking for the Indians, and he went so far as to declare that it was no use saying that native interests were paramount 'if you go and make European interests paramount in practice'. The Archbishop answered his criticism, and his letter shows once again his desire to be fair to all sides, as well as his thoroughness:

The ARCHBISHOP OF CANTERBURY *to the* REV. C. F. ANDREWS

5th September, 1923.

I tried to understand the subject to the best of my power, and I took all the pains I could to realise the Indian position as represented by yourself and by Mr. Sastri.

I appreciate the extreme importance which you feel to belong to this, as a test case, as to the genuineness of Government recognition of Indian Citizenship in the Empire. It seems to me also that this was determinedly weighed by the Colonial Office and India Office before the ultimate Document was issued.

I am inclined to think, that, if I had been drafting the ultimate decision, I should have said more about Indian Citizenship and its value, and our obligation to recognise it, but I think this was shown not inadequately by what was decided.

I do not think you are quite fair to the Settlers' side. I hold no brief for them, and I should have deplored it had the decision been to the effect that they had, so to speak, won their case all along the line. I do not think this is so at all, and I was impressed and somewhat pleased by finding how marked was the disappointment of some of those who represented the British Settlers when the decision was made public. Certainly, the Government had a most difficult course to steer, and, although I should personally have liked to see an ampler recognition of the Indian case, I felt that the Government had to look, not at the Indians in Kenya alone, but at the imperial problems of a wider sort as well. . . .

What pleased me most was the prominence given to the fundamental principle that both English and Indians who are in Africa as immigrants, are, in some measure, outsiders, and that the real people entitled to primary consideration are the Native Africans. . . .

I am afraid that all this will seem to you very disappointing, and that you would have liked me to say that India is being ruthlessly trampled upon by this Government action. I cannot think so, or say so. I should like India to have secured more, and that the security should have been more explicit, but, if I try to look at it with all the fairness possible, I am forced to the belief that the Government has, in the main, done what is right.

The race question in Kenya came up again in subsequent years, but the story of this crucial occasion has been rather fully told as an instance of the Archbishop's interest in a problem of unusual significance for the Christian statesman as well as the missionary, and of the method which he followed. The correspondence of 1923 to 1927, as well as reports of debates in the House of Lords, show that he followed the later developments with the closest attention and felt a good deal of anxiety with regard to the actual way in which the principles laid down in the White Paper were being worked out.

Two further events may be noted. On June 6, 1923, the Archbishop took part in a Conference of six Governors and ex-Governors at the Colonial Office, under the Chairmanship of Mr. Ormsby Gore, the Under-Secretary, which resulted in the establishment of an Advisory Committee on Native Education in the British Tropical African Dependencies.[1] Again, in a debate

[1] The following accepted invitations to serve on the Committee: the Bishop of Liverpool (Dr. David), Bishop Bidwell (nominated by Cardinal Bourne), Sir Frederick Lugard, Sir Michael Sadler, Sir James Currie, Mr. J. H. Oldham, Sir Herbert Read, with Major Hans Vischer as Secretary. It is perhaps interesting to observe that the Meeting of Governors and ex-Governors which led to the appointment of this Committee, took place on Derby Day, showing that the consideration of African education was regarded by those representatives of the governing classes of Great Britain as preferable to the attractions of the Derby.

on the land policy in Africa, in the House of Lords, on May 20, 1925, the Archbishop elicited from Lord Balfour, speaking for the Government, the unexpected declaration that the Government were proposing to set up an institution (later known as the Committee of Civil Research) bearing some resemblance to the Committee of Imperial Defence to deal with civilian problems, including those of Imperial development.

CHAPTER LXXVIII

EPISCOPAL APPOINTMENTS

I cannot wish well to a popular election of the clergy, when I consider that it occasions such animosities, such unworthy courting of the people, such slanders between the contending parties, and other disadvantages. It is enough to allow the people to remonstrate against the nomination of a minister for solid reasons.

BOSWELL, *Life of Dr. Johnson* (1772).

NO Archbishop of Canterbury can ever have exercised a greater influence in the appointment of the Bishops and other chief officers of the Church than Randall Davidson. That influence began even before his coming to Windsor in 1883, with his very first interview with Queen Victoria, and the part which he took in the nomination of Archbishop Benson as the successor of Tait. It continued through his tenure of the Deanery, and of the two sees of Rochester and Winchester, right down to Queen Victoria's death in 1901. It remained unchanged in the opening years of King Edward's reign, while he was still Bishop of Winchester. It is the purpose of this chapter to describe his relations with the Crown, through successive Prime Ministers, as Archbishop of Canterbury, and the manner in which his advice was given and received.

I

The personal interest which Queen Victoria took in ecclesiastical patronage was unique in its degree; and her influence was also of exceptional quality. And though the Archbishop always maintained that the exercise of such personal influence in a perfectly constitutional form was a valuable factor in securing the best nominations, it was clearly a characteristic rather specially personal to the Queen. Her two successors on the Throne, King Edward and King George, were both alive to the importance of the best Church appointments, and careful to weigh the merits of alternative names before their formal submission; but, generally speaking, they had not the same individual interest in each particular case. In any event, while Randall Davidson's counsel to Queen Victoria was rather personal than official as Dean and Bishop and Clerk of the Closet, his own official responsibility increased when he became Archbishop. It was therefore with the Prime Ministers that he was most directly and closely concerned; and it was they who asked for and received his recommendations when particular vacancies occurred.

During his Primacy seven different statesmen occupied the post of Prime Minister of Great Britain—three of them Conservatives or Unionists (Mr. A. J. Balfour, Mr. Bonar Law, and Mr. Stanley Baldwin), three Liberals (Sir Henry Campbell-Bannerman, Mr. Asquith, and Mr. Lloyd George), and one belonging to the Labour party (Mr. Ramsay MacDonald). They were very different men, with very different traditions. Indeed, three of them were Presbyterians and one a Baptist. They all, though some less strongly than others, realized their responsibilities in relation to Church patronage. They all gave careful attention to the Archbishop's recommendations, and never, in the many instances of episcopal nominations during twenty-five years, did they make a single appointment which they knew to be fundamentally objectionable to the Archbishop. This does not mean that they always took the Archbishop's advice about fitness for a particular see, but that, if the Archbishop insisted that a particular person was wholly unsuitable for the office of Bishop, no Prime Minister ever during these twenty-five years persevered with his name. Some appointments were, of course, less satisfactory than others, and some the Archbishop, left to himself, would not have made; but in every case the merits and qualifications of the person ultimately chosen were carefully and conscientiously considered; and there was no instance whatever of what could fairly be called a mere political job.

The method which the Archbishop usually followed when a vacancy occurred was this. He would, without loss of time, either speak or write to the Prime Minister about the particular bishopric. Some Prime Ministers knew much more than others about the work of a Bishop and the needs of the diocese, and about the personnel of Church leaders—and this was notably the case with Mr. Asquith. If necessary, the Archbishop would describe the general conditions of the diocese—or indicate the kind of Bishop required at a particular juncture. As a rule he would discuss both the diocese and the possible successors in conversation with the Prime Minister, as well as in correspondence. And, in all but quite exceptional cases, he would furnish the Prime Minister with some three or more names of people to be considered—only very rarely concentrating the whole of his strength on a single person. He would also make his own inquiries from various sources as to names which might have been independently suggested to the Prime Minister—whether for his own or for the Prime Minister's guidance. It may indeed be argued that there was a reluctance to suggest or to appoint extreme men in any school of thought, and that the Bench therefore lacked the presence of some eminent figures who were leaders in a particular Church party. But while party leaders did in fact become Bishops (like Bishop Gore and Bishop Knox), Bishops cannot so easily remain party leaders; and on investigation it would probably be found that the number of men *vere episcopabiles* overlooked on such grounds in the twenty-five years was smaller than might have been expected. The two general impressions left on the mind, after reading the extensive correspondence and memoranda covering this quarter of a century are, first, that though like other human beings they might not always succeed, Prime Minister and Archbishop both did their very best to find the most suitable men for the Bench of Bishops; and second, that Archbishop Davidson exercised a predominating influence upon the character of that Bench.

II

Mr. Arthur Balfour, the Prime Minister who nominated Archbishop Davidson himself, remained in office until 1905. He was an intimate friend, and the first advice actually required of the Archbishop related to the filling of the vacancy which his own appointment to Canterbury caused, and of the see of St. Albans, with the consequential nominations to Exeter and Newcastle. His first letter on the subject, after the offer of the Archbishopric is a good illustration of his attitude. He wrote on January 5, 1903, and after expressing the view that undoubtedly the Bishop of Rochester (Dr. Talbot) would be the best man for Winchester, he named six other Bishops, in favour of any of whom good arguments might be put forward, and put the pros and cons of each case separately, winding up with the Bishop of Exeter (Dr. Ryle). With regard to St. Albans he suggested the Bishop of Newcastle (Dr. Jacob)—and as the latter's successor the Suffragan Bishop of Thetford (Dr. Lloyd), or possibly (with two others)

Dr. Robertson of King's College. He went on with a word about the vacant Deanery of Winchester, and ended:

The ARCHBISHOP OF CANTERBURY *to the* RT. HON. A. J. BALFOUR

January 5, 1903.

I have said my say. I hope it is not too lengthy. Of course it is a mere contribution to your material for decision. It is hard upon you to have so much all at once to decide.

The contribution proved very effective. But difficulties arose in the way of appointing Bishop Talbot to Winchester. He was criticized as too sympathetic to the Ritualists; and the criticism found expression in a leading article in *The Times*. The Archbishop was never insensitive to public opinion on points like these.

In the end Dr. Ryle went to Winchester, to be succeeded as Bishop of Exeter by Dr. Robertson: while Dr. Jacob moved to St. Albans, and Dr. Lloyd to Newcastle. It was a good augury. Till the end of Mr. Balfour's government, the closest connexion was maintained between Downing Street and Lambeth.

III

Sir Henry Campbell-Bannerman (Prime Minister 1905–8) was more independent. He and the Archbishop were real friends, but the latter used to say that no one more constantly sought his advice and more seldom took it. Indeed, Sir Henry himself admits as much in a letter written about the vacant see of Chichester, 'an exceedingly difficult place to fill' on account of the recent passing over to Rome of 'no fewer than 17 Curates and Vicars'. . . .

The RT. HON. SIR HENRY CAMPBELL-BANNERMAN *to the* ARCHBISHOP OF CANTERBURY

Private.

5 Nov. 1907.

I am afraid you will think me very finnicky and fastidious: but I have not yet found my man for Chichester. The Bishop of Wakefield, as you expected, declined. . . .

I am using much freedom with you, in always bothering you, and, as you once said, never acting on your advice. But you will be lenient to my doubts and perplexities!

The remark brings out Sir Henry's real desire to do what he believed to be his duty, coupled with his almost fastidious conscientiousness in a field in which he was not himself specially well informed. In fact, he said on another occasion, to the private secretary (Mr. Henry Higgs) into whose department Church patronage fell, 'Our hesitation arises from our being so *méticuleux*.' Nevertheless the personal relations of Sir Henry and the Archbishop were most cordial. 'He is a most sensible man,' said Campbell-Bannerman to Arthur Ponsonby of the Archbishop, in his last days when the Archbishop visited him so often. 'I say "sensible", because he thinks just as I do!'

The next Prime Minister, Mr. Asquith, who held office altogether for nearly nine years (1908–16), had a far wider knowledge, and took a far keener personal interest in ecclesiastical appointments. 'No branch of Asquith's activities as Prime Minister', his biographers record, 'interested him more than that which relates to ecclesiastical patronage and appointments.'[1] Again, Sir Roderick Meiklejohn, one of his Private Secretaries, testifies even more clearly:[2]

> On ecclesiastical matters there can have been few laymen as well informed as he. He was well acquainted with past ecclesiastical history, had heard from his youth up many of the chief pulpit orators preach, and was on terms of friendship with many leading ecclesiastics and knew about the personalities and characteristics of very many more. . . . It was my duty to put before him a short list of the persons considered most suitable for any particular post, and he weighed their respective claims with the most scrupulous care and, while he was always ready to receive the advice of the Archbishop of Canterbury, with whom he was very intimate, it was invariably on his own unbiased selection that a name was submitted to the King.

The accuracy of this statement is fully borne out by the similar evidence in Archbishop Davidson's letters. And there can be no doubt that Mr. Asquith was the most thorough and best informed of all the Prime Ministers with whom Randall Davidson had to deal in this sphere during his Primacy. He took a special interest in the academic record of those proposed for consideration[3]—and was quite remarkably alive to the importance of the

[1] *Life of Lord Oxford and Asquith*, J. A. Spender and Cyril Asquith, ii. 378.

[2] Ibid., ii. 378–9.

[3] Writing on April 9, 1913, Mr. Asquith sent the Archbishop a list of thirteen

University posts, and the needs of the time, as to which he had exceptionally good sources of information.

Mr. Asquith, like other Prime Ministers, desired to keep a balance in the different schools of thought on the Bench. But he also had his difficulties. In 1911, five vacancies occurred in the Southern Province (Winchester, Southwark, Oxford, Salisbury, Birmingham); and one in the Northern (Ripon). The Northern Province at that time had a considerable majority of evangelical Bishops: and Dr. Lang, who had been appointed Archbishop of York in 1909, hoped for a change in this 'excessive preponderance'. But the five vacancies in the Canterbury Province had none of them been filled by Evangelical appointments. And an Evangelical for this turn was inevitable:

The ARCHBISHOP OF CANTERBURY *to the* RT. HON. H. H. ASQUITH

Oct. 5, 1911.

Ripon is, I agree, a real difficulty for you in view of recent admirable nominations which, as I gather, make you feel it to be difficult to nominate another Bishop just yet who belongs to the non-Evangelical school. And yet, you know *per contra* how utterly swamped the Northern Province is with 'Evangelical' Bishops in the party sense of a misused word. Durham[1] and Liverpool[2] and Carlisle[3] and Newcastle[4] and Manchester[5] and Sodor and Man.[6] Men of mark but all of them lacking in any wide sympathy with other forms of Churchmanship than their own. In the South we should (or *I* should) welcome such men as Liverpool or Durham—for we lack them sorely, and if only it were say, Hereford or Gloucester or Bristol or St. Albans or Lichfield or Bath and Wells, which was now vacant and not Ripon I should be all in favour of a decided Evangelical if a good enough man can be found.

In the North they do need to have the 'stronger Churchmanship' side strengthened. It is hard on the Archbishop of York to be made to look like an extreme High Churchman, merely because of the contrast with that big group.

The Archbishop, however, appreciated the Prime Minister's difficulty and tried to help him. But the number of Evangelical

Bishops in 1895 (Benson, Temple, Westcott, Ellicott, Durnford, Ridding, Stubbs, Creighton, Wordsworth, Talbot, Basil Jones, Jayne, Percival) as 'an *aperçu* of how things stood about twenty years ago': 'Without any wish to disparage the scholarship of the present Bench', he says of these thirteen, 'it is to be observed that the whole of these (except perhaps Durnford) were Headmasters, Professors or Dons.'

1 Dr. Moule. 2 Dr. Chavasse. 3 Dr. Diggle.
4 Dr. Straton. 5 Dr. Knox. 6 Dr. Drury.

Churchmen who had the necessary power of leadership was not large. He consulted, amongst others, the distinguished Evangelical Churchman, Bishop Ingham (Secretary of the Church Missionary Society), and his reply is significant:

BISHOP INGHAM *to the* ARCHBISHOP OF CANTERBURY

October 7, 1911.

It was a great responsibility to have been admitted to your confidence yesterday at Lambeth on matters so important to the good government of our Church!

The incident has powerfully impressed me with the truth of your words—that there are really so few leaders in what are known as the Evangelical ranks. . . .

The Bishop then gave a list of half a dozen names of those 'who are now, or will be in the near future, fairly representative of our side of things in the Church'. The Archbishop sent three others forward. In the end Dr. Drury, Bishop of Sodor and Man, was approved. The Evangelicals retained a majority among the Northern Bishops for a further nine years. But nothing is clearer, as one reads the large correspondence between the Archbishop and Mr. Asquith, than that the Prime Minister had unusual means of judging, and was extremely well informed—making independent inquiry where necessary—and that he desired to give to the Church as Bishops, in close consultation with the Archbishop, the best men he could find.

In December 1916, Mr. Lloyd George became Prime Minister, and remained at the head of the Government until 1922. In the handling of ecclesiastical affairs, no greater contrast could be imagined. Mr. Lloyd George had but scanty knowledge either of the conditions of Church life or of Church leaders. He had the assistance of one leading Churchman, Canon Pearce[1] of Westminster, who had helped Mr. Asquith in the smaller ecclesiastical appointments (like the less important crown livings), and beyond

[1] There was an excellent instance of the Archbishop's humour, and unfailing readiness in an awkward situation, when Canon Pearce was nominated in 1919 by Mr. Lloyd George to the bishopric of Worcester. Canon Pearce came to consult the Archbishop, with whom he was on excellent terms. He said that he had one great difficulty about the right answer to the Prime Minister's proposal. He had (he told the Archbishop) read all the files at 10 Downing Street relating to recent episcopal appointments, including all the Archbishop's letters, and never once had the Archbishop mentioned his name as a possible Bishop! The Archbishop, without a moment's hesitation, put his hand on Canon Pearce's shoulder, and replied, 'My dear Pearce, you were always in the background!'

doubt Canon Pearce wielded considerable influence. But, apart from Canon Pearce's help, Mr. Lloyd George had no such facilities for obtaining information as his predecessors had enjoyed. He was also much more interested in the preaching ability of the men proposed for high office in the Church than in their academic record.

An earlier chapter has described the controversy raging round the appointment of Dr. Henson as Bishop of Hereford. The Archbishop, as we have seen, would have preferred another appointment—but, while pointing out the difficulties which Dr. Henson's nomination might arouse, he did not reject the proposal as one that ought not to be made. The sequel, however, was interesting.

Mr. Lloyd George—so runs a Memorandum by the Archbishop dated February 24, 1918:

> admits quite frankly that he has no time for it [ecclesiastical appointments], or adequate knowledge, and is not at all averse to the idea of getting some advice regularly given by those who can be regarded as representative Churchmen.

Accordingly, a suggestion was made with perfect courtesy to Mr. Lloyd George by certain Church members of Parliament, who informed the Archbishop. They (Mr. Laurence Hardy, Sir Arthur Boscawen, Sir Robert Williams, Lord Wolmer, and two or three others) urged that it was unfair upon a non-Churchman to expect him to decide ecclesiastical appointments unaided. Mr. Lloyd George met the plea with unexpected welcome. A breakfast followed; and, after some further conference, the general principle of consultation between the Prime Minister and selected Churchmen was agreed. The Archbishop, however, pressed upon the M.P.s concerned that the consultation ought to be very informal. Certain names were suggested, three laymen, two clergy. The Archbishop in his Memorandum of March 3, 1919, wrote:

> But I pressed that they ought to be consulted, if at all, independently, and not as a committee; that the Prime Minister should not feel bound to consult all of them on every occasion, and that what passed between him and them should be regarded as wholly private, and therefore that they should not be regarded as men holding a sort of office of a representative kind. Their *raison d'être* and status would be simply this, five men whom Churchmen in

the House of Commons recognise as suitable persons to whom individually the Prime Minister might turn so as to keep himself in touch with Church opinion. With all this Boscawen agreed, and he undertook to represent it to his friends. I pointed out my fears that the whole arrangement might drift into too formal a character, which would be almost wholly mischievous, and would be fair neither to the Church, nor to me, nor indeed to the Prime Minister himself.

The Committee met occasionally, but was not in practice very much used, and gradually faded away.

A little earlier (May 1918), in view of the Hereford controversy, a joint committee of Canterbury Convocation had been appointed 'to consider various proposals for the giving of more effective expression to the mind of the Church either previously to such [Crown] nominations or before they became final'. The Joint Committee sat for a year and a half, and in February 1920 recommended as follows:

> That his Grace the President be requested to approach the Prime Minister and ask his consent to a plan whereby a Standing Committee of representative Churchmen might be empowered to bring before him the names of persons suitable for bishoprics, and might regularly be consulted by him before the submission of names to the Crown for nomination to such appointments.

This proposal was rejected by the Lower House, and the following Resolution was passed:

> That his Grace the President be requested to approach the Throne in order to secure that the two Archbishops should be officially consulted by the Prime Minister before the submission of names by him to the Crown for nomination to any diocesan bishopric.

When the plan of a Standing Committee was brought before the Upper House (February 13, 1920), an amendment was moved to agree with the Resolution of the Lower House. The Archbishop defined his attitude both to the plan of the Standing Committee and to the word 'officially' as follows, 'purposely with reserve and caution':

> This is a very difficult and delicate subject to discuss, and perhaps it is a peculiarly difficult and delicate subject for me to discuss, for more reasons than one. If I may say so, I think that the only mistake in the suggestion now made is the laying of emphasis, in asking for a Committee, on the *official* character of the advice that is given. The moment that you get that, you take away the

responsibility from those on whom it rests, and suggest that it shall be shared with others in a very undefined way. If there is a great desire that consultation shall take place and that people shall be better satisfied than they are, that is one thing; but it is a rather different thing from what is proposed. As matters at present stand —I need not say it to your lordships, but those outside do not all understand it—the theory is that the State, represented in former days by the personal voice of the Sovereign, and nowadays by the voice of the people spoken through the Prime Minister, shall itself have a large share in nomination to episcopal office. The Prime Minister is the one person who, as the representative of the nation, can speak on behalf of the nation, and he can speak where the Sovereign cannot speak with a personal voice. The theory is that the nation is speaking through the Prime Minister, and is nominating the person whom the spokesman believes to be the person best fitted to serve the nation in ecclesiastical office, and then comes in the duty of those on whom the ecclesiastical responsibility rests. I quite agree with the Bishop of Hereford that there is a good deal of exaggeration in speaking as if there was something heroic in the action of a Chapter, or of an Archbishop, in deciding that a nomination shall be resisted. The Archbishop has very large responsibility ultimately, and I have myself stated publicly in print what I feel as to the really definite responsibility resting on the shoulders of an Archbishop in such a case as that which we are considering. If the responsibility was exercised in a way which meant defiance to Crown authority, I do not think it would react personally on the Archbishop, but I think it would react on the constitutional position of the Church in this country, and would involve some change in its relationship with the State. I think the fact of that possible contingency is, in itself, a protection against occasion being given by the Prime Minister for the Archbishop to object. The Archbishop would not be a mere automaton in dealing with a case, and that fact, I think, is known. If there is a great desire to make sure that consultation is taken with those whom the Church is supposed to trust, or does trust, a Resolution to that effect would be quite harmless; but, if the consultation is made obligatory and official, I think that it must diminish the responsibility which rests on the shoulders of those who at present bear it. The original Resolution prepared by the Committee would, I think, be open to challenge in a great many ways, but the Resolution of the Lower House removes many of the drawbacks and difficulties which I feel stand in the way of passing the other Resolution. I can only myself accept this proposal in the sense that it is desired that I shall take means of conveying the wish that is felt, but if the interpretation put upon the Resolution is that it is obligatory, I cannot accept it.

The Archbishop deliberately laid great emphasis on the particular responsibility of the Prime Minister in relation to ecclesiastical appointments,[1] for he felt that this particular responsibility could not be transferred either to a committee or to any other individual, or (as was once or twice suggested, though not by a Prime Minister) to another member of the cabinet. The amendment, with the word 'officially' omitted, was passed: and the Resolution thus adopted was sent to Mr. Lloyd George on February 21, 1920, who replied:

RT. HON. D. LLOYD GEORGE *to the* ARCHBISHOP OF CANTERBURY

February 21, 1920

I thank you for your letter, enclosing a copy of the Resolution which was passed at the recent Session of the Convocation of Canterbury. As you are aware, it has been my invariable practice, since I became Prime Minister, to invite your counsel, which you have at all times been kind enough to give me, upon all important appointments in the Church. Certainly in this case of Diocesan Bishoprics my recommendations to His Majesty have only been made after careful and anxious consultation with yourself, and in the case of Sees in the Northern Province with the Archbishop of York also. It is also within your knowledge that I have in regard to all higher appointments taken the further step of seeking the opinion of a number of prominent Churchmen representing all shades of opinion. Whilst the Resolution therefore may appear to the public to partake of the nature of a criticism of the present procedure, it is in reality an expression of approval of the course

[1] The responsibility of the Prime Minister is illustrated by the following story, reported by the Archbishop in an account of a dinner party (June 28, 1895) at which he, Mr. Gladstone, John Morley, Jack Tennant, Mrs. Asquith, Mrs. Gladstone, and Mrs. Drew were present in Mr. Asquith's house. Mr. Gladstone 'told a story to Melbourne's credit (adding that it was, he thought, the only discreditable thing he had ever heard of that man of saintly dignity, Archbishop Howley). The story was this. Before Hampden was nominated to Hereford, Lord Melbourne had consulted Archbishop Howley who had recommended the appointment. Then Howley took fright, and afterwards in the House of Lords* joined the other Bishops in attacking the Government for doing it. When Melbourne rose to speak, he had in his pocket Howley's letter of recommendation, but he did not refer to it, and when asked privately why he had not, he said he had no right to shelter himself in such a manner from the responsibility which was his as a Minister of the Crown.'

* On December 21, 1837. But the occasion was actuallyHampden's appointment as Regius Professor of Divinity in the University of Oxford.

which I have adopted. You do not ask for, and I could not assent to, an action which would derogate from the well-established responsibility which rests upon Ministers of the Crown in respect of the advice which it is their duty to tender to His Majesty, but in seeking the benefit of your co-operation, and that of the Archbishop of York, I am glad to know that I am acting in accordance with the wishes of Convocation. I need hardly say that I gladly welcome such assistance, for I am deeply conscious of the vital importance of ensuring that the highest offices, upon whose functions much of the influence and power of the Church necessarily depends, shall be filled by those best qualified for the responsibility attaching to them of making the Church a great spiritual force in the life of the nation.

The Prime Minister's letter did in fact state his practice: and the practice continued to the end of his period of office. At the same time there is little doubt that the troubles of February 1918 had made him far more anxious to avoid further controversy, and as a means thereto very ready to consult the Archbishop. He persisted in his wish for Bishops with oratorical gifts, and was somewhat suspicious of headmasters. The Archbishop put the other side to a common friend, for communication to Lloyd George. In the particular instance, the Archbishop's wish did in fact prevail: but the letter is given because of its wider bearing:

The ARCHBISHOP OF CANTERBURY *to* ——

12 March, 1921.

Am I right in gathering from you that the Prime Minister has expressed to you his personal opinion on the general question of what is at present needed with regard to appointments to the Episcopate, and that he feels rather strongly that the present Bishops lack a little the sort of forcefulness of personal appeal which is specially needed at the present hour in England—i.e.—that we need men who will have the power of ready speech and arresting the attention of hearers and, if one may use the word, forcing upon them the truths of religion in a way that they cannot but attend to? With all this I am largely in agreement. I think we want such men more than ever we did, and I also think there is at present a lack of that particular sort of gift among many of our leading ecclesiastics, and not least among us Bishops. Be it remembered, however, that we have been trying to meet that difficulty in recent appointments. . . . But I want to put in a caveat. Important, indeed vital, as that power is among our ecclesiastics if they are to do their work properly, I am not certain that it is chiefly wanted among the Bishops. Some Bishops we ought to have who can sway a popular audience by the force of eloquent appeal, but the making of pulpit appeals is not the chief duty of Bishops. They have to administer the whole life of a vast organisation, and it would in my judgement be as wrong to choose a Bishop simply because he has that electric power of swaying an audience as it would be to choose a Home Secretary because he was an admirable Trafalgar Square orator. The Home Secretary has a great many things to do besides his oratory. Still more is this true of Bishops. . . .

Again, it is said—We don't want men who as schoolmasters or otherwise have shown their power of influence. We want men who will by their burning words quicken people's pulses and fire their enthusiasms. To say this is, I think, to forget that a Bishop's power in the Church is largely his indirect power—i.e.—he can, if he is a man of original thought, forceful University influence, personal glamour, and intense power of sympathy, attract young men to take Orders in the Church of England. See how this was done by men like Lightfoot and Westcott—neither of them orators, but both of them men who drew to the North of England the best type of younger men to ordain them as clergy and set them going with enthusiasm in the great cities. . . .

The power of popular oratory by itself will no more constitute a good Episcopate than it would constitute a good Cabinet.[1]

A further and milder controversy arose in 1921 on an interesting point. The Bishop of Salisbury (F. E. Ridgeway) died in May 1921. The Archbishop set his heart on securing the appointment of Dr. Donaldson, Archbishop of Brisbane. Mr. Lloyd George agreed, and a cablegram was sent out to Australia, through the Governor of Queensland. On June 3, Archbishop Donaldson cabled back to ask the Archbishop of Canterbury whether acceptance would involve his return from Brisbane before the meeting of the General Synod of the Church of England in Australia and Tasmania, in October. The Prime Minister wished to insist that Dr. Donaldson must either return to take up his

[1] By a curious coincidence, on the day after the writing of this letter, Mr. Silas McBee, a thoughtful American well known in religious circles on both sides of the Atlantic, reported at Lambeth a conversation between himself and two eminent French Roman Catholic scholars, P. Batiffol and Grandmaison. Mr. McBee asked them if they had any message for the Archbishop of Canterbury. They thought for a moment, and then Grandmaison said, 'Tell him to make more Bishops like Lightfoot.' Batiffol agreed and added Chase—to which Grandmaison replied, 'Let us also add Gore!'

duties in Salisbury almost at once, or refuse the offer—and so informed the Archbishop. This put the Archbishop on his mettle.

The Archbishop of Canterbury *to the* Rt. Hon. D. Lloyd George

13th June 1921.

You sent to me on the 3rd June a telegram from the Governor of Queensland saying—'Please communicate following from Archbishop of Brisbane to Archbishop of Canterbury. Offer received. Would acceptance involve movement before General Synod October?' This means that Archbishop Donaldson wished to know my view as regards the date when his work at Salisbury must begin. It appears to me that this enquiry on the part of Archbishop Donaldson was exactly right. You will not think me disrespectful if I say that, while of course it rests with the Prime Minister on behalf of the Crown to nominate to a vacant See, it rests with the Archbishop to decide at what date he is to take up his work in the new office. Supposing the man to be not yet a Bishop, it is for the Archbishop to decide when he will consecrate him, and when he is to begin his work. This is absolutely right, because the Archbishop administers the See during the vacancy and is responsible for its due care. I have taken very great pains about the care of the Diocese of Salisbury. An admirable Bishop is doing the work under my Commission, and in the peculiar characteristics of the Diocese of Salisbury, which I need not here discuss, I have no reason to think that any detriment will arise by the technical vacancy continuing through the Autumnal weeks, when the rural areas are not very amenable to rounds of Episcopal ministration....

Looking then at all the circumstances, I venture with the utmost respect to urge that you should let Donaldson be informed that, in the Archbishop of Canterbury's judgement (for which he has asked) he may, after accepting the post, remain until the Synod. But, as I have said, I am willing, if you feel a difficulty about this, to telegraph myself to Donaldson giving him my personal advice.

I know you well enough to believe that you will not regard me as discourteous in having thus told you plainly how the matter strikes me. I have very grave responsibilities in these matters. I accept them and try to carry them to the best of my ability. One of them relates to the date at which men duly nominated can, under my authority, take up the work assigned to them. I have given to the point in this particular case abundant thought, and I am quite convinced that I am advising rightly, and am ready to accept full responsibility for so doing.

Mr. Lloyd George immediately gave his consent in the following letter:

The Rt. Hon. D. Lloyd George *to the* Archbishop of Canterbury

Criccieth, 14th June, 1921.

In urging that Archbishop Donaldson should be asked immediately to take up his duties as Bishop of Salisbury, I was only apprehensive of the criticism, and, as it appeared to me, the legitimate criticism, which might ensue from delay, that the important diocese of Salisbury had been left without a shepherd 'except a provisional one' for a period extending over several months.

Your experience and authority in these matters, however, are paramount, and, if you think there is nothing in that criticism, I am willing to defer to your counsel, and, although the appointment is not yet made, and will not be made, until I have actually signed the recommendation to the King, I am prepared to do so at any moment following the course which you recommend. But kindly let me know what your final view is on the subject. I am only sincerely anxious to discharge to the best of my ability one of the greatest responsibilities entrusted to me as Prime Minister, and one to which I have always given, even when burdened with immense anxieties, the most concentrated care. I have always realised how much the spiritual well-being of England depends upon the choice of the right men for these exalted and sacred functions.

So all was well.

Mr. Bonar Law was Prime Minister for less than a year (October 1922–May 1923). On the first occasion on which the Archbishop saw him about any appointment (November 30, 1922), that of Dr. Headlam to the see of Gloucester, he found him very friendly. Indeed Mr. Law volunteered the promise that he would always consult the Archbishop about appointments, though naturally he would not undertake always to agree.

In 1923, Mr. Baldwin succeeded. He held the office for two periods: 1923–4, and again 1924–9. In the first of these periods, he had an exceptionally large number of bishoprics to fill. With regard to them all, he put himself in close touch with Archbishop Davidson; and paid great attention to his views. Consultation was constant. One of the most interesting appointments made by Mr. Baldwin, at the Archbishop's urgent request, was that of Dr. Frere to Truro. There is a long and important correspondence between the Archbishop and Dr. Frere on the question of acceptance. Here it is sufficient to print a single paragraph from the Archbishop's letter of August 28, 1923:

The ARCHBISHOP OF CANTERBURY *to the* REV. DR. W. H. FRERE

August 28, 1923.

It is not lightly that I have pressed upon the Prime Minister the conclusion I had reached after quiet consultation with Ebor, with Winton, and with others. For a long time past I have felt strongly that the Church had been suffering from the fact that among Diocesan Bishops there was no-one who could speak with responsibility on behalf of what is called, however inadequately, Anglo-Catholicism, and yet be able to regard these questions largely, sanely, and with the equipment of scholarly knowledge. Men who can do this can certainly be found. But that is not enough. We need someone whom the Prime Minister can fairly be urged to nominate, as a man who carries the confidence of Churchmen generally, whether they are of his school or not. It would be both futile and unfair were I to urge the Prime Minister to nominate to the Episcopate some admirable men whose virtues and capacities I myself know, but who would be neither known nor trusted by the rank and file of Churchmen of all schools. There is one man who does possess the qualifications which—when I think it all out before GOD—seem to me to be essential, and you are the man. This is no fad of mine, as you must know well. It is the view, so far as I can judge, of all those whom you would specially trust or who have a special claim on your attention. I have acted with a deep conviction in what I have done, and I unhesitatingly believe that I am right.

Mr. Ramsay MacDonald was Prime Minister for less than a year (January to November 1924) while Dr. Davidson was Archbishop. He hardly knew the Archbishop before, and it was at dinner in Lord Parmoor's house that they first met to discuss the general question of ecclesiastical appointments.

The Archbishop, in a letter to his host, again emphasized the Prime Minister's personal responsibility with regard to nominations, a responsibility which could not properly be handed over to any other individual, or any committee.

The ARCHBISHOP OF CANTERBURY *to the* RT. HON. THE LORD PARMOOR

February 1st, 1924.

My own view of the matter, and I think you share my opinion, is this: nothing must be done which will weaken in any degree the responsibility of the Prime Minister in regard to these nominations. Nothing must happen which would allow a notion to become current that the Prime Minister had handed over his responsibilities to other people. I perfectly understand that he has no intention of doing so, but I am anxious that in whatever is done the facts should be made clear. Next (and here I am sure both you and the Prime Minister will agree with me) the independence of the Crown in the matter must remain obviously unimpaired. I suppose that, as a matter of fact, the Sovereign has always taken a rather more independent position of personal 'say' with regard to ecclesiastical appointments than with regard to other appointments, though the ultimate responsibility rests essentially with the Prime Minister.

I should therefore express the position somewhat thus: the Prime Minister's nominations to the Crown must be based on adequate information which he has obtained in such way as he thinks best. The procedure he follows in obtaining that information is of his own planning and carrying out, and the Crown has, so to speak, no direct concern in it, but simply receives from the Prime Minister advice which is based upon the Prime Minister's own enquiries. The Prime Minister may courteously tell us privately that the procedure he means to follow is the consulting of the two Archbishops and some others, but, if I may say so, I think that the Sovereign should have no *official* cognizance of this, but should simply receive the nominations as coming from a well-informed Prime Minister. What you told me as to the present Prime Minister's probable choice of advisers seems to me a very sound plan, but it ought, in my judgement, to be an unofficial, not an official, plan. I would of course co-operate to the utmost of my power in helping the Prime Minister in the matter. I hope I have now put the matter fairly before you.

It was quite clear to the Archbishop that Mr. MacDonald wished to exercise his responsibilities in the best interests of the Church—and Mr. MacDonald showed that he was eager to receive and consider the Archbishop's advice. He might indeed, and on occasion did, feel a wish that the appointments of bishops did not fall to the lot of a jaded politician like the Prime Minister; but, having the duty to perform, he fulfilled it to the best of his power, and with the same impartiality as his predecessors. Some of his colleagues in the Labour party were at first perturbed because he did not appoint clergy who had served the Labour party in their parishes; but he soon made it plain that service to the

Labour party was an insufficient qualification for the office of a Bishop—and that some of the clergy who had been good Labour men were not in fact in possession of the experience or special abilities required for the government of a diocese.

Mr. MacDonald's principal appointment during his first term of office was that of Dr. Barnes as Bishop of Birmingham.

CHAPTER LXXIX

THE MALINES CONVERSATIONS

I have heard say, that when cardinal Lorrain saw our Prayer-book in Latin, or in French, he should answer, that he liked well of that order, 'if', saith he, 'they would go no further'. Sept. 16th, 1572. *The* ARCHBISHOP OF CANTERBURY *to* LORD BURGHLEY. (*Correspondence of Archbishop Parker.*)

To frame a common confession of faith, or liturgie, or discipline, for both Churches, is a project never to be accomplished. But to settle each so that the other shall declare it to be a sound part of the Catholic Church, and communicate with one another as such; this may easily be done without much difficulty by them abroad, and I make no doubt but the best and wisest of our Church would be ready to give all due encouragement to it. ARCHBISHOP WAKE *to the* REV. W. BEAUVOIR, Feb. 14th, 1717–18.

I

IN October 1921 the Archbishop received a letter from Lord Halifax informing him of a visit which he was proposing to pay, in company with the Abbé Portal, to Cardinal Mercier at Malines. Lord Halifax was eighty-two, and Fernand Portal sixty-six. They had been associated thirty years before, as already described,[1] in an unsuccessful mission to Archbishop Benson about Rome and Anglican Orders. They had not met for many years, and it was now proposed by Portal that they should visit Cardinal Mercier together, and talk of the Reunion of Christendom. Lord Halifax welcomed the idea with enthusiasm, and at once wrote to the Archbishops of Canterbury and York for a letter of introduction to the Cardinal. In this letter he hoped that they would also state their own great desire for the healing of the divisions of Christendom, and their readiness to promote conferences between the Church of England and the Church of Rome to that end. The Archbishops consulted, and a letter was written by the Archbishop of Canterbury. It was the easier for him to write, as he had already sent the Cardinal a copy of the Report of the Lambeth Conference 1920, and the Appeal to All Christian People, which his Eminence had cordially acknowledged, as himself an ardent advocate of unity. 'May God', the Cardinal said (May 21, 1921), 'hearken to the prayers we con-

[1] See p. 229 f.

tinually offer for the union of all Christian believers, and crown with success your efforts to attain their goal.'

But the Archbishop's commendation was very guarded. He said:

The Archbishop of Canterbury *to* Cardinal Mercier

12 October, 1921.

Lord Halifax does not go in any sense as an ambassador or formal representative of the Church of England, nor have I endeavoured to put before him any suggestions with regard to the possibilities of such conversations as might take place between Your Eminence and himself. Anything that he says therefore would be an expression of his personal opinion rather than an authoritative statement of the position or the endeavours of the Church of England in its corporate capacity. I cannot but think however that you would find a conversation with him consonant with the thought expressed in Your Eminence's letter to me of May 21st, and of the visions set forth in the Lambeth Conference Appeal.

The visit was duly paid, and the Cardinal received Lord Halifax and the Abbé Portal with the warmest sympathy. But when Lord Halifax asked the Cardinal if he would consider the possibility of conferences between Anglicans and Romans, His Eminence was a little astonished. 'Why do you not address yourselves first', he asked, 'to the English Catholic authorities?' Lord Halifax replied, 'Because their disposition is against it' (*l'état des esprits s'y oppose*). After reflection the Cardinal agreed, and said that if Lord Halifax came to Malines with two trusted and competent theologians prepared informally to discuss the situation, he would gladly receive them, and if necessary go himself to Rome and talk the matter over with the Pope.

On his return to England, Lord Halifax made a report to the Archbishops, and, on his own responsibility, invited two distinguished theologians to go with him very quietly to Malines in December. The two men were Dr. Armitage Robinson, Dean of Wells, and Dr. Walter Frere, Superior of the Community of the Resurrection, Mirfield. The former was a churchman who leaned to no party, the latter was Anglo-Catholic in his sympathies. The whole event was kept most private—and the Archbishop himself, except for knowing the bare fact, remained entirely outside.

This first Conversation at Malines was of an exploratory character—to see whether there was a case for the holding of conferences between Romans and Anglicans, with some real, though at first informal, encouragement from the highest authorities on both sides. It lasted three days (December 6–8, 1921). The Cardinal presided, and with him were his Vicar-General, Mgr. van Roey,[1] and the Abbé Portal, to meet the three Anglicans. The general basis of the conversation was (1) a Memorandum prepared by Lord Halifax dealing with the constitution of the Church, and the nature of the Sacraments, and (2) the Lambeth Appeal. The discussion was mainly theological, dealing in a preliminary way with the *maximum* common ground of agreement, and also with the difference between fundamental and non-fundamental dogmas. It was noteworthy that the question of the validity of Anglican Orders no longer proved the forbidding, if not fatal, barrier which it had been in Archbishop Benson's day. And the reason was that the statement contained in the Lambeth Appeal, intended for non-Episcopalians but capable of application to Rome, was felt to get over the difficulty. It ran as follows:

> If the authorities of other Communions should so desire, we are persuaded that, terms of union having been otherwise satisfactorily adjusted, Bishops and clergy of our Communion would willingly accept from these authorities a form of commission or recognition which would commend our ministry to their congregations, as having its place in the one family life.

It was a beginning full of hope—and both parties to the Conversation were agreed that there was plenty to encourage the holding of a conference, with some kind of sanction by authority.

II

Nine months, however, passed before any further move was made. Meantime, in February 1922, a new Pope had been elected, Cardinal Ratti, Archbishop of Milan, as Pius XI. He was well known to Cardinal Mercier, and believed to be deeply interested in Christian unity.

In September 1922, Cardinal Mercier told Lord Halifax that their exchanges of view had been approved at the Vatican, which would like them continued. But under what authority?

[1] Afterwards Cardinal van Roey, Archbishop of Malines.

Lord Halifax hoped that the Cardinal's initiative would be sufficient authority on the Roman side to justify the English Archbishops in naming their spokesmen. But the Archbishops were clear that this was not enough. The Archbishop of Canterbury said privately at the time (October 31, 1922) that an authoritative request from the Vatican, or at least an authoritative endorsement of Cardinal Mercier by the Vatican, was indispensable. If Mercier died, it would be perfectly possible for the Vatican to disclaim all responsibility for Mercier's action with the observation that he was certainly 'a very good man, but a little weak in his old age'. If, however, the Vatican were committed, it would be a very different matter. He and the Archbishop of York were ready to encourage the Conversations, but on certain conditions. The Archbishop wrote to Lord Halifax:

The ARCHBISHOP OF CANTERBURY *to* VISCOUNT HALIFAX

30 October, 1922.

I could not lend myself to giving authoritative 'mission' to spokesmen of the Anglican Church for conferring with spokesmen of the Church of Rome unless there be an authorisation on the part of the Vatican corresponding to that which is given from Lambeth. It is not for me to prescribe the exact manner in which that authorisation should be conveyed—whether by a letter from His Holiness the Pope, or the Cardinal Secretary of State on his behalf, or otherwise. But it must emanate from the centre and not from any ecclesiastical leader, however distinguished he be in person or in office. If any one goes from England, as sent by me or by the Archbishop of York and myself, to take part in such conference, those with whom he confers must hold credentials not less authoritative. I repeat that it does not follow from this that what such emissaries might agree to say would be binding upon those who send them or upon the Church at large. They would go to confer and to make suggestions—nothing more. The suggestions would have to be considered by those whose responsibility is of a central kind. I feel it necessary to make this clear at the outset of any new discussions or arrangements which may be in contemplation.

Cardinal Mercier was determined to see the matter through, and succeeded in securing the necessary authorization from the Vatican. He told Lord Halifax. The Archbishop asked that the Cardinal should write direct to him—'A three cornered correspondence, though in some cases useful, is never quite satisfactory; it has always an element of possible misconception and mistake' (December, 24 1922). The following letter was the result:

CARDINAL MERCIER *to the* ARCHBISHOP OF CANTERBURY

Malines. 10 January, 1923.

I am aware that Lord Halifax has kept your Grace informed of the private conversations ('informal') which were held at Malines from the 6th to the 8th December, 1921, between three Anglicans, Lord Halifax, Dr. Armitage Robinson and the Rev. W. Frere, and three Catholics, l'Abbé Portal, Mgr. Van Roey, Vicar General, and the Archbishop of Malines, with the object of promoting, if possible, the reunion of the Anglican Church with the Church of Rome.

Those conversations have seemed to you matters of such grave importance that you have desired still further to enforce that importance.

The Lambeth Conference, over which you presided, has already proclaimed its desire to search out means which may further the realization of the prayer for unity so expressly uttered by our Divine Saviour. You have therefore welcomed the renewal of the conversations begun at Malines in December 1921, and have been willing to add to their weight by being ready to name persons who should take part in them.

On our side we have the pleasure of being able to inform you that His Eminence the Cardinal Secretary of State has been authorised to inform me that the Holy See approves and encourages such conversations and prays God with all its heart to bless them.

If you are able to name as your delegates the three persons with whom we have had a first exchange of views, and possibly to add to them others selected by yourself, we should, on our side, be ready to name an equal number of friends to collaborate in our effort for reunion.

So arranged, the fresh conversations, without being authoritative, would be invested with more importance and weight.

I should esteem it a pleasure and an honour to offer to all these gentlemen, those on your side as well as on ours, at such a date as we might arrange, a simple but cordial hospitality.

Accept, my Lord, the expression of my highest regard and religious consideration.

The ARCHBISHOP OF CANTERBURY *to* CARDINAL MERCIER

Lambeth Palace. 2nd February, 1923.

I am now able to write to Your Eminence in reply to your important letter of January 10th, for which I have already thanked you.

I note with great interest the assurance which Your Eminence is authorised to transmit from the Cardinal Secretary of State 'que le Saint Siège approuve et encourage [les] conversations, et prie de tout son cœur le bon Dieu de les bénir'.

This enables our arrangements to go forward with the knowledge that the position of the members of the Church of England who take part as your guests in the discussions to which Your Eminence invites them, corresponds to the position accorded to the Roman Catholic members of the group, and that the responsibilities, such as they are, which attach to such conversations are thus shared in equal degree by all who take part in them.

With regard to the persons, and the number of persons, who are thus to meet, I think I am not mistaken in believing that, although Your Eminence is graciously willing to receive, if it be really requisite, one or two others in addition to the three who attended before, Your Eminence would on the whole prefer that, for the present at least, we should content ourselves with Lord Halifax and the Dean of Wells and Dr. Frere, the three representatives who enjoyed the privilege of Your Eminence's hospitality on the former occasion, the informal Conference thus consisting of six persons. With this opinion I cordially agree. Should the conversations be prolonged, and should those who confer express a wish for the addition of others to the number, I should of course be willing, like Your Eminence, to give attention to such request.

As regards the subjects of discussion, the Archbishop of York and I are in agreement in thinking that it would be better on all accounts that those who take part in the conversations should themselves arrange beforehand the subjects or headings for conversation, as any agenda otherwise arranged might unduly limit rather than facilitate satisfactory discussion.

I presume I am right in understanding that the arrangements as to date of meeting and any other particulars will now be in the hands of Your Eminence and Lord Halifax.

I need not assure Your Eminence how cordially I unite in the prayer to which expression is given on the part of the Holy See that the blessing of God may rest upon these conversations.

There were rocks ahead for both Cardinal and Archbishop. The

Abbé Portal told Lord Halifax that Cardinal Bourne (to whom Cardinal Mercier had shown Cardinal Gasparri's authorization embodied in the letter just given) had already indicated his disapproval—and that the conflict of rival influences would soon begin at Rome. And the Archbishop, apart from other difficulties, had the growing anxiety of the Prayer-Book controversy, and the fear lest any rash act, in even a tentative conversation with a representative of Rome, should wreck the revision. The Archbishop indeed was exceptionally cautious. In strict confidence he informed the Bishops of what was commencing—and not all of them approved. He annoyed the Abbé Portal by the emphasis which he laid, when speaking in Convocation in February 1923, on the increasing connexions between the Church of England and the Eastern Orthodox Church, through the recent recognition of Anglican Ordinations by the Patriarch of Constantinople. More disappointing still, he steadily set his face against any addition to the personnel of the Anglican members of the Second Conversation, due to be held at Malines in March. The Cardinal, after reading the carefully phrased letter announcing this refusal, felt constrained to speak of 'la grande réserve des deux archevêques de Cantorbéry et d'York'.

The caution was necessary—for it was from this, the first semi-official conversation, that the document concerning the *pallium* emerged, with the signatures of Anglicans as well as Roman Catholics, which so greatly disturbed the Archbishop. Moreover, while the Anglicans regarded the Archbishop of Canterbury as the chief of a great Christian communion allowing them to meet the representatives of the Head of the Roman Church, the Roman Catholics, except Portal, could not get rid of the idea, at least at first, that the proper analogy for the Anglican approach to the question of Reunion with Rome was the return of the prodigal. The same six persons met at Malines for this second Conversation (March 14 and 15, 1923) as had met in 1921. But the Anglicans now came with the friendly cognizance of the Archbishops of Canterbury and York, and the Romans with the knowledge of the Holy See. Archbishop Davidson had written out certain points which he wished to be remembered on the Anglican side of the debate, such as:

> Don't detract from the importance of the XXXIX Articles. Don't budge an inch as to the necessity of carrying the East with us in

ultimate Reunion steps. Bear constantly in mind that in any admission made as to what Roman leadership or 'primacy' (?) may mean, we have to make quite clear too that which it must not mean—i.e. some of the very things which the Cardinal's Pastoral claims for it.[1]

As a matter of fact, however, the memorandum which formed the basis of discussion, prepared by the Anglicans, dealt not with doctrine but with possible methods of a practical kind by which, supposing a reasonable measure of agreement on doctrinal matters were reached, the Anglican Communion as a whole might be brought into union, more or less complete in the first instance, with the Holy See. This leaving aside of dogmatic controversy surprised the Cardinal, as he afterwards confessed, but he agreed to the wishes of the Anglicans, who, after the preliminary doctrinal discussions of their previous visit, desired to explore the important questions of jurisdiction.

By way of introduction to the second Conversation, a good deal was said by the Anglicans about the geographical and numerical extent of the Anglican Communion in 1920, as compared with the condition of the Church of England in the sixteenth century, when, before the Reformation, there were only twenty-one Bishops occupying English and Welsh sees. The chief problems which would now arise, if the Anglican Communion were to be united as a world-wide communion with the Church of Rome, would be the relation of the Archbishop of Canterbury to the Holy See—the authority of the Pope in connexion with the Anglican Communion and its Bishops—the position of the existing Roman Catholic hierarchy in England—and the retention of certain characteristic Anglican rites and customs. In the Memorandum which had been prepared by the Anglicans it had been suggested that possibly a grant of the *pallium* by the Pope to the Archbishop of Canterbury might serve as an act of

[1] e.g. 'When, on Monday, February 6th, about noon, wireless telegraphy conveyed to all the nations of the world the news that a Pope, yesterday still unknown to the majority, had ascended the seat of Peter, under the name of Pius XI, three hundred million people instantly acclaimed Cardinal Ratti as their Chief and Father. In the intimacy of their conscience and in their full personal independence, they paid him the complete homage of their faith, and the submission of their intellect, will, and filial affection, ready to accept death if need be, rather than to infringe, I do not say one of his commands, but the least of his wishes.' From Cardinal Mercier's Pastoral Letter to his Diocese on the Papacy and the Election of H.H. Pius XI, printed in *A Call to Reunion* by Viscount Halifax, 1922, p. 28.

recognition which would thus determine the relation of the latter to the Holy See.

There was a good deal of discussion and division on the Memorandum submitted by the Anglicans. In the end each side agreed to submit a statement on the points debated to their respective authorities.

The French statement put the fundamental proposal in a clear and challenging form:

The French Statement

Cette fois,[1] la question examinée par nous revient à ces termes: Suppose que l'assentiment des esprits soit accompli sur le terrain doctrinal, dans quelles conditions pourrait s'opérer l'union de l'Église Anglicane à l'Église Romaine?

La préoccupation dominante de l'Église Anglicane est de garder, dans la mesure du possible, son organisation et sa hiérarchie actuelles, son rite, sa discipline.

Puisqu'il s'agit non d'un retour de personnalités isolées à l'Église de Rome, mais d'un retour collectif, cette préoccupation est toute naturelle.

Il est naturel que l'Archevêque de Cantorbéry, considéré par les évêques, par le clergé, par les fidèles de l'Église Anglicane, comme leur chef, soit considéré aussi comme devant continuer à leur égard l'exercice de son autorité.

Moyennant cet exercice, les rites et la discipline seraient suffisamment maintenus. L'entrée en masse dans le giron de l'Église Romaine serait ainsi facilitée. Certaines mesures, d'ailleurs, pourraient avoir un caractère temporaire.

Alors, la question fondamentale qui se pose paraît être la suivante:

Le Saint-Siège approuverait-il que l'Archevêque de Cantorbéry, acceptant la suprématie spirituelle du Souverain Pontife et le cérémonial jugé par lui nécessaire à la validité de la consécration de l'Archevêque, fût reconnu comme le Primat de l'Église Anglicane rattachée à Rome?

Le Saint-Siège consentirait-il à accorder à l'Archevêque de Cantorbéry et aux autres métropolitains le pallium comme symbole de leur juridiction sur leurs provinces respectives?

Permettrait-il à l'Archevêque de Cantorbéry d'appliquer aux

[1] i.e. the second Conversation, March 13–15, 1923. For the text of these statements, and for the full minutes and other documents, see *The Conversations at Malines, 1921–5*, Original Documents edited by Lord Halifax. Philip Allan, 1930.

autres évêques Anglicans le cérémonial de validation accepté par l'Archevêque?

Permettrait-il enfin à chaque Métropolitain de confirmer et de consacrer à l'avenir les évêques de sa province?

Tant que cette question primordiale n'aura pas été résolue, il nous serait malaisé de poursuivre nos négociations. Si elle était résolue affirmativement, la voie serait aplanie qui pourrait nous conduire à l'examen de questions ultérieures d'application.

We accept the above for submission to the respective authorities.[1]

Halifax.
J. Armitage Robinson.
Walter Howard Frere, C.R.

✠D.-J. Card. Mercier.
E. Van Roey, vic. gén.
F. Portal, p.d.l.M.

The English statement, which was more reserved, ran as follows:

The English Statement

The Anglican representatives being in hearty agreement with the statement drawn up by His Eminence desire on their part to sum up the position in the following terms.

As a result of the recent conversations at Malines it was agreed by those who were present that, supposing the doctrinal differences now existing between the two Churches could be satisfactorily explained or removed, and further supposing the difficulty regarding Anglican Orders were surmounted on the lines indicated in the Lambeth Appeal, then the following suggestions would form a basis of practical action for the reunion of the two Churches.

1. The acknowledgement of the position of the Papal See as the centre and head on earth of the Catholic Church, from which guidance should be looked for, in general, and especially in grave matters affecting the welfare of the Church as a whole.

2. The acknowledgement of the Anglican Communion as a body linked with the Papal See in virtue of the recognition of the jurisdiction of the Archbishop of Canterbury and other Metropolitans by the gift of the Pallium.

3. Under the discipline of the English Church would fall the determination of all such questions as:

The English rite and its use in the vernacular,
Communion in both kinds,
Marriage of the clergy.

4. The position of the existing Roman Catholic Hierarchy in

[1] In the original text the words '*We accept . . . authorities*' are in the handwriting of Viscount Halifax.

England with their Churches and congregations would for the present, at any rate, remain unaltered. They would be exempt from the jurisdiction of Canterbury, and, as at present, directly dependent on the Holy See.

Accepté pour être soumis aux autorités respectives.[1]

✠D.-J. Card. Mercier, arch. de Malines.
E. Van Roey, vic. gén.
F. Portal, p.d.l.M.

Halifax.
J. Armitage Robinson.
Walter Howard Frere, C.R.

The two documents were brought home to England. In haste, on the last morning, its authors signed each document before they separated, the Anglicans adding their signatures to the French statement as attesting its correctness as a document, and the Romans similarly attesting the English statement. The first sight of the statements, and especially of the three Anglican signatures on the French statement, filled the Archbishop of Canterbury with alarm. And the Dean of Wells, bringing the documents from Malines to Lambeth on March 16, and failing clearly to explain the difference between the signing and the attesting, was a good deal disturbed by His Grace's dismay. The Archbishop knew something of the latent feeling in England about Papal supremacy—and he saw at once what disastrous use could be made of such a proposal to give the *pallium*. The *pallium* was originally a cloak, made of the wool of lambs fed at the church of St. Agnes outside the walls of Rome, embroidered with four crosses and laid for a night on the tomb of St. Peter. In itself the history of the *pallium* represented the growth and extension of papal claims. Originally granted by the pope as an honour without further significance (and even worn by bishops), it was then restricted to metropolitans. The oath to the Papacy with which it was later associated first made an appearance in the days of Gregory VII (Hildebrand); and from the eleventh century onwards the insistence that it must be sought in person and the requirement that before reception the recipient should take an oath of obedience to the Pope gave occasion to represent the possession of it as requisite for the execution of the office. Finally, the papal lawyers, extending the claims of jurisdiction, claimed

[1] In the original text the words '*Accepté . . . respectives*' are in the handwriting of Cardinal Mercier.

to deprive the candidate not merely of metropolitical but even of diocesan jurisdiction until he had complied with the requirements. The *pallium* as received by Augustine of Canterbury from Gregory the Great was therefore very different in significance from that received from Hildebrand and his successors by the later archbishops in England.[1]

Whatever practical arrangement might be derived for determining future relationship in the field of administration, it was essential, in the Archbishop's judgement, that the great doctrinal issues which divided England and Rome should be considered *first* and in some measure solved. The Archbishop, therefore, wrote a long letter to the Dean of Wells (which he hoped that the Dean would send to the Cardinal). This letter, he directed, must be kept inseparably with the other papers, as recording his own view of the situation. The Dean referred to it afterwards, with a chuckle, as an instance of the Archbishop's method of insurance by memoranda against posthumous misunderstanding! After reference to the origin of the conversations and the difficulties 'which do not to my eyes grow less' he wrote thus:

The ARCHBISHOP OF CANTERBURY *to the* DEAN OF WELLS

19 March, 1923.

I take no exception whatever to your plan of discussing first some of the administrative questions you have dwelt upon, provided it is kept always in mind that there are great outstanding questions of a doctrinal sort which would require deliberate discussions and some measure of settlement before administrative problems would even arise.

I should personally place among the foremost of these the doctrine of the Roman Catholic Church as to the position, the jurisdiction, and the powers of the Papal See. The deep significance of that matter may very easily be slurred over in common talk by admitting as an historical and practical matter of so-called general knowledge the 'primacy' of the Bishop of Rome. In certain senses this is an indisputable historical fact. But as used by Roman Catholics his primacy means a great deal more. Though the Vatican Council emphasised and increased what we deem the false doctrine of the Pope's independent and autocratic status as sole Vicar of Christ, the claim had of course been made for many centuries. Its recognition is virtually, and is now even technically,

[1] See J. P. Whitney, 'The National Church and the Papacy', pp. 40–4, in *The Anglican Communion*, ed. H. A. Wilson (London, 1929).

de fide. It therefore affects in the widest way, both doctrinally and administratively, the whole question of the relation of the Church of Rome to the rest of Christendom. It bears upon almost every problem that can come up for discussion. If we are bound—as I certainly believe we are—to discard as untrue the theory that the Bishop of Rome holds *jure Divino* in the Church of Christ a position of distinct and unique authority, operative everywhere, and perhaps even—though here I speak with reserve—that, directly or indirectly, it is through that channel alone (at all events in the West) that the Ministerial Commission can be rightly or validly exercised, there is an obvious inappropriateness in discussing other Church questions until that fundamental question has been brought to a clear issue. I have not tried to express myself in technical terms, and the words I have used may be open to legitimate criticism. But I hope that I have, for the purpose of this letter, made my meaning sufficiently clear.

There are also, as your conversations have shown, large differences between us, with which the question of Papal status is only indirectly concerned, and these would call of course for full and far-reaching discussion. I refer, for example, to such questions as the dogma of Transubstantiation, or the dogma of the Immaculate Conception of the Blessed Virgin: and of course there are others. But the point I have referred to lies so clearly *in limine* that I would urge you, when you next meet, (and I hope your conversations will be resumed ere long) to let it be placed in the arena of your deliberations with a view to some sort of definite statement on either side. Such statements may of course in the first instance be provisional only. But the question is so vital a one that it is really essential to the whole.

At the same time he did not rule out the whole possibility of the proposal brought him by the Dean:

I have given you my view of the situation as disclosed in the memoranda with signatures appended. It is a situation full of difficulty and calling for the utmost circumspection and caution, but it calls also for quiet perseverance, and the gates towards a pathway which may lead unionwards are certainly not peremptorily closed. Subject to what I have said as to the attainment of agreement on the large *doctrinal* questions, I am ready to say that the suggestions which the two Memoranda contain are well calculated to furnish the basis for future discussion and conference.

This letter greatly disturbed Lord Halifax, whose 'enthusiasm (so the Archbishop declared) enabled him to override the really grave questions which lie at the root of the matter'. And it cannot be denied that the Archbishop's alarm was encouraged by Bishop Gore:

BISHOP GORE *to the* ARCHBISHOP OF CANTERBURY

March 19, 1923.

I am only writing to say that the concessiveness of our delegation to Malines, apparently at the first Conference and certainly at the second, seems to me more disastrous and perilous the more I think of it. It astonished me to hear from the Dean what he was prepared to admit as to Roman supremacy, and that he is prepared to contemplate the (conditional) reordination of the Anglican clergy from top to bottom.

The Archbishop wrote also to the Cardinal:

The ARCHBISHOP OF CANTERBURY *to* CARDINAL MERCIER

24 March, 1923.

I have now seen the Archbishop of York, and I am in a position to write further to Your Eminence with regard to the recent conversations at Malines.

The Archbishop of York unites with me in thanking Your Eminence for the kindly care you are taking in this whole matter, and for the clearness with which you have set forth the position taken by yourself, and by those with whom you act, as regards certain fundamental questions, doctrinal and administrative.

We clearly understand the wish which those who represented the Anglican Church expressed, that attention should be given at this early stage to the administrative questions relating to the course of practical action which might conceivably be followed if an agreement had, after discussion, been provisionally reached on the large doctrinal matters which underlie the whole. It was right that these practical matters should not, even at this early stage, be left wholly in the air. They must be reduced to more or less definite form.

I do not want at this stage to say of any proposal of a merely administrative sort whether it is or is not out of the question. For it would be necessary first to know what the administrative act implies. The obtaining of that knowledge will, I hope, be the task of the further conferences.

I do not doubt that Your Eminence will agree with me in thinking that, after all, the really fundamental question of the position of the Sovereign Pontiff of the Roman Catholic Church must be candidly faced before further progress can be made. The ambiguity of the term 'primacy' is well known to us all. It has an historic meaning which can be accepted without difficulty. If, however, it is understood as implying that the Pope holds *jure divino* the unique and solemn position of sole Vicar of Christ on earth, from whom as Vicar of Christ must come directly or indirectly the right to minister validly within the Church, there ought to be no delay in discussing that implication and expounding its essential bearings. For it would not, in my judgement, be fair to Your Eminence or to others that I should encourage further discussion upon subordinate administrative possibilities without expressing my conviction that such a doctrine of papal authority is not one to which the adherence of the Church of England could be obtained. I say this simply for clearness' sake, and not as meaning that I desire these conversations to end. There may be explanations forthcoming on Your Eminence's part of which I have no knowledge. If such there be, it would certainly be well that the discussions should go on.

I have explained to my three Anglican friends what I feel upon this anxious and difficult matter, and have encouraged them to look forward to a resumption of the conferences. So great is the importance of this matter and its issues, that no effort on the part of any of us should be spared which may contribute towards the ultimate attainment of Unity within the Church of Christ.

It might be possible to augment to a small degree the numbers of those who take part in further deliberations. Such addition would have obvious difficulties of its own. But on this, and on any other points, I should of course be most anxious to hear further from Your Eminence to whose Christian courtesy we owe so much.

CARDINAL MERCIER *to the* ARCHBISHOP OF CANTERBURY

The Archbishop's Palace, Malines. 11th April 1923.

Your kind letter of 24th March has reached me safely, but a ten days' absence from Malines has prevented me from replying to it immediately.

Please accept my thanks for it and find herewith the reflections which it has suggested to me.

It is very gratifying to me to learn that the Archbishop of York and yourself have taken note of the memoranda which your three delegates have brought back from Malines; that you have both given them a sympathetic reception; and that you both wish for the continuation of the conferences inaugurated at Malines.

Since the first conference, in December 1921, it has seemed to us that we ought at once to concentrate our attention on the fundamental question of the primacy of the Roman Pontiff.

Lord Halifax, who suggested to me this meeting at Malines, and his two companions, were in agreement with my Vicar-General, with the Abbé Portal, and with myself on this point.

But then, when, this year, there came to us, from Dean Robinson and his two colleagues, the memorandum for discussion in the course of our second conference, I was surprised to see that the projected conversation deviated from the original doctrinal point of view, and invited us to consider questions of a rather more practical and 'administrative' kind.

Since our sole desire was to comply with the appeal of the loyal and generous souls who had of their own accord come to meet us, we felt that we ought, without making any objections, to agree to the proposition which was put before us. Also, these administrative questions, perhaps of secondary importance, ought none the less, sooner or later, to be submitted to the examination of the authorities and, in addition, the memorandum of the Dean of Wells contained the formal declaration that the solutions which should be given now to these disciplinary questions, would not be put into practice until the day when agreement should be reached in the realm of doctrine.

That is to say, my dear Lord, that I share your opinion and that of the Archbishop of York, when you shew yourselves anxious to bring back the conversation to what we call with you 'the large doctrinal matters which underlie the whole'.

I believe, nevertheless, that I am voicing the deep desire of all the members of the Conference in expressing to you here a wish: Since, as a matter of fact, 'administrative' questions have formed, at the request of your delegates, the object of our second conference, and the two groups face to face have pledged in the examination of these questions their responsibility at the same time personal and collective, would you not feel yourself able to let us know your opinion and that of your colleague of York on the conclusions to which our conference has come, and which are to be found recorded in the report of the meeting and in the two memoranda which your delegates have had the honour of placing in your hands?

You will agree, in fact, my dear Lord, that if we were able to reciprocate to the two Archbishops of Canterbury and York the complimen which they have had the kindness to address to us with gratitude 'for the clearness with which we have set forth the position taken by ourself and by those with whom we act' the two groups engaged in the conference would take up their task again with more assurance and on firmer ground.

Having said that, in all frankness and in the interest of the cause in which we are collaborating, I come readily to the 'fundamental' question of the position accorded to the Sovereign Pontiff in the Roman Catholic Church.

The logical train of our conferences, as well as the mutual duties of loyalty on the part of the members who meet there, oblige us to take up again this examination of the primacy of the Bishop of Rome, successor of Peter, defined as a dogma of the catholic faith by the Vatican Council.

Our third conference, which like you I hope may be soon and, to a certain extent, enlarged, will assume then the task of studying this doctrine more thoroughly, and will apply itself, in accordance with your desire, to making more precise its significance.

Meanwhile, I make it my personal duty to tell you what I believe to be the Roman Catholic doctrine on the special point about which you wish to question me.

You ask me if the Primacy accorded to the Sovereign Pontiff signifies or entails this consequence, that alone, by divine right, the Pope is the Vicar of Christ on earth, in this sense that from him alone derives, directly or indirectly, all legitimate power to exercise validly a ministry in the Church: 'If the term "primacy" is understood as implying that the Pope holds *jure divino* the unique and solemn position of sole Vicar of Christ on earth, from whom as Vicar of Christ must come directly or indirectly the right to minister validly within the Church.'

Certainly, the Pontiff of Rome is, in a special sense, the Vicar of Christ on earth, and the piety of the faithful is accustomed to bestow on him this title by choice. But Saint Paul states that all the apostles are the ministers of Christ: '*Sic nos existimet homo ut ministros Christi.*' The Roman Liturgy, in the Preface to the Mass for Apostles, calls all the apostles the 'Vicars' put in charge by the eternal Shepherd of the pastoral direction of his work: '*Gregem tuum, pastor aeterne, non deseras, sed per beatos apostolos tuos continua protectione custodias: ut iisdem rectoribus gubernetur, quos operis tui Vicarios eidem contulisti praeesse pastores.*' Still more, of the simple priest in the exercise of his ministry, we say readily that he is the representative of Christ, 'another Christ', '*sacerdos, alter Christus*'. If he did not occupy the place of Christ, '*vices gerens Christi*', '*Vicarius Christi*', how could he truthfully say of the Body and of the Blood of our Saviour: '*Hoc est Corpus meum*: *hic est calix Sanguinis mei*'; how could he, in remitting sins, which God alone can absolve, say: '*Ego te absolvo*', '*I* absolve thee'?

The ordinary application of the title 'Vicar of Christ' to the Sovereign Pontiff does not involve therefore as a consequence, that *alone* the Bishop of Rome possesses powers coming direct from Christ.

The powers of the Bishop refer for one part to the Body, real, historical, of our Lord Jesus Christ—'Power of Order'—for the other part, to his mystical Body—'Power of jurisdiction'.

The power of 'Order', power of consecrating the Body and Blood of our Saviour in the Holy Eucharist, power of conferring on someone else the fulness of the priesthood, including in that the ability to transmit it with a view to perpetuating the Christian life in the Church, was given by Christ to all his apostles. It belongs fully to the bishops, their successors, inalienably; no human authority whatever could break its validity.

Is it not well known, for example, that the Church of Rome recognises the persisting validity of the Orders and Sacraments in the Eastern Orthodox Church, which, nevertheless, has been separated for a thousand years from the Roman Primacy?

The power of 'jurisdiction', power of ruling the Church, the mystical body of Christ, belongs by divine right to the episcopate, that is to say to the bishops, successors of the apostles, in union with the Sovereign Pontiff.

The episcopate, regarded as the whole institution of government, is of divine right and it would not be in the power of the Bishop of Rome to abolish it.

The power of 'jurisdiction' devolved upon each bishop is also of divine right; it is ordinary and immediate within the limits of the diocese assigned to the bishop by the Sovereign Pontiff.

The peace and the unity of the Christian Society demand, in fact, that at the head of the government of the Church there should be a supreme authority, itself ordinary and immediate, over the whole Church, over the faithful and their pastors;[1] to this supreme authority belongs the prerogative of assigning to each bishop the portion of the Christian flock which he is called to rule in union with the Pontiff of Rome and under his authority.

The bishop's power of jurisdiction over his flock is of divine right, but when the theologians ask how this divine origin ought to be interpreted, their counsels are divided.

One party holds that this power of jurisdiction comes immediately from God, like the power of 'Order'. According to this conception, the Pope nominates the bishop, assigns to him his subjects, but the jurisdiction over these subjects comes from God, without human intermediary. This opinion, in the words of Benedict XIV, has on its side solid arguments, '*validis fulcitur argumentis*'.

[1] '*Si quis dixerit Romanum Pontificem . . . non habere plenam et supremam potestatem jurisdictionis in universam Ecclesiam . . . aut hanc ejus potestatem non esse ordinariam et immediatam sive in omnes ac singulas ecclesias, sive in omnes et singulos pastores et fideles, anathema sit.*' *Conc. Vaticanum Sess. IV*, Cap. III.

But, he adds, to this opinion is opposed another, according to which the jurisdiction comes from Christ, as principal source, but is granted to the bishop through the intermediary of the Roman Pontiff. According to this conception, episcopal consecration gives to the bishop the qualification for jurisdiction, but the actual complete jurisdiction is dependent on the mandate of the Sovereign Pontiff.

This opinion, says Benedict XIV, seems to have on its side better arguments of reason and authority: '*rationi et auctoritati conformior videtur sententia*.'[1]

No further decision, which commands universal assent, has settled the controversy.

Neither does the *Codex juris canonici* edited by Pope Benedict XV, the word of which is law in the Catholic Church, settle it. It sums up in these words the general doctrine of the Roman Church concerning the episcopate: '*Episcopi sunt apostolorum successores atque ex divina institutione peculiaribus ecclesiis praeficiuntur quas cum potestate ordinaria regunt sub auctoritate Romani Pontificis*.'[2]

This universal authority of the Sovereign Pontiff, say the Fathers of the Vatican Council, ought not to be considered by the bishops as a menace or a danger. It is, on the contrary, for the authority of the bishop over against his flock, a support, a strength, a protection. '*Tantum abest, ut haec Summi Pontificis potestas officiat ordinariae ac immediatae illi episcopalis jurisdictionis potestati, qua Episcopi, qui positi a Spiritu Sancto in Apostolorum locum successerunt, tanquam veri pastores assignatas sibi greges, singuli singulos, pascunt et regunt, ut eadem a supremo et universali Pastore asseratur, roboretur et vindicetur*.'[3]

More than once, in the course of my episcopal career, my experience has confirmed the truth of this conciliar declaration.

But this is not the time for me to enlarge on this subject. I must confine myself to replying briefly to the question about which your valued letter has engaged for the moment my attention. The conference which we shall, shortly, please God, have occasion to resume, will have to examine more closely the question which surpasses all the others in importance both christian and social, of the Primacy of the Pope.

I hope that you will not think it unfitting that in bringing to a close these lines, I should express to you the feeling which is prompted in my heart by my love for our Saviour Jesus Christ, my love for His Church: We are engaged in collaborating for the re-establishment of peace in the world by the drawing together

[1] *De Synodo diocesana*, Lib. I, Cap. IV, n. 2.
[2] Titul. VIII, Cap. I, *de episcopis*, Can. 329.
[3] *Conc. Vat. Sess. III*, Cap. III.

of the souls baptized in the same sheep-fold, under the crook of the same shepherd, '*ut fiat unum ovile et unus pastor!*' Let us pray with all our heart unceasingly for one another for the realization of this great ideal of unity for which Christ prayed and suffered and gave His life. Let us quicken ourselves with Christian power and with the spirit of charity, in order that among us all may be fulfilled the prayer of our holy Liturgy: '*Ut et ea quae agenda sunt videant et ad agenda quae viderint, convalescant.*'

Please accept, my dear Lord, and convey to your revered colleague, the Archbishop of York, the assurances of my respectful esteem and of my religious zeal.

P.S. Allow me to make you a present of a Pastoral letter relating to the Encyclical *Ubi Arcano Dei* of His Holiness Pope Pius XI, and an attempted translation of this weighty document.

The Archbishop acknowledged the letter, but the correspondence with Lord Halifax and others shows that he was full of questions; and the Cardinal frankly said to Lord Halifax:

CARDINAL MERCIER *to* VISCOUNT HALIFAX

April 24, 1923.

Speaking quite confidentially I may and ought to tell you that in my opinion the danger at the present moment is lest the Archbishops should be unwilling to take in hand the fundamental question at issue and the question of opportunity and of its application.

They are the guides of their flocks, and they ought to form clear ideas and personal convictions as to the line of their spiritual government. That done, there will be time to ascertain how to induce others to accept what their conscience will have told them is the truth and the end to be pursued.

At length the Archbishop sent the following reply:

The ARCHBISHOP OF CANTERBURY *to* CARDINAL MERCIER

May 15th, 1923.

I owe apologies to Your Eminence for delay in replying further to your very important letter, dated 11th April, for which I briefly thanked you on April 13th. During these weeks my work has been even exceptionally onerous, and it has been difficult to find time for other than urgent correspondence.

I have now considered with great care all that Your Eminence was good enough to write in the letter of 11th April, and I have had opportunity also of taking counsel with the Archbishop of York, as well as with the Dean of Wells.

In the light of your letter and of these conversations, I desire to assure Your Eminence that we perfectly understand how it was that in the two Conferences at Malines the course of proceeding was followed which you have described to me. After recounting the order of proceeding, Your Eminence asks 'Ne jugeriez-vous pas pouvoir nous faire connaître votre appréciation et celle de votre collègue de York sur les conclusions auxquelles notre conférence a abouti et qui se trouve consignées dans le procès-verbal de la réunion et dans les deux memorandums que vos délégués ont eu l'honneur de déposer en vos mains?' The difficulty we find in expressing an opinion about these conclusions is this:—

The administrative suggestions are not only hypothetical in themselves (depending as they do on the condition that some measure of general agreement should first have been reached upon the large doctrinal question we have referred to), but the actual suggestions as they stand can only be interpreted aright if we know what the words imply; and this knowledge we cannot have until the preliminary discussions have resulted in some positive statement. To take an example of what I mean, an example which I select because it is obvious and simple, I find in the Memorandum drawn up by the Roman Catholic Members of the Conference the following suggestion for consideration:

'Le Saint Siège consentirait-il à accorder à l'Archevêque de Cantorbéry et aux autres Métropolitains le pallium comme symbole de leur juridiction sur leurs provinces respectives?'

It is impossible to express an opinion upon this suggestion without a clear knowledge of what is meant or implied by the giving of the pallium. I should feel it to be impossible to express even provisional assent to such a suggestion until it has been made clear:

(1) whether the Act of the Holy See in giving the pallium as a symbol of jurisdiction did or did not imply that the recipient was recognized as being already the holder of Valid Orders, and,

(2) whether the Act of the Archbishop in receiving the pallium did or did not imply an acceptance of the doctrine that his jurisdiction must, if it is to be valid, be conferred by the Pope. It is of course obvious that these questions would require careful discussion, involving the consideration of large problems, both doctrinal and historical. In this connexion, I note with the utmost interest the opinion expressed by Your Eminence:

'La conférence que nous aurons, s'il plaît à Dieu, bientôt, l'occasion de reprendre, aura à examiner de plus près la question, qui prime toutes les autres en importance chrétienne et sociale, de la Primauté du Pape.'

Your Eminence has been good enough to set out with admirable clearness in the same letter the distinction which must be borne in mind between Questions of Order and Questions of Jurisdiction. And I have purposely taken as an example of my difficulty one question only, a question belonging to the subject of jurisdiction. There are of course very many other large and far-reaching problems belonging to every branch of the subject, and it would, I hope, be possible to deal with some of these when the Conferences are resumed.

My point to-day is simply to make clear to Your Eminence why it is that I cannot at present meet the desire which you express when you say 'Ne jugeriez-vous pas pouvoir nous faire connaître votre appréciation . . . sur les conclusions', etc.

It has probably been an excellent thing to set forth examples in the form of suggestions, as to some of the practical and administrative details which might hereafter emerge if the greater matters had received solution, and I find no difficulty in saying that if upon the large preliminary questions both of Order and Jurisdiction a really satisfactory agreement had been reached, the actual process of outward arrangement suggested in the signed paper might well form the subject of friendly and hopeful consideration. To make such a statement, however, at this juncture, would seem to me to have little significance while the underlying questions of a fundamental character remain quite unsolved. Your Eminence has explained to me that on some of those great questions there are different, and it would seem rival, theories of interpretation which have a place, more or less authoritative, within the Church of Rome, and, if the discussions go forward, as I hope they may, in further Conferences, it would be of supreme interest to us to understand whether both sets of opinion are now permissible among you and may be taught without breach of loyalty. But all this lies in the future, and I am not asking Your Eminence for an answer now to such enquiry. I thank Your Eminence for the generous readiness with which you have been willing, notwithstanding the responsibilities of your great office, to write and speak with so much freedom upon the solemn and difficult points of controversy which have emerged during the discussions. My sole desire at this moment is to make it clear that there must be further discussion upon the great question underlying the series of suggestions formulated at Malines, and that until preliminary elucidation has been given to it I am not in a position to say more than I have said.

In again thanking Your Eminence for your unwearied kindness in this grave matter, I desire to express my concurrence in what you have said as to the advantage of some addition, when the Conference is resumed, to the number of those who take part in it. I should like to invite Bishop Gore or another of our leading theologians to associate himself with the Dean of Wells and with Dr. Frere, and I hope I am not mistaken in thinking that this would be welcomed by Your Eminence.

It is I think obvious that no advantage would arise from our making public at present anything which has passed in the conversations at Malines. Such partial and fragmentary statement as would alone be possible would, I think, inevitably lead to misunderstanding. If I find it to be desirable to make a brief reference in general terms to the fact of our having taken advantage of your gracious invitation to Malines, I would venture to submit beforehand to Your Eminence a copy of anything which I propose to say.

The reply was not very satisfactory to the Cardinal, who told Lord Halifax that 'the writer seems to me to be refraining from expressing his mind. His words in spite of himself betrayed an uneasiness which inevitably communicated itself to others.' (July 10.)

The Archbishop's uneasiness was increased when the Bishop of Zanzibar, as president of the Anglo-Catholic Congress, telegraphed the respectful greetings of 16,000 Anglo-Catholics to the Pope humbly praying that the day of peace might quickly dawn. The Archbishop had already written to Lord Halifax strongly dissuading him from a public meeting on the subject of Reunion with Rome. It had been proposed that the Bishop of Oxford (Dr. Burge) should take the chair. But the Archbishop maintained his objections.

When Lord Halifax suggested the Bishop of Zanzibar in his place, the Archbishop replied:

The ARCHBISHOP OF CANTERBURY *to* VISCOUNT HALIFAX

13 July, 1923.

I am afraid that I should feel even more apprehension about the meeting under those conditions. To invite people to attend such a meeting would be, in my judgement, to open the door to discussions which I should regard as being not only inopportune but mischievous, as they must quite inevitably lead to misapprehension about what has passed, about what is now happening, and about what might now be encouraged or expected. If I felt this strongly, as I did when I read your letter, I feel it far more strongly now when the Bishop of Zanzibar has, to the consternation of all sorts of reasonable men, compromised things by his action in telegraphing to the Pope on behalf of the Anglo-Catholic Congress, without even telling the Bishop of London, as its President, or Dr. Frere and others who are so largely responsible for the Congress and its well-being. I yield to no one in my personal regard for the Bishop of Zanzibar, but I do look upon him as a source and centre of real danger to the Church at present owing to the unguarded way in which he writes and speaks. I have seen several people who were in the Albert Hall last night, and there is not one of them who has not told me of the disquietude caused by some of Bishop Weston's words.

Lord Halifax replied with a distress he made no attempt to conceal. He said he would obey the Archbishop's wishes, but:

The VISCOUNT HALIFAX *to the* ARCHBISHOP OF CANTERBURY

July 17, 1923.

What causes my great trouble now is that, after reading Your Grace's letter to me of July 13 as carefully as I can several times, I cannot help seeing that I have misled the Cardinal as to Your Grace's real mind and wishes; nor can I conceal from myself, in view of the whole tenor of the letter, that Your Grace would be relieved if the present attempt to promote the reunion of the Church of England with Rome came to an end.

It is a most painful reflection that Cardinal Mercier should seem more anxious for that reunion, and more ready to consider methods by which it may be brought about, than Your Grace.

III

Meantime preparations went forward for a third Conversation. It was agreed that the number should be enlarged on either side. The Archbishop was most anxious to secure the help of Bishop Gore, who, though gravely pessimistic, agreed to go.

BISHOP GORE *to the* ARCHBISHOP OF CANTERBURY

31 July, 1923.

I think it is of such immense importance—with a view to your retaining your present position in real mental vigour as long as possible—that you should be relieved of any anxiety in whole or in part, that if you seriously believe my joining the party for Malines would relieve you, I cannot doubt that I ought to agree to go.

There was some talk of obtaining another Anglican, representing a moderate or evangelical point of view: but it came to nothing. In the end Bishop Gore and Dr. Kidd (Warden of Keble), the Church historian, were chosen. The Archbishop's own hesitations were abundantly evident throughout these months. A long memorandum is preserved in which he set out his doubts and difficulties. In the course of it he wrote:

August 19, 1923.

> There is, I suppose, no conceivable subject of controversy so inflammatory as the position of the Church of Rome in English, Scottish, or Irish life, and red-hot Protestants on one side, or intractable and uncompromising Papists on the other, would instantly distort and misrepresent, however unintentionally, any broken or isolated facts which might reach them. This would have the result not merely of bringing to an abrupt and perhaps fiery close any attempt to reach a roadway towards reconciliation, but it might, not unnaturally, arouse suspicion among different sections of our own Churchmen. Far easier, perhaps I ought to say far safer, it would be to let the matter severely alone and refuse to take any steps whatever upon so uncertain or treacherous a quagmire. Yet to take that course would mean the deliberate turning of a deaf ear to the little whisper of tentative enquiry or approach which reaches us from the Roman side. That I am determined I will not do. Of course it will be said that we cannot entertain any strong hopes of ultimate success attending any effort at present to bridge a chasm due to, or indicative of, fundamental differences as to modes of faith and worship. But I will not attempt to estimate the chances of success. I cannot consistently with the obligations, first, of our common Christianity, and, next, of the special resolves and hopes to which the Lambeth Conference gave expression three years ago, refuse to participate in any genuine and pious endeavour towards reaching a goal which ought not in the nature of things to be unattainable by Christian men who believe in the reality of Our Master's Prayer and in the present day guidance of God the Holy Spirit. So, if our Roman Catholic friends are ready to co-operate, try we must and will.

The memorandum referred to the importance, at this stage, of facing fundamental matters:

> The position and authority of Holy Scripture, the meaning and authority of Tradition, the existence or non-existence of a Supreme Authority upon earth, a Vicariate of Christ, and what it means

as regards both doctrine and administration: then further, the introduction of such dogmas as that of the Immaculate Conception, or again, and in another field, the definite teaching of the Church of Rome as to Transubstantiation and the attendant or consequent doctrines and usages. . . . If, when the representatives next meet, they will thus put the first things first in discussion, as they have always been first in their thoughts, then the deliberations which have already taken place may prove to have been wholly advantageous. If, however, it should appear that there are great doctrinal questions (or even great administrative questions like the claim of unchallengeable papal autocracy) upon which no modification or explanation is possible, I can myself see very small gain in continuing discussions which would be foredoomed to failure. For it ought to be made clear on the Anglican side, beyond possibility of doubt, that the great principles upon which the Reformation turned are our principles still, whatever faults or failures there may have been on either side in the controversies of the sixteenth century. It would be unfair to our Roman Catholic friends to leave them in any doubt as to our adherence, on large questions of controversy, to the main principles for which men like Hooker or Andrewes or Cosin contended, though the actual wording would no doubt be somewhat different to-day. What those men stood for, we stand for still, and I think that in some form or other that ought to be made immediately clear.

Lord Halifax tried to reassure the Cardinal—but His Eminence could not but be aware of the Archbishop's reserve. In a strictly personal letter to Lord Halifax he made this comment upon it:

CARDINAL MERCIER *to* VISCOUNT HALIFAX

Sept. 10, 1923.

Ma pensée n'est pas du tout de me retirer; au contraire, j'ai le vif désir de reprendre et de poursuivre nos conversations, même dans un cercle élargi. Mais il ne me paraît pas possible que les *Autorités* ecclésiastiques soient engagées d'un seul côté.

L'Archevêque de Cantorbéry attend, garde le silence, s'abstient. Plusieurs personnes, qui le connaissent, disent en parlant de lui: 'He is cautious, very cautious.'

Si nous voulons collaborer à des conversations qui ne soient pas purement 'individuelles', il importe que l'autorité ne se retranche pas, d'un côté, dans le réserve, presque l'abstention, tandis que, de l'autre côté, elle serait invitée à s'avancer toujours davantage. Pour qu'il y ait rencontre fraternelle, il faut qu'elles s'avancent l'une vers l'autre.

What Cardinal Mercier failed to observe was the far greater reserve of the Pope, who never emerged from the background on the Roman side; while the Archbishop of Canterbury, on the Anglican side, did emerge. The Archbishop saw the Anglican emissaries at Lambeth before they went to Malines, and called on a few advisers (the Bishop of Ripon,[1] Canon Storr, Canon Quick, Dr. Jenkins) to discuss the programme with him. He explained the points, and quoted various documents in elucidation.

The third Conversation took place at Malines on November 7–8, 1923. The Roman Catholics were the same as before, with the addition of two French scholars, Monsignor Pierre Batiffol and Père Hippolyte Hemmer. The discussion was wholly confined to the position of St. Peter, on the basis of full memoranda prepared beforehand by theologians of both sides. It was recognized by the Anglicans that St. Peter was the accepted chief or leader of the Apostles in the New Testament, and that he was so accepted because he was treated so by our Lord: but the Anglicans maintained that the power given to St. Peter in Matthew xvi, while so given to him as chief leader of the apostolic company, was fulfilled to all the twelve:

> so that all constitute the foundation of the Church, all have the keys of the kingdom, and all have the authority to bind and to loose. St. Peter's special position, therefore, we hold to have lain, not in any jurisdiction which he alone held, but in a leadership among the other Apostles.

The Anglicans after some discussion expressed their readiness to say

> that the sayings of the Gospel—notably the *Tu es Petrus* and the *Pasce agnos*—express a prerogative of Peter as the foundation of the Church and the principle of its unity.
>
> We consider that the events of history have thrown light on these texts which has brought out more clearly their true significance.
>
> The Vatican Council defines as of the Catholic Faith the primacy of universal jurisdiction conferred on Peter, grounding itself on the two texts *Tu es Petrus* and *Pasce oves*. It declares that the denial of the primacy is contrary to the plain sense of Holy Scripture as the Catholic Church has always understood it.
>
> The Council does not indicate the numerous testimonies which prove the tradition in the interpretation of the texts, and which are to be found in the patrology and ancient Christian literature.

[1] Dr. Drury.

The question, however, to be faced was in their view 'What constitutes primacy?' And 'What is the relation of the Pope to other Bishops?' The Anglicans agreed:

> That he has a primacy among all the Bishops of Christendom; so that, without communion with him, there is in fact no prospect of a reunited Christendom.
>
> That to the Roman See the churches of the English owe their Christianity through 'Gregory our father' (Council of Clovesho, A.D. 747) 'who sent us baptism' (Anglo-Saxon Chronicle, *anno* 565).

The third Conversation gave pleasure to all who attended—and Bishop Gore expressed himself charmed with the gracious entertainment and wise chairmanship of the Cardinal. It was not so sensational as the second, but it reached a greater measure of agreement on doctrinal matters, and secured the admission that the doctrine underlying the Papal claim might be further probed.

The next question to be considered was how far the public could be taken into the confidence of the promoters of the Conversations. It was felt that complete silence was dangerous, yet the manner and the amount of communication involved difficulties. In the end, the Archbishop decided to issue at Christmas a Letter to the Metropolitans of the Anglican Communion, informing them generally of the results of the Lambeth Appeal, and giving a large section to the Malines Conversations. He drafted a letter and circulated it to the Anglican members of the Conference and also to Cardinal Mercier. There were several criticisms, all of which the Archbishop took well. The Cardinal secured certain modifications in the reference to the authorization by the Vatican, and he also expressed a wish for a warmer and more religious conclusion. Lord Halifax pointed out what he considered the difference in tone between the first part of the letter dealing with the Protestant bodies, and the second part dealing with Rome, and he could not refrain from a general criticism of the final document:

The VISCOUNT HALIFAX *to the* ARCHBISHOP OF CANTERBURY

29 December, 1923.

I wish also that the letter contained some acknowledgment that the statements of Anglican theologians of the sixteenth and seventeenth centuries are not the only statements the rulers of the Church of England have to consider. I wish also very much that it had contained a sentence or two which would have appealed to the heart. The heart and the imagination are more compelling forces than any which appeal only to the head. I fully recognize the need of emphasizing the reality of the difficulties that stand in the way of reunion, but if the balance is to be kept true, it should surely be redressed by allusion to the glory of the vision which would be presented by the reunion of the Church of England with the Church of St. Gregory and St. Augustine, if it should please God in His good providence to allow that reunion to be helped forward by our means. Would not such an utterance have put the matter in a light that would have disarmed criticism? I venture to enclose to Your Grace the copy of a note I made at Malines, which may serve to illustrate the difficulties which may arise from the attenuated account contained in Your Grace's letter. They are difficulties which might conceivably make it necessary, in order to avoid misunderstanding, that some supplemental account should be given of the conversations at Malines.

Your Grace is to forgive me for what I have ventured to say in this letter. I have many misgivings about sending it, but it is not the first time that I have had to trust to the generosity and forbearance of the *alterius orbis Papa*, who, I know, would wish that what is felt should be expressed, and would be sure that in saying 'I should esteem it the greatest misfortune for the English Church, were he not here to guide its fortunes', I am speaking from the depths of my heart.

It is unnecessary to print the full text of the Archbishop's letter here, for the facts which it records have been related above in an ampler form. The section dealing with Malines began by recognizing the special difficulty which Rome presented, and also Dr. Davidson's full sense of his responsibility:

The ARCHBISHOP OF CANTERBURY *to the* ARCHBISHOPS *and* METROPOLITANS OF THE ANGLICAN COMMUNION

Christmas, 1923.

You will agree with me in regarding that subject as separate from other reunion problems, not only by the history of centuries of English life, but by present-day claims and utterances. And the plain fact confronts us that in relation to that subject there exist both at home and in the overseas Dominions, passions, dormant or awake, which are easily accounted for, but which, when once aroused, are difficult to allay. I have myself been repeatedly warned that to touch that subject is unwise. Men urge that 'even if the opportunity be given' it is easier and safer to let it severely alone. That may be true, but you and I are party to the 'Appeal to all Christian People', and I, at least, find it difficult to reconcile that document with an attitude of apathy or sheer timidity as to our touching the Roman Catholic question. Not only are we pledged to the words and spirit of the 'Appeal' itself, but we have before us what was said on the subject by the Committee of the same Lambeth Conference in 1920. We there express our readiness to welcome any friendly discussion between Roman Catholics and Anglicans for which opportunity may be given.[1] I have no right to say that the utterances of the Lambeth Conference have influenced Roman Catholic opinion, but I am certain that they have increased our own responsibilities in the matter.

It stressed the importance of the historic Anglican position:

I found, as I anticipated, that our visitors to Malines were not likely to forget what the historical Anglican position and claims have been in the past, as set forward for example by the great theologians of the sixteenth and seventeenth centuries—a position which we have no thought of changing or weakening to-day. It seemed to me to be fair to the Roman Catholic members of the Malines Conference, now augmented by the addition of Monsignor Batiffol and the Abbé Hemmer, that the firmness and coherence, as we believe, of our Anglican doctrine and system should be unmistakably set forward.

And it defined the limitations of the proceedings:

There has not yet been time [since the third conference] to weigh adequately the record of the conversations which took place, still less the unsolved differences which they exhibit, but I may say at once that, as was inevitable, the discussions are still in a quite

[1] The words are as follows: 'Your Committee feels that it is impossible to make any Report on Reunion with Episcopal Churches without some reference to the Church of Rome, even though it has no Resolution to propose upon the subject. We cannot do better than make our own the words of the Report of 1908, which reminds us of "the fact that there can be no fulfilment of the Divine purpose in any scheme of reunion which does not ultimately include the great Latin Church of the West, with which our history has been so closely associated in the past, and to which we are still bound by many ties of common faith and tradition". But we realize that—to continue the quotation—"any advance in this direction is at present barred by difficulties which we have not ourselves created, and which we cannot of ourselves remove". Should, however, the Church of Rome at any time desire to discuss conditions of reunion we shall be ready to welcome such discussions.'

elementary stage, and that no estimate, so far as I judge, can yet be formed as to their ultimate value. Needless to say, there has been no attempt to initiate what may be called 'negotiations' of any sort. The Anglicans who have, with my full encouragement, taken part, are in no sense delegates or representatives of the Church as a whole. I had neither the will nor the right to give them that character. This is well understood on both sides. They have sought merely to effect some re-statement of controverted questions, and some elucidation of perplexities. And to me it seems indubitable that good must in the Providence of God ensue from the mere fact that men possessing such peculiar qualifications for the task should, in an atmosphere of good-will on either side, have held quiet and unrestrained converse with a group of Roman Catholic theologians similarly equipped. No further plans are yet prepared, but it is impossible, I think, to doubt that further conversations must follow from the careful talks already held. At the least we have endeavoured in this direction, as in others, to give effect to the formal recommendation of the Lambeth Conference that we should 'invite the authorities of other Churches to confer with [us] concerning the possibility of taking definite steps to co-operate in a common endeavour . . . to restore the unity of the Church of Christ'.

The Letter aroused a storm of controversy. Both the Archbishop and the Cardinal were the victims of attack. Resolutions from many societies were forwarded to Lambeth denouncing the Archbishop's betrayal of the Protestant religion. And it is interesting to observe, in view of later developments, that one of the first critics was Sir William Joynson-Hicks.

The substance of Sir William Joynson-Hicks's letter is sufficiently shown by the following extract from the Archbishop's public reply:

The ARCHBISHOP OF CANTERBURY *to the* RT. HON. SIR WILLIAM JOYNSON HICKS

January 28, 1924.

I think you take much too circumscribed and even petty a view of the great fact in our contemporary religious life that we are solemnly trying in the faith and fear of God to press upon the Christian people of our time a bolder and truer view of what Christian unity means, as something for which our Divine Lord prayed on the last evening of His earthly life. It is this endeavour 'to meet the demands of a new age with a new outlook' which finds expression in our 'Appeal to All Christian People'. You, as I gather, would rule as out of consideration any idea that we should contemplate the possibility of a united Church of Christ on earth. For you deem it to be clear that the distinctive teaching of the Church of Rome is immutable. If it is once admitted that certain distinctive doctrines of that Church are falsified by their lack of Scriptural foundation, an opinion which I presume we all hold, we must, according to your view, as you deem them to be immutable, leave it so, and take no steps, except perhaps as private individuals, to understand better the position which Roman Catholics take, or to explain to them our own. You would wish this to hold good even if there be a readiness on the part of prominent Roman Catholic leaders and theologians to converse with us on the subject with a view to the removal of possible misunderstandings or confusions. The result to which such conversations are directed must, in your view, precede the conversations. Such is not my view of what is desirable. I do not believe it to be our Lord's Will that I should say—'We will discuss our differences with those Protestant theologians to whom our doctrines seem mistaken. We will discuss them with theologians of the Eastern Churches, but we will not, even when encouraged to do so, discuss them with theologians belonging to the Church of Rome. The members of that Church are ruled out, unless, prior to any conversation on the subject, they begin by admitting their errors and withdrawing from the position for which they contend.'

He made a more formal rejoinder to the critics in the Upper House of Canterbury Convocation, on February 6, 1924. Two passages may be quoted. After describing again the origin of the Conversations, arranged 'almost fortuitously', he said:

Though I had no responsibility with regard to this, it is doubtless the fact that had I desired to do so I might, so to speak, have stamped out the very suggestion of such a conversation taking place, however informally; or at least I might have refused to know anything whatever about it. Such action on my part—and this seems to me to be self-evident—would have belied the Appeal which the Lambeth Conference had made in the widest possible terms 'to All Christian People' for the furtherance of a wider unity of the Church of Christ on earth. It would, further, have been contrary to every principle which I have entertained in religious matters. I have always believed that personal intercourse is of the very highest value for the better understanding of matters of faith or opinion whereon people are in disagreement, however wide or even fundamental the disagreement may be. To me the quenching of smoking flax by the stamping out of an endeavour to discuss, thus privately, our differences, would, I say it unhesitatingly, have seemed to be a sin against God.

And again:

. . . there have been no negotiations whatever. We are not at present within sight of anything of the kind. Cardinal Mercier emphasizes this as strongly as I do. There are whole sentences about it in his Pastoral. They were private conversations about our respective history and doctrines and nothing more. The critics of our action urge that before any such conversation can be rightly allowed to take place we ought to insist that the Church of Rome must confess the error of its doctrines and repudiate the Declaration about Anglican Orders. I think your lordships will agree with me when I say that to describe the conversations as being useless or harmful unless we secure a preliminary surrender shows a fundamental misconception of what is meant by the sort of conversations which can be held to elucidate our respective positions. Where should we be, my lords, if, in all matters of controversy, conversations were to be pronounced useless or hurtful unless the conclusion or even conversion which on either side is hoped for has been already secured?

He repeated, for the statement had been questioned in Rome, that the Vatican had cognizance of the Conversations exactly corresponding to the cognizance extended by himself.

The Cardinal also had to defend himself from attack, in a letter to his Clergy. He gave the facts, referring to the 'de-Christianization of the masses, and the swiftness with which the failing of faith in the supernatural leads to the denial of all religion'. He pointed out the private character of the Conversations:

Our discussions were thus in no sense 'negotiations'. To negotiate, it is necessary to hold a mandate, and neither on one side nor on the other were we invested with a mandate. And I, for my part, had asked for no such commission; it was enough to know that I was acting in agreement with the supreme Authority, blessed and encouraged by It.

We set to work, inspired by a like desire for mutual understanding and brotherly aid, firmly resolved to banish the spirit of barren controversy.

Obviously, the disagreement of both sides on several fundamental questions was notorious; we all knew that. But we also knew that if truth has its rights, charity has its duties; we thought that, perhaps, by dint of open-hearted converse, and the intimate conviction that in a vast conflict centuries old, all the wrongs were not on one side; by a precise enunciation of certain controverted points, we might break down preconceptions, dispel ambiguities, smooth the way along which loyal souls, aided by grace, might discover, if it pleased God, or recover, the truth.

As a matter of fact, at the close of each of our three meetings, we all felt closer to, more trustful towards, one another, than at the start. Our guests told us so; wrote it to us; we said as much to them, and I am happy to repeat it here.

Need I add, nevertheless, that neither my friends nor I, when essential questions were mooted—such as the Primacy of the Pope, defined by the Vatican Council, which was the first and the last to be moved—did we give away, in a wild craving for union at all price, one single article of our Catholic, Apostolic, and Roman Creed.

He also rebuked the critics in England who had criticized the Conversations as being inopportune 'because they think it is wise to let the separated Churches go to complete decay', and ineffective 'because individual conversion only must be sought for'. And he explained what it was that made him take the opportunity so unexpectedly presented:

For the whole world, I would not that one of our severed brethren should have the right to say that he knocked trustfully at the door of a Roman catholic bishop, and that this Roman catholic bishop refused to open it.

A great nation was, for more than eight centuries, our beloved sister; this nation gave the Church a phalanx of saints whom to this day we honour in our liturgy; astonishing reserves of Christian life have been maintained in its vast empire; from it numberless missions have gone out far and wide; but a gaping wound is in its side. We catholics, kept safe, by the grace of God, in the whole truth, we weep over the criminal sundering which tore it away, four centuries ago, from the Church our Mother; and forsooth there are catholics who would that, like the Levite in the parable of the Good Samaritan, a catholic bishop should pass his way, superbly unfeeling, and refuse to pour oil in this gaping wound, to tend it, and try to lead the invalid to God's House whither God's mercy calls him.

I must needs have pleaded guilty had I been so cowardly.

So far as other Churches with which a *rapprochement* was in any way proceeding were concerned, it is of interest to note that the Free Church members of the Joint Conference of Anglicans and Free Churchmen, meeting regularly at Lambeth, were re-assured after a conversation with the two Archbishops. One Free Churchman indeed went so far as to say that he did not see how the Archbishop could have acted otherwise. It is equally interesting to observe that the Patriarch of Constantinople, Gregory, writing to the Archbishop in June 1924, when thanking him for a copy of his letter to Metropolitans, used these words:

> The recent efforts for fraternal communion with the Church of Rome appear to us also to be such a righteous and godly endeavour.

IV

The question soon arose of a further Conversation. The Archbishop was definitely in favour of postponement, while the Cardinal and Lord Halifax desired greater speed. Already the shadow of the Prayer Book controversy appeared in the background, as may be seen from the following letter:

The RT. HON. LORD HUGH CECIL *to* VISCOUNT HALIFAX

22 May 1924.

> I do not quite agree with you about going on with the Malines conversations in October. My reason is one with which you are familiar, that the Malines conversations are a dangerous complication while the Prayer Book controversy is going on. I am afraid I think that controversy very formidable, and that serious mischief might easily be done if it took a wrong turn. Unquestionably, if there were a conference at Malines in October, great alarm and dissatisfaction would be caused among the whole Evangelical party at a moment when it is most important that they should be soothed and tranquillized.

Cardinal Mercier did not understand such complications. In fact, as his own friends said, there was a certain simplicity about him which sometimes landed him in difficulties which might have been avoided, in other fields, as when he intervened unwisely in Ireland and had a clash with his own Walloon clergy as well as with the English Roman Catholics. As M. Portal put it, 'His greatness was likely to be better recognized in the next world than it is in this.'

It was natural, therefore, that he should be disappointed, and think that all the warmth was on the Roman Catholic side. There was a great deal of warmth in the breast of Lord Halifax, and it was difficult for the Cardinal to realize why the Archbishop could not rise to the same temperature. Lord Halifax wanted the Archbishop to invite the Pope to express his views on the subject of corporate reunion, but the Archbishop refused to take such an initiative, to the disappointment also of the Cardinal. In writing to Lord Halifax a little later, the Cardinal could not refrain from saying:

Cardinal Mercier *to* Viscount Halifax

6 March, 1925.

In proportion as the Sovereign Pontiff, and the Cardinal Secretary of State at the Vatican, affirm with increasing distinctness their confidence in our humble efforts, and thus indirectly disavow certain oppositions of the English Roman Catholics, it would seem as if on our side the nearer hopes of re-union seemed likely to be realized, the more sensitive the good Archbishop of Canterbury seems to grow as to his responsibilities to his own people, and to desire to put off, rather than to hasten, the definite bringing together of both sides.

The fourth and last Conversation took place at Malines in May 1925, with the same membership as before. There had been similar preparation of memoranda beforehand on either side. The main subject discussed was that of the relation of the episcopate to the Holy See, resumed from the previous occasion. It was claimed by the Romans that the Pope had a supremacy over the whole of the Church. The Vatican decree of infallibility was mentioned,[1] and the Anglicans felt obliged to reply

[1] Vatican Decree of Infallibility: *Si quis itaque dixerit, Romanum Pontificem habere tantummodo officium inspectionis vel directionis, non autem plenam et supremam potestatem iurisdictionis in universam Ecclesiam, non solum in rebus, quae ad fidem et mores, sed etiam in iis, quae ad disciplinam et regimen Ecclesiae per totum orbem diffusae pertinent; aut eum habere tantum potiores partes, non vero totam plenitudinem huius supremae potestatis; aut hanc eius potestatem non esse ordinariam et immediatam sive in omnes ac singulas ecclesias sive in omnes et singulos pastores et fideles; anathema sit.* Conc. Vatican: *Pastor Aeternus*, Caput III, ad fin.

Itaque Nos . . . docemus et divinitus revelatum dogma esse definimus: Romanum Pontificem, cum ex Cathedra loquitur, id est, cum omnium Christianorum Pastoris et Doctoris munere fungens, pro suprema sua Apostolica auctoritate doctrinam de fide vel moribus ab universa Ecclesia tenendam definit, per assistentiam divinam, ipsi in beato Petro promissam, ea infallibilitate

that it was this supremacy which constituted so grave a difficulty. It was, however, agreed by the Roman Catholics that a union between the Church of England and Rome would assist in bringing about instances and forms of decentralization useful to the whole Church. In the course of the discussion a warm recognition was given by the Cardinal to the reinforcement which the Church of England would bring to the Roman Church if union came about. Bishop Gore had already emphasized the fact that the Church of England and the Orthodox Church and the Protestants preserved certain spiritual elements belonging to the original Christianity of the New Testament, and also in accord with what was best in modern critical and democratic movements, elements which had been more or less eliminated by the Roman Church: and the Dean of Wells had spoken of the logical completeness of the Latin system as a very terrifying thing.[1] There was also a discussion on the distinction between what was *de fide* and what was not *de fide*: the Anglicans claiming that the basis of faith in any union should be the Oecumenical Faith of the Councils, with a tolerance of diversity determined by the distinction between what was *de fide* and what was not *de fide*.

The most interesting part of the discussion, however, was based

pollere, qua divinus Redemptor Ecclesiam suam in definienda doctrina de fide vel moribus instructam esse voluit; ideoque eiusmodi Romani Pontificis definitiones ex sese, non autem ex consensu Ecclesiae irreformabiles esse. Ibid., Caput IV, ad fin.

From *Pastor Aeternus* (Constitutio Dogmatica Prima de Ecclesia Christi): Mansi: *Collectio Conciliorum*, tome 52, col. 1330 et seq.; *Collectio Lacensis Conciliorum recentiorum*, tome vii, col. 482 et seq.

[1] '*At Malines, 19 May 1925.* [A note by Dean Robinson, shown only to the Abbé Portal.] These are logical conclusions deduced from certain premises. We distrust logical conclusions *as such*. Moreover we don't admit *all* the premises.

'Further we see that the resulting system has issued in isolating the Latin element in Christendom, which has pursued its own course of development. The Greek element and the Anglo-Saxon element have come to be practically ignored, and the development has been what we now see and cannot possibly accept as final. We are crying out for a larger, more comprehensive, conception of the Catholic Church.

'We feel that under Providence we exist to bear this witness. Our position can perhaps hardly be understood except by ourselves. It is a protest for mental liberty—a protest against settling things by logical deductions in a world in which there is more than logic.

'We are a very unruly element from the ecclesiastical point of view. In a complete and comprehensive Church we should have our place and no more. We should be a stimulus to thought and movement: but our eccentricity would be counterbalanced by other elements. Our exclusion is bad for ourselves (though we may not think it), and it is certainly bad for the Church as a whole.'

on a private paper not previously circulated, read by the Cardinal as the work of a canonist, furnished to him from Rome.[1] It was anonymous. Its title was 'L'Église Anglicane unie non absorbée'. It called attention to the long history of the Church of England and the special position of the Archbishop of Canterbury, drawing the conclusion that an Anglican Church *absorbed by* Rome and an Anglican Church *separated from* Rome were both equally inadmissible. The really historical formula was 'The Anglican Church united to Rome'. The memorandum proposed in brief that the Anglican Church should be under a Patriarch, the Archbishop of Canterbury, who could receive his investiture from the successor of St. Peter by the historic imposition of the *pallium*: that it should have its own rites, liturgies, canon law, discipline (including a non-celibate clergy), subject only to the indispensable link of subordination to the Universal Church of which the centre of unity was at Rome. The memorandum was not discussed in any detail, though it aroused the deepest interest. It may well prove to be not the least enduring result of Malines.[2] The conversation, after its reading, returned in the main to the programme which it had set before itself concerning questions of doctrine.

The subject of doctrinal discussion was a paper by Bishop Gore entitled 'On Unity with Diversity',[3] together with a paper written in reply to Bishop Gore by Monsignor Batiffol.[4] The discussion waxed hot at times without ceasing to be friendly. Bishop Gore put the root difficulty in the dogmatic field as follows:

> I write as an Anglican who has not the slightest desire to submit himself as an individual to the Roman authority, but with all his heart would desire to see his own Anglican communion, and the

[1] The canonist was Dom Lambert Beauduin (of Amay).

[2] This important Memorandum deals in detail with questions of jurisdiction. When it was published by Lord Halifax in 1930, with other Original Documents as *Annexe XIII*, Cardinal van Roey stated in the *Libre Belgique* that Cardinal Mercier made certain reserves. Lord Halifax therefore wrote a letter to *The Times* which appeared on February 27, 1930, and included the following words: 'Cardinal Mercier entirely approved of Dom Beauduin's paper, otherwise he would not have read it. But, if further proof be needed, Dom Beauduin has already replied to his critics in *Irenikon*, 1927, p. 150, where he publishes a letter of Cardinal Mercier's praising his work and saying that it is sure to do good.'

[3] *Concedit (Cyprianus) salvo jure communionis . . . diversum sentire.* Aug. *De bapt.* iii. 5. See for the full text *Recollections of Malines*, by Walter Frere, 1935, pp. 110–19.

[4] For full text see *The Conversations at Malines, 1921–1925*, Original Documents, Lord Halifax, 1930, pp. 263–87.

communion of the Orthodox Churches, reunited to the Holy See of Rome. The at present insuperable obstacle to such reunion, in either case, is the demand for submission, as to *de fide* dogmas, to certain doctrines, which, as claiming to be part of the essential faith, seem to us to conflict with history and with truth. I must speak with simple frankness. It seems to us illegitimate to yield that faith which we give to the fact of the virginal conception of our Lord, or His resurrection, or His ascension, to the immaculate conception of Mary. The former group of accepted facts rest upon original witness and good evidence: the latter on nothing that can be called historical evidence at all. But to believe in a *fact* on the mere ground of *a priori* reasoning as to what is suitable, without any evidence of the fact, seems to us to alter the fundamental character of the act of faith. It also makes with the other doctrines just specified, a claim for the authority of the church, as centralized and absolute, which the ancient church never made. It frees it from all those restrictions of universal agreement and unvarying tradition and scriptural authority—which in our judgment make the fact of faith rational. It seems to us quite clear that the existing Roman demand, as we understand it to be made, is and remains quite unacceptable.

Thus the two essential problems, both of discipline—including jurisdiction (in the Canonist's Memorandum)—and of doctrine (in Bishop Gore's paper), were both faced with great frankness, and the Conversations thus reached the climax which was possible at the moment.

Before the meeting closed, the following document was read. It had been drawn up by the Anglicans in conference among themselves:

Some considerations following on the discussion about relations between the Pope and the Bishops.

The Church is a living body under the authority of the bishops as successors of the Apostles: and from the beginnings of Church History a primacy and leadership among all the bishops has been recognized as belonging to the Bishop of Rome. Nor can we imagine that any reunion of Christendom could be effected except on the recognition of the primacy of the Pope.

But while we think that both the Eastern Orthodox and the Anglican Churches would be prepared to recognize such primacy, we do not think it likely that they would be ready to define it more closely.

However, the following points may be usefully stated:

1. The authority of the Pope is not separate from that of the episcopate; nor in normal circumstances can the authority of the episcopate be exercised in disassociation from that of its chief.

2. In virtue of that primacy the Pope can claim to occupy a position in regard to all other bishops which no other bishop claims to occupy in regard to him.

3. The exercise of that primacy has in time past varied in regard to time and place: and it may vary again. And this adds to the difficulty of defining the respective rights of the Holy See on the one side, and of the episcopate upon the other.

This was, as it turned out, the last conference to be held. The Roman Catholics, said Bishop Gore, showed a surprising concessiveness in matters of organization, but were adamant on dogmatic issues. He deprecated any plan of going to Malines again. The Archbishop of Canterbury, however, after reflection, decided in favour of continuing. His letter to the Cardinal gives a summary of the whole discussion:

The ARCHBISHOP OF CANTERBURY *to* CARDINAL MERCIER

Lambeth Palace. 1st August, 1925.

Following upon my recent letter to Your Eminence, in which I asked permission for a short delay owing to the stress of work, I am now glad to be able to assure Your Eminence that I have read attentively the papers and memoranda relating to the last group of Conversations at Malines. I cannot when thus writing refrain from again thanking Your Eminence for the unbroken courtesy and kindness with which you have facilitated during these years the Conversations which have attracted, both in England and on the Continent, an attention due in large measure to the personality and kindness of Your Eminence.

Looking back now along these years to the beginning of the matter in 1921, I am increasingly persuaded that the gatherings under Your Eminence's roof at Malines have been fruitful of good. Whatever misunderstanding may at first have arisen in England has now I think been largely or wholly removed from the minds of thoughtful and well-informed men. The mere fact that such Conversations after long centuries during which they would scarcely have been possible, should now have taken place must I think be a source of thankfulness.

I have given close attention to the Memoranda and *procès-verbal* of the meeting in May and I have compared these with previous records and memoranda relating to the earlier meetings. The question obviously arises whether the Conversations have now reached a stage when a longer interval for consideration is desirable or whether they should be speedily resumed, and if so at what date. Articles or notices in the Belgian Press which have been sent to me appear to indicate that Your Eminence favours the idea of resuming the Conversations at an early date, whether for a single gathering to sum up what has already been said, or with a view to a series of further meetings. If such is Your Eminence's wish, it is certainly desirable that it should be acceded to, and this accords I think with what is felt by the Anglican Group which has taken part in the Conversations.

It seems to me that what will then emerge is that explanations have been given of exaggerations or misunderstood phrases current both popularly and in theological literature as to what in England is called Popery and as to what in Roman Catholic circles is summed up as Protestantism. Recent discussions have (if I may use the figure) built piers which would be useful if we were able to construct the bridge. The arches, however, remain unconstructed, and in honesty I am bound to say that I do not at present see the vision of their taking any substantial shape.

The meetings under Your Eminence's care have undoubtedly brought about a better and more sympathetic understanding, on either side, of the position occupied by the other. The documents which have passed, and the records of the Conversations place this, to my mind, beyond doubt. While I rejoice to say this, I dare not in honesty adopt the phrase suggested by Your Eminence that we have made 'progress in agreement'.

In studying the papers before me, I do not find any indication of a readiness on the part of those whom Your Eminence associated with yourself at Malines to show or suggest the possibility of any modification by re-statement or otherwise of what are commonly regarded as irreducible doctrinal requirements to which expression has been given. The same may doubtless be said of the views expressed by the Anglican ecclesiastics who have shared in the Conversations. I am far from criticizing, still less blaming, either group on that account, but I feel bound to say that I think the ordinary members of our respective Churches would be misled, were I now to present the position as one in which there was evidence of any nearer agreement upon the fundamental questions at issue.

I go back along the story of the four Conversations. In the first, there was a general discussion of subjects so fundamental and far-reaching as The Nature of the Church, The Doctrine of the Sacraments, and The Authority attaching to Holy Scripture. These discussions naturally raised questions rather than handled them with any thoroughness. They were basic questions, and were among those referred to when, in the Lambeth Appeal to All Christian People, words were used to the effect that there must be agreement on fundamentals before discussion of details can be fruitful.

The second 'Conversation' deliberately dealt with administrative possibilities which might become practicable if on the doctrinal basis agreement had been reached.

At the third 'Conversation' those conferring rightly went back, as I ventured to urge they should, to the great doctrinal question of the position of the Papacy, which is now an article *de fide* in the Roman Catholic Church. The question was dealt with on the ground of the New Testament and in connexion with the history both of the Early Church and of the Sixteenth Century.

At the fourth, the recent 'Conversation', attention was still fixed in the main on this outstanding question of the Papacy and the place it has held and holds in the history of the Christian Church.

I need not remind Your Eminence that on all these questions there was not merely verbal discussion, but that literary contributions of the most valuable kind were made available. I have myself studied both the record of the Conversations and the material furnished to aid them. Your Eminence will I think agree with me when I say that they afford no evidence of a departure on either side from the doctrinal principles which you or we maintain.

A question necessarily arises as to the next step which can usefully be taken. I share the opinion of Your Eminence that those who have met under your presidency should meet again. I take it for granted that at such a meeting an attempt would be made to formulate some statement (or perhaps two statements emanating from the two sides in the discussion) both as to the matters on which misunderstandings may have been removed, and as to the points which still remain obdurately outstanding as unremoved obstructions. It would be misleading were these latter to be treated lightly or described in general terms only. I am inclined to think that we require both a somewhat fuller statement of the kind I have indicated, for the use of those who have been conferring, and also a briefer and more general statement capable of being usefully made public. So far I venture to hope that we should all be in agreement. It corresponds with what Your Eminence said on the last occasion at Malines, when you advocated the preparation of some brief statement and deprecated, as I also deprecate, the publication of the documents which have been used. A short statement for publicity ought, however, to make mention of the subjects I have above referred to as having been under discussion during these years.

A further question arises, whether, as some of my friends certainly desire, there should be fresh discussion of some of the doctrinal difficulties which have remained unresolved—for example, the Doctrinal Decrees of the Council of Trent might possibly be considered. The question, however, of this further discussion is one which I should like to leave for the consideration and decision of those who take part in the Conversations.

May I, in conclusion, recur to the thought to which I have more than once given expression during these years. The vision which we set before ourselves in issuing the Lambeth Conference Appeal to All Christian People was a very wide one embracing Christians throughout the world. It was a vision (I quote the words) 'of a Church, genuinely Catholic, loyal to all Truth, and gathering into its fellowship all "who profess and call themselves Christians". . . . To all other Christian people whom our words may reach we make the same appeal. We do not ask that any one Communion should consent to be absorbed in another. We do ask that all should unite in a new and great endeavour to recover and to manifest to the world the unity of the Body of Christ for which He prayed.'

The difference between Your Eminence's view and my own, where it exists, may be not so much a difference of faith or charity in dealing with the same problem, as a difference in our conception of what the problem is and what its solution involves.

Even Lord Halifax was pleased with what the Archbishop had written, and reported the Cardinal as remarking 'It is not what we could have hoped, but it might have been worse (*moins bon*)'. The Cardinal himself made a long reply later, proposing a fifth meeting for January, though confessing to a certain uneasiness at the diminution of confidence which he noticed in the letter of the Archbishop. He begged him not to give way to the solicitations of either 'the inveterate optimists' or the 'obstinate pessimists' which, as in both their flocks, demanded the one an immediate success, the other an immediate abandonment:

CARDINAL MERCIER *to the* ARCHBISHOP OF CANTERBURY

October 25, 1925.

But do you not think it would be weakness on our part if we gave way to their solicitations? We have responsibilities which they do not have and do not understand. Our situation imposes upon us the duty to consider the general situation from a higher standpoint, according to standards more deeply supernatural. We have graces in virtue of our position for directing consciences and acting with authority.

The Cardinal expressed his agreement with the proposal to make a statement on the conclusions which both sides had reached in common, but did not favour a statement of disputable points:

> Negative conclusions, whatever they may be, would inevitably provoke polemics in the press, reawaken ancient animosities, and accentuate divisions, thus harming the cause to which we have resolved to devote ourselves.

The Archbishop replied at some length:

The Archbishop of Canterbury *to* Cardinal Mercier

Old Palace, Canterbury, 9th December 1925.

Your Eminence has I fear been for some time past expecting a letter from me following upon what I wrote to you on October 29th. Your experience I know corresponds to my own as to the difficulty which urgent daily duties interpose in the way of writing our important letters on the larger and more general questions of our time.

It gives me real satisfaction to know that, on Your Eminence's hospitable invitation, the interrupted 'conversations' are to be resumed at Malines on January 25th. The fact that this is so, and that I have been in touch with our Anglicans who will be with you on that day, renders it I think unnecessary that I should now write at any length in continuance of our recent correspondence. I have, as Your Eminence I believe knows, taken care that your very important letter of October 25th should be quietly considered by those who share in the 'conversations'. They all, I think, agree with Your Eminence in desiring that next month some record should be compiled of what has already taken place, and the Dean of Wells is already occupied in the preparation of a summary account of it. This will, as I understand, be submitted for Your Eminence's consideration before it is discussed in the gathering at Malines.

I have myself considered with the utmost care the opinion expressed by Your Eminence about what should be contained in, or omitted from, any published record. Unless I misunderstand you, your opinion is that the record, while it tells of the endeavour, successful as I hope, to remove or diminish misunderstandings upon several points of difference between us (points which though important are really minor), should make no reference to the larger and more fundamental question or questions upon which no approach towards agreement has been made or appears possible. I refer specially to the vital question of the Papacy. I of course realize that upon questions such as the rights of Diocesan Bishops and the source of their authority or upon the varieties of rule or usage which may be permissible in Uniat Churches (to mention only two examples out of many), there has been, and there may increasingly be, removal of mutual misunderstanding, and for this reason among others I believe the Malines 'conversations' to have been wholesome and profitable. But prior to all these, and far outweighing them in importance, stands the fundamental question —Is there, or is there not, a Vicar of Christ upon earth, who possesses *jure divino* a distinctive authoritative position in relation to the whole of Christendom?

Upon that great question, if it has in its largest aspect been discussed at all, there has been, so far as I know, no approach to agreement, and that fact must beyond question be set forth clearly in any record which is made public.

I claim to know something about the Church and People of this Country, and I have no hesitation in saying that to publish a record or summary of the discussions without making outspoken reference to that great unremoved mountain of difficulty would be worse than useless. The outcry which would immediately arise would certainly retard instead of promoting the cause for which we care—the cause of removing misunderstandings and contributing to the wider reunion of Christendom.

It is possible that I may have misunderstood Your Eminence, and that you would share my opinion that, in anything that is to be published, the position upon the point I have mentioned must in a few words be made clear. Granted that this is done, I rejoice to repeat to Your Eminence the assurance that in my belief some record of what has taken place may suitably be made public, and by promoting the preparation of such a record Your Eminence will add yet another to the services which you have by your generous action rendered to the whole Church of Christ at this juncture in its history.

The Cardinal replied on December 22, 1925. He had been ill, and his health was giving ground for anxiety. He agreed generally that some intimation of the divergence between Romans and Anglicans, especially as to the Primacy of the Pope, was inevitable, but the precise character of the statements to be issued would have to be discussed.

A few days later, news came that the Cardinal was worse and that the Conversation would have to be postponed. The Archbishop was kept informed of the progress of the illness. It soon became clear that the Cardinal could not live, and Lord Halifax went out to say farewell. On January 21, 1926, the Cardinal wrote his last letter to Lambeth:

CARDINAL MERCIER *to the* ARCHBISHOP OF CANTERBURY

Archevêché de Malines Bruxelles: Le 21 Janvier, 1926.

Monseigneur,

Dans l'épreuve que la Divine Providence m'a envoyée ces dernières semaines, ce m'a été un réconfort sans pareil de recevoir la visite de notre vénéré ami Lord Halifax.

J'ai appris par lui le désir persévérant d'union qui vous anime; et suis heureux de cette assurance qui me fortifie à l'heure présente.

'Ut unum sint,' c'est le vœu suprême du Christ, le vœu du Souverain Pontife; c'est le mien, c'est le vôtre. Puisse-t-il se réaliser dans sa plénitude.

Les temoignages de sympathie que Votre Grandeur a bien voulu me faire transmettre m'ont vivement touché; je vous en remercie de grand cœur, et prie Votre Grandeur d'agréer les assurances de mon religieux dévouement.

✠ D. J. CARD. MERCIER, Arch. de Malines.

Two days later he died. The Archbishop at once dispatched a telegram to Canon Dessain, the Cardinal's secretary:

23rd January 1926.

We receive with sorrow the intimation that the earthly life of the venerated Cardinal Archbishop has reached its close. We thank God with you for the long years of devoted and heroic service and for his untiring effort in the cause of unity and peace.

V

With the passing of the Cardinal, the main inspiration of the Conversations came to an end. The news of his death had reached the Archbishop while he was absorbed in a long session of the House of Bishops on Prayer Book revision, now reaching a closing and difficult stage. That subject was destined more and more to occupy the foreground of Randall Davidson's thoughts, and it is not to be wondered at if, in the circumstances, he showed himself a little unwilling to throw fresh hostages to fortune. He had not been happy about the draft of the statement which was to be discussed at Malines, even after he had expressed his criticisms to the Anglicans severally; and he told Dr. Kidd that he feared lest the document when published should look like 'truckling to the Roman See'. But on the Cardinal's death, the difficulties connected with any report or reports became very clear. Lord Halifax had one report which he wished to publish. The other Anglicans had another. It was uncertain what the Romans would do. Mgr. van Roey was a little later appointed Archbishop of Malines. This seemed hopeful, but there were bitter blows to the cause of *rapprochement* to follow. The Abbé Portal died on June 19, 1926—an irreparable misfortune. On October 25, 1926, a fifth conference was held at Malines under the new Archbishop's presidency, but simply for the purpose of drawing up a Report. Two Reports were discussed, an Anglican and a Roman, and a desire was expressed that both should be issued, the one supplementing the other, the Roman particularly emphasizing the points of agreement. The results were communicated to the Archbishop of Canterbury, and the question of publication became more urgent. In December 1926 Lord Hugh Cecil wrote to the Archbishop, after reading the draft:

LORD HUGH CECIL *to the* ARCHBISHOP OF CANTERBURY

December 11, 1926.

I return the pamphlet which I have read with the deepest interest. From the general point of view of Christian unity I think its publication will in the long run do a great deal of good: but *any* publication about Malines will frighten some people just now—though there is little to cause reasonable alarm in this. The really striking thing is the concessions the Romans seem ready at least to consider: I expect the Ultramontanes will be extremely angry. But, as I said, what people fear is that Malines is meant to lead to our all 'going over to Rome' as a body. And any reminder of Malines is therefore unfortunate, just while Prayer Book revision is going on. Apart from that the fears would not matter and would soon disappear. But some Protestants will now certainly think and say that Malines and P.B.R. are two parts of the same conspiracy. It would have been better to put off the publication till P.B.R. is over, but I suppose that is now hardly possible.

In February and March, the all but final text of the Revised Prayer Book was published. On Easter Day, Cardinal Bourne went to York and delivered an elaborate attack on the Church of England. On April 30, the Archbishop wrote the following letter to the Bishop of Truro:

The ARCHBISHOP OF CANTERBURY *to the* BISHOP OF TRURO

30 April, 1927.

I have to-day your important letter of yesterday about the Malines publication. It came opportunely, for I have been troubling my mind rather sorely on the subject during the last few days. Various things have combined to concentrate attention on the subject of our attitude towards Rome. The controversy between Cardinal Bourne and the Bishop of Durham is, as you have perhaps seen, occupying almost the whole of the 'Tablet', and the 'Record', and other similar publications have been ventilating the matter with vigour. The conversations I have had with Members of the Government and leading M.P.s about the Parliamentary atmosphere on the Prayer Book question are not altogether re-assuring. The Prime Minister had a talk with me about it yesterday. I am to address such Members of the House of Lords as care to attend a Meeting convened by Salisbury, Beauchamp, Haldane, Asquith (Oxford), Parmoor, and the Lord Chancellor, and one or two more, on May 12th, and to speak about the Prayer Book and answer questions. The 'Record' has a sermon preached by young Chavasse, at Oxford, to which a good deal of attention is certain to be given. A good deal of the excitement or disquiet among unecclesiastical people turns on the Roman question.

In these circumstances there can be no doubt that the publication just now of our Malines paper will be eagerly used by men of the honest Inskip school to strengthen their hands in the speeches they are going to make at Meetings in London and in the Provinces.

There was, at the same time, a great hesitation on the Roman side as to the publication of their version of the proceedings. Yet in Lord Halifax's view it would have been most undesirable to publish the English version alone. A change had taken place in the official Roman attitude. The Archbishop became all the more anxious to postpone, until the Prayer Book Measure had been through the ordeal of Parliament, and in the end he persuaded Lord Halifax both to acquiesce in the postponement, and also to publish nothing himself. He agreed out of respect for the Archbishop, though he had, he said, no sort of interest in the passing of the Prayer Book. The Prayer Book Measure was rejected by the House of Commons on December 15, 1927.

Further delay of the Report was seen to be impossible, and on January 19, 1928, it was published to the world.[1]

The Report itself expressed the hope that further conversations might be held to elucidate the statements which had been made, and to help in the removal of misunderstandings. The Archbishop of Canterbury, as we have seen, was not very clear that further conference would prove of value. But it was Rome that brought the Conversations to an end. A new spirit was now dominant in the Vatican, and there was no Cardinal Mercier to stand forth as the champion of a *rapprochement*. On January 6, 1928, Pope Pius XI, who had on March 24, 1924, expressed to the Sacred Consistory his satisfaction and gratitude for these very conferences, launched his Encyclical, *Mortalium Animos*, in which he repeated the doctrine of the Papal Supremacy in unmistakable terms, and condemned many Churches and many movements towards unity. The *Osservatore Romano* (quoted in *The Times*, January 21, 1928) definitely announced that the Conversations were to cease. To Cardinal Mercier they had been, as he wrote to the Dean of Wells, the great consolation of his life. To the Archbishop of Canterbury, so much more cautious, they were a matter of deep interest, but not without their embarrassing side. Of their effect on the Church as a whole, who can speak? There has been progress in understanding, in charity, in desire. So far as the longed-for *rapprochement* was concerned, the fundamental difficulties remain unsolved. But channels of thought and methods of study have been started, from which perhaps in later days some great gain may result.

[1] *The Conversations at Malines, 1921–1925.* Published in English and French.

A FOOTNOTE IN VERSE

(*With apologies to A. A. Milne, 'Punch'*, Jan. 23, 1924, p. 81. W. F. N.)

H. H. Hensley Hensley
Hereford and Dunelm
took great
care of the Church
though he was not at th' helm.

H. H. Hensley, Hensley
said to the Church, said he,
you must never be seen
on the way to Malines
without consulting me.

Armitage Armitage, Robinson, Gore,
Halifax, Frere and Kidd
were sometimes seen
on the way to Malines
though they tried to be hid.

Herbert Herbert Hensley Hensley
said to the Arch, said he,
What the dickens you mean
By this game at Malines
is more than I can see.

R. R. Cantuar
said to H. H. D.
I mean that we mean to
be seen at Malines, .
so please leave that to me.

Armitage Armitage, Robinson, Gore,
Halifax, Frere and Kidd
are constantly seen on the
way to Malines
and no longer try to be hid.

W. F. N.[1]

[1] W. F. Norris, Dean of Westminster 1925–37.

CHAPTER LXXX

THE GENERAL STRIKE

Hold your hands,
Both you of my inclining, and the rest:
Were it my cue to fight, I should have known it
Without a prompter.

SHAKESPEARE, *Othello*, I. ii.

FEW actions in the whole of his life created so much stir, or aroused so much surprise, as the Appeal from the Churches, which the Archbishop issued during the General Strike of May 1926. It was the first time in English history that a General Strike had been declared; and its issue was watched with the keenest interest not only in England, but all over the world. Communists and Fascists alike, and the colonies of all schools of political thought, followed its progress with enthusiasm, contempt, or dismay. The General Strike arose out of a dispute in the mining industry. On March 10, 1926, the Coal Commission under Sir Herbert Samuel presented a unanimous report. Amongst other things it recommended that the coal subsidy (it amounted to £10,000,000) paid by the State should cease on April 30; that costs of production must be reduced, which meant a reduction of wages, subject to safeguards to the worst-paid men; and that the industry should be reorganized. On March 24, the Government announced its acceptance of the Report, provided the miners and owners accepted it too. The miners and the owners were unable to come to terms. A deadlock ensued—the owners offering new wages settled by districts, which the miners declared impossible of acceptance. The Industrial Committee of the Trades Union Congress agreed with the miners, and told the Prime Minister, Mr. Baldwin, that the whole Trade Union movement would be obliged to stand by the miners till the end against such acceptance. A conference of both sides with the Prime Minister, on April 22, produced no result. The new wage offers, as the owners called them—'lock-out notices' in the eyes of the miners—had by now been posted by the owners, to take effect on April 30. A special Conference of about 1,000 Trade Union delegates meeting in London on April 29 endorsed the action of its Committee, and desired negotiations to continue, provided the new wage offers or lock-out notices were withdrawn. There was no withdrawal—and on April 30 a complete national stoppage of the coal industry took place. On May 1, a Royal Proclamation declared a state of emergency; and the same afternoon the General Council of the Trades Union Congress decided to order a General Strike to begin at midnight on May 3, if the notices to the miners had not been withdrawn. The Prime Minister, in spite of the threat, continued negotiations. But, just before midnight on Sunday, May 2, when he heard that strike notices had already been issued and that some compositors in the *Daily Mail* office had refused to print in the Monday paper certain sentences with which they disagreed, he brought the negotiations to an end. At midnight on Monday, May 3, the General Strike began.

We now turn to the Archbishop. In a Memorandum of May 23, 1926, he wrote:

> During the last week of April the possibility of a General Strike had been in everybody's mind and I had discussed it very fully with many people, notably with Hugh Cecil at Clovelly, and with Baldwin himself, in at least one interview. . . . On Thursday 29th, I lunched with Asquith and there discussed with him and Birrell and Sir Donald Maclean the possibility of a Strike.

On Saturday May 1, he dined at the Royal Academy.

> Notwithstanding the fact that it had been announced by the Trade Unionists that a Strike would be called for Monday night May 3rd, people seemed for the most part to believe that it would be averted. The Sunday papers were on the whole hopeful, and in the evening we learned by wireless that the Prime Minister was at that hour (9.30) receiving the T.U.C. leaders. On Monday morning, therefore, the depression was all the greater when we learned that the Prime Minister's negotiations had broken down and that the strike would go forward.

He had more talk with some Churchmen and others on May 3, heard the Prime Minister's pronouncement in the Commons, and dined at Mr. Runciman's that evening.

On May 4:

> I went from there [a missionary meeting] to the House of Lords, where Salisbury, Haldane, Parmoor, and Asquith spoke. Asquith excellent—very strong about the iniquity of the Strike.

On May 5, he spoke himself in the House of Lords, and made it perfectly clear that in his view the Government was only doing its duty in using all its resources to bring the Strike to an end:

> As regards the Strike itself [he said] I do not think that among thoughtful people there is very great difference of opinion as to its unwisdom and its mischievousness. . . . [This Strike is] so intolerable that every effort is needed, is justifiably called for and ought to be supported, which the Government may make to bring that condition of things as speedily as possible to an end. The thing does not seem to me really to bear discussion or to admit of argument, so obvious do the facts seem to be.

At the same time he expressed the belief that the real motive behind the General Strike was a fear that, unless the strike had been called, efforts would be made to lower the standard of living for poorer people in all industries. Therefore he pressed for further efforts for a settlement:

> I hope [he concluded] that every possible effort will continue to be made, even as I say with the risk of an apparent illogicality, to reach a solution on the part of those who have done so much already to carry the matter through. We want to see that they are undaunted in face of the present perplexity, as they have been persevering and untiring in their efforts hitherto.

On May 6, the Bishops of London and Southwark, with Dr. Scott Lidgett and a strong deputation of Nonconformists, came to Lambeth, and issued an appeal, transmitted by the B.B.C. and published in the press on May 7, asking for prayers and assuring Christian people that they were 'anxiously considering possible ways by which Christian opinion may be brought effectively to bear towards the solution of the grave problems of the hour'.

On Friday, May 7, after rejecting a proposal brought from Liverpool to back a big special fund (apparently started by a rich capitalist) to take the place of the subsidy for men returning to work, the Archbishop had a long interview with a group of Churchmen and Nonconformists about issuing a conciliatory appeal. Those present included the Bishops of Ripon and Southwark,[1] Canon Woodward, the Rev. E. S. Woods, Dr. Scott Lidgett, Dr. R. F. Horton, the Rev. H. Carter, and the Rev. P. T. R. Kirk; and, while it was taking place, the Archbishop was called out to

[1] Dr. E. A. Burroughs and Dr. C. F. Garbett.

see a coal-owner, Lord Londonderry, who wished to help. There was a keen discussion about the character of the appeal. Should it be trenchant? Should it demand conciliation and retreat, independent of the withdrawal of the strike? Should the owners be asked to withdraw their notices? Should the Government be pressed to continue their subsidy? All or any of these? And which should come first?

> Finally we agreed upon using the words 'Simultaneously and concurrently'.

It was then arranged with the B.B.C. that the Archbishop should broadcast the appeal that night.

> Then I went to the House of Commons. I first saw Ramsay MacDonald, who was enthusiastically in favour of the appeal exactly as we had drafted it. He thumped the table and said, 'It is inspired, for it puts the thing exactly in the right way—only would you not make the withdrawal of the Strike No. 1 instead of No. 3 in your suggestions?' I replied that I was certain we should all agree with this. We had only given it a lower place for the sake of him and his friends.

He next went to the Prime Minister's room; but, as the Cabinet was sitting, could only get at him through a secretary, who went to and fro.

> Baldwin entirely approved of the appeal except for the words 'simultaneously and concurrently'. He thought he must himself adhere to his declaration that the complete withdrawal of the strike must precede the beginning of negotiations by him. It was awkward having tc speak to him through a secretary, but we did it.

While the Archbishop was consulting Ramsay MacDonald and the Prime Minister, his chaplain (the Rev. F. D. V. Narborough) went to see Cardinal Bourne.

> During my absence from Lambeth that afternoon, Narborough called at Cardinal Bourne's with a copy of the Appeal, asking for his concurrence. The Cardinal was out, but on his return he caused a message to be sent expressing his agreement with the document, but asking (like Ramsay MacDonald) that the withdrawal of the Strike should be the first of the three suggestions.

The form in which the Appeal stood, as finally approved by the

Archbishop, the President of the Free Church Council, Cardinal Bourne, and the others named above, was as follows:

The Crisis. Appeal from the Churches

After full conference with leaders of the Christian Churches in this country the Archbishop of Canterbury desires to make public the following expression of considered opinion:—

Representatives of the Christian Churches in England are convinced that a real settlement will only be achieved in a spirit of fellowship and co-operation for the common good, and not as a result of war. Realising that the longer the present struggle persists the greater will be the suffering and loss, they earnestly request that all the parties concerned in this dispute will agree to resume negotiations undeterred by obstacles which have been created by the events of the last few days. If it should seem to be incumbent on us to suggest a definite line of approach, we would submit, as the basis of a possible Concordat, a return to the status quo of Friday last. We cannot but believe in the possibility of a successful issue. Our proposal should be interpreted as involving simultaneously and concurrently—

(1) The cancellation on the part of the T.U.C. of the General Strike;

(2) Renewal by the Government of its offer of assistance to the Coal industry for a short definite period;

(3) The withdrawal on the part of the mine owners of the new wages scales recently issued.

7th May 1926.

All was thus ready for the Archbishop to broadcast the appeal that night. Suddenly, however, a message came from the B.B.C. that the permission was withdrawn. The Director-General, Mr. Reith, a personal friend of the Archbishop, rang up to say that, on reading over the words of the appeal, he felt that to broadcast it would 'run counter to his tacit arrangement with the Government about such things'. But on being challenged by the Archbishop, 'Then you have had a hint from Downing Street not to accept the Appeal for broadcast', Mr. Reith replied, 'No. Downing Street knows nothing about it. I am speaking entirely on my own responsibility.' He also assured the Archbishop that a letter which the Archbishop had just received from Lord Gainford, who happened to be a coal-owner and was Chairman of the B.B.C., objecting to certain crucial points in the Appeal, had nothing to do with the refusal.

The message, therefore, was not broadcast that night. The Archbishop, however, wrote the following letter next day to Mr. Reith:

The ARCHBISHOP OF CANTERBURY *to* J. C. W. REITH, ESQ.

8th May 1926.

I feel it my duty to write to you about what happened yesterday. I have no wish to raise difficulties, still less to make formal complaint, but I am honestly puzzled as to what the position is. It would have been quite unsuitable to discuss it yesterday on the telephone when you were communicating with me in the afternoon.

The position is that yesterday morning the authorities of the Churches in England, not sitting formally but carrying the imprimatur of the two Archbishops, several Bishops, the Leaders of the Free Churches, and all, in short, who could be got together to represent what may be called official Church opinion in this country, agreed upon a statement which they desired me to put forth in their names. Cardinal Bourne has expressed his full concurrence in it. It was fully believed, indeed rather taken for granted, that it would be possible for this to be done by a broadcast message from your headquarters, and I was willing to go myself and say it in order to give additional weight. You, or I suppose your Committee, decided, when you saw the words, that this could not be done, though you had up to that time welcomed my speaking at so grave an hour. You will see how serious a matter this is. It is impossible to tell what may be the further developments of the Strike problem. Are we to understand that if the Churches desire to put something forth their grave utterance must be subject to the approval of its wording by the Broadcasting Committee, and that without such approval we are confined, as we were yesterday, to utilising the scraps of publicity available by means of the few newspapers which have their limited circulation? I ask because it is impossible to foresee what may be the developments of the Strike question during the next week or fortnight, and I do not want to hold out erroneously such expectations as were entertained yesterday by the Church leaders throughout the country that a message which we wished to make public may, as yesterday happened, be declined by the Broadcasting Authorities. I am of course conscious of the difficulties which confront you in these matters and the great responsibility which rests upon the Broadcasting Committee for wise arrangements at such an hour. I am asking for elucidation of the situation for my own information and that of my friends to whom, of course, I have had to say that the Broadcasting Authorities declined to let the Message of the Churches be made public yesterday through your Agency.

I purposely say nothing about any opinion entertained personally by the Prime Minister, or about the letter from Lord Gainford which reached me in the afternoon, as you have assured me that these had nothing to do with the decision to which you came.

A further point I ought to mention. You are, I know, arranging that my address to-morrow night in St. Martin's-in-the-Fields is to be broadcast. Am I to understand that in the view of your authorities I should be precluded from making any reference to the publication in to-day's papers of our Joint Message?

The whole matter is of such importance that I must know before speaking to-morrow how things stand. If you desire to see me I shall be at home between 2.30 and 4.30 to-day. This would give time to communicate with St. Martin's.

Pray understand that I write all this in the friendliest way and with a genuine desire to co-operate in all that is really right.

An interview followed the same afternoon:

At three o'clock on Saturday, May 8th, 1926, Mr. J. C. W. Reith called to discuss the incident of the British Broadcasting Company in declining yesterday to let me give out from Savoy the Churches' Message. The matter has evidently distressed him terribly, and he certainly squirmed somewhat at what I said in my letter this morning about the Churches being refused a hearing at a great historic juncture. But he repeated again what he had frequently told me before about the great danger of the B.B.C. being commandeered by the Government and made a mere Government agency.[1] He said that Birkenhead and Churchill were eager for this, but that Baldwin had resisted it because of his confidence in the power shown by Reith and his friends of managing the matter wisely. He thought that if the Churches' utterance of yesterday had been broadcast it would have accentuated the trouble and weakened Baldwin's hands in resisting his colleagues. It evidently distressed him greatly to say this and to have had to act as he had acted. The responsibility is his, not a Committee's, and Gainford had nothing whatever to do with it; nor had he heard anything from the Government. He quite saw the almost intolerableness of the position as I had sketched it—namely, that the Churches

[1] A clause in the Licence of the Company from the Postmaster-General made it lawful for the Postmaster-General to take possession of all broadcasting stations 'if and whenever in the opinion of the Postmaster-General an emergency shall have arisen in which it is expedient for the public service that His Majesty's Government shall have control over the transmission of messages by the licensed apparatus'. The Postmaster-General, May 1926, was Sir William Mitchell Thomson.

should be muzzled at a time when they ought to be speaking to the Nation, but he appeared to me to realise the difficulty of his own position. It would of course be easier for him to let the Government commandeer the B.B.C., but he thought it would be harmful in the public interest.

The importance of the refusal was accentuated by the fact that the B.B.C. was at that time the main, and often the only, source of news about public events all over England.

The Appeal was, however, printed in *The Times*, which managed to survive in a diminished form. But it was refused a place in the official journal—the *British Gazette*—edited by Mr. Winston Churchill from the *Morning Post* offices.

Once the text was out, an immense excitement was created. The excitement was increased when it became known that the Appeal had been suppressed by the B.B.C., and also by the *British Gazette*.

Messages and telegrams came pouring in to Lambeth, and there were many offers to circulate the message on the Archbishop's behalf; but the Archbishop refused to sponsor such circulation, being content to have spoken and let others distribute as they pleased. There were, as was inevitable, plenty of objections. Amongst those whom the Archbishop saw was Col. Lane Fox, the Minister of Mines (May 8):

> His object was to point out that in his view the utterance to-day published on behalf of the Churches, suggesting simultaneous action on the part of the parties concerned, was harmful and might be gravely detrimental to the cause of peace. We were asking, he said, impossibilities and suggesting that the Government should weaken the declaration it had made that it was impossible to deal with the Unions until the ground had been cleared by the calling off of the Strike. The Government go that length in view of all that has been said and of all that they feel, and it would be very unfortunate if the Church were to insist as a bounden duty upon negotiations being attempted until the Strike was cleared away.

Col. Lane Fox was also fearful of what the Archbishop might say in his sermon to be broadcast from St. Martin's-in-the-Fields the next evening (Sunday):

> But I reassured him quite definitely about to-morrow's Sermon to the effect that I should not think of trying in a Sermon to deal with

> the economic question, even to the small extent that we tried to deal with it in our utterance. My object would be a spiritual one and an assurance that the Church was alive and awake to what is happening, and that its leaders were doing their best.

The sermon was preached to the immense invisible audience, and followed the lines just sketched.

On Monday more interviews followed with all sorts of people, politicians and others. That afternoon Mr. Lloyd George raised the question of the Appeal in the House of Commons, and commented strongly on the refusal of publication by the B.B.C. and the *British Gazette*. The intervention of the Archbishop beyond doubt had made a profound impression on all classes—not least because, as Mr. Lloyd George said in his speech, the Archbishop 'is known to be a very wise, a very cautious man, who certainly has never been guilty of any charge of impetuous interference in business not his own'. The impression made in the Labour world as a whole was astounding—for they felt themselves to be receiving sympathy and support from a quarter where (mistakenly enough) they had least expected it. But there were others who objected that the Archbishop's action was a grave embarrassment to the Government which, they said, it was the first duty of all citizens at such a juncture to support. In many circles the Archbishop's attitude was unfavourably compared with that of Cardinal Bourne, who on Sunday at High Mass in Westminster Cathedral issued a very decided pronouncement that the Strike was 'a sin against the obedience which we owe to God . . . and against the charity and brotherly love which are due to our brethren'. As a matter of fact, as we have seen, Cardinal Bourne had given his name (though the Archbishop never published it) to the Appeal for conciliation. The following encounter at Westminster with a Conservative M.P., Sir Joseph Nall, shows the strength of the feeling:

> Nall was very angry with me for our message and thought with Major Kindersley, who was with him, that we had done great harm and that the Church would suffer discredit. They were very outspoken, but quite reasonable too. I showed them that they did not really understand what had passed and assured them that I was quite unrepentant about the message, believing it to have done good. They amused me by saying, 'What a contrast—your attitude and that of Bourne'. I asked, 'Are you aware that Bourne wholly

approved of all that we said and himself suggested some of the words we had inserted?' This staggered them and amazed them. I think they felt a little abashed.

Whatever may be urged about the duty of supporting the Government as such at all costs in the time of a General Strike, it must be remembered that there were two views of the nature of the strike, and as men held one or other they tended to be against or for conciliation. One party said that it was a revolution, an attack on the constitution. The other claimed that it was simply an industrial dispute. The latter was the claim of the Trades Union Council itself, which incidentally returned a cheque of many thousands of pounds to the All Russian Central Council of Trades Unions. But Mr. Baldwin met the claim by the remark that 'their method of helping the miners is to attack the community'. The Archbishop would not have differed from Mr. Baldwin in his view of the attack on the community. He had condemned it already in the House of Lords. But when Mr. Baldwin said, 'The general strike must be called off absolutely and without reserve. The mining industry dispute can then be settled', the Archbishop declared that the calling off of the strike must be 'simultaneous and concurrent' with steps for settling the mining dispute. The Archbishop did not want the issue to be one of 'victory' and 'defeat'—with the sore memories which it was bound to leave. He was conscious of mistakes on sides other than that of the miners and the Trades Union Congress, and wished to do what he could to help the Prime Minister 'to weld together again all the family thus disordered'. He went to see the Prime Minister:

Interview at 12 o'clock on Tuesday, 11th May 1926 at Downing Street with Mr. Baldwin whom I had asked to let me call.

I was afraid that he might be drifting into the same position as other people and regard me as hostile to him and his whole policy and as having raised an antagonistic flag which I was prepared to nail to the mast, and to regard him as stupidly hostile that he did not conform to what our Appeal on behalf of the Churches had said. I told him that was not my position and that we had very deliberately come to the conclusion we had formulated as a suggestion for the Government to consider, but that the responsibility must now be his as to whether or not they turn our suggestion down and go forward on what they believe to be a sounder and more excellent line. I pressed on him that the responsibility must be his and that we had definitely said our say. I showed him that

I appreciated his difficulties as well as my own. I found him perfectly friendly about it and appreciative of our difficulties and he repeated more than once that he thought I had done all that was possible for me to do in issuing that Appeal, and he told me what I had not before known, that it was to be broadcasted an hour later.

I took the opportunity of pressing a little upon him the distrust we have in the truculent and fighting attitude not of himself but of some of his colleagues. He did not in the least deny it and spoke of his difficulties as hourly very great. He took on the whole a rather more sanguine view of the situation from the Government point of view than I should be prepared to take at the present moment. We parted in the friendliest way.

Many factors contributed to the termination of the strike. Such were the speech of Sir John Simon, and the judgement of Mr. Justice Astbury, on the illegality of the action taken, in breach of contracts, by the strikers; the Government's meeting of the general situation, and the rallying of the public in unprecedented ways to its support; and the general good humour and common sense of the people. But there can be no doubt that the Archbishop's appeal wrought a real change in the atmosphere—and in particular had a very great influence on the attitude of the working classes.

On May 12, following unofficial but very important discussions between Sir Herbert Samuel and the General Council of the Trades Union Council, the General Strike was terminated by the Council. There were no conditions; but the Prime Minister immediately promised to do his best to bring about the resumption of the negotiations between miners and owners. Mr. Baldwin had prevailed; but in prevailing he begged that there might be no recriminations, and 'that the whole British people should not look backward but forward, and resume their work in a spirit of co-operation and goodwill'. The Archbishop wholeheartedly endorsed the Prime Minister's appeal, in a message made public the following day. He also wrote a personal letter to the Prime Minister, saying how much he had been impressed by the combination of firmness, persistent conciliatoriness, and solid practical counsel which he had shown; and expressing his sense 'of the value and strength—I would say the *Christian* spirit—of your leadership of the nation in a very difficult hour'. Mr. Baldwin replied:

The RT. HON. STANLEY BALDWIN, *to the* ARCHBISHOP OF CANTERBURY

23rd May 1926. 10 Downing Street, Whitehall, S.W. 1.

I cannot tell you how I value your most kind and generous letter.

We are not yet through these troublous times but such appreciation as yours is a great encouragement and will help me to face the future with serenity.

Thank you from my heart.

Among great numbers of other letters received by the Archbishop from M.P.s, Professors, Free Church leaders, Bishops, were the following:

SIR HENRY CRAIK *to the* ARCHBISHOP OF CANTERBURY

5A Dean's Yard, Westminster. 12 May 1926.

Few letters in my long life of 80 years have caused me more pain than this—addressed to one of my oldest friends, and to one who certainly came after none of my friends in the regard and reverence in which I have always held him. But Your Grace's last pronouncement has struck a grievous blow at that regard and reverence. You ask me to express my agreement with your pronouncement. Were I to do so, I would, in my judgement, commit not only an error, but a grievous crime.

By this post I have written to convey my deep admiration to Principal Martin of the U.F.C. for his courageous letter in the *Scotsman* of May 10th. You may imagine my feelings, in sending these two letters after all that I recall in the past.

PROFESSOR GILBERT MURRAY *to the* ARCHBISHOP OF CANTERBURY

Yatscombe, Boar's Hill, Oxford. 20th May 1926.

May I, now that the crisis is over, send a line to thank you for the magnificent lead which you gave to the forces of peace throughout the Strike. As you know, many of us in Oxford helped you as best we could, but it was through your action that the whole movement had its authority and force.

I do not think I have ever known such a manifestation of the spirit of peace and goodwill rising through the whole nation and triumphantly asserting itself. And certainly the Church led the conscience of the country.

Please do not answer: you must be overwhelmed with letters.

The Bishop of Durham *to the* Archbishop of Canterbury

Auckland Castle, Bishop Auckland. June 9, 1926.

. . . Your Grace knows that I regard with great apprehension the present tendency to centralize government in the Church of England, a process which is tending to destroy the independence of the Diocesan Bishops and to reduce them to mere deputies of the Primate, a position which conflicts with the authority of episcopal office, with the traditions of the Church of England, and with the primary condition of sound administration. I certainly for one, can not, and will not accept such a position. In the particular instance of the General Strike, the normal difficulty was greatly increased by the gravity of the issue at stake. Your Grace knows how strongly I feel on the national character and responsibility of the Church of England. Surely that character and that responsibility did require at such a crisis as the General Strike created, a clear and imperative call to fundamental civic duty. What could be more unfortunate—I might almost say grotesque—than a procedure which made it possible for Cardinal Bourne to become the mouthpiece of national sentiment and civic duty—a role which belongs pre-eminently to the National Church, and therein conspicuously to the Primate. As to the practical mischiefs which have followed and will follow Your Grace's action, I have no doubt whatever. On this point of course, opinions will vary, and the value attached to them will vary. That the clear and vital issue which the General Strike presented, has been in many minds obscured, cannot, I think, be doubted, nor yet that a great impetus has been given to the tendency, already dangerously active, of many parochial clergymen—and they often the least equipped with knowledge or character—to substitute for religious teaching, a declamatory, sentimental socialism as far removed from sound economics as from Christian morality. . . .

I have been following closely during these weeks of compulsory inactivity, the course of events, and I should fasten upon the speeches of Mr. Baldwin and Lord Grey as beyond comparison the wisest and best worth consideration. It seems to me very unfortunate that the weight of the National Church should not be frankly placed behind statesmen (since God has been good enough to give them to us) whose utterances are both patriotic, and in the best sense, Christian. . . .

Your Grace will make allowance for the circumstances in which I write, and believe that amongst so many things which at this time perplex and sadden me, there is none which does so more than the inability under which I labour to applaud and support the public course which Your Grace adopts. But you are as magnanimous as you are wise, and will compassionate my folly, while you condone my independence.

RT. HON. J. RAMSAY MACDONALD, M.P., *to the* ARCHBISHOP OF CANTERBURY

Upper Frognal Lodge, Hampstead, N.W. 12th May 1926.

I am afraid you are having to suffer for the fine Christian stand you have taken, but will you give me the great pleasure of allowing me, as one who has striven from the beginning for peace . . . to thank you for what you have done and to assure you that it contributed greatly to the events of this day? You had the support of earnest minded Christians of all sects and of no sect, and I hope you have much consolation of soul to reward you.

On May 13, members of the Trades Union Council, including Mr. Ben Turner and Miss Margaret Bondfield, came to Lambeth to thank the Archbishop, and to plead with him to use his influence against victimization.

In spite of the calling off of the General Strike, the coal stoppage continued for nearly seven months. But the Archbishop took no further part in the dispute, except to make an announcement in the Church Assembly in July with regard to the attitude of the Ecclesiastical Commissioners—very large owners of mining royalties—as trustees for an immense number of poorer incumbents. He said that in the previous March the Estates Committee and the royalty owners as a body made it known to the Government that if the Government deemed it desirable in the interests of the whole country that the royalties should be acquired by the State, the Commissioners, together with other royalty owners, raised no objection to such a plan. Later in the summer a number of Bishops and Free Church leaders, led by the Bishop of Lichfield, took an active part in further negotiations with the miners, even going so far as to frame a Memorandum of Terms which, though accepted by the Miners' Executive and a Delegates' Conference, was rejected by the Prime Minister, and on August 11 by the miners themselves on a ballot vote by districts. The Archbishop was kept informed of the progress of the proceedings, but took no part in them himself. Indeed, he was not specially pleased that the Bishops should engage in the detailed work of finding a precise economic solution. He stood up strenuously—as he wrote to the Bishop of Lichfield on August 9—for the duty of Church officers as such to be prominent on the side of conciliation and peacemaking. But he said:

The ARCHBISHOP OF CANTERBURY *to the* BISHOP OF LICHFIELD

August 9, 1926.

What I dread, and I find that others dread (notably dear old Bishop Talbot, who has always been on the Liberal side), is that in a short time we shall find it stated that the arrayed forces consist of the Church plus the Miners on the one side and the Government on the other side—a hopelessly unreasonable statement, but one which is certain to be made. If you can devise modes of preventing this the gain will be great. I am not in the least afraid of opposing a Government when I am certain of my own ground and that they are wrong, but if the forces were rallied into the opposite camps I have described I should feel it difficult to say where my allegiance lay.

CHAPTER LXXXI

THE ARCHBISHOP AND BISHOP BARNES

... Then said the cardinal to them, 'Is this Dr. Barnes your man that is accused of heresy?' 'Yea, and please your grace; and we trust you shall find him reformable, for he is both well learned and wise.' 'What! master doctor,' said the cardinal; 'had you not a sufficient scope in the Scriptures to teach the people?' ... And Barnes answered, 'I spake nothing but the truth out of the Scriptures, according to my conscience, and according to the old doctors.' And then did Barnes deliver him six sheets of paper written, to confirm and corroborate his sayings. The cardinal received them smiling on him, and saying, 'We perceive then that you intend to stand to your articles and to shew your learning.' 'Yea,' said Barnes, 'that I do intend, by God's grace, with your lordship's favour.'

JOHN FOXE, *Acts and Monuments*, vol. v, pp. 416 ff.

ON Thursday morning, October 20, 1927, the public was startled by reading in the Press an open letter from the Bishop of Birmingham to the Archbishop of Canterbury. The purpose of the letter (so the Bishop told the Primate) was to give vent to certain reflections upon an interruption to the service in St. Paul's Cathedral on the previous Sunday, when the Bishop was preaching. It was a curious way for a Suffragan to address his Metropolitan, but it had the great advantage, from the writer's point of view, of securing the widest possible public for his views. Moreover, the succession of utterances of which it formed the centre were peculiarly embarrassing not only to the Archbishop but to all those responsible authorities in the Church who desired to see the last stages of Prayer Book Revision happily fulfilled. It can hardly be doubted that the Bishop's action at this juncture, whatever its intention, had the effect of heightening the fears of Low and Broad Churchmen and generally strengthening the adversaries of the Revised Prayer Book.

The Bishop of Birmingham had long been known as a militant liberal Churchman. He was a mathematician and a scientist, and an outspoken champion of the evolutionary view of the origin of man; and he claimed a freedom to remodel Christian theology on that basis. He was also a most decided opponent of distinctively Anglo-Catholic teaching about the Sacraments; and his opposition to certain important proposals with regard to the revision of the Order of Holy Communion was widely known.

On Sunday, September 25, 1927, preaching in Westminster Abbey, he made a vigorous pronouncement on the first of these points. Taking as his text the recent Presidential Address to the British Association by Sir Arthur Keith, he proclaimed in trenchant terms the necessity of accepting the biological doctrine of evolution. He accepted the evolution of man, 'possibly a million years ago from a tangle of apes', and greeted the gorilla as man's first cousin. He added that the Darwinian discovery and its triumph had destroyed the whole theological scheme, dependent on the story of the creation of Adam and Eve and their fall. The sermon aroused a good deal of attention, mainly, it must be supposed, from the vigour of the style in which the Bishop's thoughts were expressed, as well as the pungency of his references to Christians (unlike himself) obsessed by 'traditional theology'—for the thoughts were by no means new or unfamiliar in themselves. A fortnight later (October 6), at a lunch-hour service at Birmingham, he delivered an address on Sacramental Teaching. In language which was bound to cause offence, he derided the doctrine of the Real Presence. He said that there were men and women to-day whose sacramental beliefs were not far from those of the cultured Hindu idolater. 'They pretend that a Priest using the right words and acts can change a piece of bread so that within it there is the real presence of Christ. The idea is absurd and can be disproved by experiment.' He also, in the spirit of the most naïve materialism, expressed his readiness to believe in the doctrine of transubstantiation, 'when I can find a person who will come to the Chapel of my house and tell me correctly whether a piece of bread which I present to him has undergone the change for which believers in transubstantiation contend'. This address was bitterly resented by multitudes of Churchmen. On Sunday, October 16, as Dr. Barnes was preparing to preach in St. Paul's Cathedral, a leading Anglo-Catholic incumbent of the London diocese, Canon Bullock-Webster, appeared with a large body of laymen and made a public protest against his false and heretical teaching about the Sacraments of the Holy Catholic Church. He appealed to the Bishop of London to inhibit the Bishop of Birmingham, and to the Archbishop of the Province to try him. After making his protest, Canon Bullock-Webster celebrated what he called a 'Reparation Mass' in the Church of St. Michael Royal, hard by.

Such was the painful scene—the 'interruption in the service'—and such were the causes which led the Bishop of Birmingham to address his Open Letter to the Archbishop.

In the letter, the Bishop referred to his experience as Master of the Temple—and the 'wistful agnosticism' of his congregation, 'probably the most intellectual in England'. He told of his wide reading and plain speech—his teaching 'positive and unreported', and referred to a sermon, preached when the British Association met at Cardiff in 1920, which 'travelled round the world and brought me over a thousand letters'. This was in comment on his statement that 'one cause of weakness of the Church has arisen from the apparent determination of religious teachers to ignore scientific discovery, though all competent biologists accept man's evolution from an ape-like stock'. He then went on to declare that 'the second main reason for the present alienation of educated men and women from the Church of England is the growth of erroneous sacramental doctrines during and since the War'. He maintained that he was upholding the traditional sacramental doctrine of the Church of England, while his critics held to the sacramental errors which that Church repudiated. He reaffirmed his statement that the doctrine of transubstantiation was untrue, referred again to the impossibility of discriminating by spiritual discernment between consecrated and unconsecrated bread, and after declaring 'No man shall drive me to Tennessee or to Rome', ended thus:

The Bishop of Birmingham *to the* Archbishop of Canterbury

I invite Your Grace to consider what steps can be taken to help those of us who are giving of our best to fit the Church to be in the future the spiritual guide of an educated nation. This letter, of course, calls for no public reply.

The Archbishop saw the letter for the first time in the Press, though a telegram from the Bishop had warned him that a letter was coming. In spite of the fact that it had not called for a public reply, His Grace sent an immediate answer to the Bishop of Birmingham. It was very courteous, it showed a real sense of humour and dignity, but it was of a kind (said a writer at the time) to give Dr. Barnes very small and cold comfort. It was as follows:

The ARCHBISHOP OF CANTERBURY *to the* BISHOP OF BIRMINGHAM

Lambeth Palace, S.E. 22nd October 1927.

I have read with great care your open letter to myself published two days ago. You will not doubt my condemnation of the unseemly incident in St. Paul's Cathedral which you have taken as an occasion for writing to me. Not by action of that sort can the cause of truth be reasonably set forward.

But, speaking generally, I think that you mistake what it is that has evoked from cultured men, with scientific and philosophical as well as theological knowledge, vehement reprobation of some of your recent utterances. With regard to these I have probably received, publicly or privately, more communications than any one except yourself.

I do not attach great weight to the denunciations of what I have heard described as 'the gorilla sermons'. I believe that you overrate the adherence of thoughtful people to Creation theories of fifty to a hundred years ago, and I scarcely think that among those who listen to you there are a great number who hold the opinions which you satirize. For myself, at least, I can say that your position on the biological question, in outline and so far as I understand it, is one with which I personally have been familiar for more than fifty years. Believe me, this teaching, however admirable, is to most of us not novel, and I do not think that those who hear you on the subject with interest and advantage would recognise themselves as 'wistful agnostics'. As far as I can judge, it is not on what you have said with regard to that branch of science or theology that the attention of thoughtful men has been centred. It is too familiar. You may, I am certain, dismiss, my dear Bishop, the fear that anyone in England desires to lead or drive you either to Rome or to Tennessee.

The words which give rise to the sort of indignation I refer to are the words which you use in dealing with the Sacrament of Holy Communion. It is on what you have said respecting Sacramental doctrine that intelligent and large-minded Churchmen, lay as well as clerical, have approached me day by day.

I have an intense dislike to the use of the daily Press for the discussion of such subjects. I purposely refrain from trying in such a letter as this to discuss the profound and life-giving doctrines involved, but, of course, I am more than ready to go into the matter with yourself at any time should you so desire. But your open letter forces me, however reluctantly, to some reply. Formally and publicly you invite me 'to consider what steps can be taken to help those of us who are giving of our best to fit the Church to be in the future the spiritual guide of an educated nation'. That is a large and difficult matter, needing time and care, but I can say at once that in my judgment one of the first steps is to secure the scrupulous use of the most careful language possible in dealing with doctrinal matters of deep solemnity which affect the devotional thoughts and prayers of Christian people. That duty, obligatory upon every Christian teacher, is peculiarly incumbent upon us Bishops, who have to weigh the effect of our words upon all sections of the great body to whom we desire to be Fathers in God. We promised on our consecration day 'to be ready with all faithful diligence to banish and drive away all erroneous and strange doctrine contrary to God's Word', and while, as you have truly said, 'smooth unctuous platitudes' are not enough, yet in all the range of our duties there is none which calls more clearly for the exercise of tender and fatherly carefulness in word and act.

Now in your open letter to myself you assure me that what you have been lately doing, and have been denounced for doing, is as 'a Bishop of the Church of England' to 'uphold its traditional Sacramental doctrine' and to 'affirm'—as we all affirm—that 'the doctrine of Transubstantiation is untrue'. Do not suppose me to be unmindful of our duty to stem whatever trend there is that way. The duty is clear. But when I turn to the Birmingham sermon which aroused criticism I find that the statement you make to me fails to describe fairly what you there said. In your natural and legitimate desire to denounce the few in the Church of England who hold or teach the doctrine of Transubstantiation you were led to speak of the Sacrament of Holy Communion in a way which—quite reasonably as I think—gives real offence to the great body of devout Churchmen and Churchwomen, and not least to those who are able to give scholarly as well as reverent consideration to the Sacramental doctrines which our Church upholds.

I do not believe that you had any intention of wounding the souls of honest and faithful English Churchmen, but you ignore or belittle the position and teaching of those within our Church who stand in the tradition of such English Bishops as Andrewes or Ken or Wilson or, in our own day, Edward King or Charles Gore. Nay, more. Your words seem to me capable of being so interpreted as to include in reprobation or almost in contempt the position of the great mass of Churchmen who would associate themselves with the teaching of such leaders as, say, my own great masters Bishop Lightfoot or Bishop Westcott, or who have caught the devotional spirit of the hymns of Charles Wesley.

I prefer to think that if you re-read your Birmingham sermon in the light of such criticism as your letter has drawn from me, you will feel that what I have said is not unfair.

You say in your letter that your teaching is 'positive and unreported'. Your Birmingham sermon, however, contains some such positive teaching. And as I read your words about the grace of Our Saviour's presence through the whole act of worship they leave me wondering whether, if you were to consider what are their implications, you would not find further cause to modify the width and scope of your negative and destructive statements.

We have all been impressed in these recent months by the self-restraint and the considerateness for others shown by many of the clergy and laity who have been foremost in our Prayer Book discussions. To the larger tasks which lie beyond these discussions we Bishops must lead the way. But we shall lead only if we walk 'with all lowliness and meekness, with long-suffering, . . . giving diligence to keep the unity of the Spirit in the bond of peace'.

The Bishop of Birmingham was unrepentant. He wrote another Open Letter on October 26, but he added little to what he had already said. The main part of his letter dealt again with errors of sacramental doctrine. He still spoke of his desire for 'experimental tests to be reverently carried out in a suitable place, which would show that no man, in his spiritual capacity, can distinguish consecrated from unconsecrated bread'. He emphasized his conviction that 'most of the irregularities which have crept into our Churches in recent years' had followed from these erroneous sacramental beliefs. The Archbishop gave no further public answer. The correspondence closed. But the controversy had added to the embarrassment attending the Church's spokesmen in defending the Revised Prayer Book in Parliament.

CHAPTER LXXXII
THE PRAYER BOOK

I will not dispute it here, what power a lay assembly (and such a Parliament is) hath to determine matters of religion, primely and originally by and of themselves, before the Church hath first agreed upon them. Then indeed they may confirm or refuse. And this course was held in the Reformation.

ARCHBISHOP LAUD, *Answer . . . to the Speech of Lord Saye and Sele, touching the Liturgy.*

It must be own'd, that this Bill hath met with very hard Fortune, and yet that doth not in the least diminish the value of it. MARQUESS OF HALIFAX, *Some Cautions offered to the consideration of those who are to chuse Members to serve for the ensuing Parliament.*

I

THE first public act of the Archbishop at Lambeth, after his enthronement, in 1903 had been to receive a deputation of over 100 Unionist M.P.s on ecclesiastical disorders. They came to him then in order to urge effective action against 'ritualism' in the Church of England. He agreed that 'the sands had run out', and that 'stern and drastic action' was required in the case of those men—very few—who were guilty of flagrant and definite illegality and disobedience. The result of the deputation, and of the contemporary agitation in the House of Commons, was the Royal Commission on Ecclesiastical Discipline, with its recommendations that Letters of Business should be issued to the Convocations for rubrical reform and for modification in the existing law relating to the conduct of Divine Service—'with a view to their enactment by Parliament'.

It was the Archbishop's fate, twenty-five years later, at the end of his primacy, to witness the refusal of Parliament to enact the very measures which had been so long and carefully planned as a result of the Royal Commission. But before we describe the final scenes of the drama in the House of Commons in 1927 and 1928, we must go back to the closing stages of Prayer Book Revision in the Convocations.

Before the War, the general policy followed by the Bishops had been to confine the revision of the rubrics to comparatively small dimensions. The critical question then was that of Eucharistic vestments, and by 1914 there seemed fair reason to believe that a way to answer it could be found. Besides this, there were the use of the *Quicunque Vult*, a few modifications in the occasional services, some cautious recognition of reservation 'for the sick person', a few not very important adjustments in the order of Holy Communion (involving no change of structure, or alteration in the Prayer of Consecration), and a measure of general enrichment.

With the War, however, there came a considerable change. The Eucharist became more and more prominent in the worship of Churchmen, and so more and more prominent in public discussions on the Prayer Book. The debate on Reservation in the Upper House of Canterbury Convocation in 1917 (already described) marked a significant stage.[1] The debate in the same place in February 1918, accepting the proposals of the Lower House for an alteration of the central part of the Communion Service (refused in April 1915), was also significant. It was then that the question of an Alternative Order of Holy Communion first took a definite place in the Bishops' proposals for Prayer Book Revision. By October 1918, agreement on all matters except this had been practically secured, with the help of representatives of both Convocations; and the Archbishops were asked to call a special conference to deal with this single issue. Before the conference could meet, a Memorial was presented to their Graces, signed by nine Bishops[2]—six of them in the Northern Province—3,000 clergy, and 100,000 laymen, to protest against any such changes in the Communion Service. The Conference, however, produced an agreed solution, proposed by the Evangelical Bishop of Ripon (Dr. Drury) and the Anglo-Catholic Dr. Frere. It included an invocation of the Holy Spirit.[3] It was accepted by Canterbury Convocation

[1] See p. 811.

[2] Durham (Dr. Moule), Chester (Dr. Jayne), Liverpool (Dr. Chavasse), Manchester (Dr. Knox), Carlisle (Dr. Diggle), Sodor and Man (Dr. Denton Thompson), Llandaff (Dr. Hughes), Bath and Wells (Dr. Kennion), Chelmsford (Dr. Watts-Ditchfield).

[3] 'I.—That the Prayer of Humble Access be moved so as to follow immediately after the Comfortable Words.

'II.—That in the Prayer of Consecration the following words be added after the Words of Institution:—

> '"Wherefore, O Father, we thy humble servants, having in remembrance before thee the precious death of thy dear Son, his mighty resurrection and glorious ascension, looking also for his coming again, do render unto thee most hearty thanks for the innumerable benefits which he hath procured unto us. And we pray thee of thine almighty goodness to send upon us and

on February 11, 1920—when the Archbishop thus defined his own position, a position which he consistently maintained to the end:

> Speaking as to my own personal inclination, I should prefer to have no alternative Service at all, but I am loyally prepared to abide by the outcome of the Conference and to commend to the Church the acceptance of the proposal.

It was rejected by York Convocation, where the Bishops who had signed the Memorial had a clear majority in the Upper House.

With this single exception, both Convocations concurred with the rest of the Proposals for the Revision of the Book of Common Prayer. And on April 29, 1920, both Archbishops and Prolocutors signed their Answer to the Royal Letters of Business with the Appended Schedules; the Schedules from Canterbury Convocation being set out as follows:

1. Proposals for the Revision of the Book of Common Prayer as approved by the Convocation of Canterbury. April, 1920.
2. Table of Lessons, as approved by the Convocation of Canterbury. April, 1920.
3. The Prayer Book Psalter revised,[1] as approved by the Convocation of Canterbury. April, 1920.
4. The Athanasian Creed in a Revised Translation,[2] as approved by the Convocation of Canterbury. April, 1920.

> upon these thy gifts thy holy and blessed Spirit, who is the Sanctifier and the Giver of life, to whom with thee and thy Son Jesus Christ be ascribed by every creature in earth and heaven all blessing, honour, glory, and power, now henceforth and for evermore. *Amen.*"

'III.—That the Lord's Prayer be placed after the Prayer of Consecration, prefaced by the words:—

> ' "As our Saviour Christ hath commanded and taught us, we are bold to say, *Then shall the people join with the Priest, and say,* Our Father . . . for ever and ever. Amen."

'IV.—That the Prayer of Oblation be not moved from its present position; that the rubric before it shall read, *Then shall be said one or both of the following*; and that the present rubric before the Thanksgiving be omitted.'

[1] This was the Prayer Book Psalter revised in accordance with the proposals of a Committee appointed by the Archbishop of Canterbury together with Amendments made by Convocation of Canterbury. The Committee was presided over by Bishop Jayne of Chester and reported in 1916 (S.P.C.K.).

[2] This was a translation made by a Committee, appointed by the Archbishop in 1909 (Chairman, Bishop John Wordsworth) at the request of the Lambeth Conference of 1908, and revised in 1917 under the Chairmanship of Bishop Robertson (S.P.C.K.).

The Archbishop officially communicated the Answer to the Home Secretary, who replied.

The ARCHBISHOP OF CANTERBURY *to the* RT. HON. EDWARD SHORTT

Lambeth Palace, S.E.1. 22nd May 1920.

It is my duty to transmit to you, as I do herewith, for submission to His Majesty the King, the Answer of the Convocation of Canterbury to the Royal Letters of Business on the Rubrics of the Book of Common Prayer, to which our attention was directed in His Majesty's Royal Letter of Business.

Should legal effect be hereafter given to the recommendations we have made, I presume that the process followed would be that which is laid down in the recent Act of Parliament respecting Ecclesiastical legislation.

The RT. HON. EDWARD SHORTT *to the* ARCHBISHOP OF CANTERBURY

Home Office, Whitehall, S.W. 6th July, 1920.

I have the honour to inform Your Grace that I have laid before His Majesty the answers of the Convocations of Canterbury and York to the Royal Letters of Business on the Rubrics of the Book of Common Prayer.

I agree with Your Grace that for the purpose of giving legal effect to the recommendations of the two Convocations the procedure to be followed should be that laid down by the Church of England Assembly (Powers) Act, 1919, and I would suggest that steps should be taken by Your Grace to bring the proposals before the National Assembly of the Church of England.

II

It will be seen that procedure by means of the new Church Assembly (Powers) Act, 1919, was taken as a matter of course. This was natural because the Letters of Business had been originally issued, according to the Recommendations of the Royal Commission, 'with a view to enactment by Parliament'; and the Archbishop had expressly stated in the House of Lords, in the debate on the Enabling Act, that the revision of the Prayer Book would fall under its provisions. Moreover, the Church Assembly also contains its House of Laity, which was bound to be consulted, as the Archbishop had promised from the start. It was perhaps hardly expected, after the exhaustive deliberations in the Convocations—lasting fourteen years (1906–20) that the Church

Assembly would want to spend a further prolonged period on the same business. Even in 1918 Bishop Gore said 'the delay of our revision . . . is becoming a universal jest!' But so it was. The Church Assembly met for the first time for a brief two days in the summer of 1920—yet in the autumn (to quote Lord Hugh Cecil), with the zest and self-confidence of extreme youth, it appointed a committee of all three Houses to consider and report upon the Answers of the Convocations to the Royal Letters of Business. In June 1922 the Committee presented its Report, adopting the greater number of the Convocations' proposals substantially unchanged. But a warning note was struck with regard both to the Order of Holy Communion and to Reservation. Of the ten lay members on the Joint Committee, one, Mr. Athelstan Riley, an Anglo-Catholic, presented a Minority Report of his own dealing especially with the alternative Eucharistic Office, and five others, all Evangelical, printed a Note of objection to the proposals for Reservation. In October 1922, the House of Bishops introduced the Revised Prayer Book (Permissive Use) Measure (N.A. 84) into the Assembly, simply attaching a Measure to the Committee's Proposals unaltered. General Approval was given in all three Houses, sitting separately, in January and April 1923, with three dissentients in the House of Bishops—Bristol (Dr. Nickson), Norwich (Dr. Pollock), and Worcester (Dr. Pearce); and for the next two years the Houses of Clergy and Laity, sitting separately, went steadily through the stage of Revision.

Had the members of the Assembly been left to deliberate on the proposals of Convocation by themselves, their task would have been comparatively simple. But from the moment when the Report of the Prayer Book Revision Committee (N.A. 60) was published in the summer of 1922, a torrent of rival proposals poured in from right and centre and left. The most valuable productions were severally known as the Green Book, the Grey Book, and the Orange Book. The first of these was a very thorough Anglo-Catholic presentation of a series of amendments by a Committee of the English Church Union; the second a series of alternative services and prayers, from a liberal point of view, with a preface by the Bishop of Manchester (Dr. Temple); the third consisted of scholarly pamphlets of a moderate English Catholic type, produced by the Alcuin Club. In addition to this, the floodgates of criticism, comment, and protest were already opening. On October 20, 1925, when the House of Bishops began its own task of revision, the Archbishop stated that he had received 800 different memorials, most of them dealing with the Order of Holy Communion: including an important document from Cambridge University, praying for no change in that service; another organized by Bishop Knox and numbering 308,000 signatures, to a similar effect; and, not least important, a statement signed by nine diocesan Bishops[1] (June 13, 1925) that they were 'definitely opposed at the present time to any change being made in the Order of Administration of Holy Communion after the Creed, or to any alternative form of service'.

The revision stage began in October 1925, with a sitting in public, very much against the Archbishop's wish. But from January 1926 to the conclusion in 1927, the House of Bishops met privately at Lambeth Palace, where the drawing-room was transformed and placed at their disposal. The idea of Lambeth Palace being the meeting-place had been due to Mrs. Davidson, and beyond doubt made a very great difference to the harmony of the proceedings, with many Bishops staying in the house, and all meeting at meals:

> It not only softens asperities, but it gives opportunities for consultation and practical talk which, though only side dishes, contribute a great deal to the central fare. (Feb. 13, 1927.)

During the sessions (between forty and fifty full days) the Bishops not only went through the amendments of the other two Houses, but also made such a substantial remodelling that the result not unfairly produced the impression that they were addressing themselves to the improvement of the Prayer Book for the first time. From the start the Bishops of Norwich, Birmingham, and Worcester were seen to be in opposition.

It was proposed at the outset (October 1925) that the Revision should be effected in two stages, leaving all that concerned the Holy Communion until the rest of the Prayer Book had been revised. But this proposal was defeated by 24 votes to 9. The main differences throughout were with regard to the Order of Holy Communion and Reservation. In the former service the

[1] Norwich (Dr. Pollock), Sodor and Man (Dr. Thornton-Duesbery), Exeter (Lord W. Cecil), Worcester (Dr. Pearce), Birmingham (Dr. Barnes), Gloucester (Dr. Headlam), St. Edmundsbury and Ipswich (Dr. Whittingham), Bradford (Dr. Perowne), and Bristol (Dr. Nickson). None of these had signed the previous Nine Bishops' Memorial of 1919—all of whom had vacated their sees.

movement for an alternative order had steadily grown. The House of Clergy desired it—and the House of Laity were prepared to acquiesce if the Bishops said it would 'promote peace and order in the Church'. The real reason behind the desire for an alternative order was dissatisfaction with the abrupt close of the Prayer of Consecration in the Book of Common Prayer, which ends with the words of institution, and a desire to revert to the older form, as seen in the Prayer Book of 1549, where the Prayer of Consecration included (1) the prayer for the Church, (2) the present prayer of consecration, with some variation, including an invocation of the Holy Spirit, (3) the memorial and oblation. It was argued by some of those who advocated in particular the introduction of an invocation of the Holy Spirit (*epiklesis*) that this would help in guarding against a tendency to lay all the weight of consecration on the actual words of institution. Some, again, maintained that once an Anglican Canon thus enlarged was permitted, the use of the Roman Canon, secretly or otherwise, could be brought to an end. One Bishop, at least, Dr. Headlam, Bishop of Gloucester, who had signed the Memorial against an Alternative Canon, changed his mind during the meetings of the House of Bishops. In view of the fact that in other parts of the Christian Church alternative forms were permitted, like the Liturgy of St. Basil and the Liturgy of St. Chrysostom in the Orthodox Church, he expressed his willingness to recognize the use of two Communion Offices side by side in the Church of England. The proposal for an alternative Canon was approved in June 1926 by 29 votes to 5.

What was the Archbishop's own attitude? Throughout the sessions of the House of Bishops his role was the role of chairman. Looking through the verbatim report, we hardly find a single occasion on which he gave a decided lead on a critical issue. The truth is that he was not really sufficiently interested; he took a lay point of view. His sympathies were on the whole with the moderate layman, and he did not understand the imaginative or romantic or perhaps even the sacramental side of the Anglo-Catholic party. To him it was a question, in the good sense of the word, of expediency:

January, 1926.

I have found it very difficult to know what, speaking generally, ought to be my own line in regard to proposals for changing the

Communion Office. On the one hand my own instinct would have been for leaving that Office alone and adhering to what has satisfied English people for more than three centuries. And I am certain that such is the view of the overwhelming majority of English Churchmen throughout the country. The average M.P. or County Councillor, or local squire, or man of business, says emphatically, 'let it alone'. Ought it to be one's policy to fall in with that wish or give leadership in that direction, and practically refuse what the ecclesiastically minded folk want in the way of change or reform or reversion to older usage? The answer is not easy. These people who have given their thoughts to the structure of a service which to many of them means more than anything else on earth, have been working for years at trying to bring about the sort of changes which they think would make our Office more Catholic without impairing its really English character. The majority of Churchmen want no change. But the people who do want the change are the people who have studied the subject and care about it most. Their views are for the most part not my views, but they are entitled to respect, and some people believe that by yielding in a reasonable degree to the wishes those folk express, we should allay present disorder and unruliness and that they would accept half the loaf they are eager for, rather than go on as things are, and that accepting it they would be peaceable. I am by no means sure that this is the case, but on the whole it seems certain that some experiment in that direction must be made, and, so far as I am personally concerned, I feel that it could honestly be made without impairing our Anglican orthodoxy at all. But such is not the view of the majority of the Protestants, who, under the leadership of Bishop Knox, or again of milder folk like Canon Storr, may so frighten the public mind as to make the peaceable carrying of a reforming measure impossible.

In the end, in June 1926, he agreed to an alternative canon, though unable to disguise from his brother Bishops, when the final form[1] was presented, that he found it 'very difficult to attach

[1] The final form of the Prayer of Consecration, as approved by the House of Bishops, differed from that of 1662 in the following way. The opening words were 'All glory be to thee, Almighty God our heavenly Father, for that thou of thy tender mercy. . . .' Then came the rest of the Prayer of 1662 unchanged. Immediately afterwards there followed (1) a Memorial, and (2) an Invocation of the Holy Spirit, thus:

'Wherefore, O Lord and heavenly Father, we thy humble servants, having in remembrance the precious death and passion of thy dear Son, his mighty resurrection and glorious ascension, according to his holy institution, do celebrate, and set forth before thy Divine Majesty with these thy holy gifts, the memorial

the importance that some attach to questions like the order of the paragraphs in a long prayer'—more particularly at the very time when, as he noted in his Papers, 'the outstanding thing dominating all else' was 'the strike—first general, then coalfields'.

With regard to Reservation, this was a practice, as we have already seen,[1] which had grown in a very remarkable way as a result of the War. It was 'An Alternative Order for the Communion of the Sick'. According to this Order, the consecrated bread and wine were set apart at the open communion in church and reserved only for the communion of the sick. This method of communicating the sick person in his own home was recognized in the Prayer Book of 1549, but did not appear in the Prayer Book of 1662. Its reintroduction after a long interval, in which it had been unknown, had been condemned in the Court of Arches as unlawful:[2] and Archbishops Temple and Maclagan had both given opinions from Lambeth in 1900 condemning its use in the Church of England. It was, however, lawful in the Scottish Episcopal Church, in the Province of South Africa, and in other branches of the Anglican Communion. Its danger was supposed to be a danger of superstitious use. The problem before the Bishops was how to regulate the Reservation of the consecrated elements in such a way as to rule out anything in the nature of corporate devotions in connexion with the Reserved Sacrament: in other words, how to distinguish sharply in practice between Reservation for Communion and Reservation for adoration. They decided that the distinction could be made by means of Rubrics prescribing the purpose, and of Rules settling the method, of Reservation; and that this distinction, which was easy to make when Reservation was intended for certain known persons (for it ceased when they

which he hath willed us to make, rendering unto thee most hearty thanks for the innumerable benefits which he hath procured unto us.

'Hear us, O merciful Father, we most humbly beseech thee, and with thy Holy and Life-giving Spirit vouchsafe to bless and sanctify both us and these thy gifts of Bread and Wine, that they may be unto us the Body and Blood of thy Son, our Saviour, Jesus Christ, to the end that we, receiving the same, may be strengthened and refreshed both in body and soul.'

The Prayer ended with the words of the Prayer of Oblation of 1662, but commencing, 'And we entirely desire thy fatherly goodness', and ending, 'world without end', then '*Amen*'; followed by the Lord's Prayer said by the Priest and people together. After the Communion of the Priest and people, the Prayer of Thanksgiving of 1662 came with these prefatory words: 'Having now by faith received the precious Body and Blood of Christ, let us give thanks unto our Lord God.'

[1] See p. 806. [2] *Bishop of Oxford* v. *Henly*, [1907] P. 88, [1909] P. 319.

had received the Sacrament), could also be made when Reservation was continuous (in order to secure that 'any sick person' may not lack the benefit of the Sacrament), but in that case it must be definitely with the permission and under the control of the Bishop. Further 'there shall be no service or ceremony in connexion with the Sacrament so reserved, nor shall it be exposed or removed except in order to be consumed in Communion, or otherwise reverently consumed'. It was this continuous Reservation which became the heart of the difficulty: for the opponents of the Bishops maintained that with continuous Reservation 'superstitious uses' were inevitable.

The proposal for Continuous Reservation was approved by the House of Bishops in June 1926. The first Rubric (approved with one dissentient) dealt with Reservation at a particular celebration for a particular sick person on the same day. The second and third Rubrics are as follows:

> If further provision be needed in order to secure that any sick person may not lack the benefit of the most comfortable Sacrament of the Body and Blood of Christ, the Priest, if licensed by the Bishop so to do, may, to that end, when the Holy Communion is celebrated in the church, reserve so much of the consecrated Bread and Wine as is needed for the purpose. And the Bishop shall grant such licence if satisfied of the need, unless in any particular case he see good reason to the contrary.
>
> The consecrated Bread and Wine set apart under either of the two preceding rubricks shall be reserved only for the Communion of the Sick, shall be administered in both kinds, and shall be used for no other purpose whatever. There shall be no service or ceremony in connexion with the Sacrament so reserved, nor shall it be exposed or removed except in order to be received in Communion, or otherwise reverently consumed. All other questions that may arise concerning such Reservation shall be determined by rules, framed by the Archbishop and Bishops of the Province, or by Canons lawfully made by the Convocation of the Province, and subject to any such rules and Canons, by the directions of the Bishop.

The second Rubric was approved by 19 votes to 11; the third Rubric by 25 votes to 6.

The Rules referred to in the second of the above Rubrics required that the consecrated Bread and Wine should be reserved 'in an Aumbry set in the North Wall of the Sanctuary or of the

Chapel; or, if need be, shall be reserved in some other place approved by the Bishop'.

On February 7, 1927, a Draft Book was presented to the Convocations, with speeches from both Archbishops. The main work was done, but, in view of the large number of amendments introduced, it was felt desirable to give the Lower Houses the opportunity of making their own comments and suggestions before the Revised Prayer Book was submitted to the Church Assembly in its final form. The Archbishop records his impression of the situation and of the propaganda in the press a few days later (February 13) in revealing sentences:

> I intensely dislike the wretchedness of getting these things (some of them too sacred, and some of them too petty, for public discussion) bandied about as though they were the things which absorbed the Church's interest, as, indeed, for the moment they do absorb clerical interest to the detriment of wider things. In my heart I cannot honestly say that I very greatly long for any of the changes, or that they are of supreme deep-down importance. I cannot get myself to feel warmly about such things as order of the Canon, or the Saints' days' Collects, or other matters and I have to admit that with regard to Reservation my line of action is based upon the conviction that in the present unsettled conditions in London and some other places, the only chance of peace is by allowing some degree of Reservation-liberty, guarding it scrupulously against abuses.

The Lower House met on February 22, 1927, and made a number of proposals. After further revision in the House of Bishops the final form was presented to the Convocations, March 29 and 30, and by them commended to the Church Assembly by large majorities.[1]

Meantime, the champions of the revised Prayer Book and its adversaries marshalled their forces. The extremists of both parties in the Church were against it. The extreme Protestants were opposed to Reservation and to any Alternative Order of Holy Communion. The extreme Anglo-Catholics were opposed to the

	For	*Against*
[1] Canterbury Upper House	21	4
,, Lower House	168	22
York Upper House	unanimous	
,, Lower House	68	10

(March 29–30, 1927.)

limitations attached to Reservation, requiring permission from the Bishop for continuous Reservation as well as prohibiting 'devotions'; and to the form of the Alternative Canon—with its inclusion of an Invocation of the Holy Spirit in the Prayer of Consecration *after* the Words of Institution, which (they averred) belonged to the Eastern liturgies and was a sudden reversal of 'the tradition of the English Church since its beginning 1400 years ago'.

In addition, the Protestants, led by Sir William Joynson Hicks, then Home Secretary, wished to have a positive assurance from the Archbishop as to how the Bishops would treat clergy who still disobeyed, supposing the new Prayer Book became lawful. On February 24, 1927, Joynson Hicks asked the Archbishop a number of questions and reminded him of a Memorial signed by 1,000 Anglo-Catholic clergy in 1917 refusing to obey any Regulation which forbade adoration. The Archbishop saw Joynson Hicks on March 7, but obviously took too sanguine a view of the conversation. He replied as follows:

The ARCHBISHOP OF CANTERBURY *to the* RT. HON. SIR W. JOYNSON HICKS

12th March 1927.

I must ask your pardon for a little delay on my part in fulfilling the promise I made in our recent interview that I would write to you a reply to your letter of February 24th. In that letter you ask, as you say, for further light upon certain points.

(1) You are anxious to know 'what steps the Bishops propose to take in order to secure obedience to the provisions expressed or implied in the issue of the new Book'. I am not surprised that this question should be asked, as it constantly is asked at present, in connexion with the new proposals. But I think you agree with me that the subject of how best to promote clerical discipline is a different one from the providing of Rubrics as to the conduct of Divine Service, and you have told me emphatically that you are not in favour of the institution of prosecutions where it can possibly be avoided. I can assure you that it is the earnest hope of myself and other Bishops that when the new provisions are in operation we may be able to secure much more effectively a reasonable adherence within the enlarged limits to the directions of the Church in regard to the conduct of Divine Service. I had the advantage of discussing this with you and I will not expand upon it now, for I think we are fairly in agreement about it. Our hope and belief are that if we can carry successfully some new

scheme like that which is under consideration for the improvement of our Ecclesiastical Courts with general consent, all disciplinary questions will be more happily and harmoniously handled.

(2) You next ask 'To what extent is the Composite Book to be regarded as a final settlement of the matter?' 'Finality' is of course an impossible and even a wrong thing to promise in the life of a living Church. You are thinking I suppose of a relative 'finality' and so far as I personally am concerned I am quite ready to say that if the provisions of the present Measure and the Book appended to it become law I should not anticipate any re-opening of the matter at any early period in our future history.

(3) You next ask 'To what extent is the new book to be understood as excluding unauthorised teaching and practice now prevalent and not authorised by the new book, though not explicitly condemned by it?' I hope that what I have said in answer to your first two questions affords a reply to this also.

Fourthly, you enquire whether it is contemplated that the Bishops, either individually or acting together, would continue giving permission for the use of practices plainly illegal. This again goes over the same ground as what I have tried to deal with, and we traversed it pretty fully in conversation. Once the new Book has been legalised I do not think that we shall experience the same difficulty as hitherto with regard to sanctions given or implied for practices which are not actually legal.

You have shown me that you appreciate fully what has been our difficulty in that matter and the prospect of its removal by degrees if the new Book becomes law. At the same time your experience enables you to realise the inability of Bishops to make a positive declaration that the observance of ritual rules in all their details will be everywhere and uniformly enforced. We shall do our best. We shall act I hope unitedly, or at least shall endeavour to do so, but these can never be matters upon which specific and binding undertakings can be given in black and white and be penally enforced. Nor, I am sure, would you desire it.

I hope I have succeeded in showing you that the conditions which you look for if the new Book is accepted are, so far as I can judge, likely to be reasonably attained.

The reply was unsatisfactory. Indeed the letter might be described as a kind of climax to the danger that lay in the Archbishop's habit of mind, especially when engaged upon an uncongenial subject. His method worked extraordinarily well when his interest was aroused, that is when the strong force of his character and his personal convictions were behind it. It was much less likely to succeed when these were lacking.

Sir William's rejoinder has an ominous tone:

The RT. HON. SIR W. JOYNSON HICKS *to the* ARCHBISHOP OF CANTERBURY

70, Queen's Gate, London, S.W. 7.
18th March, 1927.

I have received your letter of the 11th instant in reply to mine of the 24th February. Will you forgive me if I say it does not seem to deal with the matter quite as fully as you did in your conversation with me last week.

I had hoped that I had convinced Your Grace of the very grave and unhappy position in which many of the Evangelicals like myself are placed. We have been all our lives opponents of vestments and reservation; we honestly do not believe in them, but some of us might have been willing for the sake of peace in the Church to waive our objections—not altering our beliefs—if we could have been satisfied on the points raised in my letter.

We should have still felt sore and, of course, we should never attend any Church in which these practices were adopted, but, at the same time, speaking at all events for myself, I should have gone a long way in the cause of peace if you had met me with a full and frank acceptance of the points raised in my letter—if you had been able to say to me—'Of course, this is a concordat which will be carried out in the letter and spirit on both sides; those Anglo-Catholics who desire to use the Reserved Sacrament for the purposes of Adoration can have no part or lot in the future of the Church of England; and we, as Bishops, give you a frank assurance that not only will we not consent to going any further but we will use our utmost endeavours to deal with men who in the future may really be considered as defying every law, canonical, Ecclesiastical or political'.

Alas, you have not given me this assurance. You refer to the fact that I do not want wholesale prosecution. I agree; I always have agreed, but as long ago as the Royal Commission I suggested a way out of that difficulty, namely, not to promote the offenders and the Diocese of London has been flooded with them by the Bishop of London since the Commission made its report.

I am deeply sorry; I thought there might have been as the outcome of our interview and our correspondence a hope for peace in the Church, but as I write it seems to me to recede into the distance.

The Archbishop replied again—but he was still insufficiently definite:

The ARCHBISHOP OF CANTERBURY *to the* RT. HON. SIR W. JOYNSON HICKS

21 March, 1927.

Every case would have to be considered on its merits. So far as I am myself concerned I can say unhesitatingly that I should regard any man who deliberately flouts the directions explicitly laid down not two hundred years ago but to-day as a very grave offender. How an 'offender' should be treated is a question quite separate from the Rubrics, and you have expressed to me in no doubtful terms your own opinion of its difficulty, but the fundamental thing to remember is that the number of offenders will be, as we firmly believe, comparatively few and the difficulty of the situation proportionately reduced.

The interest in the country was extraordinary. All through the year the papers were full of news, speeches, and letters: and an immense flood of pamphlets was produced besides. There were four Bishops against the Book—Norwich, Birmingham, Worcester, and also Exeter. The Bishop of Norwich advocated a division of the measure into two portions, the controversial and the uncontroversial—which had the fatal defect of leaving the substantial problem with which the Assembly was asked to deal unsolved. There were objections to the Book from very different camps—that it was too modernist, too old-fashioned, too rigid, too loose, that there were too many prayers for the dead, and too few prayers for the King. But the crucial charges were briefly that the new Prayer Book changed the doctrine of the Church of England so as to be untrue to the Reformation, and that, even if it became lawful, it would not be obeyed. The debate in the Church Assembly took place on July 5 and 6, 1927. The measure authorized the use of the Revised Prayer Book, known as the Deposited Book (because deposited with the Clerk of the Parliaments for purposes of identification). The use was to be optional. The old Prayer Book remained as before: it was not superseded. The Deposited Book was not a compilation of additions and deviations by themselves but, as desired by the House of Laity, a *Composite* Book, containing within its covers both the proposed additions and deviations, and also the whole of the existing Book of Common Prayer with a few slight exceptions. The Archbishop himself moved the final approval of the Prayer Book Measure. His crucial words were:

> You may take it from me as absolutely certain that the bishops will require obedience to the new rules and will do their utmost to secure it.

But he again refused to specify the methods. With regard to doctrine he repeated what he said in Convocation:

> If I thought that what we are suggesting to-day would mean or involve any marked re-setting of the distinctive position of the Church of England, I should not be standing here to advocate your acceptance of what we lay before you. My Churchmanship is the Churchmanship which has found it possible, yes, and desirable, to include Hooker and Jewel and Andrewes, and Cosin and Waterland and Simeon and Keble, and I am persuaded that we are not departing therefrom to the right hand or to the left.

The attack was led by Dr. Darwell Stone for the extreme Anglo-Catholics, and by Sir William Joynson Hicks, the Bishop of Norwich, and Sir Thomas Inskip for the Evangelicals. It was strong and determined—and Dr. Stone's quotation of a statement by 700 Anglo-Catholic priests of their most complete and uncompromising opposition, afforded a further argument for the Evangelicals. In the end the measure was passed by a very large majority in all three Houses as follows:

	For	*Against*
Bishops	34	4
Clergy	253	37
Laity	230	92
	517	133

III

The next step lay with Parliament. But in the meantime the agitation to influence the votes of members of both Houses grew apace. The Archbishop of Canterbury addressed a private meeting of Peers: and the Archbishop of York a private meeting of M.P.s. Dr. Stone and some of his Anglo-Catholic colleagues, as well as the extreme Evangelicals, alike did their best to persuade Parliament to reject the measure. An attempt was made to prohibit the measure in the High Court, which Sir John Simon successfully resisted on behalf of the Church Assembly. Nonconformist opposition also grew in spite of the friendly attitude of Dr. Carnegie Simpson and Dr. Scott Lidgett. And fuel was added by a declaration on behalf of 1,400 Anglo-Catholic members of the Federation of Catholic Priests, that, if the Prayer Book Measure passed in its present form, they would feel justified in the following practices: Communion from the Reserved Sacrament of the whole, as well as the sick; corporate Devotions; Reservation in one kind; and perpetual Reservation in spite of the prohibition of the diocesan.

The Archbishop was again pressed on the question of the Bishops' attitude to clergy who might still refuse obedience supposing the Prayer Book Measure were approved by Parliament and received the Royal Assent. After consulting the whole body of Bishops he obtained their consent to the publication of a letter, containing a new assurance, to Canon V. F. Storr, who had written on behalf of a number of Liberal Evangelicals. This letter repeated the pledge given in the Church Assembly. It was the strongest statement made by the Archbishop during the whole discussion, and though he still declined to state the methods by which obedience was in fact to be secured, he made the important announcement that the Bishops would act together in the matter. The letter appeared in *The Times* on October 31:

The ARCHBISHOP OF CANTERBURY *to the* REV. CANON V. F. STORR

29 October 1927.

I did not speak lightly when, on July 6, I publicly used the words:

> You may take it from me as absolutely certain that the Bishops will require obedience to the new rules and will do their utmost to secure it.

I was sure at the time that I was speaking correctly, but I have now, in conjunction with the Archbishop of York, had an opportunity of meeting or communicating with all the diocesan Bishops of both Provinces, 43 in number, and I am able to tell you that I have obtained the concurrence of every one of them (except the Bishop of Norwich) in reiterating the announcement I have referred to. It is obvious that the methods by which this clear and definite intention will be fulfilled cannot be specified in detail beforehand; but those whom you represent and indeed all others who are interested in the matter, may rest assured that what is laid down in the new Book will, if the Measure receive the Royal Assent, be faithfully administered, and that the Bishops will act together in the matter.

On November 24, 1927, the Ecclesiastical Committee in a lengthy report advised the Houses of Parliament that in their opinion the measure should proceed. The most important passage in the Report was as follows:

> The Committee would not recommend any interference with the decisions of the Church Assembly on matters so clearly lying within the province of that Assembly as the doctrines and ceremonial of the Church, unless persuaded that any proposed change of doctrine were of so vital a description as materially to alter the general character of the National Church as recognised in the Act of Settlement and by the oath sworn by His Majesty at his Coronation, whereby His Majesty has promised to maintain the Protestant Reformed Religion established by law.
>
> The Committee have carefully examined the Measure and the Deposited Book from this point of view, as well as the arguments of the objectors in relation thereto, and the replies of the Bishop of Chelmsford and other authorities of the Church. Without entering into argument on doctrinal questions, but having considered all that has been laid before them and the expressed opinion of the Archbishops and Bishops as to the doctrinal position of the Church of England, the Committee take the view that no change of doctrine of constitutional importance is involved, that accordingly the 'constitutional rights of all His Majesty's subjects' are not in this respect prejudicially affected, and there is nothing to modify the purport of the Coronation Oath.

On December 12, the Archbishop moved in the House of Lords 'that the Prayer Book Measure be presented to His Majesty for Royal Assent'. The House was crowded and interest intense. The Archbishop spoke for over an hour, and in most persuasive manner. He began by referring to the position of Parliament:

> We hear words which I think windy and even foolish, to the effect that this is not really a matter for Parliament, that the Church has spoken its own voice decidedly and that the duty of Parliament is to endorse what the Church has said. I dissent altogether from that view and dissociate myself from those statements. We are acting under what is known as the Enabling Act. . . . Every member of this House has, in my view, his absolute right to vote

freely upon a matter of this kind and it would be impertinence on my part to suggest anything else.

It seemed a strong—perhaps too strong a statement: but he qualified it in a moment by insisting on the moral aspect of the matter, the need of a man before voting exercising 'very extreme care' and reflecting 'what would be the consequence in the country of the rejection of a united wish officially given by a united Church'. (It must of course be remembered that the successful opposition afterwards claimed that the Church was not united.) He struck a personal note:

> The attack has been largely against myself. I am an old man. I have been a Bishop nearly 35 years and an Archbishop for nearly 25 years and my life has not been lived in private or silently or unrecorded. Standing here I assure your Lordships to-day that I am absolutely unconscious of any departure from the principles of the reformed Church of England to which I declared allegiance at my ordination 52 years ago and I have striven to maintain them ever since.

He then recounted the history of the revision, calling attention once more to the words of the Royal Commission that 'the law of public worship in the Church of England is too narrow for the religious life of the present generation': and emphasized the representative character of the Church Assembly and its laity:

> They do not profess to represent the people of England, but they do profess to represent the Church of England, the people who care about these matters and go to church, who want to use their Prayer Book, who care about the form that Book should take, who understand the question and who are the people really qualified to speak.

He gave an account of the main parts of the revision, including the Order of Holy Communion and Reservation, where the most important difference lay—but refusing to 'go into such profound doctrine as the presence of our Lord, in argument on the floor of this House'. And as to doctrine he said again:

> In my deliberate judgment nothing that we have suggested makes any change in the doctrinal position of the Church of England. The balance of emphasis may here and there be somewhat altered, but that mere fact will disquiet no one who remembers

what different aspects of the truth have been emphasized by recognised Church leaders during the last four hundred years.

He pleaded that the adoption of the Book would 'enormously facilitate the work of the Bishops'; and repeated his public promise 'that the Bishops mean to act together in this matter, and that they intend this Book to be obeyed and intend to use all their efforts to secure that it shall be obeyed'. And finally—and most characteristically of his whole attitude to Prayer Book Revision and the work of the Church—he took still larger ground and urged 'that the giving to us of this Book would mean the liberation of the Church from the great mass of those petty strifes which have troubled us up and down the country in the past'.

We have talked about rubrics and special prayers and differences of view on important questions, but in my personal opinion there is a larger issue at stake than any of these. The Church of England, for which to-night I am spokesman, has a trust immeasurably great and sacred. From the depths of our hearts we want to use it aright. We want to use for the bettering of English life every ounce of the strength which by God's benediction is ours. We want that strength so consecrated and so united that it shall be irresistible for what we desire to effect in our country's life.

The debate lasted three days. All through it, Privy Councillors and M.P.s were coming to and fro, and the public galleries were thronged. There had been nothing like it for years. It had been feared that the Lords would be more difficult to win than the Commons. Nearly all the speeches reached a high standard, but the honours easily lay with the Archbishop and his supporters.

In the end, the Resolution was carried by 241 votes to 88.

The last act of the drama was played next day, December 15, in the House of Commons. The large majority in the House of Lords seemed of good omen. The Archbishop himself had left the choice of speakers and the whole conduct of the debate to the House of Commons supporters; and by their wish he invited Mr. Bridgeman to move the required Resolution, as a popular country gentleman who had done well for the Government in difficult waters as First Lord of the Admiralty.

That afternoon the House and the galleries were crowded; and there was an extraordinary buzz of excitement everywhere. The Archbishop sat over the clock, and surveyed the scene. Near him was the Archbishop of York, and not far away sat Free Church leaders. Soon after three-thirty, the debate began. But it was an unhappy start. Mr. Bridgeman had been told to present the measure in its broad issues, leaving others to go into detail should it prove necessary. No one could have predicted the course the debate would take. He was irritated by interruptions into saying: 'I can imagine that those who dislike the Church of England may wish to reject this measure.' These unfortunate words provoked the first sign of the coming turmoil; and Mr. Bridgeman sat down almost without having attempted any real explanation of the case.

Sir W. Joynson Hicks followed—and at once directed the debate to far more controversial ground. He did the very thing which the Archbishop had refused to do—on the floor of the house. He turned the occasion into one of high doctrinal dispute. Before ten minutes had passed, he had kindled the first sparks of the fire which was to consume the new Book, the fire of the fear of Rome:

> It may be quite true that the new scheme is right. It may be equally true that the doctrines of the Church of Rome are right; but it is quite clear that the doctrines of the Church of Rome, or any doctrines approximating to those of the Church of Rome, are not the doctrines which were established by us at the time of the Reformation. I do not propose to say one word against the doctrines of the Church of Rome; they are not in dispute here. All I have to say is that they are not the doctrines of our Church, and that there are many things done in our Church to-day which, as the Royal Commission itself said, are 'on the Romeward side of the dividing line'.

Yet it was the old Prayer Book quite as much as the new which taught the doctrines which Joynson Hicks deplored. And, so far as Romanist tendencies were concerned, no notice was taken of the fact that the Romanizers were in league with his supporters. But the attack proved abundantly successful, the speaker (so the Archbishop notes afterwards) 'marshalling his facts with facility, and producing unanswerable conclusions if only his premises could be accepted as reasonable and accurate'. And it was aided by the reproaches which Joynson Hicks cast at the Archbishop, as he looked up at him over the clock, weighting them with quotations from former charges or speeches or reports, because episcopal authority had not been exercised either sternly or decisively (as the Archbishop had promised, when Bishop of Winchester, thirty years ago)—'The sands are still running out to-day, and nothing has been done. We are asked to trust the Bishops. Therein lies the difficulty.'

The speech of the evening, so far as votes were concerned, was made by Mr. Rosslyn Mitchell, member for Paisley. It was extraordinarily eloquent. The Archbishop noted:

> The most effective speech of all as regards votes was, I think, Rosslyn Mitchell's. It was a simply ultra-Protestant harangue, with no real knowledge of the subject, but owing its power to a rhetorical presentment of no-Popery phrases and arguments of the sort which are to be found in *Barnaby Rudge*, when the Lord George Gordon Riots set London aflame.

There were other speeches, effective in their way, against the measure, like Sir John Simon's: and some speeches of a thoughtful character for the measure. But the Archbishop, in the gallery, listened to the debate with increasing dismay. There was no one to argue—nor even to explain. All hopes lay on Lord Hugh Cecil. But in vain:

> For some reason or other he completely failed. He was nervous and obviously was bitterly chagrined when the House began to thin.

The Prime Minister spoke in support, but the tide against the measure was too strong, and when Sir Thomas Inskip closed for the opposition, its fate was sealed. The measure was rejected by 238 votes to 205.[1]

The defeat was sensational. Sympathy for the Archbishop was universal, and many letters, private and public, came assuring him of admiration and affection. And he himself never once spoke a wounded, much less a bitter word; and though his disappointment was keen, he immediately issued an appeal 'that

[1] Considerable confusion exists as to the division figures in this case. The *Journals of the House of Commons* (vol. clxxxii, p. 378) give the figures as Yeas 205, Noes 247. With this the Day to Day series of the *Parliamentary Debates* (vol. 211, No. 139, col. 2662) agrees; as does *The Times* of Friday, 16 December 1927. But the *Parliamentary Debates, Official Report* (vol. 211, 5th series, col. 25652) gives Ayes 205, Noes 230; and prints a detailed division list, in which the number of names voting with the Noes totals 238. With this figure of 238 *The Times* of 17 December 1927 agrees, giving also a list of persons voting. It seems safe, therefore, to regard 238 as the accurate figure of the Noes.

patience and charity may be exercised, and precipitate words and acts avoided'.

What should be the next step?

In a single hectic night the House of Commons had apparently destroyed the work of more than twenty years. But it could not quite be left there: for thirty-nine out of forty-three Bishops, most of the clergy, the representative laity from the dioceses, almost all the Diocesan Conferences, a majority of English M.P.s[1] and a majority of the House of Lords had recommended the changes; and whatever else might be the result of the Prayer Book Measure, its existence, thus recommended, made it quite impossible for any Bishop to discipline a clergyman who adopted those parts of the Revised Book which were considered objectionable. There was therefore much to be said, as Lord Birkenhead and others argued, for allowing the Book, and letting the next step rest with the Legislature.

The Bishops, however, decided otherwise. On December 23, the two Archbishops issued a statement on behalf of the Bishops, containing the following words:

> It was within the right of the House of Commons to reject the Measure. On the other hand, mere acquiescence in its decision would be in our judgment inconsistent with the responsibilities of the Church as a spiritual society.
>
> The Bishops fully recognize that there are circumstances in which it would be their duty to take action in accordance with the Church's inherent spiritual authority. We realize this duty, and are ready, if need be, to fulfil it. But we believe that the recent decision of the House of Commons was influenced by certain avoidable misunderstandings as to the character of the proposals before it, and we cannot, therefore, take the responsibility of accepting as final the vote of December 15.
>
> The House of Bishops has accordingly resolved to re-introduce the Measure into the Church Assembly as soon as possible, with such changes, and such changes only, as may tend to remove misapprehensions and to make clearer and more explicit its intentions and limitations.

Such a reintroduction was a hazardous measure, and the removal of avoidable misunderstandings involved many heart-

[1] The Division list showed that amongst members representing English constituencies there was a clear majority in favour of the measure. (Roman Catholics abstained from voting.)

burnings, and lost the support of certain Anglo-Catholics without much pacifying of Evangelicals. The debate in the House of Commons had certainly revealed curious misunderstandings of what were by comparison details, which the Bishops believed they could meet. The Bishops had, however, miscalculated the amount of Protestant prejudice behind the adverse vote, which they could not hope to satisfy. The crux of the matter was perpetual Reservation. The Archbishop was himself very nervous about retaining it—and many of his friends begged him to let it disappear. Sir Thomas Inskip also saw the Archbishop, at the latter's request (January 18, 1928). The Archbishop noted:

> I found him greatly troubled about the Prayer Book situation and I think quite genuinely anxious to get things settled, if it can possibly be done, without compromising what he regards as fundamental principles. He told me that he had come to the conclusion that, on the whole, he would be prepared to assent to a great deal that he dislikes in the new Book provided we could get rid of the continuous Reservation which the Book, under certain conditions, sanctions. I pressed him as to Vestments, the Alternative Communion Office, and even the Reservation for the Sick under the first rubric. All of these he said that he would, though somewhat reluctantly, be prepared to agree to, and I think he went so far as to say that he would press those who act with him in the Assembly or in Parliament to take the same view. But on the question of continuous Reservation he could not possibly give way.

The suggestion, however, was really impossible. If Reservation were to be included in any form, some provision for continuous Reservation was inevitable. Otherwise, not only would the general body of Anglo-Catholics, extreme and moderate alike, have been irretrievably alienated, but in the opinion of large numbers of thoughtful church-people, as well as critics and observers, too great a surrender would have been made to Parliament in a spiritual matter. 'We give not to our Princes', says the 37th Article, 'the ministry either of God's Word, or of the Sacraments.' The Archbishop did, however, persuade the Bishops to make the conditions of Continuous Reservation more definite, with the result that they appeared more rigorous. He also persuaded the Bishops to insist on the arrangements with regard to Reservation being incorporated in Rubrics instead of Rules. The relevant Rubrics, thus amended and extended, are as follows—attention should be specially drawn to the opening words of the first of these three Rubrics:

> If the Bishop is satisfied that in connexion with hospitals, or in time of common sickness, or in the special circumstances of any particular Parish, the provisions of the preceding rubrick are not sufficient, and that there is need of further provision in order that sick and dying persons may not lack the benefit of the most comfortable Sacrament of the Body and Blood of Christ, he may to that end give his licence to the Priest, to reserve at the open Communion so much of the consecrated Bread and Wine as is needed for the purpose. Whenever such licence is granted or refused, the Minister, or the people as represented in the Parochial Church Council, may refer the question to the Archbishop and Bishops of the Province.
>
> The consecrated Bread and Wine set apart under either of the two preceding rubricks shall be reserved only for the Communion of the Sick, shall be administered in both kinds, and shall be used for no other purpose whatever. There shall be no service or ceremony in connexion with the Sacrament so reserved, nor shall it be exposed or removed except in order to be received in Communion, or otherwise reverently consumed.
>
> The consecrated Bread and Wine thus set apart shall be reserved in an aumbry or safe. The aumbry shall (according as the Bishop shall direct) be set in the North or South wall of the sanctuary of the church or of any chapel thereof, or, if need be, in the wall of some other part of the church approved by the Bishop, provided that it shall not be immediately behind or above a Holy Table. The door of the aumbry shall be kept locked, and opened only when it is necessary to move or replace the consecrated Elements for the purposes of Communion or renewal. The consecrated Bread and Wine shall be renewed at least once a week.

With these and a few other modifications (including the insertion of the Black Rubric at the end of the Alternative Order of Holy Communion), the new Measure was submitted first to the Convocations and then to the Church Assembly.

At the time, there were many heartburnings on account of the haste with which the policy of going to Parliament again was adopted; and there was a curious want of consultation between the House of Bishops and leaders of either of the other Houses or of leading Churchmen of different schools outside the Church Assembly. The imposition of fresh limitations was resented by Anglo-Catholics—while some Evangelicals who had supported the old Book now changed their minds. And in the end the majorities in both Convocations and the Church Assembly were appreciably smaller.[1] The fusillade of pamphlets continued—and the Archbishop himself contributed to their number,[2] though, perhaps because too late in the day, his own brochure, while straightforward and disarming, did not influence votes.

On June 13, 1928, the Solicitor-General, Sir Boyd Merriman, opened the debate in the House of Commons—in a clear and excellent speech. This time the debate lasted two days. The Archbishop again listened in the gallery, though unwell:

> I sat through the debate in the Commons notwithstanding my rather invalid condition, and in the face of grumbled remonstrance from Barlow and Cassidy, but I felt it rather vital to see the discussion through to a finish. I consider that the debate of this last week was in every respect superior to the debate on Dec. 15th. The tone was on the whole higher, the mere rodomontade was less, and there were speeches of general excellence, notably Hugh Cecil's, the Duchess of Atholl's, and Lady Iveagh's. Joynson Hicks was necessarily, I suppose, rather unfair, for he had to make the best of what I honestly think was not a very good case. And the same applies to Inskip, but I have no real ground of complaint against either of them, except in one matter of Inskip's speech about which I have written to him.

The particular point which Sir Thomas Inskip, winding up for the opponents, made with icy effect at the close of his speech was this:

> We have been challenged to produce a policy. The hon. Member who spoke immediately before me challenged me to refer to what I said in the previous Debate as to accepting nine-tenths of this Book. He asked me what I would do. I will tell him a little piece of history—it is hardly right to call it history, but a statement of what I have done in that connection. I was prepared to take a great responsibility upon myself, which perhaps I had no right to

[1]

	For	*Against*
Canterbury Upper House	20	6
,, Lower House	126	48
York Upper House	unanimous	
,, Lower House	50	19

Church Assembly	*For*	*Against*
Bishops . . .	32	2
Clergy . . .	183	59
Laity	181	92
	396	153

[2] *The Prayer Book: Our Hope and Meaning*, Hodder and Stoughton.

> do. I ran the risk of being told I was sacrificing my principles to expediency. With the concurrence of the Home Secretary and the present Lord Chancellor, I went to the Archbishop of Canterbury and told him that, with whatever influence we had, we were prepared to assent to a Measure passing through this House provided it did not include this perpetual Reservation, which is the keystone of the system. In his wisdom the Archbishop of Canterbury perhaps thought that offer unworthy of further consideration. It was honestly made. I believe if the Home Secretary and the Lord Chancellor and myself—I hope the House will not think this is taking too much upon us—had expressed that opinion, I believe that we should have had enough of our hon. friends to go with us to ensure the passage of such a Measure through this House of Commons.

As a matter of fact the Archbishop had not so understood Sir Thomas, even when he had again visited Lambeth, after the first interview described above, though Sir Thomas clearly felt that he had made the offer plain. But for reasons already given, acceptance of such offer was not practicable. It was in fact—though in a different sense from the speaker's—'the keystone of the system'. Still the making of the point at the very last minute, and the suggestion which it contained that something had been concealed by the Archbishop, was decisive—and, what made it especially unfortunate, there was no means of replying. The Prime Minister followed, and had the last word, but he did not succeed in averting defeat.

In the end, the House of Commons rejected the second Prayer Book Measure by 266 votes to 220—a slightly larger majority.

Once again the House of Bishops met to consider the results of the defeat. There were some who urged that the Convocations and Church Assembly and Bishops should ignore the Commons' verdict and should arm the new Prayer Book with the fullest Church authority in their power, and see what happened. In the end the Bishops agreed unanimously to the following statement:

> It is a fundamental principle that the Church—that is, the Bishops together with the Clergy and the Laity—must in the last resort, when its mind has been fully ascertained, retain its inalienable right, in loyalty to our Lord and Saviour Jesus Christ, to formulate its Faith in Him and to arrange the expression of that Holy Faith in its forms of worship.

The Archbishop, commending the statement to the Assembly, said:

> I venture to believe that no one can challenge that principle as a principle however loyal he be to the true relation which that principle bears in a Christian land, and ours is a Christian land, to the recognised constitutional rights of the State or nation as such. I do not regard that principle of our fundamental loyalty to Christ and its full expression as in the least inconsistent with, or traversed by, the national position which the life-history of England has, thank God, accorded to our Church and has steadily maintained under all the changes of Parliamentary conditions. But whatever may have been the intentions of those who voted, the recent decision has troubled many consciences and has raised anxious questions.
>
> It is our firm hope that, when the facts have been quietly considered, some strong and capable committee of statesmen and Churchmen may be appointed to weigh afresh the provisions of the existing law in order to see whether any readjustment is required for the maintenance, in the conditions of our own age, of the principle which we have here and now reasserted.

In reality such a statement, thus delivered by the Archbishop, was a courageous statement for one with Dr. Davidson's past traditions to make at the end of a long life; but it did not go so far as some would have liked, and in particular the Bishop of Durham considered that the fact that it could be accepted by the Bishop of Norwich, the principal opponent of the Prayer Book Measure, deprived it of all vital meaning. The Archbishop read it to the Church Assembly on July 9. His speech introducing it was ordered to be entered in the Minutes. That speech again was too calm and moderate to satisfy those who felt that the authority of the Church had been desperately challenged. The Archbishop realized the deep interest in the faith and worship of the Church which the discussions in Parliament had shown —he recognized the seriousness of the consequences, and the impossibility of drifting. But he refused to believe that the House of Commons was 'arrogantly claiming to take in hand the absolute control of the belief and worship of the Church of England':

> I venture, while carefully regarding the matter with all the gravity that it demands, to express my own judgment that no such far-reaching challenge was intended. If the House of Commons, by

its vote on June 14th—a vote which I deplore—is supposed to have flouted or violated the well-proven working arrangement of Church and State, the House did it with no intent of a constitutional kind. Many of those who rejected the resolution believed, however mistakenly, that they were voicing the real underlying wish of a majority of Church folk in England.

The root of the trouble was that, in exercising its unquestionably legal power, the House of Commons had 'departed, lamentably as it seems to me, from the reasonable spirit in which alone the balanced relationship of Church and State in England can be satisfactorily and harmoniously carried on':

> While claiming to appraise what can be called Church opinion, it deliberately traversed the declared desire of the Church's official and representative bodies—Bishops, Clergy, and Laity. It declined to respect the wishes of the solid central body of Church opinion duly expressed and recorded both centrally and locally throughout the land, and allowed itself, on the contrary, to be influenced by the representations of the strange combination of vehement opposite groups or factions of Churchmen united only in their resolve to get the Measure and the Book defeated.

But the Archbishop refused to admit that all the wearisome work was wasted. He appealed to the younger members of the Assembly to see that its very perplexities made it fruitful, and reminding them how, years hence 'across years which I shall not see', they would look back on 1928 as a year almost unique in English Church History, he added:

> I pray God that in that backward look you may find nothing in your record of here and now to be sorry for, nothing of narrowness or of obstinate self-will either as individuals or as groups, nothing of the spirit 'it must be my way or no way at all', nothing but the memory of a whole-hearted resolve to go forward unitedly in God's service as Christ's men, strong in the power of prayer and conscious of His Captaincy alone. If that spirit can permeate our whole ranks now, and if we can welcome close to our side, shoulder to shoulder, in the onward march, those who like ourselves have made their sectional preferences—even cherished preferences—give place to the larger unity, then, if that come true, our efforts, our sore disappointments, even our unhappy rivalries, may prove to have been not in vain.

It was the last session of the Church Assembly over which the

Archbishop presided, and the closing words of this speech fitly express the spirit which he had sought to make prevail during the whole of his twenty-five years as Primate of all England.

IV

Why did the Prayer Book Measures fail? We are perhaps still a little too near to give a satisfactory reply. But two or three reflections may be of service.

First and most strong was the ancient fear of Rome—a fear which flares up in an astonishing way at intervals in our history. It was the fear men felt at the time of the Gunpowder Plot; the fear which inspired the Lord George Gordon riots; the fear which lay behind Lord John Russell's Ecclesiastical Titles Bill, 1851, and the agitation against the restoration of the Roman hierarchy. It was behind the heated controversies about ritualism with which the present century opened—when Sir William Harcourt clashed his armour and Parliament was stirred. And the Archbishop was under no illusion about its influence in the House of Commons debates of 1927 and 1928. After the second rejection he wrote:

> One kept asking as the talk went on, 'what are really the facts or motives which will affect the issue?' I think they are not to be sought within the House of Commons, but in the country at large. I suppose there is no force on earth so determined and uncompromising as the force of the No-Popery cry in England, and it does not need any knowledge of history for backing it except the general sense with which England is impregnated. We suffered so much from Rome that everything which can be depicted, however unfairly, as having a Romeward trend is condemned *ipso facto* without need of argument. I honestly think that that spirit is much more answerable for our defeat than any detailed attacks upon the Prayer Book in its various parts. The purveyors of literature on the subject, and especially the Protestant Alliance, played down to this prejudice in the literature they produced, and they were wise in their generation.

The fear was strong enough: it showed the deep Protestantism of English people; but it was very irrational.

The second reason was the disunity of Churchmen. Time after time it was said that, if only the Church could present a united demand, there would be no question but that Parliament would grant it. This reasoning appears more plausible. But its substance is not as great as it seems at first sight. In a matter of such profound religious interest, division was inevitable. The majorities in favour of the revision were composed of the instructed Church leaders and communicants—those, that is to say, who knew something of the problem and what was at stake, and had the responsibilities; although it must in fairness be added that not a few distinguished liturgical scholars, such as Dr. F. E. Brightman, were not altogether happy about the liturgical quality of important parts of the new Book.

The real question was whether a vital religious movement was to be given an honourable place in the Church of England. Did Sir Thomas Inskip and his friends really wish the members of this movement to be driven from the Church, as the Methodists had been driven? It was a question which was never fairly and openly faced—as the Archbishop's own Memorandum shows, though he realized its importance:

> My own thoughts turn to a time nearly 200 years ago, when the vagaries and excitements of Methodists irritated the Bishops and clergy so much that they made no real effort to prevent those enthusiasts from going off at a tangent and fashioning a new Church or Churches of their own, Methodists and Independents and Wesleyan Methodists and Primitive Methodists and so on. Nearly every one now says—'Surely if the Bishops of that time had taken a larger view the splendid work which evangelists have done outside the Church for 150 years might have been done inside the Church to the steadying of vagaries and the infusion of spiritual life into the Church.' I want to ask Inskip whether he thinks a similar criticism might be current in the year 2000, if he and his friends can get the Church authorities of to-day so to act as to force Anglo-Catholics of an advanced kind to form some kind of organisation of their own, and weld together men of intensest devotion, great pastoral effectiveness, and deep piety, whom the Church ought never to have lost. I think of saying something to that effect when I have to debate the matter, if we reach a really critical stage. The problem may reduce itself to this—'Will you support the inclusion within the Church of a body of deeply devout men who by temperament or training or belief are irrevocably tied to a view of the Holy Communion which seems to you quite erroneous? You say nothing will induce you to do so. Are you sure that you are thus acting in accordance with the Holy Spirit, or that your action would be justified when the history of this

century is completed?' I have not said this publicly, and hardly to any one privately, for it is the kind of argument which, if vulgarised, might become I think untenable, but after abundant thought it is the direction in which my own thoughts tend when I am trying to frame in the sacred sense a policy pleasing to God, and consonant with loyalty to the principles of the Church of Christ. It may all look differently a few months hence. That is how it suggests itself to me at this Epiphany. [January, 1928.]

The fact that the Archbishop did not himself bring this argument forward, which was really the most powerful argument, in a vigorous way, forces us to ask how far his own leadership was responsible for the failure. It must be admitted at once that the Archbishop's lack of personal interest in the main question at issue—which has been already brought out in the extracts from his papers—was itself a great handicap. Considering the complexities of the subject, the keen passions on either side, profound conviction or deep enthusiasm were necessary to successful generalship. He lacked them. He had great experience, ample memory—and was a first-rate chairman. But he had not the interest in the subject itself which was necessary for effective command and direction. It was too much a matter of expediency (in the right sense of the word): and when passions are aroused on either side, expediency is not enough. The Archbishop could not bring himself to believe that the revision of the Prayer Book was in fact a vital matter to the Church. Not believing it himself, he lacked the fire to convince others, and especially the House of Commons. To acknowledge this is not to say that the Archbishop was wrong, because of this lack of interest or conviction. His religious interests were of a more general, even a broader character. But his inability to devote his best mind to what was first the Rubrics, and then the Prayer Book question, prevented him from giving a decided lead to the Church itself, and from pressing for a swifter and much less ambitious revision—when this was possible, in the earlier stages before the War. That want of deep interest and fire also made it impossible for him to go to Parliament and say that the Church, in its deliberative assemblies, had made up its mind after twenty-two years of labour, and claimed from Parliament the statutory ratification of the Church's measure if it wished that kind of Church to remain the Established Church.

There was another reason which played an important part in the rejection of the measure in Parliament. This was the Archbishop's unwillingness to give definite pledges with regard to the enforcement of obedience. He knew the importance of the reform of Ecclesiastical Courts: he had pressed it indeed ever since he had been chaplain to Archbishop Tait. He would in some ways himself have preferred the reform to have been carried through before the revision of the Prayer Book. And a very valuable Report of a Special Commission on Ecclesiastical Courts of which the Archbishop of York was chairman was published in 1926. He acquiesced, however, in its consideration being postponed till after the Revision, accepting the argument that the law which the Courts must administer ought to be settled before the Courts were reformed. But apart from the Courts he was asked by Joynson Hicks to give the pledges with regard to discipline which we have noted. Under pressure he went a certain distance, but not far enough to be of service. He would not say that the Bishops either (as Joynson Hicks desired) would refuse to promote men who were disobedient, or (as Dr. Carnegie Simpson desired) 'would unitedly withdraw all spiritual episcopal recognition from any plain transgressors of the limits laid down in this book'. One reason for the Archbishop's unwillingness to give such pledges was, no doubt, the belief, whether right or wrong, that they would be regarded by the Anglo-Catholics as a threat, and involve the withdrawal of the support which all but the extremists gave.

But, when all this is said, something more fundamental remains. The deepest reason for the failure was that the whole method was from the very beginning wrong. The revision of Church services and the enforcement of ecclesiastical discipline are different things. A revision of worship, of common prayer, which is intended from the start to be used as an instrument for stopping disobedience is at any rate not likely to produce the happiest results in the realm of worship! And side by side with this, the recommendation of the Royal Commission to consider the preparation of a new Ornaments Rubric 'with a view to its enactment by Parliament'—and to frame modifications in Church services 'with a view to their enactment by Parliament'—started all on a false track. Before ever he became Archbishop, Dr. Davidson had declared his abhorrence of detailed discussion by Parliament of proposed changes in Church Services.[1] A year after he succeeded to the Primacy he made a strong appeal to Mr. Balfour as Prime Minister against a proposed reference of ritual questions to a Parliamentary Select Committee. He did this on the ground that it was on sacramental questions that ritual difficulties ultimately turned. He quoted the argument of leading clergy that the strain between the Parliament and the Church 'might become intolerable and preponderate over the national gain of Establishment if Parliament were to exercise its undisputed rights to the full extent that it logically can'. By such arguments he persuaded Mr. Balfour to appoint a Royal Commission on Ecclesiastical Discipline instead of a Parliamentary Select Committee.[2] Again, when the Royal Commission reported in favour of issuing Letters of Business to the Convocations with instructions to consider the preparation of an Ornaments Rubric and to frame modifications in the existing law relating to the conduct of Divine Service, 'with a view to their enactment by Parliament', the Archbishop, who was mainly responsible for those recommendations, reminded Convocation that it was the requirement of Parliamentary sanction that was 'the very crux of our difficulties'. At the time, the Archbishop hoped that some method might be found for securing Parliamentary sanction 'without involving discussions which would be quite obviously and manifestly unsuited to Parliament if they necessitated discussions there upon the details either of worship or of doctrine'.[3] The Archbishop's fears were more than confirmed. The very discussions on worship and doctrine which he so earnestly deprecated, took place in a most vehement form. And if one thing is clearer than another, it is that the present parliamentary method of legislation in questions of public worship is not and cannot be a satisfactory method.

NOTE

To carry the record of the Prayer Book controversy beyond Archbishop Davidson, it should be said that at the end of 1928 the Prayer Book of 1928 was published by the privileged presses as an ordinary book, with a note stating what had happened in the Church Assembly and Parliament, adding, 'The publication of this Book does not

[1] See p. 328. [2] See p. 460. [3] See p. 652.

directly or indirectly imply that it can be regarded as authorised for use in churches'. Between the autumn of 1928 and July 1929, most of the Bishops consulted the clergy and laity in their Diocesan Conferences. As a result, in July 1929 (with the support of the Lower House), the Upper House of Convocation of Canterbury recognised the impossibility of bringing back the conduct of public worship strictly within the limits of the Prayer Book of 1662, and resolved 'that in the exercise of their administrative discretion they will in their respective dioceses consider the circumstances and needs of parishes severally, and give counsel and directions' in conformity with the following principles:—

'(1) That during the present emergency and until further order be taken the Bishops, having in view the fact that the Convocations of Canterbury and York gave their consent to the proposals for deviations from and additions to the Book of 1662, as set forth in the Book of 1928, being laid before the National Assembly of the Church of England for Final Approval, and that the National Assembly voted Final Approval to these proposals, cannot regard as inconsistent with loyalty to the principles of the Church of England the use of such additions or deviations as fall within the limits of these proposals. For the same reason they must regard as inconsistent with Church Order the use of any other deviations from or additions to the Forms and Orders contained in the Book of 1662.

'(2) That accordingly the Bishops, in the exercise of that legal or administrative discretion, which belongs to each Bishop in his own Diocese, will be guided by the proposals set forth in the Book of 1928, and will endeavour to secure that the practices which are consistent neither with the Book of 1662 nor with the Book of 1928 shall cease.

Further—

'(3) That the Bishops, in the exercise of their authority, will only permit the ordinary use of any of the Forms and Orders contained in the Book of 1928 if they are satisfied that such use would have the good will of the people as represented in the Parochial Church Council, and that in the case of the Occasional Offices the consent of the parties concerned will always be obtained.'

It is on these lines that Bishops have been administering their dioceses since 1928, 'during the present emergency, and until further order be taken'. In the meantime with a view to such further order being taken, the Archbishops have appointed a Commission on the relations between Church and State in pursuance of a Resolution passed by the Church Assembly of February 5, 1930. The Resolution, which contained the Terms of Reference of the Commission, was as follows:

> 'That whereas, in the words addressed to the Church Assembly on July 2nd, 1928, by Archbishop Davidson, with the concurrence of the whole body of the Diocesan Bishops, "it is a fundamental principle that the Church, that is, the Bishops, together with the Clergy and Laity, must in the last resort, when its mind has been fully ascertained, retain its inalienable right, in loyalty to our Lord and Saviour Jesus Christ, to formulate its faith in Him and to arrange the expression of that Holy Faith in its form of worship";
>
> 'It is desirable that a Commission should be appointed to enquire into the present relations of Church and State, and particularly how far the principle, stated above, is able to receive effective application in present circumstances in the Church of England, and what legal and constitutional changes, if any, are needed in order to maintain or to secure its effective application; and that the Archbishops be requested to appoint a Commission for this purpose.'

Viscount Cecil was appointed Chairman of the Commission. The Report of the Commission (which was unanimous) was published in 1935, under the title *Church and State* (2 vols.).

CHAPTER LXXXIII

RESIGNATION

> Let me not live . . .
> After my flame lacks oil, to be the snuff
> Of younger spirits.
>
> SHAKESPEARE, *All's Well that Ends Well*, I. ii.

IF any one were to look through the newspaper-cutting books at Lambeth for the ten years after the War, he would find an almost regular reference in the autumn and winter months to the impending resignation of the Archbishop of Canterbury, and queries as to his successor. The Archbishop made it a practice to remain quite indifferent to these recurrent speculations. He had one large guiding principle with regard to the whole matter: and it is deeply significant. The Lambeth Conference was due again in 1930. Its deliberations would affect the life of the whole Anglican Communion for another ten years. The chairman, therefore, of that Conference must be an Archbishop of Canterbury who, on all ordinary reckoning, would be able to play his part in following up the policy of that Conference for some while at least after it had taken place. So the Archbishop wrote in his private papers—after resignation:

> I had repeatedly said, and most of the Bishops had heard me say it, that I should not preside over another Lambeth Conference, and that I must in fairness to my successor have left Lambeth in good time to allow him to make the Conference arrangements. (*Jan. 5, 1930.*)

It is true that the formal announcement of his decision to resign came only a few weeks after the second rejection of the revised Prayer Book. And in some quarters his resignation was attributed to that rejection. But the facts are quite otherwise. To quote his private papers again:

> I tried to forestall this misinterpretation of my action by announcing to the Canterbury Diocesan Conference in June, some days before the second Prayer Book debate in the House of Commons, that another man would be in my place in 1930. Had I been ten or fifteen years younger, I should have treated the defeat of the Prayer Book as an episode in the life of the Church—and in my own life —an important episode no doubt, but not one that called for heroic

measures or a drastic resignation. I wish to leave on emphatic record that this episode had no influence on my action. My mind was really made up, I might almost say, in 1920, that the Lambeth Conference of 1930 would not find me as its President. (*Jan. 5, 1930.*)

The Archbishop was now eighty years old, and though astonishingly hale and alert in comparison with most octogenarians, he could not disguise the fact that he was no longer able to do all that he had been accustomed to do as a matter of course. He got more easily tired in the evenings; and he suffered especially in the last year or two from intermittent attacks of a serious form of headache. Moreover, while he could tackle the big occasions which came his way—important speeches and sermons—the constant strain of everyday work, with its unceasing demands of all kinds, was proving too severe for his strength. To put it in another way, and in his own words while talking at Canterbury to the wife of Canon Bickersteth, on January 5, 1928, just after the first rejection of the Prayer Book, he said quite plainly that it was his intention to resign that year whether the Prayer Book passed or not, and gave as his reason, 'While my mind can grasp one thing, it cannot grasp six or seven almost simultaneously, as it ought to be able to do, and as it had been able to do in the past.' Naturally enough, before 1928, the question of the Archbishop's duty as well as the date of any resignation was often in his mind, and formed the subject of discussion with some of the most intimate of his friends. It is possible that if the Archbishop or those nearest to him had realized the greatness of the danger that the Prayer Book Measure should suffer defeat, he might have entrusted its final piloting in 1926–7 to the hands of his successor. But though the Archbishop was anxious at times as to the issue, he believed, rightly enough, that his own influence would count for a great deal. And therefore it was not unnatural that he should wish to see the long labour of Revision brought to an end while he was still at Lambeth. In any case, rightly or wrongly, it was not the Revision of the Prayer Book and the tasks which it would inevitably bring for the two Provinces of Canterbury and York, but the unknown responsibilities which the next Lambeth Conference must involve for the whole Anglican Communion, which formed the determining factor.

At first, as the Archbishop's age advanced, the arguments against resignation, brought by people of very different schools, were very strong. Men relied on him so much, and, while he held the helm, the ship, it was said, would steer a steady course. Was not the archbishopric itself a trust which could not be forsaken? And to the very end there were those who regarded his resignation as almost a sin against God—on the grounds that an Archbishop of Canterbury ought not to resign in any event. Indeed, the plain fact that no Archbishop of Canterbury had resigned and the strong sense of a trust were both facts which would weigh with Archbishop Davidson himself to a peculiar degree. And there were many others, both laymen and Bishops from overseas, who disapproved of the idea and when the decision was finally made expressed keen disappointment. There were all sorts of reasons why the Archbishop should never resign. And, as every one who has had to do with the question of resignation in even the smallest sphere knows, resignation is extraordinarily difficult to face—and though it may be discussed for months or years, its achievement is a very different matter. But the Archbishop's own sense of duty, and his and Mrs. Davidson's most careful guardianship of the good of the Church, proved stronger than all the reasons on the other side. The most trusted of his friends whom they both consulted agreed that resignation would be right. He had his hesitation, it is true. He was not quite sure that his nearest friends based their thought on adequate knowledge. But his recognition that he could not efficiently discharge so continuous a strain of work, as well as the counsel of his friends, prevailed on the other side. Thus the decision was taken—though none but the Archbishop himself could ever have realized the wrench which it meant—and he fixed the actual date for November 12, the day of his golden wedding. It was the most difficult thing that he had ever had to do: it was the end, the voluntary laying down, of his life.

The resignation itself had to be accomplished in proper form. A commission was accordingly appointed by the King consisting of the Archbishop of York and the Bishops of the three principal sees. The formal announcement was made in the Press as follows:

10, Downing Street,
Whitehall, S.W. 1. 25th July, 1928.

The King has received with great regret an intimation from the Archbishop of Canterbury that he is desirous of resigning his high office. His Majesty, on the recommendation of the Prime Minister, has, by Royal Warrant, appointed a Commission consisting of the Archbishop of York, the Bishop of London, the Bishop of Durham, and the Bishop of Winchester, for the purpose of receiving the resignation.

The Commission have reported their acceptance of the Archbishop's resignation to take effect on November 12 of this year and this has been approved by His Majesty.

The Archbishop also, later, wrote to the Dean of Canterbury to intimate formally to the Dean and Chapter of Canterbury the fact of his impending resignation on November 12, adding:

The ARCHBISHOP OF CANTERBURY *to the* DEAN OF CANTERBURY

25 October 1928

It is right that you and the Chapter of Canterbury should be thus made formally cognisant of the fact and of the consequent obligations which will devolve upon you and the Chapter.[1]

II

The announcement of the Archbishop's resignation was the signal for a quite extraordinary outburst of gratitude and affection on all sides. It is literally true to say that no one was more surprised than the Archbishop himself. He said at the time to an intimate friend, with complete sincerity:

I honestly don't understand it; I am speaking, as I should to you, absolutely freely—and if I was describing myself I should say I was a funny old fellow of quite mediocre, second-rate gifts and a certain amount of common sense—but that I had tried to do my best; I have tried—and I have tried to stick to my duty; but that is really all there is about it.

The fact remained that the appreciation and reverence were felt and expressed very widely indeed. Already in the earlier part of the year, on the actual completion of the twenty-fifth year of the primacy, and again on his eightieth birthday, the opportunity had been taken by old friends, by the public at large, and by the clergy of the diocese, to express their admiration; and the Mayor and Corporation of Canterbury presented him on the birthday

[1] The receipt of this letter was duly referred to by the Dean and Chapter in their petition to the Crown for a *congé d'élire*. An attempt was made in connexion with the election of Archbishop Davidson's successor to maintain that the Archbishop had not canonically resigned: but the Dean and Chapter (after taking the Opinion of Mr. F. H. L. Errington, the Commissary-General of Canterbury and Chancellor of London), rejected the plea, and gave their reasons.

itself with the Freedom of the City. There can be no doubt that a special warmth was added to these and later expressions by a feeling of deep sympathy for the Archbishop personally in the fate of the revised Prayer Book. The whole volume of thankfulness, however, found a special focus in what came to be known as the Tribute to Archbishop Davidson, organized by a special committee including the Archbishop of York (as Chairman), the Prime Minister, Lord Stamfordham, Lord Harris, Dr. Scott Lidgett, the Headmaster of Harrow and other representatives of public life, the Church, the county and diocese, and having Mr. Arthur Sheppard[1] as secretary. The response to the appeal (issued June 29, closed October 31) was astonishing. It came from the widest circles—and from all ranks: at least 15,000 subscribers: and it included not only substantial sums from the well-to-do but very many a widow's mite. The total reached was £17,117. Of this a portion was spent on a stone cross, the work of W. Reynolds Stephens, the sculptor, with the architectural assistance of W. Tapper, set up in the middle of the courtyard of Lambeth Palace—while the main portion was to be used in such ways as would enable the Archbishop and Mrs. Davidson to end their days in peace and comfort. The gift made possible the purchase of a house in Cheyne Walk.[2]

The announcement of the Archbishop's successor followed swiftly after the announcement of his resignation. He was taken fully into the Prime Minister's confidence over this—and the consequential appointments. There was, indeed, not a moment's doubt in the Archbishop's mind as to who that successor should be—Cosmo Gordon Lang, Archbishop of York since 1908. The Archbishop's record is as follows:

> Baldwin has been kindness itself, and has come repeatedly to Lambeth to talk things over, besides seeing me in the House of Commons and in Downing Street. . . . There is no parallel, I am sure, to the speed with which these things have been settled. But the speed did not in the least mean carelessness or lack of trouble, for we have given hours to the matter and Baldwin has honestly grappled with the difficulties. . . . His (Ebor's) appointment was really dramatic. I saw Baldwin at the King's Garden Party on

[1] Formerly private secretary to the Archbishop.

[2] The Archbishop left the bulk of the Tribute ultimately to his successors, as a fund of which the interest could be used at their discretion to meet special calls such as commissions or conferences at home or abroad.

Thursday, July 26, and he told me that he wanted some quiet talk at Lambeth. I was able to tell him that Ebor had come to London that day and he would sleep at Lambeth. We accordingly arranged that Baldwin should come to Lambeth at 9.30 p.m. and that I would have Ebor there ready for a talk. This was a great relief to me for I had been rather set in a tremble by rumours during the previous 48 hours to the effect that Baldwin had in some way changed his mind; apparently there was no foundation for this. He came at night and I left him alone with Ebor for half an hour and then we all three discussed the other appointments—to York, to Manchester, to Chelmsford, supposing these to be the men promoted. Wonderful to relate, the whole thing was carried out within the week. Baldwin came again to Lambeth and saw Temple, on the Monday night, July 30th, Temple being on his way for a holiday in France. It was all arranged then and there, though of course Temple had thought it all over carefully owing to the popular expectation. Temple . . . approved of Chelmsford being his successor, and Chelmsford accordingly met Baldwin on Wednesday, came straight from Baldwin to me, and the matter was clinched.

In August, the Archbishop went for his regular holiday to Scotland, going the familiar round with the omission of Cloan, since Lord Haldane had died. He returned at the end of September, and then came a winding up both at Canterbury and Lambeth. Interspersed with it all were 'the large and deep things attaching to the great laying down of an office after a quarter of a century of leadership':

One had little time, I fear, for adequate quiet thought about it all, and yet I do not think that on any single day I began it lightly or prosaically—so far as my own thoughts went.

The last Bishops' Meeting which he attended was held on September 25–7. It was an important meeting and concerned the future policy of the episcopate in the matter of Prayer Book Revision; but, while present, he left the guidance of the discussion to the Archbishop of York. On October 22, he received the freedom of the City of London at the Guildhall—and this honour, given in the presence of a great and representative assembly, pleased him much. Never before (he said) had any ecclesiastic thus been honoured *qua* ecclesiastic, and he took the 'unexpected honour' characteristically enough as a tribute to the interweaving of the Church and national life, and the Church's task to witness to righteousness as above denominational interests.

Another honour which gave him still greater satisfaction when it was announced on November 3 was his nomination to a peerage. For thirty-three years he had been one of the spiritual peers, and throughout that time he had taken an active part in Parliamentary work. There was a widespread feeling that means ought to be found by which his experience and advice would still be at the service of the country in the House of Lords. Accordingly the King, on the advice of the Prime Minister, created him a Baron, and he took the title of Lord Davidson of Lambeth. There were some, like Lord Rosebery, who felt that, if he were to take his place in the House of Lords after resignation of the office which made him First Subject of the Crown, he should be given a Dukedom. There were others who felt that, having been in the House of Lords as Archbishop of Canterbury, he could not fitly return there in any lesser capacity. But the Archbishop himself did not see any anomaly in re-entering the House of Lords as a temporal peer. He quite clearly wished still to have his place in that Chamber; but he also quite clearly only desired the qualification for entry and he did not trouble his head about the question of rank in the peerage. The possession of a barony supplied the qualification, and that was all that was requisite.

On November 3, he went to Canterbury for the last time as Primate. Here he dedicated a Memorial to Viscount Milner, in the Cathedral, where the Chapel of S. Martin of Tours had been restored by Lord Milner's personal friends.

On Sunday, November 4, he preached his farewell sermon from the Cathedral pulpit. The crowds all day were very large, craning for a sight of the old Archbishop, as he went to and from the Cathedral and his home. His sermon (which was broadcast) was simple and full of hope. Its keynote was struck in the following sentences:

> An old man has the gain of being able to look back. He can think not only, as we all think within these walls, about the varied blessings and the fruitful captaincies of former centuries. He thinks, too, about what in the long years his own eyes have seen. At fourscore I look back along 50 years of serious service—25 of special trust and answerableness. So looking, I say to you to-night, as my firm conviction, that the Church of England to-day, whatever her difficulties, is far stronger, far more zealous, has a truer vision of God's purpose, and is more united—yes, more united in effort

and in prayer—than it was when my working years began. It may seem to be a paradox, but it is true that these Prayer Book discussions in themselves—until some jarring notes, relating to a few points only, raised trouble at the close—have evolved a deeper and more thoughtful spirit of unity in purpose and in prayer than any we have known before.

But that unity in extended prayer is only one of the firm foundations we have for thankful confidence and high hope. Who shall measure the growth and deepening of our sense that God has been increasingly giving us a great trust as a Missionary Church in contemporary life? A Missionary Church, too, which is extending with free development throughout the world. Who again shall measure our growth in understanding other parts of the Church of Christ in East and West? Are we not beginning to see on a new scale how to embrace different types of Christian saintliness and thus perchance to have a pivot-place in a United Christendom? Think of the wider sense we have of the Church's obligation in the leavening of social and industrial life. You find little or no word of that in former days. And that we may do our enlarged work better our whole organic life has been made stronger and its touch closer with our brothers overseas. But underlying all that, I note with yet greater thankfulness in how many ways our spiritual life grows deeper, not least in a sounder and better reasoned appreciation of sacramental grace. On every one of these lines I am persuaded that our Church has been growing from strength to strength. God, not man, has been at work, both to will and to do of His good pleasure. And the old man whose duty it has been to mark and further the advance along all these lines and to compare the present with the past must surely bid you remember those much greater things when with penitence and resolve you are noting what is amiss.

On the Monday afternoon came the final departure for Lambeth. The Archbishop left the Old Palace quietly walking, as was so often his wont, to Canterbury East Station. Earlier in the day, when arrangements were being discussed, he remarked, 'I wish to avoid any dramatic departure.' Mrs. Davidson left two hours later, also by train. The friend of many years, Canon Thory Gage Gardiner, was at the station for the departure of each train to bid them farewell.

November 12 was the day of the golden wedding. It began with a celebration of the Holy Communion in Lambeth Palace Chapel, at the very altar before which Randall Davidson and

Edith Tait had been joined in matrimony fifty years before. Joining with them in deep thanksgiving for the blessings of that long married life were members of their family and many intimate friends. All day long deputations, gifts, and good wishes poured into the house, the gifts including a golden bowl from the King.

During the afternoon the Archbishop and Mrs. Davidson received a large number of the inner circle of their friends, and at 5 o'clock these assembled in the Chapel for a final act of praise and thanksgiving. Achievements and disappointments, joys and sorrows, the love of friends, and all the varied associations of fifty years were gathered together on that afternoon of golden memories. The Archbishop by the light of a silver candlestick held in his own hand read the words from Philippians i. 3, 'I thank my God upon every remembrance'.

At 6 p.m. the Prime Minister, Mr. Stanley Baldwin, came as the representative of the Nation to present the Nation's gift. He was accompanied by other members of the Tribute Committee, including the Archbishop of York, Lord Stamfordham, Sir Thomas Inskip, Lord Cornwallis, Dr. Scott Lidgett, and Dr. Carnegie Simpson. The Archbishop and Mrs. Davidson received them in the study, some intimate friends being also present. The Archbishop of York read the address, which closed with these words:

> It is our earnest prayer, and we are confident it is the earnest prayer of all who offer you this tribute, that God may crown the many gifts which He has bestowed upon you and upon Mrs. Davidson in your fifty years of united service, with the gift of His abiding peace.

The Prime Minister followed with words which while touching in their simplicity were significant by their insight—for in dwelling on the admiration he felt for the Archbishop's character he declared that what he had chiefly learnt from him was the power of love unfeigned.

Then came a gift from the Diocese of Canterbury, consisting of a cheque, together with bookshelves for the study in his new home bearing the inscription "ΞΥΛΙΝΑ ΑΝΤΙ ΧΡΥΣΕΙΩΝ"

In the evening, Bishop Brent and the Rev. Dr. Ogilby brought the gift from the Episcopal Church in the United States of America—a golden inkstand together with a cheque.

At midnight the resignation took effect, and Randall Davidson ceased to be Archbishop of Canterbury.

CHAPTER LXXXIV
THE END

For life, with all it yields of joy and woe,
And hope and fear,—believe the aged friend,—
Is just our chance o' the prize of learning love,
How love might be, hath been indeed, and is.[1]

ROBERT BROWNING, *A Death in the Desert.*

On November 14, the Archbishop and Lady Davidson left Lambeth Palace, and stayed as the guests of General Sir Neville Lyttelton at the Governor's House, Chelsea, while their new house in Cheyne Walk was being made ready. The same day he took his seat in the House of Lords as Baron Davidson of Lambeth. He sat on the Cross benches, and from time to time took part in debate, while further assisting on certain committees. He also had the happiness of still being able to attend the meetings of the Trustees of the British Museum, which had been one of his most prized public duties ever since 1884. His note is as follows:

> One very pleasing incident is perhaps worth recording.
>
> I have been a Trustee of the British Museum since Queen Victoria appointed me in 1884. That position came to an end when as Archbishop I became ex-officio a 'Principal Trustee'. That again came to an end by my resignation, but I could not revert to the former post, as it is now held by Lord Esher. Thereupon the Trustees decided to get a vacancy made somehow to elect me. Lord Kilbracken most generously resigned and I was elected, and then they revived the use of an ancient statute allowing for the increase of the number of the Standing Committee—they increased it by one so as to give me a place thereon. It was a remarkable testimony, and to me a very pleasant one, for though I am not in the Chair at meetings I am practically carrying on as before, and must do it with thoroughness if I am to justify all their kindness.[2]

Another event which gave him pleasure was his entertainment

[1] These lines from *A Death in the Desert* were printed on the letter of thanks sent by Archbishop and Lady Davidson to the many friends who sent them messages in their 'going out from Lambeth', November 1928.

[2] See p. 1199.

as the guest of honour by the Athenaeum Club on December 11, 1928. Twenty-five years before, at the opening of his Primacy, some twenty-four members, nearly all laymen, and a brilliant representation of the Club, had given him a dinner, in circumstances already described,[1] the Prime Minister, Mr. Balfour, being in the chair. On the present occasion the Club desired to do honour to Lord Davidson and Lord Balfour together, as senior trustees, on the attainment of their eightieth birthdays. Lord Balfour was unable to attend, owing to ill health. Over a hundred and fifty members were present, with the junior trustee, Lord Warrington of Clyffe, as chairman. The only speeches were those of the chairman, proposing the Archbishop's health, and his Grace's reply.

But the transformation of daily life and interest which resignation brought, was indeed profound. Unlike statesmen accustomed to the spells of comparative idleness and detachment which a change of government brings, the Archbishop never had been out of office, and he found it difficult to realize the full gravity of the difference which twenty-four hours could bring to the whole habit of his life. Looking back four months later—the first time he dictated a Memorandum about himself after his resignation—he described the position as follows:

> Anyhow, after several months have passed, I am able better to judge and to consider quietly what the change means. So far as I am personally concerned, the position is different from what I had visualized beforehand. I had thought of getting quietly out of things, yet being for some time in a position of a good deal of responsibility, and instead of that it looks to me as if a shutter has come down with a run, like a draper's shop on a Saturday afternoon—and that lo and behold I was somewhere outside it—out of all touch and out of all responsibility—and all in the space of a few hours. Perhaps this sounds, even to oneself, like a want of appreciating the kindness of everybody. It is not so. I do not know what more either the new Archbishop or his friends could have done. It was my own misunderstanding of how things shaped themselves at such a juncture.

In the other memoranda written intermittently during the next twelve months, similar thoughts find expression. And though the change for Lady Davidson was different in character it was

[1] See p. 406.

perhaps no less great—as the Archbishop fully understood. He wrote:

> What it has meant to Edith I can hardly put into words. I have been intensely impressed by her quietness and courage throughout it all. . . . It is all of a piece with what she has been for 50 years.

The new house at 10 Cheyne Walk was thoroughly comfortable. It had a little chapel where family prayers were regularly said. And the study, furnished with book-cases, specially designed by Mr. T. F. W. Grant, a gift from the Diocese, was admirably equipped, and, thanks to Lady Davidson, everything was done to make the new house home. But there is no denying that the Archbishop felt the difference between it and Lambeth, and the whole change which it symbolized to him, patient as he never ceased to be. He found it hard to have so little to do—and not to be wanted:

> I will not deny that I have found the adjustment to the new life intensely difficult. I have felt the comparative smallness of the house: I have missed what was I suppose the unconscious stimulus of intercourse with men of all shades of opinion. I have felt the lack of the spur of a daily round of work which had then and there to be done. This is a little different from the help given by the greater stimulus and invigoration of being in the centre of 'affairs'. And it has been strange not to have the sense of being 'wanted' at every hour of the day, and sometimes night. (*Jan. 5, 1930.*)

The pang was all the keener, as, within three weeks of his enthronement on December 4, the new Archbishop fell dangerously ill at Canterbury, and was out of action till the summer, while he himself was or felt comparatively hale. The early weeks of resignation were also overshadowed by the King's grave illness, which he felt intensely.

His relations with his successor were as frank and intimate as ever. There was no sort of nervousness on the part of the new Archbishop about the old Archbishop intervening in troublesome ways. His advice was welcomed though 'it is obvious that there are a great many details of administration on which he [Archbishop Lang] will act on lines differing widely from my own'; and 'certainly he will be free from what some of those dearest to me regard as my temptation, or weakness, of consulting too many people'.

His advice was still sought by many, both at home and overseas; and his old talent of giving the whole of his mind and will to the needs of those who consulted him was not suffered to rust. He entertained many friends; and nothing pleased him and Lady Davidson more than seeing and welcoming Bishops and others on their journeys to London. One of the visits he himself most enjoyed was a visit he paid to Archbishop Lang, at Bognor, in March 1929, when he had long talks with the Archbishop of Canterbury and the King, who were both convalescent from grave illness within a mile of one another at Aldwick.

He was much in request for speeches and sermons, and was not unwilling to accept such invitations. On June 9, 1929, he and Lady Davidson went for two nights to the Deanery, Canterbury, in order to take part in the consecration of his former chaplain (G. K. A. Bell) as Bishop of Chichester. In the summer of 1929, he took an active part in the difficulties which had arisen over the proposed new sacristy which had been designed by Walter Tapper as an additional building on the north-east side of Westminster Abbey, and became chairman of the committee formed by the Dean of Westminster to give advice. But though he took the greatest pains, going over the whole of the Abbey buildings more than once, his labour was in vain, as the money offered to build the sacristy was withdrawn in view of the controversy which the proposal caused.

One task loomed ahead as likely to claim a good deal of his time. This was the sorting of his papers, and in particular the handling of the piles of Memoranda he had made at nearly all stages of his public life. On March 16, 1929, he wrote:

> I do want intensely to get forward with the papers of the past in my own life, and to leave rough-hewn behind me some kind of history of the last 50 years, wherein during that period I have been for the latter half principal, and for the former half cognisant of and sharing, in all that was taking place.

And many were the people, both friends and acquaintances, who pressed upon the Archbishop that his really urgent duty was the preparation of a biography, and that the other things he was doing were comparatively unimportant. It is true that a good deal of work was done towards compiling the book—especially for the earlier part of his life before 1900—but on February 23, 1930 (the date of his last dictated Memorandum), he admitted that 'Mary[1] and I have not been making very rapid progress with biographical work'. It was not very easy, especially at eighty-one, to apply the mind in a systematic way to autobiographical toil; and the whole task proved more exacting than a stranger might suppose.

The last big event in his life was his visit to Scotland to take part in the final act of the Union of the Church of Scotland and the United Free Church of Scotland, by speaking at the final evening session of the first reunited General Assembly, held in the large Hall in Annandale Street, Edinburgh, on October 3, 1929. The Duke of York[2] sat in the Royal Throne as Lord High Commissioner, and the Right Reverend Dr. John White presided as Moderator. In introducing Lord Davidson, the Moderator referred to his previous visit to their separate Assemblies in 1921 when he addressed them on the Lambeth Conference's Appeal for the Reunion of Christendom; and, in the name of all, he welcomed him now alike for his work's sake and for his own sake. Lord Davidson spoke both as a Scotsman and as a great leader of the Church. He described the nature of the discussions about Church truth and Church order over many years 'as more or less peculiar to us Scotsmen'. He spoke of Walter Scott, 'that most Scottish of Scotsmen', and the strong brush which he used in *Old Mortality*, *The Heart of Midlothian*, and elsewhere in his tales of Scottish history. He spoke also of the understanding which every Scotsman for generations had, more or less, of questions which would be quite unmeaning to ordinary folk elsewhere. And then he went on:

> If you will pardon a personal note, I was myself, in years not far after the Disruption, brought up in Scotland, and though I flitted early across the Tweed for training and education and work of quite another kind and allegiance, I have vivid memories of the talk of my elders in those days, and had heard of Auchterarder and Strathbogie long before I can have had a glimmer of what they stood for, and I regarded it as a kind of adventure when I was taken once in a way to listen to such men as Candlish and Guthrie at their best. Such memories come flooding in upon me now.

But his speech took a wider range than Scotland. He spoke of the

[1] Mary C. S. Mills, the Archbishop's cousin, and Secretary to Lady Davidson for many years.

[2] Now King George VI.

Lambeth Appeal, and the responses received, of the first World Conference on Faith and Order held in Lausanne in 1927, a babe conceived in Edinburgh at the World Missionary Conference of 1910. He referred to the new efforts in Christian Unity being made by the great Churches in the East and to the one great exception, Rome, 'no helpful word or act comes from the City of the Seven Hills'. He emphasized the significance of the Scottish union, and of the part which Scottish thought must play in the whole field of Christian Unity. And he ended, first reminding the Assembly of the greatness of the Christian calling, and the war in which all Christians were enlisted and armed and united—a war to the death against the impurities and the laziness and the greed which mar and corrupt the common life: and then, in a final word, he commended to his younger brothers the lesson of hope which his eighty-one years had brought to him, and appealed to them, with their vigour of manhood and buoyancy of youth, to bring to its accomplishment the vision of unity which those whose course was wellnigh run had seen. It was a noble close, and received the loud applause of its hearers.

The speech, however, proved a severe tax, and on his return to London he was exhausted and over-tired.

> Dr. Cassidy declared the curious form of headache, together with rheumatism and lumbago, which was prostrating me, was due to over-fatigue, and that I must give up for the time being sermons and speeches to big audiences. (*Jan. 9.*)

He was obliged to cancel a further visit to Edinburgh and Glasgow in November, where he had promised to preach and speak for the Scottish Episcopal Church. During the latter weeks of 1929 he was only fairly well—and suffered at times from the same peculiar form of headache which in the last two or three years of his life was so real a trial.

On Friday, January 3, 1930, he went with Lady Davidson to the Exhibition of Italian Pictures at Burlington House, and was there taken with sharp pain due to old surgical troubles. He stayed a few days in bed, and the discomfort passed off. But in the next few weeks there were many ups and downs—days in bed, varied with short visits to the Italian Exhibition (which he much enjoyed), and some special committee work for the British Museum, besides seeing friends, and the sorting of papers. On Sunday, January 26, he celebrated Holy Communion for the last time in the little chapel at Cheyne Walk. On February 15, he attended church for the last time in the Old Church, Chelsea—for the christening of a grandson of an old friend, Tom Gordon Duff. The same day, and again on February 28, he and Lady Davidson went to Horsted Keynes to see Miss Tait who was in poor health. During this fortnight, he was suffering acutely from a whitlow on his finger, which had been giving trouble for some time. He was still, however, eagerly thinking about his next big task. On February 23 he wrote:

> I have a few big things ahead which may or may not admit of ultimate accomplishment. The biggest will be the Lambeth Conference Sermon at St. Paul's Cathedral at the opening of the Conference. I have full hopes of being able to do it, and should be disappointed were it not to come off. At present unhappily I have no vision of what ought to be said.

His own share in the Lambeth Conference—though as a spectator from outside—occupied a good deal of his thought; and he looked forward to afternoons in Lambeth Palace garden during July when he could see and talk to Bishops from overseas. On Friday, March 7, and Saturday, March 8, he was at the British Museum. Lady Davidson and Mary Mills fetched him in the car on the Saturday. Mary Mills writes:[1]

> Though in pain and with his arm in a sling, he had enjoyed the meeting of the Trustees, and some talk he had had with the Archbishop of Canterbury. Before leaving we all three (together with the Archbishop of Canterbury) looked at the Luttrell Psalter and Bedford Book of Hours, which were on view. This was his last visit to the British Museum. In the evening he dined with Lord Stamfordham. This was the last time he left the house.

During the next few days he was partly in bed, and partly in the study, but in much pain and general discomfort. On March 17, it became clear that a nurse was necessary, the Archbishop, owing to the whitlow on his finger, being crippled in all his movements. The next day an emergency meeting of Harrow School Governors was held in his bedroom:

> The Archbishop was too unwell to come down to the study, and the Harrow Governors who came that morning, the 18th, met round his bed. The Warden of All Souls was there, Mr. Stanley Baldwin, Mr. Amery, Mr. Grenfell and several more. The Arch-

[1] The passages which follow describing the stages of the Archbishop's illness are from a memorandum written at the time by Mary Mills.

bishop was in pain and discomfort and got through the meeting with much difficulty.

The Archbishop's illness grew worse, and two regular nurses, from St. John's and St. Thomas's Home, Nurse Amsden and Nurse Higgins, took up their quarters in the house. Both were carefully chosen.

No better choice could have been made, and to our great comfort and help they stayed with us to the end. We soon settled down into a routine. In the morning after his quiet time of prayer with E.M.D., letters and reading—as of old the newspapers first; then the morning letters, which of course grew less and less as the weeks ran on; the reading of old journals and diaries—sometimes a friend would come in for a talk before luncheon time. After lunch he would rest, while E.M.D. and I went out for an hour or hour and a half.

Each day Lady Davidson would try to arrange that some one, preferably a man, should come to tea and have a talk with him afterwards. The Archbishop of Canterbury was among these visitors, who included Bishops and many old friends and chaplains: and every Sunday the Holy Communion was celebrated in his room, or the little chapel. On April 3, he became a little better and was able to lie on the sofa in his study. April 7, was his eighty-second birthday, and he was much touched by the many messages which reached him, including a visit paid the following day on the King's behalf by Lord Stamfordham.

We had much reading aloud, including portions of his favourite *Waverleys*. We also read Stephen Gwynn's *Life of Walter Scott*, a book which gave him much pleasure. Easter Day, April 20th, was a great disappointment to him; his head was very bad and he suffered much discomfort. Bishop Montgomery celebrated and the maids sang 'The strife is o'er' outside his room. Later in the day he saw the Bishop of London and Bishop Gore. He came down as usual to the study. He stayed for prayers in the evening and blessed us all from his chair by the fire.

The next day he was again in the study and stayed up for prayers, giving the Blessing as on the previous evening. Earlier in the day we had read him the closing chapters of Scott's life, and he was much moved at the description of Sir Walter's last home-coming to the Border country.

After this the Archbishop seemed to get worse. As the days passed he seemed both depressed and often confused.

Friday April 25th, St. Mark's Day, his Consecration day—was an anxious one. He slept most of the morning. In the afternoon when we returned from our walk we found him unhappy and tired and confused. He was very weak and went to bed early. This was the last time he came downstairs.

Sir Thomas Barlow was away for a month, but Dr. Maurice Cassidy, who had been attending him with Sir Thomas for some time, kept a steady watch on his patient. All these days were days of long summer sunshine.

On Wednesday Sir John Rose Bradford came for a consultation with Dr. Cassidy. The Archbishop quite understood from the doctors that they wanted him to give himself up to rest. He saw Mr. Ellison for a few minutes. We read him *Old Mortality*.

On May 1st he was much interested in Edward Woods' Consecration as Bishop of Croydon in the Abbey. We had much reading of papers and some old journal-reading too. George and Hettie Bell saw him, and John Macmillan. E.M.D. had quiet talk with him about what to expect and plan for the future—a quieter life: preparation of papers: helping friends by counsel etc.

As the days slipped by, though there were occasional rallies, the Archbishop got weaker; though he still enjoyed seeing old friends, and appreciated the gifts they brought, sometimes conversations about passing events, sometimes spiritual help. He was always thankful for the prayers which were said beside him. And all the time he displayed a quite extraordinary patience and courage: and was consistently courteous and grateful to those about him.

There were times of real pain and much discomfort and weariness, but not one complaint ever crossed his lips. His nurses marvelled at it.

Nurses Amsden and Higgins nursed him devotedly; nor could anything exceed the care and solicitude of Sir Thomas Barlow and Dr. Cassidy. In the earlier stages when surgical help was required Mr. Eric Pearce Gould gave every help in his power, and Miss Lloyd Still, of St. Thomas's Hospital, a friend of many years, was always ready with help of all kinds.

Then there was, again as ever, the strong determination to work just so long as strength endured, the morning's letters must be dealt with promptly, the papers read, and in the early days of the illness interviews arranged.

Every day up to the very last, he would ask each morning (using the phrase so often on his lips in full working days) 'What are my duties to-day'—or 'what are my obligations' to-day—and in increasing weakness, each morning this question would be asked, sometimes almost in a whisper. And every morning the hand would be stretched out for the pocket book always by his side, the accusation being made sometimes that it was not being kept up to date.

One morning, not very long before the end, he handed it to me saying 'Tell me what we have to do to-day; there is so much written, but I cannot read it.'

Sunday May 18th, his last Sunday on earth—was very anxious. Mervyn Haigh celebrated in the little Chapel and took the Communion to him. He was very weak. After Mervyn Haigh and I had left the room and he was alone with E.M.D., in a clear voice he said part of the words of the Administration of the Bread: and then 'the Blessing of God the Father, God the Son, and God the Holy Ghost be upon you all'. E.M.D. asked if the blessing included Lucy; he replied 'Of course; it was *all.*' E.M.D. said that he spoke the words of blessing looking right *out*, and she was sure that he meant it to go far beyond his bedroom.

The same afternoon:

The Archbishop of Canterbury came and prayed with him. We read him little bits of *Beside the Bonnie Briar Bush*, and though he had been much confused and restless, the Scottish words and phrases seemed to soothe him. The third Nurse came.

On May 20 he saw the Archbishop of Canterbury for the last time.

The Archbishop of Canterbury asked for his blessing; he knelt by the bedside and asked him to put his hands on his head: then the words came

'God give you judgment [repeated twice],
God give you mercy,
God give you peace.'

After that he was quiet for a little. Later in the evening he blessed his household. At the close of his blessing he added very faintly 'We come to Thee in thankfulness and love; we come in trustfulness, simplicity and peace—but always simplicity.'

During the next few days, as his weakness increased, he saw several of his family and friends. On Friday evening, May 23, Sir Thomas Barlow returned from abroad and came straight from the station.

About midnight he became very restless. We stayed beside him. Dr. Cassidy came about 3 a.m. He was unconscious and breathing was difficult. We watched and prayed beside him. Mr. Ellison came about 7 a.m., Sir Thomas Barlow soon after breakfast. All day long the difficult breathing. The Archbishop of Canterbury called and many others and beautiful flowers poured in for him. Sir Thomas and Dr. Cassidy were with us watching. We had the blinds up so that the evening light shone in upon him. And so the hours went on; we said prayers and hymns at intervals, and Mr. Ellison said the Commendatory Prayer; at about 12.30 the breathing grew quieter, and at 1.5 a.m. on Rogation Sunday morning it gently ceased.

When we saw him again a few hours later, dressed in his robes, he lay wrapped in peace, looking so young, so quiet, so 'satisfied'.

As the Archbishop himself wished, he was buried at Canterbury. The Dean of Westminster had at once offered Westminster Abbey, a fitting mark of the national esteem. But the Archbishop's own known wish was observed. The first part of the funeral was held in the Abbey on Ascension Day, Thursday, May 29. The Duke of Gloucester attended on behalf of the King, and all the main branches of public life were represented by the Pallbearers.[1] The same evening the body was borne by car to Canterbury. A few moments' pause was made outside Lambeth Palace, where were gathered the Bishops of Southwark and Kingston and a group of South London clergy. The little procession was met at the Westgate of Canterbury by the Mayor and Corporation, the City Clergy, and the students of St. Augustine's College. It passed through the crowded but silent streets, reaching the West Doors of the Cathedral at 9.15 p.m. in the after-glow of a lovely sunset. There it was met by the Dean and Chapter and Choir, and, to the singing of 'I am the Resurrection and the Life', the coffin was carried through the Nave, down to the Crypt, where it lay all night before the Altar in the Undercroft Chapel of Our Lady, the Chapel linked to the Archbishop and Lady Davidson by special associations. Here next morning the Holy Communion was celebrated in the presence of a large congregation. Then the coffin was taken to the Choir below the High Altar.

The Burial Service in the afternoon was taken by the Archbishop of Canterbury, the Bishop of Dover, and the Dean of Can-

[1] The Pallbearers were Mr. Stanley Baldwin, Mr. Ramsay MacDonald, Lord Stamfordham, the Earl of Selborne, Sir Lewis Dibdin, Sir Frederic Kenyon, the Rev. J. Scott Lidgett, D.D., and Sir Thomas Barlow.

terbury. A very large number of Bishops and clergy were present. There was a remarkable gathering of the Archbishop's former chaplains, the Bishop of Chichester carrying the Crozier given to the Archbishop in 1920 by the Bishops attending the Lambeth Conference. The Cathedral was crowded, and those who could followed the procession to the Cloister Garth. The grave is opposite the Chapter House, under the shadow of Bell Harry Tower, and near to the Old Palace. It was lined with flowers, as also were the Cloisters and the Garth.

Lady Davidson and those nearest to her stood on the South side of the grave, the bishops facing her, and the chaplains gathered near by.

As the Archbishop of Canterbury read the words of Committal the rain fell in torrents. But it was a day of peace and thanksgiving for a long life nobly, patiently, and courageously lived in the service of the Church of England, and indeed of the whole Catholick Church of Christ.

APPENDIX I

PRINCIPAL DATES

1848 Randall Thomas Davidson born in Edinburgh (April 7).
1857 The family moved to Muirhouse.
1862 Entered Harrow.
1866 Serious shooting accident (August).
1867 Entered Trinity College, Oxford. (First Lambeth Conference.)
1868 Dr. Tait appointed Archbishop of Canterbury.
1871 B.A. Third Class Law and Modern History.
1872 Italian Tour. Commenced training for ordination at the Temple.
1872–3 First visit to Palestine.
1874 Ordained Deacon (March 1). Curacy at Dartford.
1875 Ordained Priest (February 21).
1876 Second visit to Palestine.
1877 Went to Lambeth Palace as Resident Chaplain to Archbishop Tait.
1878 Second Lambeth Conference.
1878 Married Edith Tait (November 12).
1882 Death of Archbishop Tait (December 3).
1882 First interview with Queen Victoria (December 9).
1883 Dr. Benson appointed Archbishop of Canterbury.
1883 Installed Dean of Windsor (June 25).
1888 Third Lambeth Conference.
1888–90 Trial of Bishop of Lincoln (Edward King).
1889 Publication of *Lux Mundi* (*editor* Charles Gore).
1891 Consecrated Bishop of Rochester (April 25). Serious illness (May 6). Publication of *Life of Archbishop Tait* (R. T. D. and W. Benham).
1894 Viscount Halifax and Abbé Portal: first attempt at rapprochement with Rome.
1895 Appointed Bishop of Winchester. Resignation of Rev. R. R. Dolling.
1896 *History of the Lambeth Conferences, 1867, 1878, 1888* published.
1896 Death of Archbishop Benson (October 11). Dr. Temple appointed Archbishop of Canterbury.
1897 Fourth Lambeth Conference.
1898–1900 Ritual Controversy. Sir William Harcourt's Letters.
1899 Charge to Diocese of Winchester.
1899–1902 South African War.

1900 Archbishop Temple's Decision on Reservation (Lambeth Hearing).

1901 Death of Queen Victoria (January 22). Accession of King Edward VII. Dr. Winnington Ingram appointed Bishop of London.

1902 Canon Charles Gore consecrated Bishop of Worcester. Education Act. Death of Archbishop Temple (December 23).

1903 Appointed Archbishop of Canterbury (confirmed February 6).

1904 Visit to Canada and U.S.A. *The Christian Opportunity* (Addresses and Sermons) published.

1904–6 Royal Commission on Ecclesiastical Discipline.

1906 Royal Letters of Business issued to Convocations (Prayer Book Revision).

1906 Mr. Birrell's Education Bill. Rejection by House of Lords.

1907 Deceased Wife's Sister's Marriage Act.

1908 Fifth Lambeth Conference.

1908 Mr. Runciman's Education Bill withdrawn.

1909 Dr. Lang became Archbishop of York.

1909 Mr. Lloyd George's Budget rejected by House of Lords.

1910 Death of King Edward VII (May 6).

1911 King George V crowned (June 22).

1911 *Captains and Comrades in the Faith* (Addresses and Sermons) published.

1911 Parliament Act.

1912 Charge to the Diocese of Canterbury. *The Character and Call of the Church of England.*

1912 Publication of *Foundations* (*editor* B. H. Streeter).

1913 Conference at Kikuyu, East Africa.

1914 Canterbury Convocation. Resolution on Clerical Orthodoxy (April).

1914 European War commenced (August 4).

1916 National Mission of Repentance and Hope.

1916 Canterbury Convocation. Resolution on Reprisals (February).

1916 Archbishop's visit to the Front (May).

1917 Canterbury Convocation. Resolution on Reservation (February).

1917 Russian Revolution.

1918 Dr. Henson consecrated Bishop of Hereford.

1918 European War ceased (November 11).

1919 Archbishop's second visit to the Front (January).

1919 *The Testing of a Nation* (Addresses and Sermons) published.

1919 National Assembly of the Church of England (Powers) Act.

1920 Convocations' Answers to Royal Letters of Business completed.

1920 Appointment of Committee of the Church Assembly to report on the Answers.

1920 Disestablishment of the Welsh Church took effect.

1920 Mr. H. A. L. Fisher's Proposals (Elementary Schools) published.

1920 Lord Buckmaster's Matrimonial Causes Bill carried in House of Lords (June).

1920 Sixth Lambeth Conference.

1921 Irish Settlement.

1921 The Malines Conversations began under presidency of Cardinal Mercier.

1922 Oecumenical Patriarch, Meletios, enthroned at Constantinople.

1922 Russian Patriarch Tikhon arrested. Archbishop's Protest to Lenin.

1922 Archbishop preached at Geneva before the opening of Third Assembly of League of Nations.

1922 Appointment of Archbishops' Doctrinal Commission.

1923 Treaty of Lausanne.

1923 Duke of Devonshire's White Paper on Indians in Kenya.

1925 House of Bishops commenced Revision Stage of Prayer Book Assembly Measure (October).

1926 Death of Cardinal Mercier.

1926 General Strike (May 3–12).

1927 Prayer Book Measure approved by Church Assembly (July 6).

Prayer Book Measure approved by House of Lords (December 14).

Prayer Book Measure rejected by House of Commons (December 15).

1928 Prayer Book Measure (amended) approved by Church Assembly (April 27).

Prayer Book Measure (amended) rejected by House of Commons (June 14).

Received Freedom of City of London (October 22).

Resignation (November 12).

1929 Addressed first Reunited General Assembly of the Church of Scotland (October 3).

1930 Death (May 25).

APPENDIX II

A LIST OF APPOINTMENTS TO DIOCESAN SEES IN THE PROVINCES OF CANTERBURY AND YORK BETWEEN FEBRUARY 6, 1903, AND NOVEMBER 12, 1928

Date of Confirmation of Election or Investiture	*See*	*Name of Bishop*	*Name of Prime Minister*
1903			
April 3	Winchester	Herbert Edward Ryle	The Rt. Hon. A. J. Balfour
April 30	Exeter	Archibald Robertson	,,
May 12*	St. Albans	Edgar Jacob	,,
June 4	Newcastle	Arthur Thomas Lloyd	,,
November 26	Manchester	Edmund Arbuthnott Knox	,,
1904			
November 14	Southwell	Edwyn Hoskyns	,,
1905			
January 27	Birmingham	Charles Gore	,,
February 1	Carlisle	John William Diggle	,,
February 24	Worcester	Huyshe Wolcott Yeatman-Biggs	,,
May 24	Southwark	Edward Stuart Talbot	,,
May 30	Gloucester	Edgar Charles Sumner Gibson	,,
May 30	Llandaff	Joshua Pritchard Hughes	,,
July 5	Rochester	John Reginald Harmer	,,
October 17	Ely	Frederic Henry Chase	,,
1906			
November 29	Truro	Charles William Stubbs	The Rt. Hon. Sir Henry Campbell-Bannerman
1907			
September 2	Newcastle	Norman Dumenil John Straton	,,
November 30*	Sodor and Man	Thomas Wortley Drury	,,
1908			
January 24	Chichester	Charles John Ridgeway	,,

Date of Confirmation of Election or Investiture	*See*	*Name of Bishop*	*Name of Prime Minister*
1909			
January 20	York	Cosmo Gordon Lang	The Rt. Hon. H. H. Asquith
1910			
April 22	Norwich	Bertram Pollock	,,
June 23	Lincoln	Edward Lee Hicks	,,
1911			
May 1	Winchester	Edward Stuart Talbot	,,
May 25*	Southwark	Hubert Murray Burge	,,
October 17	Oxford	Charles Gore	,,
October 17	Salisbury	Frederic Edward Ridgeway	,,
October 28*	Birmingham	Henry Russell Wakefield	,,
1912			
January 19	Ripon	Thomas Wortley Drury	,,
March 25*	Sodor and Man	James Denton Thompson	,,
July 24	Truro	Winfrid Oldfield Burrows	,,
1913			
June 13	Lichfield	John Augustine Kempthorne	,,
1914			
February 24*	Chelmsford	John Edwin Watts-Ditchfield	,,
February 24*	St. Edmundsbury and Ipswich	Henry Bernard Hodgson	,,
March 21	Sheffield	Leonard Hedley Burrows	,,
June 12	Bristol	George Nickson	,,
1915			
November 30*	Newcastle	Herbert Louis Wild	,,
1916			
September 20	Peterborough	Frank Theodore Woods	,,
December 20	Exeter	Lord William Gascoyne Cecil	,,
1918			
January 23	Hereford	Herbert Hensley Henson	The Rt. Hon. D. Lloyd George
October 23	Coventry	Huyshe Wolcott Yeatman-Biggs	,,
1919			
February 19	Worcester	Ernest Harold Pearce	,,
July 9	Chichester	Winfrid Oldfield Burrows	,,
July 31	Chester	Henry Luke Paget	,,
August 6	Oxford	Hubert Murray Burge	,,

Date of Confirmation of Election or Investiture	*See*	*Name of Bishop*	*Name of Prime Minister*
1919			
October 8	Truro	Frederic Sumpter Guy Warman	The Rt. Hon. D. Lloyd George
October 18*	Southwark	Cyril Forster Garbett	,,
1920			
January 2	Lincoln	William Shuckburgh Swayne	,,
February 2*	Bradford	Arthur William Thomson Perowne	,,
April 19	St. Albans	Michael Bolton Furse	,,
July 27	Durham	Herbert Hensley Hen-son	,,
August 23	Carlisle	Henry Herbert Williams	,,
August 23	Ripon	Thomas Banks Strong	,,
October 5	Hereford	Martin Linton Smith	,,
1921			
January 24	Manchester	William Temple	,,
July 25*	St. Edmundsbury and Ipswich	Albert Augustus David	,,
October 31	Bath and Wells	St. John Basil Wynne-Willson	,,
December 16	Salisbury	St. Clair George Alfred Donaldson	,,
1922			
June 24*	Coventry	Charles Lisle Carr	,,
1923			
January 24	Gloucester	Arthur Cayley Headlam	The Rt. Hon. A. Bonar Law
October 9	Chelmsford	Frederic Sumpter Guy Warman	The Rt. Hon. S. Baldwin
October 18	Liverpool	Albert Augustus David	,,
October 26	Truro	Walter Howard Frere	,,
November 1*	St. Edmundsbury and Ipswich	Walter Godfrey Whitting-ham	,,
December 28	Winchester	Frank Theodore Woods	,,
1924			
January 30	Peterborough	Cyril Charles Bowman Bardsley	,,
March 24	Ely	Leonard Jauncey White-Thomson	,,
Sept. 29*	Birmingham	Ernest William Barnes	The Rt. Hon. J. Ramsey Macdonald

Date of Confirmation of Election or Investiture	*See*	*Name of Bishop*	*Name of Prime Minister*
1925			
February 24*	Sodor and Man	Charles Leonard Thornton-Duesbery	The Rt. Hon. S. Baldwin
October 13	Oxford	Thomas Banks Strong	,,
1926			
January 5	Ripon	Edward Arthur Burroughs	,,
March 25*	Southwell	Bernard Oliver Francis Heywood	,,
1927			
January 26	Blackburn	Percy Mark Herbert	,,
February 15	Leicester	Cyril Charles Bowman Bardsley	,,
March 23	Peterborough	Claude Martin Blagden	,,
June 28	Guildford	John Harold Greig	,,
July 13	Portsmouth	Ernest Neville Lovett	,,
October 5	Newcastle	Harold Ernest Bilbrough	,,
October 12	Derby	Edmund Courtenay Pearce	,,
1928			
June 11*	Sodor and Man	William Stanton Jones	,,
September 27	Southwell	Henry Mosley	,,
November 1*	Wakefield	James Buchanan Seaton	,,

NOTE

The date given in the foregoing Table is that of the Confirmation of the Election of the Bishop-designate, or of his Investiture, except where the date is marked by *, which signifies the date of consecration. Confirmation on behalf of the Archbishop of the Province takes place after an election by the Dean and Chapter. In dioceses where there is no Dean and Chapter, and the Bishop-designate is being translated from another see, the Archbishop invests the Bishop-designate. The material parts of the Investiture consist of the Bishop-designate taking the oaths of Allegiance and Canonical obedience, and making the Declarations of Assent and against Simony. The Archbishop then formally accepts the Bishop-designate as Bishop of the new see, and invests him so that he may enjoy all the rights, privileges, jurisdictions, and emoluments belonging to the Bishopric. In dioceses where there is no Dean and Chapter, and when the Bishop-designate is a priest, there is no investiture; the Bishop-designate becoming Bishop of his see by his consecration.

SUMMARY

Number of Diocesan Bishops appointed Feb. 6, 1903–Nov. 12, 1928 . . 80

under King Edward VII 20

under King George V 60

EPISCOPAL APPOINTMENTS 1903–28

Number appointed in Premiership of		Mr. A. J. Balfour	14
"	"	Sir H. Campbell-Bannerman	4
"	"	Mr. H. H. Asquith	19
"	"	Mr. D. Lloyd George	20
"	"	Mr. A. Bonar Law	1
"	"	Mr. S. Baldwin	21
"	"	Mr. J. Ramsay Macdonald	1

APPENDIX III

PORTRAITS OF RANDALL DAVIDSON

1. As Dean of Windsor (1890). Rudolf Swaboda. Windsor Castle.
2. As Bishop of Winchester (1904). A. S. Cope, R.A. Wolvesey, Winchester.
3. As Archbishop of Canterbury (1905). Hugh Rivière. Trinity College, Oxford.
4. As Archbishop of Canterbury (1910). J. S. Sargent, R.A. Lambeth Palace.
5. As Archbishop of Canterbury (1926). Philip de Laszlo. Church House, Westminster.

Recumbent Effigy in Bronze (1934). Cecil Thomas. Canterbury Cathedral.

APPENDIX IV

THE CORONATION OF KING GEORGE V

Second Gentleman. May I be bold to ask what that contains,
That paper in your hand?
First Gentleman. Yes; 'tis the list
Of those that claim their offices this day
By custom of the coronation.

SHAKESPEARE, *Henry VIII*, IV, i.

THE Coronation of King George V and Queen Mary took place in Westminster Abbey on June 22nd, 1911. Although Archbishop Davidson was intimately concerned both with the event and with the long preparations which preceded it, he has left no description of either behind him. Indeed the Coronation, significant and solemn as it was, provided only a brief interlude of peace amid the anxieties of the political crisis, of which the last scene was laid in the House of Lords, in the famous debate on the Parliament Bill on August 10th[1]. But there are certain points of more than passing interest connected with the Coronation Service itself which are worthy of record.

I

In 1902 the Archbishop of Canterbury (Dr. Temple) crowned King Edward VII, and the Archbishop of York (Dr. Maclagan) crowned Queen Alexandra. This recent precedent led many to expect that the Coronation of Queen Mary would be the privilege of Dr. Lang, who had succeeded Dr. Maclagan as the Northern Primate. The circumstances of 1902, however, were altogether exceptional, and in 1911 the Archbishop of Canterbury crowned both the King and the Queen. The facts are as follows:

In the latter part of 1901 Archbishop Maclagan presented a Petition[2] to the Court of Claims for a special place in the ceremony of the Coronation of King Edward VII and Queen

[1] See chap. xxxvii *supra*.

[2] For the text of the Petition see Note, p. 1402. See also G. Woods Wollaston, *Coronation Claims* (second edition, 1910), p. 150.

Alexandra. He made no definite request as to the particular part to be taken, but only that it should be appropriate to the position and history of his office. At the same time he quoted authorities in favour of his contention that the privilege of crowning the Queen Consort, when both Archbishops were present, belonged to the Archbishop of York.[1] When, however, the claim was heard, the Archbishop of York stated that he need not trouble the Court, as the King had accepted the suggestion of the Archbishop of Canterbury that he, as Archbishop of York, should crown Queen Alexandra. The President announced the opinion of the Court that, in these circumstances, no claim of right being before the Court, it was not necessary for the Court to come to any decision, and that His Majesty's pleasure must be conclusive on such a matter.

Dr. Davidson, as Bishop of Winchester, writing to Archbishop Temple at the time, referred thus to the decision that the Archbishop of York should crown the Queen:

The Bishop of Winchester to the Archbishop of Canterbury

Farnham Castle, Surrey.
Private. January 4, 1902.

With regard to Coronation arrangements—the King wishes me to tell you *privately* that if you propose, as he understands you probably will, to delegate the duty of crowning the *Queen* to some one other than yourself, he would entirely approve of your asking the *Archbishop of York* to be your deputy. I know little of the actual precedents in the matter of such delegation, and I do not know how much the King knows about it! nor from whom he has learnt what he does know! But I said I would tell you that he approves of your asking Ebor if you think well so to do.

Presumably you may have said something about it in your draft Form of Service. But at all events it is well that you should be forewarned as to the King's personal view of the matter. I should think he is right in believing that delegation to Ebor (so far as the *Queen* is concerned) would be both regular, appropriate, and popular. But I am only a conduit to convey to you the King's expression of his view.

The two Primates were both old men, Archbishop Temple being 81, and Archbishop Maclagan 76.

[1] Dean Stanley, *Historical Memorials of Westminster Abbey*, p. 41; Sir W. R. Anson, *Law and Custom of the Constitution*, ii. 416.

Eight years later, Dr. Davidson, as Archbishop of Canterbury, writing to Sir Arthur Bigge, gave the following explanation of the reasons:

The Archbishop of Canterbury to Sir Arthur Bigge

November 24th, 1910.

I have found the letters (or some of them) which passed when Archbishop Maclagan was invited by Archbishop Temple to crown Queen Alexandra and King Edward approved; but I know also that King Edward's approval was due to the fact that he had fears that Archbishop Temple would be physically unequal to the duties of the day.

And in a later letter to the same correspondent the Archbishop added:

The Archbishop of Canterbury to Sir Arthur Bigge

24th March, 1911.

It is most fortunate that it did so happen because, as you will remember, Temple collapsed as soon as he had done Homage to the King, and he could not have crowned the Queen at that moment even if he had intended to do so.

It was not unnatural that, when preparations for the Coronation of King George were being made, the new Archbishop of York should hope for the same privilege as had been granted to his predecessor. He did not claim it, however, on account of the ancient rights of the See. Only once since the Conquest had an Archbishop of York crowned the Queen Consort. The single instance was the Coronation of William the Conqueror's wife, Queen Matilda of Flanders, who was crowned by Aldred, Archbishop of York, in 1068 at Winchester, eighteen months after the Coronation of King William I, who had himself been crowned by Aldred in Westminster Abbey on Christmas Day, 1066. But the reason for the choice of the Archbishop of York by King William I was that Stigand, Archbishop of Canterbury,[1] had ousted his predecessor, and was therefore not recognized by the Pope.

[1] See *On the Right of the Archbishop of York to Crown the Queen Consort*, L. G. Wickham Legg, from the *Transactions of the St. Paul's Ecclesiological Society*, 1902. Mr. Wickham Legg shows that on every recorded occasion of the Coronation of the Queen Consort in England since 1066, with two exceptions, she was crowned by the Archbishop of Canterbury. In the two exceptions, the same Prelate crowned both King and

Archbishop Lang based his request on quite different grounds. He pointed to the immense increase in the importance of the North of England, and the propriety of recognizing that fact by the assigning of the Coronation of the Queen Consort to the Northern Primate. But Archbishop Davidson, while admitting the great change in the circumstances of the North of England, could not agree to the proposal. He saw and corresponded with Archbishop Lang and with Sir Arthur Bigge, and with others. And he successfully maintained that it would be sufficient recognition if the Archbishop of York preached the Sermon.

There is a memorandum signed by the Archbishop of Canterbury, and dated December 13, 1910, which was presented to the King through Sir Arthur Bigge. It contained various points, and amongst them:

> May I understand that I may now go forward preparing the Service for submission to the King on lines that—
> 1. The Archbishop of Canterbury crowns both King and Queen?
> 2. The Archbishop of York preaches the (*very* short) sermon?

This Memorandum was returned to the Archbishop with this autograph comment by King George:

App^{d} *G.R.I.*

The following letters passed between the Archbishop of Canterbury and the Archbishop of York:

The Archbishop of York to the Archbishop of Canterbury

Private. Bishopthorpe, York. December 24th, 1910.

With regard to the Coronation. I send you two letters (*which please return*) which will explain themselves. The first (which I ought to have communicated to you before) is in answer to a memorandum which I sent through Bigge, in which I urged as in duty bound some weighty reasons why the Archbishop of York should *now*, in view of the modern position of the North of England as compared with what it was at all Coronations previous to that

Queen, Archbishop Aldred of York crowning William I and Queen Matilda; and the Bishop of Winchester (Henry Woodlock) crowning Edward II and Queen Isabella of France under a commission from the Archbishop of Canterbury, who was abroad. See also generally, for the claims of the Archbishop of York at a Coronation, *A History of the English Coronation*, P. E. Schramm (trans. by L. G. Wickham Legg), Clarendon Press, 1937, pp. 40, 42–5, 60.

of Queen Victoria or even with what it was then, be allowed to crown the Queen. I put the case as strongly as I could: it *is* a strong one: never till Edward VII's Coronation had 'the North' become in English life what it is now: and *then* the Archbishop of York did crown the Queen. I think it was unfortunate that my predecessor was allowed to do this, if it was not intended to set a precedent. It would have been much more satisfactory under these circumstances if the Archbishop of Canterbury had deputed part of his functions to one of his own Suffragans. But of course I loyally accept the King's decision: as it was a matter for grace, not for claim: and I will do my best in the *very* difficult ordeal of the Sermon.

This is what I said in the reply to Bigge's letter of 8th to which he in turn replies in the second letter I send: and I added that I thought it was most important that some announcement should be made as to the reasons which account for the fact that the precedent of 1901 is not to be followed, and as to the place now given to York. It may allay some of the disappointment which I know will be widely felt in this highly sensitive North Country.

As you know, I have no personal feeling in the matter whatever: I am only sorry that in this respect the arrangements of the Coronation cannot be adapted to a remarkable and most important change in English life and history.

The Archbishop of Canterbury to the Archbishop of York

Private. Old Palace, Canterbury. Dec. 27, 1910.

I return Bigge's two letters on the Coronation matter. I share your view that our honoured Predecessors both in North and South, *muddled* this business sadly, and that their arrangement was such as inevitably to bequeathe a legacy of difficulty. My *belief* (though I have no direct evidence) is that dear Temple, who in his rugged way disregarded, or despised history, tradition or precedent, had been misled as to the facts by trusting Stanley's curiously careless statement, and had in conversation with W. Ebor taken for granted that such was the right arrangement, and that subsequently when the error was pointed out, he, or they, fell back on the *personal* grounds, and on these grounds [*this* is fact, not conjecture] King Edward assented! But most certainly it ought to have been made clear at the time. We must see that it is made publicly clear soon, by some official pronouncement.

Bigge comes here for Sunday next, and I will talk it over with him. The usages of Feudal times don't fit well into a Democratic age!

The official pronouncement followed a few weeks later (*The Times*, March 25, 1911). It ran as follows:

> In regard to the arrangements for the Coronation Service, we are authorized to state that the King has decided that the Archbishop of Canterbury shall, in accordance with continuous precedent from early times, crown the Queen as well as the King. Practically the only exception to this was at the Coronation of King Edward VII, when Queen Alexandra was crowned by the Archbishop of York.
>
> By his Majesty's command the Sermon at the approaching Coronation will be preached by the Archbishop of York.

II

The preparation of the Coronation Service required and received a great deal of thought. According to custom the duty of overseeing the Service, and if possible shortening it, belonged to the Archbishop of Canterbury. At the time of the Coronation of Queen Victoria in 1838 liturgical study was little considered in England, and the Order then provided is the least satisfactory in the series. When preparations were being made for the Coronation of King Edward VII in 1902, Dr. Armitage Robinson,[1] Canon of Westminster, and a very eminent liturgical scholar, desired to secure an improved and enriched Form. In this he was strongly supported by Dr. Randall Davidson, then Bishop of Winchester and Clerk of the Closet. But the position was delicate, as Archbishop Temple wanted to make still further changes, which would have had the result of even more whittling away. For example he desired that the anointings should be reduced to one only. The King, however, himself said flatly that, if he were going to be anointed at all, he wished the anointing to be done properly. And in this and other points, mainly through Dr. Robinson's persistence, the Form prepared for Edward VII was a real improvement. It will be remembered, however, that on account of the illness of the King, the Coronation was postponed from June 26, 1902, to August 9, 1902; and to spare His Majesty as much as possible, the Form actually used at the Coronation, though only privately printed,

[1] Dr. G. G. Bradley was Dean of Westminster at the Coronation in 1902. He resigned on 29th September 1902, and was succeeded by Dr. Robinson.

was a good deal shorter than the Form which had been originally authorized.

When a new reign began and the time came to make ready for the Coronation of King George V, the original King Edward VII Form became the basis for the new Form. Dr. Robinson[1] noted the following points in a private memorandum which he made for Archbishop Davidson:

> The last Coronation Service, as originally drawn up, was very much shorter than the Service of 1838.
>
> The form then settled was the only form officially presented to the public, and was in the hands of the Congregation at the time of the Service.
>
> When it became necessary yet further to shorten the Service, the abbreviations were as follows:
>
> 1. The omission of the Shortened Litany.
> 2. The omission of the Sermon.
> 3. The singing of *Te Deum* after the King had gone to St. Edward's Chapel.
> 4. The abbreviation of the Homage.
> 5. Time was saved by the King's not going before the Altar for the Oath, and not returning to His Throne, but to His Chair, after receiving the Holy Communion.
>
> In this way the whole Service (apart from Processions), from the time when the Archbishop began to the time when he ended, occupied exactly an hour and a half.

In the preparation of the Form of 1911 further improvements were introduced. Much of the work was entrusted to the Lambeth Librarian, the Rev. Claude Jenkins, who went through it stage by stage, comparing it with earlier Forms, and going behind the alterations introduced by Bishop Compton for William III and Mary, and by Archbishop Secker for George III, in an effort to get back to the older simpler Forms. The improvements were real, though they did not go as far as the Lambeth Librarian would have liked. His suggestions were checked by Dr. Robinson, the Archbishop agreeing that those emendations which Dr. Robinson approved could all be em-

[1] Dr. Ryle (formerly Bishop of Winchester) accepted the Deanery of Westminster on 22nd December 1910, in succession to Dr. Robinson, who was appointed Dean of Wells. His installation on 29th April 1911 took place in the choir by special permission, because the Abbey was in the hands of H.M. Office of Works, and preparations for the Coronation were far advanced.

bodied. The scrutiny was strict and a good many suggestions failed to pass the test. Dr. Robinson, for example, refused to sacrifice some of the eighteenth-century alterations in phrasing on the ground that, 'like the monuments in the Abbey' they were date marks, but he warmly supported the most important change, viz. the restoration of the prayer 'God crown you with a crown of glory and righteousness' in its simpler form at its proper place in connexion with the putting on of the Crown (sec. xii).

The principal changes in the Order of 1911 from the Order of 1902 are set out by Archbishop Davidson as follows:

Principal Changes in Order of Coronation Service

Sec. 5. Introit 'Let my prayer come up', Purcell, sung as the Offertorium in 1902, takes the place of 'O Hearken thou unto the voice' (Sullivan) transferred to the Offertory with a setting by Elgar.

Collect after the Lord's Prayer omitted.

Sec. 12. Form of exhortation after Crowning reverts to ancient use.

Sec. 14. Te Deum removed to separate section (19) before the Recess.

Sec. 16. Homage Anthem Ps. xxxiii. 1, 12–16, 18–22. Substituted for Isa. xlix. 7–12.

Sec. 18. Offertorium reduced to the words 'O Hearken thou' (see above) with a setting by Elgar.

Preface to the Sanctus enlarged by seven lines.

A further change worthy of notice was the restoration of the word *Churches* in place of the word *Church* in the question put to the King.

> And will you preserve to the Bishops and Clergy of *England*, and to the *Churches* there committed to their charge, all such rights and privileges as by law do, or shall, pertain to them or to any of them?

The change from *Churches* to *Church* had been made in 1902 under a misapprehension. Since the Church of Ireland was disestablished in 1869 the Sovereign was no longer required to promise to preserve their lawful rights unto 'the Bishops and Clergy of England and Ireland', but the alteration in King Edward's Form of *Churches there* to *Church therein* was a mistake, due to the supposition that the Churches indicated in the phrase were corporate bodies, whereas the plural number really referred to the Churches (or Dioceses) under their

Bishops, and reflected the organization of the Church in the ninth century, when this phraseology was first drawn up.

It should also be observed that the Recognition of the King in sec. iii was called for at all the four sides of the theatre, instead of only at one side, as had been required by the illness of Edward VII. A minor change was the removal of those rubrics, or portions of rubrics, which were merely concerned with what Peers and Peeresses and State Officials were to do.[1] More important, though not exactly concerned with the Form and Order, was the allocation of a special place for the first time to the Prime Minister, for whom a precedence had been recently established, by a Sign Manual Warrant of Edward VII, dated December 2, 1905, by which the King decreed that the Prime Minister 'shall have place or precedence next after the Archbishop of York'. It is further of some interest to note that while certain representatives of the Evangelical Free Churches were present, no question of their being allowed any special prominence seems to have been raised.

III

The Service, when complete, was, according to precedent, first submitted to the Committee of the Privy Council, and by them ordered to be presented for the approval of the King in Council, the Archbishop of Canterbury being in attendance on both occasions. It was then issued by the King's printers at the end of March.

[1] In ancient ceremonials the Archbishop of Canterbury is mentioned as 'attended by two gentlemen', but no names are given before 1902. There is no mention of a Cross-bearer in the Ceremonial of the Coronation of King Edward VII. In writing to the Archbishop on April 4, 1911, the Duke of Norfolk said, 'In the performance of your duties at the solemnity of the Coronation . . . you will require to be attended by two gentlemen, and to be preceded by your Cross-bearer.' In reply to an inquiry as to whether 'gentlemen' necessarily meant laymen (the Rev. J. V. Macmillan being Cross-bearer), the Duke of Norfolk said (April 11, 1911):

> 'With regard to the Gentlemen to attend upon you, I can find no precedent for any one but a layman filling this office, but I see no objection to your nominating any one in Holy Orders if you think fit.'

The Archbishop had supposed that the term 'gentlemen' was used in 1902 'in order that the two sons of Archbishop Temple might be covered by it, neither of them being in Holy Orders'. In fact Archbishop Temple was following precedent, while Archbishop Davidson was creating a new precedent, which was followed by Archbishop Lang at the Coronation of King George VI. In 1911 the Archbishop was attended by the Rev. E. L. A. Hertslet and the Rev. C. Jenkins.

It is well known that the King's printers are entitled under the terms of their Letters Patent to execute the printing of all Forms of Prayer issued by command of His Majesty. A new point, however, arose in connexion with the publication of the Forms of Prayer commended by the Archbishops of Canterbury and York 'for general use' on the day of the Coronation. The King's printers (Messrs. Eyre & Spottiswoode) appealed to the Clerk of the Privy Council (Sir Almeric Fitzroy) on the ground that these Forms had not been issued through them, but through the Society for Promoting Christian Knowledge, a procedure contrary to that followed in the case of the Form and Order of Service recommended for use in the Churches on the occasion of the Coronation of King Edward VII. They claimed that they were entitled to execute the printing of these Forms under the terms of their Letters Patent. In a letter to the Archbishop of Canterbury Sir Almeric Fitzroy made the following inquiry:

Sir Almeric Fitzroy to the Archbishop of Canterbury

19th April, 1911.

I shall be glad if Your Grace will be so good as to inform me, in order that I may deal with the complaint in the proper way, under what authority the present Forms of Prayer were issued, since it would not appear that Section 3 of the Act of Uniformity Amendment Act, 1872 (35 and 36 Victoria, cap. 35) which authorizes the use of special forms of service upon special occasions when approved by the Ordinary applies in this case.

The Archbishop of Canterbury replied as follows:

The Archbishop of Canterbury to Sir Almeric Fitzroy

21st April, 1911.

This Form of Service does not claim to be 'issued by command of the King' which was the imprint on the Forms of Service issued by Archbishops Temple and Maclagan in 1902. I do not know what was the exact significance of that imprint, or the channel or process of that command.[1] On this occasion the two Archbishops

[1] Sir Almeric Fitzroy, writing to the Archbishop of Canterbury on February 18, 1911, i.e. before the question had been raised by the King's printers, said:

> There is no record here of any direction of the Privy Council dealing with the use of the Order of Service in Parish Churches, and I presume therefore the observance of the day on the last occasion was ordained by ecclesiastical authority alone.

It would appear, therefore, that the use of the words 'By The King's Command' was misleading.

have themselves recommended a particular set of Forms of Prayer for general use, subject of course to Diocesan or other sanction which may be necessary. It is not put forth by order of the Privy Council or by formal command of the King, and I think that Messrs. Eyre & Spottiswoode are under some misapprehension on that point. They would not, I imagine, claim to be the sole, or even the ordinary, printers of all special Prayers or Forms of Service issued at any time by the Archbishops or Bishops for use on some particular occasion.

The King's printers were informed of the Archbishop's reply by Sir Almeric Fitzroy, who added:

Sir Almeric Fitzroy to Messrs. Eyre & Spottiswoode Ltd.

4th May, 1911.

In these circumstances this Department is advised that you are not entitled, under your Letters Patent, to claim the execution of the printing of the Forms in question.

I have to add, however, that if prints of the Forms should happen to be issued hereafter bearing the imprint 'Issued by Command of The King', or words of like or similar significance, other considerations would arise, and it might then be that you would have ground of complaint.

IV

It is not necessary to add here any description of the actual Coronation gathered from the contemporary press. Yet, in the light of the later experience of the use of the cinematograph and of broadcasting at the Coronation of King George VI, it may be of interest to note that in 1911 there was a considerable discussion as to the desirability of photographs being taken of the Coronation Service, for which Sir Benjamin Stone was appointed the official photographer. The Archbishop was not in favour of any photographs being taken of the actual Service, holding that photography should cease from the moment that prayers began. But both the King and the Duke of Norfolk were in favour, and it was agreed to allow photographs, from a concealed place, of four central scenes—the Recognition; the Presenting of the Sword; the Presenting of the Bible; the Homage.

On the evening of June 22, when all the ceremonies of the Coronation were over, the Archbishop of Canterbury wrote the following letter to the King. It is reproduced here because of its prophetic character. Before the letter reached the King a telegram had already been dispatched by His Majesty himself to the Archbishop.

The Archbishop of Canterbury to H.M. the King

Lambeth Palace, S.E.

To His Majesty the King. 22 June, 1911.

Sir,

I hope that I am not doing wrong, after all the strain and fatigue to Your Majesty of such a day as this, in writing a few loyal and dutiful lines to express my grateful sense of the privilege which has to-day been mine in being allowed to be the spokesman of a Christian people which desires to invoke the blessing of the Lord God Himself upon its Sovereign. I cannot help thinking that in ancient times, or even a century ago, it must sometimes have been a little difficult for an Archbishop to use quite whole-heartedly or without some measure of anxiety and foreboding the terribly solemn and significant words of *expectant* and *hopeful* prayers which our historic 'Coronation Service' provides. To-day—Your Majesty will pardon me if I speak quite frankly—there are no such forebodings. We have said our solemn prayers, Sir, with you and for you,—and I have been allowed, in the name, and on behalf of the whole Empire to 'consecrate' our Sovereign to his great task; a task which might well daunt any man who did not believe that he has a right to count upon and to use the direct help which GOD will give him every day.

If our 'Coronation Service' means anything, it means the promise of that help, a promise accompanied by the knowledge on the King's part that his people are in almost every English-speaking home praying for him and expecting that their prayers will be answered, and that GOD will indeed grant them at their head a 'consecrated' man, not in any pedantic or over-wrought sense of that word—but a man who deliberately means, by the help of God, to lead a life of 'service', a life of straight forward devotion to some of the most important duties on earth, a life of manly purity and justice and truth.

I suppose it has seldom happened in English history—at all events in 'Constitutional' times—that an English King has, on his Coronation Day, had a more anxious and complicated *outlook* before him, as he tries to gauge the currents of public opinion among his people, and to judge what his action ought to be, and how far he is justified in using personal influence in public affairs.

To those of us who have thought much over the present situation in Parliament and in the country, these difficulties of our Sovereign loom large. It gave all the more meaning to our prayers to-day in Westminster Abbey, and for myself I can say that at the moment when I used over Your Majesty the grave but inspiring words which follow the *anointing* ['Our Lord Jesus Christ . . . pour down upon &c.'], or the vigorous appeal which follows the *girding* of the sword ['with this Sword do justice &c.'] I had in my thoughts at the very moment, the problems which may soon have to be faced. It is because we do in our hearts believe that Your Majesty shares with us these thoughts and hopes and prayers, that we can tonight 'Rejoice and be glad'.

I have the honour to be
Your Majesty's most loyal and devoted servant,
RANDALL CANTUAR:

His Majesty the King to the Archbishop of Canterbury

7.15 p.m., June 22, 1911.

It is difficult to find words to express adequately the deep appreciation of myself and the Queen of the beautiful and sacred service of to-day so much due to you personally. We thank you from our hearts and shall never forget what a comfort you have been to us on this the greatest and most solemn day of our lives.

GEORGE R. & I.

NOTE

Text of Archbishop Maclagan's Petition to the Court of Claims

To the Right Honourable
The Commissioners appointed to hear, receive, and determine the Petitions and Claims concerning the Services to be done and performed at their Majesties Coronation.

The Petition and claim of
William Dalrymple
Archbishop of York
Bishopthorpe York

Sheweth
That by reason of

1. The great antiquity of the See of York.
2. The position and rank of the Archbishop of York both in the Church of England and in the Constitution of the Realm.

3. The connexion of the Archbishops of York from ancient times, both historically and legally, with the Coronation of the Sovereigns of England.

Your Petitioner claims

That in the ceremony and Service at the coming Coronation of their Majesties a place and part should be assigned to the Archbishop of York consistent with his rank in the Church and Realm and with the traditions of his Archiepiscopal See.

1. Of the two Archbishoprics, York is the older See, although the later Archbishopric.

It probably dates, as a Bishopric, from the second century.

Its Bishops were present at several of the earliest Councils of the Christian Church; as at Arles A.D. 314; Nicea A.D. 325; and others.

After the temporary suppression of the See during the invasions of the fifth and sixth centuries, it was restored early in the seventh; and was shortly raised to an Archbishopric, soon after the original constitution of the Archiepiscopal See of Canterbury.

2. The Archbishop of York holds the second place in the Church of England.

He is the Archbishop of an independent Province. After centuries of strife and contention the relative position of the two Archbishops was personally decided by the adjudication of the Sovereign in the presence and with the consent of both Archbishops, at the Palace of Westminster in the year 1353. It was there determined that the Archbishop of York might bear his Archiepiscopal cross erect within the Province of Canterbury. In Parliaments and Councils a seat on the right hand of the King was to be assigned to the Archbishop of Canterbury, and a seat on the left to the Archbishop of York; each with his cross erect. In a procession the two Archbishops were to walk abreast; each having his cross borne. When from the narrowness of the way this should be impossible, the precedence was to be given to the Archbishop of Canterbury. This precedence was also certified by the titles bestowed upon the two Archbishops. Both were Primates and Metropolitans; but while the title of the Archbishop of York was and is 'Primate of England', the title of the Archbishop of Canterbury is 'Primate of all England'.

As regards precedence in the Kingdom the Archbishop of York holds the third place, after the Royal Family, among the subjects of the Realm.

3. To the Archbishop of Canterbury belongs the indefeasible right and privilege of crowning the Sovereign; but from the earliest times,

in the absence of the Archbishop of Canterbury, the Archbishop of York, if present, has taken his place. So it was, for example, that the Archbishop of York officiated at the Coronation of William the Conqueror, and at a later date crowned his Queen. It was also the Archbishop of York who was called upon to crown the son of King Henry the 2nd during the absence of the Archbishop of Canterbury.

But it is further enacted in a Statute of the first year of William and Mary c. VI. s. 2 (a Statute still in force) that the oath to be administered in the Coronation Office to these Sovereigns and 'to every King or Queen who shall succeed to the Imperial Crown of this Realm of England shall be administered by the Archbishop of Canterbury or the Archbishop of York, or either of them, or any other Bishop of this Realm whom the King's Majesty shall thereunto appoint'; implying a primary right and privilege as appertaining to either of the two Archbishops, and only failing both of them, is an appointment to be made, by the Sovereign, of any other Bishop.

It has been frequently stated by persons of authority and it has been very commonly believed that the privilege of crowning the Queen Consort when both Archbishops are present belongs to the Archbishop of York. In the Church Dictionary, a standard work compiled by Dr. Hook, the well known Church Historian, it is stated that 'by ancient custom the Coronation of the Queen Consort belongs to the Archbishop of York'. The same statement has also a place in the *Historical Memorials of Westminster Abbey* by Dean Stanley. It is also to be found in a Manuscript of the 17th Century, now in the Bodleian Library (M.S. Rawlinson B 102. fo: 506). Finally in the learned work of Sir William Anson on *The Law and Custom of the Constitution of England* this matter is referred to as follows: 'The Archbishop of Canterbury has the privilege of crowning the King, or the Queen regnant; while the Archbishop of York may crown the Queen Consort.'

Your Petitioner therefore claims

That in the Ceremony and Service at the coming Coronation of their Majesties a place and part should be assigned to the Archbishop of York consistent with his rank in the Church and Realm and with the traditions of his Archiepiscopal See.

AND your Petitioner will ever pray &c.

WILLELM: EBOR:

INDEX

Note. To facilitate identification and to avoid confusion, some of the *dramatis personae*, variously designated in the text of the book, are entered in this Index under their original names, and their chief subsequent titles or positions are added—e.g. 'Gore, Charles (successively Canon of Westminster, Bp. of Worcester, Bp. of Birmingham, and Bp. of Oxford)'. For the same reasons, and also to save space, frequent use is made, in the earlier part of the Index, of the initials 'R.T.D.' to indicate the principal *persona* of the book. Various contractions are also employed, e.g. 'Q. Victoria' for Queen Victoria.

The entries in the Index under Randall Davidson's name, while they are primarily pointers to the pages of the text, are also intended to form a brief summary of his whole life.

R. T. D.'s apptmt. to a bpric., i. 184, but presses him upon Ld. Salisbury for the See of Winchester, i. 187, and on Ld. S. refusing to nominate him thereto, ultimately agrees that R. T. D. should be offered the choice of the Sees of Rochester and Worcester, i. 191; but is anxious about his health, i. 197; H.M.'s partial blindness, i. 244; on death of Bp. Thorold (1895), H.M. again asks Ld. Salisbury to consider R. T. D. for the See of Winchester and is gratified by his acquiescence and by the apptmt. being made, i. 245–6; a year later, on death of Abp. Benson, presses for the apptmt. of R. T. D. to the Primacy, but is overruled by Ld. Salisbury, and by R. T. D.'s strong advice that Bp. Temple of London should be apptd., i. 285; objects, on grounds of health, to R. T. D.'s being nominated as Temple's successor in the See of London, i. 285; H.M.'s Diamond Jubilee (1897) and the service outside St. Paul's, i. 308–10; R. T. D. accompanies H.M., as Chaplain, to Cimiez, and describes the place and the life there, i. 311; H.M. officially issues a 'Queen's Letter' to the Abp. of Canterbury 'for a general collection in the Churches of Eng. and Wales on behalf of sufferers in the S. African War', i. 312; but is opposed to the suggestion that a special day for intercession should be apptd., urging that the necessity for special prayer and praise—not humiliation—should be inculcated generally 'not on one day, but throughout these times of national anxiety', i. 313–14; expresses to Lady Audrey Buller her sympathy and her faith in Sir Redvers Buller, despite the reverses he had met with in the S. African War, i. 315–16; H.M.'s last effort—an hour's talk with Ld. Roberts—before her death (on Jan. 22, 1901), i. 351; R. T. D.'s account of her illness, death, and funeral, i. 351–7; *Letters of Q. Victoria* (frequently quoted and referred to in this biography), i. 412; her wish that the Prince Imperial should be buried in Westr. Abbey recalled, ii. 1177; Abp. Davidson writes for *The Times* a short article on the Queen on the eve of the publication of the Second Series of H.M.'s *Letters* (postscript by Ld. Rosebery), ii. 1215–17.

Villiers, Henry, i. 74–5.

Wace, Dr. Henry (afterwards Dean of Canterbury), i. 150, 153, 395, 486, 534 *et seq.*, 722; ii. 863–5, 1040.

Wake, W., Abp. of Canterbury (1716), i. 444.

Wakefield, H. Russell (afterwards Bp. of Birmingham), i. 402.

Wales, Abp. of (*see* 'Edwards, A. G.').

Walpole, Sir Spencer, Secy. to the Post Office, i. 244.

Walsh, W., successively Bp. of Mauritius and Bp. Suffragan of Dover, i. 415; death, ii. 914.

Walton, Rev. J. L., ii. 1032.

Ward, Mrs. Humphry, her novel *Robert Elsmere*, i. 122.

Warre, Rev. Dr., headmaster of Eton, i. 205.

Warrington of Clyffe, Lord, as junior trustee of the Athenaeum Club, presides at banquet given by the Club in honour of Ld. Davidson after his resignation of the Primacy, ii. 1371.

Washington, Booker, negro leader, i. 446.

Waterpark, Lady, i. 79.

Watkins, H. W., Archn. of Durham, i. 169.

Watson, Arthur, asst.-master at Harrow, i. 14, 15, 17.

Watts-Ditchfield, J. E., Bp. of Chelmsford, ii. 1040.

Wayte, Rev. Samuel, Pres. of Trin. Coll., Oxford, i. 21.

Webster, Sir Richard, Attorney-General, i. 103, 135.

Wellesley, Dean of Windsor, i. 50, 61, 69, 76, 77, 82, 163, 202.

Wellwood, Sir Hy. Moncrieff, i. 3.

Welsh Bprics., correspce. about apptmts. to, i. 178–9.

Welsh Church Disestablishment, i. 224–5, 504–5, 640–4; ii. 981–90.

Wesley, John, said to have visited Thomas Randall (the elder) at Inchture in 1768, i. 3.

West, Sir Algernon, as vice-chairman of the R. Commn. on the Liquor Licensing Laws, i. 324*n*.

Westcott, Dr. Foss, Bp. of Chota Nagpur, the problem of German Missions in his Dio. during and after the War, ii. 926–8.

Westcott, B. F., asst.-master at Harrow (afterwards Bp. of Durham), i. 14–17, 19, 68, 103; apptd. to the Bpric. of Durham, i. 179–81, 187, 227, 250, 325*n*, 662; ii. 1248.

Westminster Abbey, Abp. Davidson's views on questions of burial in, ii. 1177.

PRINTED IN GREAT BRITAIN
AT THE UNIVERSITY PRESS, OXFORD
BY CHARLES BATEY, PRINTER TO THE UNIVERSITY